Related Titles for College-Bound Students

SAT

SAT with CD-ROM

SAT for Super Busy Students

SAT 1600

SAT Math Workbook

SAT Verbal Workbook

Titles for the New SAT starting March 12, 2005

The NEW SAT

The NEW SAT with CD-ROM

NEW SAT 2400

The NEW SAT Critical Reading Workbook

The NEW SAT Math Workbook

The NEW SAT Writing Workbook

Vocabulary-Building for the SAT

Extreme SAT Vocabulary Flashcards Flip-O-Matic

SAT Vocabulary Flashcards Flip-O-Matic

SAT Vocab Velocity

Frankenstein: A Kaplan SAT Score-Raising Classic

The Ring of McAllister: A Score-Raising Mystery Featuring 1,046 Must-Know SAT Vocabulary Words

SAT for Native Spanish Speakers

Domina el SAT: Prepárate para Tomar el Examen para Ingresar a la Universidad

College Life and Admissions

Broke!: A College Student's Guide to Getting By on Less

Once Upon a Campus: Tantalizing Truths about College from People Who've Already Messed Up

Parent's Guide to College Admissions

Sharing Spaces: Tips and Strategies on Being a Good College Roommate, Surviving a Bad One, and Dealing with Everything in Between

Scholarships

Straight Talk on Paying for College

THE
UNOFFICIAL, ~~UNBIASED~~
GUIDE
TO THE
331
MOST INTERESTING
COLLEGES

2005 Edition

By the Staff of Kaplan Test Prep and Admissions

Simon & Schuster

NEW YORK · LONDON · SYDNEY · TORONTO

Kaplan Publishing
Published by Simon & Schuster
1230 Avenue of the Americas
New York, New York 10020

Contributing Editor: Seppy Basili

Editors: Eileen Mager, Jessica Shapiro

Educational Research Manager: Jessica Shapiro

Contributors: Eileen Mager, Jessica Shapiro, Larissa Shmailo, Angela Cress, Ruth Baygell, Déa Alessandro, Rodolfo Robles

Cover Design: Brad Foltz

Interior Page Layout: Hugh Haggerty

Production Manager: Michael Shevlin

Managing Editor: Déa Alessandro

Senior Managing Editor: Eileen Mager

Executive Editor: Jennifer Farthing

Special thanks to: Derek Clark

Manufactured in the United States of America
Published simultaneously in Canada

July 2004
10 9 8 7 6 5 4 3 2 1

ISBN 0-7432-5199-7

TABLE OF CONTENTS

kaptest.com/publishing

The data in this guide is compiled from surveys sent to schools each year. Kaplan is not responsible for errors in reported data. Be sure to contact the schools directly for more information on application deadlines and requirements.

If there are any changes or corrections to the data in this book, we will post that information online at **kaptest.com/publishing**.

kaplansurveys.com/books

What did you think of this book? We'd love to hear your comments and suggestions. We invite you to fill out our online survey form at **kaplansurveys.com/books**. Your feedback is extremely helpful as we continue to develop high-quality resources to meet your needs.

It's our firm belief that there's more than one "perfect" college out there for each and every student; the hard part is matching your needs and desires with what a college has to offer. This book will help you figure out exactly what you want in a college and determine which schools are right for you.

How We Created This Book

The Most Interesting Colleges

First, Kaplan's unofficial, unbiased panel of experts worked together to compile a list of the most interesting schools. We needed to determine the "most interesting" colleges and universities. Why "most interesting," you ask? Because profiling colleges based only on selectivity—as many other college guides do—leaves you with a fairly homogenous group of schools and excludes schools that might have something unique to offer.

So what makes a college "interesting"? Well, highly selective schools are admittedly interesting, if only for the quality of academics they can offer. Unique programs and academic strengths are other obvious criteria. In some cases, having lower admissions standards or being relatively unknown can make a particular college an interesting alternative to a high-profile school. The student body can also certainly make a school interesting: for example, if a state school draws a majority of out-of-state students, or if the student body at a school is highly diverse.

Of course, this is not a comprehensive collection of all the schools in the country that are worth checking out; there are some perfectly good schools that are not included in this guide. But we hope that our selections will give you an idea of the breadth of choices available. Whatever your finances, academic interests, geographical location, and personality type, there is a college that's right for you.

Inside Information

After deciding which colleges we wanted to profile, we turned to a wide assortment of "insiders" for information. We surveyed current students, recent graduates, high school guidance counselors, and college officials in order to find out about each college from different angles. We sent a lengthy open-ended survey to students, another open-ended survey to the school administration, yet another survey to the administration to collect institutional data, and we conducted a scientific survey of guidance counselors. The in-depth, narrative answers we received, particularly from the student surveys (no leading multiple-choice questions here!), allowed us to see what daily life is really like for undergraduates at each of these schools. From academics to campus safety, housing availability to Greek life, faculty accessibility to alcohol and drug use, this "unofficial" information is vital in determining whether or not you would be happy at a particular college.

We then used the information from *all* of these surveys—as well as info we gathered from various media outlets—to write the candid college profiles in Section II of this guide. And we couldn't resist adding our own opinions, mostly featured as quotes in the separate "The Experts Say . . ." box near the end of each profile (though our opinions also wormed their way into the profile text at times—after all, it is an "unbiased" guide!).

How to Use This Book

Step One: Decide What You Want in a College

Before you can find the right college, you need to know what it is that you want in a college, in terms of academics, campus environment, and student life. The self-assessment tools in our Introduction will help you to do that.

Step Two: View the Lists of Recommended Schools, Organized by Specific Features

Do you want to go to a school with unconventional, "outside the box" academics? Or a school with a low student/faculty ratio? Or a school that's a good value for your tuition dollar? Our lists in Section I are a good place to start your college search.

Step Three: Read the College Profiles to Get the Facts and the Inside Scoop

You'll find useful, detailed information on the 331 most interesting colleges and universities in Section II: College Profiles. If you feel overwhelmed by the number of profiles, use our indexes in Section III to sort all 331 profiled schools by location, size, and cost.

Colleges are not one-dimensional. When evaluating a college, you can't look at just the academics, just the facilities, or just the social scene. You need to take a look at the whole picture to see whether the college is a good match for you, and vice versa.

But before you look at what the various colleges can offer, stop and think about what you want out of a school. What are your likes and dislikes? Your dreams and goals? Don't forget: You are the consumer here. The power is in your hands. If you do a good job of deciding what you want out of a college, and find the college that matches your needs and expectations, there's an excellent chance that you'll be admitted and spend a happy and productive four years at the best college for you.

Use the following self-assessment quiz to establish exactly what you want out of a college—inside the classroom, around campus, and from your fellow students. If some of these criteria are unimportant to you, fine. But you'll probably come across some important factors that you've never even considered before.

The Kaplan Self-Assessment Quiz

Inside the Classroom

- Do you want to go to a college that will prepare you for a specific career? A college that will give you a solid liberal arts education? Or one that will help you to grow as a person? (Of course, these are not necessarily mutually exclusive!)

- Are you the type of student who thrives under pressure and can handle a heavy workload? Or would you prefer a lighter workload in a very laid-back environment?

- Are you a top student who can't wait to go head-to-head against the cream of the crop in a highly competitive environment? Are you a good student who shies away from competition and might even prefer being "a big fish in a small pond," intellectually speaking?

- Think about class size. Will you mind being "just a number" in large lecture-based courses? Or will you feel "put on the spot" in small, discussion-based seminars?

- Is it important for you to go to a school with renowned faculty? Or is it more important to you that your professors are approachable and know you by name?

- How important is it for you to have a wide range of courses and majors from which to choose? Do you already know what you want to major in, or do you want to explore different areas before officially declaring a major?

- Do you want the freedom to create your own academic program, without having to fulfill extensive core requirements? Or do you like the idea of having core requirements to keep you on track and provide you with a broad liberal arts background?

- Are you mainly interested in a traditional, classroom-based education, or do you want to participate in co-ops, internships, and study-abroad opportunities?

- How important is it that you go to a school with cutting-edge facilities? Do you plan to conduct independent research or participate in faculty research?

Campus Environment

- Do you want to attend a large university, with tons of activities and the opportunity to meet lots of new people? A small, close-knit college, where everyone knows each other? Or a medium-sized school, where you won't get bored but also won't feel overwhelmed?

- Do you want to be in a big city with lots of cultural offerings? Would you prefer a small town, where the school is an important part of the community? Or do you want to be surrounded by nature?

- What kind of weather do you prefer? Are you a snow-lover or a sun-worshipper?

- Would you mind going to a school where everyone is required to live on campus all four years? Would you panic if went to a school that forced you to move off campus after a year or two?

- Do you want to be able to have a car at school, even during freshman year? If you don't have a car, will you go stir-crazy?

Student Life

- Do you want to be part of a diverse student body and make friends with people from very different backgrounds? Or would you feel more comfortable surrounded by students who are very similar to you, in terms of cultural, religious, and/or economic background?

- Do you want to be in a socially conservative environment, where the rules governing student behavior are respected and enforced? Or a very open environment, where you can feel free to express your opinions about anything and everything?

- Do you want to be on a politically active campus, either conservative or liberal? Or is political apathy fine with you?

- Do you plan to spend most of your free time on campus and want a wide variety of school-sponsored activities to choose from? Or maybe you plan to spend most of your free time off campus and want the surrounding community to offer plenty of diversions?

- Are you a party animal who wants easy access to parties, clubs, and bars seven days a week? Do you plan to limit your partying to weekends? Or are you a teetotaler?

- Do you dream of joining a fraternity or sorority? Or is the idea of Greek life so unappealing to you that you'd prefer a school with no Greek organizations at all?

- If you're an athlete, do you want to play only on a top-ranked intercollegiate team? Would you play on any intercollegiate team, even if it's not highly ranked? Or do you love to play sports just for fun and want to play on a club or intramural team?

The Sky's the Limit

You might have noticed that questions about your finances were conspicuously missing from the self-assessment quiz above. We do have a Tuition Index in Section III of this guide, and we encourage you to use it.

However, when starting their initial college search, too many families limit their choices by looking only at colleges that have a tuition the family can readily afford. We encourage you to "think outside the box." Consider all of the possibilities when trying to find colleges that are a good match. If you then fall in love with a college that seems out of your price range, thoroughly investigate all financial aid options, including both need-based and non-need-based aid. You can find information on tuition and financial aid in each college's sidebar data in their profiles in Section II of this guide.

Now that you are aware of what you want in a college, it's time to begin your college search. Good luck, and happy hunting!

THE UNOFFICIAL, ~~UN~~BIASED COLLEGE LISTS

Choosing a college is not easy. The key is to find out all you can about a school before you apply. By buying this guide, you've taken the first step towards finding the right school for you. You'll find inside information on 331 select colleges and universities, covering admissions, selectivity, financial aid, student life, and academics. But numbers don't tell the whole story. Which school really has that "special something" that will make it the best school for you? Your own high school guidance counselor can give you lots of information about various colleges, including qualities most college guides don't measure. But even your guidance counselor's knowledge may be limited to those schools he or she has visited or dealt with in the past.

To give you the scoop on schools you may not be familiar with, Kaplan's panel of experts has assembled a series of lists based on this guide's "interesting" schools. These lists refer to specific characteristics of schools and range from colleges for the wallet-conscious—with a high percentage of financial aid—to quirkier lists that show you some famous alumni of selected schools. If getting out of school in four years flat is a top priority for you, check out our "Out the Door in Four Years" list. If getting outside in the sun for four years straight is your main goal, take a look at our "Outdoor Activities" lists of schools for sun-worshippers and snow-lovers.

Lists of Recommended Schools

- Schools with Enviable Yield Rates
- Schools that Provide a Large Percentage of Students with Non-Need-Based Gift Aid
- Schools that Provide Laptops or Computers to Students
- Schools with High Percentages of Fraternity and Sorority Participation
- Schools that See a High Percentage of Grads Enter Graduate School Within a Year
- Schools with Impressive Graduation Rates
- Schools that are Innovative or Unconventional
- Schools where a High Percentage of Students Complete More than One Major
- Schools with a Low Student/Faculty Ratio
- Schools with Very Selective Acceptance Rates
- Schools that See a High Percentage of Grads Accepting Jobs at the Time of Graduation
- Schools that Have Had Movies or TV Shows Filmed on Campus
- Schools with a High Percentage of Young Alumni Contributions
- Schools with High Average Loan Debt per Student
- Great College Towns
- Schools in Locations for Students Interested in the Great Outdoors
- Schools that Provide a High Percentage of Students with Institutional Aid
- Schools with Celebrity Alumni

LISTS OF RECOMMENDED SCHOOLS

Enviable Yield Rates

Check out these popular schools that students obviously find desirable: Their yield rates (% of admitted applicants who actually enroll) are through the roof!

United States Naval Academy	83% enroll	Brigham Young University	74% enroll
Harvard University	79% enroll	Princeton University	73% enroll
Juilliard School	78% enroll	Kansas State University	73% enroll
United States Merchant Marine Academy	78% enroll	United States Coast Guard Academy	71% enroll
Deep Springs College	76% enroll	Flagler College	71% enroll
Berea College	75% enroll	Stanford University	70% enroll

Merit-Based Financial Aid

Admit it: You dream of someone handing you a big scholarship or award, not because you need it but because you deserve it. Your dream could come true! Here are some schools that give non-need-based scholarship or grant aid to a large percentage of their students:

	% FT Undergrads Receiving Merit-Based Aid	Avg Award Per Student
Denison University	51%	$10,732.00
Birmingham-Southern College	48%	$10,425.00
New College of Florida	46%	$3,247.00
DePauw University	45%	$12,134.00
Kalamazoo College	44%	$9,500.00
University of South Carolina Columbia	43%	$4,037.00
University of Florida	43%	$3,622.00
Clemson University	43%	$6,495.00
Hendrix College	42%	$12,567.00
Hampden-Sydney College	42%	$14,307.00
Berry College	41%	$11,228.00
Flagler College	40%	$4,262.00
Illinois Institute of Technology	40%	$10,106.00

Laptops Included

Do many schools with 25,000 undergrads just hand out valuable computer equipment to each student, free of charge? No. But here are some schools that provide each student with a laptop or desktop computer:

Berea College	University of California-Davis
Drew University	Ursinus College
Rhode Island School of Design	Villanova University
United States Coast Guard Academy	Wake Forest University
United States Naval Academy	

Rush Out to Rush: Joining Fraternities & Sororities

Whether it's for the social opportunities or future career connections, going Greek is the thing to do at these colleges:

	% of men join frats		% of women join sororities
Washington and Lee University	75%	Washington and Lee University	70%
DePauw University	74%	DePauw University	70%
Wabash College	62%	Wofford College	64%
Birmingham-Southern College	57%	Centre College	60%
Wofford College	54%	Rhodes College	58%
Millsaps College	55%	Rose-Hulman Institute of Technology	58%
Ripon College	55%	Birmingham-Southern College	56%
Rhodes College	51%	Millsaps College	56%

The Road to Success: Grad School

If you're thinking of going to grad school for professional training after college, here are some colleges where you will be in good company. A large percentage of students at these colleges go to graduate or professional school within a year of graduating:

American University	73% within a year	Oberlin College	50% within a year
Trinity College	68% within a year	Xavier University of Louisiana	49% within a year
Reed College	65% within a year	Gallaudet University	47% within a year
California Institute of Technology	60% within a year	Harvey Mudd College	47% within a year
Illinois Institute of Technology	55% within a year	St. Mary's College of Maryland	46% within a year
Northern Arizona University	51% within a year	Bard College	45% within a year
Kettering University	50% within a year	Howard University	45% within a year

Out the Door in Four Years: Impressive Graduation Rates

Yes, it can be done! The vast majority of students at these schools manage to graduate in four years (or less):

Deep Springs College	100% in four years	Duke University	87% in four years
United States Air Force Academy	97% in four years	College of the Holy Cross	87% in four years
Williams College	92% in four years	Wellesley College	86% in four years
Princeton University	91% in four years	Pomona College	86% in four years
Georgetown University	90% in four years	United States Naval Academy	86% in four years
Amherst College	89% in four years	Dartmouth College	86% in four years
Haverford College	89% in four years	Washington and Lee University	85% in four years
Davidson College	88% in four years	Cornell University	85% in four years
Yale University	88% in four years	Carleton College	85% in four years
Brown University	88% in four years		

Outside the Box: Innovative Schools

In high school, it's not hip to be square. But at these colleges, anything goes! These schools are good options for students seeking a more innovative and unconventional academic environment:

Hampshire College	MA	Bard College	NY
Brown University	RI	Virginia Polytechnic Institute and State University	VA
Antioch College	OH	University of Texas—Austin	TX
University of California—Santa Cruz	CA	University of California—Berkeley	CA
Evergreen State College	WA	Washington University in St. Louis	MO
New College of Florida	FL	Saint John's College	NM
Oberlin College	OH	Northwestern University	IL
Colorado College	CO	Reed College	OR
New York University	NY	Boston University	MA
Cornell College	IA	Deep Springs College	NV
Duke University	NC		

"Curious George" Schools: Multiple Majors

If your intellectual curiosity is so great that you can't imagine limiting yourself to only one major, check out these schools, where a large number of students pursue more than one major:

Hastings College	53% more than 1 major	Muhlenberg College	28% more than 1 major
Claremont McKenna College	52% more than 1 major	Centre College	28% more than 1 major
Cornell College	49% more than 1 major	Columbia University-Columbia College	27% more than 1 major
Lake Forest College	42% more than 1 major	Syracuse University	27% more than 1 major
St. Olaf College	33% more than 1 major	Austin College	26% more than 1 major
Amherst College	32% more than 1 major	Georgetown University	26% more than 1 major
Wellesely College	32% more than 1 major	University of Pennsylvania	26% more than 1 major
Macalester College	31% more than 1 major	Bowdoin College	25% more than 1 major
Ripon College	31% more than 1 major	Trinity University	25% more than 1 major
Middlebury College	28% more than 1 major	Valparaiso University	25% more than 1 major

Close Contact with Faculty: Student/Faculty Ratio

Why take the chance of getting into trouble at a bar when you could be having a nice dinner at your prof's house? Students at these schools may be able to develop close relationships with their professors, thanks to their cozy student/faculty ratios:

Deep Springs College	2:1	University of Pennsylvania	6:1
California Institute of Technology	3:1	Columbia University-Columbia College	7:1
Juilliard School	4:1	Gallaudet University	7:1
University of Chicago	4:1	Northwestern University	7:1
Princeton University	5:1	Stanford University	7:1
Rice University	5:1	Sweet Briar College	7:1
Emory University	6:1	United States Naval Academy	7:1
Massachusetts Institute of Technology	6:1	Washington University in St. Louis	7:1
Sarah Lawrence College	6:1		

Intimidatingly Selective: Acceptance Rates

You could be a valedictorian, a sports star, a third-generation legacy… but you'll still have to fight tooth and nail to get accepted into these schools, which admit only a tiny percentage of their applicants:

Juilliard School	7% of applicants admitted	College of the Ozarks	14% of applicants admitted
United States Coast Guard Academy	7% of applicants admitted	United States Military Academy	14% of applicants admitted
Princeton University	10% of applicants admitted	United States Air Force Academy	15% of applicants admitted
United States Naval Academy	10% of applicants admitted	Massachusetts Institute of Technology	16% of applicants admitted
Harvard University	11% of applicants admitted	Brown University	17% of applicants admitted
Columbia University	11% of applicants admitted	California Institute of Technology	17% of applicants admitted
Deep Springs College	11% of applicants admitted	Amherst College	18% of applicants admitted
Yale University	11% of applicants admitted	Dartmouth College	18% of applicants admitted
Stanford University	13% of applicants admitted		
Cooper Union	13% of applicants admitted		

Prepped for Success: Job Offers

A high percentage of students at these schools had already accepted a job offer at the time they graduated:

United States Air Force Academy	100% accepted job offer	Carnegie Mellon University	82% accepted job offer
United States Naval Academy	99% accepted job offer	SUNY Binghamton University	82% accepted job offer
United States Military Academy	98% accepted job offer	Citadel	75% accepted job offer
Kettering University	90% accepted job offer	Beloit College	74% accepted job offer
College of the Atlantic	89% accepted job offer	Providence College	74% accepted job offer
Lewis and Clark College	88% accepted job offer	CUNY John Jay College of Criminal Justice	72% accepted job offer
Michigan Technological University	88% accepted job offer	University of Houston	72% accepted job offer
Evergreen State College	87% accepted job offer		
Berea College	85% accepted job offer		

I'm Not a College Student, But I Play One on TV

Movies and TV shows find locations for their cameras at various colleges and universities. These schools welcome the spotlight:

University of Texas–Austin   *The Life of David Gale*

Berry College   *Remember the Titans*

UC Berkeley   *The Hulk*

Wellesley College   *Mona Lisa Smile*

Columbia University   *Spiderman*

Princeton University   *A Beautiful Mind*

SUNY University at Buffalo   *MTV's Fraternity Life* and *Sorority Life*

Drew University   *The Sopranos*

University of the Pacific   *Dead Man on Campus*

Carnegie Mellon   *Wonder Boys*

Satisfied Customers: Young Alumni Contributions

Alumni contributions can reflect a couple of things: a certain degree of postgraduate success (after all, the alum can afford to contribute) and a high degree of satisfaction with the undergraduate experience. A large percentage of young alums (who graduated between 1992–2002) at these schools have made financial contributions to their alma mater since graduating:

Claremont McKenna College	95% contribute	Tuskegee University	75% contribute
Scripps College	88% contribute	Colby College	73% contribute
Princeton University	86% contribute	Rhodes College	73% contribute
Washington and Lee University	83% contribute	Kenyon College	72% contribute
Ripon College	82% contribute	Rose-Hulman Institute of Technology	72% contribute
Knox College	81% contribute	Stanford University	71% contribute
Trinity College	78% contribute	Hobart and William Smith Colleges	70% contribute
Wabash College	78% contribute	Hollins University	70% contribute
Wofford College	78% contribute		

Deep in Debt: Average Loan Debt Per Student

You'd better be sure that the school you choose is worth every single penny, or you'll regret it when it's time to start paying back your loans. The average loan debt carried by undergrads at these schools is a bit intimidating:

Embry-Riddle Aeronautical University	$36,022	University of Puget Sound	$23,782
Kettering University	$33,605	Allegheny College	$23,735
Pepperdine University	$31,179	Rensselaer Polytechnic Institute	$23,725
Villanova University	$30,178	Case Western Reserve University	$23,534
University of Miami	$29,046	Vanderbilt University	$23,334
Rose-Hulman Institute of Technology	$27,000	University of Vermont	$23,167
George Washington University	$25,943	Wagner College	$23,144
Santa Clara University	$25,492	University of Denver	$23,138
Parsons School of Design	$25,226	St. Lawrence University	$23,091
Fairfield University	$25,194	Hampton University	$23,000
New York University	$24,620	Marquette University	$22,924
Wake Forest University	$24,549		

Great College Towns

You won't be going to college in a bubble! Location is one of the most important factors in choosing a college. Here are some of our favorite college towns, where you'll never run out of interesting people to meet and interesting things to do:

Austin, TX	Athens, GA
Washington, DC	Charlottesville, VA
Madison, WI	San Diego, CA
Ann Arbor, MI	Chapel Hill, NC
Portland, OR	New York, NY
Berkeley, CA	Boston-Cambridge, MA

Outdoor Activities

If you just can't get enough of the great outdoors, keep that fact in mind when you're choosing a college. Here are some colleges where you'll find lots of opportunities to join in many kinds of outdoor activities, whether on a beach or on a mountain top.

Sun-Worshippers	Snow-Lovers
University of Hawaii—Manoa	Middlebury College
University of Miami	University of Colorado—Boulder
San Diego State University	University of Utah
Arizona State University	Bates College
Pepperdine University	University of Vermont

Generosity Begins at School: Institutional Aid

The best-case scenario: A generous great-uncle who offers to pay for your full tuition and room and board. The second-best scenario: A college that helps you to fund your own education. These schools give some form of institutional aid to a huge percentage of their students:

Berea College	100% receive institutional aid	Hanover College	86% receive institutional aid
Ursinus College	96% receive institutional aid	Culinary Institute of America	83% receive institutional aid
Fisk University	94% receive institutional aid	Saint Anselm College	82% receive institutional aid
Morehouse College	93% receive institutional aid	Catholic University of America	81% receive institutional aid
Hiram College	92% receive institutional aid		
Chatham College	90% receive institutional aid	Alfred University	80% receive institutional aid
College of the Ozarks	90% receive institutional aid	Xavier University of Louisiana	80% receive institutional aid
Spelman College	90% receive institutional aid		
College of the Atlantic	86% receive institutional aid	Bradley University	80% receive institutional aid

Celebrity Alumni

Ah, the allure of stardom. We can't guarantee you a talk show, but wouldn't it be fun to be able to say that you went to the same college as Jon Stewart? If you want to walk the same hallways that your favorite *People* magazine regulars once did, check out these schools:

Jon Stewart—College of William and Mary

Hillary Rodham Clinton—Wellesley College

Maggie Gyllenhaal—Columbia University

Spike Lee—Morehouse College

Meg Ryan—New York University

Denzel Washington—Fordham University

Natalie Portman—Harvard University

P. Diddy—Howard University

James Gandolfini—Rutgers College

Brooke Shields—Princeton University

Tim Robbins—UCLA

SECTION II:

COLLEGE PROFILES

The information about each school in this college guide follows a basic format. The facts are broken down into sections that give you all the crucial information at a glance.

The Profiles

The profiles are divided into three sections, each covering a different aspect of college life.

Inside the Classroom

Since you are going to college to get an education (presumably), this section contains some of the most important information you'll need in your college search. Read this section to find out what's available to undergrads in terms of majors, undergraduate colleges (as part of a larger university), research opportunities, and internships. You'll also find insights on which programs of study are among the strongest (or weakest). We'll tell you what you can expect as a new student regarding the workload, the level of intensity and competitiveness, class size and faculty accessibility, and core requirements.

Campus Environment

If you're spending four (or more) years at a school, you'd better be comfortable with your surroundings. This section discusses the physical layout of the campus and the surrounding areas off campus. We'll tell you what the school's campus housing policies are and give you insights about the availability and quality of both on-campus and off-campus housing. We'll also discuss the transportation options available to students in general and freshmen in particular (since many colleges prohibit freshmen from having cars on campus).

Student Life

The key to finding the right college often lies in matching your personality, interests, and lifestyle to those of the college's student body. Read this section to determine how you'll "fit in." Besides a description of the student body, you'll find information on popular and unpopular student clubs and organizations, including athletics and Greek organizations. We'll also discuss the overall social scene, such as the amount of partying that goes on both on and off campus. School traditions and major events are covered in this section as well.

The Experts Say ...

To get our own, admittedly biased impressions of these colleges, check out the "Experts" box on the right-hand page of each profile. Among other things, we may describe a school's pros or cons, the type of student who should apply to a certain school and the type who shouldn't, and alternative schools a student should investigate.

The Data

If statistical data is what you're looking for, you'll find plenty of facts in the sidebar columns of each school profile. Colleges vary in how thoroughly they report data, so some schools may list more information than others do. Here's the overview:

General Info

Type of School: Here you'll find out whether the school is coed or single sex, public or private, and whether or not it is affiliated with any religious organization.

Setting: Under this heading, you'll find information on the campus surroundings—urban, suburban, small town, or rural. Keep in mind, though, that a campus may have quite a different feel to it than the area that immediately surrounds it.

Academic Calendar: A **semester** schedule is divided into two terms, fall and spring. A **trimester** schedule is divided into three terms, generally one before winter break and two after. A **quarterly** schedule has four terms, including one quarter usually offered during the summer. A **4-1-4** calendar consists of semesters divided by a month-long special term. Some schools also have specialized calendars.

Student Body

These figures are meant to reflect enrollment for fall 2003. (However, in some cases, where more recent numbers were unavailable, schools provided 2002 data.)

Undergraduate Enrollment (Full-Time and Part-Time): One of the most important decisions you face is whether you want to attend a large or a small school. This category tells you how many full-time and part-time degree-seeking undergraduate students are at the school, including information about the male-female breakdown. Adding the number of full-time and part-time students will give you the total number of degree-seeking undergraduate students.

Total Undergraduate Population: This section breaks down important information about the student body, including ethnicity, international status, how many students are from out of state, how many live off campus, how many are involved in Greek life, and how many graduate and first-professional students are on campus.

> *African American, Asian American, Latino, Native American, Caucasian:* The figures in these categories tell you the percentage of the school's total (full-time and part-time) U.S. resident degree-seeking undergrad population from these ethnic backgrounds. The Asian American category also includes Pacific Islanders. (Remember, however, that many students do not report ethnicity.)
>
> *International:* This refers to the number of undergraduate students who reside outside the United States but have come to the school to study. This figure is also reported as a percentage of the school's total degree-seeking undergraduate population.

Out-of-State Residents: Some schools draw students from across the nation; at other schools the bulk of the students come from the local area. This category tells you the percentage of degree-seeking undergraduate students who are from a different state than the one the college is in.

Living Off Campus: This is the percentage of degree-seeking undergraduates who live off campus and not in campus residence halls. Keep in mind that even if the percentage looks large, many schools require that freshmen (and sometimes even sophomores) live on campus.

In Fraternities/Sororities: The percentage of undergraduate men who join a fraternity and the percentage of undergraduate women who join a sorority are reported here.

Graduate and First Professional Students: This figure will give you an indication of whether the school focuses primarily on undergraduate studies or offers substantial graduate and/or first professional degree programs.

Academics

Note: We asked for data to reflect the specific years indicated below. However, in some cases, where more recent numbers were unavailable, schools provided data for the most recent year available (generally one year prior to the year indicated).

Faculty: Under this heading you'll find figures on the number of full- and part-time instructional faculty for fall 2003. We also provide the percentages of full-time and part-time faculty members who have Ph.D.s, first professional, or other terminal degrees.

Student/Faculty Ratio: Here you can see the ratio of the number of full-time equivalent students to the number of full-time equivalent instructional faculty. Faculty and students in stand-alone graduate or professional programs are excluded, as are student teaching assistants. This is also for fall 2003.

Most Popular Majors (% Student Body in Major): We've listed the schools' top majors and the percentage of the undergraduate student body in those majors. This is generally for the 2002–03 school year. We've also included the percent of students graduating in spring 2003 who completed two or more majors.

Freshmen Retention Rate: This figure indicates the percentage of freshmen who had entered in 2002 that returned for their sophomore year in fall 2003. This can be very useful in comparing overall freshman satisfaction at different schools.

Graduation Rates: How many full-time degree-seeking students from the freshman class of 1997 graduated within four years? Within six years? These numbers will give you an idea of how many students complete the requirements for a degree and how long it takes them.

Computers: Here you'll see which schools require individual students to have their own laptop or computer, as well as which schools provide students with their own laptop or computer.

Admissions

Note: Deadlines change from year to year and may vary for different programs within a school. While this book provides general guidelines and endeavors to provide the most up-to-date information, you must check with the individual school to ensure that you are applying on time.

Regular Application Deadline: This is the date by which you must submit all your application materials in order to be eligible for fall admission. Be aware that many schools have earlier deadlines for application to special programs or for particular groups of students such as international students.

Early Decision/Early Action Deadline: Some schools offer Early Decision programs in which applicants are notified of their acceptance earlier than regular applicants. Early Decision generally comes with the stipulation that students withdraw all other college applications if accepted, or that the student apply only to the institution in question. The deadline for such applications tends to be earlier than the regular application deadline provided above. Some schools offer an Early Action option, which is a nonbinding version of Early Decision. We've provided the application deadlines for both when applicable.

Transfer Application Deadlines: If you're transferring in from another college for the fall or spring semester, you'll need to know the relevant application deadline(s).

Total Number Applied/Admitted/Enrolled: Here you can see the number of first-time students who applied, the number who were admitted by the school, and the number who actually chose to enroll. (Keep in mind, however, that many high quality schools have a more self-selecting pool of applicants; that is, fewer people believe they have a chance of admission, so fewer people apply to them. Thus, their seemingly high acceptance rates may be deceptive.) These numbers will be for freshmen entering in fall 2003 (or the most recent year available).

Waitlisted Students: Waitlisted students have met admission requirements, but are only offered a place in the entering class if space becomes available. You can see how many were offered a place on the list, how many accepted it, and how many eventually were admitted for fall 2003 (or the most recent year available).

Applied/Admitted Early Decision: You can find out how many applicants applied for Early Decision for fall 2003 (or the most recent year available) and how many were actually accepted.

Test Scores: The SAT Verbal, SAT Math, and/or ACT composite and individual test scores listed here will give you an indication of your chances of admission by allowing you to compare your test scores to those of the school's most recent freshman class. Using both of these scores, you can tell whether your test scores fall within, above, or below the test score spread for the middle 50 percent of freshmen at the school. (But remember: 25 percent scored above this range, and 25 percent scored below.) These scores are for the fall 2003 entering class (or the most recent year available).

H.S. Rank of Entering Freshmen: This listing provides the percentages of enrolled freshmen for the fall 2003 entering class (or the most recent year available) who ranked in the top 10, 25, and 50 percent of their high school class.

Average GPA of Freshmen Enrolled: Here is the average high school grade point average of those providing class rank information for the entering freshman class for 2003 (or the most recent year available). Since the meaning and measure of GPA differ so much from school to school, you should use this information with caution, as it may not be very reliable in predicting your admissions chances.

Costs

Tuition & Fees: In most cases, we've provided tuition costs for a year of undergraduate study. Tuition figures are the most recent available at the time of data collection; you will see the year indicated (*est.* means *estimated*). Public colleges and universities generally charge less for in-state students; we have listed both in-state and out-of-state tuitions, and have also indicated schools that offer a regional or "good neighbor" tuition. Private institutions usually do not differentiate between state residents and nonresidents. Required fees that all students must pay are included in the tuition figures provided. Usually they include activity, health, and registration fees, among others. Expenses like books and optional fees like parking costs are not included. Some schools may have special work-study programs, or full scholarship programs, that alleviate or eliminate the burden of paying for tuition. Other special situations may also be indicated.

Total Annual Expenses: Comprehensive fees are provided where a breakdown of tuition & fees and room & board is not available.

Room & Board: Here we provide estimated average costs for on-campus room and board for undergraduate students sharing a room with another student over a one-year period.

Tuition, Room & Board Paid by U.S. Government: This is seen with United States military schools. Usually the student pays a one-time fee, but their major expenses are paid by the government.

Payment Plan(s): Some schools have indicated if they have special payment plans: installment, deferred, and prepayment.

Institutional Aid

These numbers reflect data for 2002–3 or estimated for 2003–4, as indicated. Special cases may also be indicated.

Institutional Aid, Need-Based: This is the total dollar amount of need-based institutional aid (and external funds awarded by the college) available (including non-need-based aid used to meet need). It does not include athletic awards and tuition waivers. These funds include endowment, alumni and other funds.

Institutional Aid, Non-Need-Based: This is the total dollar amount of non-need-based institutional aid (and external funds awarded by the college) available (excluding non-need-based aid used to meet need). It does not include athletic awards and tuition waivers. These funds include endowment, alumni and other funds.

Full-Time Undergrads Receiving Aid, and Average Amount per Student: This is the percent of full-time degree-seeking undergraduates who receive any financial aid, and the average financial aid package per student.

Full-Time Undergrads Receiving Non-Need-Based Scholarship or Grant Aid, and Average Amount per Student: This is the percent of full-time degree-seeking undergraduates who did not have financial need and who received gift aid that was non-need-based, and the average amount of such aid awarded to those students.

Receiving Need-Based Scholarship or Grant Aid, and Average Award: This is the percent of those students receiving any aid (see above) who received gift aid based on financial need, and the average gift award.

Receiving Need-Based Self-Help Aid, and Average Award: This is the percent of those students receiving any aid (see above) who received self-help aid based on financial need, and the average award. Keep in mind that self-help includes loans, which must be repaid, as well as jobs, which involve time commitment.

Average Loan Debt per Student: This is the average amount graduating students owe in loan debt (not including what you may owe your parents!). This number is usually for the 2003 graduating class, but in some cases may be from the class of 2002.

Financial Aid Deadline: This is the date by which you must submit your financial aid application, including priority dates for aid consideration where available. (Deadlines may vary for different programs within a school, and change from year to year. While this book provides general guidelines, and endeavors to provide the most up-to-date information, you must check with the individual school to ensure that you are applying on time.)

Graduates

Continued to Grad School: This indicates what percentage of students who graduated in 2002 chose to pursue a higher degree within one year of graduation.

Accepting Job Offer at Time of Graduation: One factor that you should be taking into account while making your college decision is how easy or difficult it will be for you to land a job after graduation. This percentage will help you to ascertain how strong the school's career placement program is and how highly its graduates are regarded in the working world. However, many students do not stay in contact with college placement offices, so the numbers reported may not be completely accurate. These numbers reflect students graduating in 2002, (or the most recent year available).

Companies Recruiting on Campus: Here you'll get the number of companies and organizations that came on-campus to actively recruit students for job positions in the 2002–2003 school year.

Alumni Giving: This is the percent of young alumni (those who graduated between 1992 and 2002) who have made any voluntary financial contribution to the school since graduation.

Note: The data for schools that did not respond to our survey this year will usually be from a year or two earlier than the data for those schools that did respond to our survey. We have indicated which schools did not respond to our survey this year by including a notation at the top of a school's data column ("Note: Info. not verified by school").

For many college guides sold in bookstores, colleges have paid fees that affect how the school is covered in the book. Kaplan does not solicit or accept fees of any kind for its coverage of the schools profiled in this book.

AGNES SCOTT COLLEGE

141 East College Avenue, Decatur, GA 30030
Admissions Phone: (404) 471-6285; (800) 868-8602 Fax: (404) 471-6414
Email: admission@agnesscott.edu   Website: www.agnesscott.edu
Application Website: www.agnesscott.edu/onlineapplication/login.asp

General Info

Type of School: private, all women, Presbyterian USA

Setting: urban

Academic Calendar: semester

Student Body

Full-Time Undergrads: 824
  Women: 100%

Part-Time Undergrads: 21
  Women: 100%

Total Undergrad Population:
  African American: 20%
  Asian American: 5%
  Latino: 4%
  Caucasian: 57%
  International: 7%
  Out-of-State: 42%
  Living Off-Campus: 18%

Graduate and First-Professional Students: 25

Academics

Full-Time Faculty: 77
  With Ph.D.: 96%

Part-Time Faculty: 34
  With Ph.D.: 56%

Student/Faculty Ratio: 10:1

Most Popular Majors:
  psychology (15%)
  economics and business (12%)
  history (7%)
  international relations (6%)
  biology (6%)

Completing 2 or More Majors: 16%

Freshmen Retention Rate: 84%

Graduation Rates:
  58% within four years
  63% within six years

Admissions

Regular Application Deadline: 3/1
  (Priority)

Early Decision Deadline(s): 11/15

Transfer Admission Deadline: rolling

Total # of Students Applied: 782
  Admitted: 514
  Enrolled: 213

# of Students Waitlisted: 34
  Students Accepting Place: 18
  Waitlisted Students Admitted: 3

Inside the Classroom

Agnes Scott College provides a strong liberal arts education for women, with emphasis on "research, independent experiences, and international education." As you might expect from a small school, course offerings are somewhat limited—students choose from among 30 majors, but also have the opportunity to design their own courses of study. Over the years, Agnes Scott has established a reputation for its strong writing and English literature program. The college also boasts an increasingly impressive science program.

One of the great advantages of Agnes Scott is its small class size. The student/faculty ratio is a mere 10:1, and classes average 15 students. This means that students get to know faculty members very well. A guidance counselor from Tennessee showers praise on Agnes Scott's "dynamic faculty with strong commitment to excellence in teaching and global perspectives." A philosophy major tells us that "professors are very accessible," and that they keep "satisfactory office hours." Most professors live close to campus and are involved with the college community. According to one woman, "The faculty are truly interested in your skills and progress."

Students are serious but not terribly competitive. An alum tells us, "Everyone is really there to learn, and the small class size is fabulous." Students work relatively hard, and seem happy doing so. One junior notes that "the workload varies from major to major," with heavier workloads for science, Spanish, and English majors.

Students can cross-register with nearly 20 other colleges in the Atlanta area, thereby considerably broadening their options for study. Students can enroll in a dual-degree program in engineering with Georgia Institute of Technology and a dual-degree program in architecture with Washington University in St. Louis. Through a program called the Atlanta Semester, students can engage in internships and research in Atlanta organizations and gain a full semester's credit upon completion. Global learning and international experiences are key at Agnes Scott; recently, nearly half of students have studied abroad through the faculty-led Global Awareness Program, Global Connections, and independent experiences. There are over 100 international study programs in which students can participate.

Campus Environment

Agnes Scott is well endowed financially, which means that students can get some great financial aid packages. The deal is especially sweet for Georgia residents, through the HOPE Scholarship program. And thanks to the endowment, the quality of life at Agnes Scott is better than you'll find at most colleges, with great dorms, good food, and plentiful parking. You've probably already seen Agnes Scott without realizing it: The movie *Scream 2* was filmed on campus. In general, the administration is well respected and works hard to make life comfortable for students. A new $36.5 million Science Center recently opened. (One very odd feature: a large double helix that rises three stories on the atrium's east wall, representing the actual DNA sequence of Agnes Scott, the woman for whom the college was named. The sequence was derived from a direct female descendent of Agnes Scott.) A school official describes other recent campus renovations: "New tennis courts have recently opened… The new Delafield Planetarium has a computer-controlled Zeiss projector, one of only nine in the United States, as well as its 30-inch Beck telescope, one of the largest in the Southeast. A new Alston Campus Center, which includes meeting rooms, a 24-hour-access Cyber Café, and a computer lab, opened during 2000–01 academic year. Another recent renovation involves the completely renovated McCain Library, which has doubled in size, and has access to the Internet available at every seat."

Seven dorms and three "theme houses" provide housing for Agnes Scott's students, almost all of whom live on campus, where housing is guaranteed for all students. Two dorms are reserved for first-year students. Students give high marks to the dorms, many of which have hardwood floors, huge windows, antique-filled lobbies, and relaxing porch swings. One junior tells us that "Agnes Scott has some of the nicest and most comfortable housing available," with "quite a variety of room types ranging from traditional dorm rooms, to loft rooms, tower rooms, and apartments." Another student raves, "All the dorms far surpass national campus standards." Housing is allotted by a lottery system that is "very democratic," and allows students to choose not just dorms but individual rooms. A new campus center houses many activities as well as a snack bar, bookstore, and post office. The recently renovated dining hall is "beautiful" with "huge vaulted ceilings" and a great variety of tasty offerings. Says one recent grad, "The food is good and the atmosphere is special."

Then there's Atlanta, a great college town only six miles away. Notes one student, "Many women's colleges are in very small towns. Agnes Scott has a great location. It's so nice to have the city of Atlanta available." Students—even first-years—can have cars on campus, and parking passes are included in general student fees. We hear that parking is convenient and plentiful.

Student Life

"Scotties" are "all very friendly," we hear, and since the college is so small "every face becomes a familiar one and you are often greeted by a smile from one of your peers." The student body is quite diverse, with women from many cultures and countries represented. Minority groups constitute approximately one-third of the student population. About half of the students are from Georgia, and a significant number come from neighboring Florida.

Despite the small student body, Agnes Scott students participate in about 70 campus organizations, including seven intercollegiate sports, nine intramural sports, and several cultural organizations and political groups. Service organizations are popular, including Habitat for Humanity and several programs that partner students with people with mental and developmental disabilities.

For better or worse, the social life on campus is rather quiet—"rowdiness is almost unheard of on campus," reports a student. There are no sororities. Drinking is not much of a problem on campus, students say, and "it is rare to hear of any drinking incidents." Notes one woman, the college is "not for those who wish to major in beer bashes." Agnes Scott students often mix with students from other area colleges and universities; says one woman, "You get the benefits of a small college while still being able to take advantage of the opportunities offered at larger universities."

Other schools to check out: Hollins, Randolph-Macon Woman's, Sweet Briar, Chatham, Spelman.

Applied Early Decision: 37
Early Decision Admitted: 34

Test Scores (middle 50%):
SAT Verbal: 550–690
SAT Math: 530–630
ACT Comp: 24–30

HS Rank of Entering Freshmen:
Top 10%: 47%
Top 25%: 79%
Top 50%: 97%

Avg. HS GPA: 3.64

THE EXPERTS SAY...

" Hopefully, as more people recognize what this college has to offer (such as an appreciation of diverse cultures and a commitment to justice), Agnes Scott's name recognition outside the region will improve. "

" The best of all worlds: a small, supportive, diverse community of women, plus all the museums, theater, shopping, and other advantages of Atlanta. "

Costs (2004–5)

Tuition and Fees: $22,050

Room & Board: $8,200

Payment Plan(s): installment plan

Inst. Aid (est. 2003–04)

Institutional Aid, Need-Based: $7,108,479

Institutional Aid, Non-Need-Based: $2,758,239

FT Undergrads Receiving Aid: 64%
Avg. Amount per Student: $21,264

FT Undergrads Receiving Non-Need-Based Scholarship or Grant Aid: 26%
Avg. Amount per Student: $10,451

Of Those Receiving Any Aid:

Rec. Need-Based Scholarship or Grant Aid: 100%
Average Award: $15,043

Rec. Need-Based Self-Help Aid: 85%
Average Award: $5,461

Upon Graduation, Avg. Loan Debt per Student: $20,321

Financial Aid Deadline: 5/1, 2/15 (priority)

Graduates

Going to Graduate School: 22% Within One Year

Companies Recruiting On Campus: 21

Alumni Giving: 48%

ALBERTSON COLLEGE OF IDAHO

2112 Cleveland Boulevard, Caldwell, ID 83605-4432
Admissions Phone: (800) 224-3246; (208) 459-5305 Fax: (208) 459-5757
Email: admission@albertson.edu
Website: www.albertson.edu

General Info

Type of School: private, coed, Presbyterian

Setting: suburban

Academic Calendar: 13–6–13

Student Body

Full-Time Undergrads: 786
Men: 46%, Women: 54%

Part-Time Undergrads: 17
Men: 41%, Women: 59%

Total Undergrad Population:
African American: <1%
Asian American: 3%
Latino: 3%
Native American: 1%
Caucasian 79%
International: 1%
Out-of-State: 26%
Living Off-Campus: 48%
In Fraternities: 20%
In Sororities: 15%

Graduate and First-Professional Students: 9

Academics

Full-Time Faculty: 57
With Ph.D.: 91%

Part-Time Faculty: 12
With Ph.D.: 75%

Student/Faculty Ratio: 13:1

Most Popular Majors:
biology (15%)
business (14%)
education (11%)
psychology (9%)
politics and economics (7%)

Freshmen Retention Rate: 77%

Admissions

Regular Application Deadline: 6/1; 2/15 (priority)

Early Action Deadline: 11/15

Fall Transfer Deadline: 8/1, 2/15 (priority)

Spring Transfer Deadline: 1/15, 12/15 (priority)

Total # of Students Applied: 777
Admitted: 610
Enrolled: 197

Inside the Classroom

Albertson College is a tiny gem of a school where students are the number one priority: Defying the national trend of steadily escalating tuition costs, Albertson announced a plan in December 2002 to reduce its tuition by 30 percent in order to help bridge the gap between deserving students' desire for a quality liberal arts education and their ability to pay. And this is in spite of the fact that the school is battling a serious budget crisis. "Our school is missing money and is trying to cut costs to make up this deficit," explains a sophomore history/secondary ed major. "They are doing this with as little effect to students as possible, but of course with this being such a small school, we all feel the effects of any cost to staff and faculty."

Albertson offers B.A. and B.S. degrees in 25 majors. According to the college website, nearly 80 percent of Albertson prelaw and premed students who applied to professional schools in recent years were accepted. The school admits, "Many of our students didn't get straight A's in high school. Yet Albertson College has a long history of transforming students of all levels into extraordinary performers."

Students here simply rave about the quality and accessibility of their professors. "Many of your professors also become your friends," says a sophomore biology major. "I thought that only happened in the movies, but one of my professors invited me over to dinner and I am treated as an equal."

"The workload is fairly intensive," admits a junior studying business marketing and theater. Besides taking courses in their major and elective courses, students must fulfill the general graduation requirements, which fall into three categories: Foundations of Knowing (writing, math, and culture and civilization), Disciplines of Knowing (nature, society, and physical education), and Meaning and Values (literature, philosophy, and religion).

Albertson may be tiny, but it has more than its share of outstanding special programs. Students who are accepted into the Gipson Honors Program develop individual program contracts and work within the spirit of the college's liberal arts objective without having to meet general graduation requirements. Albertson's extensive study abroad options allow students to study in more than 70 countries around the world, in practically any discipline; all students are strongly encouraged to study overseas for an academic year, semester, or summer.

In 2001, Albertson started a program that places new laptop computers into the hands of students every two years so that students can access the college's wireless LAN from anywhere on campus. A portion of the laptop's cost is factored into tuition, and students have an opportunity to buy the machines at reduced rates once the school year starts.

Campus Environment

Albertson has five coed residence halls and one female-only residence hall. The Village, a newly-built residence hall community that merges dormitory and apartment living, opened in fall 2002. All freshmen and sophomores are required to live on campus (unless they live in the immediate area with their family), and there

KAPLAN

is no freshmen-only housing. "In the case of overcrowding, rooms that are currently double or single capacity become triple or double capacity," explains a school official.

Caldwell is a city of more than 25,000 people located about 30 minutes from Boise. A sophomore admits, "The location is one of the only complaints I have of the school. Caldwell is not pretty, nor does it offer a ton to do." (Another sophomore complains about "the smell of the sugar beet factory from the next town over.") However, the campus is located within an hour of some of the best skiing, mountain biking, hiking, fishing, and whitewater in the West. Students tell us that having a car is convenient but not necessary: there's a grocery store right across from campus, and Dairy Queen, Taco Bell, McDonald's, and Subway are all within walking distance.

Student Life

A senior reflects on the social scene at Albertson: "Students go to films, go to events in Boise, or ski. There are always social events going on like parties, campus programs, comedians, etc. People are really physically conscious here, also—everyone works out." When asked about alcohol, he replies, "Drinking is not a big factor, but it is something that is enjoyed by a majority of students." A sophomore adds, "During the week, a lot of students hang out watching movies in each other's rooms, and some go clubbing Wednesday night because that is the all-age night."

Among the most popular campus organizations are ALAS (Albertson Latino Americano Students), Circle K International, Equestrian Club, Scarlet Masque (student theater group), and HOSA (Health Occupation Students of America). The sororities and fraternities are also very active; a sophomore biology major muses, "I think they are so popular because they have a large range of activities that they participate in, from hosting Toga to raising money for kids suffering from cancer." Approximately one-third of the student body competes in the five men's and seven women's NAIA intercollegiate sports. "Athletic events are sacred here," claims a senior English major. "Soccer and basketball are the fan favorites."

"The Albertson College community embodies the values of the American West—independent, resourceful, hard working, diverse, progressive, and adventuresome," says a school official. Of course, given Albertson's size and location, the campus lacks real diversity. A freshman acknowledges, "The average student is a middle- to upper-class, white Idahoan. Students as a group are pretty conservative and, if pressed, would have to admit to being Republican or Independent, which is due to living in Idaho more than anything else." But students love the fact that their campus is extremely close-knit. A sophomore tells us, "The people on campus are very friendly. That was part of the reason I came here. You can walk from class to class and almost be late because people just want to talk to you!"

In terms of style, says a freshman, "most people take themselves pretty seriously: personal grooming is prevalent, clothes without holes dominate, and if there was an average dress I'd have to say 'preppy' more than anything else. Not that the guys are wearing sweater vests, though!" But fashion takes a backseat to frolicking fun during the annual "Finney Fun Run": Every winter, on the night of the first significant snowfall, students don their summer clothes and run in a group between residence halls, beginning at Finney Hall.

Other schools to check out: University of Puget Sound, Whitman, Willamette, Gonzaga, Pacific Lutheran.

THE EXPERTS SAY...

" You'll never feel anonymous in Albertson's close-knit community of high achievers. "

" Kudos to Albertson for putting students first and actually *reducing* the cost of tuition. "

ALBION COLLEGE

611 East Porter Street, Albion, MI 49224
Admissions Phone: (517) 629-0321; (800) 858-6770 Fax: (517) 629-0569
Email: admissions@albion.edu Website: www.albion.edu
Application Website: www.albion.edu/admissions/apply

General Info

Type of School: private, coed, Methodist
Setting: small town
Academic Calendar: semester

Student Body

Full-Time Undergrads: 1,706
    Men: 44%, Women: 56%

Part-Time Undergrads: 26
    Men: 31%, Women: 69%

Total Undergrad Population:
    African American: 2%
    Asian American: 2%
    Latino: 1%
    Native American: <1%
    Caucasian 87%
    International: 1%
    Out-of-State: 9%
    Living Off-Campus: 4%
    In Fraternities: 40%
    In Sororities: 40%

Academics

Full-Time Faculty: 123
    With Ph.D.: 93%

Part-Time Faculty: 34
    With Ph.D.: 44%

Student/Faculty Ratio: 13:1

Most Popular Majors:
    economics/management (14%)
    psychology (12%)
    English (10%)
    biology (9%)
    history (6%)

Completing 2 or More Majors: 22%

Freshmen Retention Rate: 86%

Graduation Rates:
    64% within four years
    68% within six years

Admissions

Regular Application Deadline: 7/1

Early Action Deadline: 12/15

Fall Transfer Deadline: 8/1,
    5/1 (priority)

Spring Transfer Deadline: 12/15,
    12/1 (priority)

Total # of Students Applied: 1,534
    Admitted: 1,332
    Enrolled: 487

Inside the Classroom

Founded in 1835, Albion College offers B.A. and B.F.A. degrees in 27 distinct majors, plus numerous special programs. "Liberal arts at work" is the catch phrase for Albion's brand of education. Albion's core curriculum includes requirements in environmental, ethnic, gender, and global studies. A first-year seminar uses small class sizes and personalized instruction to nurture academic skills, creativity, and inquiry methods. Students can select from a variety of seminar topics, and participate in out-of-class experiences that supplement the formal discussion. At the end of each student's studies is a "capstone experience," taking the form of a research paper, dramatic presentation, musical piece, or other format that applies what was learned during the student's years at Albion.

The latest improvements to Albion academics are the Centers for Interdisciplinary Study, a series of separately endowed programs that create opportunities for students and faculty to collaborate on special projects and mentoring experiences and develop new learning experiences inside and outside the classroom. The four centers established to date also enrich Albion's curriculum with interdisciplinary subjects like contemporary expression in the arts; ethnic, gender, and global issues; history and culture; and meaning and value.

Students wanting coursework in a preprofessional field or specialty area can enroll in one of Albion's four institutes for environmental studies, public policy and service, professional management, and honors. Institute studies involve a specific curriculum of courses and can include internships, a capstone experience, a research project, or independent study.

A history major states, "I really find the academic environment here has fostered a deeper understanding of the subject. The great thing is how accessible the professors are, and how well run and interactive the classes are." On the downside, says a recent graduate, "majors do not get priority of their own classes. As a Speech Communication major, I was often unable to get the classes I needed during registration."

Campus Environment

Albion's pretty campus is located on the east branch of the Kalamazoo River in the town of Albion, a community of 10,000. Students and "townies" don't interact much, we hear. The original campus, which was once limited to the buildings around the central Quadrangle, has expanded to include over 30 buildings. A scenic annex to the campus is the Whitehouse Nature Center, a 135-acre preserve with nature trails that are used for both pleasant strolls and out-of-class science instruction. The hub of campus activity is the five-story Kellogg Center, which houses the Eat Shop (a grill and snack bar), all campus mailboxes, study spaces, and areas where concerts, speakers, parties, dances, tournaments, and other student activities are staged.

Dormitories for undergrads include Wesley, Seaton, Twin Towers, and Whitehouse Halls. On the ground floor of Wesley Hall is Kresge Commons, a multipurpose center for entertainment and educational programming. All dorms are coed with separate sections for men and women, except for Dean Hall, which is all-female. For upperclassmen, apartment-style housing is also available in the new Karro Residential Village, and in the Briton House and Burns Street Complexes. Greek housing is another option for men, but the sorority houses are designated for meetings and functions only and have no bedrooms. Off-campus housing is strongly discouraged: "People do apply to Residential Life to live off campus, but few are granted permission and they jump through many hoops to get there," says an alum.

One campus standout is the Bobbitt Visual Arts Center, home to the art and art history department. In addition to two galleries, the center also contains studios for painting, sculpture, ceramics, and printmaking, and houses Albion's permanent collection of more than 4,000 pieces. Included in this collection are over 2,000 prints by artists such as Matisse, Picasso, Goya, and Rembrandt.

The Dow Recreation and Wellness Center, located adjacent to the school stadium, is devoted to educational and recreational purposes, including individual and group sports activities, physical conditioning, and health and wellness programs. The building's fieldhouse contains flexible court space for intramural basketball, volleyball, badminton, and tennis, as well as a 1/9-mile track. Also included in the facility are two racquetball courts, a weight room with fitness equipment, and areas for training and rehabilitation.

Student Life

Albion's student body, while not diverse, is close-knit. "We have a nice atmosphere where people are friendly," says one student. A senior offers a different perspective: "Everyone here is bright and intelligent. However, the campus is full of in-state white rich kids who can be materialistic. The running joke is that the campus mascot should be a J. Crew or Banana Republic catalog." A recent grad agrees, noting that female students all "followed the same J. Crew/Nordstrom/Express fashion trends and flipped their hair in the same direction."

The five fraternities and six sororities on campus drive much of Albion's social life. However, "it is not necessary to be in a Greek organization to be 'popular' or 'have a social life,'" insists one sorority member. "Most Greek events are open to the entire campus." More social activities are provided by the Union Board, which sponsors entertainment in the form of music, comedians, special events, movies, lectures, and off-campus excursions. Other interesting student organizations include Da Yooper Club, which celebrates "da land, da people, and da lifestyle of da Upper Peninsula of Michigan"; the Albyonne Medievalist Society, which recreates medieval life in the form of period feast each semester and costuming and dance; and SISTAHS, a support group for black women. Of course, anyone who just wants to share a nice latte with some friends can stop in at The Coffee House.

The Albion Britons play in NCAA Division III sports; teams for both men and women include cross country, golf, soccer, basketball, swimming, diving, tennis, and track and field. Men can play football and baseball, while women can play volleyball and softball. In addition to varsity sports, the college also offers intramural competition in basketball, badminton, canoe racing, flag football, golf, floor hockey, soccer, softball, tennis, volleyball, walleyball, and long distance running. Intramurals attract large numbers of players, and rivalries between residence hall floors and among student organizations are reported to be intense.

Other schools to check out: Calvin, Kalamazoo, College of Wooster, Cornell College, Ripon.

Test Scores (middle 50%):
SAT Verbal: 530–640
SAT Math: 530–650
ACT Comp: 23–28
HS Rank of Entering Freshmen:
Top 10%: 32%
Top 25%: 62%
Top 50%: 91%
Avg. HS GPA: 3.54

Costs (2003–04)

Tuition and Fees: $21,948
Room & Board: $6,262
Payment Plan(s): installment plan, deferred payment plan, pre-payment plan

THE EXPERTS SAY...

"Albion's educational approach emphasizes creative problem-solving and critical thinking."

"Go Greek or go stir-crazy at this small, remotely located school."

Inst. Aid (est. 2003–04)

Institutional Aid, Need-Based: $13,062,103
Institutional Aid, Non-Need-Based: $5,416,296
FT Undergrads Receiving Aid: 65%
Avg. Amount per Student: $18,945
FT Undergrads Receiving Non-Need-Based Scholarship or Grant Aid: 32%
Avg. Amount per Student: $11,177
Of Those Receiving Any Aid:
Rec. Need-Based Scholarship or Grant Aid: 100%
Average Award: $15,556
Rec. Need-Based Self-Help Aid: 78%
Average Award: $3,865
Upon Graduation, Avg. Loan Debt per Student: $19,802
Financial Aid Deadline: rolling, 2/15 (priority)

Graduates

Going to Graduate School:
41% Within One Year
Companies Recruiting On Campus: 62

ALFRED UNIVERSITY

One Saxon Drive, Alfred, NY 14802-1205
Admissions Phone: (607) 871-2115; (800) 541-9229 Fax: (607) 871-2198
Email: admwww@alfred.edu
Website: alfred.edu Application Website: admissions/html/apply.html

General Info

Type of School: private, coed
Setting: rural
Academic Calendar: semester

Student Body

Full-Time Undergrads: 1,930
  Men: 48%, Women: 52%

Part-Time Undergrads: 39
  Men: 44%, Women: 56%

Total Undergrad Population:
  African American: 5%
  Asian American: 2%
  Latino: 4%
  Native American: 1%
  Caucasian 77%
  International: 2%
  Out-of-State: 35%
  Living Off-Campus: 33%

Graduate and First-Professional
  Students: 312

Academics

Full-Time Faculty: 186
  With Ph.D.: 89%

Part-Time Faculty: 28
  With Ph.D.: 43%

Student/Faculty Ratio: 12:1

Most Popular Majors:
  art and design (25%)
  business administration (10%)
  ceramic engineering (7%)
  psychology (6%)
  elementary education (5%)

Completing 2 or More Majors: 7%

Freshmen Retention Rate: 82%

Graduation Rates:
  44% within four years
  63% within six years

Admissions

Regular Application Deadline: 2/1
  (priority)

Early Decision Deadline(s): 12/15

Fall Transfer Deadline: 8/1

Spring Transfer Deadline: 12/1

Total # of Students Applied: 2,169
  Admitted: 1,493
  Enrolled: 474

Applied Early Decision: 58
  Early Decision Admitted: 44

Inside the Classroom

"We have the greatest ceramics program ever!" boasts a student, and with cause: Whether it's the arts or materials science engineering you're interested in, Alfred is the premier school in the nation for the study of ceramics and glassworks. Alfred's unique College of Ceramics has a School of Art and Design and a School of Ceramic Engineering and Materials Science. The schools are funded in part by the State University of New York, which means New York State residents can attend for reduced tuition. Alfred's other schools are the College of Business and the College of Liberal Arts and Sciences.

At this "friendly little school," "every one is accessible from the professors to the janitors," a senior remarks. The student/faculty ratio is 12:1, and class sizes are small. "You are very close with your professors," says one student, adding: "Our faculty, although good, is not 'diverse.'" The school is considered a "best value" in the region: "You don't have to be a millionaire to go to our school because we have a generous financial aid program," a political science major asserts.

For a small school, Alfred offers a diverse range of programs (over 60). For the engineers, there are programs in bioceramics, composites, photonic and optical materials, plus cutting-edge research on superconductivity. For artists, programs include ceramic art, electronic arts, glass art, and wood design. The business programs have a solid reputation, and English and sciences are also good. In Alfred's "Centers for Excellence," undergraduates work with professors and are mentored by graduate students.

Cooperative education at Alfred is the real deal, "not an internship or a summer program," say college officials. Students work for five to eight months, receiving pay and/or credit for their hands-on experience. Opportunities range from the fields of ceramic engineering to journalism, with participating companies such as IBM, Walt Disney World, and the Alfred Sun newspaper. A recent school survey of Alfred graduates showed that 97 percent of all respondents were either employed or in graduate school a year after graduation, with many programs achieving a 100 percent placement rate.

Campus Environment

The 232-acre campus is set in the village of Alfred in the foothills of the Allegheny Mountains in Western New York. "Our location is breathtakingly beautiful," says a senior, but "it's in the middle of nowhere." The village of Alfred is quaint, with sweet shops, children's parks, and bicycle collections. The collegiate restaurant "The Jet," an Alfred hangout since 1924, has walls lined with hand-painted fraternity/sorority "paddles"; the university granted honorary doctorates to the restaurant's founders for their service to its students. The town atmosphere is quiet, "but quieter when Alfred State (the other local college) has a vacation," says a senior.

Alfred has "the safest campus ever." The campus is residential, with the majority of its 2,400 students living in 23 residence halls. Students must live on campus for four semesters. Housing ranges from traditional corridor style dorms to apartments.

Single rooms are available to new students on a limited basis. "There is enough of it (housing) but you need to have five friends to get into a suite or apartment," says a student. "The singles are very small but the freshman dorms are big." Common Interest Housing (CIH) is available to upperclass students, with themes like tae-bo, engineering, poder latino, and outdoor enthusiasts.

"It is quite popular to live off-campus but also very expensive," cautions a student. "It is crazy what they charge for housing." You "do not need a car to get around campus or town," but claustrophobia can set in quickly without one, especially in the long, cold, upstate winters.

Students take day trips to the nearby mountains, but closer to home are the Pine Hills Trails just behind the AU campus where students camp and hike, and Kanakadea Creek for boat-floating and rock skipping. In the winter, sledding is big, especially on the hill next to McLane Athletic Center. But, laments a student, "We have no ski resorts nearby."

Student Life

A senior describes the student body at Alfred: "The art students don't shower much and like weed. The engineers are smart and like to work. The business kids like to party and are most likely to join a frat or sorority. The Liberal Arts kids are usually laid-back." The student body is fairly homogeneous, being predominantly white and upper-middle class with a majority of New Yorkers. About ten percent of students are minorities. "The administration thinks that people are discriminated against but I think that's a bunch of hooey," says one College of Liberal Arts student. Art students tend to be more liberal, standing out in the conservative Alfred region.

Although isolated on the Alfred campus, students find many ways to have fun. "You study during the week from about Sunday evening to Tuesday evening," explains a senior. "Partying starts Wednesday but you don't have to join in. There are tons of clubs and activities on campus because there isn't much around our area. Comedians and 'small act' bands come to us starting on Thursday evening." Frats are a presence on campus. "They are popular because they give away free beer," a student observes. As for substances: "There is a considerable amount of drinking done," reports a student. "Drinking is much more popular than drugs. The only drug found on campus is pot. There is no call for anything harder."

There are over 100 clubs and organizations at Alfred. Reports one student. "Popular: Habitat for Humanity, Student Volunteers for Community Action, Rugby, Student Activities Board, African Dance, Poder Latino, Spectrum. Not popular: Gamer's Guild, College Republicans, College Democrats." WALF, Alfred's student radio station, is the school's largest student organization. The Fiat Lux, the school newspaper, is one of the oldest, continuously published student newspapers in the country. "All varsity sports are popular," our student informs us. "Intramural sports are also quite popular." The AU Saxons compete in 23 NCAA Division III sports. About 20 percent of all undergrads play a varsity sport, and half of all students participate in either intramural or club sports.

Test Scores (middle 50%):
SAT Verbal: 500–600
SAT Math: 500–600
ACT Comp: 23–28

HS Rank of Entering Freshmen:
Top 10%: 23%
Top 25%: 51%
Top 50%: 87%

Costs (2003–04)

Tuition and Fees: $20,656
note: Tuition figure is a blended average.

Room & Board: $8,478

Payment Plan(s): installment plan

THE EXPERTS SAY...

" Alfred is the top school in the nation for ceramics engineering. There's a great mix of scientists, artists, and business kids. "

" Making ceramics, testing ceramics, sculpting ceramics, selling ceramics: If you don't like ceramics, don't come here! "

Inst. Aid (est. 2003–04)

Institutional Aid, Need-Based: $15,757,000

Institutional Aid, Non-Need-Based: $2,070,000

FT Undergrads Receiving Aid: 80%
Avg. Amount per Student: $19,352

FT Undergrads Receiving Non-Need-Based Scholarship or Grant Aid: 12%
Avg. Amount per Student: $6,300

Of Those Receiving Any Aid:

Rec. Need-Based Scholarship or Grant Aid: 99%
Average Award: $14,264

Rec. Need-Based Self-Help Aid: 90%
Average Award: $5,844

Upon Graduation, Avg. Loan Debt per Student: $18,000

Financial Aid Deadline: rolling

Graduates

Going to Graduate School:
32% Within One Year

Companies Recruiting On Campus: 79

ALLEGHENY COLLEGE

520 North Main Street, Meadville, PA 16335
Admissions Phone: (814) 332-4351; (800) 521-5293 Fax: (814) 337-0431
Email: admissions@allegheny.edu Website: www.allegheny.edu
Application Website: www.commonapp.org

General Info

Type of School: private, coed, United Methodist

Setting: small town

Academic Calendar: semester

Student Body

Full-Time Undergrads: 1,808
  Men: 49%, Women: 51%

Part-Time Undergrads: 14
  Men: 36%, Women: 64%

Total Undergrad Population:
  African American: 2%
  Asian American: 2%
  Latino: 1%
  Caucasian: 94%
  International: 1%
  Out-of-State: 33%
  Living Off-Campus: 3%
  In Fraternities: 26%
  In Sororities: 29%

Academics

Full-Time Faculty: 134
  With Ph.D.: 90%

Part-Time Faculty: 13
  With Ph.D.: 23%

Student/Faculty Ratio: 13:1

Most Popular Majors:
  economics (12%)
  psychology (10%)
  political science (10%)
  English language and literature (9%)
  biology (8%)

Completing 2 or More Majors: 15%

Freshmen Retention Rate: 85%

Graduation Rates:
  60% within four years
  67% within six years

Admissions

Regular Application Deadline: 2/15

Early Decision Deadline(s): 1/15

Fall Transfer Deadline: 7/1

Spring Transfer Deadline: 11/1

Total # of Students Applied: 2,438
  Admitted: 2,001
  Enrolled: 478

# of Students Waitlisted: 62
  Students Accepting Place: 62
  Waitlisted Students Admitted: 14

Inside the Classroom

Allegheny, one of the oldest colleges in America, prides itself on its strong academic tradition and its personalized undergraduate program. The individual attention begins even before you start your first semester. Incoming freshmen choose just one course, a First Seminar, to attend during orientation. (These seminars tend to be more offbeat, with titles such as "Why People Believe Weird Things," "From Ricky (Ricardo) to Ricky (Martin)," and "Eating Poetry.") The professor of the seminar becomes your first academic adviser, helping to select the semester's classes and map out an education plan in general.

Students here love the emphasis the school puts on personal education—the small classes (the average size is 22), the flexible curriculum, and the myriad opportunities for independent research and collaborative research with faculty. "Every Alleghenian completes at least one independent research project," we're told, probably in the form of the Capstone project, which all seniors, regardless of major, must complete before graduating. The Allegheny College Center for Experiential Learning (ACCEL) is a major selling point for those looking for a college that's dedicated to its students' success: ACCEL coordinates all "experiential learning programs" such as study abroad and off-campus programs, career services, leadership development, and thousands of internship opportunities. Co-op programs are also available in the engineering, education, arts, medical technology, and nursing fields.

There are three academic divisions at Allegheny: humanities, natural sciences, and social sciences. All students must choose a major in one, a minor in another, and eight additional credit hours from the third. Students may design their own major or minor, or select from one of 30 offered. All fields are strong; popular programs include psychology, environmental science/studies, economics, English, political science, and biology. Nearly 40 percent of first-year students expect to major in one of the natural sciences; 15 percent anticipate a career in a health field. There are also three interdisciplinary majors in international studies, neuroscience, and women's studies.

As you can imagine, the workload is intense and challenging. The school says students spend three hours a day working in class, and five hours a day working outside class. Students gladly take an earnest, hands-on approach to their studies, and they're happy that the faculty and administration at Allegheny take their education as seriously as they do. It pays off quite well, too: Allegheny grads boast excellent acceptance rates to medical, law, and business school, and the college ranks in the top 7 percent of all liberal arts colleges in the number of graduates who go on to earn Ph.Ds.

Campus Environment

Allegheny's beautiful, historic campus consists of 38 buildings on a 72-acre central campus, a 182-acre outdoor recreation complex, and a 283-acre nature preserve. A number of buildings "on the hill" were constructed in the 19th century, including two that are listed on the National Register of Historic Places. One of the prettiest and most storied spots on campus is the Rustic Bridge ravine. (As part of an annual tradition during Orientation Week, freshmen race to see who can be the first to steal the famous 13th plank of the bridge.)

Seventy-five percent of the student body lives on campus; all freshmen are required to, as are sophomores who do not commute from home. First-year students live in traditional residence halls—coed or single-sex—while upperclassmen have the additional option of living in apartment-style units, in their frat house, or in one of 20 college-owned houses, 12 of which are deemed "special interest." Juniors and seniors may live off campus.

Students warn that the weather tends to be dreary, particularly in the winter. (After all, the guy who "developed the wind chill factor" went here.) They also complain that the school's location in Meadville, Pennsylvania is in the middle of nowhere. It's 90 minutes north of Pittsburgh, two hours east of Cleveland, and two hours southwest of Buffalo. There's not a whole lot to do in this small town (pop: 14,000), and unless you have a car for weekend trips, you'll probably stay close to campus like most students do. Parking permits are available to all undergrads for a fee.

Student Life

Students here are serious-minded and studious; they're also fairly religious, which is not surprising considering that the school maintains a historic affiliation with the United Methodist Church (though it welcomes those of all faiths, of course). There's very little diversity at Allegheny; only about 5 percent of students are minorities. These are not necessarily your typical upper-class college coeds, however, as an overwhelming majority of undergrads receive some form of financial aid to attend.

We hear that Alleghenians follow a "work hard, play hard" philosophy, although some say life here is a little too focused on the "work hard" portion of the equation. Greek life is popular, with about a quarter of the students pledging one of four fraternities and four sororities. Frat parties are the social highlight of the average weekend at Allegheny, and are perhaps the only option for students who are under 21 but looking for a party. Students also tap kegs in off-campus apartments.

There are more than 100 other clubs and organizations to choose from, including the student government group, the activities programming committee, a Christian outreach organization, and several performing arts groups. We're also told that "Allegheny students consistently devote approximately 26,000 hours to community service each year." The student activities center hosts a variety of entertainment including movies, concerts, dances, comedians, etc. And Allegheny offers 20 varsity sports: 10 for men and 10 for women. It's a Division III school, and nearly all of its teams have won a conference championship or received a national ranking in the last two decades. The new $13 million Wise Sport & Fitness Center is the home of basketball and volleyball games as well as individual recreation and intramural competition. There are at least nine IM sports per semester for men and women, with 70 percent of all Allegheny students participating.

Other schools to check out: Gettysburg, Denison, College of Wooster, St. Lawrence, Wittenberg.

Applied Early Decision: 88
Early Decision Admitted: 69

Test Scores (middle 50%):
SAT Verbal: 540–650
SAT Math: 550–650
ACT Comp: 23–28
ACT English: 22–28
ACT Math: 21–27

HS Rank of Entering Freshmen:
Top 10%: 41%
Top 25%: 72%
Top 50%: 92%

Avg. HS GPA: 94%

THE EXPERTS SAY...

" If you want to get into to medical, law, or business school, and are willing to work hard to get there, Allegheny can get you in. "

" Get ready to work five hours a day outside of class for your grades. 4.0 isn't high enough here. "

Costs (2004–5)

Tuition and Fees: $25,550
Tuition, room and board paid by U.S. Government

Room & Board: $6,160

Payment Plan(s): installment plan, pre-payment plan

Inst. Aid (est. 2003–04)

FT Undergrads Receiving Aid: 74%
Avg. Amount per Student: $19,624

FT Undergrads Receiving Non-Need-Based Scholarship or Grant Aid: 22%
Avg. Amount per Student: $8,883

Of Those Receiving Any Aid:

Rec. Need-Based Scholarship or Grant Aid: 100%
Average Award: $13,733

Rec. Need-Based Self-Help Aid: 85%
Average Award: $5,843

Upon Graduation, Avg. Loan Debt per Student: $23,735

Financial Aid Deadline: rolling, 2/15 (priority)

Graduates

Going to Graduate School:
31% Within One Year

Accepting Job Offer:
27% at time of graduation

Companies Recruiting On Campus: 40

Alumni Giving: 50%

AMERICAN UNIVERSITY

4400 Massachusetts Avenue N.W., Washington, DC 20016-8001
Admissions Phone: (202) 885-6000 Fax: (202) 885-1025
Email: afa@american.edu Website: www.american.edu
Application Website: admissions.american.edu

General Info

Type of School: private, coed, United
   Methodist
Setting: urban
Academic Calendar: semester

Student Body

Full-Time Undergrads: 5,401
   Men: 38%, Women: 62%

Part-Time Undergrads: 230
   Men: 39%, Women: 61%

Total Undergrad Population:
   African American: 6%
   Asian American: 5%
   Latino: 5%
   Native American: <1%
   Caucasian: 62%
   International: 7%
   Out-of-State: 99%
   Living Off-Campus: 32%
   In Fraternities: 17%
   In Sororities: 18%

Graduate and First-Professional
   Students: 5,225

Academics

Full-Time Faculty: 492
   With Ph.D.: 95%

Part-Time Faculty: 473

Student/Faculty Ratio: 14:1

Most Popular Majors:
   international studies (19%)
   business administration (15%)
   political science (11%)
   public communication/
      public relations (6%)
   communication/legal
      institutions/econ/govt.
      interdisciplinary (5%)

Completing 2 or More Majors: 13%

Freshmen Retention Rate: 86%

Graduation Rates:
   65% within four years
   72% within six years

Admissions

Regular Application Deadline: 2/1

Early Decision Deadline(s): 11/15

Fall Transfer Deadline: 7/1, 3/1
   (priority)

Spring Transfer Deadline: 11/1
   (priority)

Inside the Classroom

American University has five undergraduate units: the College of Arts and Sciences, Kogod School of Business, School of Communication, School of International Service, and School of Public Affairs. Not surprisingly, given the Beltway location, international studies and political science are among AU's strongest and most popular majors; broadcast journalism and other communications programs are also well regarded.

With an average class size of 19 students and a student/faculty ratio of 14:1, students say it's easy to form relationships with their instructors. Many faculty members are nationally and internationally recognized in their fields and bring a real-world perspective to the classroom. One example: Professor Akbar Ahmed, Chair of Islamic Studies, is well known for interfaith dialogue and the study of global Islam and has been interviewed extensively in the national media. Students often work alongside faculty members on research projects. A college official notes, "Our Career Center's Office of Merit Awards actively searches out current students who are good candidates to pursue research… In addition, the College of Arts and Sciences, School of International Service, and the University Honors Program sponsor student research conferences each year that showcase the academic and creative accomplishments of undergraduates."

Internship opportunities are widely available; certain majors even require internships as part of the curriculum. A college official says students have been able to land internships "in any field—from the arts/humanities and sciences through international relations, government, and communication/media. Internships both here and overseas can be arranged through individual faculty and through the AU Career Center." Roughly 65 percent of AU students complete at least one internship before they graduate.

A Maryland guidance counselor tells us that "individual attention comes into play tremendously" at AU. The university's Academic Support Center is widely respected for its many one-on-one programs, especially those for learning-disabled students.

Campus Environment

AU's 84-acre campus is in a "*very* nice part of DC," students assure us, "in a residential area near embassies, so most people feel very safe." The North Side of campus is considered "more quiet," while the South Side has "more of the party dorms." While freshmen are not required to live on campus, a college official tells us that about 99 percent do so (and many are put in temporary triples, say students). AU has six coed residence halls, some of which have single-sex floors, and all of which have been renovated within the last ten years. "The dorms are *awesome*!" exclaims a frosh. "However, you definitely pay for it!" The university recently entered into a ten-year lease with a luxury apartment building in Maryland, about a mile and a half from campus; this facility can house around 730 seniors and grad students. Still, many upperclassmen choose to move off campus, despite the high cost of living in the DC area.

KAPLAN

Freshmen are not permitted to have cars on campus or to even park them in the area surrounding the school. Upperclassmen may have cars as long as they register the car with Public Safety and pay the annual parking fee. However, even upperclassmen are discouraged from parking in surrounding areas, so most students choose to use American University's free shuttle bus service and public transportation. AU also provides van service to students with internships.

In 2002, AU implemented its plans to become the nation's leading wireless university by converting its campus to a wireless system to handle voice, data, and messaging. The system provides two different services using the same technology: wireless LAN access for laptops and PDAs, and enhanced cell phone reception for phones from certain carriers. The system is accessible throughout key areas of the AU campus, including residence halls.

Student Life

AU is home to a proudly diverse student body. "Every race, religion, sexuality, and class is represented here, and it's one of the main reasons I came here," claims a sophomore visual media/American studies major. Students come from all 50 states and more than 150 foreign countries. In general, AU students tend to be upper-middle class (some say "snobby"), career-oriented, and politically active. All views are represented: "AU seems on the surface to be liberal, but there are a lot of less vocal conservatives, too," confides a sophomore majoring in broadcast journalism.

A Division I Patriot League school, AU offers 10 women's sports and 9 men's. AU has no football team, so basketball and soccer pick up the slack. There are also more than 30 intramural and club sports. AU also has a new Jacobs Fitness Center with a wide range of both cardiovascular and strength training equipment and group exercise classes including step aerobics, kickboxing, and yoga.

AU offers more than 150 student clubs and activities, and most students become actively involved—"people who do nothing do not fit in here," notes a sophomore. The award winning, student-run Kennedy Political Union brings speakers to the AU community; past speakers include Bill Clinton, the Dalai Lama, Charlton Heston, Jesse Jackson, and Coretta Scott King. Other popular groups are the Student Confederation (student government), *The Eagle* (student newspaper), and DC Reads (tutoring group). Roughly one-fifth of the student body joins the 10 fraternities and 12 sororities, but there's no Greek housing and students say Greeks don't much influence campus life. It's a dry campus: No alcohol is allowed on campus, even for students who are 21: "If caught, there are serious consequences," a sophomore warns.

Community service is a part of life at AU. "AU feels that its mission is summed up in the phrase, 'Ideas into action, action into service,'" says a university official. In the Freshmen Service Experience, roughly half the incoming freshman class arrives on campus before the beginning of fall semester to do several days of community service in the DC area.

Needless to say, AU students eagerly take advantage of everything DC has to offer. Nightlife is fun and varied, with tons of restaurants, bars, and clubs in the area and surrounding neighborhoods such as Georgetown. And there are more than enough social, political, cultural, and sporting events to keep students constantly busy.

Other schools to check out: GWU, Georgetown, Syracuse, Boston U, Clark.

Total # of Students Applied: 10,282
 Admitted: 6,107
 Enrolled: 1,283

Waitlist Available

Applied Early Decision: 380
 Early Decision Admitted: 196

Test Scores (middle 50%):
 SAT Verbal: 570–670
 SAT Math: 560–650
 ACT Comp: 25–29

HS Rank of Entering Freshmen:
 Top 10%: 36%
 Top 25%: 74%
 Top 50%: 97%

Avg. HS GPA: 3.42

THE EXPERTS SAY...

" Anyone with a keen interest in world affairs should definitely check out AU's School of International Service. AU is also a good destination for students with learning disabilities. "

" It's every teen's dream: a university that encourages you to use your cell phone! "

Costs (2004–5)

Tuition and Fees: $26,694

Room & Board: $10,260

Payment Plan(s): installment plan, pre-payment plan

Inst. Aid (est. 2002–03)

FT Undergrads Receiving Aid: 44%
 Avg. Amount per Student: $24,370

FT Undergrads Receiving Non-Need-Based Scholarship or Grant Aid: 13%
 Avg. Amount per Student: $12,410

Of Those Receiving Any Aid:

Rec. Need-Based Scholarship or Grant Aid: 83%
 Average Award: $12,699

Rec. Need-Based Self-Help Aid: 93%
 Average Award: $9,175

Upon Graduation, Avg. Loan Debt per Student: $18,716

Financial Aid Deadline: 3/1

Graduates

Going to Graduate School:
 73% Within One Year

Companies Recruiting On Campus: 200

Alumni Giving: 37%

AMHERST COLLEGE

P.O.Box 5000, Amherst, MA 01002-5000
Admissions Phone: (413) 542-2328 Fax: (413) 542-2040
Email: admission@amherst.edu
Website: www.amherst.edu

General Info

Type of School: private, coed
Setting: small town
Academic Calendar: semester

Student Body

Full-Time Undergrads: 1,617
  Men: 52%, Women: 48%

Total Undergrad Population:
  African American: 10%
  Asian American: 12%
  Latino: 8%
  Native American: <1%
  Caucasian: 45%
  International: 6%
  Out-of-State: 81%
  Living Off-Campus: 2%

Academics

Full-Time Faculty: 182
  With Ph.D.: 93%
Part-Time Faculty: 37
  With Ph.D.: 81%
Student/Faculty Ratio: 8:1
Most Popular Majors:
  English (16%)
  economics (14%)
  psychology (14%)
  political (10%)
  LJST (16%)
Completing 2 or More Majors: 32%
Freshmen Retention Rate: 96%
Graduation Rates:
  89% within four years
  97% within six years

Admissions

Regular Application Deadline: 12/31
Early Decision Deadline(s): 11/15
Fall Transfer Deadline: 2/1
Spring Transfer Deadline: 11/1
Total # of Students Applied: 5,631
  Admitted: 1,001
  Enrolled: 413
# of Students Waitlisted: 940
  Students Accepting Place: 411
  Waitlisted Students Admitted: 72
Applied Early Decision: 374
  Early Decision Admitted: 130

Inside the Classroom

"The top liberal arts school in the country," proclaims a New York guidance counselor. But if you're looking for a traditional, structured curriculum, Amherst College is not the place for you. For highly motivated students with an independent streak and intellectual thirst, however, it's absolute Nirvana.

With no core curriculum or distribution requirements to get in the way (the only school-wide required class is the freshman seminar), Amherst's open curriculum "allows for a lot of in-depth exploration in many areas of study," says an English major. Of course, there's a flip-side to all this academic freedom: The workload here is one of the heaviest in the nation. This is the result of several factors: the emphasis placed on individual study and personalized discipline areas, the challenging instructional style of the faculty, and the "very intense" pressure brought on by being in an environment of highly motivated students. However, one student says, "there are a lot of guidance resources (advisors, profs, class deans) for students who may feel overwhelmed or want a little more direction."

Classes at Amherst are exceptionally small, even by liberal arts college standards. Students have a great deal of interaction with their professors, and department chairs and top professors teach all levels of classes, including freshmen. The faculty make it a point to be accessible, and as one student puts it, "There's almost as much learning going on in one-on-one meetings with faculty as there is in the classroom." Another student says, "Often after a semester is over, the relationship between a professor and a student continues, with professors taking an active interest in the futures and subsequent endeavors of their students." Unfortunately, as is common with such talented and in-demand faculty, "when the professors go on sabbatical, lots of classes are omitted."

While Amherst students tend to be well-rounded perfectionists (and proud of it), most students insist that they are not overly competitive with each other. "I've heard time and again that the Amherst students are only in competition with themselves, i.e., their own goals, aspirations, and standards," states a senior.

Amherst pioneered the interdisciplinary American studies program, and it remains one of the most popular majors on campus; other interdisciplinary programs are also hot, including Asian Languages and Civilizations and Women's and Gender Studies. Amherst's standing as one of the Five-College Consortium—an affiliation that includes UMass-Amherst, Smith, Hampshire, and Mount Holyoke—substantially increases the number and kinds of courses and programs students may enroll in. If you don't find what you're looking for at Amherst, you can attend a class at one of these other top schools.

Campus Environment

The 1,000-acre campus, which includes a wildlife preserve and forest, is situated on a hill overlooking the town of Amherst. "It's a safe campus," we are told. Students have good things to say about the local restaurants, which they flock to once they tire of the "mediocre" food served in the school's recently renovated dining hall.

First-year students live together, and upperclassmen live in mixed-class residence halls. Housing is guaranteed for four years, and virtually no one lives off-campus. The 33 residence halls offer many different living options: singles, doubles, triples, suites, and several popular theme houses. The administration has plans to construct new housing, which is a good thing, since "sophomores get shafted" in the existing system ("they are at the bottom of the room draw," a student explains). However, most students do describe the housing as "comfortable."

The town of Amherst, one of those quaint New England towns, doesn't offer much in the way of excitement, but the neighboring town of Northampton is a major regional cultural center, with clubs, movie theaters, and dozens of restaurants that give the area a cosmopolitan feel. The college is a 90-minute drive from Boston and a three-hour drive from New York.

Student Life

"Amherst has a very liberal atmosphere," says one student, "but there are strong conservative voices on campus, both in the student body and in the poly sci department." This politically active campus held both a peace rally and a patriotism rally ("I think in response to the peace rally," says one student) after the September 11 terrorist attacks, and students say there was "heated political debate" on related issues for months afterward.

Students at Amherst work hard and work a lot; even a large portion of the weekend is spent studying. "There's not much to do off-campus, so partying on campus is the primary social outlet," a student tells us. Dorms sponsor their own parties and activities, but with no fraternities or sororities on campus, "the social scene is pretty pathetic," one student complains. A few "unofficial" Greek organizations exist off campus and "they do provide some social events." Drugs aren't used much on campus ("except for pot"), but students claim that alcohol is prevalent at parties. However, the social scene really is pretty tame compared to many other schools. As one student quips, "If you enjoy standing around a keg for a few hours and then possibly making a trek up to some dorm for a dance party with 300–400 people, then this is the place for you."

If social opportunities are few, there are, however, a healthy number of extracurricular activities and organizations on campus, including several student newspapers and journals, various music, dance and theater companies, political and professional clubs, and a host of a cappella singing groups. Athletics are "huge" at Amherst, with decent Division III varsity teams in hockey, soccer, baseball, basketball, and lacrosse. "Club sports are also big, such as rugby and crew," says one student. The school's location particularly lends itself to outdoor sports and activities, including hiking, biking, and jogging. There are also several school-wide social events, such as Casino Night.

Other schools to check out: Williams, Bates, Swarthmore, Bowdoin, Bennington, Haverford.

Test Scores (middle 50%):
  SAT Verbal: 660–770
  SAT Math: 660–770
  ACT Comp: 29–34
HS Rank of Entering Freshmen:
  Top 10%: 86%
  Top 25%: 100%

Costs (2003–04)

Tuition and Fees: $29,730

Room & Board: $7,740

Payment Plan(s): installment plan, pre-payment plan

THE EXPERTS SAY...

" The perfect destination for independent-minded workaholics who love a challenge. "

" If you have even the slightest tendency towards laziness, stay away: There are plenty of other prestigious colleges out there with much lighter workloads. "

Inst. Aid (est. 2003–04)

Institutional Aid, Need-Based: $17,665,237

FT Undergrads Receiving Aid: 48%
  Avg. Amount per Student: $25,366

Of Those Receiving Any Aid:

Rec. Need-Based Scholarship or Grant Aid: 98%
  Average Award: $23,703

Rec. Need-Based Self-Help Aid: 90%
  Average Award: $3,424

Upon Graduation, Avg. Loan Debt per Student: $10,787

Financial Aid Deadline: 2/15 (priority)

Graduates

Going to Graduate School:
  44% Within One Year

Companies Recruiting On Campus: 50

Alumni Giving: 57%

ANTIOCH COLLEGE

795 Livermore Street, Yellow Springs, OH 45387
Admissions Phone: (937) 543-9436; (800) 543-9436 Fax: (937) 769-1111
Email: admissions@antioch-college.edu Website: www.antioch-college.edu
Application Website: www.antioch-college.edu/admissions/apply-antioch.htm

General Info

Type of School: private, coed

Setting: rural

Academic Calendar: trimester

Student Body

Full-Time Undergrads: 571
  Men: 38%, Women: 62%

Total Undergrad Population:
  African American: 5%
  Asian American: 1%
  Latino: 4%
  Native American: 1%
  Caucasian: 58%
  International: <1%

Graduate and First-Professional
  Students: 10

Academics

Full-Time Faculty: 50
  With Ph.D.: 56%

Part-Time Faculty: 7
  With Ph.D.: 71%

Most Popular Majors:
  cultural and interdisciplinary
  studies (11%)
  environmental & biological
  sciences (4%)
  arts (4%)
  self-designed major (4%)
  languages, literature & culture
  (4%)

Freshmen Retention Rate: 66%

Graduation Rates:
  27% within four years
  41% within six years

Admissions

Regular Application Deadline: 2/1

Early Decision Deadline(s): 11/15

Early Action Deadline: 11/15

Fall Transfer Deadline: 2/1 (priority)

Spring Transfer Deadline: 11/1
  (priority)

Total # of Students Applied: 467
  Admitted: 348
  Enrolled: 144

Inside the Classroom

For many students, the experience of graduating from college and entering the work force is akin to being hit on the head with an anvil. They suddenly realize that, in their insular, protected, collegiate environment, they haven't been prepared at all for life and work in the real world. Students at Antioch, however, experience the real world early on, thanks to the school's innovative co-op program.

The program requires students to fulfill five co-op placements before they graduate. Students study for several months on campus, then take off to work in some field of interest for which they receive college credit. Each student has a faculty advisor who helps in the selection of a co-op, guides the student through the application process, and evaluates the related paper or project that the student must complete by the end of each co-op experience. Students are able to use co-op jobs to try out different fields before deciding on a major, or to make sure that their choice of major is right for them. And while all majors require that at least one co-op job be field-related, students do have other co-op options, such as volunteer work or study abroad.

The co-op requirements also force students to become independent quickly. As one student explains, "Application to the co-op department compels us to lead creative lifestyles, since we must learn to succeed in big-city environments where we do our internships. Students become more motivated, too, once they find out what awaits them after graduation." Finding the right co-op can take some effort, and one student offers advice to incoming freshmen: "Choose co-ops based on the work you would be doing, or on the experience you would have. I once chose one based pretty much on its location, and it didn't work so well."

Core requirements are few, allowing students room in their schedules to experiment with different subjects. All majors are interdisciplinary and require completion of a senior project. Emphasis is placed on reading original texts, which students are asked to analyze and deconstruct. An advantage to Antioch's small population is that classes are relatively small and professors get to know students well. Instead of grades, students receive extensive evaluations directly from their professors.

While on campus, students become deeply immersed in their studies. Undergraduates describe the workload at Antioch as "heavy." These hardworking students don't have the luxury of hanging out at the pool all summer long; they get only a short break between the spring and summer semesters, with co-op and classroom work filling most of the calendar year. One senior said, "My advice to new students: Take breaks. You really just have to get out of here and get some perspective so you can keep coming back and doing your work. And cheesy as it sounds, do whatever you have to do to get time and space to yourself. Antioch has a million ways of stealing it."

Campus Environment

The Yellow Springs campus is now part of a far-flung network of schools that operate under the banner of Antioch University. In addition to the college, the system also includes the Antioch New England Graduate School in Keene, New Hampshire, as well as branches in Los Angeles, Santa Barbara, and Seattle.

Although located in a rural region, many Antioch students have good things to say about Yellow Springs, a town with a "real granola" population that includes vegetarian eateries, health food stores, folk art galleries, New Age shops and boutiques, and Birkenstocks galore. Many students are nature lovers, and the campus has enough open spaces, fresh air, and expansive woods to keep them happy; if not, they can just amble over to Glen Helen, a thousand-acre nature preserve adjacent to campus.

Student Life

Diversity—of race, of opinions, of creeds, of everything—is lived and breathed at Antioch. According to one student, "The joke is, 'Hi, I go to Antioch, and it takes me 15 minutes to explain my sexuality.' That's not far off." Students feel a deep sense of belonging to a community where acceptance of all points of view is the only thing carved in stone. Drug use doesn't raise many eyebrows around here. The student population tends to be, as one student puts it, "pretty radical." For most Antioch students, causing a ruckus in the name of conviction is nothing new: People who enroll here expect to challenge popular ideas and break out of social constraints. As one student puts it, "We tend to be out on the edge of what's acceptable and what isn't."

With so many students leaving campus for their internships, there's inevitably a certain amount of instability in the college's social scene. Many alternate semesters between on-campus study and off-campus co-ops. The majority of students live in on-campus residence halls, and they tend to socialize at intimate get-togethers and informal parties rather than at huge bashes. Students also become committed to the school's clubs and organizations, many of which are politically oriented. Some standouts include the Third World Alliance, the Antioch Environmental Group, the Gay/Lesbian/Bisexual Center, the Womyn's Center, and the Anarchist Study Group.

Other schools to check out: Hampshire, Reed, Bennington, Marlboro, Warren Wilson.

Costs (2004–5)

Tuition and Fees: $24,260

Room & Board: $6,413

Payment Plan(s): installment plan

THE EXPERTS SAY...

" For motivated students who enjoy living on the edge, Antioch offers the educational and real-world experiences needed for postgraduation success. "

" 'Experimentation' is the keyword at Antioch—both academically and socially (and perhaps pharmaceutically). "

Inst. Aid (est. 2003–04)

Institutional Aid, Need-Based: $5,745,620

Institutional Aid, Non-Need-Based: $936,168

FT Undergrads Receiving Aid: 74%
Avg. Amount per Student: $19,214

FT Undergrads Receiving Non-Need-Based Scholarship or Grant Aid: 26%
Avg. Amount per Student: $7,520

Of Those Receiving Any Aid:

Rec. Need-Based Scholarship or Grant Aid: 96%
Average Award: $11,293

Rec. Need-Based Self-Help Aid: 100%
Average Award: $4,198

Financial Aid Deadline: 3/1, 2/16 (priority)

ARIZONA STATE UNIVERSITY

Box 870112, Tempe, AZ 85287-0112
Admissions Phone: (480) 965-7788 Fax: (480) 965-3610
Email: ugradinq@asu.edu Website: www.asu.edu
Application Website: www.asu.edu/admissions

General Info

Type of School: public, coed

Setting: suburban

Academic Calendar: semester

Student Body

Full-Time Undergrads: 30,792
  Men: 48%, Women: 52%

Part-Time Undergrads: 6,544
  Men: 49%, Women: 51%

Total Undergrad Population:
  African American: 4%
  Asian American: 5%
  Latino: 12%
  Native American: 2%
  Caucasian: 70%
  International: 3%
  Out-of-State: 23%
  Living Off-Campus: 85%
  In Fraternities: 6%
  In Sororities: 7%

Graduate and First-Professional
  Students: 10,274

Academics

Full-Time Faculty: 1,722
  With Ph.D.: 84%

Part-Time Faculty: 122
  With Ph.D.: 43%

Student/Faculty Ratio: 23:1

Most Popular Majors:
  business (11%)
  interdisciplinary studies (5%)
  journalism/mass
    communication (5%)
  psychology (4%)
  communication (3%)

Freshmen Retention Rate: 77%

Graduation Rates:
  26% within four years
  52% within six years

Admissions

Regular Application Deadline: 4/15
  (priority)

Early Action Deadline: 11/1

Fall Transfer Deadline: 4/15
  (priority)

Spring Transfer Deadline: 11/15
  (priority)

Total # of Students Applied: 19,785
  Admitted: 17,490
  Enrolled: 7,126

Inside the Classroom

ASU's undergraduate colleges include: architecture and environmental design, business, education, engineering and applied sciences, extended education, liberal arts and sciences, nursing, public programs, fine arts, and the Barrett Honors College. "They offer everything that you could possibly want to take for a major or minor," says a student. Guidance counselors praise the "honors college and the opportunity for undergraduate research" as well as the "excellent communication department."

ASU does have problems typically found at large schools. Classes at introductory levels can be huge, and the more popular courses may be difficult to access—"Good luck getting into classes," snorts one disgruntled student. Another calls registration "a nightmare," and advises prospectives to "make sure you preregister as early as possible." The administration is reputed to be less than responsive, and students grouse about red tape.

Despite the school's size, one student tells us that "for the most part, the professors are really good and seem to care about the students' well being." Another agrees, citing "the strong faculty" as one of the school's greatest strengths. While the quality of the educators is high, a pre-business major tells us that "professors know that most students don't care about education, so they take it easy on them." Other students complained that teaching assistants aren't all that knowledgeable. ASU's resources and facilities, particularly for programs in the sciences, engineering, and performing arts, are generally good. One student praised the "state-of-the-art computer lab in the center of campus."

The workload, we hear, is "moderate," and one senior psychology major told us that "the intensity is minimal." Arizona's students are reputed to be laid back; a few students noted a less-than-intellectual atmosphere. A former political science major told us, "the school is easy to get in to, and that shows in the quality of the students." One disillusioned sophomore puts it this way: "A student who enjoys school and seeks academic challenges might not fit in at Arizona State because the classes are just way too easy and most of the students don't care." However, ASU's Barrett Honors College is designed to provide about 2,500 qualified students with a more intensive and challenging academic experience.

The Arizona Univerisity System is implementing an overhaul, called "Changing Directions," to allow the separate univeristies to specialize more in their individual academic strengths and to decide on different admissions standards (traditionally, any in-state resident need only meet certain class rank, standardized test score, or GPA requirements to be guaranteed admission). Along with these changes, tuition hikes are also in the works. While some feel this will negatively affect those who cannot pay as much out-of-pocket, more money will be diverted toward financial aid. Purported advantages to the Changing Directions program are higher quality students and academics, and better graduation rates.

Campus Environment

"The campus is absolutely beautiful," we are told. "It is clean and well kept, and the auditorium designed by Frank Lloyd Wright is stunning." Tempe is hot for much of the year, and a few students noted that walking around the huge campus in "120-degree weather" is less than fun. Still, others love basking in the sun and studying and hanging out outdoors nearly every day. "Where else can you study by the pool?" asks one happy student.

A former student tells us that campus housing is "touch and go" and that "some of the rooms are great, some are the size of a closet." Freshmen are not required to live on campus. The university's Off-Campus Student Services Office will help students get started in a search for off-campus housing. A large percentage of students have cars, and we are told that "you can live anywhere in the valley, and still be to school in half an hour." While parking is fairly plentiful, some lots are way more desirable than others. A free shuttle service or the city bus system are other alternatives to getting around; a sophomore explains that "the Phoenix bus sytem is adequate" but "could be improved on weekends."

Students looking to enjoy outdoor recreation will certainly find it on Arizona State's "country club" campus. The warm weather and excellent sport and recreational facilities make outdoor activities—from golfing and tennis to swimming and sunbathing—possible year round. There is a "plethora of opportunities away from the school," raves one senior, including "the mountains, the lakes, the beaches of California, Las Vegas, and the Grand Canyon." A student praises Tempe as a "college town with lots of clubs and bars. There are also a lot of local bands that play around here." Says one former student, "*Girls Gone Wild* films constantly at a club less than one block from campus."

Student Life

Among the many notable ASU alums are comedian David Spade, baseball players Barry Bonds and Reggie Jackson, and Pepsi chairman and CEO Craig Weatherup. The student body is fairly diverse in terms of ethnicity (though a Michigan guidance counselor groused that the administration is "more concerned about the number of minorities and meeting quotas instead of their academic programs"). Because ASU is so large, and so many students commute to school, some students say there is little "cohesive sense of community." Not everyone agrees with this; one gay student reports that the atmosphere is supportive.

Greek life is prevalent and one student says that it "tends to control student elections, so they always have a large say in the social events that take place with student funds." But other students say that Greeks don't really dominate social life. As you might expect from a school this size, there are more than 400 clubs, organizations, and extracurricular activities available.

Sports are big at Arizona State: ASU's NCAA Division I athletics program is a member of the Pac-10 Conference and offers 21 varsity sports. One member of the university's administration boasts that "ASU's physical plant for athletics is second to none on the West Coast and is in the top five nationally." Also, the NFL's Arizona Cardinals play in ASU's Sun Devil Stadium. Intramural sports are popular, with over 7,000 students participating annually. One guidance counselor noted that ASU is a hot pick "for sports more than academics."

"ASU is always depicted as a party school," notes a California guidance counselor. Tempe is "filled with teen and young-adult oriented activity," raves one student, and folks seem to take full advantage of it. "If you're bored at ASU," jokes another student, "[it must be because] you can't find your way out of your dorm room."

Test Scores (middle 50%):
SAT Verbal: 480–600
SAT Math: 490–620
ACT Comp: 20–26
ACT English: 19–26
ACT Math: 20–27
HS Rank of Entering Freshmen:
Top 10%: 26%
Top 25%: 53%
Top 50%: 84%
Avg. HS GPA: 3.36

Costs (est. 2004–05)

Tuition and Fees, In-State: $3,595
Tuition and Fees, Out-of-State: $12,028
Room & Board: $6,453

THE EXPERTS SAY...

" 'Changing Directions' could bring a lot of good to ASU's academic reputation (hopefully not at the expense of economically disadvantaged students)."

" Sun, sports, parties... No wonder nobody wants to leave after only four years! "

Inst. Aid (2002–03)

Institutional Aid, Need-Based: $13,420,238
Institutional Aid, Non-Need-Based: $14,012,167
FT Undergrads Receiving Aid: 39%
Avg. Amount per Student: $7,225
FT Undergrads Receiving Non-Need-Based Scholarship or Grant Aid: 11%
Avg. Amount per Student: $4,043
Of Those Receiving Any Aid:
Rec. Need-Based Scholarship or Grant Aid: 82%
Average Award: $4,175
Rec. Need-Based Self-Help Aid: 78%
Average Award: $4,057
Upon Graduation, Avg. Loan Debt per Student: $17,780
Financial Aid Deadline: 3/1 (priority)

Graduates

Companies Recruiting On-Campus: 515

AUBURN UNIVERSITY

202 Mary Martin Hall, Auburn University, AL 36849-5145
Admissions Phone: (334) 844-4080; (800) AUBURN9 (in-state)
Email: admissions@auburn.edu Website: www.auburn.edu Application Website:
auburn.edu/student_info/student_affairs/admissio/admissform.html

General Info

Type of School: public, coed
Setting: small town
Academic Calendar: semester

Student Body

Full-Time Undergrads: 17,572
  Men: 51%, Women: 49%

Part-Time Undergrads: 1,573
  Men: 63%, Women: 37%

Total Undergrad Population:
  African American: 7%
  Asian American: 1%
  Latino: 1%
  Native American: <1%
  Caucasian: 88%
  International: 1%
  Out-of-State: 37%
  Living Off-Campus: 85%
  In Fraternities: 18%
  In Sororities: 34%

Graduate and First-Professional
  Students: 3,901

Academics

Full-Time Faculty: 1,171
  With Ph.D.: 93%

Part-Time Faculty: 143
  With Ph.D.: 47%

Student/Faculty Ratio: 16:1

Most Popular Majors:
  business (19%)
  engineering (15%)
  education (8%)
  health sciences (7%)
  psychology (3%)

Completing 2 or More Majors: 1%

Freshmen Retention Rate: 84%

Graduation Rates:
  37% within four years
  68% within six years

Admissions

Regular Application Deadline: 8/1

Early Decision Deadline(s): 11/1

note: Rolling first or only decision
  plan notification date

Total # of Students Applied: 12,439
  Admitted: 9,653
  Enrolled: 3,706

Waitlist Available

In the Classroom

Auburn University is the oldest four-year coeducational school in Alabama and the second oldest in the Southeast. Auburn students choose programs of study from a range of schools and colleges, including agriculture; education; engineering; forestry; human sciences; liberal arts; nursing; pharmacy; and sciences and mathematics. One student tells us that departments at Auburn "have the same equivalent quality education as many 'more prestigious schools.'" Strong research programs are in agricultural sciences, natural resources, biological sciences, engineering, and physical sciences. An Alabama guidance counselor praises Auburn's "outstanding engineering school, school of veterinary medicine, and school of architecture," while a Georgia counselor observes, "They offer programs not easily found." Auburn brags that it is one of the top five universities in the nation for producing NASA scientists and astronauts.

With over 19,000 undergrads, Auburn is a very large institution. However, the school tries to keep the class size as low as possible: "The median class size for core curriculum courses is 25 students. Upper-division classes tend to have fewer students … Some survey courses are larger. For example, Freshman History courses are generally taught in sections of 150 students." But freshman comp classes cap at 25 students. Like many large universities, you may have to do some legwork to reach professors (who can occasionally be more involved in research than teaching). The core curriculum covers "everything from the basics of math, English and science to philosophy, fine arts and sociology," according to the school.

A chemical engineering major describes their workload as "very hard, intense, and competitive." Like many large universities, this kind of thing varies from major to major and we are told that some programs have "light" and "uncompetitive" workloads. One complaint we heard was that "funding for university components does not seem to be distributed in a logical way (e.g.: the athletic department receives lots of money while many academic departments are desperate for funds)." An Alabama guidance counselor agrees: "Auburn gives very few freshman scholarships; the only recruiting I have observed them to do is for athletics."

Campus Environment

There are many housing options here. Freshmen are not required to live on campus. Apartments are available even for freshmen, in units of varying size with varying perks (sharing the bathroom with 3 people instead of 30, community pool table). There are also various coed and women's residence halls. Getting AC and a single room is not unheard of here. One student tells us, "The on-campus housing is generally easy to get. Some dorms are old and falling apart, but most have been renovated and are very nice." Most Auburn students live off-campus, and we're told that "off-campus housing is available whenever demanded and is often pretty nice."

"Most students get around by car," says one student. "A problem Auburn will probably always have is a lack of parking spaces for the thousands of students who drive to campus every day." The good news is that even freshmen are allowed to bring a car to campus, after obtaining a permit. Tiger Transit also offers transportation "to most living locations, but is often unreliable." A junior explains that "the general off-campus atmosphere is friendly" and "the town [of Auburn] is very supportive of the university and friendly to students." Auburn is kind of small, but "there are many places to eat, dancing clubs, bars, etc." As always, stay aware of your surroundings. While "the safety is generally pretty good" on campus, "many parts of the campus are not well lit at night and seem spooky."

Student Life

The school explains, "Auburn's official mascot is a tiger ['Aubie'], but the school's battle cry is 'War Eagle,' dating back to the late 1800s, when, according to legend, a former soldier from the Civil War brought a rescued eagle to a football game." In 1892, Auburn beat the University of Georgia 10-0 in what is the oldest football rivalry in the South. Today, Auburn is an NCAA powerhouse and member of the Southeastern Conference (Charles Barkley and Bo Jackson played here).

Students praise "the friendly environment" and "social acceptance" here, along with the fact that "no matter how different you are from the typical student, there will be a group of people who are just like you." A guidance counselor explains Auburn's popularity among applicants: "It is easier to get into and there are a lot of opportunities socially." Students range from those who "work hard at school and setting the stage for careers" to those who "strive to make social achievements on campus (fraternities, sororities, SGA, etc.)" to the "many athletic people who are committed to sports," and "some that are there just to party and have fun." A junior explains, "The one type of student that might not be like all the other students is somebody who is there to simply to do school work and nothing else."

According to students, drinking on weekends is pretty big—"People do it at fraternity/sorority parties, bars and dance clubs, and house parties." We learned that "there doesn't seem to be a lot of pressure on non-drinking students to drink, but there is a big temptation for those students who are neutral about drinking." One student also tells us that in the dorm "many people have been arrested and kicked out for smoking marijuana in their rooms." On weekends, students also go to the beach, bowling, movies, and restaurants. A healthy number of students join fraternities and sororities at Auburn, and Greeks "seem to have a big influence on campus on the social and political atmosphere." A student complains that "they seem to be popular because they make it seem like 'all cool people at Auburn are in a fraternity or sorority' and that is not true."

One odd tradition here from the '50s and '60s, then revived in the '80s, is called Hey Day: "a day on which all students wear name tags and say 'hey' to everyone they pass. Leaders on campus join forces and pass out nametags to revive this tradition and prove that Auburn University has the friendliest campus around." One student also told us proudly that "no matter what trial comes around, the faculty, students, etc. always do their best and never give up at making it a great university." Hey.

Test Scores (middle 50%):
  SAT Verbal: 510–600
  SAT Math: 520–620
  ACT Comp: 22–27
  ACT English: 21–28
  ACT Math: 20–26

HS Rank of Entering Freshmen:
  Top 10%: 31%
  Top 25%: 54%
  Top 50%: 85%

Avg. HS GPA: 3.51

THE EXPERTS SAY...

" We all do our part: Auburn University professors formulated a special dog food that's now used by the U.S. Department of Defense's Military Working Dog School, the only site in the nation that certifies dogs for airport bomb-detection duty. "

" Sports, cheerleading, fraternities: Hot. Living on campus, graduating in four years: Not. "

Costs (2003–04)

Tuition and Fees, In-State: $4,430

Tuition and Fees, Out-of-State: $12,886

Room & Board: $5,970

Payment Plan(s): installment plan

Inst. Aid (2002–03)

Institutional Aid, Need-Based: $3,276,940

Institutional Aid, Non-Need-Based: $1,439,208

Upon Graduation, Avg. Loan Debt per Student: $18,535

Financial Aid Deadline: 3/1 (priority)

Graduates

Going to Graduate School: 35% Within One Year

Accepting Job Offer: 29% at time of graduation

Companies Recruiting On Campus: 500

Alumni Giving: 23%

AUSTIN COLLEGE

900 N. Grand Avenue, Suite 6N, Sherman, TX 75090-4400
Admissions Phone: (800) 442-5363; (903) 813-3000 Fax: (903) 813-3198
Email: admission@austincollege.edu Website: www.austincollege.edu
Application Website: www.austincollege.edu/admis/applyingforadmis.htm

General Info

Type of School: private, coed, Presbyterian

Setting: small town

Academic Calendar: 4-1-4

Student Body

Full-Time Undergrads: 1,278
Men: 44%, Women: 56%

Part-Time Undergrads: 6
Men: 50%, Women: 50%

Total Undergrad Population:
African American: 4%
Asian American: 10%
Latino: 7%
Native American: 1%
Caucasian: 76%
International: 2%
Out-of-State: 9%
Living Off-Campus: 29%
In Fraternities: 21%
In Sororities: 19%

Graduate and First-Professional Students: 38

Academics

Full-Time Faculty: 92
With Ph.D.: 99%

Part-Time Faculty: 30
With Ph.D.: 63%

Student/Faculty Ratio: 13:1

Most Popular Majors:
business administration (8%)
psychology (7%)
biology (5%)
political science (5%)
English (4%)

Completing 2 or More Majors: 26%

Freshmen Retention Rate: 86%

Graduation Rates:
68% within four years
74% within six years

Admissions

Regular Application Deadline: 8/15; 3/1 (priority)

Early Decision Deadline(s): 12/1, 1/10

Early Action Deadline: 1/15

Total # of Students Applied: 1,328
Admitted: 960
Enrolled: 338

Inside the Classroom

Austin College, affiliated with the Presbyterian Church, may be a small school, but guidance counselors insist that this hidden treasure deserves wider recognition. Among AC's best programs are premed, prelaw, biology, psychology, economics, business administration, international education, and other international majors. About two-thirds of students pursue an advanced degree within five years of graduation.

AC students (or "Aussies") can earn a B.A. degree in 28 majors, including interdisciplinary studies for students who want to develop their own majors. While AC is devoted to educating undergraduates, a master's degree program in teaching is also available. Students don't need to formally declare a major until the spring of sophomore year. The general degree requirements involve students showing proficiency in a foreign language, written communication skills, quantitative competency, and passing a physical fitness class.

Guidance counselors praise the "caring faculty," and students here love their professors and say there's never a problem with accessibility. "Faculty members are encouraged— if not required—to take an active role in campus life," says an alum. The average class holds fewer than 23 students, and the rare larger classes regularly break into smaller groups and labs. All classes are taught by professors, as there are no teaching assistants.

Research opportunities abound at AC, thanks in part to the school's superb resources. A college official says, "Austin College is fortunate to own three pieces of property in Grayson County that serve as research areas, field laboratories, and nature preserves. The proximity of these sites to campus and to one another facilitates comparative studies and long-term research projects." There's also the Robert L. Snider Memorial Social Science Lab, which enables students to "observe political and social behavior, formulate hypotheses about human behavior, test these hypotheses by field research techniques, acquire a more immediate and realistic sense of the structure and needs of the community."

Students get a chance to experiment with courses outside their major during Austin College's January Term. Students must complete three Jan Term courses. There are also ample opportunities for individual, off-campus study in the forms of field studies and internships. There is a Washington Internship Program that gives students the opportunity to be selected for internships in Washington, DC. There are a number of institutional co-op programs available to promote "the enrichment and improvement of graduate and undergraduate teaching and research." And studying abroad is very popular; in fact, more than 60 percent of Austin College students study abroad before graduating.

Campus Environment

Freshmen, sophomores, and juniors are required to live on campus in one of the six residence halls (unless they're married or living with their families). Seniors may live in the dorms, the on-campus apartments, or may find off-campus housing. Of the six residence halls, Caruth and Clyce Halls are women-only; Baker and Luckett are male-only; and Dean Hall and Jordan Family Language House are coed. The dorms are integrated for all year levels, though there are freshman floors and wings. Housing is guaranteed for all four years. The college-owned Bryan Apartments consist of 16 two-bedroom apartments that are typically occupied by 3–4 upperclassmen or grad students.

The campus offers an assortment of facilities. For art lovers, the Ida Green and Craig Hall Galleries offer new exhibits regularly, and give students a forum for showing off their talents. There are also two theaters, an indoor swimming pool, science laboratories, and athletic facilities. The recently completed Robert J. and Mary Wright Campus Center serves as a social and meeting area for students. There's also a new gym, the Verde Dickey Fitness Pavilion, as well as the 30-acre Robbie Kubela Rogers Lake Campus on Lake Texoma "for recreational activities, retreats, meetings, and camping."

Students without cars could have a hard time. They'll need to rely on the charity of friends in order to get around town, since Sherman does not offer a formal public transportation system. Cars are definitely not needed to get around campus, though: All residence halls are no more than a 5-minute walk from any classroom.

The town of Sherman receives a thumbs-down from students. "It's a small town and [there is] basically nobody interesting to get to know, so you're confined to the 800 or so students that live on-campus," complains one student. While perhaps not the most exciting place, Sherman does offer some attractions: The city has four golf courses, 12 public parks, an 11,000-acre wildlife refuge, and Lake Texoma, one of the largest man-made lakes in the state. And Sherman is only 60 miles north of the Dallas/Fort Worth area, so students are able to enjoy the cultural and social activities of a big city as well.

Student Life

The student body is pretty darn diverse for a small, Texas college (though one student describes his fellow Aussies as "mostly white, upper- and middle-class Texans from small towns and suburbs"). Students say that you have to make your own fun on the weekends—that's where the "very cliquey" Greeks come in. Thirty percent of students join one of the ten local fraternities and seven local sororities on campus, though there is no Greek housing or special facilities. According to the school website, "Any AC student in good standing who has completed at least one semester at Austin College and meets the Rush guidelines may participate in Rush. Formal Rush takes place every year in February."

Austin College offers more than 70 student clubs and organizations including music, religious, and theater groups, student publications, student government, academic societies, service organizations, and Greek organizations. A college official lists the Fellowship of Christian Athletics, Campus Activity Board, Indian Cultural Association, Student Development Board, and International Relations Club as the most popular groups. There are chapters of Amnesty International and Habitat for Humanity on campus, and the Student International Organization serves both foreign students as well as students who have completed or are preparing to participate in the study abroad program; the group exposes students to foreign cultures. The Saturday Morning Program enables students to become involved in the Sherman community by becoming friends with low-income children between the ages of six and ten.

AC competes at the NCAA Division III level and is a member of the American Southwest Conference. Around 20 percent of the student body compete in the eight men's and seven women's intercollegiate sports teams, the Kangaroos. There are 14 intramural sports as well, which draw around 30 percent of the student body.

Other schools to check out: Southwestern, Southern Methodist, Trinity, Texas Christian, Baylor.

# of Students Waitlisted: 34
Students Accepting Place: 19
Waitlisted Students Admitted: 8

Applied Early Decision: 31
Early Decision Admitted: 30

Test Scores (middle 50%):
SAT Verbal: 568–680
SAT Math: 570–660
ACT Comp: 22–28

HS Rank of Entering Freshmen:
Top 10%: 45%
Top 25%: 73%
Top 50%: 96%

Avg. HS GPA: 3.39

THE EXPERTS SAY...

" AC has lots to offer, including dedicated faculty, great preprofessional programs, and a friendly, ethnically diverse student body. "

" To those who complain that Sherman isn't exactly one of the best college towns in the country: It's got a big lake and is within a kangaroo's hop of Dallas/Fort Worth, so quit whining. "

Costs (2004–5)

Tuition and Fees: $19,140

Room & Board: $7,089

Payment Plan(s): installment plan, deferred payment plan, pre-payment plan

Inst. Aid (est. 2003–04)

FT Undergrads Receiving Aid: 60%
Avg. Amount per Student: $17,454

FT Undergrads Receiving Non-Need-Based Scholarship or Grant Aid: 36%
Avg. Amount per Student: $8,473

Of Those Receiving Any Aid:

Rec. Need-Based Scholarship or Grant Aid: 99%
Average Award: $11,753

Rec. Need-Based Self-Help Aid: 77%
Average Award: $5,479

Upon Graduation, Avg. Loan Debt per Student: $22,085

Financial Aid Deadline: 4/1 (priority)

Graduates

Going to Graduate School:
32% Within One Year

Accepting Job Offer:
44% at time of graduation

Companies Recruiting On Campus: 32

Alumni Giving: 56%

BABSON COLLEGE

Office of Undergraduate Admission, Babson Park, MA 02457
Admissions Phone: (781) 239-5522; (800) 488-3696 Fax: (781) 239-4006
Email: ugradadmission@babson.edu Website: www.babson.edu
Application Website: www2.babson.edu/babson/babsonugp.nsf/Public/applynow

Note: Info. not verified by school.

General Info

Type of School: private, coed

Setting: suburban

Academic Calendar: semester

Student Body

Full-Time Undergrads: 1,735
  Men: 61%, Women: 39%

Total Undergrad Population:
  African American: 3%
  Asian American: 9%
  Latino: 4%
  Native American: <1%
  Caucasian: 46%
  International: 19%
  Out-of-State: 44%
  Living Off-Campus: 19%

Graduate and First-Professional
  Students: 1,672

Academics

Full-Time Faculty: 169
  With Ph.D.: 90%

Part-Time Faculty: 78
  With Ph.D.: 37%

Student/Faculty Ratio: 13:1

Freshmen Retention Rate: 92%

Graduation Rates:
  77% within four years
  83% within six years

Admissions

Regular Application Deadline: 2/1

Early Decision Deadline(s): 11/15

Early Action Deadline: 11/15

Fall Transfer Deadline: 4/1

Spring Transfer Deadline: 11/1

Total # of Students Applied: 2,402
  Admitted: 1,153
  Enrolled: 402

# of Students Waitlisted: 535
  Students Accepting Place: 268
  Waitlisted Students Admitted: 19

Applied Early Decision: 122
  Early Decision Admitted: 71

Test Scores (middle 50%):
  SAT Verbal: 550–630
  SAT Math: 600–690

Inside the Classroom

Babson College is a business specialty school in which students not only start their own business freshman year, but they are able to self-design their own business curriculum. What type of student would thrive at Babson? A college official replies: "An entrepreneurial-minded student who seeks a diverse learning environment in which they can delve into the visual and creative arts while pursuing their business degree. Babson students 'think outside the box' to solve business problems, and put their entrepreneurial skills to work doing this."

The nine academic divisions at Babson include accounting/law, arts and humanities, economics, entrepreneurship, finance, history and society, management, marketing, and math and science. The undergraduate curriculum uses an interdisciplinary approach to learning experience in management and the liberal arts, with an emphasis on field-based learning and the acquisition of business skills. Each student is expected to become competent in five broad areas: rhetoric; numeracy; ethics and social responsibility; international and multicultural perspectives; and leadership, teamwork, and creativity. All classes are taught by professors (they use no teaching assistants). The largest class at Babson has only 60 students, while the average class size is 27.

First-year students become CEOs immediately through the Foundation Management Experience (FME), a program that allows students to found and manage their own businesses. Each student project is funded by the college, and profits are donated to charity. Names of companies started by Babson students in spring 2004 include Renegade Promotions, Babsonopoly, Solemates Jewelry, and The Cup Co. The program also ties in a community service requirement, where students can donate time towards causes like helping the Special Olympics organization and serving meals for the homeless in Harvard Square.

Out-of-class learning experiences are also available to students, including a selection of over 1,000 internships. An impressive selection of study abroad programs is also available, in which students can select from 30 institutions in 18 countries. Both internships and study abroad programs are résumé stuffers for graduates looking to impress M.B.A. programs and future employers.

A new partnership with the nearby Franklin W. Olin College of Engineering also gives students the opportunity to cross-register for courses. This allows Olin students to strengthen their business and entrepreneurial skills while Babson students broaden their knowledge of technology-based business.

Campus Environment

Babson's manicured, 370-acre campus in Wellesley, Massachusetts features plenty of woods and rolling hills. Located about 14 miles west of Boston, the school is within easy reach of both the businesses and the distractions of the big city. "Believe it or not, even though we're in close proximity to Boston, students may have cars on campus for all four years," a college official tells us. "They are required to obtain a parking permit, which costs just $50 per year for students living in on-campus housing and $25 for commuters… There is a shuttle that runs on Saturdays for students who do not have cars."

All freshmen are required to live on campus, in one of the 12 residence halls. Options for students include single-, double-, triple-, and quadruple-person rooms, with special areas set aside for substance-free housing and multicultural group living. Most freshmen (90 percent) are assigned to one of two all-freshmen dorms; the remaining 10 percent of freshmen are in integrated dorms all over campus. Residence halls may contain kitchens, study lounges, meeting rooms, and "hatcheries"—work space set aside for freshmen to manage their fledgling FME businesses. The main eatery is Trim Dining Hall, with its variety of food stations and an extensive vegan bar.

An alternative to the dining hall is the Crossroads Café, which serves grilled food, snacks, and sandwiches in the Reynolds Campus Center. The center serves as the hub of student life at Babson, housing the bookstore, a coffee bar called Woody's, a food court, vendor carts, meeting and reading rooms, a television lounge, a student mailroom, and a games room. Places for students to socialize include Roger's, the campus pub, which serves nonalcoholic beverages as well as beer and wine for students over 21.

One fairly recent campus addition that adds variety to Babson's offerings is the the Sorenson Center for the Performing Arts, where many arts and entertainment events are held, including student performances, creativity programs, touring artist presentations, and community arts groups. The facility includes the 450-seat Carling-Sorenson Theater, a "black box" rehearsal space, individual practice rooms for musicians, a clay studio, a darkroom, and a drawing studio.

Student Life

The Babson social life is understated; an article in the April 2, 2002 *Boston Globe* described a student survey that showed a majority of students voicing dissatisfaction with their entertainment and social options. One senior cited the administration's tough anti-alcohol policies as a contributing reason: A strict three-strikes rule presides over alcohol violations, and there is a limit of 15 students for each gathering or party that's held in the suites. Another student suggested the prevailing business culture as a possible cause: "People are so focused on the end result, they forget they have four years here. Spirit activities aren't as important as the marketing club bringing speakers to campus." The *Globe* article does mention some signs of improvement lately, most notably a campus-wide outpouring of support for the men's basketball team.

The Babson Beavers compete at the NCAA Division III level. Sports for men and women include basketball, golf, lacrosse, track and field, soccer, tennis, swimming, alpine skiing, and cross country. Men can compete as Babson Beavers in baseball and ice hockey, while women can play field hockey, softball, and volleyball. Intramural sports include floor hockey, basketball, soccer, racquetball, squash, tennis, volleyball, squash, flag football, and coed softball.

Many of the student clubs and organizations on campus are centered around business, such as the Asia Business Forum, the marketing club, and the Babson College Fund, which is a mutual fund managed by undergraduate and graduate students. Other groups are more diversionary, like the Babson Barbecue Forum (BBQ), the outdoor committee, and the Buffoonery Committee—an annual variety show produced by graduate students. In addition, "the Babson Dance Ensemble almost always sells out their dance performances, and the Babson Players put on numerous plays and musicals each year," we are told.

HS Rank of Entering Freshmen:
Top 10%: 44%
Top 25%: 81%
Top 50%: 100%

THE EXPERTS SAY...

" Babson's stellar reputation in business and entrepreneurial studies makes it the perfect stepping stone for an M.B.A. "

" Until the administration's measures to improve school spirit kick in, the social life for students is all business, too. "

Costs (2003–04)
Tuition and Fees: $27,248
Room & Board: $9,978

BARD COLLEGE

Po Box 5000, Annandale-On-Hudson, NY 12504-5000
Admissions Phone: (845) 758-7472 Fax: (845) 758-5208
Email: admission@bard.edu
Website: www.bard.edu

General Info

Type of School: private, coed
Setting: small town
Academic Calendar: 4-1-4

Student Body

Full-Time Undergrads: 1,310
  Men: 44%, Women: 56%

Part-Time Undergrads: 55
  Men: 38%, Women: 62%

Total Undergrad Population:
  African American: 3%
  Asian American: 4%
  Latino: 5%
  Native American: <1%
  Caucasian: 79%
  International: 6%
  Out-of-State: 75%
  Living Off-Campus: 1%

Graduate and First-Professional
  Students: 202

Academics

Full-Time Faculty: 113
  With Ph.D.: 97%

Part-Time Faculty: 101
  With Ph.D.: 86%

Student/Faculty Ratio: 8:1

Most Popular Majors:
  languages and literature (19%)
  studio art (8%)
  film (7%)
  political studies (6%)
  music (5%)

Freshmen Retention Rate: 89%

Graduation Rates:
  59% within four years
  71% within six years

Admissions

Regular Application Deadline: 1/15

Early Action Deadline: 11/1

Fall Transfer Deadline: 1/15

Spring Transfer Deadline: 11/1

Total # of Students Applied: 3,118
  Admitted: 1,107
  Enrolled: 343

# of Students Waitlisted: 235
  Students Accepting Place: 216
  Waitlisted Students Admitted: 37

Inside the Classroom

Students at Bard create "an active plan for learning," choosing and pursuing their academic interests with care and faculty support. This small and progressive liberal arts school prides itself on rigorous, if untraditional, academics and a responsive faculty. All first-year students at "the place to think" participate in the Workshop in Language and Thinking, an intensive, three-week writing program that begins in early August, and the First-Year Seminar. Freshmen also take part in a structured program of first-year advising and a series of elective courses in which they are encouraged to "experiment with the unfamiliar."

Lower College, as Bard calls freshmen and sophomore years, focuses on general education with a multidisciplinary flavor; Upper College (junior and senior years) involves advanced study of specific subjects and a lot of independent work. During Upper College, tutorials, one-on-one classes with professors, are the norm. The Senior Project is considered the capstone of a Bard education and can be a research paper, a translation, findings from fieldwork, original art, a performance, or other approved work. A student moving from Lower to Upper College "moderates" by assessing his or her first two years and preparing a statement identifying goals and a proposed study plan for the next two years.

Students have great things to say about Bard faculty, who are all full professors and "teachers first." Students work in small seminars and one-on-one with professors, so close relationships form, and it's not uncommon for students to visit with professors at their homes. Class size in the Lower College averages at about 14 students, and 8 in the Upper College; the student-faculty ratio is 8:1.

Many of Bard's academic programs are interdisciplinary in nature. Distribution requirements include a course from each of these categories: philosophical, aesthetic, and interpretive study; literary texts and linguistics; social and historical study; foreign language and culture; natural sciences, empirical social sciences, and mathematics; performing and visual arts; and a "quantitative" course designated as having a significant mathematical component.

Bard's best and most popular divisions are in the arts and in language and literature, particularly the writing program, but social sciences are also strong. Bard is also a great place to study photography. Bard is in the midst of a wide-ranging science initiative to improve facilities and programs and there are places reserved for Bard students in Rockefeller University's Summer Undergraduate Research Program. Bard attracts strong students, even though it doesn't require the SAT, and the Excellence and Equal Cost Program (EEC) cuts Bard's high tuition to state school prices for academic achievers. Bard oversees Simon's Rock College of Bard in Massachusetts, the only liberal arts college for 15- and 16-year-olds.

Bard's academic focus may be better preparation for grad school than for the job market, but students say that the writing and thinking skills developed here are highly transferable to the "real world." During the six-week winter intercession, students pursue internships and study in language immersion classes in places like Heidelberg, Bologna, Tours, Oaxaca, St. Petersburg, and Tianjin.

Campus Environment

Bard's 540-acre campus is located in Annandale-on-Hudson in the Hudson Valley, about 90 miles north of New York City. The Hudson River borders the campus on the west and the Catskill Mountains are nearby; the campus is adjacent to 1,400 acres of nature preserve. ("Very woodsy. . .great for creative writing," a guidance counselor muses).While the area is breathtakingly beautiful, with historic mansions and gorgeous scenery, there is no real college town for students, and isolation is a complaint. Students say a car is essential, although the campus provides a shuttle to nearby Redhook, Rhinebeck, and Tivoli. The Amtrak to New York City is about nine miles away.

Recently Bard trustees made a $120 million donation to the college, a gift that roughly doubled the school's endowment overnight. As a result, the college has undertaken a number of new construction projects, including much-needed new housing to replace the "Ravine" dorms, a source of student gripes. New additions are the Alumni Houses (known individually as Shelov, Bluecher, Bourne, Leonard, Obreshkove, and Wolff), and the Village Dormitories, nine environmentally friendly residence halls designed with Bard student input; these new "green" dormitories make use of timber from non-virgin sources and are heated and cooled using a geothermal heat exchange system. Another new addition is the Performing Arts Center, designed by the internationally acclaimed architect Frank O. Gehry.

Student Life

Artsy, academically-focused Bard is not a party school by any stretch of the imagination. There are no fraternities or sororities (not PC, say some), and athletics don't draw crowds. Come weekends, many students escape to New York City or the artist's colony at Woodstock, half an hour away, to find fun. Still the campus isn't dead. There are parties and dances, and a cinema on campus, plus student coffee shops in the neighboring towns. The Winter Carnival raises money to fight world hunger, and the annual Drag Race ("Dress in drag or don't dress at all!") is a festival of cross-dressing. The Bard Music Festival takes place each summer on campus and at Lincoln Center in New York City as part of the latter's Great Performers Series. With so many drama majors, it's not surprising that theater is very big on campus.

Students agree that Bard isn't a school for jocks, but many like to keep fit. The Hudson Valley offers a range of outdoor sports including skiing, snowboarding bicycling, hiking, rock climbing and kayaking. Bard fields six varsity teams in Division III and offers eight club and nine intramural sports; women's varsity soccer is strong.

Bard students are eclectic, original, and very liberal. The student body is diverse for a small school. This nontraditional school is "not for everyone," a guidance counselor warns. The artistic temperament runs high here, and some complain that the atmosphere can be cold and cliquish. Political correctness is the norm, and the small conservative contingent on campus can feel outnumbered and outgunned. Bard students are deeply engaged by their studies and their art. The best way to break through social barriers, students say, is to talk: The sensitive Bard student will surprise you.

Other schools to check out: Eugene Lang, Sarah Lawrence, Bennington, Marlboro, SUNY Purchase.

Test Scores (middle 50%):
SAT Verbal: 650–750
SAT Math: 590–690

HS Rank of Entering Freshmen:
Top 10%: 64%
Top 25%: 90%
Top 50%: 99%

Avg. HS GPA: 3.5

THE EXPERTS SAY...

" Bard is a unique mixture of classical and progressive education designed to create clear thinkers and writers."

" If independent study isn't your bag, neither is Bard. "

Costs (2003–04)

Tuition and Fees: $27,680

Room & Board: $8,134

Payment Plan(s): installment plan, pre-payment plan

Inst. Aid (est. 2003–04)

Institutional Aid, Need-Based: $10,894,679

Institutional Aid, Non-Need-Based: $664,808

FT Undergrads Receiving Aid: 61%
Avg. Amount per Student: $21,466

Of Those Receiving Any Aid:

Rec. Need-Based Scholarship or Grant Aid: 94%
Average Award: $17,724

Rec. Need-Based Self-Help Aid: 85%
Average Award: $4,244

Upon Graduation, Avg. Loan Debt per Student: $15,400

Financial Aid Deadline: 2/15, 2/1 (priority)

Graduates

Going to Graduate School: 45% Within One Year

BARNARD COLLEGE

3009 Broadway, New York, NY 10027
Admissions Phone: (212) 854-2014 Fax: (212) 854-6220
Email: admissions@barnard.edu
Website: barnard.edu

General Info

Type of School: private, all women
Setting: urban
Academic Calendar: semester

Student Body

Full-Time Undergrads: 2,232
  Women: 100%
Part-Time Undergrads: 49
  Women: 100%

Total Undergrad Population:
  African American: 5%
  Asian American: 19%
  Latino: 6%
  Native American: 1%
  Caucasian: 66%
  International: 3%
  Out-of-State: 64%
  Living Off-Campus: 11%

Academics

Full-Time Faculty: 186
  With Ph.D.: 94%
Part-Time Faculty: 107
  With Ph.D.: 84%
Student/Faculty Ratio: 10:1

Most Popular Majors:
  psychology (13%)
  English (12%)
  economics (12%)
  political science (9%)
  history (7%)

Completing 2 or More Majors: 7%
Freshmen Retention Rate: 93%

Graduation Rates:
  75% within four years
  84% within six years

Admissions

Regular Application Deadline: 1/1
Early Decision Deadline(s): 11/15
Fall Transfer Deadline: 4/1
Spring Transfer Deadline: 11/15
Total # of Students Applied: 4,034
  Admitted: 1,254
  Enrolled: 554
# of Students Waitlisted: 766
  Students Accepting Place: 507
  Waitlisted Students Admitted: 36
Applied Early Decision: 337
  Early Decision Admitted: 153

Inside the Classroom

"The atmosphere throbs with intellectual excitement and curiosity," raves a member of Barnard's class of 2006. Barnard's location in New York City and its status as one of the four undergraduate schools of Columbia University give its students amazing academic offerings. An independent college of liberal arts and sciences for women, Barnard has its own campus, faculty, and administration. But thanks to the Columbia-Barnard partnership, Barnard students can take all the courses they want across the street at Columbia—without dealing with Columbia's infamous registration procedures.

Courses at Barnard, though, tend to be much smaller (the student/faculty ratio is about 10:1), and are taught by professors, not TAs. This lets students work closely with Barnard's prestigious faculty, a high percentage of whom are women, although a senior protests "the fact that so few female professors are given tenure. All the Barnard department heads are men!" A sociology-political science major calls students "driven" and "competitive," but a math major counters: "Far from a competitive 'grind,' Barnard is a supportive community that encourages all of its members to succeed. Professors often linger after class, arrange to meet in campus eateries, and provide extra support via email." However: "I can scarcely imagine how the unmotivated would survive here, without handholding and academic leniency."

Students choose from among about 50 different majors or create their own; programs in English, creative writing, psychology, economics, and the performing arts are strong. During their first year, students take a writing course and an interdisciplinary seminar. General education requirements (called "Ways of Knowing") are rigorous and include courses across a broad spectrum of disciplines. Seniors must complete a major project or take a comprehensive examination. During the first two weeks of each semester, classes are "open," so that students can get a first-hand look at them before enrolling.

The world-famous Center for Research on Women provides a venue for feminist scholarship and activism. A guidance counselor rightly calls the city a "lab" for students: a senior praises the "great job and internship opportunities"—there are over 2,500 internships in Manhattan. Barnard also offers accelerated joint-degree programs with Columbia's graduate divisions in law, engineering, dentistry, and international and public affairs. Music students may qualify for a Barnard B.A. and a Master's in Music from Juilliard, or attend classes at the nearby Manhattan School of Music. Students also may take programs in Arizona at Biosphere 2.

Campus Environment

"The campus itself appears deceptively serene and cozy for one that houses over 2,000 women," remarks a student. Most freshwomen live in the Quad, four residence halls facing an enclosed courtyard, in doubles or triples; upperclasswomen can live in apartment-style housing or suites. Security is considered good. Drugs, alcohol, and smoking are all taboo in the dorms. Housing is guaranteed for all four years; numerous meal plans are available. About 90 percent of students live on campus.

Barnard's upper-Manhattan neighborhood, Morningside Heights, has gentrified considerably from its rougher days. "NYC rent is expensive, but most people seem to enjoy living in the apartments around Barnard. The location is safe, clean, and collegiate-feeling," comments a student. Another student quips: "If you get off-campus housing you're either a) rich, b) sharing with 10 people, or c) living in a closet." Barnard students know better than to even think of bringing a car to Manhattan. "No car—I'm a slave to the subway system!" jokes a student (subway and bus lines stop right on campus).

Student Life

"Places of interest?" a student asks. "It's New York. That said, I didn't stray a block from campus for the first two months of school, and I never had a dull moment." The hub of campus life is the McIntosh Student Center—with a cafeteria, music practice rooms, an art exhibit area, a bowling alley, and offices for Barnard's 80-plus student organizations; many activities enlist members from both Columbia and Barnard. "Barnard students are never more passionate than when they dance to cherished ballet music, debate public policy in the library cafe, or compete for a vacancy in the dorms' musical practice rooms," a math major declares.

"Weeknights revolve around campus: studying at the library, socializing, studying in dorms," reports a freshwoman. "Weekends: New York City is our playground. For the cost of round-trip subway fare, students descend on the city for a day at the museums, parks, and people-watching." A sociology-political science major says, "There are some who always stay in either because of money or because they study too much, but most people get out a decent amount," adding: "People who don't like the city will hate it here." With coed Columbia across the street, a senior states, "Barnard feels more like a coed university than a 'girls' school'" but laments: "I feel like I missed out on a real college experience (no campus life, female dorms)." Also rankling: "Columbia assertions that we are not as smart as they are."

Barnard students compete in the NCAA Division I in 14 teams. "Intramural sports are all the rage, but we don't have enough 'athletes' for serious varsity victories," a first-year student explains. Sororities, claims a student, "have nothing to do with popularity, and could in fact hurt popularity for some." In addition to the usual campus work, the Barnard Bartending Agency, Barnard Babysitting Service, and Barnard Store all provide jobs. Drugs aren't big: "If there are drugs and alcohol at Barnard, they must be kept somewhere dark and secret," says a freshwoman.

The student body is heterogeneous by social background, but 36 percent are minority students, and there are active Jewish, Asian, African American, and Arab communities. Post-9/11 race issues and the war on Iraq have been hot topics recently—a senior complains about the "pervasive left-wing, politically correct dogma." "The typical Barnard student is politically aware, financially and socially savvy, and confident, with a grasp of writing skills as firm as her handshake," says a frosh. "Intellectually aroused, creative, high-energy... humbling." However, a senior bemoans the "attempts at school spirit (we have none)," "closed communities," and "bitchy girls" ("very NYC"), and warns: "It is also not the friendliest campus, so you have to be pretty resilient and aggressive." But another student counters, "One cannot pass through the Barnard gates without returning on the arm of a friend."

Other schools to check out: Columbia, Brown, Wesleyan, Cornell, Bryn Mawr.

Test Scores (middle 50%):
SAT Verbal: 650–730
SAT Math: 630–700
ACT Comp: 28–31
HS Rank of Entering Freshmen:
Top 10%: 82%
Top 25%: 99%
Top 50%: 100%
Avg. HS GPA: 3.86

Costs (2003–04)

Tuition and Fees: $26,528
Room & Board: $10,462
Payment Plan(s): installment plan, deferred payment plan, pre-payment plan

THE EXPERTS SAY...

" Barnard alumnae range from world-famous authors like Zora Neale Hurston to entrepreneurs like Martha Stewart. "

" Combine PC ideas with a no-nonsense NYC attitude, and you've got Barnard. "

Inst. Aid (est. 2003–04)

Institutional Aid, Need-Based: $15,311,995

FT Undergrads Receiving Aid: 42%
Avg. Amount per Student: $26,045

Of Those Receiving Any Aid:

Rec. Need-Based Scholarship or Grant Aid: 94%
Average Award: $21,533

Rec. Need-Based Self-Help Aid: 100%
Average Award: $5,192

Upon Graduation, Avg. Loan Debt per Student: $16,275

Financial Aid Deadline: 2/1

Graduates

Going to Graduate School:
24% Within One Year

Companies Recruiting On Campus: 90

Alumni Giving: 45%

BATES COLLEGE

2 Andrews Road, Lewiston, ME 04240
Admissions Phone: (207) 786-6000 Fax: (207) 786-6025
Email: admissions@bates.edu Website: www.bates.edu
Application Website: www.commonapp.org

General Info

Type of School: private, coed
Setting: small town
Academic Calendar: 4-4-1

Student Body

Full-Time Undergrads: 1,746
 Men: 48%, Women: 52%

Total Undergrad Population:
 African American: 2%
 Asian American: 3%
 Latino: 2%
 Native American: <1%
 Caucasian: 83%
 International: 6%
 Out-of-State: 88%
 Living Off-Campus: 9%

Academics

Full-Time Faculty: 163
 With Ph.D.: 95%

Part-Time Faculty: 27
 With Ph.D.: 81%

Student/Faculty Ratio: 10:1

Most Popular Majors:
 psychology (11%)
 economics (11%)
 political science (9%)
 biology (7%)
 English (6%)

Completing 2 or More Majors: 10%

Freshmen Retention Rate: 93%

Graduation Rates:
 84% within four years
 89% within six years

Admissions

Regular Application Deadline: 1/15

Early Decision Deadline(s): 11/15,
 1/1

Fall Transfer Deadline: 3/1

Spring Transfer Deadline: 11/1

Total # of Students Applied: 4,089
 Admitted: 1,254
 Enrolled: 487

# of Students Waitlisted: 844
 Students Accepting Place: 211
 Waitlisted Students Admitted: 22

Applied Early Decision: 432
 Early Decision Admitted: 187

Inside the Classroom

Years ago, the faculty at Bates voted to make submitting SAT scores an optional part of the admissions process because they felt that test scores don't accurately represent a student's individual strengths and potential. As a result, writing samples, school transcripts, and personal interviews hold much greater weight in the selection process. That's just one of the many ways Bates has maintained its ideal as a place where students are treated as individuals in an open, tolerant academic environment.

Bates offers 32 majors, including interdisciplinary programs which have grown increasingly popular. While Bates is strong in the liberal arts and the social sciences, the college truly shines in the natural sciences. A few years ago, the college instituted an advising system for students interested in health professions that kicks in during their first year. The system seems to be working: In 2001, 100 percent of the Bates students and alumni who applied to med schools were admitted.

For all students, the core curriculum includes courses in the humanities, social sciences, natural sciences, quantitative techniques, and physical education. Nearly all freshmen take a first-year seminar—limited-enrollment courses in a wide variety of offbeat subjects such as "Ethics and Human Rights in Sports," "Anatomy of a Few Small Machines," and "Doing It, Getting It, Seeing It, Reading It" (about sex and sexuality).

With an average class size of 15, classes at Bates tend to focus on discussion and debate. Some classes are team-taught by three or four professors who challenge students to articulate and rethink their opinions. While Bates professors are known as harsh graders who make strict demands on students, students still describe their profs as being friendly and accessible: "While A's are nearly impossible to receive, so are F's," a student tells us. "The profs will do everything they can to help you make it through."

All Batesies must take two "short terms" before they graduate. The short term is a special five-week period in May when students can take it a bit easier by studying something more unconventional. Some short-term courses involve field trips (studying marine biology on the coast of Maine or theater in New York City) or more extensive travel (learning about art history in Italy or politics in Mexico). More than half of the student body participates in a study abroad program at some point. For year-long programs, studying at the prestigious London School of Economics is the most popular choice; during the winter semester, Australia is number one on students' lists. Bates also participates in the Colby-Bates-Bowdoin Study Abroad Program, where faculty from the three colleges host programs in London, Cape Town, and Quito each year.

Nine out of ten seniors complete a thesis. The thesis—where students spend their final semester or year undertaking a project related to their major—is offered in all departments and is required by most. In an article about the senior thesis in *The Bates Student*, a political science major warns, "This is something you are going to be working on for a long time, and it has to be something you are really interested in, otherwise you will hate every moment of it."

Campus Environment

An hour from the stunning Maine coastline, Bates's beautifully maintained 109-acre campus has an impressive mixture of old and new structures. All freshmen are assigned to one of 13 mostly coed dormitories, which tend to be small but are otherwise pretty good. Nine in ten Batesies remain on campus for all four years; nearly half live in one of 25 restored Victorian houses. Several of these absolutely charming residences are "theme houses." The six theme houses for 2002–03 were: Human Rights, Mentoring Leadership, Fine Arts, Chemical-Free Activities, Performance, and Russian.

The gorgeous Maine forest and coastline are perfect for various outdoor activities. All Bates students are official members of the Outing Club (the oldest such organization in the country), which sponsors activities such as hiking, camping, mountain biking, and skiing. And if you twist an ankle during an outing, fear not: The Bates Health Center is open 24/7 during the academic year—one of the few college health centers open at all hours.

Student Life

Founded in 1855 by abolitionists, Bates was established as an institution of higher learning open to people of any race, religion, nationality, or sex. "Students can affect just about anything here, from policy to play," states a senior. One example: In 1998, in response to student protests over the inadequate response to a string of alleged sexual assaults on campus, the administration decided to start alerting the student body to sexual assault allegations once the alleged victims file charges with the dean's office.

About one-tenth of the student body come from Maine, and a significant portion of the remainder hail from other parts of New England, especially Massachusetts. While the school tends to attract a lot of white, upper-class, prep school graduates, Batesies are generally tolerant and open to new experiences and viewpoints, and many involve themselves in political organizations and causes. Bates has never had fraternities or sororities, following the principle that all student organizations are open to all students. "Everyone is welcome in pretty much everything," shrugs one student.

Almost every Bates student is into playing some sport or activity, either on an intercollegiate or intramural team. There are 15 varsity sports for men and 16 for women, plus 12 club sports. About half of all students participate in service-learning, and about a third of the faculty include a service component in their courses. In a recent year, students provided 59,381 hours of service to 139 nonprofit groups and government agencies.

Bates may not be a raucous party school, but no student can live by books alone. "Sleep seems optional because, to borrow a cliché, we work and play so hard," says a senior. Small parties are frequent and a number of large, annual campus-wide events, like Winter Carnvial, are eagerly anticipated. Another fun (if not dangerous) winter tradition is "puddle jumping," when students attempt to pole vault over a hole in the frozen campus lake.

Other schools to check out: Bowdoin, Colby, Middlebury, Amherst, Williams.

Test Scores (middle 50%):
SAT Verbal: 630–700
SAT Math: 640–710

HS Rank of Entering Freshmen:
Top 10%: 65%
Top 25%: 92%
Top 50%: 100%

THE EXPERTS SAY...

" Changes may be in store for Bates: On July 1, 2002, Elaine Tuttle Hansen, formerly provost at Haverford College, assumed office as the seventh president of Bates College. "

" The admissions office really wants to get to know you, so send in those essays, portfolios, and videotapes (though no one wants to see your baby pictures). "

Costs (est. 2004–05)

Comprehensive Fees: $37,500

Payment Plan(s): installment plan, pre-payment plan

Inst. Aid (est. 2003–04)

Institutional Aid, Need-Based: $13,157,456

FT Undergrads Receiving Aid: 40%
Avg. Amount per Student: $24,457

Of Those Receiving Any Aid:

Rec. Need-Based Scholarship or Grant Aid: 95%
Average Award: $21,234

Rec. Need-Based Self-Help Aid: 90%
Average Award: $4,716

Upon Graduation, Avg. Loan Debt per Student: $14,401

Financial Aid Deadline: 2/1, 11/15 (priority)

Graduates

Alumni Giving: 32%

BAYLOR UNIVERSITY

One Bear Place #97056, Waco, TX 76798-7056
Admissions Phone: (254) 710-3435; 800-229-5678 Fax: (254) 710-3436
Email: Admission_Serv_Office@Baylor.edu
Website: www.baylor.edu

General Info

Type of School: private, coed, Baptist

Setting: small town

Academic Calendar: semester

Student Body

Full-Time Undergrads: 11,203
  Men: 42%, Women: 58%

Part-Time Undergrads: 409
  Men: 46%, Women: 54%

Total Undergrad Population:
  African American: 6%
  Asian American: 5%
  Latino: 8%
  Native American: 1%
  Caucasian: 75%
  International: 1%
  Out-of-State: 15%
  In Fraternities: 15%
  In Sororities: 17%

Graduate and First-Professional
  Students: 2,225

Academics

Full-Time Faculty: 777
  With Ph.D.: 75%

Part-Time Faculty: 144

Student/Faculty Ratio: 16:1

Most Popular Majors:
  pre–business (15%)
  biology (7%)
  psychology (5%)
  teacher education (4%)
  journalism (3%)

Freshmen Retention Rate: 84%

Graduation Rates:
  40% within four years
  70% within six years

Admissions

Regular Application Deadline:
  3/1 (priority)

Total # of Students Applied: 8,968
  Admitted: 7,342
  Enrolled: 2,678

Test Scores (middle 50%):
  SAT Verbal: 530–630
  SAT Math: 540–645
  ACT Comp: 22–27
  ACT English: 21–27
  ACT Math: 20–26

Inside the Classroom

Baylor University is comprised of 10 schools and colleges. These include the College of Arts and Sciences; George W. Truett Theological Seminary; Hankamer School of Business; Louise Herrington School of Nursing; School of Education; School of Engineering and Computer Science; School of Music; School of Social Work, as well as the Graduate School and Law School. 158 baccalaureate degree programs are offered at the undergraduate level. Even though Baylor is a large school with almost 14,000 students, the student-to-faculty ratio is still only roughly 16:1, and the average class size is around 30 students. Additionally, practically all classes (around 93%) are taught by faculty members as opposed to graduate assistants.

The Baylor Interdisciplinary Core (BIC) is an alternative type of core curriculum. While still meeting students' general degree requirements, the school states that the BIC "offers an interdisciplinary curriculum of course sequences that replaces traditional courses in the humanities, fine arts, social sciences, and physical sciences." The BIC strives to provide coherence and a sense of purpose to learning, enlarge students' perspectives of the world, and to foster a sense of commitment to the community and connection to the outside, or "real," world. The program is meant to accomplish all of these goals through courses that build upon and complement each other, and through the development of relationships among students and faculty through open forums for discussion. The program is composed of five sequences of courses— World Cultures, The World of Rhetoric, Social World, Natural World, and The Examined Life. A student's major or program of study may influence which specific courses he or she takes within the BIC.

Baylor has high aspirations for the future as well. The school boasts that under the their innovative 10-year plan, known as Baylor 2012, "Baylor intends to enter the top tier of American universities while reaffirming and deepening its distinctive Christian mission. Baylor will build a faculty and a student body to provide leadership in a period of change and conflict. It will strengthen and expand its traditional sense of community. It will pursue athletic excellence with integrity. In doing all these things, it will take its place among the finest colleges and universities in the world."

Campus Environment

Freshmen at Baylor are not required to live on campus, although it is encouraged. Single-sex dorms for women and men are available, as well as apartment complexes and housing for married, graduate, law and seminary students. One of the goals of Baylor 2012 includes building new residence halls and renovating older ones.

Baylor has recently modified its dorm visitation hours, since the issue had been a major student gripe for some time. Previously, men were allowed to visit women's dorms (and vice versa) for 10 hours total per week for freshmen and 12 for upperclassmen; these hours have been increased significantly. The issue comes down to a struggle between the administration's desire to keep students happy (and keep them living on campus), and not compromising the values of this Baptist university. In fact, some students have disapproved of the administration's decision to make male-female mingling in the dorms more convenient.

KAPLAN

Baylor is a 432-acre campus in Waco, Texas. Waco is situated nicely for road trips, being a mere 100 miles south of the Dallas/Fort Worth area and 100 miles north of Austin. Attractions in Waco include Fort Fisher, the Texas Ranger Hall of Fame and Museum, the Dr. Pepper Museum, the Brazas River, and the historic suspension bridge. Waco also offers ample opportunity for outdoor activity: bike trails and golf courses can be found at Cameron Park; fishing, swimming and skiing can be done at Lake Waco—the largest urban lake in Texas; and there are fishing and hunting preserves as well as camping areas. The Heart O'Texas Fair and Rodeo and the Baylor Homecoming are two major Waco events that occur each year.

Baylor is a small enough campus that you can walk from one side to the other within 10 minutes. However, a car is generally the way to get around town. Parking on campus can be tight, but there are both parking lots and garages to help alleviate the problem. For students without the luxury of a car, however, city buses are available that service various areas of the city. The school also offers a trolley system that transports students in and around the school, as well as to many of the nearby apartments. Though Waco does have its own airport, there's also a shuttle available to the Dallas/Fort Worth airport.

Student Life

Baylor offers 260 student organizations on campus. Greek life is available, as well as academic, honor, music/performance, religious, ethnic, and political groups. Fifty percent of the student body is involved in intramural sports, and there are 19 club sports.

Community service is important at Baylor. One annual tradition among students is called Steppin' Out; this involves setting aside one Saturday each semester to 'step' into the Waco community to help improve the area and provide assistance to its people. The school also features the first collegiate chapter of Habitat for Humanity.

Students can take advantage of the historic downtown entertainment district, which has featured live concerts on the banks of the Brazos, great Texas musicians at Oktoberfest, and the work of local artists at the Open Door Arts Fest. The area also offers its share of bars and nightclubs.

Other schools to check out: Texas Christian, Southern Methodist, Belmont, Austin College.

HS Rank of Entering Freshmen:
Top 10%: 38%
Top 25%: 67%
Top 50%: 91%

Costs (2004–5)

Tuition and Fees: $19,780

Room & Board: $5,713
note: Board is 11-meal plan

Payment Plan(s): installment plan

THE EXPERTS SAY...

" This traditional Baptist school offers enough programs to satisfy anyone. Baylor is a real educational value. "

" The Baylor Interdisciplinary Core is the only 'alternative' aspect of this clean-cut, traditional university. "

Inst. Aid (est. 2003–04)

Institutional Aid, Need-Based: $20,147,456

Institutional Aid, Non-Need-Based: $15,507,162

FT Undergrads Receiving Aid: 46%
Avg. Amount per Student: $12,282

FT Undergrads Receiving Non-Need-Based Scholarship or Grant Aid: 28%
Avg. Amount per Student: $5,419

Of Those Receiving Any Aid:

Rec. Need-Based Scholarship or Grant Aid: 92%
Average Award: $7,954

Rec. Need-Based Self-Help Aid: 77%
Average Award: $5,441

Financial Aid Deadline: rolling, 3/1 (priority)

BELMONT UNIVERSITY

1900 Belmont Boulevard, Nashville, TN 37212-3757
Admissions Phone: (615) 460-6785; Fax: (615) 460-5434
Email: buadmission@belmont.edu
Website: belmont.edu

General Info

Type of School: private, coed, Baptist
Setting: urban
Academic Calendar: semester

Student Body

Full-Time Undergrads: 2,638
  Men: 40%, Women: 60%

Part-Time Undergrads: 291
  Men: 31%, Women: 69%

Total Undergrad Population:
  African American: 4%
  Asian American: 1%
  Latino: 2%
  Native American: <1%
  Caucasian: 89%
  International: 1%
  Out-of-State: 51%
  Living Off-Campus: 43%
  In Fraternities: 3%
  In Sororities: 3%

Graduate and First-Professional
  Students: 640

Academics

Full-Time Faculty: 199
  With Ph.D.: 67%

Part-Time Faculty: 222

Student/Faculty Ratio: 11:1

Most Popular Majors:
  music business (30%)
  commercial music (9%)
  business administration (7%)
  nursing (7%)
  English (2%)

Completing 2 or More Majors: 2%

Freshmen Retention Rate: 78%

Graduation Rates:
  39% within four years
  55% within six years

Admissions

Regular Application Deadline: 5/1;
  3/15 (priority)

Fall Transfer Deadline: 8/1, 5/1
  (priority)

Total # of Students Applied: 1,607
  Admitted: 1,207
  Enrolled: 603

Test Scores (middle 50%):
  SAT Verbal: 520–620
  SAT Math: 510–620

Inside the Classroom

Belmont University provides a strong liberal arts and professional education in a nurturing, service-oriented Christian community. One of the largest private colleges in Tennessee, Belmont nonetheless offers a personal education with small class sizes and a terrific faculty/student ratio (11:1) in so-called "Music City, USA." It's "an excellent combination of a small school within a large, urban setting," a school official tells us. Students interested in entering the music industry—either the performing side or the business side of things—benefit from one of the best and largest programs in the country. (Trisha Yearwood, Lee Ann Womack, and Brad Paisley are just a few of Belmont's talented alumni.) The opportunities for music and music business majors abound: Recently, the university acquired Ocean Way Nashville, a recording studio on Music Row, and it has also just partnered with the Country Music Hall of Fame to restore and operate RCA's Studio B.

But Belmont is more than just a music school. It also boasts excellent business programs, which were recently awarded the highest level of accreditation. In all, there are approximately 57 major areas of study in five undergraduate colleges: College of Arts and Sciences, College of the Business Administration, College of Health Sciences, College of Visual and Performing Arts, and the School of Religion. Students must take a host of core curriculum courses in various areas: fine arts, humanities, social sciences, oral communication, written communication, world civilization, biological sciences, math, physical science, wellness, and religion. In an effort to encourage well-rounded thinking and lifelong (and out-of-classroom) learning, Belmont also has a "Convocation" requirement, which students fulfill by attending a specific number of cultural, social, academic, and spiritual programs, or "experiences."

Facilities and academic opportunities rival those of schools twice Belmont's size. The Belmont Undergraduate Research Symposium (BURS) affords students the opportunity to conduct independent research and present it to a community of peers. The Office of Career Services gets raves for its helpfulness and success rate. The faculty is praised as smart, helpful, and accessible. An enrollment of around 3,000 allows for much interaction between professors and students, as well as between students and students. It's a competitive but Christian environment.

Campus Environment

The university is ideally situated in the best of both worlds: it's in the city of Nashville but virtually all traffic skirts the 62-acre campus, so it remains quiet and feels almost secluded. Once the grounds of a 19th century estate, Belmont's beautiful, historic campus is dotted with Victorian gardens, statues, and gazebos and features the antebellum Belmont Mansion, the university's social center and historical museum which is a must-see for Nashville tourists.

All freshmen and sophomores from outside of Nashville are required to live on campus. There is one coed, two men's, and two women's halls; rooms are arranged either suite-style (two rooms joined by a bathroom) or traditional-style (double rooms with community bathrooms). Other housing options include furnished, four-bedroom townhouses; unfurnished, two-bedroom apartments; and the recently built

KAPLAN

Hillside apartment complex, which features furnished two- and four-bedroom apartments. There are also "Special Emphasis Houses" next to campus that center around a specific theme or culture. Most juniors and seniors move off-campus to one of the many living options in Nashville.

Belmont allows all students, even freshmen, to bring cars to campus, provided they fork over registration and parking fees. Although most undergrads walk or bike between classes, cars are a popular mode of transportation around town. The large off-campus/commuter population only enhances the feeling that everyone has his own car here. The school is in the process of building a parking garage, in an attempt to alleviate the shortage of space.

Student Life

Belmont undergrads tend to be serious about their studies, their careers, and their faith. The Honor System—which defines the university's emphasis on being a trustworthy, honest, and academically and socially responsible community—is wholeheartedly followed. It's a friendly, serene environment, if not a very diverse one. Most students come from well-to-do families from the Southeastern U.S. Less than 300 students on campus are minorities.

More than 50 clubs and organizations are available, but some students complain about the lack of extracurricular activities on campus. There is a small but growing Greek system—about 3 percent each of men and women join one of a handful of fraternities and sororities—but no Greek houses. Religious and campus ministry organizations such as the Baptist Student Union and the Campus Crusade for Christ are among the most popular, as are music and honor societies. Belmont is a full member of NCAA-I in the Atlantic Sun Conference, offering eight women's sports and seven men's (but no football). Intramurals, including billiards, sand volleyball, and floor hockey, are also organized, but we hear that students aren't enthusiastically joining these teams.

A dry campus, Belmont gives its student body plenty of "drug-free" things to do, usually involving musical performances and activities. Popular annual events include Fall Follies, a student-run variety show; Musical Showcases, which feature auditioned student musicians and technicians; and the Mistletoe Ball, a formal holiday dinner and dance. Everyone looks forward to the Vince Gill Event, a school fundraiser where many of country music's finest performers come to campus to "participate in a basketball game followed by a concert called 'Vince Gill and Friends.'"

Belmont undergrads can check out the action on a number of other campuses, too. Nashville, a notoriously friendly town, has been called "the city of students," with more than a dozen colleges and universities in the area. Nashville's historic riverfront district boasts a lively nightlife, with bars, clubs, restaurants, coffeehouses, and shops. For a more cultured night on the town, the Tennessee Performing Arts Center has a full roster of performances. Sports fans can catch NFL and NHL games as well.

Other schools to check out: Baylor, Berry College.

ACT Comp: 22–27
ACT English: 22–30
ACT Math: 21–27
HS Rank of Entering Freshmen:
Top 10%: 34%
Top 25%: 63%
Top 50%: 91%
Avg. HS GPA: 3.43

THE EXPERTS SAY...

" Belmont can help you break into the music industry and get into the Country Music Hall of Fame. "

" Country music and campus ministry are the main extracurriculars. If your tastes run to Eminem or 50 Cent instead of Vince Gill, skip Nashville and head straight for L.A. "

Costs (2003–04)

Tuition and Fees: $15,954
Room & Board: $8,138
Payment Plan(s): deferred payment plan

Inst. Aid (2002–03)

Institutional Aid, Need-Based: $2,051,995
Institutional Aid, Non-Need-Based: $4,284,698
FT Undergrads Receiving Aid: 49%
Avg. Amount per Student: $2,796
FT Undergrads Receiving Non-Need-Based Scholarship or Grant Aid: 22%
Avg. Amount per Student: $4,792
Of Those Receiving Any Aid:
Rec. Need-Based Scholarship or Grant Aid: 71%
Average Award: $2,161
Rec. Need-Based Self-Help Aid: 83%
Average Award: $3,088
Upon Graduation, Avg. Loan Debt per Student: $15,954
Financial Aid Deadline: rolling, 3/1 (priority)

Graduates

Going to Graduate School: 15% Within One Year
Accepting Job Offer: 44% at time of graduation
Companies Recruiting On Campus: 150
Alumni Giving: 27%

BELOIT COLLEGE

700 College Street, Beloit, WI 53511
Admissions Phone: (608) 363-2500; (800) 9BELOIT
Fax: (608) 363-2075
Website: www.beloit.edu

General Info

Type of School: private, coed
Setting: small town
Academic Calendar: semester

Student Body

Full-Time Undergrads: 1,226
  Men: 39%, Women: 61%

Part-Time Undergrads: 19
  Men: 47%, Women: 63%

Total Undergrad Population:
  African American: 3%
  Asian American: 3%
  Latino: 3%
  Native American: <1%
  Caucasian: 83%
  International: 5%
  Out-of-State: 81%
  Living Off-Campus: 7%
  In Fraternities: 15%
  In Sororities: 5%

Academics

Full-Time Faculty: 103
  With Ph.D.: 96%

Part-Time Faculty: 23
  With Ph.D.: 87%

Student/Faculty Ratio: 11:1

Most Popular Majors:
  psychology (11%)
  creative writing (8%)
  sociology (7%)
  history (6%)
  biology (6%)

Completing 2 or More Majors: 23%

Freshmen Retention Rate: 91%

Graduation Rates:
  60% within four years
  72% within six years

Admissions

Regular Application Deadline: 1/15
  (priority)

Early Action Deadline: 12/15

Fall Transfer Deadline: 2/1 (priority)

Spring Transfers Deadline: rolling

Total # of Students Applied: 1,901
  Admitted: 1,321
  Enrolled: 346

# of Students Waitlisted: 62
  Students Accepting Place: 30

Inside the Classroom

Beloit (pronounced "buh-loyt," rhymes with "Detroit") was founded in1846 "to serve a society at its frontier by preparing people who were capable of change and who valued learning for its own sake." Beloit offers 45 academic majors in 19 departments, with particularly strong programs in creative writing and the natural sciences. The college claims to be ranked as one of the top 50 undergraduate colleges for producing the nation's leaders in science. Classes are "rigorous and comprehensive," according to one student, and class size is nearly always small—average class size is 15 students, and many classes have fewer than 10. With an 11:1 student/faculty ratio, most students find professors involved, interesting, and supportive. Students say that relationships between students and faculty are very comfortable, and professors are often called by their first names. Even the administration is praised as approachable and supportive of students.

Beloit has a focus on internationalism, which translates in part to the huge number of students—nearly half of the student body—who study abroad during their college years. Study abroad programs are varied, and include those in Europe, Asia, Africa, South America, and Australia; there are also lots of domestic exchange programs. General requirements, which are very flexible, include study of a language and/or culture other than your own, as well as a sampling of natural science, arts and humanities, and social science courses. Students must also demonstrate writing proficiency or take an intensive writing course.

Learning by doing is big at Beloit, and there are many opportunities for research projects, internships, and field study. A highlight at Beloit is Symposium Day, when classes are cancelled and students and professors all check out students' presentations of their research projects, on subjects ranging from environmental issues to literature to social problems. Beloit offers cooperative education opportunities in engineering, nursing, environmental management, and health sciences, among others.

Beloit is clearly not for everyone; you'll either see it as an amazingly flexible haven that gives you the rare opportunity to "invent yourself," or as a weakly-structured place where it's too easy to make wrong choices. Beloit students report that their school is not for people who need lots of hand-holding; but if you want plenty of freedom in a supportive setting that encourages you to take risks, consider Beloit. Most students who end up choosing Beloit seem to love it, and appreciate its challenging academics, intimate environment, and malleable structure. Students praise Beloit's First-Year Initiatives ("FYI") program as a great way for freshmen to get to know the Beloit community. "It is the springboard to everything that is Beloit: interdisciplinary approaches, creative teaching and learning, community service, and enterprising actions," the college explains. Each year, FYI has a theme, and during the summer, all entering first-year students complete a common FYI theme.

Campus Environment

Students call the wooded campus "gorgeous." Scattered about the campus are 23 conical, linear, and animal effigy mounds built between A.D. 700 and 1200. One, in the form of a turtle, inspired the symbol (and unofficial mascot) of the College.

Over 90 percent of students live on campus; only seniors are allowed to move to off-campus digs, but most choose to stay on. Dorms are "very clean" and numerous single rooms give students the chance to enjoy some privacy in a dorm setting. Most dorms mix all classes, but a few are reserved for upperclass students only. There are also several small theme houses, and a few Greek houses. Most of the dorms are renovated, but a few are more "rustic."

Like Beloit itself, the food in the dining hall ("Café Belwah") is "a mix of all cultures," a bit different from your typical college fare. Students can also grab snacks on campus at DKs, the Java Joint, and the Coughy Haus ("C-Haus").

Student Life

Beloit has greater diversity than many small colleges: more than three quarters of students come from out of state (20 percent from Illinois), and more than 12 percent of students are minorities. There's also a substantial international contingent, with over 50 countries represented. A guidance counselor says the "interesting students" are among the best things about Beloit. Beloit is a tolerant place: We hear that students coexist pretty peacefully. Most students are decidedly liberal in their political bent, but seem to be open to lively debate with students with other points of view.

Beloit College has 18 NCAA Division III varsity athletic teams and is a member of the Midwest Athletic Conference; club sports are popular, too. Student activities are varied, with clubs ranging from the "Society for Creative Anachronisms" to "Cigar Aficionado," and there's usually something interesting happening on campus. There's a popular student-run radio station, as well as a public service TV station on campus.

Greek life draws about 15 percent of men and less than half as many women. While word is that there is plenty of drinking and drug use at Beloit, there is, as one clean-living student tells it, "no pressure to partake in it." Be warned, though: Students say that it's pretty easy to party a bit too much if you're at all inclined. Nearly all socializing goes on in the "bubble" of Beloit's campus, since there's not much going on in the little town of Beloit. Stir-crazy students drive to Madison, Milwaukee, or Chicago for a change of pace.

Other schools to check out: Colorado College, Carleton, College of Wooster, Ripon, Lawrence.

Test Scores (middle 50%):
 SAT Verbal: 580–690
 SAT Math: 550–660
 ACT Comp: 25–30
 ACT English: 25–31
 ACT Math: 22–28

HS Rank of Entering Freshmen:
 Top 10%: 34%
 Top 25%: 64%
 Top 50%: 94%

Avg. HS GPA: 3.51

THE EXPERTS SAY...

" Beloit students are ready for a global society. The study abroad options are fantastic, and you can 'invent yourself' by shaping your own education. "

" If you hate independent study and need a structured program to do well, look elsewhere. "

Costs (2004–5)

Tuition and Fees: $25,736

Room & Board: $5,696

Payment Plan(s): installment plan

Inst. Aid (est. 2003–04)

Institutional Aid, Need-Based:
 $13,198,894

Institutional Aid, Non-Need-Based:
 $2,034,552

FT Undergrads Receiving Aid: 73%
 Avg. Amount per Student: $18,635

FT Undergrads Receiving Non-Need-Based Scholarship or Grant Aid: 15%
 Avg. Amount per Student: $8,372

Of Those Receiving Any Aid:

Rec. Need-Based Scholarship or Grant Aid: 100%
 Average Award: $14,026

Rec. Need-Based Self-Help Aid: 100%
 Average Award: $4,609

Upon Graduation, Avg. Loan Debt per Student: $18,783

Financial Aid Deadline: 3/1, 1/15 (priority)

Graduates

Going to Graduate School:
 25% Within One Year

Accepting Job Offer:
 74% at time of graduation

Companies Recruiting On Campus: 40

Alumni Giving: 43%

BENNINGTON COLLEGE

One College Drive, Bennington, VT 05201
Admissions Phone: (800) 833-6845; (802) 440-4312 Fax: (802) 440-4320
Email: admissions@bennington.edu
Website: www.bennington.edu

General Info

Type of School: private, coed

Setting: rural

Academic Calendar: semester;
Standard fall/spring terms, winter work term

Student Body

Full-Time Undergrads: 635
Men: 33%, Women: 67%

Part-Time Undergrads: 5 Women: 100%

Total Undergrad Population:
African American: 1%
Asian American: 1%
Latino: 3%
Native American: <1%
Caucasian: 85%
International: 6%
Out-of-State: 95%
Living Off-Campus: 5%

Graduate and First-Professional Students: 153

Academics

Full-Time Faculty: 64
With Ph.D.: 69%

Part-Time Faculty: 23
With Ph.D.: 30%

Student/Faculty Ratio: 8:1

Most Popular Majors:
interdisciplinary studies (43%)
visual arts (14%)
literature (9%)
social sciences (9%)
drama (7%)

Freshmen Retention Rate: 80%

Graduation Rates:
58% within four years
67% within six years

Admissions

Regular Application Deadline: 1/1

Early Decision Deadline(s): 11/15, 12/1

Fall Transfer Deadline: 6/1

Spring Transfer Deadline: 1/1

Total # of Students Applied: 773
Admitted: 526
Enrolled: 172

Inside the Classroom

Having tossed out traditional grading policies and final examinations, Bennington encourages its students to learn for the sake of learning. Working closely with advisors, with whom they meet on a regular basis, students map out their academic programs according to their own interests. They can immerse themselves in a single field, say biology or drama, or dabble in several, no matter how strange the combination. A college official says, "By developing individualized plans of study, Bennington students learn what it means to discover and pursue an intellectual identity and to replace imposed discipline with self-discipline."

The fine arts programs at Bennington are particularly well regarded. Because Bennington is such a small school, fewer courses are offered than at other liberal arts colleges. However, small classes allow undergrads to receive undivided attention from their professors, who often develop real friendships with their students. Instead of letter grades, students receive in-depth written evaluations from their teachers. Additionally, research opportunities are not lacking. Students work on research projects in nearly every discipline, since the faculty are actively engaged in their own professional work and they routinely incorporate that work in the classroom.

Bennington has a unique curriculum, known as the Plan. Each academic year consists of three terms: two 14-week, on-campus terms during the fall and spring, and an eight-week winter term of fieldwork off campus. Students must provide approved written documents that comprise the Plan, and their overall course of study must "reflect breadth and depth in the liberal arts." Students must also demonstrate competency in writing, quantitative reasoning, and computer/multi-media technology. The Field Work Term involves students taking "their academic interests to the world beyond Bennington, where they pursue jobs and internships in areas that complement their studies in fields ranging from publishing to politics, from arts administration to teaching, from medical research to social work." The result of this innovative program, according to a school official, is that at the end of their four undergraduate years, Bennington students "have acquired a body of work experience, a significant set of references, a network of professional contacts, and, most important, the confidence that they can make their way in the world."

Campus Environment

Bennington's campus covers 550 rolling acres at the foot of the Green Mountains in southwestern Vermont. You couldn't find a more rustic environment if you tried; the campus used to be a working farm, and some of the buildings that now house classrooms, studios, and offices were once barns and stables.

Student housing at Bennington mixes freshmen with returning students in houses that accommodate about 30 students each. A college official says, "Student housing at Bennington consists of 12 colonial-style clapboard houses arranged around a common lawn that stretches towards what students call the 'End of the World,' and offers a spectacular mountain view." Additional student houses were opened in 2001 to prevent overcrowding. Most houses come with "cooking spaces and elegant living rooms with fireplaces," and "Sunday evening coffee hours offer a chance to discuss specific house issues as well as matters of wider campus concern." Each house has its own personality and serves as a focal point for socializing. The school's permissiveness is apparent in its roommate policy: Students of the opposite sex may share rooms if they both request it. Housing is guaranteed for all four years.

All students are permitted to have cars on campus, and permits are required. For students without cars, a school official says, "Shuttle service is available during set times to the Vermont towns of Bennington, North Bennington, and Manchester, and to Williamstown, Massachusetts."

Student Life

Though Bennington doesn't offer the most diversified student body, it still offers a community feel and a general air of tolerance and open-mindedness. Students claim to be on a first-name basis with much of the school staff as well, which they feel adds to the homey atmosphere.

Because they're given so much freedom, Bennington students must be extremely self-motivated to complete their academic programs. The school attracts individuals who are independent, individualistic, and proud of it. The social scene at Bennington reflects the diversity of the students' experiences and interests. There are no fraternities or sororities on campus. Even though there are several campus-wide social events a year, students tend to hang out in small circles, often with their housemates or with those who share similar interests.

Although students venture off campus for outdoor sports in the Vermont area, the social life is generally centered on campus. Fortunately, with all the talented student performers and artists here, finding a good concert, play, or dance recital is never difficult. Of the activities available on campus, a college official lists the following campus groups as among the most popular: Student Council, the Campus Activities Board, the Outing Club, the Film Society, and the Student Action Network.

Bennington students take advantage of opportunities for physical and outdoor recreation. The Meyer Recreation Barn is "a fully equipped facility for cardiovascular, aerobic, and weight-resistance activities, and also includes an expansive rock climbing wall. Outdoor activities, including hiking, camping, snowshoeing, and others, are coordinated through the Recreation Barn and the Office of Student Life." During the fall, many students participate in a coed, intercollegiate soccer league with colleges from Vermont and Massachusetts; players of various skill levels participate. Other intramural sports include basketball, volleyball, flag football, and ultimate Frisbee. Additionally, a college official says, "Bennington's Outdoor/Weekend Program offers students an opportunity to experience and learn a wide range of outdoor activities, including canoeing, hiking, caving, rock climbing, cross-country skiing, white-water rafting, and so on."

The school offers some unique campus traditions: There's a surprise Midnight Breakfast served to students by staff and faculty, and Rollerama, roller-skating disco parties. Holiday caroling is another Bennington tradition.

Other schools to check out: Bard, Oberlin, Sarah Lawrence, Reed, Hampshire, Brown.

# of Students Waitlisted: 25
Students Accepting Place: 15
Waitlisted Students Admitted: 12

Applied Early Decision: 38
Early Decision Admitted: 38

Test Scores (middle 50%):
SAT Verbal: 600–700
SAT Math: 530–650
ACT Comp: 24–30
ACT English: 23–31
ACT Math: 18–26

HS Rank of Entering Freshmen:
Top 10%: 23%
Top 25%: 62%
Top 50%: 87%

Avg. HS GPA: 3.48

THE EXPERTS SAY...

" You can create your own plan of study at Bennington. The winter term is great for students who want real-life, off-campus experiences. "

" No grades, no finals, and you can room with members of the opposite sex. Now that's a great school! "

Costs (2003–04)

Tuition and Fees: $28,770

Room & Board: $7,140

Payment Plan(s): installment plan

Inst. Aid (est. 2003–04)

Institutional Aid, Need-Based:
$5,669,658

Institutional Aid, Non-Need-Based:
$389,011

FT Undergrads Receiving Aid: 65%
Avg. Amount per Student:
$21,821

FT Undergrads Receiving Non-Need-Based Scholarship or Grant Aid: 14%
Avg. Amount per Student: $4,929

Of Those Receiving Any Aid:

Rec. Need-Based Scholarship or
Grant Aid: 99%
Average Award: $17,520

Rec. Need-Based Self-Help Aid: 95%
Average Award: $4,772

Upon Graduation, Avg. Loan Debt
per Student: $17,558

Financial Aid Deadline: 2/1, 3/1
(priority)

Graduates

Alumni Giving: 18%

BENTLEY COLLEGE

175 Forest St., Waltham, MA 02452-4705
Admissions Phone: (781) 891-2244; (800) 523-2354 Fax: (781) 891-3414
Email: ugadmissions@bentley.edu
Website: www.bentley.edu

General Info

Type of School: private, coed
Setting: suburban
Academic Calendar: semester

Student Body

Full-Time Undergrads: 3,918
    Men: 58%, Women: 42%

Part-Time Undergrads: 355
    Men: 54%, Women: 46%

Total Undergrad Population:
    African American: 3%
    Asian American: 7%
    Latino: 4%
    Native American: <1%
    Caucasian: 71%
    International: 8%
    Out-of-State: 43%
    Living Off-Campus: 21%

Graduate and First-Professional
    Students: 1,329

Academics

Full-Time Faculty: 260
    With Ph.D.: 83%

Part-Time Faculty: 196
    With Ph.D.: 31%

Student/Faculty Ratio: 13:1

Most Popular Majors:
    management (23%)
    marketing (16%)
    finance (12%)
    accounting (10%)
    information design and corporate
    communications (8%)

Completing 2 or More Majors: 0%

Freshmen Retention Rate: 93%

Graduation Rates:
    66% within four years
    77% within six years

Computers: Computer Required

Admissions

Regular Application Deadline: 2/1

Early Decision Deadline(s): 11/15

Early Action Deadline: 12/1

Fall Transfer Deadline: 5/1 (priority)

Spring Transfer Deadline: 11/15
    (priority)

Total # of Students Applied: 5,474
    Admitted: 2,529
    Enrolled: 955

Inside the Classroom

Bentley is the largest business school in New England, offering undergrads a business education with strong areas in accountancy, finance, marketing, management, computer information systems, and information design and corporate communication. Students here get all the benefits of a business education while still getting a balance of other subjects. The school explains: "Liberal arts courses build skills in critical thinking, decision-making, communication, and other areas essential to becoming a well-rounded, contributing member of the community." Also, the themes of ethics and social responsibility are part of the Bentley curriculum. A management major boasts, "I am learning how to be a well-rounded, thoughtful, ethical member of the business world."

One perk at this school of "world-class technology facilities" is that every entering freshman receives a laptop. Students rave about the technology at Bentley. As one senior explains, "The school is completely wireless; you can literally go anywhere on campus with your laptop and be connected to the world via the web."

Half of students' classes are completed in the arts and sciences, making up the General Education Core. There are 18 majors and 20 minors, and all freshmen take the First-Year Seminar, a one-credit program that covers topics like academic planning, individual learning styles, diversity, and faculty expectations. Students we surveyed had only good things to say about their "eager to help" professors, who have real-world experience in their fields. "Professors are always available for students," notes a management major, "one professor gave us his cell phone number and another has office hours from 10–11 PM!"

The workload at Bentley can be pretty intense, and "many kids are talented and are not afraid to show it off." But the student-faculty ratio is an intimate 13:1, and there are tutoring resources available to help. Students are competitive and driven—within 6 months of graduation, 93% of students are either employed or enrolled in grad school. A senior tells us "the classes here challenge you and require you to think outside of the box to find the best possible solution." Another offers this perspective: "Classes are challenging but very empowering, with an emphasis on hands-on, real world applications."

Campus Environment

"The best part of Bentley's campus is that you get the small-town campus feel while being only 10 miles from Boston," a management major tells us. The school is located in suburban Waltham, but provides a shuttle to Harvard Square in Cambridge, from which students can also go anywhere in Boston via the subway system. Students agree that the 163-acre campus is very safe, clean, and attractive. A management major/finance minor tells us, "Last year my friends all lived in a different dorm than I did and I would walk across campus at like 2 AM and I would feel completely safe."

There are 26 student residences, which include traditional dorms (where all freshmen live), apartments, and suites. All rooms have basic cable and a college-funded movie channel. Housing is guaranteed for four years. The newest residence

KAPLAN

halls opened in 2001, and one is scheduled to open in fall 2004. A junior says that housing is "not bad, but it's not the Hilton, either," and other students note that housing gets more comfortable after your first year or two. Most Bentley students stay on campus throughout their college career, and an international studies major jokes, "off campus often means at home."

The student center opened in 2001, featuring a dining hall and a pub that offers entertainment nearly every night. Also, in the past few years Bentley has seen new soccer and baseball fields, a track, and lighted tennis courts added to the campus, along with two new parking decks.

Student Life

Students are described as "really friendly" within the small student body. However, we are also told that students "tend to be very cliquey" and that "once groups are established it is quite hard to cross over to another one." According to students, the student body tends to dress more professionally than their pajama-clad peers at some other schools. Perhaps this is in relation to the "real-world," career-oriented atmosphere at Bentley. One student describes the "typical male" as "dressed as if they were 40 years old in dress shoes, shirts, and pants." Dressing down includes "brand name apparel such as from Ralph Lauren and Diesel" and "making sure the logos are very visible" (hey, those logos represent successful business people!). The same sophomore tells us that women "dress up, too, or look like they are in a club," adding, "high heels to college classes are just annoying."

There are over 80 student clubs and organizations, and a freshman tells us "outside of the classroom Bentley students are usually very busy. They are involved in several clubs, which meet on weeknights. There are always several other events going on during the week such as movies in the Pub, concerts, comedians, sporting events, plays, and other shows." Bentley boasts 23 varsity teams (12 men's, 11 women's) in NCAA Divisions I and II, and is a member of both the Northeast-10 Conference and the Division I Atlantic Hockey League. Greek life has a place at Bentley, but students seem to agree that it is not overly influential. One student explains, "Popularity has NO relation to sororities or fraternities. People are popular based on how many people they get to know, and how they get involved."

When students want to leave the Bentley campus, they can go into the town of Waltham where Moody Street is the place to go for restaurants and bars. A marketing major tells us, "John Brewers (home of 10-cent wings and free lunch buffets during halftime of Pats games) is a great place to go." Otherwise, students take the quick shuttle ride to Harvard Square, where they can explore all that student-friendly Boston and Cambridge have to offer.

Other schools to check out: Boston College, Boston U., Babson College, Northeastern U., U. Penn, Carnegie Mellon U.

# of Students Waitlisted: 952
  Students Accepting Place: 807
  Waitlisted Students Admitted: 60

Applied Early Decision: 197
  Early Decision Admitted: 124

Test Scores (middle 50%):
  SAT Verbal: 530–610
  SAT Math: 570–660
  ACT Comp: 22–28

THE EXPERTS SAY...

" Bentley offers talented business students a strong basis in liberal arts and business ethics. And a laptop! "

" If getting dressed up for first-period class doesn't sound like your kind of college experience, you probably don't belong at Bentley. "

HS Rank of Entering Freshmen:
  Top 10%: 37%
  Top 25%: 72%
  Top 50%: 97%

Costs (2003–04)

Tuition and Fees: $24,324

Room & Board: $9,580

Payment Plan(s): installment plan, deferred payment plan

Inst. Aid (2002–03)

FT Undergrads Receiving Aid: 51%
  Avg. Amount per Student: $22,573

FT Undergrads Receiving Non-Need-Based Scholarship or Grant Aid: 10%
  Avg. Amount per Student: $10,651

Of Those Receiving Any Aid:

Rec. Need-Based Scholarship or Grant Aid: 91%
  Average Award: $13,530

Rec. Need-Based Self-Help Aid: 93%
  Average Award: $6,486

Upon Graduation, Avg. Loan Debt per Student: $19,560

Financial Aid Deadline: 2/1

Graduates

Going to Graduate School:
  13% Within One Year

Accepting Job Offer:
  64% at time of graduation

Companies Recruiting On Campus:
  440

BEREA COLLEGE

CPO 2220, Berea, KY 40404
Admissions Phone: (859) 985-3500; (800) 326-5948 Fax: (859) 985-3512
Email: admissions@berea.edu
Website: www.berea.edu/admissions

General Info

Type of School: private, coed,
Nonsectarian (Inclusive Christian)

Setting: small town

Academic Calendar: 4-1-4

Student Body

Full-Time Undergrads: 1,510
Men: 39%, Women: 61%

Part-Time Undergrads: 1
Men: 100%

Total Undergrad Population:
African American: 17%
Asian American: 1%
Latino: 1%
Native American: 1%
Caucasian: 70%
International: 8%
Out-of-State: 59%
Living Off-Campus: 19%

Academics

Full-Time Faculty: 130
With Ph.D.: 91%

Part-Time Faculty: 22
With Ph.D.: 55%

Student/Faculty Ratio: 11:1

Most Popular Majors:
business administration (12%)
child family studies (8%)
technical/industrial arts (8%)
biology (7%)
educational studies (6%)

Completing 2 or More Majors: 3%

Freshmen Retention Rate: 80%

Graduation Rates:
29% within four years
49% within six years

Computers: School provides
individual computer/laptop

Admissions

Regular Application Deadline: 4/30;
11/30 (priority)

Early Action Deadline: 11/30

Fall Transfer Deadline: 4/30, 12/30
(priority)

Spring Transfer Deadline: 12/30,
11/1 (priority)

Inside the Classroom

Berea provides a high-quality, tuition-free education for students from the Appalachian region who have limited financial resources but demonstrate high academic potential. With a three-part mission of "learning, labor, and service," Berea requires all students to work 10–15 hours per week in a campus job while still carrying a full academic course load. "Students are employed in administrative offices, health care, academic departments as teaching assistants, craft areas, college operations, campus sales, or community service programs, to name a few," a college official tells us. Freshmen are given specific assignments, but continuing students compete for jobs and sign contracts with the appropriate departments for each academic year. An evaluation of each student's work every semester builds an insightful record of performance.

Academically, Berea is known for its strong programs in business administration, child and family studies, technology/industrial arts management, English, and biology. Berea's programs in nursing, agriculture, education, and music are also popular. Students can earn a B.A. degree in one of 22 liberal arts majors, or a B.S. degree in one of 4 preprofessional majors.

A guidance counselor recommends Berea because "they work more one-on-one with their students." All classes are taught by faculty, not by teaching assistants; with an 11:1 student/faculty ratio, students receive a great deal of individual attention.

Berea recognizes the value of providing both a "hands-on" education and a strong liberal arts background. Its broad core curriculum includes: two first-year courses emphasizing reading and writing; two cultural area courses; one social science course; two arts courses; two or three natural science courses; two Western traditions courses; one course in recent world issues; one seminar in contemporary Christianity; and three courses "emphasizing the concept of wellness."

During the four-week January Term, students may take a course on campus, or they may travel abroad, either alone or with groups of students and faculty. Additionally, students may spend January Term at Middlebury College (Vermont) or Gustavus Adolphus College (Minnesota). There are also many opportunities for internships and faculty-mentored undergraduate research.

Campus Environment

Berea's campus, located 42 miles south of Lexington, features some unique facilities. The Boone Tavern Hotel has 58 guest rooms and is known for its traditional Southern dishes such as spoon bread. The Appalachian Center directs more than a dozen services for the region. The Log House Craft Gallery features the work of students and local artisans. And the Hutchins Library houses the Weatherford-Hammond Appalachian Collection, one of the finest in the nation for Appalachian research.

The design phase has been completed for the development and construction of a $9 million EcoVillage: a residential and teaching facility which will provide 50 one-, two-, and three-bedroom apartments and townhouses, a Sustainability and Environmental Studies House, a Child Development Lab for 120 children, a permaculture food forest, and an urban garden. Ecological performance goals include a 75 percent reduction in energy use, a 75 percent reduction in water use, recycling at least 50 percent of the waste stream, on-site treatment of sewage and storm water to swim quality, and on-site generation from renewable resources of 10 percent of electricity use.

Freshmen are assigned to freshmen-only residence halls in an attempt to emphasize the "first year experience." There are three freshmen residence halls for women and two freshman halls for men. Residence hall staff members (student labor positions) are very involved with freshmen through programming and interaction, to a greater degree than in halls for upperclassmen. When overcrowding occurs, freshmen are housed temporarily in other rooms in residence halls, such as lounges and study areas, until space becomes available.

Students are definitely not thrilled with the small town of Berea—"a quiet town with more churches than restaurants." And escape is difficult because most students are not allowed to have cars on campus. "Permission to have cars on campus is allowed on an as-needed basis, such as distance from home, medical reasons, or family commitments. Seniors who meet certain requirements have student priority," a college official informs us.

Student Life

The student body is said to be "friendly," "approachable," and "like a large family." Although 80 percent of Berea students hail from Kentucky and the Southern Appalachian region, there's also a sizable international population, resulting in an unusually diverse student body for a small Southern school. Founded in 1855, Berea was actually the first school in the South to admit both blacks and whites, men and women. In fact, the founder of Berea College and a few of his supporters were tarred (but not feathered) for attempting to establish Berea as a coed interracial school in the pre-Civil War era.

Students say there's little to do on- or off-campus besides college-sponsored events or just hanging out with friends. Each student is expected to attend seven Convocations each term; these may include lectures, concerts, or dance or theater performances. There are approximately 72 campus organizations open to students. Some of the most popular are: service oriented organizations, national honorary societies, speech and debate clubs, music groups, and departmental/major clubs. Berea College offers 17 varsity sports for men and women, and nearly 500 students participate in intramural sports. Berea does not have fraternities or sororities, and alcohol is strictly forbidden.

Each fall since 1875, the college has celebrated "Mountain Day." Classes and student labor are cancelled so that students and staff can hike, relax and enjoy the college's mountain trails. "Labor Day" is another Berea College tradition. Celebrated each spring, classes and regular labor assignments are suspended for the day. In the early years, students competed in various labor-related campus activities; today, the "Labor Day" activities have evolved to adopting community service projects which students, staff and faculty perform.

Total # of Students Applied: 2,119
Admitted: 530
Enrolled: 396
Avg. HS GPA: 3.37

Costs (2003–04)

Fees: $507

Every student receives a full tuition scholarship

Room & Board: $4,523

THE EXPERTS SAY...

" Berea offers an amazing opportunity for low-income kids to receive a high-quality education, valuable work experience, and continued exposure to people from different cultures. "

" How can Berea not be a great value? It's _free_! "

Inst. Aid (est. 2003–04)

Institutional Aid, Need-Based: $29,102,789

FT Undergrads Receiving Aid: 100%
Avg. Amount per Student: $24,668

Of Those Receiving Any Aid:

Rec. Need-Based Scholarship or Grant Aid: 100%
Average Award: $23,110

Rec. Need-Based Self-Help Aid: 100%
Average Award: $1,558

Upon Graduation, Avg. Loan Debt per Student: $6,275

Financial Aid Deadline: 8/1, 4/15 (priority)

Graduates

Going to Graduate School: 25% Within One Year

Accepting Job Offer: 85% at time of graduation

Companies Recruiting On Campus: 100

Alumni Giving: 21%

BERKLEE COLLEGE OF MUSIC

1140 Boylston Street, Boston, MA 02215
Admissions Phone: (800) BER-KLEE; (617) 747-2222 Fax: (617) 747-2047
Email: admissions@berklee.edu
Website: www.berklee.edu

General Info

Type of School: private, coed
Setting: urban
Academic Calendar: semester

Student Body

Full-Time Undergrads: 3,799
  Men: 76%, Women: 24%

Total Undergrad Population:
  African American: 6%
  Asian American: 4%
  Latino: 6%
  Native American: 1%
  Caucasian: 73%
  Out-of-State: 82%
  Living Off-Campus: 80%

Academics

Full-Time Faculty: 193
Part-Time Faculty: 280
Student/Faculty Ratio: 8:1
Most Popular Majors:
  performance (11%)
  music business/management
    (10%)
  professional music (8%)
  film scoring (6%)
  music production & engineering
    (5%)
Computers: Computer Required

Admissions

Regular Application Deadline:
  2/1 (priority)
Fall Transfer Deadline: Rolling; 2/1
  (priority)
Total # of Students Applied: 2,123
  Admitted: 1,680
  Enrolled: 746
Waitlist Available

Costs (2003–04)

Tuition and Fees: $22,166
Room & Board: $10,280
Payment Plan(s): installment plan

Inst. Aid (est. 2003–04)

Institutional Aid, Need-Based:
  $7,925,332

Inside the Classroom

So you want to study music, but you can't find a music school that understands the fact that your tastes run more to Bono than to Beethoven? Welcome to Berklee. Berklee College of Music in Boston is the world's largest independent music college and the premier institution for the study of contemporary music. Alumni include Living Colour drummer Will Calhoun; singer/songwriter Paula Cole; singer/guitarist Melissa Etheridge; Steely Dan leader Donald Fagen; pop singer/keyboardist Bruce Hornsby; producer/arranger Quincy Jones; jazz singer/pianist Diana Krall; and Natalie Maines of The Dixie Chicks.

Berklee employs a rigorous and pragmatic educational approach to teach jazz, pop, rock, and other forms of world music, including classical music. "Berklee is neither just a jazz school, or just a rock/pop school, but a college offering all styles of contemporary music for today's music industry," says the college. The 12 majors leading to a bachelor of music degree are: composition; contemporary writing and production; film scoring; jazz composition; music business/management; music education; music production and engineering; music synthesis; music therapy; performance; professional music; and songwriting.

Berklee's Admissions Office advises that all applicants have at least two years of formal instruction on their principal instrument, along with knowledge of basic music theory. Note that all students must play an instrument—even students majoring in music business or production. Berklee's philosophy is that anyone interested in a successful career in the music industry must gain training on an instrument and have a sound background in music theory. This is why a core music curriculum (including harmony, arranging, ear training, music technology, ensemble, and private instruction) is required in any major.

Berklee also recognizes the value of a liberal arts background: General education courses (in English, history, mathematics, languages, philosophy, and social and physical science) make up approximately 25 percent of the bachelor's degree program. (A Professional Diploma program is available to students who want to focus exclusively on music, but this diploma is not equivalent to a college degree.)

Berklee is "a microcosm of the music industry," and networking with other musicians begins immediately upon enrollment. The Office of Experiential Learning (OEL) provides the opportunity for qualified upper semester students to gain professional experience in the music industry while building career contacts in their field of study. More than 100 companies participate in the program, including Universal, WEA, Sony Music, Zildjian, Jive, and Virgin. Another option for graduates of Berklee's music business/management major: a special, accelerated M.B.A. program at Boston's Suffolk University, which waives nearly a semester's worth of requirements.

Campus Environment

Berklee has recently opened a new, state-of-the-art student practice facility with over 12,000 square feet of rehearsal space, providing students with 55 new practice rooms. Other facilities include ten professionally equipped recording studios; more than 100

MIDI-equipped workstations; 230 acoustic pianos; and hundreds of synthesizers. The Film Scoring Department houses six fully equipped film/video scoring and editing labs. The Berklee Library holdings include 10,500 recordings and 17,300 musical scores. The 1,200-seat Berklee Performance Center hosts student and faculty concerts along with numerous performances presented by major concert promoters.

Berklee houses approximately 800 students in three residence halls in Boston's Back Bay/Fenway neighborhood. "Residence hall space fills up very quickly, and not everyone who wants to secure on-campus housing will be able to do so," the college warns. A dining hall serves three meals a day Monday through Friday and two meals on Saturday, Sunday, and holidays; after 10 P.M., the Dining Hall becomes Berklee's own nightclub, hosting student performances, revues and all-out parties. Although the college does not have a full-fledged fitness facility on campus, the fitness room at nearby Massachusetts College of Art is available to Berklee students at a small cost.

Popular hangout spots include the student mailboxes, the 150 Mass. Ave. lobby, and the sidewalk in front of the 150 Mass. Ave. building—dubbed "the Berklee Beach." Some of the hot spots around Berklee where students play gigs include Wally's, Bob the Chef's, the Linwood Grille, and Bill's Bar. Students mostly use public transportation to travel to gigs—or anywhere else, for that matter. "Students are not encouraged to have cars while at the college," says a Berklee official.

FT Undergrads Receiving Aid: 55%

FT Undergrads Receiving Non-Need-Based Scholarship or Grant Aid: 25%
Avg. Amount per Student: $6,608

Of Those Receiving Any Aid:

Rec. Need-Based Scholarship or Grant Aid: 43%

Rec. Need-Based Self-Help Aid: 97%
Average Award: $3,785

Financial Aid Deadline: 3/1 (priority)

THE EXPERTS SAY...

❝ Berklee provides comprehensive music and career preparation—not to mention great contacts throughout the industry. ❞

❝ Classical performers may receive better training elsewhere, but anyone else who is passionate about music should give Berklee serious consideration. ❞

Student Life

Of all U.S. colleges and universities, Berklee has the largest percentage of undergraduate students from outside the U.S., representing more than 70 countries. Approximately 17 percent of students are from Asia, and 12 percent are from Europe.

Each year over 350 student and faculty ensembles present over 700 concerts in the college's five performance halls. Every concert is open to the public. Popular ensembles include the Jazz/Rock Ensemble, the Thelonious Monk Ensemble, Vocal Summit, the Commercial Pop/Rock Recording Ensemble, and the Gospel Choir.

While Berklee does not provide a typical collegiate experience, students can still enjoy some of the same activities as their peers at "normal" colleges. Popular student organizations include: The Groove (student newspaper), Berklee C.A.R.E.S., the Music Business Association, and the Council of Students (student government). Students can also play on intramural teams for basketball, football, and soccer.

BERRY COLLEGE

2277 Martha Berry Highway, NW, Mount Berry, GA 30149-0159
Admissions Phone: (706) 236-2215 Fax: (706) 290-2178
Email: admissions@berry.edu Website: www.berry.edu
Application Website: www.berry.edu/admissions/printapp.html

General Info

Type of School: private, coed
Setting: suburban
Academic Calendar: semester

Student Body

Full-Time Undergrads: 1,848
    Men: 36%, Women: 64%

Part-Time Undergrads: 37
    Men: 46%, Women: 54%

Total Undergrad Population:
    African American: 3%
    Asian American: 1%
    Latino: 1%
    Native American: <1%
    Caucasian: 91%
    International: 2%
    Out-of-State: 14%
    Living Off-Campus: 25%

Graduate and First-Professional
    Students: 150

Academics

Full-Time Faculty: 148
    With Ph.D.: 87%

Part-Time Faculty: 27
    With Ph.D.: 41%

Student/Faculty Ratio: 12:1

Most Popular Majors:
    business administration (13%)
    communication (8%)
    early childhood education (8%)
    psychology (7%)
    biology (6%)

Completing 2 or More Majors: 5%

Freshmen Retention Rate: 76%

Graduation Rates:
    50% within four years
    62% within six years

Admissions

Regular Application Deadline: 7/23;
    2/1 (priority)

Fall Transfer Deadline: 7/23,
    2/1 (priority)

Spring Transfer Deadline: 12/6

Total # of Students Applied: 1,846
    Admitted: 1,531
    Enrolled: 505

Test Scores (middle 50%):
    SAT Verbal: 540–650
    SAT Math: 530–630

Inside the Classroom

"Berry stresses academic excellence, student work opportunity, and religion-in-life: the education of the head, hands and hearts of our students," says a college official. Berry consists of four schools: The Campbell School of Business, the Charter School of Education and Human Sciences, the Evans School of Humanities and Social Sciences, and the School of Mathematical and Natural Sciences. The most popular majors are business administration, biology, communication, early childhood education, psychology, animal science, and music; the program in animal science is said to be particularly strong. Dual degree programs are available in engineering with Georgia Institute of Technology and Mercer University, and in nursing with Emory University.

Berry was founded with the intent of developing students' work ethic, and work is an integral part of the Berry experience. The college's work-opportunity program employs well over 70 percent of the student body in any given semester. A college official explains, "Most entering students will work in departments that provide basic services for the college community. Upperclassmen are encouraged to seek out their own jobs that often are related to academic or personal interests of the students." In addition, Berry is dedicated to "Christian values" and the "interdenominational Christian commitment found in its tradition."

General education requirements are rigorous, and include rhetoric and writing; public speaking; arts; sciences; social sciences; mathematics; health; and phys ed. One student reports that "the academic program is pretty rigorous, no matter what major you choose to pursue." Class sizes are small, so students have ample opportunity to interact with faculty members. Notes one student, "The professors are very accessible, always willing to take time to get to know you and to offer extra help if you need it." According to a recent graduate, "The staff and faculty at Berry will devote themselves to you when they see that you're devoted to your education." And a guidance counselor stresses, "Teachers at Berry are hired to *teach*, not conduct research."

Independent study or research courses are available in majors throughout the college. The college's Honors program offers students the opportunities to complete a senior thesis under the direction of a faculty mentor. The college sponsors a Symposium on Student Scholarship each spring where students from across disciplines present scholarly papers or posters or creative presentations. The School of Mathematical and Natural Sciences particularly fosters faculty-student research projects throughout its programs.

Campus Environment

Berry's 28,000-acre campus is "the largest campus in the world" and includes mountains and a large lake. The campus is also a wildlife refuge, where deer, wild turkey, and other wildlife are abundant. Students call the campus "breathtaking," and one enthusiastic student raves, "Berry has the most beautiful campus on earth." The Gothic-style architecture of the buildings complement the beauty of the natural surroundings; a guidance counselor adds, "There are four chapels on campus, all uniquely beautiful."

Students are housed in ten dorms and several on-campus apartment complexes, including traditional dorms, suites, and townhouse garden apartments furnished with microwaves and dishwashers. While Berry's dorms have traditionally been single-sex, a student tells us that "Berry is just starting to have coed housing." About 75 percent of students live on campus. Freshmen live on freshmen-only floors within the dorms. Students are required to live on campus until they accumulate 60 hours of academic credit, which means that freshmen and sophomores generally live on campus. While housing is guaranteed for all four years, some juniors and seniors choose to move off campus, where "you can find decent, affordable housing fairly easily."

Freshmen can have cars on campus, and students can park their vehicles for a reasonable annual fee of five dollars. Many students get around on bikes. In addition, the college runs a shuttle bus service across the expansive campus, and students take Rome city buses from school to town, three miles away. The nearest cities are Atlanta and Chattanooga, each about 65 miles away.

Construction projects are ongoing. Recently, Berry saw the dedication of a totally renovated classroom/office building that houses the Charter School of Education and Human Sciences, the dedication of a new alumni center within the college's historic Ford Complex, and the groundbreaking for a new apartment-style residence hall.

Student Life

Berry is not a paragon of diversity: most students are white and from Georgia. This might change, as the Atlanta-based Goizueta Foundation recently awarded the college a $1.5 million grant, part of which will be used to establish and endow a scholarship for Hispanic and Latino students. About 60 percent of the students at Berry are female. A junior notes, "The typical student you find at Berry College is a middle-class white of the traditional college age (18–22). Most students are well-dressed and drive nice cars."

The overall atmosphere at Berry is quite conservative. "Christian values are still strong on campus," notes a Georgia guidance counselor. Religious organizations on campus are active and popular. "If your beliefs are not mainstream, you probably won't be happy at Berry," cautions one recent graduate. A junior says, "While Berry is a welcoming school, any student who is too far out there in any direction (dress, politics, religious beliefs, etc.) would probably find it difficult to become a part of life at Berry."

One major drawback of this small town school is the "limited" social life. Thursday night is party night; "many students go to Tropicana, which is a club that has a college night on Thursdays," says one student. A freshman's warning: "Think twice before coming here" if you're heavy into partying. However, a junior disagrees: "Drinking is a pretty big factor around here. Many students joke that we're the 'wettest dry campus.'" One student notes that while Berry sponsors weekend activities, they are not terribly well attended, mostly because so many students go home for the weekend.

Naturally, outdoor recreation is popular on Berry's huge, splendid campus. "You can hike, mountain bike, and roam around for hours upon hours and never see the same sites twice," raves one recent grad. Intramural sports are popular—nearly 80 percent of students participate—and include ultimate Frisbee, flag football, and "pickle polo." "There is no football team at Berry, which makes the fall semester a little boring," notes a student.

Other schools to check out: Belmont, Birmingham-Southern, Furman, Millsaps.

THE EXPERTS SAY...

" Berry offers a good education and a beautiful and safe environment to students who are willing to work hard. "

" Wildlife abounds on this picturesque campus, but don't try the old 'A wild turkey ate my homework' excuse. "

BIRMINGHAM-SOUTHERN COLLEGE

900 Arkadelphia Road, Birmingham, AL 35254
Admissions Phone: (205) 226-4698; (800) 523-5793 Fax: (205) 226-3074
Email: admission@bsc.edu Website: www.bsc.edu
Application Website: www.bsc.edu/admission/

General Info

Type of School: private, coed, United Methodist
Academic Calendar: 4-1-4

Student Body

Full-Time Undergrads: 1,276
  Men: 42%, Women: 58%

Part-Time Undergrads: 27
  Men: 48%, Women: 52%

Total Undergrad Population:
  African American: 6%
  Asian American: 2%
  Latino: 1%
  Native American: <1%
  Caucasian: 90%
  International: <1%
  Out-of-State: 25%
  Living Off-Campus: 16%
  In Fraternities: 57%
  In Sororities: 56%

Graduate and First-Professional
  Students: 85

Academics

Full-Time Faculty: 96
  With Ph.D.: 95%

Part-Time Faculty: 25
  With Ph.D.: 32%

Student/Faculty Ratio: 12:1

Freshmen Retention Rate: 82%

Graduation Rates:
  63% within four years
  75% within six years

Admissions

Regular Application Deadline:
  1/15 (priority)

Early Action Deadline: 12/1

Transfers Admission Deadline: rolling

Total # of Students Applied: 1,080
  Admitted: 956
  Enrolled: 357

Test Scores (middle 50%):
  SAT Verbal: 550–670
  SAT Math: 540–660
  ACT Comp: 24–30

HS Rank of Entering Freshmen:
  Top 10%: 53%
  Top 25%: 82%
  Top 50%: 95%

Avg. HS GPA: 3.35

In the Classroom

As one of the best liberal arts colleges in the South, Birmingham-Southern attracts some of the brightest students in the region. BSC has a strong dedication to the liberal arts, and fosters an intimate environment that sends high percentages of prepared students off to medical and law school (not to discount the large numbers entering grad programs in business, economics, English and history as well). The school recently opened the state-of-the-art Elton B. Stephens Science Center, "one of the top undergraduate science teaching facilities in the country." (What happened to the old science building? It's been renovated into a new Humanities Center—nobody gets left out here!) Also, BSC "has long put a strong emphasis on the fine and performing arts." One student complains, however, "You know that course catalog they sent you? Half of those courses haven't been offered in the past four years."

BSC's general education plan is called "Foundations," emphasizing practice, theory, and real-world applications with requirements spread throughout the academic disciplines. "BSC is a school for the intense student seeking a quality education in a challenging atmosphere," says a junior, adding that "students are competitive, always trying to be at the top." A senior English major notes, "Academically, this school is what you make of it. Extracurricular activities like the over-hyped 'service learning' program are far more competitive than the academics." However, hard work pays off here: "Certainly it's tough, but you know that whatever grade you earned was what you deserved."

BSC's student/faculty ratio is a low 12:1, and many faculty members even live on campus. Students work closely with their professors, who almost always know students by name. Professors, according to students, are "probably the best real feature of this campus," "an amazing resource for achieving post-graduate goals," and "always available for help, clarifying assignments, or just having a cup of coffee." It's not uncommon to establish relationships with professors that extend beyond the classroom. "I have been spending a lot of time with my biology professor," says a student. "He has been teaching here for 30 years. He is so smart, and I really respect him. But he's also down-to-earth."

Campus Environment

Freshmen are typically housed together in single-sex dorms, but suite-style housing is available after that, and is described by one student as "amazing!" A music and political science major adds, "Everything is pretty plush, with cable, Internet, phones, and air and heating units. Plus, we have a cleaning service that cleans everything daily!" Most students live on campus (a requirement for everyone under 21). Off-campus housing is available, but not too practical, as living on-campus is "beautiful, safe, and convenient." A senior explains about living off-campus: "You need to live at least 15 minutes away to be in a safe area. It's basically not worth it."

Campus safety is somewhat akin to a Disney movie. A student tells us, "You can leave your car unlocked. You can walk anywhere on campus anytime of the day or night by yourself." Another student explains that BSC is a "very safe school, with only one entrance onto the campus," noting also that "campus security officers are probably the most popular people on campus—they not only always check your tires and your oil, but give rides to class in the rain, and pick you up if your car breaks down and you're stranded off campus."

You can bring a car, so long as you register it with the school, but the campus itself is pretty small and walkable. Students "car pool to Wal-Mart, the mall, and other places of interest—someone is always leaving, and asks if you need a ride." The city of Birmingham is just about three miles away, linking the small campus to a cultural and entertainment center. In Birmingham, you can find music history at the Alabama Jazz Hall of Fame, explore the Birmingham Civil Rights Institute, visit the Birmingham Zoo or Botanical Gardens, or get out of student mode and wander around one of the city's many major shopping malls.

Student Life

With such a small enrollment, almost all the students know one another, creating a sense of community. Most students come from a similar background and share similar, usually conservative values. "The typical student is a white, Republican, religious conservative from in-state who is fairly bright, fairly well-off... but not at all cultured," says one student. However, the same student adds, "As stereotypical as many people here are, I think everyone would feel welcome. People have a lot of promise, they just don't have many opportunities to expand their horizons." Another tells us, "Most of the student body are middle-class Caucasians, but in terms of attitude and style, you have literally everything." The student body is open and warm: "the Southern hospitality that you expect is exactly what you get."

The social life here is dominated by the Greek system, which attracts much of the student population. The school tells us that it recently completed building a new Fraternity Row, with houses for its six national Greek fraternities. However, one student notes that the administration "lately seems to have it out for Greek life. They are constantly trying to punish fraternities in particular." The administration is "completely clueless as to how much they depend on the Greek system." The senior explains that fraternities are a big help in recruiting men to BSC, and that sororities have a big impact on campus activities like "faculty appreciation day," Earth Day, and open houses. Independents and Greeks alike are involved in extracurriculars like volunteer work and community service, theater, religious fellowship services, and service learning. Drinking is typical for a college campus: "most people drink on campus," but "there is absolutely no pressure to partake." "Many times, designated drivers are established," says a student, "Also, the school provides a shuttle service on weekend nights, lovingly called 'the Drunk Bus.'"

BSC participates in NCAA Division I and Big South Conference sports for men's and women's basketball, cross-country, golf, soccer, and tennis, as well as men's baseball; and women's softball, volleyball, and rifle. There is no football team; a double major theorizes, "I think that's what makes the academic atmosphere so unique—because athletes are very academically minded as well." Students tell us that intramural sports are also very popular, especially with Greeks.

Other schools to check out: Rhodes, University of the South, Centre, Millsaps, Hendrix.

Costs (2003–04)

Tuition and Fees: $19,109
Room & Board: $6,634

Inst. Aid (est. 2003–04)

Institutional Aid, Need-Based:
$13,100,490

FT Undergrads Receiving Aid: 41%
Avg. Amount per Student: $16,015

FT Undergrads Receiving Non-Need-Based Scholarship or Grant Aid: 48%
Avg. Amount per Student: $10,425

Of Those Receiving Any Aid:

Rec. Need-Based Scholarship or
Grant Aid: 100%
Average Award: $7,342

Rec. Need-Based Self-Help Aid: 68%
Average Award: $5,404

Upon Graduation, Avg. Loan Debt
per Student: $12,200

Financial Aid Deadline: 8/1,
3/1 (priority)

THE EXPERTS SAY...

" Nearly half of BSC's graduating class continues on to grad school within one year. "

" A small, friendly, Greek-oriented, Southern campus: Either it works for you, or it doesn't. "

BOSTON COLLEGE

140 Commonwealth Avenue, Devlin Hall 208, Chestnut Hill, MA 02467-3809
Admissions Phone: (617) 552-3100; (800) 360-2522 Fax: (617) 552-0498
Email: ugadmis@bc.edu   Website: www.bc.edu

General Info

Type of School: private, coed,
  Roman Catholic/Jesuit

Setting: suburban

Academic Calendar: semester

Student Body

Full-Time Undergrads: 8,851
  Men: 48%, Women: 52%

Total Undergrad Population:
  African American: 5%
  Asian American: 9%
  Latino: 6%
  Native American: <1%
  Caucasian: 75%
  International: 2%
  Out-of-State: 72%
  Living Off-Campus: 22%

Graduate and First-Professional
  Students: 4,760

Academics

Full-Time Faculty: 639
  With Ph.D.: 98%

Part-Time Faculty: 568

Student/Faculty Ratio: 14:1
  (from 2002)

Most Popular Majors:
  communications (11%)
  English (9%)
  finance (8%)
  political science (8%)
  Psychology (7%)

Freshmen Retention Rate: 95%

Graduation Rates:
  82% within four years
  87% within six years

Admissions

Regular Application Deadline: 1/2

Early Action Deadline: 11/1

Fall Transfer Deadline: 4/1

Spring Transfer Deadline: 11/1

Total # of Students Applied: 22,424
  Admitted: 6,896
  Enrolled: 2,208

# of Students Waitlisted: 5,000
  Students Accepting Place: 2,000
  Waitlisted Students Admitted: 200

Test Scores (middle 50%):
  SAT Verbal: 600–690
  SAT Math: 630–710

Inside the Classroom

Each of Boston College's four undergraduate schools has its own admissions procedures. A New England guidance counselor's opinion of BC's admissions: "Way too competitive! Their admissions practices are inconsistent—making it hard to advise students." But a young alum argues that the admissions process at BC is unusually humanistic: "I felt they made a real effort to help me determine whether or not the school was a good fit for me, and not the other way around." And a California counselor notes that "financial aid is fair for all; scholarship practices are being geared to many more students than in past years."

BC has a "national academic reputation," brags a Massachusetts guidance counselor. Another notes, "Job placement after college is excellent." The schools of business, education, and nursing all have excellent reputations, while arts and sciences, the largest school at BC, has strong departments in a number of areas, including English, political science, history, economics, and philosophy. Not surprisingly, "premed, business, and prelaw majors tend to be the most competitive," says a psychology/theology double major. Students in all areas carry "fairly substantial" workloads, and the environment is said to be "very competitive, but not cut-throat."

The rigid, "pretty intense" core curriculum can take much of the first two years to complete and reflects the classical Jesuit emphasis on the liberal arts. It includes required courses in several basic academic fields: natural and social science, history, philosophy, theology, English, math, fine arts, and cultural diversity. Freshmen take a writing seminar and all students must be proficient in a foreign language to graduate. In addition to BC's own extensive course offerings, students can also cross-register at several other schools, including Boston University.

Because of the heavy core curriculum, some of the introductory courses can have hundreds of students. But as students progress in their major, class sizes get smaller. One student tells us, "I've gotten to know a majority of my professors personally," and several other students agree that most professors are "very accessible."

Campus Environment

The expansive campus, located in "one of the ritzier suburbs of Boston," has a number of high-quality, well-maintained facilities, including the recently constructed theater arts center, sports complex, state-of-the-art chemistry center, and ultramodern O'Neill Library. Students agree that "safety usually isn't an issue"— "the campus police do a great job of alerting students of any potentially dangerous circumstances," says a young alum.

Residence halls are scattered in several locations around campus. Most first-year students live together in the dorms, while juniors frequently move off campus. Senior year, many students choose to return to BC housing and live in the Mods—blocks of student townhouses complete with yards for barbecues and parties. During study days for final exams, BC imposes 24-hour "quiet hours" in the dorms. However, from 11 to 11:15 P.M. is "Primal Scream," when students blast loud music and scream out their windows to relieve stress.

The school's proximity to Boston greatly enhances entertainment options. Students frequently head to popular hangouts and restaurants in the city or to visit friends at other area schools. "Cars are not prevalent on campus, as parking is very limited," says a recent grad. Other students agree, but add that cars are really not necessary anyway, since it's so easy to just take the "T" (Boston's user-friendly subway system) or a bus.

Student Life

Students here definitely enjoy an active social life. There are no fraternities or sororities, but alcohol is "a major factor" on- and off-campus, "particularly in the fall, when BC has home football games." Although the wildest parties won't necessarily be found on-campus, where alcohol policies are strictly enforced, many people regularly head off-campus to popular local bars or keg parties thrown by everyone from "the sports teams to the Irish Society to the campus newspaper." Students say that while there are "a good number" of people who smoke marijuana, hard-core drugs are not used at BC.

One of the main attractions at BC is unquestionably the Division I athletics—"very competitive, extremely popular," says one student. BC offers 14 men's and 17 women's varsity teams. A Connecticut counselor theorizes that BC's "big school spirit" and "good athletics program" are a big draw for applicants. Crowds of enthusiastic fans come to watch BC's football, hockey, and basketball teams. Also, as an alum points out, "Boston is a very health-conscious city, so many students are active, whether through varsity, intramural, or self-motivated activities. The school gym is always busy, [and] running is also very popular."

Much of BC's popularity is based on word-of-mouth: "Students always return home to tell friends how much fun they had there!" exclaims one guidance counselor. BC also boasts a large number of "legacy" students—"I know of many families, including my own, that have more than one BC student/alum in them," says a recent grad. The flip-side of this is a lack of diversity among the mainly upper-middle-class, J. Crew/Abercrombie-wearing student body. An alum tells us that one of the ongoing jokes at BC is that "a great percentage of the student body is very physically attractive and is up-to-date with the fashions simply because of the money they have and can spend on clothes, makeup, gyms, etc." Some less happy (and less wealthy) students find the population to be a bit snobbish and shallow to that end. And BC students tend to be fairly conservative, both politically and socially. "Anyone looking for 'a cultural awakening' should look elsewhere," warns another alum.

As a Roman Catholic school, BC incorporates religion into many aspects of campus life. The innovative and popular PULSE program, for instance, combines community service with the study of theology, ethics, and philosophy. But religion isn't forced down anyone's throat. "While there are so many opportunities to become religiously or spiritually involved on-campus, students are not required to, and should not feel uncomfortable if they choose not to," says one recent grad. And BC students are not shy about comparing themselves favorably to other Catholic universities: "Many would argue that Notre Dame is the Catholic university in the U.S.," says another grad, "but BC alums would argue that Notre Dame is in the middle of nowhere and is boring, while BC offers the cultural attractions of the city of Boston."

Other schools to check out: Georgetown, Notre Dame, Villanova, Boston University, Holy Cross.

HS Rank of Entering Freshmen:
Top 10%: 73%
Top 25%: 93%
Top 50%: 98%

Costs (2004–5)

Tuition and Fees: $29,396

Room & Board: $9,620

Payment Plan(s): installment plan, pre-payment plan

THE EXPERTS SAY...

" Part of the holy triumvirate of Catholic higher education, along with Georgetown and Notre Dame. "

" Great academics, top-ranked sports, and an active party scene make BC the place to be... if you can stomach the overly preppy atmosphere. "

Inst. Aid (est. 2002–03)

Institutional Aid, Need-Based: $43,902,200

Institutional Aid, Non-Need-Based: $3,117,012

FT Undergrads Receiving Aid: 38% Avg. Amount per Student: $22,859

FT Undergrads Receiving Non-Need-Based Scholarship or Grant Aid: 2% Avg. Amount per Student: $7,561

Of Those Receiving Any Aid:

Rec. Need-Based Scholarship or Grant Aid: 90% Average Award: $16,820

Rec. Need-Based Self-Help Aid: 94% Average Award: $6,231

Upon Graduation, Avg. Loan Debt per Student: $17,517

Financial Aid Deadline: 2/1 (priority)

BOSTON UNIVERSITY

121 Bay State Road, Boston, MA 02215
Admissions Phone: (617) 353-2300 Fax: (617) 353-9695
Email: admissions@bu.edu; intadmis@bu.edu (Int.) Website: www.bu.edu
Application Website: www.bu.edu/admissions/apply/index.html

General Info

Type of School: private, coed

Setting: urban

Academic Calendar: semester

Student Body

Full-Time Undergrads: 15,463
  Men: 40%, Women: 60%

Part-Time Undergrads: 317
  Men: 53%, Women: 47%

Total Undergrad Population:
  African American: 2%
  Asian American: 13%
  Latino: 5%
  Caucasian: 60%
  International: 7%
  Out-of-State: 78%
  Living Off-Campus: 26%
  In Fraternities: 3%
  In Sororities: 5%

Graduate and First-Professional
  Students: 11,367

Academics

Full-Time Faculty: 2,500

Part-Time Faculty: 992

Student/Faculty Ratio: 14:1

Most Popular Majors:
  communication/journalism (13%)
  business administration and
    management (11%)
  engineering (8%)
  psychology (5%)
  health and rehabilitation
    services (4%)

Completing 2 or More Majors: 7%

Freshmen Retention Rate: 90%

Graduation Rates:
  62% within four years
  75% within six years

Admissions

Regular Application Deadline: 1/1

Early Decision Deadline(s): 11/1

Fall Transfer Deadline: 4/1

Spring Transfer Deadline: 11/1

Total # of Students Applied: 29,356
  Admitted: 15,191
  Enrolled: 3,961

Inside the Classroom

A psych major at BU tells us, "I have a lot of friends who go to schools that may be better ranked, but they don't seem to have nearly as much work… BU is much, much harder than anyone thinks!" The largest university in Boston, BU's extensive facilities and academic offerings attract thousands of students from across the country and around the world. A guidance counselor notes, "Students love the entire atmosphere of the school."

With more than 250 majors and minors available, students can find almost any program of study they want in BU's undergraduate schools: the College of Arts and Sciences, College of Communication, College of Engineering, College of Fine Arts (made up of the schools of music, theatre arts, and visual arts), Metropolitan College, Sargent College of Health and Rehabilitation Sciences, School of Education, School of Hospitality Administration, and School of Management. Some of BU's most distinguished programs are in the departments of physics, astronomy, economics, anthropology, biomedical engineering, and physical therapy. The communications and music programs are also well regarded.

Students claim that the workload at all BU schools is "heavy but manageable," and say that the academic atmosphere is "very competitive," particularly in the School of Management and the Sargent College of Health. "People are pretty competitive because they are trying to get into med schools or are looking to apply to Ph.D. programs in the future," explains a biochemistry/molecular biology student.

Core requirements are different for each undergraduate college. All freshmen are required to complete the two-semester Freshman Writing Program; class size in these writing seminars is limited to 18 students. Students tell us that most professors at BU are "accessible" and "have high standards and love to teach."

While the faculty at BU receives high marks from students, the administration sometimes does not. Several students complain about the "lack of action by the administration" and object to the rising tuition costs (which were already exorbitant). As at many large universities, BU students are pretty much on their own when it comes to cutting through all the red tape. "A student who wants the administration to walk them through every step of his or her college career would not fit in here," a psych major warns us. "There are definitely ways of getting questions answered and help sought out here, but you have to find these things on your own."

Campus Environment

Around 70 percent of BU students live in on-campus housing, which is said to be decent, particularly in the smaller, renovated brownstones. BU is excited over the construction of its new Student Village—"a 10-acre hub of activity" featuring three new residence halls, a new fitness center, and a new 6,200–7,200-seat sports arena. The extra housing is desperately needed: "This past year, they over-enrolled and many students were forced to stay in hotels for the first semester," says a freshman. "After first semester, many were moved out and put into dorms where exchange students or transfer students used to live." Most freshmen live in the 14-story Warren Tower, which houses more students than the entire populations of some small liberal arts colleges. Although this environment does help freshmen meet other students, the massive tower doesn't create an especially cozy environment. For upperclassmen, Boston has plenty of living spaces off-campus, but not always of the best quality; students need to watch out for overpriced dumps in bad areas.

The residence halls have tight security, as befits an urban campus. "Many students find the security measures to be excessive and ridiculous," says one freshman, but a more appreciative frosh declares, "BU security is fantastic! It's a pain in the @#! at times, but I have never felt unsafe anywhere on campus." Still, students complained so much about the strict policy regarding after-hours visitors that the administration has finally eased up a bit.

Student Life

Although attending a large, urban university like BU does mean sacrificing a sense of togetherness, it has its social advantages, such as a diverse student body ("there are a lot of rich foreign kids," notes a junior). A recent grad says, "Since BU has been dubbed the 'UN' of colleges, you meet a wide spectrum of people." A freshman adds, "Everyone who goes here has the opportunity to find his or her niche within this community." Most BU students are upper-middle-class and moderately liberal. "Girls have a style that looks like it's from Banana Republic, the GAP, Express, Guess, and French Connection," observes a 2002 graduate. "Black pants or Diesel jeans with high–heeled, pointy-toed boots is a very popular look on campus."

"The typical student is the above-average, good student, who still really likes to socialize, and gets involved with stuff because he or she wants to," says a freshman. BU offers nearly 400 activities, from playing on one of the many "strong" varsity teams (though BU has no football team) or "highly popular" intramural teams to joining a fraternity. There's no real pressure to go Greek: "Not very many people take part in the organizations themselves, but everyone goes to their parties," says one student. Another student explains, "BU is in the city, so if anyone wants a good party scene, they go downtown, not to some frat or sorority."

"Weeknights, and especially Sunday night, all people do is study, so the libraries are packed," says an international relations/biology double-major. But from Thursday to Saturday night, the campus can get "pretty rowdy." "BU is located right next door to a multitude of clubs and other nightspots," says a young alum. Drinking is popular ("not as big as at big Greek schools or state schools," claims one student), but "not a lot of people do drugs here—the school's policies are extremely tough on drugs so it probably discourages a lot of that here," another student explains.

What do students find most appealing about BU? Try *location*. Says one student, "Boston is the ultimate place for a student. It's awesome. Period." Set directly on the Charles River in the historic Back Bay district, BU's campus virtually blends into the city. The "T", Boston's subway system, links the school to any of the city's social, cultural, and culinary attractions that form the basis of the BU student's social life.

Other schools to check out: NYU, Boston College, Tufts, Syracuse, George Washington U.

# of Students Waitlisted: 2,871
  Students Accepting Place: 1,324
  Waitlisted Students Admitted: 1,214

Applied Early Decision: 502
  Early Decision Admitted: 249

Test Scores (middle 50%):
  SAT Verbal: 600–690
  SAT Math: 620–690
  ACT Comp: 26–30
  ACT English: 26–31
  ACT Math: 26–30

HS Rank of Entering Freshmen:
  Top 10%: 60%
  Top 25%: 92%
  Top 50%: 100%

Avg. HS GPA: 3.5

THE EXPERTS SAY...

" Many applicants may not know that Martin Luther King Jr. was a BU alum, and Nobel Peace Prize Laureate Elie Weisel is a BU professor. "

" If you don't get lost in the crowds of grad and undergrad students, or drown in the sea of red tape, you can get a lot out of BU. "

Costs (2004–5)

Tuition and Fees: $30,402

Room & Board: $9,680
  note: expenses vary

Payment Plan(s): installment plan, pre-payment plan

Inst. Aid (est. 2003–04)

FT Undergrads Receiving Aid: 47%
  Avg. Amount per Student: $25,338

FT Undergrads Receiving Non-Need-Based Scholarship or Grant Aid: 13%
  Avg. Amount per Student: $14,324

Of Those Receiving Any Aid:

Rec. Need-Based Scholarship or Grant Aid: 94%
  Average Award: $16,953

Rec. Need-Based Self-Help Aid: 91%
  Average Award: $5,921

Upon Graduation, Avg. Loan Debt per Student: $17,535

Financial Aid Deadline: 2/15 (priority)

Graduates

Going to Graduate School: 25% Within One Year

Companies Recruiting On Campus: 325

Alumni Giving: 18%

BOWDOIN COLLEGE

5700 College Station, Brunswick, ME 04011-8448
Admissions Phone: (207) 725-3100 Fax: (207) 725-3101
Email: admissions@bowdoin.edu Website: www.bowdoin.edu
Application Website: www.bowdoin.edu/admissions/apply

General Info

Type of School: private, coed

Setting: small town

Academic Calendar: semester

Student Body

Full-Time Undergrads: 1,636
  Men: 51%, Women: 49%

Total Undergrad Population:
  African American: 5%
  Asian American: 10%
  Latino: 5%
  Native American: 1%
  Caucasian: 74%
  International: 3%
  Out-of-State: 87%
  Living Off-Campus: 8%

Academics

Full-Time Faculty: 154
  With Ph.D.: 97%

Part-Time Faculty: 25
  With Ph.D.: 64%

Student/Faculty Ratio: 10:1

Most Popular Majors:
  government (21%)
  economics (12%)
  history (9%)
  English (8%)
  biology (8%)

Completing 2 or More Majors: 25%

Freshmen Retention Rate: 93%

Graduation Rates:
  81% within four years
  90% within six years

Storngly Recommend Students
  Have Own Computers

Admissions

Regular Application Deadline: 1/1

Early Decision Deadline(s): 11/15,
  12/31

Fall Transfer Deadline: 3/1

Transfer Closing Date for
  International Students: 1/1

Total # of Students Applied: 4,719
  Admitted: 1,154
  Enrolled: 467

Waitlist Available

Applied Early Decision: 552
  Early Decision Admitted: 167

Inside the Classroom

Bowdoin (pronounced "Bo-dun") is one of a growing number of top schools that don't require SAT or ACT scores in the admissions process—an option used by approximately one-third of admitted applicants. The administration claims to be much more interested in examining the whole student than in looking at test scores. This humanistic attitude is evident throughout the school, particularly in its doctrine of "the Common Good"—putting one's education to work for the betterment of society.

The school attracts "independent and intellectually inquisitive" people. Students rave about the opportunities for independent study, and about 60 percent are involved with some form of individualized work, such as a custom major or a for-credit research project not connected with any course but under a professor's (or department's) guidance. As you would expect, this requires an active and accessible faculty, something Bowdoin has in spades. Most, if not all faculty members, are there when you need them and are "willing to help students one on one." "There may be a couple of visiting professors who aren't always around when you'd like, but they are the exception, rather than the rule," confirms one student.

By the end of sophomore year, students must complete the general curriculum requirements by taking classes in natural science and math, social and behavioral sciences, humanities and fine arts, and non-Eurocentric studies. The workload obviously varies a bit, but is generally "intense and heavy." There are opportunities for many different kinds of academic experiences, including renowned interdisciplinary programs from Asian Studies to Arctic Studies, and an inexpensive study abroad program, in which over half the student body participates. Utilizing cutting-edge facilities and resources, Bowdoin's science departments are excellent, particularly in chemistry (the school is known for its microscale labs), biology, and environmental studies. The programs in government, history, English, and economics are also strong. In addition to an impressive main library, Hawthorne-Longfellow, students are also able to use specialized libraries in art history, science and mathematics, music, women's studies, and Africana studies.

Campus Environment

Visit Bowdoin's 110-acre campus, surrounded by beautiful Maine wilderness, and you might feel you've stepped into a nature preserve, complete with pine tree groves, one of Maine's largest rivers, and the rocky Atlantic coast just a few miles away. The school's location makes it a haven for outdoor lovers, and it gets high marks for safety.

All first-year students live on campus in one of six red brick dorms, known collectively as "The Bricks." Depending on the dorm assignment, each first-year student also becomes a full-fledged member of one of the five upperclassmen social houses. Here, students can participate in their house's activities, ranging from shared meals to educational programs to parties and performances. "It's a great way to meet people," says one student; another adds that there's no pressure, since students can "change their affiliation without any difficulty." All members of the faculty are automatically connected to one of the brick dorms as advisers, and they may dine at that dorm's affiliated house with students. There are no fraternities or sororities. About 12 percent of upperclassmen move off-campus—the lucky ones find "beautiful ocean-front housing" that's a short drive away. All students are permitted to bring cars, but having one isn't a necessity. The campus is small, and downtown Brunswick is an easy walk.

Bowdoin is rare in that it receives almost universal praise for its on-campus food; it ranks among the top 10 in national surveys of colleges. "The food is everything you've heard about and more—it's amazing," one student boasts.

Student Life

Although "all types are accepted at Bowdoin," the typical student can be described as a "white, upper-class, boarding-school graduate," a recent grad tells us. While it's true that a significant number of students come from upper-class New England prep schools, almost half graduated from public high schools. The resulting mix seems to be a "very friendly," hardworking crowd of scholars who get along pretty easily. Bowdoin students are smart and devoted to their studies; a large percentage plan on going on to graduate or medical school. Yet the "very academically focused" atmosphere is markedly relaxed and free of cutthroat competition—perhaps a holdover from the days when Bowdoin didn't give out grades. "Students act like colleagues, not competitors," says one government major. A high school guidance counselor compliments the "good balance between academics and social life" on campus. About 70 percent of Bowdoin students volunteer in the community, and many participate in one of several student organizations seriously committed to the environment.

Since the nearest city, Portland, is more than 30 minutes away, most social activities take place on campus or in the town of Brunswick, which has restaurants, stores, a movie theater, and a popular bar. Drinking is, of course, a common weekend activity ("What else is there to do in Maine?" one student jokes), but Bowdoin isn't a big party school. Athletics are popular, and "play a large role in the social scene." Thirty-five percent of the student body play on one of 31 NCAA teams (14 men's, 15 women's, 2 coed), and another 30 percent participate in intramural or club sports. Hockey is the number-one sport, and students regularly crowd the 2,400-seat Dayton Arena to cheer on the Polar Bears. The Outing Club, the largest and most popular student organization, organizes weekend trips centering on a variety of outdoor experiences, from canoeing and skiing to biking and rock climbing. As one sophomore puts it, "The best thing here is that it's a small college atmosphere that gives you the chance to be involved with an incredible number of activities."

Bowdoin is a proud and tradition-rich college. During their first week on campus, students sign the same Matriculation Book as alumni Nathaniel Hawthorne and Henry Wadsworth Longfellow. Other traditions include Ivies Weekend, Winter's Weekend, and a campus-wide lobster bake that welcomes back students every fall. And each winter, the town of Brunswick floods its downtown park to make an outdoor skating rink.

Other schools to check out: Williams, Amherst, Dartmouth, Middlebury, Bates, Colby.

THE EXPERTS SAY...

" This selective school looks at the whole student. The science programs are exceptional. "

" Welcome to Walden Pond! If you don't want to change the world, change schools. "

BRADLEY UNIVERSITY

1501 West Bradley Avenue, Peoria, IL 61625
Admissions Phone: (309) 677-1000; (800) 447-6460 Fax: (309) 677-2797
Email: admissions@bradley.edu
Website: www.admissions.bradley.edu

General Info

Type of School: private, coed
Setting: suburban
Academic Calendar: semester

Student Body

Full-Time Undergrads: 4,926
  Men: 46%, Women: 54%

Part-Time Undergrads: 362
  Men: 42%, Women: 58%

Total Undergrad Population:
  African American: 5%
  Asian American: 3%
  Latino: 2%
  Native American: 1%
  Caucasian: 83%
  International: 1%
  Living Off-Campus: 31%
  In Fraternities: 34%
  In Sororities: 37%

Graduate and First-Professional
  Students: 832

Academics

Full-Time Faculty: 332
  With Ph.D.: 83%

Part-Time Faculty: 196

Student/Faculty Ratio: 15:1

Most Popular Majors:
  communications (11%)
  business management (5%)
  elementary education (5%)
  psychology (5%)
  mechanical engineering (5%)

Completing 2 or More Majors: 10%

Freshmen Retention Rate: 89%

Graduation Rates:
  23% within four years

Admissions

Total # of Students Applied: 5,207
  Admitted: 3,570
  Enrolled: 1,105

# of Students Waitlisted: 137
  Students Accepting Place: 48
  Waitlisted Students Admitted: 21

Test Scores (middle 50%):
  ACT Comp: 23–28

HS Rank of Entering Freshmen:
  Top 10%: 25%
  Top 25%: 61%
  Top 50%: 90%

Inside the Classroom

Bradley University provides large school opportunities in a mid-size school environment, with a distinctive dose of real-world experience. A research institution that gives a lot of individualized attention to its students, Bradley offers more than 90 programs through its five undergraduate schools: education and health sciences, engineering and technology, liberal arts and sciences, business administration, and communications and fine arts. The school prides itself on a low student/faculty ratio, early and continuous field experiences, and excellent job and grad school placement rates. (However, one senior tells us, "The accessibility of professors in the freshman- and sophomore-level classes is very difficult. The upper-level classes are more accessible.") Bradley has high rankings among schools in the Midwest and is considered a regional "best value."

Bradley is best known for its programs in business, engineering, and natural sciences. There's even a new degree in music business. General education requirements are designed "to develop students, regardless of major or professional aspiration, who are able to understand and participate in society as responsible human beings." The core curriculum includes courses in English composition, speech, mathematics, Western civilization, non-Western civilization, fine arts, human values, social forces, science and technology, and computer usage. Bradley emphasizes teaching, and faculty serve as academic advisors, mentors, and career guides to undergrads. Class size averages less than 24 students.

Bradley's small size enables it to provide students with many special programs. About 30 percent of students take part in study abroad programs in Europe and Mexico. Hands-on experience is what Bradley is about, and co-ops and internships start in sophomore year. Students can choose from an alternating schedule of full-time work and full-time study, or work and study part-time. All students in the schools of business, engineering, education, and the health sciences are required to take semester-long hands-on practicum courses in their fields. Senior-level business students work on projects with central Illinois businesses as part of their curriculum requirements. Every semester more than 750 students in the College of Education and Health Sciences perform field work at education and health care agencies.

The real-world experience pays off: The overall job placement rate for Bradley graduates in a recent school-sponsored survey was 97 percent; the placement rate for graduates with cooperative education experience was 99 percent. In recent years, 82 percent of Bradley students applying to medical schools have been accepted, 93 percent to dental schools, and 99 percent to graduate schools in the natural sciences.

Campus Environment

In the biggest capital project of its history, Bradley completed renovation on the Olin Hall of Science in 2002, adding 59,000 square feet of new classroom and lab space. Bradley's 41 buildings are located on a 75-acre campus in Peoria, a city with a metro area of about 350,000 residents. Freshmen may have cars but may not park them on campus. The campus is self-contained, and many students walk or bike. "The campus is located in a 'rough' neighborhood, but the campus itself is safe," explains one student. While not the most exciting college town, Peoria does provide the amenities like shopping, restaurants, and a few cultural attractions; a city bus system goes to major shopping centers and downtown Peoria.

Bradley has several residence halls; the university also owns a student apartment building a block from campus. Singles are reserved for sophomores, juniors, and seniors in the school's three-building Singles Complex. Students may express (but not always get) their housing preferences in the assignment process. Freshmen and sophomores are required to live on campus; sophomores may live in fraternity housing. About 30 percent of students live off-campus, where housing is expensive and you need "6–8 people before it's affordable. Also, the surrounding neighborhood consists of old, run-down houses." Comparatively, on campus there is "lots of housing," which is "pretty comfortable."

Student Life

Braves basketball is huge at Bradley. The men's basketball team, long a favorite of students and enthusiastic Peoria fans alike, has played in Carver Arena in downtown Peoria ever since winning their fourth NIT in 1982. One student tells us, though, that "even though we have a typically successful basketball team, sports are not huge because we do not have the facilities. Fans have to travel to various areas in Peoria to attend events." Men's and women's athletic teams compete at NCAA Division I level. Intramurals are also popular, with 70 percent of students participating in competition or other fitness programs.

With 16 fraternities and 12 sororities, the Greek scene is massive, and the Greeks provide a steady flow of entertainment and parties. "The frats are a huge part of the social life at Bradley because they all have their own house," says one student. "The parties are well-advertised and every weekend." The student further explains that drinking is "a major 'hobby' at Bradley." Although some students complain that everyone at Bradley is either a Greek or a jock ("the artsy, bohemian student population is very small; alternative lifestyles are not the norm," notes a senior), the arts are not neglected, and art exhibits and recitals (including performances by the Basketball Band) are frequent. Guest speakers and artists have included Maya Angelou, Susan Sontag, David Halberstam, the National Theater of the Deaf, John Updike, and Stephen J. Gould. The student radio and television stations serve all of Central Illinois.

Bradley has over 220 student organizations. The Engineering Club goes back to 1898, 22 years before there was an engineering program. Popular organizations include the Center for Student Leadership and Public Service, the Activities Council, and the Student Senate. The Bradley speech team has won nationals over 30 times since 1980.

The typical Bradley student is white and from the suburbs of Chicago. A communications/public relations major tells us, "The students are generally 'preppy' and from money." College officials say that the kind of student who would thrive at Bradley would enjoy its balance between academics and social life, and would want to take advantage of the co-ops, internships and practicums offered. The Bradley student gets the best of all worlds—recognition rather than anonymity among peers, small school attention from faculty, and large school resources.

Other schools to check out: Marquette, University of Dayton, DePaul, DePauw, Illinois Wesleyan.

Costs (2003–04)

Tuition and Fees: $16,930

Room & Board: $5,980

Payment Plan(s): installment plan, deferred payment plan

Inst. Aid (est. 2003–04)

Institutional Aid, Non-Need-Based: $7,244,669

FT Undergrads Receiving Aid: 80%
Avg. Amount per Student: $11,545

FT Undergrads Receiving Non-Need-Based Scholarship or Grant Aid: 20%
Avg. Amount per Student: $9,614

THE EXPERTS SAY...

" A nice choice for Mid-westerners who are interested in business, engineering, or the natural sciences. "

" If you want to go to an urban Illinois school, Chicago has a heck of a lot more to offer than Peoria. "

Of Those Receiving Any Aid:

Rec. Need-Based Scholarship or Grant Aid: 91%
Average Award: $8,907

Rec. Need-Based Self-Help Aid: 52%
Average Award: $5,208

Upon Graduation, Avg. Loan Debt per Student: $15,941

Financial Aid Deadline: 3/1 (priority)

Graduates

Going to Graduate School: 18% Within One Year

Companies Recruiting On Campus: 369

Alumni Giving: 20%

BRANDEIS UNIVERSITY

415 South Street, Waltham, MA 02454
Admissions Phone: (781) 736-3500; (800) 622-0622 (out-of-state) Fax: (781) 736-3536
Email: sendinfo@brandeis.edu
Website: www.brandeis.edu

General Info

Type of School: private, coed

Setting: suburban

Academic Calendar: semester

Student Body

Full-Time Undergrads: 3,137
  Men: 44%, Women: 56%

Part-Time Undergrads: 38
  Men: 47%, Women: 53%

Total Undergrad Population:
  African American: 2%
  Asian American: 8%
  Latino: 3%
  Native American: <1%
  Caucasian: 68%
  International: 7%
  Out-of-State: 76%
  Living Off-Campus: 16%

Graduate and First-Professional
  Students: 1,810

Academics

Full-Time Faculty: 335
  With Ph.D.: 98%

Part-Time Faculty: 106
  With Ph.D.: 80%

Student/Faculty Ratio: 8:1

Most Popular Majors:
  economics (15%)
  biology (12%)
  politics (10%)
  psychology (9%)
  sociology (9%)

Freshmen Retention Rate: 94%

Graduation Rates:
  80% within four years
  84% within six years

Admissions

Regular Application Deadline: 1/31

Early Decision Deadline(s): 1/1

Fall Transfer Deadline: 4/1

Spring Transfer Deadline: 11/1

Total # of Students Applied: 5,770
  Admitted: 2,524
  Enrolled: 823

# of Students Waitlisted: 755
  Students Accepting Place: 367
  Waitlisted Students Admitted: 108

Applied Early Decision: 297
  Early Decision Admitted: 215

Inside the Classroom

"Brandeis is driven by the academic stature of its students—there is a true passion for learning and knowledge which extends across the majors," states a recent grad. But with this passion comes pressure: "The intensity and competition within every field are extreme," says another Brandeis alum.

Brandeis is virtually unrivaled in Near Eastern and Judaic studies, with the largest faculty in the field outside of Israel. The biochemistry, chemistry, neuroscience, and physics programs are top-notch; over two-thirds of Brandeis undergrads who apply to medical school are accepted. Premeds receive personalized attention with special advisors, internships, and their own Berlin Premedical Center, with specialized laboratories designed to provide aspiring MDs with research opportunities. Competition is intense: "They weed out premeds like crazy," says a psychology/biology double major. Departments such as English, history, and political science offer nationally ranked graduate programs. A number of interdisciplinary programs, including Internet Studies ("the first in the nation"), Peace and Conflict Studies, and Women's Studies, add spice to the academic menu. Brandeis also maintains a commitment to the creative arts, with strong theater offerings and a theory-based music program founded by the late Leonard Bernstein.

A guidance counselor tells us, "Brandeis uses generous merit aid to attract top scholars." With a student/faculty ratio of 8:1 and a median class size of 16, students have the opportunity to interact with some of the top minds in their fields. Although the "intermittently brilliant professors" may often be immersed in their own work ("many seem to be in a rush to go to meetings and go on to more important, exciting things," notes a junior), students tell us they are "generally friendly" and "very easy to approach."

Campus Environment

The school charges a high tuition and receives a great deal of money in grants and donations; the funding allows the school to maintain cutting-edge facilities, such as the $41.5 million Volen Natural Center for biological, cognitive, and computational research. The brand-new, $22 million Shapiro Campus Center includes "new offices, entertainment, and places where the students can hang out," a student informs us.

The campus features a mix of architectural styles, including several striking contemporary structures ("like the auditorium shaped like a top hat and the music building shaped like a piano"). Housing arrangements are equally eclectic in style ("You can live in a replica of a Scottish castle with pie-shaped rooms and stairways leading to nowhere!"). First-year students are usually housed together in two residence quads, Massell and North. Housing is guaranteed for freshmen and sophomores only, and overcrowding is a problem: "Many first-year students begin in 'unnatural triples,' which bring together three people in a room that barely fits two," complains a young alum. Luckily, "The Village," a new 220-room residence hall for juniors and seniors, recently opened. Off-campus housing "is easy enough to find if you have the right connections," we are told. And the unsponsored frats maintain their own "'frat houses' (no letters on the houses, but consistently lived in by fraternity members)."

Waltham is known for its great dining—"It has the best restaurants, many which rival the great tastes of Boston," says a recent grad. Students head to Moody Street for Thai, Japanese, and Indian food. For less exotic fare, "Lizzie's is a student favorite for homemade ice cream." Another student's take on Waltham: "Not much to do except eat ice cream, but Boston is about half an hour away." Or, as a senior puts it: "Basically, the town really doesn't want to have much to do with Brandeis, and Brandeis doesn't want to have much to do with the town, and everyone's okay with that." Student safety is not a problem: "Waltham doesn't look very safe, but it is safe, even late at night," a student assures us.

Student Life

Although the school maintains no religious affiliation, the majority of students are Jewish. The typical Brandeis student: "a reformed Jew (not actively religious), upper-middle class, premed wannabe," according to one Asian American student. Another student's take: "neatly-dressed, Jewish, politically liberal, morally conservative, nonathletic, studious, hard-working." (One Connecticut guidance counselor believes Brandeis "could use more diversity.") "There is a mutual understanding among students to practice open-mindedness," we are told. When an anti-Arab flier was circulated in one of the dorms in fall 2002, students and administrators were quick to condemn it.

Brandeis students "are very friendly and helpful, but somewhat guarded at first appearance," says a junior. A young alum agrees, saying students "often wear a social mask when interacting with one another." Cliques are common, and "most people tend to remain within their own social circles." The unsponsored fraternities "are the agreed source of all things social on campus," a student tells us. "You don't need to be Greek to have a social life, but you need to deal with them."

The 175+ campus organizations reflect the range of students' interests; theater, media, activism, student government, and community service are among the most active campus groups. A recent grad specifies: "The most popular school-sponsored group is Hillel, the Jewish religious group. This is followed only by a cappella groups—singing without music, for some reason, has appeal." As a Division III school, Brandeis offers 11 intercollegiate sports for men and 11 for women. Says a senior, "Athletics aren't so popular. Most students have never attended a varsity game." But around 1,500 students participate in intramurals, and more than one-third of Brandeis students participate in club sports.

"Brandeisians aren't a very rowdy bunch, although they do like having fun," says one student. Another student notes, "Weekends tend to be fairly low-key (although almost everyone stays around on campus—people don't go home on the weekend). Friday night, the big thing is Shabbos and a big communal Shabbat dinner (that draws probably about 300 people a week)." Students also enjoy hanging out at Brandeis University's campus coffeehouse, Cholmondeley's (pronounced "Chumley's"), which is rumored to be the inspiration for *Friends'* Central Perk (*Friends* creators Marta Kauffman and David Crane are Brandeis alumni, as are actress Debra Messing, producers Gary David Goldberg and Marshall Herskovitz, and Pulitzer Prize-winning journalist Thomas Friedman).

Other schools to check out: Tufts, Washington University in St. Louis, Columbia, Brown, Emory.

Test Scores (middle 50%):
  SAT Verbal: 620–720
  SAT Math: 630–720
  ACT Comp: 28–33
  ACT English: 28–33
  ACT Math: 26–32

HS Rank of Entering Freshmen:
  Top 10%: 69%
  Top 25%: 95%
  Top 50%: 100%

Avg. HS GPA: 3.82

THE EXPERTS SAY...

" At Brandeis, your values, beliefs, and opinions will constantly be tested and critically examined through open dialogue. "

" Focused, confident, politically active preprofessionals can thrive here. If that doesn't describe you, look elsewhere. "

Costs (2004–5)

Tuition and Fees: $29,875
Room & Board: $8,612

Inst. Aid (est. 2003–04)

Institutional Aid, Need-Based:
  $20,621,203
Institutional Aid, Non-Need-Based:
  $8,795,320
FT Undergrads Receiving Aid: 48%
  Avg. Amount per Student: $22,199
FT Undergrads Receiving Non-Need-Based Scholarship or Grant Aid: 23%
  Avg. Amount per Student: $16,883

Of Those Receiving Any Aid:

Rec. Need-Based Scholarship or Grant Aid: 96%
  Average Award: $16,420
Rec. Need-Based Self-Help Aid: 90%
  Average Award: $7,238
Financial Aid Deadline: rolling, 1/31 (priority)

Graduates

Going to Graduate School:
  29% Within One Year
Accepting Job Offer:
  70% at time of graduation

BRIGHAM YOUNG UNIVERSITY

A-153 ASB, BYU, Provo, UT 84602-0002
Admissions Phone: (801) 422-2507; (801) 422-2500 Fax: (801) 422-0005
Email: admissions@byu.edu Website: www.byu.edu
Application Website: ar.byu.edu/admissions

General Info

Type of School: private, coed, Church of Jesus Christ of Latter–Day Saints

Setting: urban

Academic Calendar: semester

Student Body

Full-Time Undergrads: 26,586
 Men: 50%, Women: 50%

Part-Time Undergrads: 3,346
 Men: 53%, Women: 47%

Total Undergrad Population:
 African American: <1%
 Asian American: 3%
 Latino: 3%
 Native American: 1%
 Caucasian: 87%
 International: 3%
 Out-of-State: 72%
 Living Off-Campus: 80%

Graduate and First-Professional Students: 3,076

Academics

Full-Time Faculty: 1,269
 With Ph.D.: 81%

Part-Time Faculty: 472
 With Ph.D.: 60%

Student/Faculty Ratio: 21:1

Most Popular Majors:
 elementary education (3%)
 psychology (3%)
 English (3%)
 nursing (2%)
 marriage, family, and human development (2%)

Completing 2 or More Majors: 4%

Freshmen Retention Rate: 93%

Graduation Rates:
 27% within four years
 71% within six years

Admissions

Regular Application Deadline: 2/15

Fall Transfer Deadline: 3/15 (priority)

Spring Transfer Deadline: 3/15 (priority)

Total # of Students Applied: 9,300
 Admitted: 7,227
 Enrolled: 5,331

Inside the Classroom

Founded and run by the Church of Jesus Christ of Latter-Day Saints (whose members are commonly known as Mormons), Brigham Young University is firmly rooted in the doctrines of the LDS church. A senior majoring in philosophy tells us, "The well-rounded education students receive here—not only in academics, but also in spiritual matters—is the best there is."

BYU offers 212 academic programs in its schools of management and education, and colleges of biology and agriculture; engineering and technology; family, home, and social sciences; fine arts and communications; health and human performance; humanities; nursing; and physical and mathematical sciences. Most departments are excellent, with business, engineering, and education considered particularly strong. "Any student going into graduate school has a real advantage with a BYU education," states a senior heading to medical school. BYU also provides an unusually diverse language instruction program, with 66 languages offered to students.

Strict general education requirements include courses in English and writing, foreign languages, math, natural sciences, social sciences, arts and letters, physical education, and several religion courses. (Full-time undergraduate students need to take the equivalent of one religion class each semester of enrollment.) Such stiff requirements make the workload somewhat heavy. As one student told us, "Trying to balance the burden and load of required classes and major classes is almost impossible." Additionally, many students leave campus to do the missionary work required by the Church, which makes graduating in four years almost impossible.

Students call the academic environment at BYU "extremely competitive." "Everyone is there to learn," says an accounting major. Although some courses have hundreds of students, most are kept to under 30 students, and professors are said to be "extremely approachable." First-year students have the option of participating in "Freshman Academy," in which freshmen in "learning communities" attend a cluster of three classes with a small group of others living in the same housing area.

Campus Environment

More than 80 percent of freshmen live on campus. With such a large student population, campus housing is a crunch, and many upperclassmen are forced to move off campus, which can be expensive. The campus is "very safe" and is kept absolutely pristine, from the flawless landscaping to the modern buildings. BYU has several excellent facilities. The BYU Regional Family History Library accesses the approximately 100,000 books and more than 800,000 rolls of microfilm contained in the Church's Family History Library in Salt Lake City. There's also the Monte L. Bean Life Science Museum, the Museum of Peoples and Cultures, the Museum of Art, and the Harris Fine Arts Center.

Provo is "the epitome of 'college town,'" says one senior. Another senior tells us, "Provo is small, but it's mostly geared toward BYU students so there are many things to do." If you're looking to get out of town, the Wasatch Mountains overlook BYU on the east, and to the west lies Utah Lake. Salt Lake City is 45 miles away, and within an hour's drive are several canyons and ski resorts.

According to the BYU Housing Office, skateboards and in-line skates are not allowed on campus "because of an increase in accidents and damage to university facilities," although bicycles are still permitted. A student informs us, "You don't need a car to get around, but most people have one."

Student Life

Before enrolling, all BYU students agree to strictly follow the Honor Code "at all times and in all places"—which means both on AND off the school campus, 365 days a year. Among other things, the Honor Code strictly forbids the use of alcohol, drugs (including caffeine), and tobacco; swearing; cohabitation; and extramarital relations. A dress and grooming code is also in place. Violations of the Honor Code can result in the student being suspended or expelled from school (and if you don't think they're serious about this, remember all the trouble *The Real World: New Orleans*'s Julie got into because of her cozy coed living arrangements!). But the Honor Code does create a close-knit community in which students trust and respect one another, which is no mean feat considering there are close to 30,000 full-time undergrads.

Obviously, this type of environment is not for everyone. "The liberal-minded rebel who rejects authority and does not live up to commitments (i.e., the Honor Code) would not fit in very well, since an atmosphere of respect and obedience permeates student life," explains a senior. Since the Church provides funding support for BYU, students who are members of the Church pay about 30 percent less in tuition fees than those who are not members of the faith. But BYU's strong academic reputation and relatively low tuition do attract some non-Mormon students. As one student says, "Everyone comes from different backgrounds, and yet most people have similar values and goals."

"There are a lot of fun activities to keep students busy and out of trouble," says a student. As explained above, alcohol and drugs cannot be found on or off campus. "Very, very few people break that commitment due to integrity, as well as peer pressure to abstain and the academic consequences of being caught," a student tells us. But students do get together for (dry) parties, and they enjoy many of the same activities as students at many other colleges across the country—including watching videos, eating out with friends, playing Ultimate Frisbee, bowling, "disco-skating," etc.

Sports are a very important part of the social life at BYU—"there is no escaping it," says one student. Varsity and intramural teams are very popular, and students take full advantage of BYU's extensive facilities, which include an indoor track, basketball, volleyball, and racquetball courts, and a swimming pool. BYU has several very strong varsity teams that compete in the Western Athletic Conference. Students crowd Cougar Stadium to watch football games—which, after church services, are among the most highly attended events on campus. Additionally, the school's location lends itself to a number of popular outdoor sports, especially hiking and skiing.

Test Scores (middle 50%):
SAT Verbal: 550–660
SAT Math: 560–670
ACT Comp: 24–29
ACT English: 24–30
ACT Math: 24–29
Avg. HS GPA: 3.71

Costs (2003–04)

Tuition and Fees: $3,150

Room & Board: $5,354

Payment Plan(s): deferred payment plan

THE EXPERTS SAY...

" BYU offers Mormon students a fantastic opportunity to receive a superb education in an environment singularly supportive of their lifestyle and beliefs. "

" Chances are, unless you're a Mormon, this isn't the place for you. "

Inst. Aid (2002–03)

Institutional Aid, Need-Based: $1,505,000

Institutional Aid, Non-Need-Based: $17,658,000

FT Undergrads Receiving Aid: 34%
Avg. Amount per Student: $4,157

FT Undergrads Receiving Non-Need-Based Scholarship or Grant Aid: 27%
Avg. Amount per Student: $2,862

Of Those Receiving Any Aid:

Rec. Need-Based Scholarship or Grant Aid: 80%
Average Award: $2,446

Rec. Need-Based Self-Help Aid: 41%
Average Award: $1,711

Upon Graduation, Avg. Loan Debt per Student: $11,301

Financial Aid Deadline: rolling, 4/15 (priority)

Graduates

Companies Recruiting On-Campus: 320

Alumni Giving: 28%

BROWN UNIVERSITY

Box 1876, Providence, RI 02912
Admissions Phone: (401) 863-2378 Fax: (401) 863-9300
Email: admission_undergraduate@brown.edu
Website: www.brown.edu

General Info

Type of School: private, coed

Setting: urban

Academic Calendar: semester

Student Body

Full-Time Undergrads: 5,705
 Men: 46%, Women: 54%

Part-Time Undergrads: 101
 Men: 39%, Women: 61%

Total Undergrad Population:
 African American: 6%
 Asian American: 14%
 Latino: 6%
 Native American: 1%
 Caucasian: 50%
 International: 6%
 Out-of-State: 95%
 Living Off-Campus: 20%
 In Fraternities: 5%
 In Sororities: 0%

Graduate and First-Professional
 Students: 1,862

Academics

Full-Time Faculty: 738
 With Ph.D.: 94%

Part-Time Faculty: 124
 With Ph.D.: 69%

Student/Faculty Ratio: 9:1

Most Popular Majors:
 biological and biomedical
  sciences (8%)
 international relations and
  affairs (6%)
 history (6%)
 business economics (5%)
 economics (5%)

Freshmen Retention Rate: 97%

Graduation Rates:
 88% within four years
 95% within six years

Admissions

Regular Application Deadline: 1/1

Early Decision Deadline(s): 11/1

Fall Transfer Deadline: 7/5

Total # of Students Applied: 14,612
 Admitted: 2,464
 Enrolled: 1,458

Inside the Classroom

Brown's curriculum is the most nontraditional and flexible in the Ivy League. There is no core curriculum or any universal requirements; all required courses at Brown are within your academic major, or 'concentration.' Students are allowed to take any class 'pass/fail' and are given the opportunity to be the "architects of their educational experience." Students create their own experience based on self-imposed limits, and they "set extremely high standards for themselves." A senior tells us that "anyone who needs *structure*" may have a hard time at Brown. "Unless you're an engineer or getting a B.S., then most of your classes are your own choice. If you can't take responsibility to give yourself a broad education, then don't apply." A recent grad agrees: "Those who are excessively grade-oriented and competitive may feel outnumbered by people who take a more balanced view of education."

Students can freely pick and choose courses that interest them from Brown's extensive course offerings. "This allows people to take classes they otherwise wouldn't take (because they had to get requirements out of the way or because they were afraid of dropping their GPA)," says one student. Another student tells us that Brown has "the only History of Math department in the country," and that there is even "a course on Circumcision in the Judaic Studies department."

Students need to pass only 30 courses to graduate. As mentioned, Brown has an atypical grading policy with 2 options: A, B, C, No Credit or Satisfactory/No Credit. (Be warned, though, that the higher-ups do notice too many 'no credits.') In return for all the freedom afforded them, students are expected to do their work and come to class well prepared. According to a senior, "You only get out of a class what you put into it. Most people work hard because they're in a class to learn, not just to get a grade." Professors are very accessible, and a high school guidance counselor says of Brown: "They have an excellent school president, and their alumni has a strong network."

Campus Environment

Providence is something of a college town, with Brown, Providence College, RISD, and URI all in the immediate area; Boston is 45 minutes away and makes a popular road trip destination. Downtown Providence is a 10-minute walk, and students head there for movies, theater, and restaurants. "Providence gets lots of good concerts, has lots of nice restaurants, a huge mall, and has other good entertainment options (once you learn where to look)." Another student says, "Students from big cities tend to dislike Providence, while students from small towns love it." Brown may seem to dominate Providence to some extent: "Relations can get testy when Brown wants a new building, but in general the east side is campus and everyone knows it."

Students are required to live on campus for their first three years with guaranteed housing. Students seem to consider the dorms comfortable, if not perfect. "As far as the Ivies go, we're not that good. As far as other places go, we're really good." Another student agrees, saying, "Some dorms are much better than others. People complain of the concrete and dark quality of the towers of the graduate center, while others rejoice at the large size of their single bedroom in Sears." Freshmen are assigned to double rooms, and sophomores and juniors enter a lottery—which is not popular. "The housing lottery stinks!" one junior tells us. "It's confusing and people (especially sophomores) rarely get what they want." Students are allowed to live off-campus only senior year, "due to housing shortages in the neighborhood. The cost is pretty much equivalent thanks to a gentrified neighborhood, but it's still popular." A recent grad tells us that "rent runs from $400–$650 per month for old New England houses with hard wood floors, creaky staircases and bath tubs with feet."

Student Life

Brown students come from a variety of backgrounds and tend to be liberal and socially conscious; gay rights, feminism, multiculturalism, fair labor and the environment are among the many hot topics on campus. A student says, "Although I hesitate to say it, extremely politically conservative students might have trouble finding others like them at Brown." Another student goes further, saying that "a conservative, straight, male, Christian athlete frat brother from the Midwest/South who wants to make lots of money in a consulting firm when he graduates" simply would not fit in. Other students, however, feel that there is "lots of political correctness and squelching of certain ideas" and that "the student body, because it is so wealthy on average, can have a hard time understanding what low-income living entails. This makes students appear self-righteous and hypocritical at times."

Students spend a lot of time studying and are generally active in community service, though some of the "bazillion" school-sponsored clubs can "absorb your life." The most popular ones include Habitat for Humanity and College Democrats; "Young Republicans are probably the least popular."

Though there is a large "straight edge population," Brown is a wet campus; a student states that "people drink a fair amount, although the administration tries to cut it out. Brown's policy was that if you're here you're an adult… but they seem to be changing that. I think that should be reinstated." Greek life is not too popular: "People like to make fun of the Greek system, but they enjoy the frat parties, so the relationship is kind of up and down." Athletes tend to join fraternities, while the two sororities have a hard time attracting members ("I think Brown just doesn't attract the typical sorority girl.") Freshmen often use frat parties to make friends; after this has been accomplished, "the hot and sweaty appeal wears off."

Sports are not overwhelmingly popular, either. One student tells us that school spirit is "restricted to a select few," and another says, "I did not attend a single sporting event at Brown and imagine several other students have had the same experience."

Other schools to check out: Barnard, Yale, Swarthmore, Oberlin, Middlebury.

# of Students Waitlisted: 1,450
  Students Accepting Place: 450

Applied Early Decision: 1,918
  Early Decision Admitted: 526

Test Scores (middle 50%):
  SAT Verbal: 640–750
  SAT Math: 650–750
  ACT Comp: 26–32

HS Rank of Entering Freshmen:
  Top 10%: 87%
  Top 25%: 97%
  Top 50%: 100%

THE EXPERTS SAY...

" At Brown, students get to map out their own curriculum and experiment with new fields, without the pressure of grades and requirements. "

" Brown students get an awesome combo: the quirkiness of a liberal arts college with the cachet of an Ivy League degree. "

Costs (2003–04)

Tuition and Fees: $29,846
Room & Board: $8,096
Payment Plan(s): installment plan

BRYN MAWR COLLEGE

101 N. Merion Avenue, Bryn Mawr, PA 19010-2859
Admissions Phone: (610) 526-5152; (800) 262-1885 Fax: (610) 526-7471
Email: admissions@brynmawr.edu
Website: www.brynmawr.edu

General Info

Type of School: private, all women

Setting: suburban

Academic Calendar: semester

Student Body

Full-Time Undergrads: 1,282
  Men: 2%, Women: 98%

Part-Time Undergrads: 28
  Women: 100%

Total Undergrad Population:
  African American: 4%
  Asian American: 12%
  Latino: 3%
  Caucasian: 50%
  International: 8%
  Out-of-State: 80%
  Living Off-Campus: 5%

Graduate and First-Professional
  Students: 447

Academics

Full-Time Faculty: 146
  With Ph.D.: 97%

Part-Time Faculty: 52
  With Ph.D.: 71%

Student/Faculty Ratio: 8:1

Most Popular Majors:
  English (11%)
  political science (10%)
  biology (10%)
  mathematics (8%)
  anthropology/economics (6%)

Completing 2 or More Majors: 13%

Freshmen Retention Rate: 95%

Graduation Rates:
  78% within four years
  85% within six years

Admissions

Regular Application Deadline: 1/15

Early Decision Deadline(s): 11/15,
  1/1

Fall Transfer Deadline: 3/15

Total # of Students Applied: 1,748
  Admitted: 899
  Enrolled: 352

# of Students Waitlisted: 207
  Students Accepting Place: 176
  Waitlisted Students Admitted: 1

Applied Early Decision: 146
  Early Decision Admitted: 78

Inside the Classroom

Ask any Bryn Mawr undergrad about the workload, and she won't kid you: it's not for the faint at heart. "The atmosphere is pretty work-intense," a chemistry major tells us. "We work all the time." However, most find it ultimately rewarding. "You can go as far as your intellect will take you," a student says. Although Bryn Mawr is one of the few all-women's liberal arts colleges to offer extensive graduate programs, the focus remains on undergrads. Students find the faculty dedicated and "incredibly accessible"; professors have been known to hand out their home phone numbers. Classes are purposely kept small, inviting a high level of one-on-one interaction.

Bryn Mawr boasts many impressive academic statistics, including ranking first in the nation for the percentage of its graduates earning Ph.D.s in humanities and third in all fields. The academic programs are very rigorous and outstanding across the board, from the liberal arts standbys to more unusual programs such as "growth and structure of cities." The science programs are excellent; over one-third of the women here major in math or science. In fact, the number of women majoring in physics at Bryn Mawr is second only to the number at MIT. There are several fine interdisciplinary concentrations available, including environmental studies and feminist and gender studies.

Though its enrollment is entirely female, Bryn Mawr participates in the "Quaker Consortium" with three nearby coed institutions: Haverford College, Swarthmore College, and the University of Pennsylvania. The relationship with Haverford is especially close; many programs are offered jointly by the two schools, and undergrads at either college may take courses or pursue majors at the other. This "bi-college community" has expanded to a "tri-college community" including Swarthmore, so as a Bryn Mawr student, you are free to take undergrad courses there as well. Penn's agreement with Bryn Mawr includes reciprocal tuition and allows student access to its impressive resources.

The core curriculum includes courses in social sciences, humanities, lab sciences, and quantitative work; students must also fulfill English composition, foreign language, and physical education requirements, and pass a swim test. First-year students take an intense interdisciplinary writing seminar in which they meet regularly with their professors. Studying abroad is another popular option, with 30 percent of the junior class choosing to spend a semester or a year in one of 50-plus study abroad programs in 26 countries around the world.

Campus Environment

The 135-acre campus is filled with trees and dotted with "Collegiate Gothic"–style buildings. Don't be surprised to see men roaming around the dorms, thanks to the school's relationship with Haverford, which includes limited housing exchange. (A few Mawrtyrs are permitted to live on the Ford campus as well.) Nearly all undergrads (98 percent) live on campus, and all residence halls mix the classes together. All 14 residence halls, which ranging from renovated older buildings with fireplaces and hardwood floors to more modern structures, receive raves for comfort, style, and uniqueness. Many juniors and seniors have single rooms, and "you are

KAPLAN

pretty much guaranteed a single by sophomore year if you want one." There are four dining rooms, plus those at Haverford and Swarthmore, and the food is first-rate, particularly the vegetarian specialties.

Although the town of Bryn Mawr is just a five-minute walk from campus, students say it "is not too college-oriented … it is a very rich town with rich stores." Students looking for city action take the train seven stops to Philadelphia to enjoy its rich and diverse cultural offerings, but we hear the "fares are sort of expensive and the train stops at midnight."

Freshmen are not permitted to bring cars; there is a small registration fee for the upperclassmen who choose to park on campus. Not many students have cars, however, as there is a train station steps away for trips into Philadelphia and beyond, and the school runs the "Blue Bus," which travels between Bryn Mawr and Haverford as often as twice an hour.

Student Life

In spite of its small, single-sex population, Bryn Mawr has a fairly diverse student body, featuring a sizable percentage of both Asian Americans and international students. One student's description: "The typical student at BMC is a hard worker and overachiever. Ethnicity, religion, political views, and interests are all very diverse, but we all work hard and put too many eggs in one basket." They are proud of their honor code that allows them to schedule their own examinations and monitor themselves. The honor code, in addition to the all-female environment, fosters a tight-knit yet independent community. "Students respect one another socially and academically," we hear. The students work hard but there's no cutthroat competition; each individual establishes her own level of excellence.

As most Mawrtyrs are singularly focused on their academic pursuits, their social life tends to suffer. "Don't come here looking for parties," warns a junior. "The social scene is pretty bland." Weeknights are spent studying, and those in search of lighter times—and drinking—generally head for Haverford, Swarthmore, or Penn on the weekends.

On campus, there are a number of literary, performing arts, political, ethnic, religious, and preprofessional clubs that students throw themselves into; Haverford clubs are available as well. Among the more vocal and prominent organizations are lesbian and feminist groups, which some say contribute to the stereotype of the "typical" Bryn Mawr student. Athletics are also popular, with 11 varsity teams (including a badminton team that's "a force to be reckoned with," says one student) and six intramural sports available.

Bryn Mawr takes great pride in its traditions, and these events are the highlights of the social calendar. Major events include "Lantern Night," an elaborate initiation for first-year students at which "the lamp of knowledge" is passed along to them, and "May Day," a festival featuring "hoop races" and a feminist parody of the maypole dance, first held at Bryn Mawr in 1900. During finals week, students litter the ground beneath the statue of Pallas Athena, the goddess of wisdom, with "sacrificial gifts" in hopes of good luck.

Other schools to check out: Haverford, Smith, Wellesley, Swarthmore, Mount Holyoke, Vassar.

Test Scores (middle 50%):
SAT Verbal: 620–720
SAT Math: 580–680

HS Rank of Entering Freshmen:
Top 10%: 56%
Top 25%: 92%
Top 50%: 100%

Costs (est. 2004–05)

Tuition and Fees: $28,610

Room & Board: $9,700

Payment Plan(s): installment plan

THE EXPERTS SAY...

" Bryn Mawr has a supportive community of extremely intelligent women, without the isolation that turns some people away from single-sex colleges. "

" You've got scholars and activists, lesbians and Haverford men. Something for everyone! "

Inst. Aid (est. 2003–04)

Institutional Aid, Need-Based: $13,003,391

FT Undergrads Receiving Aid: 62%
Avg. Amount per Student: $25,139

Of Those Receiving Any Aid:

Rec. Need-Based Scholarship or Grant Aid: 94%
Average Award: $21,583

Rec. Need-Based Self-Help Aid: 79%
Average Award: $6,172

Upon Graduation, Avg. Loan Debt per Student: $17,827

Financial Aid Deadline: 2/2

Graduates

Going to Graduate School:
20% Within One Year

Companies Recruiting On Campus: 175

BUCKNELL UNIVERSITY

Freas Hall, Lewisburg, PA 17837
Admissions Phone: (570) 577-1101 Fax: (570) 577-3538
Email: admissions@bucknell.edu Website: www.bucknell.edu/
Application Website: www.applyweb.com/aw?buckn

General Info

Type of School: private, coed
Setting: small town
Academic Calendar: semester

Student Body

Full-Time Undergrads: 3,445
 Men: 50%, Women: 50%

Part-Time Undergrads: 12
 Men: 58%, Women: 42%

Total Undergrad Population:
 African American: 3%
 Asian American: 6%
 Latino: 2%
 Native American: <1%
 Caucasian: 85%
 International: 2%
 Out-of-State: 68%
 Living Off-Campus: 11%
 In Fraternities: 38%
 In Sororities: 38%

Graduate and First-Professional
 Students: 192

Academics

Full-Time Faculty: 291
 With Ph.D.: 96%

Part-Time Faculty: 19
 With Ph.D.: 53%

Student/Faculty Ratio: 12:1

Most Popular Majors:
 management (11%)
 biology (7%)
 economics (6%)
 mechanical engineering (4%)
 accounting (4%)

Completing 2 or More Majors: 19%

Freshmen Retention Rate: 95%

Graduation Rates:
 83% within four years
 89% within six years

Admissions

Regular Application Deadline: 1/1

Early Decision Deadline(s): 11/15,
 1/1

Fall Transfer Deadline: 4/1

Spring Transfer Deadline: 11/1

Total # of Students Applied: 7,706
 Admitted: 2,961
 Enrolled: 906

Inside the Classroom

Approximately 80 percent of students are enrolled in Bucknell's College of Arts and Science; the rest are part of the College of Engineering. Students can choose from 52 majors and 72 minors, ranging from Latin American studies to cell biology. A good number of Bucknellians (around 20 percent) go on to grad school or professional school within a year of graduation, so courses that pave the way for law, business, and medical school are particularly popular.

The requirements in both colleges are rigorous. In the College of Arts and Sciences, students must take courses in humanities, social sciences, and natural science and math, and all freshmen take a "foundation seminar." Seniors must complete a Capstone project, which can be a thesis, internship, or independent project, in order to graduate. In the College of Engineering, all first-year students take the same course load, helping to develop a sense of camaraderie. Bucknell has been called a "Baby Ivy," and the general academic atmosphere bears this out. Students describe their workload as heavy, but manageable. It depends pretty strongly on your major—science and engineering undergrads may find themselves working longer and harder than English or humanities majors. Bucknell's big on studying abroad, too: Nearly 40 percent of each graduating class takes advantage of the opportunity to live and study in places such as France, London, and Barbados.

Class sizes are kept to a minimum, although popular introductory courses might be somewhat larger. There are only nine classes for which over 100 students are allowed to sign up—other than that, groups are small. (Official school literature plugs its student/faculty ratio of 12:1.) Small classes reinforce the close-knit environment of the school. "In class, you frequently come across the same people," remarks one student. Professors get high marks, too, for being "extremely accessible" and "passionate about what they teach." The school boasts that all classes are taught by professors, never TAs, and students claim that "the majority of the faculty establish good working relationships" with them.

Campus Environment

The 400-acre campus is often ranked as one of the country's most beautiful, so living in the dorms, as all freshmen must, isn't such a bad thing. And the school offers a nice variety of living arrangements. Besides traditional residence halls (which don't include a single-sex men's dorm), freshmen may choose to live in one of six residential colleges organized around common academic interests: arts, environmental, humanities, international, social justice, and technology and society. For upperclassmen, living off campus almost seems more trouble than it's worth: students must fill out an application and attend an information session before a committee approves their move.

Cars for freshmen are out of the question, but upperclassmen recommend having one if you want to go to the mall, the grocery store, or home for the weekend. As is often the case with schools in small towns, you'll feel safe here. Aside from the rowdy frat party or two, it's a pretty quiet place to be. "The overall atmosphere is pretty appealing," a student says.

Student Life

Students affectionately refer to the school's secluded atmosphere as the "Bucknell Bubble," where about 3,400 undergraduates work and play. The joke is that you can spend four years without a clue as to what's going on in the "real" world. Located in Lewisburg—touted as one of the best small towns in America—Bucknell is three and one-half hours from a city of any size ("in the middle of nowhere," students moan), so there's little room for outside distraction. While some people might go stir-crazy in such conditions, most who live under the Bubble seem to like it just fine. "This place really is a country club, or a retreat center," says one student. "It is a great place to get focus."

The small, isolated feel of the school also creates a family-like environment: "Because there is nothing around, everyone stays on campus—it's not like half the students are leaving and half are staying," a student says. Diversity, however, is not among Bucknell's many strengths. The stereotypical Bucknell student has been described as "conservative" and "preppy," and students we talked to were hard put to argue with that. "Pretty white, pretty well off," agrees one student; another admits, "you'd like to meet some different kinds of people." But some defend the makeup of the friendly student body, as this junior attests: "Our school is not very diverse, but it is not hard to find people like you."

Alcohol plays a huge role in students' extracurricular lives. Apparently, "there's not a lot to do otherwise." If you're not 21, forget about hitting the Lewisburg bars. For the rest of campus, fraternities and sororities dominate the social scene, providing "a constant source of entertainment." After the first year, students can go Greek if they wish; roughly half the eligible students do. The fraternity houses host many all-campus parties, "which adds to the drinking atmosphere." So on any given weekend and many weeknights—particularly Wednesdays, since most classes start later on Thursdays—there's bound to be some kind of party going on somewhere. Students also hang out in their dorms, at the Bison student center, or at the on-campus café. Sporting events always draw big crowds, and about one-fifth of the student body plays on one of 28 varsity sports teams (14 men's and 14 women's teams).

Students who want to make the trek to an actual city do have the opportunity: "The university provides free shuttle buses to different cities; that gets good attendance," a student informs us. But many are content to stay right where they are. "The 'Bucknell Bubble' lives on," said one undergrad when asked about her school. "That can sound like a negative thing, but it's actually really good. We love it."

Other schools to check out: Colgate, Lehigh, Lafayette, Villanova, Dartmouth.

# of Students Waitlisted: 1,768
Students Accepting Place: 688
Waitlisted Students Admitted: 46

Applied Early Decision: 643
Early Decision Admitted: 323

Test Scores (middle 50%):
SAT Verbal: 600–670
SAT Math: 630–700

HS Rank of Entering Freshmen:
Top 10%: 69%
Top 25%: 93%
Top 50%: 99%

THE EXPERTS SAY...

" Bucknell students are hardworking preprofessionals who also know how to relax. "

" If you want to escape the real world, the 'Bucknell Bubble' is your place. If you don't like preppies, booze, or frats, stay clear. "

Costs (2004–5)

Tuition and Fees: $30,730

Room & Board: $6,578

Payment Plan(s): installment plan

Inst. Aid (est. 2003–04)

Institutional Aid, Need-Based: $40,581,400

Institutional Aid, Non-Need-Based: $61,000

FT Undergrads Receiving Aid: 51%
Avg. Amount per Student: $19,000

Of Those Receiving Any Aid:

Rec. Need-Based Scholarship or Grant Aid: 89%
Average Award: $16,500

Rec. Need-Based Self-Help Aid: 100%
Average Award: $1,600

Upon Graduation, Avg. Loan Debt per Student: $16,695

Financial Aid Deadline: 1/1

Graduates

Going to Graduate School: 22% Within One Year

Accepting Job Offer: 68% at time of graduation

Companies Recruiting On Campus: 290

Alumni Giving: 58%

CALIFORNIA INSTITUTE OF TECHNOLOGY

Mail Code: 1-94, Pasadena, CA 91125   Admissions Phone: (626) 395-6341
Fax: (626) 683-3026   Email: ugadmissions@caltech.edu   Website: www.caltech.edu
Application Website: admissions.caltech.edu/

General Info

Type of School: private, coed

Setting: suburban

Academic Calendar: quarter

Student Body

Full-Time Undergrads: 891
Men: 67%, Women: 33%

Total Undergrad Population:
African American: 1%
Asian American: 31%
Latino: 7%
Native American: 1%
Caucasian: 51%
International: 8%
Out-of-State: 60%
Living Off-Campus: 10%

Graduate and First-Professional
Students: 1,281

Academics

Full-Time Faculty: 285
With Ph.D.: 98%

Part-Time Faculty: 33
With Ph.D.: 70%

Student/Faculty Ratio: 3:1

Most Popular Majors:
engineering (50%)
physical sciences (26%)
mathematics (11%)
biological/life sciences (10%)
social sciences & liberal arts (3%)

Completing 2 or More Majors: 10%

Freshmen Retention Rate: 95%

Graduation Rates:
79% within four years
89% within six years

Admissions

Regular Application Deadline: 1/1

Early Action Deadline: 11/1

Fall Transfer Deadline: 3/1

Total # of Students Applied: 3,071
Admitted: 520
Enrolled: 191

# of Students Waitlisted: 386
Students Accepting Place: 315
Waitlisted Students Admitted: 45

Test Scores (middle 50%):
SAT Verbal: 700–780
SAT Math: 760–800

Inside the Classroom

Do you have what it takes to become a "Techer"? "It's very, very challenging," one student says, then quickly adds, "but I wouldn't want to be anywhere else." Getting accepted at Cal Tech isn't easy; more than one-third of the undergrads here were high school valedictorians. Once in, students become immersed in a demanding program that combines intense academic study with heavy-duty research. The focus, of course, is on science, math, and engineering. It's not unheard of for students to publish academic papers before graduation. When they do graduate, Cal Tech students go on to prestigious graduate programs or receive top positions in their chosen fields. Not surprisingly, the school has graduated 15 Nobel Prize–winning scientists. A recent endowment of $600 million, the largest academic donation in history, is helping the school to expand new opportunities of research, such as the next generation of space telescopes.

With an undergraduate enrollment of only around 900 and grad enrollment at 1,100, Cal Tech offers a much more intimate environment than most other science and technical schools, without sacrificing top-notch research assets. With a shocking 3:1 student-to-professor ratio, there are more research opportunities than there are students to take advantage of them. Arguably the most popular of these opportunities is SURF, a summer program that allows undergrads to work closely with a mentor on an individual research project. Everyone agrees that the academics are brutally intense, but the experience you gain is incomparable.

The majority of students' credits are devoted to their majors. The core curriculum can take up to two years to complete, so there's not much room for elective study. Students take required courses in math, physics, chemistry, biology, several labs, humanities, social sciences, and even phys ed—resulting in an unusually well- rounded education.

Cal Tech is on a quarter system, and each session is crammed. The schedule alone increases the academic pressure as exams and deadlines come up frequently. The level and amount of work for each class also create a high-pressure environment. Each class can take 15 to 20 hours of work a week. However, freshmen are graded on a pass/fail basis, providing a transition to the tough coursework, and students rely on each other for support. Additionally, collaborative work is often encouraged so students don't have to feel isolated.

The environment around campus is an interesting if not academic one, and even downtime can take on an intellectual bent. For one, Cal Tech manages NASA's Jet Propulsion Lab, the leading U.S. center for robotic planetary exploration. And while most students are well rounded, the "nerd" factor applies here: Weekend talks commonly center around "who discovered what" rather than "what beach you went to or what movie you saw." After all, this is the place where the principles of jet flight, left and right brain functions, and Richter scale measurements were discovered. People are genuinely excited about science, and perhaps aren't as gregarious as you'd find on other college campuses. One of the most eagerly awaited events is the Engineering Design Competition, where undergrad mechanical engineering students compete in a design contest with robotic rovers they have designed and built. The machines, which must perform an assigned task, are judged on design and effectiveness.

Campus Environment

Each fall, incoming freshmen are gently introduced to the rigors of Cal Tech through "Frosh Camp"—the entire freshman class goes to the San Jacinto Mountains for a fun-filled, three-day orientation to student life. Then comes Rotation Week, when students select a residential "House" in which to live for freshman year. The Houses aren't really dorms or frats, though they do tend to serve as the focal point of a student's social life. A closer description might be "self-governing living group" that brings together 65–100 undgrads from all four classes (though one House also has grad students and faculty members). Students can change Houses at any time, or can remain in one House until they graduate.

Given the huge endowment of the school, campus facilities are always being renovated. NASA's newest window on the universe, the Center for the Space InfraRed Telescope Facility, was recently built, as was a new aeronautics lecture hall. Along with MIT, Cal Tech has launched the "Voting Technology Project," to develop new technology to prevent a recurrence of the problems that threatened the 2000 presidential elections. As for getting around campus, most students walk, bike, or use the campus van, though all students may bring a car.

Student Life

At Cal Tech, the men far outnumber the women, which, depending on your point of view, may help or hurt your social chances. However, one student tells us, "It can be tough finding dates around campus, but then there are other scenes. After all, this is Southern California!" The campus, with its Spanish architecture and courtyards coupled with the temperate California weather, keeps students from feeling like they're in a pressure cooker. Most significantly, Cal Tech's strict honor code—to which everyone enthusiastically adheres—reduces competition among students and fosters a sense of camaraderie.

Cal Tech students are far from being workaholic drones. Their notorious pranks, such as "Ditch Day" (when seniors ditch their classes for the day and leave complex, imaginative puzzles, called "stacks" for underclassmen to solve), indicate their sense of fun as well as their creativity. Other social outlets include informal parties, hanging out on campus or in rooms, and going to movies. Intramural sports and athletics are also very popular, and anyone who wants to play usually can. The accessibility to Los Angeles provides an abundance of social and cultural alternatives to the study grind. As for sports, Cal Tech is an NCAA Division III school, and the attitude isn't terribly competitive. About 30 percent of students participate in 18 intercollegiate sports, and there are 9 intramural sports.

Other schools to check out: MIT, Stanford, Harvey Mudd, Harvard, Princeton.

HS Rank of Entering Freshmen:
Top 10%: 94%
Top 25%: 100%

Costs (2004–5)

Tuition and Fees: $25,551

Room & Board: $8,013

Payment Plan(s): installment plan, deferred payment plan, pre-payment plan

THE EXPERTS SAY...

" With a 3:1 student-faculty ratio, Cal Tech offers more research opportunities than there are undergrads. The faculty and alumni have won more than two dozen Nobel Prizes. "

" You could go to MIT, but with Cal Tech's unbelievable 3:1 student/faculty ratio, why would you want to? "

Inst. Aid (est. 2003–04)

Institutional Aid, Need-Based: $12,332,001

Institutional Aid, Non-Need-Based: $3,016,590

FT Undergrads Receiving Aid: 58% Avg. Amount per Student: $26,285

FT Undergrads Receiving Non-Need-Based Scholarship or Grant Aid: 22% Avg. Amount per Student: $15,630

Of Those Receiving Any Aid:

Rec. Need-Based Scholarship or Grant Aid: 100% Average Award: $23,853

Rec. Need-Based Self-Help Aid: 76% Average Award: $2,873

Upon Graduation, Avg. Loan Debt per Student: $7,906

Financial Aid Deadline: 1/15 (priority)

Graduates

Going to Graduate School: 60% Within One Year

Accepting Job Offer: 17% at time of graduation

Companies Recruiting On Campus: 103

Alumni Giving: 39%

CALIFORNIA POLYTECHNIC STATE UNIVERSITY

1 Grand Avenue, San Luis Obispo, CA 93407
Admissions Phone: (805) 756-2311 Fax: (805) 756-5400
Email: admissions@calpoly.edu Website: www.calpoly.edu

General Info

Type of School: public, coed
Setting: small town
Academic Calendar: quarter

Student Body

Full-Time Undergrads: 16,425
 Men: 56%, Women: 44%

Part-Time Undergrads: 832
 Men: 56%, Women: 44%

Total Undergrad Population:
 African American: 1%
 Asian American: 11%
 Latino: 10%
 Native American: 1%
 Caucasian: 63%
 International: 1%
 Out-of-State: 6%
 Living Off-Campus: 79%
 In Fraternities: 10%
 In Sororities: 8%

Graduate and First-Professional
 Students: 1,046

Academics

Full-Time Faculty: 730
 With Ph.D.: 72%

Part-Time Faculty: 497
 With Ph.D.: 21%

Student/Faculty Ratio: 19:1

Most Popular Majors:
 business (11%)
 mechanical engineering (6%)
 agriculture business (5%)
 civil & environmental engineering
 (4%)
 electrical engineering (4%)

Freshmen Retention Rate: 89%

Graduation Rates:
 81% within six years

Admissions

Regular Application Deadline:
 11/30; 11/1 (priority)

Early Decision Deadline(s): 10/31

Fall Transfer Deadline: 11/30

Spring Transfer Deadline: 8/31

Total # of Students Applied: 20,827
 Admitted: 7,989
 Enrolled: 2,828

Applied Early Decision: 2,717
 Early Decision Admitted: 513

Inside the Classroom

Cal Poly takes a practical, career-oriented approach to education. You'll find no dreamy undecided majors here. Students must select a major at the time of application, and as soon they arrive, they jump right into required classes (called an "upside-down curriculum"). Recommended by guidance counselors as having a "great hands-on technical curriculum," you won't see much theory at Cal Poly. Instead, you'll get the nuts and bolts of your discipline.

Originally established as a vocational high school, Cal Poly has evolved into a major university. Offering bachelor's and master's degrees, it still focuses on occupational and professional fields (agriculture, architecture and environmental design, business, engineering, science and math, and teacher education), though today it incorporates liberal arts as well. Its architecture program is particularly well known, as are agriculture and engineering. Cal Poly's five-year architecture program educates an estimated one out of every five architects in California. Explains one senior, "Though this isn't the place to get a 'great college experience,' it is simply the best when it comes to engineering. Industry knows it, and companies actively recruit here."

With over 16,000 full-time students, the classes at Cal Poly tend to be large, particularly the general education classes, averaging about 40 students. Students say that it's not uncommon to experience "difficulty to enroll in courses you need because of low availability." We're also told that changing majors "is a pain!" Graduating from Cal Poly in five years is typical for most, and with such a large student body, this has had a significant impact on the school. In 2001, the administration reduced the number of required units for bachelor's degrees in several majors, hoping to increase what it calls "through put" at the university.

With a guiding philosophy of "Learn by Doing," Cal Poly students rank high in community service. In 2002, the *Washington Monthly* cited almost 30 percent of Cal Poly students with federal work-study jobs working in education or social service departments. Many students tutor in the nearby school district. Others work in after-school programs through the city's Housing Authority. Labs and internships are what students rave about here, as well as the highly personalized teacher-student relationship.

"The primary mission of the Cal State Universities is undergraduate education," says an ecology/systematic biology student. "Consequently, the professors are less tied up in their own research or in working solely with graduate students." He continues, "The professors expect high quality performance from their students. They give difficult and challenging exams and assignments, especially in the sciences."

Campus Environment

As one student tells us, "Cal Poly is a beach school: Enough said. Outside of class the atmosphere is very relaxed. The sun is always shining and people are always playing Frisbee, going to the beach, and having fun." Located on the coast in tiny San Luis Obispo, halfway between Los Angeles and San Francisco, the 1,321-acre main campus lies at the northeast edge of town. The Pacific Ocean is about 10 miles in one direction, the Los Padres National Forest in another, and wine country in yet another.

KAPLAN

"Housing is a huge issue on campus. There is none," says one student. No one—and that includes freshmen—is guaranteed on-campus housing. Believe it or not, there's only enough space to house 2,700 of the school's over 16,000 students on campus. That means many freshmen lose out on the experience of dorm living. The on-campus housing situation is so tight that some undergrads must live in converted dorm lounges, laundry rooms, and nearby hotels until new residence halls are completed. The campus is safe, and one California guidance counselor notes that "parents love Cal Poly!" On-campus parking is very limited, but most students have their own car, anyway, but since they live off-campus. If not, "the town is small and the bus system is great for getting to class," notes a student.

Student Life

The student body at Cal Poly is almost entirely from in-state. One student tells us, "It's not very diverse, and there's the biggest Christian group I have ever seen here. Someone very alternative would probably not fit in here." A young alum's opinion: "Cal Poly's typical student is white and upper-middle class. There are also a notable amount of students from rural/agricultural areas who have a distinct style." The school has struggled with diversity issues since affirmative action was eliminated in 1995, and perhaps because of its location away from the main urban centers, has been at a disadvantage when trying to attract minority students. We hear that many minority students feel like they don't fit in. In a push to increase these numbers, Cal Poly has formed partnerships with many high schools to help them strengthen student skills for college. The "Building an Engineer" program brings adolescent girls to campus to teach them about engineering (currently, the engineering school is about 84 percent male).

"'Stuff to do' is always an issue here," one senior explains. "The nightlife in the city is almost nonexistent. People who love having a busy, exciting nightlife might not fit in." An alum agrees: "Sunday through Wednesday nights are mellow (though Thursday, Friday, and Saturday night, you can usually find a party going on somewhere)." The school has 11 sororities and 23 fraternities (including specialized ones for African Americans, Asians, and Latinos), and while some say they contribute by far the most in terms of nightlife, others disagree. "The largest parties are usually hosted by Greeks, but the most enjoyable parties usually are not," notes an astute young alum.

With so little to do at night, students focus more on the 350 extracurricular clubs, many of which are related to specific majors, such as the agribusiness club. As a Division I school, Cal Poly has a vast array of varsity sports and intramural sports—it even has an intercollegiate rodeo team. There's a prize-winning student newspaper, and radio and television stations. In 2001, students approved a fee increase, on the condition that the additional monies would go solely to students, so now there's more room for extracurricular events.

Other schools to check out: CSU Chico, UC Irvine, UC Davis, University of the Pacific, Virginia Tech.

Test Scores (middle 50%):
SAT Verbal: 520–620
SAT Math: 570–660
ACT Comp: 23–27
ACT English: 22–28
ACT Math: 24–29

HS Rank of Entering Freshmen:
Top 10%: 42%
Top 25%: 78%
Top 50%: 96%

Avg. HS GPA: 3.71

THE EXPERTS SAY...

" The upside-down curriculum is perfect for students who know what they want coming into Cal Poly. "

" It's a beautiful setting, but it's kind of isolated in the no-man's-land between LA and San Francisco. "

Costs (2003–04)

Fees: $3,459

Room & Board: $7,479
note: Non-residents pay an additional per-unit tuition

Payment Plan(s): installment plan, deferred payment plan, pre-payment plan

Inst. Aid (est. 2003–04)

Institutional Aid, Need-Based: $3,963,620

FT Undergrads Receiving Aid: 35%
Avg. Amount per Student: $6,998

Of Those Receiving Any Aid:

Rec. Need-Based Scholarship or Grant Aid: 72%
Average Award: $1,448

Rec. Need-Based Self-Help Aid: 82%
Average Award: $4,060

Upon Graduation, Avg. Loan Debt per Student: $12,781

Financial Aid Deadline: 6/3, 3/2 (priority)

CALIFORNIA STATE UNIVERSITY— CHICO

400 West First Street, Chico, CA 95929-0722 Admissions Phone: (530) 898-4428;
(800) 542-4426 Fax: (530) 898-6456 Email: info@csuchico.edu
Website: www.csuchico.edu Application Website: www.csumentor.edu

General Info

Type of School: public, coed

Academic Calendar: semester

Student Body

Full-Time Undergrads: 12,580
  Men: 46%, Women: 54%

Part-Time Undergrads: 1,323
  Men: 45%, Women: 55%

Total Undergrad Population:
  African American: 2%
  Asian American: 5%
  Latino: 10%
  Native American: 1%
  Caucasian: 66%
  International: 2%
  Out-of-State: 1%
  Living Off-Campus: 88%
  In Fraternities: 7%
  In Sororities: 6%

Graduate and First-Professional
  Students: 1,613

Academics

Full-Time Faculty: 528
  With Ph.D.: 88%

Part-Time Faculty: 330
  With Ph.D.: 34%

Student/Faculty Ratio: 20:1

Freshmen Retention Rate: 80%

Graduation Rates:
  11% within four years
  47% within six years

Admissions

Regular Application Deadline:
  11/30; 10/1 (priority)

Fall Transfer Deadline: 11/30
  (priority)

Spring Transfer Deadline: 8/30
  (priority)

Total # of Students Applied: 9,157
  Admitted: 6,718
  Enrolled: 2,001

Test Scores (middle 50%):
  SAT Verbal: 460–570
  SAT Math: 470–570
  ACT Comp: 19–24
  ACT English: 18–24
  ACT Math: 18–24

Inside the Classroom

Chico State is among CSU's most popular campuses. The number of applications has been increasing, and the administration reports that the average entering freshman GPA jumped by one-tenth in 2002. "Any student with a curiosity for learning, who also enjoys goal-oriented projects, will do very well at Chico," states a university official.

Chico State offers undergraduate programs in seven colleges (agriculture; behavioral science; business; communication and education; engineering, computer science, and technology; humanities; and natural science) and three schools (nursing; social work; and the arts). Of its 39 B.A. degree programs and 29 B.S. degree programs, liberal studies (elementary teaching), business, computer science, mechatronic engineering, journalism, and agriculture are among the strongest. Graduates of Chico's special ed, speech pathology, nursing, and construction management programs reportedly enjoy a near 100 percent employment rate.

The average class size is 22 students—not bad for a state university. Says a sophomore, "The professors are all down-to-earth and are willing to help you." A school official explains, "Chico faculty don't just teach and go home—they care about their students and do the extra things to help them succeed."

In addition to completing coursework for a specific major, students must complete an extensive General Education program. Freshmen have the option of enrolling in the General Education Courselink Program, where they share three GE courses with 24 other students. Another option is the General Studies Thematic program: 36 freshmen enroll in a two-semester common curriculum of intensive study in the humanities, arts, and social sciences, satisfying many of their GE requirements.

Chico is a leader in distance learning, including open university and noncredit classes and workshops, in addition to master's degree programs for working professionals. Liberal Studies Online, preparation for elementary teaching, has been offered since spring 2002 to California students studying to be elementary school teachers.

Campus Environment

Chico State's 119-acre main campus is known for its beauty. (The university also manages 800 acres of farmland and 240 acres of rangeland.) "I cannot say enough about how beautiful and natural this campus is," raves an alumna. The campus is actually an arboretum with more than 200 different varieties of trees and other plants, some dating back to the school's founding in 1887. Nine walking bridges cross Little Chico Creek, which winds through the center of campus. But beware: Students get slapped with a fine if they are caught picking flowers from the George Petersen Rose Garden. (A campus myth says there are even hidden cameras inside the three stone statues overlooking the flowers to help enforce this rule.)

Besides being beautiful, the campus is also functional. The Bell Memorial Union (student union) recently underwent a $32 million expansion and renovation, adding many recreation rooms, lounges, computer labs, and other facilities. Yolo Hall, a new $12 million physical education classroom building that includes the latest sports sciences equipment, was completed in January 2003. The campus also features six art galleries, along with museums of anthropology and natural history.

KAPLAN

The university provides more than 1,700 living spaces in six on-campus residence halls and one off-campus apartment complex (University Village). University housing is not required, nor is it guaranteed. A university official explains, "We house approximately 1,600 out of 2,000 freshmen—about 80 percent of the freshman class. (About 90 percent of the rest of the student body lives within one mile of campus.) The university priority is to house freshmen; new transfer students would be next priority." Off-campus housing is reportedly "plentiful and affordable," and the university housing office is very helpful in helping students find housing off campus.

Located 90 miles north of Sacramento and 174 miles northeast of San Francisco, the town of Chico (population 65,000) is only two miles from the foothills of the Sierra Nevada. *Bicycle* magazine named Chico "America's Best Bike Town" in 1997. Students enjoy going to the movie theaters in town and the numerous music and dance clubs in the area.

Student Life

The university sponsors more than 240 student organizations each year. All students are members of the Associated Students of CSU Chico—a multi-million dollar corporation managed by students, responsible for the student government, the student bookstore, Adventure Outings, the student union, and other services. Other popular (and award-winning) student organizations: Students in Free Enterprise (SIFE) wins national awards almost annually for its community outreach programs. Chico's powerful Model United Nations club was asked to represent the United States in 2002 following the tragedy of 9/11. Chico's campus newspaper, *The Orion*, has won numerous awards, including best non-daily college newspaper in the nation in 2002 by the National Newspaper Association.

Chico has top-flight Division II intercollegiate athletic teams and participants. In 2002, the men's baseball team went to the College World Series for the fourth time in six years (where twice it has won it all), and individual athletes won NCAA championships in golf and track and field. Additionally, more than half of the students at Chico participate in recreational sports.

The university has done a lot recently to battle its "party school" image, with much success. Chico State is enforcing its "dry campus" policy, and fraternities are not allowed to have any kind of alcohol function at their fraternity houses (a few years back, a fraternity pledge at Chico died after ingesting too much alcohol). The Campus Alcohol and Drug Education Center (CADEC) hosts alcohol-free events on campus, trains peer educators, holds classes for violators of campus alcohol policies, provides transportation for inebriated students, and even mails birthday cards with words of advice to students turning 21. CADEC also has assisted with increased enforcement of no-drinking rules in residence halls and improved coordination with the local community. (But even without alcohol, tragedy keeps hitting Chico's Greek system: In November 2002, a senior committed suicide in his frat house bedroom.)

CSU's most recent Student Needs and Priorities Survey ranks Chico number one in the CSU system for undergraduate and graduate student satisfaction. A university official tells us that students with "an adventuresome spirit and a love of the outdoors" can thrive at Chico, and notes that many Chico students "grow to love Chico so much they find it hard to leave when they graduate."

Other schools to check out: San Diego State U, California Polytechnic State U, UC Davis, Arizona State U.

HS Rank of Entering Freshmen:
  Top 10%: 35%
  Top 25%: 76%
  Top 50%: 100%
Avg. HS GPA: 3.27

Costs (2003–04)

Tuition and Fees, In-State: $2,796

Tuition and Fees, Out-of-State: Additional $282 per unit

Room & Board: $7,245

Inst. Aid (2002–03)

Institutional Aid, Non-Need-Based: $874,522.00

Financial Aid Deadline: rolling, 3/2 (priority)

THE EXPERTS SAY...

" Chico's 800-acre University Farm offers lab experience in beef, swine, and sheep production, among other things. "

" If animal husbandry doesn't do it for you, go work out at one of Chico State's gyms or dance the night away at one of the many local clubs. "

CALVIN COLLEGE

3201 Burton Street S.E., Grand Rapids, MI 49546
Admissions Phone: (616) 526-6106; (800) 668-0122 Fax: (616) 526-8513
Email: admissions@calvin.edu Website: www.calvin.edu
Application Website: www.calvin.edu/admin/admissions/

General Info

Type of School: private, coed, Christian Reformed

Setting: suburban

Academic Calendar: 4-1-4

Student Body

Full-Time Undergrads: 4,085
    Men: 44%, Women: 56%

Part-Time Undergrads: 93
    Men: 55%, Women: 45%

Total Undergrad Population:
    African American: 1%
    Asian American: 3%
    Latino: 1%
    Native American: <1%
    Caucasian: 85%
    International: 8%
    Out-of-State: 43%
    Living Off-Campus: 44%

Graduate and First-Professional
    Students: 34

Academics

Full-Time Faculty: 305
    With Ph.D.: 83%

Part-Time Faculty: 77
    With Ph.D.: 18%

Student/Faculty Ratio: 13:1

Most Popular Majors:
    elementary education (13%)
    nursing (5%)
    English (4%)
    psychology (4%)
    business (4%)

Completing 2 or More Majors: 10%

Freshmen Retention Rate: 87%

Graduation Rates:
    56% within four years
    74% within six years

Admissions

Regular Application Deadline: 8/15

Total # of Students Applied: 1,933
    Admitted: 1,906
    Enrolled: 1,042

Test Scores (middle 50%):
    SAT Verbal: 540–660
    SAT Math: 540–660
    ACT Comp: 23–28
    ACT English: 22–29
    ACT Math: 22–28

Inside the Classroom

Located in Grand Rapids, Michigan, Calvin College offers a liberal arts education with a Reformed Christian flavor. Named for the 16th-century reformer John Calvin, the college maintains the largest scholarly collection on its namesake in the country.

Calvin's core curriculum, entitled "An Engagement with God's World," is central to each student's experience. Both course content and student learning are guided by three broad areas: core knowledge, core skills, and core virtues. Although each major's required courses are important, the ultimate goal is to provide an education that equips students to live and serve effectively in contemporary society.

Over 90 academic options are available, with popular majors being business, English, history, philosophy, music, mathematics, engineering, teacher education, natural sciences, and communication arts. Internships and practicum experiences are required by many academic programs, but the college encourages all students to participate in internships regardless of major. Through the school's career services office, students can be placed in a variety of internships: Some offer credit while others don't, and some offer monetary compensation.

"The workload is doable," says one student. "Profs push you but not to an unrealistic point." Part of what makes the Calvin experience so rewarding for students is the dedication of the faculty to the students, and of the students to each other. "Most are very willing to sit down and talk with you about anything, whether you need extra help or just want to talk about life. There really isn't much competition between students—we all want each other to do well and help each other out."

Calvin also offers a large selection of study abroad programs for a school of this kind; students can study in Hungary, Japan, Mexico, the Netherlands, and Spain.

Campus Environment

Most of Calvin's compact campus is arranged around a circular road, with the academic buildings and dorms inside the circle and the sports facilities and theological structures right outside it. Priority for dormitory housing is given to freshmen and sophomores, with most of the seven residence halls structured as four-person suites. The school tries to match two freshmen with two sophomores per suite, and if any suites are left over, juniors and seniors may choose from the rest.

Since housing isn't guaranteed after sophomore year, however, nearly 40 percent of students live off campus in rented apartments. "The dorms are nice," says one upperclassman, "but the freshman classes get so big every year that housing is becoming scarcer. Off-campus housing is pretty popular, and cheaper than the dorms."

The city of Grand Rapids, with a population of around 250,000, offers restaurants, music, theater, and other distractions for students, who pay only a quarter to ride pubic GRATA buses into town. According to one student, however, public rides into town are scarce: "Grand Rapids has a decent amount of interesting places but the public transportation system is virtually nonexistent. One needs a car to get around. If you live off campus, it's very easy to feel like you are not part of the college."

Another student agrees: "If you don't have a car, make friends with someone who does or you'll get very bored."

Student Life

"The typical Calvin student is Dutch, Christian Reformed, from Grand Rapids, wealthy, and shops at Abercrombie," says one senior. "However, since Calvin tries to challenge students' beliefs, very few leave with the same world view they arrived with." Religion does play a role on campus, but as one student puts it, "While it's a Christian school, it's not a 'Bible college.'"

The social life at Calvin is understated; as one psych major puts it, "Since we have a dry campus with no Greek system, there are very few wild parties on campus." Another student paints a different picture, saying, "Calvin students party a lot, with lots of alcohol. We just do it off campus." A nonalcoholic campus hangout is the Cave Café, where folk music, poetry readings, and other coffee-friendly entertainment is offered.

Many student organizations have spirituality and community service as themes, taking names like Calvin Students for Christian Feminism and Youth Excited to Serve (YES). Others are more secular in nature, including a historical simulations club, an anime club, and a visual arts guild.

One biology major says, "We have no football team, much to the dismay of me and many others, but we do have a very good basketball team and many students enjoy supporting them." Basketball and cross-country tend to be the perennial sports standouts, sometimes winning state and national championships. The nine sports for women and eight sports for men also include baseball, softball, soccer, golf, tennis, volleyball, rack and field, and swimming. Club sports are offered in crew, ice hockey, lacrosse, rugby, and ultimate Frisbee. In addition to these options, over 40 intramural sports are enjoyed by nearly 2,000 students.

Fun Calvin traditions include Airband, an annual, student-directed lip-sync contest; Chaos Day, an event during fall orientation when the seven residence halls compete for top honors; and the Cardboard Canoe Contest, a race around the campus pond by engineering students who build their own canoes from cardboard.

HS Rank of Entering Freshmen:
Top 10%: 25%
Top 25%: 53%
Top 50%: 79%

Avg. HS GPA: 3.54

THE EXPERTS SAY...

" Calvin College offers an interesting mixture of real-world liberal arts and Christian values. "

" The religious influence and its accompanying conservatism may prove stifling to the liberal- and secular-minded. "

Costs (2003–04)

Tuition and Fees: $16,775

Room & Board: $5,840

Payment Plan(s): installment plan, pre-payment plan

Inst. Aid (2002–03)

Institutional Aid, Need-Based: $13,281,900

Institutional Aid, Non-Need-Based: $3,706,000

FT Undergrads Receiving Aid: 64%
Avg. Amount per Student: $12,252

FT Undergrads Receiving Non-Need-Based Scholarship or Grant Aid: 26%
Avg. Amount per Student: $3,884

Of Those Receiving Any Aid:

Rec. Need-Based Scholarship or Grant Aid: 99%
Average Award: $7,922

Rec. Need-Based Self-Help Aid: 72%
Average Award: $6,201

Upon Graduation, Avg. Loan Debt per Student: $17,000

Financial Aid Deadline: rolling, 2/15 (priority)

Graduates

Going to Graduate School: 39% Within One Year

Companies Recruiting On Campus: 36

Alumni Giving: 48%

CARLETON COLLEGE

100 South College Street, Northfield, MN 55057
Admissions Phone: (507) 646-4190; (800) 995-2275 Fax: (507) 646-4526
Email: admissions@acs.carleton.edu Website: www.carleton.edu
Application Website: www.carleton.edu/admissions/application

General Info

Type of School: private, coed

Setting: small town

Academic Calendar: 3 courses for
each of three 10–week terms

Student Body

Full-Time Undergrads: 1,927
Men: 48%, Women: 52%

Total Undergrad Population:
African American: 5%
Asian American: 9%
Latino: 4%
Native American: 1%
Caucasian: 77%
International: 4%
Out-of-State: 76%
Living Off-Campus: 18%

Academics

Full-Time Faculty: 196
With Ph.D.: 95%

Part-Time Faculty: 24
With Ph.D.: 63%

Student/Faculty Ratio: 9:1

Most Popular Majors:
biology
political science/international
relations
English
history
economics

Freshmen Retention Rate: 97%

Graduation Rates:
85% within four years
89% within six years

Admissions

Regular Application Deadline: 1/15

Early Decision Deadline(s): 11/15,
1/15

Fall Transfer Deadline: 3/31

Total # of Students Applied: 4,737
Admitted: 1,414
Enrolled: 488

# of Students Waitlisted: 1,212
Students Accepting Place: 272
Waitlisted Students Admitted: 8

Applied Early Decision: 459
Early Decision Admitted: 200

In the Classroom

"Carleton is a place where people are eager to learn. There is a lot of hardcore studying that goes on," a senior explains. A young alum agrees: "Carleton attracts a student who wants an excellent education in a non-Ivy League setting." Students describe the academic climate as "intense," but at the same time, "noncompetitive" and "friendly." The challenging academics and the dedication to learning explains why so many Carls go on to top grad schools—and why top grad schools are eager to get Carleton alumni. Of all liberal arts colleges in the U.S., Carleton ranks first in the number of students that have gone on to get a Ph.D. in the natural sciences and mathematics.

Carleton's academic year is divided into three 10-week terms with a 6-week break that extends from mid-November to the first part of January. Students take only three courses per term, allowing them to focus on a limited number of subjects. However, students point out that this schedule means exams and deadlines creep up frequently.

The faculty is regarded as among the best in the nation, but, as one student says, they didn't get that way by being "softies." They're tough, but they're accessible and committed to teaching. Professors often meet with students outside of class for extra help or informal discussions over meals and coffee. Says one student, "This is an open academic environment. The professors are always willing to help students out." The average class size at Carleton is 17, and 65 percent of the classes have 20 or fewer students.

The extensive graduation requirements are designed to ensure "not only rigor and depth, but also sufficient breadth," according to the college's catalog. Students must meet distribution requirements in the arts and literature, the humanities, the social sciences, and mathematics and natural sciences. In addition, there are writing, second language, and phys ed requirements, and students must take at least one course in a non-Western culture. To graduate, seniors complete a comprehensive examination or complete an independent project within their chosen field.

About two-thirds of Carleton students study abroad for at least one of their 12 terms at Carleton. Most students go abroad with other Carleton students and professors, but many also go through programs sponsored by other organizations or universities.

Campus Environment

Carleton is located in the "quaint, charming, and safe" small town of Northfield, 45 miles south of Minneapolis-St. Paul. Of course, Northfield's idea of a fun time, is, shall we say, a bit quirky: "One can't miss the Jesse James Day celebration which includes cheese curds galore and a reenactment of Jesse James getting busted at the First National Bank of Northfield," a young alumna reminisces.

Carleton's peaceful 900-acre campus includes a 400-acre arboretum. The tree-covered campus revolves around a grassy field called the "Bald Spot," which in winter is transformed into two lighted ice-skating rinks. Carleton's Gould Library is one of the largest undergraduate libraries in the nation. In 2002, the library introduced art exhibits and public literary events—including a marathon reading of the *Odyssey* and a Shakespeare birthday celebration filled recitations from sonnets and plays.

All students (except those who are married or have children) are required to live in college housing, although an application can be made to arrange your own housing arrangements off campus. Freshmen are placed in residence halls; returning students also have the options of living in a shared interest community or in one of the coveted college apartment buildings. Shared interest communities are based on a shared interest or cultural background and are housed in residence halls or one of the college's houses.

"While attending Carleton College, students are not permitted to drive or possess motor vehicles within the city limits of Northfield…" begins the college's motor vehicle policy. Few exceptions apply, although students may apply for permission to use a car to get to college, but then it must be parked in "dead storage" until the end of the term. Instead, the college provides shuttle services that offers transportation to the Twin Cities on weekends, the airport at the beginning and end of each term, and around town on weekdays. In addition, the "Love Bus," sponsored by the student governments of Carleton and St. Olaf College (also in Northfield), provides transportation to movie theaters and shopping centers on Friday and Saturday nights.

Student Life

Carleton embraces multiculturalism, and the minority population is slowly growing. Still, says a math and physics double major, "we are almost entirely white, upper-middle-class kids." Adds another student, "The student body is pretty geographically diverse, but not very racially diverse." Nevertheless, you'll find small but active Asian American, African American, Jewish, Latino, and GLBT organizations on campus.

As one Idaho guidance counselor puts it, Carleton is truly a "*liberal* liberal arts college." "The Republican club is just about the only group with 'sore thumb' status," says an alum, adding, "Sometimes the liberal minds tend to forget that openness includes accepting things that aren't 'leftist' or 'PC.'" Carleton students love debating complex topics, and in fall 2002, the college introduced the Program in Ethical Reflection at Carleton (PERC), which is "designed to encourage students to grapple with personal and social ethical issues."

Carls are often overcommitted and insanely busy. When there is downtime, Carls may go out for a night on the town, take in a campus party or event, or attend an event at nearby St. Olaf College, with whose students Carls frequently socialize. With the college administration, the academic departments, the student government, the student clubs and organizations, the dorms and shared interest communities, and the athletic department all actively organizing campus activities, there is always something going on at the college. There are no fraternities or sororities.

While Carleton's NCAA Division III intercollegiate teams aren't too popular, club and intramural sports draw large numbers of participants. The school's best-known teams are its men's and women's Ultimate Frisbee club teams. Ultimate Frisbee also dominates intramural competition both in spring and fall, with most dorm floors fielding teams organized into leagues of varying skill levels. In winter, the same enthusiasm is channeled to broomball—after all, there's nothing like a spirited game of broomball beneath a clear night sky to warm you up in winter.

Other schools to check out: Grinnell, Oberlin, Macalester, Haverford, Pomona.

Test Scores (middle 50%):
  SAT Verbal: 650–750
  SAT Math: 650–730
  ACT Comp: 28–32

HS Rank of Entering Freshmen:
  Top 10%: 71%
  Top 25%: 95%
  Top 50%: 99%

THE EXPERTS SAY…

" A degree from Carleton commands respect from businesses and from graduate and professional schools nationwide. "

" Safety isn't an issue on this friendly Minnesota campus—but frostbite sure is. Still, if you're the type who thrives on cramming 36 hours' worth of activity into a 24-hour day, Carleton could be the place for you. "

Costs (2003–04)

Tuition and Fees: $28,527

Room & Board: $5,868

Payment Plan(s): installment plan, pre-payment plan

Inst. Aid (2002–03)

Institutional Aid, Need-Based: $15,059,898

Institutional Aid, Non-Need-Based: $425,541

FT Undergrads Receiving Aid: 55%
  Avg. Amount per Student: $19,933

FT Undergrads Receiving Non-Need-Based Scholarship or Grant Aid: 9%
  Avg. Amount per Student: $2,533

Of Those Receiving Any Aid:

Rec. Need-Based Scholarship or Grant Aid: 98%
  Average Award: $14,722

Rec. Need-Based Self-Help Aid: 99%
  Average Award: $4,944

Upon Graduation, Avg. Loan Debt per Student: $15,689

Financial Aid Deadline: 2/15 (priority)

Graduates

Going to Graduate School: 20% Within One Year

Companies Recruiting On Campus: 27

CARNEGIE MELLON UNIVERSITY

5000 Forbes Avenue, Pittsburgh, PA 15213
Admissions Phone: (412) 268-2082 Fax: (412) 268-7838
Email: undergraduate-admissions@andrew.cmu.edu Website: www.cmu.edu
Application Website: www.cmu.edu/enrollment/admission

Note: Info. not verified by school

General Info

Type of School: private, coed

Setting: urban

Academic Calendar: semester

Student Body

Full-Time Undergrads: 5,084
  Men: 62%, Women: 38%

Part-Time Undergrads: 110
  Men: 69%, Women: 31%

Total Undergrad Population:
  African American: 4%
  Asian American: 22%
  Latino: 5%
  Caucasian: 44%
  International: 11%
  Out-of-State: 76%
  Living Off-Campus: 28%
  In Fraternities: 15%
  In Sororities: 11%

Graduate and First-Professional
  Students: 3,278

Academics

Full-Time Faculty: 799
  With Ph.D.: 98%

Part-Time Faculty: 81
  With Ph.D.: 99%

Student/Faculty Ratio: 10:1

Most Popular Majors:
  computer science (10%)
  business administration (9%)
  electrical and computer
    engineering (9%)
  information systems (6%)
  mechanical engineering (6%)

Freshmen Retention Rate: 93%

Graduation Rates:
  63% within four years
  79% within six years

Admissions

Regular Application Deadline: 1/1

Early Decision Deadline(s): 11/1,
  11/15

Fall Transfer Deadline: 3/15
  (priority)

Spring Transfer Deadline: 11/1
  (priority)

Inside the Classroom

The one factor at Carnegie Mellon that most distinguishes students is their different academic disciplines. "The student body gets polarized" between science/engineering students and fine arts students, we are told. A sophomore states, "The school is very specialized in terms of majors, and most students come in knowing what it is they want to do and are thus very determined." But no matter what program they're in, CMU students are some of the hardest workers you'll find anywhere. "Students take a lot upon themselves," agrees a student. "One can describe the typical CMU student as very driven, knowing what they want."

The six undergraduate colleges at CMU are the College of Fine Arts, the College of Humanities and Social Sciences, the School of Computer Science, the School of Industrial Management, the Carnegie Institute of Technology, and the Mellon College of Science. The engineering, computer science, and drama programs are unquestionably among the best in the nation. Other programs in the arts, sciences, and architecture are also excellent. According to the university, applications for undergraduate admission have more than doubled in the past 10 years. Each college has its own admissions process and core requirements. Transferring between the schools can be difficult, we're told, but such an event is rare given most students' motivation, direction, and serious attention to studies.

Almost all programs provide students with opportunities for hands-on, practical experience. In the drama program, students work with experienced theater personnel to put on professional-quality shows. Engineering, computer, and science students utilize superb facilities as they become immersed in independent projects. (Interesting fact: "The Pentagon has a backup of their computer system in our school computers," reveals an information systems major.) A business administration major proudly states, "We have amazing technology available at our fingertips —the largest wireless network in any institution worldwide."

"People almost universally acknowledge they're getting a quality education here," says one student. "We have some of the best professors in the country. Academically speaking, this school is top-notch." Another student stresses that the workload is very heavy—"probably more than a lot of the Ivy League schools." The school attracts top-level faculty, who teach both graduates and undergrads. Unfortunately—despite an impressive 10:1 student-teacher ratio—students describe their professors as "not very accessible" and "hard to approach." "Students mostly approach TA's for help," explains an undergrad.

Campus Environment

Students are guaranteed housing for all four years—a real advantage in a city school. "Variety in housing is great, ranging from very comfortable to the other extreme," says one student. But she complains that "availability for on-campus housing is increasingly limited as the freshman classes get bigger" and it is "very difficult for most students to get a decent room." But things may get better now that the university is building a new "environmentally friendly" residence hall for first-year students, scheduled to open in spring 2003. (Another environmentally friendly

KAPLAN

policy affecting the whole campus: Beginning in fall 2004, smoking will be banned in all on-campus housing, including private student rooms.)

While freshmen are required to live on campus, many upperclassmen choose to live off-campus: "Most people prefer this because it is cheaper." However, a student warns us that "availability is limited for the better apartments." Students tell us that you'd be "wise to get a car"—"public transportation is free for students, yet it is hard to get around," says a sophomore.

Carnegie Mellon's 103-acre campus is located in the Oakland neighborhood of Pittsburgh, five miles from the downtown area. "The city of Pittsburgh is small and not a friendly city towards students," says one student, adding that safety "is not too great." A senior goes into more detail: "Even a block or two off campus there have been incidents of flashing, rape, and people being held at gunpoint." But another student insists, "There are some great, fun parts of town within walking distance, and the school borders one of the largest parks in the city."

CMU has been doing its best to turn this city into an East Coast Silicon Valley: More than 70 startup companies in the Pittsburgh region have emerged from research conducted by Carnegie Mellon faculty and students in fields such as computer science, software engineering, and robotics. And one student tells us that one of the best things about CMU is the "good opportunities for internships."

Student Life

The student body is "very diverse, yet they all seem to fall into one category or another, creating many cliques," says one student. Another student muses, "I think that a large percentage of our school's students are quite affluent, but this is obvious, since our school doesn't help out much with financial aid and a large percentage do come from international schools." Fraternities and sororities "are not a big influence on the overall social life of the school." However, a senior notes that "the introduction of all the recent Asian interest groups, fraternities, and sororities" has been a pretty big topic on campus lately.

The caffeine-dependent workload really doesn't accommodate a party atmosphere; students agree that "the social life is lacking." One student moans, "People spend an awful lot of time working. There are some who spend 30 hours a week on homework. I don't think they do anything for fun here." But another student tells us that "drinking is very common both on and off campus." "Most people usually stay in their dorms, especially during the long winters in Pittsburgh, yet once the weather is nice, many students will start to come out," says one student. "On weekends, students can either go to the fraternity houses or join the activities organized by the school or by the different organizations on campus. These include parties, snowboarding trips, etc. Most students will also go out to shop or watch movies."

While CMU does offer a variety of Division III varsity teams, it's not exactly a sports powerhouse, and students allude to a resulting "lack of school spirit." But there are club sports and more than 40 intramural sports, plus lots of quirky traditions to keep students amused and occupied. Some examples: painting "the Fence" (used as a billboard, students may paint messages on it only at night and then must guard their handiwork until sunrise), having buggy races during Spring Carnival, and "traying" (using cafeteria trays as sleds).

Other schools to check out: U of Pittsburgh, Cornell, U of Rochester, Case Western Reserve, Cooper Union.

Total # of Students Applied: 16,696
  Admitted: 5,211
  Enrolled: 1,318

# of Students Waitlisted: 3,265
  Students Accepting Place: 715
  Waitlisted Students Admitted: 73

Applied Early Decision: 281
  Early Decision Admitted: 104

Test Scores (middle 50%):
  SAT Verbal: 600–700
  SAT Math: 680–770
  ACT Comp: 27–31
  ACT English: 27–31
  ACT Math: 28–32

HS Rank of Entering Freshmen:
  Top 10%: 72%
  Top 25%: 94%
  Top 50%: 99%

Avg. HS GPA: 3.62

THE EXPERTS SAY...

" You'd better hope your college degree is worth its weight in gold: In recent years, the price of tuition at CMU has jumped a whopping 37 percent. "

" In a recent year, a student used a $1,000 university grant to construct a wood-frame house on campus in which he planned to live for three months, maintaining a vow of silence while dressed in a lobster costume. This is where your money is going??? "

Costs (2003–04)

Tuition and Fees: $29,410

Room & Board: $9,978

Payment Plan(s): installment plan

Graduates

Going to Graduate School:
  23% Within One Year

Accepting Job Offer:
  82% at time of graduation

Companies Recruiting On Campus:
  860

CASE WESTERN RESERVE UNIVERSITY

103 Tomlinson Hall, 10900 Euclid Avenue, Cleveland, OH 44106-7055
Admissions Phone: (216) 368-4450 Fax: (216) 368-5111
Email: admission@case.edu Website: case.edu Application Website: admission.case.edu/admissions/

General Info

Type of School: private, coed

Setting: urban

Academic Calendar: semester

Student Body

Full-Time Undergrads: 3,302
  Men: 61%, Women: 39%

Part-Time Undergrads: 162
  Men: 68%, Women: 32%

Total Undergrad Population:
  African American: 5%
  Asian American: 15%
  Latino: 2%
  Native American: <1%
  Caucasian: 71%
  International: 5%
  Out-of-State: 45%
  Living Off-Campus: 27%
  In Fraternities: 34%
  In Sororities: 17%

Graduate and First-Professional
  Students: 5,599

Academics

Full-Time Faculty: 598
  With Ph.D.: 96%

Student/Faculty Ratio: 8:1

Most Popular Majors:
  management (10%)
  biology (9%)
  mechanical engineering (8%)
  psychology (7%)
  computer science (6%)

Completing 2 or More Majors: 18%

Freshmen Retention Rate: 93%

Graduation Rates:
  55% within four years
  78% within six years

Admissions

Regular Application Deadline: 1/15

Early Action Deadline: 11/15

Fall Transfer Deadline: 5/15

Spring Transfer Deadline: 10/15

Total # of Students Applied: 4,680
  Admitted: 3,525
  Enrolled: 878

Students Accepting Place on
  Waitlist: 243
  Waitlisted Students Admitted: 117

Inside the Classroom

As one of the leading independent research institutions in the nation, CWRU offers outstanding preprofessional programs. The Case School of Engineering is the strongest and most renowned of CWRU's four undergraduate schools (the other three: the College of Arts and Sciences, the Weatherhead School of Management, and the Frances Payne Bolton School of Nursing). Other strong undergraduate programs are premed, accounting, anthropology, biology, chemistry, math, music (a joint program with the Cleveland Institute of Music), nursing, psychology, and physics. The B.S. program in polymer science is one of a few such undergraduate programs in the country. A major perk of attending CWRU is the Pre-Professional Scholars Program, in which participants who maintain a high GPA and certain other standards are automatically admitted to the appropriate CWRU professional school (law, medical, dental, or social work).

Although they are outnumbered by graduate and professional students, undergrads do receive individual attention here, with an undergraduate student/teacher ratio of only 8 to 1. "The workload tends to be heavy at times, but no one that comes to this school expects it to be less," notes a premed student. Another premed student breaks it down by major: "Engineering gets the most work, second is premed, and third is everyone else."

A university official tells us, "Our goal is to have a freshman class that reflects a mix of the following qualities: strong record of academic performance; academic promise and enthusiasm for learning; willingness to contribute to school or community; distinctive achievements or talents; and knowledge of self and appreciation for individual differences." Both students and guidance counselors applaud the "generous financial assistance" CWRU often offers.

To help with the transition to college life, incoming freshmen may apply to the First Year Experience Program, a residential college program in which a close-knit group of students live on the same floor and take Freshman English class together. Another residential college option is the College Scholars Program, a three-year honors program (sophomore through senior year) focusing on interdisciplinary learning and leadership. Approximately 20 students are accepted into the program each year. Six of the College Scholars went to Kenya as sophomores in fall 2000 to experience the African nation firsthand; they returned to Kenya as seniors and used skills learned in their classes to improve conditions at a Kenyan primary school.

An estimated 65 to 75 percent of undergrads participate in some form of independent research (all engineering students do, as they are required to complete a senior research project for graduation). The Office of Undergraduate Studies compiles a directory of undergraduate research opportunities that you can use to match your interests with those of faculty who are willing to oversee undergraduate research. CWRU offers co-op opportunities for majors in engineering, computer science, management, accountancy, and the sciences (except astronomy). "More than 650 companies across the country ask for CWRU co-op students, and salaries range from $1,900 to $4,000 a month," says a school official.

Campus Environment

CWRU's main campus consists of 128 acres in Cleveland's University Circle, a concentration of various cultural, religious, and other institutions in the center of the city. "Walking alone at night is not advisable," say several students. But another student assures us that "escorts are readily available at any time to accompany anyone who is uncomfortable walking alone. Students are made aware of security alerts through email." In a highly unusual occurrence in May 2003, a CWRU graduate went on a shooting rampage on campus, killing one man and wounding two others.

CWRU has a strict four-year residency requirement: All undergrads, except for those living with a parent or guardian, must live on campus. Seniors who are 21 or older may apply to live off campus. While some may find this policy restrictive, it does create a strong sense of community. All freshmen are housed in one of 11 North Village residence halls, which have double rooms, with a few scattered single rooms available for third- and fourth-year students. Students from other classes live in the South Village halls, which have small single rooms grouped in suites. Some Greek chapters have their own houses; others live in groups in the residence halls. Students must have sophomore standing before they can move into a chapter house.

A university official informs us, "CWRU's North Campus will be getting a makeover that includes new residence halls with apartment-style housing, a new student center, and a new field house. Students have been involved in the planning for the project, and their input has resulted in changes to the original concept."

Parking is extremely limited, and new students are discouraged from bringing cars on campus. The University Circle "greenie" buses (they're actually white, but used to be green, and the nickname remains) provide free shuttle service around the campus and University Circle, as well as evening service to Cleveland Heights's Coventry neighborhood, an area of eclectic shops and restaurants popular with students. Free, unlimited use of Cleveland's public transportation system (bus and subway) is also included with the student activity fee.

Student Life

"A typical student at Case is somewhat introverted in one way or another," a sophomore admits. "No matter how hard they may try to avoid it, they are not usually the most social and popular person." A freshman's assessment of her fellow students: "Everyone is very odd in their own way. We have people who wear shorts and people who wear galoshes ALL of the time."

"Many people find that if they want to be social at Case, it is sort of hard to find what to do and who to do it with because many people stay at home staring at their computers all day," gripes one student. Not surprisingly, several of the campus clubs and organizations are premed- or engineering-oriented. However, there are also a number of arts, ethnic, community service, and special interest groups. Several nights each week, CWRU students enjoy going to Movies on the Quad. Students also go "downtown to go shopping or go to dinner or dancing if the students are of age. Sometimes on Thursdays or Wednesday nights, students go to the flats to go dancing on college ID night."

CWRU offers NCAA Division III varsity teams in eleven sports for men and nine for women. While varsity sports don't get a lot of support from students, about 70 percent of CWRU undergrads participate in at least one intramural sport.

One-third of the men and one-fifth of the women are involved in Greek life, and "they have great influence on the social life, because there is not much else to do around here," says one student. There are occasional frat parties, but "Case parties never get very rowdy." The whole school turns out for Greek Week, a food drive with fun competitions like the Root Beer Chug and the Rope Pull. Other fun events are the Winter Carnival and the Spring Olympics.

Other schools to check out: Brandeis, Carnegie Mellon, U of Rochester, Washington U of St. Louis, Emory.

Test Scores (middle 50%):
 SAT Verbal: 590–700
 SAT Math: 630–730
 ACT Comp: 26–32
 ACT English: 25–31
 ACT Math: 26–32
HS Rank of Entering Freshmen:
 Top 10%: 63%
 Top 25%: 87%
 Top 50%: 98%

THE EXPERTS SAY...

" Even if you don't get into the Pre-Professional Scholars Program, a huge percentage of CWRU undergrads go on to top graduate or professional programs upon graduating. "

" You'll need to make a conscious effort to put away your lab coat, pull your roommate away from his computer screen, and go out and have some fun. "

Costs (2004–5)

Tuition and Fees: $26,762

Room & Board: $8,202

Payment Plan(s): installment plan

Inst. Aid (est. 2003–04)

Institutional Aid, Need-Based: $23,029,930

Institutional Aid, Non-Need-Based: $12,989,240

FT Undergrads Receiving Aid: 55%
 Avg. Amount per Student: $23,571

FT Undergrads Receiving Non-Need-Based Scholarship or Grant Aid: 34%
 Avg. Amount per Student: $12,352

Of Those Receiving Any Aid:

Rec. Need-Based Scholarship or Grant Aid: 100%
 Average Award: $15,695

Rec. Need-Based Self-Help Aid: 89%
 Average Award: $6,498

Upon Graduation, Avg. Loan Debt per Student: $23,534

Financial Aid Deadline: 2/1 (priority)

Graduates

Going to Graduate School:
 42% Within One Year

Companies Recruiting On Campus:
 150

Alumni Giving: 21%

CATHOLIC UNIVERSITY OF AMERICA

Office of Enrollment Services, Washington, DC 20064-0002
Admissions Phone: (800) 673-2772; (202) 319-5305 Fax: (202) 319-6533
Email: cua-admissions@cua.edu Website: www.cua.edu
Application Website: admissions/cua.edu/application/

General Info

Type of School: private, coed, Roman Catholic

Setting: urban

Academic Calendar: semester

Student Body

Full-Time Undergrads: 2,461
  Men: 45%, Women: 55%

Part-Time Undergrads: 263
  Men: 35%, Women: 65%

Total Undergrad Population:
  African American: 7%
  Asian American: 3%
  Latino: 4%
  Caucasian: 73%
  International: 2%
  Out-of-State: 94%
  Living Off-Campus: 34%
  In Fraternities: 1%
  In Sororities: 1%

Graduate and First-Professional
  Students: 2,981

Academics

Full-Time Faculty: 336
  With Ph.D.: 96%

Part-Time Faculty: 340

Student/Faculty Ratio: 8:1

Most Popular Majors:
  engineering (11%)
  architecture (10%)
  politics (9%)
  business (8%)
  nursing (7%)

Freshmen Retention Rate: 85%

Graduation Rates:
  59% within four years
  69% within six years

Admissions

Regular Application Deadline: 2/15

Early Decision Deadline(s): 12/1

Fall Transfer Deadline: 8/1

Spring Transfer Deadline: 12/1

Total # of Students Applied: 2,748
  Admitted: 2,251
  Enrolled: 673

Test Scores (middle 50%):
  SAT Verbal: 530–640
  SAT Math: 520–630
  ACT Comp: 22–28

Inside the Classroom

The Catholic University of America (CUA) is a perfect example of how a strong religious affiliation by no means limits a school's educational possibilities. The official university of the Roman Catholic Church in the United States, Catholic University has first-rate academic programs in such diverse areas as music, drama, nursing, and politics, to name just a few.

There are six undergraduate schools at CUA: Architecture and Planning, Engineering, Music, Nursing, Philosophy, and Arts and Sciences. Students can choose from among 92 undergraduate programs of study. And because CUA is a member of the Consortium of Universities of the Washington Metropolitan Area, students can take courses not offered on campus through other member institutions and enjoy online access to the library holdings of the Washington Research Library Consortium.

A rigid liberal arts core curriculum includes courses in philosophy, literature, natural and social sciences, foreign language, and, of course, religion classes taught by clergy. Preprofessional programs are among the most popular at CUA, and many students go on to graduate and professional schools. Washington also offers plenty of internship and work experiences; being located in the heart of the U.S. capital certainly gives CUA students in the political department an unbeatable advantage. A college official says there are "many internships available in the Washington Metropolitan Area, including government, media, private sector, the arts, and so forth. We generally have more offers of internships than we have students available to fill them."

A Florida guidance counselor praises the school and administration, saying, "They've done more with a personal outreach program to recruit students, such as visiting high schools more often." Current students praise the accessibility of their teachers, who are generally friendly and approachable. After introductory level courses, most students' classes will be small and manageable. Some classes are taught by graduate students, but undergraduates will have the opportunity to study with and get to know full professors. A college official states that "undergraduates are encouraged to participate in faculty research" and adds, "Our professors have won the Professor of the Year award for DC universities in seven of the past 12 years." The Honors Program is described as "first rate and interdisciplinary" and the school boasts that "the faculty fully utilizes the resources of the Washington Metropolitan Area for class assignments, field experiences, and internships."

Campus Environment

Although the school isn't located in the safest part of the city, the 145-acre campus itself is self-contained and secure. As one student says, "The kids who get into trouble are generally just not being smart." The campus is beautiful, with a mixture of Gothic stone and contemporary buildings neatly arranged along tree-lined paths, adjacent to Washington's impressive National Shrine of the Immaculate Conception.

Housing is available for undergraduate and grad students in seven residence halls and in Centennial Village, a cluster of eight colonial-style houses. A school official tells us, "All freshmen and sophomores, except commuters, are required to live on campus. For freshmen, options include freshmen-only or integrated with students from all classes. A freshmen residential college is available." Additionally, two apartment-style residence halls were completed in August 2001.

CUA's Washington location makes it truly cosmopolitan and enables students to enjoy an active off-campus social life. A college official tells us that while "freshmen are permitted to have cars on campus and parking permits are required," most students opt for public transportation. "Most students use the Metro (subway)," he says. "The station on the edge of campus provides easy access to downtown Washington, museums, galleries, restaurants and movies at Union Station, and Reagan National Airport."

Student Life

While the vast majority of CUA students are Catholics from the East Coast, not all CUA students are strictly religious. For some, going to church every so often and taking the required religion courses amount to the entire scope of their personal religious duties. "People from other religions are very accepted," says a student. For those who want to maintain or strengthen their religious ties, however, there are plenty of opportunities to do so, both in CUA's excellent religious studies courses as well as in a variety of church-related programs and activities.

On-campus organizations, activities, and events provide opportunities for students beyond the classroom. "Community service is a big thing here," says one student. Both intramural and intercollegiate sports benefit from the use of a $10 million sports facility. A school official says, "The University offers over 20 intercollegiate sports in which about 25 percent of the undergraduates participate. There is also a full array of intramural and club sports." Students enjoy watching movies on the campus mall and take part in the popular school-sponsored retreat program. Additionally, because of the acclaimed drama and music programs, there are frequent high-quality student productions on campus. A school official describes a staging of *Romeo and Juliet* "by an interracial cast of Catholic University and historically black Howard University students, for a vision of Shakespeare's play set in medieval West Africa." This school official also lists the Campus Ministry, College Republicans, College Democrats, Undergraduate Student Government, and Students for Life as the most popular clubs and organizations on campus.

And much like students in all DC-area colleges and universities, students make the most of the lively nightlife available in DC and the surrounding areas, as well as the many cultural, educational, and artistic attractions.

Other schools to check out: Fordham, Marquette, Loyola (MD), American U, Loyola of New Orleans.

HS Rank of Entering Freshmen:
 Top 10%: 24%
 Top 25%: 57%
 Top 50%: 91%
Avg. HS GPA: 3.36

Costs (2004–5)

Tuition and Fees: $24,750

Room & Board: $9,498

Payment Plan(s): installment plan, deferred payment plan

THE EXPERTS SAY...

" You can pick and choose your Washington, DC internships at Catholic University. "

" An option for those who can't let go of the impossible dream of attending Georgetown. "

Inst. Aid (est. 2003–04)

Institutional Aid, Need-Based: $18,497,768

Institutional Aid, Non-Need-Based: $2,028,167

FT Undergrads Receiving Aid: 81%
 Avg. Amount per Student: $14,945

FT Undergrads Receiving Non-Need-Based Scholarship or Grant Aid: 10%
 Avg. Amount per Student: $8,533

Of Those Receiving Any Aid:

Rec. Need-Based Scholarship or Grant Aid: 27%
 Average Award: $4,478

Rec. Need-Based Self-Help Aid: 54%
 Average Award: $5,506

Financial Aid Deadline: 2/1, 1/15 (priority)

Graduates

Going to Graduate School:
 36% Within One Year

Accepting Job Offer:
 41% at time of graduation

Companies Recruiting On Campus: 125

Alumni Giving: 17%

CENTRE COLLEGE

600 West Walnut Street, Danville, KY 40422
Admissions Phone: (859) 238-5350; (800) 423-6236 Fax: (859) 238-5373
Email: admissions@centre.edu Website: www.centre.edu
Application Website: www.centre.edu/admission/admission.html

Inside the Classroom

"There's a little college down in Kentucky which in 60 years has graduated more men who have acquired prominence and fame than has Princeton in her 150 years." So said former president Woodrow Wilson back in 1903, and a century later, Centre College is still the pride of Kentucky. Freshmen are particularly well looked after: The 2001 National Survey of Student Engagement ranked Centre number one in the category of supportive campus environment for first-year students at a national liberal arts institution. Accordingly, the top Kentucky high school students are drawn here; the test scores of incoming freshmen are higher than those of any other school in the state.

Centre offers 25 undergraduate majors plus preprofessional programs in law, medicine, dentistry, optometry, pharmacy, physical therapy, veterinary medicine, and education. One unique aspect of Centre's academics is its encouragement of self-designed majors; some recent examples include American political culture, physics and metaphysics, and medieval studies.

General education requirements include establishing basic skills in expository writing, foreign language, and mathematics; a two-course humanities sequence; two social studies courses; two natural science courses with a lab; two courses in the area of "fundamental questions" (for the less high-minded: religion and philosophy); and a fluency requirement in either foreign language, mathematics, or computer science.

About two-thirds of Centre students participate in a study abroad program of some sort—a rate that's among the ten highest in the country. The school has permanent semester-long programs in Ecuador, France, Mexico, and the United Kingdom, as well as three- to five-week programs in Africa, the Bahamas, Israel, and Vietnam.

Centre also has one of the few arts departments offering glass blowing. This drew national attention at the 2002 Winter Olympics in Salt Lake City, where a group of Centre faculty, alumni, and students staged a glass-blowing exhibition at the World Party celebration. One of the elaborately colored vessels was reportedly given to Jacques Rogge, president of the International Olympics Committee.

Campus Environment

The rolling bluegrass region that surrounds the historic town of Danville is one of the most attractive parts of the country. Centre, too, is both scenic and antique: Its 115-acre campus has 60 buildings, 21 of which are on the National Register of Historic Places. Drive there from anywhere else, and you'll pass some of the many thoroughbred horse farms that breed contenders in the Kentucky Derby.

First-year students are assigned to freshmen-only dorms. This isn't necessarily a bad thing, since Nevin Hall, the freshmen men's dorm, underwent a major renovation in summer 2002. Apartments and townhouse-style living quarters are also available for upperclassmen. Don't worry about getting to know all of your dormmates—with a student population of little more than 1,000, you'll probably know everyone by the time you graduate.

A campus favorite with students is the Combs Center, a converted hemp warehouse that's referred to by students—predictably—as "The Warehouse." Located at the end of Greek Row, the center houses a grill and coffeehouse and plays host to dances, mock game shows, debates, and other get-togethers. The center also contains pool tables, a jukebox, and meeting space for student organizations.

The Norton Center for the Arts, one of the largest buildings on campus, is a performing arts center that houses two theaters and a 1,500-seat concert hall. The center is active all year long as the site of dramatic productions, dance recitals, and concerts by symphonies and musical groups. In October 2000, the building became the focus of national attention when Dick Cheney and Joe Lieberman descended on Danville for the vice-presidential debate.

Painted on the side of the campus post office building is the last vestige of a remarkable occasion: The upset of Harvard University by Centre College's football team in 1921. Totally unexpected, the victory received national press attention and drove Centre students into such a frenzy that they painted the final score—C6–H0—on everything they got their hands on... walls, greenery, and even (according to one newspaper article) a cow. (Reportedly, Harvard was offered a rematch on the 75th anniversary of the game, but it declined. Perhaps that was for the best, considering what happened last time.)

Student Life

The social life at Centre could almost be described as cozy: Knowing everyone by face, if not by name, is practically inevitable. This reinforces a strong sense of community among students, but of course being visible has its price. "The Walk of Shame is an integral part of the Centre rumor mill," said one student. "My favorite thing to do is to go into Cowan [Commons] on Monday afternoon and find out what went on Friday and Saturday night." For the less nosy, Centre offers a remarkable variety of other distractions, including concerts, volunteer projects, coffeehouses, movies, plays, game shows, parties, and concerts.

Six fraternities and four sororities throw the most visible parties on campus, but the fun isn't as out-of-control as it might be at a larger school, and the negatives associated with Greek societies aren't quite as evident. "The Greek community isn't exclusive like some larger schools," said one recent graduate. "It's really diverse here. It's also a great way to get involved with Centre and the Danville community."

Centre also has its share of oddball traditions. Former Supreme Court justice Fred Vinson regularly attends Centre's sports games, even though he's been dead since 1953. Turns out the judge was a three-sport athlete at Centre and a member of the Phi Delta Theta fraternity, so today's Phi Delts bring a portrait of "Dead Fred" to every home football and baseball game. Another tradition is the Senior Women Serenade, when fourth-year women march to Craik House wearing bath towels to serenade the college president and his wife. Like many campus traditions, how this one got started is anyone's guess.

Other schools to check out: Kenyon, Rhodes, DePauw, Hendrix, University of the South.

THE EXPERTS SAY...

" Centre's academics, and its academic flexibility, make it the premier liberal arts institution in Kentucky. "

" You know your sports teams have a small fan base when dead judges sit in the bleachers. "

CHATHAM COLLEGE

Woodland Road, Pittsburgh, PA 15232
Admissions Phone: (412) 365-1290; (800) 837-1290 Fax: (412) 365-1609
Email: admissions@chatham.edu
Website: www.chatham.edu

General Info

Type of School: private, all women
Setting: urban
Academic Calendar: 4-1-4

Student Body

Full-Time Undergrads: 400
    Women: 100%

Part-Time Undergrads: 45
    Women: 100%

Total Undergrad Population:
    African American: 13%
    Asian American: 1%
    Latino: 1%
    Native American: 1%
    Caucasian: 75%
    International: 6%
    Out-of-State: 33%
    Living Off-Campus: 40%

Graduate and First-Professional
    Students: 552

Academics

Full-Time Faculty: 71
    With Ph.D.: 89%

Part-Time Faculty: 4
    With Ph.D.: 25%

Student/Faculty Ratio: 12:1

Most Popular Majors:
    biology/biochem (15%)
    psychology (15%)
    business (15%)
    social sciences/history (12%)
    English (10%)

Freshmen Retention Rate: 65%

Graduation Rates:
    54% within four years
    60% within six years

Admissions

Regular Application Deadline:
    3/15 (priority)

Total # of Students Applied: 243
    Admitted: 149
    Enrolled: 78

Test Scores (middle 50%):
    SAT Verbal: 490–620
    SAT Math: 430–550
    ACT Comp: 19–26
    ACT English: 18–26
    ACT Math: 18–22

Inside the Classroom

Chatham College holds the trademark (literally) on higher education for women, with its mission to turn out "World Ready Women™"—women who, says a school official, are "confident, assertive, knowledgeable, articulate, responsible, creative, and passionate." That may be a tall order, but Chatham women are more than up to the task. Indeed, students at Chatham are bright and studious, and take immense pride in their school's tradition of educating women who want to change their world.

Established in 1869, Chatham, formerly known as the Pennsylvania College for Women, is one of the oldest women's liberal arts colleges in the United States. (At Chatham, bachelor degrees are offered to women only, though the master's degree, continuing education, and teacher certification programs are open to both men and women.) The college offers 37 undergraduate majors, with particularly strong programs in biology, English, and psychology. Students also have the opportunity to cross-register at nearby Carnegie Mellon University and the University of Pittsburgh.

Small class sizes give the school an intimate, caring atmosphere. More than half of the faculty is female, and there are no TA's. Chatham students report that being in a classroom with all women is empowering, and that they aren't as intimidated to speak up and speak out as they might be in a coed class. And that's a good thing, since at Chatham, courses are largely discussion-based (as opposed to traditional lecture style), so you'd better come to class prepared, we're told.

"Chatham's general education curriculum includes seven required interdepartmental courses to prepare students to think scientifically, globally, and ethically," the school tells us. In addition, all Chatham students bookend their studies with the first-year writing seminar and the senior tutorial, "a one-on-one year-long academic project with a faculty mentor." Many opportunities exist for nontraditional learning opportunities. The well-respected Global Focus Program focuses on one country or region of the world each year to study and incorporate into special programs, courses, and cultural events. There's a great deal of emphasis on the environment at Chatham, largely due to the influence of alumna Rachel Carson, the author of *Silent Spring* and the founder of the modern environmental movement; at the Rachel Carson Institute, students study the environment and environmental policy. Chatham's Center for Women in Politics in Pennsylvania is "the first organization in the state to focus specifically on women's political participation in Pennsylvania," a school official says. Both the Carson Institute and the Center "complement the college's commitment to women in leadership, global awareness, and environmental awareness."

Campus Environment

It's a small school, all right: just 32 acres in a trendy area of Pittsburgh. But perhaps its large endowment (at $52.5 million, it's among the largest per student in the nation) allows Chatham to offer facilities not usually seen at schools of its size. All campus facilities have been remodeled or upgraded in the past decade, we're told, "with the most significant investment made in fully wiring every residence hall room for the Internet and campus network." As a result, the student-to-computer ratio has been bumped up to 3 to 1. The new $10 million science complex is finished, with a new greenhouse, labs, computer suites, modern scientific instruments, and an open glass atrium that highlights a stunning Tiffany window. An $18 million athletic and fitness center is scheduled to open fall 2004.

Chatham's campus is quite lovely—it's a registered arboretum, in fact. At the center of campus is the quad, which often serves as the social hub of Chatham on sunny days. The library, art facilities, theaters, and the outdoor amphitheatre overlook the quad. On-campus housing is guaranteed for all, and is a requirement for first-year students. Not that they mind: Many students live in beautiful residence halls that are the "restored mansions of Pittsburgh industrialists." There are also "modern apartments" for upperclassmen.

The campus is less than a mile from Carnegie Mellon University and the University of Pittsburgh, so there are plenty of student-friendly activities in the area. (There's a free shuttle van between the schools.) Within a 10-minute walk, students find the cafés, bookstores, restaurants, and shops of the hip Squirrel Hill and Shadyside neighborhoods. Downtown Pittsburgh is easy to get to by bus or car, and students flock there to enjoy the city's many cultural offerings.

Student Life

With such a tiny undergrad population, Chatham really does feel like one big family. Chatham women are friendly and supportive of one another. (Beware of the gossip, though, we hear.) "Research has shown that women's college students participate more fully in and out of class than their coed counterparts, report greater satisfaction with their classes, develop higher levels of self esteem, and score higher on achievement tests," a college official tells us. "They are more likely to graduate and are more successful in their careers."

Students can participate in more than 30 school-sponsored clubs, including everything from academic organizations to volunteer and community service groups to arts clubs and outdoor activities. Among the more popular organizations are the International Student Organization, the Black Student Union, Students Against Sexual Oppression, Green Horizons (an environmental club), and the Student Government and Chatham Activities Board, which plan on-campus events and entertainment. Chatham also offers six Division III varsity sports teams: basketball, soccer, softball, tennis, volleyball, and the first women's varsity collegiate ice hockey team in Pennsylvania. Varsity women's swimming was added in 2003. Intramural sports include badminton, basketball, cross-country, fencing, football (non-tackle), golf, karate, skiing, soccer, softball, swimming, table tennis, volleyball, and weightlifting. Crew is also available as a club sport.

From Opening Convocation to Closing Convocation, "traditions are an integral part of life at Chatham College," we're told. Indeed, there seems to be at least one Chatham-wide event each month. There's the Fall Serenade, Fallfest Weekend (an Octoberfest-type celebration), Family Weekend, the Haunted Hayride, Halloween Dinner, a weeklong Battle of the Classes (which "culminates with Song Contest, a tradition at Chatham for more than 70 years"), Thanksgiving Dinner, a semiformal Holiday Ball, and May Day. Best of all may be Spring Fling, with lip-synch contests, a bonfire into which seniors throw their tutorials, and something called "Toe Dabbling Day."

Other schools to check out: Sweet Briar, Agnes Scott, Hollins, Mills, Simmons.

HS Rank of Entering Freshmen:
Top 10%: 15%
Top 25%: 34%
Top 50%: 79%
Avg. HS GPA: 3.24

Costs (2003–04)

Tuition and Fees: $20,552

Room & Board: $6,714

Payment Plan(s): installment plan

THE EXPERTS SAY...

" Chatham women put their training in leadership, global awareness, and environmental awareness to good use. "

" Chatham is about preparing for the future while still valuing traditions from the past. If you think you're too cool to go on a Haunted Hayride or sing in the Fall Serenade... well, it's your loss, not theirs. "

Inst. Aid (est. 2003–04)

Institutional Aid, Need-Based: $2,770,219

Institutional Aid, Non-Need-Based: $1,949,943
note: above figures do not include loans or work study

FT Undergrads Receiving Aid: 90%
Avg. Amount per Student: $22,742

FT Undergrads Receiving Non-Need-Based Scholarship or Grant Aid: 16%
Avg. Amount per Student: $5,717

Of Those Receiving Any Aid:

Rec. Need-Based Scholarship or Grant Aid: 100%
Average Award: $7,158

Rec. Need-Based Self-Help Aid: 100%
Average Award: $5,700

Upon Graduation, Avg. Loan Debt per Student: $18,655

Financial Aid Deadline: 5/1, 3/15 (priority)

Graduates

Going to Graduate School: 36% Within One Year

Companies Recruiting On Campus: 62

Alumni Giving: 33%

CITADEL

171 Moultrie Street, Charleston, SC 29409-0204
Admissions Phone: (843) 953-5230; (800) 868-1842 Fax: (843) 953-7036
Email: admissions@citadel.edu Website: citadel.edu
Application Website: www.citadel.edu/admission/cadmission/cadapplication.html

General Info

Type of School: public, coed
Setting: urban
Academic Calendar: semester

Student Body

Full-Time Undergrads: 2,037
  Men: 94%, Women: 6%

Part-Time Undergrads: 113
  Men: 56%, Women: 44%

Total Undergrad Population:
  African American: 8%
  Asian American: 3%
  Latino: 4%
  Native American: <1%
  Caucasian: 82%
  International: 2%
  Out-of-State: 49%

Graduate and First-Professional
  Students: 1,545

Academics

Full-Time Faculty: 149
  With Ph.D.: 95%

Part-Time Faculty: 72
  With Ph.D.: 49%

Student/Faculty Ratio: 15:1

Most Popular Majors:
  business administration (35%)
  criminal justice (12%)
  political science (10%)
  civil engineering (7%)
  history (7%)

Completing 2 or More Majors: 1%

Freshmen Retention Rate: 78%

Graduation Rates:
  62% within four years
  72% within six years

Admissions

Total # of Students Applied: 1,919
  Admitted: 1,286
  Enrolled: 553

Test Scores (middle 50%):
  SAT Verbal: 500–600
  SAT Math: 503–610
  ACT Comp: 20–25

HS Rank of Entering Freshmen:
  Top 10%: 11%
  Top 25%: 34%
  Top 50%: 74%

Avg. HS GPA: 3.31

Inside the Classroom

The Citadel, the Military College of South Carolina and the oldest such college in the country, offers young men and women a unique opportunity to earn a well-respected degree in a very structured environment. In an effort to turn out strong leaders, The Citadel strives to develop the "whole" person—mind, body, and spirit. Character-building is just as important as résumé-building. Cadets pledge to solemnly and fervently abide by the Honor Code, which states that "A Cadet does not lie, cheat, steal, nor tolerate those who do." This code is the cornerstone of The Citadel experience; cadets cherish the principles of honor and pride above all else.

Military service is not required upon graduation, though cadets are required to complete four years of ROTC. In fact, more than half of all graduating seniors use their Citadel degrees to pursue careers in the private sector. About one-third accept a military commission, and most of the rest go on to grad school. Famous alumni range from high-ranking military officers and government officials to pro football players and a best-selling author.

The core curriculum is extensive. In general, all students must complete four semesters each of English, science, and a foreign language, and two semesters each of math, history, and social science, as well as a comprehensive physical education requirement (two semesters in health and two semesters in activity courses). The first-year experience course, Citadel 101, is designed to help freshmen adjust to the unique academic and social environment of a military college. And cadets must know all about their new home. "Knob Knowledge," another requirement of sorts, is a collection of Citadel lore and trivia which grew out of the tradition of upperclassmen asking "knobs" (freshmen or fourth classmen) questions to enhance their knowledge of The Citadel and "to build esprit de corps."

There are 21 majors and 19 minors offered, with business degrees being the best and most popular. The college is also known for its criminal justice, engineering, and education programs. As you may imagine, it's an extremely intense atmosphere, academically and otherwise. You have to work hard for your grades; no one's going to hold your hand. Most cadets report that there's a lot of pressure—coming from within and from without—to excel. Graduates proudly wear their hard-earned Citadel rings, which certainly have opened more than a few doors.

Campus Environment

All students live in the dorms (barracks) as "citizen-soldiers." Residences are coed and integrated with cadets of all classes. Campus life is regimented from "Reveille" to "Taps." Cadets must sport the standard haircut, ensure their shoes are always shined, and don a uniform nearly all the time. ("Civilian clothes" are allowed only when departing for or returning from furlough or on special occasions such as a job interview.) There are specified study periods, SMIs (Saturday morning inspections), and countless drills and pushups. Life isn't easy, particularly during the first year spent as a lowly knob, but we hear it does improve as students move through the classes.

The picturesque campus, located on a piece of land near the Ashley River, features 27 buildings surrounding a large grass parade ground. Freshmen are not permitted to have cars, but the campus is easy to navigate on foot and the school is located in a "walking city." Charleston is a beautiful, historic town with much to offer its guests. For its part, Charleston reveres The Citadel and considers it one of its foremost assets.

Student Life

As an institution dedicated to serve the citizens of the area, The Citadel mainly attracts students from the South, and approximately half of each entering class hails from South Carolina in particular. The female population is slowly growing; there are about 100 women in the Corps of Cadets today. It's still a male-dominated environment, however, and even though women have been present at The Citadel since 1996 and sexual harassment and discrimination are officially prohibited, it's not as if they roll out the welcome mat for females. However, the college is eager to point out that women command two of its companies, and that the women's athletic program has significantly increased its offerings—from zero to seven NCAA teams in just five years—and a new women's athletic facility is nearing completion. Half of all female cadets are varsity athletes, many playing more than one sport. As for the men, athletics are hugely popular: nearly every male cadet plays on one team or another. There are nine intercollegiate men's teams, 15 club sports, and 25 IMs.

Let's face it, students don't come here to party. (Citadel literature even puts quotation marks around the phrase "free time.") Dating is difficult—only seniors, for example, may bring a date to a Bulldog football game. Most cadets look to sports and campus organizations for socializing. Military societies are quite popular, of course, as are choral groups. All major religions are represented on campus, and, given The Citadel's emphasis on moral fortitude, it's not surprising that religious organizations report decent memberships. Most students volunteer in the community, whether it be cleaning up the beaches, working with Habitat for Humanity, or mentoring local youth through the Bulldog-Bullpup Program. Charleston is a great town to live and play in, and when cadets are granted weekend leave, there are plenty of local options to keep them busy. There are bars, restaurants, cultural venues, festivals, golf courses, and beaches, plus several area schools to go to for "more traditional" college fun.

The Citadel is steeped in tradition—even the uniforms are reminiscent of the Civil War. Indeed, school officials can't even list all the unique traditions for us, as "there are too many." Parades are certainly the most obvious, and a popular tourist attraction. Touted as "the best free show in Charleston," Citadel parades occur most Friday afternoons during the school year on the parade ground of Summerall Field. It's quite an experience, seeing and hearing hundreds of cadets proudly marching, shouting, and bearing arms.

Costs (2003–04)

Tuition and Fees, In-State: $4,999

Tuition and Fees, Out-of-State: $13,410

Room & Board: $4,778

THE EXPERTS SAY...

" This Southern military college has many of the benefits of West Point without the military service obligation. "

" After classes and homework (a lot of it), there's marching, drilling, and preparing your room for inspection. After that, you get to recite 'Knob Knowledge' to a cadet first class. If you value your free time, don't come to The Citadel. "

Inst. Aid (est. 2003–04)

Institutional Aid, Need-Based: $1,743,977

Institutional Aid, Non-Need-Based: $1,921,476

FT Undergrads Receiving Aid: 51% Avg. Amount per Student: $7,992

FT Undergrads Receiving Non-Need-Based Scholarship or Grant Aid: 8% Avg. Amount per Student: $7,438

Of Those Receiving Any Aid:

Rec. Need-Based Scholarship or Grant Aid: 72% Average Award: $4,980

Rec. Need-Based Self-Help Aid: 69% Average Award: $5,000

Upon Graduation, Avg. Loan Debt per Student: $14,396

Financial Aid Deadline: rolling, 2/28 (priority)

Graduates

Going to Graduate School: 27% Within One Year

Accepting Job Offer: 75% at time of graduation

Companies Recruiting On Campus: 92

CITY UNIVERSITY OF NEW YORK— BARUCH COLLEGE

One Bernard Baruch Way Box H-0720, New York, NY 10010-5585
Admissions Phone: (646) 312-1400 Fax: (646) 312-1361
Email: admissions@baruch.cuny.edu Website: www.baruch.cuny.edu

General Info

Type of School: public, coed
Setting: urban
Academic Calendar: semester

Student Body

Full-Time Undergrads: 8,985
  Men: 45%, Women: 55%

Part-Time Undergrads: 3,237
  Men: 38%, Women: 62%

Total Undergrad Population:
  African American: 15%
  Asian American: 26%
  Latino: 18%
  Native American: <1%
  Caucasian: 32%
  International: 9%
  Out-of-State: 3%
  Living Off-Campus: 100%
  In Fraternities: 10%
  In Sororities: 10%

Graduate and First-Professional
  Students: 2,664

Academics

Full-Time Faculty: 473

Part-Time Faculty: 522

Student/Faculty Ratio: 17:1

Most Popular Majors:
  finance (24%)
  accounting (20%)
  STA/CIS (19%)
  marketing (15%)
  management (10%)

Freshmen Retention Rate: 89%

Graduation Rates:
  18% within four years
  52% within six years

Admissions

Regular Application Deadline: 4/1;
  3/1 (priority)

Early Decision Deadline(s): 12/13,
  1/7

Early Action Deadline: 12/15

Fall Transfer Deadline: 3/1,
  2/1 (priority)

Spring Transfer Deadline: 11/1,
  10/1 (priority)

Total # of Students Applied: 9,446
  Admitted: 3,425
  Enrolled: 1,674

Inside the Classroom

Baruch College grads get into the best M.B.A. programs and often outearn peers that attend private schools—and all for a low public school price. Baruch ranks among the top colleges for the number of its graduates who serve as senior executives of America's major corporations. *Money* magazine listed Baruch among the top 20 nonresidential colleges nationwide, and Baruch tied Harvard University in 1999 in *Accounting Today*'s "100 most influential people in accounting" for graduates with bachelor's degrees.

Baruch is one of the senior, more selective schools of the City University of New York (CUNY). Its strengths are accounting and business. Eighty-five percent of its students major in business subjects; although a full range of liberal arts majors are available, these are largely geared to the business world. Baruch has three schools: the Zicklin School of Business, the largest collegiate school of business in the nation; the Mildred and George Weissman School of Arts and Sciences, which offers interdisciplinary programs such as business journalism and corporate communications; and the School of Public Affairs, founded in 1994, which also offers a B.S. in real estate.

Accounting, computer information systems, and marketing are the most popular majors. Core requirements include courses in communication, quantitative skills, humanities, natural sciences, and social sciences. Additional coursework in mathematics, economics, foreign languages, and statistics is required for the Bachelor of Business Arts (B.B.A.) degree. Combined degree programs include preparation for the CPA exam and a five-year M.S. in accountancy. Classes are offered at night and on weekends to accommodate working students. Workload, reports a junior, "is reasonable given that a lot of the students here have part-time and even full-time jobs."

Baruch faculty combine academic credentials with significant real-world business experience. Says a finance major: "We have professors that teach at Columbia and NYU that teach exactly the same course at Baruch. Same text and everything, but our credits are probably one-quarter the price of either of these schools." However, with nearly 13,000 undergrads and a student-faculty ratio of 17:1, it can be hard to get to know your professors, or even your TA. A junior comments, "There is hardly any accessibility to professors outside of class and maybe two hours a week during conference hours... Fortunately, we have some professors that are amazing." Instructional facilities are high-tech and include a simulated Wall Street trading environment. Career development is excellent, and internships are often lucrative; the Black and Latino Alumni Association is an active source for minority students.

"The students frown upon the administration for their inability to do anything remotely out of their way for the students," gripes a student. "We have so much red tape to go through it's ridiculous." Thumbs are down for "the registration process, anyone that works in the Registrar's office, elevators that never, ever work!" but up for "location, affordability, and good solid education for business majors."

Campus Environment

Baruch's facilities are clustered between East 22nd and 25th Streets in the upscale Gramercy Park section of Manhattan. A finance major comments, "There is no campus, really, which limits any type of socializing to club hours, which are once a week." To compensate, Baruch College's "Vertical Campus" opened for classes August 2001. The 17-story building is a series of stacked atriums which substitute for traditional college quads (a dramatic glass curtain offers views of Lower Manhattan) and houses hundreds of classrooms, a three-level sports center, a 500-seat auditorium, a food court, and a bookstore. Across the street is Baruch's William and Anita Newman Library, named the best college library in the country by the Association of College and Research Libraries (ACRL).

Baruch is nonresidential and the school is of little help in locating off-campus housing. "If you want an apartment near Baruch, you should be willing to shell out at least $1,200 [a month]," a student advises, "And that's the size of a closet." And: "Don't bring a car, parking is ridiculous." However, the school is close to many subway and bus lines, Penn Station, and Grand Central Terminal, making it a convenient commute from the five boroughs and their suburbs.

Student Life

Baruch's being a commuter school does affect the social atmosphere. A majority of the students are there to receive their degrees and aren't particularly interested in socializing, or have jobs and can't. But people do manage to meet one another in the student centers and the libraries, or in one of the more than 100 clubs, which include *The Ticker* (the undergraduate student newspaper paper), the Accounting Society, Hillel, the Asia Cultural Association, and the Caribbean Students Society.

Enthuses a junior, "The school is at the center of everything. Anything and everything that is interesting can be seen either by walking or taking the train a few stops." "Students spend their time drinking in bars, going to the movies, shows (since we can get student tickets on Broadway), and museum hopping," we're told. "We have great bars right around the corner from our library; people don't get trashed at school, we go across the street. People do drugs, but most of the students don't seem to be crackheads that go to Baruch."

There are no fraternities or sororities, but there are honor societies such as Beta Alpha Psi for accounting and Beta Gamma Sigma for business. Baruch's Vertical Campus is home to the ARC (Athletics and Recreation Complex), a state-of-the-art facility opened in 2002. The College has 12 varsity teams; 700-plus students participate in intramural sports, but a student says the latter are "not encouraged."

U.S News and World Report has ranked Baruch College the most diverse school in the nation. A substantial number of students are 25 or older; many are the first in their families to attend college. The Baruch Volunteer Income Tax Assistance (VITA) team annually pitches in to help New Yorkers with their taxes, especially in underserved immigrant areas, since many Baruch students are bilingual and the children of recent immigrants. While the vast majority are New York staters, a junior explains, "Baruch is as much a cultural melting pot as New York City is. There are young people, old people, rich people (international students), poor people, everything."

Other schools to check out: CUNY Brooklyn College, Hofstra, SUNY Buffalo, SUNY Stony Brook, Wagner.

\# Applied Early Decision: 22
Early Decision Admitted: 3

Test Scores (middle 50%):
SAT Verbal: 460–570
SAT Math: 520–630

HS Rank of Entering Freshmen:
Top 10%: 22%
Top 25%: 52%
Top 50%: 82%

Avg. HS GPA: 3.0

THE EXPERTS SAY...

" Baruch is the second most selective campus for under-graduate admissions among public schools in New York State (after the U.S. Military Academy at West Point) and fifth among all New York institutions (after Juilliard, Cooper Union, and Columbia). "

" The Baruch Bearcats? Don't they mean the Baruch Bureaucrats? "

Costs (est. 2003-4):

Tuition and Fees, In-State: $4,300

Tuition and Fees, Out-of-State: $8,940

Payment Plan(s): installment plan, deferred payment plan

Inst. Aid (est. 2003–04)

Institutional Aid, Need-Based: $644,000

Institutional Aid, Non-Need-Based: $1,339,550

FT Undergrads Receiving Aid: 76%
Avg. Amount per Student: $4,930

FT Undergrads Receiving Non-Need-Based Scholarship or Grant Aid: 7%
Avg. Amount per Student: $1,800

Of Those Receiving Any Aid:

Rec. Need-Based Scholarship or Grant Aid: 92%
Average Award: $4,300

Rec. Need-Based Self-Help Aid: 45%
Average Award: $3,700

Upon Graduation, Avg. Loan Debt per Student: $10,100

Financial Aid Deadline: 4/30, 3/15 (priority)

Graduates

Companies Recruiting On-Campus: 350

CITY UNIVERSITY OF NEW YORK— BROOKLYN COLLEGE

2900 Bedford Avenue, Brooklyn, NY 11210-2889
Admissions Phone: (718) 951-5001 Fax: (718) 951-4506
Email: adminqry@brooklyn.cuny.edu Website: www.brooklyn.cuny.edu

General Info

Type of School: public, coed
Setting: urban
Academic Calendar: semester

Student Body

Full-Time Undergrads: 7,665
  Men: 42%, Women: 58%

Part-Time Undergrads: 2,898
  Men: 37%, Women: 63%

Total Undergrad Population:
  African American: 28%
  Asian American: 10%
  Latino: 11%
  Native American: <1%
  Caucasian: 45%
  International: 5%
  Out-of-State: 1%
  Living Off-Campus: 100%
  In Fraternities: 2%
  In Sororities: 2%

Graduate and First-Professional
  Students: 4,553

Academics

Full-Time Faculty: 509
  With Ph.D.: 91%

Part-Time Faculty: 444

Student/Faculty Ratio: 13:1

Most Popular Majors:
  business management and
    finance (15%)
  education (7%)
  accounting (6%)
  psychology (5%)
  computer information science (5%)

Completing 2 or More Majors: 1%

Freshmen Retention Rate: 84%

Graduation Rates:
  14% within four years
  39% within six years

Admissions

Regular Application Deadline: 3/1
  (priority)

Total # of Students Applied: 7,128
  Admitted: 2,595
  Enrolled: 1,349

Test Scores (middle 50%):
  SAT Verbal: 460–570
  SAT Math: 480–580

Inside the Classroom

A part of the City University of New York, the nation's leading public urban university system, Brooklyn College offers "a superior education at a low cost," a college official says. She's right: Brooklyn College undergrads may choose from nearly 100 programs, with economics, computer and information science, speech communication arts and sciences, psychology, education, and film, television, and radio being among the most popular majors. Brooklyn's professors are perhaps the school's strongest feature; many have impressive credentials. Regularly included on the staff are Pulitzer Prize–winners, world-famous researchers, and internationally known artists and composers. "Three alumni and a professor have close connections to 31 of this year's Academy Award nominations," we're told. The alumni list is equally as impressive: Michael Lynn (co-chairman and CEO of New Line Cinema), Barbara Boxer (U.S. Senator), Alan Dershowitz (defense attorney and legal scholar), and Jimmy Smits (actor) all have Brooklyn College diplomas.

The nationally renowned core curriculum, instituted in 1981, is comprised of a 14-course foundation program "that offers a comprehensive overview of a variety of subjects [such as art, Western culture, computer programming, literature, political science, philosophy, and the life sciences] and provides a broad background in the liberal arts and sciences," according to the school. There is a foreign-language requirement as well. Some students gripe about the rigorous curriculum, but overall, Brooklyn undergrads tend to be serious about their studies. Students have the opportunity to distribute their core coursework over three years in order to immediately sign up for classes in their major or for some electives. Even freshmen can take classes in their major field. Indeed, the college helps first-year students jump right in with its award-winning Freshman Year College, "designed to help new students make the transition to college life by offering advisement, support services, and specially designated course sections for first-time freshmen," says a school official. The On-Course Advantage is a fast-track program for academically strong first-year students who are "willing to commit to full-time study to accelerate their progress towards graduation."

Exceptional students may reap the benefits of the Honors Academy, with its bevy of special programs, including the CUNY Honors College, the Scholars Program, the B.A.-M.D. program (through which students are guaranteed entrance to the SUNY Downstate College of Medicine), Dean's List Honors Research program, the Mellon Minority Fellowship, the Engineering Honors Program, and MARC, a program in the sciences for minority students.

Campus Environment

Brooklyn College's 26-acre, tree-lined campus, with its Georgian-style buildings and large, green quad, is considered one of the most attractive urban campuses in the country. (Interesting factoid: The present Midwood campus was built in 1930 "on the former circus ground for the Barnum & Bailey Circus," we're told. Perhaps this is par for the course at a campus that's infested with parakeets—yes, parakeets in Brooklyn. If you look up at the lights and utility poles on campus, you'll see a colony of wild South American Monk Parakeets that have established residence there.) There is no on-campus housing, so between classes, students hang out at SUBO, the seven-story student union building offering a panoramic view of New York City as well as pool and ping-pong tables, video games, TVs, a study lounge, and a computer lab. In addition to extensive recreational and athletic resources, Brooklyn students take advantage of a 150-workstation microcomputer lab, a dining complex featuring a kosher dairy bar, a radio production facility, and fine arts and performing arts facilities, including a television studio.

The college has embarked on a major capital improvement program; in the last decade, it has secured more than $275 million in funding from the state. A good portion of this money has gone to expand and renovate the library, a $72 million wonder that's the largest and "most technologically advanced" library in the CUNY system. The other new facility on campus is the Morton and Angela Topher Library Café, a state-of-the-art facility that's open 24/7 for students "to browse the World Wide Web, complete online assignments, plug in a laptop, or have a cup of Starbucks coffee and a bite to eat," the school says.

As for the off-campus environment, Brooklyn College is "less urban" than some of its CUNY brethren. A multitude of stores, eateries, bars, clubs, and cultural venues are within reach, and Midtown Manhattan is just 30 minutes away by subway. Students who are wary of wandering the urban neighborhood at night can try to arrange for campus security to escort them to their cars or public transportation. There's also a shuttle van service to a few key transportation points.

Student Life

"The student body represents the cultural and ethnic diversity of the borough of Brooklyn," a school official says, and rather accurately. Students of every race, religion, socioeconomic background, and age (nearly one-third of the student body is older than a "typical" college undergrad) harmoniously gather at Brooklyn College, lending a unique feel to every classroom. Since no one lives on Brooklyn College grounds, and few live in the immediate surroundings, campus is pretty quiet after class. But "Brooklyn College has a vibrant and growing student club body," we're told.

There are more than 150 academic, special interest, and social clubs; four student newspapers; and a student-run radio station. Among the more popular clubs are the CLAS Student Government, the Golden Key International Honor Society, the New York Public Interest Research Group, and various religious (Hillel Club, Newman Center) and cultural (Puerto Rican Alliance, West African Students Association, Dominican Student Movement, Asian Outreach Committee) organizations. Fraternities and sororities, of which there are quite a few, often hold parties at local bars, we hear. Each spring, Volunteer Week gets students, staff, and faculty "to don aprons and get out the gardening tools and paint brushes to spring-clean the campus and surrounding neighborhood." Students also gather for movies, theater performances, art shows, and concerts by well-known and on-campus artists alike.

Brooklyn College's Division III athletic teams include men's soccer and women's softball, and men's and women's tennis, basketball, swimming, volleyball, indoor and outdoor track, and cross country. The intramural program "varies each semester," with such programs as Bowling Night, racquetball, and table tennis being offered in the fall, and Swimfest, Mini Golf Night, chess, and billiards appearing in the spring.

Other schools to check out: CUNY Baruch, SUNY Binghamton, NYU, Hofstra, Wagner.

HS Rank of Entering Freshmen:
Top 10%: 14%
Top 25%: 37%
Top 50%: 69%
Avg. HS GPA: 3.0

Costs (est. 2003-4):

Tuition and Fees, In-State: $4,353
Tuition, Out-of-State: $360 per credit
Payment Plan(s): installment plan

THE EXPERTS SAY...

" Brooklyn College offers a nicer campus, a more active social scene, and more highly regarded bachelor's degree programs than most commuter schools do. "

" Looking for cultural diversity and real-world experience? There are many private liberal arts colleges in the boonies that claim to offer these things, but Brooklyn College is the real deal. "

Inst. Aid (est. 2003–04)

Institutional Aid, Need-Based: $800,000

Institutional Aid, Non-Need-Based: $900,000

FT Undergrads Receiving Aid: 78%
Avg. Amount per Student: $5,400

FT Undergrads Receiving Non-Need-Based Scholarship or Grant Aid: 10%
Avg. Amount per Student: $4,000

Of Those Receiving Any Aid:

Rec. Need-Based Scholarship or Grant Aid: 91%
Average Award: $3,300

Rec. Need-Based Self-Help Aid: 89%
Average Award: $2,200

Upon Graduation, Avg. Loan Debt per Student: $13,500

Financial Aid Deadline: rolling, 4/1 (priority)

Graduates

Going to Graduate School: 39% Within One Year

Companies Recruiting On Campus: 115

CITY UNIVERSITY OF NEW YORK—
JOHN JAY COLLEGE OF CRIMINAL JUSTICE

445 West 59th Street, New York, NY 10019-1128
Admissions Phone: (212) 237-8865 Fax: (212) 237-8777
Email: admiss@jjay.cuny.edu Website: www.jjay.cuny.edu

General Info

Type of School: public, coed
Setting: urban
Academic Calendar: semester

Student Body

Full-Time Undergrads: 8,412
  Men: 37%, Women: 63%

Part-Time Undergrads: 2,875
  Men: 43%, Women: 57%

Total Undergrad Population:
  African American: 28%
  Asian American: 5%
  Latino: 37%
  Caucasian: 28%
  International: 2%
  Living Off-Campus: 100%

Graduate and First-Professional
Students: 1,517

Academics

Full-Time Faculty: 322
  With Ph.D.: 76%

Part-Time Faculty: 500

Most Popular Majors:
  criminal justice (20%)
  police science (16%)
  forensic psychology (15%)
  legal studies (7%)
  forensic science (7%)

Freshmen Retention Rate: 74%

Graduation Rates:
  13% within four years
  36% within six years

Admissions

Regular Application Deadline: 1/1
  (priority)

Total # of Students Applied: 5,750
  Admitted: 4,137
  Enrolled: 2,261

Test Scores (middle 50%):
  SAT Verbal: 430–530
  SAT Math: 420–520

John Jay may have an inside track into what may be the next hot academic major: terrorism studies. Applications to Jay are up since 9/11 as more students become interested in careers in the F.B.I., Secret Service, the INS, security management, and the uniformed services. Traditionally a training ground for police and fire personnel looking to climb the ranks, Jay has plans to significantly expand its curriculum, adding courses in bioterrorism and terrorist literature, and beefing up current offerings in toxicology, terrorist groups, and risk management. A recent conference hosted by the college, the Urban Hazards Forum, had topics like Nuclear Terror in Urban Areas, Mind of a Terrorist, Hostage Taking, and Chemical and Biological Terrorism.

Founded in 1964, John Jay is one of the senior colleges of the City University of New York (CUNY). Designed to graduate practitioners rather than theorists, the school is becoming known for its forensics courses and its deviant behavioral psychology program. Majors are offered in computer information systems in criminal justice and public administration, correctional studies, criminal justice, criminology, deviant behavior and social control, fire science, fire and emergency services, forensic psychology, forensic science, government, international criminal justice, judicial studies, legal studies, police studies, public administration, and security management. Freshmen get to sample majors and meet professors workshops during the Freshmen Forum.

John Jay has a new center wholly dedicated to cybercrime ranging from worms to child pornography to Internet fraud, as well as a criminal justice center that provides consultation and training to professionals. There are exchange programs with Bramshill Police Command College in the United Kingdom, and in An Garda Siochana, Ireland. Career services are good, with an active career development center on campus.

Despite its dedication to criminal justice, Jay is a liberal arts school with the traditional general education requirements, which include English, speech and mathematics, history, literature, philosophy, ethnic studies, social sciences, fine arts, natural sciences, and physical education (phys ed requirements can be satisfied by police or fire academy programs). As part of the CUNY system, John Jay is one of 20 colleges in a massive and often frustrating bureaucracy, and problems with the central administration are common. Class sizes can be large, and professors sometimes inaccessible. However, with 110 students and alumni killed in the World Trade Center attacks, many involved in rescue efforts, education at Jay has taken on a new meaning. Course content across the curriculum reflects a new urgency and sense of responsibility as students train to become leaders in crime prevention, threat management, and emergency response.

Campus Environment

John Jay is located on Tenth Avenue and West 59th Street in Manhattan. The neighborhood once known as "Hell's Kitchen" is mixed: posh Lincoln Center is a stone's throw away, as are complexes of low income housing. There is no central campus: Jay's facilities are separated by busy New York streets, with a major New York hospital dominating its landscape. While the facilities are not attractive, they seem to

KAPLAN

suit the tough-minded John Jay students, most of whom are preparing to deal with the grittier side of life anyway.

Jay does not provide housing for students, nor is it much help in finding apartments. There is limited space available at Long Island University in Brooklyn, and a few apartments in the campus neighborhood, although the housing quality of affordable digs is not considered the best. Most students commute from the greater New York area, using the many subway lines of the nearby Columbus Circle Station to take them to and from school and into the greater city.

Student Life

Being an urban commuter school puts a crimp into campus social life. Most of John Jay's 11,000 students are at the school to train for their professions in criminal justice; many work or have family responsibilities, and most have little time for socializing. There is no social scene on weekends. However, there is a professional camaraderie among students that gives the campus some cohesion, and students hook up in study groups, at the library, and at nearby coffee shops.

The John Jay student body is multicultural and diverse, and economically mixed. There's a large percentage of first-generation college students. The average John Jay student is athletic, often for professional rather than recreational reasons. The college competes in varsity teams and clubs in cross country, soccer, tennis, volleyball, basketball, rifle, swimming, baseball, softball, karate, judo, Tae Kwon Do, and track and field. Like many native New Yorkers, John Jay students might be too busy or blasé to take advantage of the cultural attractions of New York, but they are always available. Shopping, Central Park, hundreds of restaurants, and miles of riverside track for biking, blading, and jogging are just nearby the school.

The central recent event for most Jay students has been 9/11. Students, faculty, and staff wrote a play called "What Happened: The September 11 Testimony Project," based on collected oral histories to commemorate the event. The school's extensive counseling network has a photograph of the Twin Towers on its website, helping students deal with the personal loss of classmates and friends. Most John Jay students deal with the trauma, however, by rededicating themselves to the professions on the front lines.

Costs (2003–04)

Tuition and Fees, In-State: $4,259

Tuition and Fees, Out-of-State: $8,899

Payment Plan(s): installment plan, deferred payment plan

THE EXPERTS SAY...

" Feeling patriotic? John Jay can train you for the F.B.I., Secret Service, or a police detective's shield. And the school has new courses that address the how-to of fighting terrorism. "

" John Jay has a campus only a cop could love. "

Inst. Aid (est. 2003–04)

Institutional Aid, Non-Need-Based: $814,000

FT Undergrads Receiving Aid: 66%
    Avg. Amount per Student: $5,100

Of Those Receiving Any Aid:

Rec. Need-Based Self-Help Aid: 45%
    Average Award: $2,500

Upon Graduation, Avg. Loan Debt per Student: $10,000

Financial Aid Deadline: 6/1 (priority)

Graduates

Going to Graduate School:
    30% Within One Year

Accepting Job Offer:
    72% at time of graduation

CLAREMONT MCKENNA COLLEGE

890 Columbia Avenue, Claremont, CA 91711
Admissions Phone: (909) 621-8088 Fax: (909) 621-8516
Email: admission@claremontmckenna.edu Website: www.mckenna.edu
Application Website: www.commonapp.org

General Info

Type of School: private, coed
Setting: suburban
Academic Calendar: semester

Student Body

Full-Time Undergrads: 1,041
  Men: 54%, Women: 46%

Part-Time Undergrads: 9
  Men: 67%, Women: 33%

Total Undergrad Population:
  African American: 4%
  Asian American: 16%
  Latino: 10%
  Native American: 1%
  Caucasian: 66%
  International: 3%
  Out-of-State: 52%
  Living Off-Campus: 4%

Academics

Full-Time Faculty: 137
  With Ph.D.: 94%

Part-Time Faculty: 22
  With Ph.D.: 5%

Student/Faculty Ratio: 8:1

Most Popular Majors:
  economics (19%)
  government (16%)
  international relations (15%)
  sciences (12%)
  psychology (7%)

Completing 2 or More Majors: 52%

Freshmen Retention Rate: 94%

Graduation Rates:
  80% within four years
  86% within six years

Admissions

Regular Application Deadline: 1/2;
  12/20 (priority)

Early Decision Deadline(s): 11/15,
  1/2

Early Action Deadline: 11/1

Spring Transfer Deadline: 4/15
  (priority)

Total # of Students Applied: 2,892
  Admitted: 897
  Enrolled: 284

# of Students Waitlisted: 675
  Students Accepting Place: 275

Applied Early Decision: 182
  Early Decision Admitted: 55

Inside the Classroom

Claremont McKenna is "designed to prepare students for leadership in business, the professions, and government," an admissions counselor tells us. And apparently, it succeeds in its mission: One in eight alumni is a CEO, CFO, or holds a top management or leadership position. The school places strong curricular emphasis on public affairs within a strong liberal arts program. Known for its excellent programs in economics, government, and international relations (though one student complains that, unfortunately, "other areas of study are not as developed as these three"), its joint science department with other members of the Claremont Colleges system is also reputedly excellent.

Unlike most other schools with a preprofessional bent, CMC offers students a high level of individual academic attention. One guidance counselor from California recommends CMC as unique for its "small size and personal attention." Of course, the small student body helps—the student/faculty ratio is only 8:1. With just over 1,000 undergrads, you'll find few large lecture classes. Here, most classes are small—so small, you'll be expected to participate and interact with professors on a regular basis. Professors are "very accessible, within the classroom as well as with office hours," says a junior. It's not unusual to see professors at a campus sporting event or lecture. "Most of my profs put their home numbers on the syllabus, and I've been over to many of their houses for dinner," confirms a senior. With nine research institutes on campus, students often begin collaborating with faculty in their freshman year.

The atmosphere at CMC is academically intense. To guard against grade inflation, grades are awarded on a 12-point scale instead of the typical 4-point scale: A's are equal to 12 grade points, B's are worth 9, C's are worth 6, etc. But this is not a problem for CMCers, who are very focused and driven to achieve, well-read, and determined in their academic goals. In fact, 70 percent of students eventually go on to graduate school. As one student says, "we don't do busy work." While one student tells us there's "quite a hefty workload," another student explains that "the workload is what you want it to be, but if you want to get the grades, you'll be putting the hours in." Even downtime can be intellectually challenging: The typical student likes to engage in political discussions, is outspoken about current events, and, as one student claims, "reads several newspapers before breakfast." That's not to say that students don't relax, though; it's just that they "work hard and play hard."

Campus Environment

CMC can be as large or as small as students want to make it. While the McKenna campus is a compact 50 acres, it is part of the much larger Claremont Colleges system, which makes it feel much bigger. Students can freely take advantage of the facilities, clubs, and social events at the four other participating schools (Pomona, Scripps, Pitzer, and Harvey Mudd).

The McKenna campus itself is very quiet and subdued, at least during the week. But "on weekend evenings, certain parts of campus can get rowdy as parties are going on," reveals a student. Nearly all CMC students live in the 13 residence halls, all of which are mixed with freshmen, sophomores, juniors, and seniors. According to one student, "It's a general consensus that of the five Claremont colleges, CMC has the best dorms."

The campus is compact enough that students can easily walk to wherever they need to go ("most people roll out of bed five minutes before class and still get there on time"), but you'll need to use a car, a bike, or public transportation to get around town. However, "it's not a big deal if you don't" have a car, says one student, who adds that "rides are always available."

The surrounding town of Claremont is considered quaint and "a nice place to get a cup of coffee, but not much more"—a subdued community with many retirees and commuter families. Overall, the entire area is considered extremely safe. And while many students enjoy the weather and proximity to Los Angeles (35 miles), they also complain about the heavy traffic and smog.

Student Life

If there is one complaint that CMC students have, it is regarding the social life. One student reported that the place can get "claustrophobic," and most students do make a point of getting away from Claremont, if only on occasion. The social scene tends to be dominated by the "jocks," and as there's no Greek system, parties on campus tend to be small. Students tell us that "drinking is huge" at weekend parties, but drugs are not at all a factor.

Sports are hugely popular at CMC—nearly one-third of students play a varsity sport, and nearly two-thirds play an intramural sport. "For a game against a rival school, you'll get most of the school out cheering," says one student. Additionally, as most students are civic-minded and politically aware, the model UN club, debate team, and summer internships are popular; the school also sponsors a one-semester internship in Washington D.C.

A significant portion of the student body comes from California, and though the school isn't as well-known in the East, it does attract students from across the country and throughout the world. "There's a whole range of students here in terms of conservatives and liberals, although conservative voices are louder," a student reports. The school also draws a large number of Asians and Latinos, resulting in an unusually diverse student body for such a small college. "Pretty much everyone fits in at CMC," says a junior. "The only student who might not enjoy it would be someone who's looking for a huge, loud, university-like atmosphere."

Though located in trendy California, CMC has some quaint traditions, such as tea being served every weekday from 3:00–4:30 ("besides tea, they have Rice Krispie treats, chocolate-covered strawberries, and lots of cool snacks, all made by our in-house pastry chef"). And the admissions office tells us about another tradition: "On a person's birthday, they are 'ponded' in one of our fountains on campus."

Other schools to check out: Pomona, Williams, Georgetown, University of Pennsylvania, Stanford.

Test Scores (middle 50%):
SAT Verbal: 670–740
SAT Math: 670–740
ACT Comp: 28–31

HS Rank of Entering Freshmen:
Top 10%: 84%
Top 25%: 95%
Top 50%: 100%

THE EXPERTS SAY...

" If you're considering Georgetown, take a look at CMC's economics, government, and international relations programs. "

" If you don't enjoy political debate or getting 'ponded,' you won't be happy here. "

Costs (2003–04)

Tuition and Fees: $27,700

Room & Board: $9,180

Payment Plan(s): installment plan, deferred payment plan, pre-payment plan

Inst. Aid (est. 2003–04)

Institutional Aid, Need-Based: $10,785,015

Institutional Aid, Non-Need-Based: $470,650

FT Undergrads Receiving Aid: 56%
Avg. Amount per Student: $23,920

FT Undergrads Receiving Non-Need-Based Scholarship or Grant Aid: 9%
Avg. Amount per Student: $5,620

Of Those Receiving Any Aid:

Rec. Need-Based Scholarship or Grant Aid: 100%
Average Award: $20,446

Rec. Need-Based Self-Help Aid: 40%
Average Award: $3,767

Upon Graduation, Avg. Loan Debt per Student: $14,500

Financial Aid Deadline: 2/1, 1/1 (priority)

Graduates

Going to Graduate School:
25% Within One Year

Accepting Job Offer:
60% at time of graduation

Companies Recruiting On Campus:
180

Alumni Giving: 95%

CLARK UNIVERSITY

950 Main Street, Worcester, MA 01610
Admissions Phone: (508) 793-7431 (in-state); (800) GO-CLARK (out-of-state)
Fax: (508) 793-8821 Email: admissions@clarku.edu Website: www.clarku.edu
Application Website: www.clarku.edu/prospective/undergrads/

General Info

Type of School: private, coed
Setting: urban
Academic Calendar: semester

Student Body

Full-Time Undergrads: 1,994
  Men: 39%, Women: 61%

Part-Time Undergrads: 81
  Men: 40%, Women: 60%

Total Undergrad Population:
  African American: 3%
  Asian American: 4%
  Latino: 3%
  Caucasian: 65%
  International: 7%
  Out-of-State: 63%
  Living Off-Campus: 33%

Graduate and First-Professional
  Students: 817

Academics

Full-Time Faculty: 167
  With Ph.D.: 98%

Part-Time Faculty: 108

Student/Faculty Ratio: 10:1

Most Popular Majors:
  psychology (19%)
  government and international
    relations (10%)
  biology (7%)
  history (7%)
  communication and culture (7%)

Completing 2 or More Majors: 11%

Freshmen Retention Rate: 85%

Graduation Rates:
  60% within four years
  67% within six years

Admissions

Regular Application Deadline: 2/1

Early Decision Deadline(s): 11/15

Fall Transfer Deadline: 4/15

Spring Transfer Deadline: 11/1

Total # of Students Applied: 3,950
  Admitted: 2,488
  Enrolled: 541

# of Students Waitlisted: 160
  Students Accepting Place: 60
  Waitlisted Students Admitted: 8

Applied Early Decision: 78
  Early Decision Admitted: 55

Inside the Classroom

Free thinkers are the end product of Clark, a small school in Worcester, Massachusetts that respects its students' opinions of what their education should be. In fact, according to its website, "undecided" is the most popular major of the student body because the school allows students to sample the various disciplines without declaring a major until the end of sophomore year. According to one student, "A friend who visited once described it as 'magical.' It's a place where students are free to be individuals, to think, and to challenge convention."

Clark is unusually humanistic for a research-oriented school. A California college admissions counselor loves the fact that "'numbers' aren't the only criteria for acceptance … [they] really examine student potential." A Massachusetts guidance counselor recommends Clark for the "impact" it can make on students' lives and for the grants it gives to qualified students "who have lived in the neighborhood for at least five years prior."

Psychology is a particularly strong department here, owing to the school's heavy emphasis on research and its early connections with Sigmund Freud, who is immortalized with a statue on campus. The first I.Q. tests in the United States were developed here, and the first person to begin a study by dropping a rat into a maze was a graduate student at Clark. Originally founded as a research school, Clark still recognizes the importance of research in academic pursuits and gives its undergrads plenty of opportunities to participate. Research is also a prime reason why some guides rank Clark's geography program number one in the nation. Another reason is that more Ph.D.s in geography have been earned from Clark than from any other school in the nation.

The core of each degree is a flexible Program of Liberal Studies that includes coursework in broad areas of the liberal arts. Categories include perspectives on aesthetics, comparative studies, history, language and culture, natural science, and values. An interesting option for students is the International Studies Stream, in which students can enhance their degree program with an international perspective through courses, internships, and study abroad.

The options available to students aren't limited to those on campus: Clark is a member of the Worcester College Consortium, a group of 14 schools in the area that share resources and facilities. Clark students can share in other schools' libraries, and after their freshman year they may register for one course per semester at another consortium member school.

Campus Environment

Clark's campus is cheek-by-jowl with the rest of Worcester, which doesn't seem to inspire student affection. According to one student, "Clark is really squashed into the surrounding neighborhood … not the best neighborhood, but I've seen worse. There isn't a single inch of space to build anything new on campus, except maybe a large phallic symbol dedicated to Freud." Another student grumbles, "We may have 12 other colleges in the area, but Worcester is not a college town."

All students at Clark must live on campus for their first two years, with the majority of freshmen living in Wright and Bullock Halls. Most of the other six halls have standard, double-occupancy rooms for mixed classes: Dodd Hall is all-female, and the rest are coed by floor, wing, or suite. A number of special-interest houses are also available for students who prefer, for example, a quiet living environment or an environment of "substance awareness."

Much of the campus is arrayed around or near the Campus Square, where the statue of Freud can be seen. The square is a favorite student hangout between classes. A picturesque part of campus is Woodland Street, which is lined with finely preserved Victorian houses. The street and its surrounding neighborhoods are looked after by a partnership that includes the university, local businesses, residents, churches, and city government.

Student Life

There are no fraternities or sororities at Clark. Alcohol is frowned upon, too, although as one student puts it, "If you and your friends want to party, you will." The small student body means you'll be bumping beers with the same people fairly often, however. Fortunately, school-sponsored social functions, movies, and other small-scale events keep students entertained. Boston is also a fairly short drive away, for special nights when there's no substitute for big-city fun.

Clark students are certainly active: 65 percent of undergraduate students participate in intercollegiate, intramural, club, wellness, and recreational programs. Varsity squads are known as the Cougars, with teams for both sexes including crew, soccer, basketball, swimming, diving, and tennis. Sports for men include baseball and lacrosse, while sports for women include field hockey, tennis, volleyball, and softball. In recent years the basketball teams for both sexes earned the right to participate in NCAA Division III national tournaments. Student activities and clubs are also popular, especially the Clark Bars, an a cappella group that has released CDs of its performances.

One event that's looked forward to on campus is the annual Academic Spree Day in mid-spring. A mix of academic showcasing and social fun, Academic Spree Day serves as a celebration of undergraduates' research and creative work. Papers are presented, panel discussions are held, music is listened to, art is exhibited, and spring is enjoyed by all.

Test Scores (middle 50%):
SAT Verbal: 550–660
SAT Math: 540–640
ACT Comp: 22–27

HS Rank of Entering Freshmen:
Top 10%: 30%
Top 25%: 69%
Top 50%: 96%

Avg. HS GPA: 3.41

THE EXPERTS SAY...

" Clark's psychology program commands national respect, and its research opportunities are unheard of for such a small school. "

" If you're in the Boston area checking out the big-name colleges, swing by Clark's campus to learn more about this hidden treasure. "

Costs (2003–04)

Tuition and Fees: $26,965
note: tuition discount for students from local area

Room & Board: $5,150

Payment Plan(s): installment plan, pre-payment plan

Inst. Aid (est. 2003–04)

Institutional Aid, Need-Based: $14,845,235

Institutional Aid, Non-Need-Based: $6,977,244

FT Undergrads Receiving Aid: 60%
Avg. Amount per Student: $23,136

FT Undergrads Receiving Non-Need-Based Scholarship or Grant Aid: 8%
Avg. Amount per Student: $12,056

Of Those Receiving Any Aid:

Rec. Need-Based Scholarship or Grant Aid: 99%
Average Award: $18,012

Rec. Need-Based Self-Help Aid: 94%
Average Award: $4,991

Upon Graduation, Avg. Loan Debt per Student: $18,375

Financial Aid Deadline: 2/1 (priority)

Graduates

Going to Graduate School:
36% Within One Year

Accepting Job Offer:
21% at time of graduation

Companies Recruiting On Campus:
100

Alumni Giving: 47%

CLEMSON UNIVERSITY

106 Sikes Hall, Clemson, SC 29634-5124
Admissions Phone: (864) 656-2287 Fax: (864) 656-2464
Email: cuadmissions@clemson.edu Website: www.clemson.edu
Application Website: www.clemson.edu/admission/

General Info

Type of School: public, coed
Setting: small town
Academic Calendar: semester

Student Body

Full-Time Undergrads: 12,809
  Men: 55%, Women: 45%

Part-Time Undergrads: 872
  Men: 59%, Women: 41%

Total Undergrad Population:
  African American: 7%
  Asian American: 2%
  Latino: 1%
  Native American: <1%
  Caucasian: 83%
  International: <1%
  Out-of-State: 28%
  Living Off-Campus: 54%
  In Fraternities: 16%
  In Sororities: 30%

Graduate and First-Professional
  Students: 3,203

Academics

Full-Time Faculty: 952
  With Ph.D.: 88%

Part-Time Faculty: 155
  With Ph.D.: 48%

Student/Faculty Ratio: 15:1

Most Popular Majors:
  general engineering (9%)
  business (5%)
  mechanical engineering (4%)
  marketing (4%)
  nursing (3%)

Graduation Rates:
  39% within four years
  72% within six years

Computers: Computer Required

Admissions

Regular Application Deadline: 5/1;
  12/1 (priority)

Total # of Students Applied: 11,419
  Admitted: 6,945
  Enrolled: 2,749

# of Students Waitlisted: 436
  Students Accepting Place: 436
  Waitlisted Students Admitted: 181

Inside the Classroom

Those who think of Clemson University as just a school for football fans and parties may want to take a second look at its impressive academic offerings. Guidance counselors we spoke to raved about this "top-rated public university," pointing out "outstanding" programs in engineering, graphic communications, and architecture, among others. The university offers more than 80 undergraduate degrees through five academic colleges: agriculture, forestry, and life sciences; architecture, arts and humanities; business and behavioral science; engineering and science; and health, education, and human development. More than one-quarter of all undergrads pursue a business degree, often in marketing or management. The school boasts the leading engineering program in South Carolina, and its Department of Food Science (home of the famous Clemson blue cheese) is the only one of its kind in the state.

Clemson is proud of its innovative Communication-Across-the-Curriculum (CAC) program, a teaching method designed to inspire students to be better writers, speakers, thinkers, and problem-solvers. Reportedly, more than half the professors here implement this style in their classrooms. CAC encourages less multiple-choice tests and lectures and more interactive (and practical) learning. Students love this idea—and who wouldn't rather write in a journal or work in groups than fill up a blue book or type a 10-page essay? Clemson continues to emphasize communication skills in its general education requirements. In addition to the standard math, physical/biological science, humanities, and social science requirements, students must take courses in English, oral communication, writing, and computer skills.

Due to the sheer size of the school (more than 13,000 undergrads), it's not surprising that some classes can be quite large and impersonal, especially the intro courses, and apparently, it's getting worse. The student/faculty ratio is 15:1, and although we hear that some professors are more interested in their own research than in teaching, this psychology major has only praise: "Professors always make time for me even if their schedules are just as, if not more hectic than mine."

Campus Environment

Clemson's 1,400-acre campus is situated on a former plantation on the shores of Lake Hartwell, a huge manmade lake that stretches to Georgia. Its beautiful blue waters offer every water sport imaginable. "On clear days or during a sunset when the sky is bluish pink, there is no better place to be," one student gushes. From campus you can also see the spectacular Blue Ridge Mountains.

Clemson is less than three hours from Atlanta, Columbia, and Charlotte. "Most students have cars," we're told, "but that does not mean they are a necessity." Those who don't want to deal with parking—a major gripe—take advantage of the public transportation system, and almost everything is within walking distance: classes, dorms, and downtown restaurants, shops, and bars. Clemson is described as a pure "college town"—friendly, safe, and dedicated to the university. It can be a little boring, though, especially for students who are looking for a more urban way of life.

On campus, there are 21 residence halls and, for upperclassmen, four apartment complexes and the unique "Clemson House." All freshmen must live on campus. The dorms vary in quality and size (just a tip: one hall is nicknamed "The Shoeboxes"), and can be single-sex or coed. "The dorms are not that impressive," one high school guidance counselor tells us. Housing options include the "Tiger Fitness" center, where students have access to exclusive workout facilities, and the First-Year Experience program, which provides activities and resources to help students adjust to college life. "Despite the many new dormitories and on-campus apartments," a senior says, "many students elect to move off-campus." Indeed, over half the student body lives in apartments right in town or a few miles down the road.

Student Life

You'd be hard-pressed to find a school with more school spirit than Clemson. Students and townies love their football team, and during the season the Tigers are foremost in everyone's mind. "Check out the orange tiger paws around the town!" laughs a Georgia guidance counselor. On game day, the campus and the whole town are transformed from a sleepy, "slow pace" city to one packed with students, alumni, fans, and, of course, beer, as thousands pour into the Clemson Memorial Stadium, a.k.a. "Death Valley," one of the 10 largest on-campus stadiums in the country. We hear that the fall often feels like one nonstop party. (Football mania may even help explain Clemson's not-too-impressive four-year graduation rate: We hear that some seniors try to come back for a fifth fall just to get football tickets!) Sports fans have plenty of other cheering opportunities, with 19 varsity sports to root for, including a nationally ranked basketball team and a strong soccer program. Those who'd rather play than watch can participate in excellent intramurals of "nearly every sport." More than 40 sports clubs—including sky diving, sailing, and rugby—complete the exhaustive rec offerings.

Drinking is the main pastime on the weekends and most weeknights. Students party in dorms and frats or head to the local bars. A junior explains, "Downtown Clemson does have bars that students frequent on Thursday nights through the weekend, but they are very strict about underage drinking." About 20 percent of the population go Greek. For less intoxicating activities, students turn to campus for movies, bowling, or a variety of entertainment events and major concerts (U2, OutKast). There are also hundreds of organizations to join. "Pretty much anything you would be interested in doing is offered," one student agrees. As a testament to how sports-crazy Clemson is, behold the wildly popular club IPTAY, which stands for "I Pay Ten a Year." IPTAY is an athletic support group which, in exchange for a donation that goes toward athletic scholarships and building and maintaining campus sports facilities, offers discounts for local businesses and, more importantly, opportunities for better seats at games. "Practically every student is a member," we're told.

Clemson students are a friendly, easygoing bunch. It's a politically conservative campus, and a Southern one—students who aren't from South Carolina generally hail from Georgia or North Carolina. Nearly all of the small minority population is African American. Students generally love their school and the warm family atmosphere here. "Clemson is a family," states one happy undergrad. And Tiger pride runs deep: One South Carolina guidance counselor tells us, "Many generations attend this legacy school."

Test Scores (middle 50%):
 SAT Verbal: 550–630
 SAT Math: 570–660
 ACT Comp: 24–29

HS Rank of Entering Freshmen:
 Top 10%: 42%
 Top 25%: 77%
 Top 50%: 97%

Avg. HS GPA: 3.99

Costs (2003–04)

Tuition and Fees, In-State: $7,144

Tuition and Fees, Out-of-State: $14,742

Room & Board: $5,038

Payment Plan(s): installment plan

THE EXPERTS SAY...

" South Carolina guidance counselors tell us that Clemson's academic reputation has improved lately since their admissions standards have risen. "

" The dorms aren't impressive, but the beautiful scenery and great school spirit keep Clemson students happy. "

Inst. Aid (est. 2003–04)

Institutional Aid, Need-Based: $2,089,170

Institutional Aid, Non-Need-Based: $3,879,889

FT Undergrads Receiving Aid: 43%
 Avg. Amount per Student: $9,405

FT Undergrads Receiving Non-Need-Based Scholarship or Grant Aid: 43%
 Avg. Amount per Student: $6,495

Of Those Receiving Any Aid:

Rec. Need-Based Scholarship or Grant Aid: 31%
 Average Award: $3,331

Rec. Need-Based Self-Help Aid: 60%
 Average Award: $3,636

Upon Graduation, Avg. Loan Debt per Student: $15,125

Financial Aid Deadline: 4/1 (priority)

Graduates

Alumni Giving: 26%

COLBY COLLEGE

4800 Mayflower Hill, Waterville, ME 04901-8848
Admissions Phone: (207) 872-3168; (800) 723-3032 Fax: (207) 872-3474
Email: admissions@colby.edu Website: www.colby.edu
Application Website: www.colby.edu/admissions

General Info

Type of School: private, coed
Setting: small town
Academic Calendar: 4-1-4

Student Body

Full-Time Undergrads: 1,768
  Men: 46%, Women: 54%

Total Undergrad Population:
  African American: 2%
  Asian American: 5%
  Latino: 3%
  Native American: <1%
  Caucasian: 83%
  International: 7%
  Out-of-State: 87%
  Living Off-Campus: 6%

Academics

Full-Time Faculty: 157
  With Ph.D.: 97%

Part-Time Faculty: 45
  With Ph.D.: 69%

Student/Faculty Ratio: 10:1

Most Popular Majors:
  biology (14%)
  English (13%)
  economics (12%)
  government (11%)
  history (8%)

Completing 2 or More Majors: 21%

Freshmen Retention Rate: 93%

Graduation Rates:
  84% within four years
  86% within six years

Admissions

Regular Application Deadline: 1/1

Early Decision Deadline(s): 11/15,
  1/1

Fall Transfer Deadline: 3/1

Spring Transfer Deadline: 12/1

Total # of Students Applied: 4,126
  Admitted: 1,388
  Enrolled: 474

# of Students Waitlisted: 651
  Students Accepting Place: 322
  Waitlisted Students Admitted: 6

Applied Early Decision: 505
  Early Decision Admitted: 201

Inside the Classroom

The liberal arts are alive and well at Colby College, which prides itself on the range and quality of its special study options. The college offers a B.A.degree in 54 majors. The science and premed programs are particularly strong, along with the programs in international studies, government, and economics. Notable alumni include historian and author Doris Kearns Goodwin, historian Alan Taylor, and novelist Annie Proulx.

In 2002, Colby adopted a strategic plan that will guide the expansion of college programs and campus facilities over the coming decade. All Colby undergrads must now complete 128 credits to graduate, up from 120 in the past. Students must fill distribution requirements in six areas: one course each in the arts, historical studies, literature, quantitative reasoning, and social sciences; and two courses (one with a lab component) in natural sciences. Other general education requirements include English comp, foreign language, cultural diversity, and non-credit "wellness" lectures.

Colby's "Jan Plan" was one of the first of its kind in the Northeast, and it soon became all the rage at many other schools. Students devote the month of January to something that interests them but that they may not necessarily have room for in their schedules during the fall and spring semesters—say, learning to play the harpsichord or speaking Russian. While freshmen are limited to the specific January courses offered by Colby, upperclassmen have the options of independent study, internships, or field experience.

Colby has earned national recognition as a leader in research-based learning, and research opportunities for students are abundant. One example: Colby was a founding partner of the Biological Research Infrastructure Network (BRIN), partnering with Jackson Labs and other institutions to advance genomics research and to create research opportunities for Colby students.

More than two-thirds of the student body studies abroad at some point, and Colby is unique in offering entering freshmen the opportunity to study French or Spanish in Europe during their first semester. Another unique study option is Colby's senior scholars program, in which a select group of seniors work independently on a research topic of particular interest and merit.

The spirit of independent work carries through to the regular courses, which average only around 17 students per class, making it "easy to pursue personal interests and work closely with faculty," according to one student. The professors are often cited by students as the best thing about the school: We hear they're totally accessible and sincerely interested in students' goals and concerns.

Campus Environment

Colby's 714-acre campus is considered one of the most beautiful in the nation. The entire campus is a Maine Wildlife Management Area, including the 128-acre Perkins Arboretum and Bird Sanctuary. In September 2002, Colby received the Maine Governor's Award for Environmental Excellence, recognizing a long-term commitment to environmentally friendly practices on campus and its attention to the environment in the curriculum.

While the price for a Colby education looks exorbitant at first glance, it seems more reasonable once you realize the comprehensive fee covers tuition, room, and board. As a "residential college," the school strongly encourages students to live on campus. Except for the Alfond, an apartment complex reserved for seniors, campus residences are not segregated by class year; however, quiet housing and chemical-free housing options are available. Much of the social life centers on the Commons—three small, self-sufficient communities formed out of the 31 residence halls. The Commons make an already close community even closer, providing a family-like atmosphere in which friendships are quickly and easily formed. (Or, as some students put it, the Commons setup is perfect for big parties.) The food is "above average," and many faculty members drop in at the Commons, eating meals and mingling with students.

As far as Waterville, Maine, is concerned, students regard it as quaint and safe, but none too thrilling. Having a car is a good idea, since there's no real public transportation system (though the school runs a jitney to and from town). All students, including freshmen, are allowed to bring their cars; parking permits are required but are free of charge.

Student Life

"Students most likely to thrive at Colby are individuals who are intelligent, curious, independent, and energetic," says a college official. A typical Colby undergrad could be described as a white, progressive New Englander who enjoys study, debate, and outdoor sports. This homogeneity makes for a very "friendly, welcoming atmosphere" on campus. But the administration has made progress toward its goal of creating a more diverse campus community: "In 2002–03, a record number of international students represent[ed] more than 60 countries," says a college official. "Partnering with The Posse Foundation helped us assemble a diverse first-year class." Colby students have taken an active role in championing diversity on campus: In the last year, students have campaigned for multicultural housing and an academic "queer studies" program.

There are no fraternities or sororities (these were abolished in the late '80s), but Colby students are very adept at throwing parties anyway. Although the administration has been cracking down on drinking, we hear that alcohol still flows freely here. But for students looking for other social outlets, there are various school-sponsored events such as dances and concerts, and more than 90 student organizations, including government groups, a radio station, and the Powder and Wig (theater) troupe. About 40 percent of Colby students play on one or more of its 32 varsity teams; all teams compete in Division III, except for alpine and nordic skiing, which are in Division I.

Volunteering is big on this socially aware campus, and on one Saturday in spring, students go out into the community for Colby Cares Day. Colby Cares About Kids (CCAK) is a mentoring program whose goal is to provide a consistent, reliable adult presence in the lives of children. The Oak Institute for the Study of International Human Rights, located on campus, brings a human rights practitioner to campus for a semester-long fellowship involving lectures, research, and writing.

While Maine winters can be harsh, the setting is perfect for outdoor sports, including skiing, white-water rafting, and ice skating. Expeditions and activities are regularly hosted by such student organizations as the Outing Club, Mountaineering Club, and the Colby Woodsmen. Students looking for adventure further off-campus head to nearby Bates and Bowdoin, or to Portland, the coast, or the mountains, all about an hour's drive.

Other schools to check out: Bowdoin, Dartmouth, Middlebury, Hamilton, Bates.

Test Scores (middle 50%):
 SAT Verbal: 630–710
 SAT Math: 640–710
 ACT Comp: 27–30
 ACT English: 26–30
 ACT Math: 26–30

THE EXPERTS SAY...

" Strong academic programs in the social sciences, combined with an emphasis on human rights and multiculturalism, make Colby a perfect choice for tomorrow's historians and political activists. "

" Colby students know how to seize the day, giving their all in the classroom, on the playing field, and in their private lives. Not a place for couch potatoes. "

HS Rank of Entering Freshmen:
 Top 10%: 62%
 Top 25%: 90%
 Top 50%: 99%

Costs (2003–04)

Comprehensive Fee: $37,570

Inst. Aid (est. 2003–04)

Institutional Aid, Need-Based:
 $13,488,997

FT Undergrads Receiving Aid: 40%
 Avg. Amount per Student: $24,111

Of Those Receiving Any Aid:

Rec. Need-Based Scholarship or
 Grant Aid: 92%
 Average Award: $22,766

Rec. Need-Based Self-Help Aid: 79%
 Average Award: $3,862

Upon Graduation, Avg. Loan Debt
 per Student: $17,809

Financial Aid Deadline: 2/1

Graduates

Going to Graduate School:
 18% Within One Year

Companies Recruiting On Campus: 47

Alumni Giving: 73%

COLGATE UNIVERSITY

13 Oak Drive, Hamilton, NY 13346
Admissions Phone: (315) 228-7401 Fax: (315) 228-7544
Email: admission@mail.colgate.edu
Website: www.colgate.edu

General Info

Type of School: private, coed

Setting: rural

Academic Calendar: semester

Student Body

Full-Time Undergrads: 2,766
Men: 50%, Women: 50%

Part-Time Undergrads: 2
Men: 100%

Total Undergrad Population:
African American: 4%
Asian American: 5%
Latino: 4%
Native American: <1%
Caucasian: 79%
International: 5%
Out-of-State: 69%
Living Off-Campus: 10%
In Fraternities: 35%
In Sororities: 32%

Graduate and First-Professional
Students: 4

Academics

Full-Time Faculty: 241
With Ph.D.: 97%

Part-Time Faculty: 49
With Ph.D.: 59%

Student/Faculty Ratio: 10:1

Most Popular Majors:
political science (13%)
English (12%)
economics (11%)
sociology/anthropology (8%)
history (7%)

Completing 2 or More Majors: 19%

Freshmen Retention Rate: 96%

Graduation Rates:
84% within four years
89% within six years

Admissions

Regular Application Deadline: 1/15

Early Decision Deadline(s): 11/15

Fall Transfer Deadline: 3/15

Spring Transfer Deadline: 11/1

Total # of Students Applied: 6,789
Admitted: 2,126
Enrolled: 726

Inside the Classroom

The breadth and depth of Colgate's academic programs are unusual for a small liberal arts college. Of the 50 majors offered, programs in the natural sciences and social sciences are particularly strong. Several majors are interdisciplinary, such as Peace Studies, Environmental Economics, and Native American Studies. Colgate also offers an honors program for each concentration. A professor says that most people at Colgate have "two, three, or five passions," and 22 percent of Colgate students are double majors; an additional 28 percent have a major and a minor.

The core curriculum includes a unique four-course general education requirement, taught by faculty members in various disciplines and fields, that includes the study of Western civilization, non-Western culture, and the impact of science and technology on society; a First-Year Seminar serves as an introduction to both college and the liberal arts. Many first-year students take linked courses, in which they study two different subjects together as a group.

Students have terrific things to say about the academic environment at Colgate. "I love the small classes because there is so much individualized attention," says one freshman. Average class size is 19 and the student-faculty ratio is 10:1, and even introductory classes are small. There are no teaching assistants: faculty teach, advise, and mentor students from day one. First-Year Seminar professors serve as advisors until students choose a major and pick a new one. There's also a "Link" system which pairs freshmen with a peer advisor. Students praise their professors for being incredibly accessible and clearly concerned about their students. Career services are excellent due to strong alumni ties. 96 percent of Colgate freshmen return for their sophomore year.

Although Colgate is a university, there are only a handful of graduate students, and the school's focus is unquestionably on its undergrads. Undergraduate research is strongly encouraged, and summer research assistantships are granted to 100 undergrads each year. This funding enables students to work full-time on their own research or on scholarly projects with one or more faculty members. It's not unusual for Colgate students to collaborate on presentations for professional conferences and journal articles.

Fifty-five percent of Colgate students study off-campus, either abroad or in the United States There are 22 semester-long study groups led by professors to Australia, China, India, Japan, Russia, Switzerland, Wales, and Trinidad and Tobago, as well as Santa Fe, Washington, DC, and the National Institutes of Health in Bethesda, among many other locations. Accompanying some courses are month long extension programs in places like South Africa and New York City. Other special programs include the Sea Semester, maritime studies at Mystic Seaport, the Swedish program, and honors programs through Colgate's Center for Ethics and World Societies. Colgate also has its own quarry.

Campus Environment

Don't let the New York state address fool you—Colgate is about as far away from Manhattan's urban mayhem as you can get. The campus offers rich natural beauty (trumpeter swans grace Lake Taylor), but the rural small town of Hamilton offers few amenities for students besides the university-owned Barge Canal coffeehouse, a popular student hangout. One junior reflected, "Colgate is very isolated—the nearest city, Syracuse, is one hour away. The university's isolation focuses everyone's attention on campus life and creates a strong sense of community." Luckily, students are permitted to have a car on campus for all four years, making the occasional weekend trip to Syracuse or even NYC possible.

Nearly all Colgate students live on campus in residence halls or houses. There are a variety of housing options including corridor-style halls, suites, college theme houses such as Ecology House and Harlem Renaissance Center, and fraternities and sororities, although only juniors and seniors are allowed to live in Greek houses. Substance-free housing is also available. All first-year students live "on the hill" near academic buildings and dining halls (when students go "up the hill" at Colgate, they usually mean that they are going to study or to class). Lab facilities at the university are state-of-the art, and *Yahoo! Internet Life* recently rated Colgate as one of the most wired colleges in the nation.

Student Life

Colgate students love the school's location for its beauty and accessibility to outdoor sports, including backpacking and activities on nearby Lake Moraine. Colgate's Outdoor Adventure program draws hundreds of students and freshmen can come to campus early for the Wilderness Adventure orientation. The Greek system remains a major presence here, with more than one-third of the students joining (rush is restricted to sophomores, juniors, and seniors). The Greeks create an active party scene, even though Colgate's reputation as a party school has waned in recent years. Greeks and non-Greeks are compatible here, with people making friends throughout the campus.

After Greek-related events and parties, sports are the activity of choice for most students. Colgate is a charter member of the Patriot League, which leads the NCAA Division I in graduation rates for student athletes, and fields 25 teams; 17 percent of students participate in varsity sports. Colgate's extensive athletic facilities enable students to participate in sports of all kinds, even in the dead of winter, and 80 percent play in 23 intramural and 20 club sports. Other popular campus activities include Comedy Nights in the Pub—Broken Lizard, a Colgate University-bred comedy troupe that the *Village Voice* calls "a sort of Monty Python for the Rolling Rock-and-Pringles set," produced the movie *Super Troopers*. Casino Nights, dance parties, and movies are also popular. There are also more than 100 student clubs.

The school that began with "13 men with 13 dollars and 13 prayers" boasts students that are intellectual, athletic, and outgoing; a guidance counselor calls them "the happiest students in the world." While one-third of the student body is from New York, there's a 16 percent minority population and students from 48 states and 47 countries. One senior described his experience at Colgate in the following way: "It's a small school with a unique culture. The classes are good, the social scene is strong, and the athletic facilities are great. You know everyone on campus and grow together with your peers and professors for the four years you spend here."

Other schools to check out: Bucknell, Lafayette, Lehigh, Hamilton, Dartmouth.

# of Students Waitlisted: 895
  Students Accepting Place: 416
  Waitlisted Students Admitted: 47

Applied Early Decision: 657
  Early Decision Admitted: 357

Test Scores (middle 50%):
  SAT Verbal: 620–710
  SAT Math: 650–720
  ACT Comp: 29–32
  ACT English: 28–33
  ACT Math: 26–32

HS Rank of Entering Freshmen:
  Top 10%: 64%
  Top 25%: 88%
  Top 50%: 100%

Avg. HS GPA: 3.54

THE EXPERTS SAY...

" Colgate is great for students with many interests. The professors really care, and students are really happy. "

" The nearest city is an hour away, and it's Syracuse. No wonder half the students study abroad. "

Costs (2003–04)

Tuition and Fees: $29,940

Room & Board: $7,155

Payment Plan(s): installment plan, pre-payment plan

Inst. Aid (est. 2003–04)

Institutional Aid, Need-Based: $24,767,434

FT Undergrads Receiving Aid: 44%
  Avg. Amount per Student: $25,421

Of Those Receiving Any Aid:

Rec. Need-Based Scholarship or Grant Aid: 95%
  Average Award: $22,956

Rec. Need-Based Self-Help Aid: 73%
  Average Award: $4,064

Upon Graduation, Avg. Loan Debt per Student: $11,104

Financial Aid Deadline: 2/1

Graduates

Going to Graduate School: 16% Within One Year

Companies Recruiting On Campus: 126

Alumni Giving: 52%

COLLEGE OF CHARLESTON

66 George Street, Charleston, SC 29424
Admissions Phone: (843) 953-5670 Fax: (843) 953-6322
Email: admissions@cofc.edu
Website: www.cofc.edu

General Info

Type of School: public, coed

Setting: urban

Academic Calendar: semester, 3-week May interim session

Student Body

Full-Time Undergrads: 8,921
    Men: 36%, Women: 64%

Part-Time Undergrads: 903
    Men: 44%, Women: 56%

Total Undergrad Population:
    African American: 8%
    Asian American: 1%
    Latino: 1%
    Native American: <1%
    Caucasian: 84%
    International: 2%
    Out-of-State: 33%
    Living Off-Campus: 74%
    In Fraternities: 12%
    In Sororities: 17%

Graduate and First-Professional
    Students: 1,712

Academics

Full-Time Faculty: 487
    With Ph.D.: 86%

Part-Time Faculty: 366
    With Ph.D.: 32%

Student/Faculty Ratio: 14:1

Most Popular Majors:
    business administration (13%)
    communication (11%)
    biology (10%)
    psychology (7%)
    elementary education (6%)

Completing 2 or More Majors: 7%

Freshmen Retention Rate: 84%

Graduation Rates:
    36% within four years
    56% within six years

Admissions

Regular Application Deadline: 4/1;
    12/1 (priority)

Early Action Deadline: 11/15

Fall Transfer Deadline: 4/1

Spring Transfer Deadline: 11/1

Total # of Students Applied: 7,606
    Admitted: 4,560
    Enrolled: 1,874

Inside the Classroom

The College of Charleston is the oldest academic institution in South Carolina, the 13th oldest in the nation, and the first municipal college in America. The school was founded in 1770 to promote the liberal arts, and continues that pledge through its demanding core curriculum consisting of required courses in English, history, modern and classical languages, math, science, the arts, and the social sciences. There are five undergraduate schools: arts, business and economics, education, humanities and social sciences, and sciences and mathematics. Its science programs, particularly marine biology, are quite strong; the school enjoys a "close relationship with [nearby] Medical University," where many graduates continue their education. A high school guidance counselor compliments the school's "strong" fine arts program, where students enjoy close working relationships with the local symphony orchestra, art museum, and ballet, and the Spoleto Music Festival.

With about 10,000 undergrads enrolled, the college has classes that range in size but tend to stay small. Most students agree that their professors are "easily accessible." One Honors Program student tells us, "I am often amazed by the quality of the teaching staff here, and feel confident that I will be well prepared for grad school/law school."

The college is academically challenging, but not overwhelmingly so (one student boasts that, in fact, the "workload is pretty easy"). Students are not too competitive or intense, and they like their relatively pressure-free academic environment just fine. A psych major sums it up: "This is the South, it's a liberal arts school near the beach—no one takes themselves that seriously here, even if he or she takes their education seriously."

Campus Environment

"Charleston is the most charming town in the U.S.," one student says proudly. And most of her peers would agree wholeheartedly. People love it here—the Southern hospitality, the history, the food, the culture … and the beach. "Since our institution is located so close to numerous beaches, there is a growing number of students who have interest in the coast, whether it be marine biology or weekend surfers," says one college official.

The "beautiful campus," located in the heart of Charleston, embraces its rich past in the many historic structures that house students and administrators. "It's like walking into the 18th century when you walk onto campus," one student says. The open green space of the Cistern, which provided water for the campus in the 1800s, is the site of graduation, where the men wear white tuxedoes and the women wear white dresses with roses ("it's really quite lovely," we hear). Unfortunately, as one guidance counselor laments, there is "limited dorm space." With only about 2,000 beds, less than one-quarter of all undergrads, mostly freshmen, choose to call the dorms home. All classes are mixed in six "comfortable" residence halls (a seventh hall is upperclassmen only). There are also 22 historic residence houses, typically reserved for upperclassmen only.

Most students opt to live in and around Charleston. Downtown is a very popular and convenient spot; it's "cool but pricey," and the consensus seems to be, if you can afford it, move there. If not, there are many less expensive options outside the city, including beach areas, and the opportunities keep expanding. "There is a lot of urban renewal going on here," a student tells us, "so neighborhoods that today I would not consider living in will be nice, safe, and probably expensive in just a few years." Parking is a universal complaint, and even the school warns: "Due to the nature of downtown Charleston, parking is rather costly." Walking or biking is the transportation of choice.

Student Life

Ask any student to describe his fellow classmates—or the school in general—and you'll probably hear, "laid back." The campus is notoriously friendly and relaxed (when asked to name typical student activities, one undergrad replies, "Most students here like to sleep"). Two-thirds of the student body are South Carolinians, and it's almost 90 percent white. "I would say the campus is split between black and white. You don't see much intermingling," one student tells us. But, she continues, "even if you are a minority, everyone is pretty friendly and welcoming."

Perhaps it's the easygoing, fun-loving atmosphere of the students and the city, but the College of Charleston has quite a reputation for partying. Most students spend their weekends—and most weeknights—with a drink in hand. "There is more partying than studying that goes on here," a senior says. Students hang out at friends' apartments or at one of the many downtown bars. "Everyone has a fake ID and when you're younger there's always keg parties." It's mostly drinking, though we hear that some pot smoking goes on as well. Some students (and certainly the administration) take issue with the "party school" rep, however, saying, "It detracts from the fact that it really is a great school." Indeed, with the majority of students living all over the city, it's a bit difficult to define a typical weekend here. As usual, it depends on your personal social circle. "I think it is easy to avoid the alcohol/drug scene here if you want," a sophomore tells us. If clubs aren't your speed, Charleston offers a wide variety of restaurants, movies, music, art galleries, theaters, and shopping. Students also hit the beach for everything from surfing to sunbathing.

On campus, undergrads run for student government offices, work at the campus newspaper and radio station, participate in leadership programs, or join one of the other 100-plus special-interest clubs and organizations. Greek life is a popular option, with around 15 percent of men and women pledging fraternities and sororities, but students we spoke to say the Greeks don't run the show. "Their influence is definitely limited," one undergrad asserts. The College Activities Board brings various entertainment acts to campus throughout the school year. There are eight men's and eight women's varsity sports, plus a top-rated coed sailing team. Cougars basketball games are far and away the fan favorite; the others "do not have as large a turnout," we hear.

Test Scores (middle 50%):
  SAT Verbal: 560–640
  SAT Math: 560–640
  ACT Comp: 22–25

HS Rank of Entering Freshmen:
  Top 10%: 28%
  Top 25%: 62%
  Top 50%: 93%

Avg. HS GPA: 3.67

THE EXPERTS SAY...

" This great old Southern school has a strong marine biology program, plus an inside track to South Carolina med schools. "

" If students here were any more laid back, they'd fall over. But you won't find a more charming city anywhere. "

Costs (2003–04)

Tuition and Fees, In-State: $5,770

Tuition and Fees, Out-of-State: $13,032

Room & Board: $6,117

Payment Plan(s): installment plan

Inst. Aid (2002–03)

Institutional Aid, Need-Based: $1,119,457

Institutional Aid, Non-Need-Based: $3,689,089

FT Undergrads Receiving Aid: 36%
  Avg. Amount per Student: $8,324

FT Undergrads Receiving Non-Need-Based Scholarship or Grant Aid: 20%
  Avg. Amount per Student: $7,389

Of Those Receiving Any Aid:

Rec. Need-Based Scholarship or Grant Aid: 64%
  Average Award: $2,794

Rec. Need-Based Self-Help Aid: 82%
  Average Award: $3,333

Upon Graduation, Avg. Loan Debt per Student: $15,135

Financial Aid Deadline: rolling, 3/15 (priority)

Graduates

Alumni Giving: 43%

COLLEGE OF NEW JERSEY

Paul Loser Hall 228, P.O. Box 7718, Ewing, NJ 08628-0718
Admissions Phone: (609) 771-2131; (800) 624-0967 Fax: (609) 637-5174
Email: admiss@vm.tcnj.edu Website: www.tcnj.edu
Application Website: www.admissions.tcnj.edu/apply_online.html

General Info

Type of School: public, coed
Setting: suburban
Academic Calendar: semester

Student Body

Full-Time Undergrads: 5,614
  Men: 40%, Women: 60%

Part-Time Undergrads: 324
  Men: 40%, Women: 60%

Total Undergrad Population:
  African American: 6%
  Asian American: 5%
  Latino: 6%
  Caucasian: 78%
  Out-of-State: 5%
  Living Off-Campus: 4%

Graduate and First-Professional
  Students: 973

Academics

Full-Time Faculty: 325
  With Ph.D.: 90%

Part-Time Faculty: 338
  With Ph.D.: 20%

Student/Faculty Ratio: 12:1

Most Popular Majors:
  business general (13%)
  elementary education (9%)
  psychology (9%)
  biology (8%)
  English (8%)

Completing 2 or More Majors: 23%

Freshmen Retention Rate: 95%

Graduation Rates:
  62% within four years
  81% within six years

Admissions

Regular Application Deadline: 2/15

Early Decision Deadline(s): 11/15

Fall Transfer Deadline: 2/15

Spring Transfer Deadline: 11/1

Total # of Students Applied: 6,373
  Admitted: 3,070
  Enrolled: 1,178

# of Students Waitlisted: 217
  Students Accepting Place: 217
  Waitlisted Students Admitted: 98

Applied Early Decision: 508
  Early Decision Admitted: 178

In the Classroom

With a small undergraduate population for a public institution, students at The College of New Jersey get the feel of a smaller private college at the price of a public education. Guidance counselors note that in recent years, TCNJ (formerly Trenton State College) has been increasing its selectivity standards, thus attracting more academically competitive students and, in fact, becoming the top choice for many New Jersey high school seniors. Undergrads may select academic programs from seven schools: Art, Media, and Music; Business; Culture and Society; Education; Engineering; Nursing; and Science. Established in 1855 as a teacher training school, TCNJ's education program is highly respected, and the school now offers over 50 liberal arts and professional programs for students.

All undergraduate classes here are taught by professors, not graduate students, and the classes are generally small. One student tells us, "Unlike most larger colleges and universities, the small class size allows the professors to not only learn the names of every student in the class but also to learn their students' academic patterns and talents." There is no giant lecture class culture in which to hide and avoid participation. A senior explains, "[The] attention to students' individuality leads the classroom at The College of New Jersey to be an intense and competitive place. The intensity stems from the small number of students and allows for strong debate and the ability to show one's professor that one has done the work." "Since certain majors have small enrollments, people within specific majors all come to know each other and turn into a family," says one student. We are told that it's "necessary to complete work and be prepared to express oneself in debate" in class. A student sums up the academic atmosphere of The College of New Jersey: "The faculty pushes students to perform and overall dedication and intelligence of TCNJ students makes the classroom atmosphere one of cooperative learning instead of apathy."

On the downside, a graduating student complains of "the zeal in which the administration foists its pet projects on the students in the General Education department. It seems as though whenever a professor comes up with a 'revolutionary' idea for a class it is implemented and forced upon all majors to suffer through. The administration frowns upon people who feel this way about Gen Ed requirements, as well as those who complain about the parking situation for commuting students."

Campus Environment

And there's reason to complain about parking: "The administration ... sells too many permits and students must constantly fight for parking." TCNJ is rather isolated geographically, positioned in a suburb of Trenton, New Jersey. "A car is key in Ewing if one wants to go anywhere," explains a political science major, "because Mercer County's mass transit system is not very accommodating nor is there anything within walking distance of the college."

We are told by students that "the college lies beside two small lakes and is surrounded by a thick ring of trees that cuts it off from suburban Ewing. This semi-isolation leads to a greater sense of community among the students." Also, "Most students tend to regard the campus as a little town that they live in or commute to and generally treat the campus well." The isolation and feeling of community on campus makes it pretty safe. A student tells us that police "make regular patrols around campus and keep a close eye on everything. In general the campus is safe and the most common crimes are petty theft and auto break-ins from outside agitators." Students tell us about off-campus safety: "Ewing is a very boring place," and while it is pretty safe, "Ewing's neighbor, Trenton [the state capital], is dangerous in some parts."

Most students live on campus, and new full-time freshmen are guaranteed housing for two years. Housing runs the gamut, explains one upperclassman (with a bit of sarcasm): "They range from traditional-style dorms to condo-like housing where four students share a floor and live in luxury." As for living off-campus, we are told, "In general, Ewing has many properties to rent and they usually range from $550 for a two-bedroom apartment and up" and "basically it is easy to find inexpensive off-campus housing."

Student Life

"The typical student wears clothes that would best be suited for exercising or relaxing indoors," laughs one student. "However, when students decide to dress normally they usually are the typical Abercrombie types that populate the majority of America's colleges these days." Says a senior, "It's a New Jersey crowd, so Bible Belt politics ... would not be well accepted here." Greek life exists, but does not dominate. "They [fraternities and sororities] are popular but have little influence over social life. The campus has a limited scope and their impact is low because of the amount of commuters and people who are disinterested in that kind of activity." Students tell us that the school newspaper (*The Signal*) and activist groups are also popular. There are over 120 student organizations.

TCNJ has a lot of commuters and local students who leave campus on weekends, but there is still a campus social life for those that stick around. The student center has its own bar called "The Rat" where bands often perform. One student tells us that in recent years, "Duncan Sheik performed and TV's John Amos performed a one-man play." "The students who live on campus or in Ewing find that there is little to do in the immediate area," says a student. "Most students drive to the local bar scenes of Trenton, Ewing, or Philadelphia [about a half hour away] for entertainment." Locally students frequent bars and clubs such as Katmandu, and Perry's Club 88. The quaint town of Princeton, New Jersey is also a short drive, with access to more restaurants and coffeehouses (one student sighed that "the coffee on campus is poor").

TCNJ plays at Division III level in 21 sports. "TCNJ has a great sports program in its division and many teams have won championships," raves one student. However, while sports are "popular for some," "half the campus leaves in the afternoon, leaving a small fan base for events." Intramural sports are also popular.

THE EXPERTS SAY...

" TCNJ is a school that's been growing rapidly in quality and selectivity. "

" TCNJ doesn't yet have a national reputation. Console yourself with that fact if you're denied admission. "

COLLEGE OF THE ATLANTIC

105 Eden Street, Bar Harbor, ME 04609
Admissions Phone: (207) 288-5015; (800) 528-0025 Fax: (207) 288-4126
Email: inquiry@ecology.coa.edu Website: www.coa.edu
Application Website: www.coa.edu/admissions/appprocess.html

General Info

Type of School: private, coed

Setting: small town

Academic Calendar: trimester

Student Body

Full-Time Undergrads: 229
  Men: 46%, Women: 54%

Part-Time Undergrads: 21
  Men: 52%, Women: 48%

Total Undergrad Population:
  African American: 1%
  Asian American: 1%
  Latino: 1%
  Caucasian: 22%
  International: 17%
  Out-of-State: 63%
  Living Off-Campus: 60%

Graduate and First-Professional
  Students: 11

Academics

Full-Time Faculty: 18
  With Ph.D.: 94%

Part-Time Faculty: 10
  With Ph.D.: 90%

Student/Faculty Ratio: 10:1

Freshmen Retention Rate: 91%

Graduation Rates:
  4% within four years
  53% within six years

Admissions

Regular Application Deadline: 2/15;
  4/1 (priority)

Early Decision Deadline(s): 12/1,
  12/15

Fall Transfer Deadline: 4/25,
  4/1 (priority)

Total # of Students Applied: 270
  Admitted: 186

Waitlist Available

Applied Early Decision: 38
  Early Decision Admitted: 35

Test Scores (middle 50%):
  SAT Verbal: 570–680
  SAT Math: 520–640
  ACT Comp: 27–31

Inside the Classroom

Given its name, it's probably no surprise that College of the Atlantic specializes in ecological issues. It was founded in 1969 to provide an interdisciplinary education in ecology, combining academic rigor with practical application. There is only one major here, Human Ecology, but it is investigated and studied by students and faculty from many viewpoints and approaches.

At COA, education is self-directed. Students have a great deal of academic freedom, planning their programs according to their individual interests. Within the degree focus, undergrads may concentrate on one or more of the following areas: design, environmental science, landscape and building, architecture, marine studies, natural history museum studies, public policy, teacher education and certification, and selected humanities studies.

The core curriculum includes course offerings in the three resource areas of environmental science, human studies, and arts and design. Students are also required to fulfill a 10-week internship, participate in community service, and complete a senior project. Additionally, they must turn in a Human Ecology Essay in the spring of junior year or fall of senior year. Students are given the opportunity to spend a winter term in the Yucatan, Mexico, and COA has established an exchange program with Palacki University in the Czech Republic.

Students give their professors (and their school as a whole) incredibly high marks. COA is so small and specialized, faculty-student interaction—and student-student interaction—is key, and everyone works closely in small classes and on special projects. Students receive individual evaluations of their work and get grades only if they ask for them. Not surprisingly, self-motivation is the cornerstone of success at COA.

Campus Environment

COA's breathtaking 26-acre campus (it only takes about five minutes to walk end to end) is located on Maine's Mount Desert Island, facing Frenchman Bay. It's easily one of the most beautiful campuses in the country. A 120-foot pier provides easy access to the water for both research and recreation, as well as a starting point for the annual Bar Island Swim (at a barbecue during the first week of classes, students and faculty jump off the pier and swim one-third of a mile in 60-degree waters to Bar Island while being cheered on by their peers). Acadia National Park is also within walking distance, with miles of trails, mountains, forest, and rocky shoreline to explore and enjoy. The park is also home to many different kinds of wildlife. Of course, living in Bar Harbor may be too confining and isolated for some; it's a seasonal community, and we hear that practically everything in town shuts down in the winter.

The on-campus housing is just like the rest of the college: cozy, personal, and largely self-directed. There are five small residences, with quaint names like "Peach House" and "Cottage House." All are coed, and include community living space and furnished kitchens. Freshmen must live in campus housing, where they share chores and cook weekend meals together. The dining hall, with the help of the college's community garden and organic farm, serves surprisingly excellent dishes. The school practices what it preaches: everything and everyone is environmentally friendly, using recycled paper and bicycles whenever possible. After their first year, most students live off-campus in reasonably priced rented houses somewhere on the Island, usually within walking or biking distance to campus.

Student Life

The liberal student body is activist, intelligent, and tolerant (it's reportedly a very gay-friendly campus). With just over 250 students, close friendships are the norm. It's a warm, supportive environment, and the overall atmosphere is that of a relaxed, cohesive communal retreat. COA's "self-government" system fosters a strong sense of commitment and responsibility to the school. Students serve on all college committees, from Academic Affairs to Personnel, with full voting rights. At the monthly assembly, the work of the committees is reviewed by the community as a whole.

The social scene at COA reflects the casual attitudes of the students and primarily revolves around the school's natural surroundings. It isn't your typical school, so don't except to find typical "collegiate" activities. There are no fraternities or sororities, no reports of wild keg parties (although we hear that pot is always on hand), no football tailgates ... no varsity sports at all, actually. There are intercollegiate soccer teams affectionately called "The Swarm," though they've yet to win a game, we hear. A pick-up game of Frisbee, volleyball, horseshoes, and the like is more along the lines of a COA "organized" sport. Ice skating, cross-country skiing, and sledding are all popular winter pastimes. Students can take advantage of their waterfront location by using COA's recreational fleet, which includes ocean and river kayaks, whitewater and lake canoes, and sailboats; a sailing class is offered each fall term, and scuba-diving is popular as well. As part of the activity fee, students receive membership to the YMCA, where they can workout or join basketball, indoor soccer, and underwater hockey games.

When students want a break from all that activity, there are plenty of more sedentary things to do, including pool tournaments, open-mike nights, movies, or just hanging out in the Student Lounge. The village of Bar Harbor is within walking distance, where students enjoy a wide variety of shops, restaurants, and nightspots, as well as art shows, concerts, and numerous summer activities. COA isn't home to very many student organizations—just a handful, in fact, and they generally revolve around outdoor activities (Outing Club, Dive Club) or political activism (Social Environmental Action, World Citizens for Social, Environmental, and Economic Justice). Students are proud of their active role in community service, through local social programs or environmentally related work at Acadia National Park. There is an active artistic community on the island, and exhibitions at COA's Blum Art Gallery have received critical acclaim.

Other schools to check out: University of Maine—Orono, Lewis and Clark, Marlboro, Hampshire, Antioch.

HS Rank of Entering Freshmen:
Top 10%: 23%
Top 25%: 42%
Top 50%: 75%
Avg. HS GPA: 3.4

Costs (2003–04)

Tuition and Fees: $23,961
Room & Board: $6,543
Payment Plan(s): installment plan

THE EXPERTS SAY...

" If you really care about the environment, College of the Atlantic will prepare you to do something about it. The major in Human Ecology can take you in a lot of different directions. "

" There are only 250 students, and they're all seriously Green. Don't come here wearing your fur coat. "

Inst. Aid (est. 2003–04)

Institutional Aid, Need-Based: $1,820,579
Institutional Aid, Non-Need-Based: $16,000
FT Undergrads Receiving Aid: 86%
Avg. Amount per Student: $21,823
FT Undergrads Receiving Non-Need-Based Scholarship or Grant Aid: 1%
Avg. Amount per Student: $2,250
Of Those Receiving Any Aid:
Rec. Need-Based Scholarship or Grant Aid: 88%
Average Award: $18,900
Rec. Need-Based Self-Help Aid: 86%
Average Award: $4,664
Upon Graduation, Avg. Loan Debt per Student: $13,882
Financial Aid Deadline: 2/15, 2/15 (priority)

Graduates

Going to Graduate School:
2% Within One Year
Accepting Job Offer:
89% at time of graduation
Companies Recruiting On Campus: 3
Alumni Giving: 27%

COLLEGE OF THE HOLY CROSS

1 College Street, Worcester, MA 01610-2395
Admissions Phone: (508) 793-2443; (800) 442-2421 Fax: (508) 793-3888
Email: admissions@holycross.edu Website: holycross.edu
Application Website: www.applyweb.com/apply/hc/menu.html

General Info

Type of School: private, coed,
  Society of Jesus, Roman Catholic

Setting: suburban

Academic Calendar: semester

Student Body

Full-Time Undergrads: 2,748
  Men: 46%, Women: 54%

Part-Time Undergrads: 25
  Men: 36%, Women: 64%

Total Undergrad Population:
  African American: 3%
  Asian American: 4%
  Latino: 5%
  Native American: <1%
  Caucasian: 77%
  International: 1%
  Out-of-State: 65%
  Living Off-Campus: 13%

Academics

Full-Time Faculty: 228
  With Ph.D.: 95%

Part-Time Faculty: 59

Student/Faculty Ratio: 11:1

Most Popular Majors:
  economics (17%)
  psychology (13%)
  political science (12%)
  English (12%)
  history (12%)

Completing 2 or More Majors: 13%

Freshmen Retention Rate: 98%

Graduation Rates:
  87% within four years
  89% within six years

Admissions

Regular Application Deadline: 1/15

Early Decision Deadline(s): 12/15

Fall Transfer Deadline: 5/1

Spring Transfer Deadline: 11/1

Total # of Students Applied: 5,035
  Admitted: 2,131
  Enrolled: 704

# of Students Waitlisted: 1,097
  Students Accepting Place: 374
  Waitlisted Students Admitted: 88

Applied Early Decision: 361
  Early Decision Admitted: 221

Inside the Classroom

"Of the 28 Jesuit colleges and universities in the United States, Holy Cross stands alone in its exclusive commitment to undergraduate education," states a school official. Holy Cross believes strongly in the benefits of a strong liberal arts education. Even its excellent premed, predental, and prelaw programs are grounded in a broad liberal arts background. And according to a Massachusetts guidance counselor, Holy Cross has started "thriving academically" in recent years, strengthening an already solid academic reputation.

All students must complete at least one course each in the arts, literature, religion, philosophy, history, and cross-cultural studies; and two courses each in language, social science, and natural and mathematical science. The workload can be pretty heavy at Holy Cross, but, as one student explains, "it's not at all competitive or cutthroat." And the environment is very supportive: "Students are really down-to-earth and the professors are friendly and approachable."

Class sizes are always kept small to enable students to interact with their professors. You can't hide at the back of the room here; be prepared to become involved in class discussion and to answer questions. "The faculty encourages perfection," notes a high school guidance counselor out in Arizona. Incoming freshmen are given the option of participating in the First-Year Program, a residential college program that brings students and teachers together inside and outside the classroom.

One of the most popular special study options at Holy Cross is their Washington Semester Program. "The Holy Cross reputation of sending the best and brightest to D.C. made acceptance into the more sought-after positions much easier," comments a satisfied program grad. Holy Cross also sponsors a highly regarded study abroad program that operates in 23 countries throughout Europe, Asia, and the Americas. Because Holy Cross is a member of the Worcester Consortium for Higher Education, students can also cross-register at nine nearby schools.

Campus Environment

The majority of students live in one of the nine residence halls on the 174-acre campus. Those high school students who have never operated a vacuum in their lives will be relieved to learn that all dorms feature maid service. In addition to a traditional residence hall environment, freshmen can choose to live in a special living-and-academic-learning dormitory. On-campus housing is guaranteed for all four years.

Students awarded work-study as part of their financial aid package have a wide variety of options available on campus. Positions include the support of all academic departments as well as many administrative functions such as Information Technology Services. Students may also take advantage of employment opportunities in Dining Services without regard to financial assistance.

Recent construction projects on campus include the 56,000-square-foot Smith Hall, completed in 2001 at a cost of $19 million (home to the Center for Religion, Ethics, and Culture), the Rehm Library, and various academic and administrative offices.

The college has also completely renovated and expanded O'Neil Hall, which houses the biology department.

"There's no need for a car, everything is within walking distance, and since the entire school is on a gigantic hill, you will never get overweight," quips one student. Campus parking is limited to juniors and seniors; parking permits are required. A free shuttle is available to 13 other Worcester Consortium institutions.

Off campus, the city of Worcester doesn't offer all that much that appeals to students other than a few bars, restaurants, and movie theaters. However, the school is about an hour away from the cities of Boston, Providence, and Hartford, making weekend road trips possible.

Student Life

The religious influence of the Jesuits at Holy Cross, while not pervasive, is evident in different ways. The school recently received a $2 million grant from the Lilly Endowment "to create or enhance programs enabling young people to draw upon the resources of religious wisdom as they consider their vocational choices." Most students are Irish Catholic, but they're not necessarily strictly religious. For those who want it, however, there are opportunities to be spiritually active by attending church services and going on retreats with Jesuit teachers. Upon graduation, a substantial number of Holy Cross students traditionally begin their professional lives by serving in wide variety of volunteer organizations, including Americorps, the Peace Corp, and the Jesuit Volunteer Corps.

Holy Cross students work hard, but they also like to have fun. Although there are no fraternities or sororities and the alcohol policy is strictly enforced on campus, it's not hard to find parties in dorm rooms or at off-campus apartments. Many students also head to local bars. "Drinking's pretty big here. We are predominantly Roman Catholic and have a reputation to keep up," jokes one student.

But at Holy Cross, athletics are the most popular diversion. Anyone who attends a Holy Cross football or basketball game and hears the crowds of rowdy student fans roaring in support of their team can get a sense of how deep the school spirit runs here. Many of the varsity teams have strong records, and Crusaders games are all very well attended. And with the extensive range of intramural teams to choose from, almost every student finds some sport to play. "While the actual number of teams will vary with the level of interest, last year approximately 1,200 students participated in 6 separate intramural sports and another 200 took part in 12 different club teams," we are told.

Other schools to check out: Boston College, Colgate, Trinity (CT), Bucknell, Wake Forest.

Test Scores (middle 50%):
SAT Verbal: 580–680
SAT Math: 630–670

HS Rank of Entering Freshmen:
Top 10%: 68%
Top 25%: 92%
Top 50%: 99%

THE EXPERTS SAY...

" The Jesuit tradition of 'being men and women for others' shines at Holy Cross. "

" If you don't want to be a 'Crusader,' consider Trinity or Boston College. "

Costs (2004–5)

Tuition and Fees: $29,686

Room & Board: $8,860

Payment Plan(s): installment plan, pre-payment plan

Inst. Aid (2002–03)

Institutional Aid, Need-Based: $13,002,178

Institutional Aid, Non-Need-Based: $1,805,693

FT Undergrads Receiving Aid: 56%
Avg. Amount per Student: $21,917

FT Undergrads Receiving Non-Need-Based Scholarship or Grant Aid: 2%
Avg. Amount per Student: $10,951

Of Those Receiving Any Aid:

Rec. Need-Based Scholarship or Grant Aid: 73%
Average Award: $14,858

Rec. Need-Based Self-Help Aid: 85%
Average Award: $7,520

Upon Graduation, Avg. Loan Debt per Student: $17,253

Financial Aid Deadline: 2/1

Graduates

Going to Graduate School: 24% Within One Year

Accepting Job Offer: 35% at time of graduation

Companies Recruiting On Campus: 42

Alumni Giving: 59%

COLLEGE OF THE OZARKS

P.O. Box 17, Point Lookout, MO 65726
Admissions Phone: (417) 334-6411; (800) 222-0525 Fax: (417) 335-2618
Email: admiss4@cofo.edu
Website: www.cofo.edu

General Info

Type of School: private, coed, Presbyterian

Setting: small town

Academic Calendar: semester

Student Body

Full-Time Undergrads: 1,278
  Men: 44%, Women: 56%

Part-Time Undergrads: 70
  Men: 43%, Women: 57%

Total Undergrad Population:
  African American: <1%
  Asian American: 1%
  Latino: 1%
  Native American: <1%
  Caucasian: 83%
  International: 2%
  Out-of-State: 33%
  Living Off-Campus: 16%

Academics

Full-Time Faculty: 87
  With Ph.D.: 53%

Part-Time Faculty: 32
  With Ph.D.: 22%

Student/Faculty Ratio: 15:1

Most Popular Majors:
  business
  education
  agriculture
  computer science
  criminal justice

Freshmen Retention Rate: 76%

Graduation Rates:
  29% within four years
  48% within six years

Admissions

Regular Application Deadline: 8/20; 2/15 (priority)

Fall Transfer Deadline: 8/20, 2/15 (priority)

Total # of Students Applied: 2,076
  Admitted: 290
  Enrolled: 149

# of Students Waitlisted: 100

Test Scores (middle 50%):
  ACT Comp: 17–26

Inside the Classroom

"Getting out of college debt-free is a wonderful thing," sighs a CofO student. The College of the Ozarks ("Hard Work U.") is a Christian college that offers a great bargain: You work on campus 15 hours per week (during the school year), plus two 40-hour workweeks (during school breaks), and your tuition is FREE. Even better, you can work 6 or 12 weeks during the summer to pay for your room and board for the upcoming semester or year. And we're not talking the usual typing and filing work, either: Work opportunities are available in the campus airport, the Child Development Center, the Fruitcake and Jelly Kitchen, and dozens of other interesting sites on campus.

Sounds too good to be true? Well, there are some catches: The school admits only a small percentage of applicants, and heavily favors applicants with modest financial means from southern Missouri, northern Arkansas, and limited areas in Illinois, Kansas, and Oklahoma. And the school's mission to encourage "academic, spiritual, vocational, cultural, and patriotic growth" is set in an intensely Christian, "Big Brother" atmosphere that many would find stifling. A junior explains: "The administration frowns upon disobedience and on students taking their near-free education for granted. Examples: not attending class or not attending work." A senior agrees: "At this school, we don't sleep in, we can't skip class or work. If we are slacking, someone notices immediately."

Because students must carry a full academic load of at least 12 semester hours while working on campus, the workload can seem "heavy," "intense," and "difficult to manage," students tell us. "It takes a lot of work/studying to make A's," says a junior. Another junior notes, "Lazy students would not fit in here." But the professors are understanding and very accessible and are among the school's most appealing features, students say. "The professors here are great! Every one of my professors knows me by my first name, and I feel that I can approach them with class problems as well as personal issues," says a phys ed/secondary education major.

Students can choose from 31 majors and many more minors. CofO is known for strong programs in business, elementary education, animal sciences, psychology, and broadcast journalism. But there are also a number of more unusual programs that draw students, such as aviation maintenance technology, forensic science, and dietetics.

Campus Environment

CofO's beautiful 1,000-acre campus overlooks Lake Taneycomo—a popular hangout in warm weather. Students compliment the campus landscaping, but complain about an unusual regulation: Walking on the grass is not allowed on campus. A junior explains: "Appearance is a big deal to our administrators. Since our institution depends so much on outside donations, they really care about the outer impression." Recent campus construction projects include The Keeter Center for Character Education, which will house conference facilities and a media center.

On-campus housing is guaranteed for four years; in fact, you can live off-campus only if you are over 21. The four women's halls and three men's halls are strictly off-limits to the other sex 24/7 ("Girls and guys are only allowed in each other's dorm rooms two times a year each," explains a premed student). While the dorms are integrated with students from all classes, students tell us that first-year women in particular usually end up in rooms that are "tiny, crowded, and hot, but very social" (but men's and upperclasswomen's dorms are said to be "very nice").

"You don't need a car to get around campus, which is good considering freshman cars are locked up," a student comments. Yes, freshmen must keep their cars in a special lot, which is closed from 1 A.M. on Sundays through noon on Fridays—strongly encouraging freshmen to stay on campus during the week. But students agree that cars are only necessary to get around town, and "you can always get a ride" from other students. The college also provides transportation to the local Wal-Mart and other stores.

The campus is right next to the "busy tourist town" of Branson, which draws lots of families and "older folks" in the summer and fall. While some students seem to enjoy the wholesome entertainment Branson provides, others grumble that Branson's offerings "are only interesting if you enjoy country music shows or Glen Miller." As an English/secondary education major notes, "most college students would rather go see a movie and go out to eat than see a show."

Student Life

Both the town and the campus are "very quiet, very safe, and very religious." Students "go out of their way to say hello" and are generally "low-key and serene." "We are not a diverse population," admits a senior majoring in history/English. "However, we reflect the Ozarks region—white, conservative, and rural." Unfortunately, some students "don't seem to see past the gates at the top of the hill," says another senior. "They don't realize there is a world outside of CofO." Another student agrees, worrying that CofO "may shelter students too much from the real world."

The rules governing students' lives are very strict, extending to clothing, body piercings, and hairstyles (long hair on men is not allowed). As one student warns, "Be conservative, or keep your mouth shut, or get kicked out." There are also curfews, room checks, and a required number of convocations and chapel meetings each semester. But as one student points out: "The school has lots of strict rules that make lots of students mad, but you know those rules when you apply."

In their free time, "students go to on-campus Christian organizations like the Baptist Student Union for worship meetings or Bible study," a junior tells us. While varsity sports other than basketball are not all that popular ("most people are too busy"), approximately 500 students participate in intramurals. On the weekends, many students head home, but some students take the 45-minute drive to Springfield, where they can "dance, shop, or see a movie." While drugs are nonexistent on- and off-campus, and alcohol cannot be found anywhere on campus, students do admit that off-campus drinking "occurs, but it is usually done discreetly."

Other schools to check out: Berea, Berry, Warren Wilson.

THE EXPERTS SAY...

" This is a nice choice for regional students looking to go to school in a nurturing, Christian environment. Plus, you'll come away with four solid years of work experience and no debt. "

" 'Devil-worshippers,' outspoken liberals, and Britney Spears lookalikes need not apply. "

HS Rank of Entering Freshmen:
Top 10%: 19%
Top 25%: 50%
Top 50%: 89%
Avg. HS GPA: 2.99

Costs (2004–5)

Fees: $250
Room & Board: $3,550

Inst. Aid (est. 2003–04)

Institutional Aid, Need-Based:
$8,798,018

Institutional Aid, Non-Need-Based:
$114,925

FT Undergrads Receiving Aid: 90%
Avg. Amount per Student: $12,446

FT Undergrads Receiving Non-Need-Based Scholarship or Grant Aid: 10%
Avg. Amount per Student: $12,446

Of Those Receiving Any Aid:

Rec. Need-Based Scholarship or Grant Aid: 57%
Average Award: $7,716

Rec. Need-Based Self-Help Aid: 57%
Average Award: $2,884

Upon Graduation, Avg. Loan Debt per Student: $6,060

Financial Aid Deadline: 3/15 (priority)

Graduates

Going to Graduate School:
15% Within One Year

Accepting Job Offer:
70% at time of graduation

Companies Recruiting On Campus: 72

Alumni Giving: 26%

COLLEGE OF WILLIAM AND MARY

P.O. Box 8795, Williamsburg, VA 23187-8795
Admissions Phone: (757) 221-4223 Fax: (757) 221-1242
Email: admiss@wm.edu Website: www.wm.edu
Application Website: wm.edu/admission/new/index.html

General Info

Type of School: public, coed

Setting: suburban

Academic Calendar: semester

Student Body

Full-Time Undergrads: 5,652
    Men: 44%, Women: 56%

Part-Time Undergrads: 34
    Men: 50%, Women: 50%

Total Undergrad Population:
    African American: 6%
    Asian American: 7%
    Latino: 3%
    Native American: <1%
    Caucasian: 68%
    International: 2%
    Out-of-State: 33%
    Living Off-Campus: 25%
    In Fraternities: 33%
    In Sororities: 34%

Graduate and First-Professional
    Students: 2,001

Academics

Full-Time Faculty: 563
    With Ph.D.: 91%

Part-Time Faculty: 166
    With Ph.D.: 57%

Student/Faculty Ratio: 12:1

Most Popular Majors:
    business (13%)
    psychology (11%)
    English (9%)
    government (8%)
    biology (8%)

Completing 2 or More Majors: 21%

Freshmen Retention Rate: 94%

Admissions

Regular Application Deadline: 1/5

Early Decision Deadline(s): 11/1

Fall Transfer Deadline: 2/15

Spring Transfer Deadline: 11/1

Total # of Students Applied: 10,161
    Admitted: 3,488
    Enrolled: 1,326

# of Students Waitlisted: 1,534
    Students Accepting Place: 736
    Waitlisted Students Admitted: 9

Applied Early Decision: 1,046
    Early Decision Admitted: 499

In the Classroom

William and Mary was created as a liberal arts college, and traditional arts and sciences remain its primary focus. Undergraduate programs are offered through the schools of Arts and Sciences and Business Administration. Undergrads can also apply to the School of Education during their sophomore year. Biology, English, and government are considered particularly good, as is the history department, which benefits from the school's proximity to major historic sites. In addition to liberal arts, the business school has an excellent reputation, although it's extremely competitive.

William and Mary students adhere to a strict honor code, and students tell us "the administration takes the Honor Code very seriously, but the students do also, so it is not a major problem." Students are definitely serious about academics here, and "you will find an alarming number in the library on the weekends and during holidays," one junior says. The "academic atmosphere is pretty intense," "there is lots of work," and "most students are competitive." Guidance counselors stress that W&M is "highly selective."

Freshman Seminars cap at 17 students in a class. "Professors are mostly great though, very accessible and they really like to teach. There is definitely a focus on undergraduate education here." Another student tells us, "Most professors expect hard work from their students but they understand that the workload from other classes keeps you busy." Also, as another student explains, "the real focus is on undergraduate teaching. Professors almost always teach the classes, not TAs, and are available to undergrads. There are also lots of opportunities for undergrads to work with profs on research projects, etc."

Campus Environment

"All freshmen must live on campus," says one student. Another adds, "There are a few apartment complexes fairly nearby and some students rent houses near campus, but living on campus is more popular." A junior describes dorms: "[They] are typical of most universities: small and not particularly nice, but they serve their purpose. Many of the dorms have had recent renovations. Freshman dorms have been quite crowded in the past couple of years. All dorms have ethernet connections which is really fast—much better than an Internet modem."

W&M is the second oldest college in the country and has the oldest academic building in continual use. A students explains that "the campus is right beside colonial Williamsburg so many of the tourists from that area are also seen checking out the college." Also: "Police are around all the time and most students feel very safe walking at night." A junior tells us that the city "is relatively safe. There is not much to do in the area except for sightseeing at colonial Williamsburg and Jamestown. There is one shopping outlet 10–15 minutes from campus."

A student describes one of the best attributes of William and Mary as "the fact that there is not much to do around the area to distract you from studying," and one of the least appealing as "not much to do in Williamsburg." "Williamsburg is beautiful, but definitely geared more towards the tourists than the students. There is not a whole lot to do at night. Busch Gardens [an amusement park] is nearby and has a college day every fall where students can get tickets for a reduced price."

And you'll need a car to get there. An upperclassmen explains, "Freshmen and sophomores are not allowed to have cars on campus ... Many juniors and seniors have cars, but not all. It is nice to have one, there is not really any public transportation in Williamsburg. But it is fairly easy to get rides from people you know or from the college ride board on the Internet." Besides, one student says, "Parking is a big issue. Many students complain about the cost of parking permits and the lack of spaces."

Student Life

"I think the stereotype of William and Mary is the J. Crew-wearing preppy type. While this is true of some students, definitely not all. There is diversity in the sense that students have many different interests and styles (not so much in the sense of racial diversity). Dyed hair and body piercing is not at all thought of as bizarre or uncommon," says one student. The "student body is in general really friendly, there is a real sense of community on campus."

The social world is not as rowdy as it is at some institutions. A student explains: "Sunday through Wednesday is mostly spent on work and campus activities. Thursday is a popular weeknight to go out to the delis (Williamsburg's version of bars). Friday and Saturday many people go out to the delis or frat parties (which are generally open to all students). Sometimes people go out during the week, but it is not uncommon for them to then stay in on a weekend night to catch up on work."

About 30 percent of students go Greek. "Greek life is huge," agrees one student. "However, it is not essential to meeting people. Most parties are open to everyone and most Greeks have good friends who are not Greek and are involved in activities on campus outside of their fraternity or sorority." A psychology major tells us the Greek organizations "have a tremendous amount of influence on the social life because they the major source of parties. They are popular because of the parties." Students tell us that a lot of drinking takes place during parties, but drugs are generally not used.

"Varsity sports aren't very popular. Intramural sports are popular because many of the students who are not good enough to play on the varsity teams have a chance to compete," we are told. However, "going to football and basketball games is becoming more popular in the past couple of years. Homecoming is popular, although this is mostly because of other, non-football activities that accompany it, like alumni visits ... and parties."

Other schools to check out: University of Virginia, James Madison, Wake Forest, Rice, Gettysburg.

Test Scores (middle 50%):
SAT Verbal: 630–730
SAT Math: 630–710
ACT Comp: 30–32
ACT English: 28–33
ACT Math: 28–31

HS Rank of Entering Freshmen:
Top 10%: 85%
Top 25%: 97%
Top 50%: 100%

Avg. HS GPA: 4.0

THE EXPERTS SAY...

" An over 300-year-old tradition of excellence in education at a public school price; truly a 'public Ivy.' "

" Williamsburg can be a little old-fashioned— three cornered hats and fife and drum old-fashioned. No word on if honors-system violators are placed in the stocks. "

Costs (2003–04)

Tuition and Fees, In-State: $6,430

Tuition and Fees, Out-of-State: $21,130

Room & Board: $5,794

Payment Plan(s): installment plan, pre-payment plan

Inst. Aid (2002–03)

Institutional Aid, Need-Based: $4,025,744

Institutional Aid, Non-Need-Based: $947,321

FT Undergrads Receiving Aid: 26%
Avg. Amount per Student: $8,664

FT Undergrads Receiving Non-Need-Based Scholarship or Grant Aid: 17%
Avg. Amount per Student: $7,173

Of Those Receiving Any Aid:

Rec. Need-Based Scholarship or Grant Aid: 87%
Average Award: $6,963

Rec. Need-Based Self-Help Aid: 80%
Average Award: $3,218

Upon Graduation, Avg. Loan Debt per Student: $19,952

Financial Aid Deadline: 3/15, 2/15 (priority)

Graduates

Going to Graduate School: 31% Within One Year

Companies Recruiting On Campus: 200

COLLEGE OF WOOSTER

847 College Avenue, Wooster, OH 44691
Admissions Phone: (330) 263-2322; (800) 877-9905 Fax: (330) 263-2621
Email: admissions@wooster.edu
Website: www.wooster.edu

General Info

Type of School: private, coed
Academic Calendar: semester

Student Body

Full-Time Undergrads: 1,822
  Men: 47%, Women: 53%

Part-Time Undergrads: 16
  Men: 56%, Women: 44%

Total Undergrad Population:
  African American: 5%
  Asian American: 2%
  Latino: 1%
  Native American: <1%
  Caucasian: 78%
  International: 7%
  Out-of-State: 42%
  Living Off-Campus: 3%
  In Fraternities: 9%
  In Sororities: 10%

Academics

Full-Time Faculty: 134
  With Ph.D.: 97%

Part-Time Faculty: 45
  With Ph.D.: 71%

Student/Faculty Ratio: 12:1

Most Popular Majors:
  English (10%)
  history (10%)
  communication (6%)
  psychology (6%)
  biology (5%)

Completing 2 or More Majors: 5%

Freshmen Retention Rate: 87%

Graduation Rates:
  61% within four years
  68% within six years

Admissions

Regular Application Deadline: 2/15

Early Decision Deadline(s): 12/1,
  1/15

Fall Transfer Deadline: 6/1

Spring Transfer Deadline: 12/1

Total # of Students Applied: 2,560
  Admitted: 1,780
  Enrolled: 559

# of Students Waitlisted: 249
  Students Accepting Place: 66

Applied Early Decision: 75
  Early Decision Admitted: 70

Inside the Classroom

The needs of the individual are given prime importance at the College of Wooster, a small liberal arts and sciences college in Wooster, Ohio. Offering 39 undergraduate majors (students can also design their own major with faculty guidance), the college provides intensive small-class study where the student's independent work serves as the heart of each student's academic experience.

Requirements for graduation include a first-year seminar for students, one to three courses in global and cultural perspectives, a course in religious perspectives, a course in quantitative reasoning, six interdisciplinary courses, and seven to nine courses in the student's major. The centerpiece of the curriculum, however, is three courses of independent study for upperclassmen. Referred to on campus simply as "I.S.," the study involves working one-on-one with a faculty member to produce an original work of research. What the student produces is less important than how he produces it: I.S. is designed to teach students how to think, and much attention is paid to the choices each student makes during the study. According to one alumnus, another byproduct of I.S. is the confidence instilled in the student by tackling and finishing an endeavor like this alone.

Another important component of a Wooster education is the first-year seminar. Held in small classes and centered around a writing-intensive course of critical inquiry, the seminars engage students with issues, questions, and ideas of an interdisciplinary nature. The faculty member who teaches each seminar also serves as the advisor for every student in the seminar.

Fortunately for students, individual attention from faculty doesn't diminish after freshman year. According to one psychology major, "Faculty are always there for you, know you personally, and are willing to bend over backwards to help you in your academic pursuits. Of course, this is provided you at least extend the facade of academic seriousness; slackers who are identified as such may have more difficulty in this regard."

Wooster also encourages students to incorporate a study abroad program into their educational experience, and approximately 20 percent of each takes advantage of the opportunity. Some programs are run by the college under the direction of faculty members. Programs like Wooster in Greece, Wooster in Kenya, and the Study-Travel Seminar in India are offered approximately every three years. Other programs directly sponsored by the College, such as Wooster in Besanon, are available every semester.

Campus Environment

Wooster's nicely laid-out campus is festooned with greenery and makes for a pleasant walk when the workload is light. The Quad is a giant field located in the center of campus and adjacent to five of Wooster's residence halls. The hub of student life is the Lowry Student Center, with its dining hall, a snack bar called Mom's Truck Stop, meeting rooms, lounges, bookstore, bowling alley, meeting rooms, and game room. One nice feature for students is the dining hall's flexible hours: Students can stop in any time between 7:30 A.M. and 6:45 P.M. for a meal. The center also houses the Java Hut, a campus coffeehouse.

Residence halls at Wooster are varied in quality and type. Most freshmen are housed in Armington Hall according to the principle that interaction with each other helps to smooth the transition to university life. Juniors and seniors are housed in Luce Hall and Kenarden Lodge, the latter of which is most coveted by students for its generously sized rooms and picturesque appearance. Stevenson Hall is all-male, and Compton Hall houses women only. Attached to Compton is Kittredge Hall, one of two campus dining halls and home of the "No Fry Zone," an eatery serving only vegan foods (those with no meat or animal byproducts). Kittredge is also home to the school's Soup and Bread Program, a volunteer service opportunity for students. In addition to the more conventional housing options, students can also choose to live in small houses that are set aside for groups with a common interest.

Bissman Hall is the home of the school's improvised fraternity system. There are no national fraternities or sororities at Wooster; however, there are local equilavents referred to as "sections" (for men) and "clubs" (for women). The groups got this name because they once were housed in sections of Kenarden Lodge. Participating students now live in different sections of Bissman instead of in off-campus houses.

Student Life

The sections and clubs drive much of the party scene, attracting a significant number of students. Since individuality is valued here, however, many choose to go their own way when it comes to socializing. Perhaps those students have a point, since one club member says of them, "If independents make fun of us then so be it, but they miss a hell of a good time shotgunning beers, talking to Ralph on the big white phone, and then making fun of each other."

Students can also hang out at The Underground, Wooster's campus pub, which provides a variety of entertainment, food, and drink. Live bands, comedians, and dance parties are organized by the student activities board for all students to enjoy, and on quieter nights students can always use the pool tables, darts, and video games.

The Wooster Fighting Scots compete at the NCAA Division III level. Sports for both sexes include basketball, soccer, indoor track, swimming, diving, lacrosse, golf, tennis, and track. Men may also compete in football and baseball, while women can compete in field hockey, volleyball, and softball. Clubs that complement the sports teams include cheerleading, a marching band, and a bagpipe band.

One of the big highlights each fall is the Party on the Green, a campus-wide event held under a huge tent. Elaborately staged, the party features a live band and many other forms of entertainment, often eclipsing Homecoming in its popularity with Wooster students. Another tradition is the Bacchanalia Festival, named in honor of the Greek god of wine for good reason.

Other schools to check out: Denison, Kenyon, Allegheny, Hiram, Beloit.

Test Scores (middle 50%):
SAT Verbal: 540–660
SAT Math: 550–650
ACT Comp: 23–28
ACT English: 22–29
ACT Math: 23–28

HS Rank of Entering Freshmen:
Top 10%: 36%
Top 25%: 68%
Top 50%: 94%

Avg. HS GPA: 3.58

THE EXPERTS SAY...

" The College of Wooster allows independent-minded students to forge their own course of study in a small-class setting. "

" The I.S. component takes initiative and gumption. Students lacking in discipline could flounder if they don't change their ways. "

Costs (2004–5)

Tuition and Fees: $26,560

Room & Board: $6,640

Payment Plan(s): installment plan, deferred payment plan

Inst. Aid (est. 2003–04)

Institutional Aid, Need-Based: $16,051,932

Institutional Aid, Non-Need-Based: $7,301,264

FT Undergrads Receiving Aid: 64%
Avg. Amount per Student: $21,812

FT Undergrads Receiving Non-Need-Based Scholarship or Grant Aid: 34%
Avg. Amount per Student: $10,643

Of Those Receiving Any Aid:

Rec. Need-Based Scholarship or Grant Aid: 100%
Average Award: $15,970

Rec. Need-Based Self-Help Aid: 84%
Average Award: $5,251

Upon Graduation, Avg. Loan Debt per Student: $19,494

Financial Aid Deadline: rolling, 2/15 (priority)

Graduates

Going to Graduate School: 44% Within One Year

Accepting Job Offer: 32% at time of graduation

Companies Recruiting On Campus: 35

COLORADO COLLEGE

14 East Cache La Poudre, Colorado Springs, CO 80903
Admissions Phone: (719) 389-6344; (800) 542-7214 Fax: (719) 389-6816
Email: admission@coloradocollege.edu
Website: www.coloradocollege.edu

General Info

Type of School: private, coed

Setting: urban

Academic Calendar: Block Plan:
Students take 1 course at a time
for $3\frac{1}{2}$ weeks

Student Body

Full-Time Undergrads: 1,929
Men: 45%, Women: 55%

Total Undergrad Population:
African American: 2%
Asian American: 4%
Latino: 7%
Native American: 2%
Caucasian: 78%
International: 2%
Out-of-State: 72%
Living Off-Campus: 24%

Graduate and First-Professional
Students: 27

Academics

Full-Time Faculty: 166
With Ph.D.: 96%

Part-Time Faculty: 45

Student/Faculty Ratio: 9:1

Most Popular Majors:
biology (10%)
economics (8%)
psychology (8%)
political science (6%)
international political economy (6%)

Completing 2 or More Majors: 4%

Freshmen Retention Rate: 92%

Graduation Rates:
70% within four years
77% within six years

Admissions

Regular Application Deadline: 1/15

Early Action Deadline: 11/15

Fall Transfer Deadline: 3/1

Spring Transfer Deadline: 11/1

Total # of Students Applied: 3,533
Admitted: 1,975
Enrolled: 593

# of Students Waitlisted: 467
Students Accepting Place: 186
Waitlisted Students Admitted: 14

Inside the Classroom

Colorado College, the only national liberal arts and science college in the Mountain Time Zone, is one of two colleges in the nation to use the Block Plan (the other is Cornell College in Iowa). CC's Block Plan divides the academic year into eight three-and-a-half week segments, or blocks. All students take just one course at a time and professors teach just one. Some courses may last for one block, others for two or three. In three and a half weeks, students must cover as much material as you would in a conventional semester. "The successful Colorado College student is a self-directed learner, has a sense of adventure (both in the classroom and in the co-curricular), wants a voice in his own education, has commitment, and desires immersion in their academic studies," says one college official. A Colorado student admits that "the work is intense," but says the benefit is that "you get completely absorbed in what you are studying, and you become close friends with your professor and peers since you're with them so often."

CC isn't the place to sleep in class: Active participation is required. Procrastination can be lethal, and missing one class can feel like missing a week. A student cautions that another drawback to the Block Plan is limited long-term retention, since the material is learned in such a short period of time. "You either love the Block Plan or hate it," he claims.

In this intensive academic environment, where class size is limited to 25 people, a special kind of bonding takes place between students and faculty. Students rave about their caring teachers, who often give out their home phone numbers. To help break up the monotony of the classroom setting, many professors take their classes out for breakfast or lunch, one student told us. But Colorado offers other ways of breaking the potential boredom of the block. The First-Year Program for freshmen, designed to inspire creativity and multidisciplinary thinking, approaches coursework under broad thematic rubrics. Themes for the 2002–03 academic year were "Order and Chaos" and "Frontiers and Boundaries."

CC's interdisciplinary programs include American cultural studies, Southwest studies, and environmental studies, and take advantage of the college's location in the Rocky Mountain west, as do field-based anthropology, biology, and geology programs; other classes travel to more exotic locations like the Caribbean. Outdoor classes are held at the college's Baca campus in the San Luis Valley, as well as at CC's mountain cabin. There are also team-taught courses with two faculty of different disciplines co-teaching courses.

Distribution requirements include courses in the natural sciences, social sciences, humanities, and foreign languages. Half of student body takes part in community service. Fifty percent of students also study abroad; 40 percent take part in independent study and grants are awarded for students to collaborate in faculty research or to conduct original research.

Campus Environment

CC's 90-acre campus in downtown Colorado Springs is located on the front range of the Rocky Mountains; the landscape, with stunning Pike's Peak nearby, inspired "America the Beautiful." While some feel Colorado Springs doesn't have much for students, a growing city population and a thriving downtown near campus have made for more alternatives in dining, entertainment, and outdoor activities in recent years. When students want a quick getaway, Denver is an hour away and offers more options for food, music, shopping, and culture.

First-year students may be integrated with students from all classes, but two dorms are primarily for freshmen. Housing is guaranteed for all four years, but overcrowding has sometimes occurred. However, the new Western Ridge complex, an apartment-style and theme-house dorm, has alleviated some space problems. There is no housing in fraternity/sorority buildings. Only upperclassmen are allowed to have cars; parking permits are required. For transportation, most students use bicycles, the city bus system, and their feet (downtown is just six blocks south of campus).

Student Life

The social scene at Colorado College flourishes, even in the midst of the cold of winter. Student-sponsored dances, parties, comedy nights, and music festivals like the annual Llamapalooza keep campus life happening. People also check bulletin boards for dorm parties and off-campus bashes. The Greek system is small, but accounts for its share of weekend fun since students say there are no good bars close to campus.

At the end of each block, students are given a four-day "block break," and many take advantage of the outdoor activities offered by the school's Rocky Mountain location. Skiing, mountain climbing, hiking, and camping are favorite sports, and CC's freshman outdoor orientation program introduces new students to all the options. There are usually several student-organized outdoor trips in the fall breaks. Others use their block breaks for community service.

The most active school-sponsored clubs include the Center for Community Service, student government, Outdoor Recreation Committee, arts and crafts organizations, and the Theater Workshop. There are nine intercollegiate sports for women and nine for men; men's ice hockey and women's soccer are NCAA Division I. There are 18 intramural sports, and 80 percent of the student body participates.

Colorado College is a liberal school, despite its location in one of America's most conservative bastions. While the student body is largely homogeneous, increasing the school's diversity is a concern shared by the administration and students alike. "Most of us are upper-middle class and white," commented a junior. "Despite our homogeneity, we are very open-minded—after all, granolas, hippies, and preppy alternative thinkers live together in relative harmony." A significant number of students join politically oriented organizations or clubs. "The students are interested in what's going on around them, both inside and outside the classroom," observes one student. But some say that many students get caught up in the "CC Bubble" and lose touch with the real world. "You should expect to see a lot of students in thrift store clothing driving $40,000 cars," a former student notes.

Other schools to check out: Middlebury, Whitman, Colby, Evergreen State, Cornell College (IA), Beloit.

Test Scores (middle 50%):
 SAT Verbal: 580–690
 SAT Math: 580–670
 ACT Comp: 24–30
 ACT English: 25–30
 ACT Math: 24–29

HS Rank of Entering Freshmen:
 Top 10%: 44%
 Top 25%: 77%
 Top 50%: 94%

Costs (2004–5)

Tuition and Fees: $28,644

Room & Board: $7,216

Payment Plan(s): installment plan

THE EXPERTS SAY...

" The Block Plan is perfect for students who love to delve into a subject, learning all they possibly can about it, before moving on to the next thing. "

" Not the best place to prepare for the real world, where multitasking is king. "

Inst. Aid (est. 2003–04)

Institutional Aid, Need-Based:
 $14,015,955

Institutional Aid, Non-Need-Based:
 $1,856,305

FT Undergrads Receiving Aid: 45%
 Avg. Amount per Student: $23,278

FT Undergrads Receiving Non-Need-Based Scholarship or Grant Aid: 14%
 Avg. Amount per Student: $16,100

Of Those Receiving Any Aid:

Rec. Need-Based Scholarship or Grant Aid: 94%
 Average Award: $19,275

Rec. Need-Based Self-Help Aid: 90%
 Average Award: $4,717

Upon Graduation, Avg. Loan Debt per Student: $13,850

Financial Aid Deadline: 2/15 (priority)

COLUMBIA UNIVERSITY— COLUMBIA COLLEGE

212 Hamilton Hall, Mail Code 2807, 1130 Amsterdam Avenue, New York, NY 10027
Fax: (212) 854-1209 Website: www.columbia.edu
Application Website: www.studentaffairs.columbia.edu/admissions/applications/

General Info

Type of School: private, coed
Setting: urban
Academic Calendar: semester

Student Body

Full-Time Undergrads: 4,181
  Men: 49%, Women: 51%

Total Undergrad Population:
  African American: 8%
  Asian American: 12%
  Latino: 8%
  Native American: <1%
  Caucasian: 52%
  International: 6%
  Out-of-State: 75%
  Living Off-Campus: 2%
  In Fraternities: 7%
  In Sororities: 5%

Academics

Full-Time Faculty: 689
  With Ph.D.: 95%

Student/Faculty Ratio: 7:1

Most Popular Majors:
  political science (14%)
  economics (12%)
  English (11%)
  history (10%)
  psychology (6%)

Completing 2 or More Majors: 27%

Freshmen Retention Rate: 97%

Graduation Rates:
  84% within four years
  92% within six years

Admissions

Regular Application Deadline: 1/2

Early Decision Deadline(s): 11/1

Fall Transfer Deadline: 3/15

Total # of Students Applied: 14,665
  Admitted: 1,643
  Enrolled: 1,011

# of Students Waitlisted: 1,706
  Students Accepting Place: 1,143
  Waitlisted Students Admitted: 64

Applied Early Decision: 1,802
  Early Decision Admitted: 467

Inside the Classroom

Columbia University is the smallest of the Ivies in terms of undergrad enrollment. Columbia College is the home of Columbia University's arts and sciences division. Many Columbia undergrads are preparing for further education in medical school, law school, or Columbia's acclaimed Graduate School of Journalism.

Columbia's core curriculum, which many guidance counselors cited as one of the best things about the university, is heavy with requirements. All students are required to take courses in literature, art, music, philosophy, contemporary civilization, logic and rhetoric, science, non-Western culture, foreign language, and phys ed. These classes are kept small and are discussion-oriented.

Columbia offers 106 majors, with strength in the English, political science, linguistics, Asian, and Russian studies departments. Internships in Manhattan abound, and many students conduct individual or faculty-sponsored research. In this "community of learners and thinkers," the academic atmosphere is "competitive and stimulating." "The struggle to stay ahead can get rather intense," a junior reports. Another student observes that the workload is "fairly rigorous, but only because of the quality of the student population. Assignments are reasonable… [students] help each other to all do equally superbly." At least one student complains of grade inflation.

Columbia draws A-list faculty, many of whom hold top positions in their field while teaching on the side. This can make reaching profs outside of class difficult. "If you see your faculty advisor more than once after orientation, you're lucky," we hear. Others say that you can get close to your advisor: "You have to be determined and make the effort," says one student. There's no coddling of students at Columbia: "Students are expected to be independent," states a high school guidance counselor.

Campus Environment

Columbia's small campus is located at 116th Street and Broadway, on the edge of Harlem in Morningside Heights. While some guidance counselors fret over the "absence of a self-contained campus," students insist that the concern over the safety of the neighborhood is way overrated. "Columbia has a great location," a student explains. "It's in Manhattan but not in the center so much like NYU. You can go out for a night on the town and then come to a nice neighborhood like Columbia's. It becomes your home away from home." More than half of the school's faculty live in Morningside Heights.

The quality of the 15 dormitories varies, and most students live in the dorms for all four years. "Anything off-campus would be so expensive it's inconceivable," shudders a junior. Housing is guaranteed, and more than 65 percent of Columbia undergrads live in singles. The freshman food plan, while not the highest quality, is plentiful. Transportation is definitely not by car: "This is New York, baby!" a classics major exclaims. "It's all about public transportation. The subway and bus system is one of the best in the world! There are also cabs for those with more money and less energy/patience."

Student Life

Columbia students are known to be independent-minded and many are politically active. "Columbia is a very liberal-minded school," notes a student. "If you're a Republican, think twice." A junior describes the "typical" student: "Dark neo-'60s style glasses, a plaid sweater vest, army boots, and corduroys." Columbia is much more diverse than any other Ivy League school—approximately 30 percent of students are minorities. "There are a lot of different people of every race, religion, and sexual orientation and someone who cannot accept that would likely feel very lonely," a student observes.

Most students socialize in the dorms or head out with friends to nearby bars and coffeehouses (the Hungarian Pastry Shop is a favorite), or hang out on Low Library steps. Butler Library is "the social scene on campus... don't expect to get work done," a junior comments. On weekends, students make "a mass exodus from the 116th Street subway station" to other parts of the city. "Outside the classroom, the overall atmosphere is actually rather dull," a junior observes. "Since it's such a big city, it seems like people will find things to do outside of campus rather than on it." The Greek scene is small, and has minimal influence on social life ("You have New York City... What do you need cheap beer for?" asks one student.) Drugs, according to students, can be easily found: "No, not the five-fingered leaf . . . we're talking serious drugs," says one student.

The most popular clubs include the College Democrats, African American and Asian American associations, volunteer groups, and the *Columbia Spectator*. "A capella groups are everywhere!" says a student. "There is always a play, or two, or three playing somewhere." "There is a constant battle for more funding for student groups," a student informs us. "The school has an endowment of over five billion dollars, but undergraduates see very little of it."

Columbia competes in NCAA Division I sports. "Our football team sucks miserably and intramural sports struggle as the university provides no funding," a junior complains. "Everyone must take two semesters of physical education... without which most students may never see the gym."

The atmosphere at Columbia is infamous for seeming cold. "People at 'Baby Blue' can be friendly, but be prepared to climb some psychological walls," warns a political science major. Extra support is available for those who seek it: In recent years, Columbia's counseling center reported a 40 percent increase in use since the 1994–95 academic year, and has extended its hours, nearly doubled its staff, and set up offices in dormitories. Still, another student observes, "Someone who is not ready for a big experience in a big city may want to look elsewhere." Another cautions: "New York City is an incredible place, but a future student needs to know what she or he is getting into." A junior sums it up: "You get as much out of Columbia as you put in. The school will not hold your hand... You have to know who you are and what you want."

Other schools to check out: Barnard, University of Pennsylvania, Brown, NYU, Tufts.

Test Scores (middle 50%):
 SAT Verbal: 650–750
 SAT Math: 660–750
 ACT Comp: 26–32
 ACT English: 26–33
 ACT Math: 26–32

HS Rank of Entering Freshmen:
 Top 10%: 81%
 Top 25%: 96%
 Top 50%: 100%

Avg. HS GPA: 3.8

THE EXPERTS SAY...

" Columbia is a wonderful choice for extremely bright students who appreciate the classics and who thrive under pressure. "

" Exciting and stimulating, yes. Warm and fuzzy bonding experience, no. Know what you want out of your college experience before coming to Columbia. "

Costs (2003–04)

Tuition and Fees: $29,788

Room & Board: $8,802

Payment Plan(s): installment plan, pre-payment plan

Inst. Aid (est. 2003–04)

Institutional Aid, Need-Based: $33,048

FT Undergrads Receiving Aid: 42%
 Avg. Amount per Student: $27,079

Of Those Receiving Any Aid:

Rec. Need-Based Scholarship or Grant Aid: 97%
 Average Award: $23,555

Rec. Need-Based Self-Help Aid: 93%
 Average Award: $6,106

Upon Graduation, Avg. Loan Debt per Student: $16,085

Financial Aid Deadline: 2/10

Graduates

Companies Recruiting On-Campus: 370

CONNECTICUT COLLEGE

270 Mohegan Avenue, New London, CT 06320-4196
Admissions Phone: (860) 439-2200 Fax: (860) 439-4301
Email: admission@conncoll.edu Website: www.connecticutcollege.edu
Application Website: www.conncoll.edu/admissions

General Info

Type of School: private, coed

Setting: suburban

Academic Calendar: semester

Student Body

Full-Time Undergrads: 1,701
  Men: 42%, Women: 58%

Part-Time Undergrads: 26
  Men: 15%, Women: 85%

Total Undergrad Population:
  African American: 4%
  Asian American: 3%
  Latino: 4%
  Native American: <1%
  Caucasian: 72%
  International: 9%
  Out-of-State: 84%
  Living Off-Campus: 2%

Graduate and First-Professional
  Students: 12

Academics

Full-Time Faculty: 151
  With Ph.D.: 89%

Part-Time Faculty: 72
  With Ph.D.: 11%

Student/Faculty Ratio: 10:1

Most Popular Majors:
  economics (11%)
  English (10%)
  government/international
    relations (10%)
  psychology (10%)
  history (8%)

Completing 2 or More Majors: 21%

Freshmen Retention Rate: 92%

Graduation Rates:
  83% within four years
  87% within six years

Admissions

Regular Application Deadline: 1/1;
  11/15 (priority)

Early Decision Deadline(s): 11/15,
  1/1

Fall Transfer Deadline: 4/1 (priority)

Spring Transfer Deadline:
  11/1 (priority)

Total # of Students Applied: 4,396
  Admitted: 1,536
  Enrolled: 511

Inside the Classroom

Connecticut College has exceptional academic programs set in a comfortable environment. The college offers more than 1,000 courses and 65 majors, including zoology, astrophysics, dance, gender and women's studies, film studies, religious studies, neuroscience/psychobiology, theater, and medieval studies. CC takes "a holistic approach" to the admissions process: interviews are "strongly recommended," and a California guidance counselor approves of the fact that submission of the SAT I is optional (though submitting three SAT IIs or the ACT is required).

The academics are first-rate in almost all departments, from the performing arts to the social sciences and the natural sciences. CC is particularly known for interdisciplinary studies, innovative international programs, paid internships, and its Honor Code. The Honor Code gives students control over their own education. One student said that being able to take self-scheduled exams under the Honor Code was "what Connecticut was all about." A young alum comments, "The Honor Code creates a more communal atmosphere; self-scheduled exams also reduce stress levels."

The academic atmosphere is "subtly intense, but not overbearing," says one student. Another student's opinion: "Conn Coll is competitive and challenging, although it is not at the Ivy League level." The student body is small, creating a comfortable, warm, mutually enriching environment for students and faculty. "We get to know our peers, professors, and administrators," notes one student. As with the top liberal arts schools, tales of students being invited to professors' homes for dinner are common. Conn students say they admire their professors' commitment, both inside and outside the classroom: In March 2003 (before the war started), 139 Connecticut College faculty and staff signed and released a statement opposing the preemptive war against Iraq.

More than half of the student body study abroad at some point during their college career. In addition, students of any major can apply during their sophomore year to the highly respected Center for International Studies in Liberal Arts (CISLA). This unique program works to "internationalize any major." Students study a particular country's language, culture, and business practices, and get a funded summer internship in that country. Participants must also complete a senior seminar and an integrative project.

Campus Environment

Overlooking the Atlantic Ocean, the Conn campus stretches out over 700 acres, a large portion taken up by an arboretum, instilling a natural beauty that can also calm the nerves and reduce stress. The Crozier-Williams student center—with a bar, snack shop, game room, and coffeehouse—provides a great hangout for students who want to relax and take a break from their books.

If you're looking for comfort and privacy, CC's housing certainly fits the bill. The school has 14 residential houses where all classes and both sexes are integrated (and most bathrooms are coed, too!). Freshmen are placed in doubles, triples, or quads (but Web junkies shouldn't panic: Internet hookups are available for each occupant of every dorm room). According to the college, approximately 90 percent of upperclassmen live in singles; the remaining 10 percent (usually sophomores) are in doubles. Seniors can file an application to move off-campus, where "there a few perennially rented homes, but not many."

The industrial town of New London has never held much appeal for students; many complain about the shortage of "college bars." There have been recent attempts to turn it into "a hip little city," however. One student remarks, "We're seeing every empty building turn into a store or coffee shop." Students find nearby Mystic "a cute town to go out to eat or go shopping."

All students are permitted to bring cars, although parking rules follow a hierarchical system. Freshmen lots are in a more remote location (about a 10-minute walk) while seniors have spots in the center of campus. It's mostly a walking campus, anyway. Take this senior's advice: "One of your friends will have a car, so you don't need to bring one."

Student Life

"The school tends to draw primarily New England-based, relatively affluent white students," a student tells us. Another student notes, "The school is generally preppy in clothing style, music style, among other things… Students that are 'gothic' or 'thugs' may not fit in well." Students tend to be "fairly left-leaning" and concerned about a variety of issues, including human rights and the environment. While there are a good number of international students, the minority population is small; in February 2003, the college chose to provide "a mandatory lesson on diversity and acceptance" in response to a string of racially-charged incidents on campus.

Most students study about three to four hours a night and are very concerned about their grades. But starting on Thursday nights, things get "very lively" for the weekend, we hear. "There is a lot of beer drinking," admits one student, who adds that hard cider is also a local favorite. A senior claims that marijuana is "a big factor" among certain populations and that some students have been known to abuse prescription drugs (then again, "substance-free" housing is available and popular here, too). On the weekends, there's usually a selection of dorm parties and school events, such as the "dress like your favorite superhero" dance, as well as a series of classic and current films.

Athletics are "quite popular, but not dominant in social life," a student says. About 80 percent of the student body participate in intercollegiate, club, or intramural sports. There are 26 Division III teams, with hockey and basketball (there is no football) being among the more popular. Although CC has no fraternities or sororities, there are over 100 student clubs and organizations, including community service, government, and multicultural groups. One popular club is UFO, the Undisputed Funk Organization, dedicated to reliving '70s funk. The theater and dance departments produce numerous quality performances that draw students.

Some Conn Coll students say they quickly tire of being stuck on campus with the same people and the same social options every weekend. But at least one student believes having such a close-knit community is "a blessing in some respects." He continues, "It's nice to be able to walk around the campus and know and recognize people. It gives you a sense of belonging… You're not just a face in a crowd."

Other schools to check out: Bates, Haverford, Bowdoin, Colby, Manhattanville.

# of Students Waitlisted: 852
  Students Accepting Place: 275
  Waitlisted Students Admitted: 37

Applied Early Decision: 324
  Early Decision Admitted: 210

Test Scores (middle 50%):
  SAT Verbal: 603–695
  SAT Math: 602–695

HS Rank of Entering Freshmen:
  Top 10%: 46%
  Top 50%: 97%

Costs (2004–5)

Comprehensive Fees: $39,975

THE EXPERTS SAY...

" Connecticut College's low acceptance rates make it one of the most selective liberal arts colleges in the country. The rigor of your high school program carries the most weight in Conn's holistic admissions process. "

" CC is a great school, in spite of the fact that their mascot is a camel. (What's their motto—'We can hold our water'???) "

Inst. Aid (est. 2003–04)

Institutional Aid, Need-Based: $13,945,090

FT Undergrads Receiving Aid: 46%
  Avg. Amount per Student: $24,120

Of Those Receiving Any Aid:

Rec. Need-Based Scholarship or Grant Aid: 91%
  Average Award: $21,414

Rec. Need-Based Self-Help Aid: 87%
  Average Award: $5,332

Upon Graduation, Avg. Loan Debt per Student: $18,375

Financial Aid Deadline: 1/15

Graduates

Alumni Giving: 43%

COOPER UNION FOR THE ADVANCEMENT OF SCIENCE AND ART

30 Cooper Square, New York, NY 10003
Admissions Phone: (212) 353-4120 Fax: (212) 353-4342 Website: cooper.edu

---

Note: Info. not verified by school

General Info

Type of School: private, coed
Setting: urban
Academic Calendar: semester

Student Body

Full-Time Undergrads: 846
    Men: 65%, Women: 35%

Part-Time Undergrads: 10
    Men: 60%, Women: 40%

Total Undergrad Population:
    African American: 5%
    Asian American: 28%
    Latino: 7%
    Native American: <1%
    Caucasian: 49%
    International: 8%
    Out-of-State: 44%
    Living Off-Campus: 80%
    In Fraternities: 10%
    In Sororities: 5%

Graduate and First-Professional
    Students: 12

Academics

Full-Time Faculty: 56

Part-Time Faculty: 196

Most Popular Majors:
    fine art (30%)
    architecture (17%)
    electrical engineering (15%)
    mechanical engineering (13%)
    chemical engineering (11%)

Freshmen Retention Rate: 90%

Graduation Rates:
    63% within four years
    79% within six years

Admissions

Early Decision Deadline(s): 12/1

Total # of Students Applied: 2,210
    Admitted: 297
    Enrolled: 202

HS Rank of Entering Freshmen:
    Top 10%: 80%
    Top 25%: 100%

Avg. HS GPA: 3.3

Inside the Classroom

"We are the best-kept secret in New York, and maybe in the college world," confides one Cooper Union student. And it's a wonder why. For a great education at a great price in a great location, Cooper Union is hard to beat. Cooper Union's three renowned schools—the School of Art, the Irwin S. Chanin School of Architecture, and the Albert Nerken School of Engineering—are completely focused on preparing students for professions in their respective areas. And perhaps the most unbelievable part: All students receive full-tuition scholarships.

This is not to say Cooper Union is a free ride. It's tough to get in—Cooper accepts about 150 architecture students, 250 art students, and 450 engineering students out of a huge applicant pool—and it's tough to stay in. Don't even apply if you're unsure of what you want to do; the only flexibility you'll find is in the engineering school, and there you can switch only to different disciplines of engineering. Applicants to the art and architecture schools must submit "home tests"—a number of projects to be completed within one month and returned to the admissions committee for review. Each "home test" contains its own instructions to be followed explicitly. You have to know what you want and be ready to show you can do it to get into Cooper Union.

It doesn't get any easier upon acceptance. Students are immediately thrust into an intensive, structured program that combines academic study with practical, hands-on projects. The workload is heavy, and students spend the bulk of their hours committed to schoolwork. Students at Cooper Union bond quickly, however, in part because the workload is intense and support is needed, and in part because teamwork is encouraged by the faculty. "You won't make it through here unless you learn to work as a team. They tell you that from day one, and you find out quickly it's true," says one student. "There's no room here for arrogance or timidity. And, frankly, there's no room for it in these fields once you go on to the outside world. In a way, it's the best training."

Students have mixed reviews of the professors and their accessibility; some question the teaching skills of these experts. However, everyone is taught by full professors, and class sizes are small. All students in the first two years take a core curriculum of four required courses in the humanities and social sciences, giving students a rare chance to interact with those outside their own program. Third- and fourth-year students continue to explore the humanities and social sciences through elective courses. While the facilities of nearby NYU are available to Cooper students (such as the library), cross-registration is an irregular arrangement. "Some semesters it's available, some not," said one student. Career services are said to be excellent for the schools of engineering and architecture, and so-so for the school of art.

Campus Environment

Cooper Union doesn't have a campus so much as a cluster of four buildings in the East Village, the bohemian downtown section of New York City. The school's historic Great Hall has witnessed the birth of the NAACP, the women's suffrage movement, and the American Red Cross, and has hosted over a century's worth of serious discussion and debate, with speakers ranging from Abraham Lincoln to Bill Clinton.

Cooper housing is very limited and guaranteed only to freshmen. Dorm rooms have kitchenettes; when students tire of cooking, they can eat at the school cafeteria or grab a bite from the hundreds of delis, bistros, pizzerias, and coffee shops within blocks of school. Off-campus housing—well, this is New York: people aren't joking when they talk about scanning the obituaries for vacancies. Transportation is by bus, subway, and taxi. Cars are a liability in the city, and students are strongly advised to leave theirs home.

Student Life

Cooper Union's Village location provides social opportunities by the thousands, if the busy Cooper student can find any time to enjoy them. The school is within easy walking distance of Washington Square Park and the numerous bookstores, galleries, and film houses of Greenwich Village, and students can easily travel to other sections of the city via bus or subway. Art and architecture students especially take full advantage of the city's many museums and historic landmarks since it complements their coursework.

Since Cooper Union is small, campus social offerings are limited, but students are allowed to participate in NYU's extracurricular activities. The typical Cooper student is sleepy from pulling all-nighters, but does usually have enough energy for billiards, ping-pong, or bowling; intercollegiate sports play little role in campus life, and intramural participation is low. Some indicate that the lack of a central campus makes for a diffuse college community; others say that the atmosphere at Cooper is close-knit, at least within each school. The school's academic divisions sometimes complicate things: engineers are described as "nerds," architects as "stuck-up," and art students as "self-absorbed." Over 40 percent of Cooper's students are minority students; of them, well over half are Asian, but racial divisions don't seem to cause the problems that academic ones do at Cooper.

There is Greek life at Cooper, but the frats don't have houses, nor are they particularly noted for parties or events. A relatively high percentage of Cooper students join professional clubs. Students do occasionally venture out into the East Village to explore its bars and clubs, and go to apartment parties, but Cooper isn't by any stretch of the imagination a party school. While there may not be much by way of traditional campus life, Cooper offers its sometimes offbeat students top-notch preparation in their fields and fast friendships formed in late-night study groups.

Other schools to check out: NYU, Carnegie Mellon, Parsons School of Design, Rhode Island School of Design.

Costs (2003–04)

Tuition and Fees: $27,400

Every student receives a full-tuition scholarship

Room & Board: $9,000

Institutional Aid

Financial Aid Deadline: 6/15, 4/15 (priority)

Graduates

Going to Graduate School: 43% Within One Year

Accepting Job Offer: 57% at time of graduation

Companies Recruiting On Campus: 80

THE EXPERTS SAY...

" It's hard to get into Cooper Union, but for architects, artists, and engineers, the preparation and the price—free—are hard to beat. "

" The East Village is designed for fun—too bad you'll be pulling all-nighters instead. "

CORNELL COLLEGE

600 First Street West, Mount Vernon, IA 52314-1098
Admissions Phone: (319) 895-4477; (800) 747-1112 Fax: (319) 895-4451
Email: admissions@cornellcollege.edu
Website: www.cornellcollege.edu

General Info

Type of School: private, coed, Methodist

Setting: small town

Academic Calendar: Nine $3\frac{1}{2}$ week terms

Student Body

Full-Time Undergrads: 1,093
  Men: 41%, Women: 59%

Part-Time Undergrads: 8
  Men: 13%, Women: 88%

Total Undergrad Population:
  African American: 2%
  Asian American: 1%
  Latino: 3%
  Native American: 1%
  Caucasian: 88%
  International: 1%
  Out-of-State: 69%
  Living Off-Campus: 9%
  In Fraternities: 30%
  In Sororities: 32%

Academics

Full-Time Faculty: 85
  With Ph.D.: 85%

Part-Time Faculty: 16
  With Ph.D.: 69%

Student/Faculty Ratio: 12:1

Most Popular Majors:
  psychology (15%)
  economics and business (11%)
  secondary education (9%)
  English (8%)
  history (8%)

Completing 2 or More Majors: 49%

Freshmen Retention Rate: 81%

Graduation Rates:
  63% within four years
  68% within six years

Admissions

Regular Application Deadline: 3/1

Fall Transfer Deadline: 3/1

Spring Transfer Deadline: 12/1

Total # of Students Applied: 1,555
  Admitted: 1,067
  Enrolled: 369

# of Students Waitlisted: 137
  Students Accepting Place: 137
  Waitlisted Students Admitted: 23

Inside the Classroom

Cornell College, a small, liberal arts school, is unusual in that it offers a "One-Course-At-A-Time" framework. This means that students study one topic intensively for three and a half weeks; the school year is comprised of nine such terms, with about 60 courses offered each term. Four-day breaks between terms let students chill out and regroup before hitting the next topic. Students say that taking one course at a time allows you to "immerse yourself fully in the subject." According to one student, "If you love a class, you are able to devote yourself to the class, and nothing else is going to slip. If you hate a class, it's over in 18 days." And for better or worse, "it's impossible to procrastinate" when the entire term lasts 18 days. Classes are small, averaging 14 students; it's the rare class that has more than 25. According to Cornell, "Meaningful interaction with professors is the rule, not the exception." Professors are extremely accessible, often inviting students to their homes. One recent grad calls the learning environment "spectacular." We do hear of some grousing that too many professors are part-timers, which may be a product of Cornell's One-Course-At-A-Time framework.

Cornell is very flexible; it "encourages the creative structuring of a student's educational experiences by offering a choice of four degree programs within the framework of a liberal education." Programs include Bachelor of Arts, Bachelor of Music, Bachelor of Philosophy degrees, as well as the Bachelor of Special Studies. All students are placed in the B.A. program upon entering Cornell, until they choose another degree program. The B.A. program has 10–14 course requirements, distributed over natural sciences, social sciences, humanities, mathematics, foreign languages, and fine arts. There are preprofessional programs in medicine, law, dentistry, medical technology, nursing, social work, and theology. The most popular majors are psychology, biology, economics, and education. Nearly half of all Cornell graduates finish with more than one major, and many students design their own major.

Internships are big at Cornell: According to one college official, in a recent class, almost two-thirds of students participated in one or more internships while attending the college.

Campus Environment

Students say the Cornell campus is "absolutely beautiful." The college rests on a wooded hilltop and is listed on the National Register of Historic Places. Students who live on campus—and more than 90 percent do—are housed in single-sex residence halls, coed residence halls, and apartments. About half of the first-year students live in freshmen-only dorms, with the rest scattered among all of the other residence halls. Dorm rooms are about average in size and retain "the charm from years ago." All students are allowed to have cars on campus. The campus is fully wired, and students have access to the Internet from every residence hall room. Another perk is free cable-TV hookup in each dorm room.

A number of facilities have recently been renovated or are currently under construction, including the largest residence hall and several academic buildings. There's also a brand-new technology center.

Student Life

Word is that Cornell feels like a "real community," in part because nearly all students live on campus. Students seem to be happy at Cornell, even if they do report a bit of claustrophobia in this small, sheltered environment. Cornell participates in the Iowa Intercollegiate Athletic Conference, and about a quarter of students participate in one or more intercollegiate sports; wrestling is particularly popular and well-regarded. More than half of students participate in one or more of the 66 intramural sports offered. About two-thirds of students get involved in volunteering. There are 14 non-national Greek "social and service groups" on campus, which about 30 percent of students join. Of Cornell's nearly 1,000 students, nearly 70 percent are from out of state.

Most of the social life goes on on campus, and the school sponsors frequent concerts, lectures, and activities. Tiny Mount Vernon, Iowa is a pretty town with a population of less than 4,000 and one stoplight. As you might guess, there's not much going on in town, but Iowa City and Cedar Rapids are each less than 20 miles away, and Chicago is a doable weekend road trip.

Other schools to check out: Colorado College, Hiram, Hastings, Evergreen State, Allegheny.

Test Scores (middle 50%):
SAT Verbal: 560–670
SAT Math: 530–660
ACT Comp: 23–29
ACT English: 23–30
ACT Math: 22–28

THE EXPERTS SAY...

" With the One-Course-at-a-Time plan, you can immerse yourself in a subject for month without any distractions, then try something completely new. "

" You can get the One-Course-at-a-Time plan at Colorado College—and you won't have to be in Iowa. "

HS Rank of Entering Freshmen:
Top 10%: 29%
Top 25%: 57%
Top 50%: 87%

Avg. HS GPA: 3.54

Costs (2004–5)

Tuition and Fees: $22,650

Room & Board: $6,240

Payment Plan(s): installment plan

Inst. Aid (est. 2003–04)

Institutional Aid, Need-Based: $11,210,559

Institutional Aid, Non-Need-Based: $2,684,733

FT Undergrads Receiving Aid: 77%
Avg. Amount per Student: $19,455

FT Undergrads Receiving Non-Need-Based Scholarship or Grant Aid: 23%
Avg. Amount per Student: $11,210

Of Those Receiving Any Aid:

Rec. Need-Based Scholarship or Grant Aid: 100%
Average Award: $15,585

Rec. Need-Based Self-Help Aid: 79%
Average Award: $4,858

Upon Graduation, Avg. Loan Debt per Student: $17,850

Financial Aid Deadline: 3/1 (priority)

Graduates

Going to Graduate School:
31% Within One Year

Companies Recruiting On Campus: 10

Alumni Giving: 50%

CORNELL UNIVERSITY

410 Thurston Avenue, Ithaca, NY 14850
Admissions Phone: (607) 255-5241 Fax: (607) 255-0659
Email: admissions@cornell.edu Website: www.cornell.edu
Application Website: admissions.cornell.edu

General Info

Type of School: private, coed

Setting: small town

Academic Calendar: semester

Student Body

Full-Time Undergrads: 13,616
  Men: 50%, Women: 50%

Total Undergrad Population:
  African American: 5%
  Asian American: 16%
  Latino: 5%
  Native American: <1%
  Caucasian: 60%
  International: 7%
  Out-of-State: 62%
  Living Off-Campus: 42%
  In Fraternities: 27%
  In Sororities: 24%

Graduate and First-Professional
  Students: 5,965

Academics

Full-Time Faculty: 1,643
  With Ph.D.: 91%

Part-Time Faculty: 153
  With Ph.D.: 74%

Student/Faculty Ratio: 9:1

Most Popular Majors:
  biological/life sciences (17%)
  engineering (16%)
  agriculture (10%)
  social science/history (9%)

Completing 2 or More Majors: 1%

Freshmen Retention Rate: 96%

Graduation Rates:
  85% within four years
  92% within six years

Admissions

Regular Application Deadline: 1/1

Early Decision Deadline(s): 11/10,
  12/11

Fall Transfer Deadline: 3/15

Spring Transfer Deadline: 11/1

Total # of Students Applied: 20,441
  Admitted: 6,334
  Enrolled: 3,135

# of Students Waitlisted: 1,983
  Students Accepting Place: 1,632
  Waitlisted Students Admitted: 4

Inside the Classroom

"Choices, choices, choices!" raves a guidance counselor about this "all-encompassing school." Cornell has seven undergraduate schools, but three—agriculture and life sciences; human ecology; and industrial and labor relations—are funded by New York State, so New Yorkers can attend for just above SUNY tuition. While tuition at these so-called "contract schools" is going up, it's still an incredible bargain that sets Cornell apart from the other Ivies. Cornell's four private schools—hotel administration; engineering; architecture, art, and planning; and arts and sciences— are considered among the best in the nation. Each school has its own admission and core requirements, but all students live together and share many other facilities. Students can choose from more than 4,000 courses in any of the seven schools.

While most students call Cornell's atmosphere "fiercely competitive" ("I've seen more than my share of people crying on the steps of the chemistry building after receiving their organic chemistry exam grades..."), others insist that "students and profs help each other." A California guidance counselor notes that programs in the "sciences are very intense." "Don't expect the grade inflation that is so rampant at other Ivies to be duplicated at Cornell," a bio major warns. "Professors expect blood, and most of the time get it." Is the effort worth it? It "definitely prepares you for the real world," says another guidance counselor. A senior concludes, "A Cornell degree is worth much more than its weight in gold."

There's a popular saying that it may be easier to get into Cornell than other Ivies, but it's the hardest one to stay in. Of course, even if you think you've gotten in, you need to make sure it's for real: The *New York Times* reported that in February 2003, Cornell emailed acceptance letters to 1,700 high school students who had submitted early-decision applications—including nearly 550 applicants who had already been rejected in December. (Within a couple of hours, the admissions staff followed with an "oops" email message to those 550 applicants, admitting that they had made a mistake and offering their apology "for any confusion and distress this message has caused.")

Cornell recently announced a sweeping $400 million 10-year plan to become the finest research institution for undergraduates in the nation. Freshmen are now guaranteed good housing, get to work with sophisticated classroom technologies, and are getting faculty attention (theoretically) on par with graduate students. Even with Cornell's new focus on undergrads, finding your way among 13,500 of them "can be overwhelming," notes a New York City guidance counselor, warning that "one can get lost." Forming relationships with the faculty can be another challenge; a lot of advising goes on by email. But a senior says that professors are "demanding but accessible."

Jeffrey S. Lehman, former dean of the University of Michigan Law School and a Cornell alum, took office as Cornell's eleventh president on July 1, 2003. Lehman recently gained national prominence for his leading role in Michigan's defense of its race-conscious admissions policies.

Campus Environment

While one student calls Ithaca "a friendly hippie town" and a guidance counselor says that it "has everything you need," most students find it dull. "Ithaca is generally a dead town," explains a student. "Kmart is often the source of amusement." Transportation is by foot if you live in the dorms. "You really *can* tell your kids that you walked up a hill through ten feet of snow just to get to class," a student quips. There is a bus system, which students rate from "awful" to "excellent." A car isn't necessary, say students, but it's nice to have for trips to Syracuse and Manhattan.

As part of its undergrad initiative, freshmen and sophomores are now guaranteed housing, with all freshmen living on North campus. "North has nicer dorms… bigger rooms, nicer design," a history major explains. Students who live off campus mainly move to Collegetown, adjacent to Cornell's campus, where there are affordable apartments, inexpensive restaurants, and popular bars and coffeehouses.

The food at Cornell is rated among the best in the nation. There are a variety of dining plans, and several times a year, chefs from the country's best restaurants prepare their signature dishes for students. Cornell's own dairies make homemade ice cream, served every night.

Student Life

Cornell students are as passionate about social causes as they are about their schoolwork; rallies for a variety of causes are common on campus. There are literally hundreds of clubs. "You will find every single interest you can think of at this school and a group of people who share that interest," declares one student. "There are hippies, punks, preppies, trendy New Yorkers, nerds, jocks, and so many more. Everyone can find their niche at Cornell." While a senior tells us that Cornell students tend to be "rather conservative (as college students go)," another student insists, "While many Cornellians tend to be wealthy, I have never found that money gets in the way of friendships." A junior agrees: "The great thing about Cornell is that no one judges you. I am friends with all kinds of people… Everyone is unique and gets respected for it."

On weekend nights, Cornellians hit the Collegetown bars or house parties. A senior adds, "Collegetown is pretty rowdy from Thursday–Saturday, but Uris Library is the main social scene Sunday–Wednesday." There are more than 50 fraternities and sororities, which are responsible for a lot of the social life. In warm weather, students head to the gorges and the Cornell Plantations (3,000 acres of woodlands, streams, and nature trails) to tan, swim, hike, and play frisbee; during the winter, many head to nearby Greek Peak to ski.

As far as varsity sports go, one student comments, "Cornell varsity athletics are pretty pathetic, but what do you expect from a bunch of academic overachievers?" The exception is men's hockey, where "you have to sleep out just to get tickets," a senior complains. Students tend to vent any pent up aggression at hockey games, especially against Harvard: "Lynah Rink has been voted as the rink most disliked by visiting teams because the fans are so rabid." Though varsity sports are a little uneven, a junior informs us, "Cornell has the largest intramural sports program in the Ivies. You can find a sport and someone to play with at your level, guaranteed."

Other schools to check out: University of Pennsylvania, Harvard, Johns Hopkins, University of Chicago, University of Rochester.

Applied Early Decision: 2,730
Early Decision Admitted: 1,709

Test Scores (middle 50%):
SAT Verbal: 610–700
SAT Math: 622–720
ACT Comp:

HS Rank of Entering Freshmen:
Top 10%: 87%
Top 25%: 93%
Top 50%: 100%

THE EXPERTS SAY…

" Ezra Cornell wrote: 'I would found an institution where any person can find instruction in any study.' Today, Cornell continues to take its commitment to diversity seriously. "

" The low in-state tuition at its three state-funded colleges makes Cornell far more affordable for many students than its peer institutions. And who can resist homemade ice cream? "

Costs (est. 2004–05)

Tuition and Fees: $28,754

Room & Board: $9,580

Payment Plan(s): installment plan

Inst. Aid (est. 2003–04)

Institutional Aid, Need-Based: $79,300,000

FT Undergrads Receiving Aid: 48%
Avg. Amount per Student: $24,500

Of Those Receiving Any Aid:

Rec. Need-Based Scholarship or Grant Aid: 94%
Average Award: $17,100

Rec. Need-Based Self-Help Aid: 95%
Average Award: $8,800

Upon Graduation, Avg. Loan Debt per Student: $20,277

Financial Aid Deadline: 2/11

Graduates

Going to Graduate School: 32% Within One Year

Accepting Job Offer: 45% at time of graduation

Companies Recruiting On Campus: 578

CREIGHTON UNIVERSITY

2500 California Plaza, Omaha, NE 68178-0001
Admissions Phone: (402) 280-2703; (800) 282-5835 Fax: (402) 280-2685
Email: admissions@creighton.edu Website: www.creighton.edu
Application Website: www.applyweb.com/apply/creightn/menu.html

General Info

Type of School: private, coed, Catholic Jesuit

Setting: urban

Academic Calendar: semester

Student Body

Full-Time Undergrads: 3,444
  Men: 40%, Women: 60%

Part-Time Undergrads: 292
  Men: 31%, Women: 69%

Total Undergrad Population:
  African American: 3%
  Asian American: 7%
  Latino: 3%
  Native American: 1%
  Caucasian: 84%
  International: 2%
  Out-of-State: 56%
  Living Off-Campus: 55%
  In Fraternities: 21%
  In Sororities: 28%

Graduate and First-Professional Students: 2,801

Academics

Full-Time Faculty: 622
  With Ph.D.: 92%

Part-Time Faculty: 238
  With Ph.D.: 92%

Student/Faculty Ratio: 14:1

Most Popular Majors:
  nursing (18%)
  biology (9%)
  psychology (8%)
  finance (8%)
  journalism (7%)

Freshmen Retention Rate: 86%

Graduation Rates:
  58% within four years
  71% within six years

Admissions

Regular Application Deadline: 8/1;
  1/1 (priority)

Fall Transfer Deadline: 8/1

Total # of Students Applied: 3,199
  Admitted: 2,813
  Enrolled: 937

Test Scores (middle 50%):
  SAT Verbal: 530–650
  SAT Math: 540–650
  ACT Comp: 23–28

Inside the Classroom

"As a Jesuit Catholic university, Creighton emphasizes *cura personalis*, care for the whole person—mental, spiritual, and physical," a Creighton official informs us. Creighton students are groomed for personal and professional success in an atmosphere of personal academic support.

Creighton's three undergraduate colleges provide a sound education in arts and sciences, business administration, and nursing. Majors and special programs include conventional war horses like history, physics, economics, business leadership, and fine arts, as well as some more unusual options like Irish studies, justice and peace studies, Native American studies, and electronic commerce. For all undergrads, core curriculum requirements include courses in five categories: theology, philosophy and ethics; cultures, ideas, and civilizations; the natural sciences; social and behavioral sciences; and skills like writing, speech, and mathematics.

Preprofessional programs are extremely popular at Creighton. The real powerhouse programs are the medical and nursing degrees, so it's not surprising that the premed program is so strong. "It's well deserved and worth the price students pay to associate themselves with it," says a premed student. "The quality of instruction at this level is fantastic." Fortunately for Creighton undergrads, the professional schools give them preference when it comes to admissions. Creighton University faculty members are internationally recognized for research in such diverse areas as cancer genetics, respiratory diseases, osteoporosis and hard tissue research, laser dentistry and implantology, and health policy and ethics.

"The teachers are very helpful and concerned with student progress," states a junior majoring in public relations, who also points out that "classes at Creighton are so small that they are hard to skip because teachers notice." Another student's take on Creighton classes: "Some classes don't require students to do more than read the text and memorize the facts. This is an effective method, but it's usually not built upon with meaningful lectures or talked about in discussion groups." Still, this student adds, "The classes that were good were very, very good."

Campus Environment

A picturesque, tree-lined mall runs down the middle of Creighton's 92-acre campus, which is a reasonable walk from downtown Omaha. A junior tells us, "Creighton is a very down-to-earth campus. When it is nice out, most of the students are sitting on the lawn studying between classes." "The campus is very friendly," agrees a sophomore. "Everyone knows everybody else, somehow. In a way, that's a good thing, but when you want some down time for yourself, it can be hard to get away." While a Jesuit campus in Nebraska might seem like the safest place on earth, common sense precautions should still be taken: In December 2002, a Creighton custodian was fired after stealing students' names and Social Security numbers out of the trash to set up fraudulent phone accounts.

All freshmen are assigned to freshmen-only residence halls. Two new dorms were recently built to accommodate the university's recent growth. "We have great on-campus housing," said one junior. "The dorms were refurbished and remodeled in the past few years, and they're very comfortable." Another junior elaborates: "At Creighton, you have to live in the dorms freshman and sophomore year. The dorms freshman year have a great sense of community and allow people to make lots of friends. Sophomore year, the dorms are suite-style and there are four people to a room (two bedrooms and a bathroom)."

Off-campus housing is popular among upperclassmen, and the university sends daily shuttles to designated spots where high concentrations of students live. Yet living too far away has its drawbacks, according to one nursing student. "If you live more than a mile away, you need a car. The Omaha transportation system sucks … it rarely works, and if it does, it's late. And it closes early."

As for the city of Omaha … well, one student puts it this way: "There's a saying my friends and I have: Omaha is what you make of it, and not what it makes of you. You have to look for the fun things, not wait for them." As Nebraska's largest city, Omaha offers students some shopping and entertainment options, as well as opportunities for internships and employment in city government and leading industries, including telecommunications, insurance, banking, and health care.

Student Life

When asked to consider what the typical Creighton student is like, one student says, "White, Catholic, upper-middle class, and from the Midwest. The only student I don't see fitting into our school is one who's extremely liberal. Even though we're open to new avenues of thought and cultural experiences, a forward thinker may not be taken very well in a school grounded in tradition. That would include Goths or an anarchist-type person."

Creighton weekends, which begin unofficially on Thursday, offer the usual types of college fun. "Partying is a way to relax and release tensions from the week," says one recent graduate. "Drinking is big on campus but not so big off campus. A lot of us get together at one another's houses for potluck dinners and stuff, and then we go to the bars." The five fraternities and four sororities are popular and "throw great parties." "Most of our student-elected congress and board of directors are members of the Greek system," notes a student. Lately, more students have been ending their weekend on a wholesome note by attending Candlelight Mass at 10 P.M. on Sundays.

Relatively small schools like Creighton usually get stomped in NCAA sports, but Creighton's Division I Bluejays—particularly the men's basketball team—are very successful and have a loyal fan base. "They play with such enthusiasm; it's awe-inspiring," says a starry-eyed fan. Intramural sports are also big: "Most of the student organizations have a team, and each of the dorms has multiple teams that play. The interest has been so great that they had to expand the program to meet demand."

When asked what sets Creighton apart from other schools, a senior sums it up this way: "The fact that we're Jesuit, and that we're one big family. All members of the Creighton community are in tune with this point. It makes us what we are." A Jesuit priest agrees: "I think that more students are coming to Creighton looking for something spiritual; more students are listening to a voice to find a new dimension in life that was missing."

Other schools to check out: Marquette, DePaul, Loyola of Chicago, Saint Louis University, University of Dayton.

HS Rank of Entering Freshmen:
Top 10%: 38%
Top 25%: 69%
Top 50%: 90%
Avg. HS GPA: 99%

Costs (2004–5)
Tuition and Fees: $19,922
Room & Board: $6,826

THE EXPERTS SAY...

" Creighton's motto of 'cura personalis' isn't just for show: Each year, the varsity basketball team spends the Thanksgiving holiday serving meals to the homeless at a local shelter. "

" The acceptance rate is absurdly high, making Creighton a shrewd choice for premed wannabes who might get weeded out of the premed program at a more selective school. "

Inst. Aid (est. 2003–04)

Institutional Aid, Need-Based:
$13,584,266

Institutional Aid, Non-Need-Based:
$8,653,783

FT Undergrads Receiving Aid: 50%
Avg. Amount per Student: $18,340

FT Undergrads Receiving Non-Need-Based Scholarship or Grant Aid: 28%
Avg. Amount per Student: 7,568

Of Those Receiving Any Aid:

Rec. Need-Based Scholarship or Grant Aid: 18%
Average Award: $11,637

Rec. Need-Based Self-Help Aid: 86%
Average Award: $7,131

Upon Graduation, Avg. Loan Debt per Student: $20,920

Financial Aid Deadline: rolling, 4/1 (priority)

Graduates
Alumni Giving: 30%

CULINARY INSTITUTE OF AMERICA

1946 Campus Drive, Hyde Park, NY 12538
Admissions Phone: (800) 285-4627; (845) 452-9430 Fax: (845) 451-1068
Email: admissions@culinary.edu Website: www.ciachef.edu
Application Website: https://www.applyweb.com/aw?ciachef

General Info

Type of School: private, coed

Setting: suburban

Academic Calendar: continuous,
Progressive Learning Year

Student Body

Full-Time Undergrads: 2,404
Men: 65%, Women: 35%

Total Undergrad Population:
African American: 1%
Asian American: 3%
Latino: 4%
Native American: 1%
Caucasian: 62%
International: 7%
Out-of-State: 71%
Living Off-Campus: 22%

Academics

Full-Time Faculty: 131

Part-Time Faculty: 59

Student/Faculty Ratio: 18:1

Most Popular Majors:
culinary arts
baking and pastry arts
culinary arts management
baking and pastry arts management

Admissions

Total # of Students Applied: 1,173
Admitted: 788
Enrolled: 531

Waitlist Available

HS Rank of Entering Freshmen:
Top 10%: 9%
Top 25%: 25%
Top 50%: 50%

Avg. HS GPA: 2.98

Costs (2003–04)

Tuition and Fees: $18,540

Room & Board: $6,320

Payment Plan(s): installment plan

Inside the Classroom

Are you upset because you think you have to choose between cooking and college? Between bouillabaisse and a bachelor's degree? Don't be. The Culinary Institute of America, the country's premier training facility for the food service industry, offers bachelor's degrees in culinary arts management and in baking and pastry arts management. (The CIA also offers popular associate's degree programs in culinary arts and in baking and pastry arts.) And you won't find finer faculty anywhere: The largest concentration of Certified Master Chefs in the country is found among the CIA's 130 faculty members.

It gets better: Because the CIA's calendar is based on a unique Progressive Learning Year, you can enroll during any one of the CIA's 16 entry dates throughout the year and go on to earn your bachelor's degree in only 38 months. The Progressive Learning Year is a "building block system," where students take only one kitchen course at a time for three weeks and then progress to the next intensive three-week class. "Students must have the ability to multitask, while concurrently focusing on a specific subject or skill," explains a CIA staff member. "Effective stress management, creative thinking, and an analytical mind are also trademarks of successful students at the college. These attributes help students to excel during their tenure at the CIA, as well as when they enter their professional careers."

The first two years of the bachelor's degree programs are identical to those for the associate's degree, featuring instruction in cooking, baking, liberal arts, and management. Students leave campus for five months between freshman and sophomore years for their 18-week, paid "externships." Junior- and senior-year courses expand upon earlier courses, with marketing, communications, finance, foreign language, humanities, and advanced culinary and management classes. Between junior and senior year, students get to participate in a highly anticipated, month-long "intercession"—a Wine and Food Seminar in California.

The college boasts that there are approximately 7–8 job opportunities per CIA graduate. "With the CIA on your résumé, you will be instantly networked with the more than 35,000 CIA alumni," says the school. "Our alumni are chefs and executive chefs, bakers, pastry chefs, caterers, research and development chefs, educators (nationally, 35 percent of the instructors in culinary programs are CIA graduates), food stylists, food journalists, authors, media celebrities, marketers, corporate leaders, restaurateurs, and entrepreneurs."

The CIA requires that you have at least six months of food service experience before entering the program. "The experience requirement is designed to help you understand the realities of working in the food service industry before you enroll." (Note that you don't need this experience to *apply* for admission; the requirement must be met before *entering* the CIA.)

Academics are taken seriously here. The Learning Strategies Center (LSC) offers peer tutoring, workshops, supplemental practice materials, computer-assisted instruction, and one-on-one sessions with staff. Tutoring for writing and math is available in the Writing Center and Math Lab. In addition, you can receive guidance through the Faculty Mentor Program, which pairs faculty members with students who are experiencing difficulties during their freshman year.

Campus Environment

The CIA's 150-acre residential campus is located in Hyde Park (population: 29,000), approximately three miles north of Poughkeepsie in the beautiful Hudson Valley. It's a region rich in food and wine, with many local producers supplying fresh, seasonal products and ingredients that you will work with in your classes. It's the best of both worlds—only minutes from the mountains and less than two hours away from New York City. A car is not necessary but can make traveling easier. Public transportation options (taxis, buses, trains) are available for off-campus travel.

New students are guaranteed on-campus housing, if they request it. The four residence halls and modular cottages house more than 1,200 students. This summer, construction begins on new townhouse-style residence halls. Three of the four residence halls feature private baths; students under 21 are assigned to the alcohol-free residence hall. Most rooms are doubles; temporary triples may be set up in cases of overcrowding. All rooms are air-conditioned and wired for phone and TV service. The campus features a wireless network accessible from all residence halls, classrooms, and key public spaces.

The facilities, which include 41 kitchens and bakeshops and five award-winning public restaurants, are outstanding. The Colavita Center for Italian Food and Wine opened in 2001, with classrooms, kitchens, and the Ristorante Caterina de Medici. Farquharson Hall, the main student dining facility and former Jesuit chapel, underwent a $1.4 million renovation in 2002.

CIA students can just sit back and laugh as they listen to their peers at other colleges complain about cafeteria food. All the food at the CIA, whether it's being served to freshmen or to four-star generals, is always divine. The students themselves have a hand in this: For example, students in the sophomore-level Banqueting and Catering class prepare and serve food for the incoming freshmen during the new students' first three weeks on campus. And the incredible food isn't confined to campus: Recently, the U.S. Navy began a program in which new recruits attend the CIA for basic training as "mess specialists" prior to deployment on ships.

Student Life

The CIA has a very diverse student body that ranges in age from 17 to 60 (the average age is 23), hails from all across the United States and 30 countries, and includes recent high school graduates, food service professionals, and career changers. "Whatever your background, you'll fit right in here," says the college.

Students have the chance to participate in many campus clubs, most of which are food-oriented. You must be at least 21 years old to join the Ale and Lager Educational Society, which "examines the science, art, and business of brewing through tours, presentations, tastings, and hands-on brewing." The Cigar Society "explores the culture and culinary traditions of cigar smoking including pairing with food and spirits, table service, etiquette and other restaurant issues." Other popular organizations: Culinary Christian Fellowship, Black Culinary Society, and Women Chefs and Restauranteurs.

About 700 CIA students participate in at least one of the school's nine intramural or four club sports. Students also have on-campus movies, parties, casino nights, dances, stand-up, and other campus events to keep them entertained. In addition, the Office of Student Activities regularly sponsors trips to places like New York City, Boston, malls, and ski resorts.

Other schools to check out: Cornell, Drexel, Syracuse, Texas Tech, Kansas State.

Inst. Aid (2002–03)

Institutional Aid, Need-Based: $5,457,618

Institutional Aid, Non-Need-Based: $1,710,324

FT Undergrads Receiving Aid: 83%
Avg. Amount per Student: $8,500

FT Undergrads Receiving Non-Need-Based Scholarship or Grant Aid: 4%
Avg. Amount per Student: $2,000

Of Those Receiving Any Aid:

Rec. Need-Based Scholarship or Grant Aid: 66%
Average Award: $2,000

Rec. Need-Based Self-Help Aid: 100%
Average Award: $5,715

Financial Aid Deadline: rolling

Graduates

Companies Recruiting On-Campus: 320

THE EXPERTS SAY...

" This year, the CIA doubled the enrollment of its baking and pastry degree programs due to the growing demand for qualified bakers and pastry chefs. "

" It sounds so tempting: Get a highly respected degree, working with world-class chefs on a beautiful, residential campus. Is it too late to change careers? "

DARTMOUTH COLLEGE

Dartmouth, Hanover, NH 03755
Admissions Phone: (603) 646-2875 Fax: (603) 646-1216
Email: admissions.office@dartmouth.edu Website: www.dartmouth.edu
Application Website: app.commonapp.org

General Info

Type of School: private, coed
Setting: rural
Academic Calendar: quarter

Student Body

Full-Time Undergrads: 4,006
  Men: 51%, Women: 49%

Total Undergrad Population:
  African American: 6%
  Asian American: 12%
  Latino: 6%
  Native American: 3%
  Caucasian: 59%
  International: 5%
  Out-of-State: 96%
  Living Off-Campus: 19%
  In Fraternities: 26%
  In Sororities: 23%

Graduate and First-Professional
  Students: 1,585

Academics

Full-Time Faculty: 477
  With Ph.D.: 91%

Part-Time Faculty: 113
  With Ph.D.: 27%

Student/Faculty Ratio: 8:1

Most Popular Majors:
  economics (13%)
  government (10%)
  psych & brain science (8%)
  history (8%)
  English (6%)

Completing 2 or More Majors: 13%

Freshmen Retention Rate: 97%

Graduation Rates:
  86% within four years
  95% within six years

Computers: Computer Required

Admissions

Regular Application Deadline: 1/1

Early Decision Deadline(s): 11/1,
  12/15

Fall Transfer Deadline: 3/1

Total # of Students Applied: 11,855
  Admitted: 2,155
  Enrolled: 1,092

# of Students Waitlisted: 1,296
  Students Accepting Place: 840
  Waitlisted Students Admitted: 54

In the Classroom

At Dartmouth, students may design programs using the college's unique Dartmouth plan ("D-plan"), which divides the academic calendar into four 10-week terms. This "provides greater flexibility for vacations and for the 40 study-abroad programs in 21 countries," explains the college. A recent grad states, "The 10-week terms make things fairly intense, and we would often joke that midterms would end just days before finals were due to begin."

Students discuss their academics: "The workload is rather intensive but students are not cutthroat and are willing to help one another," says one biology major. A recent grad elaborates: "There was more an atmosphere of cooperation among students as opposed to competitiveness (except perhaps for premeds)." Competition among students is affected by "a code of silence that makes it a faux pas to talk about grades outside of class," but "there is still a lot of personal ambition." In addition to your major, you must take 10 courses spread over eight intellectual fields, plus three courses in world culture, and a multidisciplinary or interdisciplinary course. You also need to become proficient in a foreign language.

Professors are highly accessible and "perhaps the college's greatest resource" says one student; they "do incredible research but still have time for their students. No courses are ever taught by a TA." A government major gets personal: "I've made four friends on the faculty … and every prof I've had knows me by name and says hi to me when we pass." A student also tells us that "Dartmouth was the last school in the Ivy League to become coeducational, but it currently has more tenured women faculty than any other Ivy." There is a lot of opportunity for undergraduate research and undergrads work side-by-side with their dedicated professors.

Campus Environment

Students talk about the surrounding area: "Hanover is the ideal college town and the locals get along very well with the students." Another adds that it's "a tiny town and the nearest city (Boston) is close to three hours away. The town caters to the students, though, and there are plenty of good restaurants and coffee shops. Only two bars, and they close at midnight." The downside to the quaintness of an isolated campus and a small town atmosphere: "Being in the middle of nowhere may be scenic at first, but it gets boring very quickly."

While a student claims that the "campus is very safe," another explains that "people assume that because our campus is literally in the middle of nowhere that there are absolutely no safety concerns. Unfortunately, this is not the case … Many students are reluctant to admit that there are safety problems, and they even leave their personal doors unlocked. This unfortunately leads to problems such as laptop theft. Student-to-student sexual assault is a problem as well, but that is probably true on just about any college campus." Dartmouth's seeming tranquility was shattered in early 2001 by the double murder of two of its professors.

"Most people live on campus because there aren't many other places to go. Quality varies widely. There are a lot of really tiny rooms, and you'll probably be stuck with those your first two years. But most seniors can get pretty nice singles," explains one student. Off-campus housing is less available and "more expensive." One student asks, "What off-campus housing?"

"The entire campus is walkable. No cars are needed, though they are convenient for leaving town when Advance Transit is not running," says a junior. Another student tells us, "You can walk to the one commercial street in Hanover easily as well. The parking situation stinks, so I think it is better to have a friend with a car than to actually have a car yourself. You really only need a car for the one or two trips you may have to make to Wal-Mart per term." Generally, freshmen cannot keep their cars at Dartmouth.

Student Life

The "typical" student at Dartmouth? A junior tells is that they are "smart, but well rounded and fun-loving." An American government major says, "smart and ambitious, but not overly consumed by work. He [the typical student] is white, upper-middle class, and politically conservative." Guidance counselors note that the student body has "steadily become more diverse." Another government major tells us the typical Dartmouth student "played sports in high school, is smart, tested well, drinks a fair bit, and works hard." Notable alums run the gamut from Daniel Webster to Dr. Seuss.

"During the week people do all sorts of extracurricular activities," says one student. "Intramural sports are very popular, and there are all sorts of different clubs that are always having meetings or events—cultural organizations, student government, political groups. There are also lots of publications people write for, and all sorts of student performing groups—a cappella, dance, music, drama." The same student describes weekends: "Friday and Saturday nights are pretty much dominated by frat parties—beer pong in the basement, dancing on the main floor, and hooking up in the rooms upstairs." "Drugs are practically unheard of with the exception of pot," says another student.

According to some students, a cause of friction with the administration seems to be the planned phasing out of fraternities and sororities. One student notes, "Dartmouth students feel like they're very smart and successful, so how dare anyone try to tell us how to spend our free time." Another student tells us, "The administration wants to get rid of the Greek system…[It] aims to eliminate drinking, which, aside from being a pipe-dream, is a source of tension."

A senior explains that "varsity sports are extremely popular, but in recent years, Dartmouth has done terribly in the 'big three' men's sports. Intramural sports are popular, too, due to Dartmouth having so many high-school athletes." According to another student, "PE classes are required, but there is something for everyone. You can do anything from soccer and baseball to ballroom dancing and yoga. A lot of our varsity teams aren't very good, but people love to go watch games and cheer anyway. It is fun to be at a place with such good school spirit. People are always wearing Dartmouth sweatshirts, t-shirts, etc." As one biology major puts it when asked why he chose Dartmouth, "This school had the warmest atmosphere of all the Ivy League schools I visited. Students here are smart but not weird."

Other schools to check out: Princeton, Duke, Northwestern, Brown, Williams.

Applied Early Decision: 1,216
Early Decision Admitted: 397

Test Scores (middle 50%):
SAT Verbal: 660–760
SAT Math: 670–770
ACT Comp: 27–33

HS Rank of Entering Freshmen:
Top 10%: 83%
Top 50%: 100%

Avg. HS GPA: 3.66

THE EXPERTS SAY...

" A top-notch faculty and plenty of research opportunities make it an excellent school for undergraduate attention. "

" Slowly but surely, Dartmouth's president is teaching students to embrace diversity. "

Costs (2003–04)

Tuition and Fees: $29,145

Room & Board: $8,625

Payment Plan(s): installment plan, pre-payment plan

Inst. Aid (2002–03)

Institutional Aid, Need-Based: $32,574,271

Institutional Aid, Non-Need-Based: $3,700

FT Undergrads Receiving Aid: 49%
Avg. Amount per Student: $24,538

Of Those Receiving Any Aid:

Rec. Need-Based Scholarship or Grant Aid: 93%
Average Award: $20,563

Rec. Need-Based Self-Help Aid: 95%
Average Award: $5,698

Upon Graduation, Avg. Loan Debt per Student: $16,922

Financial Aid Deadline: 2/1

Graduates

Going to Graduate School: 18% Within One Year

Accepting Job Offer: 27% at time of graduation

Companies Recruiting On Campus: 125

Alumni Giving: 64%

DAVIDSON COLLEGE

P.O. Box 7156, Davidson, NC 28035
Admissions Phone: (800) 768-0380; (704) 894-2230 Fax: (704) 894-2016
Email: admission@davidson.edu
Website: www.davidson.edu

General Info

Type of School: private, coed, Presbyterian (USA)

Setting: suburban

Academic Calendar: semester

Student Body

Full-Time Undergrads: 1,711
  Men: 50%, Women: 50%

Part-Time Undergrads: 1 Woman: 100%

Total Undergrad Population:
  African American: 6%
  Asian American: 2%
  Latino: 3%
  Native American: <1%
  Caucasian: 81%
  International: 3%
  Out-of-State: 78%
  Living Off-Campus: 8%
  In Fraternities: 41%

Academics

Full-Time Faculty: 162
  With Ph.D.: 99%

Part-Time Faculty: 8
  With Ph.D.: 88%

Student/Faculty Ratio: 11:1

Most Popular Majors:
  English (14%)
  political science (13%)
  history (12%)
  biology (12%)
  economics (8%)

Completing 2 or More Majors: 9%

Freshmen Retention Rate: 96%

Graduation Rates:
  88% within four years
  89% within six years

Admissions

Regular Application Deadline: 1/2

Early Decision Deadline(s): 11/15, 12/15

Fall Transfer Deadline: 3/15

Spring Transfer Deadline: 11/15

Total # of Students Applied: 3,927
  Admitted: 1,249
  Enrolled: 492
  Waitlisted Students Admitted: 2

Applied Early Decision: 374
  Early Decision Admitted: 208

Inside the Classroom

"Davidson is no walk in the park," says one Davidson College student. "I don't know of a more difficult school .... and yes, I have friends at Harvard and MIT and they have it easier." The liberal arts curriculum here has a stellar reputation in the South, and a degree from Davidson can be considered an intellectual pedigree. While aspiring to provide its students with the same high level education of an Ivy League school, Davidson is a bit less competitive and not quite as expensive as many comparable schools. Once you get in, though, you will study hard. As another student puts it, "If you've never gotten a C in a class, you probably will here."

The choice of 21 majors in the liberal arts, social sciences, natural sciences, math, and theater are relatively small, but the quality of the programs makes up for the quantity. Interdisciplinary studies are also quite good at Davidson, including such acclaimed and innovative programs as gender studies, medical humanities, and a program that takes a nontraditional, broad approach to the study of Western civilization. The extensive core requirements include courses in literature, history, natural sciences, math, social sciences, fine art, philosophy, writing, foreign language, and a class on non-Western thought. Because of Davidson's Presbyterian affiliation, a course in religion is also required.

Academics at Davidson also have a distinctive international flair. The international studies program is one of the most renowned in the country, and the school's foreign language departments are highly acclaimed. Many students opt to check out other countries in one of the school's overseas programs. As one junior said, "Had I not chosen this school, I would have not only missed out on wonderful friendships, but interesting cultural experiences as well."

Small classes and the faculty's devotion to individual attention mean that education at Davidson is a personal matter. One student says, "In only two months of school, I've been invited to a professor's home for a fried chicken dinner, tagged along to drop off a professor's daughter at theater class, and spent countless hours in their offices for extra help." Many students report professors giving out their home phone numbers and enjoying meeting with students over coffee at the cafes in town.

Like many schools of this caliber, Davidson has an official student honor code that's taken very seriously. Exams aren't proctored, work is done honestly, and even the doors to students' dorm rooms remain (reportedly) unlocked. "The honor code is awesome," said one junior. "Students looking for college to be easy, or who are dishonest, won't fit in here."

Campus Environment

The beautiful, 106-acre campus is located on the shores of Lake Norman. With its sprawling lawns, looping paths, and heavily wooded areas, the campus is extremely safe, making for a peaceful atmosphere. Red brick and white columns are the themes holding Davidson's buildings together, presenting a unified and collegiate appearance.

The stately Chambers Building, the main landmark on campus, is located in the dead center of everything and contains classrooms, faculty offices, and the Love Auditorium, where guest speakers can often be seen. The largest building on campus is the 142,000-square foot Baker Sports Complex, which houses the 6,000-seat arena, an eight-lane pool, workout facilities, racquetball and squash courts, and studios for aerobics and dance. Another impressive campus landmark, the Grey Building, once served as the college library and later as the college union. After recent renovations, it now houses the college's music department.

Dorms at Davidson are decidedly above average in quality, with free laundry drop-off service and controllable heat and air conditioning in most. Options for all classes include smoke-free dorms; substance-free areas within dorms; suites in West Residence and Duke Halls, where two single rooms share a bathroom; "pods," in which eight single rooms share a common room and two bathrooms; and clusters, in which two double rooms are grouped together. The five-dorm apartment buildings in the Martin Court complex are for seniors and are the most prized commodity.

Student Life

Most of the students are from the South and tend to come from upper-middle class, conservative backgrounds. Many are also religious. This combination creates a distinctive atmosphere that some describe as "typically Southern," although one psychology major sees it differently: "Many students are closed-minded and tend to be dorky. Girls have blond hair and wear pearls and black pants, while boys wear khakis and collared shirts with rolled-up sleeves." By and large, however, students are friendly, respectful of one another, and concerned about honesty and moral issues.

The social life on campus centers on the eating clubs and the fraternities, which draw well over half the student population. Located at Patterson Court, the ten eating clubs are a unique facet of Davidson life and an alternative to meal-plan dining at Vail Commons. Each one, with its own dining room and cook, not only provides a place for members to eat, but also hosts special events and parties. Each club is also required to have parties open to the entire school. According to one student, "Fraternities and eating houses are the social life. There's not much else to do other than attend their events. And drinking is huge."

In the world of sports, Davidson is one of the smallest NCAA Division I colleges in the nation. Both men and women can compete as Davidson Wildcats in basketball, soccer, swimming, diving, track and field, cross country, and tennis. Men can also compete in baseball, football, golf, and wrestling, while women can compete in field hockey, lacrosse, and volleyball. Club sports include crew, fencing, rugby, sailing, ultimate frisbee, and waterskiing. Many students play some type of intramural sport, the most popular one being a variation on touch football called flickerball.

For Davidson students, friendly peers and a community environment make Davidson as comfortable a place to live and work as their hometowns. "The tremendous academic reputation, Divison I athletics, the sense of hometown community, and the Carolina blue skies are what brought me here," said one student. "What's kept me here are the people."

Other schools to check out: Wake Forest, Rhodes, University of the South, Vanderbilt, Washington and Lee.

Test Scores (middle 50%):
SAT Verbal: 630–720
SAT Math: 640–720
ACT Comp: 27–31

HS Rank of Entering Freshmen:
Top 10%: 76%
Top 25%: 96%
Top 50%: 100%

THE EXPERTS SAY...

" Davidson offers an Ivy League-caliber education without the ultracompetitive admissions process. "

" The arts may be liberal, but the students aren't. Left-leaning students may have a hard time sharing their values. "

Costs (est. 2004–05)

Tuition and Fees: $25,903
Room & Board: $7,371

Inst. Aid (2002–03)

Institutional Aid, Need-Based: $8,135,559

Institutional Aid, Non-Need-Based: $2,360,413

FT Undergrads Receiving Aid: 33%
Avg. Amount per Student: $17,432

FT Undergrads Receiving Non-Need-Based Scholarship or Grant Aid: 24%
Avg. Amount per Student: $6,652

Of Those Receiving Any Aid:

Rec. Need-Based Scholarship or Grant Aid: 94%
Average Award: $14,710

Rec. Need-Based Self-Help Aid: 83%
Average Award: $4,262

Upon Graduation, Avg. Loan Debt per Student: $21,350

Financial Aid Deadline: 2/15 (priority)

Graduates

Going to Graduate School: 26% Within One Year

Companies Recruiting On Campus: 482

DEEP SPRINGS COLLEGE

HC 72 Box 45001, Dyer, NV 89010
Admissions Phone: (760) 872-2000 Fax: (760) 872-4466
Email: apcom@deepsprings.edu
Website: www.deepsprings.edu

General Info

Type of School: private, all men

Setting: rural

Academic Calendar: semester

Student Body

Full-Time Undergrads: 26
  Men: 100%
  Out-of-State: 88%

Academics

Full-Time Faculty: 15
  With Ph.D.: 93%

Student/Faculty Ratio: 2:1

Most Popular Majors:
  liberal arts (100%)

Freshmen Retention Rate: 96%

Graduation Rates:
  100% within four years

Admissions

Regular Application Deadline: 11/15

Total # of Students Applied: 150
  Admitted: 17
  Enrolled: 13

# of Students Waitlisted: 4
  Students Accepting Place: 4
  Waitlisted Students Admitted: 4

Test Scores (middle 50%):
  SAT Verbal: 740–800
  SAT Math: 660–770

Costs (2004–5)

Fees: $1,000

In the Classroom

Deep Springs College, an all-male school, makes its home in a Nevada desert valley and the nearest town, Bishop, is 40 miles away. Just 26 students study, labor (the school runs a working ranch), and occasionally play in this isolated college community. While Deep Springs only offers an Associate's Degree in liberal arts, students find that the in-depth education they receive helps them to transfer to top-tier four-year schools to continue their educations (think Harvard, Brown, Swarthmore, Oxford) after their two years in the desert. Every student gets a full tuition scholarship.

The average class size here is four students—there's no disappearing into the crowd here if you aren't prepared! There are three long-term professors (one each in social sciences, humanities, and natural sciences and mathematics), and three visiting faculty members each semester. Required courses are Composition and Public Speaking, the latter of which is learned and practiced for both years. Additionally, students choose from seminars as diverse as "Thermodynamics," "Constitutional Law," "Epic Literature," and "Horsemanship." Students may also embark on "Directed" (designed by a professor) or "Independent" (more student-designed) studies.

"The quality of classes is mixed," says one student, "I've had very intense, academically rigorous classes here. I've also had classes that I could have aced asleep (and occasionally did). On the whole, the classes fall more toward the rigorous than the pathetic end of the spectrum." Another student tells us, "We are constantly required to analyze and evaluate what we read and hear. It is very difficult to complete all of your reading and also reflect on it meaningfully in preparation for each class, especially with all of our labor and self-governance responsibilities." But Deep Springers sure do try—it is not unusual to find students at work on their academics at any hour of the night. The school really functions as a community, and while there is a lot of work, there is not really any cutthroat competition, according to students. Faculty members live on campus, eat with their students, and are readily available: "If I really need to talk to them, I can get them out of bed at night."

Environment

At Deep Springs, besides the regular school facilities, which include one dorm, three classrooms, the library, and the boarding house (food!), you will find cows, horses, tractors, and acres of alfalfa. There is also a music room, piano room, laboratory, blacksmith shop, darkroom, ceramics studio, auto shop, woodshop, and a saddle and leatherworking shop. More spontaneous classrooms include faculty members' houses and "the irrigation ditch." Campus safety? "The campus is safe unless you do stupid things with farm implements," quips one Deep Springer.

The dormitory houses all 26 students, who rave about their "enormous dorm rooms with awesome furniture." Living off-campus? "There's a lot of desert you can pitch a tent in. Of course, you have to share it with rattlesnakes, scorpions, black widows, hanta-carrying mice, and plague-bearing coyotes." Housing choices aren't limited to your bed or the desert, though, since "rarely does a night go by that students will not be sleeping everywhere but their rooms (the porches, the main living room, the lawn)." Students eat food prepared by their peers in the Boarding House. Students are not permitted to leave campus, except for the student driver's weekly trip to Bishop for supplies. But to get around their many acres, students "walk or bike around campus; sometimes you might even ride a horse."

Student Life

"Student life" is woven into the fabric of the school's three basic pillars of academics, labor, and self-governance. Everybody works, and everybody is involved with committees for governing of the school (including assisting in hiring faculty and school policies such as whether to remain a dry campus). "Sometimes we get rowdy at SB [student body] meetings," one student says, "but it is always in good spirits and usually involves impromptu wrestling matches." Over their two-year stay, students milk, brand, or slaughter cows, dig ditches, scrub toilets, do repairs, operate heavy farm machinery, and cook for the community, just to name a few jobs. Titles include "student cowboy," "office cowboy," "student gardener," and "dairy boy."

The typical student here is described as white, upper-middle class, and liberal-leaning. Also, he usually has first-rate secondary school records and very high test scores. The intimacy and community of the student body and isolation of the campus make for close relationships, and we are told "we are not best friends with all of our classmates, but most of us like most of them and are true friends with a number of them." Friends spend their precious free hours talking, playing guitar, playing chess, and watching taped episodes of *The Simpsons* (no regular TV here). They also march through the desert on the annual Death March, a weeklong hike "along mountain ridges of the entire valley perimeter," before which food and water are placed in various locations along the route.

There are no organized clubs or sports, and no fraternities. One student notes the "the Deep Springs Student Body is like one big frat that runs an institution instead of planning parties." Students may start an impromptu game of soccer or ultimate Frisbee. Just a sampling from one student of how Deep Springers may amuse themselves during down time: "We ride bikes naked off a ramp into the reservoir. We talk about Heidegger until four in the morning. We read *Harry Potter* and *Lord of the Rings* aloud to one another. We curse one another. We commiserate with each other about absent or more often non-existent girlfriends. Or occasionally boyfriends." Moreover, friendships here "are cemented by a common purpose, a common way of being at Deep Springs, a mutual interest in improving the community and the mutual sacrifices we must make in order to spend time together."

Other Schools to Check Out: Antioch College, Hampshire College, St. John's College, Bard College, Evergreen State College

DENISON UNIVERSITY

Denison University Admissions Offiice, Box H, Granville, OH 43023
Admissions Phone: (800) DENISON; (740) 587-6276 Fax: (740) 587-6306
Email: admissions@denison.edu
Website: www.denison.edu

General Info

Type of School: private, coed
Setting: small town
Academic Calendar: semester

Student Body

Full-Time Undergrads: 2,113
    Men: 45%, Women: 55%

Part-Time Undergrads: 80
    Men: 26%, Women: 74%

Total Undergrad Population:
    African American: 5%
    Asian American: 2%
    Latino: 3%
    Native American: <1%
    Caucasian: 84%
    International: 4%
    Out-of-State: 56%
    Living Off-Campus: 2%
    In Fraternities: 28%
    In Sororities: 40%

Academics

Full-Time Faculty: 180
    With Ph.D.: 96%

Part-Time Faculty: 11
    With Ph.D.: 36%

Student/Faculty Ratio: 11:1

Most Popular Majors:
    economics (10%)
    communication (10%)
    biology (9%)
    psychology (8%)
    political science (7%)

Completing 2 or More Majors: 20%

Freshmen Retention Rate: 90%

Graduation Rates:
    73% within four years
    77% within six years

Admissions

Regular Application Deadline: 2/1

Early Decision Deadline(s): 11/15,
    1/15

Fall Transfer Deadline: 7/1

Spring Transfer Deadline: 12/1

Total # of Students Applied: 3,141
    Admitted: 2,125
    Enrolled: 629

# of Students Waitlisted: 433
    Students Accepting Place: 164
    Waitlisted Students Admitted: 13

Inside the Classroom

The term "university" in Denison's name is rather misleading—master's programs were once part of its curriculum, but since the late 1920s, Denison has devoted itself to educating undergrads only. But this small school offers all the resources and research facilities you'd see at a much larger institution.

"The workload is pretty heavy … We cover a lot of material in a semester," says one Denison student, while another admits, "I have found my classes harder than I expected they would be, and more work." Professors are loved by students, and the feeling is mutual—"most of the professors seem to genuinely care about us," says an English major. A premed student agrees: "The academic atmosphere is pretty intense overall, but the professors go out of their way to make it more bearable by offering their help any way they can."

For a small liberal arts college, Denison offers an unusual number of unique academic programs. "The college places a premium on students doing both independent and collaborative research with faculty," states one college official. The interdisciplinary Environmental Studies Program benefits from Denison's well-maintained, 350-acre Biological Reserve and the state-of-the-art Anderson Field Station. The Certification in Organizational Studies includes a set of courses integrated with an intensive summer seminar and a paid internship in such fields as finance, marketing, and private and non-profit management. Other unique programs are the Richard G. Lugar Program in American Politics and Public Service and the Media Technology and Arts major.

Approximately 30 percent of Denison's students participate in the four-year Honors Program. Honors students participate in honors seminars and complete a senior project, allowing them to engage, one-on-one, in graduate-level research with faculty members. Incoming honors students also benefit from the Mentor Program, in which current honors students help the new students make the transition to college life.

Guidance counselors have high praise for Denison's May Term—an optional program to provide students with a variety of opportunities for exploring careers. It offers students over 200 internship sites around the country in a broad array of careers: business, education, government, law, medicine, etc. Denison also offers more than 20 service-learning courses year-round that incorporate community-based experience as their subject matter.

Campus Environment

The picturesque, 250-acre main campus is set on a hill above the "adorable" and "very safe" little town of Granville. Approximately 65 percent of the first-year class are housed in "freshman-only" residence halls, with the rest of the first-year students residing in housing with other classes. "In the event additional space is needed for student housing, convertible lounges are utilized; the occupancy of rooms is not increased," a school official informs us. There's no separate housing for fraternities and sororities, and students were pretty upset with Denison's recent decision to "take away all off-campus housing after years of slowly dwindling the number of students who were allowed to live off." It "kind of ruined the party scene," laments a student. (That was kind of the idea, we think!)

All students are allowed cars on campus (as long as they obtain a parking permit). "You don't really need a car to get anywhere except if you want to go to a big city," says a junior. A university shuttle service, "The Big Red Express," offers transportation each weekend to malls in nearby Newark and in Columbus, approximately 25 miles from the campus (though a student tells us that these trips "are not very popular").

The campus is undergoing major construction, including work on a new common to be framed by a new life science building, Samson Talbot Hall of Biological Science, and the Morgan Center for student, faculty, and alumni-related activities. Beneath the new common will be an underground parking garage for approximately 385 cars.

Student Life

"The students here are very friendly, people you barely know will say hello when passing on the academic quad," says one student. Another student tells us, "You really get to know people, and groups of friends are very tight. People gossip and know everyone's business, but it is fun that way." Guidance counselors tell us that the close-knit feeling does not end upon graduating; Denison has a very active alumni network and enjoys a large endowment. Notable alums run the gamut from Michael Eisner, CEO of the Disney Company, to Jennifer Garner, star of ABC-TV's hit series, *Alias*.

"Sunday, Tuesday, and Thursday are usually study nights, when even the hardcore partiers can be spotted in the library," says a student. The other four nights of the week are the "party nights." Even though students are angry that there's no longer any off-campus housing where they can party, there are two 21-and-over bars in Granville and several 18-and-over bars in neighboring towns that students flock to. Although the administration has been cracking down on Greek organizations for the past few years, even kicking some groups off campus, most students still believe that "certain sororities and fraternities seem to run the social scene." A student explains, "Freshman guys always say that they would never join a house, but come Rush in January, every guy who likes to party ends up pledging something."

Sports are popular at Denison: More than 50 percent of the students participate in intramurals, more than 30 percent of students participate in club sports (crew is the most popular), and approximately 20 percent of women and 30 percent of men participate in Division III intercollegiate athletics. In 2001, the Denison Women's Swimming and Diving team won the NCAA Division III National Team Championship.

Other schools to check out: Kenyon, Hamilton, DePauw, Centre, Illinois Wesleyan.

Applied Early Decision: 124
  Early Decision Admitted: 124

Test Scores (middle 50%):
  SAT Verbal: 560–650
  SAT Math: 570–660
  ACT Comp: 24–29

HS Rank of Entering Freshmen:
  Top 10%: 46%
  Top 25%: 82%
  Top 50%: 100%

Avg. HS GPA: 3.6

THE EXPERTS SAY...

❝ Denison students receive a great deal of individual attention and wonderful opportunities for research. ❞

❝ A school on the rise. Denison's administration has been raising their admissions standards and really cracking down on the once-rampant partying. ❞

Costs (2003–04)

Tuition and Fees: $25,760

Room & Board: $7,290

Regional or "good neighbor" tuition available

Payment Plan(s): installment plan, deferred payment plan

Inst. Aid (est. 2003–04)

FT Undergrads Receiving Aid: 49%
  Avg. Amount per Student: $22,756

FT Undergrads Receiving Non-Need-Based Scholarship or Grant Aid: 51%
  Avg. Amount per Student: $10,732

Of Those Receiving Any Aid:

Rec. Need-Based Scholarship or Grant Aid: 99%
  Average Award: $16,786

Rec. Need-Based Self-Help Aid: 75%
  Average Award: $5,405

Upon Graduation, Avg. Loan Debt per Student: $15,009

Financial Aid Deadline: rolling, 2/15 (priority)

Priority Deadline for Major Scholarship Consideration: 1/1

Graduates

Going to Graduate School:
  22% Within One Year

Companies Recruiting On Campus: 40

Alumni Giving: 45%

DePaul University

1 East Jackson, Suite 9100, Chicago, IL 60604
Admissions Phone: (312) 362-8300; (800) 4DEPAUL Fax: (312) 362-5749
Email: admitdpu@depaul.edu Website: www.depaul.edu
Application Website: www.depaul.edu/admission/apply-online.asp

General Info

Type of School: private, coed, Catholic

Setting: urban

Academic Calendar: differs by program, all UG & grad progs. use quarter system; law uses semester

Student Body

Full-Time Undergrads: 10,823
 Men: 42%, Women: 58%

Part-Time Undergrads: 3,202
 Men: 39%, Women: 61%

Total Undergrad Population:
 African American: 11%
 Asian American: 9%
 Latino: 13%
 Native American: <1%
 Caucasian: 60%
 International: 2%
 Out-of-State: 13%
 Living Off-Campus: 80%

Graduate and First-Professional Students: 9,025

Academics

Full-Time Faculty: 805

Part-Time Faculty: 711

Student/Faculty Ratio: 17:1

Most Popular Majors:
 communication (11%)
 psychology (8%)
 computer sicence (7%)
 political science (6%)
 finance (6%)

Freshmen Retention Rate: 63%

Graduation Rates:
 44% within four years
 63% within six years

Admissions

Regular Application Deadline: 2/1 (priority)

Transfer Deadline: rolling

Early Decision Deadline(s): 12/15

Early Action Deadline: 1/15

Total # of Students Applied: 9,464
 Admitted: 6,904
 Enrolled: 2,261

Inside the Classroom

DePaul is the largest Catholic university in the nation and the largest private university in Chicago, but students say that the atmosphere is "like a small school." Students report a high degree of satisfaction with DePaul—a real achievement for what's largely a commuter school. And guidance counselors from Ohio and New York have told us that they appreciate the generous scholarships DePaul offers to minorities and students from underprivileged backgrounds.

Of DePaul's eight campuses—Lincoln Park, Loop, Lake Forest, Barat, O'Hare, Rolling Meadows, Naperville, and Oak Forest—Lincoln Park and the Loop are the largest. The Loop in downtown Chicago is home to the schools of commerce, computer science, telecommunications, and information systems, and the School for New Learning, which offers distance learning programs and experiential learning credits. Loop students are primarily preprofessionals who take advantage of the school's location in downtown Chicago by participating in a number of work and internship opportunities. The Lincoln Park campus, located in a more affluent region of Chicago, is the home of the schools of arts and science, education, theater, and music. And for those seeking a small-college atmosphere, the Barat campus is located along the scenic shore of Lake Michigan.

Offering more than 130 undergraduate and graduate areas of study, DePaul is known for its business and prelaw programs, but the schools of theater, music, and computer sciences are also exceptionally strong. "The 10-week quarters go by really fast," says a fourth-year biology student. "I like this because it keeps you on your toes, since there is really no time to slack off."

DePaul recently restructured its freshman programs to focus on the school's location in Chicago. Freshmen enroll in a variety of experiential learning courses designed to explore diversity and urban identity. In courses such as "Love and Committed Relationships, Chicago Style" and "Blue Collar Chicago: People with Big Shoulders," students reflect on their experiences through intensive reading, writing, and discussion.

Teaching is highly valued at DePaul, taking precedence over professors' personal research. Students report that class sizes are getting larger and getting into the courses you want is getting a bit more difficult than in the past. Most classes, however, still average 20–30 students. Professors teach all courses; there are no graduate TA's. Students have high praise for their professors, who "communicate with the students on an individual basis" and speak out on political and social issues.

Campus Environment

The school has added half a dozen buildings in the last few years, including a $25 million student center, a far cry from its beginnings as a small urban campus called "the little school in the shadow of the L tracks." While DePaul is primarily a commuter school, about 2,500 undergrads live on DePaul's Lincoln Park campus (a bonus: each residence hall room is equipped with a networked computer furnished by the university); the majority of Barat's 900 students live in its three campus residence halls. While lack of housing is a frequent student complaint, the dorms that are available are considered good. "The security in the dorms is tight: every guest must be signed in with a picture ID, and every resident has to show their ID to an attendant and then swipe it in a verifier before entering," a senior informs us.

Many students live off campus in the Lincoln Park area. "Off-campus housing is more readily available and affordable," a recent grad reports. A senior explains, "There are tons of apartments in the near area, but these are very expensive. Many students opt for apartments that are a few train stops away (and a couple hundred dollars cheaper a month)." Students have great things to say about the neighborhood surrounding the Lincoln Park campus, where there are "many young people around," as well as nice shops and cafés. Transportation is primarily by mass transit, and the school provides discounts on fare cards. "The location cannot be beat," raves a student. "We are a ten-minute train ride from the heart of the city, four blocks from the lake, and five minutes from Wrigley Field."

Student Life

DePaul student social life is centered around Chicago itself. "Students often go to various music venues for concerts, poetry readings... go to museums, the theater, see films, visit coffee shops or jazz/blues clubs, bars, and visit the lakefront." Favorite student hangouts include the cavernous bars and clubs lining Rush, Lincoln, and Halstead Streets. True to the DePaul mission, however, community service and volunteer work are as popular as bar hopping for many students. One sums the atmosphere up this way: "DePaul maintains a relatively calm social environment yet connects readily with Chicago's vast cultural and political agendas and events."

Students unite to cheer on their NCAA Division I men's basketball team, and the stadium is packed whenever the Blue Demons play Notre Dame. Athletics are popular due to DePaul's state-of-the art fitness centers. There are more than 100 student organizations. One shrewd student notes, "There are plenty of organizations here to help advance your networking potential." Fraternities and sororities are not a major presence, but there are a good number of African American and Latino chapters on campus. A sorority member explains, "Because of the fact that we don't have Greek houses, there is not a lot of emphasis on Greek life as being party-oriented and the like."

Diversity is celebrated at DePaul. "You cannot be a DePaul student and have not heard the word 'diversity' a hundred times, but I think it's great that every student is valued here no matter what. The way the entire DePaul community is accepting of differences is what makes it a nice place to be," a senior says. One-third of the students are members of minority groups. Although the school is a Catholic institution, less than half of all students are Catholic, and "there is little sense of forced Christianity," according to a philosophy major. While a majority of DePaul students come from Chicago and its suburbs, the school is actively recruiting more out-of-state students. The campus is "liberal and stimulating," says a graduate, and students are generally "urban-minded and laid-back," with an unusual sense of community. According to DePaul's website, approximately 45 percent of its full-time freshmen are the first in their families to attend college.

Other schools to check out: Loyola University of Chicago, Marquette, University of Dayton, Fordham, Duquesne.

Test Scores (middle 50%):
SAT Verbal: 500–620
SAT Math: 490–600
ACT Comp: 21–26
ACT English: 20–27
ACT Math: 19–26

HS Rank of Entering Freshmen:
Top 10%: 17%
Top 25%: 41%
Top 50%: 74%

Avg. HS GPA: 3.3

THE EXPERTS SAY...

" DePaul's admissions office should be applauded for actively seeking students with diverse special talents, interests, and socioeconomic backgrounds. "

" A commuter school with a heart. "

Costs (2003–04)

Tuition and Fees: $18,790
Room & Board: $8,790
Payment Plan(s): installment plan

Inst. Aid (est. 2003–04)

Institutional Aid, Need-Based: $25,000,000

Institutional Aid, Non-Need-Based: $11,700,000

FT Undergrads Receiving Aid: 75%
Avg. Amount per Student: $13,691

FT Undergrads Receiving Non-Need-Based Scholarship or Grant Aid: 2%
Avg. Amount per Student: $7,070

Of Those Receiving Any Aid:

Rec. Need-Based Scholarship or Grant Aid: 80%
Average Award: $8,989

Rec. Need-Based Self-Help Aid: 87%
Average Award: $5,729

Upon Graduation, Avg. Loan Debt per Student: $21,695

Financial Aid Deadline: 5/1 (priority)

Graduates

Going to Graduate School: 8% Within One Year

Companies Recruiting On Campus: 334

DEPAUW UNIVERSITY

101 East Seminary St., Greencastle, IN 46135
Admissions Phone: (765) 658-4006; (800) 447-2495 Fax: (765) 658-4007
Email: admission@depauw.edu Website: www.depauw.edu
Application Website: www.depauw.edu/admission/applyonline/

General Info

Type of School: private, coed, United
  Methodist
Setting: small town
Academic Calendar: 4-1-4

Student Body

Full-Time Undergrads: 2,315
  Men: 45%, Women: 55%
Part-Time Undergrads: 4
  Men: 25%, Women: 75%
Total Undergrad Population:
  African American: 6%
  Asian American: 2%
  Latino: 3%
  Native American: <1%
  Caucasian: 86%
  International: 2%
  Out-of-State: 49%
  Living Off-Campus: 7%
  In Fraternities: 74%
  In Sororities: 70%

Academics

Full-Time Faculty: 209
  With Ph.D.: 94%
Part-Time Faculty: 42
  With Ph.D.: 48%
Student/Faculty Ratio: 10:1
Most Popular Majors:
  English (15%)
  communications (14%)
  economics (9%)
  computer science (7%)
  biology (6%)
Completing 2 or More Majors: 12%
Freshmen Retention Rate: 93%
Graduation Rates:
  71% within four years
  75% within six years

Admissions

Regular Application Deadline: 2/1;
  12/1 (priority)
Early Decision Deadline(s): 11/1
Early Action Deadline: 12/1
Fall Transfer Deadline: 3/1
Spring Transfer Deadline: 12/1
Total # of Students Applied: 3,651
  Admitted: 2,296
  Enrolled: 581

Inside the Classroom

Some liberal arts institutions fill their students' heads with lofty ideas before sending them out as fodder for the business world. Others, like DePauw, take pains to ensure their graduates can thrive in today's professional job market. "Personally and professionally, if you're searching for what you want to do, Depauw is a great place to start," says one student.

Offering over 50 study programs and 11 preprofessional options, DePauw is a wholly undergraduate school where the most popular majors are biological sciences, communications, computer science, economics, elementary education, English, history, music, political science, and psychology. "The difficulty of classes depends on the desires of the student," says a recent graduate. "There are easier majors—which will remain unnamed—but all disciplines produce solid performers."

The education DePauw offers is specifically designed to hone students' analytical skills, perfect their writing ability, and ensure that they can think and speak effectively. All students must pass core requirements in six areas: natural sciences and mathematics, social and behavioral sciences, literature and the arts, historical and philosophical understanding, foreign language, and self-expression. "DePauw places high expectations on its students," says a grateful senior. "Academically, I got what I paid for."

Another fine aspect of DePauw is the approachability and quality of its faculty. An Indiana high school guidance counselor approves of the way DePauw "works individually with students," giving each one personal attention. "I've found the personal attention to be the largest incentive possible to study and do well," agrees a senior. "The professors are open to suggestions, if you think something is simply not working well in class. I've even been invited by one of my professors to help reorganize a class I just finished, and to help her develop a second-level class to follow it up. It's a really good feeling to have so much say in your education, and not just be led by the hand."

Over 80 percent of students complete at least one internship before graduation, and honors students can secure semester-long paid internships through a fellows program that also includes intense coursework. About a quarter of the student body participates in international study programs, choosing both DePauw's own programs and those offered by other schools in Africa, Asia, Europe, Latin America, North America, and the Middle East.

Campus Environment

DePauw's campus is compact, as befitting a school with around 2,000 undergrads (though one guidance counselor views the small size of the campus as a drawback). The small-town atmosphere builds a strong sense of community that can sometimes be too strong for some: "If you have a problem with a person for whatever reason, it may be difficult to avoid them." Residence halls are divided into the North Quad and the South Quad. All first-year students must live on campus, and most of them are herded into the five dorms in the South Quad. After freshman year, students can enter a lottery system where the winning ticket is an apartment-style living unit or theme house.

An ongoing boom in construction and renovation has made a big impact on campus. Two freshmen dorms, Bishop Roberts and Longden Halls, were completely renovated, with the improvements including long-requested air-conditioning systems. A $9 million indoor tennis and track center opened in 2001, and four times that amount is being spent on a three-year renovation and expansion of DePauw's mathematics and science center. Rounding out the list is a new $12 million art building.

DePauw is a wired college. The Lilly Endowment awarded the school a $20 million grant to launch its "361 Degrees" program. Using a new technology center in the math and science building as its base, the program will prepare DePauw students for the use of information technology in all aspects of their careers and lives. It will also provide more than 100 additional internships to the school's long list, as students and faculty work with businesses and other schools in technological outreach programs.

Student Life

About 70 percent of the student body belongs to one of 12 fraternities and 9 sororities, which get mixed reviews from students. "The Greek system presents many opportunities for a student to develop character, discipline, and confidence," says a recent graduate. Another student has sour grapes: "Sorority girls are only into frat boys. What's the deal with that? One day I'm not good enough for you; then I pledge a frat, and now you wanna go out?" Another junior grumbles, "They justify their high dues by saying it pays for the community activities they volunteer for. We all know the real reason is to pay for the neverending parties. Seriously, who joins a frat for the community activities they're involved in? 'Hey Fred, are you gonna pledge Alpha?' 'No, man, I'm pledging Kappa. They help feed the homeless.'"

If the Greeks' dedication to community service is less than genuine, the school's certainly isn't. According to an admissions official, about 75 percent of the student body participate in DePauw Community Service (DCS), which enables students to volunteer with many local and national organizations. "This is one of our best selling points," exclaims one sophomore. "A lot of programs are student-run, providing more leadership experience for interested students."

One of the most beloved campus activities is the annual Monon Bell football game with Wabash College. Continuing for over 100 years, it's one of the nation's oldest and fiercest football rivalries. Whoever wins gets to keep the antique locomotive bell—painted half red and half gold—until the next clash. "The contest draws alumni from many generations and is quite an event," said one student. The other 11 varsity sports include baseball, basketball, cross-country, golf, soccer, swimming, tennis, and track and field. Club sports and intramurals are also popular.

Other schools to check out: Bradley, Denison, Centre, Illinois Wesleyan, Trinity University (TX).

# of Students Waitlisted: 181
 Students Accepting Place: 39
 Waitlisted Students Admitted: 12

Applied Early Decision: 56
 Early Decision Admitted: 40

Test Scores (middle 50%):
 SAT Verbal: 560–660
 SAT Math: 570–660
 ACT Comp: 25–29
 ACT English: 24–29

THE EXPERTS SAY...

" DePauw's extensive internship opportunities and attention to marketable knowledge and skills bode well for anyone looking to beat the competition before their careers even begin. "

" Being well-rounded isn't everything. Someone who goes to a big state university and specializes may get more schooling in your field than you'll get here. "

HS Rank of Entering Freshmen:
 Top 10%: 57%
 Top 25%: 85%
 Top 50%: 99%

Avg. HS GPA: 3.66

Costs (2004–5)

Tuition and Fees: $25,460

Room & Board: $7,300

Payment Plan(s): installment plan, deferred payment plan

Inst. Aid (est. 2003–04)

FT Undergrads Receiving Aid: 58%
 Avg. Amount per Student: $20,208

FT Undergrads Receiving Non-Need-Based Scholarship or Grant Aid: 45%
 Avg. Amount per Student: $12,134

Of Those Receiving Any Aid:

Rec. Need-Based Scholarship or Grant Aid: 60%
 Average Award: $16,693

Rec. Need-Based Self-Help Aid: 65%
 Average Award: $5,392

Upon Graduation, Avg. Loan Debt per Student: $15,635

Financial Aid Deadline: 2/15

Graduates

Going to Graduate School: 37% Within One Year

Companies Recruiting On Campus: 38

Alumni Giving: 59%

DICKINSON COLLEGE

P.O. Box 1773, Carlisle, PA 17013-2896
Admissions Phone: (717) 245-1231; (800) 644-1773 Fax: (717) 245-1442
Email: admit@dickinson.edu Website: dickinson.edu
Application Website: app.commonapp.org

General Info
Type of School: private, coed
Setting: suburban
Academic Calendar: semester

Student Body
Full-Time Undergrads: 2,227
 Men: 44%, Women: 56%
Part-Time Undergrads: 8
 Men: 13%, Women: 88%
Total Undergrad Population:
 African American: 3%
 Asian American: 3%
 Latino: 2%
 Native American: <1%
 Caucasian: 90%
 International: 2%
 Out-of-State: 65%
 Living Off-Campus: 8%
 In Fraternities: 23%
 In Sororities: 24%

Academics
Full-Time Faculty: 166
 With Ph.D.: 96%
Part-Time Faculty: 36
 With Ph.D.: 53%
Student/Faculty Ratio: 13:1
Most Popular Majors:
 English (10%)
 political science (10%)
 international studies (10%)
 biological sciences (9%)
 international business (7%)
Completing 2 or More Majors: 21%
Freshmen Retention Rate: 90%
Graduation Rates:
 76% within four years
 79% within six years

Admissions
Regular Application Deadline: 2/1
Early Decision Deadline(s): 11/15, 1/15
Early Action Deadline: 12/15
Fall Transfer Deadline: 4/1
Spring Transfer Deadline: 11/1
Total # of Students Applied: 4,633
 Admitted: 2,394
 Enrolled: 624

Inside the Classroom

Dickinson College is best known for its impressive study abroad program and its outstanding programs in international studies and foreign languages. Dickinson is a national leader in terms of foreign language majors, and currently teaches 11 languages, from Chinese to Hebrew to Latin to Portuguese. Well over half the student body studies abroad—the highest rate in the state and one of the highest in the country—and over one-third of these students participate in programs that take them overseas for a full academic year. The college sponsors 13 international programs (for the year, semester, or summer) in places such as Japan, Spain, England, Korea, Cameroon, and Germany. Students who study abroad have nothing but raves for their experience and for their school that gave them such terrific opportunities. The international studies program is arguably the school's best and toughest offering. It's an interdisciplinary major, with students studying all aspects of their chosen area. Russian Studies majors, for instance, enroll in courses relating to Russia's politics, art, religion, economy, and language, and then would go study in Russia for at least a semester. All international studies majors must also complete an intense oral exam before graduating. (We've heard of students dropping their major during their senior year out of fear of taking this exam.)

In all, there are 37 fields of study: 15 arts and humanities programs, 14 in the social sciences, and 8 in the natural sciences. There's also a special 3-3 program in cooperation with Dickinson School of Law, enabling students to earn a bachelor's and law degree in six years. Guidance counselors compliment Dickinson's "strong liberal arts program." The general education requirements are rigorous, and include courses in arts and humanities, social sciences, quantitative reasoning, lab sciences, foreign language, diversity, and comparative civilizations. Students must also fulfill the writing requirement, take a small freshman seminar, and complete four phys ed classes. Dickinson also has an interesting "Community Experience" policy, requiring students to volunteer off-campus or perform community service, in Carlisle or beyond. While students appreciate the well-rounded education they receive at Dickinson, many gripe about the size and intensity of the core curriculum.

One high school guidance counselor calls the school "very competitive," and students admit they have to work hard for their grades. Campus can be quiet on weeknights, with many undergrads studying in the library, the computer lab, or their rooms. Classes are small (on average, 15 students), and there are approximately 13 students for every faculty member. Professors are given good marks all around: they're reportedly personable, accessible, and always willing to give extra help. Many students point to the close interaction with their teachers as the best part of attending a small school like Dickinson.

Campus Environment

Students brag that Dickinson's "breathtaking" campus looks like those in the movies. "Just gorgeous," concedes a high school guidance counselor. One of the oldest colleges in the nation (founded in 1783), Dickinson boasts many old, but beautifully restored, buildings on its 103 green acres.

Dickinson prides itself on being a residential college, and "expects" all students to live and eat on campus. (A few seniors are "awarded" permission to move off-campus.) There is a variety of options, ranging from residence halls housing 40 to 200 students to suites, apartments, and small homes, including special interest and Greek houses. Most residences are coed, and are arranged as doubles, triples, or quads. There are just a handful of single rooms. We heard few complaints from students about the housing conditions.

Carlisle, a small rural town in the "middle of nowhere," is far from exciting. The town is historical but has little to offer college students, and what's worse, town-gown relations are reportedly pretty terrible. Harrisburg is a half-hour away, and though we don't hear of many students heading there for nightlife or culture, it does have a train station and an airport.

Student Life

The student body is overwhelmingly white and middle- to upper-middle class. Students tend to be conservative, studious, and career-minded. It's often described as being a very friendly, close-knit campus, which isn't surprising when you consider that there are just over 2,000 undergrads enrolled, most of whom live within walking distance of one another. Some feel it's a little too close for comfort, and grow tired of seeing the same people, day in and day out. On the other hand, some complain that, with the majority of students going abroad junior year, the campus lacks the cohesiveness found at many colleges of Dickinson's size.

Around a quarter of Dickinson students join one of the eight fraternities or four sororities. Men may rush in the spring of their freshmen year, but women must wait until the fall of their sophomore year. There is no pressure to join per se, but the Greeks exert a pretty hefty influence on campus. Even for non-Greeks, frat parties are at the epicenter of Dickinson social life. We hear that just about the only thing to do on weekends is drink at fraternities, except for those who can legally (no fake IDs here) go to the handful of local bars. The alcohol policy is strict and well enforced, but students still manage to party a good deal.

For the nondrinkers, there are more than 120 clubs and activities, including music and drama groups, student publications, and religious, political, special-interest, and community service organizations. The Campus Activities Board regularly organizes movies, comedians, concerts, and dances on weekends. Annual events include Springfest and Greek Week. Sports are also popular to play and to watch. Dickinson, a Division III school, offers 23 varsity sports, 11 for men and 12 for women, as well as a host of club and IM sports.

Other schools to check out: Trinity College, Hamilton, Gettysburg, Muhlenberg, Franklin and Marshall.

# of Students Waitlisted: 292
Students Accepting Place: 292
Waitlisted Students Admitted: 17

Applied Early Decision: 389
Early Decision Admitted: 286

Test Scores (middle 50%):
SAT Verbal: 590–680
SAT Math: 590–680
ACT Comp: 25–30

HS Rank of Entering Freshmen:
Top 10%: 50%
Top 25%: 83%
Top 50%: 97%

THE EXPERTS SAY...

" Dickinson teaches 11 foreign languages and has 13 international programs. "

" Forget about the Greek language: Greek organizations form the social life at this small school in a small town "

Costs (2004–5)

Tuition and Fees: $30,300
Room & Board: $7,600
Payment Plan(s): installment plan

Inst. Aid (est. 2003–04)

Institutional Aid, Need-Based: $17,178,889
Institutional Aid, Non-Need-Based: $3,391,496
FT Undergrads Receiving Aid: 53%
Avg. Amount per Student: $22,973
FT Undergrads Receiving Non-Need-Based Scholarship or Grant Aid: 12%
Avg. Amount per Student: $10,842

Of Those Receiving Any Aid:

Rec. Need-Based Scholarship or Grant Aid: 96%
Average Award: $18,568
Rec. Need-Based Self-Help Aid: 89%
Average Award: $5,890
Upon Graduation, Avg. Loan Debt per Student: $19,207
Financial Aid Deadline: 2/1

Graduates

Going to Graduate School: 20% Within One Year
Companies Recruiting On Campus: 34
Alumni Giving: 64%

DREW UNIVERSITY

36 Madison Ave., Madison, NJ 07940-1493
Admissions Phone: (973) 408-DREW Fax: (973) 408-3068
Email: cadm@drew.edu
Website: www.drew.edu

General Info

Type of School: private, coed, United
  Methodist
Setting: suburban
Academic Calendar: semester

Student Body

Full-Time Undergrads: 1,511
  Men: 39%, Women: 61%
Part-Time Undergrads: 35
  Men: 26%, Women: 74%
Total Undergrad Population:
  African American: 4%
  Asian American: 6%
  Latino: 5%
  Native American: <1%
  Caucasian: 63%
  International: 1%
  Out-of-State: 43%
  Living Off-Campus: 13%
Graduate and First-Professional
  Students: 915

Academics

Full-Time Faculty: 120
  With Ph.D.: 97%
Part-Time Faculty: 46
Student/Faculty Ratio: 12:1
Most Popular Majors:
  political science (14%)
  psychology (12%)
  economics (11%)
  English (10%)
  sociology (6%)
Completing 2 or More Majors: 18%
Freshmen Retention Rate: 87%
Graduation Rates:
  71% within four years
  75% within six years
Computers: School provides
  individual computer/laptop

Admissions

Regular Application Deadline: 2/15
Early Decision Deadline(s): 12/1,
  1/15
Fall Transfer Deadline: 8/1
Spring Transfer Deadline: 1/1
Total # of Students Applied: 2,746
  Admitted: 1,894
  Enrolled: 420

In the Classroom

Drew University was the first liberal arts college in the country to provide personal computers to all of its students as part of tuition, showing itself to be dedicated to helping its students to develop skills for the post-graduation "real" world. Academics are not taken lightly here, and one senior explains, "Drew does its best to foster an academically aware environment."

Few undergraduates arrive at Drew with a career, or even a major, already decided. While there are 27 majors in the College of Liberal Arts, from anthropology to computer science to women's studies, the political science program is a real standout (not surprising, as Drew's president is former NJ governor Tom Kean). Everyone must complete at least 32 credits from eight different areas as a general requirement, in addition to their major and a required minor. One student notes, "I've found the classes themselves to be highly competitive, although there is certainly room for improvement." Another student states, "The professors grade fairly, and trust me, nobody is just given a grade—they must earn it."

Drew students can take full academic advantage of the school's proximity to New York City (just 30 miles away) by enrolling in special semester-long programs. The Wall Street Semester brings students to the financial district to develop a deeper understanding for the role of Wall Street and the economy. During the Semester on the United Nations students get the opportunity to spend two days a week in New York at the UN, attending presentations and conducting research for individual projects. The New York Semester on Contemporary Art is a mandatory course for all art majors, but other interested students can participate. Students travel into the city twice a week to partake in the art scene, viewing exhibits, visiting museums, and even meeting prominent artists. There is also the yearlong Drew International Seminars program, where students combine on-campus classwork with three- or four-week seminars in international locations. Drew foots the bill for travel, room, and board, and the student pays for tuition and incidentals.

Professors are very active in Drew life. "Drew's biggest asset lies in the fact that its professors are almost always accessible. Professors go out of their way to make it known that they can be reached at almost any time," says one student. A junior majoring in chemistry agrees: "The professors here are spectacular. They are great to work with on a professional and personal level. For almost all of the students, the professors are both mentors and friends."

Campus Environment

Most undergraduates live on campus. The on-campus housing situation is fairly traditional (double rooms, single-sex or coed floors), but there are other options such as cooperative housing and special housing for international students, and theme houses for sophomore-through-senior year students. One student tells us, "There are a number of race/religion-based theme houses that students can choose to live in after their first year. While these houses serve an important programming purpose that often benefit[s] the whole student body, they also tend to segregate some of the minority students." Upperclassmen can apply for parking permits to keep a car in campus lots.

"Drew is extremely quiet, and it isn't uncommon to hear one of the thousands of squirrels dropping an apple out of a tree onto the ground," comments a junior. The school's large wooded campus ("The Forest") is quite safe. "I, for one, feel comfortable walking around any part of the campus at any time of day," says another student. Students say the town of Madison is pretty boring. "While Madison is an extremely beautiful and outwardly friendly town, there is very little in the way of town-gown relations," says a senior. "Considering Madison is the home to three different colleges, much more should be done in terms of making the town student-friendly."

Drew has fine facilities for such a small school. Drew is proud of its wireless network, "where you can take your laptop about anywhere on campus and connect to the Internet." Drew's Simon Forum seats 4,000 people and hosts concerts, athletic events, and also presentations by notables such as President George W. Bush, Shimon Perez, and Colin Powell. Also, Drew's Kirby Theater is home to the annual New Jersey Shakespeare Festival. In April 2003, Drew celebrated the newest addition to campus: a multimillion dollar music wing which will become part of the Dorothy Young Center for the Arts.

Student Life

One student tells us, "The typical student at Drew is a white, upper middle-class female from New Jersey. She dresses moderately in some of the latest styles from Gap." One student tells us that political conservatives would not fit in on campus, while another student says that openly gay students might have trouble in what's basically a "don't ask-don't tell" social environment. "A person looking for anything but the 'small-school atmosphere' would be well advised to look elsewhere," another student warns us. Even guidance counselors mention that "some students might want a larger school." But while the small size can limit the social scene, it also breeds a friendliness and openness among students: "It's the kind of place where you know everyone by face, if not by name," claims one student. Another student adds, "Even people I don't know tend to flash smiles."

A junior states, "The students are almost never rowdy. The only exception is on Thursday nights when about 50–100 students meet in one of the dorms and have a party." Parties, says another student, "are typically open to the entire campus, and there is little to no pressure to drink at any of them." As for the absence of Greek organizations, we are told that "nobody misses them. People with the same interests tend to form their own cliques anyway." The university participates in NCAA Division III athletics and offers numerous clubs and organizations.

When the campus feels too small, Drew is still just an hour from New York City, and an hour from New Jersey beaches, so the occasional weekend getaway or day trip is easy. "The best part of Drew for me and most other students is the proximity to New York City," says a junior. "In under an hour and for only $5, a student can go into one of the biggest cities in the world, crammed with everything imaginable!"

Other schools to check out: College of New Jersey, Wagner, Manhattanville, Fairfield, Juniata.

# of Students Waitlisted: 61
  Students Accepting Place: 47
  Waitlisted Students Admitted: 10

Applied Early Decision: 102
  Early Decision Admitted: 99

Test Scores (middle 50%):
  SAT Verbal: 560–670
  SAT Math: 550–650

HS Rank of Entering Freshmen:
  Top 10%: 41%
  Top 25%: 71%
  Top 50%: 91%

THE EXPERTS SAY...

" You can choose a school with a bigger reputation, but it may not have such unique programs as Drew's Wall Street Semester, Semester on the United Nations, New York Semester on Contemporary Art, and International Seminars. "

" Ah, the Forest, where there are three female Drewids for every two males, plus thousands of apple-dropping squirrels. Bring on those international seminars! "

Costs (2003–04)

Tuition and Fees: $27,906

Room & Board: $7,644

Payment Plan(s): deferred payment plan, pre-payment plan

Inst. Aid (2002–03)

FT Undergrads Receiving Aid: 50%
  Avg. Amount per Student: $19,955

FT Undergrads Receiving Non-Need-Based Scholarship or Grant Aid: 26%
  Avg. Amount per Student: $11,421

Of Those Receiving Any Aid:

Rec. Need-Based Scholarship or Grant Aid: 99%
  Average Award: $14,972

Rec. Need-Based Self-Help Aid: 82%
  Average Award: $5,196

Upon Graduation, Avg. Loan Debt per Student: $16,381

Financial Aid Deadline: 2/15

Graduates

Going to Graduate School:
  23% Within One Year

Companies Recruiting On Campus: 27

Alumni Giving: 62%

DREXEL UNIVERSITY

3141 Chestnut Street, Philadelphia, PA 19104-2875
Admissions Phone: (215) 895-2400; (800) 237-3935 Fax: (215) 895-5939
Email: enroll@drexel.edu Website: www.drexel.edu
Application Website: www.drexel.edu/em/undergrad/apply/

General Info

Type of School: private, coed

Setting: urban

Academic Calendar: semester, quarter

Student Body

Full-Time Undergrads: 9,338
Men: 61%, Women: 39%

Part-Time Undergrads: 1,673
Men: 56%, Women: 44%

Total Undergrad Population:
African American: 10%
Asian American: 13%
Latino: 2%
Native American: <1%
Caucasian: 61%
International: 5%
Out-of-State: 39%
Living Off-Campus: 63%
In Fraternities: 12%
In Sororities: 8%

Graduate and First-Professional
Students: 4,772

Academics

Full-Time Faculty: 653

Part-Time Faculty: 655

Student/Faculty Ratio: 10:1

Most Popular Majors:
information systems (7%)
computer science (6%)
mechanical engineering (4%)
marketing (4%)
finance (4%)

Freshmen Retention Rate: 82%

Graduation Rates:
13% within four years
39% within six years

Computers: Computer Required

Admissions

Regular Application Deadline: 3/1

Fall Transfer Deadline: 8/15
(priority)

Spring Transfer Deadline: 2/15
(priority)

Total # of Students Applied: 10,390
Admitted: 7,285
Enrolled: 2,127

Waitlist Available

Inside the Classroom

Drexel offers more than 50 bachelor's degree programs in the colleges of arts and sciences, business, engineering, information science and technology, and media arts and design; and the schools of biomedical engineering, science, and health systems; education; environmental science, engineering, and policy (SESEP); and hospitality management. Engineering is indeed Drexel's forte (often to the exclusion of other departments, we hear): Drexel has the third largest private engineering school in the country, and its engineering curriculum has been designated a national model by the National Science Foundation. Drexel also has one of the best information systems programs in the country; business is a strong and popular field of study, as well.

The hallmark of a Drexel education is its excellent co-op program, "The Ultimate Internship." Co-ops are a mandatory part of most degree programs at Drexel. All freshmen must take a co-op orientation, where they'll learn how the program works, along with gaining invaluable résumé-writing and interviewing skills. Starting sophomore year, the job search begins. There are two different bachelor's degree schedules: a four-year program (students complete one co-op), and the more popular five-year program (students complete three different co-ops). The university works on a quarter system, enabling undergrads to alternate classroom work with paid professional internships. Students are assigned a co-op cycle, so, for example, those on a Fall/Winter cycle would work during the Fall/Winter term and attend classes in the Spring and Summer quarters. All internships are six months, and, with little exception, they're salaried. Drexel boasts connections with almost 3,000 employers in 26 states and 12 foreign countries. Students love the fact that, armed with a diploma and up to a year and a half of work experience, they graduate with a serious leg up on the competition. A graphic design major states, "Drexel makes you get a job and prepares you to have a career—not weave baskets and be hippies." Two-thirds of co-op students get job offers from their co-op employers.

The average class size is around 20–25 students. We didn't hear many great things about the professors and the administration, however. "If you need help, most professors will direct you to their graduate assistants," says an engineering student. "The most distinguished professors have the most limited time because of research and guest lecturing." Classes are challenging, especially for engineering, and the school's quarter system often makes it feel like a "pressure cooker." Students grow weary of cramming a semester's worth of material into a 10-week period. They must learn, and learn fast, how to budget and manage their time. "Someone who likes things done for them will not survive here. This is a school for motivated people," comments one student.

The general education requirements and the workload vary across the curriculum. A senior majoring in mechanical engineering tells us, "For engineering, the workload for the first two years is out of control—it is used more as a weeding tool, rather than time to teach the basics (by overloading perspective engineering students, the true engineering students will emerge and the fakes will change majors). In terms of workload, after engineering, art and design students have the most, then computer science and IS majors, arts and sciences next, and last in workload is business and finance majors."

Campus Environment

Drexel is located on 49 acres in University City near the heart of Philadelphia, with a campus of 45 academic and research buildings, a student center, a phys ed center, several recreational fields, and seven residence halls. A self-described "Cyber Campus," Drexel was the first major university to go completely wireless—students and faculty can access the Internet from anywhere on campus.

Housing is limited. All freshmen are required to live on campus their first year unless they live at home; many upperclassmen live in one of ten frat houses or other homes adjacent to campus in the historic Powelton Village section of the city. Only about one-quarter of the student body resides in on-campus housing; it's guaranteed for your freshman year only, and after that students participate in a lottery.

"Safety is a big concern around here," says a senior. "The savvy Drexel student learns the first week to stay close to campus." Though the campus is not in the greatest or safest of areas, security on campus is reportedly excellent. In fact, some describe the security team, the "Yellow Jackets," as overbearing at times. Walking escorts are available at all times on campus. The campus borders the University of Pennsylvania's, and all sorts of public transportation are just steps away. (Drexel also offers a shuttle service.) All students are permitted to bring cars, but parking is pricey, and the school's city location makes it accessible to everything imaginable.

Student Life

Drexel's student body is fairly diverse, with significant numbers of Asian Americans and African Americans on campus. But a senior points out, "Unfortunately, many students are 'cliquey' and only hang out with people of the same ethnic origin or the same academic major. It's easy to meet people within your major or within your ethnic background." The population skews male (there are about two men for every woman), and students in general tend to be focused on their studies and their careers.

The social life at Drexel doesn't garner much praise. Students bemoan the lack of things to do on campus and the virtually nonexistent school spirit. (The fact that hardly anyone lives on campus certainly contributes to this.) This is not a party school by any stretch of the imagination, although the frat houses on Greek Row do try their best to keep the alcohol flowing. Most freshmen, we hear, depend on the Greeks for weekend activity, and around ten percent of the population eventually join a sorority or fraternity.

There are more than 100 student organizations, including a campus newspaper, a radio station, and a local cable TV station. Drexel offers nine men's and nine women's varsity teams, as well as numerous club and intramural sports. (Students aren't the most voracious or attentive fans, however.) Luckily, Drexel's Philly location guarantees a wide variety of things to do: restaurants, bars, clubs, museums, arts and entertainment venues, and beautiful waterfront and historic areas.

Other schools to check out: Temple, Northeastern, American U, University of Pittsburgh, University of Cincinnati.

Test Scores (middle 50%):
SAT Verbal: 540–630
SAT Math: 560–660
HS Rank of Entering Freshmen:
Top 10%: 31%
Top 25%: 64%
Top 50%: 93%
Avg. HS GPA: 3.52

Costs (2003–04)

Tuition and Fees: $21,105
Room & Board: $9,600
Payment Plan(s): installment plan

THE EXPERTS SAY...

" Students seeking multiple co-op placements should definitely check out Drexel's fruitful (though expensive) five-year program. "

" Forget 'the City of Brotherly Love'—with both Drexel and Temple inside its borders, Philly should be called 'the City of Preprofessional Education.' "

Inst. Aid (est. 2003–04)

Institutional Aid, Need-Based: $1,569,679

Institutional Aid, Non-Need-Based: $52,742,990

FT Undergrads Receiving Aid: 70%
Avg. Amount per Student: $10,266

FT Undergrads Receiving Non-Need-Based Scholarship or Grant Aid: 17%
Avg. Amount per Student: $6,469

Of Those Receiving Any Aid:

Rec. Need-Based Scholarship or Grant Aid: 52%
Average Award: $4,873

Rec. Need-Based Self-Help Aid: 99%
Average Award: $5,912

Upon Graduation, Avg. Loan Debt per Student: $22,234

Financial Aid Deadline: 2/15

DUKE UNIVERSITY

2138 Campus Drive, Durham, NC 27708
Admissions Phone: (919) 684-3214 Fax: (919) 684-8941
Email: ugrad-admissions@duke.edu Website: www.duke.edu
Application Website: www.admissions.duke.edu

General Info

Type of School: private, coed, United Methodist Church

Setting: suburban

Academic Calendar: semester

Student Body

Full-Time Undergrads: 6,065
  Men: 51%, Women: 49%

Part-Time Undergrads: 21
  Men: 57%, Women: 43%

Total Undergrad Population:
  African American: 10%
  Asian American: 12%
  Latino: 7%
  Caucasian: 60%
  International: 5%
  Out-of-State: 85%
  Living Off-Campus: 17%
  In Fraternities: 29%
  In Sororities: 42%

Graduate and First-Professional
  Students: 5,975

Academics

Full-Time Faculty: 949
  With Ph.D.: 94%

Student/Faculty Ratio: 11:1

Most Popular Majors:
  economics (18%)
  public policy (9%)
  biology (8%)
  psychology (8%)
  political science (7%)

Freshmen Retention Rate: 97%

Graduation Rates:
  87% within four years
  93% within six years

Admissions

Regular Application Deadline: 1/2

Early Decision Deadline(s): 11/1

Fall Transfer Deadline: 3/15

Total # of Students Applied: 16,729
  Admitted: 3,873
  Enrolled: 1,619

Waitlist Available

Applied Early Decision: 1,423
  Early Decision Admitted: 471

Test Scores (middle 50%):
  SAT Verbal: 660–750
  SAT Math: 670–770

Inside the Classroom

Ask a Duke student to compare his beloved school to the Ivy League, and you'll hear, "Harvard: The Duke of the North." Few schools excel in so many different areas. "We have an unbelievable combination of top-quality sports and top-quality academics," states one proud student. "The whole atmosphere is perfect," agrees an Ohio guidance counselor. "The programs are great, the facilities look good, and the campus is wonderful." Of course, as a North Carolina guidance counselor points out, it's "tough to get admitted unless the student is truly stellar or has a special talent or 'hook.'"

Duke's two undergraduate schools, the School of Engineering and the College of Arts and Sciences, are both considered excellent. The strongest academic programs include the sciences (biology, ecology, neuroscience), political science, economics, literary studies, and public policy (for which undergrads can study at the prestigious Institute of Policy Science). "It's a premed standout," raves one Virginia guidance counselor. All students may apply for funding for research apprenticeships beginning in their first year.

Duke attracts driven types, and one student claims that fellow classmates are "career- and goal-oriented from when they get off the bus" (though an Arizona counselor complains of a "lack of career guidance, lack of job placement assistance"). There's a substantial workload, but most describe the competition as "more internal than external." While the rivalry among premeds is admittedly more intense, students say the campus is "too laid-back" to support much cutthroat competition among students. "We have a difficult, intense curriculum, but at the same time, we don't allow ourselves to be consumed by the amount of work we have," offers a psych major.

While faculty members are top-notch in their fields, opinions vary as to the quality of their teaching. An English major we spoke to says that she had only one class taught by a TA. We've heard from a few students that some profs "are too involved in their research to concern themselves with students." And others complain that some professors don't have the greatest command of the English language.

Campus Environment

"Duke's academic reputation was what initially grabbed my interest. But it was my campus visit that actually hooked me," says a junior. Duke's beautiful campus is one of its great strengths. "The campus is one of the reasons the students are relaxed," explains one student. "The climate is very temperate, and the campus is so big, it is easy to find some space to yourself when you need it."

The campus is divided into East and West Campus. East Campus is where all freshmen live: "One of the best things about Duke is having a separate campus for freshmen," a junior tells us. "Having them all together creates a friendly, open environment that plays a huge role in creating a positive first-year experience." After freshman year, students move to West Campus, where the Gothic-style buildings are beautifully preserved. It's also the more socially active of the two, since it houses the fraternities and the student center. Dorms here are all considered nice; old buildings have been renovated, and August 2002 saw the completion of a huge new residence hall. Students are required to live on campus for three out of four years, so off-campus housing isn't much of an issue.

The town of Durham doesn't offer much ("There's a feeble attempt at a college 'strip,'" explains one junior), but recently, more clubs and restaurants catering to students have opened up. Students warn that the area immediately surrounding campus isn't a place you'd want to be after dark.

Student Life

As one recent grad bluntly puts it, "A typical Duke student is a rich, white, preppy person with a wild, party side, but with enough money to fix any indiscretions that might ensue." Many students admit that's not far off the mark. "Most students are pretty well off, and most females are probably pretty image-conscious," agrees a coed. One student's pet peeve is the overly conservative campus environment, and another feels the student body breaks on economic lines: "We could use some children of cops or firemen here. Just once, I'd like to hear one of my classmates say his parents worked for a living." Many of the students and guidance counselors we spoke to griped about the lack of diversity at Duke, and we hear that students of the same race or ethnicity tend to stick together. Yet one undergrad tells us, "Though it's pretty homogeneous and conservative, I feel that students can still easily stand up for their beliefs without fearing rejection or narrow-mindedness by others."

Supporting the sports teams is a huge component of being a Duke undergrad. There is "incredible school spirit," raves a North Carolina guidance counselor. Of Duke's 26 varsity teams, the most popular by far is men's basketball—lots of bonding goes on at Cameron Indoor Stadium. Students frequently camp out for tickets to Blue Devil games against favorite rivals. Kryzewskiville, as it is commonly known (named after the school's coach), is the "tent city" erected outside the stadium several weeks prior to these games. "There are several people in a tent," we're told. "Students rotate to take showers." Intramural sports are extremely popular, and almost everyone participates in some activity, even if it's just Frisbee out on the quad.

At Duke, as one student puts it, "Students drink. Heavily." Another reports that "drinking is a must." Recently, the administration closed the campus bar and has begun to really crack down on drinking, but that hasn't put too much of a crimp in alcohol consumption. Fraternities—which clearly dominate the social scene—may have fewer parties on campus now, but they're renting space in Durham restaurants to throw their bashes. Around one-third of all students belong to the Greek system, though the sororities don't have their own housing.

For those who aren't into sports, frats, or beer, it can be difficult to find a niche. Still, it's not impossible, especially with the hundreds of clubs and extracurricular activities that often form their own social networks. As one student says, "There is an emphasis on being both an academic institution *and* a place kids go for fun."

Other schools to check out: Dartmouth, University of Pennsylvania, Cornell, Stanford, Georgetown.

ACT Comp: 29–34

HS Rank of Entering Freshmen:
Top 10%: 88%
Top 25%: 97%
Top 50%: 100%

Avg. HS GPA: 3.93

Costs (2004–5)

Tuition and Fees: $30,720

Room & Board: $8,520

Payment Plan(s): installment plan, pre-payment plan

THE EXPERTS SAY...

" Duke offers a balance of work and play that many other top-tier schools lack. But guidance counselors are split on whether it's underrated or overrated. "

" Great for extroverts who can thrive in a whirlwind of challenging academics, competitive athletics, and an always active social scene. "

Inst. Aid (2002–03)

Institutional Aid, Need-Based: $39,969,165

Institutional Aid, Non-Need-Based: $4,498,398

FT Undergrads Receiving Aid: 39% Avg. Amount per Student: $26,250

FT Undergrads Receiving Non-Need-Based Scholarship or Grant Aid: 14% Avg. Amount per Student: $9,321

Of Those Receiving Any Aid:

Rec. Need-Based Scholarship or Grant Aid: 100% Average Award: $20,700

Rec. Need-Based Self-Help Aid: 86% Average Award: $6,392

Upon Graduation, Avg. Loan Debt per Student: $19,737

Financial Aid Deadline: 2/1

Graduates

Alumni Giving: 44%

DUQUESNE UNIVERSITY

600 Forbes Avenue, Pittsburgh, PA 15282-0201
Admissions Phone: (412) 396-5000 Fax: (412) 396-5644
Email: admissions@duq.edu Website: www.duq.edu
Application Website: www.duq.edu/index.html

Note: Info. not verified by school

General Info

Type of School: private, coed,
  Roman Catholic

Setting: urban

Academic Calendar: semester

Student Body

Full-Time Undergrads: 4,951
  Men: 42%, Women: 58%

Part-Time Undergrads: 381
  Men: 44%, Women: 56%

Total Undergrad Population:
  African American: 4%
  Asian American: 1%
  Latino: 2%
  Native American: <1%
  Caucasian: 82%
  International: 3%
  Out-of-State: 18%
  Living Off-Campus: 55%
  In Fraternities: 14%
  In Sororities: 14%

Graduate and First-Professional
  Students: 4,047

Academics

Full-Time Faculty: 408

Part-Time Faculty: 444

Student/Faculty Ratio: 14:1

Most Popular Majors:
  liberal arts
  business
  pharmacy
  helath professions
  education

Freshmen Retention Rate: 85%

Admissions

Regular Application Deadline: 7/1;
  11/1 (priority)

Early Decision Deadline(s): 11/1

Early Action Deadline: 12/1

Fall Transfer Deadline: 7/1, 12/1
  (priority)

Spring Transfer Deadline: 12/1

Total # of Students Applied: 3,139
  Admitted: 3,018
  Enrolled: 1,191

# of Students Waitlisted: 20
  Students Accepting Place: 20
  Waitlisted Students Admitted: 20

Inside the Classroom

Founded in 1787 by the Congregation of the Holy Ghost, Duquesne University roots itself firmly in its moral and spiritual values and its academic excellence in liberal arts and professional education. Students here have several fine undergrad schools to choose from: liberal arts; business administration; education; natural and environmental sciences; pharmacy; nursing; health sciences; and music. Sciences, especially the pre-health fields, are the school's strong suit, and the pharmacy program is its shining star, boasting a 100 percent job placement record. More than one-quarter of the student body majors in business and management, and the physical therapy and sports medicine programs are top-notch as well. The school of music recently became one of the nation's few prestigious "All Steinway Schools."

All students must take 27 credits in the University Core curriculum. The specifics depend on the academic college, but most courses revolve around such fields as writing, problem solving, philosophy, arts, history, the sciences, and theology. The workload varies across the board; pharmacy and pre-health majors are worked particularly hard. "You must be willing to put in the time outside of class in order to excel," a student majoring in accounting tells us. There are numerous opportunities for internships, work-study, research, and study abroad, including Duquesne's very own campus in Italy.

Although many students compliment the school for not shoving religion down their throats, Duquesne remains true to its Roman Catholic roots. As the university likes to say, it provides "education for the mind, the heart, and the soul." The faculty and administration is committed not just to their students' education but their spiritual growth as well. With approximately 5,000 undergrads, Duquesne, as its personnel puts it, "is large enough to enjoy the benefits of a comprehensive university . . . but small enough to assure that students are not simply numbers." The average class has less than 50 students, and the student/faculty ratio is about 14:1. Professors are generally applauded for their accessibility and willingness to work on a one-to-one basis when necessary. "They take the time to get to know you," says a junior. "The faculty and students develop personal relationships that help the students succeed in school and in their careers."

Campus Environment

Located on the "Bluff" overlooking the city of Pittsburgh, Duquesne's self-enclosed 40-acre campus is often touted as one of the safest in the nation. Its unique perch ("it is somewhat isolated, but you are minutes from the city," one student marvels) is pretty to look at as well, with its Victorian décor, flowers, fountains, and the beautiful, pedestrian-only Academic Walk that cuts through the center of campus. "The campus is kept clean and nice-looking," we hear. The school claims that every one of its buildings is either new or totally refurbished, but students still complain that the library is seriously lacking.

There are five dormitories (or "living-learning centers," as the school likes to call them); all freshmen are assigned to St. Ann's or St. Martin's, which offer double rooms and community bathrooms. Those in the Honors College live together on a floor in another hall, Assumption. About half the school lives on campus. Upperclassmen move to apartments nearby or houses in the nearby South Side neighborhood. As a large chunk of the student body comes from the Pittsburgh area, the commuting population is pretty big here. Parking is a universal gripe, and even though all students are permitted to bring their cars to campus, the cost of parking is prohibitively expensive (a garage permit can run $75 a month). Take this junior's advice: "A car is convenient sometimes, but you can definitely live without it." The campus is small enough to walk, and downtown Pittsburgh is really just steps away. There is also a bus and light-rail transit system.

Student Life

Duquesne students, on the whole, are a serious and career-minded bunch. The overwhelmingly white (and Catholic) population has been described by some as friendly, but cliquish. "Most students tend to stick with their group of friends," one student says, "but you can always just go up to someone and talk to them." Most coeds hail from Pittsburgh and its environs, and head home often, so don't expect to find much of a social scene on weekends. Duquesne is definitely a "suitcase school." (Some students even call it "The Social Black Hole of Pennsylvania.") Many in search of a collegiate party trek to University of Pittsburgh or Carnegie Mellon. But students who stay at Duquesne find ways to entertain themselves at small dorm gatherings, house parties, and downtown clubs. On campus, the student union center hosts NiteSpot, a "recreation/lounge/cyber-cafe area." The city of Pittsburgh is rich in culture and nightlife, offering symphonies and rock concerts, jazz and dance clubs, and museums and theaters, as well as Penguins hockey, Steelers football, and Pirates baseball.

There are more than 100 student clubs available, including social, honor, professional, cultural, literary, special interest, religious, political, and departmental groups. Campus ministry, which opens its membership to all faiths, has a strong, spiritual voice on campus. Fraternities and sororities are popular, attracting about 15 percent of men and women, although we hear that "you do not feel excluded if you are not in one." The Greeks are largely responsible for Carnival, an annual charity event with student stage performances, raffles, and food and game booths. Other popular organizations include the Student Government Association; the Duquesne Program Council, which is responsible for bringing entertainment to campus; and the Commuter Council, which sponsors an Annual Halloween Masquerade Ball. The DUV (Duquesne University Volunteers) also draws its fair share of undergrads—in fact, Duquesne students rank among the top five percent of all university students in volunteer efforts. There are a wide range of intramural and club sports, and 19 intercollegiate athletic teams, with football and men's and women's basketball getting the most notice.

Other schools to check out: Drexel, Marquette, Fordham, DePaul, University of Dayton.

Applied Early Decision: 182
Early Decision Admitted: 182

Test Scores (middle 50%):
SAT Verbal: 490–590
SAT Math: 490–590
ACT Comp: 23–25
ACT English: 20–26
ACT Math: 19–26

HS Rank of Entering Freshmen:
Top 10%: 22%
Top 25%: 43%
Top 50%: 71%

Avg. HS GPA: 3.4

THE EXPERTS SAY...

" Duquesne pharmacy students get 100 percent job placement. The science programs are standouts. "

" Duquesne is a suitcase school, and students are too busy thinking about their careers to have fun. "

Costs (2003–04)

Tuition and Fees: $19,425

Room & Board: $7,482

Payment Plan(s): installment plan, deferred payment plan

Graduates

Going to Graduate School:
25% Within One Year

Accepting Job Offer:
60% at time of graduation

Companies Recruiting On Campus:
140

EARLHAM COLLEGE

801 National Road W., Richmond, IN 47374-4095
Admissions Phone: (765) 983-1600; (800) 327-5426 Fax: (765) 983-1560
Email: admission@earlham.edu Website: www.earlham.edu
Application Website: www.earlham.edu/~adm/apps.html

General Info

Type of School: private, coed, Society of Friends

Setting: small town

Academic Calendar: semester

Student Body

Full-Time Undergrads: 1,108
  Men: 44%, Women: 56%

Part-Time Undergrads: 17
  Men: 53%, Women: 47%

Total Undergrad Population:
  African American: 6%
  Asian American: 2%
  Latino: 2%
  Native American: <1%
  Caucasian: 82%
  International: 4%
  Out-of-State: 74%
  Living Off-Campus: 18%

Graduate and First-Professional Students: 92

Academics

Full-Time Faculty: 96
  With Ph.D.: 84%

Part-Time Faculty: 15
  With Ph.D.: 27%

Student/Faculty Ratio: 11:1

Most Popular Majors:
  biology (11%)
  English (8%)
  sociology/anthropology (7%)
  psychology (6%)
  human development and social relations (6%)

Completing 2 or More Majors: 7%

Freshmen Retention Rate: 84%

Graduation Rates:
  53% within four years
  70% within six years

Admissions

Regular Application Deadline: 2/15

Early Decision Deadline(s): 12/1

Early Action Deadline: 1/1

Fall Transfer Deadline: 4/1, 2/15 (priority)

Spring Transfer Deadline: 11/15

Total # of Students Applied: 1,410
  Admitted: 1,088
  Enrolled: 351

Inside the Classroom

Earlham's liberal arts programs are held in high regard. English and history are very popular among students, and some unusual interdisciplinary majors—like peace and global studies—attract a sizable percentage of students looking to broaden their academic horizons. Biology and the sciences are also very strong, and Earlham's Japanese studies program ranks among the nation's best.

The Earlham graduate is nothing if not well-rounded: General education requirements include coursework in humanities, languages, religion and philosophy, natural sciences, social sciences, fine arts, athletics and wellness, and multiculturalism. This makes for lofty academic goals, but it also means a lot of hard work. "I thought living up to Earlham's high expectations would be difficult," says one student, "but by dedicating myself and working closely with my professors I was able to achieve goals beyond my dreams."

A special humanities program for first-year students sets the tone for the next four years, with all students taking three classes that allow them to learn learn individually and cooperatively. Heavy on the classics, these courses develop the reading, writing, and analytical skills that students need in a liberal arts school.

Earlham's size translates into small classes, allowing students and faculty to communicate in a more seminar-like manner. No student is just a number here:... but on the flip side, wallflowers in class will be noticed. A high-school guidance counselor describes Earlham's environment as "a good balance between challenging and nurturing."

Earlham's small size and emphasis on community mean that faculty are very accessible and, more important, very supportive. "I knew I could always walk into my teachers' office and they'd know who I was and I'd be welcome," one student says. It also makes for an environment that values an educational work ethic without an unpleasant edge of competitiveness.

Campus Environment

Surrounded by hundreds of acres of woods, the Earlham campus is tranquil, yet distinctively collegiate. The vast majority of students live in one of the seven residence halls or 27 college-owned student houses, including many theme residences. Freshmen are integrated with students from all classes, and their options include halls with a special focus on quiet, living and learning, and wellness.

A construction boom in recent years has paid off for today's Earlham students. The Landrum Bolling Center for Interdisciplinary Studies and Social Sciences features high-tech classrooms that are hard-wired right down to the individual seats. The renovations of Dennis and Stanley Halls in 2001 also improved classrooms and laboratories, and the $13 million Athletics and Wellness Center built in 1999 remedied a real sore point for athletically inclined students.

Students praise the Earlham library, which is impressive for a school of this size. Developing research skills is a key element of an Earlham education; incoming freshmen are taught at the outset the basics of using the library's books and periodicals and are later taught how to use more sophisticated electronic and print information services. Earlham grads say that their strong research skills often put them ahead of their peers in graduate or professional school.

The town of Richmond seems to be what the student makes of it. The Wayne County website says that Richmond has "a varied industrial background" and serves as "a retail center for several counties." A different point of view is provided by a recent Earlham grad, who says, "Richmond is a pit of despair—make a friend who has a car."

Student Life

Earlham is a small school founded in 1847 by the Quakers. Only a minority of today's students belong to that religion, but its values still permeate the campus: Meetings of faculty, staff, and students—well, perhaps not all students—continue to begin with a moment of silence, and the college places a high value on consensus in its decision-making. However, as an Indiana guidance counselor points out, "doing things by consensus is a slow, painful process."

The typical Earlham student leans toward the liberal and plays an active role in the college community. The emphasis on community and cooperation makes for a friendly atmosphere, but one student reports that the exchange of ideas can sometimes be a bit much: "Some students lean heavily towards reactionary behavior, and you need to get used to hearing 'That offends me' a lot."

The sports scene is surprisingly active for a small liberal arts school. About a third of the students participate in varsity sports, and fully half take part in intramural sports like basketball, football, men's lacrosse, racquetball, soccer, softball, tennis, and volleyball. Club sports are also popular, and include cheerleading, lacrosse, equestrian, rugby, and volleyball.

For anyone looking for the wild life, caveat emptor: No frats, no sororities, and no booze. "That's not to say that nobody drinks here," one student equivocates. "But it's usually done off-campus or in closed and quiet groups." The Earlham brand of fun more involves movies, campus events, concerts, and hanging out with good friends.

If people tire of the campus social scene, there are ways to get away. Study abroad is huge at Earlham, with about three-quarters of the students going overseas at some point. Destinations include England, France, Germany/Austria, Greece, Japan, Kenya, Martinique, Mexico, the Middle East, Northern Ireland, and Spain. A three-week wilderness program in the mountains of Utah is also open to incoming freshmen. "Our faculty and student leaders directed us toward being more aware of being in nature," said one happy participant. "They reminded us to stay focused in the present."

Back on campus, there are several major events that bring the entire student body together, including an annual autumn reggae festival and an International Fest. And when all else fails, students can always go looking for the mummy that's stored in the science library.

Other schools to check out: Oberlin, Grinnell, Guilford, Carleton, Lewis and Clark.

THE EXPERTS SAY...

" Here's a small liberal arts school with a real Quaker sense of community. Earlham is great for students who want an academically challenging but supportive environment. "

" Earlham is a dry, frat-free campus. Party animals will definitely feel out of place. "

ECKERD COLLEGE

4200 54th Avenue South, St. Petersburg, FL 33711
Admissions Phone: (727) 864-8331; (800) 456-9009 Fax: (727) 866-2304
Email: admissions@eckerd.edu
Website: www.eckerd.edu

General Info

Type of School: private, coed, Presbyterian

Setting: suburban

Academic Calendar: 4-1-4

Student Body

Full-Time Undergrads: 1,606
  Men: 45%, Women: 55%

Part-Time Undergrads: 25
  Men: 48%, Women: 52%

Total Undergrad Population:
  African American: 3%
  Asian American: 2%
  Latino: 4%
  Native American: <1%
  Caucasian: 77%
  International: 9%
  Out-of-State: 69%
  Living Off-Campus: 24%

Academics

Full-Time Faculty: 102
  With Ph.D.: 94%

Part-Time Faculty: 46
  With Ph.D.: 39%

Student/Faculty Ratio: 13:1

Most Popular Majors:
  marine science (8%)
  international studies (business, relations) (8%)
  management (7%)
  psychology (5%)
  enrvironmental studies (5%)

Completing 2 or More Majors: 8%

Freshmen Retention Rate: 84%

Graduation Rates:
  60% within four years
  65% within six years

Admissions

Regular Application Deadline: 2/5 (priority)

Fall Transfer Deadline: 4/1 (priority)

Spring Transfer Deadline: 11/1 (priority)

Total # of Students Applied: 2,046
  Admitted: 1,569
  Enrolled: 433

# of Students Waitlisted: 115
  Students Accepting Place: 70
  Waitlisted Students Admitted: 15

Inside the Classroom

Many colleges claim to be unique, but Eckerd College really is. Innovation and creativity are vital at this small liberal arts school, where majors are grouped not by academic divisions but by interdisciplinary "collegia"—where, for example, you could find yourself taking dance classes to satisfy your physics major. If you've ever been tempted to calculate the vectors of a pirouette, this is your big chance.

Eckerd's Collegia and majors include:

- Comparative Cultures Collegium: Seven majors including foreign languages, anthropology, international business, and international studies

- Creative Arts Collegium: Seven majors including art, the fine arts, human development, and literature

- Letters Collegium: Seven majors including American studies, communications, philosophy, and religion

- Natural Sciences Collegium: Seven majors including the natural sciences, mathematics, computer science, and premedicine

- Foundations Collegium: Two majors including composition and Western heritage in a global context

To help mentor students in their pursuit of knowledge and careers, Eckerd established an Academy of Senior Professionals, a corps of 350 retired professionals from around the world who provide advice and guidance to students starting out in their professions. Academy members deliver lectures, lead discussions in classes, assist with grad school applications, and often befriend students they interact with on campus.

Eckerd also has a dazzling record in study abroad, with well over 50 percent of its students participating in either a semester or month-long winter program in another country. The many options include Eckerd's own program in the United Kingdom; reciprocal exchange programs in Japan, South Korea, the United Kingdom, Hong Kong, France, and Northern Ireland; a winter program that takes place in a different country each year (past countries have included China, Ecuador, France, Ireland, Italy, Madagascar, Mexico, Micronesia, Morocco, Peru, Singapore, and Spain); and programs in dozens of other countries that are administered by organizations that have partnerships with Eckerd. One biology major raved about her experience: "Going abroad allowed me to combine my love of biology with my interest in the Spanish language and Latin American culture. It was a life-changing experience full of people and places that I will never forget."

The school's innovation doesn't stop at graduation. Departing students get an official cocurricular transcript in addition to their academic transcript, so that future employers and grad schools receive a full record of the student's out-of-class achievements. Items listed include volunteer activities, team and intramural sports, leadership positions, and involvement in student government and clubs. At least one recent alumnus is grateful for this service: "I majored in economics and minored in mathematics, but found that while I was getting some great educational experiences in the classroom, my experiences outside of the classroom were even more important and more educational to me in the long run."

Campus Environment

Eckerd is right on the waterfront: Its 280-acre campus overlooks Boca Ciega Bay with direct access to the Gulf of Mexico and the Intercoastal Waterway. The college has its own marina where students can check out sporting and fishing equipment, sailboats, sailboards, kayaks, and canoes for no charge. A waterside beachwalk wraps around the campus perimeter, with a number of hammocks and benches on the side for students to use on nice days.

Dorms at Eckerd are built in clusters that are called complexes and referred to by Greek alphabetical letters. Freshmen are interspersed with students of other years in a variety of options that include singles, doubles, double-singles, and suite-style apartments. The most coveted dorms are the two most recently built, Nu Complex and Omega Complex. These have apartment-style living units with balconies, and if you're lucky enough to live in Omega, you'll have a sweeping view of Boca Ciega Bay from your balcony all year.

One Eckerd facility that few other campuses have is a marine sciences lab, where those majors can benefit from hands-on research opportunities often conducted side-by-side with faculty. The center's features include two large holding tanks underneath the building that have bay water constantly pumped into them, so that marine life can be studied. Campus laboratories for computer science and physics are also very well equipped.

The nearby city of St. Petersburg, in conjunction with the city of Tampa, provides a metropolis where students can seek big-city fun as well as internship opportunities. However, one student says that although Tampa is a fine place to start a business or career after graduation, St. Petersburg is stuck in the first stages of an economic recovery effort that began years ago.

Student Life

Fraternities and sororities don't exist at Eckerd… but with the beach nearby and a warm climate year-round, you probably won't care. Dorm complexes fill the void, with each one sponsoring a campuswide social event in its designated month. Intramural sports are also inter-complex sports, with fierce but friendly competition between complexes. Other major activities for students are the annual Spring Ball, movies, comedians, hypnotists, concerts, and trips to area theme parks.

There is not a huge student body here, and since it's hard not to run into the same people each day, making pals is the most important activity. "The most important part of Eckerd was all of the friends that I made," said one recent alumna. "I do miss having them around, but I know that they will always be there and that along with family, there is very little else that you can ask for in the world."

The Eckerd Tritons compete at the NCAA Division II level and in the Sunshine State Conference. According to one student, college sports events are one of the few things that make Eckerd's diverse student population feel truly united.

Another interesting organization is Eckerd College Search and Rescue (ECSAR), an entirely student-run maritime rescue operation that provides assistance to boaters in the bay. Serving as Eckerd's private coast guard, ECSAR maintains its own fleet of rescue and fire-prevention vessels. Members undergo intensive training and must pass tests before they can serve.

Other schools to check out: Rollins, New College of Florida, University of Miami, Occidental, Pitzer.

Test Scores (middle 50%):
  SAT Verbal: 510–630
  SAT Math: 510–630
  ACT Comp: 20–27
HS Rank of Entering Freshmen:
  Top 10%: 27%
  Top 25%: 51%
  Top 50%: 85%
Avg. HS GPA: 3.3

Costs (2003–04)

Tuition and Fees: $22,774
Room & Board: $5,670

THE EXPERTS SAY…

" Eckerd's interdisciplinary focus produces well-rounded students who are creative and think for themselves. "

" With beach access and tropical weather year-round, the undisciplined will have a rude awakening around final exam time. "

Inst. Aid (2002–03)

Institutional Aid, Need-Based:
$6,684,000

Institutional Aid, Non-Need-Based:
$4,456,000

FT Undergrads Receiving Aid: 57%
  Avg. Amount per Student: $17,800

Of Those Receiving Any Aid:

Rec. Need-Based Scholarship or
  Grant Aid: 100%

Rec. Need-Based Self-Help Aid: 83%

Upon Graduation, Avg. Loan Debt
  per Student: $17,800

Financial Aid Deadline: 4/1 (priority)

Graduates

Going to Graduate School:
  31% Within One Year

Accepting Job Offer:
  56% at time of graduation

Companies Recruiting On Campus:
570

Alumni Giving: 26%

ELON UNIVERSITY

2700 Campus Box, Elon, NC 27244-2010
Admissions Phone: (336) 278-3566; (800) 334-8448 (out-of-state) Fax: (336) 278-7699
Email: admissions@elon.edu Website: www.elon.edu
Application Website: www.elon.edu/admissions/apply.asp

General Info

Type of School: private, coed, United Church of Christ–UUC

Setting: suburban

Academic Calendar: 4-1-4

Student Body

Full-Time Undergrads: 4,309
Men: 39%, Women: 61%

Part-Time Undergrads: 122
Men: 34%, Women: 66%

Total Undergrad Population:
African American: 6%
Asian American: 1%
Latino: 1%
Native American: <1%
Caucasian: 88%
International: 1%
Out-of-State: 70%
Living Off-Campus: 39%
In Fraternities: 26%
In Sororities: 43%

Graduate and First-Professional Students: 153

Academics

Full-Time Faculty: 252
With Ph.D.: 85%

Part-Time Faculty: 72
With Ph.D.: 35%

Student/Faculty Ratio: 15:1

Most Popular Majors:
communication (17%)
business (16%)
elementary education (6%)
psychology (6%)
biology (5%)

Completing 2 or More Majors: 10%

Freshmen Retention Rate: 87%

Graduation Rates:
62% within four years
71% within six years

Admissions

Regular Application Deadline: 1/10 (priority)

Early Decision Deadline(s): 11/15

Fall Transfer Deadline: 6/1 (priority)

Spring Transfer Deadline: 12/1 (priority)

Inside the Classroom

Elon's specialty is experiential education: In addition to traditional studies, undergrads at this school undertake types of learning that are more active and engaging. Internships, volunteer service, undergraduate research, and study abroad are strongly encouraged by the administration. About 78 percent of Elon students complete an internship (more than twice the national average); past students have written scripts for MTV, worked in the White House, and learned how mutual funds work at Merrill Lynch. The participation for volunteer projects is far above average, too, at 82 percent. Another impressive figure: More than half of each class's population completes a study abroad experience before graduation. Winter, summer, semester, and yearlong programs take place in France, Spain, Italy, the United Kingdom, Australia, Belize, Ecuador, Ghana, Japan, and other sites.

When students finally get a chance to bear down on their formal studies, they're working toward their choice of 46 majors in Elon's four undergraduate schools: The College of Arts and Sciences, the School of Education, the School of Communications, and the Love School of Business. "Much of the overall academic concentration is on global issues and thinking outside of just the United States," notes a senior majoring in business and economics.

"Professors are very accessible, usually giving students their home phone number to get in touch with them," states a junior majoring in communications. A senior journalism major takes it a step further: "My professors have become my friends; I know their families. One professor fed my fish when I went home for break!" A sophomore poly sci/international studies major says, "Professors are readily available to discuss school work, world news, or your last ski trip. Professors go by first names, not 'Dr. so and so.'" And a senior business major observes, "The faculty at Elon is mostly liberal, where the students are mostly conservative. This causes a bit of political debate, but that makes the whole education better."

Research facilities at Elon are high quality and well used. Facilities at the McMichael Science Center and Belk Library contain sophisticated equipment that isn't ordinarily found in undergraduate schools. A day in the spring semester is set aside for presentations at the Student Undergraduate Research Forum—classes are suspended, so you're either presenting or discussing. Last year, an expanded Fellows Program was launched, providing increased merit-based scholarships and a wide range of academic opportunities for top Honors Fellows and new Elon College Fellows. A grant from the William R. Kenan, Jr. Charitable Trust will fund a prestigious scholarship for the top Honors Fellow entering each year.

An Ohio guidance counselor approves of Elon's "hands-on approach to learning" and "innovative teaching methods." A Florida counselor's opinion: "It has a strong atmosphere and good faculty-student interaction." And another guidance counselor says that Elon "embraces an open-minded, liberal arts approach to education," but adds that the "transition from a very small, isolated attitude to a more progressive school is still in progress."

Campus Environment

The campus is situated in Elon, North Carolina, between the Appalachians to the west and the beaches to the east. The 502-acre grounds are heavily wooded (*elon* is the Hebrew word for *oak*) and remarkably beautiful. "Elon spends a lot of time on grooming the campus," said one student. "The lawn is always trimmed and green. We even have flowers in the winter."

An ongoing construction boom means that these are times of change for Elon's campus. New facilities on campus in 2002 included the first two buildings in the new Academic Village (a living-learning complex dedicated to the liberal arts and sciences), the Isabella Cannon Centre for International Studies, new residence halls in Danieley Center, a new dance studio, and Belk Track in the athletics complex.

Housing options are very good for freshmen, since the university disperses them throughout the residence halls instead of shoving them together in one dorm. Housing options include traditional rooms, suites, and flats. A senior's description: "There is no old, stained carpeting or broken sinks in the dorms, but they *are* dorm rooms, not rooms at the Plaza." Continuing the hotel theme, a sophomore disagrees: "Compared to some of the dorms I have seen at other schools, I live in the Waldorf Astoria." Greek housing is available but limited: Up to 12 students can live in each house, with preference given to members with the highest GPAs.

"Elon is located in a small town, with little more than a post office and two bars to occupy students' time," says a senior. "For 'adventurous' students, the nearby towns of Burlington, Greensboro and Raleigh offer more entertainment." Having a car is useful, according to another student, since "the nearest store is about five miles away."

Student Life

While nearly three-quarters of the students are from out-of-state, "Elon is the epitome of Southern hospitality," says a sophomore. A senior agrees: "You couldn't find a place friendlier than Elon… If you lose something, it's most likely to show up in Lost and Found." The student body is overwhelmingly white and fairly affluent, but we're told that "the student body and the administration are working closely together to celebrate diversity on campus and to recruit a diverse student body."

Nine fraternities and nine sororities exist on campus, with 13 organizations living in college-owned houses in the Loy Center, which serves as Elon's Greek Row. The administration's rules on alcohol use are strict, but according to one student, "Drinking runs rampant around rush time." Other students say that drinking on weekends is common but not out of control, and that "drugs harder than marijuana" are rarely seen.

Elon's Phoenix sports teams begin the 2003–2004 season as the newest members of the NCAA Division I Southern Conference. However, a senior says, "Varsity sports are not popular. The school just built a new football stadium, but most games find the stands nearly empty. Instead of attending varsity events, students participate in intramural sports." A special aquatics program offers students year-round swimming opportunities, including water aerobics and special events like Swim to Florida.

Interesting Elon traditions include College Coffee, in which faculty, students, and staff gather every Tuesday morning around Fonville Fountain for refreshments and conversation. A more symbolic tradition is the distribution of acorns to incoming freshmen. Graduating seniors are then given an oak sapling at commencement, and are encouraged to plant it wherever their paths lead them.

Other schools to check out: University of Richmond, Furman, Rollins College, Wake Forest, College of Charleston.

Total # of Students Applied: 7,053
   Admitted: 3,205
   Enrolled: 1,227

# of Students Waitlisted: 2,149
   Students Accepting Place: 1,150
   Waitlisted Students Admitted: 52

Applied Early Decision: 454
   Early Decision Admitted: 348

Test Scores (middle 50%):
   SAT Verbal: 530–620
   SAT Math: 540–630

HS Rank of Entering Freshmen:
   Top 10%: 24%
   Top 25%: 57%
   Top 50%: 92%

Avg. HS GPA: 3.6

THE EXPERTS SAY...

" Experiential education and a supportive community on a gorgeous campus. This treasure won't remain hidden for long. "

" Freshmen receive an acorn at Freshmen Convocation and graduates receive an oak sapling at Commencement. Talk about a sappy tradition! "

Costs (2003–04)

Tuition and Fees: $16,570

Room & Board: $5,670

Inst. Aid (est. 2003–04)

FT Undergrads Receiving Aid: 35%
   Avg. Amount per Student: $11,368

FT Undergrads Receiving Non-Need-Based Scholarship or Grant Aid: 19%
   Avg. Amount per Student: $3,512

Of Those Receiving Any Aid:

Rec. Need-Based Scholarship or Grant Aid: 90%
   Average Award: $5,779

Rec. Need-Based Self-Help Aid: 82%
   Average Award: $5,589

Upon Graduation, Avg. Loan Debt per Student: $18,102

Financial Aid Deadline: 2/15 (priority)

Graduates

Going to Graduate School:
   18% Within One Year

Companies Recruiting On Campus: 205

Alumni Giving: 25%

EMBRY-RIDDLE AERONAUTICAL UNIVERSITY—FLORIDA

600 South Clyde Morris Boulevard, Daytona Beach, FL 32114-3900
Admissions Phone: (386) 226-6100; (800) 862-2416 Fax: (386) 226-7070
Email: dbadmit@erau.edu Website: embryriddle.edu

General Info

Type of School: private, coed
Setting: suburban
Academic Calendar: semester

Student Body

Full-Time Undergrads: 4,153
  Men: 83%, Women: 17%

Part-Time Undergrads: 335
  Men: 81%, Women: 19%

Total Undergrad Population:
  African American: 5%
  Asian American: 3%
  Latino: 6%
  Native American: <1%
  Caucasian: 67%
  International: 9%
  Out-of-State: 71%
  Living Off-Campus: 60%
  In Fraternities: 9%
  In Sororities: 9%

Graduate and First-Professional
  Students: 408

Academics

Full-Time Faculty: 207
  With Ph.D.: 64%

Part-Time Faculty: 67
  With Ph.D.: 16%

Student/Faculty Ratio: 19:1

Most Popular Majors:
  aeronautical science (34%)
  aerospace engineering (27%)
  aviation business admin. (6%)
  aerospace studies (5%)
  engineering physics (4%)

Freshmen Retention Rate: 77%

Graduation Rates:
  21% within four years
  48% within six years

Admissions

Early Decision Deadline(s): 12/1

Fall Transfer Deadline: 7/1, 3/1
  (priority)

Spring Transfer Deadline: 12/1,
  11/1 (priority)

Total # of Students Applied: 3,073
  Admitted: 2,507
  Enrolled: 1,017

Applied Early Decision: 288
  Early Decision Admitted: 151

Inside the Classroom

Most colleges and universities say the sky is the limit for their graduates. Embry-Riddle actually means it. With two campuses in the United States—Daytona Beach, Florida and Prescott, Arizona—Embry-Riddle is the oldest, largest, and most prestigious university specializing in aviation and aerospace. Its undergraduate professional pilot program is the largest in the nation, with as many students as the other top 10 U.S. collegiate flight programs combined. Astronauts and pilots aren't the only products of an Embry-Riddle education, however: Majors available at the larger Daytona Beach campus (which this profile focuses on) include aeronautical science, aerospace engineering, aviation business administration, aerospace studies, and engineering physics.

As the professional marketplace has become more international in recent years, so has Embry-Riddle. The school offers study abroad programs in Denmark, France, Russia, and the United Kingdom. Exchange-student options are also available for students who wish to trade places with a student in another country, for the purpose of developing their foreign language abilities, cross-cultural skills, and overseas experience.

Core requirements at the Daytona Beach campus include coursework in communication theory and skills, mathematics, computer science, physical and life sciences, humanities, and social sciences. A distance-learning option is also available, allowing professors from one campus to teach to students at the other campus, and also allowing students to enroll in some courses from other states and countries.

An annual Career Expo serves the purpose of hooking Embry-Riddle students up with employers. The event is a smash hit with students and employers alike: The school's career services department maintains a waiting list for companies wishing to attend. "It's not to be missed," said one student who attended. "The underlying reason for attending an institution of higher learning is to become gainfully employed when your studies are completed. We're no exception."

Campus Environment

Immediately adjacent to the international airport, the Daytona Beach campus has some of the finest flight-training facilities anywhere. A recently built simulation center contains two full-motion simulators: One for a Boeing 737-300 and the other for a Beech 1900D. Actual flight instruction is done in the school's fleet of Cessna 172 and Piper Seminole aircraft, as well as in simulators for single-engine, multi-engine, and turbine aircraft. Most of the smaller simulators are found in the Wilson Aviation Technology Center, which also contains classrooms, a weather room, and dispatch headquarters.

The Lehman Engineering and Technology Center houses laboratories, wind tunnels for subsonic and supersonic testing, and a smoke tunnel. A new stereolethography unit was also recently purchased for the center, allowing students to build and test prototypes of aircraft structures quickly. Instruction on the maintenance and repair of fixed-wing and helicopter airframes, powerplants, and avionics is provided in the

Goldman Aviation Maintenance Technology Center, which also features avionics repair stations that simulate workplace environments.

Perhaps the crown jewel of Embry-Riddle facilities is the multimillion-dollar Airway Science Simulation Laboratory, which simulates the elements of the U.S. National Airspace System. Here students will find state-of-the-art equipment used for instruction in air traffic control, flight simulation, weather information, airports and airways, and pilot and aircraft performance.

The hub of student activity in the off hours is the Riddle Student Center, where grounded flyers can find the school cafeteria, the Flight Deck Grill, the Landing Strip snack bar, student activities offices, and a special Student Success Center where students can go for academic help.

All freshmen and transfer students with fewer than 27 credits must live on campus for their first academic year. Residence halls are completely furnished, and upperclass students can choose from a variety of campus housing, including suites and apartments. First-year students are housed in their own dorm. Campus housing isn't guaranteed for all four years, although upperclass students may live on campus when space permits.

Student Life

The Daytona Beach campus has over 100 clubs, including those for sports, special interests, honor societies, and religion. Many of the groups on campus are preprofessional or professional in nature, and membership carries a great deal of prestige. It's a fact that Embry-Riddle's Naval Aviation Club furnishes the U.S Navy with the second-largest number of naval aviation officers—second only to the U.S. Naval Academy. The school also has one of the largest all-volunteer Air Force ROTC detachments in the country, as well as the fastest-growing Army ROTC detachment. Social and professional fraternities exist, but no one comes to Embry-Riddle for the partying… they are here to earn their wings, either literally or figuratively.

The team nickname for Embry-Riddle sports is, predictably, the Eagles. Sports for both men and women include cross country, soccer, golf, and tennis. Men can also compete in baseball, while women can compete in volleyball. Student athletes also participate in a variety of club and intramural sports, including lacrosse, wrestling, flag football, rugby, sailing, crew, and softball. The area surrounding Daytona Beach is also conducive to hiking, camping, fishing, sailing… and, of course, just lying on the beach.

Test Scores (middle 50%):
  SAT Verbal: 490–600
  SAT Math: 520–630
  ACT Comp: 21–27
  ACT English: 20–26
  ACT Math: 22–28
HS Rank of Entering Freshmen:
  Top 10%: 20%
  Top 25%: 48%
  Top 50%: 78%
Avg. HS GPA: 3.25

THE EXPERTS SAY...

" Embry-Riddle's reputation in the aerospace industry is unsurpassed, and many of its facilities can't be found at any other school in the U.S. "

" Be sure of your career ambitions before enrolling at Embry-Riddle, because there's not much else to choose from if you aren't sky-bound. "

Costs (2004–5)

Tuition and Fees: $22,190

Room & Board: $6,630

Payment Plan(s): installment plan, deferred payment plan

Inst. Aid (est. 2003–04)

Institutional Aid, Need-Based: $6,745,409

Institutional Aid, Non-Need-Based: $3,044,176

FT Undergrads Receiving Aid: 66%
  Avg. Amount per Student: $12,563

FT Undergrads Receiving Non-Need-Based Scholarship or Grant Aid: 14%
  Avg. Amount per Student: $3,588

Of Those Receiving Any Aid:

Rec. Need-Based Scholarship or Grant Aid: 37%
  Average Award: $3,727

Rec. Need-Based Self-Help Aid: 86%
  Average Award: $5,794

Upon Graduation, Avg. Loan Debt per Student: $36,022

Financial Aid Deadline: rolling, 4/15 (priority)

Graduates

Going to Graduate School:
  4% Within One Year

Accepting Job Offer:
  42% at time of graduation

Companies Recruiting On Campus:
  120

EMERSON COLLEGE

120 Boylston Street, Boston, MA 02116-4624
Admissions Phone: (617) 824-8600 Fax: (617) 824-8609
Email: admission@emerson.edu
Website: www.emerson.edu

General Info

Type of School: private, coed
Setting: urban
Academic Calendar: semester

Student Body

Full-Time Undergrads: 2,904
   Men: 40%, Women: 60%

Part-Time Undergrads: 105
   Men: 45%, Women: 55%

Total Undergrad Population:
   African American: 2%
   Asian American: 4%
   Latino: 5%
   Caucasian: 85%
   International: 4%
   Out-of-State: 65%
   Living Off-Campus: 52%
   In Fraternities: 5%
   In Sororities: 4%

Graduate and First-Professional
   Students: 984

Academics

Full-Time Faculty: 136
   With Ph.D.: 79%

Part-Time Faculty: 209
   With Ph.D.: 43%

Student/Faculty Ratio: 15:1

Most Popular Majors:
   visual and media arts (22%)
   performing arts (20%)
   writing, literature, and publishing
      (11%)
   journalism (9%)
   marketing and advertising (8%)

Freshmen Retention Rate: 83%

Graduation Rates:
   63% within four years
   66% within six years

Admissions

Regular Application Deadline: 1/15

Early Action Deadline: 11/1

Fall Transfer Deadline: 5/1, 3/1
   (priority)

Spring Transfer Deadline: 12/15,
   11/1 (priority)

Total # of Students Applied: 4,321
   Admitted: 2,090
   Enrolled: 700

Inside the Classroom

As one of the country's premier colleges for the study of communication and the performing arts, Emerson is truly unique. Undergrads in Emerson's School of the Arts and the School of Communication can choose from a range of strong programs: visual and media arts (including film, TV/video, audio/radio, and new media); the performing arts; communication disorders; journalism; marketing communications; and writing, literature, and publishing. Approximately 900 courses are offered each semester.

A small student/teacher ratio ensures that students are connected to the accomplished, professional faculty. A student majoring in theater education tells us, "The professors are always there for us and encourage us to come to them with any kind of problem. I am an international student and always find help when I have problems understanding things or when I need more time to finish work." A student studying integrated marketing communications says the professors "are experienced and have thorough knowledge about subjects"—an important consideration for a hands-on, preprofessional school.

Students describe the workload as "challenging" but "manageable." A sophomore elaborates: "The coursework is very intense, but it helps to prepare us for jobs in the future." As is often the case with career-minded students, the atmosphere is rather competitive—"Because people are so focused around here, it's only natural," a freshman explains.

If you (or more likely, your parents) are worried about not getting a strong liberal arts background, don't despair: All B.A. and B.S. students must take approximately one-third of their coursework in the liberal arts. (A B.F.A. program is also available for those students seeking intensive conservatory training.) Emerson also requires a communication core of speech and writing classes balanced by at least one course each from a selection of global and multicultural perspectives, interdisciplinary studies, and ethics and values.

Emerson is known for its many "hands-on" opportunities that help prepare students for the real world. "A lot of our work happens outside of class," says a junior. "We have a lot of group projects to do." Students are given opportunities to showcase original work at film festivals, in publications, on the airwaves and Internet, and in journalism or marketing competitions. Internships for academic credit are available in every academic program, and hundreds of opportunities exist throughout Boston and in cities across the country. The school also sponsors a study abroad program in the Netherlands and an intensive study and internship program in L.A.

Campus Environment

Emerson's state-of-the-art facilities are among the school's strongest features. The 950-seat Emerson Majestic Theatre (rumored to be "haunted") heads an extensive list of outstanding educational facilities, including two on-campus radio stations, TV studios, DVD authoring and digital editing suites, an online journalism news service, and seven facilities and programs to observe therapy in communication disorders. The new 11-story Tufte Performance and Production Center houses expanded performance and rehearsal space, a theater design/technology center, makeup lab, and television studios with editing and control rooms. Plans are also underway to build a 10-story college center and residence hall across from the Boston Common, which should correct what one West Coast guidance counselor views as Emerson's biggest drawbacks: "too spread out and no feeling of a campus."

Emerson's four residence halls house some students in special living/learning clusters such as the Writers' Block and Digital Culture. Although the school cannot guarantee housing for all freshmen, "every effort is made to accommodate first-year students who request housing," states a university official. Off-campus housing is expensive "but very available, and Emerson's Off-Campus Student Services [office] is *so* helpful in obtaining housing in your price range and distance," a junior tells us.

Emerson's campus on Boston Common in the heart of the city's theater district allows students to experience all kinds of opportunities in the country's most popular college town. "Boston is full of colleges and college students," a student points out. "There are so many things to do—concerts, clubs, shopping, theater, etc." Students report that they feel safe on campus and in the surrounding area: "Our campus police and the BPD [Boston Police Department] do a great job of keeping the area safe for students," says a sophomore.

"As an urban campus, Emerson does not have private parking facilities, and students are encouraged not to bring automobiles," states a college official. Students agree that cars aren't needed. "A T pass is all that is necessary!" exclaims one student. Luckily, Emerson's "front door" is opposite the Green Line's Boylston Station, and students are eligible for mass transit discount passes for all city subway, bus, and commuter rail routes.

Student Life

The atmosphere at Emerson is "very open and artsy." "If you have a problem with gay people, black people, foreign people, eccentric people, etc., you would have a problem here," states a junior. Who else wouldn't fit in at Emerson? "Someone who wants to party," answers a sophomore. "People here are way too focused to fool around." On the other end of the spectrum, a freshman notes that "a bookworm" might also feel left out, "because subjects like communications or theater involve practical participation."

Students keep very busy during the week with schoolwork and activities related to their majors, and many don't slow down on weekends, either. "On the weekends, many kids work on co-curricular activities and do production work such as film shoots, stage plays, and radio shows," says a student double-majoring in TV/video and marketing.

There are more than 50 student organizations, including WERS-FM, the Film Arts Society, EIV (Emerson Independent Video), the Society of Professional Journalists, and Musical Theatre Society. While Emerson is a Division III school offering 12 intercollegiate teams, sports are "not too popular" among the arts-focused student body. Greek life is relatively unpopular as well.

Among the most appealing benefits of attending Emerson are "the opportunities that the alumni give us in Hollywood," say students. Notable alums include Jay Leno, Henry Winkler, Denis Leary, *Friends* producer Kevin Bright, and cosmetics entrepreneur Bobbi Brown. Hollywood hotshots also show up on campus throughout the school year for various projects, such as the EVVY award show ("an annual spectacular of student performance, new media, video, print, and film projects"). Students were thrilled when Whoopi Goldberg recently visited the campus for a week, teaching workshops and even attending some classes.

# of Students Waitlisted: 773
  Students Accepting Place: 314

Test Scores (middle 50%):
  SAT Verbal: 570–660
  SAT Math: 540–640
  ACT Comp: 24–28
  ACT English: 24–30
  ACT Math: 22–28

HS Rank of Entering Freshmen:
  Top 10%: 34%
  Top 25%: 77%
  Top 50%: 98%

Avg. HS GPA: 3.5

THE EXPERTS SAY...

" Networking is the key to success in any industry, and Emerson students have a leg up on the competition because of their amazing alumni network. "

" Yes, the students are driven, but will swimming in such a small pond really prepare you for the reality of competing against thousands in the cutthroat world of show business? "

Costs (2003–04)

Tuition and Fees: $22,663
Room & Board: $9,858
Payment Plan(s): installment plan

Inst. Aid (est. 2003–04)

Institutional Aid, Need-Based:
  $13,684,301

Institutional Aid, Non-Need-Based:
  $1,626,132

FT Undergrads Receiving Aid: 60%
  Avg. Amount per Student: $11,820

FT Undergrads Receiving Non-Need-Based Scholarship or Grant Aid: 16%
  Avg. Amount per Student: $12,322

Of Those Receiving Any Aid:

Rec. Need-Based Scholarship or Grant Aid: 76%
  Average Award: $9,631

Rec. Need-Based Self-Help Aid: 87%
  Average Award: $4,625

Upon Graduation, Avg. Loan Debt per Student: $10,550

Financial Aid Deadline: 3/1 (priority)

Graduates

Going to Graduate School:
  4% Within One Year

Companies Recruiting On Campus:
  125

Alumni Giving: 14%

EMORY UNIVERSITY

200 B. Jones Center, Atlanta, GA 30322
Admissions Phone: (404) 727-6036; (800) 727-6036 Fax: (404) 727-4303
Email: admiss@learnlink.emory.edu Website: www.emory.edu
Application Website: www.emory.edu/ADMISSIONS

General Info

Type of School: private, coed, Methodist

Academic Calendar: semester

Student Body

Full-Time Undergrads: 6,157
  Men: 44%, Women: 56%

Part-Time Undergrads: 61
  Men: 38%, Women: 62%

Total Undergrad Population:
  African American: 9%
  Asian American: 16%
  Latino: 3%
  Native American: <1%
  Caucasian: 61%
  International: 3%
  Out-of-State: 70%
  Living Off-Campus: 32%
  In Fraternities: 27%
  In Sororities: 26%

Graduate and First-Professional Students: 5,336

Academics

Full-Time Faculty: 1,076
  With Ph.D.: 100%

Part-Time Faculty: 143
  With Ph.D.: 99%

Student/Faculty Ratio: 6:1

Freshmen Retention Rate: 93%

Graduation Rates:
  84% within four years
  88% within six years

Admissions

Regular Application Deadline: 1/15

Early Decision Deadline(s): 11/1, 1/1

Fall Transfer Deadline: 6/1 (priority)

Spring Transfer Deadline: 11/1 (priority)

Total # of Students Applied: 10,372
  Admitted: 4,357
  Enrolled: 1,296

# of Students Waitlisted: 500
  Students Accepting Place: 500
  Waitlisted Students Admitted: 70

Applied Early Decision: 735
  Early Decision Admitted: 452

Inside the Classroom

Emory University is "a very old, revered school—the most prestigious university in the South," a Florida guidance counselor states. In addition to Emory College (the undergraduate college of arts and sciences), the University has a graduate school of arts and sciences and professional schools of medicine, theology, law, nursing, public health, and business. Another undergraduate option is Emory's two-year Oxford College, located 30 miles east of Atlanta; students can spend their first two years in Oxford's "friendly," "intimate," and "beautiful" environment before transferring to the main campus.

Undergrads can choose from a total of 65 majors. Emory's prelaw and premed programs are renowned, and many Emory students are on a preprofessional track. A senior creative writing major offers her perspective: "Emory is a very pragmatic school. It's a place where people go to prepare themselves for careers, which can leave those of us who aren't 'pre-anything' feeling a little lost."

Students call the workload "heavy," and some report that the environment is pretty competitive. "Everyone basically does what they need to do to graduate and get a 4.0," a senior tells us. Another senior paints a slightly less frenzied picture: "Studying is typically an afternoon and *very* late night thing, usually at the library or at Dunkin' Donuts."

The school attracts many big-name faculty members, partly because of the research opportunities it affords them. Students give mixed reports about relations between students and faculty. One student comments that professors are "brilliant" and "eager to interact with students." But a self-censoring sophomore psych major claims she's not the only one who feels that many professors "don't give a ding dang." Freshmen can make valuable faculty contacts through their Freshman Advising and Mentoring at Emory (F.A.M.E.) group. Each freshman in F.A.M.E. is assigned to a group that has its own faculty, staff, and student leader; the faculty leader also serves as the student's academic advisor during her first two years at Emory.

Campus Environment

Due to an enormous endowment the school receives from the Coca-Cola Co., Emory (a.k.a. "Coca-Cola U") offers outstanding resources and facilities, both academic and recreational. The campus is undergoing major construction and renovations, including the 2002 opening of the Schwartz Center for Performing Arts and the opening of the "live-learn-play community" at Emory's Clairmont Campus.

Campus housing is reputed to be better than average; in fact, one senior calls the housing situation "wonderful, and getting better." A school official states, "First-year freshmen are required to live in on-campus housing and are assigned to freshmen-only residence halls, with one exception—we have one building that is mixed with freshmen and upperclass themes." Freshmen are not allowed to live in fraternity or sorority housing. A senior tells us that "while off-campus housing is still popular, that popularity is dropping as better housing comes on-campus, and off-campus housing around Emory has exploded in price."

The 631-acre campus is located 15 minutes from downtown Atlanta. "The best thing about Emory is its proximity to downtown Atlanta and yet its isolation from what would otherwise become a constant distraction," says one student. The city is spread out in many different, distinctive sections, each with its own character and social attractions. Buckhead is the more collegiate area, where there's "bar after bar after bar, perfect for dancing," while the funkier Little Five Points and Midtown areas draw mixed crowds where you're more likely to find "a wide variety of quirky restaurants and hole-in-the-walls." Having a car is helpful for tooling around Atlanta, though freshmen are not allowed to have cars on campus. Opinions vary widely on public transportation: some students think it's great, while others warn that it's unreliable and unsafe.

Student Life

While Emory has long been known regionally as one of the top academic institutions in the South, its excellent reputation is now attracting students from all across the country: Approximately 60 percent of the student body comes from areas outside the South. One student paints this portrait of the typical Emory student: "Wealthy, Jewish, and from New York; liberal without really thinking about it; member of a sorority; and a psychology major." A New York guidance counselor explains that Emory has a "good comfort level for Northeasterners." The student body is ethnically diverse, which students view as a big plus: "Because we have such high numbers of minorities and international students, you get a broad range perspective of life from people you never even dreamed of," comments a senior. But in general, as another senior bluntly puts it, "Emory students are known for having gorgeous expensive cars and lots of money, and are in the business school or college to make the amount of money that daddy does." Prominent alumni include fashion designer Kenneth Cole, former U.S. Senators Sam Nunn and Max Cleland, and Amy Ray and Emily Saliers of the Indigo Girls.

Fraternities and sororities are very popular on campus, with one-third of the students joining in Greek life. Drinking, especially at frat parties, is "huge," and one student reports that students do use drugs but never enough to affect their academic performance. However, the administration has recently cracked down hard on the partying: "They have closed many frat houses and have banned all Greek Row parties," says one student. "This has caused a *lot* of tension because the age to get into all clubs in Atlanta was recently raised to 21."

Though Emory is an NCAA Division III school and a founding member of the University Athletic Association, intramurals outstrip varsity sports in popularity (and there's no football team). "Athletes looking for more exposure should look into bigger schools," notes an athlete who otherwise raves about Emory's athletic facilities. Even nonathletes spend a lot of time working out: "Most Emory students are very skinny and work out a lot; they care about their appearances," another student observes.

"Whatever your interests are," says one student, "you will be able to find an outlet for them." More than half of the student body participates in Volunteer Emory; other popular clubs are Hillel and Outdoor Emory. Still, many students seem to feel that Emory is "fragmented" and "lacks a feeling of unity on campus." A poly sci major's analysis: "Emory is not necessarily apathetic, but students do not care about anything beyond their own areas. Because of that, we have too many clubs and too many leaders, but not enough students attending events."

Other schools to check out: Duke, Georgetown, University of Pennsylvania, Vanderbilt, Washington U in St. Louis.

Test Scores (middle 50%):
 SAT Verbal: 640–720
 SAT Math: 660–740
 ACT Comp: 29–33
HS Rank of Entering Freshmen:
 Top 10%: 90%
 Top 25%: 99%
 Top 50%: 100%
Avg. HS GPA: 3.8

Costs (est. 2004–05)
Tuition and Fees: $27,952
Room & Board: $8,920

THE EXPERTS SAY...

" Former U.S. President Jimmy Carter is a University Distinguished Professor at Emory; his nonprofit Carter Center is a partnership with the university. "

" No Pepsi machines here—just the real thing. And your classmates are more likely to be from New York than the Old South. "

Inst. Aid (est. 2003–04)
Institutional Aid, Need-Based:
 $31,917,055

Institutional Aid, Non-Need-Based:
 $7,371,812

FT Undergrads Receiving Aid: 38%
 Avg. Amount per Student: $25,238

FT Undergrads Receiving Non-Need-Based Scholarship or Grant Aid: 6%
 Avg. Amount per Student: $16,422

Of Those Receiving Any Aid:

Rec. Need-Based Scholarship or
 Grant Aid: 94%
 Average Award: $18,962

Rec. Need-Based Self-Help Aid: 88%
 Average Award: $6,309

Upon Graduation, Avg. Loan Debt
 per Student: $18,803

Financial Aid Deadline: 4/1, 2/15
 (priority)

EUGENE LANG COLLEGE, NEW SCHOOL UNIVERSITY

65 West 11th Street, New York, NY 10011-8963
Admissions Phone: (212) 229-5665; (877) 528-3321 Fax: (212) 229-5166
Email: Lang@newschool.edu Website: www.lang.edu

General Info

Type of School: private, coed
Setting: urban
Academic Calendar: semester

Student Body

Full-Time Undergrads: 719
 Men: 32%, Women: 68%

Part-Time Undergrads: 14
 Men: 50%, Women: 50%

Total Undergrad Population:
 African American: 5%
 Asian American: 4%
 Latino: 5%
 Caucasian: 52%
 International: 3%
 Out-of-State: 55%
 Living Off-Campus: 64%

Academics

Full-Time Faculty: 35
Part-Time Faculty: 79
Student/Faculty Ratio: 12:1

Most Popular Concentrations:
 cultural studies (28%)
 writing (25%)
 arts in context (12%)
 social and historical inquiry (10%)

Freshmen Retention Rate: 71%

Graduation Rates:
 33% within four years
 48% within six years

Computers: Computer Required

Admissions

Regular Application Deadline: 2/1

Early Decision Deadline(s): 11/15

Fall Transfer Deadline: 5/15

Spring Transfer Deadline: 11/15

Total # of Students Applied: 862
 Admitted: 560
 Enrolled: 187

# of Students Waitlisted: 70
 Students Accepting Place: 35
 Waitlisted Students Admitted: 21

Applied Early Decision: 47
 Early Decision Admitted: 38

Test Scores (middle 50%):
 SAT Verbal: 570–670
 SAT Math: 510–610

Inside the Classroom

Although Eugene Lang College has an undergraduate enrollment of fewer than 600, its connection to other institutions makes it seem much larger. Lang is the undergraduate college of the prestigious New School University (previously called the New School for Social Research). After their first year, Lang students are able to enroll in courses at the New School's graduate facility, which attracts a faculty of international renown. Students can also take courses and enroll at other New School divisions, including Parsons School of Design, Mannes College of Music, and the famed Actors Studio.

Programs in political and social sciences are strong at Eugene Lang, as are urban studies and education. Writing, particularly poetry, is well regarded, as are the performing arts. Unlike traditional college majors, you don't have to take a large number of required courses in a single academic discipline: The Advising System permits students to create the curriculum that best fits their educational goals. With the help of an advisor, students design their program within one of the following five broad interdisciplinary concentrations: cultural studies; literature, writing, and the arts; mind, nature, and value; social and historical inquiry; or urban studies.

Eugene Lang College grew from a highly progressive Freshman Year Program developed at the New School in 1973. The school was originally called the Seminar College, reflecting the style of teaching Lang is known for today. With such a small student body, there's no need for large courses and lectures. Most classes have fewer than 15 students, creating an open intellectual atmosphere in which students test out and question themselves and one another. The seminars also enable students and the faculty to get to know each other, fostering an easygoing familiarity among the campus population. "I'm on a first-name basis with teachers and members of the administration," says a transfer student. "I love being able to ask for help so easily and having teachers care about what I think."

Some students thrive on the intellectual independence and the opportunities to think outside the box that Lang's self-designed programs offer (though a Bronx guidance counselor says that the "loose structure" is not for everybody). Other students wonder about the ultimate value of their unorthodox degree in the eyes of more traditional graduate school admissions committees and in the marketplace. But there are a number of joint degree programs available through the New School itself. In addition to the Bachelor of Arts degree, Lang offers a Bachelor of Arts/Bachelor of Fine Arts degree in conjunction with Parsons School of Design and the Jazz & Contemporary Music Program. Accelerated B.A./M.A. degree programs are available through the Graduate Faculty in liberal studies. B.A./M.A. programs are also offered in media studies and secondary school education with the Adult Division and in urban policy analysis and management with the Robert J. Milano Graduate School of Management and Urban Policy. There's also an exchange student program with equally progressive Sarah Lawrence College.

Campus Environment

Located in Greenwich Village, one of New York City's most interesting neighborhoods, Eugene Lang College offers students a campus of infinite opportunities—New York City itself. The Village is the home of New York's funkier shops, restaurants, bars, and night spots, and is a playground for young people from all parts. Lacking a central campus, the New School has buildings clustered around brownstones and busy city avenues; most Lang classes are located in a building on West 11th Street. Students share housing with nonuniversity tenants in many buildings. Loeb Hall is the only residence for students only, housing undergraduates from all divisions of the university; it offers suites for four, with a resident advisor located on every other floor. The building is officially dry, and drinking policies are enforced. Older students tend to head off campus to cheaper apartments in the East Village or to the outlying borough of Brooklyn.

New York City traffic and parking are nightmarish anywhere, but nowhere more so than in the Village. Students walk (the brave will even face the street traffic as they bike or rollerblade), or use public transportation, which is easily accessible. While a food plan is available, most students eat out and take out from the Village's many bistros, salad bars, delis, and pizzerias.

Student Life

Lang is not the school you want to come to if you want a traditional college experience with sports, fraternities, and homecomings. Social life at Lang is centered around New York City itself, the reason most students came to the school in the first place, and the campus community can seem a bit diffuse. The student body at Lang is diverse in age and ethnicity, with a number of older students and almost a quarter of the students belonging to a minority group or from abroad. Over a third are from New York City. The student body is extremely liberal, with a healthy radical fringe, and PC is the norm in and outside the classroom.

First-year students tend to hang out together in the dorms. Once students move off-campus, however, they are likely to form their own social circles. The school does sponsor activities, but students are often more interested in doing their own thing. "We have a lot of events going on, mostly poetry readings, but we have to compete with the city events," a staff member tells us. There are no varsity sports (or even sports facilities), and there's limited space for on-campus activities; the students consider all of Greenwich Village their greater campus, shopping on punked-out Bleecker Street, dining in the literally thousands of restaurants, club hopping to hear the latest bands and dance, and, of course, going to the bars. When you add in the rest of the city, Lang students have endless social and cultural opportunities.

Other schools to check out: Bard, NYU, Sarah Lawrence, SUNY Purchase, St. John's College (MD).

HS Rank of Entering Freshmen:
Top 10%: 21%
Top 25%: 47%
Top 50%: 81%
Avg. HS GPA: 2.99

Costs (2004–5)

Tuition and Fees: $24,130
Room & Board: $10,810
Payment Plan(s): installment plan

Inst. Aid (est. 2003–04)

Institutional Aid, Need-Based: $5,759,567

Institutional Aid, Non-Need-Based: $225,120

FT Undergrads Receiving Aid: 68%
Avg. Amount per Student: $17,793

FT Undergrads Receiving Non-Need-Based Scholarship or Grant Aid: 2%
Avg. Amount per Student: $6,610

THE EXPERTS SAY...

" Both academically and socially, Lang is for students who want the freedom and opportunity to shape their own experiences. "

" Unless you like poetry and political correctness, there's not a lot of student activity. Sports fans, go elsewhere. "

Of Those Receiving Any Aid:

Rec. Need-Based Scholarship or Grant Aid: 98%
Average Award: $14,857

Rec. Need-Based Self-Help Aid: 83%
Average Award: $4,411

Upon Graduation, Avg. Loan Debt per Student: $20,093

Financial Aid Deadline: rolling, 3/1 (priority)

EVERGREEN STATE COLLEGE

2700 Evergreen Parkway NW, Olympia, WA 98505
Admissions Phone: (360) 867-6170 Fax: (360) 867-6576
Email: admissions@evergreen.edu Website: www.evergreen.edu
Application Website: www.evergreen.edu/admissions/apply.htm

General Info

Type of School: public, coed

Setting: small town

Academic Calendar: quarter

Student Body

Full-Time Undergrads: 3,537
  Men: 44%, Women: 56%

Part-Time Undergrads: 301
  Men: 45%, Women: 55%

Total Undergrad Population:
  African American: 5%
  Asian American: 4%
  Latino: 4%
  Native American: 4%
  Caucasian: 66%
  Out-of-State: 23%
  Living Off-Campus: 79%

Graduate and First-Professional
  Students: 277

Academics

Full-Time Faculty: 157
  With Ph.D.: 85%

Part-Time Faculty: 62
  With Ph.D.: 45%

Student/Faculty Ratio: 21:1

Most Popular Majors:
  liberal arts and sciences (100%)

Freshmen Retention Rate: 75%

Graduation Rates:
  37% within four years
  51% within six years

Admissions

Regular Application Deadline: 3/1

Fall Transfer Deadline: 3/1

Spring Transfer Deadline: 12/1

Total # of Students Applied: 1,521
  Admitted: 1,422
  Enrolled: 460

Test Scores (middle 50%):
  SAT Verbal: 520–650
  SAT Math: 480–590
  ACT Comp: 20–26

HS Rank of Entering Freshmen:
  Top 10%: 12%
  Top 25%: 35%
  Top 50%: 67%

Avg. HS GPA: 3.15

In the Classroom

Since there are no grades, no tests, no required courses, no tenured professors, no majors, and no large classes, it's obvious that Evergreen offers something different. But don't think that all the freedom accorded students makes it an easy route to a college degree. One of the most highly regarded public liberal arts colleges in the nation, TESC (the T stands for "The") is designed for students passionate about pursuing their educational goals and serious about making a difference in the world. "Evergreen believes in preserving and articulating differences of ethnicity, race, gender and sexual orientation, rather than erasing them or pushing them to the sidelines, and this belief is reflected in the design and content of our programs," reads a statement on the school website.

Evergreen disregards the traditional college curriculum, taking instead an interdisciplinary approach to higher education. All B.A. and B.S. degrees are awarded in Liberal Arts, rather than specific majors. Students enroll in "programs" rather than classes or majors. Students take team-taught, interdisciplinary programs that may be one quarter, two quarters, or yearlong. Programs are team-taught by professors representing different disciplines and focus on broad topics such as The Computer in Society or Imaging the Body. Seminars averaging about 25 students are the predominant learning mode. Although not organized by department, the school is known for its strength in the arts (Matt Groening, creator of *The Simpsons*, and Craig Bartlett, creator of Nickelodeon's *Hey Arnold!*, are alumni) and in the environmental sciences.

Instead of letter grades, students write self-evaluations and professors complete a detailed evaluation of each student. College officials call the student evaluation process "rigorous" and "analytical," and most students find the detailed feedback more useful and insightful than letter grades. However, the unorthodox structure does cause some problems outside the TESC community. With courses that don't fit readily into traditional academic disciplines and no student grades, transferring to another school can get complicated; many colleges simply consider all Evergreen credits electives. One student says, "Unless you want to start over as a freshman, once you go to Evergreen, you're stuck there." A recent graduate notes that companies don't know what to think of a job applicant who leaves the GPA line blank—it usually raises doubts not only about the applicant's capabilities but also the school. (However, since many Evergreen students go on to grad school, the school does have a process for converting narrative evaluations to a GPA.)

A college official states, "Evergreen is unique in its expectation that students take responsibility for their own learning." With education focused on interdisciplinary seminars and independent study, students have a lot of freedom. "Learn what you want to learn, at your own pace, show effort, and you get credit," a recent grad states. But another cautions those looking for an easy route to a college degree: "With maybe 30 students in seminar groups, there was no place to hide. You had to attend class regularly. You had to participate. You couldn't copy another person's work because the student–teacher ratio was so low." The involvement of the faculty with the students is an important part of the Evergreen experience. "Students and professors are on a first-name basis," a senior says. Most students can identify a professor who "really made a difference" in their education and in their life.

Campus Environment

Located a few miles outside Olympia, TESC occupies a stunning 1,000-acre site that encompasses preserved forest, wetlands, and beachfront on Puget Sound. Campus trails provide jogging and bicycling opportunities, as well as access to swimming, boating, and beachcombing. The campus also serves as a field research laboratory where faculty and students monitor plant and animal life from the tidal pools to the top of the forest canopy. The campus includes a small organic farm.

Renowned for their environmental sensitivity, TESC students, called "Greeners," prefer to walk, ride bikes, carpool, and take public transit when possible. However, there are no restrictions on bringing cars on campus (which is good, given the fact that most students commute to school).

While only one out of four students lives on campus, a variety of housing options is available, including traditional residence halls, apartments, and facilities that offer separate bedrooms with shared common space. Generally, students find their rooms compare favorably with, as one student says, "the little cubbyhole dorms my friends have" at other state schools. There is no requirement that first-year students live on campus—however, all students who do are required to purchase a meal plan.

Student Life

The open-minded nature of the academic programs carries over to the social environment. While the school is regarded (sometimes with a bit of derision) as "different," students and faculty are proud of those things that make them nontraditional. For example, at graduation, a samba band leads the graduation procession. Diversity in backgrounds, outlooks, and personalities is not just tolerated—it's welcomed. While the word "Greeners" comes from the school's name, it also describes the student political atmosphere, which is liberal and strongly environmentalist. One student unapologetically explains that Greeners are "more interested in protesting nuclear waste being trucked through our state or freedom of speech violations than in [getting] more upper-level business courses or fielding a football team."

Although Olympia is the home of Olympia beer, drinking is not a popular student activity. Most students, however, say drugs are readily available and popular among some groups. In general, the atmosphere is, in the words of a senior, "pretty mellow," with the most popular activities being campus events and hanging out in dorm rooms or coffeehouses. For a lively club scene, Greeners head for Seattle, a little over an hour away.

The Evergreen Geoducks (pronounced "gooey-duck," the geoduck is a large clam indigenous to the waters of Puget Sound) participate in NAIA Division II women's volleyball and men's and women's basketball, swimming, soccer, and cross country. Evergreen also offers intramural programs in kung fu, crew, lacrosse, softball, and rugby. In addition, students enjoy popular recreational programs that include hiking, camping, skiing, and rock climbing.

Other schools to check out: Reed, St. John's College (NM), Antioch, UC Santa Cruz, New College of Florida.

Costs (2003–04)

Tuition and Fees, In-State: $3,804

Tuition and Fees, Out-of-State: $13,485

Room & Board: $5,772

Payment Plan(s): installment plan

Inst. Aid (2002–03)

Institutional Aid, Need-Based: $613,436

Institutional Aid, Non-Need-Based: $124,783

FT Undergrads Receiving Aid: 55% Avg. Amount per Student: $10,006

FT Undergrads Receiving Non-Need-Based Scholarship or Grant Aid: 1% Avg. Amount per Student: $3,862

Of Those Receiving Any Aid:

Rec. Need-Based Scholarship or Grant Aid: 76% Average Award: $5,406

Rec. Need-Based Self-Help Aid: 82% Average Award: $4,233

Upon Graduation, Avg. Loan Debt per Student: $13,000

Financial Aid Deadline: 3/15, 2/15 (priority)

THE EXPERTS SAY...

" With its interdisciplinary programs and narrative evaluations, Evergreen is for passionate students who are comfortable setting their own pace and direction. "

" It's not easy being Green... especially if you try to transfer to another college. And Evergreen's low 6-year graduation rate shows that many students aren't ready to handle so much academic freedom. "

Graduates

Going to Graduate School: 17% Within One Year

Accepting Job Offer: 87% at time of graduation

FAIRFIELD UNIVERSITY

1073 North Benson Road, Fairfield, CT 06824-5195
Admissions Phone: (203) 254-4100 Fax: (203) 254-4199
Email: admis@mail.fairfield.edu
Website: www.fairfield.edu

General Info

Type of School: private, coed,
    Roman Catholic/Jesuit

Setting: suburban

Academic Calendar: semester

Student Body

Full-Time Undergrads: 3,357
    Men: 41%, Women: 59%

Part-Time Undergrads: 291
    Men: 51%, Women: 49%

Total Undergrad Population:
    African American: 2%
    Asian American: 3%
    Latino: 5%
    Native American: <1%
    Caucasian: 87%
    International: 1%
    Out-of-State: 75%
    Living Off-Campus: 20%

Graduate and First-Professional
    Students: 1,033

Academics

Full-Time Faculty: 222
    With Ph.D.: 93%

Part-Time Faculty: 204
    With Ph.D.: 51%

Student/Faculty Ratio: 13:1

Most Popular Majors:
    communications (8%)
    psychology (6%)
    finance (6%)
    English (6%)
    biology (6%)

Completing 2 or More Majors: 11%

Freshmen Retention Rate: 85%

Graduation Rates:
    74% within four years
    78% within six years

Admissions

Regular Application Deadline: 1/15

Early Decision Deadline(s): 11/15

Fall Transfer Deadline: 6/1

Spring Transfer Deadline: 11/15

Total # of Students Applied: 7,655
    Admitted: 3,782
    Enrolled: 789

# of Students Waitlisted: 1,988
    Students Accepting Place: 773
    Waitlisted Students Admitted: 121

Inside the Classroom

At Fairfield University, the Jesuits strive to offer an education that is "both theoretical and practical." As such, students here are treated to a wide variety of research and internship opportunities coupled with a demanding core curriculum. While not well-known outside the Northeast, Fairfield is "up and coming," insists a Massachusetts guidance counselor. Students at each of Fairfield's undergrad schools—arts and sciences, business, nursing, and engineering—claim their school is the best. The business programs, particularly accounting and finance, are excellent, as are biology, nursing, English, and religious studies. Another guidance counselor also noted Fairfield's "exciting new program in Judaic studies."

Students spend most of their first two years fulfilling the general education requirements, distributed among five areas of study: math and the natural sciences; history and the social and behavioral sciences; English and fine arts; modern and classical languages; and philosophy, religious studies and applied ethics. Students give faculty high marks all around. "Professors are generally very accessible, and anyone who takes class seriously should have no trouble getting over a 3.0," says one triple(!) major.

In keeping with the Jesuit tradition of active service in the world, many undergrads travel to Central and South America to help develop self-sustaining enterprises for host countries. Every qualified junior or senior at Fairfield is guaranteed an internship in his field of study, we hear, and with New York City just an hour away, the opportunities are top-notch. One student tells us, "Fairfield provides good opportunities for employment and has a growing reputation. Anyone willing to put in work will walk out of FU with a good education and many opportunities." Also, high percentages of Fairfield students are accepted to med and law schools.

Campus Environment

Students rave about the beauty of the campus and its location on the Long Island Sound. Fairfield University is "five minutes from the shore, 10 minutes from the countryside, [and] an hour from New York City." The town of Fairfield, while pretty, doesn't have a whole lot to offer besides the beach, and even that's changing for the worse. Relations between the community and the student body are tense, and a couple of years ago, residents of Fairfield Beach were able to persuade the university administration to enforce tougher penalties for students' off-campus drinking, loud partying, and other offenses. An upperclassman weighs in: "The town of Fairfield has money. The students do not. We live next door to one another. We hate each other."

Despite recent events—in February 2002, a Fairfield alumnus held a religion class hostage but ultimately harmed none of the 27 people involved—the campus is generally thought of as safe and secure. We are even told by a student that the university has an "overly 'safe' campus," and that "Fairfield has security and police everywhere and anywhere, so as soon as you are about to have fun, 'secure-seekers' will be sure to make those thoughts of amusement a distant memory." The library and the campus center each received significant upgrades recently as part of a $110 million construction and renovation plan currently taking place on campus.

KAPLAN

Freshmen and sophomores must live on campus unless they commute from home. First-years are housed either in traditional residence- or suite-style dorms. A junior complains, "Dorms are small, and freshmen are tripled into double-sized rooms. The Quad (5 dorms centrally located) do provide a good opportunity to meet people, but living with two other roommates is hard." The student adds that juniors "have the opportunity to live in an on-campus townhouse or apartment… but many juniors are forced to live in a dorm again." Sophomores have the opportunity to participate in the Ignatian Residential College, a program that integrates prayer, service, and residential life. Only juniors and seniors selected by lottery may move off campus (to one of the highly coveted beach houses, most likely). One student explains that "off-campus dwellers live at Fairfield Beach. Houses are small and uncomfortable and ridiculously expensive, but you are living on the beach in Fairfield County." Freshmen are not allowed to have cars, but "the campus is pedestrian- and bicycle-friendly."

Student Life

Although the school has increased its multicultural enrollment in recent years, the campus remains overwhelmingly white. Most Fairfield students hail from the Northeast, but only one-quarter are from Connecticut itself. "There are a lot of Long Islanders on campus, which brings the overall friendliness down a bit (come on, it's true)," jokes a student. He continues, "This is a Catholic school, so by default, most students are Catholic, which means they are therefore Irish or Italian, white, and conservative. People not fitting that mold may or may not fit in at FU."

At this Division I school, men's and women's basketball receive the most attention, with a "Red Sea" student cheering section in their new state-of-the-art area in neighboring Bridgeport. "Our men's basketball team is the only team with any promise," we are told. There are 9 IM programs and 12 club sports available; more than 60 percent of the student body plays on one team or another. Overall, though, we hear that there isn't as much of an emphasis on athletics as you might find at a "typical" Catholic university.

What you *can* expect at this Jesuit school is a focus on community service. Nearly one-third of the student body participates in volunteer programs, helping out at soup kitchens or health centers or local elementary schools. The Literacy Volunteer and Hunger Cleanup programs attract large numbers of students as well.

The campus activities office also organizes trips to Broadway shows and events such as "I Still Love Bowling," when students flock to the lanes on select Thursday nights for free bowling. Mostly, though, when they aren't studying, Fairfield students party. There are no fraternities or sororities, "but the beach acts like Frat Row, as the countless houses are all named and all have rotating parties, only without the cover charge." A student tells us, "There is not a whole lot going on in Fairfield, CT, so we throw our own parties and do it ourselves." The Clam Jam, a.k.a. "The Luau," is an annual event in the spring that draws thousands of rowdy undergrads to the beach for a raucous, alcohol-soaked weekend. (Despite the crackdown on off-campus partying and the increased fines for drinking, students still manage to pull it off, much to the chagrin of the locals.)

Other schools to check out: Villanova, Providence College, Fordham, Loyola College in Maryland, College of the Holy Cross.

Applied Early Decision: 205
Early Decision Admitted: 135

Test Scores (middle 50%):
SAT Verbal: 550–630
SAT Math: 560–650
ACT Comp: 25–27

HS Rank of Entering Freshmen:
Top 10%: 35%
Top 25%: 74%
Top 50%: 99%

Avg. HS GPA: 3.39

Costs (2003–04)

Tuition and Fees: $26,135
Room & Board: $8,920

THE EXPERTS SAY...

" Fairfield offers a well-rounded education with emphasis on service to the community—a winning combination for today's world. "

" Community service, yes. Too bad the surrounding community doesn't offer much for Fairfield's students. "

Inst. Aid (est. 2003–04)

Institutional Aid, Need-Based:
$14,067,828

Institutional Aid, Non-Need-Based:
$5,919,432

FT Undergrads Receiving Aid: 53%
Avg. Amount per Student: $17,603

FT Undergrads Receiving Non-Need-Based Scholarship or Grant Aid: 8%
Avg. Amount per Student: $9,483

Of Those Receiving Any Aid:

Rec. Need-Based Scholarship or Grant Aid: 84%
Average Award: $10,642

Rec. Need-Based Self-Help Aid: 84%
Average Award: $4,659

Upon Graduation, Avg. Loan Debt per Student: $25,194

Financial Aid Deadline: rolling, 2/15 (priority)

Graduates

Going to Graduate School:
20% Within One Year

Accepting Job Offer:
57% at time of graduation

Companies Recruiting On Campus:
160

Alumni Giving: 24%

FASHION INSTITUTE OF TECHNOLOGY

Seventh Avenue @ 27th Street, New York, NY 10001-5992
Admissions Phone: (212) 217-7675
Email: fitinfo@fitnyc.edu Website: www.fitnyc.edu

General Info

Type of School: public, coed
Setting: urban
Academic Calendar: semester

Student Body

Full-Time Undergrads: 6,363
  Men: 16%, Women: 84%

Part-Time Undergrads: 1,158
  Men: 19%, Women: 81%

Total Undergrad Population:
  African American: 7%
  Asian American: 11%
  Latino: 10%
  Native American: <1%
  Caucasian: 43%
  International: 12%
  Out-of-State: 29%
  Living Off-Campus: 84%

Graduate and First-Professional
  Students: 112

Academics

Full-Time Faculty: 209

Part-Time Faculty: 753

Student/Faculty Ratio: 17:1

Most Popular Majors:
  fashion merchandising management (28%)
  fashion design (19%)
  communication design (10%)
  advertising & marketing communication (8%)
  interior design (6%)

Freshmen Retention Rate: 82%

Graduation Rates:
  44% within four years
  57% within six years

Admissions

Regular Application Deadline: 1/1
  (priority)

Early Decision Deadline(s): 11/15

Early Action Deadline: 11/15

Fall Transfer Deadline: 1/1 (priority)

Spring Transfer Deadline: 10/1 (priority)

Total # of Students Applied: 3,187
  Admitted: 1,482
  Enrolled: 860

Waitlist Available

Inside the Classroom

Founded in 1944, the Fashion Institute of Technology is a college of art and design, business and technology within the SUNY system. In setting out to create "the MIT for the fashion industries," FIT's founders were clearly onto something. "FIT is fashion," reads a statement on the school's website. "We are also design, fine arts, packaging, computer animation. We are technology, and also marketing, advertising, merchandising, production. And more."

FIT is comprised of the School of Art and Design, School of Business and Technology, School of Continuing and Professional Studies, School of Graduate Studies, and School of Liberal Arts. Students can major in more than 30 different subjects at FIT's eight-building campus. You must select one, and only one, major on your application for admission. A portfolio evaluation is required of all students who apply for an art or design program. While fashion merchandising management and fashion design are by far the most popular majors at FIT, its other design programs are also excellent. And FIT is one of only a handful of colleges in the country to offer a major in toy design.

FIT offers Associate of Applied Arts degrees, Bachelor of Science degrees, Bachelor of Fine Arts Degrees, Master of Arts degrees, and Master of Professional Studies degrees, along with a number of professional certificates. It's important to note that FIT operates on a "2 + 2 system": a two-year associate (A.A.S.) degree ("lower division"), followed upon the student's request by a two-year bachelor's (B.S. or B.F.A.) degree ("upper division"). This means that if you're applying to enter FIT right out of high school, you'll actually be applying to FIT's two-year associate's program. If you've already earned an associate's degree (or at least 60 credits towards a U.S. college degree in an appropriate major), then you may be eligible to go right into FIT's two-year bachelor's degree program.

FIT students must fulfill SUNY's General Education Requirements. Lower-division students who are pursuing a bachelor's degree must take courses in math, natural sciences, social sciences, Western civilization, humanities, the arts, and basic communication. Upper-division students must meet requirements in American history, foreign language, and non-Western civilizations.

FIT's Presidential Scholars program is an honors program that "provides academically-gifted students with an opportunity to nurture their intellectual interests through creative instruction and educational enhancements." Among the program's perks: advanced classes, an annual merit stipend, priority registration, and the ability to substitute honors classes for required introductory liberal arts courses.

One of the greatest things about attending FIT is its internship program. In many majors, internships are a required part of the student's course of study and academic credit is earned. In other programs, students may take an internship on a supplemental credit or non-credit basis. The Internship Center has a roster of more than 1,800 participating sponsor companies representing all industry areas, including such big-name companies as Tommy Hilfiger, Donna Karan, Bloomingdale's, Disney, and more. The school claims that 40 percent of these internships turn into full-time jobs—a great advantage for students in today's tight job market. Numerous study abroad options are also available.

"Approximately 88–90 percent of FIT graduates are placed in industry," says the school. Most of the faculty reportedly have at least ten years of industry experience. And all of FIT's departments have advisory boards with connections in the industry.

Campus Environment

FIT is located in Chelsea, a safe area of Manhattan. (For anyone who is truly worried about safety, FIT posts detailed crime statistics on its website.) Each residence hall has a security officer posted in its lobby 24 hours a day. Residents are required to show their hall identification card to enter the buildings. All visitors must be signed in, at the security desk, by a resident.

FIT's three on-campus residence halls— Nagler, Coed, and Alumni— house approximately 1,250 students. Nagler and Coed primarily consist of doubles, plus a very limited number of apartment/suite spaces. There are common area kitchen facilities in the Coed basement and on the first floor of Nagler Hall. Alumni Hall consists of quad apartments/suites with their own kitchen and bathroom facilities. To be considered eligible for campus housing, students must be enrolled in a full-time degree program and have a permanent address outside a 35-mile radius of New York City. ("Ineligible" applicants will only be considered for housing after all eligible applicants have been accommodated.) Space in the residence halls is limited, and no student is guaranteed housing. Students are forced to seek off-campus housing after two consecutive semesters of living on campus. Help in finding off-campus housing is available through the Residential Life Department.

FIT is known for having cutting-edge facilities. The library provides resources not found in conventional academic libraries, including holdings of more than 138,000 volumes and non-book materials such as fashion forecasting services, fashion design-related clippings files, periodicals from around the world, and special collections. The Style Shop, FIT's on-campus student-run boutique, offers merchandise designed by FIT students, faculty, and alumni. FIT also has a world-class museum—"the repository for one of the world's most important collections of costume and textiles, with particular strength in 20th-century fashion."

Student Life

FIT students are, obviously, a creative, career-driven bunch. About half of the students hail from New York City. The average age of full-time students at FIT is 23. *Women's Wear Daily* described the FIT "look" in a May 2003 special college issue: "In their jeans and sweatshirts, FIT students would look right at home on just about any liberal arts campus. However, it's not uncommon to see fashion-driven types in stilettos paired with Seven jeans and Louis Vuitton handbags."

Students can participate in more than 50 campus clubs and organizations. While some of these are industry-oriented, many are not: there are several ethnic and religious clubs, performing arts organizations, and recreational organizations available. WFIT, the campus radio station, and *W27*, the student newspaper, are popular. Students looking to give of themselves can contact FIT's Student Volunteer Community Service Bank for information regarding local organizations requesting volunteers. FIT's varsity teams include men's basketball, women's basketball, men's tennis, women's tennis, women's volleyball, cheerleaders, men's bowling, and women's bowling. Free classes are offered in such areas as aerobics, boxing, yoga, martial arts, self-defense, and dance (including African, hip-hop, jazz, mambo, salsa, and swing). Various clubs regularly sponsor dances, concerts, outings, flea markets, and other events throughout the year.

Other schools to check out: Parsons, Rhode Island School of Design, Cooper Union, NYU, SUNY Purchase.

Applied Early Decision: 597
  Early Decision Admitted: 379

HS Rank of Entering Freshmen:
  Top 10%: 8%
  Top 25%: 32%
  Top 50%: 75%

Avg. HS GPA: 85%

THE EXPERTS SAY...

" FIT gives you elite Seventh Avenue connections and conservatory-type training at a public school price. "

" Notable alumni include Calvin Klein and Norma Kamali. (Perhaps it's the CK aesthetic that inspired FIT to design its whole website in khaki.) "

Costs (2004–5)

Tuition and Fees, In-State: $4,620

Tuition and Fees, Out-of-State: $10,570

note: Tuition varies by degree

Room & Board: $6,549

Payment Plan(s): installment plan, deferred payment plan, pre-payment plan

Inst. Aid (est. 2003–04)

Institutional Aid, Need-Based: $621,671

Institutional Aid, Non-Need-Based: $72,500

FT Undergrads Receiving Aid: 42%
  Avg. Amount per Student: $6,936

FT Undergrads Receiving Non-Need-Based Scholarship or Grant Aid: 2%
  Avg. Amount per Student: $1,069

Of Those Receiving Any Aid:

Rec. Need-Based Scholarship or Grant Aid: 78%
  Average Award: $3,915

Rec. Need-Based Self-Help Aid: 69%
  Average Award: $4,007

Upon Graduation, Avg. Loan Debt per Student: $10,242

Financial Aid Deadline: rolling, 2/15 (priority)

Graduates

Companies Recruiting On-Campus: 110

FISK UNIVERSITY

1000 17th Ave North, Nashville, TN 37208-3051
Admissions Phone: (800) 443-3475 Fax: (615) 329-8774
Email: admit@fisk.edu Website: fisk.edu
Application Website: www.fisk.edu

General Info

Type of School: private, coed
Setting: urban
Academic Calendar: semester

Student Body

Full-Time Undergrads: 821
  Men: 31%, Women: 69%

Part-Time Undergrads: 29
  Men: 45%, Women: 55%

Total Undergrad Population:
  African American: 91%
  Asian American: <1%
  Latino: <1%
  Caucasian: <1%
  International: 3%
  Out-of-State: 72%
  Living Off-Campus: 32%
  In Fraternities: 27%
  In Sororities: 26%

Graduate and First-Professional
  Students: 23

Academics

Full-Time Faculty: 52
  With Ph.D.: 75%

Part-Time Faculty: 37
  With Ph.D.: 51%

Student/Faculty Ratio: 13:1

Most Popular Majors:
  psychology (15%)
  biology (14%)
  business (13%)
  political science (6%)
  dramatics and speech (4%)

Freshmen Retention Rate: 84%

Graduation Rates:
  54% within four years
  72% within six years

Admissions

Regular Application Deadline: 3/1

Fall Transfer Deadline: 6/1

Spring Transfer Deadline: 12/1

Total # of Students Applied: 1,122
  Admitted: 743
  Enrolled: 231

Test Scores (middle 50%):
  SAT Verbal: 410–520
  SAT Math: 390–510
  ACT Comp: 16–21

Inside the Classroom

Fisk was founded in 1866 (making it the oldest university in Nashville) as an institution committed to educating newly freed slaves. Fisk is a small, private, predominantly African American university whose goal is to equip students of all backgrounds for intellectual and social leadership in the modern world. The school says that one in six African American doctors, lawyers, and Ph.D.s currently practicing in the United States is a Fisk graduate. Among its famous alumni are W. E. B. DuBois, one of the founders of the NAACP; Nikki Giovanni, a modern poet and author; John Hope Franklin, eminent historian; and Hazel O'Leary, former Secretary of Energy.

Fisk offers approximately 25 academic programs within the main divisions of business administration, humanities and fine arts, natural science and mathematics, and social sciences. Fisk students are very focused and usually declare a major by the end of their freshman year, earlier than most schools. Professional degree tracks, such as prelaw and premed, attract a large percentage of the student body. Joint-degree programs are available with Vanderbilt University, Rush Medical Center, and Howard University. Fisk also boasts an excellent music department, which offers a bachelor of music degree in piano, vocal, or instrumental performance. The core curriculum consists of specific courses (rather than a choice of courses) in the following areas: freshman orientation, oral and written communication, natural science, creative arts, mathematics, humanistic experience and thought, the world and its peoples, and African American heritage.

Fisk students say that the personal attention they receive from their professors is the school's greatest strength. They give faculty high marks for their personal expertise, teaching skills, mentoring, and accessibility. Fiskites also take pride in knowing that Fisk was the first HBCU accredited by the Southern Association of Colleges and Schools, and the first to be granted a chapter of Phi Beta Kappa.

Campus Environment

Fisk's campus, dotted with gardens and beautiful old buildings, is listed as a historic district in the National Register of Historic Places, and draws many visitors looking to catch a glimpse of black history. Fiskites are particularly proud of the tradition of excellence that was begun by its first students, who formed a singing troupe to raise money for their school. Known as the Fisk Jubilee Singers, the group preserved Fisk's future and funded the construction of Jubilee Hall, a national historic landmark that is recognized as the first permanent campus structure built for the education of African Americans. In this beautiful Victorian Gothic building hangs a ceiling-to-floor portrait of the original Singers, commissioned by Queen Victoria of England. Since 1871, the Jubilee Singers have performed throughout the United States and Europe; they were recently inducted into the Gospel Hall of Fame.

Arts and history are indeed big at Fisk. Besides the Jubilee Singers, the school's other claim to fame is its art gallery that houses world-famous works and one of the nation's most respected collections of African American art. The university's library contains some of America's most priceless first editions, letters, and diaries.

The 40-acre campus is situated on a hill overlooking downtown Nashville, the capital of Tennessee known for its legacy of American music. Although city life has its attractions, and Fiskites are in good company (there are 16 institutions of higher learning in Nashville, four of which are historically or predominantly African American), students here aren't too keen on their surroundings. Indeed, it's not in the best of neighborhoods and we hear that sticking to campus grounds is the smartest and safest bet.

All dorms are single-sex, and impose strict rules—quiet hours are from 8 P.M. to 8 A.M., Sunday through Sunday. About 40 percent of Fisk students live off campus or commute. Most freshmen and sophomores call the dorms home, while juniors and seniors tend to move to nearby apartments.

Student Life

The student body is almost entirely African American, and largely from the South or the Midwest. Fiskites tend to be serious about their studies, their school, and their heritage. Socializing certainly takes a back seat to studying, but students here still have a good time on campus. There's a strong sense of community here. The Greek system plays a tremendous role in uniting the student body by organizing social activities and parties. People hang out in the student center, with its TV, video games, pool tables, and cafeteria. Students also enjoy extracurriculars such as student government, the college radio station, intramural sports, dances, and theater productions. Fisk's Race Relations Institute hosts summer sessions on racism and its social, economic, political, and psychological effects, bringing highly respected and accomplished African and African American activists to campus. Recent speakers have included Dr. Joycelyn Elders, Erinn Cosby, Naomi Tutu, and James Earl Jones.

A Division III school, Fisk is a member of the Great South Athletic Conference, offering 15 varsity sports—seven for men and eight for women—but few athletic facilities as compared with other schools. Sports are generally not among Fisk's strong points.

Occasionally, students leave their intimate campus to head for downtown, where they enjoy the city's many bars, clubs, and music venues. However, for most students, social life takes second priority to Fisk's competitive academic environment. As a junior reflected, "We are here to learn, not only about our studies but about ourselves and our history. When we graduate from Fisk, we will leave with strong self-esteem and a great deal of pride for the black community."

Other schools to check out: Howard, Morehouse, Spelman, Xavier, Tuskegee.

HS Rank of Entering Freshmen:
Top 10%: 26%
Top 25%: 44%
Top 50%: 66%
Avg. HS GPA: 2.99

Costs (2004–5)

Tuition and Fees: $12,450
Room & Board: $6,230
Payment Plan(s): installment plan, pre-payment plan

THE EXPERTS SAY...

" This small HBCU has graduated more African American doctors, lawyers, and Ph.D.s than many schools twice its size. "

" Fisk is more study than socializing. Be prepared to obey strict dorm rules and shut off your stereo at 8 P.M. "

Inst. Aid (2002–03)

Institutional Aid, Non-Need-Based: $2,573,838

FT Undergrads Receiving Aid: 94%
Avg. Amount per Student: $13,650

FT Undergrads Receiving Non-Need-Based Scholarship or Grant Aid: 3%
Avg. Amount per Student: $8,200

Of Those Receiving Any Aid:

Rec. Need-Based Scholarship or Grant Aid: 99%
Average Award: $3,700

Rec. Need-Based Self-Help Aid: 98%
Average Award: $3,700

Upon Graduation, Avg. Loan Debt per Student: $20,000

Financial Aid Deadline: 6/1, 3/1 (priority)

Graduates

Alumni Giving: 27%

FLAGLER COLLEGE

P.O. Box 1027, St. Augustine, FL 32085-1027
Admissions Phone: (904) 819-6220; (800) 304-4208 Fax: (904) 829-6838
Email: admiss@flagler.edu
Website: www.flagler.edu

General Info

Type of School: private, coed
Setting: small town
Academic Calendar: semester

Student Body

Full-Time Undergrads: 1,986
  Men: 38%, Women: 62%

Part-Time Undergrads: 48
  Men: 35%, Women: 65%

Total Undergrad Population:
  African American: 2%
  Asian American: 1%
  Latino: 3%
  Native American: <1%
  Caucasian: 90%
  International: 2%
  Out-of-State: 32%
  Living Off-Campus: 36%

Academics

Full-Time Faculty: 66
  With Ph.D.: 67%

Part-Time Faculty: 90
  With Ph.D.: 4%

Student/Faculty Ratio: 31.5:1

Most Popular Majors:
  business administration (22%)
  education (16%)
  communication (15%)
  psychology (7%)
  sport management (6%)

Completing 2 or More Majors: 7%

Freshmen Retention Rate: 74%

Graduation Rates:
  41% within four years
  55% within six years

Admissions

Regular Application Deadline: 3/1,
  1/15 (priority)

Early Decision Deadline(s): 12/1,
  1/15

Fall Transfer Deadline: 3/1, 1/15
  (priority)

Spring Transfer Deadline: 10/15,
  9/1 (priority)

Total # of Students Applied: 1,897
  Admitted: 628
  Enrolled: 443

# of Students Waitlisted: 323
  Students Accepting Place: 141
  Waitlisted Students Admitted: 6

Inside the Classroom

Flagler College offers a quality private school undergraduate education for an astonishingly low price: With tuition around $8,000, and room and board another $6,610, total yearly costs are under $15,000. How is the school able to keep expenses low and quality high? By not addressing every academic discipline; offering a limited number of programs; and serving the full-time undergraduate student.

With 20 majors ranging from accounting to graphic design, as well as preprofessional programs in fashion merchandising, human services, and prelaw, the school offers bachelors of arts degrees in selected liberal arts and preprofessional studies. The most popular majors are business administration and education. There's a very strong program in deaf education, and one guidance counselor recommends Flagler for its great communications department. The fine arts department is excellent, and for those artists looking for their special niche, Flagler offers the only stained glass program in the country.

With fewer than 2,500 students, admission to Flagler is tough. In the last few years, it has been bombarded with applications. As one guidance counselor tells, the school is a "hidden treasure," and clearly the message is getting out. Once in, students must complete two courses in freshman composition; one course in speech communication; six semester hours in math, and computer literacy. In addition to these requirements, students must choose a minimum of two courses in humanities, two courses in social sciences, and one course in humanities, social sciences, mathematics, or natural sciences.

The student/faculty ratio isn't that great, but the average class size is only 21 students, and the professors are said to be dedicated and available. "One-on-one faculty attention is a hallmark of Flagler education," the college insists. The administration is student-focused, as well: We hear that Flagler's Admissions Office staff maintain extensive communication with students prior to the time that applications are submitted.

Approximately three out of four Flagler students conduct internships in fields such as business, graphic design, sports management, and youth ministry. Students may enroll in a course of archaeological studies under the direction of the Florida Museum of Natural History, which currently explores the excavation of the first successful European colony in the United States. Job opportunities are available both on the college campus and at the Florida School for the Deaf and the Blind. Assigned to those with financial need, the standard work award for these jobs is $400–$500 per semester.

Campus Environment

Flagler is located in St. Augustine, a famous historic tourist center in northeast Florida, between Jacksonville and Daytona Beach. Originally built as the grand Hotel Ponce de Leon, this is a majestic yet extremely compact campus. Many of the original painted ceilings and mosaic floors have been maintained, not to mention the stunning stained glass windows designed by Louis Tiffany. All classes are held in one building, historic Kennan Hall.

Freshmen are required to live in dorms, but in total, the majority of students live off-campus. There are two dorms, one for women and one for men. Since there are more women than men at the school, the women's dorm is twice as big, housed in the main structure from the original hotel, a masterpiece of Spanish Renaissance architecture. (Thankfully, this dorm has just been refitted with air conditioning.) Though there are a few suites, most dorm rooms house two or three students, with pay phones in the halls. The administration "believes in sensible regulations with regard to student life and conduct." We hear that the administration is rather strict about its "no interdorm visitation" policy, which means no members of the opposite sex hanging out in your room.

Just four miles from the beach and one block from the town's shopping district, students are smack in the middle of a quaint and relaxed—if touristy—community. This is the oldest continuous European settlement in the country, and most of the area (including a 17th century fort) has been restored. The town looks more like a picturesque European village than anything else, complete with horse-drawn carriages. Since tourism is St. Augustine's main industry, students must learn to share space with travelers from all over the world.

Student Life

The atmosphere at Flagler is politically and socially conservative. There are no fraternities or sororities on campus, and students are expected to behave responsibly. "The students most likely to thrive at Flagler College are those with a great deal of self-knowledge and awareness," a college official tells us. Flagler has been coed since 1971; today, two-thirds of the students are women. About 53 percent are from Florida.

As far as nightlife in town goes, it's mostly small bars. Flagler is a dry campus, but alcohol can usually be found at parties nearby. There are four honor societies and 20 clubs on campus, ranging from Surf Team to Spirit, a performance group that combines sign language, music and choreography. The art gallery, theater, campus newspaper, radio station and literary journal also provide creative outlets and preprofessional experience. Two of the more popular clubs are The Home Team, an organization that helps to repair and refurbish homes of needy local residents, and Students in Free Enterprise, which addresses issues of leadership and teamwork in free enterprise (recent programs have focused on young entrepreneurs, money issues facing students, and start-up businesses for at-risk high school students). The Student Government Association participates in work days to assist the homeless. And once a semester, there's Common Ground—an Intervarsity Christian Fellowship-sponsored party that brings together those of different faiths. With over 500 students in attendance, it's one of the most popular events on campus.

The athletics program is small, though solid: For both men and women, there are varsity teams in basketball, cross country, golf, soccer, and tennis. Additionally, for men, there's baseball, and for women, volleyball. Surfing is very popular, of course, given the school's proximity to the beach, and there's a great tennis team.

A college official describes a Flagler tradition: "Flagler College established a Single Ring Tradition as an opportunity and privilege for students who have proven that they can meet the College's standards. The Single Ring Tradition involves a candlelight procession across the campus, a ring ceremony in which the president of the College personally presents each student with his/her ring, and a reception for family and friends."

Applied Early Decision: 826
Early Decision Admitted: 436

Test Scores (middle 50%):
SAT Verbal: 530–610
SAT Math: 510–600
ACT Comp: 22–26
ACT English: 21–27
ACT Math: 20–25

HS Rank of Entering Freshmen:
Top 10%: 20%
Top 25%: 52%
Top 50%: 96%

Avg. HS GPA: 3.22

THE EXPERTS SAY...

" Flagler is an educational value with a select number of interesting programs, like deaf education and stained glass arts. "

" It's Florida, but don't bring your party hat, because the Flagler social atmosphere is 'responsible.' "

Costs (2004–5)

Tuition and Fees: $8,000
Room & Board: $4,760
Payment Plan(s): pre-payment plan

Inst. Aid (2002–03)

Institutional Aid, Need-Based:
$107,615

Institutional Aid, Non-Need-Based:
$209,363

FT Undergrads Receiving Aid: 39%
Avg. Amount per Student: $7,285

FT Undergrads Receiving Non-Need-Based Scholarship or Grant Aid: 40%
Avg. Amount per Student: $4,262

Of Those Receiving Any Aid:

Rec. Need-Based Scholarship or Grant Aid: 59%
Average Award: $2,751

Rec. Need-Based Self-Help Aid: 85%
Average Award: $3,413

Upon Graduation, Avg. Loan Debt per Student: $14,971

Financial Aid Deadline: rolling, 5/4 (priority)

Graduates

Alumni Giving: 31%

FLORIDA STATE UNIVERSITY

UCA-2500, Tallahassee, FL 32306-2400
Admissions Phone: (850) 644-6200; (850) 644-3420 Fax: (850) 644-0197
Email: admissions@admin.fsu.edu Website: www.fsu.edu/
Application Website: admissions.fsu.edu/online/

General Info

Type of School: public, coed

Setting: urban

Academic Calendar: semester

Student Body

Full-Time Undergrads: 25,879
 Men: 43%, Women: 57%

Part-Time Undergrads: 3,250
 Men: 46%, Women: 54%

Total Undergrad Population:
 African American: 12%
 Asian American: 3%
 Latino: 10%
 Native American: <1%
 Caucasian: 73%
 International: 1%
 Out-of-State: 13%
 Living Off-Campus: 84%
 In Fraternities: 15%
 In Sororities: 13%

Graduate and First-Professional
 Students: 7,254

Academics

Full-Time Faculty: 1,086
 With Ph.D.: 92%

Part-Time Faculty: 317
 With Ph.D.: 92%

Student/Faculty Ratio: 23:1

Most Popular Majors:
 business (8%)
 criminology (5%)
 biological science (4%)
 political science (3%)
 exercise science (3%)

Completing 2 or More Majors: 13%

Admissions

Regular Application Deadline: 3/1;
 12/31 (priority)

Fall Transfer Deadline: 7/1 (priority)

Spring Transfer Deadline:
 11/1 (priority)

Total # of Students Applied: 31,264
 Admitted: 13,037
 Enrolled: 6,101

Test Scores (middle 50%):
 SAT Verbal: 520–620
 SAT Math: 530–630
 ACT Comp: 22–27
 ACT English: 21–27
 ACT Math: 21–26

Inside the Classroom

"FSU is a large, research university that feels much smaller, where students find administrators and professors eager to help them, and whose parents routinely write letters expressing appreciation for the attention their sons and daughters receive," states a university official. With nearly 200 majors, Florida State University offers a comprehensive range of options within its 17 major academic divisions: the Colleges of Arts and Sciences, Business, Communication, Education, Engineering, Human Sciences, Law, Medicine, and Social Science; and the Schools of Criminology and Criminal Justice, Film, Information Studies, Music, Nursing, Social Work, Theatre, and Visual Arts and Dance. FSU's academics are strong across the board, with the sciences, the performing arts, criminology, and information studies among the real standouts.

FSU's general educations requirements, called the Liberal Studies Program, involves 36 credits distributed across five areas: math, English comp, history/social science, humanities/fine arts, and natural sciences. Students report that the workload at FSU can be surprisingly tough. "When I went to high school, I never had to study and still graduated in the top 5 percent of my class. Here, I am challenged not only by my professors, but also by my fellow students," reflects one junior. Another junior says, "FSU is an institution where lots of learning and interaction occurs, so if a student is not willing to live up to those standards set by the university, then I would say he/she would not fit in."

"The professors are always willing to go that extra mile to help you with something," says a senior poly sci major. A senior criminology major agrees, "The professors are easily accessible." This is nice to know, considering the major research and other projects that FSU's busy faculty members are always engaged in. One example: In February 2003, English Professor Mark Winegardner, director of FSU's heralded Creative Writing Program, was chosen by Random House to write a sequel to *The Godfather* by Mario Puzo.

Campus Environment

Florida State's main campus is located in Tallahassee, the state capital. Many campus buildings were built with a castle-like theme and are surrounded by the lush foliage typical of Florida. The state's year-round sunshine definitely plays a role in the choice of some students to enroll here, but you should know that while the FSU campus does include a beach on a lake, the Gulf Coast beaches are actually 45 minutes away.

Of the 16 undergraduate residence halls, all but two are available to first-year students. However, a school official warns, "University Housing is unable to accommodate all entering students interested in on-campus living. Admitted students are encouraged to apply for housing as early as possible to increase the likelihood of an on-campus assignment." In recent years, FSU has launched a series of special programs designed to more directly tie the residence hall experience to students' academic work. The Living/Learning Communities provide students with an opportunity to live with students engaged in similar coursework. Some residence halls are "dedicated" to students who are interested in arts and science, social sciences, music, or education, and those who have an interest in leadership training; there is also a Wellness Hall for students electing a living environment and lifestyle free of any tobacco or alcohol. Students who can't find what they want can always look off campus: "There are places all over town, and at all price ranges, as well. The most popular are Campus Lodge, Polos on Park, and The Gathering," says a political science major. Note that freshmen are permitted to live off-campus or in Greek housing.

"FSU is in a building boom," says one university official in an understatement. The National Weather Service recently relocated to the FSU campus, building a state-of-the-art addition to the meteorology building, and other research facilities were also upgraded. And FSU has built an impressive new Student Life Building (complete with movie theater), renovated the Oglesby Student Union, built parking garages, built a beautiful new women's softball/soccer complex, renovated the Leach Recreation Center, completely refurbished the Mike Long track, and built a new basketball practice facility.

Student Life

According to the university's website, minority student enrollment at FSU has increased by 33 percent in recent years. Students tell us that there is no "typical" FSU undergrad, and with nearly 300 student organizations, students from all walks of life have no trouble finding others who share a common interest. Clubs range from the academic to the religious, and some that are truly unique. FSU is one of the few schools in existence with its very own circus, run entirely as a club by students: The Flying High Circus features acts in flying trapeze, juggling, and high wire, and has traveled to other countries to stage its performances.

Football reigns supreme at Florida State, with the Seminoles in championship contention nearly every season. "One of the most recognized football traditions in the country happens at the beginning of Florida State football games, when a student dressed as Chief Osceola, a proud symbol of the courage of the Seminole Indians, rides an Apaloosa horse, Renegade, onto the 50-yard-line in Doak Campbell Stadium and plants a flaming spear into the field," a university official tells us. FSU competes in a total of 17 intercollegiate sports within the NCAA and Atlantic Coast Conference (eight men's and nine women's sports). Additionally, during any given year, more than 7,000 students compete in intramurals, with most students active in more than one event.

Students can also venture off campus for recreational activities. "Tallahassee is a big town," says a junior. "There are a lot of places off campus that are fun to go to, and a lot of those places are geared towards students."

While guidance counselors still harp on the student body's reputation for partying, students tell us that the administration has worked very hard in the past few years at calming that down, and it appears to have worked. "We have some people who study all the time, and then we have the opposite end. Most students fall in the middle: We know how to have fun, but school is also very important. A lot of students here on campus support themselves entirely," one student observes. Fraternities and sororities are popular, but as one student describes, "They play a role in our social life, but they don't dominate it."

Other schools to check out: U of Florida, U of Miami, U of Georgia, Georgia Tech, Clemson.

HS Rank of Entering Freshmen:
Top 10%: 55%
Top 25%: 93%
Top 50%: 100%
Avg. HS GPA: 3.8

Costs (est. 2004–05)

Tuition and Fees, In-State: $2,860

Tuition and Fees, Out-of-State: $13,888

Room & Board: $6,168

Regional or "good neighbor" tuition available

THE EXPERTS SAY...

" FSU is constantly growing and improving. Its new medical school is the first to be established in the United States in 20 years. "

" What a fun place to spend four (or more) years! Take full advantage of the sunshine, Seminoles, and circus acts. "

Inst. Aid (est. 2003–04)

Institutional Aid, Need-Based: $10,079,969

Institutional Aid, Non-Need-Based: $6,288,535

FT Undergrads Receiving Aid: 41%
Avg. Amount per Student: $5,512

FT Undergrads Receiving Non-Need-Based Scholarship or Grant Aid: 10%
Avg. Amount per Student: $2,454

Of Those Receiving Any Aid:

Rec. Need-Based Scholarship or Grant Aid: 76%
Average Award: $3,812

Rec. Need-Based Self-Help Aid: 80%
Average Award: $3,526

Upon Graduation, Avg. Loan Debt per Student: $17,112

Financial Aid Deadline: 2/15 (priority)

Graduates

Going to Graduate School: 35% Within One Year

Alumni Giving: 21%

FORDHAM UNIVERSITY

441 East Fordham Rd., Thebaud Hall, New York, NY 10458-9993
Admissions Phone: (800) 367-3426; (718) 817-4000 Fax: (718) 367-9404
Email: enroll@fordham.edu Website: www.fordham.edu
Application Website: www.fordham.edu/prospective/admissions/applications_forms1339.html

General Info

Type of School: private, coed, Catholic (Jesuit)

Setting: urban

Academic Calendar: semester

Student Body

Full-Time Undergrads: 6,688
Men: 41%, Women: 59%

Part-Time Undergrads: 556
Men: 34%, Women: 66%

Total Undergrad Population:
African American: 6%
Asian American: 6%
Latino: 11%
Caucasian: 58%
International: 1%
Out-of-State: 41%
Living Off-Campus: 42%

Graduate and First-Professional
Students: 7,328

Academics

Full-Time Faculty: 625

Part-Time Faculty: 653

note: faculty numbers from 2002

Student/Faculty Ratio: 11:1

Most Popular Majors:
business/marketing (24%)
social sciences/history (22%)
communications (14%)
psychology (8%)
visual/performing arts (7%)

Freshmen Retention Rate: 90%

Graduation Rates:
68% within four years
73% within six years
note: 5-year programs affect rates

Admissions

Regular Application Deadline: 2/1

Early Decision Available

Early Action Deadline: 11/1

Fall Transfer Deadline: 7/1 (priority)

Spring Transfer Deadline: 12/1 (priority)

Total # of Students Applied: 12,801
Admitted: 6,862
Enrolled: 1,701

# of Students Waitlisted: 1,300
Students Accepting Place: 700
Waitlisted Students Admitted: 151

Inside the Classroom

"Fordham's strength lies in its diversity," declares a young alum. And this diversity is found not only in the student body, but also in the unique strengths of Fordham's undergraduate schools on three separate campuses. Fordham College at Lincoln Center is known mainly for its arts programs, especially theater. Fordham College at Rose Hill in the Bronx is Fordham's largest undergraduate school, offering traditional liberal arts and sciences programs; the English, history, theology, political science, and sociology departments are considered particularly strong and are favored by the many students who plan to go to law school. The College of Business Administration, also at Rose Hill, offers good programs in accounting, finance, and marketing, among others. And at the new Tarrytown Campus, a small number of undergrads attend the all-women's Marymount College of Fordham University (established in 2002 when Marymount College consolidated with Fordham).

Fordham is known for its extensive core curriculum: approximately 18 courses in philosophy, theology, history, literature, and other liberal arts and sciences. "The atmosphere was pretty much noncompetitive except for those few overachievers who were workaholics and made everyone else in the class look bad," says one former student. However, the school has become much more selective over the past few years: "They have raised admissions requirements so it is harder to get in," explains a New York guidance counselor. Many liberal arts classes at Rose Hill are taught by Jesuits, most of whom live on campus. "The professors are mostly good, except for a few with heavy heavy accents and a few that are just plain old," says one student.

Fordham has a number of special academic programs. Upperclassmen—particularly communications and business majors—clamor to participate in Fordham's internship program featuring a base of more than 2,000 New York City employers, including several major television programs, networks, and production companies. The CEO Breakfast Club gives select business students the opportunity to attend breakfast meetings hosted by chief executive officers of major firms in the NYC area. And qualified juniors may apply to the 3-3 program offered by the widely respected Fordham University School of Law.

In July 2003, Rev. Joseph M. McShane, S.J., former dean of Fordham College at Rose Hill and president of the University of Scranton, becomes Fordham's 32nd president. Father McShane is known for his accessibility and for his commitment to helping students secure prestigious fellowships.

Campus Environment

Each of Fordham's two main campuses has its own unique style and atmosphere. The Lincoln Center campus consists of only a few buildings on a city street, but it's located right in the bustling cultural heart of Manhattan—perfect for the many theater and dance students who are enrolled there. The 85-acre Rose Hill campus, on the other hand, is adjacent to the Botanical Gardens and the Bronx Zoo and features beautiful landscaping and Gothic architecture which help turn this Bronx campus into a picturesque Jesuit retreat. Movies with scenes filmed on the Rose Hill campus include *The Exorcist* and *Quiz Show*.

The majority of Fordham's student body lives on campus. Freshmen can choose from a few freshmen-only dorms at Rose Hill, including Queen's Court Residential College, in which the close-knit residents take some of their core courses together. Most Rose Hill upperclassmen live in university-owned apartments, both on- and off-campus. Lincoln Center offers one "very nice" apartment-style residence hall for all of its students.

Fordham's campuses are considered "extremely safe"—"They've really done a good job with security," says an enthusiastic guidance counselor from Connecticut. The "Ram Van" shuttles students back and forth between the two campuses, and "is safer than the subway, which is several blocks away," says one student. Nearby Arthur Avenue ("the Little Italy of the Bronx") is lined with some fabulous Italian restaurants and bakeries and is a safe and convenient place for food shopping, banking, and other errands.

Fordham's new wireless network, launched in February 2003, allows laptop users to connect to the Web using wireless/radio-frequency technology. Access points have been installed in most buildings on the Rose Hill and Lincoln Center campuses, including study lounges, cafeterias, and libraries. Although there is no service charge to connect to the wireless network, users do need to register for access.

Student Life

The overall atmosphere on campus is "close-knit" or "cliquey," depending on your perspective. "Everyone basically forms their little groups in the dorms or in classes and stays with that group no matter what they are doing, whether going out or going to dinner or watching TV in rooms," explains one student. The student body is culturally diverse, although most students hail from New York, New Jersey, and Connecticut, and many head home on weekends.

With more than 120 student organizations (cultural clubs such as the Gaelic Society and the International Black Students Union are particularly popular at Rose Hill), each campus offers plenty of activities to keep students involved. The student productions at Lincoln Center are of near-professional quality. Rose Hill's weekly movie showings and comedy nights are popular with students. Athletes can choose from 21 intercollegiate sports and 12 club sports, and Rams football and basketball games are always well attended.

As a recent grad points out, "At Fordham, you've got the benefits of a tight campus community when you're starting out, and the benefits of Manhattan when you get sick of campus activities and seeing the same faces by senior year." Outings to the latest Broadway musical or art exhibition are a regular feature of student life. Many students head to bars, clubs, and off-campus parties on weekends. "The bars are the place to be every Thursday–Sunday," confirms a Rose Hill student. "Even though they have strict rules about alcohol in the dorms, everyone just floats on out to the bars." Since roaming around the city at night is not always safe, students usually go out in groups. In nice weather, Rose Hill students often enjoy studying or sunbathing on the quad, called Edward's Parade ("Eddie's").

The Jesuit influence is definitely more apparent at Rose Hill, where students are generally more conservative than their Lincoln Center counterparts. Sunday night Mass is practically considered a social event at Rose Hill; non-Catholic students who enjoy the feeling of community sometimes accompany their Catholic friends. The community service program is a strong presence on campus; more than 600 undergrads each semester participate in community service projects, including a Global Outreach program that takes student volunteers to poverty-stricken places around the world.

Other schools to check out: NYU, George Washington U, Boston U, Hofstra, Holy Cross.

Applied Early Decision: 221
Early Decision Admitted: 129

Test Scores (middle 50%):
SAT Verbal: 540–642
SAT Math: 550–640
ACT Comp: 23–28

HS Rank of Entering Freshmen:
Top 10%: 35%
Top 25%: 70%
Top 50%: 95%

Avg. HS GPA: 3.64

Costs (2003–04)

Tuition and Fees: $24,647

Room & Board: $9,700

Payment Plan(s): installment plan

Inst. Aid (est. 2003–04)

FT Undergrads Receiving Aid: 65%
Avg. Amount per Student: $17,427

FT Undergrads Receiving Non-Need-Based Scholarship or Grant Aid: 9%
Avg. Amount per Student: $7,824

THE EXPERTS SAY...

" Fordham has successful alumni in all walks of life, including Lincoln Center alum Denzel Washington, Rose Hill alum Alan Alda, and Marymount alum Susan Lucci. "

" Lincoln Center students can just walk up the street to the New York City Ballet, while Rose Hill students can just cross the street to the Bronx Zoo. (But remember: Please don't feed the dancers.) "

Of Those Receiving Any Aid:

Rec. Need-Based Scholarship or Grant Aid: 95%
Average Award: $12,974

Rec. Need-Based Self-Help Aid: 81%
Average Award: $4,990

Upon Graduation, Avg. Loan Debt per Student: $16,274

Financial Aid Deadline: 2/1 (priority)

Graduates

Going to Graduate School:
24% Within One Year

Accepting Job Offer:
40% at time of graduation

Companies Recruiting On Campus:
500

FRANKLIN AND MARSHALL COLLEGE

P.O. Box 3003, Lancaster, PA 17604-3003
Admissions Phone: (717) 291-3953 Fax: (717) 291-4389
Email: admission@FandM.edu Website: www.FandM.edu

General Info

Type of School: private, coed, Nonsectarian

Setting: urban

Academic Calendar: semester

Student Body

Full-Time Undergrads: 1,874
  Men: 52%, Women: 48%

Part-Time Undergrads: 11
  Men: 100%

Total Undergrad Population:
  African American: 2%
  Asian American: 4%
  Latino: 3%
  Caucasian: 78%
  International: 9%
  Out-of-State: 64%
  Living Off-Campus: 33%

Academics

Full-Time Faculty: 167
  With Ph.D.: 97%

Part-Time Faculty: 28
  With Ph.D.: 50%

Student/Faculty Ratio: 11:1

Most Popular Majors:
  government (20%)
  business administration
    (management) (10%)
  English (8%)
  business administration
    (accounting/finance) (7%)
  psychology (7%)

Completing 2 or More Majors: 16%

Freshmen Retention Rate: 90%

Graduation Rates:
  80% within four years
  84% within six years

Admissions

Regular Application Deadline: 2/1

Early Decision Deadline(s): 11/15,
  1/15

Fall Transfer Deadline: 5/1

Spring Transfer Deadline: 12/1

Total # of Students Applied: 3,616
  Admitted: 2,085
  Enrolled: 503

# of Students Waitlisted: 686
  Students Accepting Place: 686
  Waitlisted Students Admitted: 59

Inside the Classroom

In contrast to its peaceful Pennsylvania Dutch surroundings, Franklin and Marshall has one of the most rigorous and intensive academic programs in the country. Students complain about the "extremely heavy" workload and the difficulty of getting A's, but also take pride in their perseverance. Surviving the academic rigors of F&M means they can handle just about anything. The school boasts that "two-thirds [of students] have the clear intention of going on to graduate school immediately."

Almost everything about the academic programs at F&M is designed to encourage students to engage actively and intellectually with their studies. The extensive general education program includes distribution requirements, a writing requirement, and "Foundations" courses (an introduction to various systems of knowledge and belief). Students then progress to "Explorations" courses, in which they delve into a particular area more fully. Of course, students also take classes in their major, as well as any electives they manage to squeeze in. Professors, while notoriously tough graders, are "generally attentive and helpful," students report. The average class size is around 20, adding credence to one student's assessment that "professor accessibility is excellent."

Almost all freshmen (90 percent) fulfill their writing requirement right off the bat with a First-Year Residential Seminar. These seminars, which vary widely in subject area (the 2001–2002 offerings featured "Shakespeare's Comedies," "Growing Up Is Hard To Do," and "Saving Rainforests," among others), are limited to 16 students and emphasize participation and discussion. The groups live together on coed freshman floors, creating an instant support system. The seminar professor doubles as the student's academic adviser; additional guidance and support also comes from the Preceptor, an upperclassman teaching assistant.

Some of the best-known departments are in the premed sciences, which benefit from state-of-the-art facilities that undergraduates can use in their own research. However, one student warned that while many people begin by studying premed, a lot also wind up changing majors once faced with the difficult science courses. Those who stick with it, though, are more than well prepared for medical school; F&M students' acceptance rate to health profession schools over the past few years has ranged from 83 percent to 95 percent. The prelaw program has also been "historically strong." Programs in business, geology, government, and English are also strong and have high enrollments.

Campus Environment

The school's location in the Pennsylvania Dutch country provides a safe and serene setting for the picturesque campus. While the Amish country is popular among tourists and visiting parents, the novelty of it quickly wears off for most students, who choose to stick close to the 52-acre main campus for social activity. About two-thirds of the student body lives on campus, and as a freshman and sophomore, you'll simply have no choice (unless you stay with nearby family). For upperclassmen, there is "lots of cheap off-campus housing" available. The quality of the living facilities varies. In recent years, several fraternity houses were condemned for violations by the city and declared unfit to live in.

You can bring your car to campus, and for a fee, park it safely (though students complain of the limited availability of spaces). "Many students have cars," although downtown Lancaster is "within walking distance" of campus, and there are local buses to get around. Some people make an occasional road trip to Philadelphia, just over an hour away.

While some of the college's facilities receive criticism, students praise the computer accessibility. There are ongoing renovations and construction, especially where the arts are concerned. The school unveiled a concert hall in 2000, and a modern mainstage theater and dance studio in 2004.

Student Life

The student body of fewer than 2,000 makes the campus seem like one big family . . . which can be both good and bad. You'll get to know your fellow classmates fairly quickly and easily, particularly if you participate in a Residential Seminar, but you won't find too much deviation from the "white, upper-middle-class" coed. As one student succinctly describes his fellow classmates: "People are very friendly, but not very diverse."

F&M students may work harder than students at most other schools, but they do manage to enjoy themselves. And outside the classroom, Greek life rules. Considered by the school to be independent social organizations, fraternities and sororities "dominate much of the social scene," a student notes; about 40 percent of the men and 30 percent of the women join in their junior or senior year. "It's because the school is so small and frats have alcohol," explains a junior. For those tired of the frat scene, there are just a handful of bars close by where 21-year-olds gather. Nondrinkers look to school-sponsored venues such Ben's Underground, a late-night café, or the Bessie Smith Society, which brings in live jazz performances, for weekend fun. Each year, F&M throws a "Senior Surprise" party in a mysterious location; other annual events include the Blizzard Bash, the college formal, and Spring Arts, a weekend of outdoor entertainment.

Between 25–30 percent of the student body plays intercollegiate sports; there are 12 men's and 12 women's varsity teams, as well as an assortment of club and intramural organizations. But students complain of the lack of support—on the part of the student body and the school itself—for athletics at F&M. Over 120 clubs and organizations, ranging from a TV and radio station to music, drama, and ethnic groups, provide students with "a lot of opportunity to get involved in extracurricular activities," but many students don't become involved, says one undergrad, for fear of detracting from their academics. Indeed, the school's PR office suggests keeping a scholarly focus: students are advised to "participate in extracurricular activities, but with academics as their first priority."

Other schools to check out: Dickinson, Gettysburg, Lafayette, Colgate, Muhlenberg.

Applied Early Decision: 274
Early Decision Admitted: 179

Test Scores (middle 50%):
SAT Verbal: 570–670
SAT Math: 580–680

THE EXPERTS SAY...

" Law school and med school acceptance rates are very impressive at Franklin and Marshall. "

" There's no grade inflation at F&M—and it's tough to get an A here in Amish country. "

HS Rank of Entering Freshmen:
Top 10%: 45%
Top 25%: 76%
Top 50%: 97%

Costs (2004–5)

Tuition and Fees: $30,440

Room & Board: $7,540

Payment Plan(s): installment plan

Inst. Aid (est. 2003–04)

Institutional Aid, Need-Based:
$11,641,467

Institutional Aid, Non-Need-Based:
$2,675,736

FT Undergrads Receiving Aid: 47%
Avg. Amount per Student: $20,915

FT Undergrads Receiving Non-Need-Based Scholarship or Grant Aid: 20%
Avg. Amount per Student: $13,067

Of Those Receiving Any Aid:

Rec. Need-Based Scholarship or Grant Aid: 90%
Average Award: $17,205

Rec. Need-Based Self-Help Aid: 91%
Average Award: $5,903

Upon Graduation, Avg. Loan Debt per Student: $18,370

Financial Aid Deadline: 3/1, 2/1 (priority)

Graduates

Going to Graduate School:
25% Within One Year

Alumni Giving: 36% (for fiscal 2003 only)

FURMAN UNIVERSITY

3300 Poinsett Highway, Greenville, SC 29613
Admissions Phone: (864) 294-2034 Fax: (864) 294-3127
Email: admissions@furman.edu Website: www.furman.edu
Application Website: www.engagefurman.edu

General Info

Type of School: private, coed

Setting: suburban

Academic Calendar: 3 months–2
  months–3 months

Student Body

Full-Time Undergrads: 2,693
  Men: 43%, Women: 57%

Part-Time Undergrads: 105
  Men: 42%, Women: 58%

Total Undergrad Population:
  African American: 6%
  Asian American: 2%
  Latino: 1%
  Native American: <1%
  Caucasian: 86%
  International: 1%
  Out-of-State: 69%
  Living Off-Campus: 5%
  In Fraternities: 30%
  In Sororities: 35%

Graduate and First-Professional
  Students: 506

Academics

Full-Time Faculty: 216
  With Ph.D.: 98%

Part-Time Faculty: 37
  With Ph.D.: 16%

Student/Faculty Ratio: 12:1

Most Popular Majors:
  political science (12%)
  business administration (11%)
  history (7%)
  health and exercise science (7%)
  biology (5%)

Freshmen Retention Rate: 90%

Graduation Rates:
  78% within four years
  84% within six years

Admissions

Regular Application Deadline: 1/15

Early Decision Deadline(s): 11/15

Fall Transfer Deadline: 6/1

Spring Transfer Deadline: 2/1

Total # of Students Applied: 3,773
  Admitted: 2,259
  Enrolled: 687

# of Students Waitlisted: 501
  Students Accepting Place: 168

Inside the Classroom

Furman University offers a solid liberal arts education with a special emphasis on "engaged learning"—in other words, students are encouraged to be active participants in the learning process, both in and out of the classroom. Most Furman undergrads, in all disciplines, participate in at least one experiential learning activity at some point in their college careers, whether it be studying abroad, working as an intern, or undertaking collaborative research with professors. Furman boasts one of the most active undergraduate summer research programs in the nation, including the acclaimed Advantage Research Fellowship Program. Hundreds of undergrads choose to study abroad in one of 16 programs in six continents.

Poly sci and business are among the most popular programs, and music majors rave about the education they're getting at Furman. Preprofessional students fare rather well here; on average, 40 percent of each class goes directly to graduate or professional school. Classes are challenging and instructors are tough but fair and always accessible. There's a great deal of faculty-student interaction, and the typical class enrolls just 20.

We hear the academic atmosphere is pretty intense, probably due in large part to the unusual school schedule. FU's academic calendar is set up on a 3-2-3 basis: students take three courses during the fall and spring terms, and two courses during the eight-week winter session.

Most of your freshman and sophomore year at Furman will be spent completing the core curriculum, which includes one course in the "Asian–African Program" as well as those in four broad subject areas: fine arts, humanities, math and natural science, and social science. Students must also attend three events per term as part of the mandatory Cultural Life Program (CLP). The events—concerts, lectures, plays, films, etc.—are approved by a committee made up of faculty, administrators, and students.

Campus Environment

Furman, nestled at the base of the Blue Ridge Mountains, is widely considered one of the loveliest and most beautifully landscaped campuses in the country, with a rose garden, a Japanese garden, fountains, and a huge lake filled with swans. (It also has an 18-hole golf course, which certainly adds to the country-club feel.) Most buildings, spread over 750 lush acres, have the "Old South" look, complete with bricks and columns and porches. Students can't say enough about how gorgeous their home away from home is—indeed, campus aesthetics is often the first thing both students and administrators will mention about Furman.

The housing policy was recently amended, and now all unmarried students who don't commute from their parents' homes must live on campus for all four years. Students are housed in eight single-sex halls and four coed dorms; they're all fairly traditional in style and setup. Most rooms are doubles. Juniors and seniors have the additional option of living in one of four lakeside cottages or in the popular North Village apartment complex.

All students may have cars, but most enjoy simply strolling around the bucolic grounds. As part of a new, environmentally friendly service, bright green bicycles have been placed around campus for students to ride between classes and then leave at a bike rack. There's also a shuttle service that runs every half-hour or so. Downtown Greenville is about five miles away. For the most part, students like Greenville, and Greenville likes them right back. It's a beautiful town, with tons of shops, restaurants, bars, and cultural venues. Farther off-campus, there are rivers for white-water rafting, mountains for hiking, and beaches for relaxing. Students also take day and weekend trips to the cities of Atlanta, Asheville, and Charlotte.

Student Life

Although the university has officially broken its 166-year affiliation with the South Carolina Baptist Convention, a distinct spiritual, religious atmosphere persists. The school "encourages" church affiliation and participation, and many students consider themselves religious. It's a friendly campus, full of Southern hospitality (the majority of Furman coeds hail from the South Atlantic region). Only about a tenth of the population is not white, and the majority of undergrads are from well-to-do families. And, while it's hardly a haven for liberals, many argue that labeling Furman as an "ultraconservative" university is unfounded.

Although the campus is officially dry, students still manage to party off-campus on weekends, with the Greeks often playing host. More than one-third of the student body belongs to one of seven sororities and eight fraternities. Beyond those groups, there are over a hundred clubs and organizations to join. Community service is big—the CESC (Collegiate Educational Service Corps) is touted as one of the top volunteer programs in the country, with thousands of students assisting the Greenville community in some capacity. The Student Activities Board is charged with planning all sorts of entertainment on campus, such as concerts, movies, Homecoming activities, and trips. Annual events keep the campus buzzing. Students handcraft boats and race them in the Boat Float; escape to the South Carolina coast during Beach Weekend; set up their roommates with their dream dates for the My Tie dance; and turn the campus into a carnival for May Day Play Day. Plus, we hear that each student gets tossed into the lake on his birthday.

With all the athletic facilities available, it's no surprise that sports are popular here. Over two-thirds of the student body participates in some form of athletics. Furman, which offers 17 varsity sports, is one of the smallest Division I schools in the nation. About 20 percent of Furman students play on the intercollegiate level. The men's soccer team dominates the Southern Conference, and the women's golf program has produced six current LPGA players. The overall women's athletic program has been named the best in the conference five years in a row. Frats, sororities, residence hall groups, and other student groups compete in spirited, competitive IM sports.

Waitlisted Students Admitted: 10

Applied Early Decision: 666
Early Decision Admitted: 389

Test Scores (middle 50%):
SAT Verbal: 600–690
SAT Math: 590–680
ACT Comp: 26–30
ACT English: 26–31
ACT Math: 25–29

THE EXPERTS SAY...

" 'Engaged learning,' internships, study abroad, and one of the largest undergrad research programs in the country are the Furman difference. "

" If Furman's too religious or conservative for you, try Wake Forest, Vanderbilt, or the University of Richmond. "

HS Rank of Entering Freshmen:
Top 10%: 68%
Top 25%: 92%
Top 50%: 99%
Avg. HS GPA: 3.8

Costs (est. 2004–05)

Tuition and Fees: $24,408
Room & Board: $6,272
Payment Plan(s): installment plan

Inst. Aid (est. 2003–04)

Institutional Aid, Need-Based:
$10,541,792

Institutional Aid, Non-Need-Based:
$6,736,881

FT Undergrads Receiving Aid: 43%
Avg. Amount per Student: $19,647

FT Undergrads Receiving Non-Need-Based Scholarship or Grant Aid: 24%
Avg. Amount per Student: $10,875

Of Those Receiving Any Aid:

Rec. Need-Based Scholarship or
Grant Aid: 100%
Average Award: $16,061

Rec. Need-Based Self-Help Aid: 63%
Average Award: $3,586

Upon Graduation, Avg. Loan Debt
per Student: $19,170

Financial Aid Deadline: 1/15

Graduates

Going to Graduate School:
32% Within One Year

Companies Recruiting On Campus: 39

Alumni Giving: 50%

GALLAUDET UNIVERSITY

800 Florida Avenue NE, Washington, DC 20002
Admissions Phone: (202) 651-5750; (800) 995-0550 Fax: (202) 651-5744
Email: admissions@gallaudet.edu Website: www.gallaudet.edu
Application Website: www.gallaudet.edu/applicationforms.htm

General Info

Type of School: private, coed

Setting: urban

Academic Calendar: semester

Student Body

Full-Time Undergrads: 1,120
  Men: 46%, Women: 54%

Part-Time Undergrads: 73
  Men: 49%, Women: 51%

Total Undergrad Population:
  African American: 11%
  Asian American: 5%
  Latino: 7%
  Native American: 2%
  Caucasian: 61%
  International: 11%
  Out-of-State: 99%
  Living Off-Campus: 42%
  In Fraternities: 9%
  In Sororities: 10%

Graduate and First-Professional
  Students: 405

Academics

Full-Time Faculty: 218
  With Ph.D.: 79%

Student/Faculty Ratio: 7:1

Most Popular Majors:
  communication arts (9%)
  art (9%)
  psychology (7%)
  social work (7%)
  education (6%)

Freshmen Retention Rate: 60%

Graduation Rates:
  7% within four years
  20% within six years

Admissions

Regular Application Deadline: 8/15,
  5/1 (priority)

Fall Transfer Deadline: 6/15
  (priority)

Total # of Students Applied: 603
  Admitted: 426
  Enrolled: 238

Inside the Classroom

"Gallaudet is the world's only university that brings together deaf, hard of hearing, and hearing students as well as faculty in the common pursuit of education." That's how Gallaudet University officials describe their university, which is designed exclusively for deaf and hard of hearing students and offers a visually accessible environment. The Gallaudet community lives by the tenets set forth in its "Commitment to Sign Communication." This states that everyone has the right and responsibility to understand and be understood; that the sign language style of every individual is to be respected and practiced; and that all members of the Gallaudet community should make a sincere and assertive effort to become proficient in attaining sign language proficiency. Clear, understandable signing is considered everyone's responsibility at Gallaudet, and the school ensures an inclusive, "bilingual" community where both English and American Sign Language thrive and visual communication is the norm.

Gallaudet consists of the College of Liberal Arts, Sciences, and Technologies, and the Graduate School and Professional Programs. There are more than 30 majors offered at the undergraduate level, but students are also free to create their own majors through the Self-Directed Major program. Graduation requirements for a B.A. or B.S. include satisfactorily completing the General Studies Curriculum and major requirements, 80 hours of approved community service, a cumulative GPA of 2.0, and residency for at least the senior year. Gallaudet offers an intimate academic environment and personal attention. With a total student body of less than 2,000 students, the average class size holds 11 students, and the student/faculty ratio is an intimate 7:1.

The goals of the undergraduate curriculum include improving one's communication and literacy skills, improving critical thinking skills, exploring the human experience, and realizing self-awareness and social responsibility. Students say that although the workload can be heavy, the coursework is not very challenging. "Most of the classes bear an eerie resemblance to those taken in high school," notes one student. Some students worry that the educational standards may be lower at Gallaudet than at other colleges, and that the school might not expect enough from its students in deference to their deafness.

Opportunities are available for student research projects, student co-op work experience and internships, study abroad, and collaboration with faculty and students at other institutions. Through the Consortium of Universities of the Washington Metropolitan Area, students can supplement their Gallaudet education by taking courses (roughly 7,000 are offered) at 11 other institutions of higher learning.

Campus Environment

Gallaudet offers coed dorms, freshman dorms (Cogswell and Krug), and housing for disabled students. The university has constructed three buildings and renovated 13 others since 1992, and has spent millions on maintaining its facilities. The university offers shuttle buses that transport students to and from classes, to and from extracurricular activities, and to and from Union Station. Though all students are permitted to have cars on campus, the Metro is always a popular option for DC students to make their way around town, especially considering the always congested parking situation. The school also offers a vehicle lease program and a messenger service for the DC metropolitan area.

Gallaudet University Press is the world's largest publisher of books relating to deafness, and the University is one of the DC area's largest businesses, with salaries, wages, and benefits totaling more than $80 million annually. The DC location of the school is a major plus. There, students can take advantage of all the restaurants, malls, bars, clubs, museums, and other cultural attractions, not to mention the great nearby neighborhoods.

Student Life

Students at Gallaudet make up a diverse population. They come from all 50 states and there's a very large international contingent. Most students hail from out-of-state, a large percentage from the Northeast. But Gallaudet students tend to be "cliquish" ("Can you spell junior high?" quips one student), which can, to some extent, hinder the overall feel of diversity on campus. Students say that the Gallaudet campus isn't always the most exciting place to be on weekends (actually, "like death," is how several describe it), and so many head off-campus for a good time.

Gallaudet offers a number of student clubs and organizations, including ethnic clubs, publications, student government, academic and preprofessional groups, a wilderness club, social awareness clubs, religious groups, and Greek organizations. The university also welcomes guest speakers and holds lectures, in addition to throwing parties and alumni celebrations.

Gallaudet's 14 varsity teams compete at the Division III level. These sports include football, baseball, soccer, volleyball, cross-country, swimming, basketball, wrestling, softball, track and field, and tennis. No scholarships are offered. Intramural sports are quite popular here as well, and these feature the familiar favorites, such as flag football, basketball, softball, floor hockey, and indoor soccer. Students play intramural sports for fun and to keep in shape.

Students enjoy performances by the arts groups on campus as well. These include the Gallaudet Dance Company, which is a performance group of approximately 15 student dancers. The dancers rely on their vision as their primary mode of communication, and express themselves through their dancing, which ranges in style—one of these styles of dance is founded upon American Sign Language. There's also a Theatre Arts Department that puts on a number of performances, and exhibitions through the art department.

Costs (2003–04)

Tuition and Fees: $9,660

Room & Board: $8,030

Payment Plan(s): installment plan

THE EXPERTS SAY...

" *Gallaudet offers a broad range of opportunities for deaf and hard of hearing students in a supportive, family-like environment.* "

" *If you're extremely independent, Gallaudet's coddling may rub you the wrong way.* "

Inst. Aid (est. 2003–04)

Institutional Aid, Need-Based: $2,249,087

Institutional Aid, Non-Need-Based: $85,000

FT Undergrads Receiving Aid: 73% Avg. Amount per Student: $14,057

FT Undergrads Receiving Non-Need-Based Scholarship or Grant Aid: 4% Avg. Amount per Student: $10,996

Of Those Receiving Any Aid:

Rec. Need-Based Scholarship or Grant Aid: 98% Average Award: $12,342

Rec. Need-Based Self-Help Aid: 53% Average Award: $3,118

Upon Graduation, Avg. Loan Debt per Student: $10,273

Financial Aid Deadline: rolling, 7/1 (priority)

Graduates

Going to Graduate School: 47% Within One Year

Accepting Job Offer: 40% at time of graduation

Companies Recruiting On Campus: 39

Alumni Giving: 19%

GEORGE MASON UNIVERSITY

4400 University Drive, MSN 3A4, Fairfax, VA 22030-4444
Admissions Phone: (703) 993-2400 Fax: (703) 993-2392
Email: admissions@gmu.edu Website: www.gmu.edu
Application Website: admissions@gmu.edu/onapps.html

Note: Info. not verified by school

General Info

Type of School: public, coed

Academic Calendar: semester

Student Body

Full-Time Undergrads: 11,301
  Men: 43%, Women: 57%

Part-Time Undergrads: 4,011
  Men: 45%, Women: 55%

Total Undergrad Population:
  African American: 10%
  Asian American: 16%
  Latino: 8%
  Native American: <1%
  Caucasian: 62%
  International: 5%
  Out-of-State: 5%
  Living Off-Campus: 81%
  In Fraternities: 3%
  In Sororities: 3%

Graduate and First-Professional
  Students: 9,095

Academics

Full-Time Faculty: 847
  With Ph.D.: 84%

Part-Time Faculty: 665
  With Ph.D.: 14%

Student/Faculty Ratio: 16:1

Freshmen Retention Rate: 79%

Graduation Rates:
  26% within four years
  47% within six years

Admissions

Regular Application Deadline: 2/1

Fall Transfer Deadline: 3/15

Spring Transfer Deadline: 11/1

Total # of Students Applied: 8,106
  Admitted: 5,519
  Enrolled: 2,146

# of Students Waitlisted: 701
  Students Accepting Place: 377
  Waitlisted Students Admitted: 134

Test Scores (middle 50%):
  SAT Verbal: 480–580
  SAT Math: 490–590
  ACT Comp: 19–23
  ACT English: 18–24
  ACT Math: 18–23

Avg. HS GPA: 3.2

Inside the Classroom

George Mason University, named after the Virginia statesman who was instrumental in adding the Bill of Rights to the U.S. Constitution, is a diverse metropolitan teaching and research university serving the region of the nation's capital. The university offers over 50 undergraduate degree programs in its divisions: the College of Arts and Sciences, the School of Management, the School of Information Technology and Engineering (the first engineering school in the United States to focus on information technology rather than the traditional engineering sciences), the College of Nursing and Health Sciences, School for Computational Sciences, and the College of Visual and Performing Arts.

Freshmen may compete for the university's new Honors Program, featuring an interdisciplinary curriculum. There is also a collaborative, interdisciplinary, and self-reflective program where small groups of faculty and students concentrate on intellectual problems, stressing an integrative learning experience. The most popular majors are economics, public policy, nursing, and information technology.

All undergraduates are required to take a general education core curriculum, completing 30 credits worth of coursework from the arts and sciences. There are no teaching assistants here; faculty members teach all classes. Instructors are reasonably accessible. "They care about their students and go out of their way to ensure that their students are thriving in and out of the classroom," raves a student about her teachers.

Campus Environment

The main campus sits on 677 acres of wooded land in Fairfax, Virginia, offering the best of both urban and rural worlds. About an hour to the west lie the majestic Blue Ridge Mountains, perfect for hiking, camping, and skiing. A 30-minute subway ride to the east takes you to the historic Mall area of downtown Washington, DC, and its throngs of museums, monuments, theaters, art galleries, and fine restaurants. There are also two smaller satellite campuses in Arlington (five acres) and Manassas (124 acres), each about 30 minutes away.

The greater DC metropolitan area and Fairfax County's Fortune 500 companies combine to give GMU students hundreds of internship and cooperative education opportunities in all areas of study. As the University is just a 45-minute drive from other DC area colleges such as Georgetown and Howard, GMU students can easily interact with students at these institutions and may even take courses there through a consortium of area schools.

George Mason University guarantees housing for freshman and requires them to live in a cluster of traditional-style residence halls known as Presidents Park. Most students living on campus reside in townhouse-style housing built during the last ten years. Two new residence halls, which would accommodate a total of 1,000 students, are expected to be completed by 2005. But GMU is basically a commuter campus. The Student Government holds a lot of activities throughout the year to help maintain a sense of community.

At the center of the Fairfax campus, the George W. Johnson Center combines students' academic and nonacademic lives. The facility has four floors with eight acres of space and serves as the university's social center while also providing academic resources and quiet space for study. The Johnson Center holds a state-of-the-art library, academic offices, technology resources, a bookstore, student union, and dining services all under one roof. Campus recreation and sports complexes include the 10,000-seat Patriot Center Arena, a 64,000-square-foot recreation center, and the 3,000-seat Physical Education Building.

One thing that George Mason University students don't like is the parking situation. "Finding a parking space is always a challenge," says a student. "Just think of it this way: There are 12,000 students and faculty on campus at one time but only 11,900 parking spaces. And 900 of those are in obscure places that are impossible to find." But the school is planning on building another parking garage.

Student Life

The Johnson Center is the focal point for many of the university's 200 clubs and organizations, which range from academic and professional organizations to international organizations to a very active Student Government Association. Nearly 60 percent of GMU students participate in campus and community service programs, while about six percent are involved in Greek organizations. The school does not permit its six sororities and eight fraternities to maintain university-affiliated houses. Because of this, fraternity parties are usually held way off-campus.

George Mason University is a member of the NCAA Division I. Men's teams include soccer, basketball, baseball, track and field, golf, tennis, cross-country, volleyball, and wrestling. Women's teams include soccer, basketball, track and field, tennis, lacrosse, cross-country, volleyball, and softball. GMU participates in the Colonial Athletic Association. Club sports include men's rugby, women's rugby, men's and women's crew, football, and men's lacrosse. Nearly 70 percent of GMU students participate in a variety of intramural sports. The Patriot Center is where the GMU basketball games, concerts, sporting events, and fairs are held throughout the year.

Diversity is celebrated at GMU. One of the favorite traditions is International Week, when students from around the world have a chance to share their country's culture and traditions with the campus community.

Costs (2003–04)

Tuition and Fees, In-State: $5,122

Tuition and Fees, Out-of-State: $14,952

Room & Board: $5,881

Payment Plan(s): installment plan

THE EXPERTS SAY...

" Location, location, location: There are hundreds of DC-area internships for George Mason students, and the school is right in the middle of all of Fairfax's Fortune 500 companies. You can even take courses at Georgetown and Howard. "

" George Mason is the new kid on the block as far as area schools go. For depth, check out James Madison or Virginia Tech. "

GEORGE WASHINGTON UNIVERSITY

2121 I Street, NW, Suite 201, Washington, DC 20052
Admissions Phone: (202) 994-6040; (800) 447-3765 Fax: (202) 994-0325
Email: gwadm@gwu.edu Website: www.gwu.edu
Application Website: gwired.gwu.edu/adm/apply/index.html

General Info

Type of School: private, coed
Setting: urban
Academic Calendar: semester

Student Body

Full-Time Undergrads: 9,280
    Men: 42%, Women: 58%

Part-Time Undergrads: 1,156
    Men: 50%, Women: 50%

Total Undergrad Population:
    African American: 6%
    Asian American: 9%
    Latino: 4%
    Native American: <1%
    Caucasian: 63%
    International: 5%
    Out-of-State: 98%
    Living Off-Campus: 32%
    In Fraternities: 16%
    In Sororities: 13%

Graduate and First-Professional
Students: 12,981

Academics

Full-Time Faculty: 807
    With Ph.D.: 92%

Part-Time Faculty: 1,115
    With Ph.D.: 38%

Student/Faculty Ratio: 14:1

Most Popular Majors:
    international affairs
    business administration
    psychology
    political science
    computer science

Freshmen Retention Rate: 93%

Graduation Rates:
    69% within four years
    75% within six years

Admissions

Regular Application Deadline: 1/15;
    12/1 (priority)

Early Decision Deadline(s): 12/1, .
    1/15

Total # of Students Applied: 18,442
    Admitted: 7,103
    Enrolled: 2,266

# of Students Waitlisted: 1,601
    Students Accepting Place: 770
    Waitlisted Students Admitted: 178

Inside the Classroom

George Washington University offers a total of 85 majors in its six undergraduate schools: Columbian College of Arts and Sciences, Elliott School of International Affairs, School of Business and Public Management, School of Engineering and Applied Science, School of Medicine and Health Sciences, and School of Public Health and Health Services. A school official brags, "GW offers the breadth of courses, programs, and academic options that are more often seen at institutions twice our size." Many GW students are on a preprofessional track, heading for careers in medicine, law, business and, of course, politics. The school's politically oriented departments and programs—such as political communication and international affairs—are among its greatest assets, particularly because of the prestige and experience of the faculty. The professors are not only teachers of politics, they're political practitioners; your advisor may also be advising some of the most powerful people in government.

Along with its highly regarded academic offerings, GW's location in the heart of the nation's capital makes for a unique educational experience. "It's an exciting place to be, even if you're not interested in politics," comments one student. Opportunities for internships and career-related experience are abundant in DC, and students make the most of it. A senior tells us, "The availability of quality internships is unsurpassable." A recent grad raves, "I completed internships on the Hill, the Department of State, Department of Education, and studied abroad. I wouldn't change a thing."

If you're looking for a laid-back academic environment, GW isn't it. One grad explains, "GW is competitive: Students here generally think they are going to be the next Senator from their state." When asked what type of student wouldn't fit in, a senior responds, "Someone who is lazy and apathetic. Those who achieve at GW are students who take the initiative."

Campus Environment

"The location is very attractive to kids," says a New York guidance counselor of George Washington University. Students describe their campus as being very safe, with "tons of security." However, in light of 9/11 and the ongoing fear of terrorism, "safety" in DC has taken on a new meaning: "As the Federal government works closely with GW in making it a safe place to live and learn, students are always conscious of what it means to go to class four blocks from the White House," comments a senior.

Freshmen and sophomores must live on campus, which is fine with them since the dorms are so spacious and clean and offer perks such as maid service. Most rooms include private bathrooms, and upperclassmen get apartment-style housing complete with kitchens. The only problem with on-campus housing is that there simply isn't enough of it. A senior says, "GW always has housing problems, constantly admitting more people than it can house." In 2001, GW leased a luxury hotel to accommodate an unexpectedly large number of students who requested housing.

Many upperclassmen opt for off-campus housing. Unfortunately, apartments in the DC area are expensive, especially in the Foggy Bottom neighborhood of the school. "Off-campus housing is limited, unless you're looking to move into Virginia," notes a junior. Most students use the Metro to get around. "There is virtually no parking on campus and if you do get a spot, you'd better be ready to pay for it," a student warned us.

GW's campus is the permanent home for CNN's popular political debate program, *Crossfire*. The program is broadcast live each weeknight from the Media and Public Affairs Building's Jack Morton Auditorium. Tickets are free and are available to the public. "Many students attend each night, and incoming freshmen have said it is one reason why they were interested in attending GW," a college official tells us.

Student Life

The population of GW is ethnically and culturally diverse, with a real international flavor; students come from all over the United States and about 100 foreign countries. A recent grad states, "Almost everyone has managed to find a place at GW. We have the quiet loners and we have the hippie activists." Students do complain about the fact that the women outnumber the men and that the campus tends to be "cliquey." "The typical student at GW is very well-off, moderate in politics and expensively dressed," says one student. "People get more dressed up here to go to class than people in my hometown get dressed for weddings."

"Students soak up every aspect of Washington, DC—nightclubs, museums, sports events, parties, festivals, national events, etc.," says a senior majoring in finance. GW students regularly hang out at bars like the Madhatter or the Lion, or go to the nearby Georgetown and Adams Morgan neighborhoods, which offer a plethora of bars, restaurants, and chic lounges. A junior warns, "Don't be so quick to use your fake ID, especially on a Thursday, Friday, or Saturday night." Another student elaborates: "Bars and clubs are 21-and-up, and they scan IDs looking for fakes in most places now, and MPD has arrested a lot of students for underage drinking." (And, by the way, GW's administration is known for coming down equally hard on on-campus partying.)

GW students actively participate in a wide variety of campus clubs and organizations. Political clubs such as the College Democrats and College Republicans are popular, obviously. And students tell us that the Student Association (student government) is extremely important (and "hated" by many) since they "organize a lot of what goes on at GW." Except for basketball, intercollegiate sports aren't big, but intramurals are popular with students.

Greek life hasn't been a major force on campus, but this might change: In fall 2003, the university opened eight brand-new townhouses ("Townhouse Row"), giving five sororities and three fraternities a place to call home. This project is part of an unusual effort by school officials to encourage more undergrads (!) to go Greek. (A possible reason: "Students simply don't feel connected... Many feel no sense of community, and therefore don't give money back to the university," explains a senior.) The president reportedly would like the school's fraternities and sororities to comprise as much as 25 percent of the student body, up from the current 13 percent. But with the thriving DC nightlife and the high-powered internships available to them, many GW students say they don't need to go Greek to spice up their busy social lives or to make professional connections.

Other schools to check out: Boston University, Boston College, NYU, American U, Georgetown.

Applied Early Decision: 1,749
Early Decision Admitted: 875

Test Scores (middle 50%):
SAT Verbal: 590–690
SAT Math: 590–680

HS Rank of Entering Freshmen:
Top 10%: 65%
Top 25%: 92%
Top 50%: 100%

THE EXPERTS SAY...

" Students at GW are ambitious and benefit from impressive internships and professional opportunities, as well as from faculty members who are practitioners and leaders in their fields. "

" If you enjoy watching 'Girls Gone Wild' instead of 'Crossfire,' you should probably look elsewhere. "

Costs (2004–5)

Tuition and Fees: $34,030
Room & Board: $10,210

Inst. Aid (2002–03)

Institutional Aid, Need-Based:
$55,427,584

Institutional Aid, Non-Need-Based:
$18,215,113

FT Undergrads Receiving Aid: 38%
Avg. Amount per Student: $27,413

FT Undergrads Receiving Non-Need-Based Scholarship or Grant Aid: 22%
Avg. Amount per Student: $11,318

Of Those Receiving Any Aid:

Rec. Need-Based Scholarship or Grant Aid: 97%
Average Award: $15,891

Rec. Need-Based Self-Help Aid: 91%
Average Award: $7,858

Upon Graduation, Avg. Loan Debt per Student: $25,943

Financial Aid Deadline: 2/1 (priority)

GEORGETOWN UNIVERSITY

37th and O Streets, NW, Washington, DC 20057
Admissions Phone: (202) 687-3600 Fax: (202) 687-5084
Website: www.georgetown.edu
Application Website: georgetown.edu/undergrad/admissions

General Info

Type of School: private, coed,
   Roman Catholic—Jesuit

Setting: urban

Academic Calendar: semester

Student Body

Full-Time Undergrads: 6,125
   Men: 47%, Women: 53%

Part-Time Undergrads: 143
   Men: 32%, Women: 68%

Total Undergrad Population:
   African American: 7%
   Asian American: 10%
   Latino: 5%
   Native American: <1%
   Caucasian: 70%
   International: 5%
   Out-of-State: 97%
   Living Off-Campus: 20%

Graduate and First-Professional
   Students: 6,614

Academics

Full-Time Faculty: 694
   With Ph.D.: 92%

Part-Time Faculty: 342
   With Ph.D.: 58%

Student/Faculty Ratio: 11:1

Most Popular Majors:
   international politics (7%)
   biology (6%)
   English (6%)
   nursing (5%)
   government (5%)

Completing 2 or More Majors: 26%

Freshmen Retention Rate: 95%

Graduation Rates:
   90% within four years
   93% within six years

Admissions

Regular Application Deadline: 1/10

Early Action Deadline: 11/1

Fall Transfer Deadline: 3/1

Total # of Students Applied: 15,420
   Admitted: 3,505
   Enrolled: 1,528

# of Students Waitlisted: 2,039
   Students Accepting Place: 1,216
   Waitlisted Students Admitted: 138

Inside the Classroom

Georgetown University truly is "in the center of the Mecca of politics," as one high school guidance counselor notes. Prominent alumni include Bill Clinton, 42nd President of the United States; Antonia Novello, former U.S. Surgeon General; Antonin Scalia, Supreme Court Justice; Maria Shriver, NBC-TV News commentator; and Mark Gearan, former Director, Peace Corps.

Georgetown's four undergraduate schools—Georgetown College (liberal arts and sciences), Robert E. McDonough School of Business, Edmund A. Walsh School of Foreign Service, and the School of Nursing and Allied Health Studies—offer excellent academics across the board, though many of the most highly rated programs have an international emphasis. The world-famous School of Foreign Service is particularly competitive; combining study of history, politics, economics, and foreign language, the school prepares diplomatic hopefuls for overseas careers. Georgetown College is also highly competitive with many outstanding departments, including psychology, English, history and premed. The Faculty of Languages and Linguistics (FLL), a separate division of Georgetown College, is also well regarded. Even the business school has an international focus and includes programs in global economics.

Students must apply to a specific undergraduate school, which means there's not much opportunity to explore various subjects before choosing a major. Transferring between schools is possible after the first year, but is generally discouraged. A college official tells us that students in all four undergraduate schools "are required to take two semesters each of English, philosophy and theology. Other core requirements are set for students by each undergraduate school."

The Capitol offers innumerable study and internship opportunities, enabling students to experience government and politics in action. A college official tells us that the MBNA Career Education Center offers students a range of services to help them take full advantage of the school's DC location: "Students have significant opportunities to intern in a variety of business, government and nonprofit organizations." Research opportunities also abound. "The Georgetown Undergraduate Research Opportunities Program (GUROP) offers interested students the opportunity to learn the discipline and experience the rewards of scholarly research by working with faculty on their research projects... Students receive a monetary research award for their work, and the transcript notation 'Georgetown Undergraduate Research Assistant.'"

Georgetown's esteemed faculty includes politicians, political advisors, journalists, and ambassadors. The average class size is under 40 students, and about 30 percent of the student body takes advantage of Georgetown's far-reaching study abroad program in over 20 countries around the world.

Campus Environment

On-campus housing is guaranteed for the first two years; upperclassmen may live on campus as space permits. A college official tells us, "First-year students live together in several residence halls on campus. Halls are coeducational, contain Internet connections, are secured around the clock and have resident assistants living on the corridor. Most halls contain kitchens in floor lounges." Apartment complexes are available for upperclassmen, some of which are quite large and feature full kitchens with one or two full bathrooms. The university is currently in the process of constructing a new facility called the Southwest Quadrangle, which is set to open in 2003. A college official says, "The new facility will include a residence hall to house an additional 780 students, a 1,200-person dining hall, multipurpose space for academic and cocurricular activities, an underground parking facility and a new home for Georgetown's Jesuit community."

Students who live in university housing may not park a car on campus, but there are certainly other ways of getting around town. A fleet of shuttle buses provides students with regular service to and from Metrorail and other locations in Washington, DC and Northern Virginia.

Student Life

Georgetown was founded in 1789 and is the oldest Roman Catholic academic institution in the United States. It continues to be affiliated with the Jesuit tradition of the Church, embracing a holistic educational philosophy. A little more than half the student body is Catholic, but there's enough diversity both on campus and in the surrounding city to make students of all backgrounds feel comfortable. The school welcomes students from all 50 states and more than 100 countries.

Ever since a young basketball hotshot named Patrick Ewing began to show off his moves for the Georgetown Hoyas, the Division I athletics at Georgetown have been a beloved schoolwide obsession. While several of Georgetown's Big East varsity teams are high ranked, the basketball and football teams are fanatically followed: Games usually turn into social events with rowdy pre- and post-game parties. There are over 15 intramural sports as well.

There is no Greek system at Georgetown, so students hang out and socialize in dorm rooms, off-campus apartments, or local bars. There's also the occasional large block party, and semiformal or formal events, including the super-posh annual Diplomatic Ball. And, of course, there's always something going on in the exciting global village of Washington, DC. The Georgetown neighborhood itself is historic and charming, and features countless shops, restaurants, bars, and clubs. Its lively nightlife makes for a true college town.

Even if it didn't enjoy such a wonderful location, there would be no shortage of things to do on campus. In fact, a number of students report that the variety of activities is the school's best asset. There's a club for just about every culture, activity, and professional and political interest, from an Intercultural Relations Club to the many student service groups organized by the Volunteer and Public Service Center. A college official lists the Student Association, the student news organizations (publications and TV station), the Lecture Fund (arranges forums on political and cultural issues), Program Board, and volunteer/public service groups as the five most popular organizations on campus. The modern Leavey Center is a huge student union and conference facility that is used as a home base by over 100 clubs.

Other schools to check out: University of Pennsylvania, Duke, Stanford, Boston College, Notre Dame.

Test Scores (middle 50%):
SAT Verbal: 640–730
SAT Math: 650–730
ACT Comp: 28–32
ACT English: 28–33
ACT Math: 27–32

HS Rank of Entering Freshmen:
Top 10%: 83%
Top 25%: 96%
Top 50%: 100%

Avg. HS GPA: 3.87

THE EXPERTS SAY...

" If politics and international affairs are your passion, Georgetown is your place. The faculty are what they teach—political movers and shakers. "

" Talk about hard workers! 89% of students graduate in four years, and nearly a quarter of the students pursue a double major. "

Costs (2004–5)

Tuition and Fees: $30,163

Room & Board: $10,554

Payment Plan(s): installment plan, deferred payment plan

Inst. Aid (est. 2003–04)

FT Undergrads Receiving Aid: 41%
Avg. Amount per Student: $22,344

FT Undergrads Receiving Non-Need-Based Scholarship or Grant Aid: 0%
Avg. Amount per Student: $3,500

Of Those Receiving Any Aid:

Rec. Need-Based Scholarship or Grant Aid: 86%
Average Award: $15,663

Rec. Need-Based Self-Help Aid: 88%
Average Award: $5,906

Upon Graduation, Avg. Loan Debt per Student: $21,500

Financial Aid Deadline: 2/1 (priority)

Graduates

Going to Graduate School:
26% Within One Year

Accepting Job Offer:
64% at time of graduation

Companies Recruiting On Campus:
985

Alumni Giving: 50%

GEORGIA INSTITUTE OF TECHNOLOGY

225 North Avenue, Atlanta, GA 30332-0320
Admissions Phone: (404) 894-4154 Fax: (404) 894-9511
Email: admissions@gatech.edu Website: www.gatech.edu Application Website: apply.gatech.edu

General Info

Type of School: public, coed

Setting: urban

Academic Calendar: semester

Student Body

Full-Time Undergrads: 10,345
  Men: 72%, Women: 28%

Part-Time Undergrads: 763
  Men: 73%, Women: 27%

Total Undergrad Population:
  African American: 7%
  Asian American: 15%
  Latino: 3%
  Native American: <1%
  Caucasian: 70%
  International: 5%
  Out-of-State: 35%
  Living Off-Campus: 50%
  In Fraternities: 22%
  In Sororities: 24%

Graduate and First-Professional
  Students: 5,386

Academics

Full-Time Faculty: 807
  With Ph.D.: 95%

Part-Time Faculty: 11
  With Ph.D.: 82%

Student/Faculty Ratio: 13:1

Most Popular Majors:
  computer science (11%)
  mechanical engineering (11%)
  business management (10%)
  industrial engineering (9%)
  electrical engineering (8%)

Freshmen Retention Rate: 90%

Graduation Rates:
  24% within four years
  69% within six years

Computers: Computer Required

Admissions

Regular Application Deadline: 1/15

Fall Transfer Deadline: 2/1 (priority)

Spring Transfer Deadline: 10/1
  (priority)

Total # of Students Applied: 8,573
  Admitted: 5,386
  Enrolled: 2,235

Inside the Classroom

A senior civil engineering/premed student sums up the reason for attending Georgia Tech: "It's a great buy, and by choosing Georgia Tech you are choosing both to have fun and to have a future." The undergraduate colleges within the institute include the College of Architecture, College of Engineering, College of Computing, Ivan Allen College of Liberal Arts (Tech's "fabulous, best-kept secret," according to one guidance counselor), College of Sciences, and College of Management. Georgia Tech is primarily known for its acclaimed programs in engineering, architecture, and computer science.

No doubt about it: Academics at Georgia Tech are hard. "We bust our butts," a senior economics major confirms. "We work for long periods of time devoting full concentration on our schoolwork. The bad news is this does take time away from other pursuits. The good news is you learn how to work hard early on and mature tremendously in that respect—which is great both personally and for professional marketability." Students are competitive, "but not cutthroat." "Once you get accustomed to people asking what you got on a test—just to see if they did better than you or not—the sense of competition can go away," offers one student. But teamwork is also big at Tech: "Tech students rely upon the help of fellow classmates to tackle the often daunting challenges given to them," says the econ major. And what type of student has no chance of thriving here? "Someone who is afraid of hard work. Seriously, don't even bother applying."

Georgia Tech's location in Atlanta makes it accessible to a number of internships in various fields. More than one-third of the undergraduate student body participate in Tech's co-op program, "the largest optional co-op program in the country," according to the institute. This does add at least one extra year of school time, but you graduate with impressive experience on your resume that can make it easier to get a job—a pressing concern for these practical-minded Techies. "Almost everyone is here for the same reason: to get a productive job and graduate," observes one student. Another student agrees: "Tech doesn't have one typical student, except for the fact that every student is goal-oriented."

While Georgia Tech's faculty consists of many brilliant, highly experienced researchers, the teaching quality varies. A few students complain that a fair number of professors and TA's are not native English speakers and are difficult to understand. But a senior civil engineering/premed student counters, "You have the opportunity to sit down with faculty that you might have heard on NPR or seen on the Discovery Channel. They are every bit as impressive in person." Accessibility can be a problem in some of the larger core courses, but "the professors of classes within your major always make the time if you need it," insists a management student.

Campus Environment

Aside from a few complaints about the ongoing construction, students seem to enjoy Georgia Tech's campus. Despite the school's location in downtown Atlanta, "there are trees and squirrels and lots of red brick," notes one student. "Students actually want to live on campus." Dorms and campus apartments were greatly improved to house

Olympic athletes in 1996, and students are reaping the benefits; an aquatic center, coliseum, sports complex, and seven new residence halls were built. Of the 32 residence halls on campus, 12 are reserved for the Freshman Experience, an option involving partnerships with faculty members, tutorials, separate meal plans, peer leaders, a one-hour credit course to help with the transition to college, and a freshman activities board. Also, unlike most other schools, Georgia Tech allows freshmen to live in Greek housing.

The campus is designed so that walking from residence halls to an academic building will never take more than 15 minutes. Freshmen cannot have a car on campus for the first semester, and students complain that parking is scarce (a common problem for urban campuses). However, the university offers an on-campus shuttle bus service (the "Stinger"), and Atlanta's public transportation system is another option.

Student Life

A senior management major tries to debunk a popular stereotype: "Tech students are *not* nerds, and we *do* like to go out and have a good time on the weekends." Adds a senior chemical engineering student, "There is a dominant 'work hard, play hard' mentality at Georgia Tech, and many students use the week to earn their weekend of fun." Greek life is certainly very popular at Tech. "The Greek life at Tech provides much of the social life here with band parties and such. However, the institute has recently begun a program called Ramblin' Nights… These are alcohol-free events for students that attract large-scale performers to campus to provide a social outlet for the general student," says a senior computer science major. And students often head into Atlanta to see a play or movie or to cruise the local bar scene (but you've really got to be 21 to get in, students warn).

The athletic program also enlivens the social scene: "On the weekends during football season, almost everyone is focused on tailgating and preparing for the game," comments a senior. Georgia Tech's football and basketball teams compete in the NCAA Division I's tough Atlantic Coast Conference, and both draw large crowds of student fans to games. A large athletic complex also serves as a center for a thriving intramural program.

"The campus atmosphere is very diverse. It's not uncommon to hear several different languages on the way to class," notes a sixth-year electrical engineering student. But because Georgia Tech is an urban campus, and because students are so devoted to their studies, there isn't always an obvious sense of campus community. "It's not the kind of place where strangers just say hello in passing," another senior admits, adding, however, "We complain amongst ourselves, but when we leave the campus, we are proud to be Tech students."

Other schools to check out: Virginia Tech, Purdue U, Duke, University of Georgia, California Polytechnic State U.

# of Students Waitlisted: 163
  Students Accepting Place: 85
  Waitlisted Students Admitted: 35

Test Scores (middle 50%):
  SAT Verbal: 600–690
  SAT Math: 650–740
  ACT Comp: 26–30

HS Rank of Entering Freshmen:
  Top 10%: 58%
  Top 25%: 88%
  Top 50%: 99%

Avg. HS GPA: 3.72

THE EXPERTS SAY...

" Georgia Tech offers a prestigious degree at an affordable price, but students must know, or learn, how to manage their time wisely. "

" The intense workload and competition are balanced with an intense social scene! "

Costs (2003–04)

Tuition and Fees, In-State: $4,076

Tuition and Fees, Out-of-State: $16,002

Room & Board: $6,264

Inst. Aid (est. 2003–04)

Institutional Aid, Need-Based: $4,381,469

Institutional Aid, Non-Need-Based: $2,413,540

FT Undergrads Receiving Aid: 32%
  Avg. Amount per Student: $7,444

FT Undergrads Receiving Non-Need-Based Scholarship or Grant Aid: 8%
  Avg. Amount per Student: $3,201

Of Those Receiving Any Aid:

Rec. Need-Based Scholarship or Grant Aid: 54%
  Average Award: $3,499

Rec. Need-Based Self-Help Aid: 76%
  Average Award: $3,872

Upon Graduation, Avg. Loan Debt per Student: $16,972

Financial Aid Deadline: 3/1

Graduates

Going to Graduate School:
  23% Within One Year

Accepting Job Offer:
  65% at time of graduation

Companies Recruiting On Campus: 800

Alumni Giving: 33%

GETTYSBURG COLLEGE

300 North Washington Street, Gettysburg, PA 17325
Admissions Phone: (800) 431-0803; (717) 337-6100 Fax: (717) 337-6145
Email: admiss@gettysburg.edu
Website: www.gettysburg.edu

General Info

Type of School: private, coed
Setting: suburban
Academic Calendar: semester

Student Body

Full-Time Undergrads: 2,553
  Men: 48%, Women: 52%

Part-Time Undergrads: 44
  Men: 39%, Women: 61%

Total Undergrad Population:
  African American: 4%
  Asian American: 1%
  Latino: 1%
  Native American: <1%
  Caucasian: 91%
  International: 2%
  Out-of-State: 72%
  Living Off-Campus: 7%
  In Fraternities: 35%
  In Sororities: 26%

Academics

Full-Time Faculty: 186
  With Ph.D.: 92%

Part-Time Faculty: 73

Student/Faculty Ratio: 11:1

Most Popular Majors:
  management (15%)
  psychology (8%)
  political science (7%)
  history (6%)
  English (5%)

Completing 2 or More Majors: 14%

Freshmen Retention Rate: 91%

Graduation Rates:
  70% within four years
  75% within six years

Admissions

Regular Application Deadline: 2/15
  (priority)

Early Decision Deadline(s): 11/15,
1/15

Fall Transfer Deadline: 4/15
  (priority)

Spring Transfer Deadline: 12/1
  (priority)

Total # of Students Applied: 5,017
  Admitted: 2,317
  Enrolled: 695
  Waitlisted Students Admitted: 20

Inside the Classroom

Located right near Cemetery Ridge, where the tide of the Civil War infamously turned, Gettysburg College is literally surrounded by history. In fact, one of the campus' oldest buildings was used as a hospital during the battle, and many claim the place is haunted by army ghosts. So it should come as no surprise that history is one of the most popular majors here, but it's by no means the extent of the great programs available. Students may choose from more than 30 degree programs, fulfill a double major, pursue an interdisciplinary or self-designed major, and take a minor concentration (including a minor in Civil War era studies). Business is a very popular program, as is poly sci. Science majors are treated to state-of-the-art facilities including electron microscopes, spectrometers, and a planetarium. The school, and particularly the English department, is very proud of its association with The Gettysburg Review, and recently, the college was awarded a grant to strengthen its Asian studies program.

Students are required to complete the Liberal Arts Core—one course in the arts, three in the humanities, one in English comp, one in a non-Western culture, two in the natural sciences, two in the social sciences, and one in quantitative reasoning. Students must also fulfill the foreign language and phys ed requirements.

In their small classes, students get to know their professors, who are "friendly and accessible," one student reports. The average class size is 18. Students are encouraged to undertake independent research projects, with the help and guidance of faculty advisers. Nearly 45 percent of the student body participates in some sort of off-campus study during their time here. Internships are extremely popular, and Gettysburg students have good acceptance rates at professional schools (seven percent of the student body goes on to law school, seven percent to business school, and six percent to medical school).

Gettysburg uses a College Navigation (CNAV) Web tool to keep the college community connected and informed about curricular and extracurricular offerings. With the students' permission, parents can even use CNAV to access their children's course schedules and academic transcripts(!). Incoming students are strongly encouraged to bring personal computers with at least Windows 98 and MS Office 2000.

Campus Environment

The 200-acre campus is next to Gettysburg National Park, and the town reportedly draws close to two million visitors per year. (Students, for the most part, say they could do without all the tourists.) Otherwise, the school is fairly isolated, but Harrisburg, Baltimore, and Washington, DC are all an easy drive away for students who want a taste of city life.

All freshmen must live on campus—actually, all sophomores and juniors must, too, which could explain why the school figures that about 90 percent of its undergrads live in campus housing (which is "excellent," according to one high school guidance counselor). There are seven first-year residence halls, most of which are associated with the popular First Year Residential College Program, where academic and residential worlds collide. Upperclassmen may choose from 18 other residences, including apartments and special-interest housing. Many men live with their "brothers" in one of close to a dozen frat houses on or near campus; there are no sorority houses.

Student Life

Gettysburg began as a Lutheran school, and its religious affiliation still carries an impact. While only 10 percent of the student body is actually Lutheran, Gettysburg students in general are religious and are concerned about moral issues and values. The school's honor code is taken with the utmost seriousness by students, who view it as a moral guidepost. Students here can be described as conservative and career-minded; the student body is also mostly white and from well-to-do families.

For those who don't have their noses in books—and don't worry, students say the "workload leaves enough time for socializing"—there's plenty of partying to be done. Unless they're drinking at the local bars, most students view the town of Gettysburg as a tourist trap and stick close to campus at night and on weekends. The Greeks dominate the social life: Many students belong to one of the 11 fraternities or five sororities. (Some students claim it feels like everyone is Greek.) The administration is fervently trying to curb drinking, especially at frat houses, where much of the student body parties. There are non-Greek social events—the school claims that there are an average of nine speakers, films, plays, recitals, concerts, and exhibits per week on campus—but clearly "the Greeks are the campus leaders," admits one student.

Students do hang out at the student center and the Junction, an on-campus club that shows movies, hosts student bands, and occasionally provides other forms of entertainment. The Attic, a campus nightclub where students may book and run their own parties, opened in March 2001. The Student Senate sponsors day trips to Washington, Baltimore, and New York, and every year there are at least two concerts by big-name acts on campus. Students may also choose from 100 organizations ranging from the College Republicans and the Pre-Health Professions Club to the Colorguard and the Civil War Club; many are involved in community service activities or religious clubs. Intramural sports are quite popular, and the school has 22 intercollegiate teams at the Division III level. We hear that school spirit is lacking here, however, and that sports events aren't as well-attended or supported as at other schools.

Other schools to check out: Dickinson, Franklin and Marshall, William and Mary, Muhlenberg, Lafayette.

Applied Early Decision: 309
Early Decision Admitted: 213

Test Scores (middle 50%):
SAT Verbal: 600–670
SAT Math: 600–670

HS Rank of Entering Freshmen:
Top 10%: 62%
Top 25%: 84%
Top 50%: 99%

THE EXPERTS SAY...

" History buffs will love the classes, the town, and the Civil War Institute. "

" If you liked the social scene at prep school, you'll love Gettysburg College. "

Costs (2004–5)

Tuition and Fees: $30,240

Room & Board: $7,354

Payment Plan(s): installment plan, deferred payment plan, pre-payment plan

Inst. Aid (2002–03)

Institutional Aid, Need-Based: $22,132,910

Institutional Aid, Non-Need-Based: $1,323,125

FT Undergrads Receiving Aid: 56%
Avg. Amount per Student: $24,317

FT Undergrads Receiving Non-Need-Based Scholarship or Grant Aid: 5%
Avg. Amount per Student: $10,930

Of Those Receiving Any Aid:

Rec. Need-Based Scholarship or Grant Aid: 96%
Average Award: $18,531

Rec. Need-Based Self-Help Aid: 88%
Average Award: $5,786

Upon Graduation, Avg. Loan Debt per Student: $16,000

Financial Aid Deadline: 3/15, 2/15 (priority)

Graduates

Going to Graduate School: 29% Within One Year

Companies Recruiting On Campus: 52

Alumni Giving: 37%

GONZAGA UNIVERSITY

502 East Boone, Admin 102, Spokane, WA 99258
Admissions Phone: (509) 323-6572; (800) 322-2584 Fax: (509) 324-5780
Email: admissions@gonzaga.edu
Website: www.gonzaga.edu

General Info

Type of School: private, coed, Roman Catholic

Setting: urban

Academic Calendar: semester

Student Body

Full-Time Undergrads: 3,766
   Men: 46%, Women: 54%

Part-Time Undergrads: 215
   Men: 38%, Women: 62%

Total Undergrad Population:
   African American: 1%
   Asian American: 5%
   Latino: 3%
   Native American: 1%
   Caucasian: 79%
   International: 1%
   Out-of-State: 48%
   Living Off-Campus: 51%

Graduate and First-Professional
   Students: 1,797

Academics

Full-Time Faculty: 304
   With Ph.D.: 87%

Part-Time Faculty: 228

Student/Faculty Ratio: 12:1

Most Popular Majors:
   business administration (20%)
   social sciences (15%)
   engineering (11%)
   biology (4%)
   psychology (4%)

Completing 2 or More Majors: 5%

Freshmen Retention Rate: 90%

Graduation Rates:
   63% within four years
   79% within six years

Admissions

Regular Application Deadline: 2/1

Early Action Deadline: 11/15

Fall Transfer Deadline: 7/1,
   3/1 (priority)

Spring Transfer Deadline: 11/1
   (priority)

Total # of Students Applied: 3,713
   Admitted: 2,846
   Enrolled: 908

In the Classroom

Gonzaga University includes five schools conferring undergraduate degrees—the College of Arts and Sciences, School of Business Administration, School of Education, School of Engineering and School of Professional Studies; together they offer degrees in 92 fields of study. The university is particularly known for its preprofessional programs, and many of its students plan to pursue graduate degrees in fields such as law, medicine, nursing, dentistry, business, and engineering.

Although Gonzaga has many of the advantages of a large university, its undergraduate liberal arts program operates like a small college. "Professors are available any day, any time and usually give out home phone numbers," a business major says. Another student says there is a real campus learning community, where professors are regarded not only as teachers, but also as friends.

This Catholic school, administered by the Jesuits, maintains a strong religious environment. Students are required to take three one-semester courses in religious studies; the prescribed sequence is scriptural studies, Christian doctrine, and applied theology. In addition, professors in other courses are encouraged to relate the content to Christianity. One student says that the school's religious character "is a turn-off to some, but I see it as a strength; I find it a way to grow in faith."

All undergrad students are required to take a core liberal arts curriculum that accounts for 31 of the 128 credits required for graduation. In addition to the religion requirement (nine credits), courses in thought and expression (seven credits), philosophy (nine credits), mathematics (three credits), and English literature (three credits) are required.

Campus Environment

There are 90 buildings on the 108-acre campus, which is set in a residential district of Spokane. The climate is drier but colder than Seattle, making cold winter weather the number one complaint of most students from outside the area. A senior says, mostly in jest, "If I were to do it again, I would choose someplace like Gonzaga, but warmer!"

Freshmen and sophomores under the age of 21 are required to live on campus. The 13 residence halls provide a variety of living options, including single, double, and triple rooms; freshmen are encouraged to have a roommate for at least the first semester. Students can choose among all-male, all-female, and coed halls. Coed dorms have same-sex floors; entry to each floor is through locked doors for which only floor residents have keys. In addition there are several university-owned apartment buildings—some on-campus and the others nearby—that provide housing primarily for juniors, seniors, and grad students. Two dorms provide "positive choice living," that is free of alcohol, tobacco, and other drugs.

A car may not be necessary since Gonzaga is within walking distance of the restaurants, shops, and theaters of downtown Spokane, but having one makes getting around town easier and opens up recreation activities, including skiing. A senior says that it you don't have a car, you'd better have a friend with one. Parking is in short supply, and parking permits must be purchased for on-campus parking.

Student Life

The student body tends to come from a white, middle-class, and Catholic background. According to one student, "Gonzaga's religious affiliation means more than just a few theology classes thrown in the graduation requirements." Another student says the school's conservative religious character "influences everything that happens on campus." For example, during the 2000–01 school year, a representative from Planned Parenthood was prevented from coming on campus to speak to a student club.

The Crosby Student Center, named after Bing Crosby, Gonzaga's most famous alum, serves as the hub of the campus community (and houses what the university calls "the world's largest public collection of Bing Crosby memorabilia"). The Student Body Association sponsors a variety of clubs and activities, including speakers, dances, street fairs, ski days and even a rodeo. The most popular club is the Kennel Klub for fans of the Gonzaga Bulldogs basketball team, and the least popular clubs are political ones.

There are no fraternities or sororities and the Zag social scene is laid back. "Weekends consist of friendly pick-up soccer or basketball games, and weekend nights are spent visiting friends," one student says. That's not to say you won't be able to find a party; GU has "its share of partiers," according to another student. Weekends, you're likely find various student parties on and off campus (although the campus is officially "dry"), and two student-oriented bars, The Bulldog and Jack & Dan's, are within walking distance of campus. While drinking is fairly common among many Zags, drug usage is relatively low.

Gonzaga offers seven men's and seven women's sports and competes in the NCAA Division I. There is no football team, but the Bulldog basketball team is legendary and deserves a paragraph of its own (see below). Men's sports include basketball, baseball, soccer, golf, tennis, cross country/track, and crew. Women's sports include volleyball, basketball, soccer, tennis, cross country/track, crew, and golf. In addition, a variety of club sports are available, including ice hockey, lacrosse, and snowboarding. About 800 students get involved in Zag intramural sports including volleyball, basketball, flag football, softball, soccer, racquetball, and ultimate Frisbee.

It's no surprise that basketball games are among the biggest events on campus. A few years ago, the basketball team transformed the school from a virtually unheard of small college into one of national fame, although many newscasters got the pronunciation wrong (it's "zag" as in "zigzag"). Since then, the Bulldogs have repeated the David-and-Goliath story and ended up at the NCAA national championships, almost always making it to the Sweet Sixteen or higher. "The smallest big-time basketball program in the country," as the *New York Times* called it, has been a major boon to both student recruitment and university fund-raising.

Other schools to check out: Santa Clara, Pepperdine, Loyola Marymount, Pacific Lutheran.

GOSHEN COLLEGE

1700 S. Main St., Goshen, IN 46526-4794
Admissions Phone: (574) 535-7535; (800) 348-7422 Fax: (574) 535-7609
Email: admission@goshen.edu
Website: www.goshen.edu

General Info

Type of School: private, coed, Mennonite Church

Setting: small town

Academic Calendar: semester, two semesters and a three week May term

Student Body

Full-Time Undergrads: 781
Men: 40%, Women: 60%

Part-Time Undergrads: 106
Men: 25%, Women: 75%

Total Undergrad Population:
African American: 4%
Asian American: 1%
Latino: 4%
Native American: <1%
Caucasian: 83%
International: 8%
Out-of-State: 43%
Living Off-Campus: 31%

Academics

Full-Time Faculty: 69
With Ph.D.: 58%

Part-Time Faculty: 55
With Ph.D.: 38%

Student/Faculty Ratio: 10:1

Most Popular Majors:
elementary education (9%)
nursing (7%)
communication (6%)
history (5%)
art (5%)

Completing 2 or More Majors: 9%

Freshmen Retention Rate: 81%

Graduation Rates:
46% within four years
66% within six years

Admissions

Regular Application Deadline: 8/15;
2/15 (priority)

Fall Transfer Deadline: 8/15

Spring Transfer Deadline: 12/15

Total # of Students Applied: 608
Admitted: 371
Enrolled: 182

Test Scores (middle 50%):
SAT Verbal: 510–660
SAT Math: 520–640

Inside the Classroom

You know a college is different when one of its most popular majors is "Peace, Justice, and Conflict Resolution." The philosophy behind the education offered at Goshen College is rooted in the pacifist Anabaptist/Mennonite tradition. The college's motto, "Culture for Service," encapsulates Goshen's mission to foster intellectual, spiritual, and social growth among its students in order to serve both the world and the church that it's affiliated with.

Goshen College is also a long-established leader in international education, offering a surprising number of study abroad options for a school so tiny. About 68 percent of the graduating seniors in 2001 studied abroad, most of whom participated in the Study-Service Term (SST), which involves spending 12 weeks in another country's capital city. Participants live with host families and study language and culture for the first six weeks, and then work alongside native residents in various jobs for the second half of the program. "What I will remember and cherish most about my time in Costa Rica is my host families," says one business major. "I hope that I'll return someday. My host mom always told me, 'You'll always have a home in Costa Rica.'"

Rooted firmly in the liberal arts, Goshen offers more than 70 programs of study leading to 36 majors. Its premedical program is considered top-notch, with graduates getting into graduate schools at twice the national average. One premed student says, "After starting classes, I quickly learned why the science department at GC has such a good reputation. The classes are challenging, but the professors do everything they can to help you succeed in the tough academic environment." The reputation extends to some other majors, too: Nursing, accounting, and English majors pass their respective exams at rates well above the national average.

Campus Environment

On-campus housing is guaranteed for all four years Three-quarters of Goshen students live in a three-dorm complex known as KMY—Kratz, Miller, and Yoder Halls. The three dorms share a lawn that plays host to an annual frisbee football tournament—a must-see, if not must-play, occasion. Kulp Hall is considered a prize, with high ceilings, original woodwork, and balconies that play host to both outdoor hymn singing and infamous student pranks. Other options for students include campus-owned houses located within a block of campus. Students interested in these can apply as a group during their junior and senior years.

Facilities include a recently completed music building that boasts a 1,000-seat performance hall and a recital hall that contains a $500,000 Taylor & Boody organ that was custom-built. The arts building contains offices and space for a number of different departments, including music. ("A hint to those musicians practicing in the northernmost rooms: if you use your music stand as a microphone to lip synch, students on the third floor of the Science building can see you," says a senior.)

No one will ever mistake Goshen, Indiana for a collegiate party playpen. Located on the western edge of Indiana's largest Amish settlement, Goshen is a quiet town of 26,000 that has shopping, movie theaters, coffee shops, and a few other distractions.

Some students take advantage of internships and jobs with businesses in the community, and Goshen Community Hospital—located right across Main Street—provides an on-the-job education for nursing students. For more nightlife options, the larger cities of Mishawaka, South Bend, and Fort Wayne are a short drive away.

A new campus athletic center offers clean, modern facilities: three full-size basketball and multipurpose courts, a 2,800-square-foot weight room, 200-meter running track, four racquetball courts, a swimming pool, a large training room, and an exercise science lab. Lighted tennis courts, soccer fields, and a brand-new track and field complex are located right next door.

Student Life

Goshen is a Mennonite school, with religion playing an important role on campus. Not every student is religious, but most students express and explore their spirituality in some way. A junior says, "I think the spiritual life on campus is right where it should be. God is not forced on students, but the opportunity to be in a religious setting is there for those who want it. Students can be wherever they need to be in their spiritual journeys." Of course, the journey is what one makes of it, as this religion major wrote in a school newspaper article: "From what I hear, attendance at Campus Worship Night is rarely in the double digits, and if my memory is correct, a survey in *The Record* last year said that only half of GC students attend church on a regular basis. For the record, I am not among them."

Intramural sports leagues and tournaments number more than a dozen, and more than half of the student population plays. GC's competitive intercollegiate teams participate in the Mid-Central College Conference. Varsity sports include basketball, baseball, soccer, softball, tennis, cross-country, track and field, volleyball, and golf.

Perhaps the most unusual Goshen tradition is SAP Day: a festival-like occasion held on Groundhog Day. Each year, a group of faculty and students calling themselves Scientists and Scholars Advocating Precision (SAP) gather at the College's official sugar maple tree to compare the amount of sap collected to a certain figure derived from that year's winter weather statistics. The resulting, um, "information," attained through the use of something called a "sapometer," is used to determine the precise day that spring will arrive. The official announcement is attended by students, faculty, local dignitaries, and news media. And the thrills don't stop there: After the announcement, everyone sits down to eat pancakes smothered with maple syrup and engage in what one admissions official describes as "plenty of light-hearted groundhog bashing." Try getting that at some other school.

Other schools to check out: Calvin, Wheaton (IL), Hanover, St. Olaf.

ACT Comp: 21–28
ACT English: 21–29
ACT Math: 20–27
HS Rank of Entering Freshmen:
Top 10%: 26%
Top 25%: 46%
Top 50%: 67%
Avg. HS GPA: 3.42

THE EXPERTS SAY...

" Few schools can provide a more perfect match for premedical students and world travelers with a spiritual side. "

" At a school this small, there's nowhere for atheists and other free thinkers to hide. "

Costs (2004–5)

Tuition and Fees: $18,200

Room & Board: $6,200

Payment Plan(s): installment plan, deferred payment plan, pre-payment plan

Inst. Aid (est. 2003–04)

Institutional Aid, Need-Based: $2,922,731

Institutional Aid, Non-Need-Based: $1,461,606

FT Undergrads Receiving Aid: 66%
Avg. Amount per Student: $15,741

FT Undergrads Receiving Non-Need-Based Scholarship or Grant Aid: 6%
Avg. Amount per Student: $7,567

Of Those Receiving Any Aid:

Rec. Need-Based Scholarship or Grant Aid: 100%
Average Award: $10,111

Rec. Need-Based Self-Help Aid: 79%
Average Award: $5,813

Upon Graduation, Avg. Loan Debt per Student: $16,319

Financial Aid Deadline: rolling, 2/15 (priority)

Graduates

Going to Graduate School: 11% Within One Year

Companies Recruiting On Campus: 234

Alumni Giving: 28%

GOUCHER COLLEGE

1021 Dulaney Valley Road, Baltimore, MD 21204-2794
Admissions Phone: (410) 337-6100; (800) 468-2437 Fax: (410) 337-6354
Email: admissions@goucher.edu
Website: goucher.edu

General Info

Type of School: private, coed

Setting: suburban

Academic Calendar: semester

Student Body

Full-Time Undergrads: 1,257
  Men: 31%, Women: 69%

Part-Time Undergrads: 30
  Men: 47%, Women: 53%

Total Undergrad Population:
  African American: 6%
  Asian American: 3%
  Latino: 3%
  Native American: <1%
  Caucasian: 63%
  International: 1%
  Out-of-State: 63%
  Living Off-Campus: 74%

Graduate and First-Professional
  Students: 1,001

Academics

Full-Time Faculty: 98
  With Ph.D.: 90%

Student/Faculty Ratio: 10:1

Most Popular Majors:
  English (13%)
  biological science (8%)
  psychology (7%)
  sociology (7%)
  communication (6%)

Freshmen Retention Rate: 69%

Graduation Rates:
  63% within four years
  69% within six years

Admissions

Regular Application Deadline: 2/1

Early Action Deadline: 12/1

Fall Transfer Deadline: 4/1 (priority)

Spring Transfer Deadline: 12/1
  (priority)

Total # of Students Applied: 2,751
  Admitted: 1,779
  Enrolled: 342

# of Students Waitlisted: 367
  Waitlisted Students Admitted: 26

Applied Early Decision: 28
  Early Decision Admitted: 22

Inside the Classroom

Goucher College is a private, coed, liberal arts and sciences college where intensive classroom study combines with extensive off-campus and international experience to put higher learning into action. Goucher offers majors in 18 different departments and six interdisciplinary areas, incorporating internships, study abroad, and service-learning programs to provide a real-world reinforcement of the lessons students learn. In fact, a number of faculty integrate service-learning into their courses, with some even making community service work a requirement.

Goucher's small student population allows faculty to work closely with students: Most classes have fewer than 20 students, and one guidance counselor tells us that personal attention is a hallmark of a Goucher education. With a small student/faculty ratio, professors really get to know their students and share their areas of expertise in class and on collaborative research projects. "My favorite class was a history class about the civil rights movement," said one senior. "How often do you have the opportunity to learn about something from someone who was actually there and is willing to share his experience? It made me think about my present generation in a whole new way." Another guidance counselor lauds the fact that Goucher "emphasizes writing throughout its curriculum."

The school's Program in General Honors allows exceptional students to complete advanced honors work in courses that cross the disciplinary boundaries of the humanities, sciences, social sciences, and arts. Honors students learn to challenge assumptions, test problem-solving skills, and gain insights into complex topics while developing their critical reading, writing, and speaking skills. Most honors courses are interdisciplinary and some are team-taught.

A thriving study abroad program at Goucher provides students with the opportunity to add international perspectives to their education. Summer, semester, and year-long programs are offered in China, Cuba, Denmark, France, Germany, Ghana, Greece, Honduras, Hungary, Israel, Italy, Japan, Russia, Scotland, South Africa, Spain, the United Kingdom, and Zimbabwe. Often, students find out more about other countries' systems of education than they expected. "You go to class the first day and you're handed a 5- or 6-page-long reading list," said one student on the London program. "Don't panic! You're not expected to read all of this. In fact, you pick and choose what you want to read, then you pick the supplementary sources that go with your chosen books. This is a system built on personal motivation, so look out."

The career development office also offers vital services, connecting students with internship placements and advising graduates and alumni in job searches. Career counselors are available throughout the academic year, and the office houses a library of career planning guides, online search programs, and directories listing countless businesses and organizations. Workshops on such topics as résumé writing, interview skills, and time management are offered monthly, and are open to all Goucher students.

According to the Goucher website, admitted applicants with a grade point average of 3.0 or higher and combined SAT I scores of 1100+ (or ACT composite scores of 25 and higher) automatically qualify for a four-year Marvin Perry Scholarship valued at $8,500 per year. And those with combined SAT scores of 1200+ (or ACT composite scores of 27 and higher) automatically qualify for $10,000 per year. For truly outstanding applicants, Trustee Scholarships provide full tuition, room, and board for four years, and Dean's Scholarships provide full tuition for four years. Goucher also offers several scholarships to applicants who have demonstrated extraordinary ability in specific areas of the arts.

Campus Environment

Goucher's wooded, 287-acre campus is located in Towson, Maryland, a few miles north of Baltimore. The campus is unique in that it melds living and learning environments: The four fieldstone residence halls located right in the center of campus also house many academic and social resources, like the student union, music practice rooms, computer and language labs, and health and counseling services. Each residence hall is subdivided into "houses," where 40 to 50 students live in a close-knit, self-governing community. The Rogers Library is the central repository of written knowledge on campus, containing 295,000 books, 1,100 journals and periodicals, and a large collection of CD-ROM, CD, and record titles. Students can also take advantage of web-based, full-text editions of more than 200 journals. Most of Baltimore's academic libraries offer reciprocal borrowing privileges, so if you can't find what you're looking for on campus, it probably isn't far away.

The city of Baltimore has experienced a rebirth in recent years, fueled by the multimillion dollar renovation of its waterfront area. A number of bars, coffeehouses, nightclubs, restaurants and stores cater to students from over 20 colleges and universities in the area, offering a wealth of distractions for students looking for off-campus fun.

Student Life

Goucher's male-female ratio has yet to reach equilibrium since the school switched from an all-women to a coed environment a few years ago. The residence houses serve many of the functions of fraternities and sororities—which don't exist at Goucher—including the planning and running of social events. The school also sponsors movies and campus-wide get-togethers as well. Trips into Baltimore are popular, as are slightly longer jaunts to Washington, DC, an hour away.

The campus boasts over 50 clubs and organizations, all founded and run by students. Some of the more colorful options include the Swing Jive-Swing Dance Club, the Ministry of Funny Walks (a footbagging club), the Street Show Collective, and Comics Anonymous. The Goucher Gophers compete with other schools at the NCAA Division III level. Sports for both men and women include basketball, cross country, soccer, lacrosse, swimming, tennis, track and field, and equestrian. Women can also compete in volleyball and field hockey. A long list of intramural sports is also available.

Other schools to check out: Agnes Scott, Simmons, Mary Washington, Elon.

Test Scores (middle 50%):
SAT Verbal: 570–670
SAT Math: 540–640
ACT Comp: 25–29

HS Rank of Entering Freshmen:
Top 10%: 27%
Top 25%: 60%
Top 50%: 88%

Avg. HS GPA: 3.23

THE EXPERTS SAY...

" Goucher takes a practical approach to liberal arts that focuses on the application of study to real-world practice. For a similar experience (but with no men at all), check out Agnes Scott College (down south) or Simmons College (up north). "

" With about 1,200 students and a disproportionate number of women, the social life at Goucher involves a determined effort. "

Costs (2003–04)

Tuition and Fees: $24,450

Room & Board: $8,200

Inst. Aid (2002–03)

Institutional Aid, Need-Based: $11,897,516

Institutional Aid, Non-Need-Based: $1,500,999

FT Undergrads Receiving Aid: 58% Avg. Amount per Student: $18,813

FT Undergrads Receiving Non-Need-Based Scholarship or Grant Aid: 8% Avg. Amount per Student: $9,363

Of Those Receiving Any Aid:

Rec. Need-Based Scholarship or Grant Aid: 99% Average Award: $0

Rec. Need-Based Self-Help Aid: 96% Average Award: $4,323

Upon Graduation, Avg. Loan Debt per Student: $16,062

Financial Aid Deadline: 2/15

GRINNELL COLLEGE

1103 Park Street, Grinnell, IA 50112-1690
Admissions Phone: (641) 269-3600; (800) 247-0113 Fax: (641) 269-4800
Email: askgrin@grinnell.edu Website: www.grinnell.edu
Application Website: www.grinnell.edu/admission/apply/

General Info

Type of School: private, coed
Setting: small town
Academic Calendar: semester

Student Body

Full-Time Undergrads: 1,475
  Men: 45%, Women: 55%

Part-Time Undergrads: 3
  Men: 33%, Women: 67%

Total Undergrad Population:
  African American: 4%
  Asian American: 5%
  Latino: 4%
  Native American: 1%
  Caucasian: 69%
  International: 10%
  Out-of-State: 87%
  Living Off-Campus: 13%

Academics

Full-Time Faculty: 139
  With Ph.D.: 98%

Part-Time Faculty: 3
  With Ph.D.: 100%

Student/Faculty Ratio: 10:1

Most Popular Majors:
  biology (11%)
  English (9%)
  economics (7%)
  history (7%)
  anthropology (7%)

Completing 2 or More Majors: 18%

Freshmen Retention Rate: 92%

Graduation Rates:
  80% within four years
  85% within six years

Admissions

Regular Application Deadline: 1/20

Early Decision Deadline(s): 11/20,
  1/1

Fall Transfer Deadline: 5/1

Spring Transfer Deadline: 12/1

Total # of Students Applied: 2,284
  Admitted: 1,443
  Enrolled: 405

# of Students Waitlisted: 244
  Students Accepting Place: 93
  Waitlisted Students Admitted: 1

Applied Early Decision: 119
  Early Decision Admitted: 94

Inside the Classroom

Grinnell College is known for its strong academics, for the freedom and responsibility students are afforded, and for a tradition of liberal social activism. With an open curriculum, students are free to design their own programs of study in conjunction with their faculty advisers. In addition, the school's policy of self-governance allows students huge input into almost every area, and places on them the responsibility of structuring their community according to "the tastes and desires of the campus community."

There is no core curriculum at Grinnell. However, there are some broad guidelines upon which each student's curriculum must be built: All students must take courses in each of the three main divisions of the curriculum: humanities, science, and social studies. The only college-wide course requirement is an intensive first-year tutorial, in which a small group of students works with a faculty tutor to study a subject of common interest. The tutor is also the academic adviser for each student in the group, so students receive advice and insights from a faculty member who sees them from week to week. These tutorials help students get to know at least one professor well from the start.

From all reports, professors at Grinnell truly care about their students and often take the time to work with them on an individual basis; the student/faculty ratio is a mere 10:1, and classes are generally limited to 20 people. One student tells us that the professors often help students "by providing guidance if people are having problems." Another student agrees, adding, "They'll make office hours whenever you need to see them, and some will even meet you at their houses." Students rate the workload extremely difficult, but not competitive. "A strong intellectual atmosphere, without being overly intense," is how one high school guidance counselor describes it. The pressure comes from the students' own desire to do their best, and as a result, many of the undergraduates feel that the student body pulls together as a community. One recent grad reports, "Everyone had their area of excellence, yet everyone seemed to focus on what they still wanted to learn."

Popular majors include biology, history, English, political science, and economics. In addition, a few hundred students pursue double majors or interdisciplinary concentrations. For a small school, Grinnell produces a large number of Ph.D.s, ranking in the top 20 of all U.S. institutions. Many Grinnell students—nearly 60 percent of every graduating class—participate in off-campus study, either abroad or in the United States.

Campus Environment

Most students live on campus in one of the 15 relatively small residence halls. A few students note that dorm rooms are small, but not unpleasant. The food in the dining halls is reputed to be pretty good and actually "good for you," and the atmosphere is more like a "cathedral" than a "mess hall." Thanks to generous alumni gifts and excellent investing, Grinnell is financially well off, as the beautiful campus shows. The Harris Center, with a theater, movie theater, and dance space, provides a site for school-sponsored special events, including frequent films, concerts, and dances.

The town of Grinnell has a population of only 8,900 and is far from any major city (Des Moines and Iowa City are each well over an hour away), and although some may find that sticking around campus gets boring, most students don't mind it at all. One student praises the community for its "clean air, no traffic, great view of the stars, and virtually no crime." Another fan of this rural enclave finds "the simplicity, safety, and security… nothing short of heaven." Still, others warn that "the location of Grinnell can be both a blessing and a curse—the sense of isolation can allow one to better focus on one's studies, but it also makes it very difficult to get away."

Student Life

"It's an open, friendly campus," says one student. "It is very accepting of differences." This policy of inclusiveness is reflected in the fact that Grinnell has never had any fraternities or sororities—social activities are open to the entire campus community. The atmosphere is "pretty liberal, both socially and politically," a student states. "There is a high percentage of students involved in community service and political activism." This spirit of activism on campus is not new: Grinnell was a stop along the Underground Railroad, and was one of the first colleges to admit African Americans and women to full degree programs. In addition, the school's travel-service program predates the Peace Corps.

Students actually praise the school's administration for its openness and responsiveness to their needs. One recent graduate says that students' voices were always heard, "whether the conversation was one-on-one or mob-on-one."

Grinnell's student body is diverse (for Iowa): 13 percent are students of color, and 10 percent hail from overseas. The atmosphere is described as tolerant, and while most students have a decidedly liberal bent, one student says that there are even a few "young Republicans" on campus. Just about everyone describes the student body as friendly and down-to-earth; one student says, "At Grinnell, there are no strangers."

Grinnell isn't a party school, but students seem to find plenty of things to do—some, rather offbeat. Each year, Grinnell throws a huge disco party, in which about 1,000 of the 1,300 students participate. Intramural sports are popular, with a large percentage of the community participating just for fun. Still, Grinnell is not a sports mecca; one student says wryly, "If you're a dedicated jock who takes competition seriously, Grinnell College is not for you."

Other schools to check out: Oberlin, Carleton, Reed, Brown, Macalester.

Test Scores (middle 50%):
SAT Verbal: 610–730
SAT Math: 630–720
ACT Comp: 25–32
ACT English: 27–32
ACT Math: 26–31

HS Rank of Entering Freshmen:
Top 10%: 62%
Top 25%: 88%
Top 50%: 100%

THE EXPERTS SAY...

" Grinnell students are deeply involved in creating their campus community; the open curriculum also lets students create their own program. "

" If you're quirky, brainy, and liberal, head on out to Iowa to take a look at Grinnell. Minorities are especially welcome. "

Costs (2004–5)

Tuition and Fees: $25,820

Room & Board: $6,870

Payment Plan(s): installment plan, pre-payment plan

Inst. Aid (est. 2003–04)

Institutional Aid, Need-Based: $12,030,246

Institutional Aid, Non-Need-Based: $4,006,514

FT Undergrads Receiving Aid: 60%
Avg. Amount per Student: $20,298

FT Undergrads Receiving Non-Need-Based Scholarship or Grant Aid: 28%
Avg. Amount per Student: $8,890

Of Those Receiving Any Aid:

Rec. Need-Based Scholarship or Grant Aid: 100%
Average Award: $15,616

Rec. Need-Based Self-Help Aid: 84%
Average Award: $5,548

Upon Graduation, Avg. Loan Debt per Student: $16,818

Financial Aid Deadline: 2/1 (priority)

Graduates

Going to Graduate School: 30% Within One Year

GUILFORD COLLEGE

5800 West Friendly Avenue, Greensboro, NC 27410
Admissions Phone: (336) 316-2100; (800) 992-7759 Fax: (336) 316-2954
Email: admissions@guilford.edu
Website: www.guilford.edu

General Info

Type of School: private, coed,
  Society of Friends (Quaker)

Setting: suburban

Academic Calendar: semester

Student Body

Full-Time Undergrads: 1,734
  Men: 41%, Women: 59%

Part-Time Undergrads: 367
  Men: 28%, Women: 72%

Total Undergrad Population:
  African American: 19%
  Asian American: 2%
  Latino: 2%
  Caucasian: 70%
  International: 2%
  Out-of-State: 34%
  Living Off-Campus: 20%

Academics

Full-Time Faculty: 91
  With Ph.D.: 74%

Part-Time Faculty: 74
  With Ph.D.: 38%

Student/Faculty Ratio: 16:1

Most Popular Majors:
  business management (13%)
  psychology (11%)
  English (7%)
  elementary education (7%)
  computer information systems (6%)

Freshmen Retention Rate: 71%

Graduation Rates:
  51% within four years
  57% within six years

Admissions

Regular Application Deadline: 2/15;
  1/15 (priority)

Early Action Deadline: 1/15

Fall Transfer Deadline: 5/1

Total # of Students Applied: 1,647
  Admitted: 1,137
  Enrolled: 298

# of Students Waitlisted: 7
  Students Accepting Place: 7
  Waitlisted Students Admitted: 1

Applied Early Decision: 38
  Early Decision Admitted: 38

Inside the Classroom

Established as a Quaker institution, Guilford College still draws on Quaker tradition to offer a liberal arts education that, according to its website, "prepares men and women for a lifetime of learning, work, and constructive action dedicated to the betterment of the world." An Oregon guidance counselor agrees: "Guilford's Quaker community orientation sets a unique tone." The road leading to the school is still named Friendly Road, and the school's commitment to philanthropic efforts is demonstrated by the popularity of its community service programs.

The roster of 33 academic majors and five cooperative preprofessional programs includes the standard liberal arts and sciences selection, plus some notable interdisciplinary majors such as African American studies, peace and conflict studies, and integrative studies. Concentrations are available in a number of areas, including some hard-to-find options like Quaker studies, interpersonal communication, applied ethics, and peace and conflict studies.

In 2002, Guilford became the first college in North Carolina to offer a forensic biology major for students interested in criminal justice careers, the FBI, and humanitarian agencies investigating human rights abuses. The forensic biology major has consistently ranked as the most-desired new major in surveys of adult students. The new major builds on Guilford's concentration in forensic science (offered since 1999), which includes procedure, introduction to forensics, forensic chemistry, and forensic anthropology.

The internship program at Guilford allows students to explore career interests, gain job experience, and build a strong résumé. Each internship carries four credits and involves a minimum of 144 hours worked, some written papers, and regular conferences with a faculty sponsor. A wide range of opportunities is available, including those in accounting, women's studies, nonprofit management, sports studies, communications, and many others.

An excellent program for first-year students helps to ease the transition from high school. Students are assisted through the special CHAOS orientation program, student mentoring, and the special Avanti program, which involves outdoor adventure and wilderness experiences. "These experiences are a lot of fun," said one student. "And they allow you to do something you never thought of doing before. It will be an experience you will never forget!"

Guilford also provides students with the opportunity to understand and appreciate diverse cultures through its study abroad programs. Current offerings include semester programs in France, Germany, England, Mexico, Italy, and Ghana. Or, students can spend a year in Japan as part of Guilford's exchange program with International Christian University.

Campus Environment

Residence halls on campus are picturesque, red-brick structures surrounded by green lawns. The inside scoop on housing: English Hall is all-male and has extended quiet hours. Hobbs and Shore Halls are all-female: Shore is a quiet hall while Hobbs allows its residents to save on expenses by sharing housekeeping duties. Upperclass students are fond of Bryan Hall, which houses both men and women in suites. The four buildings of Bryan Hall are arranged around a central courtyard where many social activities like dances are held. Special interest housing is also offered for students wishing to share their interests in language study, science, or cultural themes. Perhaps most sought after are the 24 student apartments, where four students share a fully equipped kitchen and an unfurnished dining room and living room.

The recently built Frank Family Science Center is a state of the art teaching and meeting facility that provides meeting facilities for off-campus groups and supports the college's many community service programs. The building includes laboratories, classrooms, offices, research space, a multifunctional auditorium, an observatory, and an atrium.

The athletic facilities at the Ragan-Brown Field House are remarkable for a school of Guilford's small size and contribute to the popularity of intramural and club sports on campus. The building contains a specially-designed hardwood floor, basketball, volleyball, and racquetball courts, a 25-meter pool, and a weight and training room. Adjacent to the field house are eight tennis courts, seven playing fields for baseball, soccer, and lacrosse, a 3,000-seat stadium with a running track, and a wooded running trail.

Student Life

The Guilford Quakers are quite competitive in the Old Dominion Athletic Conference (ODAC), playing at the NCAA Division III level. Sports for both men and women include basketball, lacrosse, soccer, and tennis. Men can also compete in baseball and golf, while women may play volleyball. Standout teams include men's basketball, women's tennis, and men's golf—each has won a national championship, and the Quakers have won ten conference championships since joining the ODAC in 1991. Students also participate in women's, men's and coed intramurals and club sports such as ultimate Frisbee, rugby, track and field and volleyball.

One guidance counselor told us that "for some, this school would not be preppy enough." Student clubs and organizations on the Guilford campus reflect a variety of student interests. Club themes range from the usual student fare like the school choir, the Scrabble and chess club, and the Model UN to more unusual clubs for interests like pagan mysticism and Culture Jammers. One unusual student club is the Freak Show, a troupe of students that performs contortionist acts, fire eating, juggling, and—in one controversial show last year—cricket swallowing. Student media organizations include the campus radio station, WQFS-FM, which has traditionally ranked among the top three college radio stations in the nation.

An amusing encapsulation of Guilford was written in spring 2002 by a columnist for *The Guilfordian*, the student newspaper: "Perhaps the best analogy of Guilford is that our school is like beer ... Like beer, Guilford is an acquired taste. For some people, the more they drink, the more they like it, and decide they want to make beer a regular part of their diet. To continue the beer analogy a little further, people that drink beer need to research what makes a good beer: the more you pay attention to what you drink, the more satisfied you will be."

Other schools to check out: Earlham, Warren Wilson, Antioch, Berea, Elon.

Test Scores (middle 50%):
SAT Verbal: 520–650
SAT Math: 500–620
ACT Comp: 21–26

HS Rank of Entering Freshmen:
Top 10%: 9%
Top 25%: 38%
Top 50%: 79%

Avg. HS GPA: 3.06

Costs (2003–04)

Tuition and Fees: $19,450

Room & Board: $5,940

Payment Plan(s): installment plan

THE EXPERTS SAY...

" Guilford College frames a quality liberal arts education in a setting where the improvement of all mankind is the underlying goal. "

" Guilford has the Holy Grail: a forensic biology major. "

Inst. Aid (est. 2003–04)

Institutional Aid, Need-Based:
$5,796,993

Institutional Aid, Non-Need-Based:
$2,488,990

FT Undergrads Receiving Aid: 68%
Avg. Amount per Student: $12,795

FT Undergrads Receiving Non-Need-Based Scholarship or Grant Aid: 25%
Avg. Amount per Student: $7,112

Of Those Receiving Any Aid:

Rec. Need-Based Scholarship or Grant Aid: 100%
Average Award: $9,105

Rec. Need-Based Self-Help Aid: 84%
Average Award: $4,800

Upon Graduation, Avg. Loan Debt per Student: $10,893

Financial Aid Deadline: 3/1 (priority)

Graduates

Going to Graduate School:
17% Within One Year

Companies Recruiting On Campus: 85

Alumni Giving: 26%

GUSTAVUS ADOLPHUS COLLEGE

800 West College Avenue, Saint Peter, MN 56082-1498
Admissions Phone: (507) 933-7676; (800) 487-8288 Fax: (507) 933-7474
Email: admission@gustavus.edu Website: www.gustavus.edu
Application Website: www.gustavus.edu/prospective/apply/apply.efm

General Info

Type of School: private, coed, Lutheran

Setting: suburban

Academic Calendar: 4-1-4

Student Body

Full-Time Undergrads: 2,544
    Men: 43%, Women: 57%

Part-Time Undergrads: 13
    Men: 54%, Women: 46%

Total Undergrad Population:
    African American: 1%
    Asian American: 4%
    Latino: 1%
    Native American: <1%
    Caucasian: 92%
    International: 1%
    Living Off-Campus: 15%
    In Fraternities: 27%
    In Sororities: 22%

Academics

Full-Time Faculty: 178
    With Ph.D.: 87%

Part-Time Faculty: 68
    With Ph.D.: 26%

Student/Faculty Ratio: 13:1

Most Popular Majors:
    economics/mangement (19%)
    biology (11%)
    psychology (10%)
    communication studies (10%)
    English (6%)

Completing 2 or More Majors: 20%

Freshmen Retention Rate: 89%

Graduation Rates:
    78% within four years
    82% within six years

Admissions

Regular Application Deadline: 4/1;
    2/15 (priority)

Fall Transfer Deadline: 6/1, 4/1
    (priority)

Spring Transfer Deadline: 1/1, 12/1
    (priority)

Total # of Students Applied: 2,317
    Admitted: 1,790
    Enrolled: 688

# of Students Waitlisted: 129
    Students Accepting Place: 129
    Waitlisted Students Admitted: 12

In the Classroom

Gustavus Adolphus offers a lot of choices: Its 27 academic departments offer 66 majors, the most popular of which are psychology, biology, management, communications, and political science. Besides choosing a major, students can choose between two different core curriculum options. Students in Curriculum I select courses from a wide range of disciplines to meet a more traditional liberal arts core requirement. They must also take the First-Year Seminar, a small, discussion-based course which focuses on critical thinking, writing, and speaking skills; their professor in this seminar becomes their academic advisor. Curriculum II, subject to a limitation of 60 students per entering class, is an interdisciplinary core that focuses on the great ideas that have shaped Western civilization. Curriculum II students, who represent all major fields of study, follow a prescribed series of core courses open only to them but take electives and course in their majors with Curriculum I students.

In both Curriculum I and II, classes are often small and discussion-oriented, requiring that students actively participate. This, along with the College's high academic standards, makes for a fairly demanding academic environment. Students like the fact that their professors get to know them by name and that they often get to work closely together on special projects. According to college statistics, the average class size is 17.

The college is on a 4-1-4 program and requires a minimum of eight semesters and three January terms for graduation. Many students select off-campus January programs that allow them to escape the Minnesota winter, often going abroad. For those who want a longer and richer experience abroad, the college offers its own programs in Sweden, Australia, Japan, Scotland, and Malaysia; students can also select from a number of off-campus programs administered by consortia of which the school is a member. An estimated 40 percent of Gustavus graduates have spent a January term, semester, or full year studying in another country.

Gustavus is known for its student research opportunities; since 1991, the college has ranked among the top ten schools nationally for the percentage of its students qualifying to present at the National Conference on Undergraduate Research. The school is also known for annually hosting the prestigious Nobel Conference (officially sanctioned by the Nobel Foundation that awards the Nobel prizes) that brings renowned scientists and scholars to publicly discuss contemporary issues relating to science, economics, peace, and literature.

Founded by Swedish Lutherans, Gustavus Adolphus remains an institution of the Lutheran church and requires students to take at least one religion course. The college, named after a Swedish king, also maintains its Swedish heritage through programs and events like the Nobel Conference, study abroad programs in Sweden, and even regular visits by the King and Queen of Sweden.

Campus Environment

The 340-acre campus is located on a hill outside the town of St. Peter, about an hour and a half drive southwest from the Twin Cities. The Christ Chapel, with its soaring

187-foot spire, marks the center of the campus. Given the relative isolation of the campus, access to a car can expand options for weeknight and weekend activities. First-year students are not permitted to have cars on campus, although exceptions can be granted based on student need. For those without cars, the college's "Gus Bus" provides occasional service to the Twin Cities airport, the Mall of America (in a Minneapolis suburb), and downtown Mankato (a small city 15 minutes from St. Peter).

All full-time students are expected to live in college-operated residences unless granted a specific exemption or unless college housing is not available. Nearly all students, including 99 percent of freshmen, live on campus. Most halls are coed by section or floor, and smoking floors, single rooms, and student apartments are available. There are theme-housing options, including Crossroads, a living/learning center for those sharing international and intercultural interests. The dorms are grouped into two main areas, which a sophomore describes as follows: "Inhabitants of the North side tend to be heavily involved in 'classical' college activities like athletics and fraternities and sororities, whereas Southsiders tend toward more 'geeky' activities, like gaming, theater, and foreign culture experiences."

Student Life

Gustavus Adolphus's origins as a Lutheran institution are still evident in the student body, a majority of which is Lutheran. More than 80 percent of the students come from Minnesota, and more than 90 percent are white. Although lacking in diversity, students form a closely knit, friendly community, smiling and saying hello to people they pass around campus, whether or not they already know them.

Gusties sometimes journey to St. Paul or Minneapolis for a bit of big-city culture and excitement. For the most part, though, they stick near their own campus, hanging out at such places as the student union, dorm rooms, and an on-campus club (with no alcohol) called The Dive, which often hosts bands on weekends. And thanks to the school's music and theater departments, there's usually a choice of student concerts or productions on campus. One student describes a laid-back social scene: "Many students just hang out at coffeehouses, watch videos, and sit around and talk." However, another student sees it differently: "There are tons of parties all the time." Many of the parties—on and off campus—are sponsored by fraternities and sororities, which at Gustavus have all the trappings of Greek houses … without the house (they are nonresidential social organizations). The fall rush often produces controversial activities, dividing the campus into pro- and anti-Greek sides. Just under a quarter of the students join fraternities or sororities.

In athletics, Gustavus competes in NCAA Division III and offers men's and women's varsity teams for basketball, cross-country, golf, hockey, swimming and diving, soccer, tennis, and track and field; women's teams for gymnastics, softball, and volleyball; and men's teams for baseball and football. Gustie tennis teams are particularly strong and are often contenders in Division III national championships. Superb indoor sporting facilities, including a tennis center, ice arena, 200-meter track, and huge swimming and diving pool, allow sports to triumph over the Minnesota winter. About 30 percent of the students participate in intramural sports, and a limited number of club sports are available as well. At the college intramural office you can check out everything from camping gear to skis to brooms (for broomball).

Other schools to check out: St. Olaf, Pacific Lutheran, Wittenberg, Lawrence.

Test Scores (middle 50%):
  SAT Verbal: 540–600
  SAT Math: 560–680
  ACT Comp: 23–28
  ACT English: 22–28
  ACT Math: 23–28

HS Rank of Entering Freshmen:
  Top 10%: 35%
  Top 25%: 69%
  Top 50%: 85%

Avg. HS GPA: 3.64

Costs (2004–5)

Tuition and Fees: $22,775
Room & Board: $5,780

THE EXPERTS SAY...

" This close-knit campus is famed for its friendliness and opportunities for undergrad research. You can major in Scandinavian studies here. "

" Of course the campus is friendly, it's all one person: white, Lutheran, and from Minnesota. "

Inst. Aid (2002–03)

Institutional Aid, Need-Based: $11,328,567

Institutional Aid, Non-Need-Based: $4,365,306

FT Undergrads Receiving Aid: 65%
  Avg. Amount per Student: $14,921

FT Undergrads Receiving Non-Need-Based Scholarship or Grant Aid: 32%
  Avg. Amount per Student: $6,239

Of Those Receiving Any Aid:

Rec. Need-Based Scholarship or Grant Aid: 100%
  Average Award: $11,133

Rec. Need-Based Self-Help Aid: 79%
  Average Award: $4,569

Upon Graduation, Avg. Loan Debt per Student: $17,400

Financial Aid Deadline: 4/15 (priority)

Graduates

Going to Graduate School:
  26% Within One Year

Accepting Job Offer:
  25% at time of graduation

Companies Recruiting On Campus: 43

Alumni Giving: 37%

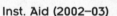

HAMILTON COLLEGE

198 College Hill Road, Clinton, NY 13323
Admissions Phone: (315) 859-4421; (800) 843-2655 Fax: (315) 859-4457
Email: admission@hamilton.edu Website: www.hamilton.edu
Application Website: www.hamilton.edu/admission/apply/default.html

General Info

Type of School: private, coed
Academic Calendar: semester

Student Body

Full-Time Undergrads: 1,755
    Men: 50%, Women: 50%

Part-Time Undergrads: 2 Women:
    100%

Total Undergrad Population:
    African American: 4%
    Asian American: 5%
    Latino: 3%
    Native American: <1%
    Caucasian: 82%
    International: 5%
    Out-of-State: 63%
    Living Off-Campus: 3%
    In Fraternities: 34%
    In Sororities: 20%

Academics

Full-Time Faculty: 183
    With Ph.D.: 91%

Part-Time Faculty: 26
    With Ph.D.: 62%

Student/Faculty Ratio: 9:1

Most Popular Majors:
    economics (12%)
    government (10%)
    psychology (7%)
    English (5%)
    computer science (5%)

Completing 2 or More Majors: 14%

Freshmen Retention Rate: 94%

Graduation Rates:
    83% within four years
    87% within six years

Admissions

Regular Application Deadline: 1/1

Early Decision Deadline(s): 11/15,
    1/1

Fall Transfer Deadline: 3/15

Spring Transfer Deadline: 1/1

Total # of Students Applied: 4,405
    Admitted: 1,457
    Enrolled: 465

# of Students Waitlisted: 514
    Students Accepting Place: 254
    Waitlisted Students Admitted: 18

Applied Early Decision: 434
    Early Decision Admitted: 197

Inside the Classroom

At Hamilton, students have the freedom to pursue their own educational interests within the broad goals of a liberal arts education. Students who graduate from Hamilton are therefore equipped with the critical thinking skills necessary to succeed in any professional or academic arena.

For a small liberal arts college, Hamilton offers a relatively wide variety of concentrations. Programs in the social sciences are among the strongest and the most popular, with public policy studies a standout. Hamilton's East Asian languages and literature department co-administers (with Williams and Oberlin) the Associated Colleges in China Program—a study abroad program involving language-intensive, cultural immersion in Beijing. Other study abroad options include the Junior Year in France, the Madrid-based Academic Year in Spain, and a program at Pembroke College of Oxford University, which allows students to experience Oxford academic life, including the famous tutorials. Students can also intern at the House or Senate through the Washington, DC semester.

One of the best things about Hamilton, a student tells us, is how committed the professors are to their students. A California guidance counselor raves about Hamilton's "individual attention" and "caring staff." The professors here aren't likely to disappear after class or hole up in their offices. "Many make it a point to eat regularly in the cafeteria," we are told. "Most know your name. It just feels very natural for them to speak to you."

Hamilton College does not reward passive learners; students are expected to contribute to classroom discussions. Class sizes are kept to around 15 students, giving the students a chance to voice their opinions and actively participate in their studies. The academic atmosphere is competitive, but not cutthroat. Students "stress," but also know how to have a good time.

Hamilton recently eliminated its traditional distribution requirements in favor of a new liberal education plan, which involves the following: first- and second-year seminars; three writing courses; a more substantive faculty advising system; and a Senior Program culminating in a research project, comprehensive exam, or other work. A new Sophomore Program takes the form of a series of interdisciplinary seminars that culminate in an integrative project with public presentation (called the "Gateway").

Campus Environment

Hamilton in located in the tiny New York town of Clinton. There's little for students to do in town, but while students from urban or suburban settings may complain that Hamilton is isolated, the many students from upstate New York are already accustomed to rural living. A car is very useful to have for the ten-minute hop to nearby Utica and for longer getaways, although a great deal of driving has to be done to get to a big city. Freshmen are not allowed to have cars.

Surrounded by acres of Hamilton-owned woodland, the campus is divided into two sections: the Hamilton campus with its ivy-covered stone buildings, and the more modern Kirkland campus, formerly an all-women's college that merged with

Hamilton. Virtually all Hamilton students live on campus; the variety of residential options has increased in recent years, and now includes an opportunity to live in a 22-room estate overlooking the valley. A student center located between the campuses provides a central socializing spot and a tasty diner popular with students.

Student Life

Speaking of their social life, Hamilton students comment that "your nights will often be spent doing the same things you did the night before." Some seniors venture into Clinton to bars, but most students remain on campus. Although the school recently cracked down on Greek houses by regulating them more stringently, fraternities are still a major force in Hamilton social life.

The school makes an effort to provide additional activities, one student tells us, by sponsoring special events and cultural performances by guest artists like the Dave Matthews Band and B.B. King. The Great Names speaker series has featured such names as Madeleine Albright, Jimmy Carter, Archbishop Desmond Tutu, Lady Margaret Thatcher, Colin Powell, Mary Matalin and James Carville, Elie Wiesel, and F.W. deKlerk. Movies, plays, and concerts are frequent on campus, and there are many music groups, both official and student-run.

Athletics are also big and students enjoy using the modern fitness center. There are 28 varsity teams as well as several junior varsity teams, and nearly 40 percent of the student body play on at least one of them. The men's basketball and hockey teams have good records and draw many enthusiastic—and rowdy—student fans to their games. At a hockey game, you can see the Hamilton spirit at its finest, as students throw oranges at the opposing team's goalie, an old Hamilton tradition. Nature lovers are sure to be happy with the mountains, lakes, and wooded areas surrounding Hamilton. Incoming freshmen are encouraged to participate in an Adirondack Adventure—an eight-day outdoors program occurring before regular orientation. Students can choose from 18 different trips featuring activities such as hiking, canoeing, rock climbing, mountain biking, and community service.

With such a small student body, students say that it's easy to meet people, and remark on the sense of community at the school. The student body leans toward conservatism, but students warn that the faculty are ultra-PC. The number of minority students is low, and some report feeling out of place. Students are predominantly white and well-to-do. However, despite Hamilton's reputation as a school for prep school kids, 57 percent of students are from public schools, and there's a wide diversity of states and foreign countries represented. If a lively intellectual community with strong faculty support and a healthy campus social scene appeals to you, Hamilton may be your school.

Other schools to check out: Skidmore, Trinity College, Bates, Middlebury, Connecticut College.

Test Scores (middle 50%):
SAT Verbal: 640–720
SAT Math: 640–720

HS Rank of Entering Freshmen:
Top 10%: 68%
Top 25%: 88%
Top 50%: 99%

THE EXPERTS SAY...

" Hamilton offers a lot of concentrations for a small school, including standout study abroad programs in Beijing and at Oxford. Hamilton professors are genuinely committed to teaching and advising students. "

" The Dave Matthews Band has come to campus, but on those other days, you won't find much to do in Clinton. If you really get stir-crazy, you could try digging a hole to China. "

Costs (2003–04)

Tuition and Fees: $30,200
Room & Board: $7,360
Payment Plan(s): installment plan

Inst. Aid (est. 2003–04)

Institutional Aid, Need-Based: $16,581,959

Institutional Aid, Non-Need-Based: $628,210

FT Undergrads Receiving Aid: 58%
Avg. Amount per Student: $22,980

FT Undergrads Receiving Non-Need-Based Scholarship or Grant Aid: 4%
Avg. Amount per Student: $9,665

Of Those Receiving Any Aid:

Rec. Need-Based Scholarship or Grant Aid: 95%
Average Award: $19,451

Rec. Need-Based Self-Help Aid: 73%
Average Award: $4,952

Upon Graduation, Avg. Loan Debt per Student: $16,894

Financial Aid Deadline: 2/1 (priority)

Graduates

Going to Graduate School: 20% Within One Year

HAMPDEN-SYDNEY COLLEGE

P.O. Box 667, Hampden-Sydney, VA 23943-0667
Admissions Phone: (434) 223-6120; (800) 755-0733 Fax: (434) 223-6346
Email: hsapp@hsc.edu Website: www.hsc.edu
Application Website: www.hsc.edu/admissions/apply/

General Info

Type of School: private, all men, Presbyterian

Setting: rural

Academic Calendar: semester

Student Body

Full-Time Undergrads: 1,033
  Men: 100%

Part-Time Undergrads: 6
  Men: 100%

Total Undergrad Population:
  African American: 4%
  Asian American: 1%
  Latino: 1%
  Native American: 1%
  Caucasian: 85%
  International: 2%
  Out-of-State: 36%
  Living Off-Campus: 5%
  In Fraternities: 34%
  In Sororities: 0%

Academics

Full-Time Faculty: 87
  With Ph.D.: 80%

Part-Time Faculty: 19
  With Ph.D.: 37%

Student/Faculty Ratio: 11:1

Most Popular Majors:
  economics (49%)
  history (17%)
  political science (15%)
  biology (7%)
  religion (7%)

Completing 2 or More Majors: 22%

Freshmen Retention Rate: 74%

Graduation Rates:
  54% within four years
  59% within six years

Admissions

Regular Application Deadline: 3/1

Early Decision Deadline(s): 11/15

Early Action Deadline: 1/15

Fall Transfer Deadline: 7/1

Spring Transfer Deadline: 12/1

Total # of Students Applied: 1,156
  Admitted: 825
  Enrolled: 306

Inside the Classroom

The ideals of honor, tradition, and character are a way of life at all-male Hampden-Sydney College, as much today as they were at the dawn of the American Revolution. The school is the ninth-oldest college in the United States (founded in 1776), and counts Patrick Henry among its early trustees. The school's founding philosophy was "to form good men and good citizens." Students live by a demanding code of honor that condemns cheating, stealing, and any other sort of dishonesty. Students who break the honor code are put in front of a court of their peers to be judged and punished.

A large part of a young man's first two years at Hampden-Sydney are spent completing the rigorous distribution requirements that include mandated courses in humanities, social sciences, and natural sciences, as well as foreign language proficiency. In addition to all of this is the challenging Rhetoric Program that centers on writing skills and critical thinking in all program areas.

The most popular majors are economics, political science, history, English, religion, and biology. The premed program is particularly exceptional; about 70 percent of Hampden-Sydney premed students are accepted to medical school,

Student research is an integral part of the academic program at Hampden Sydney. Opportunities range from the summer research program sponsored by the honors program, to independent research. All science departments require majors to participate in open-ended project-based research laboratories. This abundance of research opportunities is sponsored and even emphasized by Hampden-Sydney as essential to its inquiry-based interdisciplinary liberal arts curriculum

Class sizes are small, as there are only about 1,000 undergraduates at Hampden-Sydney. Professors are almost always available for one-on-one mentoring. Students get to know their professors and are never taught by a grad student.

Campus Environment

Hampden-Sydney sits on a pastoral campus dotted with quaint, red brick 18th and 19th century buildings and tall trees. The 600-acre campus includes a 300-acre forest with three miles of trails. Much of the campus has been designated a National Historic Preservation Zone. It is not far from the Appomattox Court House, site of Lee's surrender to Grant that ended the Civil War, and some students participate in the historical reenactments that take place in the area. The school's location just outside of Farmville, Virginia is well suited for outdoor enthusiasts, while students craving city excitement can find it as near as Richmond, 60 miles away.

All freshmen are assigned to freshmen-only dorms. Freshmen are housed first and then spaces are allotted to the upperclassmen population, but on-campus housing is guaranteed for all four years. Since freshmen are not allowed to join fraternities until the end of the first year, they do not live in fraternity houses.

Recent construction on campus includes the renovation of two fraternity houses. An ongoing project on campus is to renovate one residence hall per year, changing from traditional doubles and singles to apartments.

Student Life

Hampden-Sydney is one of only three men's colleges left in the United States. Amazingly enough, the students seem to love the all-male atmosphere. Gentlemanly conduct is expected of students, which includes saying hello to any and all other students on campus, greeting visitors, and providing service to the larger community. In practice, it means that faculty can trust students; that residence hall rooms can be left unlocked, and student books left in the library. It is not uncommon to see backpacks sitting on the grass around the dining halls at mealtime. Students drop them on the ground on the way in, confident that they won't be rifled through.

About 40 percent of the students join one of the 12 fraternities, so that the Greek system effectively constitutes almost half of the social environment. The fraternities regularly throw parties that draw women from the surrounding all-female schools such as Sweet Briar College. It may actually become difficult to notice Hampden-Sydney's all-maleness Thursday through Sunday, since we hear that the fraternity houses are usually filled with women from surrounding colleges: "I can't tell you how many parties we have had with a higher turnout of women," says a fraternity member.

Athletics and socializing are the other key facets of the Hampden-Sydney experience. Intercollegiate sports are popular, drawing in about a quarter of the students. The school is a member of the NCAA Division III and the Old Dominion Athletic Conference, with varsity teams in football, baseball, golf, tennis, soccer, cross country, basketball, and lacrosse. Over 70 percent of students participate in intramural sports such as flag football, soccer, basketball, and softball. Outdoor activities such as canoeing and rafting are also popular.

Some of the most popular school-sponsored clubs include the Union Philanthropic Society (a debate society founded in 1789 and the second-oldest literary society in America), the Glee Club, and the Outsiders Club (an outdoor recreation club).

One of Hampden-Sydney's most charming traditions is the tolling of an old hanging bell that signals the start of class each day. The bell tower itself is an historic landmark and is made from bricks taken from the homes of men instrumental in founding the school. But students admit the bell is also used for another (less charming) tradition: In the middle of winter, freshmen must run naked from their dorm to the middle of campus to ring the bell. "It is a rite of passage to finish their freshman year," explains an upperclassman.

Other schools to check out: Morehouse, Wabash, Davidson, University of the South, Washington and Lee.

THE EXPERTS SAY...

" The code of honor and gentlemanly conduct are a part of everything a Hampden-Sydney man does, in the classroom and on the playing field. "

" There's a good reason there are only three all-male colleges left: If you want to get a date, you must join a frat. "

HAMPSHIRE COLLEGE

893 West Street, Amherst, MA 01002
Admissions Phone: (413) 559-5471; (877) 937-4267 Fax: (413) 559-5631
Email: admissions@hampshire.edu
Website: www.hampshire.edu

General Info

Type of School: private, coed

Setting: small town

Academic Calendar: 4-1-4

Student Body

Full-Time Undergrads: 1,325
  Men: 42%, Women: 58%

Total Undergrad Population:
  African American: 3%
  Asian American: 4%
  Latino: 5%
  Native American: 1%
  Caucasian: 76%
  International: 3%
  Out-of-State: 86%
  Living Off-Campus: 8%

Academics

Full-Time Faculty: 115
  With Ph.D.: 90%

Part-Time Faculty: 27
  With Ph.D.: 33%

Student/Faculty Ratio: 11:1

Most Popular Majors:
  interdisciplinary
  visual and performing arts
  social sciences and history
  English

Freshmen Retention Rate: 79%

Graduation Rates:
  44% within four years
  63% within six years

Admissions

Regular Application Deadline: 1/15

Early Decision Deadline(s): 11/15

Early Action Deadline: 12/1

Fall Transfer Deadline: 3/1 (priority)

Spring Transfer Deadline: 11/15
  (priority)

Total # of Students Applied: 2,270
  Admitted: 1,246
  Enrolled: 391

# of Students Waitlisted: 389
  Students Accepting Place: 186
  Waitlisted Students Admitted: 1

Applied Early Decision: 84
  Early Decision Admitted: 62

Inside the Classroom

Students come to Hampshire College for the incredible academic freedom: You design your own interdisciplinary course of study, working closely with mentoring faculty. A young alumna states, "It's basically graduate school in an undergraduate setting." There are no grades and no majors. "Students will either hate it or love it," comments a California guidance counselor. Self-motivation is key: "It is up to each student to kick their own butt," says a student. A Hampshire official agrees: "To succeed at Hampshire, students need to be disciplined in their approach to their work in order to handle the demanding academic program."

In lieu of traditional academic departments, Hampshire is comprised of five interdisciplinary schools: social science; natural science; cognitive science; interdisciplinary arts; and humanities, arts, and cultural studies. The film, video, and creative writing programs are standouts; notable alumni include documentary filmmaker Ken Burns (*Jazz*), writer Jon Krakauer (*Into Thin Air*), and playwright Naomi Wallace (*One Flea Spare*). Hampshire's programs in the natural sciences are also very strong. As a member of the Five College Consortium, Hampshire students can also draw upon the considerable resources of nearby Smith, Amherst, Mount Holyoke, and UMass Amherst.

Hampshire students qualify for the B.A. degree by completing a full-time program composed of three levels of study. In Division I, Basic Studies, students study across Hampshire's five schools and complete four exams or projects. In Division II, the Concentration, students explore their chosen field through an individually designed program of courses, independent work, and internships or field studies. In Division III, Advanced Studies, seniors complete a major research or creative project centered on a specific topic, question, or idea. An alumnus quips, "You get not just the regular canon of college information, but also how to analyze it, absorb it, and make fun of it." In addition to these courses, students must include volunteer service to Hampshire or the surrounding community as part of their education. Students are encouraged to study off-campus or even to take time off to pursue other interests before completing their degree.

Too much freedom too fast can be overwhelming, so in fall 2002, Hampshire instituted a new first-year program (the first first-year program in the college's history) to provide a more supportive academic structure and improved advising. Every new student now enrolls in a small group tutorial, and the professor teaching the tutorial becomes the advisor to each of those students. "Emphasis is also being placed on linking academic and co-curricular activities to residential life, promoting a greater sense of community for students from their first year onward," a college official informs us.

Professors get a chance to know their students personally. Even the administrators make a real effort to connect with the students: The college president meets over breakfast with students once a week, according to one college official: "All students who would like to attend (and are willing to wake up that early) are welcome to come and talk with him about whatever is on their minds related to Hampshire."

Campus Environment

Hampshire's campus is as unconventional as its curriculum. The Eric Carle Museum of Children's Picture Book Art opened in November 2002: "It is adjacent to the Hampshire campus and is the latest addition to our 'Cultural Village' (independent institutions located on or adjacent to the campus that also provide academic and cultural opportunities for our students)," a college official informs us. She adds, "Hampshire has adopted and begun implementing a Sustainable Campus Plan, which will affect not only 'green' issues such as recycling and energy use, but also encompasses more complex issues involved in sustaining Hampshire itself—academically, socially, financially, and physically."

Residence halls are coed and are integrated with students from all classes. "Some students live in traditional residence halls and eat in the dining hall," says a college official. "Others live in 'mods' [college-maintained apartments on campus] of 8 to 12 students and do family-style cooking of their own meals." Overall, a high school guidance counselor rates the housing as "not very good," but at least overcrowding is usually not an issue. PETA has listed Hampshire among the 10 best campuses for vegans and vegetarians.

The town of Amherst is quaint but "boring." A free bus system transports students throughout the Five College system and to local areas during most of the day. All students are allowed to keep cars on campus (parking permits are required).

Student Life

The atmosphere at Hampshire is decidedly liberal. Activism is encouraged (and is looked upon quite favorably by the Admissions Office, by the way): "Many students at Hampshire are activists concerned about social justice issues; this is a tradition that goes back to the founding of the school," states a college official. And Hampshire students expect no less from their faculty and administration: Just weeks before the war with Iraq started, with the reasoning that "saying nothing models a behavior that contradicts Hampshire's mission to encourage active, well-thought-out civic engagement," Hampshire's president publicly expressed his personal opposition to the upcoming war, and the faculty passed a resolution in opposition to the impending war which they then sent to President Bush and to the senators and representatives from Massachusetts.

While sports are not big at Hampshire, the outdoors program (climbing, etc.) is pretty popular. Other popular campus organizations: Community Council ("functions like student government, only it includes all segments of campus and not just students"); Community Bike Collective ("makes 'yellow bikes' available for loan on campus"); FISH (Forum of International Students at Hampshire); and Mixed Nuts (a food co-op). The LGBT community is active on campus. If pot and acid are your thing, we hear that "it's really easy to sit around and get high" (although beer isn't the staple it is at most other colleges). However, students report that peer pressure is low.

At Hampshire, "people learn not just to make a living, but to make a life," says a college official. "They don't find jobs after graduation; they become entrepreneurial enough to create their own dream jobs."

Other schools to check out: Bard, Reed, Antioch, Bennington, Marlboro.

Test Scores (middle 50%):
SAT Verbal: 600–700
SAT Math: 560–660
ACT Comp: 25–29

HS Rank of Entering Freshmen:
Top 10%: 30%
Top 25%: 67%
Top 50%: 94%

Avg. HS GPA: 3.47

Costs (2003–04)

Tuition and Fees: $29,642
Room & Board: $7,689

THE EXPERTS SAY...

" Hampshire's signature inquiry-based, student-directed learning is not for everyone. Among other things, the admissions committee looks for evidence of writing ability, creativity, curiosity, and self-discipline. "

" Hampshire students are accepting of everything except mainstream tastes and right-wing politics. "

Inst. Aid (est. 2003–04)

Institutional Aid, Need-Based:
$11,873,765

Institutional Aid, Non-Need-Based:
$287,010

FT Undergrads Receiving Aid: 54%
Avg. Amount per Student: $24,615

FT Undergrads Receiving Non-Need-Based Scholarship or Grant Aid: 2%
Avg. Amount per Student: $4,990

Of Those Receiving Any Aid:

Rec. Need-Based Scholarship or Grant Aid: 100%
Average Award: $18,260

Rec. Need-Based Self-Help Aid: 99%
Average Award: $6,355

Upon Graduation, Avg. Loan Debt per Student: $16,975

Financial Aid Deadline: 2/1

HAMPTON UNIVERSITY

Hampton University, Hampton, VA 23668
Admissions Phone: (757) 727-5328; (800) 624-3328 Fax: (757) 727-5095
Email: admit@hamptonu.edu
Website: hamptonu.edu

General Info

Type of School: private, coed
Setting: urban
Academic Calendar: semester

Student Body

Full-Time Undergrads: 4,475
    Men: 37%, Women: 63%

Part-Time Undergrads: 323
    Men: 50%, Women: 50%

Total Undergrad Population:
    African American: 96%
    Asian American: <1%
    Latino: <1%
    Native American: <1%
    Caucasian: 3%
    International: <1%
    Out-of-State: 69%
    Living Off-Campus: 41%
    In Fraternities: 5%
    In Sororities: 4%

Graduate and First-Professional
    Students: 811

Academics

Full-Time Faculty: 284
    With Ph.D.: 83%

Part-Time Faculty: 116

Student/Faculty Ratio: 16:1

Most Popular Majors:
    biology (10%)
    psychology (9%)
    management (9%)
    mass media arts (8%)
    computer science (7%)

Freshmen Retention Rate: 85%

Graduation Rates:
    39% within four years
    58% within six years

Admissions

Regular Application Deadline: 3/1
    (priority)

Early Action Deadline: 12/1

Fall Transfer Deadline: 3/1 (priority)

Spring Transfer Deadline: 12/1
    (priority)

Total # of Students Applied: 5,696
    Admitted: 3,505
    Enrolled: 1,050

Inside the Classroom

"Hampton has the best campus of all the HBCU's (Historically Black Colleges/Universities)!" proclaims one proud student, who goes on to say that "the students here are really focused and intelligent." And they have to be, for the scenically beautiful school, steeped in history (it was founded in 1868 during the Reconstruction Period following the Civil War) offers rigorous and challenging programs for African American youth. The six schools that encompass Hampton University (business; engineering and technology; liberal arts and education; nursing; pharmacy; and science) offer 47 undergraduate majors. The most popular majors are biology, psychology, management, and mass media. Other strong programs at Hampton include computer science, prelaw, and pharmacy. Hampton has the double distinction of being the third leading producer of black medical school entrants (according to the National Network for Health Science Partnerships) in the nation as well as being the first historically black college or university to offer the Ph.D. in nursing. Many of Hampton's programs and organizations focus on issues in the African American community.

Personalized instruction and attention from the instructors at Hampton is made possible by the student to faculty ratio, which is only 16:1. Over 80 percent of full-time faculty hold doctoral degrees in their respective fields and bring a wealth of real-world experience to the classroom.

Core requirements at Hampton include: cultures and civilization, English, freshman orientation, concepts of mathematics, science and technology, social science, oral communications, health, and physical education. Foreign language is also included in the core for a number of selected majors. University 101 is a course that provides freshmen with a history of the school. Study abroad and a semester in Washington are two options many upper-division Hampton students pursue.

Campus Environment

The 204-acre campus sits on the banks of the Hampton River and is described as a "treasure in its own right," with its waterfront and historic buildings. Four buildings, including Memorial Church, the Mansion House, Virginia-Cleveland Hall, and Wigwam, are included in the Virginia Landmark Register. Fifteen acres of the campus are designated a National Historic District. Emancipation Oak was the site of the first Southern reading of President Lincoln's Emancipation Proclamation. The peaceful shade of this majestic oak on the Hampton campus served as the first classroom for newly freed men and women eager for an education. The National Geographic Society designates the Emancipation Oak as one of the 10 Great Trees of the World.

The Hampton University Museum, established in 1868, is the oldest African American museum in this country, housing African, African American, and Native American Art with over 9,000 artifacts in its collection. The library system includes the George Peabody Collection of 28,000 items by and about African Americans as well as the new Academic Technology Mall. Campus radio and cable news stations afford media majors hands-on experience in their prospective careers.

Freshmen typically live in first-year only dorms, but, as housing is allotted only on a first-come first-serve basis, only 70 percent of freshmen and 59 percent of the total student body actually live on campus. However, two brand-new residence halls (completed in February 2002) should alleviate crowding on campus. An office of off-campus housing helps students in finding other living arrangements. "Most students find off-campus housing to be cheaper and more readily available than on-campus housing," says a student.

Recent construction and additions to the Hampton campus include: additions to Armstrong Stadium, (1,800 more seats for the arena named after the university founder, Union General Samuel Chapman Armstrong), a new Student Center (completed in 2001), and the two new residence halls. The Scripps Howard Center for Journalism is currently under construction.

Student Life

A typical Hamptonian is described by one student as a "middle-class African American student, with parents that have attended college, many that are professionals." More than 4,500 undergraduates come to Hampton from 49 states and 35 territories and nations.

The social scene at Hampton is divided between on-campus activities and Greek life. "Sororities and fraternities constitute much of the social life here at Hampton," says a student. "This is because sororities and fraternities sponsor most of the social activities. Since our school is predominately African American, our African American-based sororities and fraternities ('The Divine Nine') attract many," explains another. While the frats throw many parties, the student union board also hosts on-campus functions that include movie nights and school-sponsored parties. Many students are involved in Christian or "church-related" activities such as Bible Studies, Praise Jams, Noon Day Prayer, etc. "Drinking and drugs are not a major factor because Hampton has a zero tolerance policy and you will be expelled immediately if caught with either," says a student.

There are a number of activities for students to become involved in. Student government, the college radio and TV stations, and community service programs are the most popular. Many students volunteer in the Hampton roads community, tutoring disadvantaged children or mentoring them as Big Brothers and Sisters. Sports are popular as well, with basketball and football being the big varsity draws. From 1999–2001, Hampton University was named the most winning Division I sports program in the state of Virginia. Students come to the games as much to see the Marching Force band as the players. There are intramural teams for nearly every sport, and soccer and track and field are enjoyed all year. Students also enjoy biking and rollerblading around campus in nice weather.

Homecoming weekend and parent's weekend are two big annual events that draw the Hampton University community together. The new student center which acts as a gym, conference facility, and conference hall is also a unifying force on campus. Popular student getaways include Virginia Beach, 30 miles away, or Washington DC, 2 hours away.

Other schools to check out: Tuskegee, Spelman, Morehouse, Howard, Xavier, Fisk.

Test Scores (middle 50%):
SAT Verbal: 490–590
SAT Math: 480–580
ACT Comp: 20–24
HS Rank of Entering Freshmen:
Top 10%: 20%
Top 25%: 45%
Top 50%: 95%
Avg. HS GPA: 3.0

Costs (2003–04)

Tuition and Fees: $12,864
Room & Board: $6,118
Payment Plan(s): deferred payment plan

THE EXPERTS SAY...

" This prestigious HBCU is a premed's dream: Hampton is a leader in sending African American students to med school. "

" The 'Divine Nine' fraternity social scene is hot because the campus is dry. Take care: you will be expelled if you drink or take drugs on campus. "

Graduates

Going to Graduate School:
40% Within One Year

Accepting Job Offer:
44% at time of graduation

Companies Recruiting On Campus:
376

HANOVER COLLEGE

P.O. Box 108, Hanover, IN 47243-0108
Admissions Phone: (812) 866-7021; (800) 213-2178 Fax: (812) 866-7098
Email: admission@hanover.edu
Website: www.hanover.edu

General Info

Type of School: private, coed,
  Presbyterian

Setting: rural

Academic Calendar: 4-4-1

Student Body

Full-Time Undergrads: 984
  Men: 46%, Women: 54%

Part-Time Undergrads: 5
  Men: 40%, Women: 60%

Total Undergrad Population:
  African American: 2%
  Asian American: 3%
  Latino: 2%
  Native American: <1%
  Caucasian: 89%
  International: 4%
  Out-of-State: 29%
  Living Off-Campus: 3%
  In Fraternities: 33%
  In Sororities: 44%

Academics

Full-Time Faculty: 85
  With Ph.D.: 99%

Part-Time Faculty: 6
  With Ph.D.: 50%

Student/Faculty Ratio: 10:1

Most Popular Majors:
  business administration (11%)
  psychology (11%)
  sociology (10%)
  biology (8%)
  communications (8%)

Completing 2 or More Majors: 9%

Freshmen Retention Rate: 75%

Graduation Rates:
  65% within four years
  67% within six years

Admissions

Regular Application Deadline: 5/1;
  3/1 (priority)

Transfer Application Deadline: rolling

Early Action Deadline: 12/1

Total # of Students Applied: 1,364
  Admitted: 1,073
  Enrolled: 292

# of Students Waitlisted: 92
  Students Accepting Place: 86
  Waitlisted Students Admitted: 55

Inside the Classroom

Founded in 1827, Hanover has the distinction of being the oldest private college in Indiana. Staying true to its roots as a community-oriented liberal arts college, it has never grown beyond its small size and continues to place students in either grad schools or their chosen careers at a rate well over 90 percent—significantly above the national average. The philosophy at Hanover is to instill learning in a small, intellectual community where some of the most rewarding moments in learning extend beyond the classroom.

Hanover awards the B.A. degree in 29 fields of study: Humanities, sciences, social sciences, and arts are all well represented. Preprofessional programs in law, business, dentistry, education, medicine, and divinity are also offered. The educational experience here is designed to be intensive and comprehensive. Courses are required in a number of different subject areas, and the goal of many programs is to make students not only experts but also leaders. Internships, independent study, and specialized senior projects are available in most majors.

An interesting fact cited by one student is that the college has a very good geology program—a rare find for a private college in the relatively rockless Plains states. Facilities are well equipped, and class sizes are so small after the introductory-level courses that one-on-one instruction becomes commonplace. It's also not uncommon to be asked to help professors with their own research. Another unusual aspect of Hanover for all majors is that not only are professors accessible—which is to be expected at a small school—but more than half of them live in campus housing. Try to wear something besides your ripped jeans if you're invited over for a meal—it does happen.

Hanover also has a surprising number of study abroad options for a school of its size. Students can elect to study European culture in Australia, Belgium, France, Spain, Mexico, and Turkey. Other off-campus programs are available in Washington, DC and at Stillman College in Tuscaloosa, Alabama.

Campus Environment

Located on 650 wooded acres that overlook the Ohio River, the Hanover campus is nicely landscaped, with most of its 34 buildings reflecting the Georgian style of architecture. Roads, pathways, and buildings are arrayed in a neat grid pattern, with the science buildings clustered near the river, the rest of the academic buildings and dorms in the middle of campus, and the athletic fields, track, and tennis courts forming a wide green expanse on the fringes of the college.

The Duggan Library contains over 250,000 print volumes, 200,000 documents, and 5,000 audiovisual items to support student research, as well as numerous electronic databases and full text files. If you're clueless about how to use all of these resources, don't worry: Librarians provide reference and research assistance and classroom instruction on the use of the library's resources.

Dormitories are small in size: The largest, Crowe Hall, houses 140 students, while tiny College House has a capacity of 20. Most dorms are single-sex, with Parker and Wiley Halls serving as coed dorms. The Greenwood Suites and the new Ogle Center offer suite-like living spaces for upperclassmen, and three theme houses allow students with a common interest to live in close proximity. One student wasn't pleased about the number of options available to students, citing a big demand for non-dorm living that is not satisfied by the theme and Greek houses.

The campus dining hall gets mixed reviews from students. One student cites the age-old maxim that humans will consume anything—and enjoy it—once they're hungry enough. Another says that long lines form on nights when chicken nuggets and pasta dishes are served for dinner. Variety is consistently cited as a strong point. The Underground snack bar located in the Brown Campus Center reportedly does a brisk business.

Student Life

With a small student body, greeting other students by name on the way to class is not only expected, it's inevitable. Small parties and hanging out in small groups are the norm here, as are movie-watching and school-sponsored social functions. Other parties are thrown by the Greeks, who comprise four frats and four sororities. Unlike many campuses, Hanover's fraternal organizations are blessed in that all have their own chapter houses. Hanover students are also active in student government, publications, theater, music, and a variety of special interest clubs.

In the world of sports, men and women compete in the Indiana Collegiate Athletic Conference. Teams for both men and women include basketball, cross country, golf, soccer, tennis, and track. Men can also play football and baseball, while women can compete in softball and volleyball. Men's and women's intramural choices—in which faculty have also been known to play—include flag football, physical-fitness contests, basketball, volleyball, and softball. There are also facilities on campus for swimming, racquetball, and other sports.

The neighboring town of Madison, a few minutes off campus, is historic, pretty, and worth a visit or two. Fortunately, more excitement can be found in road trips to Louisville, Cincinnati, and Indianapolis, which are 45, 70, and 95 miles from campus, respectively.

Other schools to check out: DePauw, Wittenberg, Goshen, Wheaton (IL).

Test Scores (middle 50%):
SAT Verbal: 510–630
SAT Math: 530–630
ACT Comp: 22–27
HS Rank of Entering Freshmen:
Top 10%: 42%
Top 25%: 71%
Top 50%: 95%

Costs (2004–5)

Tuition and Fees: $20,600
Room & Board: $6,200
Payment Plan(s): installment plan

THE EXPERTS SAY...

" The community experience is what Hanover is all about. Humanities, sciences, social sciences, and arts are very strong here. "

" This is no place for social claustrophobics. If you don't like who you're studying with, this could be a long four years. "

Inst. Aid (est. 2003–04)

Institutional Aid, Need-Based: $8,051,122

Institutional Aid, Non-Need-Based: $1,633,296

FT Undergrads Receiving Aid: 86%
Avg. Amount per Student: $14,788

FT Undergrads Receiving Non-Need-Based Scholarship or Grant Aid: 14%
Avg. Amount per Student: $15,625

Of Those Receiving Any Aid:

Rec. Need-Based Scholarship or Grant Aid: 100%
Average Award: $12,594

Rec. Need-Based Self-Help Aid: 57%
Average Award: $3,815

Upon Graduation, Avg. Loan Debt per Student: $11,583

Financial Aid Deadline: 3/10 (priority)

Graduates

Going to Graduate School:
31% Within One Year

Companies Recruiting On Campus: 57

Alumni Giving: 35%

HARVARD UNIVERSITY

Byerly Hall, 8 Garden Street, Cambridge, MA 02138
Admissions Phone: (617) 495-1551 Fax: (617) 495-8821
Email: college@fas.harvard.edu Website: college.harvard.edu
Application Website: adm-is.fas.harvard.edu

Note: Info. not verified by school

General Info

Type of School: private, coed

Setting: urban

Academic Calendar: semester

Student Body

Full-Time Undergrads: 6,637
  Men: 53%, Women: 47%

Part-Time Undergrads: 12
  Men: 50%, Women: 50%

Total Undergrad Population:
  African American: 8%
  Asian American: 18%
  Latino: 8%
  Native American: 1%
  Caucasian: 42%
  International: 7%
  Out-of-State: 83%
  Living Off-Campus: 4%

Graduate and First-Professional
  Students: 13,516

Academics

Full-Time Faculty: 775
  With Ph.D.: 100%

Part-Time Faculty: 180

Student/Faculty Ratio: 9:1

Most Popular Majors:
  psychology
  economics
  political science and government
  English language and literature
  biology

Freshmen Retention Rate: 96%

Graduation Rates:
  83% within four years
  92% within six years

Admissions

Regular Application Deadline: 1/1;
  12/15 (priority)

Early Action Deadline: 11/1

Fall Transfer Deadline: 3/1

Total # of Students Applied: 19,609
  Admitted: 2,066
  Enrolled: 1,627

Waitlist Available

Inside the Classroom

Harvard University is the oldest and most prestigious school in the country—as well as the most "overrated," according to many guidance counselors. "Too much money!!!" exclaims one counselor (and that was *before* Harvard announced that it's raising its tuition by 5.5 percent, the biggest percentage increase in a decade). Harvard's alumni include Nobel Prize winners, presidents, poets, and giants of industry. "My freshman class of 20 students had two Westinghouse science winners, an all-American athlete, a world-class musician, and the granddaughter of a famous professor—and me," says a young alumna. "Pretty fast company." Guidance counselors call it the school for valedictorians, but applicants with straight A's and 1600 SATs have been turned down. So what does it take to get in? Well, being a legacy helps: According to the *Wall Street Journal*, Harvard accepts 40 percent of legacy applicants (compared with an 11 percent overall acceptance rate), and the Dean of Admissions personally reads all applications from children of alumni.

Stress and competition run high at Harvard. "The premed students were ruthless, and the classroom sounded like there were constantly birds pecking at the windows because they all had these four-color pens so they could take down their notes in different colors," a grad relates. But a student points out, "There's the sense that you can get things accomplished if you try." The night before finals, to relieve the incredible stress, students remove all "nonessential" clothing, and run through campus.

Harvard is a highly decentralized university: Much of the power rests with the deans at the university's 10 schools. Classes can be enormous, and you may have trouble getting the courses you want. ("Survival of the fittest is the rule," says one student.) You may have to beg, plead, and hustle your way into the upper-level courses taught by the noted faculty. Another drawback is "finals after winter recess." Professors "can be detached from their classes." "I found that the big time profs were usually too involved in their own research to care unless you were the shining pupil," states a grad. "However, this was not universal and my chem prof, who had a Nobel prize, would eat lunch with students every Thursday."

Harvard recently installed a new president who promises to use the school's $18 billion endowment to revamp undergraduate education, hire new professors, spread financial aid more evenly, and boost science research. In a new program, Harvard will give $14 million in "presidential scholarships" to 200 to 300 graduate students interested in public service or research careers. It will also offer below-market-rate loans to all 12,000 of its graduate and professional students. The university is considering an expansion of its online course schedule—after it decides whether one needs to be physically present in the classroom to get a Harvard degree.

Campus Environment

Guidance counselors rate Harvard's old and elegant campus as one of the most beautiful in the nation, and Harvard's massive endowment keeps it that way. Most freshmen are housed together in a large building around Harvard Yard. After the first year, most students move to several "houses," each with its own appeal. Each house holds about 400 students and has its own dining room and library. "A lot of people will [complain] about housing, but it was amazing," a grad raves. "My rooms at school were so much bigger and nicer than my room at home."

Many students describe Cambridge as "the perfect college town," but "very few people live off campus and it's pretty expensive in Cambridge," an alum informs us. "Most of the people living off campus were those who deemed themselves too damn cool to live in the lowly dorms." Neighboring Somerville is a bit less expensive. Though Boston is just a quick subway ride away, many say they rarely go there, but those who do make the trip enjoy its nightlife, museums, and history.

Student Life

While Harvard prides itself on its ethnically diverse population, students claim that there's not a lot of cultural diversity. Explains a young alumna, "I thought the campus was quite WASPish, conservatively liberal, too politically correct, and teeming with nerds trying to prove to themselves that they were still smart and yet cool... There were *very, very* few 'freaks and weirdos'—the three kids with pink hair all hung together."

Because of all the studying required, the social scene is tame. One senior notes that "it's difficult to date, for many reasons." There are no fraternities or sororities (in keeping with the university policy that an organization must allow both men and women), though there are exclusive Finals Clubs ("old-school good ol' boy clubs"). There's drinking, but according to a study by the U.S. Department of Education, drug and alcohol violations at Harvard are (predictably) lower than at most other schools. When students do take time out from studying, they often go to movies or concerts instead of wild parties. Still... "Imagine the nerd of your high school," remarks a recent grad. "Then imagine a school of them. Then imagine that freshman year, they all start drinking for the first time. Nerd love ensues."

While sports may not be the first thing (or second, or third) that come to mind when you think of Harvard, the university does boast the largest Division I athletics program in the country. The men's squash team has won 31 national championships, but students say that football is the only sport that gets much attention. Some of the more popular nonathletic clubs on campus are the Institute of Politics, the Immediate Gratification Players (an improv group), the Glee Club, and the Computer Society.

"People will either drool or hate you when you say 'I went to Harvard,'" quips a grad. A student adds, "Anything amazing you can think of, there's someone here who has already done it." A guidance counselor reflects, "I expected to hate it, thinking I would find arrogance and elitism. I saw neither, but rather the best we know put into practice." An alum sums it up: "It's Harvard. You don't say no to Harvard. I think for me, I would have been happier as the shining star at a lesser known college than one of the masses at Harvard, but even knowing that, I probably still would have gone to Harvard."

Other schools to check out: Yale, Princeton, U Penn, Stanford, Georgetown.

Test Scores (middle 50%):
SAT Verbal: 700–800
SAT Math: 700–790
ACT Comp: 30–34
ACT English: 29–34
ACT Math: 30–34

HS Rank of Entering Freshmen:
Top 10%: 90%
Top 25%: 98%
Top 50%: 100%

Costs (2003–04)
Tuition and Fees: $29,060
Room & Board: $8,868

Graduates
Alumni Giving: 68%

THE EXPERTS SAY...

" A lot is happening on the Harvard campus, including tuition hikes, a new president's vision for the university, and a major new financial aid initiative for grad students. "

" Yes, it's expensive, it's cut-throat... but, at the end of the day, it's the one and only Harvard. "

HARVEY MUDD COLLEGE

301 East 12th Street, Claremont, CA 91711-5990
Admissions Phone: (909) 621-8011 Fax: (909) 607-7046
Email: admission@hmc.edu
Website: www.hmc.edu

General Info

Type of School: private, coed

Setting: suburban

Academic Calendar: semester

Student Body

Full-Time Undergrads: 700
  Men: 68%, Women: 32%

Part-Time Undergrads: 4
  Men: 75%, Women: 25%

Total Undergrad Population:
  African American: <1%
  Asian American: 18%
  Latino: 5%
  Native American: <1%
  Caucasian: 57%
  International: 3%
  Out-of-State: 57%
  Living Off-Campus: 5%

Academics

Full-Time Faculty: 83
  With Ph.D.: 100%

Part-Time Faculty: 8
  With Ph.D.: 88%

Student/Faculty Ratio: 8:1

Most Popular Majors:
  engineering (26%)
  computer science (17%)
  physics (14%)
  mathematics (11%)
  chemistry (8%)

Completing 2 or More Majors: 7%

Freshmen Retention Rate: 94%

Graduation Rates:
  72% within four years
  84% within six years

Admissions

Regular Application Deadline: 1/15

Early Decision Deadline(s): 11/15

Early Action Available:

Fall Transfer Deadline: 4/1

Total # of Students Applied: 1,773
  Admitted: 709
  Enrolled: 191

# of Students Waitlisted: 566
  Students Accepting Place: 111

Applied Early Decision: 85
  Early Decision Admitted: 47

Inside the Classroom

Question: When is a tech school more than a tech school? Answer: When it's within the Claremont Colleges system.

Harvey Mudd College is the school for science and engineering in the Claremont system, as well as one of the top schools for those fields in the nation. Undergrads can take one of six majors: biology, chemistry, computer science, engineering, math, or physics. Engineering is by far the most popular, drawing more than a quarter of the student body. While HMC specializes in technical studies, it also insists on giving students a well-rounded education. All "Mudders" take one third of their credits in humanities and social sciences. And being that the school is in the Claremont system, students can freely cross register at the other schools (Claremont McKenna, Pitzer, Pomona, and Scripps). All in all, HMC students have many more opportunities than they would otherwise have at just a tech school.

With only around 700 undergraduates, the enrollment is significantly smaller than at most tech schools. That translates into a real hands-on education. Professors teach all the classes, which often have fewer than 20 students. And for those that are larger, professors often lead small review sessions. Students must devote one-third of their study to a common technical core, which includes four semesters of math, three of physics, two of chemistry, and one of computer science, as well as two electives. The remaining third is taken in their chosen major.

The academics are rigorous here. One junior says, "In high school, I cruised through the classes. When I got to Mudd, I felt like I was starting several steps behind everyone. I struggled the entire time I was there just to catch up." Facilities are quite extensive for a college of its size. All of Harvey Mudd's full-time faculty (about 80) have Ph.D.s, and all are engaged in research in addition to their teaching responsibilities. For the college as a whole, upper-division class and lab section size averages 15–20 students. Faculty-student interaction is particularly close as students become involved in project research and design.

Most students take five courses each semester, which require long hours of problem solving, lab work, and preparation outside of class. Rather than becoming competitive with one another, the grueling labors they share foster a sense of camaraderie among the students. The school's honor code creates an atmosphere of mutual trust and respect, with most computers and labs open 24/7. As campy as that sounds, students rave about the level of trust and open access.

Students at HMC are encouraged to round out their theoretical studies with practical applications. The unique 'clinic' programs provide real-world work experience, where teams of four or five undergrads tackle problems submitted and funded by outside clients (In true HMC form, students came up with alternative landscape designs for greenery on campus that would conserve water and resources). In 2000, the school started a "Harvey Mudd Fellows" project that helps high school students from disadvantaged areas learn more about science, engineering, and math. Many students also conduct independent research, often publishing the results. Their hard work generally pays off, as about three out of four go on to graduate school; 41

percent of all HMC alumni have earned a Ph.D. (the nation's highest percentage), according to research data from the National Research Council and the U.S. Department of Education.

Campus Environment

Located in the suburb of Claremont, 30 minutes from Los Angeles, Mudd has a small town feel. In some ways, Claremont is more like a New England college town than a suburb of LA—mostly residential, espresso bars, Victorian homes—but without the frigid northeast temperatures. We hear that the campus architecture is far from beautiful (it's even ugly, many say), though efforts are made to keep the grounds lush and green.

On campus, freshmen are all mixed in with upperclass students in all residence halls. All freshmen must live on campus, and most students seem happy with their room placements. We're told that very few people move around. After the first year, housing is not guaranteed, though 96 percent of students live on campus. All dorms have been renovated within the last six years. While cars are permitted, they're not essential: You'll see lots of skateboards, rollerblades, and bikes around campus.

Certain dorms, however, are known to be "wilder" than others (of course, it's all relative). Weekend partying is not unheard of. Those who want other activities have many options, though, particularly within the other Claremont schools, which share a common 550-acre campus with HMC. Becoming involved in activities and organizations at the other schools gives students a break from their fellow HMC techies and a chance to mingle with students who have many different interests.

Student Life

One of the first things you notice here is that there are a lot more men than women here. In terms of diversity, you'll find significant numbers of Asian Americans and Latinos, though noticeably few African Americans. And yes, there are plenty of eccentric computer geeks, though most do let loose on weekends.

Because Mudders are so focused on their work, there isn't much of an active social scene on campus. Proving the point of the "eccentric" personality here, the signature Mudd group is Gonzo Unicycle Madness, a unicycle riders club. One of the most noteworthy traditions here is "Fosters Run," which occurs every spring on the switch to daylight savings time: With a free strawberry donut as their goal, students unicycle to a donut shop nearly nine miles away.

Students also hang out at the Muddhole, a student center with lounges, video games, fast food, pool tables, and table tennis. Rather than becoming involved with intercollegiate sports, more students play intramural sports against teams from other Claremont campuses. A sporting event that is entirely a Harvey Mudd tradition, though, is the Five Class competition, a goofy—if not grueling—day of bizarre relay races involving food, mathematical abilities, and occasionally a bit of physical prowess.

THE EXPERTS SAY...

" HMC offers a real hands-on education, with real-life clinic projects to put theory into practice. Plus HMC has all the benefits of cross-registration with all the schools in the Claremont system. "

" Do you really want to join the Gonzo Unicycle Madness club, or participate in doughnut races? Oh, those wacky engineers! "

HASTINGS COLLEGE

800 Turner Ave., Hastings, NE 68901-7696
Admissions Phone: (402) 461-7403; (800) 532-7642 Fax: (402) 461-7490
Email: admissions@hastings.edu Website: hastings.edu
Application Website: hastings.edu/html/admiss/admissions5.stm

General Info

Type of School: private, coed,
  Presbyterian (USA)
Setting: small town
Academic Calendar: 4-1-4

Student Body

Full-Time Undergrads: 1,054
  Men: 52%, Women: 48%
Part-Time Undergrads: 20
  Men: 35%, Women: 65%
Total Undergrad Population:
  African American: 2%
  Asian American: 1%
  Latino: 2%
  Native American: <1%
  Caucasian: 92%
  International: 1%
  Out-of-State: 23%
  Living Off-Campus: 45%
  In Fraternities: 16%
  In Sororities: 32%
Graduate and First-Professional
  Students: 39

Academics

Full-Time Faculty: 80
  With Ph.D.: 74%
Part-Time Faculty: 37
  With Ph.D.: 22%
Student/Faculty Ratio: 13:1
Most Popular Majors:
  teacher education (22%)
  business administration (20%)
  psychology (12%)
  visual and performing arts (8%)
  biology (7%)
Completing 2 or More Majors: 53%
Freshmen Retention Rate: 73%
Graduation Rates:
  51% within four years
  64% within six years

Admissions

Regular Application Deadline: 8/1;
  3/1 (priority)
Fall Transfer Deadline: 8/1,
  3/1 (priority)
Spring Transfer Deadline: 1/1,
  10/1 (priority)

Inside the Classroom

Affiliated with the Presbyterian Church, Hastings College is a small school in the heart of Nebraska. Known primarily for its liberal arts and communications programs, Hastings offers over 68 majors in the arts and sciences and a dozen programs for preprofessionals. Students can choose between a traditional course of study with core requirements and concentrations and a personalized study program where they can tailor their own major with faculty guidance. Core requirements include social sciences, the fine arts, health and wellness, a foreign language, communication, math and sciences, and the humanities. The workload is tough but manageable, and Hastings students are generally serious about their education. A sophomore says, "Competitiveness is alive and well at Hastings, but it is healthy competition."

Hastings's small size is its strength: Students receive individualized attention in their studies right from the start in its student development program. Students are trained extensively in study skills as freshmen and are counseled as they adjust to college life. This nurturing continues throughout their four years, as their development is carefully looked after by advisors and counselors. We hear this supportive atmosphere extends to the classroom as well. "Our professors are awesome!" gushes a business major. "You can get in touch with almost all of them at any time you desire."

Most students are eligible to receive lower- and upper-division credit for internship experiences. Campus departments occasionally allow students to serve as interns, and the career services department manages a service-learning program through AmeriCorps. Hastings also operates a social research center where students can receive hands-on experience that includes polling for area organizations. Additional opportunities exist for premed students, who can get on-the-job experience at the hospital in Hastings.

Campus Environment

Located two and a half hours west of Omaha, the campus features 105 acres of green landscaping and red brick buildings. McCormick Hall, which is listed in the National Register of Historic Places, is the oldest structure on the grounds, while new structures seem to be popping up everywhere. The school recently completed construction on its $14.5 million sports complex as well as a sports arena/educational center that houses up-to-date athletic facilities, offices, classrooms, and a computer lab. But perhaps the crown jewel of the campus is the Gray Center for the Communication Arts. Easily found on campus by its large satellite dishes, the center houses a computerized newsroom, two television studios, three photo labs, a radio station, classrooms, and labs for video and audio production. And if Hastings has a small, family-like feel, then the Hazelrigg Student Union serves as the students' living room: Providing eating facilities, places to relax, meeting rooms for student clubs, and a 24-hour study lounge, the building also has a new coffee room that overlooks a Japanese garden.

All students must live on campus or with local family unless they're over 21, married, or have dependents. "Most freshmen are paired with freshmen," we're told, "but some are paired with upperclassmen." The dorms are mostly three-story halls that house around 100 students. Each is single-sex except for Altman Hall, where women live on the south end of the hall and men on the north. In a nod to the college's Christian roots, there are strict guidelines that restrict the times when students of the opposite sex visit one another—much to many students' chagrin. Aesthetics of the dorms range from the elegant Georgian style of Taylor Hall to the red-brick bunker of Weyer Hall. At least one student we spoke to had major gripes about the quality of on-campus housing, calling it "terrible." She explains: "The dorms have entirely too many rules, cost entirely too much, come with terrible food, and do not have adequate adult role models living in them." Perhaps many Hastings students agree with her, as it seems most juniors and seniors jump at the opportunity to escape to houses off campus. All students may keep cars, and most do, since parking permits are free and there's no public transportation besides a train station two miles away in Hastings.

The town of Hastings is a former wagon stop on the Oregon Trail that doesn't offer much for students. "There is not much to do in Hastings from the college student's point of view," a student confirms. Locally famous as the home of the man who invented Kool-Aid, the town throws a Kool-Aid Days festival each August. And former hyperactive children and future diabetics shouldn't miss the Hastings Museum, which has a permanent exhibit where everyone can learn about the sad fate of Kool-Aid pie fillings and ice cream mixes.

Student Life

The social life at Hastings is relatively quiet. "Don't get me wrong," a student says, "Hastings College students have their fair share of fun, but they are ethical about [their] actions." With few other options to let off steam, "a lot of students drink," we're told. There are four fraternities and five sororities (no Greek housing, though) who throw some fun parties. Student organizations and clubs also chip in with their own functions. There are more than 60 of these to choose from, with a sprinkling of religious clubs adding flavor to the usual types like choral groups, student newspaper, the campus radio station, music ensembles, and theater clubs. The forensics team is consistently recognized as one of the best in the nation.

Campus traditions include the annual Boar's Head Dinner, a formal, sit-down occasion where Christmas music is played, faculty and administrators do the serving, and a student walks through the candle-lit dining hall carrying the head of a boar (best not to ask too many questions about this one). Another favorite tradition is the May Fete, a five-day festival that features an interfraternity singing competition, games, picnics, and dances.

With all the beautiful new facilities, it's no wonder that sports are important at Hastings. Football games draw big crowds, as does the excellent women's basketball team, which won the 2002 NAIA Division II national championship. Intramurals are also popular on campus, with nearly everyone playing one sport or another.

Other schools to check out: Cornell College, Hiram, Allegheny, Wittenberg, Gustavus Adolphus.

Total # of Students Applied: 1,553
  Admitted: 1,236
  Enrolled: 405

Test Scores (middle 50%):
  SAT Verbal: 460–650
  SAT Math: 490–600
  ACT Comp: 20–26
  ACT English: 20–26
  ACT Math: 20–27

THE EXPERTS SAY...

" Preprofessional programs are popular at this relatively inexpensive school. "

" Anyone who enjoys Kool-Aid (or Lord of the Flies) might get a kick out of Hastings. "

HS Rank of Entering Freshmen:
  Top 10%: 25%
  Top 25%: 35%
  Top 50%: 75%

Avg. HS GPA: 3.2

Costs (2004–5)

Tuition and Fees: $16,290

Room & Board: $4,760

Payment Plan(s): installment plan, pre-payment plan

Inst. Aid (est. 2003–04)

Institutional Aid, Need-Based: $3,299,302

Institutional Aid, Non-Need-Based: $1,500,344

FT Undergrads Receiving Aid: 73%
  Avg. Amount per Student: $11,812

FT Undergrads Receiving Non-Need-Based Scholarship or Grant Aid: 25%
  Avg. Amount per Student: $7,289

Of Those Receiving Any Aid:

Rec. Need-Based Scholarship or Grant Aid: 99%
  Average Award: $8,402

Rec. Need-Based Self-Help Aid: 83%
  Average Award: $4,203

Upon Graduation, Avg. Loan Debt per Student: $15,778

Financial Aid Deadline: rolling, 5/1 (priority)

Graduates

Going to Graduate School: 16% Within One Year

Companies Recruiting On Campus: 49

Alumni Giving: 38%

HAVERFORD COLLEGE

370 W. Lancaster Avenue, Haverford, PA 19041-1392
Admissions Phone: (610) 896-1350 Fax: (610) 896-1338
Email: admitme@haverford.edu Website: www.haverford.edu
Application Website: www.haverford.edu/admission/howtoapply

General Info

Type of School: private, coed
Setting: suburban
Academic Calendar: semester

Student Body

Full-Time Undergrads: 1,163
  Men: 48%, Women: 52%

Total Undergrad Population:
  African American: 5%
  Asian American: 14%
  Latino: 6%
  Native American: 1%
  Caucasian: 72%
  International: 2%
  Out-of-State: 83%
  Living Off-Campus: 2%

Academics

Full-Time Faculty: 108
  With Ph.D.: 98%

Part-Time Faculty: 5
  With Ph.D.: 100%

Student/Faculty Ratio: 8:1

Most Popular Majors:
  English (16%)
  biology (14%)
  history (9%)
  economics (8%)
  political science (8%)

Completing 2 or More Majors: 4%

Freshmen Retention Rate: 96%

Graduation Rates:
  89% within four years
  92% within six years

Admissions

Regular Application Deadline: 1/15

Early Decision Deadline(s): 11/15

Fall Transfer Deadline: 3/31

Total # of Students Applied: 2,973
  Admitted: 878
  Enrolled: 313

# of Students Waitlisted: 671
  Students Accepting Place: 167
  Waitlisted Students Admitted: 6

Applied Early Decision: 202
  Early Decision Admitted: 103

Inside the Classroom

Haverford is one of the best liberal arts schools in the country "The feeling at Haverford is that work is *always* being done." 'Fords do not compete academically against each other as much as they hold themselves to very high personal standards. "It is very rare to have someone ask how you did on an exam or paper, and most people, if asked that by anyone but a close friend, won't answer," observes a psych major.

The school offers a strong, general liberal arts program. The core curriculum even includes courses in phys ed and social justice. Small class size—"What's a lecture hall?" students wryly respond—fosters a great deal of interaction with faculty, whom students praise as one of the school's major assets. A recent alum tells us, "Most professors assign way more reading and writing than is possible for any human to complete." Consequently, "most students quickly learn how to pick out what reading is really important and if you can manage your time well, you'll be fine." The instructors at Haverford genuinely care about their teaching, not just their own research, and devote much of their time to working closely with students. We are told that "most professors are extremely accessible" and "they really want you to succeed, no matter what it takes." To fulfill their majors, most 'Fords complete a special project or thesis during their senior year, which gives them a chance to work closely with a chosen faculty adviser.

In addition to the academic rigor, the school's character is dominated by its "working and dynamic" Honor Code, which is fully student-run and covers not only academics, but social interaction as well. According to the code, students schedule and monitor their own exams and set and enforce many of the campus regulations; the student-run Honor Council hears all complaints and determines the proper disciplinary measures for those who break the code.

The school's close ties with nearby Bryn Mawr College also makes Haverford unique; many think of them as two parts of the same school. Students can take courses and even pursue their major at either school. Haverford students can also eat meals or even live at Bryn Mawr, which is connected by a free shuttle bus that runs frequently. Students also have the option of taking courses at Swarthmore College and the University of Pennsylvania.

Campus Environment

The parklike, 216-acre suburban (close to Philadelphia) campus includes a nature walk, a duck pond, and 400 species of trees and shrubs. Haverford is a residential college, with about 98 percent of all undergrads living in on-campus housing. All freshmen are assigned to one of three houses: Barclay, Gummere (which contains all singles and is known as more of a "party dorm"), or on-campus apartment buildings known as Haverford College Apartments, or HCA. A recent grad tells us that "none of the dorms are all that attractive and most rooms are small (though you can get lucky and get that big single or double)," but that "upperclass dorms are nice and the houses have big rooms." The housing policy is a prime example of how Haverford treats its students like adults: Men and women can share a suite with a common living room and bathroom (though there are single-sex floors and bathrooms for those who prefer them). And recently, the school has started to allow mixed gender groups of three upperclass students to share bedrooms in some apartments.

Freshmen are not permitted cars, but we hear cars aren't necessary, especially since the campus is so small and pleasant to walk through. The school runs the free "Blue Bus" twice a day to Bryn Mawr College, and Philadelphia is just a 20-minute train ride away. The campus itself is very safe, and "people leave their bags unattended and rarely is something stolen (though it is happening more and more now)."

Student Life

Haverford began as a Quaker institution, and certain Quaker values, such as strong community and hard work, are the cornerstones of life here. The Haverford campus often seems like one big family. "People are usually willing to help you out, even if they don't know you. As a freshman, upperclassmen especially will tend to take you under their wing and show you around," says an alum. A guidance counselor notes, "Students have a *very* strong sense of community." The student population is pretty diverse: Over one-fourth of 'Fords are minorities. "'Fords are like onions: they have layers, and the more you hang out with them, the more you see," claims one student.

Most students are friendly but academically focused, in large part leaving social pursuits on the back burner. A young alum's colorful description: "The typical Haverford student is probably what most would consider a typical 'dork,' is very liberal politically, semi-athletic, apathetic in general (little outward school spirit), likes quiet time, and may not possess the best social skills (sorta introverted)."

The school tends to be rather quiet during the week—and on weekends: "Haverford students don't really know how to get out of control." With no Greek organizations around, most of the social life on campus involves casual hanging out in dormitory common rooms. However, one student tells us that often there are campus-wide parties in senior dorms or houses on Thursday and Saturday nights ("Fridays are dead and are usually study nights or off-campus nights").

Although the school isn't known for its athletic teams, over 40 percent of Haverford students play one of the 21 varsity sports offered. Its track team is a steady Division III contender, and the women's lacrosse team is also strong. There are also numerous club sports available, with Ultimate Frisbee, crew, and badminton among the most popular. Some 'Fords play on Bryn Mawr rec teams as well. Students may also choose from more than 80 student clubs and organizations—plus those at Bryn Mawr—ranging from the Looney Tunes (a capella group) to the 'Fords Against Boredom (sponsor of various alcohol-free events) to the Eighth Dimension (volunteer program). "I think the school attracts a student body with a strong sense of social justice. It's certainly hard to leave without feeling some sense of obligation to give back to your community," says one 'Ford.

Other schools to check out: Bryn Mawr, Swarthmore, Amherst, Vassar, Carleton.

Test Scores (middle 50%):
  SAT Verbal: 640–730
  SAT Math: 650–720
  ACT Comp: 28–32
  ACT English: 28–33
  ACT Math: 27–33

Costs (2004–5)

Tuition and Fees: $30,270

Room & Board: $9,420

Payment Plan(s): installment plan, deferred payment plan

THE EXPERTS SAY...

" Haverford is not one of these small liberal arts colleges that will hold your hand every step of the way. The admissions committee will want to make sure you have the maturity needed to succeed here. "

" Sure, the administration will let you room with members of the opposite sex... but will Mom and Dad? "

Inst. Aid (est. 2003–04)

Institutional Aid, Need-Based: $9,395,704

FT Undergrads Receiving Aid: 43%
  Avg. Amount per Student: $25,073

Of Those Receiving Any Aid:

Rec. Need-Based Scholarship or Grant Aid: 94%
  Average Award: $22,203

Rec. Need-Based Self-Help Aid: 90%
  Average Award: $4,582

Upon Graduation, Avg. Loan Debt per Student: $15,362

Financial Aid Deadline: 1/31

Graduates

Going to Graduate School: 17% Within One Year

Accepting Job Offer: 55% at time of graduation

Companies Recruiting On Campus: 34

Alumni Giving: 53%

HENDRIX COLLEGE

1600 Washington Avenue, Conway, AR 72034
Admissions Phone: (501) 450-1362; (800) 277-9017 Fax: (501) 450-3843
Email: adm@hendrix.edu
Website: www.hendrix.edu

General Info

Type of School: private, coed, United Methodist

Setting: suburban

Academic Calendar: semester

Student Body

Full-Time Undergrads: 1,031
  Men: 43%, Women: 57%

Part-Time Undergrads: 19
  Men: 68%, Women: 32%

Total Undergrad Population:
  African American: 4%
  Asian American: 2%
  Latino: 3%
  Native American: 1%
  Caucasian: 71%
  International: 1%
  Out-of-State: 40%
  Living Off-Campus: 20%

Graduate and First-Professional Students: 9

Academics

Full-Time Faculty: 81
  With Ph.D.: 100%

Part-Time Faculty: 19
  With Ph.D.: 32%

Student/Faculty Ratio: 12:1

Most Popular Majors:
  psychology (8%)
  biology (6%)
  English (4%)
  economics/business (3%)
  history (3%)

Completing 2 or More Majors: 8%

Freshmen Retention Rate: 85%

Graduation Rates:
  56% within four years
  64% within six years

Admissions

Regular Application Deadline: 2/1
  (priority)

Fall Transfer Deadline: 8/1, 4/1
  (priority)

Spring Transfer Deadline: 12/15,
  11/15 (priority)

Total # of Students Applied: 891
  Admitted: 770
  Enrolled: 267

Waitlist Available

Inside the Classroom

Hendrix is a small, Methodist-affiliated liberal arts college where "academics are without a doubt the number one priority," according to one of its students. All in all, Hendrix offers 27 majors, but many students choose to design their own course of study, working closely with a faculty advisor. Almost a third of Hendrix College students major in the sciences. Hendrix's premed program is very well regarded: A college official has told us that one in eight licensed physicians practicing in Arkansas earned an undergraduate degree at Hendrix. The school's theater arts program also gets high marks, and the bio and psych departments are the largest on campus.

Hendrix has just returned to a semester academic calendar after more than 30 years on a trimester system. There are also new general education requirements consisting of three components: The Collegiate Center, Learning Domains, and Capacities. What this means is students learn about cultures and contemporary issues; acquire a basic understanding of various disciplines in the humanities, social sciences, and natural sciences; and exhibit fundamental skills that cross content areas. The school encourages students to study off campus, through programs such as Hendrix-in-London and Hendrix-in-Oxford. There's also a solid internship program, and Hendrix has one of the nation's largest undergraduate research programs.

Hendrix caters to undergrads; the only graduate program is in accounting. So professors, not TAs, teach all classes, which tend to be small; class size averages 15 students. One student happily reports, "You really get to know your fellow classmates and professors." Students have great things to say about their professors: "[The professors] are very helpful and push you to your maximum potential—often much higher than the standards I had set for myself," states a junior majoring in politics. While science classes can be particularly intense, the atmosphere is supportive. "The workload is strenuous but not overbearing," says a senior, "and excessive competitiveness does not get in the way of learning."

Student input is important at Hendrix. In response to students' demands, the administration is allowing them to create their own Social Events and Academic Integrity Policies, and recently the Student Senate effectively mobilized against the introduction of a plus/minus grading system. As one student says, "The fact that we are able to create our own rules reflects the respect with which we are treated by the administration and the maturity of our students to create responsibility for themselves."

Campus Environment

Most students live on campus, and freshmen are required to do so. All dorms but one are single-sex; according to one student, they "all have their unique personality and a strong bond is built among their residents." Word is the on-campus food is "very good," and the cafeteria is open all day. We hear that the head of food service tries to modify the menu based on student input—something unheard of at larger schools.

Several major construction projects have recently been undertaken, including all-new science facilities, a language and literature center, and a three-building art complex, providing new space for faculty and student studios. While this means that facilities are improving, students complain that perpetual construction is annoying.

Students often study and relax outdoors. The Pecan Court is a stretch of campus covered completely in pecan shells. With its benches and large rocks, the area makes for a great study escape and gives the Hendrix campus landscape a unique look and feel. Students often take excursions to Toad Suck, a local park located on the Arkansas River near the Toad Suck Lock and Dam, where people from across the state gather each May for a festival. Thirty miles away is Little Rock, where students can escape on weekends if they're looking for more urban thrills. The nearby Ozark Mountains present students with the chance to hike, canoe, or camp out in their spare time.

Student Life

Hendrix is small, so students report that it's easy to forge a sense of community and intimacy. The flip side is that things can get a bit cliquey, and privacy is hard to maintain. As one student complains, "If you hook up with someone at a party, everyone will know by the next morning." Although the student body could stand for more racial diversity, Hendrix is surprisingly liberal for a school in the Bible Belt. Students value tolerance; there is reputedly a sizeable and active gay community on campus. A student sums up, "The individual is celebrated above all else."

Among students we spoke to, the major complaint about attending Hendrix is its immediate surroundings. "The city of Conway is not the most fun place to live," gripes a senior. It's in a "dry" county—which means no bars—so "activity seems to center around the campus with events throughout the week and most weekends," according to one student. House parties can get wild, and plenty of drinking goes on. "Drinking is one of the major forms of social interaction and for the most part is not abused, though you always have those few," a student offers. School-sponsored activities keep things active, too. Volunteer work is popular, as are intramural sports. The Hendrix-Murphy Programs in Language and Literature bring major writers, poets, and playwrights to campus throughout the year. Live bands often play on campus, and we're told that "Hendrix students love to dance."

There are no fraternities or sororities on campus—a fact which students celebrate, literally: The Hendrix Olympix is an all-day fall term event celebrating the elimination of the Greek system on the campus over 50 years ago. Actually, Hendrix students participate in a bunch of fun campus traditions. During the first week of school there's Hendrix Shirttails Serenade, when students walk from dorm to dorm and perform song-and-dance numbers, with the guys decked out in white shirts, ties, and underwear, and the girls sporting men's white shirts and (usually) boxer shorts. Campus Kitty is a week-long series of fundraisers held in the spring each year on the Hendrix campus; the climax of Campus Kitty is the Miss Hendrix Pageant. Then, on your birthday, you can expect to be thrown into the big fountain in the middle of campus. As a student tells us, "It's the little respites like this that help Hendrix students survive the four years of hard work."

Other schools to check out: Birmingham-Southern, Centre, Rhodes, University of the South, Washington & Lee.

Test Scores (middle 50%):
SAT Verbal: 570–690
SAT Math: 570–660
ACT Comp: 24–30

HS Rank of Entering Freshmen:
Top 10%: 34%
Top 25%: 64%
Top 50%: 89%

Avg. HS GPA: 3.6

Costs (2004–5)
Tuition and Fees: $16,710
Room & Board: $5,980
Payment Plan(s): installment plan

THE EXPERTS SAY...

"Students who are afraid to have their ideas challenged (or who think there are some things that just shouldn't be challenged) won't be comfortable at open-minded Hendrix."

"Once you accept the fact that you're hanging out at a park called 'Toad Suck,' you can actually have a lot of fun at quirky little Hendrix."

Inst. Aid (est. 2003–04)

Institutional Aid, Need-Based:
$3,635,592

Institutional Aid, Non-Need-Based:
$3,098,442

FT Undergrads Receiving Aid: 53%
Avg. Amount per Student:
$13,995

FT Undergrads Receiving Non-Need-Based Scholarship or Grant Aid: 42%
Avg. Amount per Student: $12,567

Of Those Receiving Any Aid:

Rec. Need-Based Scholarship or
Grant Aid: 99%
Average Award: $9,949

Rec. Need-Based Self-Help Aid: 80%
Average Award: $5,140

Upon Graduation, Avg. Loan Debt
per Student: $14,401

Financial Aid Deadline: 2/15 (priority)

Graduates

Going to Graduate School:
40% Within One Year

Companies Recruiting On Campus: 86

Alumni Giving: 47%

HIRAM COLLEGE

P.O. Box 96, Hiram, OH 44234
Admissions Phone: (800) 362-5280; (330) 569-5169 Fax: (330) 569-5944
Email: admission@hiram.edu
Website: www.hiram.edu

General Info

Type of School: private, coed, Disciples of Christ

Academic Calendar: 12 week, 3 week: Hiram Plan

Student Body

Full-Time Undergrads: 799
  Men: 46%, Women: 54%

Part-Time Undergrads: 11
  Men: 55%, Women: 45%

Total Undergrad Population:
  African American: 10%
  Asian American: 1%
  Latino: 2%
  Native American: <1%
  Caucasian: 83%
  International: 4%
  Out-of-State: 20%
  Living Off-Campus: 13%
  In Fraternities: 8%
  In Sororities: 8%

Academics

Full-Time Faculty: 72
  With Ph.D.: 92%

Part-Time Faculty: 49
  With Ph.D.: 22%

Student/Faculty Ratio: 11:1

Most Popular Majors:
  business (18%)
  history (16%)
  computer science (9%)
  education (8%)
  biology (6%)

Freshmen Retention Rate: 76%

Graduation Rates:
  56% within four years
  59% within six years

Admissions

Regular Application Deadline: 2/1 (priority)

Early Decision Deadline(s): 12/1

Fall Transfer Deadline: 7/15

Spring Transfer Deadline: 12/1

Total # of Students Applied: 888
  Admitted: 778
  Enrolled: 226

Applied Early Decision: 32
  Early Decision Admitted: 25

Inside the Classroom

Hiram College is the sort of place that believes in design as much as content. The educational philosophy is that packaging can influence the effectiveness of a course: Some subjects work best when taught over a longer period of time, while others are better taught in a short, concentrated period. That's why Hiram's academic calendar—unlike any other institution in the U.S.—includes both formats. The school's innovative academic calendar, the Hiram Plan, combines the best aspects of a traditional semester calendar with the benefits of concentrating on a short, intensive course. Each semester is divided into two sessions of 12 weeks and three weeks. During the traditional 12-week session, students typically take three courses. Then, for the three-week session, students take just one seminar course that's more "hands on." To say it's popular is an understatement: Since the short three-week course often involves a brief internship or a study abroad "extramural," students find it a welcome break from the intensity of the longer course. Half of all students here participate in a study abroad program at some point in their college career.

A very small school in an even smaller town, Hiram offers an interdisciplinary liberal arts education leading to a bachelor of arts degree. All entering students are required to complete the following: the New Student Institute and Colloquium; the First-Year Seminar; and an interdisciplinary requirement. "We have a pretty intense workload, though the classes are small and seminar-like," an environmental studies major tells us. "Most professors know students by name, and I have had dinner at several of my professors' houses."

Students rave about the quality of education they get at Hiram. By far the most popular major is business, followed by social sciences and education. In the Cooperative Professional Programs in the Sciences, Hiram students pursue a preprofessional track in business administration, dentistry, optometry, podiatry, and veterinary medicine. It's possible for exceptional students to enter these professional school programs after the junior year at Hiram. In the dual degree engineering plan, students attend Hiram for three years and then two years at the Washington University School of Engineering in St. Louis or at the Case Western Reserve Institute of Technology in Cleveland.

Since its founding, Hiram has had a continuing relationship with the Christian Church, though today it retains only a loose affiliation (read: an optional, biweekly convocation). Far more than religion, the school focuses on ethics and life skills: The Center for the Study of Ethical Issues guides students through the "gray areas" of decision making, and the Center for Literature, Medicine and the Health Care Professions uses drama, fiction, and poetry to bring a more humanistic side to the medical profession.

One guidance counselor's opinion: If you don't mind its "out-in-the-middle-of-nowhere location, Hiram has an excellent curriculum and an appealing low teacher/student ratio." While Hiram's not cheap, the school boasts that most students come from families earning less than $60,000 per year. Between great financial aid, work-study, and scholarships, we hear that most students here are pleased with how the administration "really works with you."

Campus Environment

Hiram is located in a quiet, rural setting in the middle of Ohio. (Indeed, this region was selected by the school's founders because it was "healthful and free of distractions.") Year-round residents in the tiny town of Hiram number only 300. That means there's not much in the way of nightlife. When asked to describe the off-campus setting, one junior responded, "There is no off campus. The school is surrounded by farms and woods." To get their entertainment fix, most students travel to Kent, Akron, and Cleveland, all less than an hour away.

The campus itself is reasonably attractive, combining classic buildings with historical homes. Classroom and labs are small in scale, and you'll find no cavernous lecture halls or high-rise dorms. The variety of the seven dorms "is great, each having a different atmosphere," explains one student, though he adds that a lot of people have a problem with the school's new requirement that all students live on campus. Not long ago, the administration spent a significant amount of money on dorm renovations—to increase the number of single rooms and make double rooms larger.

The nearby biological field station, a 260-acre parcel of land with a beech–maple forest, two ponds, a nature trail, and various research stations, is maintained entirely by college students. Student workers involved with groundskeeping also gain experience with woodworking, landscaping, and trail maintenance. Students develop and lead nature education outreach programs, gaining valuable teaching experience. One current program in tarantula research has gained a lot of attention. Alumni often credit their experiences at the station as inspiration for further study in science, education, and/or environmental studies.

Student Life

Most students at Hiram are Ohio natives, though as a result of aggressive recruitment efforts, the campus also boasts around 50 international students. Given the school's history with the Christian Church, the only organized congregation is the Christian Church, but opportunities abound for students of other faiths. Special interest organizations include African American Students United; Lesbian and Gay Alliance; and Students for Environmental Action.

Although Hiram does not have national fraternities and sororities, it does have local Greek social clubs. These clubs sponsor popular events like the Harvest Halloween Haunt and Eat Out—an all-day, all-night, off-campus cookout. Students look forward to annual events like the Chili Cook-Off Fundraiser, which attracts chili creations from across campus. For the Cool Room Contest, students go to outrageous lengths to decorate the coolest dorm room. Many clubs are directly related to fields of study, such as the Chemistry Club and the Philosophy Forum. There's also a student-run newspaper, a literary magazine, a yearbook, and a radio station. While sports are popular and the school offers 17 varsity sports, the athletic facilities need an overhaul. A new tennis complex houses six hard-surface courts.

Other schools to check out: College of Wooster, Allegheny, Kenyon, Hastings, Cornell College.

Test Scores (middle 50%):
SAT Verbal: 510–620
SAT Math: 490–600
ACT Comp: 21–26
ACT English: 20–26
ACT Math: 20–26

HS Rank of Entering Freshmen:
Top 10%: 24%
Top 25%: 50%
Top 50%: 86%

Avg. HS GPA: 3.4

THE EXPERTS SAY...

"Hiram is a good choice for intellectually curious students who want to explore the liberal arts and the world around them. Other schools that might interest you are Kenyon, Allegheny, and the College of Wooster."

"If you're the type of person who takes comfort in following a routine, the 12-week/3-week Hiram Plan could be unsettling."

Costs (2003–04)

Tuition and Fees: $21,134

Room & Board: $7,100

Payment Plan(s): installment plan

Inst. Aid (2002–03)

Institutional Aid, Need-Based: $3,262,038

Institutional Aid, Non-Need-Based: $4,361,596

FT Undergrads Receiving Aid: 92%
Avg. Amount per Student: $21,218

FT Undergrads Receiving Non-Need-Based Scholarship or Grant Aid: 14%
Avg. Amount per Student: $8,635

Of Those Receiving Any Aid:

Rec. Need-Based Scholarship or Grant Aid: 100%
Average Award: $8,163

Rec. Need-Based Self-Help Aid: 100%
Average Award: $8,484

Upon Graduation, Avg. Loan Debt per Student: $17,125

Financial Aid Deadline: rolling

Graduates

Going to Graduate School:
30% Within One Year

Accepting Job Offer:
55% at time of graduation

Companies Recruiting On Campus: 20

Alumni Giving: 34%

HOBART AND WILLIAM SMITH COLLEGES

629 South Main Street, Geneva, NY 14456
Admissions Phone: (800) 857-2256; (800) 245-0100 Fax: (315) 781-3471
Email: admissions@hws.edu Website: www.hws.edu Application Website: www.hws.edu/admissions/adm_apply.asp

General Info

Type of School: private, coed

Setting: small town

Academic Calendar: semester

Student Body

Full-Time Undergrads: 1,864
  Men: 44%, Women: 56%

Part-Time Undergrads: 7
  Men: 71%, Women: 29%

Total Undergrad Population:
  African American: 3%
  Asian American: 2%
  Latino: 4%
  Native American: <1%
  Caucasian: 87%
  International: 2%
  Out-of-State: 50%
  Living Off-Campus: 8%
  In Fraternities: 15%

Academics

Full-Time Faculty: 156
  With Ph.D.: 92%

Part-Time Faculty: 33
  With Ph.D.: 88%

Student/Faculty Ratio: 11:1

Most Popular Majors:
  English (11%)
  psychology (11%)
  economics (10%)
  political science (9%)
  history (7%)

Freshmen Retention Rate: 84%

Graduation Rates:
  64% within four years
  71% within six years

Admissions

Regular Application Deadline: 2/1

Early Decision Deadline(s): 11/15, 1/1

Fall Transfer Deadline: 7/1

Spring Transfer Deadline: 11/15

Total # of Students Applied: 3,277
  Admitted: 2,045
  Enrolled: 515

# of Students Waitlisted: 362
  Students Accepting Place: 28
  Waitlisted Students Admitted: 24

Applied Early Decision: 157
  Early Decision Admitted: 123

Inside the Classroom

Imagine the supportive community of a single-sex college without the social isolation that's so often a complaint. At Hobart and William Smith Colleges, students enjoy the best aspects of the single-sex and coed campus experiences. These two colleges (Hobart for men, William Smith for women) have their own administrations, student governments, and sports programs, but share the same campus, facilities, and courses.

The academic goal for every HWS student is "a true liberal arts education," but with a purpose and some interesting twists. There's a strong emphasis on public service and on international study. Study abroad subtends 5 continents and 26 countries, including exotic locations like China, Ecuador, Iceland, India, Kenya, Korea, New Zealand, Senegal, and Vietnam. Particularly strong programs include men's studies (HWS established the first minor program in the nation), environmental studies, economics, and women's studies. Off-campus study is also available in Boston, New York, and Washington, DC. Sixty percent of HWS students study off campus for a semester.

HWS students declare an academic major and an academic minor or second major. One of these must be based in a discipline. The other must be an established interdisciplinary major or minor; a percentage of students design their own. The core curriculum is broadly written, but covers all intellectual bases: communication; critical thinking; quantitative reasoning; scientific inquiry; artistic expression; differences and inequalities of gender, race, and class; world cultures; and ethical judgment. There's room for creativity in program design, as the professors demonstrate: Associate Professor of Political Science Jodi Dean was named one of the coolest professors in America by Abercrombie and Fitch for her thesis that the widespread belief in UFOs and aliens reflects a disenchantment with political rhetoric and structures.

All classes are taught by professors. In characterizing their relationships with their faculty advisors, a school-released survey reports that 47 percent of HWS students say their advisor is a friend or mentor, and 19 percent characterize their advisor as a confidant. 82 percent of seniors had at least occasionally been a guest in a faculty member's home (25 percent "often"). A high number of students are involved in faculty research projects and assist faculty in conference presentations and scientific publications. The Colleges' HWS Explorer research vessel is used by students for environmental studies on Seneca Lake. Internships, with faculty advocates, are available both locally and in Boston.

Campus Environment

The beautiful 180-acre campus is located on the shores of Seneca Lake, the largest of the Finger Lakes. Geneva, a town of approximately 14,000 people, doesn't provide much excitement for students, and town-gown relations are somewhat strained. The Finger Lakes, however, are perfect for all kinds of outdoor sports, including sailing and hiking. The college also has a 108-acre biological field station, Hanley Preserve, located 15 miles from campus on Cayuga Lake.

Hobart and William Smith think of themselves as a residential community and require students to live on-campus for at least three years (seniors may enter a lottery for limited off-campus housing). But students are rewarded with a broad choice of campus housing, including townhouses, co-ops, and theme houses (although local legend has it that HWS residences Blackwell House, McCormick House, and Miller House are haunted). First-year students have the option of single sex or coeducational housing. There are six fraternities at Hobart, but no first-year men may live in fraternity houses; William Smith does not have any sororities. Many facilities have been renovated or added to the campus recently, with major new construction planned for the near future.

Taxis are available for travel to town, but downtown is within walking distance. The school provides shuttles in the evening for travel to and from downtown locations. All students are allowed cars on campus (daytime parking is restricted), which are useful for road trips and off-campus errands.

Student Life

Public service is a watchword at HWS (before becoming HWS's president, Mark D. Gearan was director of the Peace Corps). Not surprisingly, Students for Service is one of the most popular student organizations, and HWS has campus chapters of Habitat for Humanity and Make-A-Wish. Other active groups include America Reads, The Latin American Organization, Refuse and Resist!, NPR-affiliated WEOS (college owned and operated) radio station, and Campus Greens, among over fifty other student organizations. The President's Forum speaker series has brought such luminaries as Senator Hillary Rodham Clinton, George Stephanopolous, former New York City Mayor David Dinkins, presidential candidates Michael Dukakis and Ralph Nader, and ABC newsman Sam Donaldson to campus.

The administration encourages a "residential college" feeling ("What happens in the dining halls and residence hall rooms is as important as what happens in class," stress college officials) and encourages students to stay on campus on weekends; luckily, they provide lots of campus activities to keep students occupied. One of the biggest campus events is the annual spring Folk Fest—a three-day, student-run festival whose profits help support local children's organizations. Sports are also a major part of student life, especially men's and women's lacrosse. The superb athletic facilities at both schools, including indoor tennis and squash courts and an indoor track, make it possible to participate in just about any sport; 35 percent of students are involved in varsity sports, and many more in intramurals. Still, students admit that the long, cold winters in upstate New York can be a drag; for those who venture off campus, road trips to neighboring colleges in nearby Syracuse, Ithaca, and Rochester help break the doldrums.

Other schools to check out: Hamilton, Colgate, Union, Skidmore, Dickinson.

Test Scores (middle 50%):
SAT Verbal: 540–620
SAT Math: 540–630

HS Rank of Entering Freshmen:
Top 10%: 31%
Top 25%: 65%
Top 50%: 93%

Avg. HS GPA: 3.31

Costs (2003–04)

Tuition and Fees: $28,948

Room & Board: $7,588

Payment Plan(s): installment plan, pre-payment plan

THE EXPERTS SAY...

" Hobart and William Smith Colleges offer unparalleled opportunities for public service and study abroad. "

" If you just want a degree and not a 'residential community,' HWS isn't for you. If your middle name is 'volunteer,' go for it. "

Inst. Aid (est. 2003–04)

Institutional Aid, Need-Based: $18,042,760

Institutional Aid, Non-Need-Based: $2,983,924

FT Undergrads Receiving Aid: 63%
Avg. Amount per Student: $22,963

FT Undergrads Receiving Non-Need-Based Scholarship or Grant Aid: 14%
Avg. Amount per Student: $10,732

Of Those Receiving Any Aid:

Rec. Need-Based Scholarship or Grant Aid: 100%
Average Award: $18,717

Rec. Need-Based Self-Help Aid: 87%
Average Award: $4,961

Upon Graduation, Avg. Loan Debt per Student: $20,508

Financial Aid Deadline: 2/1

Graduates

Going to Graduate School:
25% Within One Year

Accepting Job Offer:
30% at time of graduation

Companies Recruiting On Campus: 45

Alumni Giving: 70%

HOFSTRA UNIVERSITY

100 Hofstra University, Hempstead, NY 11549-1000
Admissions Phone: (516) 463-6700; (800) HOFSTRA Fax: (516) 463-5100
Email: admitme@hofstra.edu Website: www.hofstra.edu
Application Website: www.hofstra.edu/application

General Info

Type of School: private, coed
Setting: suburban
Academic Calendar: 4-1-4

Student Body

Full-Time Undergrads: 8,323
  Men: 47%, Women: 53%

Part-Time Undergrads: 866
  Men: 46%, Women: 54%

Total Undergrad Population:
  African American: 9%
  Asian American: 4%
  Latino: 8%
  Native American: <1%
  Caucasian: 62%
  International: 2%
  Out-of-State: 25%
  Living Off-Campus: 57%
  In Fraternities: 5%
  In Sororities: 6%

Graduate and First-Professional
  Students: 3,834

Academics

Full-Time Faculty: 508
  With Ph.D.: 90%

Part-Time Faculty: 786
  With Ph.D.: 31%

Student/Faculty Ratio: 14:1

Most Popular Majors:
  psychology (7%)
  marketing (6%)
  accounting (5%)
  management (5%)
  finance (4%)

Completing 2 or More Majors: 9%

Minor required for certain schools of
  communications

Freshmen Retention Rate: 74%

Graduation Rates:
  37% within four years
  56% within six years

Admissions

Regular Application Deadline: 3/1;
  12/15 (priority)

Early Action Deadline: 11/15

Fall Transfer Deadline: 3/1 (priority)

Spring Transfer Deadline: 11/1
  (priority)

Inside the Classroom

More than 80 percent of all high school students who take a tour of Hofstra's gorgeous campus make Hofstra their first choice, and there are reasons for that. From its origins as a commuter school 30 years ago, Hofstra's galaxy of academic options has grown to include the Hofstra College of Liberal Arts and Sciences, Frank G. Zarb School of Business, School of Communication, School of Education and Allied Human Services, New College, School of Law, School for University Studies, Honors College, Saturday College, and University College for Continuing Education. Another reason Hofstra has changed for the better: "The entrance requirements have become more strict," a guidance counselor notes.

Hofstra offers about 130 programs of study, including such majors as entrepreneurship and physician assistant. Career-oriented majors in business and management, marketing, engineering, television, and computer science are popular, but the Bachelor of Fine Arts degree, with its specialization in theater arts, is also strong. "Excellent science and performing arts," raves a New York guidance counselor." Another counselor likes the "strong communications" programs. Distribution requirements vary, but most degrees require courses in the humanities, natural sciences and mathematics/computer science, social sciences, and non-European cross-cultural studies.

Word on professors is mixed, with some rated hot and others tepid. "My professors give a 20–30 point curve to the rest of the class, which I feel is extremely unfair," complains a senior. "Classes are way too easy." (High achievers take note: there's a chapter of Phi Beta Kappa on campus.) Workload varies between programs, but overall is considered manageable. The average class size is 24 students. The campus is one of *Wired* magazine's top 100 and a guidance counselor raves about "the great labs" and "computer accessibility."

Students beef about the high tuition; the administration is also a target (one student calls the latter "extremely bureaucratic"). While some complain about the school, others love it, but most agree that with the many academic opportunities, Hofstra is what you make of it.

Campus Environment

Hofstra's 240-acre Hempstead, Long Island campus, located just 25 miles east of New York City, is an accredited member of the American Association of Botanical Gardens. The campus is 100 percent accessible to persons with disabilities. Freshmen can live in any of the undergraduate residence halls or at Twin Oaks apartments; Netherlands North is reserved for freshmen only. "Singles are shoeboxes; they tripled the Towers because this school consistently accepts more students than it has housing for," a senior remarks. "If you're lucky enough to get a suite, you're all right, though." Housing is not guaranteed for all four years, but returning residence hall students do have top priority for space. Off-campus housing is expensive simply because of the location. "Long Island is one of the most expensive places to live in the country," a business major points out, adding, "You definitely need a car on Long Island."

Hofstra athletic teams play and practice in state of the art facilities, and gym facilities are extensive (the Hofstra Swim Center is adjacent to the New York Jets training complex). Hofstra is in the midst of significant expansion, with a complete renovation of a vacated courthouse for the School of Education and Allied Human Services, and major additions to theaters, arts facilities, and the Hofstra Museum. Also coming is a new residence hall for honor and graduate students and a new building for University College for Continuing Education

Student Life

The typical Hofstra student ranges from "passionate" to "not a very bright bulb." A computer major bitches about the "bunch of rich stuck-up sorority/fraternity people who think that they are smart and great because they drive Beamers." A guidance counselor puts it more delicately, saying only that the students are "very 'Long Island-like.'" The campus is said to be cliquish: "If you walk into the student center there is one section of African Americans, one section of fraternity/sorority students, a section of athletes, etc." Drinking is big: "Students drink; that's what they do," comments a senior, "Tuesday, Thursday, Friday, and Saturday." Drugs have a presence on campus. And a student reports, "A few years ago, Hofstra was ranked in the top three in having the hottest girls on campus by *Playboy*."

The most active student groups are Entertainment Unlimited, Hofstra Concerts, IFSC (Inter Fraternity Sorority Council), ALFSA (African-Latino Fraternity Sorority Alliance), and HOLA (Hofstra's Organization of Latin Americans). Alumnus Francis Ford Coppola started a theater group called The Spectrum Players that is still in existence today, and Hofstra's WRHU-FM recently won a FOLIO award for best public affairs reporting. Sororities and fraternities play a major role in social life. "It's just the 'thing to do,' or at least that's what most people are brainwashed into thinking," gripes an independent.

Sports are "extremely popular and the students that play them are well catered to," comments a computer major. Hofstra sponsors 18 intercollegiate teams that compete on the NCAA Division I level. During the past two years, the Dutchmen have captured nine conference championships and appeared in ten NCAA championship tournaments.

School traditions include the Dutch Festival, with a parade featuring Dutch costumes and a Dutch Burgher guard. The winter Sinterklass Festival begins with the lighting of one of the largest living Christmas trees on Long Island, followed by a visit from Sinterklass and Santa Claus handing out presents to all the children; Hofstra's fraternities and sororities participate by creating small villages based around a central theme. More than 700 members of the Hofstra community join hands to form a human chain in the annual Hands Across Hofstra: Participants are asked to donate $2 to charity to stand in line for a few minutes and join hands. Every other year, the spring Shakespeare festival is performed on a 3/4-scale reproduction of the famed Globe Theater. And starting a new tradition, Hofstra students slept outside recently to call attention to the issue of homelessness.

Other schools to check out: Fordham, Rutgers, SUNY Stony Brook, Syracuse, Ithaca.

Total # of Students Applied: 11,691
  Admitted: 8,000
  Enrolled: 1,877

# of Students Waitlisted: 438
  Students Accepting Place: 160
  Waitlisted Students Admitted: 49

Test Scores (middle 50%):
  SAT Verbal: 510–600
  SAT Math: 520–620
  ACT Comp: 22–27

HS Rank of Entering Freshmen:
  Top 10%: 16%
  Top 25%: 43%
  Top 50%: 76%

Avg. HS GPA: 3.08

THE EXPERTS SAY...

" Once known as a commuter school, Hofstra has been working hard to build a national reputation. The School of Communication is a rising star. "

" Does the high tuition include the price of grade inflation? "

Costs (2003–04)

Tuition and Fees: $18,412

Room & Board: $8,700

Payment Plan(s): installment plan, deferred payment plan

Inst. Aid (est. 2003–04)

Institutional Aid, Need-Based: $13,750,000

Institutional Aid, Non-Need-Based: $9,000,000

FT Undergrads Receiving Aid: 56%
  Avg. Amount per Student: $10,649

FT Undergrads Receiving Non-Need-Based Scholarship or Grant Aid: 7%
  Avg. Amount per Student: $5,400

Of Those Receiving Any Aid:

Rec. Need-Based Scholarship or Grant Aid: 63%
  Average Award: $6,897

Rec. Need-Based Self-Help Aid: 92%
  Average Award: $4,885

Upon Graduation, Avg. Loan Debt per Student: $17,763

Financial Aid Deadline: rolling, 2/15 (priority)

Graduates

Companies Recruiting On-Campus: 330

Alumni Giving: 11%

HOLLINS UNIVERSITY

P.O. Box 9707, Roanoke, VA 24020-1707
Admissions Phone: (800) 456-9595; (540) 362-6401 Fax: (540) 362-6218
Email: huadm@hollins.edu
Website: www.hollins.edu

General Info

Type of School: private, all women
Setting: suburban
Academic Calendar: 4-1-4

Student Body

Full-Time Undergrads: 768
   Women: 100%

Part-Time Undergrads: 23
   Women: 100%

Total Undergrad Population:
   African American: 7%
   Asian American: 1%
   Latino: 3%
   Native American: 1%
   Caucasian: 85%
   International: 3%
   Out-of-State: 50%
   Living Off-Campus: 9%

Graduate and First-Professional
   Students: 279

Academics

Full-Time Faculty: 74
   With Ph.D.: 97%

Part-Time Faculty: 33
   With Ph.D.: 48%

Student/Faculty Ratio: 9:1

Most Popular Majors:
   English/creative writing
   psychology
   communication studies
   art
   biology

Completing 2 or More Majors: 16%

Freshmen Retention Rate: 71%

Graduation Rates:
   59% within four years
   65% within six years

Admissions

Regular Application Deadline: 8/1;
   2/15 (priority)

Early Decision Deadline(s): 12/1

Fall Transfer Deadline: 6/1 (priority)

Spring Transfer Deadline: 11/15
   (priority)

Total # of Students Applied: 813
   Admitted: 701
   Enrolled: 202

In the Classroom

Hollins University (known as Hollins College until 1998) is a small women's school known for its nationally ranked creative writing program and extensive internship opportunities. In the innovative gen-ed program called "Education through Skills and Perspectives," students study seven areas considered to be central to a well-rounded liberal arts education. "Perspectives" includes aesthetic analysis, creative expression, ancient and/or medieval worlds, modern and/or contemporary worlds, scientific inquiry, social and cultural diversities, and global systems and languages. "Skills" teaches students to write successfully, reason quantitatively, express themselves effectively, research astutely, and be adept technologically. Each year, one-third of students do internships, and more than half of Hollins' students study abroad at some point.

There are tons of research opportunities for undergraduates. Psychology majors have computers and laboratories dedicated to their research. Biology majors work with faculty members on research projects (many also spend a semester abroad in places like Kenya, the Caicos Islands, the West Indies, and the rain forests of Australia.) One student tells us that "the science program here is very strong," and that the school has an incredibly high acceptance rate "into their first choice of medical school." Math majors complete a senior research thesis under the direction of a faculty member, history majors locate and use sources and documents creatively, and physics majors learn science through research.

One sophomore lists the "small class sizes" as one of the best things about Hollins, and notes the fact that Hollins is "very student-focused." A student tells us that professors "try to have convenient office hours and will even plan to meet up with you if you cannot make it during their scheduled office hours. Many professors will give out their e-mail addresses and even home numbers in case students need to get a hold of them in the evenings."

Campus Environment

With a few exceptions, students are required to live in campus housing, and housing is guaranteed for four years. "On-campus housing is great," says a student. "There are always plenty of rooms, and if someone really wants to get a single room, the chances of it are great!" She also explains, "There are campus apartments located across from the school that many upper classmen opt to live in."

The small campus is safe, and there is 24-hour security. "Campus Safety is constantly patrolling in their cars and on bikes." Also, the size of the school makes students familiar with each other and comfortable in their surroundings, "Most of the students here are friendly and will say hi in passing even if you don't know each other well. Having a small amount of students helps [you] to recognize faces and make a lot of friends."

Students can have cars on campus, for a fee, and they suggest you bring one, since there's not much to do within walking distance. "If you don't have a car, I highly suggest making friends with someone who does and who likes going off campus," says one.

Student Life

First of all, don't expect a big party school. There are not many students, no sororities, and no guys. This campus is pretty sedate. That's not to say that these women are totally isolated from college culture. There is drinking to be found, but "it's very discrete here … Many students do their drinking at parties at other schools or privately in their rooms." Drugs are even less frequent, or more discreet. "Many students here go to other schools on the weekends," says a sophomore, "there are five other colleges within 45 minutes and more a little farther away." If you have a friend with a car, you can drive to where the boys are. Also, we are told, the city of Roanoke offers the basics: "a dance club, bowling alley, pool hall, and other things in the city to do." However, Hollins women are students first and foremost: "many students like staying on campus to study on the weekends since it's quiet here." And put out your cigarette before coming here: The Hollins campus, inside and out, is smoke-free. The school told us about "Tinker Day," a tradition since 1896. Tinker Day occurs in October, romantically "after the first frost." After the president's official declaration, classes are canceled so students, faculty, and staff can hike Tinker Mountain attired in crazy costumes for singing and a traditional meal of fried chicken and Tinker Cake. Yes, that's right—Tinker Cake. Another Hollins tradition, Freya Walks, occurs on nights of special events or issues. Members of the secret society walk at midnight to call attention to or celebrate current events, wearing black hooded robes to protect their anonymity and carrying candles to symbolize hope. Since 1907, Freya has sought to emphasize the notion that "concern for the community is a creative and active force."

More than half of the women at Hollins participate in some sort of physical activity, recreational or intercollegiate. The school participates in NCAA Division III, and students say that field hockey, lacrosse, basketball, and swimming are popular. But the main draw, say students and guidance counselors: "Horseback riding is huge and draws a large amount of applicants to the school."

There are no sororities here. A biology major tells us, "Some of our most popular organizations are our service clubs, our political clubs … and the religious life clubs." There are students of all sorts to participate, from "the rich-pearl-wearing-daddy's-girl to the shaved-multi-colored-hair-'I don't care what you think about me'-girls to the average-Jane-Doe." A small population fosters a sense of community among a diverse group. But we are also told that a less appealing aspect of this community is the "gossip—(what do you expect from all girls?)."

Other schools to check out: Sweet Briar, Randolph-Macon Woman's, Agnes Scott, Chatham.

# of Students Waitlisted: 25
  Students Accepting Place: 13
  Waitlisted Students Admitted: 6

Applied Early Decision: 51
  Early Decision Admitted: 41

Test Scores (middle 50%):
  SAT Verbal: 540–660
  SAT Math: 500–600
  ACT Comp: 21–26

HS Rank of Entering Freshmen:
  Top 10%: 25%
  Top 25%: 59%
  Top 50%: 93%

Avg. HS GPA: 3.38

THE EXPERTS SAY...

" The unique general ed program and research opportunities make for a very broad-based liberal arts education. "

" Bring your car to this party-starved campus, or make friends with one of the male grad students who has one. "

Costs (2004–5)

Tuition and Fees: $21,675

Room & Board: $6,875

Payment Plan(s): installment plan

Inst. Aid (est. 2003–04)

Institutional Aid, Need-Based:
  $4,880,339

Institutional Aid, Non-Need-Based:
  $1,776,225

FT Undergrads Receiving Aid: 66%
  Avg. Amount per Student: $17,513

FT Undergrads Receiving Non-Need-Based Scholarship or Grant Aid: 31%
  Avg. Amount per Student: $7,558

Of Those Receiving Any Aid:

Rec. Need-Based Scholarship or Grant Aid: 100%
  Average Award: $12,402

Rec. Need-Based Self-Help Aid: 85%
  Average Award: $5,770

Upon Graduation, Avg. Loan Debt per Student: $18,167

Financial Aid Deadline: 3/15, 2/15 (priority)

Graduates

Going to Graduate School:
  22% Within One Year

Alumni Giving: 70%

HOWARD UNIVERSITY

2400 6th Street NW, Washington, DC 20059
Admissions Phone: (202) 806-2755 Fax: (202) 806-4465
Email: vlittle@howard.edu
Website: www.howard.edu/enrollmentmanagement/admissions

General Info

Type of School: private, coed
Setting: urban
Academic Calendar: semester

Student Body

Full-Time Undergrads: 6,626
    Men: 33%, Women: 67%

Part-Time Undergrads: 375
    Men: 31%, Women: 69%

Total Undergrad Population:
    African American: 69%
    Asian American: <1%
    Latino: <1%
    Caucasian: <1%
    International: 9%
    Out-of-State: 86%
    Living Off-Campus: 45%
    In Fraternities: 2%
    In Sororities: 1%

Graduate and First-Professional
    Students: 3,599

Academics

Full-Time Faculty: 1,123
    With Ph.D.: 93%

Part-Time Faculty: 475
    With Ph.D.: 66%

Student/Faculty Ratio: 8:1

Most Popular Majors:
    biology (8%)
    psychology (7%)
    marketing (6%)
    journalism (6%)
    radio/tv/film (6%)

Freshmen Retention Rate: 89%

Graduation Rates:
    37% within four years
    63% within six years

Admissions

Early Action Deadline: 11/1

Fall Transfer Deadline: 3/1

Spring Transfer Deadline: 11/1

Total # of Students Applied: 7,057
    Admitted: 3,982
    Enrolled: 1,160

Test Scores (middle 50%):
    SAT Verbal: 420–680
    SAT Math: 420–680
    ACT Comp: 19–20

Inside the Classroom

Howard is the largest and most renowned predominantly African American university in the United States. Founded in 1867, the school has a long history of providing an exceptional education to intelligent and highly motivated students while fostering a strong sense of unity. A senior tells us, "Howard is a very competitive institution. Most of the students graduated with honors when coming out of high school. The professors are very concerned with class attendance and participation. These factors create a competitive, but nurturing, academic environment."

With six schools offering undergraduate degrees, Howard's academic offerings cover a wide range of subject areas. Most students arrive at Howard set on a professional career path, and preprofessional programs are among Howard's best and most popular offerings. The schools of business, engineering, and communication obtain high enrollments each year. Those studying communications gain important hands-on experience at the university's own radio and cable television stations, and students in all three programs can take advantage of the plentiful internship and work opportunities available to them in Washington, DC. In the College of Arts and Sciences, the political science, history, and theater arts programs are particularly well regarded. The programs in African and African American studies are also excellent, with far more course offerings than at most other schools. And Howard's medical and dental schools are highly acclaimed, and attract many undergrads.

Howard's core curriculum calls specific attention to the many achievements of African Americans in literature, history, criticism, philosophy, and other areas of academic study. Teachers in all departments try to bring a multicultural perspective to bear upon the material. Most professors at Howard are highly accessible and genuinely concerned about their students, always pushing them to work harder and fulfill their potential. Class sizes vary, with general courses having as many as 75 students and most upper-level classes limited to fewer than 20.

Campus Environment

The campus centers around "The Yard," a grassy area where students may be found relaxing between classes. On-campus parking is limited and is determined through a lottery each spring, though many students feel that owning a car can be more burdensome than convenient. "Public transportation in D.C. is excellent," a student says. "Having a car is a hassle because of traffic, parking, and meters. Hop on the Metro and go!" Aside from the availability of the Metro, the university provides shuttle buses to off-campus dorms, the Shaw/Howard Metro, and other points near the campus. The urban area around the campus is not particularly safe, so students need to be careful and use common sense when leaving the property. Generally, though, students love D.C.: "There is so much to see and do. The museums, monuments, clubs, and culture are all amazing."

Howard has had its share of housing difficulties lately. Students are required to live in the dorms for their first two years; after freshmen year, all undergrads must participate in the Room Selection and Verification Plan (RSVP), which is a kind of housing lottery designed to give students an equal opportunity at preferred, on-campus housing. Dorms are pretty standard here. A student says, "On-campus housing is not the best but they do have nice features like cable television, Internet access, and voicemail phone." The main problem with Howard's campus housing is the lack of it. In recent years, increasing numbers of upperclassmen have opted to remain living on campus as opposed to moving off. Additionally, Howard faced the largest freshman class in decades a few years ago, when almost 250 extra freshmen enrolled. This has caused upperclassmen to be bumped off campus and into makeshift dorms, specifically hotels. While this has caused some frustration, it is a problem shared by other area schools such as George Washington University. Howard is continuing to find solutions to the housing shortages, including requiring earlier declarations from applicants.

Off-campus housing is a popular alternative, and Howard helps students to make arrangements. "Off-campus housing is nice and it's popular," a student says. "D.C. is a very expensive city, but many landlords rent their property at a cheaper rate to college students. I live in a 3-story, 5 bedroom, kitchen, laundry room, and patio for $300/month! Of course, not alone."

Student Life

Although overwhelmingly African American, students from across the nation and more than 100 foreign countries bring to Howard a variety of experiences, ideas, and interests that create a dynamic student body. Most students are politically liberal, and "being an involved and active student is very important." Students are also very bright and highly supportive of one another's academic and career pursuits. A senior tells us that "narrow-minded individuals would not fit in at Howard," and that "there is no 'typical' student. This is a very diverse institution. I have met people from around the world just by interacting in one class. The diversity adds to the sense of global community."

Students tend to stick to the campus for socializing. Many national African American fraternities and sororities originated at Howard and they maintain a strong, but not dominant, presence on campus. In addition to hosting the occasional party, the fraternities and sororities are also very involved in the campus community, conducting volunteer work and sponsoring special events, such as visits by guest speakers. Intramural and intercollegiate sports are both very popular. Football games are particularly well attended; the homecoming game against rival Morehouse is the highlight of the football season as well as the social event of the year, when students party in full force.

A student tells us that alcohol and drugs are not too prevalent on campus. "Reputation and self-image are very important. No one wants to be seen high or drunk," a senior says. Free time and weekends are usually spent at "popular cafés and clubs in D.C.," as well as partying in the trendy neighboring areas, such as Georgetown.

Notable alumni include Thurgood Marshall, Jessye Norman, Toni Morrison, Debbie Allen, and Phylicia Rashad.

HS Rank of Entering Freshmen:
Top 10%: 30%
Top 25%: 52%
Top 50%: 83%
Avg. HS GPA: 3.04

Costs (2003–04)

Tuition and Fees: $10,935

Room & Board: $5,570

Payment Plan(s): installment plan, deferred payment plan

THE EXPERTS SAY...

" At Howard, the faculty will encourage you to do your very best, and the multicultural curriculum will inspire you. The preprofessional tracks and the African American studies major are strengths. "

" With alums like Thurgood Marshall and Toni Morrison, it's small wonder that Howard students are image-conscious. "

Inst. Aid (2002–03)

Institutional Aid, Need-Based: $22,261,434

FT Undergrads Receiving Aid: 54%
Avg. Amount per Student: $17,111

Of Those Receiving Any Aid:

Rec. Need-Based Scholarship or Grant Aid: 76%
Average Award: $3,473

Rec. Need-Based Self-Help Aid: 59%
Average Award: $6,050

Upon Graduation, Avg. Loan Debt per Student: $17,548

Financial Aid Deadline: 2/15 (priority)

Graduates

Going to Graduate School:
45% Within One Year

Accepting Job Offer:
50% at time of graduation

Companies Recruiting On Campus:
300

ILLINOIS INSTITUTE OF TECHNOLOGY

3300 S. Federal St., Chicago, IL 60616-3793
Admissions Phone: (312) 567-3025 Fax: (312) 567-6939
Email: admission@iit.edu Website: www.iit.edu Application Website: www.iit.edu/admission/undergrad/apply.html

General Info
Type of School: private, coed
Setting: urban
Academic Calendar: semester

Student Body
Full-Time Undergrads: 1,670
  Men: 75%, Women: 25%

Part-Time Undergrads: 181
  Men: 87%, Women: 13%

Total Undergrad Population:
  African American: 5%
  Asian American: 15%
  Latino: 7%
  Native American: <1%
  Caucasian: 47%
  International: 17%
  Out-of-State: 37%
  Living Off-Campus: 42%
  In Fraternities: 21%
  In Sororities: 15%

Graduate and First-Professional
  Students: 4,226

Academics
Full-Time Faculty: 330
  With Ph.D.: 82%

Part-Time Faculty: 217

Student/Faculty Ratio: 12:1

Most Popular Majors:
  architecture (14%)
  computer science (13%)
  electrical engineering (13%)
  computer engineering (11%)
  mechanical engineering (8%)

Completing 2 or More Majors: 2%

Freshmen Retention Rate: 81%

Graduation Rates:
  28% within four years
  67% within six years

Admissions
Regular Application Deadline: 5/1
  (priority)

Total # of Students Applied: 2,538
  Admitted: 1,502
  Enrolled: 398

Test Scores (middle 50%):
  SAT Verbal: 560–680
  SAT Math: 620–730
  ACT Comp: 25–30
  ACT English: 24–30
  ACT Math: 27–32

Inside the Classroom

As one of the top engineering schools in the nation, IIT is a member of the elite Association of Independent Technological Universities, a group that includes MIT, Cal Tech, Rensselaer Polytechnic Institute, and Carnegie Mellon. IIT stresses an "interprofessional" education designed to produce "Renaissance professionals" grounded in their disciplines, capable of dealing with technological change, and able to understand the point of view of professionals in other disciplines. All IIT students participate in the Interprofessional Projects (IPRO) Program, undertaking at least two semester-long projects designed to build skills in teamwork, project management, conflict resolution, and communication. Involving students from different classes and academic disciplines, projects range from improving medical electronics to designing football stadiums. IPRO projects are often suggested by local Chicago businesses like Motorola, Commonwealth Edison, or Zebra Technologies, and can lead to co-ops, internships, and careers.

ITT has a distinguished school of architecture, once headed by Ludwig Mies van der Rohe (who designed IIT's campus), and a school of design. Computer engineering is a top major, as are computer science, architecture, electrical engineering, and mechanical engineering. ITT offers an honors premed track and an honors law program. While courses in social sciences and the humanities exist, they are not strong, although they are a required part of the core curriculum.

The IIT Leadership Academy identifies students with high leadership potential and provides full-tuition scholarships and immersion in a comprehensive leadership training program. The Ed Kaplan Entrepreneurial Studies Program encourages students to learn the principles of entrepreneurship, and develop innovative ideas that can lead to successful new ventures. Students say IIT's Career Development Center is effective in helping them find co-ops and internships.

With fewer than 2,000 full-time undergrads, there is a lot of individual attention from faculty. A chemistry major comments that "all the professors know who you are." Students get to work directly with faculty on research and other projects. Professors are described as "awesome," and there's a small student/faculty ratio. Nonetheless, the academic atmosphere is highly stressful and "competitive," with students working long hours to keep up with assignments.

Campus Environment

IIT's 120-acre main campus is located on the South Side of Chicago. "The campus is pretty safe, but not the area surrounding the campus," a student comments. Town-gown relations between IIT and the predominantly black community are reportedly strained. Students find the architecturally historic Mies van der Rohe campus largely unappealing, but love its proximity to everything that Chicago has to offer. The campus is about three miles south of the Chicago Loop, one mile west of Lake Michigan, and one block from the White Sox baseball park. "The best thing about going to school in Chicago is that you don't need a car to get around," remarks a junior. "[IIT] issues passes every semester that you can use to ride the trains and the buses as much as you want." Campus shuttles provide free transportation between the main campus and the West Loop campus.

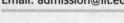

For freshmen, housing is in the McCormick Residential Village. A student remarks: "Not many single rooms available, but overall the rooms are pretty comfortable... The food's not bad." Fraternity and sorority housing is also available. Many faculty and staff live on campus in recently constructed condos and townhomes. The school has embarked on a major renewal campaign. Off-campus housing, says a junior, is "cheaper than on-campus but not very popular... due to the difficulties with commuting." About half of IIT students, many living at home with their parents, brave the commute.

Student Life

Students report that, given the IIT academic pressure, they don't have time for sleep, much less a social life. The male/female ratio doesn't make for a hot dating scene for the guys, and the fact that half the school commutes and the rest disappear on weekends leaves the campus a bit deserted after classes. Chicago is the center of student activity. "I usually study and workout at nights," a junior says. "I go downtown, or go out to explore one of the old Chicago neighborhoods for fun on weekends... I love Chicago. There are so many things to do, I don't think anybody can get bored around here."

While one student says, "I have never felt any pressure to drink or to do drugs," others say that alcohol is often used to blow off steam, and the campus bar, The Bog, is hot on Thursdays and Saturdays when it hosts bands. Greek life is big on campus and can be counted on for parties and events. A junior comments that the Student Leadership Committee is "pretty popular," and adds, "IIT was the first school to have a campus radio station, and the tape recorder was invented here." IIT isn't a sports school, but there are enthusiasts: "The most popular game is the homecoming game for the women's volleyball team," a fan claims. All the sports action in Chicago makes up for some apathy in the Scarlet Hawk following, and for somewhat shortened fitness center schedules.

Even though the campus is predominantly male and everyone is a techie, a junior asserts that there is no typical IIT student: "There are so many students here from around the United States and the world. We all have similar interests, but everyone is unique in his/her own way." Students are generally politically conservative, but more may be indifferent.

For all the stress, the campus is welcoming. "The friendliness of people here has never ceased to amaze me," one student relates, adding that one of the most appealing things about the school is " the closeness I feel to everyone here... I would most definitely choose IIT again if I had the chance to do it all over again."

Other schools to check out: Harvey Mudd, Rensselaer, Michigan Tech, Rochester Institute of Technology.

THE EXPERTS SAY...

"IIT's interprofessional education produces top-flight engineers and architects capable of teamwork, project management, and communicating with other professionals."

"IIT is as stressful as MIT—for half the starting salary."

ILLINOIS WESLEYAN UNIVERSITY

Box 2900, Bloomington, IL 61702-2900
Admissions Phone: (309) 556-3031; (800) 332-2498 Fax: (309) 556-3820
Email: iwuadmit@titan.iwu.edu Website: www.iwu.edu
Application Website: www.iwu.edu/admissions/apping.html

General Info

Type of School: private, coed
Setting: suburban
Academic Calendar: 4-4-1

Student Body

Full-Time Undergrads: 2,098
  Men: 43%, Women: 57%

Part-Time Undergrads: 8
  Men: 38%, Women: 63%

Total Undergrad Population:
  African American: 3%
  Asian American: 2%
  Latino: 2%
  Native American: <1%
  Caucasian: 86%
  International: 2%
  Out-of-State: 13%
  Living Off-Campus: 17%
  In Fraternities: 40%
  In Sororities: 32%

Academics

Full-Time Faculty: 159
  With Ph.D.: 92%

Part-Time Faculty: 49
  With Ph.D.: 49%

Student/Faculty Ratio: 12:1

Most Popular Majors:
  business administration (14%)
  biology (9%)
  psychology (8%)
  English (6%)
  music (5%)

Completing 2 or More Majors: 14%

Freshmen Retention Rate: 93%

Graduation Rates:
  70% within four years
  73% within six years

Admissions

Regular Application Deadline: 3/1
  (priority)

Fall Transfer Deadline: 3/1 (priority)

Spring Transfer Deadline: 10/1
  (priority)

Total # of Students Applied: 3,331
  Admitted: 1,431
  Enrolled: 578

# of Students Waitlisted: 837
  Students Accepting Place: 126
  Waitlisted Students Admitted: 7

Inside the Classroom

Illinois Wesleyan's academic reputation has soared in the past decade; new state-of-the-art facilities and excellence of programs have made it one of the top universities in the midwest. Next door to huge Illinois State in nearby Normal, IWU's small size and the personal attention given to students by a very involved and caring faculty are definitely among its selling points. At about 2,000 undergrads, students say the school is just the right size, offering many academic options as well as the opportunity to forge close ties with professors and fellow students. The school prides itself on extended faculty office hours, and students share anecdotes of professors working late into the night to help with coursework. Financial aid is good, although the inevitable red tape does occur.

IWU has three schools: the College of Liberal Arts, the College of Fine Arts, and the School of Nursing. The College of Liberal Arts offers 39 majors and three preprofessional programs: medical technology, predental, and pre-engineering. The College of Fine Arts includes the schools of art, music, and theater arts, and an interdisciplinary major in music theater. The School of Nursing offers a four year program and confers a bachelor of science in nursing degree. The most popular majors include business administration, biology, music, psychology, and English. The music school has a superb reputation, and the science and English departments are strong. In keeping with its liberal arts philosophy, the school encourages multiple interests and double majors in disparate fields such as physics and business administration or music and biology. While supportive, the academic atmosphere is challenging, and students really have to work for high grades.

IWU recently revamped its general education program. The core curriculum is designed to foster "intellectual independence, critical thinking, imagination, social awareness, and sensitivity to others." Freshmen are required to participate in a Gateway Colloquium, a small seminar focusing on writing, class discussion, and academic thinking on themes such as Science and Society and the Business of Business. Further distribution requirements include courses in the analysis of values; the arts; cultural and historical change; formal reasoning; intellectual traditions; literature; modern and classical languages; the natural sciences; physical education; and encountering diversity.

IWU's 4-4-1 calendar is based on two 15-week semesters, followed by a month-long May Term. Students take advantage of May Term to experiment with new subjects or to pursue traditional course matter in nontraditional ways. Students also become involved in service and experiential learning, and collaborate with faculty on research. May Term is also the time for travel, domestic and international. IWU offers study abroad programs in Australia, England, Denmark, China, and Japan, among other locales.

Campus Environment

Illinois Wesleyan University is located in Bloomington, about halfway between Chicago and St. Louis. With Bloomington's twin city Normal, the population is about 100,000. While very safe and quiet, there is little to do in Bloomington, and, after exhausting the attractions of the malls, students find the town boring. The home of

Illinois State, Normal is a bit more exciting, and IWU students find more things do to on and around the bustling ISU campus.

Students and guidance counselors love IWU's 76-acre campus for its aesthetics and for the quality of the facilities. IWU is a residential campus and first-year students are required to live in first-year residence halls. There are 19 residence halls, and the housing is mostly modern and generally good; students decorate their dorms with floor murals, painted during the school's Fall Festival. Members of frats and sororities are required to live in chapter houses after fulfilling a two-semester residence hall requirement. Several meal plan options are available. Word on the food is mixed, with some students calling it pretty good and others calling it awful. Parking permits are free and a car comes in handy for roadtrips to Chicago, Peoria, or the University of Illinois at Urbana-Champaign.

Student Life

With little to do in Bloomington or Normal, students can at least be grateful that there are not many distractions from studies in town. What entertainment is to be had is found on campus, and on the campus of nearby Illinois State. The Greeks are the main force in providing the needed fun. Frat parties liven up the weekends for Greeks and non-Greeks alike.

If you're not connected in the Greek network, life can be pretty lonely, but there is still a lot to do on campus. With a top-flight music school on campus, there are always concerts, and the theater school produces shows. Film is big, and professors introduce an International Film Series. Visiting performers have included MTV hip-hop poets, and speakers have included Gloria Steinem and Gwendolyn Brooks. There are a host of student organizations on campus. Sports are big, and the Titans compete in Division III. Basketball is king, and students turn out for the season in droves. Illinois Wesleyan is in the top ten all-time schools with the most Academic All-Americans. Intramurals are popular, and there's also a golf league.

The IWU student body is fairly moderate, leaning to the left of its surrounding area. There's a small minority population, and most Titans are concerned about the lack of diversity on this mostly white and Illinois-bred campus. Students are friendly and approachable, for the most part, and despite spending a lot of time on campus, they're still in touch with the outside world, thanks to the "social awareness" the curriculum helps instill in them.

Other schools to check out: Denison, DePauw, Bradley, Valparaiso, Lake Forest.

Test Scores (middle 50%):
  SAT Verbal: 580–690
  SAT Math: 600–690
  ACT Comp: 26–31
  ACT English: 26–32
  ACT Math: 26–31

HS Rank of Entering Freshmen:
  Top 10%: 52%
  Top 25%: 84%
  Top 50%: 99%

THE EXPERTS SAY...

" IWU's reputation is growing as the administration adds facilities, retains caring faculty, and improves programs. "

" Need we say that there is nothing to do in Bloomington-Normal? If you don't go Greek, you'll have to hope that the music majors give lots of concerts. "

Costs (2004–5)

Tuition and Fees: $25,130

Room & Board: $6,140

Payment Plan(s): installment plan

Inst. Aid (est. 2003–04)

Institutional Aid, Need-Based:
  $11,478,897

Institutional Aid, Non-Need-Based:
  $5,424,600

FT Undergrads Receiving Aid: 59%
  Avg. Amount per Student: $17,044

FT Undergrads Receiving Non-Need-Based Scholarship or Grant Aid: 29%
  Avg. Amount per Student: $7,835

Of Those Receiving Any Aid:

Rec. Need-Based Scholarship or Grant Aid: 99%
  Average Award: $11,863

Rec. Need-Based Self-Help Aid: 82%
  Average Award: $6,064

Upon Graduation, Avg. Loan Debt per Student: $20,803

Financial Aid Deadline: rolling, 3/1 (priority)

Graduates

Going to Graduate School:
  29% Within One Year

Companies Recruiting On Campus: 75

Alumni Giving: 53%

INDIANA UNIVERSITY OF PENNSYLVANIA

1011 South Drive, Indiana, PA 15705-1085
Admissions Phone: (724) 357-2230; (800) 442-6830 Email: admissions-inquiry@iup.edu
Application Website: www.iup.edu/admissions

General Info

Type of School: public, coed
Setting: small town
Academic Calendar: semester

Student Body

Full-Time Undergrads: 11,144
  Men: 44%, Women: 56%
Part-Time Undergrads: 690
  Men: 41%, Women: 59%

Total Undergrad Population:
  African American: 6%
  Asian American: 1%
  Latino: 1%
  Native American: <1%
  Caucasian: 81%
  International: 2%
  Out-of-State: 3%
  Living Off-Campus: 68%
  In Fraternities: 10%
  In Sororities: 11%

Graduate and First-Professional
  Students: 1,749

Academics

Full-Time Faculty: 632
  With Ph.D.: 82%
Part-Time Faculty: 62
Student/Faculty Ratio: 19:1

Most Popular Majors:
  criminology (8%)
  elementary education (7%)
  communications media (5%)
  nursing (4%)
  management (4%)

Freshmen Retention Rate: 73%

Graduation Rates:
  24% within four years
  49% within six years

Admissions

Regular Application Deadline: 12/31
  (priority)

Total # of Students Applied: 8,618
  Admitted: 5,136
  Enrolled: 2,761

Test Scores (middle 50%):
  SAT Verbal: 480–570
  SAT Math: 470–570

HS Rank of Entering Freshmen:
  Top 10%: 19%
  Top 25%: 38%
  Top 50%: 77%

Inside the Classroom

IUP offers its students the best of both worlds: As the university likes to say, it's big and it's small at the same time. IUP provides a strong, well-rounded education, combining a comprehensive core Liberal Studies curriculum with a wide variety of majors and minors in several undergraduate schools: the Eberly College of Business and Information Technology, the College of Education and Educational Technology, the College of Fine Arts, the College of Health and Human Services, the College of Humanities and Social Sciences, and the College of Natural Sciences and Mathematics. Students can choose from more than 100 degree programs; standouts include criminology, computer science, anthropology, education, safety science, and communications media.

All students must complete the Liberal Studies program, which includes courses in English comp, math, the humanities, fine arts, natural sciences (at least one lab), social sciences, health and wellness, and non-Western cultures. Three Liberal Studies courses are designed especially for freshmen: "College Writing," "History: The Modern Era," and one course from a list of Fine Arts selections. Before graduating, students must also take a "Senior Synthesis" course, preferably one outside of their major in order to broaden their experience.

About 90 of the university's best and brightest freshmen enroll each year in the prestigious Robert E. Cook Honors College, a four-year, university-wide program open to all majors. Students in the Honors College spend a good deal of their first two years taking an interdisciplinary core course, where they address questions such as "What do we believe?" and "How do we discern the good from the bad?"

While Honors College students rave about their professors and their classes, not all undergrads in the other schools report back so glowingly. Some complain of big, impersonal lectures. Officially, three-quarters of all undergrad courses enroll fewer than 30 students, and IUP claims that you'll always be taught by a professor, never a TA. The workload depends on the major, and students say that academic life is what you make it.

Campus Environment

The university's 340-acre main campus in Indiana (there are tiny branch campuses in Punxsutawney and Armstrong) consists of 75-plus major buildings, several of which have been entered in the National Register of Historic Places, and seven athletic fields.

All freshmen are guaranteed housing, but living on campus is not mandatory for anyone. About two-thirds of the student body live off campus or commute from home. (Many IUP students are locals.) Those who do choose dorm life have a variety of living options: coed or single-sex, smoke-free or smoking, and a couple of special-interest floors for students who wish to live with others who share a hobby, major, etc. In all, there are 13 residence halls and two apartment buildings for approximately 4,000 students to call home. Resident students are encouraged not to bring a car; parking permits are issued only to those with special or medical reasons. To get around the Indiana area, students just take the bus.

Indiana—"the Christmas Tree Capital of the World"—is a quiet, quaint country town in the heart of western Pennsylvania. The university reports that the IUP community has been ranked no. 1 in safety in the state, no. 1 in the Northeast, and no. 5 in the entire nation. Indiana is not exactly the most exciting of locations: about an hour from Pittsburgh, three from Cleveland, four from Baltimore, and five from Philadelphia. Closer to campus, students have many opportunities for outdoor activities, including hunting, fishing, skiing, biking, and golfing. The school-owned Co-op Recreational Park features a lodge and ski hut on nearly 280 acres of wooded hillsides and trails.

Student Life

A state school, IUP has a student body comprised almost entirely of Pennsylvania natives, most of whom hail from the immediate area. (The combination of low in-state tuition and great facilities makes IUP very appealing to those who live nearby.) Students here are reportedly friendly—though some say cliques abound—and easygoing. About a tenth of the student body joins one of 36 fraternities and sororities, and we hear that the Greeks are largely responsible for much of the social life on weekends, especially for freshmen looking to party. Once a well-reputed party school (IUP, students joked, stood for "I'm Usually Partying"), things have calmed down considerably in recent years, following a few alcohol-related student deaths. School and local officials have since adopted a "zero tolerance" policy toward underage and binge drinking, and we hear that the cops can be ruthless in busting up parties and arresting offenders. Nonetheless, students still find their way to a keg, either at frat parties, house parties, or, for those over 21, the local bars. There's not a whole lot else to do here—the sleepy, rural town of Indiana doesn't offer much in the way of entertainment. Restless students head home for the weekend, or drive to the bustling city of Pittsburgh to enjoy its many bars, restaurants, shops, and cultural offerings.

On campus, students hang out in the beautiful Oak Grove between classes. The new Hadley Union Building (H.U.B.) features a huge exercise center, bookstore, cybercafe, and coffee shop. The school sponsors hundreds of cultural events and activities, such as art exhibits, lectures, musicians, plays, and concerts; past visitors to the campus include Dave Matthews, Billy Joel, and Spike Lee.

Hundreds of campus clubs of all kinds give students plenty of things to do outside the classroom. A strong Division II contender, IUP offers 17 varsity sports for men and women. The men's golf program and the women's softball, basketball, and field hockey teams have all boasted great seasons of late, but it's the football games that draw the biggest crowds. The football team has been in the Division II playoffs 11 times in the past 14 years; three IUP alumni currently play in the NFL.

Costs (2002–03)

Tuition and Fees, In-State: $5,785

Tuition and Fees, Out-of-State: $12,683

Room & Board: $4,702

Regional or 'good neighbor' tuition available

Payment Plan(s): installment plan

THE EXPERTS SAY...

" You can choose from over 100 programs at IUP. Recommended for small classes and great profs: The Robert E. Cook Honors College. "

" Although officials have cracked down, 'IUP' still stands for 'I'm Usually Partying.' "

Inst. Aid (2002–03)

Institutional Aid, Need-Based: $20,000

Institutional Aid, Non-Need-Based: $2,630,672

FT Undergrads Receiving Aid: 66% Avg. Amount per Student: $7,067

FT Undergrads Receiving Non-Need-Based Scholarship or Grant Aid: 3% Avg. Amount per Student: $2,286

Of Those Receiving Any Aid:

Rec. Need-Based Scholarship or Grant Aid: 83% Average Award: $3,639

Rec. Need-Based Self-Help Aid: 91% Average Award: $3,967

Upon Graduation, Avg. Loan Debt per Student: $17,825

Financial Aid Deadline: rolling, 4/15 (priority)

Graduates

Going to Graduate School: 19% Within One Year

INDIANA UNIVERSITY—BLOOMINGTON

300 N. Jordan Avenue, Bloomington, IN 47405-1106
Admissions Phone: (812) 855-0661 Fax: (812) 855-5102 Email: iuadmit@indiana.edu
Website: www.iub.edu Application Website: www.indiana.edu/~iuadmit

General Info

Type of School: public, coed

Setting: small town

Academic Calendar: semester

Student Body

Full-Time Undergrads: 28,473
  Men: 48%, Women: 52%

Part-Time Undergrads: 1,760
  Men: 47%, Women: 53%

Total Undergrad Population:
  African American: 4%
  Asian American: 3%
  Latino: 2%
  Caucasian: 86%
  International: 4%
  Out-of-State: 33%
  Living Off-Campus: 51%
  In Fraternities: 16%
  In Sororities: 18%

Graduate and First-Professional
  Students: 8,270

Academics

Full-Time Faculty: 1,486
  With Ph.D.: 76%

Student/Faculty Ratio: 19:1

Most Popular Majors:
  business/marketing (21%)
  education (17%)
  communications/communication
  technologies (10%)
  protective sciences/public administration (10%)
  social sciences & history (7%)

Freshmen Retention Rate: 88%

Graduation Rates:
  46% within four years
  69% within six years

Admissions

Regular Application Deadline: 4/1
  (priority)

Fall Transfer Deadline: 2/1 (priority)

Spring Transfer Deadline: 11/1 (priority)

Total # of Students Applied: 22,178
  Admitted: 17,992
  Enrolled: 6,784

Inside the Classroom

Indiana guidance counselors seemingly want to shout it from the rooftops: IU Bloomington has been changing for the better. In addition to the amazing number of academic choices, guidance counselors rave about the new programs, the scholarships, the academic standards, and even the tougher admissions requirements. IU has been admitting increasing numbers of out-of-state students. This trend concerns Indiana legislators, who fear that home-state students may be edged out by the out-of-staters who typically have higher SAT scores and pay three times the in-state tuition. However, IU officials insist qualified in-state students haven't been pushed aside and won't be in the future; in fact, a new automatic scholarship for in-state students with outstanding class rank and/or test scores is being introduced.

IU's 12 undergraduate schools provide around 30,000 undergrads with hundreds of different programs of study. The undergraduate music, business, education, and journalism schools are considered to be among the best in the nation. The vocal performance program is truly outstanding: "We send more soloists to the Met than anyone else!" crows one music student. No matter what your area, landing a job after graduation should not be a problem: IU Bloomington offers not one, but 15 career and placement offices on campus, most located within a particular school or area of study.

IU Bloomington's transitional programs for incoming freshmen are among the best of their kind. Most freshmen begin their studies in the University Division and spend at least one semester taking general education classes before selecting a major and applying to one of IU's degree-granting schools. In the Freshmen Interest Groups (FIGs), up to 20 students take two or three courses on a related theme together and live on campus in close proximity. IU also sponsors an Intensive Freshman Seminar program that takes place in the summer before the student's first semester. The seminar classes are tiny, allowing students to form relationships with professors and develop critical time management skills. IU Bloomington is also renowned for its international programs and its plethora of undergraduate research opportunities.

"Our school is a very academic school," a student says. "The workload is a fair amount and challenging but it's also a lot of fun." While the university's huge size yields many academic and social options, the cattle-herd effect can be irritating (though a guidance counselor insists this is changing: "The registration and college major advising is more personal for the student."). "IU's biggest problem is the size of classes," says one student. "The teachers are very good, but in large classes it's hard to take advantage of them." But another student comments: "I love IU, I love the size because it's like living in another world."

Campus Environment

Guidance counselors call IU's sprawling campus dotted with lakes and woods one of the most beautiful in the nation. Indiana's newly passed spending plan is restoring funding to IU after massive cuts in last year's budget, including over $30 million funding for the construction of a multidisciplinary science building.

As befits a school this size, IU Bloomington has one of the most extensive dorm systems in the country. McNutt, Foster, and Teter are given the nod because "they're clean, nice, and air-conditioned." (Advises a student, "Choosing an academic floor is an easy way to get into your first choice dorm.") On-campus housing is guaranteed for all who want it, but the food "is expensive and not really worth it."

Off campus, "the apartment business is a very big business in Bloomington," we're told, and the palatial Greek houses reign. "You don't need a car because the IU Bus system is there and parking isn't great anyway," a sophomore comments. The town of Bloomington caters to the student population, and students love it right back. "The city itself is very involved with the campus," notes a sophomore.

Student Life

Explaining IU's popularity, a counselor says, "It is known as a party school and the students like the sound of it." Bill O'Reilly of Fox-TV's "O'Reilly Factor" doesn't: O'Reilly pilloried the school after the story broke in fall 2002 that a California company filmed a porn video in a "taxpayer-funded" dorm on Bloomington's campus. (Ironically, IU was reportedly selected by the filmmakers based on a questionable ranking at the time as the nation's top party school.) But applications are still on the rise. "The students want to attend because it is receiving attention," a Georgia guidance counselor observes.

Hoosiers basketball is huge and has a fanatical following, and football games draw large crowds, especially the annual game against rival Purdue. A small army of students participate in IU's powerhouse varsity teams and club and intramural sports. A longstanding campus tradition, the annual Little 500 bycicle race is broadcast on national television and over 30 teams participate each year. "It's our Tour de France," says one student. "Everywhere you look, teams are training on the roads and back roads."

For the social life, it's hard to ignore the fraternities and sororities: "Membership is a status symbol," says one sophomore, and given the mansionlike houses that some Greeks live in, it's easy to see why. Another student didn't find the frats so charming: "They might act nice to you when you first start to rush, for the sole reason of making you want to pledge. Once pledgeship starts, the fraternities then have some sort of fraternal commitment to treat you like garbage."

There are other things to do, however, outside of the Greek system, including the inevitable dorm parties, hanging out in local bars, and the many concerts and performances staged by the prestigious music school. The Indiana Memorial Union is a wonder in itself and is home to six eateries, three snack shops, a seven-story student activities tower, a 12-lane bowling alley, a 400-seat theater, and a 186-room hotel. Warns a sophomore, "There are some rude people who typically are from the East Coast," adding, "A student who wouldn't fit in at our school would be someone who doesn't like large crowds, classes, or lack of individual treatment for the first two years. Since IU is a large school, you must learn to adapt."

Other schools to check out: Miami U (OH), Purdue, U of Illinois—Urbana-Champaign, Penn State, U of Wisconsin—Madison.

Test Scores (middle 50%):
SAT Verbal: 490–600
SAT Math: 500–620
ACT Comp: 22–27
ACT English: 21–28
ACT Math: 21–27

HS Rank of Entering Freshmen:
Top 10%: 23%
Top 25%: 57%
Top 50%: 95%

Costs (2003–04)

Tuition and Fees, In-State: $5,517

Tuition and Fees, Out-of-State: $16,552

Add $1,000 for first-year students

Room & Board: $5,872

Payment Plan(s): deferred payment plan

THE EXPERTS SAY...

" IU Bloomington is becoming so diverse with out-of-staters and international students, it's hard to remember that it's a state school. "

" Enjoy the variety, but don't get trampled (and watch out for creepy California filmmakers). "

Inst. Aid (est. 2003–04)

Institutional Aid, Need-Based: $4,248,302

Institutional Aid, Non-Need-Based: $24,568,256

FT Undergrads Receiving Aid: 37%
Avg. Amount per Student: $7,425

FT Undergrads Receiving Non-Need-Based Scholarship or Grant Aid: 16%
Avg. Amount per Student: $3,586

Of Those Receiving Any Aid:

Rec. Need-Based Scholarship or Grant Aid: 56%
Average Award: $4,877

Rec. Need-Based Self-Help Aid: 43%
Average Award: $2,537

Upon Graduation, Avg. Loan Debt per Student: $18,423

Financial Aid Deadline: rolling, 3/1 (priority)

ITHACA COLLEGE

100 Job Hall, Ithaca, NY 14850-7020
Admissions Phone: (607) 274-3124; (800) 429-4274 Fax: (607) 274-1900
Email: admission@ithaca.edu
Website: www.ithaca.edu

General Info

Type of School: private, coed
Setting: small town
Academic Calendar: semester

Student Body

Full-Time Undergrads: 6,098
  Men: 43%, Women: 57%

Part-Time Undergrads: 61
  Men: 44%, Women: 56%

Total Undergrad Population:
  African American: 2%
  Asian American: 3%
  Latino: 3%
  Native American: <1%
  Caucasian: 87%
  International: 3%
  Out-of-State: 51%
  Living Off-Campus: 30%
  In Fraternities: 1%
  In Sororities: 1%

Graduate and First-Professional
  Students: 236

Academics

Full-Time Faculty: 453
  With Ph.D.: 90%

Part-Time Faculty: 180
  With Ph.D.: 58%

Student/Faculty Ratio: 12:1

Most Popular Majors:
  music (11%)
  business administration (10%)
  television–radio (10%)
  physical therapy (5%)
  cinema & photography (5%)

Completing 2 or More Majors: 3%

Freshmen Retention Rate: 88%

Graduation Rates:
  64% within four years
  73% within six years

Admissions

Regular Application Deadline: 3/1

Early Decision Deadline(s): 11/1

Fall Transfer Deadline: 3/1 (priority)

Spring Transfer Deadline: 12/1 (priority)

Total # of Students Applied: 10,650
  Admitted: 6,756
  Enrolled: 1,585

Waitlist Available

Inside the Classroom

Founded as a music conservatory in 1892, Ithaca blends a liberal arts education with preprofessional training in a highly diverse curriculum. Ithaca offers more than 100 programs in five schools: business, communications, health sciences and human performance, humanities and sciences, and its renowned music school. There's also an interdisciplinary gerontology institute. "Hands-on" is the phrase that describes education at Ithaca. Students get involved in performance, research, internships, work-study (about 2,800 students work on campus), and study abroad through a wealth of programs designed to join classroom knowledge with practical experience. The annual Whalen Academic Symposium showcases student research and creative expression in each of the College's schools.

Ithaca offers B.A., B.S., B.F.A., and B.M. degrees. The physical therapy major is one of the best in the nation, and boasts high placement rates for graduates. Television-radio, journalism, cinema, and photography are all strong, and communication students can attend programs in Los Angeles, at Nanyang Technological University in Singapore, and at the school's London Center. Theater arts and management programs are excellent, and the school of music offers incredible opportunities in music education and performance. Growing rapidly, the business school is still considered weak compared to Ithaca's other schools.

Ithaca has many of the advantages of a university like nearby rival Cornell without the disadvantages. Program offerings are large, but class size is small. Classes are taught by professors who are "very accessible and helpful" and "fair but challenging, and very good." The workload is "demanding, but not excessive," a junior says, noting that there is not "a high level of competition between students."

Campus Environment

Ithaca completely rebuilt its campus in 1960, moving from downtown location to an attractive modern environment atop a hill overlooking the city and Lake Cayuga. In recent years, Ithaca has added many new facilities to its campus, including a new music center, a state-of-the-art health-science facility, and a fitness center that has received kudos from the athletics industry. As for the city of Ithaca, a student says: "For a city of its size, there is a lot to do. It is definitely a 'college town' because of the presence of both Cornell and Ithaca College. There is an incredible diversity of restaurants, music, and culture. It is a very liberal city." Outdoor buffs can revel in the beauty of the local parks and Ithaca's fantastic waterfalls and gorges.

Ithaca is a residential college, according to the administration, which expects students to live on campus. About 70 percent of Ithacans do live in residence halls. "Usually, there is a shortage of on-campus housing due to overenrollment of incoming freshman," a student explains. "The dorms vary in age and therefore in quality, but no dorms are unreasonable." The East and West Towers are the most visible landmarks on campus and offer views of the lake, banking facilities, and a restaurant. The Terraces offer suite-style housing with an all-female building, a dining hall with fountains, and a new "Housing Offering Multicultural Experience" (HOME) program. New students may be interested in Boothroyd or Terrace 5, reserved for first-year students only. The school recently purchased an apartment complex near campus which should alleviate overcrowding. Off-campus housing is affordable and available. Freshmen, sophomores, and juniors must apply to live off-campus. Ithaca allows first-year students to bring their cars (parking permits are required). "A car is helpful, but not necessary," comments a junior. "Ithaca has a reasonable public transportation system for a city of its size, the TCAT buses, which go to most places around town."

Student Life

An Ithacan describes a typical week: "Weeknights are usually spent studying or attending meetings for clubs…On weekends, most students go out either to parties or bars or other places around town." We hear that "drinking is a big part of the weekends," but there's an "average level of drinking and drug use compared to most colleges." The administration has been eliminating traditional student blowouts on this officially dry campus, causing "a high level of friction" between students and officials. A student notes: "Like any college, there are parties but I wouldn't say it is a huge party school overall." The Greek presence is minimal, with about four percent in fraternities.

There are over 140 different clubs at Ithaca. As befits a school with an excellent communications program, the student paper, *The Ithacan*, and the campus radio and television stations are top-notch. Music students not only play in the ensemble performances required for their degrees, but also perform in organizations like the Trombone Troupe and Ithacapella. "The Community Service Network, the Student Government Association, the Ithaca College Environmental Society, and BIGAYLA are among the most popular clubs," a junior tells us. For you Twilight Zone fans, Ithaca is home to the Rod Serling Archives.

The Bombers are strong Division III competitors, with 25 varsity teams and 12 national championships, earning praise from *The New York Times*, *USA Today*, and *Sports Illustrated*. "Football and basketball are very popular and well attended," a student reports. " One of the biggest events of the year at Ithaca is the 'Cortaca' football game against Cortland State." There are 14 intramural sports and 21 club sports and about 1,700 IC students participate. Ithaca is an outdoor lover's dream, and virtually every sport is available: swimming in the gorges, skiing, sailing on the nearby lake, hiking, biking, and many more.

Ithaca is concerned about its homogeneity, but the typical student remains "white upper-middle class." The campus is fairly liberal. "A very conservative student might not fit in very well," a student observes, adding: "But I know a few very conservative students who really like Ithaca." A recent campus controversy centered around the dining service provider: "It was reported that the parent company had stock in private prisons, which led to many protests and petitions," a student tells us. Students are friendly and "there is a good level of 'school spirit' in terms of attending sporting events, etc.". While some chafe at being in the shadow of Cornell, most students appreciate their school: "[It's] big enough that there are many opportunities and options but small enough that it is easy to get involved… and class sizes are reasonable," a student concludes.

Other schools to check out: Hofstra, SUNY Geneseo, SUNY Purchase, Fordham, Syracuse.

Applied Early Decision: 259
  Early Decision Admitted: 106

Test Scores (middle 50%):
  SAT Verbal: 540–640
  SAT Math: 550–640

HS Rank of Entering Freshmen:
  Top 10%: 36%
  Top 25%: 72%
  Top 50%: 97%

Costs (2003-04)

Tuition and Fees: $22,264

Room & Board: $9,466

Payment Plan(s): installment plan

THE EXPERTS SAY…

" At Ithaca, you'll be researching, working, performing, and creating. The college offers large school programs in a small school atmosphere. "

" Get ready to spend four years tripping over Cornell students. "

Inst. Aid (est. 2003–04)

Institutional Aid, Need-Based: $42,134,119

Institutional Aid, Non-Need-Based: $8,446,507

FT Undergrads Receiving Aid: 69%
  Avg. Amount per Student: $20,381

FT Undergrads Receiving Non-Need-Based Scholarship or Grant Aid: 9%
  Avg. Amount per Student: $8,086

Of Those Receiving Any Aid:

Rec. Need-Based Scholarship or Grant Aid: 95%
  Average Award: $12,903

Rec. Need-Based Self-Help Aid: 94%
  Average Award: $6,912

Financial Aid Deadline: 2/1 (priority)

Graduates

Going to Graduate School:
  30% Within One Year

Accepting Job Offer:
  13% at time of graduation

Companies Recruiting On Campus: 111

Alumni Giving: 34%

JAMES MADISON UNIVERSITY

Sonner Hall MSC 0101, Harrisonburg, VA 22807
Admissions Phone: (540) 568-5681 Fax: (540) 568-3332
Email: gotojmu@jmu.edu Website: www.jmu.edu
Application Website: www.jmu.edu/admissions/

General Info

Type of School: public, coed

Setting: small town

Academic Calendar: semester

Student Body

Full-Time Undergrads: 14,268
　Men: 40%, Women: 60%

Part-Time Undergrads: 417
　Men: 50%, Women: 50%

Total Undergrad Population:
　African American: 3%
　Asian American: 5%
　Latino: 2%
　Native American: <1%
　Caucasian: 85%
　International: 1%
　Out-of-State: 30%
　Living Off-Campus: 60%
　In Fraternities: 10%
　In Sororities: 16%

Graduate and First-Professional
　Students: 1,212

Academics

Full-Time Faculty: 721
　With Ph.D.: 82%

Part-Time Faculty: 275
　With Ph.D.: 28%

Student/Faculty Ratio: 17:1

Most Popular Majors:
　marketing (7%)
　psychology (7%)
　health sciences (6%)
　integrated science and technology
　(5%)
　computer information (5%)

Completing 2 or More Majors: 6%

Freshmen Retention Rate: 92%

Graduation Rates:
　61% within four years
　80% within six years

Admissions

Regular Application Deadline: 1/15;
　11/1 (priority)

Early Action Deadline: 11/1

Fall Transfer Deadline: 3/1

Spring Transfer Deadline: 10/15

Total # of Students Applied: 15,056
　Admitted: 9,404
　Enrolled: 3,388

Inside the Classroom

James Madison University has exceptional academic programs set in a comfortable, amiable environment that is highly popular with Virginia high school grads and guidance counselors; almost three quarters (70 percent) of the undergraduate population come from within the state. JMU students have great pride in their school and truly believe that theirs is the best public school in the state. This conviction is reinforced by consistently being ranked among the top two or three public regional universities in the South. T-shirts seen around the campus sum up the JMU atmosphere: In traditional University of Virginia orange and blue colors, they proclaim "JMU—THE University of Virginia."

The five schools that make up this university of just under 15,000 undergraduates are arts and letters; business; education and psychology; science and mathematics; and integrated science and technology. Liberal arts, music, business, and technology programs are particularly strong at James Madison University. Outside of the General Education courses, the average class size is 29. The 17:1 student/faculty ratio makes the instructors fairly accessible. "By the end of my first semester freshman year, I knew the professors in my major's classes and they knew me," says a student.

All undergraduates at James Madison University are required to take the General Education Program, the core curriculum. In the General Education Program, students must take five different "clusters" of courses. Each cluster consists of a cross-disciplinary sequence of related courses. This constitutes 44 credit hours—a sizable piece of each student's courseload. Typical General Education class size is 36 students. Other course requirements vary by program.

Entering freshmen who graduated from high school with an unweighted grade point average of 3.5 or above, and with scores at or above 1300 on the SAT or 30 or above on the ACT, are invited to enter the highly selective Honors Program. Under the guidance of recognized teacher-scholars, the Honors Program offers students the opportunity to cultivate the habits of critical thinking, independent analysis, and creative expression through small classes and independent study.

Campus Environment

James Madison University's lovely 472-acre campus, complete with its own lake, is situated in the beautiful Shenandoah Valley, only 30 minutes from West Virginia. The school's surroundings just outside of Harrisonburg, Virginia offer plenty of opportunities for outdoor activities such as skiing, snowboarding, hiking, camping, canoeing, tubing, and horseback riding. "If you enjoy nature, you'll love it," a student says. Students craving city excitement can find it a two-hour drive away in Richmond and Washington, DC. The school also offers a weekend shuttle bus to various cities in Virginia. Montpellier, the ancestral home of the school's namesake, who served as America's fourth president and is known as the founder of the Constitution, is nearby.

On-campus housing is guaranteed only to freshmen. More than 95 percent of incoming freshmen are assigned to freshmen-only dorms. All dorms are equipped with washers and dryers, but only two are air-conditioned. Residence halls are assigned randomly to incoming freshmen; you can't choose your future residence. After the first year, students are permitted to live in fraternity/sorority housing. Upperclassmen can pick their dorm room through a lottery system. The majority of upperclassmen live in nearby off-campus apartments and in houses that are plentiful and easy to find. "I do not know of anyone who was unable to find off-campus housing," says a student. The cost of living off-campus is practically the same as living on-campus, we hear.

Student Life

James Madison University is known for its congenial and laid-back atmosphere. With a freshman retention rate of 92 percent, it's no wonder that one Virginia guidance counselor says that she has never had a student transfer from James Madison University. Students are very enthusiastic about the school and even end up recruiting their friends. "It has all the resources of a large university, yet it has the availability and friendliness of a small college," raves a student.

When asked what JMU students do for fun, one student replies, "During the week, most people spend their nights working out or just hanging out with friends in the dorms or in the apartments. On the weekends, people usually go to the apartment parties, frat parties, or the movies both on and off campus." There are several fraternities and sororities. Drinking is mostly done off campus, "since alcohol violations are taken very seriously and punished accordingly by campus police [and] RAs," a student warns.

There are plenty of activities on campus to keep students busy. JMU offers more than 230 clubs and organizations, including campus TV stations, a student magazine, religious organizations, and lots of musical groups. The most popular clubs are the student Duke club (which supports the sports teams, the JMU Dukes), the JMU Marching Band, Student Government, WMRA (campus radio station), and The Breeze (campus newspaper).

JMU sports are very strong overall, with 15 Women's NCAA Division I sports and 12 Men's NCAA Division I sports. Football and basketball programs are popular. Thirty-two club sports draw about seven percent of the student population. Some of the club sport teams play state and regional competition. There are also 30 intramural sports in which 65 percent of students compete, with soccer being the biggest draw.

# of Students Waitlisted: 1,000
  Waitlisted Students Admitted: 31

Test Scores (middle 50%):
  SAT Verbal: 540–620
  SAT Math: 540–630
  ACT Comp: 22–26

THE EXPERTS SAY...

" Virginia students really love James Madison—they recruit their friends. This public university offers terrific programs in a friendly, fun atmosphere, and is a great choice for business majors. "

" JMU is almost too perfect to be believed. Is it possible to be too well-rounded and well-balanced? "

HS Rank of Entering Freshmen:
  Top 10%: 30%
  Top 25%: 79%
  Top 50%: 99%

Avg. HS GPA: 3.66

Costs (2003–04)

Tuition and Fees, In-State: $5,058

Tuition and Fees, Out-of-State: $13,280

Room & Board: $5,966

Payment Plan(s): installment plan

Inst. Aid (est. 2003–04)

Institutional Aid, Need-Based: $64,802

Institutional Aid, Non-Need-Based: $1,582,778

FT Undergrads Receiving Aid: 29%
  Avg. Amount per Student: $6,102

FT Undergrads Receiving Non-Need-Based Scholarship or Grant Aid: 2%
  Avg. Amount per Student: $1,602

Of Those Receiving Any Aid:

Rec. Need-Based Scholarship or Grant Aid: 41%
  Average Award: $4,380

Rec. Need-Based Self-Help Aid: 79%
  Average Award: $3,761

Upon Graduation, Avg. Loan Debt per Student: $11,639

Financial Aid Deadline: 3/1 (priority)

Graduates

Companies Recruiting On-Campus: 154

Alumni Giving: 32%

JOHNS HOPKINS UNIVERSITY

3400 North Charles Street, Baltimore, MD 21218-2668
Admissions Phone: (410) 516-8171 Fax: (410) 516-6025
Email: gotojhu@jhu.edu Website: www.jhu.edu
Application Website: apply.jhu.edu

General Info

Type of School: private, coed
Setting: urban
Academic Calendar: 4-1-4

Student Body

Full-Time Undergrads: 4,103
 Men: 57%, Women: 43%

Part-Time Undergrads: 11
 Men: 73%, Women: 27%

Total Undergrad Population:
 African American: 5%
 Asian American: 21%
 Latino: 4%
 Caucasian: 64%
 International: 6%
 Out-of-State: 80%
 Living Off-Campus: 47%
 In Fraternities: 23%
 In Sororities: 22%

Graduate and First-Professional
 Students: 1,576

Academics

Full-Time Faculty: 455
 With Ph.D.: 96%

Part-Time Faculty: 23

Student/Faculty Ratio: 9:1

Most Popular Majors:
 biomedical engineering (12%)
 international studies (6%)
 biology (6%)
 public health (4%)
 computer science (4%)

Freshmen Retention Rate: 95%

Graduation Rates:
 80% within four years
 88% within six years

Admissions

Regular Application Deadline: 1/1

Early Decision Deadline(s): 11/15

Fall Transfer Deadline: 3/15

Spring Transfer Deadline: 11/1

Total # of Students Applied: 10,022
 Admitted: 3,052
 Enrolled: 1,048

# of Students Waitlisted: 1,702
 Students Accepting Place: 675
 Waitlisted Students Admitted: 84

Applied Early Decision: 610
 Early Decision Admitted: 349

In the Classroom

Undergraduate programs at prestigious JHU are offered at the Krieger School of Arts and Sciences, the Whiting School of Engineering, the School of Professional Studies in Business and Education, the School of Nursing, and the Peabody Institute. Known for its biomedical engineering and international studies programs, Hopkins has many research opportunities in which undergraduates work closely with faculty. One biology major tells us, "All students at Hopkins are intelligent and work very hard… During reading periods and finals week, our main library is open 24/7 and people literally move in. You can walk around and see students with pillows, toothpaste, contact solution, stacks of coffee cups, and pictures of their family taped up on the walls of their work station." The same student also explains, "The academics are very rigorous and you have to work really hard to stay ahead of the game." A neuroscience major says, "It is about what one makes for him/herself … if you know where you are going, Hopkins will give you all the room you need to grow. If you're clueless and hope that coming here will help you find your way, you'll be disappointed." The student continues, "if you're looking for an intimate education where you are taught by experts in the field … then Hopkins is the place." Also, the school "has one of the best premed curriculums in the country."

Top-notch faculty "are very open to students who are genuinely driven—i.e., care about the subject matter, come to office hours, and want to get more out of their classes than an A." We are also told that "the quality of the professors is very high," however, "there is no doubt that they know their stuff but students often get the feeling that professors care less about the students than they do about their research." The university describes how "the opportunity for undergraduates to learn from and work side by side with some of the most renowned faculty/researchers in the world is the most unique attribute of JHU."

Campus Environment

Housing is only guaranteed for the first two years at JHU, and for the most part freshmen and sophomores are mixed. According to the university, "Freshmen are NOT allowed to live in Greek houses." A junior describes the on-campus housing situation: "I know people that have had to triple up in rooms that were intended as doubles, until Hopkins was able to provide a place for them to move permanently." Another student tells us that "the campus accommodations are way above average in terms of amenities, space, and cleanliness." But another cautions, "not all dorms are created equal."

Many people live off campus, where housing is "readily available" but "you have to move fast to get into the more desirable apartments." Stay close to campus, though, since we are told by a student that "Baltimore was just rated the fourth most dangerous city in the United States. Having said that, the immediate area around campus is safe, but once you step outside that area, it gets pretty dangerous."

Students seem to agree that it's nice to have a car to get around here. "Bus routes run but if you want to have freedom to explore the city, invest in a car!" But we also heard, "Transportation, via school shuttle to the mall or anywhere within one mile, is convenient. Taxis are everywhere. No car is needed, plus crime is high so a car is often broken into." The university does not allow freshmen to keep cars on campus.

Student Life

"There is a stereotypical Hopkins student, though there is no true typical Hopkins student," says a senior. "Hopkins does not leave a lot of room for a wild college time," we are told. "Students go to frat parties, have on campus social activities, study, study some more, some go to D.C. [about an hour away] or the Inner Harbor [in Baltimore] or malls in neighboring suburbs" We hear that "there is drinking and drug use, but it is likely below average. Smoking is low." A student explains, "drinking was banned in the low-key bar that was located on campus and allowed drinking exploration for students who were underage; drinking was also banned on a prominent grassy knoll in front of the library called the Beach. The popular opinion is that the campus became drier without these drinking opportunities—in both senses of the word." Greek life has its place at JHU, but does not seem overbearing. "Fraternities and sororities have a very large influence on the social scene, not because they provide the ONLY entertainment, but because they provide the most accessible way to meet new people and have fun on weekends and even during the week," says one student.

"Student Council and administration do a good job of creating a diverse range of events for students in the community both for recreation and service-related activities." We are told, "this year, we had our first undergraduate research conference that was completely student-organized and student-run. Huge success." One student explains, "Alumni care a lot about undergraduates and thus we have a voice in administration." Students are active in the community. Popular school-sponsored organizations include "research [are we clear on this yet?], honor societies, and community service." According to the university, "70 percent of our students participate in at least one volunteer activity during their time at Hopkins." A student tells us, "Recent debates include student support for a higher campus minimum wage for the community workers, and grade disinflation."

"Spring Fair" is "a community/Hopkins spring event—that always draws a lot of people from the community as well as students." Also, Hopkins draws "entertainers like Shaggy and Eminem, and speakers like Janet Reno, Jerry Springer." Sports are described by students as "minimal" and school spirit "below average," but one student adds, "lacrosse is very big." Also, "A new addition to our campus has been the state-of-the-art gym that opened this winter."

Other schools to check out: Cornell, University of Pennsylvania, Duke, Carnegie Mellon, Emory.

Test Scores (middle 50%):
  SAT Verbal: 630–720
  SAT Math: 660–750
  ACT Comp: 28–32
HS Rank of Entering Freshmen:
  Top 10%: 76%
  Top 25%: 95%
  Top 50%: 100%
Avg. HS GPA: 3.66

Costs (2003–04)

Tuition and Fees: $28,730
Room & Board: $9,142
Payment Plan(s): installment plan

THE EXPERTS SAY...

" Calling all future doctors: JHU is for the serious-minded student only. Bring an extra pillow for library sleepovers. "

" At least if your car gets broken into it'll be too weighed down with books to steal. Please, put some back on the shelf and take a day trip to Baltimore. "

Inst. Aid (est. 2003–04)

Institutional Aid, Need-Based: $31,888,252
Institutional Aid, Non-Need-Based: $2,653,316
FT Undergrads Receiving Aid: 40%
  Avg. Amount per Student: $26,257
FT Undergrads Receiving Non-Need-Based Scholarship or Grant Aid: 5%
  Avg. Amount per Student: $13,096
Of Those Receiving Any Aid:
Rec. Need-Based Scholarship or Grant Aid: 89%
  Average Award: $20,599
Rec. Need-Based Self-Help Aid: 93%
  Average Award: $5,239
Upon Graduation, Avg. Loan Debt per Student: $13,300
Financial Aid Deadline: 2/15, 2/1 (priority)

Graduates

Companies Recruiting On-Campus: 200
Alumni Giving: 35%

JUILLIARD SCHOOL

60 Lincoln Center Plaza, New York, NY 10023-6588
Admissions Phone: (212) 799-5000 Fax: (212) 769-6420
Email: admissions@juilliard.edu
Website: www.juilliard.edu

General Info

Type of School: private, coed
Setting: urban
Academic Calendar: semester

Student Body

Full-Time Undergrads: 493
  Men: 48%, Women: 52%

Part-Time Undergrads: 1
  Women: 100%

Total Undergrad Population:
  African American: 13%
  Asian American: 11%
  Latino: 5%
  Native American: <1%
  Caucasian: 46%
  International: 24%
  Out-of-State: 82%
  Living Off-Campus: 49%

Graduate and First-Professional
  Students: 339

Academics

Full-Time Faculty: 120

Part-Time Faculty: 152

Student/Faculty Ratio: 4:1

Most Popular Majors:
  music – piano (14%)
  music – violin (14%)
  dance (10%)

Freshmen Retention Rate: 93%

Graduation Rates:
  63% within four years
  80% within six years

Admissions

Regular Application Deadline: 12/1

Fall Transfer Deadline: 12/1

Total # of Students Applied: 1,824
  Admitted: 124
  Enrolled: 97

# of Students Waitlisted: 48
  Students Accepting Place: 43
  Waitlisted Students Admitted: 7

Costs (2003–04)

Tuition and Fees: $21,850

Room & Board: $8,440

Inside the Classroom

At most schools, admissions are based primarily on grades and standardized test scores. At Juilliard, the decision is based mostly on a sink-or-swim audition, during which you either "have it" or you don't. Take a look at some of the accomplished alumni—Itzhak Perlman, Leontyne Price, Kevin Kline, and Robin Williams, just to name a few—and you'll get a sense of the high level of talent that is recruited and cultivated at Juilliard. Students who graduate from Juilliard are considered uniquely qualified for professional careers in their respective fields.

The programs in the school's three divisions of Music, Drama, and Dance are all grounded in the intensive study of technique. In addition to taking classes in the history and theory of their chosen disciplines, students spend hours each day practicing and working with Juilliard's renowned instructors. Each season, students present dozens of free concerts throughout New York, and more than 650 free music, dance, and drama performances at Juilliard and Lincoln Center.

Juilliard's four-year drama and dance programs lead to a bachelor of fine arts degree, and the four-year music program leads to a bachelor of music degree. (A two-year Artist Diploma program in Jazz Studies was introduced in September 2001.) In addition to their concentration, students are required to take humanities seminars during their first two years and electives during their final two years in order to guarantee they receive some kind of basic college education. Juilliard students can also take courses at Columbia University and Barnard College; a five-year, joint-degree program is available to particularly ambitious music students, leading to a bachelor of arts degree in any major through Columbia or Barnard and a master's in music at Juilliard. Music students may be allowed to major in more than one instrument, but you cannot major in more than one division (e.g., Music and Drama).

Students admit that the teaching quality varies at Juilliard. Some professors are much better teachers, both coddling and critiquing their students, while other teachers may be brilliant performers or technicians who do not demonstrate the same level of concern for their students. But no matter the teaching style, all students will receive a high level of individualized attention (though the undergraduate music students have been known to complain that graduate students receive the lion's share of attention at Juilliard). In March 2002, students and alumni were devastated by the deaths of Benjamin Harkarvy, Director of the Juilliard Dance Division, and Dorothy DeLay, a renowned violin teacher at Juilliard since 1948 whose students included Itzhak Perlman, Nadja Salerno-Sonnenberg, and Midori.

Campus Environment

Don't expect to find a homey, close-knit atmosphere at Juilliard. Students spend most of their so-called "free time" practicing their craft, not out playing Frisbee. The closest Juilliard comes to a campus is the Lincoln Center of Performing Arts, where its main buildings are located. While it may not have a central quad or lawn, the school is positioned in a prime location in terms of the New York cultural and performing arts scene. Students are just steps away from the Metropolitan and New

York City Opera, the ballet, the theater, and concerts. The school's facilities are outstanding. Students have access to 106 practice rooms, 35 private teaching studios, four large performance spaces, costume and scenery shops, a state-of-the art performing arts library, and more.

The Meredith Wilson Residence Hall is situated on the top 12 floors of the Rose Building, which is adjacent to The Juilliard School. Built in 1990, it provides students with comfortable and relatively affordable housing in pricey Manhattan and has also made it possible for students to form friendships more easily with their peers. All first-year students are required to live in the residence hall; however, on-campus housing is not guaranteed for all four years. An effort is made to house first-time college students together. The residence hall is made up of suites, each of which contains five bedrooms (three doubles and two singles), two and a half bathrooms, and a large living room with cable television. Most floors in the residence hall are equipped with two soundproof practice rooms containing Steinway L pianos. The lobby floor of the residence hall contains a lounge area (with color television and a billiard table), a community kitchen, a quiet study lounge, a typing room equipped with electric typewriters, and a laundry room. A fitness center is located on the 22nd floor. The cafeteria is located on the plaza level of the building.

Even though Juilliard is located in the heart of New York City, students say that safety is not a major concern. The school is in an upscale neighborhood with little crime. There's an electronic surveillance system at the entry of the residence hall, and no one may enter the hall without an access card.

Student Life

Be forewarned: Juilliard is a highly competitive school, and the competition extends well beyond the initial effort to get in. Of course, the pressure and competitiveness are excellent training for the rigors of the professional world. But Juilliard expects to get 100 percent of its students' time and attention; students are discouraged from doing professional engagements during their four years of conservatory training. This can be difficult for some students to accept, especially those who have already been performing professionally for years. Many students are tempted to drop out of the program after a couple of years, envious of friends with less training who are already making it big in the real world.

While a few Juilliard extracurricular activities and events draw students' attention, most turn to New York City for its incomparable cultural options. A great fringe benefit: Juilliard students can obtain free or discounted tickets for performances of the Metropolitan Opera, New York Philharmonic, New York City Ballet, Chamber Music Society of Lincoln Center, Film Society of Lincoln Center, Lincoln Center Theater, and various movie venues.

Inst. Aid (est. 2003–04)

Institutional Aid, Need-Based: $5,119,980

Institutional Aid, Non-Need-Based: $214,840

FT Undergrads Receiving Aid: 77% Avg. Amount per Student: $21,298

FT Undergrads Receiving Non-Need-Based Scholarship or Grant Aid: 12% Avg. Amount per Student: $4,689

THE EXPERTS SAY...

" With its uncompromising admissions standards and tough programs, Juilliard is the finest and most exclusive school in the country devoted entirely to the study of performing arts. "

" With its uncompromising admissions standards and tough programs, Juilliard is the finest and most exclusive school in the country devoted entirely to the study of performing arts. "

Of Those Receiving Any Aid:

Rec. Need-Based Scholarship or Grant Aid: 99% Average Award: $15,760

Rec. Need-Based Self-Help Aid: 100% Average Award: $5,856

Upon Graduation, Avg. Loan Debt per Student: $21,447

Financial Aid Deadline: 3/1

JUNIATA COLLEGE

1700 Moore Street, Huntingdon, PA 16652
Admissions Phone: (814) 641-3420; (877) JUNIATA Fax: (814) 641-3100
Email: info@juniata.edu
Website: juniata.edu

General Info

Type of School: private, coed,
  Church of the Brethren

Setting: small town

Academic Calendar: semester

Student Body

Full-Time Undergrads: 1,338
  Men: 44%, Women: 56%

Part-Time Undergrads: 58
  Men: 53%, Women: 47%

Total Undergrad Population:
  African American: 1%
  Asian American: 1%
  Latino: 1%
  Caucasian: 93%
  International: 4%
  Out-of-State: 25%
  Living Off-Campus: 16%

Academics

Full-Time Faculty: 93
  With Ph.D.: 95%

Part-Time Faculty: 35
  With Ph.D.: 43%

Student/Faculty Ratio: 13:1

Most Popular Majors:
  biology/pre–health (21%)
  education (13%)
  accounting/business (10%)
  chemistry (6%)
  psychology (5%)

Freshmen Retention Rate: 86%

Graduation Rates:
  68% within four years
  75% within six years

Admissions

Regular Application Deadline: 3/15;
  11/15 (priority)

Early Decision Deadline(s): 11/15

Fall Transfer Deadline: 6/15

Spring Transfer Deadline: 12/1

Total # of Students Applied: 1,578
  Admitted: 1,179
  Enrolled: 381

Applied Early Decision: 116
  Early Decision Admitted: 104

Test Scores (middle 50%):
  SAT Verbal: 530–630
  SAT Math: 540–640

Inside the Classroom

Juniata College offers its students a strong, challenging education that doesn't often follow a "traditional" course. Instead of choosing a preset major, students (with the help of two faculty advisors) may develop their own "Programs of Emphasis" (POEs). You may select from more than 50 already developed POEs, combine two existing ones into a third course of study, or create an entirely new program. Programs of Emphasis can lead to either a B.A. or B.S. degree and may include courses from among 17 academic departments.

More than half of all undergrads design their own POE, and approximately one-third have a POE that relates to biology in some way. The pre-health sciences are by far the biggest and best offerings here; students give these courses, facilities, and professors exceptionally high marks. A remarkable number (nearly 95 percent) of Juniata's applicants to medical, dental, optometry, podiatry, and veterinary schools have been accepted. Elsewhere, the new Information Technology program is strong, as is Environment Science and Studies, where students can research and learn at the college's nearby field station, 665 acres of watershed on Lake Raystown. Juniata's renowned PACS (Peace and Conflict Studies) program is one of very few offered in the country.

"Research opportunities are available in virtually every discipline," we hear, and almost 70 percent of all students participate in internships. The study abroad program, sending students to 14 countries worldwide, is a popular option. Undergrads may also participate in cooperative degree programs in marine biology, law, engineering, the pre-health sciences, and allied health fields.

All students must fulfill the general education requirements in each of the following five areas: fine arts, international studies, social sciences, humanities, and natural sciences. In addition, they must complete the College Writing Seminar, four communications-based courses, two courses that develop quantitative skills, and two "cultural analysis" courses. All classes are small—even the average lecture has only 21 students in it. Professors are widely praised for being tough but fair, and always accessible.

Campus Environment

Juniata College is nestled in the Appalachian Mountains of scenic central Pennsylvania. The beautiful 110-acre campus boasts, among other things, an art museum, an observatory, a ceramics studio, and various sports and recreation facilities. The school also owns a nearby nature preserve and "Peace Chapel," a serene environmental landscape site designed by Maya Lin, who also designed the Vietnam Veteran's Memorial in Washington, DC. As you may imagine, the college is basically in the middle of nowhere. Harrisburg, the closest city, is 90 miles away. Luckily, all students are permitted to have cars on campus (a small fee applies). The town is serviced daily by Amtrak train service, and bus and air transportation are available in nearby State College.

Freshmen are required to live in the dorms. Actually, all students are generally expected to live on campus unless they commute from home; a limited number of juniors and seniors move to off-campus housing. The residence halls, which range in size and style, are mostly coed (including one that's coed by room, not by floor as is the standard practice). The Cloister, the oldest and most centrally located dorm, is the one everyone wants—in fact, one campus tradition, "Vengeance Week," involves students from other halls jealously bombarding Cloister residents with water balloons. We hear that East Sunderland is the "party dorm," with a first floor once called "Thunder Alley" because—back when beer kegs weren't banned from campus, of course—when students would roll a keg down the corridor, it echoed through the dorm and sounded like thunder.

Student Life

Juniata students are bright, career-focused individuals. About three-quarters of the student body is a Pennsylvanian, and an astounding number of them are white (fewer than 30 minority students). We hear that it's a very close-knit community, which is not surprising considering the small and homogenous student population.

While there are no fraternities and sororities here, there are nearly 100 other student-run organizations. The student government, the Juniata Activities Board, Health Occupations of America, and Habitat for Humanity are among the most popular groups. International students—which comprise about five percent of the population—are a strong force on campus as well. Juniata has nine varsity men's sports and ten women's; the volleyball teams are particularly good. Intercollegiate club sports (equestrian, golf, lacrosse, rugby, and Ultimate Frisbee) are also offered. There are a total of 21 intramural and club sports, and about 60 percent of all students play on one team or another.

Juniata also has quite a few annual traditions to keep students entertained. The oldest (and the one students most look forward to) is "Mountain Day," when classes are canceled and the entire school community flocks to one of the local state parks for a day of outdoor fun. "No one knows when Mountain Day will be until the morning that it arrives," we're told. There's also the Madrigal Dinner, a formal meal and dance that hundreds of students line up for, and Springfest, which kicks off with a mud volleyball tournament and gets crazier from there. Other popular events include Lobsterfest, the Mr. Juniata Pageant, the Snowball Battle on the first snowfall of the year, and "All Class Night," where each class writes, produces, and performs an original play spoofing campus events and personalities.

Huntingdon, Pennsylvania, while lovely and quaint, is not the most happening of places. In fact, some complain that it's a virtual social black hole. Although there are a few bars and restaurants in town, students interested in something more than "lakes, mountains, fresh air, and natural beauty" may grow restless. For more "traditional" college activities and parties, Juniata students trek 30 miles (on a long, winding road, no less) to State College, home of Penn State's huge main campus.

HS Rank of Entering Freshmen:
Top 10%: 35%
Top 25%: 74%
Top 50%: 98%
Avg. HS GPA: 3.71

Costs (2004–5)

Tuition and Fees: $24,270
Room & Board: $6,770
Payment Plan(s): installment plan

THE EXPERTS SAY...

" An excellent choice for students interested in the health sciences who want a great deal of individual attention. "

" Other options for those of you determined to go to a tiny college in the middle of nowhere: Dickinson, Susquehanna, Allegheny, Ursinus, and Muhlenberg. "

Inst. Aid (est. 2003–04)

Institutional Aid, Need-Based:
$11,199,029

Institutional Aid, Non-Need-Based:
$3,528,788

FT Undergrads Receiving Aid: 79%
Avg. Amount per Student: $18,258

FT Undergrads Receiving Non-Need-Based Scholarship or Grant Aid: 30%
Avg. Amount per Student: $10,760

Of Those Receiving Any Aid:

Rec. Need-Based Scholarship or Grant Aid: 100%
Average Award: $14,190

Rec. Need-Based Self-Help Aid: 84%
Average Award: $4,729

Upon Graduation, Avg. Loan Debt per Student: $17,572

Financial Aid Deadline: 5/1, 3/1 (priority)

Graduates

Going to Graduate School:
35% Within One Year

Companies Recruiting On Campus: 16

Alumni Giving: 41%

KALAMAZOO COLLEGE

1200 Academy Street, Kalamazoo, MI 49006-3295
Admissions Phone: (269) 337-7166; (800) 253-3602 Fax: (269) 337-7390
Email: admission@kzoo.edu
Website: www.kzoo.edu

General Info

Type of School: private, coed

Setting: urban

Academic Calendar: quarter

Student Body

Full-Time Undergrads: 1,280
   Men: 44%, Women: 56%

Total Undergrad Population:
   African American: 3%
   Asian American: 4%
   Latino: 1%
   Caucasian: 80%
   International: 2%
   Out-of-State: 26%
   Living Off-Campus: 25%

Academics

Full-Time Faculty: 103
   With Ph.D.: 86%

Part-Time Faculty: 14
   With Ph.D.: 71%

Student/Faculty Ratio: 12:1

Most Popular Majors:
   psychology
   economics/business
   biology
   English
   chemistry

Completing 2 or More Majors: 11%

Freshmen Retention Rate: 86%

Graduation Rates:
   70% within four years
   77% within six years

Admissions

Regular Application Deadline: 2/15

Early Decision Deadline(s): 11/15, 12/1

Early Action Deadline: 1/15

Fall Transfer Deadline: 2/15 (priority)

Total # of Students Applied: 1,603
   Admitted: 1,127
   Enrolled: 383

# of Students Waitlisted: 38
   Students Accepting Place: 38
   Waitlisted Students Admitted: 8

Applied Early Decision: 33
   Early Decision Admitted: 27

Test Scores (middle 50%):
   SAT Verbal: 620–720
   SAT Math: 610–700

Inside the Classroom

Kalamazoo's innovative curriculum, known as the "K" Plan, combines classroom learning in the liberal arts with real-world experiences, including study abroad. A whopping 85 percent of Kalamazoo students study abroad at some point in one of 18-plus countries. Your financial assistance and scholarships transfer to the 26 "K"-sponsored programs, and due to a special endowment, your overseas airfare is also covered. In addition to studying abroad, 80 percent of students also complete at least one internship during their four years. With help from the Career Development Center, you can easily identify and participate in internships in your areas of interest.

The required Senior Individualized Project (SIP) provides students with the opportunity to work independently and immerse themselves in substantial research thesis, performance, or creative work. The school explains that the SIP project "is often compared to graduate-level work—a bonus for those going on to graduate school" and that "many SIPs are of master's-level quality, and some are even published." Students also create an electronic portfolio documenting their many and varied educational and extracurricular experiences. They can use the portfolio to determine the interconnectivity of their school experiences, while also acquiring useful Web publishing and presentation skills. If nothing else, "K" students prepare vigorously for the "real world."

Kalamazoo is known for its health science, chemistry, economics and business, and English programs, but psychology, biology, and political science are also popular. Classes are small and they're all taught by professors, not teaching assistants. Kalamazoo is on the quarter system, which enables students to balance their study abroad programs and internships with their classroom work. It also means, as a freshman was quick to point out, that students "have to cover a semester's worth of work in ten weeks." Most students, we hear, study "about six hours a day," yet a full schedule has three classes rather than the typical four at most colleges, easing the study burden somewhat. Students can also depend on very accessible faculty members for support—"The teachers give the students a lot of personal attention," a student tells us.

Campus Environment

With a few exceptions, freshmen, sophomores, and juniors must live on campus, and only two percent of students live off campus. Freshmen are "mixed throughout the entire residential system," and have "first priority in housing." Since you have to live on campus, the school tries to make it comfortable. In addition to more traditional coed residential halls, Kalamazoo offers special interest options for upperclassmen. Trowbridge Hall offers apartment-style living; Crissey Hall offers suite-style housing and has one floor for strict vegetarians (a co-op) who cook their meals in the communal kitchen (and get out of carrying a regular meal plan); and the Living Learning Housing Units include the Women's Resource Center (WRC), the Service Learning House, the Language and Culture House, the Wellness House, and the Art House.

Students are supposed to reapply for housing every quarter, but some "squatters" simply stay on from quarter to quarter. (Seriously, even the school calls it "squatting.") A student warned that when you add in the costs of the required campus housing and dining to the tuition, Kalamazoo is "a very, very expensive" school. Luckily, it also seems very generous with its scholarship money.

Freshmen are "not allowed to have a car on campus," but upperclassmen can apply for permits to keep a car there (generally issued for getting to and from off-campus jobs). And, if you're desperate to get away, "most students borrow a car if necessary." Kalamazoo's small, attractive campus is located 140 miles from Detroit and Chicago for your weekend road trip pleasure. The city of Kalamazoo is located in scenic southwest Michigan. Also, Lake Michigan is only 35 miles away, so movies, dining, and boating are all within reasonable distance.

Student Life

While the on-campus social scene might be somewhat limited, students can look forward to the many experiences and adventures awaiting them during their quarters off campus anywhere from Australia to Germany to Nepal. As a result of all the moving around students do, one student tells us, the social scene here is fractured. At any time, your friends can be studying abroad while you're in Michigan, or the other way around. There are no fraternities or sororities, so most parties spring up in people's rooms. The school's alcohol policy is based on personal responsibility and adherence to the law (so keep it quiet, and keep your door closed).

There are more than 50 clubs and organizations here. Popular choices at "K" are "Frelon," a student-run dance company, student government, and theater productions. There are also diversity-promoting groups for the fairly homogeneous population, like the Black Student Organization and the Gay/Lesbian/Bisexual Support Organization. Most people, a student said, become "seriously involved" with extracurricular activities or sports. There are 16 intercollegiate sports (eight for men and eight for women.) Kalamazoo plays at NCAA Division III level and is a member of the Michigan Intercollegiate Athletic Association, the "oldest athletic conference in the nation."

Kalamazoo students do draw together for a few on-campus traditions. Each Spring Quarter, students celebrate a "Day of Gracious Living": On a sunny day, "classes are canceled" and students are allowed to take the day to relax and enjoy the warm weather.

Other schools to check out: Macalester, Grinnell, Earlham, DePauw, Bradley.

THE EXPERTS SAY...

" Kalamazoo takes a holistic approach to your education. You will leave with a sense of accomplishment and a preparedness to tackle the 'real world.' "

" Take advantage of the study abroad program if you want to experience a social scene. "

Costs (2003–04)

Tuition and Fees: $22,908

Room & Board: $6,480

Payment Plan(s): installment plan, deferred payment plan, pre-payment plan

Inst. Aid (est. 2003–04)

Institutional Aid, Need-Based: $4,208,376

Institutional Aid, Non-Need-Based: $6,906,232

FT Undergrads Receiving Aid: 51%
 Avg. Amount per Student: $19,556

FT Undergrads Receiving Non-Need-Based Scholarship or Grant Aid: 44%
 Avg. Amount per Student: $9,500

Of Those Receiving Any Aid:

Rec. Need-Based Scholarship or Grant Aid: 99%
 Average Award: $13,126

Rec. Need-Based Self-Help Aid: 92%
 Average Award: $6,492

Upon Graduation, Avg. Loan Debt per Student: $18,782

Financial Aid Deadline: 2/15 (priority)

Graduates

Going to Graduate School:
 27% Within One Year

Accepting Job Offer:
 60% at time of graduation

Companies Recruiting On Campus: 10

Alumni Giving: 55%

KANSAS STATE UNIVERSITY

119 Anderson Hall, Manhattan, KS 66506
Admissions Phone: (785) 532-6250; (800) 432-8270 (in-state) Fax: (785) 532-6393
Email: kstate@ksu.edu Website: www.ksu.edu
Application Website: www.ksu.edu/admit

General Info

Type of School: public, coed
Setting: small town
Academic Calendar: semester

Student Body

Full-Time Undergrads: 16,285
 Men: 52%, Women: 48%

Part-Time Undergrads: 2,798
 Men: 48%, Women: 52%

Total Undergrad Population:
 African American: 3%
 Asian American: 1%
 Latino: 2%
 Native American: <1%
 Caucasian: 89%
 International: 1%
 Out-of-State: 14%
 Living Off-Campus: 67%
 In Fraternities: 20%
 In Sororities: 20%

Graduate and First-Professional
 Students: 3,967

Academics

Full-Time Faculty: 851
 With Ph.D.: 88%

Part-Time Faculty: 125
 With Ph.D.: 47%

Student/Faculty Ratio: 12:1

Most Popular Majors:
 journalism (4%)
 mechanical engineering (3%)
 animal science, general (3%)
 psychology (2%)
 elementary education (2%)

Freshmen Retention Rate: 79%

Graduation Rates:
 22% within four years
 56% within six years

Admissions

Total # of Students Applied: 7,952
 Admitted: 4,736
 Enrolled: 3,439

Test Scores (middle 50%):
 ACT Comp: 21–26
 ACT English: 20–27
 ACT Math: 20–27

HS Rank of Entering Freshmen:
 Top 25%: 56%
 Top 50%: 82%

Inside the Classroom

Thousands of students, hundreds of activities, excellent academic reputation, unparalleled research opportunities—sure, that sounds like a top-notch Manhattan school, right? But we're not talking about NYU or Columbia, here. We're describing none other than Kansas State University, located in Manhattan, Kansas.

Undergraduates at K-State can choose from more than 200 majors in eight colleges: agriculture; architecture, planning, and design; arts and sciences; business administration; education; engineering; human ecology; and technology and aviation. The college of agriculture has an outstanding reputation and offers a surprising range of programs, including such majors as golf course management, bakery science, and agricultural journalism. The college of arts and sciences has a large number of preprofessional programs, particularly in prehealth; a guidance counselor cites the strong math department. Students in K-State's excellent preveterinary program can use the resources of the graduate college of veterinary science and receive an undergraduate degree from either the college of arts and sciences or agriculture. All undergrads must complete at least 18 hours of University General Education or UGE courses (not a typo for "UGH," say officials). UGE requirements vary by college and major; students also take courses on expository writing and public speaking.

While the sheer size and scope of the university can be overwhelming, ambitious undergrads can take advantage of the unique opportunities available at a major research university. At university research centers devoted to more than 30 different subjects, students can work part-time as lab technicians, help their professors with important projects, or even fund their own projects with a university research grant through the Developing Scholars program. In recent years, K-State students have won Fulbright, Truman, Marshall, and Rhodes scholarships. "The career/employment/placement center is great," adds a guidance counselor.

A Kansas guidance counselor praises K-State's "strong student support system." Students who might need extra help making the transition to university life can participate in the PILOTS program, which uses smaller class sizes, free tutoring, and other perks to help students develop academic discipline and critical reasoning skills. Freshman Seminar introduces students to the cultural and intellectual activities on campus. Another special program is the McNair Scholars Program—a comprehensive program involving mentoring, tutoring, and summer research internships to prepare low-income and minority students for careers as professors or professional researchers.

Campus Environment

K-State's 664-acre main campus is located in the small city of Manhattan, which is also the home of Fort Riley, one of the largest Army bases in the country. With 45,000 residents and 20,000 undergrads, Manhattan is a true college town. One of the best things about the school, says a guidance counselor, is the "university-community connection." "Aggieville," a popular bar district, borders the campus, featuring many favorite student hangouts in its pizza parlors and coffee shops.

Kansas State's research facilities are first-rate. Other standouts include Bob Dole Hall, which houses the communications center; the K-State Union, a student hangout offering food, a bookstore, movies, and more; the new Colbert Hills Golf Course; and the Rec Complex with its 14 racquetball courts, 10 basketball courts, a weight/fitness area, and running tracks.

Residence halls are located on the east and west side of campus, and coed and single-sex housing is available. Single rooms are assigned on a first-come, first-served basis. Specialty housing includes intensive study, academic cluster, and leadership floors. The Smurthwaite Scholarship House is recommended for women interested in developing leadership skills. Although there are no official freshmen-only dorms, most students move off campus after their first year, so most dorms are filled with freshmen. Most fraternities and sororities have their own residences within walking distance of campus, though freshman women aren't allowed to live in sorority houses.

Student Life

While the nightlife certainly can't compare with that of the other Manhattan, K-State students say they can always find things to do. Outdoor activities are particularly popular, whether it's swimming out on Tuttle Creek Reservoir, playing a few holes on one of the area's golf courses, biking along the trail system circling the town, or just spending the day at the Sunset Zoo.

On campus, students can participate in more than 380 clubs and organizations, which run the gamut from the Opera Guild to the Quarter Scale Tractor Team. Leadership development is big, and is a theme that runs throughout many club activities and community service programs. Although a Colorado guidance counselor bemoans the "limited cultural activities," the arts have a life at K-State: the school's acclaimed theater program regularly stages professional-level productions, and the on-campus Beach Museum features the art of Kansas artists.

Sports are a way of life at K-State; around 88 percent of students participate in recreational sports. A large part of K-State social life revolves around K-State's Wildcats. The Wildcats varsity teams are part of the Big 12 Conference and draw huge, enthusiastic crowds, particularly for the championship football and basketball teams; many parties occur before, after, and during games. When students crave city life, road trips to Kansas City, especially for Chiefs and Royals action, provide more excitement.

There are 24 fraternities and 11 sororities. Around one-fifth of the student body participates in Greek organizations, which throw frequent parties but are also known for their community service efforts. While social life is usually humming, there can be cliques, especially in Greek-independent splits.

While the school offers a huge diversity of academic programs, the student population is largely homogeneous; students are predominantly white, with 81 percent from Kansas. K-State students are friendly, and it is not hard to meet people, although a guidance counselor warns that with over 20,000 students, graduate students included, the campus can be "too large and impersonal." For the incredibly low price, however, Kansas State offers quite a combination: top-notch academics, powerhouse sports, and more extracurricular activities than you could possibly fit into four years.

Costs (2003–04)

Tuition and Fees, In-State: $4,059

Tuition and Fees, Out-of-State: $11,949

Room & Board: $5,080

Payment Plan(s): installment plan, deferred payment plan

Inst. Aid (2002–03)

Institutional Aid, Need-Based: $5,543,099

Institutional Aid, Non-Need-Based: $1,590,936

THE EXPERTS SAY...

" Midwesterners brag about this world-class research university, and with good reason. There are over 30 research centers, and you probably won't find another agriculture school with journalism courses. "

" Manhattan, New York has Greenwich Village. Manhattan, Kansas has Aggieville. You pick. "

FT Undergrads Receiving Aid: 48% Avg. Amount per Student: $5,512

FT Undergrads Receiving Non-Need-Based Scholarship or Grant Aid: 5% Avg. Amount per Student: $1,538

Of Those Receiving Any Aid:

Rec. Need-Based Scholarship or Grant Aid: 65% Average Award: $1,372

Rec. Need-Based Self-Help Aid: 87% Average Award: $3,106

Upon Graduation, Avg. Loan Debt per Student: $17,000

Financial Aid Deadline: 3/1 (priority)

Graduates

Going to Graduate School: 16% Within One Year

KENYON COLLEGE

Ransom Hall, Gambier, OH 43022-9623
Admissions Phone: (740) 427-5776; (800) 848-2468 Fax: (740) 427-5770
Email: admissions@kenyon.edu Website: www.kenyon.edu
Application Website: www.kenyon.edu/admissions/apply/

General Info

Type of School: private, coed
Setting: rural
Academic Calendar: semester

Student Body

Full-Time Undergrads: 1,592
 Men: 45%, Women: 55%

Total Undergrad Population:
 African American: 3%
 Asian American: 3%
 Latino: 2%
 Native American: <1%
 Caucasian: 84%
 International: 2%
 Out-of-State: 76%
 Living Off-Campus: 1%
 In Fraternities: 27%
 In Sororities: 10%

Academics

Full-Time Faculty: 145
 With Ph.D.: 97%

Part-Time Faculty: 23
 With Ph.D.: 70%

Student/Faculty Ratio: 10:1

Most Popular Majors:
 English (15%)
 political science (7%)
 psychology (7%)
 history (5%)
 international studies (4%)

Completing 2 or More Majors: 16%

Freshmen Retention Rate: 92%

Graduation Rates:
 79% within four years
 84% within six years

Admissions

Regular Application Deadline: 2/1

Early Decision Deadline(s): 12/1,
 1/15

Fall Transfer Deadline: 6/1, 4/1
 (priority)

Spring Transfer Deadline: 11/15
 (priority)

Total # of Students Applied: 3,360
 Admitted: 1,534
 Enrolled: 454

# of Students Waitlisted: 580
 Students Accepting Place: 212
 Waitlisted Students Admitted: 59

Inside the Classroom

Kenyon's academic strengths range from the traditional liberal arts and sciences to several excellent interdisciplinary programs, including the international studies program and the integrated program in humane studies, which combines the academic study of literature, politics, and history. Boasting such talented and successful alumni as novelist E.L. Doctorow (*Ragtime*), Kenyon's English program is considered to be among the best in the nation. The performing arts also thrive here: Paul Newman and *The West Wing*'s Allison Janney are other proud Kenyon graduates. In all, students can choose from among 25 departmental majors and a growing number of interdisciplinary majors.

The average class size is only 14 students, resulting in a great deal of personal attention. "While some teachers lecture, most prefer to teach their classes through discussion, which motivates students to come prepared for class," says a senior English major. Students here become very close to their professors, most of whom live within a few miles of campus. "It would not be strange for a professor to invite a class over for dinner, or to order Chinese for a seminar class," a senior political science major tells us.

Kenyon mainly attracts applicants from the Midwest and Mid-Atlantic states who are eager for an academic challenge. A senior double-majoring in Spanish and psychology stresses, "Kenyon students have to be willing to work hard. The college has a highly academic atmosphere in the classroom and even outside of the classroom." Another senior explains, "Students take their work very seriously, but are not sitting around worrying about getting the best grades. Instead, they are learning for the sake of learning."

Kenyon's distribution requirements are not hard to fulfill: Students must choose any two courses from each of the four academic divisions: fine arts, humanities, natural sciences, and social sciences. Students also must complete a senior exercise, which may take the form of a research project, thesis, exam, or creative work.

Campus Environment

Kenyon's gorgeous campus is spread out over 800 heavily wooded acres. A number of its 50+ buildings are listed on the National Register of Historic Places, and many are arrayed along the mile-long Middle Path that serves as the main walkway. The campus features a new, state-of-the-art science quad, and construction is underway for the 263,000-square foot Kenyon Center for Fitness, Recreation, and Athletics (FRA), scheduled to open in fall 2005.

All students live on campus for all four years and participate in Kenyon's dining plan. Freshmen are housed together in a cluster of residences near the center of campus and adjacent to the Gund Commons dining hall. A senior's opinion: "Freshmen get some of the best housing. Their rooms tend to be fairly large and the dorms are usually nicer." The campus is divided into North Campus (home to many of the campus apartments) and South Campus (home to the beautiful historic dorms which are closer to classes). A limited number of single rooms are available, but the competition to secure them in the annual housing lottery is fierce. While there's no separate fraternity housing (and no sorority housing of any kind), the school allows the fraternities to fill a certain number of rooms in three of the campus dorms.

First-year students are allowed to have cars on campus, but cars aren't needed for getting around campus or around the small, friendly village of Gambier. Safety isn't a concern on or off campus: "Everyone at Kenyon is very trusting, and it is unusual to find someone who locks their door or is afraid to leave their possessions unattended during dinner or whatnot," a student informs us.

Student Life

Kenyon students tend to be "fairly well-off economically," open-minded, and intellectual. A senior tells us, "It is not uncommon to hear students talk philosophy or politics at the dinner table or at parties… Most students would rather talk about Socrates and Aristotle any day of the week as opposed to the newest hit TV show."

As for the campus environment, a senior puts it best by saying, "One word: community… There is something about returning to the village after being away—it feels like coming home." Not everyone thinks this warm and fuzzy atmosphere is a good thing: Kenyon professor and writer-in-residence P.F. Kluge caused some controversy this year with his article in the *Chronicle of Higher Education* criticizing "Kamp Kenyon" (and, to be fair, other institutions) as being too coddling, too accommodating—"a therapeutic kibbutz—ultimately compromising the purpose of a college education." But students still cite the "strong sense of community" as one of the best things about Kenyon.

Kenyon's Lords and Ladies are members of the NCAA Division III and North Coast Athletic Conference. The swimming teams have enjoyed an amazing run in the past few decades: The Lords have won 24 straight Division III championships—continuing the longest championship streak in NCAA history—while the Ladies have lost only one championship in the last 20 years. Intramural and recreational sports are also popular, as are the student newspaper, literary publications, the radio station, performance groups, and several environmental groups. "At Kenyon, every student loves being busy with something," explains a senior, "and if someone doesn't like being involved, then that person is going to get bored very fast."

Like many campuses "in the middle of nowhere," Kenyon has an active fraternity scene. The frats reportedly throw a majority of the large parties on campus, though these parties usually aren't exclusive. Kenyon's alcohol-free Late Nites program is a good alternative to the party scene, featuring comedy nights, Ping-Pong tournaments, acoustic concerts, poetry discussions, and other fun activities. Students who just want to hang out can head over to the campus bookstore, named "the best in the country" by *Rolling Stone* for its comfortable sofas and armchairs, bottomless cups of coffee, and highly sociable atmosphere.

Other schools to check out: Williams, Bowdoin, Middlebury, Carleton, Colby.

Applied Early Decision: 174
Early Decision Admitted: 146

Test Scores (middle 50%):
SAT Verbal: 620–720
SAT Math: 600–690
ACT Comp: 27–32

HS Rank of Entering Freshmen:
Top 10%: 52%
Top 25%: 88%
Top 50%: 98%

Avg. HS GPA: 3.76

Costs (2004–5)

Tuition and Fees: $32,170

Room & Board: $5,270

Payment Plan(s): installment plan

THE EXPERTS SAY...

" If you're an aspiring writer who enjoys learning for the sake of learning, you should definitely consider Kenyon. "

" Gambier in winter is awfully beautiful, but be prepared to be campus bound. "

Inst. Aid (est. 2003–04)

Institutional Aid, Need-Based:
$12,729,038

Institutional Aid, Non-Need-Based:
$4,598,564

FT Undergrads Receiving Aid: 41%
Avg. Amount per Student: $22,151

FT Undergrads Receiving Non-Need-Based Scholarship or Grant Aid: 24%
Avg. Amount per Student: $12,502

Of Those Receiving Any Aid:

Rec. Need-Based Scholarship or Grant Aid: 98%
Average Award: $18,731

Rec. Need-Based Self-Help Aid: 90%
Average Award: $4,222

Upon Graduation, Avg. Loan Debt per Student: $19,587

Financial Aid Deadline: 2/15

Graduates

Going to Graduate School:
25% Within One Year

Accepting Job Offer:
10% at time of graduation

Companies Recruiting On Campus: 31

Alumni Giving: 72%

KETTERING UNIVERSITY

1700 West Third Avenue, Flint, MI 48504
Admissions Phone: (810) 762-7865; (800) 955-4464 Fax: (810) 762-9837
Email: admissions@kettering.edu
Website: www.kettering.edu

General Info

Type of School: private, coed

Setting: suburban

Academic Calendar: each semester
is divided into 11 weeks of class
and 12 weeks of co-op experience

Student Body

Full-Time Undergrads: 2,525
Men: 83%, Women: 17%

Total Undergrad Population:
African American: 7%
Asian American: 5%
Latino: 2%
Native American: <1%
Caucasian: 74%
International: 2%
Out-of-State: 37%
Living Off-Campus: 52%
In Fraternities: 40%
In Sororities: 33%

Graduate and First-Professional
Students: 568

Academics

Full-Time Faculty: 139
With Ph.D.: 89%

Part-Time Faculty: 14
With Ph.D.: 50%

Student/Faculty Ratio: 12:1

Most Popular Majors:
mechanical engineering (54%)
electrical engineering (16%)
computer engineering (10%)
computer science (5%)
business management (4%)

Completing 2 or More Majors: 1%

Freshmen Retention Rate: 88%

Graduation Rates:
3% within four years
62% within six years

Admissions

Total # of Students Applied: 2,365
Admitted: 1,669
Enrolled: 561

Test Scores (middle 50%):
SAT Verbal: 540–640
SAT Math: 600–690
ACT Comp: 23–28
ACT English: 21–27
ACT Math: 25–30

Inside the Classroom

The practicality of a Kettering University education is evident from the moment you are accepted. Offering a range of scientific and engineering programs with a superb reputation in the industrial world, Kettering combines a rigorous academic study with career-oriented experience to produce graduates who are well ahead of their competitors in the job market. Undergraduate areas of study include applied mathematics, applied physics, computer engineering, computer science, electrical engineering, environmental chemistry, industrial engineering, management, manufacturing engineering, and mechanical engineering. In 2000, Kettering awarded more B.S. degrees in mechanical engineering than any other school in the United States.

Perhaps the greatest strength of Kettering is its cooperative education plan, in which students participate in paid professional experiences at more than 700 companies throughout the world. A unique characteristic of the co-op program is that students typically alternate 12-week terms of co-op with 11-week terms of classes starting in the freshman year. In many cases, students remain with the same employer for successive work terms, gaining both variety and depth of on-the-job experience. In addition to technical experiences, students learn what it takes to make a business successful, gaining exposure to the people, relationships, processes, and practices that make each company run. Companies with which Kettering has relationships include Ford, Xerox, General Motors, Harley-Davidson, Honeywell, Texas Instruments, Gibson Guitars, Honda, and many others.

Core study requirements at Kettering include math, physical sciences (chemistry and/or physics), humanities, social sciences, written and oral communication, and computer systems. All students participate in co-op experiences, and everyone completes a senior thesis project that may consist of either theoretical research or a topic of operational value to their co-op employer. "This place raises the bar," said one engineering major, "and its heritage says it all."

For those students seeking an international edge to their future business leadership abilities, Kettering also offers study abroad programs in the areas of mechanical engineering, business and industrial management, electrical and computer engineering, and industrial and manufacturing engineering. Countries to which students travel include Australia, the United Kingdom, France, Germany, and Spain.

The academic work at Kettering is challenging, and there's plenty of it. One senior, after referring to the regularity with which Kettering graduates become CEOs or chairs of the companies they work for, justifies the effort by saying, "It's the cost to be the boss." Perhaps the goal for endeavoring so industriously was stated more eloquently by the school's founder, patent-holder Charles F. Kettering, who once said, "Nothing ever built arose to touch the skies unless some man dreamed that it should, believed that it could, and some man willed that it must."

Campus Environment

All freshmen must live on campus, and housing is guaranteed for them. Students can live in Thompson Hall, which houses 300 to 400 students each term, or in the upper-class Campus Village Apartments if space is available. Of course, fraternity and sorority housing is also available for those who pledge, and off-campus rental apartments are another option. As with many technical schools, the male–female ratio is significantly off-kilter. According to one student, however, "There's no problem meeting friendly students from surrounding colleges and universities."

Kettering's laboratory facilities are extensive, containing state-of-the-art equipment for a wide variety of industrial technologies. Highlights include automotive, laser, radioisotope, heat transfer, electricity, and solid-state electronics as well as metallurgy laboratories. The school also features high-level computer-aided design (CAD), computer-integrated manufacturing, digital and analog computers, robotics, holography, polymer processing, injection molding, welding, foundry, and electron microscopy facilities.

Kettering's 45-acre grounds are located on the banks of the Flint River in Flint, Michigan, about 60 miles north of Detroit. The six-building campus is pretty, but students aren't kind when they describe the surrounding city of Flint. Although the industries in the city provide many co-op choices for students, one student says, "The crime rate is pretty high."

Student Life

Many student organizations on campus reflect the industrial nature of the school, including standouts like the Ethanol Team, the Amateur Radio Electronics/Computer Club, and the Society for the Advancement of Information Systems. Other clubs are more generic in nature, like the Macintosh Club, the Karate Club, and Christians in Action.

Thirteen fraternities and seven sororities exist on campus, offering the usual mix of philanthropy and intoxication. "Many students join a Greek organization in addition to the clubs and activities, so they can create an early network," said one student. With only 2,600 students enrolled, however—and a fair amount of those away on co-op experiences at any given time—the entire school can feel like one big fraternal organization.

A wide range of sports, fitness, and recreational activities is available for students who take advantage of Kettering's athletic fields, tennis courts, and recreation center. The center contains an Olympic-sized swimming pool, basketball and racquetball courts, aerobic fitness rooms, and Nautilus equipment.

Other schools to check out: Michigan Tech, Rose-Hulman, Albion, Kalamazoo.

HS Rank of Entering Freshmen:
Top 10%: 30%
Top 25%: 64%
Top 50%: 95%
Avg. HS GPA: 3.6

Costs (2004–5)

Tuition and Fees: $22,616
Room & Board: $5,110
Payment Plan(s): installment plan

THE EXPERTS SAY...

" Kettering's reputation as a proving ground for tomorrow's industrial leaders is well deserved. "

" Flint is not for the faint of heart. "

Inst. Aid (est. 2003–04)

Institutional Aid, Need-Based: $7,569,928

Institutional Aid, Non-Need-Based: $2,697,598

FT Undergrads Receiving Aid: 72%
Avg. Amount per Student: $10,740

FT Undergrads Receiving Non-Need-Based Scholarship or Grant Aid: 14%
Avg. Amount per Student: $5,385

Of Those Receiving Any Aid:

Rec. Need-Based Scholarship or Grant Aid: 98%
Average Award: $6,702

Rec. Need-Based Self-Help Aid: 78%
Average Award: $2,786

Upon Graduation, Avg. Loan Debt per Student: $33,605

Financial Aid Deadline: rolling, 2/14 (priority)

Graduates

Going to Graduate School: 50% Within One Year

Accepting Job Offer: 90% at time of graduation

Alumni Giving: 11%

KNOX COLLEGE

Campus Box 148, Galesburg, IL 61401
Admissions Phone: (309) 341-7100; (800) 678-5669 Fax: (309) 341-7070
Email: admission@knox.edu Website: www.knox.edu
Application Website: www.knox.edu/apply

General Info

Type of School: private, coed

Setting: small town

Academic Calendar: trimester (three ten-week terms)

Student Body

Full-Time Undergrads: 1,097
  Men: 47%, Women: 53%

Part-Time Undergrads: 3
  Men: 33%, Women: 67%

Total Undergrad Population:
  African American: 4%
  Asian American: 5%
  Latino: 4%
  Native American: 1%
  Caucasian: 71%
  International: 9%
  Out-of-State: 44%
  Living Off-Campus: 5%
  In Fraternities: 37%
  In Sororities: 15%

Academics

Full-Time Faculty: 92
  With Ph.D.: 95%

Part-Time Faculty: 24
  With Ph.D.: 46%

Student/Faculty Ratio: 12:1

Most Popular Majors:
  psychology (5%)
  biology (4%)
  education (4%)
  creative writing (3%)
  economics (3%)

Completing 2 or More Majors: 20%

Freshmen Retention Rate: 87%

Graduation Rates:
  71% within four years
  78% within six years

Admissions

Regular Application Deadline: 2/1

Early Action Deadline: 12/1

Fall Transfer Deadline: 4/1

Spring Transfer Deadline: 11/1

Total # of Students Applied: 1,538
  Admitted: 1,129
  Enrolled: 268

# of Students Waitlisted: 34
  Students Accepting Place: 34
  Waitlisted Students Admitted: 20

Inside the Classroom

With a student enrollment smaller than many high schools', Knox College offers a close-knit academic environment. "Knox gives careful attention to the individual," says a Missouri guidance counselor. "Students feel like they're part of a community." Students and faculty eat together, play in the same intramural sports leagues and music ensembles, and serve together on campus governance committees. A senior declares, "The professors here are just as much my friends as anyone else on campus." Another student confirms, "The faculty knows the students. They don't dress up and are mostly called by their first names."

The premedical sciences are among Knox's strongest programs, and advanced premeds may apply for early acceptance at Rush Medical College. Creative writing, education, and theater programs are also strong. In Knox's signature Repertory Theatre Term, offered every three years, students work as both actors and technicians to produce two major plays. The Open Studio term provides advanced art students with the opportunity to work intensively for an entire trimester with a faculty tutor.

During their first year, students enroll in a First-Year Preceptorial in which they work closely together in an interdisciplinary seminar focusing on writing and critical thinking. Students are required to take a second interdisciplinary seminar, called an Advanced Preceptorial, as upperclassmen. The core curriculum recently has been restructured and consists of "Foundations" in the humanities, social sciences, natural sciences, and arts, and "Key Competencies" in speaking and writing, understanding cultural differences, information technology, quantitative analysis, and a second language. "Experiential Education" (e.g., internships, original research or creative projects, study abroad, and/or service learning) is also required.

Students like the Knox trimester system for the intense focus on a few courses (three are required each trimester), but they dislike cramming a semester's worth of work into ten weeks. "It always seems like exams are just around the corner," complains a first-year student. "You've definitely got to be on top of your work." A sophomore notes, "The classes require academic drive." Class sizes at Knox are generally limited to 20 students and are always taught by professors, who teach only two classes per trimester. "The professors make sure you don't fall through the cracks if you are struggling," a junior assures us.

Knox's Honor system places students, not faculty, in charge of maintaining the academic integrity of their own work. Faculty do not proctor examinations; in fact, professors are not even allowed in the room while students are testing. It is a "great responsibility," says one student, adding, "The faculty has lots of trust in the students."

Knox emphasizes independent study, research, and original creative work across all departments. The college offers a competitive honors program for seniors to spend a year completing a thesis. Special funding is available to support independent student research projects, including overseas travel. With a solid, exceptional liberal arts background under their belts, high percentages of Knox graduates are accepted at graduate and professional schools.

Knox recently celebrated the installation of its 18th president, Roger L. Taylor, an alumnus from the class of 1963. Taylor came to the college after 30 years as a successful attorney with one of the nation's largest law firms. The new president reportedly goes by his first name and "even eats in the cafeteria, randomly sitting and chatting with students."

Campus Environment

The attractive Knox campus combines historic landmarks and modern structures; there's even an old county jail, used for psychology and philosophy classes. On-campus housing is good and is guaranteed for all four years, and nearly all students take advantage of this. Most students live in suites, but there are also several apartments, a new townhouse, and special interest and theme houses. First-year students currently live together, though a college official tells us, "There is currently a small grass roots effort to integrate first-year and upper-class housing on campus, and we may do this in the next couple of years." First-years are not allowed to live in fraternities.

Smack in the middle of Illinois farmland (complete with "those dang, smelly gingko trees"), Knox's isolated location and the Illinois winters often leave students confined to the campus. Town-gown relations reportedly are somewhat strained. Galesburg, population 33,000, does have a number of public parks, including a public beach, but students complain that there's really not much to do in this farm-and-factory town (although college officials point to the Galesburg Civic Art Center and Orpheum Theater with pride). Chicago and St. Louis, each roughly three hours away, provide good weekend escapes.

Student Life

Knox's historic Old Main was the site of the 1858 Lincoln-Douglas slavery debate, and the school is proud of its tradition of diversity. "There is an unofficial social honor code: People respect one another," notes a junior. While the plurality of students are Illinois-bred Caucasians, Knox has a high international student enrollment, a significant minority population, and an active LGBT community. "We attract the atypical," a college official states, adding, "If you come to Knox, you won't find 1,100 students like you." A sophomore agrees, "The only 'typical' part of a Knox student is individuality." So what type of student won't fit in at Knox? "Someone apathetic, someone not willing to express themselves, or someone not willing to work," a senior answers. "Too many people will challenge you."

"Although academics are always first, there is plenty of time to get involved with other activities," says a sophomore. Among the most popular clubs are the Union Board, ABLE, Habitat for Humanity, Lo Nuestro, and Alpha Phi Omega. Fraternities and sororities contribute significantly to the social scene, but there isn't fierce competition to get into houses. Knox fields teams in 21 varsity sports at the Division III level, and 25 to 30 percent of students participate; intramurals and club sports are also available.

Knox has its share of unique traditions. For 75 years, the Knox community has gathered for "Pumphandle" on the day before classes begin, to welcome each other to campus. Everyone shakes everyone else's hand, eventually forming a huge snaking line around the South Lawn. Then there's "Flunk Day" each spring, when classes are suddenly canceled and Knox students head outdoors to celebrate with bands, karaoke, and "bounce-back toys" ("boxing with huge gloves," explains one student). "Knox has history, maintains tradition, yet is utterly innovative in so many ways," a junior sums up.

Other schools to check out: Beloit, Grinnell, Lawrence, Macalester, Kalamazoo.

Test Scores (middle 50%):
  SAT Verbal: 550–690
  SAT Math: 540–660
  ACT Comp: 24–30
  ACT English: 24–31
  ACT Math: 22–29

HS Rank of Entering Freshmen:
  Top 10%: 29%
  Top 25%: 68%
  Top 50%: 92%

THE EXPERTS SAY...

" Knox students are able to celebrate their individuality in a supportive yet academically challenging environment. "

" It can be hard to tell where academic life ends and social life begins on this isolated campus. "

Costs (2004–5)

Tuition and Fees: $25,236

Room & Board: $6,102

Payment Plan(s): installment plan, pre-payment plan

Inst. Aid (est. 2003–04)

Institutional Aid, Need-Based: $9,979,041

Institutional Aid, Non-Need-Based: $2,320,463

FT Undergrads Receiving Aid: 73%
  Avg. Amount per Student: $20,770

FT Undergrads Receiving Non-Need-Based Scholarship or Grant Aid: 21%
  Avg. Amount per Student: $10,280

Of Those Receiving Any Aid:

Rec. Need-Based Scholarship or Grant Aid: 100%
  Average Award: $15,483

Rec. Need-Based Self-Help Aid: 78%
  Average Award: $6,390

Upon Graduation, Avg. Loan Debt per Student: $18,221

Financial Aid Deadline: rolling, 3/1 (priority)

Graduates

Going to Graduate School:
  30% Within One Year

Accepting Job Offer:
  27% at time of graduation

Companies Recruiting On Campus: 105

Alumni Giving: 81%

LAFAYETTE COLLEGE

Lafayette College, Easton, PA 18042
Admissions Phone: (610) 330-5100 Fax: (610) 330-5355
Email: admissions@lafayette.edu
Website: lafayette.edu

General Info

Type of School: private, coed
Setting: small town
Academic Calendar: semester

Student Body

Full-Time Undergrads: 2,213
　Men: 53%, Women: 47%

Part-Time Undergrads: 38
　Men: 66%, Women: 34%

Total Undergrad Population:
　African American: 5%
　Asian American: 2%
　Latino: 3%
　Native American: <1%
　Caucasian: 85%
　International: 5%
　Out-of-State: 71%
　Living Off-Campus: 2%
　In Fraternities: 27%
　In Sororities: 32%

Academics

Full-Time Faculty: 188
　With Ph.D.: 100%

Part-Time Faculty: 36
　With Ph.D.: 61%

Student/Faculty Ratio: 11:1

Most Popular Majors:
　engineering (21%)
　economics (20%)
　government and law (12%)
　English (11%)
　psychology (8%)

Freshmen Retention Rate: 95%

Graduation Rates:
　79% within four years
　84% within six years

Admissions

Regular Application Deadline: 1/1

Early Decision Deadline(s): 2/15

Fall Transfer Deadline: 6/1, 5/1 (priority)

Spring Transfer Deadline: 1/1, 12/1 (priority)

Total # of Students Applied: 5,835
　Admitted: 2,122
　Enrolled: 590

# of Students Waitlisted: 1,679
　Students Accepting Place: 606
　Waitlisted Students Admitted: 86

Inside the Classroom

Lafayette boasts that it's "a small-college environment with large-college resources." Indeed, with one of the largest endowments in the country, Lafayette has a lot to offer its students. More than $100 million in new academic, residential, and recreational facilities have been undertaken in the past five years, including an impressive science center that supports the chemistry, physics, and biochemistry programs. The school is also embarking on a massive renovation of its engineering facilities—engineering is, after all, its top program. Engineering majors make up more than 20 percent of the student body (the college even offers a bachelor of arts degree in engineering, exemplifying Lafayette's tradition of integrating engineering and the liberal arts). Economics and business programs are strong and popular as well, as are the psychology and liberal arts programs.

In all, students may choose from 45 areas of study across four divisions: natural sciences, humanities, engineering, and social sciences. Students may also pursue double majors, individualized majors, and dual degrees. Studying abroad is another popular option. Lafayette's offerings are considerably expanded by its participation in the Lehigh Valley Association of Independent Colleges, a consortium that allows students to take advantage of opportunities at five nearby schools.

Entering students must take the First-Year Seminar (FYS), part of Lafayette's demanding core curriculum, or "The Common Course of Study." An FYS is limited to 16 students, focuses on a special topic (everything from poetry to the Soviet Union to pop culture), and includes significant reading, writing, discussion, research, and presentation. By the end of sophomore year, students must fulfill requirements in the key areas of humanities and social sciences, natural sciences, and math. They must also take two more seminars: one on College Writing and the other on VAST (Values and Science/Technology).

The workload is quite challenging, especially for engineering students. Lafayette is big on "active learning," and students report having many opportunities to work closely with their professors. The majority of classes have fewer than 20 students (the official student/faculty ratio is 11:1), and the school boasts that 100 percent of its full-time faculty holds a Ph.D. or other terminal degree in their field.

Campus Environment

Lafayette's campus overlooking the Delaware River is located in the safe, quiet, tree-lined neighborhood of College Hill. You can pretty much get to anything on campus within a 10-minute walk: classrooms, dorms, the student center, athletic facilities, the performing arts center, and so forth. There's a bus terminal in walking distance, and an airport is 20 minutes away, which is good news for underclassmen who want to get away, since only juniors and seniors are allowed to have cars. But most students stay on campus on the weekends, and the school likes it that way: Lafayette requires all students not commuting from a parent's home to live on campus. Twelve residence halls integrate all four classes, and may be coed (by wing, floor, or room) or single-sex. First-year students usually share a double room, and we hear the conditions are nothing special. After the first year, students choose from among

KAPLAN

traditional residence halls (singles, doubles, and suites) or from townhouses, a "living group," special-interest houses, and fraternity or sorority houses. Lafayette has eight frats and six sororities, and although you may join in your sophomore year, only juniors and seniors may live in Greek housing.

Lafayette seems not to want students to even eat anywhere else: All undergrads are required to participate in some sort of meal plan. This often has the effect of making an already isolated school feel even more closed off. Town–gown relations aren't the greatest, we hear, which is interesting, considering that the college was founded by the citizens of Easton. Some describe Easton as "quaint," but it really doesn't have much to offer (unless you count the Crayola factory and the abandoned steel mills). "Easton is a pit," says one blunt guidance counselor. Lafayette students don't often wander down the hill into town unless they're going to a bar or restaurant there.

Student Life

Lafayette is one of the more competitive liberal arts schools to get into, but students generally check that competitive urge at the door. Campus is warm and friendly, if fairly homogeneous. The typical Lafayette student can be described as white, conservative, and preppie. Greek life is huge here, especially among women. To say that fraternities and sororities rule the social scene may be an understatement. You'd be hard-pressed to find a Lafayette student who didn't regularly hit the frat party circuit. The "party school" reputation is evidently well-founded; weekends start as early as Wednesday, and beer drinking and pot smoking are the favored pastimes of many an undergrad.

For drier activities on campus, students head to Gilbert's, a late-night sports bar with game tables and a sound system. LAF (the Lafayette Activities Forum) organizes such on-campus events as movies, comedians, musicians, dances, and open-mike nights, as well as the occasional big-name concert (Bela Fleck, Dave Matthews). A whopping 200-plus clubs are available: academic, community service, performing arts and publications, religious, student governance, etc.

Lafayette, a member of the Patriot League, offers 23 varsity teams and is one of the smallest schools in the country competing on a Division I level. The annual football showdown against rival Lehigh University is arguably the biggest event of the year. For intramural and rec sports, there's a fine new 110,000-square-foot athletic complex including several racquet courts, a fitness center, and a climbing wall.

The city of Easton has a historic theater, and the downtown area has some shops, cultural venues, and places to eat and drink. When students leave campus, however, they're likely to head out of town altogether. Outdoor enthusiasts have the Poconos Mountains and the Delaware Water Gap nearby; for city fans, Philadelphia and New York City are each less than two hours away.

Applied Early Decision: 367
Early Decision Admitted: 244

Test Scores (middle 50%):
SAT Verbal: 570–660
SAT Math: 610–700
ACT Comp: 25–30

HS Rank of Entering Freshmen:
Top 10%: 61%
Top 25%: 90%
Top 50%: 100%

Avg. HS GPA: 3.96

THE EXPERTS SAY...

" An excellent choice for engineering students who want to work closely with their professors and get a solid liberal arts foundation. "

" If you're looking for a smallish Pennsylvania college strong in science and engineering, Lafayette isn't your only option. Check out Lehigh, Bucknell, and Franklin & Marshall. "

Costs (2004–5)

Tuition and Fees: $28,625

Room & Board: $8,786

Payment Plan(s): installment plan, deferred payment plan

Inst. Aid (2002–03)

FT Undergrads Receiving Aid: 54%
Avg. Amount per Student: $22,407

FT Undergrads Receiving Non-Need-Based Scholarship or Grant Aid: 7%
Avg. Amount per Student: $12,445

Of Those Receiving Any Aid:

Rec. Need-Based Scholarship or Grant Aid: 94%
Average Award: $20,044

Rec. Need-Based Self-Help Aid: 71%
Average Award: $4,854

Upon Graduation, Avg. Loan Debt per Student: $17,204

Financial Aid Deadline: 2/1, 1/1 (priority)

Graduates

Going to Graduate School:
31% Within One Year

Accepting Job Offer:
65% at time of graduation

Companies Recruiting On Campus: 140

Alumni Giving: 66%

LAKE FOREST COLLEGE

555 North Sheridan Road, Lake Forest, IL 60045
Admissions Phone: (847) 735-5000 Fax: (847) 735-6271
Email: admissions@lakeforest.edu Website: lakeforest.edu
Application Website: lakeforest.edu/admissions/applying

General Info

Type of School: private, coed,
  Presbyterian

Setting: suburban

Academic Calendar: semester

Student Body

Full-Time Undergrads: 1,322
  Men: 42%, Women: 57%

Part-Time Undergrads: 10
  Men: 30%, Women: 70%

Total Undergrad Population:
  African American: 5%
  Asian American: 4%
  Latino: 4%
  Native American: <1%
  Caucasian: 77%
  International: 10%
  Out-of-State: 52%
  Living Off-Campus: 18%
  In Fraternities: 19%
  In Sororities: 15%

Graduate and First-Professional
  Students: 12

Academics

Full-Time Faculty: 87
  With Ph.D.: 97%

Part-Time Faculty: 64
  With Ph.D.: 42%

Student/Faculty Ratio: 12:1

Most Popular Majors:
  business/economics (23%)
  communications (11%)
  psychology (8%)
  English (7%)
  foreign language (7%)

Completing 2 or More Majors: 42%

Freshmen Retention Rate: 81%

Graduation Rates:
  61% within four years
  66% within six years

Admissions

Regular Application Deadline: 3/1
  (priority)

Early Decision Deadline(s): 1/1

Early Action Deadline: 12/1

Fall Transfer Deadline: 7/15
  (priority)

Total # of Students Applied: 1,835
  Admitted: 1,240
  Enrolled: 347

Inside the Classroom

For a small school, Lake Forest offers a host of academic opportunities, from independent study to self-designed majors to incredible study abroad and internship programs. Whether Foresters take advantage of these opportunities is another matter: Some do decide to coast their way through their four to six years. With a new president on board, Lake Forest is making that a little more difficult by upping academic and admission standards.

This liberal arts college boasts a faculty with a reputation for caring deeply about students. Students rave about their professors, with whom they develop close and personal ties. All freshmen must take First Year Studies programs, small intensive classes designed to foster close interaction with teachers. Students have a great deal of freedom in program design, but there are new general education requirements that include courses in the humanities, social sciences, natural and mathematical sciences, and cultural diversity. A major senior project is required for graduation.

Lake Forest offers 26 majors. The most popular are business/economics, education, psychology, English, and biology. Teacher education is top-notch, and the English department gets the nod from students. Special programs are legion. In the Richter Apprentice Scholar Program, students work one-on-one with a faculty member for a summer as junior collaborators in research, living and working with other Richter scholars and participating in weekly colloquia. Ambitious students can participate in the Independent Scholars program. Independent study topics have included sports management, graphic design, business theory, theatrical lighting design, metaphysics, and feminist theory. Student can also spend a research semester at the Oak Ridge National Laboratory.

Nearly half of all Foresters earn credit for an internship or practicum. Students have worked for the Chicago Historical Society, the Museum of Contemporary Art, Marriott Corporation, IBM, the City of Chicago, the Chicago Bears, Second City Theatre, the Consulate General of Mexico, and the Art Institute of Chicago. Twenty-five percent of Foresters study abroad. The school offers programs in Greece and Turkey, Paris, and Santiago, Chile; there's also a marine biology program in the Bahamas, and many others through cooperating institutions.

Campus Environment

Lake Forest's campus is about 30 miles north of downtown Chicago, near the shores of Lake Michigan. The campus is divided into three parts, Middle, North, and South; everything is accessible by foot, but many students use bikes. The town of Lake Forest is extremely affluent, and the campus is well-insulated from inner-city crime. The cost of living is high, however, especially rents. Consequently, 80 percent of students live on campus.

Dorms get good reviews for spaciousness from students. The women's dorm is considered the best. The freshman dorm is less attractive, but is the place to be to get hooked up into campus life. Deerpath Hall recently received a $7 million renovation, and boasts a coffee shop and a fitness center. Newly renovated Nollen Hall also has a coffee shop and brand new lounges. The International Center is also a residence hall, and offers culinary treats from around the world. All students eat together in a central dining hall.

Lake Forest officials stress that theirs is a pedestrian campus with a limited number of parking spaces available. Parking is limited to junior and senior residents and commuter students. Given the close proximity to Chicago and a train station within walking distance, students can find big-city fun using mass transportation.

Student Life

Although many Foresters are academic stars, the school hasn't shaken its image as a party school for affluent prep-school kids. The typical Forester is white and well-to-do. There are basically two types of students: those who study all the time and those who party all the time. The campus has a small minority population that often feels out-of-place in the conservatively apolitical Lake Forest environment. A 50 percent out-of-state population provides geographical diversity in an otherwise homogeneous student body. The small student body is close-knit, which can lead to gossip, a distinct lack of privacy, and a prep-school kind of atmosphere.

A common complaint is student apathy. While there are over 90 clubs, some say that the turnout for student organizations is low, even though professors are usually willing to sponsor groups. Sports are hot, however: While Lake Forest is not generally considered a big sports school, there are a lot of opportunities to participate on the club, intramural, and varsity levels, and over 65 percent of students are involved in athletics. Hockey is big, as are men's handball and tennis. With Lake Michigan a short walk away, swimming and water sports are also popular.

Frats claim 15 percent of the Forester men, and sororities 18 percent of the women. Greek life is a big force in social life, especially alcohol-related events. Drinking is a major form of recreation on campus, and pot smoking is endemic. The school has attempted to crack down on substance use, but with little effect.

Chicago is the main source of fun for students who can get away from their dorm rooms. Students visit the bars on Rush, Lincoln, and Halstead Streets, hit the music venues, museums, and the theater, shop on Michigan Avenue, and visit the Navy Pier. Others get caught up in the "Enchanted Forest" syndrome, thinking that life begins and ends on their story-book beautiful campus and its posh surroundings. The opportunities for Foresters are all there, but it's up to each student to take advantage of them.

Other schools to check out: Illinois Wesleyan, Connecticut College, Kenyon, Denison, Hamilton.

# of Students Waitlisted: 75
  Students Accepting Place: 23
  Waitlisted Students Admitted: 12

Applied Early Decision: 42
  Early Decision Admitted: 25

Test Scores (middle 50%):
  SAT Verbal: 520–640
  SAT Math: 540–640
  ACT Comp: 22–28

HS Rank of Entering Freshmen:
  Top 10%: 24%
  Top 25%: 59%
  Top 50%: 87%

Avg. HS GPA: 3.4

THE EXPERTS SAY...

" Lake Forest's caring faculty and special programs set it apart from other liberal arts schools. The gorgeous campus is just half an hour away from Chicago. "

" There are plenty of opportunities at the Enchanted Forest, but how many Foresters can stop vegging out long enough to take advantage of them? "

Costs (2003–04)

Tuition and Fees: $24,406

Room & Board: $5,764

Payment Plan(s): installment plan

Inst. Aid (est. 2003–04)

FT Undergrads Receiving Aid: 77%
  Avg. Amount per Student: $19,466

FT Undergrads Receiving Non-Need-Based Scholarship or Grant Aid: 12%
  Avg. Amount per Student: $10,606

Of Those Receiving Any Aid:

Rec. Need-Based Scholarship or Grant Aid: 100%
  Average Award: $16,147

Rec. Need-Based Self-Help Aid: 76%
  Average Award: $4,360

Upon Graduation, Avg. Loan Debt per Student: $17,285

Financial Aid Deadline: 3/1 (priority)

Graduates

Going to Graduate School:
  31% Within One Year

Accepting Job Offer:
  52% at time of graduation

Companies Recruiting On Campus: 17

Alumni Giving: 41%

LAWRENCE UNIVERSITY

P.O. Box 599, Appleton, WI 54912-0599
Admissions Phone: (920) 832-6500; (800) 227-0982 Fax: (920) 832-6782
Email: excel@lawrence.edu Website: www.lawrence.edu
Application Website: www.lawrence.edu/admissions/apply/applications.shtml

General Info

Type of School: private, coed

Setting: urban

Academic Calendar: trimester

Student Body

Full-Time Undergrads: 1,313
    Men: 47%, Women: 53%

Part-Time Undergrads: 39
    Men: 51%, Women: 49%

Total Undergrad Population:
    African American: 2%
    Asian American: 2%
    Latino: 3%
    Native American: <1%
    Caucasian: 73%
    International: 10%
    Out-of-State: 57%
    Living Off-Campus: 4%
    In Fraternities: 23%
    In Sororities: 12%

Academics

Full-Time Faculty: 130
    With Ph.D.: 74%

Part-Time Faculty: 36
    With Ph.D.: 22%

Student/Faculty Ratio: 11:1

Most Popular Majors:
    music perfomance (12%)
    government (9%)
    biology (8%)
    psychology (7%)
    English (5%)

Completing 2 or More Majors: 23%

Freshmen Retention Rate: 87%

Graduation Rates:
    49% within four years
    69% within six years
    (5-yr. program affects rates)

Admissions

Regular Application Deadline: 1/15;
    1/1 (priority)

Early Decision Deadline(s): 11/15

Early Action Deadline: 12/1

Fall Transfer Deadline: 5/15

Spring Transfer Deadline: 11/1

Total # of Students Applied: 2,044
    Admitted: 1,192
    Enrolled: 364

Inside the Classroom

Lawrence University consists of two schools: an undergraduate liberal arts and sciences college and an undergraduate music conservatory. While Lawrence offers only 37 areas of study, these aren't limited to the typical fare found at most other liberal arts colleges (although the "liberal arts majors are very good," says an Iowa guidance counselor); students can major in everything from East Asian Languages and Cultures to Biomedical Ethics to Environmental Studies. Numerous interdisciplinary programs are offered, as are preprofessional co-op opportunities.

The Lawrence Conservatory of Music offers the bachelor of music degree in performance, education, or theory-composition; the bachelor of arts degree with a major in music; or a five-year, double-degree that allows a major within the liberal arts and science curriculum and a major within the professional music degree program. Non-music majors may participate fully in conservatory ensembles, by audition.

The schedule at Lawrence is unusual: three 10-week terms, from mid-September through early June. Students generally take only three courses per term. The general education requirements for all students are fairly extensive: 10 courses spread out among foreign language; English; history, philosophy, or religious studies; the arts; math; natural sciences with lab; and social sciences. Freshmen are also required to take a two-term interdisciplinary seminar known as Freshman Studies, which is intended to help first-year students read critically, write coherently, and speak persuasively.

Lawrence encourages students to engage in at least one term of study away from the campus, and more than half of its students take advantage of one of the opportunities presented by nearly three dozen off-campus programs. A program at Lawrence's London Study Centre is particularly popular.

Students say that coursework is rigorous, but that the atmosphere is never cutthroat. The Honor Code at Lawrence is taken seriously: Students pledge that they "will not unfairly advance their own academic performance nor impede that of others." It works so well that professors have been known to give students take-home exams, trusting them not to use their textbooks or notes if so instructed. The Honor Code helps to promote a noncompetitive atmosphere among students. "No one is out there to crush other students [in order] to advance themselves," says one student. "This is wonderful because you are able to collaborate and exchange ideas without worrying that you will lose out in the end."

The faculty at Lawrence is said to be extremely accessible and supportive. "You can always go and talk to them about class or life in general," says one student about his professors. "They are here for the sake of the students, and everyone realizes that." Students get a special chance to bond with the faculty during seminars that are held each weekend at Bjorklunden, a 400-acre estate on the shore of Lake Michigan, just two hours north of Lawrence. Seminar topics are wide-ranging, from Afro-Cuban Drumming to a Model United Nations to Astronomy Observation.

Campus Environment

The 84-acre Lawrence campus is located on a bluff overlooking the Fox River in Appleton, a town in northeastern Wisconsin with a population of 69,000. Students don't need a car to get around, since the campus itself is compact and just a short walk to downtown Appleton, which offers restaurants, shops, and coffeehouses.

Nearly all Lawrence students live on campus, in one of the six residence halls, eight small houses (including "theme houses" for upperclassmen), or five frat houses. "You might not know everyone on campus but you are able to recognize them," says one student. "I never get across campus without stopping to talk to someone." Housing is varied and, by most reports, fairly pleasant. As for dining hall food, one student called in "unimaginative," but rated it pretty acceptable.

Student Life

Lawrence is a "friendly" place, and by and large, students feel good about being there. While there are divisions among students, most seem to get along. Lawrence boasts a sizable international student contingent, and students describe the overall student body as "diverse." Says one recent Lawrence grad, "The students, the faculty, and the campus life and academic environment are all top-notch, and provide for an excellent all-around experience that prepares its students for life, not just a career." The school's small size helps foster a feeling of community and intimacy. "At Lawrence, you feel like part of a family," comments one student. "I feel that if I went to a larger school, I would not give as much to the campus as I do here. Each and every person adds to the campus and shapes it into the Lawrence we all know and love."

With more than 150 student clubs, including 20 musical groups and 30 sports, a student assures us that "pretty much anytime of the day or night, you can find something to do and someone to do it with." More than one-quarter of the students join a fraternity or sorority; the frat houses and theme houses throw frequent weekend parties. Students also just like to hang and relax in the coffeehouse or the game room in the Memorial Union. Thanks to the Conservatory of Music, there are frequent music and theatre performances on campus. More than half of the students at Lawrence are involved in volunteer projects, with a particular emphasis on helping at-risk youth. And word is that the town of Appleton is "not such a bad place to spend four years of your life." Still, for students craving city life, the school organizes frequent trips to Milwaukee and Chicago.

# of Students Waitlisted: 64
Students Accepting Place: 16
Waitlisted Students Admitted: 9

Applied Early Decision: 47
Early Decision Admitted: 40

Test Scores (middle 50%):
SAT Verbal: 590–690
SAT Math: 580–690
ACT Comp: 25–30
ACT English: 24–30
ACT Math: 24–30

HS Rank of Entering Freshmen:
Top 10%: 42%
Top 25%: 71%
Top 50%: 93%

Avg. HS GPA: 3.67

THE EXPERTS SAY...

" If you like Oberlin, check out lesser-known Lawrence, another small liberal arts school with a fine music conservatory. "

" You can spend your weekends at Bjorklunden bonding with the faculty, or you make music on a more urban campus like Catholic University of America, University of Cincinnati, or Rice University. "

Costs (2004–5)

Tuition and Fees: $26,343

Room & Board: $5,559

Payment Plan(s): installment plan

Inst. Aid (est. 2003–04)

FT Undergrads Receiving Aid: 60%
Avg. Amount per Student: $21,596

FT Undergrads Receiving Non-Need-Based Scholarship or Grant Aid: 31%
Avg. Amount per Student: $9,662

Of Those Receiving Any Aid:

Rec. Need-Based Scholarship or Grant Aid: 100%
Average Award: $15,380

Rec. Need-Based Self-Help Aid: 95%
Average Award: $6,500

Upon Graduation, Avg. Loan Debt per Student: $1,796

Financial Aid Deadline: 3/15 (priority)

Graduates

Going to Graduate School:
28% Within One Year

Accepting Job Offer:
30% at time of graduation

Companies Recruiting On Campus: 10

Alumni Giving: 31%

LEHIGH UNIVERSITY

27 Memorial Drive West, Bethlehem, PA 18015
Admissions Phone: (610) 758-3100 Fax: (610) 758-4361
Email: admissions@lehigh.edu Website: www.lehigh.edu
Application Website: www3.lehigh.edu/admissions/default.asp

General Info

Type of School: private, coed

Setting: suburban

Academic Calendar: semester

Student Body

Full-Time Undergrads: 4,609
  Men: 60%, Women: 40%

Part-Time Undergrads: 47
  Men: 70%, Women: 30%

Total Undergrad Population:
  African American: 3%
  Asian American: 6%
  Latino: 2%
  Native American: <1%
  Caucasian: 77%
  International: 3%
  Out-of-State: 69%
  Living Off-Campus: 34%
  In Fraternities: 33%
  In Sororities: 39%

Graduate and First-Professional
  Students: 2,053

Academics

Full-Time Faculty: 430
  With Ph.D.: 99%

Part-Time Faculty: 117

Student/Faculty Ratio: 10:1

Most Popular Majors:
  mechanical engineering (10%)
  finance (8%)
  marketing (6%)
  industrial engineering (5%)
  psychology (5%)

Freshmen Retention Rate: 93%

Graduation Rates:
  73% within four years
  86% within six years

Admissions

Regular Application Deadline: 1/1

Early Decision Deadline(s): 11/15

Fall Transfer Deadline: 5/1, 4/1
  (priority)

Spring Transfer Deadline: 12/1,
  11/15 (priority)

Total # of Students Applied: 9,087
  Admitted: 3,678
  Enrolled: 1,125

Inside the Classroom

The College of Arts and Science, which is Lehigh University's largest undergraduate college (accounting for almost half of enrolled students), has several notable departments, including architecture, biology, government, English, and psychology. Students can minor in education in the College of Education, but most of the remaining undergrads take part in the strong programs in the College of Business and Economics or the renowned P.C. Rossin College of Engineering and Applied Sciences. The university boasts new majors in integrated business and engineering (IBE), bioengineering, and a freshman immersion program in the humanities. Lehigh also offers a unique computer science and business program, and an Integrated Product Development Program, which offers a combined curriculum of design arts, engineering, and business. Lehigh's academic programs, in general, emphasize integration of discipline. There are extensive opportunities for overseas study, co-ops, internships, externships, and part-time employment in the student's field of interest. A New York guidance counselor tells us that Lehigh makes it easy for students to combine majors.

Each college has its own requirements. The study time depends on the department and major, but many students have heavy workloads, compared to other top schools. "There are no easy courses here," a marketing major asserts. A finance major says, "Students are not out to just 'get by' but rather are out to make the dean's list and achieve A's. Lehigh students are very intense about their work and will stop at nothing to complete papers and projects."

With 4,650 enrolled undergrads, Lehigh has an average class size of about 25–30 students, and the student/faculty ratio is 10:1. Ninety-nine percent of the faculty holds a Ph.D. or other terminal professional degree in their field, and students give them high marks for accessibility and willingness to help. A large number of undergrads take advantage of distinctive research programs in which teams of students and faculty work on "real world" projects for industry and local organizations. Through these programs, students can, for example, design athletic facilities, manage financial portfolios, or participate in archeological digs. Undergrads benefit from access to graduate facilities, and qualified students can enroll in accelerated grad degree programs. The President's Scholars program allows students who graduate with a 3.75 GPA or higher to enroll in a fifth year of courses tuition-free.

Lehigh's Clipper Project allows high schoolers who have been accepted for early admission to take some freshman courses online. Students don't pay for these Web-based classes, and getting a jump-start on college can also make it easier to pursue a double major, or even graduate in less than four years.

Campus Environment

The "mountainous" 1,600-acre campus is situated on the side of a hill, providing both a view (it's "landscaped beautifully," according to one student) as well as a serious aerobic workout for anyone trekking between classes and dorm rooms. The style of campus buildings varies from traditional ivy-covered to institutional to contemporary. Freshmen are required to live in the dorms, and we heard no major complaints about the housing (outside of the usual "small, cramped, and noisy" song). As for upperclassmen, the housing options are varied: Campus Square, a new, "apartment-style" complex that includes retail space and a parking garage, opened in fall 2002. Nearly all of Lehigh's 24 fraternities and 9 sororities have their own houses, and many sophomores, juniors, and seniors live with their "brothers and sisters" there.

Freshmen aren't allowed to bring cars, but you probably won't need one on this "walking campus." The school runs shuttles if you get tired of "walking uphill all day." Most students agree that cars are helpful but not necessary. As for the city of Bethlehem, this "old steel town" has been undergoing a cultural renaissance. In the past few years, numerous shops, artist studios, and ethnic restaurants have sprung up. Safety has also become less of an issue, students report.

Student Life

The "very approachable and social" student body is one of Lehigh's main attractions. The warmth and friendliness are apparent from day one, as faculty, staff, and fellow students greet incoming families and help new freshmen unload their cars on Move-In Day. Be prepared, however, for an overwhelmingly "white," "upper middle class," "Abercrombie" student body. Diversity is not the school's strong suit, although its minority population is slowly growing. Lehigh coeds are alike in another way, as summed up by this student: "We work pretty hard, but with that we earn the right to enjoy ourselves too."

It's a very social campus. There's no denying the "tremendous influence" that the Greek system has on Lehigh social life: Approximately 40 percent of the student body belongs to a fraternity or sorority. And the Greeks make certain there's no shortage of parties on "the Hill," where most of their houses are located. Not surprisingly, drinking is a big part of the scene on the weekends (and many weeknights). On campus, alcohol policies are strict and the administration's efforts to control the party scene have been successful. A few fraternities have lost their charters and their houses on the Hill. Consequently, non-alcoholic parties, Greek and non-Greek, are gaining in popularity. "In general, our partying doesn't take away from studying and class time," one junior argues.

Students have plenty to do on campus. University Productions, a student-run group, books dozens of acts and activities each year, and Zoellner Arts Center offers world-class concerts, theatrical productions, and art exhibits. There are more than 300 clubs, activities, and intramural sports, plus a heavily used fitness center. Students support the school's 24 Division I sports, and the athletics facilities are top-notch. There is heavy student turnout for pre-game football tailgates followed by the game itself. The Mountain Hawks haven't lost a home game in four years. The Lehigh–Lafayette game is the nation's most played rivalry, attracting loyal students and alumni, both at the game and at about 50 telecast gatherings nationwide.

Other schools to check out: Cornell, Vanderbilt, Lafayette, Bucknell, Colgate.

# of Students Waitlisted: 2,264
  Students Accepting Place: 1,228
  Waitlisted Students Admitted: 51

Test Scores (middle 50%):
  SAT Verbal: 580–670
  SAT Math: 630–710

THE EXPERTS SAY...

" There's a lot to Lehigh besides engineering. Hard-working students can get an integrated, real world education, and a fifth year of courses free. "

" If you don't connect with frats, the Lehigh 'work hard–play hard' scene will just be hard work for you. "

Costs (2004–5)

Tuition and Fees: $29,340

Room & Board: $8,230

Payment Plan(s): installment plan, deferred payment plan, pre-payment plan

Inst. Aid (est. 2003–04)

Institutional Aid, Need-Based: $30,237,486

Institutional Aid, Non-Need-Based: $4,554,980

FT Undergrads Receiving Aid: 46%
  Avg. Amount per Student: $23,533

FT Undergrads Receiving Non-Need-Based Scholarship or Grant Aid: 8%
  Avg. Amount per Student: $13,193

Of Those Receiving Any Aid:

Rec. Need-Based Scholarship or Grant Aid: 95%
  Average Award: $17,403

Rec. Need-Based Self-Help Aid: 94%
  Average Award: $5,585

Upon Graduation, Avg. Loan Debt per Student: $16,774

Financial Aid Deadline: 2/1 (priority)

LEWIS AND CLARK COLLEGE

0615 SW Palatine Hill Road, Portland, OR 97219-7899
Admissions Phone: (503) 768-7040; (800) 444-4111 Fax: (503) 768-7055
Email: admissions@lclark.edu
Website: www.lclark.edu

General Info

Type of School: private, coed
Setting: urban
Academic Calendar: semester

Student Body

Full-Time Undergrads: 1,741
　Men: 39%, Women: 61%

Part-Time Undergrads: 12
　Men: 58%, Women: 42%

Total Undergrad Population:
　African American: 1%
　Asian American: 6%
　Latino: 3%
　Native American: 2%
　Caucasian: 66%
　International: 5%
　Out-of-State: 80%
　Living Off-Campus: 36%

Graduate and First-Professional
　Students: 1,279

Academics

Full-Time Faculty: 195
　With Ph.D.: 94%

Part-Time Faculty: 136
　With Ph.D.: 52%

Student/Faculty Ratio: 12:1

Most Popular Majors:
　psychology (13%)
　international affairs (10%)
　biology/biochemistry (9%)
　sociology/anthropology (8%)
　English/art (8%)

Completing 2 or More Majors: 11%

Freshmen Retention Rate: 84%

Graduation Rates:
　63% within four years
　71% within six years

Admissions

Regular Application Deadline: 2/1

Early Action Deadline: 12/1

Fall Transfer Deadline: 7/1, 2/1
　(priority)

Spring Transfer Deadline: 12/1

Total # of Students Applied: 3,405
　Admitted: 2,310
　Enrolled: 493

# of Students Waitlisted: 346
　Students Accepting Place: 122
　Waitlisted Students Admitted: 14

In the Classroom

International studies form an integral part of the total educational experience at Lewis and Clark, which has one of the oldest and largest study-abroad programs of any liberal arts college in the country. Although it's possible to satisfy Lewis and Clark's international studies and foreign language requirements by taking courses at the home campus, students are encouraged to spend at least one semester abroad. The college offers an array of study-abroad options around the world and prices them so that the total cost of participation is comparable to the cost of staying on the home campus. An average of 270 students participate in a study-abroad program each year, so that, by the time of graduation, a majority of the students have taken part in at least one of the school's off-campus programs.

On their own turf, Lewis and Clark students receive an excellent liberal arts education, choosing from 25 majors. "The academic standards are strong," one student says. "If you enroll in this school, you will learn." We are also told, "the workload can be heavy, but teachers recognize that you have other classes and can be flexible." Eighty-seven percent of the classes have fewer than 30 students, with the average having only 18 students. The small class size allows students to work closely with one another and form relationships with professors. "The professors are very accessible, and willing to help you with almost anything, from class work to recommendation letters to applications, internships, etc.," says one student. "I feel like my advisor is a good friend."

All freshmen are required to take a two-semester course called "Inventing America." According to the school, this course "will expose you to the voices that shaped the idea of America, and that continue to shape it today." Other general education requirements include courses in scientific and quantitative reasoning, creative arts, physical education, and the previously discussed areas of international studies and foreign language.

Campus Environment

The 133-acre campus sits atop Palatine Hill, overlooking the Willamette River and offering a great view of Portland's dominant landmark, Mt. Hood (although most of the time it's hidden by clouds). Lewis and Clark offers excellent facilities for a small liberal arts school, including a library that's open 24 hours on weekdays.

Students are required to live on campus for their first two years in one of the residence halls. Within these dorms, "special interest" areas give students the option of living with others who share their interests, including outdoor pursuits, multicultural, and substance-free options. After doing time in the regular residence halls, upperclassmen can apply to live in the very recently completed apartment-style buildings on campus, complete with coffee shop, rec center, and large common lounges with fireplaces. If you don't get a place in one of these three new buildings, you may have to look off campus for housing, where "rents run between $300–$500/month" according to a current student.

Freshmen are not permitted to have cars on campus. One problem for students without wheels is that the campus is situated in a quiet, secluded neighborhood without a lot going on, especially at night. Students report that one of the major drawbacks of living on campus is the lack of late-night eateries anywhere nearby (besides Maggie's, the café in Roberts Hall, which is open until midnight). Most upperclassmen have cars, although Portland's city center, located six miles away, is readily accessible via public transportation and L&C shuttle bus.

Student Life

For the most part, L&C attracts relatively affluent students from across the country who can afford the steep price tag. A senior describes the population: "In terms of the crowds, there are the nuevo-hippies who are devoted activists and environmentalists. The academics are involved in student government and other clubs (but so are the hippies). The hip-hop/snowboarder kids are pretty cool and tend to fraternize with the nuevo-hippies. Then there are the jocks in the minority, but they are not obnoxious. We have no Greek life, which is good, because it prevents some exclusivity and stupidity. All in all, people mingle among groups and all are friendly." Many students consider the lack of ethnic diversity a major drawback. But the high percentage of international students—representing over 40 countries—helps give the school a more cosmopolitan ambience. Recent school visitors include left-wing icons Ralph Nader and Michael Moore.

The social scene at Lewis and Clark tends to be casual, friendly, and low-key. There may be no fraternities or sororities, but according to the school's administration, there are more than 100 clubs and organizations on campus to get involved in. For entertainment, students typically go to small parties and gatherings in dorm rooms or off-campus apartments. "Welcome to pot central, USA, [where] non-pot-smokers are in the minority, but not discriminated against," claims one student. "Parties are usually off-campus and at student houses, fairly safe. People are usually too high to start fights, and the cops rarely interfere." This student adds, "Papachinos is a popular place to study," and "Tryon Creek Park is good for jogging and biking (right across the street from campus)." Those who want more excitement can head into Portland. The city has a lot to offer, including good restaurants, shops, coffeehouses, parks, and pedestrian malls, and an underground music scene that is coming to rival Seattle's.

The Pioneers compete in the Northwest Conference, fielding 18 varsity teams. Men's basketball is strong and many students come out to cheer the team on. Lewis and Clark plays in the NCAA Division III, and in addition to varsity athletics, there are 14 club sports and a number of intramural options that attract about 40 percent of the student body. With skiing on Mt. Hood only 50 miles away and the Pacific Coast an 80-mile trip, it's not surprising that L&C students love getting involved in outdoor activities. But to encounter nature, there's no need to travel far: Tryon Creek State Park offers 13 miles of forested trails beginning right across the street from campus.

Other schools to check out: Earlham, Reed, Eckerd, Whitman, Colorado College.

Test Scores (middle 50%):
  SAT Verbal: 600–710
  SAT Math: 580–670
  ACT Comp: 26–30
  ACT English: 25–30
  ACT Math: 24–29

HS Rank of Entering Freshmen:
  Top 10%: 41%
  Top 25%: 80%
  Top 50%: 98%

Avg. HS GPA: 3.66

THE EXPERTS SAY...

" Lewis and Clark is for the liberal-minded, hard working, liberal arts student. The countless offerings of a state park, the coast, and Mt. Hood are a bonus for outdoorsy types. "

" If you're planning to come here, consider a crash course in Phish 101. "

Costs (est. 2004–05)

Tuition and Fees: $24,686

Room & Board: $7,140 (19-meal plan)

Payment Plan(s): installment plan

Inst. Aid (est. 2003–04)

Institutional Aid, Need-Based: $13,962,395

Institutional Aid, Non-Need-Based: $2,156,411

FT Undergrads Receiving Aid: 63%
  Avg. Amount per Student: $18,654

FT Undergrads Receiving Non-Need-Based Scholarship or Grant Aid: 5%
  Avg. Amount per Student: $7,229

Of Those Receiving Any Aid:

Rec. Need-Based Scholarship or Grant Aid: 100%
  Average Award: $17,314

Rec. Need-Based Self-Help Aid: 73%
  Average Award: $5,573

Upon Graduation, Avg. Loan Debt per Student: $17,055

Financial Aid Deadline: 3/1 (priority)

Graduates

Going to Graduate School:
  22% Within One Year

Accepting Job Offer:
  88% at time of graduation

Companies Recruiting On Campus: 105

Alumni Giving: 37%

LOUISIANA STATE UNIVERSITY

110 Thomas Boyd Hall, Baton Rouge, LA 70803
Admissions Phone: (225) 578-1175 Fax: (225) 578-4433
Email: admissions@lsu.edu Website: www.lsu.edu
Application Website: appl003.lsu.edu/slas/ugadmissions.nsf/index

General Info

Type of School: public, coed
Setting: urban
Academic Calendar: semester

Student Body

Full-Time Undergrads: 23,576
　Men: 48%, Women: 52%

Part-Time Undergrads: 1,908
　Men: 46%, Women: 54%

Total Undergrad Population:
　African American: 9%
　Asian American: 3%
　Latino: 2%
　Native American: <1%
　Caucasian: 81%
　International: 2%
　Out-of-State: 10%
　Living Off-Campus: 76%
　In Fraternities: 10%
　In Sororities: 15%

Graduate and First-Professional
　Students: 5,778

Academics

Full-Time Faculty: 1,297
　With Ph.D.: 82%

Part-Time Faculty: 251
　With Ph.D.: 48%

Student/Faculty Ratio: 21:1

Most Popular Majors:
　biological sciences (8%)
　pre–business administration (4%)
　psychology (4%)
　general studies (4%)
　mass communication (3%)

Completing 2 or More Majors: 1%

Freshmen Retention Rate: 84%

Graduation Rates:
　23% within four years
　57% within six years

Admissions

Regular Application Deadline: 4/15;
　11/15 (priority)

Fall Transfer Deadline: 4/15

Spring Transfer Deadline: 12/1

Total # of Students Applied: 10,147
　Admitted: 8,171
　Enrolled: 5,428

Inside the Classroom

Louisiana State University and A&M College is the largest school in the state, with 18 colleges and schools and about 30,000 students. The school's traditional strengths lie in the sciences—particularly engineering and the natural sciences, which were given high praise by one guidance counselor from Texas—but LSU is also deeply rooted in the culture of Louisiana. It's not surprising that the study of French dialects can be found here in the heart of Creole country, and it seems only natural that one of the residence halls is named after Gen. P.G.T. Beauregard, the highest-ranking Creole officer in the Confederacy.

The first stop for most incoming freshmen is the Center for Freshman Year, a college-within-a-college that allows students to hone college-level academic skills while deciding which of the many LSU colleges to enroll in after freshman year. Orientation, counseling, and special programs are all part of the first-year program. General education requirements include nine hours of humanities courses; eight hours of natural sciences; six hours of English composition, analytical reasoning, and social sciences; and three hours of arts.

For those looking to really distinguish themselves in the liberal arts, a special Honors College provides a challenging, small-school environment within a major university. Classes are kept small to foster greater student–professor interaction: One student says, "In most of the Honors courses I've taken, the instructor has known the name of every student in the class."

LSU is both the land grant and sea grant college for the state, so students are assured of up-to-date and well-funded technical programs. In fact, at any given time, more than 2,000 sponsored research projects are underway somewhere on campus. Agricultural programs benefit from comprehensive herbariums and arboretums as well as the Burden Research Plantation. Other research and instructional programs are undertaken through the LSU Agricultural Center's Louisiana Agricultural Experiment Station.

LSU also has a very strong study-abroad selection, comprised of semester, summer, academic year study-abroad programs, work and volunteer abroad programs, and international student exchanges. Some of the many countries to which students can travel include China, Germany, Ireland, Italy, France, the United Kingdom, Senegal, Spain, and Tanzania.

Campus Environment

LSU's campus sprawls over more than 2,000 acres in the southern part of Baton Rouge, bordered on the west by the Mississippi River. Most of the 250+ buildings are grouped together on a 650-acre plateau, forming the academic heart of the campus. The school's gardenlike landscaping, studded with many oak trees, is so well-planned and beautiful that writer Thomas Gaines called it "a botanical joy" in his book, *The Campus As a Work of Art*. Fortunately for students, a free bus service is available to ferry them where they need to go.

An entire town's worth of residence halls—18, to be precise—presents students with a variety of living choices. Coed dorms include Boyd, Beauregard, East Laville, West Laville, Herget, Highland, Jackson, Lejeune, and Taylor Halls. Women-only dorms are Acadian, Blake, Evangeline, Graham, and Miller Halls, while men can enjoy the exclusive company of other men in Garig and McVoy Halls. Suite-style living is available in Beauregard, Jackson, Kirby-Smith, Lejeune, and Taylor Halls, and full apartments are open to upperclassmen in the East Campus Apartments. Honors housing is also available in East Laville Hall. Be forewarned, though: The honors dorm is so popular that students are advised to apply during their senior year of high school. Fortunately, on-campus housing isn't a requirement for students, and a majority of students find off-campus accommodations each year.

The huge LSU Student Union contains many places to eat and meet. Dining venues include the Tiger Lair Food Court, the Sidepocket Snack Bar, the Magnolia Room Restaurant, a bakery, a McDonald's, and the eCommons Café coffeehouse. Theatrical performances are staged in the Union Theater, and an improvisational comedy show called "Making It Up Again… As We Go Along" regularly cracks students up. The Union also offers "leisure classes" where students can spend their free time learning arts and crafts, photography techniques, and other nonacademic interests. A creative arts center and a bowling alley round out the Union's facilities.

Other sights to see on campus include the Louisiana Museum of Natural History, which currently holds 2.8 million specimens, objects, and artifacts that document the natural history of the state; the LSU Museum of Natural Science, which is the only comprehensive research museum in the south-central United States; and the LSU Museum of Art, which has permanent collections in ceramics, furniture, glass, lighting, paintings, prints, and silver.

Student Life

With more than 30,000 students, it's fairly easy to get lost in the crowd. LSU's strong roots in Louisiana culture may also be a bit overwhelming for the newcomer hailing from another region. "It's an excellent school for someone with deep ties to Louisiana culture," wrote one guidance counselor, "but if you don't have roots in Louisiana, you may not be interested."

Fraternities and sororities are legion on campus, providing a safe base from which students can explore socially. Of course, the Greeks provide a lot more than that: As with most big schools, parties can be both large and rowdy. "The long running joke about LSU is that it is a drinking university, and unfortunately that is true," admits one student.

The social life at LSU involves much more than that, however: Student organizations number well into the hundreds, addressing nearly every possible interest imaginable. From the Salvadoran Student Organization to the women's powerlifting team; from the Society for Players, Artists, and Tricksters to the agronomy club, there's something out there for everyone.

The LSU Tigers compete at the Division I level (Division I-A for football). A choice of 20 club sports is also available, as are intramural offerings. Sports are a major draw for the university—the football team in particular commands a large following—although one student grumbles, "I wish some of the money spent on sports would go to other places that really need it."

Test Scores (middle 50%):
ACT Comp: 22–27
ACT English: 22–28
ACT Math: 20–26

HS Rank of Entering Freshmen:
Top 10%: 25%
Top 25%: 55%
Top 50%: 85%

Avg. HS GPA: 3.49

THE EXPERTS SAY...

" LSU backs up the reputation of its engineering and sciences programs with its strong focus on research. "

" If you don't know what 'Creole' means, this is not the place for you. "

Costs (est. 2004–05)

Tuition and Fees, In-State: $3,910

Tuition and Fees, Out-of-State: $9,210

Room & Board: $5,216

Payment Plan(s): deferred payment plan

Inst. Aid (2002–03)

Institutional Aid, Need-Based: $2,422,895

Institutional Aid, Non-Need-Based: $5,764,678

FT Undergrads Receiving Aid: 45%
Avg. Amount per Student: $6,223

FT Undergrads Receiving Non-Need-Based Scholarship or Grant Aid: 37%
Avg. Amount per Student: $3,657

Of Those Receiving Any Aid:

Rec. Need-Based Scholarship or Grant Aid: 88%
Average Award: $4,190

Rec. Need-Based Self-Help Aid: 66%
Average Award: $3,852

Upon Graduation, Avg. Loan Debt per Student: $17,572

Financial Aid Deadline: rolling

Graduates

Companies Recruiting On Campus: 252

LOYOLA COLLEGE IN MARYLAND

4501 North Charles Street, Baltimore, MD 21210
Admissions Phone: (410) 617-5012; (800) 221-9107 Fax: (410) 617-2176
Website: www.loyola.edu

General Info

Type of School: private, coed
Academic Calendar: semester

Student Body

Full-Time Undergrads: 3,339
  Men: 42%, Women: 58%

Part-Time Undergrads: 48
  Men: 58%, Women: 42%

Total Undergrad Population:
  African American: 5%
  Asian American: 2%
  Latino: 2%
  Native American: <1%
  Caucasian: 88%
  International: 1%
  Out-of-State: 84%
  Living Off-Campus: 21%

Graduate and First-Professional
  Students: 2,620

Academics

Full-Time Faculty: 284
  With Ph.D.: 85%

Part-Time Faculty: 230

Student/Faculty Ratio: 13:1

Freshmen Retention Rate: 92%

Graduation Rates:
  78% within four years
  82% within six years

Admissions

Regular Application Deadline: 1/15

Fall Transfer Deadline: 7/15

Spring Transfer Deadline: 11/15

Total # of Students Applied: 6,611
  Admitted: 4,675
  Enrolled: 916

# of Students Waitlisted: 1,489
  Students Accepting Place: 782
  Waitlisted Students Admitted: 782

Test Scores (middle 50%):
  SAT Verbal: 560–650
  SAT Math: 570–660

HS Rank of Entering Freshmen:
  Top 10%: 32%
  Top 25%: 71%
  Top 50%: 97%

Avg. HS GPA: 3.41

Inside the Classroom

Loyola College is a Jesuit-run liberal arts school where academic excellence includes an education of the whole person. The school is affiliated with the Roman Catholic Church, but is open to students from all religious backgrounds. Values and character are seen as important for student development: Students are challenged to examine the ethical dimensions of personal and professional life, and to constantly reconsider their own values, attitudes, and beliefs.

Loyola awards the B.A. degree in the classics, communication, economics, education, English, the fine arts, history, modern languages, philosophy, political science, psychology, sociology, speech-language pathology and audiology, and theology. The B.S. degree is awarded in biology, chemistry, computer science, electrical engineering, engineering science, and mathematical sciences. Also, a number of interdisciplinary minors are open to students, including Catholic studies, medieval studies, and Asian studies.

For extra recognition, students can elect to take a special honors curriculum that involves 12 advanced-level courses, 8 of which take the form of seminars. The freshman seminar is an introductory writing course that substitutes for the regular writing requirement. Four of the seminars are interdisciplinary and deal with the history of Western civilization; another seminar is chosen from a selection of art history, music, and theater; the next two seminars satisfy core ethics and contemporary literature requirements; and the last seminar is a noncredit course that focuses on extracurricular components like cultural, artistic, social, and intellectual events and performances.

Loyola also has a remarkable study abroad program for a school its size. Juniors can take advantage of semester and yearlong programs at Loyola's centers in Spain, New Zealand, Thailand, China, Ireland, Belgium, Australia, and the United Kingdom.

Campus Environment

Loyola College's roughly U-shaped campus is located in Baltimore City, a suburb of Baltimore, Maryland. Both college administrators and students alike refer to the pretty grounds and buildings as the Evergreen Campus. The Donnelly Science center with its labs is a must-visit site for prospective science majors.

Choosing a residence hall at Loyola is an interesting process. The names of all 11 dorms were changed in fall 2002... a commendable move, given that the old names included Gardens A through Gardens D, Notre Dame Lane, and The Pit. Each spring, a bulletin is produced listing all of the available rooms, apartments, suites, and efficiencies designated for each class. Rooms are then chosen according to a class lottery system.

New construction on campus includes a brand-new college radio station, with state-of-the-art equipment designed to broadcast its signal over the Internet. The recent, extensive renovation of Aquinas House is also the first in a series of planned renovations for Loyola's dorms.

Student Life

Loyola's student body is well-mannered and clean-cut, if somewhat homogeneous. "The Christian values and education are attractive attributes," says one guidance counselor from Connecticut, "but the kids are all the same." Diversity was the focus of much debate in the student newspaper, *The Greyhound*, during spring 2002, with one student saying, "This semester I attended the multicultural retreat, another program geared and open to all students. How many white students showed up? None."

A special perk for first-year students is the school's Best of Baltimore program, where students are bused off campus for musical, cultural, and sports events. Transportation is free, and each event includes a special reception. The lineup of events for 2002 included trips to see a Moscow Boys' Choir concert, a Baltimore Orioles baseball game, *Riverdance*, and a production of Shakespeare's *A Winter's Tale*.

Dozens of student organizations on campus provide opportunities for students to socialize and share their common interests: Sports, religion, hobbies, nationalities, and political and academic interests are some of the common themes. Some colorfully named clubs include the Poisoned Cup Players, Roots and Shoots (an environmental club), and Girls Learning about Double Dutch and Dance (GLADD).

In the world of sports, the Loyola Greyhounds compete at the NCAA Division I level. Varsity sports for both men and women include basketball, lacrosse, soccer, crew, cross country, swimming and diving. Men can also play golf and tennis, while women can compete in volleyball. Club sports for men include baseball, ice hockey, soccer, lacrosse, volleyball, and rugby, while women's club sports are the dance team, softball, field hockey, soccer, basketball, lacrosse, and volleyball. The three coed club sports are track and field, sailing, and marksmanship. A dozen intramural sports are also available for students looking to just play for fun.

A favorite campus tradition is the Fall Football Classic, a flag football game between the freshmen and sophomore classes, with men playing the first half and women playing the second half. Loyola also sponsors a Late Night program featuring social, cultural, and athletic activities on weekend evenings. Coffeehouse entertainment is provided on Thursday nights, and a free "midnight breakfast" is served up on Fridays and Saturdays.

Costs (2003–04)

Tuition and Fees: $26,010

Room & Board: $7,800

THE EXPERTS SAY...

" Loyola College offers a strong liberal arts education within a framework of Jesuit values and ethics. "

" Solutions to the campus diversity problem have been slow in coming. For a more diverse Jesuit campus, check out Fordham or Loyola University of Chicago. "

Inst. Aid (est. 2003–04)

Institutional Aid, Need-Based: $14,259,746

Institutional Aid, Non-Need-Based: $5,037,087

FT Undergrads Receiving Aid: 48% Avg. Amount per Student: $17,370

FT Undergrads Receiving Non-Need-Based Scholarship or Grant Aid: 15% Avg. Amount per Student: $9,767

Of Those Receiving Any Aid:

Rec. Need-Based Scholarship or Grant Aid: 63% Average Award: $10,050

Rec. Need-Based Self-Help Aid: 88% Average Award: $7,320

Upon Graduation, Avg. Loan Debt per Student: $15,870

Financial Aid Deadline: 2/15

LOYOLA MARYMOUNT UNIVERSITY

One LMU Drive, Los Angeles, CA 90045
Admissions Phone: (310) 338-2750; (800) LMU-INFO Fax: (310) 338-2797
Email: admissions@lmu.edu
Website: www.lmu.edu

General Info

Type of School: private, coed, Jesuit
Setting: suburban
Academic Calendar: semester

Student Body

Full-Time Undergrads: 5,312
  Men: 40%, Women: 60%

Part-Time Undergrads: 387
  Men: 52%, Women: 48%

Total Undergrad Population:
  African American: 7%
  Asian American: 11%
  Latino: 18%
  Native American: 1%
  Caucasian: 52%
  International: 2%
  Out-of-State: 23%
  Living Off-Campus: 46%
  In Fraternities: 4%
  In Sororities: 10%

Graduate and First-Professional
  Students: 3,181

Academics

Full-Time Faculty: 419
  With Ph.D.: 87%

Part-Time Faculty: 446
  With Ph.D.: 39%

Student/Faculty Ratio: 13:1

Most Popular Majors:
  business administration (23%)
  communication studies (7%)
  liberal studies (6%)
  psychology (5%)
  political science (5%)

Freshmen Retention Rate: 90%

Graduation Rates:
  62% within four years
  73% within six years

Admissions

Regular Application Deadline: 2/1

Fall Transfer Deadline: 6/1 (priority)

Spring Transfer Deadline: 12/1 (priority)

Total # of Students Applied: 7,833
  Admitted: 4,568
  Enrolled: 1,335

# of Students Waitlisted: 371
  Waitlisted Students Admitted: 1

Inside the Classroom

Loyola Marymount, a Jesuit university just minutes from Los Angeles, offers an intimate academic experience for those also wanting the excitement of a big city. Quality programs in film and business administration, plus an emphasis on ethics, community service, and entrepreneurship, make this school an easy sell. It's no surprise that business administration is by far the most popular major, followed by communications and psychology. As one guidance counselor put it, "It's laid back but it takes a realistic attitude toward liberal arts and professional courses. Plus, it has wonderful new buildings and dorms."

Undergraduate education at LMU is provided in four colleges: liberal arts; business administration; science and engineering; and communication and fine arts. It is in the College of Communication and Fine Arts that the renowned School of Film and Television is housed: "*The* place for film production studies," says a California guidance counselor. Less cutthroat than the film schools at USC and UCLA, it provides a stellar education in a highly supportive environment, with a superb internship program—not to mention its extensive alumni network in the film and television industry (actress Beverley Mitchell from the WB's *7th Heaven* is a current student). Media ethics has become a prominent part of the curriculum.

LMU's Entrepreneurship Program also deserves special mention. Combining a formal, structured curriculum with a student's own projects, this has evolved into one of the strongest business programs for "self-directed learning" in the country. "Doing It!" defines the approach here. Indeed, several guidance counselors tell us that because LMU trains kids to be critical thinkers and leaders—not only in business but in all academic areas—it deserves more national recognition. LMU also has a fine school of education, at which undergrads can take some classes.

Most students describe the academics at LMU as "challenging but not highly rigorous." With under 6,000 undergrads, the classes are small (so small that some professors even take attendance). The student/faculty ratio is around 13:1. As one senior says, "Professors encourage visitation during office hours, and they actually get to know our names! It's highly competitive and the workload is at times a bit much, yet some professors are understanding and willing to make arrangements with students." In one of the more unusual academic programs, the engineering school trains undergrads to sniff out wasteful electricity, waste disposal, and productivity practices at nearby manufacturing plants. In another, the art department conducts Art Smart, through which 40 art majors teach art at a nearby elementary school on a volunteer basis.

The religious environment at LMU is easygoing. As one student says, "No one pushes it on you." Given the school's Catholic identity, you might think there would be required chapel or ministry, but attendance is not required at any events. In fact, the only religious requirements are two religious studies courses (such as World Religions, Buddhism, or Roots of the Catholic Tradition) and an ethics course.

Campus Environment

The 162-acre Loyola campus sits in a suburban setting just minutes from the beach and downtown Los Angeles. More specifically, it is located on a dramatic bluff facing the Santa Monica Mountains and overlooking Marina del Rey and the Pacific Ocean. The problem is, all this beauty and big city access doesn't come cheap. One of students' most common complaints is how expensive everything is here: tuition, food, books, housing, everything. After all, this is the heart of Los Angeles. With approximately 50 percent of on-campus residents in a possession of a car and all commuters needing to park, the space crunch is significant.

Thirteen residence halls house around 2,800 students. The on-campus housing situation is very comfortable, particularly since the campus has seen some major improvements recently. All the dorms and apartments underwent some type of renovation, and a new state-of-the-art recreation center was built. (At the same time, students criticized the administration for spending millions on a new fountain at the school's entrance.) All freshmen are guaranteed student housing, as are returning sophomores. We're told the availability isn't so great for juniors and seniors (for whom a lottery is held), but as one junior says, "The nearby beach communities provide great opportunities for off-campus beach living."

Student Life

Students at LMU are described as "typically wholesome and mainstream." Eighty percent of students are from in-state. "Clean cut, all American boys and good Catholic girls," is how one senior describes them. Though 60 percent of students are Catholic, and religious events are a common occurrence, the school has plenty of students of other faiths. In keeping with its mission, the school places great emphasis on diversity—and that approach has been hugely successful. With almost half the undergrad population identifying themselves as minority, there are about 1,000 Latinos, 650 Asian Americans, and 375 African American students. There are offices to support every minority group, and the Academic Persistence Program pairs incoming students of color with a peer counselor. Foreign students, who number around 110, have high enrollment in television and film programs, as well as science and business.

With six sororities and five fraternities, Greeks have a fair amount of influence on the social life. Indeed, we're told that many of those in student government are members of the Greek system. There are all types of other activities as well—campus ministry leads a monthly trip to an orphanage in Tijuana, Mexico; the campus hosts the Special Olympics each spring; and the school has a program whereby returning Peace Corps volunteers work in housing developments while earning their MBA degrees. There's even a new student record label on campus, promoting LMU diversity in song.

Loyola Marymount is a Division I member of the NCAA, sponsoring 17 varsity sports (though not football). The athletics department has produced numerous All Americans, Olympians, professional athletes and even national championships. Even so, sports on campus don't have a huge following, and it has been an area of discontent for the administration. "There's an apathy of students when it comes to supporting the athletic teams," one psychology senior explains. Club sports are popular, including rugby, men's lacrosse, women's lacrosse, and men's volleyball.

Test Scores (middle 50%):
SAT Verbal: 520–620
SAT Math: 540–630
ACT Comp: 23–27
HS Rank of Entering Freshmen:
Top 10%: 30%
Top 25%: 95%
Top 50%: 99%
Avg. HS GPA: 3.37

Costs (2003–04)
Tuition and Fees: $23,934
Room & Board: $8,260

THE EXPERTS SAY...

" Loyola Marymount has a superb film school with an environment that's actually nurturing and ethical. The internships are fabulous. "

" Media ethics? Isn't that an oxymoron? If you're ready for the cutthroat and backstabbing world of film production, also check out USC and UCLA. "

Inst. Aid
Financial Aid Deadline: 2/15 (priority)

LOYOLA UNIVERSITY NEW ORLEANS

6363 St. Charles Avenue, Campus Box 18, New Orleans, LA 70118-6195
Admissions Phone: (504) 865-3240; (800) 4-LOYOLA Fax: (504) 865-3383
Email: admit@loyno.edu
Website: loyno.edu

General Info

Type of School: private, coed, Catholic, Jesuit

Setting: urban

Academic Calendar: semester

Student Body

Full-Time Undergrads: 3,303
  Men: 39%, Women: 61%

Part-Time Undergrads: 444
  Men: 34%, Women: 66%

Total Undergrad Population:
  African American: 9%
  Asian American: 5%
  Latino: 10%
  Native American: 1%
  Caucasian: 65%
  International: 4%
  Out-of-State: 55%
  Living Off-Campus: 60%
  In Fraternities: 17%
  In Sororities: 18%

Graduate and First-Professional
  Students: 1,771

Academics

Full-Time Faculty: 293
  With Ph.D.: 88%

Part-Time Faculty: 176
  With Ph.D.: 47%

Student/Faculty Ratio: 13:1

Most Popular Majors:
  communications (15%)
  psychology (6%)
  biology (6%)
  international business (4%)
  music business (4%)

Freshmen Retention Rate: 82%

Admissions

Regular Application Deadline: 1/15
  (priority)

Total # of Students Applied: 3,609
  Admitted: 2,485
  Enrolled: 861

Test Scores (middle 50%):
  SAT Verbal: 570–670
  SAT Math: 560–640
  ACT Comp: 25–28
  ACT English: 26–30
  ACT Math: 23–27

Inside the Classroom

Like the other 28 Jesuit colleges and universities in the United States, Loyola University New Orleans is dedicated to the education of the whole person—mind, body, and soul. The goal of a Loyola education is to foster self-discovery, values, and critical thinking, ideas essential to every student's college life and career. According to one student, "Some of our better areas are communications, history, business, and philosophy."

The College of Arts and Sciences, which is the largest of the four undergraduate schools, offers 28 degree programs in 18 departments. The B.A. is offered in the fields of classical studies, communications, drama, drama/ communications, economics, English (literature or writing), history, modern foreign languages and literatures (French, German, Russian, Spanish), philosophy, political science, psychology, religious studies (Christianity or World Religions), sociology, theater arts with a minor in business administration, visual arts, and graphic arts. Students can also earn a B.S. in biological sciences, chemistry, computer information systems, computer science, elementary education, mathematics, and physics. Preprofessional programs are also offered in premedicine, predentistry, preveterinary, pre-engineering, and prelaw.

Loyola is also the only Jesuit university to offer music studies in the form of a college, as opposed to a department. With a maximum enrollment of 300 students, the music college uses small classes with intensive instruction to combine liberal studies with professional music courses. Performance is an important aspect of each student's education: Vocalists can perform with the University Chorus, the Chamber Singers, Opera Theatre, or the highly selective University Chorale, while instrumental performance opportunities include ensembles such as the University Symphony Orchestra, Loyola Chamber Orchestra, University Concert Band, Wind Ensemble, or one of the jazz bands. Students can also perform in specialized chamber ensemble experiences.

A small but thriving study abroad program exists on campus, giving students the opportunity to enroll in semester and summer programs in Belgium, Germany, Ireland, the United Kingdom, Mexico, and France.

Campus Environment

Loyola is located in the uptown section of New Orleans, a more residential neighborhood that's about 10 minutes away from the more famous downtown and the French Quarter. The entertainment and cultural options for students in the surrounding city are many; music students in particular will find many places to hear live performances of New Orleans jazz and other styles. Loyola's proximity to the French Quarter means that Mardi Gras is looked forward to with anticipation each year: Students reportedly have a great deal of fun, but campus security is also stepped up during this time and the rules governing visitors on campus are more strictly enforced.

Campus housing for students is divided into four residence halls. Biever Hall offers conventional double-occupancy rooms. Buddig Hall is a 12-story dorm of four-student suites with an honors floor on the 11th floor, while Cabra Hall has eight-student suites. The newest dorm on campus is predictably named New Hall, and offers both double rooms and suites for upperclassmen. For those who love a good tan, the roofs of Buddig and Cabra halls can be used as sundecks.

The Danna Center serves as Loyola's student union, housing the Orleans Room, the main dining hall. Other venues available here include the bookstore, post office, bank, hair salon, convenience store, and travel agency. When students tire of the standard meal plan, there's also a Pizza Hut, Smoothie King, P.J.'s Coffee, and Nawlin's Po-Boys to visit.

The Monroe Library, completed in 1999, is one of the most wired libraries in the region. Students can plug their laptop computers into one of 600 jacks on the library's tabletops, and they can also make use of special group study rooms equipped with computer hook-ups, video, and dry-erase boards. One particularly helpful department of the library is the Academic and Career Excellence (ACE) Center, which is run jointly by eight university departments and gives students the chance to get assistance from tutors in a writing lab environment.

The school's Music/Communications Complex features the Roussel Performance Hall, which is the largest auditorium on campus, as well as the Lower Depths Theater, a smaller venue for staging plays. The building also houses a writing lab and the Donnelly Center for Nonprofit Communications, a student-run organization that creates publications for nonprofit client organizations.

A pretty and well-used place on campus is the Peace Quad, a stretch of grass, pathways, and benches where special events like concerts, crawfish boils, and barbecues are thrown. Pickup games of Frisbee and soccer have also been known to break out here.

Student Life

Unlike many Jesuit schools, Loyola does have a Greek system consisting of six fraternities and six sororities. The oldest frat on campus, the Beggars, is the only non-national Greek organization and lays claim to the founding of the student government association. The administration sets limits on the size of parties, but the rules don't seem to hamper students' fun all that much. "Sobriety is not exactly our strong point," admits one student, "but the campus usually isn't too crazy."

Students can join a number of student organizations to share their interests and pastimes with other students. Some of the options include the Croquet Society, the Loyola Bowling Association, and the Friends of Magdelene. Professional organizations like the American Institute of Graphic Artists and the Society of Physics Students are also present, as well as service groups like Circle K and the Loyola University Community Action Program.

The Loyola Wolfpack athletic program competes in the NAIA (National Association of Intercollegiate Athletics) Division I as a member of the Gulf Coast Athletic Conference (GCAC). Teams are fielded for both men and women in basketball and cross country. Men also compete in baseball, while women compete in soccer and volleyball. An interesting aspect of Wolfpack sports is that they are financially self-supporting: A student fee paid by all students covers all costs, in accordance with a student referendum conducted in 1991. No athletic scholarships are offered. Club sports that compete with other schools include men's and women's rugby, men's lacrosse, and men's soccer.

HS Rank of Entering Freshmen:
Top 10%: 29%
Top 25%: 61%
Top 50%: 91%
Avg. HS GPA: 3.72

Costs (2004–5)

Tuition and Fees: $23,618
Room & Board: $7,994

THE EXPERTS SAY...

" Loyola University New Orleans upholds the Jesuit tradition of educating the whole person. Its liberal arts and music colleges are particularly strong. "

" Loyola's strong Catholic tradition may not sit well with students who prefer a nonreligious atmosphere. "

Inst. Aid (est. 2003–04)

Institutional Aid, Need-Based: $16,833,094

Institutional Aid, Non-Need-Based: $10,396,488

FT Undergrads Receiving Aid: 55%
Avg. Amount per Student: $16,895

FT Undergrads Receiving Non-Need-Based Scholarship or Grant Aid: 32%
Avg. Amount per Student: $8,868

Of Those Receiving Any Aid:

Rec. Need-Based Scholarship or Grant Aid: 98%
Average Award: $11,964

Rec. Need-Based Self-Help Aid: 73%
Average Award: $4,867

Upon Graduation, Avg. Loan Debt per Student: $18,125

Financial Aid Deadline: rolling, 2/15 (priority)

Graduates

Going to Graduate School:
22% Within One Year

Accepting Job Offer:
51% at time of graduation

Companies Recruiting On Campus: 298

Alumni Giving: 28%

LOYOLA UNIVERSITY OF CHICAGO

820 North Michigan Avenue, Chicago, IL 60611
Admissions Phone: (312) 915-6500; (800) 262-2373
Email: admission@luc.edu
Website: www.luc.edu

General Info

Type of School: private, coed, Catholic

Setting: urban

Academic Calendar: semester

Student Body

Full-Time Undergrads: 5,001
  Men: 35%, Women: 63%

Part-Time Undergrads: 2,140
  Men: 16%, Women: 31%

Total Undergrad Population:
  African American: 9%
  Asian American: 12%
  Latino: 9%
  Native American: <1%
  Caucasian: 58%
  International: 3%
  Out-of-State: 20%
  Living Off-Campus: 71%
  In Fraternities: 7%
  In Sororities: 5%

Graduate and First-Professional
  Students: 849

Academics

Full-Time Faculty: 940
  With Ph.D.: 98%

Part-Time Faculty: 1,039

Student/Faculty Ratio: 13:1

Most Popular Majors:
  biology (5%)
  business (5%)
  psychology (4%)
  nursing (4%)
  communication (3%)

Freshmen Retention Rate: 83%

Graduation Rates:
  43% within four years
  65% within six years

Admissions

Regular Application Deadline: 2/1
  (priority)

Total # of Students Applied: 4,001
  Admitted: 3,191
  Enrolled: 889

Test Scores (middle 50%):
  SAT Verbal: 520–640
  SAT Math: 520–630
  ACT Comp: 22–27

Inside the Classroom

Loyola University of Chicago has a dynamic relationship with the Windy City, integrating Chicago's vast cultural, business, and civic resources into its curriculum. Imbued with the Jesuit spirit of educating the whole person, Loyola offers thousands of academic, internship, and social service opportunities in one of the most exciting urban environments in the world. The school has unique service-learning programs, allowing students to earn credit for fighting problems like poverty, hunger, and illiteracy. Students do research and field work at the Lincoln Park Zoo, the Field Museum of Natural History, Newberry Library, Adler Planetarium and area theaters. Lake Michigan serves as a lab for biology and ecology students.

Loyola offers a total of 46 undergraduate programs in five schools: arts and sciences, business administration, education, nursing, and continuing education. There's also the Rome Center of Liberal Arts in Italy, which offers undergraduate liberal arts studies throughout the year and summer graduate programs. With a medical school on board, biology is the most popular major and the premed program offers specialties like pre-optometry, preveterinary medicine, and pre-podiatry. Business, psychology, and communication are also popular. The rigorous nursing school has a superb reputation, although students warn that the faculty is demanding.

The school of arts and sciences is the "heart" of Loyola, as well as the largest undergraduate college. The stiff core curriculum includes courses in Christian theology, philosophy, writing, foreign language, communicative and expressive arts, history, literature, mathematics, and natural sciences. A B.A. in classics is offered. Dual-degree programs are made available in many departments, and there are five-year bachelors-to-masters tracks in biology, computer science, criminal justice, environmental studies, mathematics, political science, applied social psychology, and sociology.

Loyola is home to one of the larger Jesuit communities in the world, with 100 priests, brothers, and scholastics (men studying for the priesthood). Both priests and lay faculty teach. The student/faculty ratio is 13:1 and class sizes are small. Professors are dedicated and caring, true to the Jesuit mission of seeking "the greater glory of God through the fuller growth of the human person."

Loyola's generous financial aid, spurred by the Jesuit philosophy of education for all people, makes for an economically diverse student body. Most Loyola alums remain in the Chicago area, representing a high percentage of the professionals in the city. The alumni network is strong, serving as a professional resource for students. Loyola's Career Center annually posts more than 30,000 jobs a year.

Campus Environment

Loyola has four Chicago-area campuses, each with a different atmosphere. The two undergraduate campuses are Water Tower, off North Michigan Avenue in downtown Chicago, and Lake Shore, on Chicago's North Shore. The residential Lake Shore campus is located on the shores of Lake Michigan and is home to the college of arts and sciences and the school of nursing. Lake Shore is the locus of student activity at this unconventional collection of campuses, and has more of a college feel than

Water Tower. The nonresidential Water Tower Campus is on Chicago's "Magnificent Mile," and is home to the schools of business administration and education, giving it a distinct preprofessional flavor.

The great majority of Loyola students commute, and housing is guaranteed only to out-of-state students. Freshmen dorms are the "traditional" doubles. There are also Living and Learning Centers, many equipped with computer labs. All housing is Ethernet-wired. Coed and single-sex housing for women is available, and apartment-style housing is open to upperclassmen. Cars are simply not an option given the nightmarish parking situation around the campuses, but mass transportation is convenient, taking Loyola students into the city that serves as their greater campus.

Student Life

With so many commuters, Loyola is not a big party school, and even the residential Lake Shore campus tends to empty out on weekends. Greek life exists, but is not a major presence. For entertainment, students focus on the many attractions of Chicago, like biking, blading, swimming, and boating on Lake Michigan, hitting Chicago's myriad blues and jazz clubs, visiting the museums, and checking out the ethnic restaurants.

For those who stay on campus, there are more than 140 social, cultural, ethnic, professional and academic student organizations. Varsity sports are Division I. The Ramblers make a showing in the Midwestern Collegiate Conference, but intramurals are more popular: More than 2,200 students participate in 29 intramural sports. The campus has an active speaker series, recently hosting Robert F. Kennedy Jr., George Takei (Sulu in the original *Star Trek* series), Elie Wiesel, primatologist Jane Goodall, and comedians Margaret Cho and David Spade.

Loyola is a school for students who want to meet people of all kinds: Minorities comprise nearly 30 percent of the student body, and students come from every social class and a multitude of cultures. Students are not as cliquish here as at many other colleges, and it's easy to make friends with people of different races. A fifth of the undergraduate population is over 25. While 59 percent of students are Catholics, 22 percent are from non-Christian traditions, and true to the Jesuit creed of embracing different faiths, there is a Hillel program for Jewish students, a mosque for Muslims, and chaplains for virtually every faith. There is a great deal of social consciousness, and volunteerism is extremely popular. It is in part this diversity, and part the Jesuit character of Loyola, that helps produce thoughtful, ethical graduates who contribute to the Chicago area as people and professionals.

HS Rank of Entering Freshmen:
Top 10%: 29%
Top 25%: 62%
Top 50%: 93%

Costs (2003–04)
Tuition and Fees: $20,544
Room & Board: $7,900
Payment Plan(s): installment plan

THE EXPERTS SAY...

" Taking advantage of Loyola's Jesuit education, diverse student body, and exciting Chicago backdrop can be a real opportunity for personal growth. "

" If urban Catholicism is your thing, also check out DePaul, Marquette, Fordham, and Saint Louis University. "

MACALESTER COLLEGE

1600 Grand Avenue, St. Paul, MN 55105
Admissions Phone: (651) 696-6357; (800) 231-7974 Fax: (651) 696-6724
Email: admissions@macalester.edu
Website: macalester.edu

General Info

Type of School: private, coed, Presbyterian

Setting: urban

Academic Calendar: semester

Student Body

Full-Time Undergrads: 1,834
Men: 42%, Women: 58%

Part-Time Undergrads: 15
Men: 47%, Women: 53%

Total Undergrad Population:
African American: 3%
Asian American: 5%
Latino: 3%
Native American: 1%
Caucasian: 74%
International: 14%
Out-of-State: 75%
Living Off-Campus: 31%

Academics

Full-Time Faculty: 149
With Ph.D.: 95%

Part-Time Faculty: 66
With Ph.D.: 56%

Student/Faculty Ratio: 11:1

Most Popular Majors:
economics (10%)
psychology (8%)
political science (7%)
international studies (6%)
English (6%)

Completing 2 or More Majors: 31%

Freshmen Retention Rate: 92%

Graduation Rates:
75% within four years
82% within six years

Admissions

Regular Application Deadline: 1/15

Early Decision Deadline(s): 11/15, 1/3

Fall Transfer Deadline: 4/1

Total # of Students Applied: 4,341
Admitted: 1,920
Enrolled: 513

# of Students Waitlisted: 249
Students Accepting Place: 104

Applied Early Decision: 255
Early Decision Admitted: 117

In the Classroom

Macalester is a small, highly regarded liberal arts college where individualism rules and academics are "top notch," as a student puts it. Mac students are bright and academic standards are high; expect to devote a lot of time and effort to your studies. "The academic atmosphere is rigorous but very rewarding," one student says. Another chimes in, "Do not expect grade inflation."

Close student–faculty relations are an institutionalized part of the Macalester experience. For example, freshmen must select one of 32 courses identified as a "First Year Course," each of which is a seminar limited to 16 students. The courses are far-flung in subject matter; a recent fall's offerings included such interesting titles as "Refugees, Religion, and Responses to Conflict," "Technical Theatre," and "Discrete Mathematics." The teacher of the course becomes the faculty advisor for everyone in the class, an arrangement that encourages students to establish personal relationships with their advisors right from day one. Indeed, throughout the curriculum, small class sizes and a faculty attentive to individual needs are the norm.

Students can choose from 37 majors or design an interdepartmental major of their own. The most popular majors are biology, economics, psychology, history, and political science. Students praise the selection of course offerings: "There is such a wide range of classes, and you can usually get into the ones you want." Macalester has developed a reputation for its commitment to internationalism and offers many courses, programs, and events with an international focus, including a major in geography. If you don't find what you want at Macalester, you have the option of taking courses at one of the other four schools in the Associated Colleges of the Twin Cities: Augsberg, Hamline, St. Catherine, and St. Thomas.

Many facets of the Macalester education push students to explore on their own: students are encouraged to undertake independent study projects and apply for for-credit internships. About half of all Mac students study abroad at some point during their college career. The college also believes that service is an integral part of learning and life: Each semester, about 50 percent of students volunteer with shelters, tutoring programs, Habitat for Humanity, and other programs in the Twin Cities.

Campus Environment

The campus's 53 tree-covered acres lie in a residential area midway between downtown St. Paul and downtown Minneapolis. "Even though we are in a city, it has a suburban feeling," a Mac-lover says. Students can easily venture off campus to take advantage of the cultural and entertainment opportunities of both cities—which the college administration points out are among the country's "safest and most vibrant" cities. Since a good urban bus system serves the Twin Cities, a car is not a necessity for Mac students.

For most freshmen, the First Year Course they select will determine their housing placement; they are placed in a residence hall among classmates from this course, including their roommate. A sophomore reflected on this system, saying, "I made close friends at Macalester last year because I was living and studying with the same group all year. This made it really easy to get to know them well."

Students are required to live on campus their first two years. There are 10 residence halls, five language residences, and an apartment-style building for juniors and seniors. Students choose from single-sex or coed floors, quiet floors, and nonsmoking floors. But many students find the on-campus housing situation less than ideal; one student summed up, "Macalester student housing is the pits." Many students move off-campus after their sophomore year.

Student Life

A high percentage of international students and U.S. students of color create a cosmopolitan atmosphere unusual in a small liberal arts college. The school makes a major effort not only to recruit a diverse student body, but also to ensure that students of different backgrounds play an important role in college life. A result of this diversity, according to one Mac student, is that "there is a wide range of interesting and intelligent students who enrich the community with their experience." Another says, "I didn't just read about different viewpoints and experiences; I talked to people whose lives were radically different from mine."

Although the college is officially affiliated with the Presbyterian Church, the school considers itself "nonsectarian," and free-thinking Mac students and faculty represent a wide range of views and beliefs. Guidance counselors and students alike categorized Macalester as "liberal." One student points out, "The general sentiments of the student body, faculty, and the administration lean to the left." Indeed, as a sophomore tells us, "The campus joke is that the only diversity here that is lacking is political: Republicans do not exist." (What does exist is a veggie co-op: "Students can live underneath the bleachers of the athletic field and grow their own vegetable garden for food," we're told.) Political organizations are especially popular, and students will often organize or attend various protests. One Mac undergrad goes so far as to say, "If you do not care for current events, politics, or world affairs, you might have trouble finding a conversation to join on campus."

Macalester has no fraternities (a student sniffs, "you won't have to pay people here to be your friend, they'll do it for free"), and kegs have been banned, so students tend to socialize in smaller get-togethers in rooms or at cafés and bars rather than at big parties. While we hear that drinking and smoking pot are popular pastimes, there are plenty of on-campus movies, dances, and concerts to occupy the students' time. Students also head to Grand Avenue, "a hot spot for many people," where they hang out at clubs, restaurants, bookstores, and shops. Annual events such as Spring Fest, the Scottish County Fair, and the QU dance (held by the Queer Union and featuring students dressed up in drag) draw crowds as well.

More than half of Mac students join one of the college's many student clubs, which include performing arts, service, cultural, media, recreational, religious, and volunteer groups. "Student groups are huge here," we're told, "and everyone attends their performances." As for sports, the football team has been notoriously bad, but the soccer team is a popular division leader. In general, Mac's athletic facilities are excellent.

Other schools to check out: Earlham, Carleton, Whitman, Oberlin, Grinnell.

THE EXPERTS SAY...

" Macalester students and administrators alike are environmentally conscious: In spring 2003, the college constructed an electricity-generating windmill on campus, planted just north of the school's football field. "

" Unlike at many liberal arts colleges, Mac students are actual activists, not just theoretical activists. There's a really strong connection between the school and the urban community. "

MANHATTANVILLE COLLEGE

2900 Purchase Street, Purchase, NY 10577
Admissions Phone: (800) 328-4553; (913) 323-5464 Fax: (914) 694-1732
Email: admissions@mville.edu Website: www.mville.edu
Application Website: mville.edu/admissions/undergrad_app.html

General Info

Type of School: private, coed
Setting: suburban
Academic Calendar: semester

Student Body

Full-Time Undergrads: 1,528
 Men: 32%, Women: 68%

Part-Time Undergrads: 75
 Men: 25%, Women: 75%

Total Undergrad Population:
 African American: 5%
 Asian American: 3%
 Latino: 14%
 Native American: 1%
 Caucasian: 58%
 International: 9%
 Out-of-State: 34%
 Living Off-Campus: 27%

Graduate and First-Professional
 Students: 900

Academics

Full-Time Faculty: 88
 With Ph.D.: 93%

Part-Time Faculty: 108

Student/Faculty Ratio: 12:1

Most Popular Majors:
 psychology (7%)
 management (7%)
 art (4%)
 history (3%)
 political science (3%)

Completing 2 or More Majors: 6%

Freshmen Retention Rate: 77%

Graduation Rates:
 55% within four years·
 63% within six years

Admissions

Regular Application Deadline: 3/1

Early Decision Deadline(s): 12/1,
 12/31

Fall Transfer Deadline: 3/1 (priority)

Spring Transfer Deadline: 12/1 (priority)

Total # of Students Applied: 2,450
 Admitted: 1,348
 Enrolled: 418

# of Students Waitlisted: 100
 Students Accepting Place: 84

Inside the Classroom

Manhattanville's mission is "to educate students to be ethically and socially responsible leaders for the global community." Manhattanville College offers more than 45 areas of study leading to a Bachelor of Arts, Bachelor of Science, or Bachelor of Music degree. Besides the typical liberal arts majors, Manhattanville also offers some more unusual programs, such as international management, international studies, Latin American studies, and music management. Several cooperative degree programs are also offered, some of which are in conjunction with New York Medical College, Polytechnic University, and Boston University's Goldman School of Dental Medicine. A guidance counselor raves about the "great performing arts."

Manhattanville is "student friendly," notes a guidance counselor, and the "supportive faculty and administration" are a big part of its appeal. Even the school president, charismatic Richard Berman, knows three-quarters of the students by name. A cozy environment can be felt at this small school, with most classes having fewer than 20 students. There's a student/faculty ratio of 12:1. Among Manhattanville's distinctive academic requirements is the yearlong, interdisciplinary freshman Preceptorial class, covering "basic issues of values and cultures." Emphasizing reading and writing abilities, critical thought, and library and research techniques, the Preceptorial introduces important concepts in the humanities, arts, social sciences, and natural sciences. Preceptorial topics in the past have included Community and Responsibility, Love and Family, and Wealth, Justice, and Responsibility.

The core of Manhattanville's approach to liberal arts education is its Portfolio System, whereby students are required to collect and keep a portfolio of their best work. The portfolio is evaluated periodically throughout the student's academic career, and submission and approval of that portfolio is a requirement for graduation. The Portfolio System also requires seniors to complete a research project in order to graduate, providing every student with research experience.

Many Manhattanville students volunteer or study abroad in countries like Nepal, Senegal and Mexico, or spend a semester living and studying in nearby New York City. For interesting on-campus work, students can call applicants to Manhattanville to sell the school as part of President Berman's campaign to increase enrollment.

Campus Environment

Since 1995, Richard Berman, the indefatigable president of Manhattanville College, has managed to turn the school around, increasing enrollment and bringing the school out of a financial tailspin. With less than one million dollars in endowment, Manhattanville was losing more than three million dollars a year and had sold 150 of its 250 acres of land. Dorms stood half empty and buildings were in disrepair. Today, with moneys from increased enrollment, there are Internet connections in every dorm, a computer lab with the latest computers, and a renovated gymnasium. The library, with a new electronic catalog, stays open till 4:00 A.M. every day.

Manhattanville has four coed residence halls. Spellman, a dry dorm, is the freshman hall and features double rooms, faculty/club offices, as well as classroom space.

Sophomores and juniors live in Dammann and Tenney Halls in suites that offer both doubles and singles. Founders Hall houses juniors and seniors, and primarily offers singles. By way of student request to the ubiquitous president, the dining hall serves sushi and Indian stew. On-campus housing is guaranteed and upperclassmen participate in a room lottery process. About 27 percent of the students live off-campus in Purchase and surrounding towns.

All students are permitted to have cars on campus, and a car would probably come in handy in this suburban, sprawled out Westchester County environment. For students without cars, Manhattanville provides weekly bus trips to New York City and a bus to local destinations.

Student Life

"Manhattanville is surprisingly diverse for its size," says a college official, with "undergraduates from 37 states and 53 nations." Students support this diversity and relish the community feel on campus. President Berman hosts an interfaith shabbat dinner in his home on campus several times a year, and the Black Student Union, Latin American Student Organization, and the Italian Club host open parties.

Many students are involved in community service, including working with AIDS patients, mentoring "at risk" youths, serving food to the homeless through Midnight Run, or volunteering in countries such as Mexico and Nepal. As a symbol of peace in a post 9/11 world, a Labyrinth is being built on campus. Manhattanville is also home to a Seeds of Peace chapter with more members than any other college in the U.S.; the nonprofit organization helps teenagers from regions of conflict—particularly the Middle East—learn the skills of making peace.

Students regularly take advantage of Manhattan in the form of numerous internship and work-experience opportunities, as well as recreationally through the many school-sponsored ventures into the city for plays, sports, and nightlife. There's no loss for things to do on campus, either. There are no fraternities or sororities, but Manhattanville offers a myriad of student organizations. A college official lists Amnesty International, the student radio station WMVL, the Black Student Union, and the International Student Organization as among the most popular. Quad Jam, which occurs every April, features live music and other activities. Eight of Manhattanville's NCAA Division III teams qualified for post-season tournaments and four earned conference championships; men's and women's ice hockey are nationally ranked.

Other schools to check out: Connecticut College, Skidmore, Hamilton, SUNY Geneseo, Ithaca College.

Applied Early Decision: 55
Early Decision Admitted: 34

Test Scores (middle 50%):
SAT Verbal: 490–590
SAT Math: 480–570
ACT Comp: 22–26
Avg. HS GPA: 3.0

THE EXPERTS SAY...

" In the words of its remarkable president, Manhattanville is committed to diversity and has managed its diversity 'consciously, deliberately, affirmatively, and actively.' "

" Manhattanville has come from behind to become one of the top small colleges in the nation and is in the forefront of issues like affirmative action and First Amendment Rights. For such a small school, there's a lot going on here! "

Costs (2004–5)

Tuition and Fees: $24,570

Room & Board: $10,130

Payment Plan(s): installment plan, deferred payment plan, pre-payment plan

Inst. Aid (est. 2003–04)

Institutional Aid, Need-Based: $5,968,401

Institutional Aid, Non-Need-Based: $11,979,537

FT Undergrads Receiving Aid: 65%
Avg. Amount per Student: $19,872

FT Undergrads Receiving Non-Need-Based Scholarship or Grant Aid: 22%
Avg. Amount per Student: $8,271

Of Those Receiving Any Aid:

Rec. Need-Based Scholarship or Grant Aid: 89%
Average Award: $9,137

Rec. Need-Based Self-Help Aid: 85%
Average Award: $4,689

Upon Graduation, Avg. Loan Debt per Student: $21,160

Financial Aid Deadline: 3/1 (priority)

Graduates

Going to Graduate School:
18% Within One Year

Accepting Job Offer:
64% at time of graduation

Companies Recruiting On Campus: 34

MARLBORO COLLEGE

P.O. Box A, South Road, Marlboro, VT 05301-0300
Admissions Phone: (802) 258-9236; (800) 343-0049 Fax: (802) 451-7555
Email: admissions@marlboro.edu
Website: www.marlboro.edu

Note: Info. not verifed by school

General Info

Type of School: private, coed

Setting: rural

Academic Calendar: semester

Student Body

Full-Time Undergrads: 321
  Men: 43%, Women: 57%

Part-Time Undergrads: 10
  Men: 40%, Women: 60%

Total Undergrad Population:
  African American: 1%
  Latino: 2%
  Native American: 1%
  Caucasian: 83%
  International: 1%
  Out-of-State: 89%
  Living Off-Campus: 26%

Graduate and First-Professional
  Students: 80

Academics

Full-Time Faculty: 35
  With Ph.D.: 77%

Part-Time Faculty: 17
  With Ph.D.: 29%

Student/Faculty Ratio: 8:1

Most Popular Majors:
  history
  political science
  writing
  life sciences
  visual and performing arts

Freshmen Retention Rate: 71%

Graduation Rates:
  33% within four years
  48% within six years

Admissions

Regular Application Deadline: 3/1
  (priority)

Early Decision Deadline(s): 11/15

Early Action Deadline: 1/15

Fall Transfer Deadline: 6/1, 4/1 (priority)

Spring Transfer Deadline: 12/1,
  11/1 (priority)

Total # of Students Applied: 205
  Admitted: 179
  Enrolled: 83

Inside the Classroom

Marlboro College is known for challenging academics in an "unpretentious atmosphere," combined with an emphasis on individual student attention. The school has a unique curriculum guided largely by self-directed study that promotes individuality and character within a structured program of liberal studies. The college states, "Students are expected to develop a command of concise and correct English and to strive for academic excellence informed by intellectual and artistic creativity; they are also encouraged to acquire a passion for learning, discerning judgment, and a global perspective." Students participate extensively in the planning of their own programs of study, cultivating their own self-reliance, self-confidence, and sense of civic responsibility.

Most applicants are drawn to Marlboro for its Plan of Concentration, the cornerstone of Marlboro's academic program. The college describes the Plan as an "in-depth, self-designed exploration of a field or fields of each student's choosing. The Plan culminates in a major independent project involving research, one-on-one study with faculty in tutorials, and a two- to three-hour oral examination with Marlboro faculty and an outside examiner who is an expert in the student's field."

Marlboro offers bachelor of arts and bachelor of science degrees. Graduation requirements include meeting the school's Clear Writing Requirement, completing the 50-credit Plan of Concentration, earning 120 credits with a minimum of at least a C– on the Plan of Concentration, and submitting a final copy of the Plan project to the registrar. The World Studies Program (which includes a six- to eight-month cross-cultural internship) and certain bachelor of science degree programs carry additional requirements.

Marlboro is a very small school, with around 320 undergraduates. The student/faculty ratio is an intimate 8:1, and "large" classes are those with 10–20 students. An unusually large percentage of students go on to graduate school. The college's Career Center helps students find internships and decide what to do after college. It assists students in identifying their strengths and interests and recognizing the value of their Marlboro education and what they can get out of it.

Campus Environment

Marlboro's campus consists of 350 acres in the hills of southern Vermont. Two-thirds of students live on campus; all freshmen are expected to live on campus. Campus housing ranges from dorms that typically house 12–28 people each, to apartments that are generally reserved for upperclassmen. Traditional residence halls coexist with ski-lodge-style dorms and a converted inn. Juniors and seniors can even live in cabins and cottages that are located a short walk from campus. All housing is coed except for one women's dorm. The school states that its dorms "tend to function more like homes than institutional housing," and residence life at Marlboro is similar to the academic atmosphere in that students primarily run the show. Students work together to develop and maintain policies, create a pleasant living environment, and maintain cleanliness. They collectively develop rules pertaining to the usual issues such as quiet hours, partying, and cleaning.

The community feel at Marlboro is enhanced by Town Meetings, which are based on the traditional New England Town Meeting and are loosely moderated according to Robert's Rules of Order. The Town Meetings, which are held monthly, help students to "act responsibly within a self-governing community" that abides by its own Community Constitution and bylaws. There are nine "Selectpeople" that are responsible for community leadership and that organize the Town Meetings. All students, faculty, and staff members are welcome at these meetings, and college-wide issues are addressed in an open forum. Community sentiment affects the outcomes of the meetings, and Town Meeting representatives serve on administrative committees and represent students at trustee meetings.

Marlboro's buildings don't look much like those you'll find at other colleges and universities. The dining hall is a converted barn, and the campus center was constructed about 20 years ago by students, faculty, and staff. The campus center holds a bookstore, a recreation room, and a coffee shop. The coffee shop is a social gathering spot, and serves as a site for parties, poetry readings, and rock, jazz, and folk concerts.

Student Life

The village of Marlboro is located about three miles from campus, and doesn't offer too much in the way of entertainment; there's a post office, an inn, and a meetinghouse. But Brattleboro, also nearby, offers a number of coffeehouses, bookstores and galleries, two brewpubs, two movie theaters, and a variety of restaurants. Boston is only two hours away, making it a good road trip destination, and Northampton, MA is an hour away. Northampton is a thriving city with lots of shopping, bars, and restaurants, and is the home of Smith College. It's also close to Amherst College, Mount Holyoke College, Hampshire College, and the University of Massachusetts.

There also isn't much here in the way of typical student organizations or clubs, such as Greek life or varsity sports. The school states that "students take the initiative to provide their own entertainment both with organized events and by enjoying the surrounding environment," and there are programs available to help students keep themselves busy. The Student Activities Office plans trips and campus events such as concerts and lectures. And there's also the Outdoor Program, which sponsors a variety of activities (kayaking, rock climbing), organizes local and international trips (canoeing in the Rio Grande, kayaking in Baja), and organizes an annual orientation woods trip for freshmen.

Theater has been called "the school sport of Marlboro," and each semester multiple productions are performed. These productions, held at the 300-seat Whittemore Theater, are often written and directed by students. And the new Drury Gallery serves as a place for students, faculty, and regional artists to show off their work.

Other schools to check out: Hampshire, Bard, Bennington, Antioch, Reed.

\# Applied Early Decision: 12
Early Decision Admitted: 11

Test Scores (middle 50%):
SAT Verbal: 580–690
SAT Math: 520–620
ACT Comp: 26–30
ACT English: 24–32
ACT Math: 22–29

HS Rank of Entering Freshmen:
Top 10%: 13%
Top 25%: 45%
Top 50%: 89%

Avg. HS GPA: 3.33

Costs (2003–04)

Tuition and Fees: $21,630
Room & Board: $7,425
Payment Plan(s): installment plan

THE EXPERTS SAY...

"If you like the creative life at Bard and Vassar, but can live without the attitudes, Marlboro's independent spirit and down-to-earth students might win you over."

"321 students isn't a community, it's a coffee klatch. Theater is 'the school sport.'"

MARQUETTE UNIVERSITY

P.O. Box 1881, Milwaukee, WI 53201-1881
Admissions Phone: (800) 222-6544; (414) 288-7302 Fax: (414) 288-3764
Website: www.marquette.edu
Application Website: www.marquette.edu/admissions

General Info

Type of School: private, coed,
  Catholic

Setting: urban

Academic Calendar: semester

Student Body

Full-Time Undergrads: 7,220
  Men: 45%, Women: 55%

Part-Time Undergrads: 405
  Men: 36%, Women: 64%

Total Undergrad Population:
  African American: 5%
  Asian American: 4%
  Latino: 4%
  Native American: <1%
  Caucasian: 85%
  International: 2%
  Out-of-State: 58%
  Living Off-Campus: 7%
  In Fraternities: 6%
  In Sororities: 8%

Graduate and First-Professional
  Students: 3,580

Academics

Full-Time Faculty: 578
  With Ph.D.: 87%

Part-Time Faculty: 440
  With Ph.D.: 39%

Student/Faculty Ratio: 15:1

Most Popular Majors:
  business administration (7%)
  nursing (5%)
  biomedical sciences (5%)
  mechanical engineering (3%)
  broadcast and electronic communication (3%)

Completing 2 or More Majors: 13%

Freshmen Retention Rate: 89%

Graduation Rates:
  55% within four years
  76% within six years

Admissions

Regular Application Deadline: 2/1
  (priority)

Fall Transfer Deadline: 5/1 (priority)

Spring Transfer Deadline: 12/1
  (priority)

Total # of Students Applied: 8,232
  Admitted: 6,817
  Enrolled: 1,891

Inside the Classroom

Marquette is a Jesuit school, and it focuses on educating the whole person. According to one student, Marquette offers a "well-rounded education rooted in becoming a good person and benefiting your community." The school emphasizes personal growth and community service, and provides students with "the ability to think critically, ask the right questions, formulate and support an argument, communicate clearly, and act with moral integrity." Marquette has undergraduate colleges of nursing, arts and sciences, engineering, business administration, and communication, along with a school of education. It houses the only dental school in Wisconsin, and offers a four-year degree in dental hygiene. We hear good things about engineering, business, physical therapy, nursing, and biology programs. Marquette's College of Engineering is nearly 25 percent female, which is twice the percentage of female engineering undergraduates compared to other schools in the nation. The most popular majors are business management and engineering, followed by communications and health professions. And many of you will be happy to hear that "Undecided" is a "perfectly acceptable major for freshmen and sophomores," according to the Marquette website.

"As a freshman, I heard the comment 'I came to Marquette because I didn't get into Notre Dame,' more than a couple of times," says a young alumna. She continues: "Marquette students are on average extremely bright; however, other than engineering and premed majors the academic atmosphere is very laid back. Students, in general, are not striving for straight A's. They are much more concerned with social interactiveness. The workload for classes is average relative to friends at other schools."

Students say that professors are friendly and "readily available to students." Class size is reasonably small, with fewer than 32 students in almost all first-year classes, and generally fewer than 25 students in upper-level classes. Most students say that the core curriculum—which includes classes in math, sciences, liberal arts, and religion—is challenging. Marquette offers a co-op program to engineering students, and some great internships in Milwaukee-area companies, including Harley-Davidson and Miller Brewing.

Applicants who show potential for success but do not meet Marquette's admission requirements may be selected for the Freshman Frontier Program. FFP students begin with a five-week summer session, take a reduced course load in their first year and receive academic support services throughout the summer session and freshman year.

Campus Environment

Freshmen are generally placed in four of Marquette's seven residence halls: Cobeen (women), McCormick (coed), O'Donnell (men), or Schroeder (coed). Students are required to live on campus their first two years, in either dorms or on-campus apartments. After that, many leave for private housing near campus. Housing is readily available, and according to one student we spoke with, "most students get their first choice." Word is that "rooms are decent" in the dorms, and that "apartments on campus are on average pretty nice." Each residence hall has two campus ministers—usually one Jesuit and one lay person—living in the hall to meet the spiritual and personal counseling needs of residents.

Marquette has been undergoing a period of construction and renovation, and a guidance counselor says that this has greatly improved the university. Computer facilities are top-notch, with fast Internet access in all dorm rooms. Few students have cars; most either walk to class, or take public transit around Milwaukee. Within walking distance are the Grand Avenue Mall, the Bradley Center, the Midwest Express Center, the Milwaukee Public Museum with its new IMAX theater and the Marcus Center for the Performing Arts. Parking is "ridiculously expensive" on campus, which deters students from keeping cars on campus.

One of the biggest issues at Marquette is its location. The neighborhood surrounding the campus is dicey; as one student tells it, "safety is a big concern at MU." While campus police are working to improve safety, some students grouse that the relationship between Marquette students and the Milwaukee police department could be better. Milwaukee's frigid weather also draws some complaints; as one student puts it, "the weather is horrid in the winter."

Student Life

Despite its religious underpinnings, drinking is "a major factor" at Marquette, and we hear that the administration is trying to curb excess student drinking. Says one recent grad, "Students usually start the weekend on Wednesday…. Some students head to Water Street, while others stay and head to campus bars, where they can see familiar faces and hang out." However, other than marijuana, drugs are generally not used by students. Greek life is not particularly popular at Marquette; fewer than ten percent of students join fraternities or sororities. (An alum confides, "I was correctly told before heading to MU that 'Sororities are not the thing to do.'")

Students describe the campus as friendly; one journalism major says that "everyone has the typical Midwestern friendliness." Although there is some diversity among the student body, "it is primarily upper-middle-class white kids," according to a recent grad. "MU's campus looks like a J. Crew catalog." About half the students are from Wisconsin, with many coming from the Chicago area as well. We hear that there's not a lot of socializing with students from other colleges in the area. But Marquette students are very involved in the local community; more than 60 percent of students are involved with service through student organizations and service learning, and about a third of students pursue careers in public service. Students volunteer to help the homeless, local schoolchildren, small businesses, community groups, and churches—building a more just world is integral to Marquette. As part of a national effort in mid-April, Marquette students visit more than 70 sites throughout Milwaukee, volunteering to clean up parks, paint shelters, visit the elderly and perform other tasks for pledges; the money raised is donated to fight hunger and homelessness.

Sports—particularly basketball—are huge at Marquette. Despite the team's recent losing streak, the student spirit for the basketball team has been revived, and MU home games are packed with students chanting "We are (clap, clap) Marquette (clap, clap)." Intramural sports are popular as well, and students praise the recreational facilities on campus. Incoming students have the opportunity at "O-Fest" during the first week of the fall semester to learn more about the hundreds of activities and student organizations at Marquette.

Other schools to check out: Notre Dame, Duquesne, Saint Louis, DePaul, Creighton.

Test Scores (middle 50%):
  SAT Verbal: 530–630
  SAT Math: 530–650
  ACT Comp: 23–28
  ACT English: 22–28
  ACT Math: 22–28

HS Rank of Entering Freshmen:
  Top 10%: 30%
  Top 25%: 62%
  Top 50%: 91%

THE EXPERTS SAY...

" Marquette's College of Engineering is 25 percent female, nearly twice the national average. "

" Milwaukee's weather is cold, but the people are warm and friendly, and the beer flows like tap water. "

Costs (2004–5)

Tuition and Fees: $21,932

Room & Board: $7,268

Payment Plan(s): installment plan

Inst. Aid (est. 2003–04)

Institutional Aid, Need-Based:
  $30,625,430

Institutional Aid, Non-Need-Based:
  $13,684,615

FT Undergrads Receiving Aid: 60%
  Avg. Amount per Student: $16,853

FT Undergrads Receiving Non-Need-Based Scholarship or Grant Aid: 21%
  Avg. Amount per Student: $6,674

Of Those Receiving Any Aid:

Rec. Need-Based Scholarship or
  Grant Aid: 90%
  Average Award: $10,774

Rec. Need-Based Self-Help Aid: 81%
  Average Award: $7,152

Upon Graduation, Avg. Loan Debt
  per Student: $22,924

Financial Aid Deadline: rolling, 3/1
  (priority)

Graduates

Going to Graduate School:
  26% Within One Year

Companies Recruiting On Campus:
  180

Alumni Giving: 26%

MARY WASHINGTON COLLEGE

1301 College Avenue, Fredericksburg, VA 22401-5358
Admissions Phone: (540) 654-2000; (800) 468-5614 Fax: (540) 654-1857
Email: admit@mwc.edu Website: www.mwc.edu

General Info

Type of School: public, coed

Setting: suburban

Academic Calendar: semester

Student Body

Full-Time Undergrads: 3,565
  Men: 33%, Women: 67%

Part-Time Undergrads: 474
  Men: 37%, Women: 63%

Total Undergrad Population:
  African American: 4%
  Asian American: 5%
  Latino: 3%
  Native American: <1%
  Caucasian: 88%
  International: <1%
  Out-of-State: 35%
  Living Off-Campus: 30%

Graduate and First-Professional
  Students: 572

Academics

Full-Time Faculty: 206
  With Ph.D.: 87%

Part-Time Faculty: 125

Student/Faculty Ratio: 17:1

Most Popular Majors:
  business administration (13%)
  psychology (11%)
  biology (8%)
  English (8%)
  history (5%)

Freshmen Retention Rate: 85%

Graduation Rates:
  59% within four years
  67% within six years

Admissions

Regular Application Deadline: 2/1;
  1/15 (priority)

Fall Transfer Deadline: 3/1

Spring Transfer Deadline: 11/1

Total # of Students Applied: 4,472
  Admitted: 2,676
  Enrolled: 888

Students Accepting Place on Waitlist:
  300
  Waitlisted Students Admitted: 150

Inside the Classroom

From 1944 until the early 1970s, Mary Washington College was the women's undergraduate arts and sciences college of the University of Virginia. In 1972, the College became an independent, state-supported institution for men and women. Since then, it has grown into the public undergraduate college of the liberal arts and sciences in the state, attracting a growing number of students not only from Virginia, but also from such northern states as Pennsylvania, New York and Connecticut.

Men and women enrolled at MWC can choose from among 28 undergraduate majors. The education programs in both secondary and elementary education are very strong. Proximity to the nation's capital provides students with outstanding internship opportunities, particularly in museum studies, law, political science, and international affairs. The major historical sights from the Civil War that surround Mary Washington College make history-related subjects popular (the college itself is named after the mother of the nation's first president). The Mary Washington Center for Historic Preservation is one of the best of its kind. MWC offers a unique major in historic preservation, ideal for students interested in architectural preservation, museum work, or archaeology. There are also several excellent preprofessional programs in premed, prelaw, predental, and preveterinary studies.

The general education program at MWC is extremely demanding. All students are required to complete course work in eight "goal" areas. These include writing, mathematics, science, arts and literature, Western civilization, social sciences, foreign language, and physical education. In addition, the school features a unique set of five "across-the-curriculum" requirements. These include writing intensive (5 courses), speaking intensive (2 courses), global awareness (2 courses), environmental awareness (1 course), and race/gender intensive (1 course). All Mary Washington students must subscribe to the College's Honor Code and agree to abide by the Honor System.

Unlike many other public institutions, Mary Washington College features small classes and a high level of personal attention from faculty. The average class size is 22 students, and freshman-level classes usually average 20–35 students. There are no graduate students or teaching assistants in the classrooms at MWC; all classes are taught by faculty members committed to undergraduate teaching excellence. "The classes are small enough that the professors can interact with and get to know the students," says a sophomore.

MWC provides over $60,000 annually in support of student research. Students perform their research under one-on-one supervision of full-time faculty members, in many different academic disciplines. "Our students present papers each year at state, regional, and national conferences," says a college official.

Campus Environment

Mary Washington is located in Fredericksburg, Virginia, site of one of the major battles of the Civil War. Although Richmond and Washington, DC are easy road trips, each only 50 miles away, a Massachusetts guidance counselor frets that "some students may find it too rural." All major buildings on the beautiful 176-acre campus are in neoclassical Jeffersonian design, of red brick with white columns. The campus is united by a wide brick walkway, with numerous park benches and a central fountain. Cars are restricted, leaving its brick walkways completely to pedestrians. Most of the campus is lined with trees, giving it a peaceful, park-like feel.

Students at Mary Washington rave about their housing. "From what I've seen, even our worst dorms are better than those at other colleges," boasts a freshman. Sixteen residence halls provide a variety of coed and single-sex living environments. Housing is guaranteed for freshmen and sophomores only. First-year students are housed in five freshmen-only residence halls; one houses all women and the rest are coed. The typical room setup is suite-style, with two double rooms sharing a bathroom in the middle. Upperclassmen have a choice among several types of residence halls or off-campus housing.

Student Life

"If you're looking for a party school, you'd probably do best to look elsewhere," says a student. There are no sororities or fraternities at Mary Washington. Many students in search of a more active social scene leave for the weekend to the larger schools nearby such as UVA and William and Mary. Students who stay on campus on the weekends can attend concerts, free movies, and other events. The Underground coffeehouse beneath the admissions building is a popular student hangout that hosts live music on the weekends. Campus-wide events include "Grill on the Hill," formal dances, and Westock, an outdoor music festival. In the spring, numerous dorm-sponsored picnics with great food and loud bands take place on the college lawn.

"Students need to be very self-motivated here," advises a junior. "The school has everything to offer, but it doesn't go out of its way to give it to you. You've got to find what's right for you and create your own agenda." Motivated students can become involved in approximately 90 extracurricular activities such as student government, theater production, and music groups. The most popular groups are Student Government Association, the Washington Guides (tour guide organization), Class Council, Multicultural Student Associations, and C.O.A.R (Community Outreach and Resources).

As an NCAA Division III school, MWC offers 10 varsity sports for men and 12 for women. The College plays in the Capital Athletic Conference, where it has won more conference championships than all other conference members combined. To date, the MWC Eagles have had more than 100 student-athletes achieve All-American status. Club sports include men's volleyball, women's synchronized swimming, men's and women's rugby, and men's and women's cheerleading. Some of the more popular intramural sports are aerobics, ball hockey, basketball, floor hockey, golf, soccer, table tennis, tennis, ultimate Frisbee, and volleyball.

Mary Washington's oldest and most colorful traditions are the annual Junior Ring Day and Devil Goat Day. Every spring there is a week of festivities during which juniors celebrate getting their class rings. The highlight of the week is the Junior Ring Ceremony on Friday where the president of the college presents each junior with his or her class ring. On Devil Goat Day in April (before the end of classes) the even-numbered classes play against the odd-numbered classes in a number of competitions, culminating in a concert for all students at Ball Circle.

Test Scores (middle 50%):
SAT Verbal: 570–660
SAT Math: 560–640
ACT Comp: 25–29

HS Rank of Entering Freshmen:
Top 10%: 39%
Top 25%: 88%
Top 50%: 99%

Avg. HS GPA: 3.63

THE EXPERTS SAY...

" Mary Washington offers a unique major in historic preservation. Civil War buffs will have a field day in Fredericksburg. "

" If 'Devil Goat Day' doesn't sound like loads of fun, investigate Gettysburg College, University of Richmond, College of William and Mary, and Washington and Lee University. "

Costs (2003–04)

Tuition and Fees, In-State: $4,424

Tuition and Fees, Out-of-State: $12,172

Room & Board: $5,478

Payment Plan(s): installment plan, pre-payment plan

Inst. Aid (2002–03)

Institutional Aid, Need-Based: $467,500

Institutional Aid, Non-Need-Based: $506,450

Graduates

Going to Graduate School: 23% Within One Year

Companies Recruiting On Campus: 91

Alumni Giving: 45%

MASSACHUSETTS INSTITUTE OF TECHNOLOGY

77 Massachusetts Avenue, Room 3-108, Cambridge, MA 02139-4307
Admissions Phone: (617) 253-4791 Website: web.mit.edu/admissions/www/
Application Website: web.mit.edu/admissions/www/applications/

General Info

Type of School: private, coed

Setting: urban

Academic Calendar: 4-1-4

Student Body

Full-Time Undergrads: 4,069
  Men: 58%, Women: 42%

Part-Time Undergrads: 40
  Men: 70%, Women: 30%

Total Undergrad Population:
  African American: 6%
  Asian American: 28%
  Latino: 12%
  Native American: 2%
  Caucasian: 35%
  International: 8%
  Out-of-State: 91%
  Living Off-Campus: 6%
  In Fraternities: 12%
  In Sororities: 7%

Graduate and First-Professional
  Students: 6,228

Academics

Full-Time Faculty: 1,543
  With Ph.D.: 94%

Part-Time Faculty: 639
  With Ph.D.: 88%

Student/Faculty Ratio: 6:1

Most Popular Majors:
  electrical engineering & computer science (12%)
  computer science and engineering (7%)
  management science (7%)
  biology (7%)
  mechanical engineering (6%)

Completing 2 or More Majors: 16%

Freshmen Retention Rate: 98%

Graduation Rates:
  81% within four years
  92% within six years

Admissions

Regular Application Deadline: 1/1

Early Action Deadline: 11/1

Fall Transfer Deadline: 3/15

Spring Transfer Deadline: 11/15

Total # of Students Applied: 10,549
  Admitted: 1,735
  Enrolled: 1,019

Inside the Classroom

Guidance counselors all over the country agree that MIT is the ultimate in research schools, "the paramount science and technology institute in the nation." Its faculty includes some of the world's most brilliant thinkers, several of them Nobel Prize winners. Undergrads actually get the chance to interact with these great minds, and "A-list faculty don't shy from teaching undergraduates, even at the freshman level," insists one student. "You're given the set of tools, and are expected to work your butt off with them." Of course, large lectures can make it difficult for students to form relationships with a professor. However, as one student told us, "There are some professors students adore; they are ranked up there with God. In general, most professors care about their classes."

Engineering and the sciences are obviously the standouts here; the departments of electrical engineering, computer science, and aerospace, in particular, are considered the cream of the crop. This a place where research has yielded the first chemical synthesis of penicillin and vitamin A, modern technologies for artificial limbs, and the magnetic core memory that made digital computers possible. Undergrads are expected to get their hands dirty in the labs: In a recent mechanical engineering class assignment to build a wireless, remote-controlled product, student innovations included a snowblower, a bartending machine, and a rock-climbing device. Fortunately, the core curriculum ensures that students don't become tech zombies, by requiring a range of courses, including humanities, arts, writing and physical education.

"The academics dominate students' lives," a student tells us. "People always talk about having too much work." Freshmen are graded only on a pass/fail basis, and failing grades don't show up on their transcripts, which does help students adjust to the difficulty of MIT courses. The intense workload and high-pressure environment, however, seems to draw students together, and when asked if there's a strong sense of camaraderie, one student responded, "Yes! It's us versus them!" One student described MIT as a school that's "better to be from than at," but from what we hear, that's a minority opinion. Most would agree with the student who summed up life at "the Tech" this way: "We work hard and we play hard."

Once only the ambitious students took advantage of MIT's program to earn combined bachelor's and master's degrees in five years, but it is now becoming standard, we hear. "It's pretty much expected," said one student, "and, in many cases, part of the curriculum." MIT students may also cross-register at Wellesley or Harvard.

Campus Environment

MIT is located on 154 acres that extend along the Cambridge side of the Charles River. Most undergrads live in the 10 Institute houses; as of 2002, freshmen are no longer allowed to live in frat houses and must live on campus for their first year. In an innovative program, the school has allowed students in four dorms to have cats, which is felt to improve students' well-being. While the Greeks are a huge force here, one student calls it "unusual" that MIT relies so heavily on the frats for housing. But frats here are different from those at other schools: "There's no hazing or wild orgies," says one student, "which is either regrettable or good." Another explains, "Many of the frats are located in Boston, so they're a popular place to be when you want to get away from MIT for a bit."

An "architectural metamorphosis" is now under way to renovate the campus—and in true MIT fashion, is being overseen by the Green Building Task Force to ensure maximum energy efficiency. (On the flip-side, some students complain that the constant construction is a major hassle.) The school also has a policy requiring each major construction project to include major artwork, so students can be assured of a "visual aesthetic" as well. To get around, students bike and rollerblade. "Cars are generally a liability and tough to park," says one senior.

Student Life

MIT students are not the stereotypical geeks you might imagine. They may not have all that much free time, but they make time to have fun. Having said that, no one said that students here weren't offbeat. (Point in fact: One senior told us that two things she loved about the school were the "oddity of the students," and the "highly technical view of the world.") This is a group that turned the study of material sciences and engineering into a glass blowing club and the science of numerical patterns into a student group of bellringers who travel to ring the tower bells of Boston churches. Then there's the Solar Electric Vehicle Team, in which students construct solar-powered cars; Roadkill Buffet, the improv comedy troupe; a floorball club, celebrating the most popular sport in Sweden; the Easy Rider motorcycle club; a caving club; the Quiz Bowl Team that competes in academic trivia competitions, and a ballroom dance club. Amazingly, all this creativity comes naturally to most. Explains one economics senior, the typical MIT student "cares passionately about anything he does. Beyond that, he gets a kick out of problem solving."

The arts are no less a target of students' imaginativeness: Productions range from chamber music to electronic "hyperinstrument" concerts, and classic Shakespearean plays to improvisational comedy. The range of organizations within any given area is dizzying. For political groups alone, there's the Green Party; the Student Association for Freedom of Expression; the Libertarians; the Pro-Choice Group; the Pro-Life Group; and the obscure Objectivist Club, focusing on the philosophy of author Ayn Rand.

According to the NCAA, MIT sponsors one of the broadest varsity sports programs in the country, with 41 varsity teams. But students tells us that "although a lot of people participate in varsity and intramural sports, no one makes a big deal about it." MIT is also one of the few universities to offer ROTC programs in all three branches of the military: Army, Navy/Marine Corps, and Air Force.

School traditions include the annual Mystery Hunt, a puzzle competition that challenges teams to solve puzzles leading to a hidden coin. (The prize—in typical MIT wit—is the right to organize the following year's hunt.) And students always look forward to their annual "steer roast," a two-day party hosted by the dorms, featuring a huge chunk of meat roasting over an open fire.

Other schools to check out: Cal Tech, Stanford, Harvard, Yale, Princeton.

THE EXPERTS SAY...

" MIT is home to the world's most brilliant and imaginative thinkers, faculty and students alike. "

" A lot is expected of MIT students, and despite the pass/fail system, many kids are seriously unhappy here. Even in your free time, you have to be brilliant to be cool. "

MIAMI UNIVERSITY

301 S. Campus Ave., Oxford, OH 45056
Admissions Phone: (513) 529-2531 Fax: (513) 529-1550
Email: admission@muohio.edu Website: www.muohio.edu
Application Website: www.muohio.edu/apply

General Info

Type of School: public, coed
Setting: small town
Academic Calendar: semester

Student Body

Full-Time Undergrads (2002):
  14,971
  Men: 45%, Women: 55%

Part-Time Undergrads (2002): 334
  Men: 55%, Women: 45%

Total Undergrad Population (2002):
  African American: 4%
  Asian American: 2%
  Latino: 2%
  Native American: 1%
  Caucasian: 89%
  International: 1%
  Out-of-State: 27%
  Living Off-Campus: 55%
  In Fraternities: 24%
  In Sororities: 27%

Graduate and First-Professional
  Students (2002): 1,238

Academics

Full-Time Faculty: 825
  With Ph.D.: 88%

Part-Time Faculty: 312
  With Ph.D.: 35%

Student/Faculty Ratio: 18:1

Most Popular Majors:
  marketing (8%)
  zoology (5%)
  finance (5%)
  general business (5%)
  psychology (5%)

Completing 2 or More Majors: 11%

Freshmen Retention Rate: 90%

Graduation Rates:
  67% within four years
  83% within six years

Admissions

Regular Application Deadline: 1/31

Early Decision Deadline(s): 11/1

Fall Transfer Deadline: 5/1

Total # of Students Applied: 13,859
  Admitted: 9,842
  Enrolled: 3,362

# of Students Waitlisted: 1,625
  Students Accepting Place: 543
  Waitlisted Students Admitted: 543

Inside the Classroom

A "public Ivy" that focuses on undergraduate education, Miami University is a "very tough school" that "helps students work harder," says an Ohio high school guidance counselor. Several guidance counselors complain that it's too hard to get in, but students seem to appreciate the high caliber of their Miami peers. "Most of the students come from strong academic backgrounds with excellent high school prep," says a recent grad. "I can remember my first day of orientation as a freshman when we had to describe ourselves and our backgrounds. Being the student council president or field hockey captain or homecoming queen didn't really put you above anyone else. Most of the people who surrounded me could say the same thing."

Miami students have nearly 100 majors to choose from, plus highly regarded preprofessional programs in law, medicine, and other disciplines. Undergrads enroll in the College of Arts and Science or the schools of business administration; education and allied professions; engineering and applied science; fine arts; and interdisciplinary studies. The programs in business, engineering, and education are particularly strong, but the fine arts programs tend to be weaker.

Miami has an extensive three-part core curriculum, called the Miami Plan for Liberal Education. Part One: 36 credit hours of Foundation courses in the humanities, social sciences, natural sciences, fine arts, and formal reasoning. Part Two: 9 credit hours in a Thematic Sequence outside your major. Part Three: A Senior Capstone Experience combining your broad liberal arts background with the specialized knowledge of your major.

"The workload is substantial and the school is very competitive," says an international studies major. A psych major agrees: "I think that the students are competitive in grades, but that competitiveness drives me to do better." A preveterinary student's perspective: "Other majors have less work, but even my nonscience classes have been at least somewhat challenging and definitely time-consuming. The emphasis in many classes is on group work and projects—with the main library *very* crowded in the evenings with group meetings."

A senior describes the level of interaction with faculty: "Most class sizes are small, about 50 students, and students can really get to know their professors on a better level because the one-on-one attention is great. There are some large classes, but as long as you make an effort to work hard, the professor will be very willing to help you and meet with you."

Undergraduate research opportunities abound, and Miami consistently ranks among the top 10 universities in the nation for the number of students studying abroad. While several study abroad options are available, the one that makes Miami unique is the university's own Dolibois European Center in Luxembourg.

Campus Environment

All freshmen and first-year transfers must live on campus. Students and guidance counselors agree that Miami's dorms are "clean," "comfortable," and "very beautiful." All dorm rooms are wired for computer access and cable TV, but only some are air conditioned (students with asthma may request these). Every dorm basement has study rooms, couches, a TV—"they are a favorite study or hangout destination," says a junior. Most sophomores stay in the dorms or move to a frat house, and juniors and seniors usually move to off-campus apartments or houses. Competition for off-campus housing is fierce, and students strongly advise that you start house-hunting a whole year in advance of when you'll actually move in.

The Oxford campus is located 35 miles north of Cincinnati and 45 miles southwest of Dayton. "We are surrounded by fields and cows," complains a junior. But another student sees the bright side: "The campus is gorgeous—lots of trees, grass, gardens, wonderful architecture, cute small-town atmosphere." You must obtain permission from the university if you want to bring a car to school. Luckily, students have unlimited use of the Miami Metro, a bus shuttle with routes on campus and to certain sites in town.

"Off-campus is relatively safe because, after all, Oxford is just a small campus town that survives solely on the profits made from the University," says a senior. While the administration insists that town-gown relations are great, a junior disagrees: "There is often a great disparity between the standard of living and education of the students' families and the families native to Oxford, resulting in something of a superiority complex on the part of the students."

Student Life

The typical Miami student? "One who comes from the middle to upper classes, perhaps attended private high school, is a political conservative, dresses well with all the latest trends, drives nice sporty vehicles, is involved in a Greek organization, is involved in other clubs, is fitness-oriented, good-looking, ambitious, and intelligent," answers a long-winded junior. One high school guidance counselor's pithy description of the student body: "snobby, conceited." Another junior's description: "That student would dress very nicely in Abercrombie or J. Crew. They would be in shape (we like to exercise a lot at the rec or run along the roads). They would also have a cell phone and talk in between classes." The few Miami students who don't fit into this preppy mold tend to live happily together on the Western Campus, we are told.

Students tell us that Sunday–Wednesday nights are reserved for schoolwork, and Thursday–Saturday nights are for going out to frat parties and the local bars. "Drinking is a big factor on- and off-campus," a recent grad stresses. However, another recent grad insists, "There is a lot of drinking, but there is not a lot of pressure to drink. I had many friends who didn't drink but still came to the bars or to parties with those who did drink." Students agree that drugs are not prevalent at Miami and are "not regarded as the 'cool' thing to do."

Miami has been called the "Mother of Fraternities" (four national fraternities have been founded here since 1835), and Greek life is still popular. "Rush is a huge thing, and almost every freshman does it," says one junior. But you don't need to go Greek to have a good social life. There are more than 300 student organizations on campus, including 1,800 intramural teams in 45 sports (which are much more popular than Miami's Division I varsity athletics).

Applied Early Decision: 874
   Early Decision Admitted: 668

Test Scores (middle 50%):
   SAT Verbal: 560–650
   SAT Math: 580–670
   ACT Comp: 25–29

HS Rank of Entering Freshmen:
   Top 10%: 39%
   Top 25%: 76%
   Top 50%: 98%

Avg. HS GPA: 3.7

THE EXPERTS SAY...

" Miami may draw more applicants—and become even more selective—now that it is one of the few public universities to participate in the Common Application program. "

" Be prepared for misguided beach-bum jokes: Nobody outside the Midwest and Mid-Atlantic states realizes this school is actually located in Ohio. "

Costs (2003–04)

Tuition and Fees, In-State: $8,354

Tuition and Fees, Out-of-State: $18,124

Room & Board: $6,680

Regional or 'good neighbor' tuition available

Payment Plan(s): installment plan, deferred payment plan

Inst. Aid (est. 2003–04)

FT Undergrads Receiving Aid: 32%
   Avg. Amount per Student: $7,090

FT Undergrads Receiving Non-Need-Based Scholarship or Grant Aid: 14%
   Avg. Amount per Student: $4,539

Of Those Receiving Any Aid:

Rec. Need-Based Scholarship or Grant Aid: 44%
   Average Award: $4,217

Rec. Need-Based Self-Help Aid: 84%
   Average Award: $4,117

Upon Graduation, Avg. Loan Debt per Student: $18,302

Financial Aid Deadline: rolling, 2/15 (priority)

Graduates

Going to Graduate School: 36% Within One Year

Companies Recruiting On Campus: 350

MICHIGAN STATE UNIVERSITY

250 Administration Building, East Lansing, MI 48824-1046
Admissions Phone: (517) 355-8332 Fax: (517) 353-1647
Email: admis@msu.edu Website: www.msu.edu
Application Website: admis.msu.edu/Apply.asp

General Info

Type of School: public, coed

Setting: suburban

Academic Calendar: semester

Student Body

Full-Time Undergrads: 31,023
    Men: 46%, Women: 54%

Part-Time Undergrads: 3,594
    Men: 49%, Women: 51%

Total Undergrad Population:
    African American: 9%
    Asian American: 5%
    Latino: 3%
    Native American: 1%
    Caucasian: 79%
    International: 3%
    Out-of-State: 7%
    Living Off-Campus: 58%

Graduate and First-Professional
    Students: 9,689

Academics

Full-Time Faculty: 2,312
    With Ph.D.: 94%

Part-Time Faculty: 341
    With Ph.D.: 55%

Student/Faculty Ratio: 18:1

Most Popular Majors:
    business marketing (19%)
    communications (14%)
    social sciences (10%)
    engineering (8%)
    biological sciences (7%)

Freshmen Retention Rate: 90%

Graduation Rates:
    36% within four years
    69% within six years

Computers: Computer Required

Admissions

Regular Application Deadline: 9/1

Total # of Students Applied: 24,973
    Admitted: 17,690
    Enrolled: 7,122

# of Students Waitlisted: 1,524
    Students Accepting Place: 561
    Waitlisted Students Admitted: 160

Inside the Classroom

The many academic departments at Michigan State University are organized into 14 colleges: agriculture and natural resources; arts and letters; business; communications, education, engineering, human ecology, medicine, natural science, nursing, osteopathic medicine, social science, veterinary medicine, and military. Literally hundreds of majors are offered, with the list starting at accounting and ending in zoology. Just about all preprofessional tracks are represented as well, with the exception of law.

The university's large student body means large classes, some of which are taught by teaching assistants instead of professors. One student says, "For the most part, the TAs are very helpful and resourceful; however, some of them are not able to communicate in English thoroughly." A physiology major provided this additional input: "Some of the profs are great and accessible, but there are too many TAs."

Guidance counselors point out that MSU has a top-tier career services and placement office—a necessity in a school with so many preprofessional departments. The office assists students in career advising and in finding jobs after graduation, and also offers part-time and summer employment opportunities on and off campus. Experiential learning opportunities, such as volunteer programs, are also available. Of course, for the enterprising, MSU's huge student body translates into another valuable source of employment opportunities. One alum says, "The connections I made would recommend me to their colleagues for jobs they knew were available. Every job that I've had since graduation I've received through these connections." A psychology major agrees: "I would frequently volunteer to do extra work and ended up with very good references as a result. Because of this, I have not really had to apply in the normal ways for a job."

Another professional boon for students is Michigan State's fundamental commitment to study abroad: It sends the highest number of students from a single campus than any other school in the United States. Recognizing that international perspectives are vital in the global marketplace, MSU offers over 150 programs in over 50 countries, with opportunities to spend from two weeks to an academic year in countries like Australia, Ecuador, France, Kenya, Nepal, Singapore, Thailand, and Zimbabwe. Interestingly, MSU also offers study abroad programs in academic disciplines traditionally underrepresented in international programs, including engineering, communication arts and sciences, natural science, and veterinary medicine.

Campus Environment

The campus at Michigan State is simply gigantic. Occupying 5,239 acres, the school is more like a small city than a university. But with its gently rolling grounds, more than 19,000 trees, and the Red Cedar River flowing across campus, it's an attractive site. If you get lost on campus (a likely occurrence for first-year students), Beaumont Tower, with its 47-bell carillon, is a signature landmark.

MSU has an extensive system of 26 residence halls, and the student handbook's section on the subject begins, "All students are encouraged to live in university housing ...." Then comes the kicker: "...to the extent accommodations are available." About half of the undergrads live in the dorms, with others living in Greek and co-op houses. Local residents commute, with the remainder of students living in private, off-campus apartments and houses. All of the dorms are coed, with men and women housed on separate floors or in separate sections of the same floor. All halls offer quiet areas with extended hours for silent study. There are also "living and learning communities" in certain dorms with classrooms, lecture halls, and an advising office for students sharing an academic interest.

Intramural sports and recreation are so popular on campus that four buildings, four pools, and 45 acres of outdoor space are devoted to them. The IM Sports West complex houses gyms and courts for racquetball, handball, paddleball, squash, and wallyball, among others. The IM Sports East facility features basketball, volleyball, track, and more of the same facilities housed in the West complex. Indoor soccer, roller skating, and events for the community and students are held in the Demonstration Hall arena.

Students say positive things about East Lansing, whose economy depends partly on catering to the students' need for off-campus fun. Recreational opportunities aren't limited to bars, either; one student advises, "There are some cool things to do outside of the city—other than clubs and bars every night—like rock climbing. Get a car and really get out there."

Student Life

The student body is about as big as they come, and the accompanying herd effect is not for everyone. "In a place this big, it gets lonely, people get lost and no one is concerned with what might be going on in your life," laments one junior. An automotive engineering major puts a different spin on it, saying, "Having more than 40,000 students means more opportunities to meet many different types of people... If you make the most of it, there will never be a dull moment. I promise."

If you find yourself bored on the MSU campus, it's pretty much your own fault. With about 350 student organizations, there's a club or society for nearly every interest imaginable. This includes professional organizations, including esoteric options like the Association of Black Osteopathic Medical Students, the American Association of Bovine Practitioners, and a student chapter of Packaging Professionals.

The Greek list at Michigan state reads like a Who's Who of Panhellenic organizations: There are 34 fraternities and 18 sororities, many with their own houses. "The Greeks have tons of influence on campus," says one student. "Frats and sors allow for smaller groups of friends, making it easier to have a social identity." The inevitable result, according to one happy English major, is that "this is a huge party school. If you don't drink, you don't belong here." Another student describes it a little differently: "I get tired of popping my bike tires on all the broken glass, not being able to walk my dog down the sidewalks (she'll cut her paws), and tired of the piles of puke on lawns and underwear in bushes." Perhaps this senior's opinion provides the best balance: "If you want a party you can find it, but it's just as easy to find students studying at the library every night of the week."

Test Scores (middle 50%):
SAT Verbal: 500–620
SAT Math: 520–650
ACT Comp: 22–27
ACT English: 21–27
ACT Math: 21–27

HS Rank of Entering Freshmen:
Top 10%: 28%
Top 25%: 67%
Top 50%: 95%

Avg. HS GPA: 3.58

THE EXPERTS SAY...

" Michigan State University is all things to everyone, serving as a career springboard for every kind of future professional. "

" Know what you want out of college before you enroll here. You can get completely lost on campus... and in the course catalog, along fraternity row, and just about everywhere else. "

Costs (2003–04)

Tuition and Fees, In-State: $6,703

Tuition and Fees, Out-of-State: $16,663

Room & Board: $5,230

Payment Plan(s): deferred payment plan

Inst. Aid (est. 2003–04)

Institutional Aid, Need-Based: $18,497,030

Institutional Aid, Non-Need-Based: $7,277,670

FT Undergrads Receiving Aid: 41% Avg. Amount per Student: $8,487

FT Undergrads Receiving Non-Need-Based Scholarship or Grant Aid: 23% Avg. Amount per Student: $4,172

Of Those Receiving Any Aid:

Rec. Need-Based Scholarship or Grant Aid: 87% Average Award: $3,518

Rec. Need-Based Self-Help Aid: 88% Average Award: $4,489

Upon Graduation, Avg. Loan Debt per Student: $18,814

Financial Aid Deadline: 6/30, 2/21 (priority)

MICHIGAN TECHNOLOGICAL UNIVERSITY

1400 Townsend Drive, Houghton, MI 49931
Admissions Phone: (906) 487-2335; (888) MTU-1885 Fax: (906) 487-2125
Email: mtu4u@mtu.edu Website: www.mtu.edu Application Website: www.mtu.edu/apply

Note: Info. not verified by school

General Info

Type of School: public, coed

Setting: small town

Academic Calendar: semester

Student Body

Full-Time Undergrads: 4,926
  Men: 75%, Women: 25%

Part-Time Undergrads: 864
  Men: 83%, Women: 17%

Total Undergrad Population:
  African American: 2%
  Asian American: 1%
  Latino: 1%
  Native American: 1%
  Caucasian: 85%
  International: 6%
  Out-of-State: 19%
  Living Off-Campus: 61%
  In Fraternities: 9%
  In Sororities: 16%

Graduate and First-Professional
  Students: 710

Academics

Full-Time Faculty: 377
  With Ph.D.: 88%

Part-Time Faculty: 30
  With Ph.D.: 33%

Student/Faculty Ratio: 11:1

Most Popular Majors:
  mechanical engineering (22%)
  electrical engineering (10%)
  civil engineering (8%)
  computer science (8%)
  business administration (6%)

Freshmen Retention Rate: 78%

Graduation Rates:
  29% within four years
  65% within six years

Admissions

Total # of Students Applied: 2,957
  Admitted: 2,716
  Enrolled: 1,190

Test Scores (middle 50%):
  SAT Verbal: 510–640
  SAT Math: 570–690
  ACT Comp: 23–28
  ACT English: 20–27
  ACT Math: 24–30

Inside the Classroom

Michigan Tech offers 98 majors, 42 minors, and 12 certificate programs through its five undergraduate colleges: College of Engineering, College of Sciences and Arts, School of Business and Economics, School of Forest Resources and Environmental Science, and School of Technology. Engineering is far and away the university's shining star; Tech is ranked in the top 10 in the nation in enrollment or degrees granted in chemical engineering, civil engineering, environmental engineering, geological and mining engineering, materials science and engineering, and mechanical engineering. Tech is also ranked first in the nation in enrollment in the scientific and technical communication program. And despite its overwhelmingly male student body, Michigan Tech is also No. 1 in the nation in percentage of women enrolled in biomedical engineering and environmental engineering.

The General Education curriculum includes four core courses (world cultures, communications, etc.), 15 credits of distribution courses (language, creativity, and the like), and three semester units of "co-curricular activities" (i.e., phys ed). And of course, this being Tech, students must also take 16 credits of science, engineering, mathematics, or computer science, most of which must be outside the student's major field.

The new and unique Enterprise Program "creates teams of students from different disciplines to tackle real problems posed by industry," the school says. It is, in effect, a response to the industry's need for engineers who have technical competence but who also understand the practical application of business and personal skills such as teamwork, communications, and leadership. Recent projects have included Future Truck, Aerospace, Integrated Microsystems, Baja, Robotics, Alternate Fuels, and Consumer Products.

Students here are very driven and very serious about their studies. (We hear that if you aren't, you've come to the wrong school.) Coursework can be grueling; the "Welcome" booklet for incoming freshmen advises setting aside 30–45 hours a week for studying. Classes are pleasantly small—the biggest lecture has perhaps 30 people—but some students are less than happy with their professors, especially those for whom English is not their first language. But overall, students rave about the education they're receiving, not to mention the terrific careers they're generally rewarded with after graduation. Tech's stellar reputation, extensive corporate connections, and helpful career center are major plusses in many students' books.

Campus Environment

The university—and not much else—is in Upper Michigan's Keweenaw Peninsula. The town is small and extremely safe, but offers very little to students in the way of entertainment. Winter sports enthusiasts will love it, however: With an annual average of 180 inches of snowfall, the area boasts some of the country's finest skiing. The school even has its own ski hill. "We have just improved and increased our cross-country ski trails, and our downhill ski area (across the lake from campus) features new snow-making equipment and lights for great night skiing," a school official tells us. For the unprepared, though, winter can be long, cold, and depressing. Luckily,

Michigan Tech's campus is set up so that students don't have to walk far from dorms to classrooms. First-year students are permitted to have cars, though the campus is so small and compact, you probably won't need one except for out-of-town adventures… and the closest city is Minneapolis, seven (!) hours away.

All single students who are not commuting from home must live on campus their first year. There are three residence halls: Douglass Houghton, the oldest and smallest; McNair, which is divided into the "International House" and the "Healthy Living House"; and Wadsworth, the largest of the three halls, which has some suite-style rooms. Each of the dorms offers fitness facilities, although many students take advantage of the impressive Student Development Complex, a 235,000 square-foot athletic recreational facility that features an ice arena, pool, gym, fitness center, racquetball/squash courts, dance room, music room, and a gymnastics room. The newest building on campus is the "beautiful" Rozsa Center for the Performing Arts, where the school brings internationally renowned performers to campus. (Some students, however, complain about the administration's funding of this project, implying they'd prefer laboratories to auditoriums.)

Student Life

Not surprisingly, Tech suffers from a shortage of women (although, we hear, women form nearly half the student leadership and hold several of the most responsible positions). The typical Michigan Tech undergrad is male, white, conservative, and yes, often "nerdy." Because of the time-consuming coursework, the virtually nonexistent dating scene, and the depressingly remote location, Tech students tend to keep their nose in their textbooks. But not always: We hear Tech students drink and party a lot, and are proud of it. Perhaps to combat their "nerdy" image, students often try to boast that their school is one of the heaviest drinking campuses in the country. The administration points out, however, that "according to the most recent surveys of alcohol use on campus, Michigan Tech ranks solidly in the middle in terms of frequency and volume of alcohol use on campus nationwide." Still, the "highly visible" Greek population throws many a party in their houses throughout the week.

There are 200 student groups, including professional and honor societies, cultural and religious organizations, service and special interest groups, and more than 30 sports clubs. "Undergraduate Student Government is very active on campus," we're told. The student newspaper is highly respected, and there's a campus radio station that "allows students to spin their favorite tunes in three-hour blocks of time." The men's ice hockey team is Division I; other varsity sports include men's football, women's volleyball, and men's and women's basketball, track and field, Nordic skiing, and cross-country running. Three-quarters of the student body participate in intramurals. Tech also has an indoor tennis center and its own golf course.

The biggest event of the year is Winter Carnival, the largest annual winter celebration on any campus in the country. Hosted by the Blue Key National Honor Fraternity, Winter Carnival features "huge snow statues, sports like broomball, a Division I ice hockey series, skits, and a queen coronation." There's also K-Day, when the campus heads to the shores of Lake Superior; the Parade of Nations, celebrating diversity; Spring Fling, a campus festival that takes place just before finals; and a hobo-themed Homecoming, where students "dress in their worst attire, demolish autos (then drive them through campus), and enjoy football in beautiful Sherman Field."

Other schools to check out: U of Michigan, Michigan State, U of Minnesota—Twin Cities, U of Wisconsin—Madison, Kettering.

HS Rank of Entering Freshmen:
Top 10%: 31%
Top 25%: 60%
Top 50%: 89%
Avg. HS GPA: 3.54

Costs (2003–04)
Tuition and Fees, In-State: $7,440
Tuition and Fees, Out-of-State: $18,330
note: reg. fees for lower division
Room & Board: $5,795
Payment Plan(s): installment plan

THE EXPERTS SAY…

" While these aren't the most well-rounded kids in the world, Michigan Tech students know that a little bit of nerdiness can lead to a great deal of professional success. "

" Great school, great price, great alumni network… But will city-dwelling students land more oh-so-crucial internships while you're out in the boonies with your nose stuck in a book? "

Graduates
Going to Graduate School:
30% Within One Year

Accepting Job Offer:
88% at time of graduation

Companies Recruiting On Campus:
278

Alumni Giving: 25%

MIDDLEBURY COLLEGE

The Emma Willard House, Middlebury, VT 05753-6002
Admissions Phone: (802) 443-3000 Fax: (802) 443-0256
Email: admissions@middlebury.edu Website: middlebury.edu/
Application Website: www.middlebury.edu/offices/admit/applying/apply-online.htm

General Info

Type of School: private, coed
Setting: small town
Academic Calendar: 4-1-4

Student Body

Full-Time Undergrads: 2,399
  Men: 47%, Women: 53%
Part-Time Undergrads: 25
  Men: 56%, Women: 44%

Total Undergrad Population:
  African American: 3%
  Asian American: 7%
  Latino: 5%
  Native American: 1%
  Caucasian: 69%
  International: 8%
  Out-of-State: 94%
  Living Off-Campus: 6%

Academics

Full-Time Faculty: 218
  With Ph.D.: 94%
Part-Time Faculty: 19
  With Ph.D.: 74%
Student/Faculty Ratio: 11:1
Most Popular Majors:
  economics (10%)
  psychology (9%)
  English (7%)
  political science (7%)
  environmental studies (5%)
Completing 2 or More Majors: 28%
Graduation Rates:
  82% within four years
  88% within six years

Admissions

Regular Application Deadline: 12/15
Early Decision Deadline(s): 11/15, 12/15
Fall Transfer Deadline: 3/1
Spring Transfer Deadline: 11/15
Total # of Students Applied: 5,468
  Admitted: 1,273
  Enrolled: 580
# of Students Waitlisted: 1,274
  Students Accepting Place: 665
Applied Early Decision: 767
  Early Decision Admitted: 264

Inside the Classroom

Middlebury College offers an excellent liberal arts education with a special focus on foreign languages and cultures. The general academic requirements are fairly extensive. Students must take at least one course in seven of the following eight categories: literature, the arts, religion or philosophy, history, sciences, deductive reasoning and analytical processes, social analysis and foreign language. Students must also take three courses in the areas of cultures and civilizations. All freshmen are required to take a First-Year Seminar—a thematic, discussion-oriented course with an intensive-writing component—chosen from a wide range of topics. This freshman seminar course is limited to 15 students, which creates a comfortable environment for discussion and provides the opportunity for focusing on a student's writing skills—something of great importance at Middlebury. The instructor is also a student's academic adviser until he or she chooses a major; through this program and its intimate setting, students and advisers are able to get to know each other fairly well. During an additional January term, more casual than the fall and spring semesters, students take more nontraditional courses (and also get to hang out and ski).

Students admitted to Middlebury College are very bright and motivated. Classes stay small, with a student-to-faculty ratio of roughly 11:1, and most professors encourage discussion over straight lecture. Most students report that they feel the faculty cares deeply about them, and none complain that professors didn't spend enough time with them. "However much you need, they give," reports one student. And when the warm weather does hit, many take the classes outside, "to soak up learning and sunshine in equal amounts." An Ohio guidance counselor describes Middlebury's faculty and the overall school setting as "great," and lists Middlebury among the schools with the best academic facilities.

Middlebury's foreign language programs—including Chinese, French, German, Italian, Japanese, Russian, and Spanish—are all considered superb, and most students study at least one language intensively, even if it's not required. More than half the students opt to study abroad in one of Middlebury's many overseas programs. In the summer, the school offers special immersion programs during which students eat, sleep, and breathe in a foreign language. There are also several interdisciplinary programs with an international bent, including international studies, international politics, and a unique Northern Studies program that combines study of the biological, human, and physical systems within the Northern Hemisphere.

Campus Environment

Because Middlebury has the unique feature of including room and board in the price of tuition, few students live off campus. Residence halls are grouped together to form one of five 'Commons,' each one of which is a cluster of dorms and, the school states, "a microcosm of Middlebury College as a whole." The five Commons are Atwater, Brainerd, Cook, Ross, and Wonnacott. Students of all year levels live together in the Commons, each of which is run by a team that includes a faculty head, a dean, a Commons coordinator, and two RA's. Each Commons also has its own activity fund and sponsors special events such as parties and local field trips.

Middlebury College is located in a rural and somewhat remote setting that experiences long, cold winters (sometimes described as "hellish"), and public transportation is limited. For these reasons, most students do have cars on campus, and parking can be congested. The school has been working toward improving the parking situation in recent years.

The town is quaint and charming in a quintessential New England kind of way, and its location in the heart of Vermont ski country makes it a heavenly choice for winter sports buffs. Middlebury has many inns and bed and breakfasts, as well as many interesting little shops. However, many students feel as though the town doesn't offer all that much for a college student to do. A car is required to get to the more happening Burlington, Vermont—which also happens to be where the nearest mall is located. Nonetheless, students typically describe the Middlebury campus as beautiful, the student body and townspeople as uncommonly friendly and helpful, and the campus food as outstanding.

Student Life

The winters are long and provide plenty of snowfall, but with several first-rate ski slopes nearby, students don't really seem to mind. Even if you're not a skier, there's skating, kayaking, swimming, and hiking. As far as school-sponsored athletics are concerned, about half of the student body participates, whether in club, intramural, or varsity sports. Not surprisingly, the varsity skiing and ice hockey teams at Middlebury are quite strong.

Most social activity at Middlebury happens on campus. The college also offers students clubs and organizations for exploring every interest. There are academic and cultural groups, club sports and outdoor activities, community service, media and publications, special interest/social awareness groups, spiritual and religious groups, and visual and performing arts groups.

The Winter Carnival is one of Middlebury's most popular social events. The Carnival transforms the school into a winter wonderland where students play in the snow, hold ice sculpture contests, ice skate, ski, and attend a formal dance. The Winter Carnival even features its own "night club" featuring student performances and a late-night dance party.

Students at Middlebury are culturally diverse, with an international student contingent that hails from 70 foreign countries. With that diversity comes a range of political views, from the conservative yacht-club crowd to the "raging liberals." But some students also claim the student body can be pretty homogeneous overall, describing the typical "MiddKid" as an upper-class, J.Crew–wearing skier with an expensive car. Nonetheless, despite students' differences, the atmosphere on campus remains relaxed and quite friendly.

Other schools to check out: Dartmouth, Williams, Bowdoin, Brown, Skidmore.

Test Scores (middle 50%):
SAT Verbal: 690–750
SAT Math: 680–740
ACT Comp: 28–32

HS Rank of Entering Freshmen:
Top 10%: 77%
Top 25%: 96%
Top 50%: 99%

THE EXPERTS SAY...

" For command of a foreign language, students couldn't do better than Middlebury's superb immersion, study abroad, and international studies programs. "

" If you don't ski, the cold Middlebury winters confine you to campus with a bunch of diverse-but-we-all-wear-designer-casual 'MiddKids.' "

Costs (2003–04)

Comprehensive Fees: $38,100

Payment Plan(s): installment plan, pre-payment plan

Inst. Aid (est. 2003–04)

Institutional Aid, Need-Based: $19,597,954

FT Undergrads Receiving Aid: 40%
Avg. Amount per Student: $25,899

Of Those Receiving Any Aid:

Rec. Need-Based Scholarship or Grant Aid: 100%
Average Award: $22,160

Rec. Need-Based Self-Help Aid: 91%
Average Award: $4,123

Financial Aid Deadline: 12/31, 11/15 (priority)

Graduates

Companies Recruiting On-Campus: 70

MILLS COLLEGE

5000 MacArthur Boulevard, Oakland, CA 94605
Admissions Phone: (510) 430-2135; (800) 87-MILLS Fax: (510) 430-3314
Email: admission@mills.edu
Website: mills.edu

Note: Info. not verified by school

General Info

Type of School: private, all women

Setting: urban

Academic Calendar: semester

Student Body

Full-Time Undergrads: 691
  Women: 100%

Total Undergrad Population:
  African American: 8%
  Asian American: 7%
  Latino: 8%
  Native American: 1%
  Caucasian: 56%
  International: 1%
  Out-of-State: 23%
  Living Off-Campus: 45%

Academics

Full-Time Faculty: 88
  With Ph.D.: 89%

Part-Time Faculty: 66

Most Popular Majors:
  English
  psychology
  media studies
  biology
  political, legal, and economic
    analysis

Freshmen Retention Rate: 78%

Graduation Rates:
  51% within four years
  56% within six years

Admissions

Regular Application Deadline: 8/1

Early Action Deadline: 11/15

Fall Transfer Deadline: 3/2 (priority)

Spring Transfer Deadline: 11/1 (priority)

Total # of Students Applied: 459
  Admitted: 344
  Enrolled: 123

Test Scores (middle 50%):
  SAT Verbal: 540–660
  SAT Math: 520–600
  ACT Comp: 22–27

HS Rank of Entering Freshmen:
  Top 10%: 43%
  Top 25%: 70%
  Top 50%: 99%

Inside the Classroom

Originally a seminary for young girls, Mills today offers women a wide liberal arts education within a small, strong community. "Collaborative" and "supportive" describe the environment here—not only between professors and students, but also among the students themselves. As one recent grad explains, "Mills women, in most cases, will do anything to help out other Mills women, and I've found this to be even more true once they've become alums." After a highly public decision in 1990 not to make the school coed, the school continues today with 700 undergraduate women (and an additional 400 men and women in coed graduate programs). Small classes are the norm, and professors are highly accessible. One guidance counselor cites the "sorority" environment and the strong interaction with faculty as contributing to the "very supportive atmosphere for motivated women, with lots of opportunities for leadership."

The bachelor of arts program at Mills is diverse. Students can major in the basic areas of liberal arts, and although the administration recently eliminated the communications major and many theater department offerings, it did introduce new programs in public policy and environmental science. On the preprofessional track, the school offers programs in premedicine, prelaw, and education. For business, the 4+1 B.A./M.B.A. program leverages the school's economics major into a graduate business degree with only one additional year of study, making it one of the few women's colleges to offer an M.B.A. degree. Mills also offers an outstanding 3/2 program in engineering with the University of Southern California. The school is especially noted for its education program, though many of those courses are at the graduate level. For those wanting to go the nontraditional route, the College Major allows students to integrate various curriculums, whether it's natural language communication and computers or dance in relation to anthropology. One guidance counselor recommends Mills as a great value, when weighing cost versus quality of education.

If there are any real complaints on the part of Mills students, they center around larger institutional decisions: "Often, the students don't feel listened to," notes one German Studies grad. For one, favored teachers aren't always offered tenure. For another, the recent extension in the number of class days per semester now means that some finals will be held on Saturday. But students do appreciate their many academic options: If a course isn't offered at Mills, students (with the exception of freshmen) can take it at area colleges—"one good way to meet guys," as the Mills website points out. If someone is itching to get out of California, she can spend junior year at Howard University, Mount Holyoke, or Swarthmore. And of course, studying overseas in virtually any region of the world is an option through the school's exchange programs.

Campus Environment

The Mills campus looks like a beautiful eucalyptus-tree-lined park. Everything is located within easy walking distance. Students love hanging out on campus: It's calm, cool, and small. However, certain areas off-campus aren't as nice: "As a big city, Oakland has its crime and there are a few shady places near campus, but they're really not that bad as long as common sense is practiced," explains one recent grad. Only a

30-minute bus ride away from downtown, weekends out are a given for Mills students, frequently at nearby UC Berkeley. In fact, so many students go there that there's a daily shuttle bus between the two campuses.

With regard to residential life, the good news is that housing is guaranteed for all four years (with about 60 percent of all students living on campus). The really good news is that most of the dorm rooms are singles. The four Spanish-style residence halls, each with red-tiled roofs and courtyard fountains, also have several special-interest wings: for students over 23; for those interested in the French language and culture; and for those interested in "quiet living." Apart from the dorms, there's a small housing co-op, apartments, and small units for family housing.

Students rate highly the school's extensive—and unusual—array of resources. There's a sizeable rare book library; a contemporary "music innovation" center; a multimedia lab that integrates emerging technologies with traditional art media; video production facilities; Eucalyptus Press, a small book press and bindery; and a women's leadership institute. And the school's art museum has the largest permanent collection of any liberal arts college on the West Coast.

Student Life

Three things make the Mills student population unique: First, one-quarter of undergrads are over the age of 23 ("resuming students"). Second, almost one out of every two undergrads commutes from home. And third, many entering students are in fact transfer students. While these three groups are very involved in campus activities, this fact creates an atmosphere perhaps atypical of most undergraduate schools. We hear there's not much of a social scene on campus. When parties take place, they're generally pretty small and often with UC Berkeley students. And as many students move off-campus after freshman and sophomore years, the campus social life loses focus.

The mostly native Californian community at Mills tends to be left-leaning. As one recent grad noted, "This school is more liberal and less pretentious than others like it." Diversity is an important priority here: Almost 30 percent of the student body identifies itself as minority, and there's a significant lesbian/bisexual population. One senior says, "If you're gay or bi, you will love Mills." The school has just a small handful of international students.

Community service activities are popular here, particularly since the school's CARES Center provides over 200 local offerings. In sports, Mills is a Division III school, with varsity teams in volleyball, soccer, cross country, swimming, tennis and rowing, many of whom regularly raise thousands of dollars for breast cancer research. As the school website says, "Students who have never competed on a team before can transform into athletes at Mills. Mothers, women over traditional college age, and working women have found ways to balance their academics, personal obligations, and Mills athletics." Although the school has no phys ed requirement, the classes are so popular that over half the student body enrolls in a P.E. course each semester, including classes such as massage, personal defense for women, cardio-kickboxing, core strength, fencing, sailing, cardio-samba, yoga, water exercise, and women's wellness.

Avg. HS GPA: 3.6

Costs (2003–04)

Tuition and Fees: $24,441

Room & Board: $8,930

Payment Plan(s): installment plan

THE EXPERTS SAY...

" Mills women—students and alumnae—help each other to achieve. Gay women can find an empowering environment here. "

" Great for commuters, transfers, and older students. If you want a more traditional college experience (complete with a campus social life), look at Scripps instead. "

MILLSAPS COLLEGE

1701 North State Street, Jackson, MS 39210-0001
Admissions Phone: (800) 352-1050; (601) 974-1050 Fax: (601) 974-1059
Email: admissions@millsaps.edu
Website: www.go.millsaps.edu

General Info

Type of School: private, coed, United Methodist Church

Setting: suburban

Academic Calendar: semester

Student Body

Full-Time Undergrads: 1,083
  Men: 46%, Women: 54%

Part-Time Undergrads: 40
  Men: 35%, Women: 65%

Total Undergrad Population:
  African American: 10%
  Asian American: 4%
  Latino: 1%
  Native American: 1%
  Caucasian: 82%
  Out-of-State: 43%
  Living Off-Campus: 24%
  In Fraternities: 55%
  In Sororities: 56%

Graduate and First-Professional
  Students: 77

Academics

Full-Time Faculty: 93
  With Ph.D.: 95%

Part-Time Faculty: 4
  With Ph.D.: 50%

Student/Faculty Ratio: 13:1

Most Popular Majors:
  business administration (21%)
  biology (13%)
  psychology (12%)
  accounting (7%)
  political science (7%)

Completing 2 or More Majors: 10%

Freshmen Retention Rate: 83%

Graduation Rates:
  70% within four years
  78% within six years

Admissions

Regular Application Deadline: 6/1;
  2/1 (priority)

Early Action Deadline: 12/1

Transfer Deadline, Fall & Spring: rolling

Total # of Students Applied: 1,045
  Admitted: 880
  Enrolled: 260

Inside the Classroom

Millsaps is a small, Methodist-affiliated school in the deep South that offers a liberal arts curriculum melded with ethics and social conscience. Its preprofessional majors are the most respected, and its management school has a fine reputation for pre-business studies. Since the student body is very small, so are the class sizes—allowing faculty to deliver the kind of personalized attention larger schools can't. "The faculty are very concerned," notes a guidance counselor from Tennessee who then sums up Millsaps as "a very strong academic school." Another guidance counselor agrees: "Millsaps has the most intellectual campus in the state."

One interesting aspect of Millsaps academics is the Faith and Work Initiative, a program that allows students to explore work as a "vocation" that arises from a deep sense of personal meaning. Designed to instill qualities of socially responsible leadership, the program challenges students to align their vocational goals with those of the family, community, church, economic structures, and the world.

To complete the core curriculum, ten courses in a number of general categories are required: liberal studies; the ancient, premodern, modern, and contemporary world; social, behavioral, and natural science; mathematics; and computer studies. There is also a foreign language requirement and a special exit course where seniors reflect on and synthesize what they've learned.

A small but popular study abroad option offers students the chance to study languages in Costa Rica and France, and there are multi-country programs in Europe for students in prebusiness and arts and sciences programs. "Just being in Costa Rica forced me to use Spanish skills I didn't realize I had," says one student. "The weekend trips were incredible. Hopefully, I will be able to go back next summer as well." Another student agrees: "The undergraduate college years are the best time to travel in Europe, and nothing is better than studying culture through a program like this."

Campus Environment

Campus buildings are built around the Millsaps Bowl, an expansive, gently sloping lawn where intramural sports, multicultural festivals, homecoming activities, and the annual commencement are held. At the edge of the Bowl is the school's "potted oak," a large tree surrounded by a ring of brick and cement. The ring has outlived its original purpose, which was to protect the tree's roots from the weight of displaced soil while the student union was being constructed. According to the school's website, the odd-looking "pot," which is covered by a metal grating, has taken on entirely different, though unintentional, purposes: "Over the years, various objects and small animals have been dropped and trapped beneath the grating, including an angry and difficult-to-remove dog and a number of ducks." The tree is a popular meeting place for students, if not for the local critters.

All freshmen are required to live either on campus or at home with local family. The options for first-years include Franklin, Bacot, and Galloway Halls, which have traditional rooms designed for double occupancy. Upperclassmen can live in coed, suite-style apartments in New South and Sanderson Halls, or in one of Goodman Hall's apartments. Fraternity housing is also a perk for those who pledge.

A distinctive campus landmark is the Founder's Tower, a 122-foot structure built of brick and stone. Built to honor prominent Millsaps patrons, the tower is surfaced in copper and is an impressive sight from just about anywhere on campus. Another prominent building is the Ford Academic Complex, one of the largest buildings on campus. Housing the music, art, and political science departments, the building also contains a 450-seat recital hall for concerts, special guest performances, and the popular Millsaps Arts and Lecture Series. In addition to the recital hall, the complex offers private practice rooms for students interested in vocal or instrumental music.

Student Life

Named for Major Reuben Millsaps, a Civil War veteran whose fame stems more from his donations to the college than anything he did on the battlefield, the school has a student body roughly the size of an army regiment at 1,200. Small-group dynamics is what the Millsaps social life is all about, and perhaps the most important groups leading the charge are the fraternities and sororities. A clear majority of both men and women pledge, and the usual Greek mixture of community service and beer prevails—although the balance seems tilted toward volunteerism, since some organizations have won national awards for their efforts.

Millsaps is an NCAA Division III school where men can fight as Millsaps Majors in football, cross country, golf, baseball, soccer, tennis, and basketball. Women can also don the purple and white to play volleyball, softball, basketball, soccer, tennis, cross country. A recently built fitness center houses state-of-the-art equipment to help students keep in shape.

The city of Jackson is a pocket of culture and civility in a state otherwise known for the lowest literacy rate in the nation. The town does have some entertainment and food distractions for students—most colorfully, eateries like The Squirrel on the Pearl and The Grand Catfish Races—but most students stick close to campus for recreation.

Other schools to check out: Hendrix, Rhodes, University of the South, Washington and Lee, Birmingham-Southern.

Test Scores (middle 50%):
SAT Verbal: 540–640
SAT Math: 510–630
ACT Comp: 23–28
ACT English: 23–30
ACT Math: 21–27

HS Rank of Entering Freshmen:
Top 10%: 38%
Top 25%: 65%
Top 50%: 89%

Avg. HS GPA: 3.51

THE EXPERTS SAY...

" Millsaps makes sure that tomorrow's preprofessionals are well rounded and community-minded. "

" The Faith and Work Initiative is for those believing the 'Oprah' philosophy of 'discovering your destiny.' "

Costs (2004–5)

Tuition and Fees: $19,518

Room & Board: $7,206

Payment Plan(s): installment plan, deferred payment plan

Inst. Aid (est. 2003–04)

Institutional Aid, Need-Based: $5,823,797

Institutional Aid, Non-Need-Based: $4,217,181

FT Undergrads Receiving Aid: 56% Avg. Amount per Student: $16,463

FT Undergrads Receiving Non-Need-Based Scholarship or Grant Aid: 39% Avg. Amount per Student: $11,659

Of Those Receiving Any Aid:

Rec. Need-Based Scholarship or Grant Aid: 100% Average Award: $12,512

Rec. Need-Based Self-Help Aid: 80% Average Award: $4,124

Upon Graduation, Avg. Loan Debt per Student: $15,942

Financial Aid Deadline: rolling, 3/1 (priority)

Graduates

Going to Graduate School: 34% Within One Year

Accepting Job Offer: 23% at time of graduation

Companies Recruiting On Campus: 12

Alumni Giving: 39%

MOREHOUSE COLLEGE

830 Westview Drive S.W., Atlanta, GA 30314-3773
Admissions Phone: (404) 215-2632; (800) 851-1254 Fax: (404) 524-5635
Email: admissions@morehouse.edu
Website: www.morehouse.edu

General Info

Type of School: private, all men

Setting: urban

Academic Calendar: semester

Student Body

Full-Time Undergrads: 2,716
　Men: 100%

Part-Time Undergrads: 143
　Men: 100%

Total Undergrad Population:
　African American: 93%
　Latino: <1%
　Native American: <1%
　Caucasian: <1%
　International: 4%
　Out-of-State: 73%
　Living Off-Campus: 44%
　In Fraternities: 7%
　In Sororities: 0%

Academics

Full-Time Faculty: 159
　With Ph.D.: 81%

Part-Time Faculty: 66

Student/Faculty Ratio: 15:1

Most Popular Majors:
　business administration (28%)
　engineering (10%)
　biology (10%)
　computer science (9%)
　political science (7%)

Freshmen Retention Rate: 86%

Graduation Rates:
　38% within four years
　56% within six years

Admissions

Regular Application Deadline: 2/15

Early Decision Deadline(s): 10/15

Fall Transfer Deadline: 2/15

Spring Transfer Deadline: 10/15

Total # of Students Applied: 2,225
　Admitted: 1,606
　Enrolled: 753

Test Scores (middle 50%):
　SAT Verbal: 470–580
　SAT Math: 470–590
　ACT Comp: 19–24

Inside the Classroom

Morehouse College is the nation's only historically black, private liberal arts college for men only. Founded in 1867, the college enrolls approximately 3,000 undergrads and confers bachelor's degrees on more black men than any other institution in the world. "They give a lot of individualized instruction," says a DC guidance counselor, adding that because of the school's reputation and strong alumni network, graduates usually get numerous job offers. Prominent alumni include Dr. Martin Luther King Jr., filmmaker Spike Lee, Maynard H. Jackson (the first African American mayor of Atlanta), and Nima A. Warfield, the first African American Rhodes Scholar from a historically black college or university. One student informs us, "It is normal to see celebrities walking around campus to speak to classes."

Morehouse has three academic divisions: Business and Economics; Humanities and Social Sciences; and Science and Mathematics. Preprofessional majors (business, engineering, and premed) are particularly popular, and a high percentage of students go on to graduate or professional schools. An Indiana guidance counselor praises the school's "wide curriculum," and the high quality of the business and education programs.

Comprehensive core requirements can take up the first two years of study. In addition to several courses in the sciences and humanities, students also study African and African American heritage and culture. According to the college's mission statement, "Morehouse assumes a special responsibility for teaching students about the history and culture of black people." Students can also take courses from other colleges that are part of the Atlanta University Center, including the all-female Spelman College, located across the street. Morehouse sponsors numerous exchange programs with other schools, and has a dual-degree program in engineering with Georgia Tech. Each year, several outstanding incoming freshmen are welcomed into the Project SPACE scholarship program, wherein they may participate in a paid summer internship at a NASA center.

Students have good things to say about Morehouse's "dedicated" faculty. One student notes that many of his professors are Morehouse alums with "a deep sense of love and respect for the school." Says a recent grad, "In my classes at Morehouse, I felt like the faculty and staff genuinely cared about my progress as a student and as a man. Oftentimes you will find yourself in your professor's office hours talking about everything from your family, to what you will be doing on the weekend, to the calculus problem that you just can't seem to figure out."

Campus Environment

The 61-acre campus is located in an urban area three miles southwest of downtown Atlanta. Freshmen are required to live on campus. Campus housing accommodates more than half the students, though one freshman tells us that the dorms are "small and lack variety," and that he looks forward to moving into Atlanta. The Office of Student Services hosts an annual housing fair to assist other students in securing off-campus housing.

Elsewhere on campus, the Robert W. Woodruff Library, shared by all schools in the Atlanta University Center, is ranked as one of the best libraries in the South. Overall, though, we heard complaints about the Morehouse facilities in general. The school has recently launched its most ambitious fund-raising campaign to counteract this problem, with a goal of $105 million by 2006. (It has already raised $70 million the last few years, including recent boosts in the form of a $3 million grant from the Coca-Cola Company and a promise of $5 million from Oprah Winfrey.) The money will help the school offer more scholarships, upgrade campus facilities, and more successfully compete with top colleges.

"The campus is somewhat safe but the surrounding neighborhood is very unsafe," one student tells us, although he—and most Morehouse men—agree that Atlanta is a *great* place to go to school. The city, just five minutes away, is chock-full of student-friendly things to do. And although "a car is helpful, it is not needed," we hear. (Freshmen who live on campus may not have cars.) Atlanta has a good public transportation system that many students take advantage of.

Student Life

The atmosphere at Morehouse is supportive; one man notes that students generally "want each other to succeed." There is a "unique bond between students," which helps them create a "surrogate family." In addition, students speak of the "mystique" and "sense of pride each student has in becoming a Morehouse Man." "The mindset here is greater than anywhere else," agrees one student. Although it's a friendly environment, one student we spoke to warns of "snobbish" students who make sure they're in "the latest hip-hop fashions." In late 2002, the campus erupted in controversy after one student was beaten by another in an alleged hate crime. The administration has since worked toward better dealing with diversity and tolerance.

The on-campus atmosphere is "livening back up" after being "pretty dead" for a couple of years, a student tells us. "The University Center has lots of activities." Fraternities aren't overwhelmingly popular, but Greeks do have a presence on campus, and often co-host parties with sororities at Spelman College. "Athletic events are always a big thing," a student tells us, although, according to another student we spoke to, "intramural sports are not very popular." Varsity teams compete in basketball, tennis, cross-country, track and field, and football. We hear that, regardless of how the football team performs, the Morehouse College House of Funk Marching Band is a real crowd-pleaser. Actually, fans of the performing arts will feel at home at Morehouse, with its renowned Glee Club and College Jazz Ensemble, which has been called one of the finest such ensembles in the country.

There are "not many parties on campus," and the campus—which is officially "dry"—certainly doesn't get as crazy as at some other schools. "We don't have the 'running nude' things here," laughs one student. "Not that much goes on here that is bizarre or quirky." Instead, students largely depend on downtown Atlanta ("a great city") for an active social life. "Being in Atlanta, there are many things to do," says one student. "We usually go off-campus, whether it's cultural or purely for entertainment. There is always someone coming through to give concerts."

Other schools to check out: Xavier, Howard, Fisk, Hampton, Tuskegee.

HS Rank of Entering Freshmen:
Top 10%: 22%
Top 25%: 45%
Top 50%: 82%
Avg. HS GPA: 3.14

Costs (2003–04)
Tuition and Fees: $14,310
Room & Board: $8,418

Inst. Aid (2002–03)
Institutional Aid, Non-Need-Based: $7,185,505
FT Undergrads Receiving Aid: 93%
Avg. Amount per Student: $10,950
FT Undergrads Receiving Non-Need-Based Scholarship or Grant Aid: 35%
Avg. Amount per Student: $11,120

THE EXPERTS SAY...

" 'The House' has graduated alumni like Martin Luther King and Spike Lee, so its powerful alumni network opens a lot of doors for recent grads. "

" The students are so busy being 'Morehouse Men' that they can't let themselves go and have a good, silly college time. "

Of Those Receiving Any Aid:
Rec. Need-Based Scholarship or Grant Aid: 32%
Average Award: $3,960
Rec. Need-Based Self-Help Aid: 57%
Average Award: $2,908
Upon Graduation, Avg. Loan Debt per Student: $18,000
Financial Aid Deadline: 4/1

MOUNT HOLYOKE COLLEGE

50 College Street, South Hadley, MA 01075-1488
Admissions Phone: (413) 538-2023 Fax: (413) 538-2409
Email: admission@mtholyoke.edu Website: www.mtholyoke.edu
Application Website: www.mtholyoke.edu/adm/center/applications.shtml

General Info

Type of School: private, all women

Setting: small town

Academic Calendar: semester

Student Body

Full-Time Undergrads: 2,066
  Women: 100%

Part-Time Undergrads: 31
  Women: 100%

Total Undergrad Population:
  African American: 4%
  Asian American: 10%
  Latino: 4%
  Native American: 1%
  Caucasian: 56%
  International: 15%
  Out-of-State: 64%
  Living Off-Campus: 5%

Graduate and First-Professional
  Students: 4

Academics

Full-Time Faculty: 211
  With Ph.D.: 96%

Part-Time Faculty: 43
  With Ph.D.: 51%

Student/Faculty Ratio: 10:1

Most Popular Majors:
  psychology (10%)
  English (9%)
  economics (7%)
  biological sciences (7%)
  international relations (6%)

Completing 2 or More Majors: 20%

Freshmen Retention Rate: 92%

Graduation Rates:
  72% within four years
  79% within six years

Admissions

Regular Application Deadline: 1/15

Early Decision Deadline(s): 11/15,
  1/1

Fall Transfer Deadline: 5/15, 2/15
  (priority)

Spring Transfer Deadline: 11/1

Total # of Students Applied: 2,845
  Admitted: 1,477
  Enrolled: 518

Inside the Classroom

As the first of the original Seven Sisters, Mount Holyoke has a long history of providing a superior liberal arts education. But this historic school is also a key player in the changing future of higher education: MHC's recent decision to adopt an experimental SAT-optional policy helped fuel an ongoing national debate over the college admissions process. The Class of 2005 was the first class admitted since the institution of the policy. "Our SAT-optional policy has been enthusiastically received by students and guidance counselors, and the College has taken a leadership role in the testing debate," says MHC's vice president for enrollment and college relations. "We will be carefully tracking the results over the next five years and hope to contribute substantively to the national discussion."

Students may choose from among 44 departmental and interdisciplinary majors, or they may design their own major. While many of its liberal arts and social sciences programs—particularly politics and international relations—are strong, MHC has a long tradition of strength in the natural sciences and mathematics. Each year, between one-quarter and one-third of students major in the sciences or math, and a large number of MHC students go on to receive medical degrees or doctorates in biology and chemistry. Prominent alumnae in other fields include poet Emily Dickinson, playwright Wendy Wasserstein, and Secretary of Labor Elaine Chao.

MHC's membership in the Five College Consortium—with nearby Smith, Amherst, Hampshire, and UMass Amherst—further expands the academic and social opportunities. As one student tells us, "We have access to libraries, classes, parties, and can audition at other schools. I go to a small school without the limitations of a small school."

Distribution requirements include courses in the seven different areas of the three basic divisions of humanities, social sciences, and science and mathematics. Students are also required to take a course in multicultural perspectives and fulfill foreign language and phys ed credits.

"There's a really high workload, and the professors have really high expectations of us," one student remarks. "But we get exposed to so much." While MHC's self-motivated students are very driven to succeed, this isn't a competitive, every-woman-for-herself environment. Fortunately, the attention students receive from their professors helps cut the pressure and anxiety. With a student/faculty ratio of only 10:1, professors frequently meet with students at length outside of class to give advice, talk at greater length about issues from class, or just chat.

MHC boasts several unique study options. The Speaking, Arguing, and Writing program, offered through MHC's Weissman Center for Leadership, aims to advance students' abilities to communicate effectively. January Term ("J-Term") allows students to take intensive courses with or without academic credit, devise projects of their own, or engage in a short internship. Community-based learning allows students to provide service through course projects co-designed by faculty and community partners. Study abroad and college exchanges are very popular, with 20–25 percent of students studying off-campus during their junior year. MHC is also known for its extensive internship program, offering a strong network of internship opportunities around the world.

Campus Environment

Mount Holyoke's quintessential New England campus mixes the best of old and new, with ivy-covered brick buildings standing alongside more modern facilities. "The campus is gorgeous," one student raves. "We've got ponds, trees, and everything is spread out. Everything is really well maintained."

The 17 dormitories, some older and some modern, mix all four classes and provide a small social unit in which close friendships form easily. First-year students are typically housed in doubles. In instances of overcrowding, the College uses "swing rooms"—rooms that are large enough to "swing" from a single to a double, or a double to a triple. Housing is guaranteed for all four years, and although upperclass students can apply to live off-campus, very few actually do.

Student parking decals are available on a first-come, first-served basis, with seniors having the largest allotment and first-year students having the smallest. Most students take advantage of the free Five-College bus system, which transports students among the five campuses and to local cities and towns including Amherst and Northampton. Additionally, the campus public safety office offers a RIDE van for point-to-point on-campus transportation and provides trips to local malls and shopping centers on a regular schedule.

Recent major renovations include the expansion of the Pratt Music Hall and the College Museum and Art Buiding. Construction of a new state-of-the-art Unified Science Complex is underway. And on September 13, 2001, MHC opened a new kosher/halal dining hall—one of a handful of its kind on American college campuses—"where observant Jews and observant Muslims can break bread."

Student Life

The liberal student population at Mount Holyoke is accepting of all cultures and lifestyles. "Diversity" is not just a buzzword here. In fact, MHC has the largest percentage of international students enrolled of all the national liberal arts colleges. Accordingly, a school official tells us that of the 100+ student organizations on campus, "the Association of Pan African Unity, Mount Holyoke African & Caribbean Student Association (MHACASA) and the Asian Students Association have the largest participation." (Interestingly, in spite of the diversity, a California guidance counselor tells us that MHC "still has a finishing-school image by some people.")

"Lots of students complain about the social life," one student reports. "There's this feeling that because there are no men, there's nothing to do. That's not true! If you take the initiative, rather than just sitting around complaining, you can have fun." The Five College Consortium opens up some interesting options: Nearly every first-year student at MHC will go to some big UMass party or to The Amherst Party (TAP) at Amherst College.

School traditions range from stately to homey: There's Mountain Day—"a highly anticipated day off from classes, announced without warning by the ringing of the Mary Lyon Hall bells sometime during the fall semester," a college official describes. MHC's Laurel Parade features graduating seniors carrying a laurel chain, with alumnae welcoming the grads into their ranks. And one student's favorite ritual: "M and Cs, when every night at 9:30 on the dot, a food cart is brought out with milk and cookies. This is where the old cliché of the 'freshman fifteen' originates!"

MUHLENBERG COLLEGE

2400 Chew Street, Allentown, PA 18104-5586
Admissions Phone: (484) 664-3200 Fax: (484) 664-3234
Email: admissions@muhlenberg.edu
Website: muhlenberg.edu

General Info

Type of School: private, coed, Lutheran

Setting: suburban

Academic Calendar: semester

Student Body

Full-Time Undergrads: 2,280
  Men: 42%, Women: 58%

Part-Time Undergrads: 135
  Men: 39%, Women: 61%

Total Undergrad Population:
  African American: 2%
  Asian American: 2%
  Latino: 3%
  Native American: <1%
  Caucasian: 91%
  International: <1%
  Out-of-State: 63%
  Living Off-Campus: 12%
  In Fraternities: 20%
  In Sororities: 21%

Academics

Full-Time Faculty: 157
  With Ph.D.: 87%

Part-Time Faculty: 116

Student/Faculty Ratio: 12:1

Most Popular Majors:
  business administration (14%)
  psychology (11%)
  communications (9%)
  biology (7%)
  English (7%)

Completing 2 or More Majors: 28%

Freshmen Retention Rate: 92%

Graduation Rates:
  72% within four years
  78% within six years

Admissions

Regular Application Deadline: 2/15

Early Decision Deadline(s): 1/15

Fall Transfer Deadline: 6/1

Spring Transfer Deadline: 12/1

Total # of Students Applied: 4,111
  Admitted: 1,743
  Enrolled: 589

# of Students Waitlisted: 1,000
  Students Accepting Place: 568
  Waitlisted Students Admitted: 7

Inside the Classroom

Students at Muhlenberg College tell us they feel their school truly cares. Each year, for example, incoming freshmen attend a ceremony where they write down what they hope their college years will bring; the night before graduation, the papers are returned to students to see if their expectations were met. We hear it's "quite emotional." But Muhlenberg spends as much time on the intellectual side of things: Its premed programs enjoy an excellent reputation, and an impressive percentage of 'Berg alumni go on to medical or dental school (law school, too). "Student success is high," one high school guidance counselor agrees. Another counselor lauds Muhlenberg's "great musical theater and poli sci" programs. Its education, psychology, English (especially writing), entrepreneurial studies, and biology departments are particularly strong as well, and the college has seen a surge in the popularity of its business and accounting majors in recent years.

One of Muhlenberg's strengths lies in its rigorous general education (it's a "true liberal arts setting," a guidance counselor tells us). The very broad—and very demanding—core curriculum is broken down into "skills" (writing, speaking, reasoning, and foreign language) and "perspectives," which are designated courses in the areas of Literature and the Arts, Meaning and Value, Human Behavior and Social Institutions, Historical Studies, Physical and Life Sciences, and Cultural Diversity. Freshmen must take a First-Year Seminar, a small, discussion-oriented course focused on thinking, writing, and speaking skills. A Muhlenberg education generally follows this formula: one-third core courses, one-third major courses, and one-third elective courses.

The school's small size makes the campus feel like one big family. Many classes are taught seminar-style, and the student/faculty ratio is "ideal," as one art major puts it. Students give their professors high marks, saying they're accessible, friendly, and generally excited about the subjects they teach. But professors don't mess around, as one student reports: "There is a really strict attendance policy for classes. If you miss more than three, your grade will be docked an entire letter."

But don't let the small size fool you: Students here enjoy opportunities of schools twice as large. Along with five nearby liberal arts colleges, Muhlenberg is part of the Lehigh Valley Association of Independent Colleges (LVAIC). LVAIC significantly expands opportunities for students through faculty exchanges, cross-registration, summer sessions (locally and overseas), and cultural programs. Muhlenberg students can also take advantage of cooperative arrangements with various universities around the country.

Campus Environment

Muhlenberg's campus is on about 80 acres in the residential west end of Allentown. The school also maintains a 40-acre arboretum and a 38-acre environmental field station/wildlife sanctuary. Students describe their school as beautiful and serene, with a nice mix of Gothic and modern buildings. Allentown doesn't fare as well in student opinion—we hear it's rather "blah" (listen to the Billy Joel song "Allentown" for a fairly depressing description). Muhlenberg officials like to say that Allentown has been affectionately dubbed "The Little Apple," with its theater, museum, symphony, parks, farmer's market, and various shopping and dining options—but many students would beg to differ. One senior we spoke to dismissed the surrounding area as "mundane" and "pathetic." Freshmen are not permitted to have cars on campus; there's a small fee for upperclass parking permits. The school runs a Thursday–Sunday shuttle system between the campus and downtown venues.

Student living options include traditional residence halls, special interest and Greek housing, the MILE (Muhlenberg Independent Living Experiment) program, and an apartment complex. All freshmen must live on campus; most are assigned to one of three coed dorms (since there is deferred rush, there are no freshmen in the Greek system). One student we spoke to called the on-campus facilities "beautiful" and "comfortable," but noted, "off-campus housing is really ideal."

Student Life

The 'Berg is anything but diverse. Most students are white, well-off, and conservative—the place often looks like a page from the J. Crew catalog. "This is not the school for wearing pajamas to class," one student laughs. But students are reportedly very friendly, and it's a pretty close-knit, laid-back community. The intimacy can be both good and bad, as one student puts it: "Gossip is abundant, but with the small campus size I can go anywhere and be sure to see friends." We also heard complaints about the many cliques on campus. Lending credence to this opinion is the huge Greek population: approximately 20 percent of eligible students join a fraternity or sorority, and much of Muhlenberg life outside of the classroom revolves around these groups. Students who choose not to go Greek may have a tough time, we hear.

With not much going on in town, most students stick to campus for their fun. And for the most part, "fun" means "drinking." Fraternity parties are weekend staples (with weekends usually starting on Wednesday or Thursday nights), though the frenzied drinking that used to go on has changed in recent years. The school is "encouraging" Greeks to go dry, and although none has yet to take that initiative, frats are under the tight scrutiny of the administration. Kegs are banned, parties are smaller, and more functions are "closed" to non-Greeks. One student goes so far as to say that the school "is trying to get rid of its Greek life." Indeed, more and more parties are being broken up by campus security, and students have staged rallies and protests to express their disapproval of social life. The major gripe is that the school doesn't offer enough entertainment alternatives to drinking.

That said, there are more than 100 student clubs and organizations on campus; popular ones include community service, religious, and environmental groups. The Muhlenberg Activities Council (MAC) plans campus-wide activities, such as movies, dances, comedians, and talent shows. There is a thriving "campus culture" scene, with regular plays, concerts, art exhibitions, and ethnic festivals. The regionally acclaimed Summer Music Theater stages, among other things, original productions of Broadway musicals. Sports-wise, Muhlenberg has 22 Division III varsity teams (the Mules) that compete in the Centennial Conference. Nearly three-quarters of all students play a rec or IM sport, but one student tells us, "Sporting events are poorly attended."

Other schools to check out: Franklin & Marshall, Gettysburg, Lafayette, Skidmore, Bates.

\# Applied Early Decision: 448
Early Decision Admitted: 296

Test Scores (middle 50%):
SAT Verbal: 550–650
SAT Math: 560–660

HS Rank of Entering Freshmen:
Top 10%: 39%
Top 25%: 75%

THE EXPERTS SAY...

" East Coast guidance counselors say that Muhlenberg has changed for the better in recent years, with higher admissions standards and a stronger advising program. "

" While students at some schools hold rallies to protest the war or unfair labor practices, students at Muhlenberg hold rallies in support of their right to have a good time. "

Top 50%: 97%
Avg. HS GPA: 3.45

Costs (2003–04)

Tuition and Fees: $24,945
Room & Board: $6,540
Payment Plan(s): installment plan

Inst. Aid (est. 2003–04)

Institutional Aid, Need-Based:
$11,636,268

Institutional Aid, Non-Need-Based:
$4,485,304

FT Undergrads Receiving Aid: 43%
Avg. Amount per Student: $16,847

FT Undergrads Receiving Non-Need-Based Scholarship or Grant Aid: 16%
Avg. Amount per Student: $9,718

Of Those Receiving Any Aid:

Rec. Need-Based Scholarship or Grant Aid: 97%
Average Award: $13,931

Rec. Need-Based Self-Help Aid: 70%
Average Award: $4,760

Upon Graduation, Avg. Loan Debt per Student: $16,642

Financial Aid Deadline: 2/15

Graduates

Going to Graduate School:
29% Within One Year

Companies Recruiting On Campus: 40

Alumni Giving: 46%

NEW COLLEGE OF FLORIDA

5700 North Tamiami Trail, Sarasota, FL 34243-2197
Admissions Phone: (941) 359-4269 Fax: (941) 359-4435
Email: admissions@ncf.edu Website: www.ncf.edu
Application Website: www.ncf.edu/admissions

General Info

Type of School: public, coed
Setting: suburban
Academic Calendar: 4-1-4

Student Body

Full-Time Undergrads: 671
  Men: 39%, Women: 61%

Total Undergrad Population:
  African American: 2%
  Asian American: 3%
  Latino: 7%
  Native American: <1%
  Caucasian: 83%
  International: 2%
  Out-of-State: 23%
  Living Off-Campus: 30%

Academics

Full-Time Faculty: 62
  With Ph.D.: 100%

Part-Time Faculty: 10
  With Ph.D.: 60%

Student/Faculty Ratio: 11:1

Most Popular Majors:
  psychology (5%)
  humanities (3%)
  political science (3%)
  anthropology (3%)
  sociology (3%)

Completing 2 or More Majors: 8%

Freshmen Retention Rate: 75%

Graduation Rates:
  63% within four years
  74% within six years

Admissions

Regular Application Deadline: 5/1;
  2/1 (priority)

Fall Transfer Deadline: 5/1, 2/1
  (priority)

Spring Transfer Deadline: 12/31

Total # of Students Applied: 565
  Admitted: 343
  Enrolled: 157

# of Students Waitlisted: 24
  Students Accepting Place: 21
  Waitlisted Students Admitted: 15

Test Scores (middle 50%):
  SAT Verbal: 640–730
  SAT Math: 590–680

Inside the Classroom

These are exciting times for the New College of Florida. After decades of being a separate branch of the University of South Florida system, the college was formally set apart by the Florida state legislature in July 2001. This change of governance hasn't affected the college's identity, however: Now, as it has always been, the New College of Florida is a public, liberal arts honors college with a unique and unstructured curriculum.

Academics here are designed to promote depth of thinking and one-on-one interaction with faculty. They're also highly unorthodox. Each semester, students and their advisors custom-design an academic contract with their "goals and educational activities" in mind. Although there are more than 30 arts and sciences disciplines (plus various other individualized options), there are no majors per se; students receive a liberal arts B.A. with the concentration of their choosing. Grades aren't given, either—students are evaluated in detailed narratives written by professors. What's more, students must complete a thesis or project in their senior year, and pass an oral baccalaureate examination judged by three faculty members. Who can thrive in such a free environment? "Independent students who can take responsibility for their own education and are driven to learn, not driven by grades," a college official answers. As the school's educational philosophy plainly states: "Students' progress should be based on demonstrated competence and real mastery rather than on the accumulation of credits and grades."

Each semester is divided into two seven-week modules, with one week of recess between each module. There are both semester-long and seven-week-long courses, with professors choosing the format best suited to the subject matter. There's also a separate January Interterm in which students are expected to pursue independent study.

Because the curriculum is so unstructured, students need a great deal of self-motivation to succeed here. A third-year student warns that those who are "not ready to take control of their lives and take responsibility for their actions will probably not fit in or do well at New College." But the benefit of the setup is that students can follow their own curiosity and pursue it as far as they want. The combination of small classes (average: 18 students), tutorials, and extensive advising means students get to know professors personally. The profs even take the time to give "miniclasses," brief presentations of their course offerings for the coming semester, to allow students to sample various disciplines and ensure that students are as informed as possible about their educational options. "While academics at New College are taken very seriously," a student tells us, "it is a cooperative effort on the part of everyone involved." The overall atmosphere is supportive and friendly: "The only person to compete with here is oneself."

Campus Environment

New College's bayfront campus is located in the resort city of Sarasota, which, while "not a college town in the strictest sense," is noted for its theater, art, music, and beautiful public beaches. Nearby attractions include the Ringling Museum of Art and the Asolo Theater. Most students use bicycles to travel through town and get around the 140-acre campus. We hear the SCAT (Sarasota County Area Transit) shuts down around 8 P.M., "so it is easy to get stranded."

With such a small student body, the dorm selection may be underwhelming, but the few options available are interesting. Pei Hall, a modernist complex with three courtyards, was designed by and named for famous architect I. M. Pei. Goldstein. Dort Halls are less distinctive but more sought-after by students, with suite-style apartments. Freshmen are required to live on campus, but the college scatters their living quarters among the rest of the classes instead of herding them into a separate area. We hear that students who wish to move off-campus later may find it difficult to afford decent housing in ritzy Sarasota.

College Hall, the main classroom building, is the former home of circus magnate Charles Ringling, whose tastes are still evident. Its pink marble exterior, built-in theater organ, marble floors, teak-and-mahogany music room, and frescoes depicting Pompeii (before the eruption, thankfully) provide an atmosphere that's half academia, half nouveau riche. Though we've heard complaints about the library ("small"), the school boasts some impressive facilities, including the Heiser Natural Sciences Complex and the Pritzker Marine Biology Research Center.

Student Life

As might be expected, the word that best describes student life at New College is "informal." Just as they can determine their own academic programs, students also enjoy creating their own activities, sometimes on the spur of the moment. Clubs tend to drift in and out of existence according to current interest. Activities that may (or may not) greet incoming freshmen include a bike club, an experimental dance group, a literary magazine named *Backwards and Ugly*, and a spices-and-incense club whose stated goal, according to the school's website, is to "promote the sense of smell, the neglected sense." Participatory, rather than competitive, sports and recreation predominate; with students often initiating pickup games of soccer and ultimate Frisbee. A men's softball team called "The Bones" is headed by one of the professors, and teams also exist for mountain biking, women's soccer, sailing, and aikido.

No Greek organizations are permitted on campus, although parties do exist. "New College is by no means a dry campus," a student says. Big shindigs at Palm Court are a New College tradition, as is the annual semi-formal dance named the "Semi-Normal." You can also spy a student or two relaxing under a palm tree and enjoying the beautiful surroundings.

Characterizations of the student body vary. Certainly, students here tend to be creative, left-leaning, and open-minded. The school is very small, providing a sense of community that's comforting to some and claustrophobic to others. One student raves about it being a "large family," while another warns that the free-thinking, liberal attitudes on campus may frighten the prim and proper. Either way, the small numbers permit the student government to operate as a pure democracy: Topics of campus-wide interest are discussed in "town meetings" that can be called by any student. And with the school's newfound independence and a new president in place, there's a lot to talk about at New College.

Other schools to check out: Hampshire, Evergreen State College, Oberlin, St. Mary's College of Maryland, SUNY Geneseo.

NEW YORK UNIVERSITY

22 Washington Square North, New York, NY 10011-9108
Admissions Phone: (212) 998-4500 Fax: (212) 995-4902
Website: www.nyu.edu
Application Website: admissions.nyu.edu/appprocess/

General Info

Type of School: private, coed

Setting: urban

Academic Calendar: semester

Student Body

Full-Time Undergrads: 17,494
  Men: 40%, Women: 60%

Part-Time Undergrads: 1,635
  Men: 41%, Women: 59%

Total Undergrad Population:
  African American: 5%
  Asian American: 14%
  Latino: 7%
  Native American: <1%
  Caucasian: 42%
  International: 4%
  Out-of-State: 58%
  Living Off-Campus: 45%
  In Fraternities: 4%
  In Sororities: 2%

Graduate and First-Professional
  Students: 18,682

Academics

Full-Time Faculty: 1,899

Part-Time Faculty: 2,403

Student/Faculty Ratio: 12:1

Most Popular Majors:
  business (15%)
  individualized major (9%)
  drama/theater arts (8%)
  film/cinema studies (7%)
  communications (6%)

Completing 2 or More Majors: 18%

Freshmen Retention Rate: 92%

Graduation Rates:
  71% within four years
  78% within six years

Admissions

Regular Application Deadline: 1/15

Early Decision Deadline(s): 11/1

Fall Transfer Deadline: 4/1

Spring Transfer Deadline: 11/1

Total # of Students Applied: 33,776
  Admitted: 10,843
  Enrolled: 4,219

# of Students Waitlisted: 1,987
  Waitlisted Students Admitted: 275

Applied Early Decision: 3,256
  Early Decision Admitted: 1,571

Inside the Classroom

"The best of everything!" exclaims one counselor about NYU. Students love it "because of the big city, the arts classes offered, and all the other academics are appealing as well." "New York after 9/11 has gained more popularity and now [our students] are more aware of what they have to offer," reflected another. Plus, "admission requirements [are] going up," noted a New York guidance counselor. "They have become more competitive." NYU officials have announced that a dramatic increase in the number of applicants resulted in an acceptance rate drop of two percent in 2003, raising the overall quality of the incoming freshman class.

NYU has seven undergraduate schools. The Tisch School of the Arts is one of the nation's most renowned schools of theater, dance, television, and film, with alums like Spike Lee, Oliver Stone, and Martin Scorsese. The Stern Business School is known for its Wall Street internships and excellent career placement—and competition ("Stern students kill!," a finance major warned). The College of Arts and Sciences is the largest undergraduate school, with more than 50 programs. Students at the Gallatin School of Individualized Study create their own concentrations, and the School of Continuing and Professional Studies, aimed at older students, has a new Virtual College® distance learning degree. NYU also has schools of education and social work. About 650 students, including some rejected from NYU's other divisions, are admitted yearly to the new General Studies program; students who pass the two-year "great books" curriculum are guaranteed admission to one of the university's four-year divisions.

While there are enormous lecture courses taught by graduate assistants (now unionized), there are also smaller, mostly upper-division classes whose professors make themselves available to students. "Professors are extremely accessible; we often run into them at times we'd rather not see them!" a sophomore joked. "The professors, for the most part, are very compassionate and understanding," said a senior. "Professors are hired with work experience," noted one student. "I'm a journalism major—almost all my professors were reporters or still are reporters."

The great NYU bugbear is "bureaucracy, plain and simple," commented a journalism and international relations major. "Our new president, John Sexton, is a breath of fresh air, though. He's very interested in what students have to say, unlike our former president. It seems like things are looking up!"

Campus Environment

NYU lies in the heart of Greenwich Village, site of the city's funkier dance clubs, bars, cafes, and shops. There isn't a campus so much as an enclave of buildings located within a concentrated area. Students don't seem to mind: "The city is a major part of NYU," commented a students. "We can walk around the Village as an NYU student, or we can walk around SoHo, Chinatown, or Times Square as a New Yorker." Washington Square Park lies at NYU's center and acts somewhat like a university quad. On a sunny day, you'll find students in the park with street musicians and other assorted characters (though "you can't get drugs in Washington Square Park anymore—too many cops," a student lamented).

Due to recent additions and renovations, NYU is able to guarantee students housing for four years. "Housing is all over the city, from midtown to the South Street Seaport," reported a sophomore. "Most of the dorms are right around the main part of campus (Washington Square Park). As a rule, the farther from campus, the nicer the dorm. Most of the apartments are nicer than what 90 percent of people in NYC live in. Every room has its own bathroom, which is an unbelievable bonus." Some dorms have faculty in residence. Despite the sky-high rents, a number of students head off campus, but it can be "difficult to get back into the dorms" if you move to a non-NYU apartment, a junior warned. Campus security "borders on being annoying," commented a music education major. Still, "it's New York City," said a sophomore. "You have to be smart, careful, and assertive."

Student Life

"The coolest thing about NYU is that there is no typical student," said one student. "Individuality is big here, and it's totally acceptable to be yourself." "We have an extremely diverse campus," said another. "People of all persuasions are welcomed." Added a guidance counselor, "[NYU has] become more international, drawing students from all over the world." "No matter what the affiliation, we have a political group for them," remarked a journalism major, but one student complained: "Most NYU students are insanely left-wing and liberal." "NYU students love holding demonstrations," another admitted. However, "someone who doesn't feel comfortable in the city" might not fit in. "Not everyone was meant to go to NYU," cautioned a sophomore. "Visiting campus is essential before applying." When you do visit, just be sure you're dressed right: In May 2003, *Women's Wear Daily* honored NYU as the most fashionable college in the United States.

LGBT groups are very active on campus, as are preprofessional clubs and ethnic organizations. "Sports aren't that big, we don't even have a football team," said one student." The new Cole Sports Center has state-of-the-art equipment for those who want to play. "One interesting note," remarked a sophomore, "is how NYU will give 'academic' scholarships to athletes (because we're a Division III school and can't give athletic scholarships), which can't be taken away, even if someone quits the team." Greeks "barely register on the students' radars."

"No one parties on campus since we're in NYC," commented a junior. A business major added, "There are millions of places to go, whether on MacDougal Street to bars and clubs or Broadway shows, MTV, or even shopping, since stores in NYC are open until really late." A journalism student added, "Most students have no class on Fridays, so our weekends start Thursday night. What isn't there to do? Clubs, museums, restaurants, theater, sporting events, live music… There's so much to see and do here, it's hard to go to school full-time and fit it all in four years!"

Other schools to check out: Columbia, Boston U, George Washington U, USC, UCLA.

Test Scores (middle 50%):
SAT Verbal: 600–700
SAT Math: 610–710
ACT Comp: 27–32
HS Rank of Entering Freshmen:
Top 10%: 63%
Top 25%: 92%
Top 50%: 99%
Avg. HS GPA: 3.65

THE EXPERTS SAY...

" More than a school, NYU is a microcosm of the city it calls home. Despite 9/11—or even because of it—students are drawn here. "

" No campus, no football team, and an administration based on a maze—and this is the hottest and trendiest school in the nation! "

Costs (2003–04)

Tuition and Fees: $28,496

Room & Board: $10,910

Payment Plan(s): installment plan, deferred payment plan, pre-payment plan

Inst. Aid (est. 2003–04)

Institutional Aid, Need-Based: $79,273,712

Institutional Aid, Non-Need-Based: $14,147,406

FT Undergrads Receiving Aid: 56%
Avg. Amount per Student: $18,686

FT Undergrads Receiving Non-Need-Based Scholarship or Grant Aid: 12%
Avg. Amount per Student: $6,497

Of Those Receiving Any Aid:

Rec. Need-Based Scholarship or Grant Aid: 93%
Average Award: $12,371

Rec. Need-Based Self-Help Aid: 90%
Average Award: $7,791

Upon Graduation, Avg. Loan Debt per Student: $24,620

Financial Aid Deadline: 2/15

Graduates

Going to Graduate School:
18% Within One Year

Accepting Job Offer:
68% at time of graduation

Companies Recruiting On Campus:
600

Alumni Giving: 26%

NORTH CAROLINA SCHOOL OF THE ARTS

1533 South Main Street, Winston-Salem, NC 27127 Admissions Phone: (336) 770-3290; (336) 770-3291 Fax: (336) 770-3370 Email: admissions@ncarts.edu
Website: www.ncarts.edu Application Website: www.ncarts.edu/admissions/main.htm

Note: Info. not verified by school

General Info

Type of School: public, coed

Setting: urban

Academic Calendar: trimester

Student Body

Full-Time Undergrads: 723
  Men: 59%, Women: 41%

Part-Time Undergrads: 15
  Men: 73%, Women: 27%

Total Undergrad Population:
  African American: 10%
  Asian American: 3%
  Latino: 2%
  Caucasian: 84%
  International: 1%
  Out-of-State: 52%
  Living Off-Campus: 40%

Graduate and First-Professional
  Students: 79

Academics

Full-Time Faculty: 135

Part-Time Faculty: 4

Student/Faculty Ratio: 8:1

Most Popular Majors:
  filmmaking (34%)
  design and production (22%)
  music (18%)
  drama (15%)
  dance (12%)

Freshmen Retention Rate: 75%

Graduation Rates:
  40% within four years
  48% within six years

Admissions

Regular Application Deadline: 3/1

Total # of Students Applied: 744
  Admitted: 339
  Enrolled: 200

Test Scores (middle 50%):
  SAT Verbal: 540–640
  SAT Math: 500–620
  ACT Comp: 20–25
  ACT English: 20–27
  ACT Math: 18–25

HS Rank of Entering Freshmen:
  Top 10%: 16%
  Top 25%: 45%
  Top 50%: 78%

Avg. HS GPA: 3.5

Inside the Classroom

Established in 1963 as the first state-supported residential arts school in the United States, the North Carolina School of the Arts is today part of the University of North Carolina system and has grown to include five professional schools for dance, design and production, drama, filmmaking, and music. Its unique full-education structure provides schooling in the arts from middle school through graduate school: Degrees awarded include the high school diploma, the College Arts Diploma, the Professional Artist Certificate, and bachelors (bachelor of fine arts and bachelor of music) and masters degrees.

As might be expected of an arts school, all students must audition or interview for admission. Once accepted, students attend classes taught by professionals who have had successful careers in the arts—and it isn't unusual when classes are taught by guest teachers like filmmaker Spike Lee and actor Mandy Patinkin.

The curriculum at the School of Filmmaking emphasizes hands-on experience in film and digital video in preparation for the film and television industries. The cost of each student's final senior-year project is underwritten by the university, and completed films are screened in New York and Los Angeles so that graduating students have the opportunity to make contacts with people in the profession.

Students in the School of Dance concentrate in either ballet or contemporary dance; however, they study in both areas. Students have more than 40 performance opportunities a year, including fully mounted productions such as *The Nutcracker*.

NCSA's School of Design and Production is one of a handful of independent schools of theatrical design in the country, offering programs in costume design, costume technology, lighting design, scene design, scenic painting and properties, sound design, stage automation, stage management, technical direction, and wig and makeup design. Working in conjunction with the School of Drama, design students work on more than 25 shows each year on campus.

The School of Drama provides training in acting, voice and speech, movement, singing, period and style, stage combat, and other skills, as well as business practices in the profession. College students may be admitted to the directing option in their third and fourth years of study. The school sends its graduating college seniors to New York City each spring to present a showcase for casting agents and directors.

The School of Music offers concentrations in instrumental performance, vocal performance, composition, film and music composition, and conducting. Here the basis of instruction consists of studio work with the teacher, and many students tour throughout the state, the region, and—in the case of the International Music Program—other countries.

A Division of General Studies unites the five schools by providing a broad liberal-arts education to all students. Required coursework includes languages and literature, mathematics, the humanities, and the natural and social sciences, with each area tailored to the intellectual and cultural needs of the performing artist.

Campus Environment

The showcase venue at NCSA is the Stevens Center, a 1,380-seat performance hall located apart from the campus in Winston-Salem. Built as an attractive, neoclassical structure, the Center features performances in dance, orchestra and opera performances. Dramatic performances are held in a 380-seat proscenium theater. A 200-seat arena named the Performance Place offers some structural flexibility for different types of performances. Smaller shows and concerts are staged in more intimate venues like the Agnes deMille Theater, Crawford Hall, and Recital Hall. A new chamber music hall has been completed. For film students, most of the production, postproduction, and exhibition facilities and equipment are located in Studio Village, a complex built to resemble and function like a Hollywood studio back lot. Recent construction on campus includes a brand-new fitness center and the renovated student center.

NCSA is a residential community with separate housing for high school and college students. All full-time freshmen and sophomores must live on campus in one of the six small residence halls, each of which contains eight single rooms and four doubles for a total of 16–18 students. There is also an apartment complex where four students in each apartment have single bedrooms and share a living room, kitchen, and bathroom. Most halls are coed, containing a mix of students from different classes and artistic interests. Housing options are available according to a class-based priority system, so juniors and seniors—who need not live on campus if they prefer—have the first picks. The campus coffeehouse is named "The What?" and is located between Residence Halls A and B.

Student Life

The number of students at the North Carolina School for the Arts hovers around a thousand, making the party life decidedly small-scale and the circles of friends close and long-lasting. About 275 first-year students enroll each year, and are welcomed by student leaders among the other classes who help them move in. Welcoming activities include small-group discussions, social events, and tours.

"People who attend this school should be open minded and ready for new experiences," says one student. Students tend to hang out in small groups where, as at many arts schools, drug use is not uncommon. The student activities office provides other options by scheduling regular entertainment events like karaoke night, dances, and band performances, which are listed in a special Every Thursday Calendar distributed around campus. Popular school-wide events include Fall Fest in October, Froze Arts in January, and Beaux Arts in May. Theme parties like "Weekend in Vegas" and "Jamaican Me Crazy" are also a big hit with students.

Students can also join a number of clubs and organizations on campus; many, though not all, are centered around various aspects of the performing arts. Some popular organizations include NCSA Pride, Awareness of Black Artists (ABA), and the Student Government Association.

Short road trips into Winston-Salem are also available for everyone, with free weekly transportation. Shopping malls, movie theaters, non-school arts performances in town, and local museums are among the favorite destinations. Special off-campus programs sponsored by the student activities office include trips to cultural events, amusement parks, beaches, skiing sites, paintball, and late-night bowling.

Costs (2003–04)

Tuition and Fees, In-State: $3,665

Tuition and Fees, Out-of-State: $14,795

Room & Board: $5,530

THE EXPERTS SAY...

" The North Carolina School of the Arts is a real bargain, particularly for in-state students. "

" The environment can feel more like a boarding school than a college campus. If you feel you've grown beyond hanging out with high school kids, look elsewhere. "

Inst. Aid (2002–03)

Institutional Aid, Need-Based: $734,177

Institutional Aid, Non-Need-Based: $217,592

FT Undergrads Receiving Aid: 47%
Avg. Amount per Student: $8,499

FT Undergrads Receiving Non-Need-Based Scholarship or Grant Aid: 18%
Avg. Amount per Student: $2,216

Of Those Receiving Any Aid:

Rec. Need-Based Scholarship or Grant Aid: 93%
Average Award: $4,723

Rec. Need-Based Self-Help Aid: 91%
Average Award: $2,236

Upon Graduation, Avg. Loan Debt per Student: $15,566

Financial Aid Deadline: 3/1 (priority)

NORTH CAROLINA STATE UNIVERSITY

Box 7103, Raleigh, NC 27695
Admissions Phone: (919) 515-2434 Fax: (919) 515-5039
Email: undergrad_admissions@ncsu.edu Website: www.ncsu.edu/
Application Website: www.ncsu.edu/admissions.html

General Info

Type of School: public, coed

Setting: urban

Academic Calendar: semester

Student Body

Full-Time Undergrads: 18,653
  Men: 58%, Women: 42%

Part-Time Undergrads: 1,661
  Men: 63%, Women: 37%

Total Undergrad Population:
  African American: 10%
  Asian American: 5%
  Latino: 2%
  Native American: 1%
  Caucasian: 81%
  International: 1%
  Out-of-State: 8%
  Living Off-Campus: 68%
  In Fraternities: 10%
  In Sororities: 9%

Graduate and First-Professional
  Students: 6,883

Academics

Full-Time Faculty: 1,647
  With Ph.D.: 91%

Part-Time Faculty: 176
  With Ph.D.: 66%

Student/Faculty Ratio: 15:1

Most Popular Majors:
  business (9%)
  biology (6%)
  computer sciences (5%)
  computer engineering (4%)
  mechanical engineering (3%)

Completing 2 or More Majors: 16%

Freshmen Retention Rate: 90%

Graduation Rates:
  27% within four years
  63% within six years

Admissions

Regular Application Deadline: 2/1;
  11/1 (priority)

Early Action Deadline: 11/1

Fall Transfer Deadline: 4/1 (priority)

Spring Transfer Deadline: 11/1
  (priority)

Total # of Students Applied: 12,852
  Admitted: 7,947
  Enrolled: 3,851

Inside the Classroom

With bachelor's degrees available in 92 fields of study, chances are the average undergraduate can find any area of interest at North Carolina State. Colleges open to undergrads include those for agriculture and life sciences; design; education and psychology; engineering; natural resources; humanities and social sciences; management; physical and mathematical sciences; and textiles. The university is known best for its science, engineering, and technology programs, with most of its undergraduate colleges geared toward producing competent and well-rounded professionals in industry and agriculture. And, as one guidance counselor notes, "They constantly receive grants."

Some students in other disciplines gripe that the school focuses too much on engineering. Indeed, the College of Engineering—the fifth largest in the country—ranks among the top engineering schools, offering a whopping 17 bachelor of science degree options, including biological, chemical, aerospace, industrial, and environmental engineering. Students in the college also benefit tremendously from the facilities available at the Centennial Campus, which is described below.

As with any university of this size, large classes can make professor–student interaction difficult. Some professors go the extra mile to help individual students, while others, well, don't. "I had one physics professor that did not care about the students or want to assist," says one student. "She would simply refer students to the tutorial center run by grad school volunteers. However, there was another physics professor that would bend over backwards to help a student making an effort to learn." Students' opinions about teaching styles are as varied as their thoughts on workload. We hear it's possible to slip through the cracks and squeak by doing as little work as possible in some cases, especially in large Gen Ed lectures.

Fortunately for freshmen, the administration, not wanting anyone to get lost in the fray, offers a First Year College (FYC) option for anyone unsure of his major choice. All FYC students live in one of two adjacent dormitories, allowing for social support and a chance to find a niche while taking broad-based courses that can apply toward any major. The idea is to prevent the all-too-common problem of big-university students: wasting time and money on coursework that becomes irrelevant after a change of major. "[FYC] made me appreciate that I wasn't getting a cookie-cutter education," says one junior who is now a political science major.

Campus Environment

NC State's 1,877-acre campus in Raleigh is divided into three subcampuses: East, Central, and West. A bus system called the "Wolf Line" connects them, ferrying students, faculty, and staff to both on-campus and off-campus sites. One student we spoke to warns, "The campus is a bit on the hilly side, which, although attractive, is not friendly for those with prosthetics or assisted mobility devices." Central campus, where FYC freshmen live, is home to seven residence halls; East campus has ten; and West campus has three. Housing styles and quality varies across the board. For students with the initiative to look elsewhere, off-campus housing is available. "There are many options around the Raleigh area," says one student. "There are apartments in [the nearby suburb of] Cary, and cheap houses in Garner, all within short driving distance."

The six-story Talley Student Center serves as a hub of student life, containing four separate dining facilities, a ballroom, and an 800-seat, red-carpeted theater. The Witherspoon Student Center complements Talley, offering space for a variety of educational and social activities as well as the popular Campus Cinema, which shows movies at a deeply discounted price for students.

For engineering majors, the 1,334-acre Centennial Campus—adjacent to the rest of the Raleigh campus—is a place that few other universities can match. This $340 million complex serves as a "technopolis" with facilities for undergraduates, graduates, and recent alumni alike. Research and development facilities for the university, corporations, and government can be found here, as well as business incubators for tomorrow's major firms.

Thanks to funding referendums that were recently approved, the campus will see an unprecedented amount of construction in the coming years. Classrooms, labs, residence halls, athletic fields, and parking facilities will be improved, and various new projects will be popping up all over. While the building program is certainly a boon for the school, students will have to get used to the bulldozers and the inconveniences for the next several years.

Student Life

Students from all walks of life attend NC State, enriching the cultural environment for most. Still, as one student puts it, "The stereotype for 'redneck' applies to many of the ones attending State. However, there are many friendly people with more open minds and even some rednecks have respect enough not to show their ideas in public."

Fraternities and sororities are a popular social option for students, providing the requisite keg parties but not dominating the campus social life. "Many freshmen and sophomores do rush," explains one student, "but a majority of the population doesn't. I'd say NC State is a well-rounded school, socially. So feel free to be how you want to be." Another non-Greek adds: "I think the variety of other organizations and activities keep interest [in rushing] limited. There are so many choices that include more specific common interests that facilitate stronger groups." And she's not kidding: There are literally hundreds of student organizations that cater to every student's academic, professional, recreational, religious, and societal interests.

Raleigh gets high marks from most students, who enjoy the city's welcoming restaurants, bars, and shops. There has been a crackdown on drinking of late. A prime example is Brent Road, an infamous back-to-school event where the partying often got out of hand. The city of Raleigh adopted a zero-tolerance policy, and now aggressively enforces a "nuisance party" law to cut down on student drinking and disruptions.

Being such a large school, NC State is, unsurprisingly, a sports mecca. Much of the student body voraciously supports their beloved Wolfpack (the school regularly ranks in the top 10 in the nation for home attendance). The football team often heads to Bowl games, and fans pack the new sports arena to cheer on the basketball teams. Want to do more than watch games? You can choose from nearly 50 club sports, ranging from aikido to wrestling, and a wide variety of intramural offerings.

Other schools to check out: University of North Carolina—Chapel Hill, University of South Carolina—Columbia, University of Maryland—College Park, Florida State, Clemson.

# of Students Waitlisted: 450
  Students Accepting Place: 450
  Waitlisted Students Admitted: 50

Test Scores (middle 50%):
  SAT Verbal: 530–630
  SAT Math: 570–670
  ACT Comp: 23–29
  ACT English: 21–28
  ACT Math: 24–30

HS Rank of Entering Freshmen:
  Top 10%: 40%
  Top 25%: 82%
  Top 50%: 99%

Avg. HS GPA: 4.05

THE EXPERTS SAY...

" While NC State doesn't have UNC Chapel Hill's reputation as a public Ivy, State has an excellent track record of getting premeds into medical school. "

" Shy, easily overwhelmed liberal arts students should look elsewhere. "

Costs (est. 2004–05)

Tuition and Fees, In-State: $4,344

Tuition and Fees, Out-of-State: $16,192

Room & Board: $6,496

Payment Plan(s): installment plan

Inst. Aid (est. 2003–04)

Institutional Aid, Need-Based: $17,788,759

Institutional Aid, Non-Need-Based: $9,444,230

FT Undergrads Receiving Aid: 39%
  Avg. Amount per Student: $7,497

FT Undergrads Receiving Non-Need-Based Scholarship or Grant Aid: 22%
  Avg. Amount per Student: $6,852

Of Those Receiving Any Aid:

Rec. Need-Based Scholarship or Grant Aid: 94%
  Average Award: $5,356

Rec. Need-Based Self-Help Aid: 80%
  Average Award: $3,033

Upon Graduation, Avg. Loan Debt per Student: $16,897

Financial Aid Deadline: rolling

Graduates

Going to Graduate School:
  27% Within One Year

Accepting Job Offer:
  12% at time of graduation

Alumni Giving: 25%

NORTHEASTERN UNIVERSITY

360 Huntington Avenue, 150 Richards Hall, Boston, MA 02115
Admissions Phone: (617) 373-2200 Fax: (617) 373-8780
Email: admissions@neu.edu Website: www.northeastern.edu
Application Website: www.northeastern.edu/admissions

General Info

Type of School: private, coed
Setting: urban
Academic Calendar: semester

Student Body

Full-Time Undergrads: 14,492
  Men: 50%, Women: 50%
Total Undergrad Population:
  African American: 6%
  Asian American: 7%
  Latino: 5%
  Native American: <1%
  Caucasian: 67%
  International: 5%
  Out-of-State: 64%
  In Fraternities: 4%
  In Sororities: 4%
Graduate and First-Professional
  Students: 4,268

Academics

Full-Time Faculty: 830
  With Ph.D.: 80%
Part-Time Faculty: 316
  With Ph.D.: 31%
Student/Faculty Ratio: 16:1
Most Popular Majors:
  business (29%)
  engineering (14%)
  health science (9%)
  protective services (8%)
  communications studies (5%)
Freshmen Retention Rate: 88%
Graduation Rates:
  56% within six years
  note: 5-year school

Admissions

Regular Application Deadline: 2/15;
  1/1 (priority)
Fall Transfer Deadline: 2/15
  (priority)
Spring Transfer Deadline: 5/1
  (priority)
Total # of Students Applied: 21,484
  Admitted: 10,200
  Enrolled: 3,194
# of Students Waitlisted: 2,135
  Students Accepting Place: 801

Inside the Classroom

"I think that Northeastern students have a focus that some students at other schools haven't yet found," says a recent grad. Another student agrees: "We all know we want to do something with our lives and we're just not sure what. Ahh, the lure of the co-op program."

Guidance counselors rave about Northeastern's unique model of "practice-oriented education," which blends a traditional liberal arts and sciences curriculum with an emphasis on profession-focused practical skills. This blend of skills and knowledge is then "put to the test"—through Northeastern's superb cooperative education program. "If someone is not interested in that journey, they won't appreciate what makes Northeastern special," states a young alum.

Through co-op, you alternate between periods of learning in the classroom and periods of learning in the workplace. Your work experiences are full-time, connected to your major or your personal interests, and almost always paid. "I knew what I wanted to study but I didn't know what I wanted to do with it, or even what I could do with it. The co-op program allowed me to explore a number of options in my field, and even some that weren't in my field," says a senior majoring in behavioral neuroscience. Says a recent grad: "It's great because you learn what you want and what you don't want out of a job or from that field."

Northeastern's co-op program places about 8,700 students each year with more than 3,000 employers in Boston, across the United States, and in many corners of the world. Some top co-op employers include *The Boston Globe*, Sun Microsystems, Price Waterhouse Coopers, and several renowned medical centers. Nearly 40 percent of Northeastern students go to work for their co-op employer after they graduate. "Students are more prepared to deal with life after college because of it. They have job experience," says a young alumna. "I didn't realize just how valuable it was until I graduated and realized just how far ahead of the game I was."

Northeastern has six full-time undergraduate colleges: arts and sciences; health sciences; business administration; computer science; criminal justice; and engineering. Cooperative education is required in all colleges except arts and sciences, but 80 percent of arts and sciences students do choose to participate in the co-op program. Students say that health sciences and engineering majors have the heaviest workloads, and arts and sciences students have the lightest. Most professors are "accessible" and "willing to work with you," says one student. Another student states, "They are simply great teachers and fantastic people to boot."

Starting in fall 2003, Northeastern converted from a quarterly calendar to a semester-based calendar. An alum thinks this is a big mistake: "Under the semester system, you spend more time in classes, but you have fewer classes to enjoy. It also limits the flexibility of the co-op system."

Campus Environment

Northeastern's main campus is situated on 67 acres in Boston's cultural district, between the Museum of Fine Arts and Symphony Hall. It consists of 41 academic and administrative buildings and 27 dormitory and residential buildings. The recent "revamping, upgrading, and building" have made the campus "very attractive," a Massachusetts guidance counselor tells us. The university has a full-service intranet with approximately 6,500 live network connections to all office, classrooms, labs and 4,200 student residences.

"Housing is by far Northeastern's biggest problem," states a recent grad. A senior explains: "The university guarantees you housing your first two years here… then you're basically thrown at the mercy of Boston city leasing." (However, university officials have assured us that "plans are in the works" to build more campus housing.) Most new students will share a room with one or two other students in one of 12 coed residence halls. You can also live in theme housing, such as Quiet Hall, International Hall, Wellness Hall, Engineering Hall, Honors Hall, or the Living-Learning Center. Upperclassmen who don't luck out with the campus housing lottery will find themselves looking for affordable off-campus housing—not an easy task. ("Did you ever notice that on television, even the lawyers who live in Boston have roommates? There's a reason for that," quips an alum.)

Students say they can easily get around town by walking or by using "Boston's saving grace," the T. "DO NOT bring a car into this city!" warns a senior. Parking is extremely limited, not to mention expensive. "The bus is another acceptable option at 75 cents, and a cab ride across Boston is less than $20," we are told.

Student Life

"Northeastern really fosters personal independence," states a recent grad. "You really grow up and learn how to balance friends, school, work, and finances." On the downside: "Campus clubs are not as big here as at other schools. Students tend not to be as involved in on-campus activities because they have these outside priorities." If you are interested in getting involved, however, you can choose from more than 140 student clubs and organizations.

Northeastern competes in Division I and maintains varsity teams in 9 men's and 10 women's sports. But students tell us that, except for hockey, not many students turn out to watch the games. "Northeastern students would rather be in the action than watch it," says one student, explaining why intramurals are more popular here than varsity athletics.

While they are committed to their jobs and their studies during the week, students are ready to loosen up on weekends. "Kids of age (or faking it) go to bars and clubs," says one student, who adds that drinking is "a massive portion of the social life at NU."

Students here are "hardworking" but friendly: "Doors are held, smiles are met, friends are made rather easily," says a senior. A young alum's take on students' "easygoing" attitude: "[I]n the student center or other on-campus or near-campus watering holes, you're more likely to overhear a conversation on the politics of dancing than the politics of our nation."

We're told that Northeastern's mascot—the husky—holds a special place in students' hearts. Students trek over to the bronze statue of the husky in Ell Hall before exams and rub the husky's nose for good luck. A university official explains, "As a result, the mostly dull bronze dog has a bright shiny nose."

Other schools to check out: Temple, Drexel, Syracuse, George Washington.

Test Scores (middle 50%):
  SAT Verbal: 550–640
  SAT Math: 570–660
  ACT Comp: 23–28

THE EXPERTS SAY...

" Northeastern is an exciting place for hardworking students who want to get a head start in their careers. "

" Northeastern is a frightening prospect to those who believe the whole point of college is to delay joining the real world. "

HS Rank of Entering Freshmen:
  Top 10%: 35%
  Top 25%: 70%
  Top 50%: 95%

Costs (2003–04)

Tuition and Fees: $25,840

Room & Board: $9,810

Payment Plan(s): installment plan

Inst. Aid (est. 2003–04)

Institutional Aid, Need-Based:
  $78,469,783

Institutional Aid, Non-Need-Based:
  $14,094,050

FT Undergrads Receiving Aid: 64%
  Avg. Amount per Student: $15,396

FT Undergrads Receiving Non-Need-Based Scholarship or Grant Aid: 12%
  Avg. Amount per Student: $12,627

Of Those Receiving Any Aid:

Rec. Need-Based Scholarship or Grant Aid: 93%
  Average Award: $11,050

Rec. Need-Based Self-Help Aid: 89%
  Average Award: $5,724

Financial Aid Deadline: rolling, 2/15 (priority)

Graduates

Going to Graduate School:
  18% Within One Year

Companies Recruiting On Campus: 48

NORTHERN ARIZONA UNIVERSITY

P.O. Box 4084, Flagstaff, AZ 86011-4084
Admissions Phone: (928) 523-5511; (888) 667-3628 (out-of-state) Fax: (928) 523-6023
Email: undergraduate.admissions@nau.edu Website: www.nau.edu
Application Website: www4.nau.edu.uadmissions

General Info

Type of School: public, coed
Setting: small town
Academic Calendar: semester

Student Body

Full-Time Undergrads: 11,033
  Men: 40%, Women: 60%

Part-Time Undergrads: 1,792
  Men: 40%, Women: 60%

Total Undergrad Population:
  African American: 2%
  Asian American: 2%
  Latino: 10%
  Native American: 7%
  Caucasian: 77%
  International: 2%
  Out-of-State: 15%
  Living Off-Campus: 52%
  In Fraternities: 4%
  In Sororities: 6%

Graduate and First-Professional
  Students: 5,809

Academics

Full-Time Faculty: 711
  With Ph.D.: 83%

Part-Time Faculty: 431
  With Ph.D.: 26%

Student/Faculty Ratio: 17:1

Most Popular Majors:
  elementary education (11%)
  business (9%)
  hotel, restaurant management
  (4%)
  criminal justice (3%)
  psychology (3%)

Freshmen Retention Rate: 69%

Graduation Rates:
  27% within four years
  50% within six years

Admissions

Regular Application Deadline: 3/1
  (priority)

Fall Transfer Deadline: 3/1 (priority)

Spring Transfer Deadline: 10/1
  (priority)
  Enrolled: 2,352

Test Scores (middle 50%):
  SAT Verbal: 470–590
  SAT Math: 460–590
  ACT Comp: 19–24

Inside the Classroom

Northern Arizona University is composed of the colleges of arts and science, ecosystem science and management, engineering and technology, business administration, health professions, fine and performing arts, and social and behavioral sciences, as well as the schools of communication and hotel and restaurant management and the Center of Excellence in Education. NAU offers undergraduate degrees in nearly 100 majors, including special programs in hotel and restaurant management, arts management, criminal justice, dental hygiene, forestry, and parks and recreation management. The science, business, and music programs are very good, we hear.

Whatever the major, students are required to take 35 hours of coursework in liberal studies courses, which are designed to teach students to think critically and solve problems in a variety of contexts. "The workload is heavy, but not always difficult," reports one student. Word is that students are friendly, inside the classroom and out. Notes one student, "The campus is not very competitive, but certain upper-division classes can be." The average class size is under 30 students, and can be considerably smaller in upper division classes. Professors are well-regarded and, like students, are generally friendly. "Since the classes are smaller, the professors know the students by name, and are easy to meet and chat with," reports one enthusiastic student. And "students are not looked on as numbers," says one junior—a fact that Arizona guidance counselors admire. Students also have positive things to say about NAU's advising system.

NAU offers a three-year accelerated degree program, which allows motivated students to save a chunk of money and reach professional goals more quickly. The school also offers students an opportunity to study abroad through numerous programs in Europe and Asia, as well as exchange programs with other U.S. institutions and a special Grand Canyon Semester. There's also a well-regarded honors program, and excellent opportunities for student research. Tuition is very reasonable for in-state students, making NAU even more appealing to Arizona residents.

Campus Environment

About half of the first-year students live on campus, staying in residence halls and family housing apartments. We've heard mixed reviews about the housing: While a student claims that NAU has "the best resident hall system in Arizona," one high school guidance counselor says NAU has "a limited number of dormitories for students," while another counselor complains about "their shoving freshmen in bunkbeds in the hallways." As for off-campus housing: "There are lots of apartment complexes, and condos or town houses to buy or rent, but it is kind of expensive," says a senior. Students give high marks to the food and say that there are "great meal plans and tons of choices." Overall, facilities are excellent, and students agree that the fitness center is "terrific."

The small town of Flagstaff gets mixed reviews; one student describes it as "very quaint," while another complains that there's not much going on in this "sleepy" town. Yet another student defends the town and notes there are "plenty of decent restaurants and night spots that are fun," but admits that "if you like the club scene," Flagstaff is probably "not for you."

Students report that the campus, as well as the town of Flagstaff, feels very safe (as long as you're not easily spooked—NAU is surrounded by three cemeteries). A guidance counselor praises the way the campus is laid out, adding that "it's still a university, but it's small and you feel comfortable." Many students feel that cars are not necessary on campus, "unless you have a job on the other side of town "or hate being out in cold, snowy weather." One senior notes that most people walk, ride bikes, skateboard, or take the bus around town (although one college counselor complains about the "limited bus routes").

Student Life

NAU students are very friendly; as one recent grad says, there are "smiles everywhere." The student population is quite diverse, with more than 20 percent minority students, a third of whom are Native Americans. According to one Arizona counselor, the school makes efforts to make Native American students feel welcome. In addition, about 20 percent of students are 25 or older, which creates an even greater diversity among students. Most NAU students are Arizona residents, with about 15 percent coming from out of state. One student told us that she couldn't imagine a type of person who wouldn't fit in at NAU.

How do most NAU students spend their free time? "People study in the library, go downtown to the bars (Collin's, Maloney's, and the Mad-I); they also hang out at the gym or friends' houses, and go to sorority or fraternity functions, or intramural games," answers a senior. Fraternities and sororities aren't particularly big at NAU— only about four percent of students participate—but their parties are "pretty popular." "Drinking is somewhat big, off-campus more than on," muses a student, who adds that "drugs are around, but not a huge factor."

Northern Arizona is a NCAA Division I school, but it's not obsessed with athletics. Intramural sports are popular, as are all sorts of outdoor recreational activities. One student raves about the "awesome bike trails," and notes that there's some amazing hiking in the area as well (perhaps this inspired NAU alum Mark Thatcher, CEO and Founder of Teva Sport Sandals). Lots of snow come wintertime means plenty of opportunities to ski and snowboard; the elevation of Flagstaff is 7,000 feet. Nearby natural attractions draw students on road trips, to sites such as the Grand Canyon and the red rocks of Sedona.

ACT English: 18–25
ACT Math: 18–25
HS Rank of Entering Freshmen:
Top 10%: 37%
Top 25%: 57%
Top 50%: 79%
Avg. HS GPA: 3.4

THE EXPERTS SAY...

" There are over 100 majors and the tuition is a bargain for Arizona residents. NAU has a reputation for making Native American students feel welcome. "

" If you like the NAU package, also investigate the University of New Mexico, Truman State University, and the University of Wyoming. "

Costs (2003–04)

Tuition and Fees, In-State: $3,628

Tuition and Fees, Out-of-State: $12,148

Room & Board: $5,474

Regional or 'good neighbor' tuition available

Inst. Aid (est. 2003–04)

Institutional Aid, Need-Based: $7,477,085

Institutional Aid, Non-Need-Based: $2,361,185

FT Undergrads Receiving Aid: 52%
Avg. Amount per Student: $7,898

FT Undergrads Receiving Non-Need-Based Scholarship or Grant Aid: 12%
Avg. Amount per Student: $6,039

Of Those Receiving Any Aid:

Rec. Need-Based Scholarship or Grant Aid: 80%
Average Award: $5,157

Rec. Need-Based Self-Help Aid: 78%
Average Award: $6,266

Upon Graduation, Avg. Loan Debt per Student: $16,319

Financial Aid Deadline: rolling, 4/15 (priority)

Graduates

Going to Graduate School:
51% Within One Year

Accepting Job Offer:
60% at time of graduation

Alumni Giving: 12%

NORTHWESTERN UNIVERSITY

P.O. Box 3060, Evanston, IL 60204-3060
Admissions Phone: (847) 491-7271
Email: ug-admission@northwestern.edu Website: www.northwestern.edu
Application Website: www.ugadm.northwestern.edu

General Info

Type of School: private, coed

Setting: suburban

Academic Calendar: quarter

Student Body

Full-Time Undergrads: 7,789
    Men: 47%, Women: 53%

Part-Time Undergrads: 107
    Men: 47%, Women: 53%

Total Undergrad Population:
    African American: 5%
    Asian American: 17%
    Latino: 5%
    Native American: <1%
    Caucasian: 60%
    International: 5%
    Out-of-State: 75%
    Living Off-Campus: 35%
    In Fraternities: 30%
    In Sororities: 39%

Graduate and First-Professional
    Students: 8,265

Academics

Full-Time Faculty: 900
    With Ph.D.: 100%

Part-Time Faculty: 178
    With Ph.D.: 100%

Student/Faculty Ratio: 7:1

Most Popular Majors:
    engineering (16%)
    journalism (8%)
    music (5%)
    communication studies (5%)
    economics (4%)

Freshmen Retention Rate: 97%

Admissions

Regular Application Deadline: 1/1

Early Decision Deadline(s): 11/1

Fall Transfer Deadline: 6/1

Spring Transfer Deadline: 2/1

Total # of Students Applied: 14,137
    Admitted: 4,702
    Enrolled: 1,941

# of Students Waitlisted: 776
    Students Accepting Place: 330
    Waitlisted Students Admitted: 102

Applied Early Decision: 984
    Early Decision Admitted: 451

Inside the Classroom

"Academically, Northwestern doesn't mess around," a computer science/economics major declares. Northwestern has six undergraduate schools: the Medill School of Journalism (which "boasts a nearly 100% placement rate for all of its graduates," a journalism major informs us), the McCormick School of Engineering and Applied Sciences, the School of Education and Social Policy, the School of Music, the School of Speech, and the Weinberg College of Arts and Sciences. The school offers outstanding interdisciplinary programs (like engineering and music double majors) and numerous preprofessional programs, including a seven-year B.A./M.D. program and the Teaching Media Program, which provides journalism internships. There are more than 50 research and field studies programs available.

Northwestern is hot, says a Michigan guidance counselor, because of "the caliber of students and its location." A California counselor says it's because Northwestern "has exceptionally good fine arts and avid football fans." The study abroad program's quality, however, leaves something to be desired, according to one student. Northwestern is battling the "Peter Pan" syndrome of late graduation by introducing an online system to help students figure out how close they are to graduating and how much extra time would be needed to switch majors.

Northwestern's quarter system crams four courses into ten weeks. "There are midterms starting three weeks or so into the quarter and ending not too far from finals," an international studies major complains. "Because Northwestern is a research university, professors are pretty busy, so their availability varies," another student says. "Some will ask you to go to your TA before coming to them, whereas others will try bribing students with donuts and coffee to try to get them to talk to them." While lectures tend to be large, upper-division courses may have as few as ten people.

"Most students see Northwestern as a step to graduate school, so almost everyone is striving for the limited number of A's given in each class," a senior asserts. But a learning and organizational change major states, "Things aren't really that competitive outside of the preprofessional tracks." However, "If you're not ready for a challenge, go to just about any other university," a student declares, "especially an Ivy, if you can get in."

Campus Environment

"The campus, as anyone will tell you who has stood by the lagoon and looked across at Lake Michigan and Chicago, is beautiful," rhapsodizes a computer science major. "A common complaint is that green space is becoming limited because of new academic buildings being built regularly." "Dorms are pretty standard and highly available," a math major reports. North campus dorms are "generally closer to parties and athletic facilities," and South campus dorms are "considered more artsy." The campus is "generally a very safe environment, besides the four robberies a year."

Upperclassmen mostly live in apartments just west of the school. "Off-campus housing is available but a terrible value," gripes a math major. "Cost is high and quality is extremely low." A math major reports, "Evanston and Northwestern have a terrible relationship, but it has improved slightly over the past few years with the new cinema and shopping complex." But an engineering student raves, "Off-campus life is fantastic. Great restaurants and businesses that are within walking distance provide a good place to hang out and good job opportunities. Take the train an hour south and you're in Chicago, a place that offers limitless opportunities."

Student Life

"There are a few types of students," a senior relates. "10 percent are, or think they are, jocks and hang out with athletes, 20 percent like to have a good time and act like college students, 15 percent have their close group of 4–5 friends who they only hang out with, 20 percent only spend time with their significant other, and the other 35 percent are bookworms who rarely get out because they are concerned with graduate schools." There are also those who "think that they are better than Northwestern because it wasn't their 'first choice' school, but a back-up to Harvard/Stanford." And "most of the students do come from money, and few try to hide it."

Says a senior, "Without fraternities tailgating and organizing events, this campus would seem extremely dull." Says another student, "Lately, the administration has been trying to get every fraternity to go dry and they are succeeding for the most part." Recently, there has been a crackdown on underage drinking on campus, so students head for the Keg, ("a popular local bar that doesn't card too hard," a freshman quips). "Somebody who is very serious about having a good time," a senior confides, "will tend to be frustrated at the lack of large party scene." But, says a student, "however much Northwestern is not a party school, it's not dead either." Except for the dating scene, which is "notoriously awful."

Students looking for things to do can check out The Rock—a boulder painted with event announcements. "Theater is huge on campus—there's usually three or four productions to choose from every week," a premed says. In Dance Marathon, an annual Northwestern tradition, over 500 students dance for 30 hours straight for charity. The campus newspaper, the *Daily Northwestern*, is popular, as are the Student Government and the championship Northwestern Debate Society. Students are not particularly politically active (a senior lambastes campus "apathy"), but the war in Iraq stirred debate. On weekends, students head to Chicago.

Wildcats football draws large crowds, both for the games and the tailgate parties, and basketball has a following. "Northwestern sort of makes fun of its own athletics," a biology major says. "As a Big Ten school, however, the athletic teams do enjoy some serious funding, and there are equally funded outlets for men and women." Northwestern fields 12 Division I teams, with strong men's golf and women's tennis. "Many students participate in intramural sports (mainly with their fraternity, or with their dorms if they are freshmen)," a senior tells us.

The typical Wildcat, cell phone in hand, "is involved in nine million activities and does superbly in classes." A senior sums it up: "We're a school of intelligent, studious people who actually know how to throw a party. We can go to school and still get some sleep; we don't kill each other to guarantee that perfect grade. We know how to relax."

Other schools to check out: University of Michigan, Dartmouth, Notre Dame, Georgetown, Stanford.

Test Scores (middle 50%):
SAT Verbal: 650–730
SAT Math: 660–750
ACT Comp: 29–33
ACT English: 29–34
ACT Math: 28–33
HS Rank of Entering Freshmen:
Top 10%: 83%
Top 25%: 97%
Top 50%: 99%

THE EXPERTS SAY...

" Northwestern's law school granted the first law degree to a woman in 1870 and hasn't stopped preparing great professionals since. "

" Great campus, great preprofessional programs, great performing arts, great sports, great social life... Don't they know it's no fun unless there's something to complain about? "

Costs (2004–05)

Tuition and Fees: $30,085
Room & Board: $9,393
Payment Plan(s): installment plan

Inst. Aid (est. 2003–04)

Institutional Aid, Need-Based: $51,955,485

Institutional Aid, Non-Need-Based: $139,000

FT Undergrads Receiving Aid: 44%
Avg. Amount per Student: $24,508

FT Undergrads Receiving Non-Need-Based Scholarship or Grant Aid: 0%
Avg. Amount per Student: $4,793

Of Those Receiving Any Aid:

Rec. Need-Based Scholarship or Grant Aid: 94%
Average Award: $18,857

Rec. Need-Based Self-Help Aid: 93%
Average Award: $5,652

Upon Graduation, Avg. Loan Debt per Student: $15,136

Financial Aid Deadline: 2/1

OBERLIN COLLEGE

101 N. Professor Street, Oberlin, OH 44074
Admissions Phone: (440) 775-8411; (800) 622-6243 Fax: (440) 775-6905
Email: college.admissions@oberlin.edu Website: www.oberlin.edu
Application Website: www.oberlin.edu/coladm/onlineapplication

General Info

Type of School: private, coed
Setting: rural
Academic Calendar: 4-1-4

Student Body

Full-Time Undergrads: 2,809
  Men: 45%, Women: 55%

Part-Time Undergrads: 74
  Men: 45%, Women: 55%

Total Undergrad Population:
  African American: 7%
  Asian American: 7%
  Latino: 5%
  Native American: 1%
  Caucasian: 74%
  International: 6%
  Out-of-State: 90%
  Living Off-Campus: 25%

Graduate and First-Professional
  Students: 15

Academics

Full-Time Faculty: 272
  With Ph.D.: 94%

Part-Time Faculty: 20

Student/Faculty Ratio: 10:1

Most Popular Majors:
  English (14%)
  politics (11%)
  history (9%)
  biology (9%)
  environmental studies (14%)

Freshmen Retention Rate: 90%

Graduation Rates:
  64% within four years
  81% within six years
  note: 5-year programs affect rates

Admissions

Regular Application Deadline: 1/15

Early Decision Deadline(s): 11/15,
1/2

Fall Transfer Deadline: 3/15

Spring Transfer Deadline: 12/1

Total # of Students Applied: 5,983
  Admitted: 2,159
  Enrolled: 762

# of Students Waitlisted: 890
  Students Accepting Place: 545
  Waitlisted Students Admitted: 125

Inside the Classroom

"Oberlin provides an environment that is intellectually intense for individuals, but is collectively noncompetitive," states a college official. Oberlin College is actually made up of two schools. At the College of Arts and Sciences, a high percentage of students goes on to medical school or graduate school; in fact, Oberlin has more Ph.D.s among its graduates than any other liberal arts college. The Conservatory of Music, with a student population of around 500, attracts top musicians from around the world who are intent on a professional career; the voice program in particular is considered to be among the best in the nation. For the ambitious, it's possible to study within both schools and earn a dual B.A./B.M. degree.

In both schools, the course load is demanding. Freshmen are able to get into the swing of things through Oberlin's Colloquia—seminars of around 15 students which explore some nontraditional academic themes in an interdisciplinary manner. For Arts and Science students, at least nine credit hours are required in each of the three divisions (arts and humanities, social and behavioral sciences, natural sciences and mathematics), and at least nine credit hours in courses dealing with cultural diversity. They also must satisfy writing and mathematics proficiency requirements. For Conservatory students, at least 24 credits must be in Arts and Science courses.

Three required Winter terms allow students to pursue special interests or flex their creative muscles through independent projects and special course offerings for four weeks each January. The student-run Experimental College (known as EXCO), with its unusual courses in everything from pop culture to pottery, offers students yet another opportunity to explore their interests.

"The professors are really helpful when it comes to classwork, and they are eager to get to know students on a personal level. Some professors have picnics and parties at their houses," says one student. But another student complains that classes are "occasionally tainted by the political views of the teachers." Students work extremely hard, often studying for several hours a day. However, pressure is primarily of the self-motivated kind and there's not much competition between students, at least at the College of Arts and Sciences ("but I've heard that the Conservatory students are cut-throat," a recent social sciences grad reveals).

Campus Environment

Students from both schools live and eat together and share the same facilities. Housing is guaranteed for four years, and freshmen and sophomores must live on campus. Freshmen have the option of living in an all-freshmen dorm, integrated dorms, quiet dorms, social dorms, program houses, or co-ops. Co-ops (through OSCA, the Oberlin Student Cooperative Association) are very popular with students: "Being in OSCA— cooking meals and running a cooperative collectively—can be one of the most challenging, fun, and rewarding parts of going to Oberlin," says a sophomore.

Oberlin has a number of outstanding facilities, particularly its four exceptionally well-stocked libraries—although Mudd Library is known as much for its socializing as for its resources. Recent new additions include a state-of-the-art science center and a center for environmental studies. The Allen Memorial Art Museum has an art rental for students every semester. "During the event, the museum lends students original works by well-known artists such as Picasso, Chagall, and Warhol for a mere $5 per semester. Some students even spend two nights sleeping outdoors to be first in line," a college official tells us.

Surrounded by farmland in all directions, the town of Oberlin is small and unexciting, and can feel "gloomy." "Oberlin is a small town that is finally seeing an improvement in town-gown relations. In the past, residents have resented the 'rich, privileged kids' storming into their town every summer and causing all sorts of traffic, noise, and parking problems," observes a recent grad. Now, however, "many students are increasing efforts to give back to the community." Students typically walk or ride bikes around campus and around town. All students are permitted to have cars on campus, and there is ample student parking.

Student Life

Oberlin has "a very political atmosphere." "The students are often passionate and driven young activists," says an English major. Students feel this spirit makes Oberlin vibrant, exciting, stimulating—and sometimes exhausting. "Everyone has their own opinion. Everyone is involved in some kind of organization, which sometimes results in conflict," admits one student. The students are overwhelmingly liberal ("Someone trying to start a Young Republicans club at Oberlin would have a tough time getting members," quips one student). A California college counselor cautions, "A mainstreamer might feel uncomfortable in this ultra-liberal place." Students hold "speak-outs" on the steps of the student union several times a year; part protest and part discussion, "they take theory out of the classroom and make it emotional," explains one student.

Oberlin has a history of leading the way among liberal arts schools in recruiting minorities, and was the first coed college in the United States. There is also a large and active gay and lesbian population. However, a young alum says, "There are lots of groups at Oberlin that tend to feel marginalized. That seems to be the common denominator with many Oberlin students, so there isn't as much diversity and integration as the administration likes to boast."

There are no Greek organizations at Oberlin ("Oberlin students are not the frat or sorority type, thank God!" says a sophomore), and students tend to hang out in small groups. "On the weekends, there is always a party somewhere in town, and a lot of people relax at the Feve (a coffee house/bar with a very relaxed atmosphere)," a student tells us. While one student admits there's "lots of weed smoking," another student muses, "there is a fair amount of drugs, but academic pressure lessens this." Students sometimes venture into Cleveland, particularly to go to "The Flats," an area with several bars and music clubs. Sports are not big at Oberlin, and students say that "a conservative jock or cheerleader type" would simply not fit in.

Oberlin students embrace "eccentricity." For example, each April, Oberlin holds a "drag ball"—"There's music, food, dancing, people running around naked, and a runway competition," explains a student. Successful (and suitably quirky) Oberlin alums include Jerry Greenville (cofounder of Ben and Jerry's ice cream), John Kander (award-winning composer, "Cabaret"), Jane Pratt (founder of *Sassy* and *Jane* magazines), and Liz Phair (indie rock star).

Other schools to check out: Carleton, Grinnell, Wesleyan, Pomona, Reed, Middlebury.

Applied Early Decision: 341
  Early Decision Admitted: 236

Test Scores (middle 50%):
  SAT Verbal: 630–730
  SAT Math: 610–710
  ACT Comp: 27–31

HS Rank of Entering Freshmen:
  Top 10%: 62%
  Top 25%: 89%
  Top 50%: 99%

Avg. HS GPA: 3.52

THE EXPERTS SAY...

" Oberlin is an exciting place for students passionate about both intellectual achievement and social engagement. "

" The intense Conservatory students and the laid-back college students make an interesting mix. "

Costs (2003–04)

Tuition and Fees: $29,688

Room & Board: $7,250

Payment Plan(s): installment plan

Inst. Aid (est. 2003–04)

Institutional Aid, Need-Based:
  $29,923,573

Institutional Aid, Non-Need-Based:
  $3,273,512

FT Undergrads Receiving Aid: 58%
  Avg. Amount per Student: $22,576

FT Undergrads Receiving Non-Need-Based Scholarship or Grant Aid: 10%
  Avg. Amount per Student: $11,472

Of Those Receiving Any Aid:

Rec. Need-Based Scholarship or
  Grant Aid: 91%
  Average Award: $17,488

Rec. Need-Based Self-Help Aid: 89%
  Average Award: $4,606

Financial Aid Deadline: 1/15 (priority)

Graduates

Going to Graduate School:
  50% Within One Year

Accepting Job Offer:
  50% at time of graduation

Companies Recruiting On Campus: 16

Alumni Giving: 60%

OCCIDENTAL COLLEGE

1600 Campus Road, Los Angeles, CA 90041-3314
Admissions Phone: (323) 259-2700; (800) 825-5262 Fax: (323) 341-4875
Email: admission@oxy.edu Website: www.oxy.edu
Application Website: departments.oxy.edu/admission

General Info

Type of School: private, coed
Setting: urban
Academic Calendar: semester

Student Body

Full-Time Undergrads: 1,823
  Men: 42%, Women: 58%

Part-Time Undergrads: 17
  Men: 41%, Women: 59%

Total Undergrad Population:
  African American: 7%
  Asian American: 12%
  Latino: 15%
  Native American: 1%
  Caucasian: 53%
  International: 4%
  Out-of-State: 40%
  Living Off-Campus: 30%
  In Fraternities: 5%
  In Sororities: 11%

Graduate and First-Professional
  Students: 18

Academics

Full-Time Faculty: 135
  With Ph.D.: 99%

Part-Time Faculty: 71

Student/Faculty Ratio: 11:1

Most Popular Majors:
  economics (11%)
  English (9%)
  art history & visual arts (9%)
  psychology (9%)
  diplomacy and world affairs (7%)

Completing 2 or More Majors: 5%

Freshmen Retention Rate: 91%

Graduation Rates:
  73% within four years
  78% within six years

Admissions

Regular Application Deadline: 1/10

Early Decision Deadline(s): 11/15

Fall Transfer Deadline: 3/15

Spring Transfer Deadline: 10/15

Total # of Students Applied: 4,513
  Admitted: 1,964
  Enrolled: 441

# of Students Waitlisted: 592
  Students Accepting Place: 301
  Waitlisted Students Admitted: 106

Inside the Classroom

The number of applicants to Occidental has increased 140 percent over the last six years. Occidental (or "the Princeton of the West," according to a senior) is proud of its commitment to what it calls a "total education," combining strong liberal arts programs and interdisciplinary studies with an unwavering dedication to diversity. One guidance counselor recommends Oxy as "one of the most diverse small schools with great merit scholarships and lots of individualized attention." Another guidance counselor thinks Oxy is special because of its "students who really care about classes, professors, and real learning."

Oxy offers 31 majors in the arts and humanities, sciences, and social sciences, 11 of which are interdisciplinary. The school is well-known for several programs, particularly diplomacy/world affairs, music, chemistry, economics, physics, and theater. Many students are on a preprofessional track, and some of the school's strengths are in preprofessional areas, including the prehealth sciences.

First-year Cultural Studies courses are the centerpiece of the Core Program, which encourages students to think across disciplines. All students must complete a writing seminar and an interdisciplinary colloquium in their first year. Subsequently, students must complete at least 12 units in three different geographical areas and at least 12 units of science and math, and demonstrate proficiency in a foreign language. Before graduation, every student must complete a senior "comprehensive."

With a small yet highly dynamic student body, Occidental has the atmosphere of an intimate and vibrant academic community. Says a senior with an individualized major, "You will get TONS of homework here and lots of workload. Fortunately, if you pick the right major, you're going to enjoy EVERY minute of your work and homework!" While the workload is heavy, there is an environment of cooperation, not competition. The low student/professor ratio ensures that courses are kept relatively small, and virtually all courses emphasize discussion and writing. A recent grad who'd majored in psychology tells us, "In my opinion, the best thing about Oxy is that the professors in your major all know who you are, sometimes even before you take any of their courses. Professors learn what to expect from you, and if you don't give it to them, you will probably hear about it." A junior majoring in politics adds, "Professors rarely, if ever, treat students as inferiors."

Campus Environment

The tree-laden, 120-acre campus, with its Spanish-style architecture, is situated around a central Quad, ideal for basking in the California sunshine. In fact, the campus has been used in more than 50 feature films. One movie-related fact: "When an Occidental student turns 21, he or she is lured (or taken) to the Gilman Memorial Fountain (also known as the 'Star Trek Fountain,' because of its use in the movie *Star Trek III*) and dunked," reveals a college official.

About 70 percent of students live on campus in one of 11 dorms. Residence halls vary in personality, but all are small (155 people max), and several have special theme floors. Freshmen are required to live on campus (this excludes Greek housing). All first-year students are grouped in residence halls according to their core seminars, forming what are known as "Living and Learning Communities." Most freshmen live in doubles; a small number are assigned to triples, but singles are not available for first-years. All students may have cars, and campus parking is free. A shuttle known as the Bengal Bus takes students to different locations such as the supermarket or out to local social areas such as Old Town Pasadena.

Located just eight miles north of downtown L.A., Occidental combines the close-knit community of a residential, scenic campus with all of the resources of a world-class city. Students tell us that the campus is completely safe but that you need to be careful in the surrounding area of Eagle Rock. A junior explains, "Eagle Rock is *not* a college town. If going off campus, most people tend to go to other areas of Los Angeles or other neighboring towns (Pasadena and Glendale being two of the more popular)." But no student leaves Occidental without some substantial interaction with Los Angeles, be it through coursework, an internship, or community service.

Occidental has a long history of environmental responsibility; it has worked hard to reduce energy consumption, conserve water, and develop a strong recycling program. In 2001, the school even signed a "green pledge to develop curricula, research, and outreach activities that support an environmentally sustainable future." A $16 million Physical, Earth, and Environmental Science center is scheduled to open in October 2003.

Student Life

Diversity is a big part of life here. Many students told us that they chose to attend Occidental specifically for the great cultural diversity of Oxy's student body. A junior explains that even in the admissions process, "Oxy wants to see the *whole* person, and the school tries to assemble a cross-section of different students to enrich campus life." Most students are liberal and progressive (conservatives are welcome, too, as long as they are "open-minded to other people's perspectives").

Oxy students are friendly and form a close community (the drawback: "It seems that everyone knows everyone else's business before the day is over!"). Rather than attending blowout parties, students hang out in small groups in dorms or around the campus. "Our campus safety [personnel] do an extremely good job at shooting down any sort of on-campus fun or parties that could occur," grumbles a sophomore. Fraternities and sororities draw only a small percentage of the student body, but their social events are open to everyone.

Oxy's 80 or so student clubs address a wide range of interests. Occidental fields 19 varsity teams that compete at the NCAA Division III level in the Southern California Intercollegiate Athletic Conference, but students say that, for the most part, sports are not a major focus here. Community service, on the other hand, is huge, and the school has a long tradition of community outreach: Oxy's Upward Bound program, one of the largest in California, was established as one of the country's first pilot programs in 1964. The following year, Project Amigos was established to make annual trips to Tijuana to build homes for low-income families; the ongoing project now includes alumni trips.

Other schools to check out: Pitzer, Pomona, Oberlin, Reed, Carleton.

Applied Early Decision: 106
  Early Decision Admitted: 45

Test Scores (middle 50%):
  SAT Verbal: 580–690
  SAT Math: 590–680
  ACT Comp: 25–30

HS Rank of Entering Freshmen:
  Top 10%: 59%
  Top 25%: 87%
  Top 50%: 99%

THE EXPERTS SAY...

" Oxy offers not only the personal attention typical of small liberal arts colleges, but also the cultural diversity and dynamic urban environment usually found only at large universities. "

" If you want to bury your head in the sand, find another school. Oxy's all about cultural diversity, community service, and academic involvement. "

Costs (2004–5)

Tuition and Fees: $29,692

Room & Board: $8,220

Payment Plan(s): installment plan, pre-payment plan

Inst. Aid (2002–03)

Institutional Aid, Need-Based:
  $15,611,639

Institutional Aid, Non-Need-Based:
  $2,281,537

FT Undergrads Receiving Aid: 53%
  Avg. Amount per Student: $26,676

FT Undergrads Receiving Non-Need-Based Scholarship or Grant Aid: 17%
  Avg. Amount per Student: $16,556

Of Those Receiving Any Aid:

Rec. Need-Based Scholarship or Grant Aid: 99%
  Average Award: $21,514

Rec. Need-Based Self-Help Aid: 93%
  Average Award: $6,133

Upon Graduation, Avg. Loan Debt per Student: $22,185

Financial Aid Deadline: 2/1

Graduates

Going to Graduate School:
  25% Within One Year

Accepting Job Offer:
  40% at time of graduation

Companies Recruiting On Campus: 17

Alumni Giving: 58%

OHIO STATE UNIVERSITY

110 Enarson Hall, 54 W. 12th Avenue, Columbus, OH 43210
Admissions Phone: (614) 292-3980 Fax: (614) 292-4818
Email: askabuckeye@osu.edu Website: www.osu.edu
Application Website: www.applyweb.com/aw?osu

General Info

Type of School: public, coed

Setting: urban

Academic Calendar: quarter

Student Body

Full-Time Undergrads: 33,404
   Men: 52%, Women: 48%

Part-Time Undergrads: 4,040
   Men: 52%, Women: 48%

Total Undergrad Population:
   African American: 8%
   Asian American: 6%
   Latino: 2%
   Native American: <1%
   Caucasian: 78%
   International: 4%
   Out-of-State: 9%
   Living Off-Campus: 75%
   In Fraternities: 5%
   In Sororities: 6%

Graduate and First-Professional
   Students: 13,126

Academics

Full-Time Faculty: 2,752
   With Ph.D.: 99%

Part-Time Faculty: 905

Student/Faculty Ratio: 14:1

Most Popular Majors:
   psychology (3%)
   biology (3%)
   English (3%)
   political science (2%)
   marketing (2%)

Completing 2 or More Majors: 9%

Freshmen Retention Rate: 88%

Graduation Rates:
   29% within four years
   62% within six years

Admissions

Regular Application Deadline: 2/1

Fall Transfer Deadline: 6/25

Spring Transfer Deadline: 2/1

Total # of Students Applied: 20,122
   Admitted: 14,488
   Enrolled: 6,390

# of Students Waitlisted: 669
   Students Accepting Place: 197
   Waitlisted Students Admitted: 7

Inside the Classroom

"The sky's the limit in terms of what you want to accomplish at Ohio State," a senior tells us. Another student brags, "Any program you want to study is offered at OSU." The 19 colleges that make up Ohio State University offer 174 undergraduate majors, plus 111 master degree programs and 93 doctoral programs. All of this adds up to an estimated 12,000 courses in all. Included are colleges of arts; biological sciences; business; dentistry; engineering; human ecology; nursing; optometry; and veterinary medicine; along with schools of journalism, music and architecture, among others. The majors range from the traditional (liberal arts and science, journalism, etc.) to the exotic (fisheries management, turfgrass science). Career-oriented programs such as accounting, engineering and nursing have exceptionally high enrollments.

A class at OSU "tends to be on the large side rather than on the small," says one student. Introductory classes can be huge, with 200–500 students, but they will generally have smaller recitation periods that meet once a week with a graduate TA. Higher level classes are smaller, averaging 30–40 students. This can make OSU seem intimidating, so that a student used to a small academic environment might tend to feel lost. But professors make themselves available to motivated students who seek them out. "I have found the professors generally happy to have the students come in and talk to them," says a student majoring in history. However, a finance major complains that there's "not great faculty/student interaction outside the classroom."

Core requirements in arts and humanities, natural sciences, social sciences as well as writing and foreign language are required of all students. In addition, all freshmen must take a special course called University College that introduces them to the university and gives them the chance to meet fellow new students.

"OSU puts emphasis on high academic standards," says one Ohio State student. "There are many honoraries, academic clubs and study programs." That student goes on to complain that "sometimes the workload is not consistent with the level of the class. A 100 level or broad survey class may have a bigger workload than a 400 level or junior/senior class." Guidance counselors agree that OSU's academic standards are high, and one tells us that "word of mouth is nothing but positive things."

International students are also drawn to the university. Ohio State University ranks seventh among all universities in international enrollment. Students overseas generally learn about OSU from faculty who travel to teach or conduct research abroad.

Campus Environment

With more than 30,000 undergrads, Ohio State University is a city in all but name. The 1,712-acre Columbus campus has many of the facilities and resources of one; including over 20 libraries. At its center lies the Oval—a giant grassy area where students gather to study and play Frisbee in warm weather. On-campus housing can accommodate about 20 percent of the student body. "There are about 15–20 dorms/houses on campus for students," says an Ohio State student. "There is also great variety in living arrangements; a person can choose 1, 2, 3… up to 7 other roomies!" The university is currently planning to increase on-campus housing due to its popularity with students. Off-campus housing is popular with upperclassmen. There are many houses in the campus area available at reasonable rents, although, as one student warns "utilities can be kind of surprising the first few months with initiation fees being included."

OSU is located at the edge of the city of Columbus—"all the kids like Columbus," says one guidance counselor. This location in the state capital features plenty of popular hangouts for students. Since many bars are situated around the campus and across High Street (eastern boundary of campus), "Ohio State does get rowdy on Thursday nights," says an OSU student. The campus is considered safe, since Ohio State has its own police force and also employs students as "ambassadors" to help keep the peace.

Students say that cars are not necessary and warn that finding parking spaces near campus can be a problem. They agree that the bus is the "cheapest and easiest means of travel." "All OSU students are required to pay the $9 a quarter bus fee; this includes the vast campus bus system and the city of Columbus bus system," a senior informs us.

Student Life

With so many students on campus there may not be such a thing as a "typical" Ohio State student. People from all backgrounds are represented here. "There is a surprising amount of tolerance between students of all backgrounds, "says an Ohio State student. "Even after the events of Sept 11th, there has been no open act of racism against Muslims or persons of Arab descent."

Students enjoy a rich and varied social life. There are over 700 school-sponsored clubs and organizations, including the Amateur Radio Club, the Flying Team, Habitat for Humanity, and Undergraduate Student Government. Some of the most popular organizations are Block-O (the student cheering section at OSU football games) and the Men's Glee Club (which performs concerts throughout Ohio and the rest of the country). Though there are over 20 sororities and almost 40 fraternities at Ohio State, Greek life accounts for less than 10 percent of the student body. As one student notes, "they do not play a significant role in social life unless you choose to be associated with them."

Drinking is popular at OSU, "although none of the surrounding bars/grocers sell to minors (according to my friends who have tried)," reveals a senior. "Since the frat/sor houses are across the street from campus, most underage drinking occurs there." However, students say that drugs are not popular on- or off-campus.

"Athletics are big at Ohio State," notes a student. Indeed, the school has the largest recreation and intramural program in the nation. OSU has large programs for soccer, basketball, flag football, softball, and even sand hockey in the spring. But "football is the one thing that unites every student on campus," says one student. A lot of excitement is generated when the Buckeyes play, especially against archrival University of Michigan. Every football Saturday is a party: Win or lose, the Ohio State band marches in the streets and the students go wild.

Test Scores (middle 50%):
 SAT Verbal: 530–630
 SAT Math: 550–660
 ACT Comp: 23–28
 ACT English: 22–28
 ACT Math: 23–29

HS Rank of Entering Freshmen:
 Top 10%: 33%
 Top 25%: 69%
 Top 50%: 94%

THE EXPERTS SAY...

" Nineteen colleges, 174 different majors, over 30,000 students, and the largest recreation and intramural program in the nation: If you can deal with its size, OSU has your opportunities. "

" Big school blues: Freshman classes are huge, and professors can be pretty unavailable. It may take some work to stand out from the crowd, or just avoid getting lost in it. "

Costs (2003–04)

Tuition and Fees, In-State: $6,651

Tuition and Fees, Out-of-State: $16,638

Room & Board: $6,429

Payment Plan(s): installment plan

Inst. Aid (est. 2003–04)

Institutional Aid, Need-Based: $9,475,831

Institutional Aid, Non-Need-Based: $44,710,138

FT Undergrads Receiving Aid: 50%
 Avg. Amount per Student: $8,926

FT Undergrads Receiving Non-Need-Based Scholarship or Grant Aid: 7%
 Avg. Amount per Student: $3,799

Of Those Receiving Any Aid:

Rec. Need-Based Scholarship or Grant Aid: 76%
 Average Award: $3,325

Rec. Need-Based Self-Help Aid: 88%
 Average Award: $5,034

Upon Graduation, Avg. Loan Debt per Student: $14,869

Financial Aid Deadline: 3/1 (priority)

Graduates

Alumni Giving: 26%

OHIO UNIVERSITY

120 Chubb Hall, Athens, OH 45701-2979
Admissions Phone: (740) 593-4100 Fax: (740) 593-0560
Email: admissions.freshmen@ohiou.edu Website: www.ohiou.edu
Application Website: https://applyweb.com/aw?ohiou

General Info

Type of School: public, coed

Setting: rural

Academic Calendar: quarter

Student Body

Full-Time Undergrads: 16,053
 Men: 47%, Women: 53%

Part-Time Undergrads: 1,147
 Men: 40%, Women: 60%

Total Undergrad Population:
 African American: 3%
 Asian American: 1%
 Latino: 1%
 Native American: 1%
 Caucasian: 93%
 International: 1%
 Out-of-State: 9%
 Living Off-Campus: 57%
 In Fraternities: 12%
 In Sororities: 14%

Graduate and First-Professional
 Students: 3,252

Academics

Full-Time Faculty: 866
 With Ph.D.: 88%

Part-Time Faculty: 297
 With Ph.D.: 66%

Student/Faculty Ratio: 18:1

Most Popular Majors:
 journalism (5%)
 recreation and sports sciences
  (5%)
 human & consumer sciences
  (4%)
 biological sciences (4%)
 telecommunications (4%)

Completing 2 or More Majors: 6%

Freshmen Retention Rate: 83%

Graduation Rates:
 43% within four years
 70% within six years

Admissions

Regular Application Deadline: 2/1

Fall Transfer Deadline: 5/15
 (priority)

Spring Transfer Deadline: 2/15
 (priority)

Total # of Students Applied: 12,937
 Admitted: 10,235
 Enrolled: 3,672

Inside the Classroom

There are nine undergraduate colleges that make up Ohio University at Athens: arts and sciences; business; communications; education; engineering; fine arts; health and human services; University College and Honors Tutorial. Within the College of Communication, the E.W Scripps School of Journalism is ranked among the top 10 nationally by the Associated Press Managing Editors Association, while the School of Visual Communication has more Hearst Foundation Photojournalism Competition grand champions than any other school in the history of the Hearst program.

The most interesting of the OU colleges is the Honors Tutorial, patterned after the tutorial systems of such British universities as Oxford and Cambridge. Twenty-five specialized majors are offered; students combine classes with one-on-one tutorials offered by faculty in their discipline. Students progress at their own pace and can even graduate in three years.

There are currently 285 undergraduate programs at OU. Students say the workload varies by department and college. A premed student gives us her biased opinion: "The college of engineering and the college of business contain much higher standards and harder class loads compared to the college of fine arts or the college of education."

Classes run on a quarterly basis, with each quarter lasting nine weeks. Students are on break for six weeks between Thanksgiving to New Year, and ten weeks between early June and the beginning of September. One student calls this calendar one of the most appealing aspects of OU, explaining: "I enjoy meeting new professors three different times a year and the fact that we get a six-week break between Thanksgiving and Christmas."

Students call the faculty "helpful and supportive." With an average of 22 students in a class, the faculty is fairly accessible. "It is rare not to be able to get in to see a professor within a day or two of contacting them," says a student, "and email communication is even faster (almost instantaneous)!"

Campus Environment

Ohio University—preparing to celebrate its bicentennial in 2004—is the oldest public institution of higher learning in the state of Ohio and the first in the Northwest Territory. The school is located in the town of Athens, which lies about 75 miles southeast of Columbus. An Ohio guidance counselor describes it as "a large state university in a small-town setting." The setting factored into at least one student's decision to attend Ohio U: "I chose the school over OSU in particular because it was smaller and I felt more safe in Athens than Columbus," explains a junior. "Everything is close in Athens and I didn't have to worry about a car or the bus."

The campus itself is beautiful. The university has more than 200 buildings on 1,700 acres. Students can find it "a beautiful and relaxing place" to study. However, students say there has been some controversy recently over "the fact that OU seems to spend more money on the campus landscapes than they do on the classrooms or dorm rooms."

OU has 40 residence halls (located on the East, West, South and New South College Greens) that house approximately 7,000 students. Freshmen are required to live in campus housing and participate in the food service plan. "First-year students are able to rank items such as a particular green, smoking preference, and quiet policy in order to be placed into a room" says one student. She also warns, "The campus buildings are usually at maximum capacity, so there is not much room to relocate during roommate problems." In addition to the more traditional dining hall food ("the worst food I have ever eaten," gripes one student), OU has an excellent "veggie" meal program, one that provides many food choices for avowed vegetarians.

Recent renovation projects at OU include the football stadium, where seating capacity increased to 24,000 spectators. The new athletic mall is nearing completion with the construction of a multipurpose sports facility, which includes a 400-meter running track and Astroturf field. The university also recently purchased the local movie theater and is in the process of renovating it.

Student Life

Though located in a small, rural town, OU is rich and varied, with many chances to meet people and get involved. "Although it is small, you can meet a new person every day," says one enthusiastic upperclassman. "The students are very welcoming and friendly… As an RA for two years, I really haven't seen anyone who couldn't eventually find an activity or friends."

OU has more than 350 student organizations, including 33 fraternities and sororities. A junior explains who goes Greek and who doesn't: "Many students get involved to meet people or so they can live off-campus their sophomore year. Others don't join because of the cost and time required to 'rush.'" There are so many campus and community activities to select, "there is rarely an opportunity to become bored!" says an OU student. Among the most popular clubs are the Student Senate (this group offers an internship program that helps first-year students in getting involved), Alpha Phi Omega (National Service Fraternity) and the Public Relations Student Society of America.

Sports are a big part of life at OU. There are 65 intramural teams to choose from, of which volleyball, Frisbee, basketball, baseball and broomball are popular choices. "Attendance at varsity games is very high," says one student fan, "because admission for students is free." The men's ice hockey games are crowd pleasers: The team won three national championships in the last decade, and its games routinely jam the campus ice arena.

Students and guidance counselors admit that OU has a well-deserved rep for being a party school. "The majority of students spend both weekends and weeknights drinking and going to parties," we hear. One upperclassman describes her peers: "The typical student appears to be somebody who has graduated at the top 25 percent of his/her high school class and enjoys partying every weekend." Court Street in Athens is known for the campus bar scene, locally referred to as the "Court Street Shuffle." A highlight of OU's social scene is definitely Halloween weekend. For three days, it seems that downtown Athens and campus become one continuous party. The festival draws about 10,000–12,000 on the weekend nearest Halloween, as well as some controversy. While most don't dress up, some may choose not to dress, period, and there are a number of arrests (though this has been decreasing) each year.

Test Scores (middle 50%):
  SAT Verbal: 500–600
  SAT Math: 500–600
  ACT Comp: 22–26
  ACT English: 21–26
  ACT Math: 21–26
HS Rank of Entering Freshmen:
  Top 10%: 19%
  Top 25%: 51%
  Top 50%: 89%
Avg. HS GPA: 3.3

THE EXPERTS SAY...

" Ohio University's school of journalism is outstanding— a bargain for both in-state and out-of-state students. "

" The campus is beautiful, though the population is startlingly white. Recruiting minorities should be a higher priority. "

Costs (2003–04)

Tuition and Fees, In-State: $7,128

Tuition and Fees, Out-of-State: $15,351

Room & Board: $7,320

Inst. Aid (est. 2003–04)

Institutional Aid, Need-Based: $1,341,867

Institutional Aid, Non-Need-Based: $9,926,911

FT Undergrads Receiving Aid: 48%
  Avg. Amount per Student: $6,823

FT Undergrads Receiving Non-Need-Based Scholarship or Grant Aid: 8%
  Avg. Amount per Student: $3,813

Of Those Receiving Any Aid:

Rec. Need-Based Scholarship or Grant Aid: 47%
  Average Award: $3,487

Rec. Need-Based Self-Help Aid: 87%
  Average Award: $4,115

Upon Graduation, Avg. Loan Debt per Student: $16,307

Financial Aid Deadline: 3/15 (priority)

Graduates

Companies Recruiting On Campus: 574

OKLAHOMA STATE UNIVERSITY

324 Student Union, Stillwater, OK 74078
Admissions Phone: (405) 744-6858; (800) 233-5019 (in-state) Fax: (405) 744-5285
Email: admit@okstate.edu
Website: www.okstate.edu

General Info

Type of School: public, coed

Setting: small town

Academic Calendar: semester

Student Body

Full-Time Undergrads: 16,402
  Men: 51%, Women: 49%

Part-Time Undergrads: 2,227
  Men: 51%, Women: 49%

Total Undergrad Population:
  African American: 3%
  Asian American: 2%
  Latino: 2%
  Native American: 9%
  Caucasian: 80%
  International: 5%
  Out-of-State: 13%
  Living Off-Campus: 61%
  In Fraternities: 14%
  In Sororities: 18%

Graduate and First-Professional
  Students: 4,888

Academics

Full-Time Faculty: 905
  With Ph.D.: 91%

Part-Time Faculty: 155
  With Ph.D.: 28%

Student/Faculty Ratio: 21:1

Most Popular Majors:
  animal science (3%)
  mechanical engineering (3%)
  marketing (3%)
  elementary education (3%)
  electrical engineering (3%)

Completing 2 or More Majors: 1%

Freshmen Retention Rate: 80%

Graduation Rates:
  25% within four years
  59% within six years

Admissions

Total # of Students Applied: 6,629
  Admitted: 5,930
  Enrolled: 3,484

Test Scores (middle 50%):
  SAT Verbal: 490–600
  SAT Math: 500–610
  ACT Comp: 21–26
  ACT English: 21–27
  ACT Math: 19–26

Inside the Classroom

The 15,000-plus students at Oklahoma State University's main campus in Stillwater can choose from an astounding number of degree programs. Strong, popular majors exist in each undergraduate college: management and accounting (College of Business Administration); mechanical, aerospace, electrical, and computer engineering (College of Engineering, Architecture, and Technology); animal science and agricultural economics (College of Agricultural Sciences and Natural Resources); elementary education (College of Education); early childhood education and hotel and restaurant management (College of Human Environmental Sciences); and psychology and journalism (College of Arts and Sciences). There's even a well-respected College of Veterinary Medicine here. OSU is just one of two schools that offer a unique bachelor's degree in fire protection and safety engineering technology—a program that's been internationally designated as "the West Point of Fire Service."

Although Oklahoma State is a huge, comprehensive university, the school is quick to point out that each student is given personal attention. There are a lot of undergrads, but there are also a lot of degree programs, so the average number of students majoring in any one department is fewer than 150. The school seems a lot smaller once you have declared a major, we hear. But in the meantime, you'll probably have to deal with many large lectures and teaching assistants rather than professors. The student/faculty ratio is 21:1.

All OSU undergrads must fulfill general education requirements in such areas as English comp, U.S. history, lab and natural sciences, math, humanities, social and behavioral sciences, and international studies.

A high school guidance counselor from Oklahoma tells us that OSU has changed for the better in recent years: "They have improved their business programs and have fantastic master's degree programs."

Campus Environment

The OSU campus is large, encompassing 840 acres and more than 200 permanent buildings. The Edmon Low Library is the biggest library in the state and one of the biggest in the entire Southwest. The Student Union is nothing to sniff at, either: Complete with hotel facilities, a rec center, a research center, and several performing arts venues, it's one of the largest student unions in the country. The university also owns the nearby Lake Carl Blackwell area, a huge recreational area which also serves as the region's water supply, in addition to thousands of acres throughout the state devoted to farm land or research stations.

The school has beds for more than 5,000 students, and in general, all freshmen are required to live on campus. Housing options include traditional residence halls, deluxe suites, and apartments. Greek members may also choose to live with their fraternity or sorority. High school guidance counselors give the dorms (and the food) a big thumbs-up. Chances are, you'll never tire of eating on campus, as there are more than 24 dining options in the residence halls.

After their first year, most students move off-campus to one of the many affordable apartments and other housing available for rent in Stillwater. Everyone is allowed to have a car; roughly half of the student body does. Most coeds walk, bike, or rollerblade around campus, and there's frequent trolley service as well. For trips farther away, students catch the bus in town. Stillwater is in north central Oklahoma, about an hour from Oklahoma City and Tulsa.

Student Life

Given the low in-state tuition, it's not surprising that the majority of OSU undergrads are from Oklahoma. It's a culturally diverse student body, with a sizeable minority and international population, including more than 1,400 Native Americans. Students are reportedly very nice, welcoming, laid-back… and bursting with OSU pride. Some "Cowboys" would dye themselves orange (the school color) if they could. Indeed, not many people take themselves too seriously here, and studying often takes a back seat to partying. A lot of drinking certainly goes on, although we hear that Stillwater officials rigidly enforce the alcohol laws (no drinking under 21 or in public). Fraternities and sororities are popular, attracting 14 percent of the men and 18 percent of the women, but Greek life is not necessarily the only game in town: There are literally hundreds of student-run clubs on campus.

Oklahoma State has long been admired for its successful athletic programs. OSU athletes have won over 40 national titles (only USC, UCLA, and Stanford have claimed more team championships), and its facilities are impressive and always packed. The basketball arena has been called the best in the country. There are 17 varsity teams and many more intramural and club sports offered. Football games are intense, almost religious events. Standing-room–only crowds of more than 50,000 pack Lewis Stadium. Fans are wild, especially when the "Spirit Rider" gallops across the field after each touchdown, or the revered mascot "Pistol Pete" makes an appearance. One of the biggest events of the year is the gigantic Orange Peel pep rally, where musical and comedy acts perform in the stadium before the first home game of the season to pump up the crowd even more.

Arguably the three most salient features of OSU—sports, parties, and school spirit—come together during a Homecoming unrivaled in its sheer size, magnitude, and popularity. The largest traditional homecoming in the nation, it is a weeklong celebration peppered with festivals and street fairs. At one point during the week, the campus is closed to automobile traffic so that OSU students, parents, alumni, and fans can do the "Walk-Around" to look at the colorfully decorated (in orange, no doubt) houses and lawns and vote on which is the best.

Stillwater boasts nearly a dozen shopping centers and about 100 restaurants and bars. It's a warm and friendly town, and it caters pretty heavily to the student population. Golfers can enjoy several nationally acclaimed courses, and five area lakes offer various activities including water-skiing, sailing, fishing, and camping. A number of museums and other cultural venues dot the town, and annual events such as Run for the Arts Fine Art and Jazz Festival, Tumbleweed Calf Fry, Eskimo Joe's Birthday Bash, and county fairs draw significant crowds as well.

HS Rank of Entering Freshmen:
  Top 10%: 25%
  Top 25%: 51%
  Top 50%: 83%

Avg. HS GPA: 3.49

Costs (2003–04)

Tuition and Fees, In-State: $3,748

Tuition and Fees, Out-of-State: $10,066

Room & Board: $5,468

Payment Plan(s): installment plan

THE EXPERTS SAY…

" Oklahoma State's fire protection program is groundbreaking. "

" It doesn't matter if you don't know the difference between a halfback and a fullback. Just paint yourself orange, stand up and cheer! "

Inst. Aid (2002–03)

Institutional Aid, Need-Based: $2,209,250

Institutional Aid, Non-Need-Based: $2,980,020

FT Undergrads Receiving Aid: 48%
  Avg. Amount per Student: $7,671

FT Undergrads Receiving Non-Need-Based Scholarship or Grant Aid: 24%
  Avg. Amount per Student: $2,685

Of Those Receiving Any Aid:

Rec. Need-Based Scholarship or Grant Aid: 71%
  Average Award: $3,324

Rec. Need-Based Self-Help Aid: 73%
  Average Award: $3,862

Upon Graduation, Avg. Loan Debt per Student: $16,268

Financial Aid Deadline: rolling

Graduates

Going to Graduate School:
  11% Within One Year

Accepting Job Offer:
  54% at time of graduation

Companies Recruiting On Campus:
  724

Alumni Giving: 17%

OREGON STATE UNIVERSITY

104 Kerr Administration Building, Corvallis, OR 97331-2106
Admissions Phone: (541) 737-4411; (800) 291-4192 Fax: (541) 737-2482
Email: osuadmit@oregonstate.edu
Website: oregonstate.edu

General Info

Type of School: public, coed
Academic Calendar: quarter

Student Body

Full-Time Undergrads: 13,744
  Men: 54%, Women: 46%

Part-Time Undergrads: 1,225
  Men: 52%, Women: 48%

Total Undergrad Population:
  African American: 1%
  Asian American: 8%
  Latino: 4%
  Native American: 1%
  Caucasian: 79%
  International: 2%
  Out-of-State: 11%
  Living Off-Campus: 78%

Graduate and First-Professional
  Students: 3,380

Academics

Most Popular Majors:
  business administration (13%)
  exercise and sport science (4%)
  general science (4%)
  human development and family
  studies (4%)
  liberal studies (4%)

Completing 2 or More Majors: 3%

Freshmen Retention Rate: 81%

Graduation Rates:
  29% within four years
  60% within six years

Admissions

Regular Application Deadline: 3/1
  (priority)

Early Action Deadline: 11/1

Fall Transfer Deadline: 5/1

Spring Transfer Deadline: 3/1

Total # of Students Applied: 7,410
  Admitted: 6,529
  Enrolled: 2,949

Test Scores (middle 50%):
  SAT Verbal: 470–590
  SAT Math: 490–610
  ACT Comp: 20–26
  ACT English: 18–25
  ACT Math: 19–26

In the Classroom

In some ways Oregon State feels like a small college, although it has the opportunities and facilities of a large, state-supported research university. Guidance counselors list the small-community feel, the conservative atmosphere, PAC-10 sports, and the practical, career-oriented academic programs as the most attractive attributes of OSU. Drawbacks are the large classes and reliance on TAs rather than professors to teach many courses.

A small-town friendliness pervades the campus, and students generally find the professors accessible and helpful. One student notes, "Most upper level class sizes are small and a large majority of the faculty sincerely care about their students." Even the lower level classes are not as large as you might expect; however, if you are majoring in any of the sciences or in engineering, a student says, "you can count on having many 100+ class sizes during your time at OSU."

Oregon State is composed of the following colleges: agricultural sciences; business; engineering; forestry; health and human performance; home economics; education; liberal arts; oceanic atmospheric sciences; pharmacy; science; and veterinary medicine. The university's undergraduate programs in engineering, computer science, forestry, the health professions, and business are regarded highly. Among its graduates are Linus Pauling, the only person to win two unshared Nobel prizes, and Doug Englebart, who invented the computer mouse and multiple-window computer screen. The required core curriculum emphasizes creative thinking, the arts, sciences, literature, lifelong fitness, world cultures, and global awareness. To meet core requirements, undergraduate students must obtain 48 credits (typical courses are worth 3 credits) including at least 15 credits in the category of Skills Courses, 27 credits in Perspectives Courses, and 6 credits in Synthesis Courses. In addition, students must take an intensive writing course.

Each year, nearly one-fifth of OSU undergraduates work on research projects with faculty and graduate students. The Undergraduate Research, Innovation, Scholarship, and Creativity program supports student research conducted on campus or other related research sites. The International Undergraduate Research program allows persons majoring in environmental sciences, public health, political science, or a related field to prepare a research topic on campus with a faculty mentor and conduct their research overseas.

A variety of programs offer special opportunities for OSU students. Outstanding undergraduates can participate in the University Honors College, which offers small classes taught by top professors. The International Degree program allows students to add an international component to any major offered by Oregon State. The university's internship and co-op education programs blend academic study with employment in business, industry, government, or social service agencies.

Campus Environment

OSU is a large university in a small town. Most inhabitants of Corvallis seem to either study at the university or work there. Over two-thirds of OSU students live off campus, and most of those find housing in Corvallis, although many also commute from further afield. Apartment rents depend on distance from the school, with the most expensive being those within easy walking distance. Freshmen are not required to live on campus, although housing is available for those that want to.

The university has 10 coed residence halls, including several with a special theme such as wellness, international, or honors. Within the halls you can also choose special areas such as quiet floors; all halls are smoke free. Most dorms house students from all classes, but freshmen can choose to live in a freshmen-only residence hall.

Most students have cars, including many freshmen, but parking is limited. Since many more parking permits are sold than there are parking spaces, the competition for a parking spot can get vicious. Students living off-campus are encouraged to walk, bike, or carpool to classes. Taking a bus is another option; students ride free by showing an OSU ID on city buses.

Students surveyed agreed that there isn't much going on in Corvallis. Those who found Corvallis "dead" recommended the nightlife in Salem or Portland. Others, however, used more favorable terms like "peaceful" to describe the town, and one likened it to living in a Norman Rockwell painting. Another student asserted the town does have something to offer, and pointed to "three department stores, a K-Mart, a Rite-Aid, …" Regardless of Corvallis, students agreed that the location in the Willamette Valley an hour from both the Pacific Coast and the Cascade Mountains offers access to outstanding outdoor recreation options.

Student Life

"The key to really enjoying life at Oregon State is becoming involved," one student says. With over 300 student organizations and clubs to choose from, it's not hard to find something you're interested in. Students agree that the Greek system is a key component of life at OSU. Though the number of students involved in Greek life isn't that great, those who do participate are often leaders in student government, student organizations, and campus service groups. And Greek organizations sponsor the biggest social events; however, "Even if you do not belong to a frat or sorority, you have ample opportunities to attend their parties," one nonmember explains.

Many students also get involved in sports, either as spectators or participants. OSU is an NCAA Division I school and a member of the PAC 10 conference, although the Beavers have not won many high-visibility championships in recent years. Men's varsity teams include football, basketball, crew, soccer, baseball, wrestling, and golf. Women's options are volleyball, soccer, basketball, gymnastics, swimming, softball, crew, and golf. In addition, there are various sport club teams that compete with clubs from other schools in a wide range of sports from rodeo to rugby. Completing the possibilities are more than 30 intramural sports.

Although the administration is strongly committed to increasing diversity, ethnic minorities currently do not have a large presence on campus. Moreover, the school's political climate leans toward the conservative side. One student remarked, "OSU is very welcoming to just about everyone, unless you are extremely liberal, where you might find the University of Oregon more to your liking since there are more hippies and liberal art majors."

HS Rank of Entering Freshmen:
Top 10%: 18%
Top 25%: 47%
Top 50%: 81%
Avg. HS GPA: 3.45

Costs (2003–04)

Tuition and Fees, In-State: $4,869

Tuition and Fees, Out-of-State: $17,625

Room & Board: $6,336

THE EXPERTS SAY…

" A large university with a small school feel, Oregon State is perfect for preprofessional students who like a conservative atmosphere. "

" For a less conservative climate, check out the University of Oregon and Michigan State University. "

PACIFIC LUTHERAN UNIVERSITY

Pacific Lutheran University, Tacoma, WA 98447
Admissions Phone: (253) 535-7151; (800) 274-6758 Fax: (253) 536-5136
Email: admissions@plu.edu
Website: www.plu.edu

General Info

Type of School: private, coed, Evangelical Lutheran Church in America (ELCA)

Setting: suburban

Academic Calendar: 4-1-4

Student Body

Full-Time Undergrads: 2,914
Men: 37%, Women: 63%

Part-Time Undergrads: 225
Men: 43%, Women: 57%

Total Undergrad Population:
African American: 2%
Asian American: 5%
Latino: 2%
Native American: 1%
Caucasian: 78%
International: 5%
Out-of-State: 25%
Living Off-Campus: 49%

Graduate and First-Professional
Students: 277

Academics

Full-Time Faculty: 235
With Ph.D.: 90%

Part-Time Faculty: 69
With Ph.D.: 22%

Student/Faculty Ratio: 13:1

Most Popular Majors:
business administration (9%)
nursing (6%)
psychology (4%)
communications (4%)
biology (3%)

Completing 2 or More Majors: 9%

Freshmen Retention Rate: 83%

Graduation Rates:
45% within four years
68% within six years

Admissions

Regular Application Deadline: 3/1 (priority)

Fall Transfer Deadline: rolling

Spring Transfer Deadline: rolling

Total # of Students Applied: 1,973
Admitted: 1,575
Enrolled: 694

Inside the Classroom

Although administered by the Evangelical Lutheran Church in America, PLU welcomes students of all faiths and, according to the administration, "academic integrity is never compromised by slanting education to agree with a particular religious bias." No religion courses are required; however, many students take part in at least some of the optional religious services and activities offered each week.

PLU provides a respected liberal arts program with 37 majors to choose from. The most popular majors are business, education, biology, and preprofessional health. Several specialized schools have been established within the university: a school of business administration, a school of education, and a school of nursing. These schools are largely undergraduate-oriented, although they also offer some graduate programs. Guidance counselors give the school high marks for helping students prepare for professional careers.

The "Freshmen Experience" consists of three required courses designed to help students make the transition to college-level study: the Freshman Writing Seminar, the Critical Conversation Seminar, and an approved January Term course (students choose among several options). PLU is on a 4-1-4 semester system with January Term options on and off campus that allow you to concentrate intensely on one subject for one month.

Regardless of their majors, PLU students must complete a core requirement, though they can choose between two differently defined cores: one is a distribution of courses from traditional disciplines (Core I), while the other is more interdisciplinary and international in nature (Core II). In addition, all students must satisfy requirements for courses in math reasoning, science and the scientific method, perspectives on diversity, physical education, and a senior seminar project.

One student describes the academic environment as "challenging" but notes that "teachers are very interested in your success" and the "students are also very supportive of one another." A senior says that professors "are highly accessible and they teach all the classes—teaching assistants are not part of everyday life at PLU."

Campus Environment

PLU's campus, located in a suburb six miles south of Tacoma, is typical of the Pacific Northwest, with its towering fir trees and mountain views. Seattle, with all of its cultural and entertainment options, lies 40 miles to the north, and Mt. Rainier and the Pacific Coast are both within an easy two-hour drive.

"Parkland is not the best part of Tacoma as far as safety is concerned," one student admits. A campus escort service and free classes in self-defense are among the services the college offers for those concerned about their safety. In May 2001, the murder of a popular professor as he walked on a campus walkway got nationwide media coverage. Although this was an act of random violence by a deranged person that could have happened anywhere, it has contributed to student concerns about campus safety.

Pacific Lutheran has nine residence halls; except for one female-only hall, all are coed, with men and women segregated by wing. Freshmen are integrated into all the dorms, although one dorm, containing single rooms only, is reserved for students over 20 years of age. With no fraternities or sororities and no theme housing, students generally make a selection based on which dorm offers the best facilities and where their friends are living. Dorms in the Lower Campus have a reputation for being much more rowdy than Upper Campus dorms.

The administration admits parking can be "tough" to find in campus lots and "strongly discourages" freshmen from bringing a car to campus. Bicycles are encouraged as an alternative mode of transport and bike storage is available in each residence hall. But most students consider a car a necessity on this suburban campus unless you're happy staying on campus and "don't even need to get to a grocery store," in the words of one student.

Student Life

There are two groups of students at Pacific Lutheran. A senior categorizes these as "the kids who party a lot" and "the kids who go to all the religious activities on campus." Several years ago, the university even tried separate freshmen orientations for those that did and did not want a Christian focus. And while this practice has been discontinued, the delineation remains: Both groups coexist peacefully, albeit a bit uneasily.

For those that want an active Christian religious life, there are a variety of organizations and events to consider. The biggest religious services are Jam 62 on Monday nights, Common Ground on Wednesday nights, and New Song church on Saturday nights. Student religious organizations include the Aliya Jewish Club, Baptist Student Ministries, Catholic Student Ministries, Fellowship of Christian Athletes, Intervarsity Christian Fellowship, Latter-Day Saints Student Association, Upper Room, and Young Life.

For "the kids who party a lot," there are generally several weekend parties geared to PLU students. Because PLU has a strict policy against drinking on campus, parties rarely get out of control; alcohol is more of a problem off campus. Surveyed students agreed that, while they knew of drug usage (mostly marijuana), it was not widespread and not much of a problem.

Sports are big at PLU. By the time they graduate, one-quarter of all PLU students will have competed in varsity sports and more than one-half will have been involved in intramural sports. The Lutes compete in NCAA Division III as members of the Northwest Conference—and they generally do very well! Each year the conference awards an all-sports trophy to the school with the conference's best all-round athletic program; the Lutes have earned the award for 14 of last the 15 years. Varsity sports for women are basketball, crew, cross country, golf, soccer, softball, swimming, tennis, track and field, volleyball. Men's varsity sports are: baseball, basketball, crew, cross country, football, golf, soccer, swimming, tennis, track and field, and wrestling.

Other schools to check out: Gonzaga, Pepperdine, Santa Clara, Puget Sound.

Test Scores (middle 50%):
SAT Verbal: 500–620
SAT Math: 500–620
ACT Comp: 22–29
ACT English: 21–28
ACT Math: 20–28

HS Rank of Entering Freshmen:
Top 10%: 39%
Top 25%: 70%
Top 50%: 92%

Avg. HS GPA: 3.62

THE EXPERTS SAY...

" PLU offers strong preprofessional programs in a Christian environment. "

" Whether you're religious or not, guys who want a wide range of dating options should be pleased by PLU's uneven ratio of three women for every two men. "

Costs (2004–5)

Tuition and Fees: $20,790
Room & Board: $6,410
Payment Plan(s): installment plan

Inst. Aid (2002–03)

Institutional Aid, Need-Based: $12,211,206

Institutional Aid, Non-Need-Based: $6,284,280

FT Undergrads Receiving Aid: 71%
Avg. Amount per Student: $16,210

FT Undergrads Receiving Non-Need-Based Scholarship or Grant Aid: 17%
Avg. Amount per Student: $6,320

Of Those Receiving Any Aid:

Rec. Need-Based Scholarship or Grant Aid: 83%
Average Award: $7,064

Rec. Need-Based Self-Help Aid: 92%
Average Award: $8,217

Upon Graduation, Avg. Loan Debt per Student: $20,585

Financial Aid Deadline: rolling, 2/1 (priority)

Graduates

Alumni Giving: 9%

PARSONS SCHOOL OF DESIGN

66 Fifth Avenue, New York, NY 10011
Admissions Phone: (877) 528-3321 Fax: (212) 229-5166
Email: customer@newschool.edu
Website: www.parsons.edu

General Info

Type of School: private, coed
Academic Calendar: semester

Student Body

Full-Time Undergrads: 2,313
  Men: 24%, Women: 76%

Part-Time Undergrads: 161
  Men: 21%, Women: 79%

Total Undergrad Population:
  African American: 3%
  Asian American: 18%
  Latino: 6%
  Native American: <1%
  Caucasian: 31%
  International: 32%
  Out-of-State: 47%
  Living Off-Campus: 79%

Graduate and First-Professional
  Students: 456

Academics

Full-Time Faculty: 48

Part-Time Faculty: 711

Student/Faculty Ratio: 10:1

Most Popular Majors:
  fashion design (20%)
  communication design (16%)
  design and management (12%)
  photography (11%)
  illustration (8%)

Freshmen Retention Rate: 86%

Graduation Rates:
  52% within four years
  65% within six years

Computers: Computer Required

Admissions

Regular Application Deadline: 3/1

Fall Transfer Deadline: 3/1 (priority)

Total # of Students Applied: 1,630
  Admitted: 690
  Enrolled: 309

Test Scores (middle 50%):
  SAT Verbal: 490–660
  SAT Math: 505–620

Avg. HS GPA: 3.1

Inside the Classroom

What better place to study art and design than in New York City? Parsons School of Design offers its students focused design programs in the heart of the city's most innovative neighborhood, Greenwich Village. Parsons students also benefit from the resources of its larger learning environment, New School University, which also includes Eugene Lang College, Mannes College of Music, the Jazz and Contemporary Music Program, the New School, the Graduate Faculty of Political and Social Science, the Milano Graduate School of Management and Urban Policy, and the Actors Studio.

Parsons offers bachelor of fine arts degrees in fashion design, communication design, architecture, interior design, product design, illustration, fine arts, photography, design and technology, and integrated design. Parsons digital design programs are top-notch. There's also a bachelor of business administration in design and management. Over two-thirds of the credits needed to graduate are in departmental requirements. Freshmen enroll in the Foundation program, which emphasizes drawing and a studio curriculum in two and three dimensional design, digital design, and the various professional design fields. Foundation students also take art history and other liberal arts courses.

Juniors are encouraged to begin internships in their chosen field; Parsons' busy Office of Career Services, which serves industry professionals as well as students, helps students make career-track choices. Parsons' industry partnerships are another career development program. Guided by faculty members, students take on a design assignment given by an industry partner, learning to deal with real world limitations of fixed budgets, deadlines, and materials. The Center for New Design, which opened in the fall of 1999, is a project-based design laboratory. Advanced students work with faculty on projects sponsored by commercial enterprises and the public sector. Students also have the option of study abroad in the design capitals of the world, including Paris. Parsons students regularly exhibit their work at the school's galleries on themes like New Technology in Fashion Design, the Democratic Monument in America, and Kosovo Photography.

Parsons faculty are predominantly design professionals still active and often prominent in their fields, and serve as professional contacts for students. Former alums include such luminaries as Adrian (the fashion/costume designer for *The Wizard of Oz*), Perry Ellis, Edward Hopper, Jasper Johns, Donna Karan, Isaac Mizrahi, and Norman Rockwell.

Campus Environment

New York City is the art and design capital of the world, and Parsons students make good use of its museums, galleries, and design studios. Parsons is located in Greenwich Village, one of the city's oldest and most offbeat neighborhoods, and a traditional magnet for all things creative and new. The Village is also the location of music clubs and bars frequented by students. Soho, with its galleries and chic stores, is a stone's throw away.

The New School lacks a central campus and has its buildings clustered around Village residences and busy city streets. Housing is guaranteed to freshmen only, who have the option of staying in the residence system for sophomore year. Loeb houses freshmen from all the New School divisions, and offers furnished suites with kitchenettes, dining areas and bathrooms; Loeb also has an art studio, important to the Parsons student. The Marleton House and Union Square are shared with nonuniversity tenants and offer singles, double rooms, and suites. 84 Williams Street, located downtown in the Seaport area, offers apartment style housing.

Older students look for apartments in the East Village and Brooklyn's Williamsburg and Greenpoint areas, havens for artists. The University Housing Office provides apartment listings and a comprehensive off-campus housing guide. There are four dining facilities on campus with weekday service, which students can use on a cash basis or as part of a food plan; many prefer to grab a bite from the hundreds of restaurants, delis, and pizzerias in the neighborhood. There is no campus parking in congested Greenwich Village, and students would be wise to leave their cars at home. Parsons is near all mass transit, including bus, subways, and cabs to all parts of the city. Students walk to classes; some bike (beware the traffic and bicycle theft) or rollerblade.

Student Life

Cosmopolitan Parsons is diverse, with a large number of international and minority students, but the school is predominantly female. Dating isn't a problem for Parsons women, however, with all the other university students around. Social life for first-year students is centered around dorm life, with forays out to the Village to explore the clubs and bars. Frequent exhibitions of student work, plus school projects involving the city's many museums and galleries, also keep students occupied. Freshman orientation includes a celebration on New York's Circle Line cruise around Manhattan.

Like most of their peers in New York City, Parsons students tend to be liberal and outspoken. With so many off-campus students, campus activities are limited, but there are a number of active clubs, including the feminist organization Moxie, which examines issues surrounding violence against women and body image "in a creative and artistic context." There's a popular anime screening club, numerous student zines, a Christian fellowship, and a Peter Drucker management club. There are no fraternities or sororities, and no varsity or intramural athletics. However, there are recreational programs which feature holistic and exercise-based activities such yoga, dance, Capoeira, and meditation classes.

Whether or not they are native New Yorkers, most Parsons students consider the city their home, and use its cultural resources to the max. Most become involved in the design industry, and develop a level of participation in the life of the city that is unusual for college students. Parsons students were deeply affected by 9/11: A contingent took over an abandoned Burger King near ground zero to feed the rescue workers.

Other schools to check out: Cooper Union, RISD, Fashion Institute of Technology, Eugene Lang.

Costs (2004–5)

Tuition and Fees: $25,925

Room & Board: $10,810

Payment Plan(s): installment plan

Inst. Aid (est. 2003–04)

Institutional Aid, Need-Based: $10,459,447

Institutional Aid, Non-Need-Based: $742,592

FT Undergrads Receiving Aid: 66% Avg. Amount per Student: $11,495

FT Undergrads Receiving Non-Need-Based Scholarship or Grant Aid: 4% Avg. Amount per Student: $2,972

THE EXPERTS SAY...

" There's a lot of opportunity for project-based, real world design experience at Parsons. The career services are excellent here. "

" You live, breathe, eat and sleep design here. Not the place to be if you want a liberal arts education. "

Of Those Receiving Any Aid:

Rec. Need-Based Scholarship or Grant Aid: 94% Average Award: $8,512

Rec. Need-Based Self-Help Aid: 57% Average Award: $5,063

Upon Graduation, Avg. Loan Debt per Student: $25,226

Financial Aid Deadline: 3/1 (priority)

PENNSYLVANIA STATE UNIVERSITY— UNIVERSITY PARK

201 Shields Building, Box 3000, University Park, PA 16804-3000
Admissions Phone: (814) 865-5471 Fax: (814) 863-7590 Email: admissions@psu.edu
Website: www.psu.edu Application Website: www.psu.edu/dept/admissions/apply

General Info

Type of School: public, coed

Academic Calendar: semester

Student Body

Full-Time Undergrads: 33,033
Men: 53%, Women: 47%

Part-Time Undergrads: 1,023
Men: 58%, Women: 42%

Total Undergrad Population:
African American: 4%
Asian American: 6%
Latino: 3%
Native American: <1%
Caucasian: 85%
International: 2%
Out-of-State: 25%
Living Off-Campus: 63%
In Fraternities: 13%
In Sororities: 10%

Graduate and First-Professional
Students: 6,793

Academics

Full-Time Faculty: 2,191
With Ph.D.: 77%

Part-Time Faculty: 325
With Ph.D.: 27%

Student/Faculty Ratio: 17:1

Freshmen Retention Rate: 91%

Graduation Rates:
44% within four years
80% within six years

Admissions

Regular Application Deadline: 11/30
(priority)

Transfer Application Deadline: rolling

Total # of Students Applied: 31,264
Admitted: 17,174
Enrolled: 6,048

Test Scores (middle 50%):
SAT Verbal: 530–630
SAT Math: 560–670

HS Rank of Entering Freshmen:
Top 10%: 43%
Top 25%: 80%
Top 50%: 98%

Avg. HS GPA: 3.54

Inside the Classroom

University Park—the main campus in the mammoth 20-campus Penn State system—has 10 undergraduate schools offering more than 160 academic programs, from agriculture to women's studies. High school guidance counselors rave about its "premier" engineering department. The workload tends to vary by major, running the gamut from "challenging and stimulating" classes (especially in science or engineering), to those that are "not too intense" and "not overwhelming." As one biology major puts it, "Some students are well-motivated and extremely competitive; others coast through with very easy classes and less than average grades."

Specific requirements vary by program, but all students must fulfill the broad general education requirements with classes in quantitative and communication skills, sciences, arts, physical education, and cultural diversity, among others. Large lecture classes—often numbering in the hundreds—are the norm, particularly for freshman core classes, and you'll have to work at staying involved. It's not easy to establish relationships with teachers in this kind of setting. But, assures a senior, "Once you are done with your first year, the classes are actually quite small." Regardless of class size, "smart, knowledgeable" professors are roundly praised for their accessibility and eagerness to help students, but, warns one Penn Stater, "you have to take the initiative." You may feel like just a number here, and freshmen are especially encouraged to seek out their advisers and professors, since there's "no one to check up on you." "Many freshmen take full advantage of the 24/7 party here—until they fail out," warns a senior.

Campus Environment

The "absolutely beautiful, huge" campus ("I am a senior and I still get lost") includes hundreds of classroom buildings, research facilities, athletic spaces, even farmland. There are five major housing complexes on campus "of various quality"; most are described as "comfortable" but "cramped" and "overcrowded." Chances are likely that, as a freshman, you'll be assigned to the massive East Halls area, a mini-city in itself that houses about 4,000. There are also honors dorms and special interest options, where students with similar interests, majors, or backgrounds can share a floor.

On-campus housing is guaranteed for freshmen only, so most students spend their remaining years in one of myriad apartments for rent in the surrounding community of State College, where costs are comparable to on-campus housing. "The farther you move away from campus, the better the apartment complex," we are told.

The school's remote location has its benefits—serenity, safety, a sense of community—and its pitfalls, as summed up by this junior: "I'd be lying to say there's a whole lot to do." Freshman aren't allowed cars on campus; most upperclassmen agree that having a car handy is not necessary since "everything is within walking distance," but it may be helpful for going out of town. (Beware of parking, though: it's "extremely limited and costly.")

Student Life

Even with a wonderfully diverse student body of 35,000, some complain of the homogenous, "Abercrombie" look of the population and that there is "little intermingling of blacks and whites." But with over 500 clubs and activities to choose from, "everyone can find their niche here," students assert. Those who are shy and "extremely introverted" may be overwhelmed by the sprawling 5,000-acre campus. But once you're involved, students say, you'll find yourself surrounded by resoundingly friendly and fun people ("it's a large family"). As one junior sums up her fellow coeds: "We all party hard and study hard."

And party hard they do. Penn Staters describe drinking as a "huge factor"—as a sophomore tells us, "there really isn't all that much to do on weekends other than drink." Despite the administration's continuing efforts to crack down on alcohol consumption, on "any given night of the week, there will be a party." The handful of bars in downtown State College are extremely strict about admitting minors, so undergrads under 21 make the nightly rounds of apartment parties, dorm gatherings, and fraternity bashes. With 57 fraternities and 22 sororities to choose from, even the Greek system at Penn State—the largest in the country—provides students with an overwhelming number of choices. Ten to 15 percent of the student body joins the Greek system, which some say has a "huge influence on social life." Others feel that "Greek life is simply an option." Since frat houses are often at the center of the party scene (sororities are relegated to the dorms), many new students gravitate toward them as a good way to meet people, but "the older students get, the less popular Greek life is." The Greeks are chiefly responsible for the Dance Marathon, or "THON," the largest student-run philanthropy in the country, raising over $3 million each year for kids with cancer.

The common thread among the student population is the legendary Penn State Pride—as the saying goes, the students "bleed blue and white." Probably the best sign of how deep school spirit runs here is the tremendous importance placed on the Nittany Lions football team. For most students, as well as several hundred visiting alumni and friends, football Saturdays are major social events, from pregame tailgates to postgame parties. Some feel, though, that the profitability of the renowned football team adds to the feeling that the school is run "more as a corporation than a university." The Penn State athletic program is huge and goes well beyond football—the highly ranked intercollegiate teams include men's basketball and wrestling, and women's basketball, field hockey, and lacrosse teams, just to name a few—though some gripe that they don't often receive the attention they deserve: "Every sport is a distant second to football." Innumerable intramural teams are well organized and highly competitive. "We take our athletics very seriously," proclaims one student. Another says, "So many gyms, so many intramural levels—it's mind-boggling, but crazy fun."

Costs (2003–04)

Tuition and Fees, In-State: $9,206

Tuition and Fees, Out-of-State: $18,828

Room & Board: $5,940

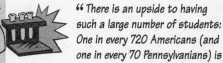

THE EXPERTS SAY...

" There is an upside to having such a large number of students: One in every 720 Americans (and one in every 70 Pennsylvanians) is a Penn State graduate—who may serve as a springboard to future career opportunities. "

" While it's unlikely you'll graduate in four years, you stand a decent chance of leaving Happy Valley in six years (as long as Mom and Dad keep signing those tuition checks). "

Inst. Aid (2002–03)

Institutional Aid, Need-Based: $17,107,383

Institutional Aid, Non-Need-Based: $13,974,382

FT Undergrads Receiving Aid: 49%
Avg. Amount per Student: $11,831

FT Undergrads Receiving Non-Need-Based Scholarship or Grant Aid: 11%
Avg. Amount per Student: $3,633

Of Those Receiving Any Aid:

Rec. Need-Based Scholarship or Grant Aid: 66%
Average Award: $4,349

Rec. Need-Based Self-Help Aid: 88%
Average Award: $4,376

Upon Graduation, Avg. Loan Debt per Student: $18,200

Financial Aid Deadline: rolling, 2/15 (priority)

PEPPERDINE UNIVERSITY

Seaver College, 24255 Pacific Coast Highway, Malibu, CA 90263-4392
Admissions Phone: (310) 506-4392 Fax: (310) 506-4861
Website: pepperdine.edu
Application Website: pepperdine.edu/seaver/admission/App.htm

General Info

Type of School: private, coed

Setting: suburban

Academic Calendar: semester

Student Body

Full-Time Undergrads: 2,608
 Men: 43%, Women: 57%

Part-Time Undergrads: 507
 Men: 47%, Women: 53%

Total Undergrad Population:
 African American: 7%
 Asian American: 9%
 Latino: 11%
 Native American: 1%
 Caucasian: 55%
 International: 6%
 Out-of-State: 48%
 Living Off-Campus: 52%
 In Fraternities: 24%
 In Sororities: 29%

Graduate and First-Professional
 Students: 4,638

Academics

Full-Time Faculty: 366
 With Ph.D.: 97%

Part-Time Faculty: 332
 With Ph.D.: 90%

Student/Faculty Ratio: 12:1

Most Popular Majors:
 business (14%)
 psychology (8%)
 international business (6%)
 political science (6%)
 biology (5%)

Freshmen Retention Rate: 89%

Graduation Rates:
 66% within four years
 78% within six years

Admissions

Regular Application Deadline: 1/15

Early Action Deadline: 11/15

Fall Transfer Deadline: 3/1, 1/15
 (priority)

Spring Transfer Deadline: 10/15

Total # of Students Applied: 5,503
 Admitted: 2,037
 Enrolled: 802

Inside the Classroom

What do you get when you cross a country club environment with conservative Christian academics? Pepperdine University. With a total of about 4,000 students enrolled in an undergraduate college (Seaver College) and graduate schools in business, education/psychology, law, and public policy, Pepperdine has great academics and personalized attention with a Christian bent.

With almost 3,000 undergraduates, Pepperdine offers bachelor's degrees in 36 majors and master's degrees in six majors. The departments of business (management); communication (advertising/journalism); and humanities (teacher education) are the school's top draws. Guidance counselors tell us that many of their most talented students are eager to study music and drama at Pepperdine. Professors here go out of their way to help you, and the academic environment is friendly and nurturing—so much so, it's common to see students dining with their professors.

"The academic standards are very high," says one California guidance counselor about Pepperdine. A student tells us, "The work here is not difficult, but it is comprehensive." For the general education (GE) requirements, students must take 16 courses in the liberal arts, which many complain take up too much time (up to four full semesters). Explains one sophomore, "All of my most challenging and time consuming classes have been GE. They tend to make it difficult to concentrate on my major." For those looking to get away, the school has programs in Florence, Heidelberg, London, and Buenos Aires for the academic year, and for the summer, several offbeat field-work options including an archaeological dig in Northern Israel; a medical mission to the jungles of Honduras; and a biblical sites visit in Egypt, Turkey, and Greece.

While the school has open admission with regard to religion, most students here identify themselves as Christian. And while some are more religious than others, most of the administrators and professors have a strong connection to the Church of Christ. In fact, the Center for Faith and Learning helps faculty to develop curriculum within a framework of Christian values. One of the biggest complaints we've heard is the required attendance at Convocation, a Christian-based seminar once a week. Though the topics tend to be more inspirational than spiritual (one student cites "anyone from a speaker against the death penalty to a hula dancer" as examples), students are graded on attendance—with the final "grade" averaged into their cumulative GPA.

Campus Environment

Guidance counselors say that the campus location—in the foothills of the Santa Monica Mountains, overlooking Malibu and the Pacific Ocean—makes Pepperdine a trendy pick for high school students. The ocean can be seen from almost every spot on campus. Though downtown Los Angeles is under an hour away, this corner of the globe seems a world apart. But as beautiful as the campus is, it's not terribly convenient for getting around: "isolated," says one student. Nor is Malibu a college town. In other words, without a car, you're bound to feel frustrated. The school is located on a hill, and there are tons—we mean tons—of stairs: As one student says, "If you have weak calves or don't like stairs, you will not survive."

All freshmen and sophomores live on campus in dorm suites or towers, each housing about 50 students. The rooms are considered nice, and so safe that many don't even lock their doors. Apart from the restriction on members of the opposite sex being in your room late at night, it's pretty standard dorm life—that is, if you call a dramatic view of the Pacific Ocean standard. Off-campus housing is incredibly tight: "It's Malibu, so housing is limited. You might end up living through the canyon, a good 45 minutes away," one student tells us.

Student Life

Vogue Magazine once called Pepperdine "the school of the suntan scholar." For the most part, there are two types of students here: wealthy students who feel that class attendance is optional, and religiously dedicated students. As for the first group, many students do in fact come from affluent families and act every bit the part ("The parking lot is lined with BMWs"). With a whopping price tag of $33,000 a year, Pepperdine doesn't come cheap—though we're told the financial aid is quite good. As for the second group, these are more academic-minded students who are fairly gung-ho about Christianity. One senior explains, "At times, religious students present an air of superiority over their sinning peers. If someone isn't rich or religious, he'll need a strong backbone to survive here." With the majority of students Caucasian, minority enrollment as a whole is sizable: seven percent African American, nine percent Asian American, and 11 percent Latino; six percent of students are international. Famous alums include actress Kim Fields, actresses Tia and Tamera Mowry, and Major League Baseball players Randy Wolf, Rick Thurman, and Mike Scott.

The social life at Pepperdine is tame and fairly low-key—with little excitement. As one sophomore tells us, "Pepperdine has a lot in common with a graveyard. It's dead. There are many weekends that I'm the only one in my dorm. And when the school tries to organize on-campus activities, no one goes." The administration manages to keep a relatively tight stronghold on the conservative tenor of the campus. That's not to say there aren't undercurrents of "liberalism," though: While you're not likely to see a protest for feminist, pro-choice, or gay rights, we're told these groups very much exist here. Greek life is huge, though there's no separate housing. In the school's attempt to defy the *Animal House* stereotype, the Greek system is dry (with strict monitoring) and has a "no hazing" policy.

Extracurriculars at Pepperdine tend to have a wholesome flavor: Lots of students volunteer, and aside from the bible study groups and retreats, there's a small a cappella gospel music group and Christian publication. Campus highlights are Riptide, where students jump in the ocean to start off the school year, and Song Fest, where students compete in song and dance routines. Athletics are also a big draw: With scores of athletic clubs and 14 Division I varsity teams to choose from (including championship golf, volleyball and water polo teams), and stellar year-round weather, it's no surprise that 99 percent of the student body participates in some type of physical fitness.

# of Students Waitlisted: 719
  Students Accepting Place: 416
  Waitlisted Students Admitted: 8

Test Scores (middle 50%):
  SAT Verbal: 540–640
  SAT Math: 550–660
  ACT Comp: 23–28

HS Rank of Entering Freshmen:
  Top 10%: 72%
  Top 25%: 95%
  Top 50%: 99%

Avg. HS GPA: 3.61

THE EXPERTS SAY...

" If you're looking for challenging academics on a conservative but diverse West Coast campus, take a close look at Pepperdine. "

" Loyola Marymount, Santa Clara, Gonzaga, and Pacific Lutheran may have Pepperdine's conservative atmosphere, but they don't have the awesome Malibu beaches. "

Costs (2003–04)

Tuition and Fees: $27,520

Room & Board: $8,270

Payment Plan(s): installment plan

Inst. Aid (2002–03)

Institutional Aid, Need-Based:
$15,881,573

Institutional Aid, Non-Need-Based:
$5,720,923

FT Undergrads Receiving Aid: 53%
  Avg. Amount per Student: $22,611

FT Undergrads Receiving Non-Need-Based Scholarship or Grant Aid: 9%
  Avg. Amount per Student: $14,042

Of Those Receiving Any Aid:

Rec. Need-Based Scholarship or
  Grant Aid: 96%
  Average Award: $16,191

Rec. Need-Based Self-Help Aid: 82%
  Average Award: $5,902

Upon Graduation, Avg. Loan Debt
  per Student: $31,179

Financial Aid Deadline: 4/1, 2/15
(priority)

Graduates

Going to Graduate School:
  33% Within One Year

Accepting Job Offer:
  25% at time of graduation

Alumni Giving: 19%

PITZER COLLEGE

1050 North Mills Avenue, Claremont, CA 91711
Admissions Phone: (909) 621-8129; (800) PIT-ZER1 Fax: (909) 621-8770
Email: admission@pitzer.edu Website: www.pitzer.edu
Application Website: www.commonapp.org

General Info

Type of School: private, coed
Setting: suburban
Academic Calendar: semester

Student Body

Full-Time Undergrads: 892
  Men: 41%, Women: 59%

Part-Time Undergrads: 50
  Men: 26%, Women: 74%

Total Undergrad Population:
  African American: 5%
  Asian American: 10%
  Latino: 13%
  Native American: 1%
  Caucasian: 45%
  International: 3%
  Out-of-State: 49%
  Living Off-Campus: 29%

Academics

Full-Time Faculty: 71
  With Ph.D.: 96%

Part-Time Faculty: 20
  With Ph.D.: 85%

Student/Faculty Ratio: 11:1

Most Popular Majors:
  psychology (14%)
  sociology (14%)
  English/World Literature (10%)
  art (9%)
  political studies (9%)

Freshmen Retention Rate: 84%

Graduation Rates:
  65% within four years
  71% within six years

Admissions

Regular Application Deadline: 1/15

Early Action Deadline: 12/1

Fall Transfer Deadline: 4/15

Spring Transfer Deadline: 10/15

Total # of Students Applied: 1,543
  Admitted: 1,215
  Enrolled: 230

# of Students Waitlisted: 195
  Students Accepting Place: 55

Test Scores (middle 50%):
  SAT Verbal: 570–660
  SAT Math: 570–670
  ACT Comp: 22–28

Inside the Classroom

With a progressive bent that emphasizes social responsibility and community involvement, Pitzer College offers an innovative academic program in a free-spirited environment, born out of the country's state of unrest in the 1960s. As a senior points out, "This is a place for alternative thinkers—if not when they first arrive here, then definitely by the time they leave."

With 900 students, Pitzer is an intimate environment that offers tremendous individualized attention and a small community feel. But it's also a part of the Claremont College system (along with Pomona, Scripps, Harvey Mudd, and Claremont McKenna), which greatly expands the school's academic and social offerings. Originally established as an all-female school, Pitzer went coed in the 1970s. The school has maintained its primary emphasis on social and behavioral sciences, which remain its strongest departments; majors in psychology, sociology, political science, media studies, and environmental studies are its main attractions. It offers a total of 42 fields of study leading to a bachelor of arts degree.

Pitzer's philosophy is to give students almost complete responsibility over the direction of their own education. Students create their own academic programs in close collaboration with faculty advisers. There are no lists of requirements to be checked off; rather, students pursue a set of "Educational Objectives" they set for themselves (and must put in writing). Community service, fieldwork, internships, and directed independent studies are strongly encouraged, and often required. More than 60 percent of Pitzer students study abroad, most in non-Western countries such as Botswana, China, Ecuador, and Nepal, where the College has programs.

Many of the courses at Pitzer stress environmental awareness in their curricula. Not surprisingly, the school was named a leading school for environmental studies by the National Wildlife Foundation in 2001. Call it offbeat—or call it crunchy-granola— Pitzer is a place where students "do their own thing" and self-motivate. With courses like "Anarchy and the Internet" and "Amerindian Psychiatry," it offers the most creative curriculum of all the Claremont Colleges. For those who want more traditional courses, there's open cross-registration with the sister schools down the street, not to mention the joint social and athletic resources.

Campus Environment

Claremont is a small town located 35 miles east of Los Angeles. Think cute New England town meets Southern California Spanish. The Pitzer campus, like the other Claremont colleges, is California in look and feel—comfortable and easy to get around, with plenty of grass for lying out and enjoying the sunshine and palm trees. There's even a swimming pool—known as a daytime party spot among students. Despite the limited size of the campus, students can freely use the other Claremont campuses, including athletic facilities, libraries, and state-of-the-art science facilities. All the campuses are adjoining and collectively comprise 265 acres within a 12-block area. Specialized facilities directly on the Pitzer campus include art galleries, an ecology center, a science center, a women's center, and an arboretum.

All full-time undergrads at Pitzer are required to live on campus until they graduate. Living communities in the three campus residence halls are arranged according to common interests. According to the school website, "Meals are usually shared in the main dining hall or at the Grove House, a classic Arts and Crafts bungalow where coffee, sandwiches and homemade cookies are available throughout the day."

Student Life

Pitzer students enjoy their studies here but don't stress out about them. Their laid-back attitudes contribute to the casual campus social scene. The progressive, friendly student body creates a community in which people from different backgrounds freely exchange ideas and opinions. Pitzer students can join clubs and organizations with students from all five Claremont schools; cultural and ethnic organizations enjoy greater popularity than those concerned with politics (though most students are decidedly left-leaning). Students here have an unusually active voice in campus governance: They are represented on all standing committees at Pitzer, "including those that deal with the most vital and sensitive issues of college life."

Beer-swillers should look somewhere else: Pitzer students aren't big drinkers (though we hear that recreational drugs aren't uncommon). Rather than going to huge bashes, students generally hang out in smaller groups around campus, in noisy dorm rooms, or in the student union, called the Gold Center. Road trips to all parts of California, from a major city to a quiet rural area or beach, are popular weekend options, and students say that owning a car is a definite plus. Many people go clubbing in Los Angeles on weekends, though we're told the traffic can be bad. Athletics are not terribly popular here, though Pitzer partners with nearby Pomona College for several Division III varsity sports teams. Pitzer students can work out at Pomona's state-of-the-art gym, which has every possible athletic facility imaginable.

Students seem to create good times for themselves all year long. One big Pitzer social event is the Kahoutek festival, named after a comet that was supposed to destroy the earth but failed to do so. The weekend-long event with its live bands, international foods, and displays by local artists has been characterized as "Woodstock meets Lollapalooza." Maybe that's representative of the Pitzer experience as a whole.

Other schools to check out: Reed, Occidental, Colorado College, UC Santa Cruz, Pomona.

HS Rank of Entering Freshmen:
Top 10%: 40%
Top 25%: 70%
Top 50%: 94%
Avg. HS GPA: 3.58

Costs (2003–04)

Tuition and Fees: $29,794
Room & Board: $7,796
Payment Plan(s): installment plan

THE EXPERTS SAY...

" Pitzer is a good choice for individuals looking for an interdisciplinary, intercultural education. Other schools to consider are Reed, Occidental, and Colorado College. "

" Mellow is good, but too mellow can make graduating difficult. If you end up going to Pitzer, be sure to follow your Educational Objectives closely so you don't get lost along the way. "

Inst. Aid (est. 2003–04)

Institutional Aid, Need-Based:
$6,672,743

Institutional Aid, Non-Need-Based:
$346,553

FT Undergrads Receiving Aid: 42%
Avg. Amount per Student: $27,950

FT Undergrads Receiving Non-Need-Based Scholarship or Grant Aid: 3%
Avg. Amount per Student: $10,000

Of Those Receiving Any Aid:

Rec. Need-Based Scholarship or Grant Aid: 100%
Average Award: $21,101

Rec. Need-Based Self-Help Aid: 97%
Average Award: $7,055

Upon Graduation, Avg. Loan Debt per Student: $20,900

Financial Aid Deadline: 2/1

Graduates

Going to Graduate School:
23% Within One Year

POMONA COLLEGE

333 N. College Way, Claremont, CA 91711
Admissions Phone: (909) 621-8134 Fax: (909) 621-8952
Website: www.pomona.edu
Application Website: www.pomona.edu/admissions

General Info

Type of School: private, coed
Setting: suburban
Academic Calendar: semester

Student Body

Full-Time Undergrads: 1,548
  Men: 49%, Women: 51%

Part-Time Undergrads: 7
  Men: 71%, Women: 29%

Total Undergrad Population:
  African American: 6%
  Asian American: 13%
  Latino: 7%
  Native American: 1%
  Caucasian: 58%
  International: 2%
  Out-of-State: 64%
  Living Off-Campus: 3%
  In Fraternities: 3%
  In Sororities: 0%

Academics

Full-Time Faculty: 160
  With Ph.D.: 96%

Part-Time Faculty: 52
  With Ph.D.: 54%

Student/Faculty Ratio: 9:1

Most Popular Majors:
  biology (14%)
  economics (12%)
  politics (7%)
  English (7%)
  psychology (6%)

Freshmen Retention Rate: 97%

Graduation Rates:
  86% within four years
  92% within six years

Admissions

Regular Application Deadline: 1/2

Early Decision Deadline(s): 11/15, 12/28

Fall Transfer Deadline: 3/15

Total # of Students Applied: 4,539
  Admitted: 968
  Enrolled: 399

Waitlist Available

Applied Early Decision: 380
  Early Decision Admitted: 110

Inside the Classroom

If you think all top liberal arts colleges are on New England campuses with golden fall foliage and gargoyle-laden Gothic buildings, check out Pomona College. Offering a liberal arts education equal to the top Northeast liberal arts schools, Pomona is located in Southern California—and that means palm trees and sunshine. And because it shares resources with the other schools in the Claremont consortium, Pomona students get the best of both worlds: a small campus community with all the resources of a large research university. Several guidance counselors told us that short of the smog, Pomona is a great small school with a superb liberal arts curriculum. With an endowment of $1 billion, few corners are cut here.

Pomona awards a bachelor of arts degree in 42 majors in the natural sciences, social sciences, humanities, and fine arts. Majors here aren't designed to prepare students for specific careers, so there are no programs in areas like accounting or marketing. Over one-fourth of all Pomona students graduate with an interdisciplinary major.

Distribution requirements ("PAC Requirements") are structured around 10 broad intellectual skill areas intended to teach critical thinking and analysis. Students must also complete a freshman seminar in critical inquiry; fulfill English language, foreign language, and phys ed requirements; and take writing- and speaking-intensive courses. Additionally, every student must complete a senior exercise, which means working one-on-one with a faculty adviser to produce a research paper, lab work, or portfolio of work.

Classes at Pomona are very small, with an average of 14 students. With a student/faculty ratio of just 9:1, it's not unusual to see students having dinner with their professors. "The professors are the best thing about Pomona," raves one senior. "They're very easy to speak with. There's a lot of individualized instruction." Professors, not graduate assistants, teach all classes, including lab sections in the sciences. With an extensive offering of overseas programs, nearly half of Pomona students study abroad before graduating. Add to that the option of taking classes at the other Claremont schools (not to mention the social and extracurriculars), and the opportunities expand immensely.

Students report that the workload is "hard, but doable." While the courses are demanding, these students, who were all near the top of their high school class, seem to enjoy the challenge. "We're all pretty smart people," acknowledges one student. However, Pomona's competitive academics don't interfere with the casual environment outside classroom; you'll usually find students hanging around on lawns and in courtyards, barbecuing, or playing Frisbee. The retention rate proves just how satisfied students are here: Well over 90 percent of freshmen return for their sophomore year.

Campus Environment

Pomona's 140-acre campus features ivy-covered courtyards and gardens, and the Spanish-style architecture contributes to the school's Western look and feel. Los Angeles is a mere 35 miles away, and though you'd think it would be a constant venue of entertainment for students, the traffic situation makes going there a nightmare. This means that during the week, the social life tends to stay on campus, while big nights out in Los Angeles are saved for the weekends.

Most of the social life happens in the 12 dormitories. Nearly all students live on campus during all four years, resulting in a close-knit student community. First-year students must live on campus, though there are no separate freshman dorms. All residence halls are coed, and two-thirds of the rooms are single-occupancy. New students are matched with a sophomore or junior "sponsor," who lives nearby and serves as an informal advisor.

Student Life

The student body at Pomona is exceptionally diverse, with minorities representing over one-third of the student body. Forty percent of students come from California, but the school is steadily attracting more students nationwide (particularly from New York, Massachusetts, and Texas). And why shouldn't it? With superior academics, sunny weather, and a motivated, friendly student body, there's plenty at Pomona to call students westward.

Being in southern California, there's no shortage of outdoor activities, but being in suburban southern California a bit inland, you're in the middle of, well, the suburbs. And since the beach is a full 45 minutes away, you can't just go for a quick dip in the ocean between classes. Cars are indispensable here. With no college town—just a bunch of on-campus parties instead—some complain it's more like "high school plus alcohol." There is some Greek life here, with two all-male fraternities and one co-ed fraternity (but strangely, no all-female groups). However, none are residential, which, members all agree, takes the pressure off of having to live up to a "typical frat mentality," and instead just focus on friendship, throwing parties, and doing community service.

Given the large number of minority groups here, there are several well-represented multicultural groups, such as the Pan-African and Chicano Students Association. The prestigious college orchestra attracts a lot of students, including a few from the other Claremont schools. There's a small organic farm, with everything from berry bushes to watermelons to fennel. As for athletics, Pomona is a Division III school, with several varsity sports for men and women.

One final note: If you're a *Star Trek* fan, this might be the perfect school for you. According to the Pomona website, the Borg vessels on *Star Trek: The Next Generation* have an uncanny resemblance to a certain labyrinthian dorm on campus. That's because one of the *Next Gen* producers attended Pomona, where he had lived in Oldenborg dorm, which is laid out like a complex maze.

Other schools to check out: Claremont McKenna, Wesleyan, Williams, Carleton, UC Berkeley.

Test Scores (middle 50%):
 SAT Verbal: 700–760
 SAT Math: 690–760
 ACT Comp: 29–33
 ACT English: 29–34
 ACT Math: 28–33

HS Rank of Entering Freshmen:
 Top 10%: 84%
 Top 25%: 91%
 Top 50%: 100%

Avg. HS GPA: 3.9

THE EXPERTS SAY...

" Pomona is considered on par with any of the elite East Coast schools. While Pomona can't draw upon graduate school resources like Harvard and Yale can, it does benefit from the combined resources of the other Claremont Colleges. "

" Hmm... A choice between spending frigid winters at Williams or Wesleyan, or relaxing in the sun at Pomona? You decide. "

Costs (2003–04)

Tuition and Fees: $27,150

Room & Board: $9,980

Payment Plan(s): installment plan

Inst. Aid (2002–03)

Institutional Aid, Need-Based:
 $13,937,664

FT Undergrads Receiving Aid: 51%
 Avg. Amount per Student: $25,700

Of Those Receiving Any Aid:

Rec. Need-Based Scholarship or
 Grant Aid: 100%
 Average Award: $20,860

Rec. Need-Based Self-Help Aid: 100%
 Average Award: $4,840

Upon Graduation, Avg. Loan Debt
 per Student: $15,000

Financial Aid Deadline: 2/1

Graduates

Going to Graduate School:
 33% Within One Year

Accepting Job Offer:
 25% at time of graduation

Companies Recruiting On Campus:
 395

PRINCETON UNIVERSITY

P.O. Box 430, Princeton, NJ 08544-0403
Admissions Phone: (609) 258-3060 Fax: (609) 258-6743
Website: www.princeton.edu
Application Website: www.princeton.edu/pr/admissions/u/appl

General Info

Type of School: private, coed

Setting: small town

Academic Calendar: semester

Student Body

Full-Time Undergrads: 4,676
  Men: 52%, Women: 48%

Total Undergrad Population:
  African American: 8%
  Asian American: 13%
  Latino: 6%
  Native American: 1%
  Caucasian: 64%
  International: 8%
  Out-of-State: 86%
  Living Off-Campus: 3%

Graduate and First-Professional
  Students: 2,012

Academics

Full-Time Faculty: 797
  With Ph.D.: 94%

Part-Time Faculty: 218
  With Ph.D.: 41%

Student/Faculty Ratio: 5:1

Most Popular Majors:
  politics (6%)
  history (5%)
  economics (4%)
  public/international affairs (4%)
  operational
  research/financial/engineering
  (3%)

Freshmen Retention Rate: 98%

Graduation Rates:
  91% within four years
  97% within six years

Admissions

Regular Application Deadline: 1/2

Early Decision Deadline(s): 11/1

Total # of Students Applied: 15,726
  Admitted: 1,601
  Enrolled: 1,176

# of Students Waitlisted: 471
  Students Accepting Place: 298
  Waitlisted Students Admitted: 27

Applied Early Decision: 2,413
  Early Decision Admitted: 591

Inside the Classroom

With fewer than 5,000 undergraduates, Princeton gives undergrads the individual attention of top liberal arts colleges—but the atmosphere is unmistakably Ivy League. One student proudly explains, "Of any major research institution, Princeton places the biggest emphasis on its undergraduates. They are a true priority here." Lectures (usually for humanities and social sciences courses) are supplemented by weekly preceptorials, which are small discussion groups. According to the university, "Members of the faculty of all ranks serve as preceptors, as do selected graduate students." For science and engineering, students work in small groups under the supervision of faculty members. Additionally, professors lead a number of seminars for first-year students. Since 1893, Princeton's honor system has allowed students take all written examinations without a faculty proctor.

"Academic reputation!" exclaims a guidance counselor, calling Princeton a hot school. Princeton offers two undergraduate degrees: the bachelor of arts (A.B.) degree and the bachelor of science in engineering (B.S.E.) degree. Concentrations (akin to majors) are offered in 35 departments, and numerous certificate programs (or minors) are also available. A California guidance counselor lauds the "old-fashioned traditional academic demands unmatched anywhere—junior-year papers and thesis required." All undergraduates do independent work, usually in the form of a junior project or paper ("J.P.") and a senior thesis. While the prestigious Woodrow Wilson School of Public and International Affairs consists mainly of graduate and post-graduate students, each year a select number of undergrads are selected for the Woodrow Wilson School Undergraduate Program, a departmental concentration for juniors and seniors.

There are some complaints about the schedule, which packs a full semester into just 12 weeks and holds first-semester exams after winter break—"A real pain," says one student. While the official reading period starts after winter break, there can be a lot of pressure to study right through your vacation. But, says a student, "It's for the most part a combination of academic intensity and having a good time. There's a balance of working hard and playing hard."

In 1998, Princeton made sweeping changes in its financial-aid policies to make the University more affordable for lower- and middle-income students. While tuition has gone up for students who pay full price, the financial aid budget has increased. In a dramatic move, grants replaced loans for undergraduates beginning in the 2001–02 academic year. Remarks a California counselor about the "no-loan" policy, Princeton "is making an effort to stop the tremendous money gouging and debt burden [on] the middle-class student." Another adds that the school is "committed to having you afford them" and gives "better financial packages to students."

In a minor scandal in 2002, Princeton admissions officials acknowledged that they gained unauthorized access to a website at Yale University containing personal information about Yale applicants. The Princeton admissions director who admitted to accessing the Yale website has since been reassigned to the department of campus life.

Campus Environment

Located in quiet and upscale Princeton, New Jersey, the university embodies the true Ivy aesthetic. The campus wins kudos from guidance counselors (except for one, who calls the campus "a bit pompous, a bit overbuilt, and too close to the 'Frank Sinatra corridor' of NJ"). Most of the housing is as romantically "Ivy" as the rest of the campus. The school explains, "All first- and second-year students at Princeton live and dine in one of five residential colleges [like 'Rockefeller,' 'Wilson,' or 'Forbes' college]." This promotes a sense of community and makes it easier to make friends, especially during those first couple of semesters. Each college "has its own dining hall, common rooms, and computer clusters, and a staff including the college master, director of studies, resident assistants (upperclass students), and faculty advisers." Juniors and seniors have separate housing.

Princeton's eating clubs are an essential aspect of Princeton life. Lined up along Prospect Street, the eating clubs began as a means of offering students alternatives to university dining—today they have essentially become the equivalent of fraternities (which were banned in 1855). Most juniors and seniors eat at one of the 11 clubs (six are open to all students on a sign-in basis; five are selective and choose members through a process called "bicker"). The clubs range in personality from clubs for jocks to clubs for the artistically inclined. A guidance counselor from New Mexico complains that the "eating clubs foster a cliquey, exclusive feel."

Student Life

The eating clubs illustrate the tendency among Princeton students to cluster together in small groups according to similar interests. "The main drawback here," one student reports, "is that there is a lot of underlying pressure to conform to what you see." Another student weighs in with, "Whether it's the eating club, or being an athlete, or joining a religious or social organization, you become known by that group really quickly." The student body is pretty homogeneous—one guidance counselor calls the student body "very preppie and elitist." But such a prestigious learning institution attracts the brightest students from around the world, and there is a "place for everyone" here, from the crew team to academic eccentrics.

Princeton offers more than 200 student organizations. The American Whig-Cliosophic Society is "the oldest college political, literary, and debating society in the United States (founded by James Madison, Class of 1771, and Aaron Burr, Class of 1772)." The Princeton Tigers play 38 varsity sports at the NCAA Division I level. There are also about 35 club sports, both single-sex and coed.

The town of Princeton is quaint and sleepy. Not much is open past 11:00 P.M. But students can be found until that time socializing over their heavy books in Small World Coffee, or even later catching some live music at Triumph Brewery, J.B. Winberie's or one of the eating clubs. On weekends, students in search of more excitement can trade Nassau Street for New York City "to check out clubs, restaurants, and stuff," according to one student. Freshmen are no longer permitted to park on campus. Luckily, the "Dinky" train stops right by campus and connects students to NJ Transit for easy access to NYC or Philadelphia.

Other schools to check out: Yale, Stanford, MIT, Dartmouth, Rice.

Test Scores (middle 50%):
SAT Verbal: 680–770
SAT Math: 690–790
HS Rank of Entering Freshmen:
Top 10%: 94%
Top 25%: 99%
Top 50%: 100%
Avg. HS GPA: 3.83

Costs (2004–5)

Tuition and Fees: $29,910
Room & Board: $8,387
Payment Plan(s): installment plan

THE EXPERTS SAY...

" Princeton's unprecedented 'no-loan' policy opens its Ivy doors to students of all income levels. "

" The admissions department at Princeton should adopt a 'no-loan' policy about borrowing info from other schools' websites. "

Inst. Aid (2002–03)

Institutional Aid, Need-Based: $42,850,000

Institutional Aid, Non-Need-Based: $0

FT Undergrads Receiving Aid: 46%
Avg. Amount per Student: $24,078

Of Those Receiving Any Aid:

Rec. Need-Based Scholarship or Grant Aid: 100%
Average Award: $22,685

Rec. Need-Based Self-Help Aid: 100%
Average Award: $1,450

Upon Graduation, Avg. Loan Debt per Student: $11,000

Financial Aid Deadline: 2/1 (priority)

Graduates

Alumni Giving: 86%

PROVIDENCE COLLEGE

549 River Ave., Harkins Hall 222, Providence, RI 02918
Admissions Phone: (401) 865-2535; (800) 721-6444 Fax: (401) 865-2826
Email: pcadmiss@providence.edu
Website: www.providence.edu

General Info

Type of School: private, coed, Roman Catholic

Setting: suburban

Academic Calendar: semester

Student Body

Full-Time Undergrads: 3,687
 Men: 42%, Women: 58%

Part-Time Undergrads: 345
 Men: 35%, Women: 65%

Total Undergrad Population:
 African American: 2%
 Asian American: 1%
 Latino: 3%
 Caucasian: 84%
 International: 1%
 Out-of-State: 80%
 Living Off-Campus: 25%

Graduate and First-Professional
 Students: 916

Academics

Full-Time Faculty: 262
 With Ph.D.: 87%

Part-Time Faculty: 75

Student/Faculty Ratio: 13:1

Most Popular Majors:
 marketing (7%)
 political science (7%)
 elementary/special education (7%)
 biology (6%)
 English (6%)

Completing 2 or More Majors: 4%

Freshmen Retention Rate: 91%

Graduation Rates:
 82% within four years
 85% within six years

Admissions

Regular Application Deadline: 1/15

Early Action Deadline: 11/1

Fall Transfer Deadline: 4/15
 (priority)

Spring Transfer Deadline: 12/1
 (priority)

Total # of Students Applied: 7,397
 Admitted: 3,906
 Enrolled: 975

Inside the Classroom

Providence College, a relatively small Roman Catholic school, is the only college in the country under the stewardship of the Dominican friars. About 10 percent of all faculty members are Dominican friars or sisters. Classes for underclassmen rarely have more than 25 students, and upperclass lectures hover around 20. This makes for a pretty cozy academic environment. "Professors are very knowledgeable and are always around to answer questions and help in any way," a student tells us. Another says, "I've never had a problem getting a teacher to meet with me. Often teachers will even give their home phone numbers." Opportunities also exist for students to conduct research one-on-one with professors. There are no graduate students or TAs teaching classes.

PC students can choose from more than 40 majors, or are free to create their own. More than half of all freshmen enroll without a declared major, so Providence offers an Undeclared Advising Center to help students identify their interests and strengths. As is often the case, the intensity of the work may depend on what you're studying. A recent humanities grad reports that "the workload can be a bit much," while a junior accounting major claims that "homework is not necessary for a solid grade in my classes."

The core curriculum requires students to take courses in theology and philosophy as well as in the usual areas of arts and sciences. Also mandatory for freshmen and sophomores is the two-year, interdisciplinary Development of Western Civilization program, which explores the history, art, literature, philosophy, and theology of Western Civilization. The school boasts that this program has been praised as one of the "finest and most academically ambitious programs in the country" and is something of a "rite of passage" among Providence students, helping them develop their study habits and other academic skills right from the start (though a student noted in an editorial in *The Cowl*: "Finding a student who has actually managed to plow through all or most of the seminar readings is kind of like finding a prophet in a Mexican brothel: it's almost too fantastic to be true").

Campus Environment

Freshmen and sophomores are required to live on campus and are guaranteed housing. Some students we spoke to complained about the availability of dorm space and the quality of the dorms themselves. (In an interesting side note, a student informs us that "certain dorms used to be part of a mental institution and there are underground tunnels connecting them.") PC has nine traditional residence halls and an apartment complex that is available to sophomores, juniors, and seniors. The on-campus apartment complex is a popular option for upperclassmen. A student tells us that "the on-campus apartments are sweet." Off-campus housing is "plentiful" and some say it's the only way to live as juniors and seniors. A recent grad warns, "Certain apartments are deemed party houses, and no matter who rents them every year, the party always ends up there."

There are five colleges and universities located in the city of Providence, making it quite the college town. The downtown area, with shops, restaurants, and historic neighborhoods, is just two miles from campus. But the area around campus has its drawbacks: "The off-campus area is not safe. We're on the outskirts of the city of Providence and we live in what seems at times like a 'ghetto,'" says one student. "You really have to go out in big groups for safety," adds another. A senior chimes in, "Walking at night is not encouraged," though the campus itself is "very safe and security guards are posted" throughout.

Students add that having a car on campus is nice, but not entirely necessary. ("Parking is a disaster at PC," we're told.) Most students walk or take advantage of the shuttle buses that head to "the local supermarket, downtown, and the mall" as well as "almost all of the local bars."

Student Life

Overall, PC students describe their campus as warm and friendly. A student says, "When you walk through the campus during the day, everyone says 'hi,' even if they don't know you. It can get a little rowdy at the end of the year. My class is infamous for multiple couch burnings on the quad. But it's never harmful."

"It is a big party school," we're told. Drinking plays a major role in out-of-classroom activities, and according to the school newspaper, there's been a recent rash of students being written up for having marijuana in the dorms. A Connecticut guidance counselor even goes so far as to say there is "too much social life for the students" at Providence. A student says, "On weekends, PC students are always at the bars or house parties. Actually, on most weeknights you can find a lot of PC students at the bars, particularly on Monday and Wednesday nights. The library gets most of its use during finals." Despite all the partying, a Massachusetts guidance counselor feels that "the atmosphere is too strict"; most students who are unhappy with the "parietal" policy (forbidding students to have members of the opposite sex in their dorm rooms past a certain hour) would likely agree.

Providence is a Division I Big East school. A junior tells us that "men's hockey and [especially] men's basketball are extremely popular. The rest of the sports don't fare as well with fans." Intramural sports attract a good number of participants, though one student we spoke to griped that IMs are "poorly run and organized." The college offers more than 100 student clubs and organizations, although there are no fraternities or sororities on campus.

Some students complain that the student body can be fairly homogenous. We heard the typical Providence student described as "white, Catholic, conservative, upper-middle class." Indeed, the general consensus is that PC could use a little diversity. "Everyone seems to dress in the same style. I've heard PC referred to as a 'J. Crew school,'" one student says. "There's very little variance from the norm... PC isn't exactly known for its multicolored hair or outlandish clothing styles." A young alum asserts, "Anyone who is outside the mainstream would have difficulty fitting in at first, but PC is a very relaxed environment and most people are very accepting."

Other schools to check out: Fairfield, Villanova, University of Scranton, Saint Anselm, Stonehill.

# of Students Waitlisted: 1,516
  Students Accepting Place: 664
  Waitlisted Students Admitted: 185

Test Scores (middle 50%):
  SAT Verbal: 550–650
  SAT Math: 560–650
  ACT Comp: 23–28

HS Rank of Entering Freshmen:
  Top 10%: 42%
  Top 25%: 82%
  Top 50%: 98%

Avg. HS GPA: 3.44

THE EXPERTS SAY...

" PC's Undeclared Advising Center can put you on the right path by helping you to identify and pursue your interests. "

" If you have mainstream tastes, style, and opinions, you'll find a home at Providence College. "

Costs (2003–04)

Tuition and Fees: $22,104

Room & Board: $8,500

Payment Plan(s): installment plan

Inst. Aid (est. 2003–04)

Institutional Aid, Need-Based: $17,727,000

Institutional Aid, Non-Need-Based: $4,432,000

FT Undergrads Receiving Aid: 55%
  Avg. Amount per Student: $15,500

FT Undergrads Receiving Non-Need-Based Scholarship or Grant Aid: 10%
  Avg. Amount per Student: $12,677

Of Those Receiving Any Aid:

Rec. Need-Based Scholarship or Grant Aid: 87%
  Average Award: $10,500

Rec. Need-Based Self-Help Aid: 97%
  Average Award: $4,900

Upon Graduation, Avg. Loan Debt per Student: $22,500

Financial Aid Deadline: 2/1

Graduates

Going to Graduate School:
  25% Within One Year

Accepting Job Offer:
  74% at time of graduation

Companies Recruiting On Campus: 100

Alumni Giving: 54%

PURDUE UNIVERSITY—WEST LAFAYETTE

1080 Schleman Hall, West Lafayette, IN 47907-1080
Admissions Phone: (765) 494-1776 Fax: (765) 494-0544 Email: admissions@purdue.edu
Website: www.purdue.edu Application Website: adpc.purdue.edu/Admissions

General Info

Type of School: public, coed

Setting: small town

Academic Calendar: semester

Student Body

Full-Time Undergrads: 29,029
  Men: 59%, Women: 41%

Part-Time Undergrads: 1,395
  Men: 56%, Women: 44%

Total Undergrad Population:
  African American: 3%
  Asian American: 5%
  Latino: 2%
  Native American: <1%
  Caucasian: 83%
  International: 6%
  Out-of-State: 25%

Graduate and First-Professional
  Students: 7,996

Academics

Full-Time Faculty: 1,918
  With Ph.D.: 99%

Part-Time Faculty: 59
  With Ph.D.: 83%

Student/Faculty Ratio: 15:1

Most Popular Majors:
  liberal arts (22%)
  engineering (21%)
  business (12%)
  engineering technology (9%)
  agriculture (8%)

Completing 2 or More Majors: 12%

Freshmen Retention Rate: 89%

Graduation Rates:
  29% within four years
  64% within six years

Admissions

Regular Application Deadline: 3/1
  (priority)

Total # of Students Applied: 22,977
  Admitted: 18,076
  Enrolled: 6,371

Test Scores (middle 50%):
  SAT Verbal: 500–610
  SAT Math: 530–650
  ACT Comp: 23–28
  ACT English: 21–28
  ACT Math: 23–29 R

Inside the Classroom

Purdue offers more than 200 specializations in its undergraduate schools of agriculture; consumer and family sciences; education; engineering; health sciences; liberal arts; management; nursing; pharmacy; science; technology; and veterinary medicine. Most students are on a preprofessional track, knowing what they want to study early on. The administration counts on that fact by requiring all applicants to officially declare a major when they apply for admission (though you're allowed to change your major later on, if needed). Applicants who are uncertain about where their interests lie can apply to the Undergraduate Studies Program (USP), a kind of voluntary liberal arts core curriculum. USP students have up to four semesters to choose an actual major, letting them explore their options. One student says, "The USP gave me time to adjust to college without being pressured to find a major. It gave me time to make important discoveries about myself."

Of all the majors, engineering and agriculture are the standouts. In fact, one guidance counselor calls the engineering program "the best thing about the school." Its graduates are certainly achievers: The corps of astronauts at NASA includes 22 alumni—including the most famous of them all, Neil Armstrong.

No matter which major you choose, you can expect a good deal of work in exchange for putting Purdue's respected brand name on your resume. "The workload is challenging but not impossible," says one student. "There's some competitiveness, and that can be sickening at times."

As a land-, sea-, and space-grant institution, Purdue expends well over $200 million annually for research, using funds received from the state and federal governments. This has obvious pros for students, in the form of 400 research laboratories on the West Lafayette campus. Not everyone, however, is so pleased with the emphasis on research. "The professors on the liberal arts side are very friendly and accessible," says one student, who is quick to add, "The professors on the science side are sometimes accessible, but half the time they're more interested in their research and they blow off undergrads. The professors expect the graduate students to do all the work, but the graduate students are too busy trying to graduate." An Indiana high school guidance counselor gripes that the school is "too high tech" with "not enough emphasis on liberal arts."

Campus Environment

The nearly 1,600 acres that comprise the West Lafayette campus lie just across the river from Greater Lafayette, a small city that doesn't have much to offer students besides a few bars. Indianapolis is a fairly easy trip (65 miles to the south), and when the urge to hit the really big city strikes, Chicago is also within reach (125 miles northwest). Freshmen generally don't have cars, since most campus parking areas are restricted, and freshmen aren't allowed to purchase a parking permit. However, the Greater Lafayette bus system allows students with Purdue ID cards to ride free of charge. And the campus's compact design, with no major roads bisecting the grounds, makes walking the preferable way to get around… at least until the winter cold sets in.

Dorm space is available, but a majority of students live off-campus, within walking distance of the school. "The dorms are okay," said one senior. "About the same as any other college's." Some rent apartments, while others form small cooperatives and rent entire houses, with each co-op member assigned certain house duties. One co-op resident raves about the experience: "Everything—from paying bills to cleaning and cooking—is done by the members. It's cheap, the atmosphere is casual, and the people are pretty cool." Fraternity and sorority houses provide yet another option. Most of the buildings on campus were built in brick, and the unified look has become a Purdue trademark. "I know some people don't like the brick buildings," said one student, "but I think it's pretty cool that everything matches and complements each other. I don't think the campus would be nearly as beautiful if the buildings didn't somehow belong together." Another student adds: "The campus becomes more and more beautiful every time I visit. They are constantly adding more trees, fountains, flowers, and parks."

The area surrounding the campus is relatively peaceful, according to one student. "Just like any town, Lafayette has its good and bad areas. The campus itself is very safe. Purdue can have its rowdy moments, but I don't think it's as bad as some other colleges."

Student Life

Part of the reason why Purdue, with over 30,000 students, feels much smaller is the presence of over 550 student clubs. For every interest you have, there's a social circle waiting to be joined. Of course, if you prefer a social life on a larger scale, the Greeks are here in full force: With 49 fraternities and 27 sororities, the Greeks enroll almost 20 percent of the student body. One recent grad waxed nostalgic about his frat, saying, "My fraternity experience obviously offered numerous chances to get lit up like Christmas Eve, but its lasting value is found in steadfast friendships and additional incentives to revisit campus as the years pass."

Another student lists other student pastimes as: "Going to sporting events, movies, dinner, and hanging out with friends. Marijuana is smoked and many people drink, but I wouldn't say more than at any other colleges."

Students looking for more excitement can attend a Boilermakers athletic event. A member of the Big Ten Conference, Purdue has nine men's and nine women's Division I NCAA teams. There's a historic rivalry between Purdue and Indiana University; one of the schools' traditions is to award the "Old Oaken Bucket" to the winner of the annual Purdue–Indiana football game. Successful though its teams may be, one student offers a word of caution: "Purdue is no place for the football or basketball fan who doesn't want his heart broken during the title stretch."

World-renowned speakers and performers regularly visit Purdue's Elliott Hall of Music. With 6,025 seats, the hall can hold more people than New York's Radio City Music Hall and plays host to large-scale musicals, operas, symphonies, ballets, comedians, and concerts by rock, country, and pop groups.

THE EXPERTS SAY...

" Purdue is a large-sized college with a small-sized feel, and its engineering programs are literally stellar. "

" The emphasis on research is a double-edged sword. If you're not a self-starter, make friends with a grad student. "

RANDOLPH–MACON WOMAN'S COLLEGE

2500 Rivermont Avenue, Lynchburg, VA 24503-1526 Admissions Phone: (434) 947-8100; (800) 745-7692 Fax: (434) 947-8996 Email: admissions@rmwc.edu
Website: www.rmwc.edu Application Website: www.rmwc.edu/admissions/apply.asp

General Info

Type of School: private, all women, United Methodist

Setting: urban

Academic Calendar: semester

Student Body

Full-Time Undergrads: 688
Women: 100%

Part-Time Undergrads: 18
Women: 100%

Total Undergrad Population:
African American: 8%
Asian American: 3%
Latino: 3%
Native American: <1%
Caucasian: 74%
International: 10%
Out-of-State: 59%
Living Off-Campus: 12%

Academics

Full-Time Faculty: 75
With Ph.D.: 91%

Part-Time Faculty: 18
With Ph.D.: 28%

Student/Faculty Ratio: 9:1

Most Popular Majors:
biology (14%)
psychology (13%)
English (12%)
political science (10%)
international relations (8%)

Completing 2 or More Majors: 16%

Freshmen Retention Rate: 79%

Graduation Rates:
59% within four years
61% within six years

Admissions

Regular Application Deadline: 3/1

Early Decision Deadline(s): 11/15

Fall Transfer Deadline: 3/1 (priority)

Spring Transfer Deadline: 12/1 (priority)

Total # of Students Applied: 716
Admitted: 615
Enrolled: 177

Applied Early Decision: 21
Early Decision Admitted: 16

Inside the Classroom

At RMWC, students are encouraged to think critically and communicate clearly. There are over 40 academic programs, including premed, prelaw, and teacher education programs, and one students tells us, "Without a doubt, the workload here is incredibly demanding." Popular majors include psychology, biology, and English. Students describe their academic atmosphere as "challenging" and "supportive." "The school sets very high standards for its students to meet," says one senior. Randolph Macon's honor system, according to the school, "demands that each student abide by the highest standards of honesty and integrity in her academic, social, and personal life."

Students are serious about their studies, and Randolph Macon fosters a nurturing and demanding environment for its all-female population. An art history major tells us, "You are judged a lot on the quality of your writing and your ability to convey ideas, even in science and math courses. Workloads are on the heavy side, but most students seem to like the challenge and feel proud of being given the responsibility."

There are only about 700 students here, and the student-faculty ratio is 9:1, which means that "you have to actually attend all your classes (hey, if there are only two other women in your course, it's obvious when you don't show)," according to a senior. "Professors are extremely accessible and responsive and go out of their way to offer students special academic opportunities," says one student. Students agree that "professors interact with students outside of the classroom" and that they are "friendly and knowledgeable and enthusiastic about what they teach."

Campus Environment

Women live on campus in one of the college's six residence halls for all four years. Each hall has its own personality: "Some have extended quiet hours, some have smoking areas, and one is restricted to seniors only." Students really, really love their dorms: "Rooms are large, with high ceilings, liberal closet space, and comfortable furnishings," says one, and they "come with the amenities of phone and Internet and TV hookups, and most dorms have hall lounges, as well as a kitchen, TV room, and 'date parlor.'" Says another, "You can get varying numbers and sizes of windows, two or three closets, or built-into-the-wall shelving and drawers." By your junior year, it's easier to get a single room; seniors enjoy this luxury in the seniors-only living of Webb Hall.

A little-known fact about RMWC: "The college's Maier Museum is a national repository for all the priceless art in the National Gallery in Washington, D.C. If ever there were to be a war in the United States, the National Gallery would ship its art to RMWC to be kept safely within the sturdy walls of the Maier Museum," boasts a student.

The campus is located in a historic area filled with brick sidewalks and beautiful manor homes. "To get anywhere really interesting (like downtown or to the mall) you definitely need a car. A car would also be a must if you wanted to go to places like Charlottesville, or D.C.," says one student. Another student disagrees: "It's certainly convenient, but you don't need a car. You can use the school-provided shopping shuttle on weekends to go to the mall, the movies, the grocery stores, whatever, and during the week you can almost always catch a ride with friends." Students agree that safety is not a huge issue here: "The campus itself is very safe, with security, administration, and residence staff keeping a friendly and watchful eye on the students."

Student Life

Says one art history major, "For the most part, the typical student is from the East Coast, particularly the states around Virginia. They are middle- to upper-class and Caucasian. And I would say the majority are from conservative backgrounds." There are over 36 clubs, and according to students, popular organizations include the Young Democrats and Young Republicans, "Circle-K" ("a community outreach type club"), Christian organizations, and fine arts clubs. There are no sororities.

Weeknights, "students usually concentrate on studying, occasionally leaving campus to go out to dinner or to a movie." On weekends, there is usually a large migration off campus. Students either go home, if they live nearby, or drive so far as Washington, DC and North Carolina to visit friends, etc. Many students regularly head for schools like Hampden-Sydney (men's college), the Virginia Military Academy, University of Virginia, or Virginia Tech to attend parties or football games. Says one student, "Boys come here, but not in droves like we might hope [Are you listening, Hampden-Sydney?]... though occasionally someone's boyfriend will bring some friends, but it's not as often as we might like. The whole locked-buildings and escort-required rule for all men seems to scare them off. But we manage just fine."

"RMWC has a strict alcohol policy that is well enforced, but a good amount of drinking still happens on campus. It really isn't a big problem though, since students are usually responsible and everything is 'kept quiet,'" explains one student. Off campus, "there aren't many good places (bars, clubs, etc.) for drinking around Lynchburg." (Hence, the weekend migration out of town.) Drugs are at a minimum: "For the most part, RMWC is completely drug-free," says a student. Another student notes, "There do seem to be an awful lot of smokers on campus, though."

Division III intercollegiate programs are offered in WildCats' basketball, field hockey, riding, soccer, softball, swimming, tennis, and volleyball. "The administration strongly supports the athletic department and coaches are serious about competition," says a student. She also explains that "RMWC has a very competitive riding team, as well as intramural riding lessons that are conducted at an impressive facility a few miles from campus."

RMWC has several unique traditions: "The sister classes and Pumpkin Parade and Ring Week and Daisy Chain and Bury the Hatchet and Tacky Party...a million things that have been going on for years and years and years," says one student. "They're awfully difficulty to explain, but they're so unusual and wonderful, and they result in a different kind of school spirit than I've ever seen anywhere. You have to visit to believe it."

Other schools to check out: Hollins, Sweet Briar, Agnes Scott, Chatham, Scripps.

Test Scores (middle 50%):
SAT Verbal: 540–660
SAT Math: 510–600
ACT Comp: 23–28
ACT English: 25–30
ACT Math: 19–26

HS Rank of Entering Freshmen:
Top 10%: 37%
Top 25%: 65%
Top 50%: 94%

Avg. HS GPA: 3.4

THE EXPERTS SAY...

" This small, intimate campus fosters a strong sense of community among its women. "

" RMWC can seem a little cloistered. Perhaps with all of those extra shelves and closets, students can work on a secret entrance for male visitors. "

Costs (2003–04)

Tuition and Fees: $19,280
Room & Board: $7,560

Inst. Aid (est. 2003–04)

Institutional Aid, Need-Based:
$5,229,645

Institutional Aid, Non-Need-Based:
$2,937,560

FT Undergrads Receiving Aid: 66%
Avg. Amount per Student: $19,958

FT Undergrads Receiving Non-Need-Based Scholarship or Grant Aid: 33%
Avg. Amount per Student: $15,351

Of Those Receiving Any Aid:

Rec. Need-Based Scholarship or Grant Aid: 100%
Average Award: $14,203

Rec. Need-Based Self-Help Aid: 85%
Average Award: $5,803

Upon Graduation, Avg. Loan Debt per Student: $21,992

Financial Aid Deadline: rolling, 3/1 (priority)

Graduates

Going to Graduate School:
35% Within One Year

Companies Recruiting On Campus:
102

Alumni Giving: 67%

REED COLLEGE

3203 SE Woodstock Boulevard, Portland, OR 97202-8199
Admissions Phone: (800) 547-4750; (503) 777-7511 Fax: (503) 777-7553
Email: admission@reed.edu Website: www.reed.edu
Application Website: web.reed.edu/apply/application.html

General Info

Type of School: private, coed
Setting: urban
Academic Calendar: semester

Student Body

Full-Time Undergrads: 1,266
    Men: 46%, Women: 54%

Part-Time Undergrads: 18
    Men: 33%, Women: 67%

Total Undergrad Population:
    African American: 1%
    Asian American: 5%
    Latino: 4%
    Native American: 1%
    Caucasian: 63%
    International: 3%
    Out-of-State: 82%
    Living Off-Campus: 45%

Graduate and First-Professional
    Students: 28

Academics

Full-Time Faculty: 120
    With Ph.D.: 88%

Part-Time Faculty: 13
    With Ph.D.: 69%

Student/Faculty Ratio: 10:1

Most Popular Majors:
    English (15%)
    biology (12%)
    psychology (9%)
    history (6%)
    anthropology (5%)

Freshmen Retention Rate: 85%

Graduation Rates:
    46% within four years
    72% within six years

Admissions

Regular Application Deadline: 1/15

Early Decision Deadline(s): 11/15,
    1/2

Fall Transfer Deadline: 3/1

Total # of Students Applied: 2,282
    Admitted: 1,044
    Enrolled: 301

# of Students Waitlisted: 551
    Students Accepting Place: 550
    Waitlisted Students Admitted: 32

Applied Early Decision: 162
    Early Decision Admitted: 100

In the Classroom

A liberal, highly progressive school, Reed College gives its students tremendous freedom, academically and socially. Bright, highly motivated nonconformists thrive here. Reed treats its curriculum like an honors program: An unusually high academic standard is the norm, and students are given almost total responsibility for the direction of their studies. "A student cannot, and will not, succeed at Reed if she does not wish and strive to learn for her own purposes," says a senior. Most classes conform to what Reed calls "the conference method of teaching," in which small classes of 10–20 students function as discussion sessions with the professor serving as facilitator. That means students must come to class well-read and ready to discuss the material. "That's what makes it fun," says one student. "If you're not ready, you're not going to be able to participate." Of course, as another student points out, these discussion-based classes can sometimes be "frustrating, because a few people monopolize the conversation, and sometimes students who are less bold may not speak at all."

Grades are de-emphasized; in fact, students are not told of their grades unless they ask for them, though grades are recorded. But students do get extensive feedback from their professors. "The student-teacher relationship is excellent," we're told. "Professors are enthusiastic about talking with you after class, and hanging out with you." But the lack of grades doesn't mean the atmosphere isn't intense. Many students accustomed to being the brightest in their high school classes have to adjust to an environment where they might have to struggle to keep up. "Some people find the atmosphere (and occasional intellectual pretension) too stressful," says one student. Another warns, "You have to be ready to work your butt off. I wouldn't recommend it if you can't do that." The intense intellectual competition among students "leads too easily to resentment and feelings of personal inadequacy, but you just have to learn to only work as hard as you need to," a student advises.

"The requirements at Reed—divisional, departmental, and major—can be very trying," says a literature/theater major. "It is not necessarily easy to complete all your required classes and take some electives, not to mention going abroad, in four years." With 22 majors plus numerous interdisciplinary fields, Reed maintains strong academic programs across the board, but its programs in the life sciences are perhaps the strongest. In this category, Reed produces more Ph.D.s than any other institution of higher learning. The science laboratories, we're told, are among the best equipped of any undergraduate college in the country. But science majors don't have all the glory—a majority of Reed's graduates go on to grad school, and the school ranks second in the number of Rhodes scholars from a liberal arts college.

Campus Environment

Recent construction at Reed has resulted in a new campus center, a renovated student union, and three new residence halls. About half of all Reedies live on campus, where students live mostly in small halls with as few as seven other people or as "many" as 30. On-campus residences are largely coed by floor or by room, and there are a surprising number of singles. Students can even request a "pet floor." Special theme housing options have recently included film, Japanese culture, outdoor recreation, and community service. First-year students are encouraged, but not required, to live on campus. There are no fraternities or sororities, but the Reed Houses offer a popular off-campus housing choice and can be unofficially "themed" (we heard of a vegan household, a rugby house, and an all-women house).

With its rolling lawns, open spaces, and "some of the largest and finest specimen trees in the Portland area," Reed's pretty 100-acre campus scores high marks with its students. At the center of campus is the canyon, a beautiful wooded upland surrounding a lake, marsh, and walking trail. The college recently built a "fish passageway" that links nearby lakes and streams. From campus, students are only a few blocks away from stores, restaurants, and various cultural venues in Portland, a city that's often touted as among the best in America. Students take advantage of living in this part of the Northwest; they're not far from innumerable parks, rivers, mountains, and the Pacific coastline. Although public transit in Portland is excellent, many Reedies have cars, and on-campus parking is free.

Student Life

The unique learning environment and individualistic culture of Reed attract a progressive student body from across the country. However, like most small colleges, Reed has difficulty attracting the racial diversity it would like. People who didn't fit in well in high school often find happiness at Reed, where being different is the norm. "Most Portlanders think of Reedies as weird, smart liberals (which, of course, most of us are), but there are a few [locals] who take that stereotype too far, to include godlessness and heathenism," says one student. "Watch out for those close-minded types!" Typically, in their free time, students get involved with like-minded students in creative endeavors, leftist political causes, or intellectual discussions. "Reed is no party school," another student says. "The emphasis is on learning pure and simple."

Of course, when Reedies do party, it can get pretty intense. For decades Reed has had a reputation for being a school for hippies and potheads. While the school has changed significantly, it's not hard to find those trying to keep the spirit alive. "Almost anyone on campus will know where to get drugs, and if they don't, they know someone who does," says one student. Another jokes, "How big a factor are drugs at Reed? That is like asking how important oil is to a car." Some see drug use as a real problem, but others argue it is no more of a problem here than any school, just more out in the open.

Reed has no intercollegiate sports teams, so "there are no jocks," one student explains, "who are not also scientists, artists, poets, mathematicians, linguists, or musicians." ("Are bongo drums a sport?" another quips.) However, intramural sports are promoted and sports clubs compete with other Pacific Northwest clubs in rugby, soccer, basketball, and squash. There is also an outdoor program that offers organized recreational activities, including ski trips to the college-owned ski cabin on Mt. Hood. Students also take part in many interesting traditions throughout the year, including Reed Arts Weekend, Renaissance Fayre, Canyon Day (wherein students work to preserve the natural ecosystem of the canyon), and Nitrogen Day (celebrating "one of the universe's most important, yet underappreciated elements").

Other schools to check out: Oberlin, Evergreen State College, Colorado College, Grinnell, Bennington.

Test Scores (middle 50%):
  SAT Verbal: 650–750
  SAT Math: 620–710
  ACT Comp: 28–32
HS Rank of Entering Freshmen:
  Top 10%: 60%
  Top 25%: 88%
  Top 50%: 99%
Avg. HS GPA: 3.8

THE EXPERTS SAY...

" Applicants and parents: Don't let the nonconformist environment distract you from the fact that Reed is one of the best liberal arts colleges in the country. "

" High academic standards, an intensely competitive atmosphere, and easy access to mind-altering substances can be a dangerous combination: Many students never get around to graduating. "

Costs (2003–04)

Tuition and Fees: $29,200

Room & Board: $7,750

Payment Plan(s): installment plan

Inst. Aid (est. 2003–04)

Institutional Aid, Need-Based: $12,822,760

Institutional Aid, Non-Need-Based: $0

FT Undergrads Receiving Aid: 54%
  Avg. Amount per Student: $24,309

Of Those Receiving Any Aid:

Rec. Need-Based Scholarship or Grant Aid: 97%
  Average Award: $20,880

Rec. Need-Based Self-Help Aid: 92%
  Average Award: $4,429

Upon Graduation, Avg. Loan Debt per Student: $13,692

Financial Aid Deadline: 1/15

Graduates

Going to Graduate School:
  65% Within One Year

Alumni Giving: 40%

RENSSELAER POLYTECHNIC INSTITUTE

110 8th Street, Troy, NY 12180-3590
Admissions Phone: (518) 276-6216 Fax: (518) 276-4072 Email: admissions@rpi.edu
Website: www.rpi.edu Application Website: admissions.rpi.edu

General Info

Type of School: private, coed

Setting: suburban

Academic Calendar: semester

Student Body

Full-Time Undergrads: 5,153
  Men: 75%, Women: 25%

Part-Time Undergrads: 11
  Men: 64%, Women: 36%

Total Undergrad Population:
  African American: 4%
  Asian American: 12%
  Latino: 5%
  Native American: <1%
  Caucasian: 69%
  International: 4%
  Out-of-State: 54%
  Living Off-Campus: 45%
  In Fraternities: 39%
  In Sororities: 18%

Graduate and First-Professional
Students: 3,055

Academics

Full-Time Faculty: 383
  With Ph.D.: 95%

Part-Time Faculty: 96
  With Ph.D.: 64%

Student/Faculty Ratio: 15:1

Most Popular Majors:
  engineering/engineering technologies (53%)
  business/marketing (13%)
  computer and information sciences (13%)
  architecture (7%)
  biological/life sciences (4%)

Completing 2 or More Majors: 20%

Freshmen Retention Rate: 93%

Graduation Rates:
  55% within four years
  81% within six years

Computers: Computer Required

Admissions

Regular Application Deadline: 1/1

Early Decision Deadline(s): 11/15

Fall Transfer Deadline: 6/1 (priority)

Spring Transfer Deadline: 11/1
  (priority)

Inside the Classroom

"When you are here, you know that your friends are going to really do amazing things in their life," a management information systems and international business major writes about RPI. The first engineering school in the nation, RPI has five divisions: engineering, architecture, management and technology, sciences, and humanities and social sciences. Most students opt for engineering tracks, but all of Rensselaer's schools are 100 percent hi-tech and emphasize the hands-on use of technology. The school of management features a virtual stock trading floor, and courses in the humanities and social sciences include engineering psychology, technical communication, and cutting-edge EMAC (electronic media, arts, and communications) programs. Remarks a student: "I decided to go to RPI because of how technologically advanced we are." In coming years, Rensselaer has ambitious plans to increase its research activity, with a focus on biotechnology and information technology.

The first year at Rensselaer, introduced by the school's "Freshman Year Experience," is "relatively easy" compared to what comes after. "It's tough," says a recent grad. The school is "intense" and a student cautions: "There is so much work that you really have to have your time management skills in check." After the first two years, students tend to work in teams. "Students usually are more collaborative than competitive," remarks one student. Professors get good marks for accessibility, and prefer seminars to lectures. "Professors [are] concerned about students, not just research," comments a junior. Undergrad research opportunities with Rensselaer's prestigious faculty are plentiful. The student/faculty ratio is 15:1.

The most popular majors are engineering, business, computer science, architecture, and biology. Computer graphics, electronic media, IT, and all engineering programs are strong—nuclear engineers have their own linear accelerator and a critical reactor. Special programs include the Incubator Program, designed to help launch technology startups, and the Center for Industrial Innovation, which offers still more opportunities for undergraduate research. Accelerated degree programs are numerous; a guidance counselor lauds the accelerated medical school program. "A lot of students go on co-op, or take a semester off for working," a junior comments. "This, and our very respected education, have companies running for us." The average starting salary of a B.S. grad from Rensselaer is $53,000.

Campus Environment

Rensselaer's 260-acre campus is located in Troy. "We are on a hill, and on the bottom of it is downtown Troy," a junior explains. " You have to know where to go and where not to. The town-gown relations are not fantastic." Another student adds: "Troy is pretty dull. The area is rather poor and some sections are dangerous. But the town is a quaint, historical place, with many cultural things."

About 55 percent of Rensselaer students live on-campus; freshmen are required to do so. A New Jersey guidance counselor calls the living conditions "terrible." "On-campus housing is very expensive and quite limited," a student gripes. "The dorms vary in quality from recently renovated and brand new to things that haven't been worked on in 20 years." Another adds: "After freshman year most people move off campus and move into apartments or Greek housing." But beware: "There are a lot of 'slum lords' that capitalize on students not being picky and with a small budget." However, " there are lots of off-campus places to live—mostly converted single family houses." Regarding transportation: "Freshman year you do not need a car, because you really are too busy to do things outside of the campus," advises an upperclassman. "You definitely should consider it later on, though."

A student reports that the school is building "an Electronic Arts Performing Theater" and "a bioinformatics building." Also, there's a new state-of-the-art gym. A student adds: "Our Student Union is wireless, and we just made it open 24 hours, and are looking to put a coffee shop inside of it, which will be a great meeting place here."

Student Life

The typical Rensselaer student is "pretty intelligent, and a bit dorky," observes a junior, adding: "We study hard but we also have a great time when we party." A chemical engineering major comments: "Most are engineers and Meyers-Briggs would probably characterize them as ISTJ (introverted, sensing, thinking, judging)." People are "very down to earth and friendly," but one student complains: "There is not that much school spirit. It is an engineering school, so that should be expected." The school is diverse, with a 21 percent minority population, but the 3:1 male/female ratio makes social life somewhat lopsided.

RPI students "work out, study, and party," comments an upperclassman. "There are bars downtown that we frequent, a mall 15 minutes away, and there is a huge fraternity scene. Which gets old when you aren't an underclassman, but you make the most of it." "Overall, the Greek leaders are same student leaders on campus," reports another student. "There is no hazing on campus, and we have a very good relationship with our Dean of Students, because we work together." Thirty percent of RPI students pledge, and frats are popular "because there's very little to do off campus. You have to drive quite a bit to reach a big city." There is "a lot of drinking, not much drugs" at the school.

Varsity sports are "pretty popular but [are] a huge commitment for students," a student explains. "Intramurals for that reason are more popular." Men's hockey is big at RPI, with the stadium filled on every opening Engineers game. "The ice hockey team is the only Division I team. The rest are Division III. Our school does not have much sports team spirit except for people that support hockey," a student remarks. There are over 130 student organizations. "There are some weird student organizations on campus…The senate is not very effective and government isn't really a big deal," a junior comments.

Students warn liberal arts majors to steer clear of RPI. Also, "someone who does not care about their future, is not hard working, or doesn't have their priorities straight" would also not fit in. A student boasts: "RPI has some of the most intelligent people in the world…We are striving to become one of the best schools in the nation, but we don't have the Ivy League bureaucracy." An IMS major concludes: "One fantastic thing about a typical student here at RPI is that we think big. People are not intimidated easily, and dare mighty things."

Other schools to check out: Rochester Institute of Technology, MIT, Lehigh, Carnegie Mellon, Illinois Tech.

Total # of Students Applied: 5,252
 Admitted: 4,216
 Enrolled: 1,341

Applied Early Decision: 168
 Early Decision Admitted: 142

Test Scores (middle 50%):
 SAT Verbal: 580–680
 SAT Math: 640–720
 ACT Comp: 24–28

HS Rank of Entering Freshmen:
 Top 10%: 58%
 Top 25%: 88%
 Top 50%: 99%

THE EXPERTS SAY…

" RPI's facilities and research programs give new meaning to the words 'cutting edge.' Watch for new developments in biotechnology and IT. "

" Brains and Greeks, no liberal arts, and there's a 3:1 male/female ratio. Try dating a critical reactor (if you haven't already). "

Costs (2003–04)

Tuition and Fees: $28,496

Room & Board: $9,133

Payment Plan(s): installment plan

Inst. Aid (2002–03)

FT Undergrads Receiving Aid: 71%
 Avg. Amount per Student: $22,791

FT Undergrads Receiving Non-Need-Based Scholarship or Grant Aid: 14%
 Avg. Amount per Student: $10,789

Of Those Receiving Any Aid:

Rec. Need-Based Scholarship or Grant Aid: 100%
 Average Award: $16,840

Rec. Need-Based Self-Help Aid: 73%
 Average Award: $7,790

Upon Graduation, Avg. Loan Debt per Student: $23,725

Financial Aid Deadline: 2/15 (priority)

Graduates

Going to Graduate School:
 20% Within One Year

Accepting Job Offer:
 32% at time of graduation

Companies Recruiting On Campus:
 129

Alumni Giving: 23%

RHODE ISLAND SCHOOL OF DESIGN

2 College Street, Providence, RI 02903
Admissions Phone: (401) 454-6300 Fax: (401) 454-6309
Email: admissions@risd.edu
Website: www.risd.edu

General Info

Type of School: private, coed
Setting: urban
Academic Calendar: 4-1-4

Student Body

Full-Time Undergrads: 1,920
    Men: 35%, Women: 65%

Total Undergrad Population:
    African American: 2%
    Asian American: 13%
    Latino: 5%
    Native American: <1%
    Caucasian: 55%
    International: 11%
    Living Off-Campus: 67%

Graduate and First-Professional
    Students: 374

Academics

Full-Time Faculty: 146
    With Ph.D.: 86%

Part-Time Faculty: 357

Student/Faculty Ratio: 10:1

Most Popular Majors:
    illustration (11%)
    architecture (11%)
    graphic design (10%)
    industrial design (9%)
    painting (7%)

Freshmen Retention Rate: 94%

Graduation Rates:
    72% within four years
    90% within six years
    note: 5-yr. program affects rates

Computers: Computer Required;
    School provides individual
    computer/laptop

Admissions

Regular Application Deadline: 2/15

Early Action Deadline: 12/15

Fall Transfer Deadline: 3/31

Spring Transfer Deadline: 11/25

Total # of Students Applied: 2,524
    Admitted: 799
    Enrolled: 392

Waitlist Available

Test Scores (middle 50%):
    SAT Verbal: 540–650
    SAT Math: 550–660

Inside the Classroom

The Rhode Island School of Design, one of the most renowned schools in the country for art, design, and architecture, offers young artists and designers the opportunity to fine-tune their talents and abilities while interacting with fellow serious students and a committed faculty. Undergraduates can choose from 17 majors, ranging from traditional fine arts such as painting and photography to less common majors such as industrial design and interior architecture.

Although the arts are the primary focus at RISD (pronounced "RIZ-dee"), there are also extensive liberal arts requirements. The school states that it recognizes the "value of a holistic education, one that balances the emphasis on the professional major with an equally important expectation that a student be versed in the humanities, literature, and the social sciences. RISD recognizes that not all students will ultimately be practicing in their professions: they may in fact choose other professional endeavors." Students must take 42 credits in art and architectural history, English composition, and history, philosophy, and social sciences. An intensive, year-long foundation studies program provides all freshmen with a common understanding of visual language, with required classes in drawing and two- and three-dimensional design. Most seniors complete some kind of major project in their field, very often completing a portfolio or putting together an exhibit.

The RISD faculty brings a wealth of knowledge and practical experience to their teaching, and they help provide students with an accurate view of the "real world" beyond the walls of the campus. The teachers can be "brutally critical" at times, a student tells us, but she praises how "they are genuinely interested in how you develop." Students often exhibit their work and receive valuable feedback from peers and teachers, getting a "hands-on education from the first year on," according to a New Jersey guidance counselor.

Although many RISD students use the six-week winter session as an opportunity to explore course offerings in disciplines outside their majors, hundreds of others choose to gain practical experience through the college's professional internship program. Internship placements range from an assistantship at Ralph Lauren to a curatorial post at the Guggenheim.

Campus Environment

Students practically live in their studios to the point of sleeping there. First-year students bond quickly because they're thrown together in studios and classes and live together in one of four freshmen-only dormitories. Freshmen are required to live on campus and are housed in the Quad, which is a series of residence halls in four interconnected, four-story buildings. The Quad offers both corridor- and suite-style living, and each floor houses between 12 and 38 students. The Quad also features the Met, RISD's main dining facility. Upperclassmen may choose the small group atmosphere of the Outer Houses, or the two apartments buildings, Colonial Houses and Dwight House. Efficiency, studio, and two- and three-bedroom apartments are offered, and they are located close to the studios. Upperclassmen usually opt to live in these apartments, or other apartments located off-campus.

RISD provides top-of-the-line working materials in all disciplines, from computer-controlled kilns used by ceramics majors to sophisticated draping software used by apparel design students. RISD even has its own museum with a collection of more than 85,000 works of art, in all media, from all cultures. The museum traces the history of art from antiquity to the present, and it is acknowledged as one of the country's best museums of its size. It sponsors a variety of lectures, gallery talks, and other events, as well as workshops for teachers and weekend classes for young artists. Students further benefit from the school's affiliation with its neighbor, Brown University, as they can cross-register and use the facilities, including Brown's library system and sports complex.

Student Life

When we talk to students at most other colleges about their social lives, they are quick to describe the on-campus parties or popular bars. The freshmen we interviewed from RISD, however, raved about the frequently attended gallery openings and exhibitions. That's just one indication of how RISD students focus on art and design in all areas of their lives. Students become so immersed in their art and projects that they shy away from most activities geared toward large groups of people, preferring instead to attend small informal parties and get-togethers.

There are more than 50 student-run organizations on campus that include social awareness, political, religious, and ethnic groups; special interest clubs; Yearbook; a fitness center; and sports. The ski team makes weekend trips to northern New England for downhill skiing at reduced student prices. There are frequent exhibitions at 11 departmental and college galleries aside from the RISD Museum. Among the popular events that feature student work are the Film/Animation/Video festival and the Apparel Design department's annual fashion show, Collection.

Although Providence isn't a large city, it fosters a large and active artistic community. There are a number of movie theaters and a repertory theater company near campus, along with several restaurants and cafés—not to mention the Rhode Island beaches and beautiful shorelines. Students can also drive out to Tillinghast Farm (better known as the RISD Farm), a 30-acre estate on Narragansett Bay that's a great place for volleyball, softball, barbecues, and other beach activities. For bigger adventures, Boston is just a short train ride away.

Other schools to check out: Cooper Union, Parsons, Fashion Institute of Technology.

HS Rank of Entering Freshmen:
Top 10%: 26%
Top 25%: 58%
Top 50%: 91%

Avg. HS GPA: 3.3

Costs (2003–04)

Tuition and Fees: $26,199

Room & Board: $7,370

Payment Plan(s): deferred payment plan

THE EXPERTS SAY...

" Unlike Cooper Union or Parsons, RISD gives you the solid liberal arts background you need to pursue professions outside of the arts, architecture, and design. "

" Unlike Cooper Union or Parsons, RISD doesn't have an exciting NYC backdrop. The social life at RISD is openings, exhibitions, and snuggling up to your computerized kiln at night. "

Inst. Aid (2002–03)

Institutional Aid, Need-Based: $8,067,000

Institutional Aid, Non-Need-Based: $15,000

FT Undergrads Receiving Aid: 47%
Avg. Amount per Student: $15,300

FT Undergrads Receiving Non-Need-Based Scholarship or Grant Aid: 2%
Avg. Amount per Student: $1,250

Of Those Receiving Any Aid:

Rec. Need-Based Scholarship or Grant Aid: 90%
Average Award: $9,400

Rec. Need-Based Self-Help Aid: 100%
Average Award: $5,900

Upon Graduation, Avg. Loan Debt per Student: $21,700

Financial Aid Deadline: 2/15 (priority)

Graduates

Going to Graduate School:
3% Within One Year

Accepting Job Offer:
1% at time of graduation

Companies Recruiting On Campus: 30

Alumni Giving: 19%

RHODES COLLEGE

2000 North Parkway, Memphis, TN 38112
Admissions Phone: (901) 843-3700; (800) 844-5969 Fax: (901) 843-3631
Email: adminfo@rhodes.edu
Website: www.rhodes.edu

General Info

Type of School: private, coed,
  Presbyterian

Setting: urban

Academic Calendar: semester

Student Body

Full-Time Undergrads: 1,518
  Men: 44%, Women: 56%

Part-Time Undergrads: 16
  Men: 44%, Women: 56%

Total Undergrad Population:
  African American: 4%
  Asian American: 3%
  Latino: 1%
  Native American: <1%
  Caucasian: 86%
  International: 1%
  Out-of-State: 71%
  Living Off-Campus: 25%
  In Fraternities: 51%
  In Sororities: 58%

Graduate and First-Professional
  Students: 12

Academics

Full-Time Faculty: 129
  With Ph.D.: 90%

Part-Time Faculty: 33
  With Ph.D.: 48%

Student/Faculty Ratio: 11:1

Most Popular Majors:
  biology (14%)
  English (12%)
  business administration (11%)
  political science (10%)
  international studies (8%)

Freshmen Retention Rate: 87%

Graduation Rates:
  71% within four years
  73% within six years

Admissions

Regular Application Deadline: 2/1

Early Decision Deadline(s): 11/1,
  1/1

Fall Transfer Deadline: 2/1

Spring Transfer Deadline: 12/1

Total # of Students Applied: 2,345
  Admitted: 1,631
  Enrolled: 680

Inside the Classroom

"A very good liberal arts school," declares a Texas high school guidance counselor. Students at Rhodes College may earn a B.A. or B.S. in one of 23 departmental or 11 interdisciplinary programs, including urban studies, American studies, Asian studies, and women's studies. Traditional liberal arts programs are generally excellent, especially in the sciences, as are the school's preprofessional fields. The distribution requirements are broad, as students take courses in four key areas: humanities, social sciences, natural sciences and mathematics, and fine arts. There are numerous opportunities for off-campus learning, and the "British Studies at Oxford" program offers students the chance to study a different period of British history and culture during a summer in Oxford, England.

One of the most important aspects (one student claims "*the* most important aspect") of life at Rhodes is the honor system. It is a student-run system that investigates charges of lying, cheating, and stealing, and can result in expulsion if the student is found guilty of the charge. Everyone takes it very seriously here: Professors leave the room during exams, and students sign a copy of the code each time they finish an unproctored test. The honor system results in an extremely safe campus. "I can be studying and leave my books and things and go to dinner and come back, and my stuff will be right where I left it," says one student, and locked doors are rare. Rhodes students truly love the honor code—they can't overemphasize its importance to them, and people we spoke to said it was "incredibly empowering" to be entrusted with so much responsibility by the administration.

Students at Rhodes feel well prepared to go out into the real world, partly because of the nurturing they receive from their teachers, and partly from the early exposure to career preparation that Rhodes emphasizes. Classes are small, with an average class size of 18 students. With one faculty member for every 11 students, it's easy to get to know professors, who are acknowledged as "excellent" by their students.

More than 60 percent of the student body participates in the internship program, working at such Memphis fixtures as St. Jude Children's Research Hospital, the Orpheum Theater, and FedEx. The school claims it has more alumni going on to complete doctoral degrees than any other college in the South. An unusually high percentage of Rhodes graduates are accepted into graduate or professional school.

Campus Environment

Rhodes students love their campus for its beauty and location. Nestled among 100 wooded acres in an attractive residential section of Memphis, the campus boasts sprawling lawns and stately Gothic academic buildings, several of which are listed in the National Register of Historic Places. Students here are within walking distance of the Memphis Zoo and the Memphis Brooks Museum of Art. However, one guidance counselor says that "safety is a concern" in certain areas near the campus.

The school, and many students, believes that keeping a majority of students on campus fosters a kind of close-knit community. So, unless they're commuting from a family home in Memphis, all freshmen and sophomores must live on campus; most juniors and seniors choose to stay put as well. In fact, more than 70 percent of undergrads live in one of 16 residence halls. Dorms are single sex—a vestige of the school's Presbyterian affiliation—and may be arranged as doubles, triples, or suites. There are Greek houses, but no one lives in them. All students may have cars on campus, and most do.

Student Life

Rhodes attracts bright students, often in the top 10 percent of their classes, from all over the country. But the majority of students are from the South and from middle- and upper-class families. Consequently, the student body is rather homogeneous in terms of ethnicity—i.e., white—and socioeconomic background. While most students share conservative religious and social values, they tend to be "middle of the road" politically. Either way, there's much tolerance among the student body. The small (1,500) population helps maintain Rhodes's reputation as a friendly, easygoing campus full of Southern hospitality, where most students readily recognize one another and greet each other with a smile.

Social life on the Rhodes campus is covered in Greek letters. We hear that if you don't join a fraternity or sorority, it's akin to social suicide. Well, it may not be that dramatic, but the Greeks do draw more half of the student body. Drinking is a part of life at Rhodes, and many students feel that the administration's new, tough policy on alcohol use (or abuse, as the school sees it) is putting a crimp in their social life. So, students often take their partying behind closed dorm doors, or off campus altogether. The event of the year is the "Rites of Spring"—a weekend of partying with live bands, food, drinks, and games.

There are also more than 80 different student-run groups, from outdoor clubs and religious groups to campus publications and multicultural organizations. "There's always a lot going on," agrees one undergrad. The popular Mock Trial team has won four national championships. Rhodes students also have an acclaimed community service record, even starting their own chapter of Habitat for Humanity. Nearly 80 percent of students are active in community service in the greater Memphis area. Sports are a fixture on campus as well. The Greeks, in addition to throwing big parties, help make the intramurals program especially active. Sixty-five percent of Rhodes students play on an IM or club sports team; 25 percent compete on a varsity level. Rhodes is a Division III school, which means no athletic scholarships are awarded.

For those venturing off campus, Rhodes students are just minutes from a revitalized, vibrant downtown Memphis, where, as the school likes to say, "Beale Street (Home of the Blues) meets the majestic Mississippi River." The city is jammed with offerings: museums, theaters, blues clubs, bars, restaurants, shops, and cultural venues. And Elvis fans don't have far to go to visit Graceland, Memphis' leading tourist attraction.

Other schools to check out: Davidson, Wake Forest, Vanderbilt, Emory, Centre.

THE EXPERTS SAY...

" The Rhodes honor code makes it possible to leave your doors unlocked on this gorgeous Memphis campus. The administration trusts the students, and the professors do not proctor exams. "

" Everyone is friendly at Rhodes— but they'll be friendlier if you go Greek. "

RICE UNIVERSITY

Post Office Box 1892, Houston, TX 77251-1892
Admissions Phone: (713) 348-7423; (800) 527-6957 Fax: (713) 348-5952
Email: admission@rice.edu
Website: www.rice.edu

General Info

Type of School: private, coed
Setting: urban
Academic Calendar: semester

Student Body

Full-Time Undergrads: 2,749
   Men: 53%, Women: 47%

Part-Time Undergrads: 20
   Men: 65%, Women: 35%

Total Undergrad Population:
   African American: 7%
   Asian American: 14%
   Latino: 11%
   Native American: 1%
   Caucasian: 54%
   International: 3%
   Out-of-State: 46%
   Living Off-Campus: 27%

Graduate and First-Professional
   Students: 1,998

Academics

Full-Time Faculty: 503
   With Ph.D.: 96%

Part-Time Faculty: 280
   With Ph.D.: 80%

Student/Faculty Ratio: 5:1

Most Popular Majors:
   economics (8%)
   biosciences (6%)
   electrical/computer
      engineering (6%)
   psychology (5%)
   English (5%)

Freshmen Retention Rate: 95%

Graduation Rates:
   75% within four years
   92% within six years

Admissions

Regular Application Deadline: 1/2

Early Decision Available

Early Action Deadline: 12/1

Fall Transfer Deadline: 4/1

Spring Transfer Deadline: 11/1

Total # of Students Applied: 7,079
   Admitted: 1,682
   Enrolled: 700
   Waitlisted Students Admitted: 54

Inside the Classroom

Thanks to an endowment per student ratio of approximately $697,000, Rice University manages to provide Ivy League-level academics and facilities at a super-bargain price (for a private school, anyway). A guidance counselor has described Rice as "a best buy for the super bright." The admissions process is very competitive, and most of those admitted are among the top five percent in their high school classes, giving Rice a smart and career-driven student population.

Although Rice is a major research university, the atmosphere tends to resemble a small liberal arts college because of its relatively small population and friendly student body. Rice has six undergraduate schools: the School of Social Sciences, the Wiess School of Natural Sciences, the Shepherd School of Music, the School of Humanities, the School of Engineering, and the School of Architecture. Rice is primarily known for science and engineering, but its humanities departments, particularly English and history, are gaining in reputation. The undergraduate programs in architecture and music are also highly rated. Requirements include four courses each in the natural sciences, social sciences, and humanities.

A student describes the academics as being "taken very seriously. Workload is intense—most students take 15+ hours a semester. Most students double- or triple-major." Another student tells us that "it's not uncommon for people to stay in on a Friday or Saturday night to study or write a paper. It's possible to pull off a C without all that much effort, but most people here are not satisfied with that and work hard for an A." Nonetheless, you won't find a cutthroat environment at Rice. A freshman says, "Rice definitely fosters an atmosphere of intelligence and creativity but without that 'Ivy League' arrogance." Another student agrees, describing the environment as being about "personal learning and accomplishment rather than intense outward competition." Additionally, professors are "easily accessible and eager to help even in larger classes." Rice is also "adjacent to several hospitals and medical centers, which is great if you're going into a health-related field or if you want to volunteer."

Campus Environment

Student life revolves in large part around the residential colleges, considered one of Rice's best assets. Each college is a small community in which students live, dine, and study together and form especially close friendships. Freshmen are assigned to a residential college when they arrive, and "form such an attachment to it they would never consider switching." They remain affiliated with the college for all four years, even if they eventually move off campus. These colleges eliminate the need for a Greek system, much to students' delight: "Rice does not have a Greek system and we like it that way. Our colleges serve as a sort of frat/sorority houses in that we throw parties, put on plays and musicals, and have events as colleges." Housing is guaranteed freshman year only; after that "there is not enough space for everyone so some people have to get bumped off campus each year. Room draw can get ugly." Though not a popular choice, off-campus housing is often comparatively cheaper and easy to find.

Although Houston isn't typically considered one of the safest cities, Rice students feel very safe on campus. "Since Rice is so small, there isn't much interaction between the city and the school." A junior says, "Almost everyone keeps their dorm rooms unlocked and I often go for runs around campus after midnight without fear for my safety."

Students enjoy Houston and claim that "saying you're a Rice student gets you instant respect in the town." Rice is close to the huge Galleria mall, an ice skating rink, a well-respected museum district, and countless restaurants. "Houston was ranked one of the fattest cities in America, which makes sense since there are tons of great places to eat," a student tells us. Since students spend most of their time on the small campus, cars are not a necessity. "Freshmen year, usually one student in a group of five friends has a car, and that's sufficient." Off-campus is another story, however. Although shuttle buses are available, "Houston has no public transportation to speak of, and you're in Texas, baby. People don't walk."

Student Life

While Rice students are ethnically diverse, students are generally apathetic when it comes to politics and social issues. "Maybe it's the stifling Houston heat or humidity, but Rice students aren't interested in being agents of change ... If you tried to create a recycling program or launch a diversity campaign, you would probably get laughed at. But then they would give you a hug and take you back."

Rice is a wet campus, which makes all those dorm parties more convenient. "Since most people live on campus we can just walk back to our rooms, which eliminates the danger of driving." Though "lots of people drink," those who don't are "certainly respected for their preference." Additionally, students praise the campus police for being "concerned more about your safety than getting you in trouble."

Rice offers a vast number of student organizations, with Rice Student Volunteer Program (RSVP) being among the most popular, but some feel that "kids don't participate in enough extracurriculars." Rice is Division I athletics but there is some "resentment of varsity athletes and a fairly strong opinion that a small, academically strong school like Rice should not spend so much of its resources" on sports. A bitter-sounding graduate says that "athletes have the dilemma of being good enough to play for a Division I school while having to blend in with a bunch of dorks ... rarely do regular students show them any respect." However, intramural sports are very popular.

On weekends, students go to Willy's, the on-campus pub, or to one of the many dorm parties. Concerts are a popular pastime, as is going off campus "to the movies, or out to dinner, or to a club." There are also "cultural things to do in Houston, such as attend the symphony or ballet." And the general consensus about Sundays is that they're for "post-party recovery and studying."

Other schools to check out: Wake Forest, William and Mary, Princeton, Duke, MIT.

\# Applied Early Decision: 488
Early Decision Admitted: 154

Test Scores (middle 50%):
SAT Verbal: 650–750
SAT Math: 670–770
ACT Comp: 28–33

HS Rank of Entering Freshmen:
Top 10%: 83%
Top 25%: 92%
Top 50%: 99%

THE EXPERTS SAY...

" After the price, the residential colleges are the best things about Rice. Lasting friendships are formed among these bright and ambitious students. "

" An affordable private school offering top-notch academics on a great campus, Rice is the perfect American university. "

Costs (2003–04)

Tuition and Fees: $19,670

Room & Board: $7,880

Payment Plan(s): installment plan

Inst. Aid (est. 2003–04)

Institutional Aid, Need-Based: $8,521,008

Institutional Aid, Non-Need-Based: $3,442,271

FT Undergrads Receiving Aid: 30%
Avg. Amount per Student: $15,498

FT Undergrads Receiving Non-Need-Based Scholarship or Grant Aid: 25%
Avg. Amount per Student: $5,932

Of Those Receiving Any Aid:

Rec. Need-Based Scholarship or Grant Aid: 100%
Average Award: $13,571

Rec. Need-Based Self-Help Aid: 86%
Average Award: $3,651

Upon Graduation, Avg. Loan Debt per Student: $12,705

Financial Aid Deadline: 3/1

Graduates

Going to Graduate School: 35% Within One Year

Accepting Job Offer: 56% at time of graduation

Companies Recruiting On Campus: 200

RIPON COLLEGE

300 Seward Street, PO Box 248, Ripon, WI 54971
Admissions Phone: (920) 748-8337; (800) 947-4766 Fax: (920) 748-8335
Email: adminfo@ripon.edu
Website: www.ripon.edu

General Info

Type of School: private, coed

Setting: small town

Academic Calendar: semester

Student Body

Full-Time Undergrads: 947
  Men: 48%, Women: 52%

Part-Time Undergrads: 1 Women: 100%

Total Undergrad Population:
  African American: 2%
  Asian American: 2%
  Latino: 4%
  Native American: 1%
  Caucasian: 86%
  International: 2%
  Out-of-State: 31%
  Living Off-Campus: 10%
  In Fraternities: 55%
  In Sororities: 21%

Academics

Full-Time Faculty: 50
  With Ph.D.: 96%

Part-Time Faculty: 25
  With Ph.D.: 48%

Student/Faculty Ratio: 15:1

Most Popular Majors:
  history (13%)
  psychology (12%)
  business (11%)
  biology (10%)
  English (9%)

Completing 2 or More Majors: 31%

Freshmen Retention Rate: 84%

Graduation Rates:
  53% within four years
  62% within six years

Admissions

Regular Application Deadline: 3/15 (priority)

Total # of Students Applied: 959
  Admitted: 809
  Enrolled: 259

Test Scores (middle 50%):
  SAT Verbal: 550–630
  SAT Math: 520–660
  ACT Comp: 22–27

Inside the Classroom

With fewer than 1,000 students, Ripon College offers a highly personalized education in a low-key and intimate environment. Classes average 11 students; labs, only 6. Even introductory classes generally have fewer than 20, so you'll never experience huge lectures. There are no teaching assistants, since the school is strictly undergrad. Students say they value getting to know their professors both in and out of the classroom. A senior says, "It is not uncommon to be invited to dinner at your professor's house or to play intramural water polo against the president of the college." Another calls the "phenomenal" professor-student relationship "one of the greatest strengths of Ripon College." Guidance counselors agree that high level of personalized attention and a strong science program make Ripon a superb value. "A small, personal gem," raves one California guidance counselor.

Ripon has produced three Rhodes Scholars over the course of its history—most recently in 2002. For such a tiny school, that's proof of its high quality academics. One double-major rates it an "8 on a scale of 10" in terms of competitiveness. Overall, however, we hear that while the academics are challenging, the workload isn't so intense or overwhelming that schoolwork is all students ever do. Many students feel they're not being worked hard enough. "Cooperative, not competitive," is how the academic environment has been described. The most popular majors are biology, business management, English, poly sci, and education.

Ripon has several interesting programs in place: In an effort to maintain a sense of campus community, the college sponsors a weekly "Golden Hour," presenting speakers and special events. The "Communicating Plus" initiative emphasizes the development of students' written and oral communication skills, as well as problem-solving abilities. There are also numerous study abroad options, and research opportunities are available in most departments beginning in a student's second or third year. We're told that students experience "immense alumni support" during job searches and internships (though we're not sure if that includes Ripon's most famous alum, actor Harrison Ford). An alumni couple recently left the school $2.5 million—the single largest gift in the college's history.

We hear that the financial situation is often a source of friction; over the past few years some operations were streamlined and faculty cuts were made. The good news is that curriculum improvements have been in the works, and more changes may be ahead, as the college has recently named a new president.

Campus Environment

Situated just an hour from Milwaukee and minutes from Green Lake, Ripon is a small, friendly community set in rural dairy-farm country. Officially a city, it is far more like a small town—one that is "very supportive of the students," according to a senior. Ripon itself is rich in history: Perhaps its most famous site is the "Little White Schoolhouse," birthplace of the Republican Party. There are local festivals and special events, though students complain there's little else in the way of everyday entertainment. Because of the remoteness of the school's location, almost everything that goes on after class happens right on campus. As one student tells us, "It's a good thing the campus is hopping, because the tiny town of Ripon isn't," though most agree that with its restaurants, movie theater, and bowling alley, it's "better than a lot of small towns." In short, the atmosphere is "charming rural." For urban fun, students can travel to Milwaukee or Madison.

All students, except for those who are married or living with their immediate family, must live on campus. We hear that some of the dorms could use improvement ("they date back to the '60s," explains one sophomore), and that Greek houses are way nicer than dorms. Certain parts of the campus, including some dorm areas, are being renovated, though we're told it's slow-going. One student points out a major perk: free laundry. "All you have to do is bring soap, no quarters!"

Overall, the campus is friendly and safe—"most people don't lock their doors." The pile of backpacks on a lobby floor is a point of pride for Ripon students, as a senior explains: "During lunchtime, everybody throws their backpacks all over the floor in the commons, no locks necessary." And you won't need a car. "When you mention you are going 'off-campus' to buy groceries for your dorm room," we're told, "it's like two blocks."

Student Life

"Ripon is one of the friendliest places that I have ever been," a senior tells us. In fact, most of the students we spoke to had nothing but raves for their fellow students and their school in general. Although according to one student, "the college prides itself on diversity," another tells us that most people he sees are "Caucasian, middle-income, jeans-wearing, and conservative." While diversity is not the school's strong suit, there are small populations of African American and Latino students. Overall, it's a nice, open environment, with a high level of tolerance. And one student defends the student body makeup, saying, "Considering the lack of racial diversity, we maintain quite a bit of diversity of background."

Greek life is huge at Ripon. "The Independents look to the Greeks to host the parties and provide a social life for everyone on campus," a student says. Indeed, fraternity "lounge parties" are the weekend activity of choice at Ripon. Sororities host a lot of activities and contribute a great deal of time and energy to charities. We've even heard some students complain that the Greeks seem to be the "favored children" of the administration.

Historically, drinking has been a problem on campus. In an area not known for its nightlife, students have typically found that drinking is the easiest way to let loose. Administrators have been trying to implement a wider range of on-campus entertainment, including movies, comedians, hypnotists, and speakers. A student says she's "impressed with the amount of activities that are available to students." And a lot of students play sports. Ripon has nine varsity teams each for men and women competing in the Midwest Conference of NCAA Division III. Intramurals are also a huge part of the Ripon experience. As one senior puts it, "The majority of students here are athletes."

Other schools to check out: Beloit, Cornell College, University of Wisconsin—Stevens Point.

HS Rank of Entering Freshmen:
Top 10%: 28%
Top 25%: 56%
Top 50%: 91%
Avg. HS GPA: 3.45

Costs (2004–5)

Tuition and Fees: $20,730
Room & Board: $5,360
Payment Plan(s): installment plan

THE EXPERTS SAY...

" While Ripon doesn't yet have a national reputation, its strong alumni network will help you to land jobs and internships. "

" Ripon's campus is so safe that students leave doors unlocked and backpacks unattended. (Try doing that in New York—your apartment would be cleaned out and your backpack would be blown up by a SWAT team.) "

Inst. Aid (est. 2003–04)

Institutional Aid, Need-Based:
$7,118,321

Institutional Aid, Non-Need-Based:
$2,524,734

FT Undergrads Receiving Aid: 77%
Avg. Amount per Student: $17,108

FT Undergrads Receiving Non-Need-Based Scholarship or Grant Aid: 22%
Avg. Amount per Student: $14,071

Of Those Receiving Any Aid:

Rec. Need-Based Scholarship or Grant Aid: 98%
Average Award: $13,810

Rec. Need-Based Self-Help Aid: 77%
Average Award: $4,629

Upon Graduation, Avg. Loan Debt per Student: $17,028

Financial Aid Deadline: rolling

Graduates

Going to Graduate School:
23% Within One Year

Accepting Job Offer:
31% at time of graduation

Companies Recruiting On Campus: 12

Alumni Giving: 82%

ROCHESTER INSTITUTE OF TECHNOLOGY

60 Lomb Drive, Rochester, NY 14623-5604
Admissions Phone: (585) 475-6631 Fax: (585) 475-7424 Email: admissions@rit.edu
Website: www.rit.edu Application Website: www.rit.edu/admissions

General Info

Type of School: private, coed
Setting: suburban
Academic Calendar: quarter

Student Body

Full-Time Undergrads: 10,636
  Men: 70%, Women: 30%

Part-Time Undergrads: 1,176
  Men: 66%, Women: 34%

Total Undergrad Population:
  African American: 5%
  Asian American: 7%
  Latino: 3%
  Native American: <1%
  Caucasian: 70%
  International: 5%
  Out-of-State: 45%
  Living Off-Campus: 40%
  In Fraternities: 5%
  In Sororities: 5%

Graduate and First-Professional
  Students: 2,304

Academics

Full-Time Faculty: 701
  With Ph.D.: 85%

Part-Time Faculty: 444
  With Ph.D.: 80%

Student/Faculty Ratio: 13:1

Most Popular Majors:
  information technology (10%)
  computer science (7%)
  mechanical engineering (5%)
  photography (5%)
  electrical engineering (4%)

Freshmen Retention Rate: 88%

Graduation Rates:
  62% within six years
  note: 5-yr. program affects rates

Admissions

Regular Application Deadline: 3/15;
  2/1 (priority)

Early Decision Deadline(s): 12/1

Transfer Application Deadline: rolling

Total # of Students Applied: 8,317
  Admitted: 5,784
  Enrolled: 2,195

# of Students Waitlisted: 150
  Students Accepting Place: 125
  Waitlisted Students Admitted: 25

Inside the Classroom

With state-of-the-art academic technologies and one of the leading co-op programs in the nation, Rochester Institute of Technology offers unparalleled career education and placement for its students, including more than 1,100 who are deaf or hearing impaired. RIT's schools are the College of Applied Science and Technology, College of Business, Thomas Golisano College of Computing and Information Sciences, Kate Gleason College of Engineering, College of Imaging Arts and Science, College of Liberal Arts, the College of Science, and the National Technical Institute for the Deaf, the world's first and largest technological college for students who are hearing impaired.

RIT offers more than 200 undergraduate degree programs, and has one of the premier schools of photography in the nation. RIT offers the nation's only Bachelor of Science degree programs in imaging science and in microelectronic engineering; RIT was also the first university in the U.S. to offer undergraduate degrees in biotechnology (1983) and information technology (1992). RIT's School for American Crafts, School of Print Media, and Center for Imaging Science offer unique academic programs rarely found at other universities, and RIT's new master's concentration in electronic game design has gotten national media coverage.

The general education curriculum includes courses in writing and literature, the humanities, and social sciences, plus a minor or concentration in a chosen area of the liberal arts. An interdisciplinary capstone course called Senior Seminar is taught by faculty from various liberal arts disciplines. As part of a focus on career education, RIT degree programs require at least one co-op work assignment to allow students to experience their chosen profession in the real world. RIT annually places 2,600 students in co-op positions with 1,300 employers. More than 450 companies visit RIT annually, conducting more than 5,000 employment interviews.

The demanding quarter system divides the calendar year into four 11-week terms and the academic pressure is high. It's not impossible to get an A, but it takes discipline, students say. A college official concurs: "Our programs are rigorous, fast-paced, and demanding, so students who succeed academically have a strong work ethic that complements their intelligence. Students who thrive at RIT have a strong orientation toward 'learning by doing' and enjoy the applied nature of our curricula and the opportunity to gain experience in their field through cooperative education and internships." Prominent alumni include Daniel A. Carp, Chairman and CEO of Eastman Kodak Company; Thomas Curley, President and Publisher of *USA Today*; Bruce R. James, CEO of the U.S. Government Printing Office; and Terrance N. Clapham, inventor of laser eye surgery for nearsightedness

Campus Environment

The RIT campus is located in suburban Rochester in Western New York, just a few hours from Niagara Falls and Toronto, and near prestigious co-op opportunities with such companies as Xerox, Kodak, and Bausch & Lomb. Except for internships, most students find business-oriented Rochester boring; a car to get away is deemed essential.

The campus design is red brick—lots of it ("Too many bricks and not enough chicks," say frustrated male students.) The weather, students warn, is not for the faint of heart—academic buildings are apart from the dorms, and long treks through snow, ice, and intense winds are inescapable. All freshmen are required to live on campus, and housing is said to have improved with recent renovations. Freshmen are housed alongside upperclassmen in all residence halls and are allowed to live in fraternity housing beginning in their second term on campus. Housing is not guaranteed for all four years, and overcrowding is an issue, causing triple occupancies in the dorms or temporary housing at the RIT Inn. About 60 percent of students live on-campus.

RIT recently built a state-of-the-art, 177,000-square-foot building to house the new B. Thomas Golisano College of Computing and Information Sciences, as well as new campus apartments and Greek houses, and a new $25 million Field House and Activities Center. RIT was recently awarded $8 million from New York state to develop a new Center for Biotechnology Education and Training, and a national Printing Industry Center has been established.

Student Life

Prospective RIT students are advised to come to this school for the education, not the social life. But for the career-oriented RIT student, struggling to keep up with the demands of the academic quarter system, the lack of a booming campus social life might not be a problem. Although the drinking age is 19 in nearby Canada, RIT is not a school for keggers. Many students leave campus on the weekends, and the rest stay in and study, creating a subdued atmosphere on campus.

Still, there are clubs and organizations for those who can find the time. The most popular student groups include the Student Government, College Activities Board, RIT Players (theater group), Student Music Association, and (of course) the Electronic Gaming Society. RIT offers 24 intercollegiate sports in NCAA Division III. More than 3,000 students each year participate in 12 different intramural sports. Club teams sponsored by RIT's student government also compete at an intercollegiate level, with the men's roller hockey and water polo clubs capturing national titles in the past two years.

The male to female ratio has gotten better, and now stands at around 3:2. About a quarter of the student body are minority students. Most students are from New York State, but international students represent 24 countries. The typical student is focused, hardworking, a bit nerdy, and, due to the long winters and the workload, sometimes a bit depressed.

School traditions include the Brick City Festival with a major speaker, a major rock band, a major family entertainer, and the Stonehurst Regatta. Spring Festival is a carnival with music and fireworks, hailing the end of the long upstate New York winter, when the campus is dormant.

Other schools to check out: Rensselear Polytechnic Institute, Cornell, Carnegie Mellon, University of Rochester, Syracuse.

Applied Early Decision: 840
Early Decision Admitted: 637

Test Scores (middle 50%):
SAT Verbal: 540–640
SAT Math: 570–670
ACT Comp: 24–29

HS Rank of Entering Freshmen:
Top 10%: 31%
Top 25%: 65%
Top 50%: 92%

Avg. HS GPA: 90%

Costs (2004–5)

Tuition and Fees: $21,804

Room & Board: $8,238

Payment Plan(s): installment plan, pre-payment plan

THE EXPERTS SAY...

" RIT's 1,100 deaf and hearing impaired students study, share residence halls, and socialize with its other 13,000 students— and enjoy a 95% career placement rate. "

" Bring your work ethic and your Chapstick. "

Inst. Aid (2002–03)

Institutional Aid, Need-Based: $45,160,900

Institutional Aid, Non-Need-Based: $7,969,600

FT Undergrads Receiving Aid: 67%
Avg. Amount per Student: $16,500

FT Undergrads Receiving Non-Need-Based Scholarship or Grant Aid: 9%
Avg. Amount per Student: $5,300

Of Those Receiving Any Aid:

Rec. Need-Based Scholarship or Grant Aid: 94%
Average Award: $10,000

Rec. Need-Based Self-Help Aid: 89%
Average Award: $5,700

Financial Aid Deadline: rolling, 3/1 (priority)

Graduates

Going to Graduate School: 15% Within One Year

Companies Recruiting On Campus: 500

Alumni Giving: 11%

ROLLINS COLLEGE

1000 Holt Avenue, Winter Park, FL 32789-4499
Admissions Phone: (407) 646-2161 Fax: (407) 646-1502
Email: admission@rollins.edu Website: www.rollins.edu
Application Website: www.rollins.edu/admission/application.shtml

General Info

Type of School: private, coed

Setting: small town

Academic Calendar: semester

Student Body

Full-Time Undergrads: 1,733
  Men: 39%, Women: 61%

Total Undergrad Population:
  African American: 4%
  Asian American: 3%
  Latino: 7%
  Native American: 1%
  Caucasian: 75%
  International: 4%
  Out-of-State: 57%
  Living Off-Campus: 38%
  In Fraternities: 38%
  In Sororities: 40%

Graduate and First-Professional
  Students: 832

Academics

Full-Time Faculty: 179
  With Ph.D.: 92%

Part-Time Faculty: 39
  With Ph.D.: 44%

Student/Faculty Ratio: 11:1

Most Popular Majors:
  psychology (13%)
  international business (12%)
  economics (10%)
  English (8%)
  elementary education (6%)

Completing 2 or More Majors: 2%

Freshmen Retention Rate: 83%

Graduation Rates:
  46% within four years
  58% within six years

Admissions

Regular Application Deadline: 2/15

Early Decision Deadline(s): 11/15,
  1/15

Fall Transfer Deadline: rolling, 4/15
  (priority)

Spring Transfer Deadline: rolling,
  11/1 (priority)

Total # of Students Applied: 2,271
  Admitted: 1,510
  Enrolled: 497

Inside the Classroom

If you're looking for a liberal arts education but are worried about finding a job in "the real world," Rollins College may be the answer. Florida's oldest college, Rollins is a small liberal arts school with a preprofessional bent. Twenty-nine majors are offered, but these are not limited to traditional areas of study—international business, environmental management/forestry, and Latin American and Caribbean affairs are among the more unusual offerings. Students can also opt for self-designed majors as well as prelaw, premed, and predental programs. Most students come to Rollins with a major, if not a future career, already in mind; only one-third of entering freshmen are undecided about which major they will select. More than half of all Rollins upperclassmen participate in the college's strong internship program.

With around 1,700 students, Rollins practically ensures your classes will be very small. Professors "truly do care," explains one senior. Another student adds: "Professors are well-educated and familiar with not only the 'textbook' answer but the real world answers also." However, "the administration has no flexibility," one student gripes.

Rollins's endowment of $125 million places it in the top 10 percent nationwide. An impressive fundraising campaign helped the school hit the jackpot in recent years, and with this money, the school has been able to boost scholarships funds, create several faculty posts, and build or improve numerous campus facilities. As such, Rollins has received a lot of "buzz," and has attracted greater numbers of students from outside the state: Its freshman classes keep getting bigger and more diverse. There are plans in the works that will further add or renovate assorted campus buildings in the near future.

All freshmen must participate in a seminar program called the Rollins Conference, designed to ensure a successful transition from high school to college. This year's RC course offerings include Sports and American Society, Spanish Eyes: Hispanic Film, and Microbes, Disease, and Humans. General education requirements, which are divided into three main areas (Skills, Cognitive, and Affective), can be met by taking a variety of courses.

Campus Environment

Located just five minutes from Orlando in Winter Park ("a very nice, upscale, and safe town," according to one recent grad), the main campus has a gorgeous lakefront setting. The buildings, on 67 tightly laid-out acres, are designed in a Spanish Mediterranean style, with stucco walls and red tile roofs. The atmosphere feels extremely safe; there's "strict campus security," we're told. One of the most distinctive features of the campus is the Walk of Fame—more than 500 stones arranged in a semicircle, each bearing the name of an admired figure, ranging from Confucius to Fred Rogers.

Housing is plentiful, and most students find on-campus accommodations comfortable. One guidance counselor names Rollins as having the best freshmen housing in the region. The school has deferred rush, so freshmen aren't eligible for Greek housing until second semester. Rollins has made a large investment in technology during the past several years—practically everything is wired to the campus network and the Internet—though we hear the library resources are lagging. Freshmen are not allowed to have cars—though with such a small campus, cars are not essential, anyway.

Student Life

Rollins can't seem to shake its reputation as a rich kids' school, though it does in fact have quite a large number of students receiving financial aid. "Cliquish" is how a few students describe the student body, and there are noticeably more women than men. Many students are fairly appearance-oriented, making it tough for alternative types. "The typical student here is a daddy's girl who gets whatever she wants," explains one student. "She talks sweetly, does all her homework (but does not push herself to speak up for herself), dresses perfectly with manicured nails, has a Tiffany bracelet, and a Coach bag… and hopes to meet her husband here." But one young alum asserts, "Anyone and everyone can fit in."

Greek life is extremely popular: Some say it's the only social life on campus, and if you aren't involved, then you're not in the loop. Social events sponsored by Greek houses seem to draw more crowds than do regular on-campus activities. One student warns of a "strict zero-tolerance" policy, so if drinking and drugs are your thing, watch out.

Rollins students love the outdoors, and greatly appreciate living in such a beautiful region. The beach is about an hour away, and the campus has a heated outdoor swimming pool. The school has no football team, but there are 21 other varsity sports, including a great water-skiing program. We hear that, despite gorgeous facilities including a brand-new basketball complex, students aren't the biggest sports fans. But almost half the student body plays some type of intramural; scuba diving, kayaking, and survival outings are other options.

When Rollins students finally do venture back indoors, they're likely to hang out at the Down Under, a coffeehouse and game room in the Student Center. Of the various clubs and organizations, one of the more interesting is the Darkness Visible Radio Theatre, a live radio drama that's broadcast weekly. Students can get academic credit for participating in these radio programs. Good theater productions are readily available in the Annie Russell Theatre. The student government is also active, establishing events such as Halloween Howl, which draws hundreds of neighborhood children for trick-or-treating in the dorms, and an anti-drinking and driving voucher program that gives students a prepaid taxi ride home when they've had too much to drink. Fox Day is an annual tradition, during which school officials surprise students with an impromptu holiday; a statue of a fox is placed at the campus flagpole, signaling no classes for the day.

Other schools to check out: U of Richmond, Southern Methodist, Denison, Eckerd, Wake Forest.

# of Students Waitlisted: 175
Waitlisted Students Admitted: 17

Applied Early Decision: 267
Early Decision Admitted: 200

Test Scores (middle 50%):
SAT Verbal: 540–630
SAT Math: 540–630

HS Rank of Entering Freshmen:
Top 10%: 38%
Top 25%: 70%
Top 50%: 87%

Avg. HS GPA: 3.4

THE EXPERTS SAY…

" A hidden treasure with a large endowment, Rollins offers very strong academic programs in business, theater, and music. "

" After spending the day at your internship at Disney's EPCOT Center, you can come back to campus and go water-skiing in Lake Virginia. We're jealous! "

Costs (2003–04)

Tuition and Fees: $26,250
Room & Board: $8,050
Payment Plan(s): installment plan

Inst. Aid (est. 2003–04)

Institutional Aid, Need-Based: $10,856,562

Institutional Aid, Non-Need-Based: $2,202,122

FT Undergrads Receiving Aid: 42%
Avg. Amount per Student: $26,005

FT Undergrads Receiving Non-Need-Based Scholarship or Grant Aid: 13%
Avg. Amount per Student: $7,982

Of Those Receiving Any Aid:

Rec. Need-Based Scholarship or Grant Aid: 96%
Average Award: $20,887

Rec. Need-Based Self-Help Aid: 85%
Average Award: $5,372

Upon Graduation, Avg. Loan Debt per Student: $14,049

Financial Aid Deadline: 3/1, 2/15 (priority)

Graduates

Going to Graduate School: 24% Within One Year

Companies Recruiting On Campus: 122

Alumni Giving: 20%

ROSE–HULMAN INSTITUTE OF TECHNOLOGY

5500 Wabash Avenue, Terre Haute, IN 47803-3999
Admissions Phone: (800) 248-7448 Fax: (812) 877-8941
Email: admis.ofc@rose-hulman.edu Website: www.rose-hulman.edu Application Website: www.rose-hulman.edu/admissions

General Info
Type of School: private, coed
Setting: suburban
Academic Calendar: quarter

Student Body
Full-Time Undergrads: 1,708
 Men: 82%, Women: 18%

Part-Time Undergrads: 2
 Men: 50%, Women: 50%

Total Undergrad Population:
 African American: 2%
 Asian American: 3%
 Latino: 1%
 Native American: <1%
 Caucasian: 93%
 International: 1%
 Out-of-State: 52%
 Living Off-Campus: 49%
 In Fraternities: 47%
 In Sororities: 58%

Graduate and First-Professional
 Students: 143

Academics
Full-Time Faculty: 139
 With Ph.D.: 99%

Part-Time Faculty: 5
 With Ph.D.: 80%

Student/Faculty Ratio: 13:1

Most Popular Majors:
 mechanical engineering (30%)
 electrical engineering (14%)
 chemical engineering (13%)
 computer science (12%)
 computer engineering (11%)

Completing 2 or More Majors: 7%

Freshmen Retention Rate: 91%

Graduation Rates:
 65% within four years
 82% within six years

Computers: Computer Required

Admissions
Regular Application Deadline: 3/1;
 12/1 (priority)

Total # of Students Applied: 3,188
 Admitted: 2,261
 Enrolled: 490

Inside the Classroom

Rose-Hulman specializes in undergraduate engineering, mathematics, and science education. Operating under the unwritten philosophy of doing few things but doing them well, the school offers its small student body only 13 majors: applied biology, applied optics (a rarity nationwide), biomedical engineering, chemical engineering, chemistry, civil engineering, computer engineering, computer science, economics, electrical engineering, mathematics, mechanical engineering, and physics. Of course, the compensation for students is that these degrees hold a prestige few other schools can match. Rose-Hulman consistently wins the title of best among engineering schools that don't have a doctoral program, and its administration reports a near-100 percent job placement for graduating seniors.

General education requirements include nine courses in humanities and social sciences, plus strong core courses in chemistry, physics, mathematics and design. Students say that the workload is heavy in most classes. "The work is very hard," said one young alum, "but very rewarding. It feels better to get a B on a hard test than an A+ on an easy test." A college official explains, "The typical Rose-Hulman student enjoys the challenge of solving problems."

The small class sizes and intimate learning environment are what attract many students to Rose-Hulman. All teaching is done by faculty, not by TA's. (Reportedly, even the college president teaches classes.) Students rave about the quality and accessibility of their professors. "The professors are always around to help, and they are very interested in what is actually going on in our lives," explains a junior majoring in mechanical engineering, adding that "they are friends and mentors more than teachers."

Another feature that makes Rose-Hulman stand out: its focus on project-based learning in a team. "Groups of students work together to solve a problem or complete a project, often for a real client," says a school official. "Students learn in a rigorous, hands-on, laboratory intensive environment where they receive personal attention from faculty, staff and administrators. Students are provided with increasing opportunities for career experiences through internships with large and small companies, and at the college's business incubator, Rose-Hulman Ventures."

Campus Environment

All freshmen who do not live at home with their families are required to live on campus in freshmen-only residence halls. Most dorms are three- or four-story brick halls that are coed by floor (although with a male population of around 80 percent, you may not notice), and students tell us they're "very comfortable." But because of the limited availability of campus housing, juniors and seniors usually move off campus (often flocking to an apartment complex about one-and-a-half miles from campus). Greek men usually live in their fraternity house sophomore through senior years (freshmen aren't allowed to live with fraternities or sororities).

Rose-Hulman isn't one of those engineering schools bunkered in gray stone buildings. Its 200-acre campus features architecture varied among several styles, forming a visually interesting mix built around two lakes. Some buildings veer into the unusual: One new addition is a 5,000-square foot nondenominational chapel with diamond-shaped, stainless steel panels forming an arched roof. Looking like an oversized band shell, the chapel also sports vertical ribbon windows and a continuous ridge skylight at the top. This past year saw the opening of Hatfield Hall, which features a state-of-the-art theater, rehearsal rooms for student performing arts groups, and a new alumni center.

The town of Terre Haute is "safe, but there's not much to do besides bowling and movies," comments a female mechanical engineering student. (A chemical engineering major's philosophical take: "There's nothing exciting about it, but there are places that are less exciting than Terre Haute.") This being Hoosier territory, the townies are typically very friendly. Students recommend having a car to get around, because the campus is on the outskirts of Terre Haute and "all stores are at least two miles away."

Student Life

The Rose-Hulman student body could be described as "nerdy," "introverted," "down-to-earth," "mostly Republican," "mostly white," ... and overwhelmingly male. "This school is definitely the place for single girls to go," said one envious male student. "They'll have no trouble finding dates, which is a big problem for us poor guys." Some of the women, like this chemical engineering major, wouldn't mind a ratio adjustment either: "I'm comfortable with all of the guys, but the number of women in engineering needs to be increased." Fortunately, Terre Haute is also home to the larger Indiana State University and the all-female St. Mary of the Woods College, so things aren't as monastic as they seem.

Anyone in search of an active social life at Rose-Hulman should seek out the Greeks. Rose-Hulman has eight fraternities and two sororities, with nearly half of the entire student body pledging. "They are popular because they offer an escape from academics," one student explains, while another student offers, "I think the relative lack of things to do in town accounts for the large numbers." Students say that, while drinking is "a moderate factor on campus," drugs are not tolerated at all.

More than 60 clubs and student organizations are available at Rose-Hulman, ranging from usual fare like the student newspaper and chess club to more curious options like the scuba club, aerial robotics club, the model railroad club, and the Solar Phantom Racing Team, which constantly tries to make aerodynamic improvements to its solar-powered car for inter-school competitions.

Varsity athletics and intramurals are headquartered in the new sports and recreation center. (And a bit of trivia for you sports fans: The Indianapolis Colts have made Rose-Hulman the site for their summer training camp for the past three years.) "The students who play varsity sports know academics come first," explains a chemical engineering student, "so naturally, our varsity teams aren't outstanding." However, intramurals are a popular way to blow off steam: An estimated 90 percent of Rose-Hulman students participate in any of the school's 13 intramural sports.

Other schools to check out: Case Western Reserve, Purdue, U of Missouri—Rolla, Michigan Tech, Kettering.

Test Scores (middle 50%):
 SAT Verbal: 570–680
 SAT Math: 640–730
 ACT Comp: 27–32
 ACT English: 25–31
 ACT Math: 28–34

HS Rank of Entering Freshmen:
 Top 10%: 62%
 Top 25%: 95%
 Top 50%: 100%

THE EXPERTS SAY...

" In this economy, any school that can boast of having a near-100 percent job placement rate for its graduating seniors should grab your attention. "

" Finding a dance partner at Rose-Hulman can be an engineering feat in itself. "

Costs (est. 2004–05)

Tuition and Fees: $26,136
 ($3,125 for laptop computer)

Room & Board: $7,065

Payment Plan(s): installment plan, pre-payment plan

Inst. Aid (est. 2003–04)

Institutional Aid, Need-Based: $8,848,717

Institutional Aid, Non-Need-Based: $3,054,389

FT Undergrads Receiving Aid: 72%
 Avg. Amount per Student: $15,261

FT Undergrads Receiving Non-Need-Based Scholarship or Grant Aid: 23%
 Avg. Amount per Student: $5,557

Of Those Receiving Any Aid:

Rec. Need-Based Scholarship or Grant Aid: 80%
 Average Award: $5,746

Rec. Need-Based Self-Help Aid: 86%
 Average Award: $6,182

Upon Graduation, Avg. Loan Debt per Student: $27,000

Financial Aid Deadline: rolling, 3/1 (priority)

Graduates

Going to Graduate School:
 19% Within One Year

Accepting Job Offer:
 60% at time of graduation

Companies Recruiting On Campus: 165

Alumni Giving: 72%

RUTGERS, THE STATE UNIVERSITY OF NEW JERSEY

65 Davidson Road, Room 202, Piscataway, NJ 08854-8097
Admissions Phone: (732) 932-4636 Fax: (732) 445-0237
Website: www.rutgers.edu Application Website: admissions.rutgers.edu

General Info

Type of School: public, coed

Setting: urban

Academic Calendar: semester

Student Body

Full-Time Undergrads: 24,707
  Men: 48%, Women: 52%

Part-Time Undergrads: 2,153
  Men: 47%, Women: 53%

Total Undergrad Population:
  African American: 8%
  Asian American: 20%
  Latino: 8%
  Native American: <1%
  Caucasian: 56%
  International: 2%
  Out-of-State: 11%
  Living Off-Campus: 55%
  In Fraternities: 10%
  In Sororities: 10%

Graduate and First-Professional
  Students: 6,671

Academics

Full-Time Faculty: 1,502
  With Ph.D.: 99%

Part-Time Faculty: 662
  With Ph.D.: 99%

Student/Faculty Ratio: 15:1

Most Popular Majors:
  business (21%)
  engineering (11%)
  biological sciences (8%)
  psychology (6%)
  pharmacy (5%)

Completing 2 or More Majors: 2%

Freshmen Retention Rate: 89%

Admissions

Regular Application Deadline: 12/1
  (priority)

Fall Transfer Deadline: 1/15
  (priority)

Spring Transfer Deadline: 11/1
  (priority)

Total # of Students Applied: 26,175
  Admitted: 14,180
  Enrolled: 4,717

# of Students Waitlisted: 1,274
  Waitlisted Students Admitted: 77

Inside the Classroom

Rutgers has more than 30,000 undergraduates, but with 17 individual colleges offering undergraduate programs, it avoids (well, in theory) the impersonal feeling typical of very large institutions. While there are additional campuses located in Camden and Newark, this profile concerns the New Brunswick campus only. Rutgers has 12 New Brunswick colleges with undergraduate programs, ranging from general liberal arts schools to a land grant/environmental school (Cook College), from the nation's largest undergraduate women's college (Douglass) to a school for the arts (Mason Gross). The schools differ in admissions standards (Rutgers College is considered the most selective and prestigious) and core requirements, but students can enroll in courses at all of them. One student notes that it is "very important to completely understand the requirements for the college you choose to attend at Rutgers because each varies greatly." Perhaps this is due to the fact that the school has "gotten too large and impersonal" recently, according to one guidance counselor—it's no longer "student-friendly."

A recent grad tells us, "It's a competitive school but if you play your cards right and keep up with what you have to do you can handle it." However, a sophomore tells us, "Mostly everyone worries about how they did and not how others did." Students describe their workloads from "moderate" and "average" to "large" and "intense." Guidance counselors respect the "fine performing arts" programs and "versatility of majors," along with the low in-state tuition, calling Rutgers a "public Ivy League" school. A freshman chimes in, "Many of us realize that this school offers just as good an education as an Ivy League, but for a third of the cost."

The separate colleges help break down the larger university, but guidance counselors warn that some new students may still find the campus too big. Lower-level lecture classes can number hundreds of students, but upper-level classes might have as few as 10 students. A young alum with an economics degree notes, "Professors are fairly accessible, but that depends on how much time they have for their research versus their students." Large enrollment can make getting into certain courses difficult and can limit personal attention, but it fosters independence and academic variety. "In order to be successful at Rutgers you need to go after what you want just like in the real world... There are people there to help you but you must find them and ask. They will not come to you unless it is to tell you that you've flunked out. The administration expects the students to be responsible for themselves," says one student.

Campus Environment

On-campus housing ranges from typical coed freshman-only double (and occasionally triple) occupancy dorm rooms to apartment-style and special interest housing (e.g., honors and language focuses). Facilities vary—a sophomore describes how "some [residences] are falling apart and some are brand new." Another student agrees, saying, "Some dorms are horrible, have no air conditioning... but then other dorms are nice." Many students choose to live off-campus at some point. "Off-campus housing can be popular but very expensive," says one student. One drawback to living off-campus is security, and even off-campus students tend to live close to campus. Students tell us that "living off campus has its benefits because there are not the same regulations as in dorms, but it is a lot less safe."

Juniors and seniors are eligible for parking permits. "There is very limited on-campus parking (especially on College Avenue)," explains one student, "and there is often excessive congestion to find parking at the meters for class if a person doesn't have a parking pass." A bus system connects the colleges, but many students complain that they spend too much time shuttling between campuses and that the buses can be overcrowded. "You can't schedule back to back classes on different campuses or you'll never make it on time trying to wait and travel on buses," agrees one student. The train station is a short walk from the Rutgers College campus and students can take the 45-minute trip to New York City. For more local trips, "to actually go out of campus, to shop, [get] groceries, go out to eat... you really need a car." Public transportation is not one of the area's finer points.

There are many bars and restaurants along nearby Easton Avenue, and a comedy club and theaters downtown. "There are certain areas [in New Brunswick] that aren't very safe and aren't very nicely kept," says one student. You can get fast food between classes (or between parties) at the "grease trucks," food trucks on College Avenue that serve variations of their famous "Fat Cat" sandwiches (a fan explains, "a sandwich can have mozzarella sticks, chicken fingers, french fries, and cheese in it").

Student Life

Besides the largely in-state student population (many students go home on weekends), it's hard to find a stereotypical Rutgers student. "There's just so much diversity it's tough to say who's a typical student," says one young graduate, "anyone with a bad attitude toward people of other cultures and backgrounds might not fit in because there's such diversity at the school." As for social life, a student tells us "drinking is a big factor, we have a large frat community. Off-campus it's tough to get alcohol because there's such a strict carding policy." A recent graduate tells us that "there is a frat row and in the spring the frat brothers put their couches in their front lawns to sit and 'chill' instead of going to class." While Greek life has its place, it does not seem to dominate extracurricular life.

There are tons of school-sponsored clubs and activities. "A lot of students join community service groups, as well as performing arts groups. There are also a lot of religious groups." We are told that "Rutgers is a politically active school with many demonstrations held, peaceful of course." As for sports, "we have many excellent teams, like soccer and basketball, but also a few bad ones," says a biology major. "Athletics are popular, but the football team is constantly derided for their awful record," explains another. The school's Scarlet Knights participate in 30 Division I sports, and RU was home to the first intercollegiate football game (in 1869, Rutgers beat Princeton).

Notable Rutgers alumni include actors Calista Flockhart and James Gandolfini, poet Robert Pinsky, economist Milton Friedman, NBA commissioner David Stern, and WNBA player Sue Wicks.

Test Scores (middle 50%):
SAT Verbal: 540–640
SAT Math: 570–670
HS Rank of Entering Freshmen:
Top 10%: 39%
Top 25%: 79%
Top 50%: 99%
Avg. HS GPA: 94%

THE EXPERTS SAY...

" The diverse student body and urban setting will allow you to learn as much outside the classroom as you will inside the classroom. "

" East Coast guidance counselors tell us that Rutgers is underrated and is a great value for your tuition dollar. They're right, of course. "

Costs (2003–04)
Tuition and Fees, In-State: $7,592
Tuition and Fees, Out-of-State: $14,106
Room & Board: $8,082

Inst. Aid (est. 2003–04)
Institutional Aid, Need-Based: $13,652,520
Institutional Aid, Non-Need-Based: $7,375,526
FT Undergrads Receiving Aid: 50%
Avg. Amount per Student: $10,288
FT Undergrads Receiving Non-Need-Based Scholarship or Grant Aid: 10%
Avg. Amount per Student: $4,954
Of Those Receiving Any Aid:
Rec. Need-Based Scholarship or Grant Aid: 67%
Average Award: $6,738
Rec. Need-Based Self-Help Aid: 86%
Average Award: $4,540
Upon Graduation, Avg. Loan Debt per Student: $15,018
Financial Aid Deadline: rolling, 3/15 (priority)

Graduates
Alumni Giving: 30%

SAINT ANSELM COLLEGE

100 Saint Anselm Drive, Manchester, NH 03102-1310
Admissions Phone: (603) 641-7500; (888) 4AN-SELM Fax: (603) 641-7550
Email: admissions@anselm.edu Website: www.anselm.edu
Application Website: www.anselm.edu/admissions/application/application03.pdf

Note: Info. not verified by school

General Info

Type of School: private, coed,
  Roman Catholic–Benedictine

Setting: suburban

Academic Calendar: semester

Student Body

Full-Time Undergrads: 1,876
  Men: 43%, Women: 57%

Part-Time Undergrads: 20
  Men: 35%, Women: 65%

Total Undergrad Population:
  African American: <1%
  Asian American: 1%
  Latino: 1%
  Native American: <1%
  Caucasian: 95%
  International: 1%
  Out-of-State: 77%
  Living Off-Campus: 15%

Academics

Full-Time Faculty: 120
  With Ph.D.: 93%

Part-Time Faculty: 45
  With Ph.D.: 47%

Student/Faculty Ratio: 14:1

Most Popular Majors:
  business (15%)
  nursing (10%)
  psychology (9%)
  criminal justice (9%)
  English (6%)

Freshmen Retention Rate: 83%

Graduation Rates:
  72% within four years
  76% within six years

Admissions

Early Decision Deadline(s): 12/1

Fall Transfer Deadline: 6/15, 5/1
  (priority)

Spring Transfer Deadline: 3/1 (priority)

Total # of Students Applied: 2,907
  Admitted: 2,113
  Enrolled: 578

# of Students Waitlisted: 27
  Students Accepting Place: 4

Applied Early Decision: 72
  Early Decision Admitted: 60

Inside the Classroom

According to the school's philosophy, Saint Anselm "challenges its students to engage in the fullest experience of a liberal arts education, to free themselves from the strictures of ignorance, illiteracy, and indecision, and to dedicate themselves to an active and enthusiastic pursuit of truth." While this may sound pretty intense (or optimistic), Saint Anselm really values your total education, and will give you the tools you need to survive when you leave.

Saint Anselm is a Catholic liberal arts college in the Benedictine tradition, so above and beyond the usual general requirements of a liberal arts education, you'll have to take some theology and philosophy courses to earn your degree. In addition to the more than 25 bachelor of arts programs, Saint Anselm offers a bachelor of science degree in nursing (a rigorous program, we hear). There's also a cooperative engineering program in conjunction with four other schools, teacher certification, and advising for coursework for pretheology (a philosophy concentration with work in the classical languages), prelaw, predental, and premed. Popular majors include business, nursing, criminal justice, psychology, and English. Saint Anselm is also known for its nationally recognized humanities program, "Portraits of Human Greatness."

"Challenging" is a word you'll often hear students ascribe to their schoolwork. Good grades are hard-earned, but one student assures us that "any student who takes the time to work hard will soon see the payoff." Coursework can be heavy, but the small student/faculty ratio helps students develop "positive and beneficial" relationships with professors. Profs are well-respected and generally accessible, though some students warn that certain teachers might over-assign readings in the tradition of assuming it's the only class you're taking. As for competition, a psych major puts it this way: "The school is fairly competitive in accepting new students, but there is no real feeling of competition on campus." Overall, the community is friendly and very supportive.

Campus Environment

Housing is a sore spot at Saint Anselm. Overcrowding is a constant problem, with some students having to double, triple, and even quadruple up in rooms meant for fewer people, although the brand-new residence hall should alleviate some cramping. Some dorms are considered almost dungeon-like, though, again, the school is working on renovations. Far and away the biggest complaint among students is the strict visitation rules imposed in the underclass residence halls. The school explains, "Saint Anselm observes and promotes Christian and Catholic standards of value and conduct. The College accepts and retains students on the condition that they respect and observe those standards." Needless to say, there are no coed dorms, and students are not allowed in the opposite sex's room except during specific hours on the weekends. Otherwise, they may "intervisit" only in the hall's common lounge, much to many students' chagrin. "Students believe these hours should be extended, especially on the weekends," a junior tells us. But the Benedictine administration is holding fast to the policy for now. Students seem to bond over these housing issues—as one regretful commuter says, "in order to develop strong relationships it seems important to live on campus." Upperclassmen may apply to live in apartment- or townhouse-style housing, and "many students look forward to their junior year in hopes of getting one," we're told.

The 400-acre campus has the picture-perfect New England vibe, especially in the fall. A prominent structure on campus is the Abbey, home to the school's Benedictine monk community as well as the liturgical center of the college. There are also various athletic arenas and fields, a library, student center, and coffee shop and pub. One thing that sets Saint Anselm apart from most colleges is its stellar dining services: students universally rave about the food quality, choices, and venues. It's "restaurant-comparable," one student says.

Downtown Manchester is minutes away, and students often venture there for shopping, bars, concerts, and various volunteer activities. You'll need a car if you want to spend a weekend in Boston, the Maine seacoast, or the White Mountains, all about an hour away.

Student Life

Guidance counselors think that Saint Anselm deserves more recognition, but somebody must know about this place: three-quarters of the students come from out of state. Other than geographically, though, diversity is not the school's strong suit. Students here are described in that all-encompassing term, "preppy." A student says, "People who are known for dressing in a unique way may not feel very comfortable in a sea of Old Navy." Of course, Catholics make up the bulk of the student body, though the school is committed to the expansion of diversity, and students of all religious backgrounds are welcome.

The Anselm Hawks play in the NCAA, the Eastern Collegiate Athletic Conference, the Northeast-10 Conference, and other sports organizations. "Athletics are very important to Saint Anselm," we hear. Intramural sports programs include basketball, flag football, soccer, hockey, softball, and volleyball; there are also various rec sports such as racquetball, tennis, aerobics, strength training, and mountain biking.

Students participate in numerous campus activities and organizations including (but certainly not limited to): the Abbey Players (theater group), the Saint Anselm Chorus, the Saint Thomas More Debate Society, *The Quatrain* (a literary magazine), *The Saint Anselm Crier* (the student newspaper), the jazz band, the Knights of Columbus and Chi Sigma Society (Christian service organizations for men and women, respectively), martial arts, a cappella, the Theological Society, and student government. The Center for Volunteers provides opportunities for students, faculty, and staff to participate in community service in the greater Manchester area.

Don't expect much hardcore partying on campus, especially with the stringent intervisitation policy in effect. Upperclass townhouses and apartments are more lenient—and also where the 21-year-olds are—so parties can pop up there as well as off-campus. We heard some gripes that Manchester offers little (except drinking) as far as weekend entertainment goes, so many students leave the books behind for a road trip into nearby Boston.

Other schools to check out: Providence, Stonehill, Fairfield, Holy Cross.

Test Scores (middle 50%):
  SAT Verbal: 510–600
  SAT Math: 510–600
  ACT Comp: 21–25
HS Rank of Entering Freshmen:
  Top 10%: 14%
  Top 25%: 47%
  Top 50%: 87%
Avg. HS GPA: 3.07

Costs (2003–04)

Tuition and Fees: $22,310
Room & Board: $8,090
Payment Plan(s): installment plan

THE EXPERTS SAY...

" Saint Anselm is great for students who value a true liberal arts education. "

" Get thee to a monastery! If your vision of college life includes Knights of Columbus meetings instead of frat parties, Saint Anselm should be right up your alley. "

Inst. Aid (est. 2003–04)

Institutional Aid, Need-Based:
  $11,657,109
Institutional Aid, Non-Need-Based:
  $3,561,436
FT Undergrads Receiving Aid: 82%
  Avg. Amount per Student:
  $21,933
FT Undergrads Receiving Non-Need-Based Scholarship or Grant Aid: 21%
  Avg. Amount per Student: $5,751
Of Those Receiving Any Aid:
Rec. Need-Based Scholarship or Grant Aid: 89%
  Average Award: $8,178
Rec. Need-Based Self-Help Aid: 64%
  Average Award: $8,543
Upon Graduation, Avg. Loan Debt per Student: $19,139
Financial Aid Deadline: 3/1 (priority)

Graduates

Going to Graduate School:
  11% Within One Year
Accepting Job Offer:
  5% at time of graduation
Companies Recruiting On Campus: 47
Alumni Giving: 51%

SAINT JOHN'S COLLEGE— ANNAPOLIS

P.O. Box 2800, Annapolis, MD 21404
Admissions Phone: (800) 727-9238; (410) 626-2522 Fax: (410) 269-7916
Email: admissions@sjca.edu Website: www.sjca.edu

General Info

Type of School: private, coed
Setting: small town
Academic Calendar: semester

Student Body

Full-Time Undergrads: 470
  Men: 54%, Women: 46%

Part-Time Undergrads: 2
  Men: 50%, Women: 50%

Total Undergrad Population:
  African American: 1%
  Asian American: 1%
  Latino: 3%
  Native American: 1%
  Caucasian: 89%
  International: 1%
  Out-of-State: 86%
  Living Off-Campus: 35%

Graduate and First-Professional
  Students: 85

Academics

Full-Time Faculty: 68
  With Ph.D.: 69%

Part-Time Faculty: 7
  With Ph.D.: 43%

Student/Faculty Ratio: 8:1

Most Popular Majors:
  liberal arts (100%)

Freshmen Retention Rate: 84%

Graduation Rates:
  58% within four years
  66% within six years

Admissions

Regular Application Deadline: 3/1
  (priority)

Fall Transfer Deadline: rolling, 3/1
  (priority)

Spring Transfer Deadline: rolling,
  12/15 (priority)

Total # of Students Applied: 531
  Admitted: 389
  Enrolled: 142

Test Scores (middle 50%):
  SAT Verbal: 660–740
  SAT Math: 600–700

HS Rank of Entering Freshmen:
  Top 10%: 36%
  Top 25%: 75%
  Top 50%: 93%

Inside the Classroom

St. John's College professes that "the way to a liberal education lies through a direct and sustained confrontation with the books in which the greatest minds of our civilization have expressed themselves." That may sound broad, but don't expect electives, or taking two years (or more) to explore your options before picking a major. The truly unique St. John's program provides for one concentration only: All students study liberal arts through the so-called "Great Books" of Western civilization.

The center of the program here is the seminar, composed of about 20 students and led by two faculty "tutors," in which students discuss the books. Tutors are not meant to feed students opinions and correct "answers," but rather to "guide the discussion, keep it moving, define the issues, raise objections, and help the students in every way possible to understand the issues, the author, and themselves." Every student is expected to participate and offer their own opinion, backing it up with argument and evidence. All students take seminars in philosophy, theology, political science, literature, history, economics and psychology. You will read such authors as Homer, Plato, Dante, Chaucer, Swift, Moliere, Kierkegaard, Marx, Freud, Heidegger, and Einstein. Dead white males? Well, Jane Austen makes the list, too.

You read the books themselves here, and not textbooks about the works. At St. John's, students go right to the source. Another component of the curriculum is the tutorial, with one tutor for 12 to 16 students. Language tutorials involve Greek for the first two years and French for the last two. There are also math and music tutorials, and a Laboratory Program that covers physics, biology and chemistry. Preceptorials—nine weeks long in your junior and senior years—temporarily replace the seminar as students select a topic or book to study in depth. This is the closest you'll get to an elective here. Typically, you finish this off with a paper, "which may be read in draft to the preceptorial and critiqued by the other members." Finally, to round out the curriculum, a formal lecture is held Fridays for the entire student body (about 472 students, sadly the size of a 101 class at some larger universities). This is your only lecture period, so you really get to sharpen your long-term listening skills. Then you can ask the lecturer all the questions you've compiled over the course of their incessant talking. The curriculum does not lend itself well to study-abroad, but some students participate in such programs during the summer months.

Campus Environment

The campus is in the colonial (since 1695) seaport town of Annapolis. The other primary student population in the area is the U.S. Naval Academy. So this historic colonial town hosts both the disciplined and uniformed training midshipmen along with the more liberal St. John's student population. (Also, there's a lot of sea fishing.) The Annapolis campus has buildings from 18th century houses to 20th century additions, "buildings designed to complement the older ones."

There are six coed-by-floor dorms, with single and double rooms. Freshmen are guaranteed housing and only about one-third of all students live off campus. There is an off-campus housing office to assist students looking to live away from the dorms. Dining services provide both regular and vegetarian menus.

When small-town life feels stifling, students can day trip to nearby Baltimore and Washington, DC. Baltimore's Inner Harbor has many bars and restaurants and a large migration of area college students on weekends. The nation's capital has the benefits of any very large city, from art museums to dance clubs to large music festivals. Students may also opt to spend time at the Santa Fe Campus, since the curricula are the same. There, they can trade the colonial East Coast sea town for the new-age and Southwestern flavors of New Mexico, complete with desert views, mountains, and adobe dorms.

Student Life

There are no fraternities or sororities at St. John's, but you will know more Greek than any frat boy by the time you graduate. While the student body is mostly white, the college explains that since everyone is working the same program, "minority and international students find that they are immediately part of mainstream campus social and academic life rather than members of some identifiable subset."

Student activities are not extremely structured. Groups kind of come and go with the students who are interested in them, and some form from interests that overflow out of regular coursework. St. John's students often incorporate their academic life into their social life. Come here if talking philosophy outside of class is more interesting to you than talking football. Of course, there are some mainstays in the college social life. "The King William Players stage one or two classical plays a year, perform one or two modern works, and produce several one-act plays," we're told. The student film club screens movies regularly and there are multiple music groups with facilities provided by the school.

College parties are attended by both students and tutors. There are rock dances, waltz parties, the Halloween Masked Ball, a Christmas party, the Mid-Winter Ball and a Spring Cotillion. Also, there is a spring festival called Reality Weekend, with student skits and parodies, and "a full day of picnicking and athletic competition." So, you are dedicated to your Great Books, but desperate for a little fresh air and muscle usage? While the school doesn't participate in intercollegiate varsity sports (surprised?), there is a large intramural program with sports like flag football, basketball, volleyball, and softball. There are rowing and fencing clubs that compete with other schools on a local level. And St. John's and the United States Naval Academy play an annual croquet match for the Annapolis Cup.

Other schools to check out: Bard, Bennington, Saint Mary's College of Maryland, Eugene Lang, Marlboro, Colorado College, Evergreen State.

Costs (2004–5)

Tuition and Fees: $30,770

Room & Board: $7,610

Payment Plan(s): installment plan

Inst. Aid (est. 2003–04)

Institutional Aid, Need-Based: $4,044,865

Institutional Aid, Non-Need-Based: $0

FT Undergrads Receiving Aid: 54%
   Avg. Amount per Student: $22,220

Of Those Receiving Any Aid:

Rec. Need-Based Scholarship or Grant Aid: 94%
   Average Award: $16,510

Rec. Need-Based Self-Help Aid: 96%
   Average Award: $5,710

Upon Graduation, Avg. Loan Debt per Student: $18,125

Financial Aid Deadline: 2/15 (priority)

THE EXPERTS SAY...

" At St. John's, you read the great works of Western Civilization, not textbooks about them. "

" Seriously consider whether the Great Books program is for you, because there are no other options at St. John's. "

Graduates

Going to Graduate School:
   19% Within One Year

Accepting Job Offer:
   37% at time of graduation

Companies Recruiting On Campus: 2

SAINT JOHN'S COLLEGE—SANTA FE

1160 Camino Cruz Blanca, Santa Fe, NM 87505-4599
Admissions Phone: (800) 331-5232; (505) 984-6060 Fax: (505) 984-6162
Email: admissions@mail.sjcsf.edu
Website: www.sjcsf.edu

General Info

Type of School: private, coed
Setting: small town
Academic Calendar: semester

Student Body

Full-Time Undergrads: 432
    Men: 54%, Women: 46%

Part-Time Undergrads: 2
    Men: 50%, Women: 50%

Total Undergrad Population:
    African American: <1%
    Asian American: 3%
    Latino: 5%
    Native American: 2%
    Caucasian: 87%
    International: 2%
    Out-of-State: 91%
    Living Off-Campus: 24%

Graduate and First-Professional
    Students: 101

Academics

Full-Time Faculty: 68
    With Ph.D.: 79%

Part-Time Faculty: 2
    With Ph.D.: 50%

Student/Faculty Ratio: 8:1

Most Popular Majors:
    liberal arts (100%)

Freshmen Retention Rate: 69%

Graduation Rates:
    53% within four years
    64% within six years

Admissions

Regular Application Deadline: 3/1
    (priority)

Total # of Students Applied: 338
    Admitted: 275
    Enrolled: 143

Waitlist Available

Test Scores (middle 50%):
    SAT Verbal: 630–710
    SAT Math: 570–670
    ACT Comp: 26–30

HS Rank of Entering Freshmen:
    Top 10%: 20%
    Top 25%: 47%
    Top 50%: 77%

Inside the Classroom

At St. John's, "great books are the teachers." Johnnies spend their entire four years reading the great works of Western civilization. The curriculum begins with ancient Greece and goes through the 20th century, and includes the study of classical mathematics, sciences, literature, philosophy, music, and foreign language (Greek and French only). For each subject, students go directly to original sources, reading the words of such great thinkers as Plato, Newton, Freud, and Einstein without textbooks and lectures. One sophomore says, "It's so exciting to see the historical process in the making as we read these original sources. The difficulty, sometimes, is pretending we don't know what the outcome of an idea is." A guidance counselor praised St. John's "integrity," but cautioned that the school may be "too intense."

Enrollment at the Santa Fe campus is limited to about 440 students. Classes are small, discussion-oriented tutorials during which everyone delves directly into the texts; students are not lectured to, but are taught in true question-and-answer Socratic method. The teaching faculty are called "tutors" instead of "professors," not lecturing but "guiding the students through the program of study." Tutors are expected to be able to lead classes in any subject, and do.

Because the seminars are so dependent upon discussion, students read extensively in preparation, often three to four hours a night. Class attendance is a must; missing more than a few classes is grounds for dismissal. "Our tutors give us a great deal of respect by valuing our ideas and encouraging us to speak out. We show our respect for them by studying hard and keeping prepared," comments a junior. Except for a required algebra test, there are no written exams; students write papers that they present and discuss in class, and seniors sit for oral examinations. St. John's students don't receive grades but meet directly with their tutors for evaluation of their work. The curriculum is almost completely laid out for the students, leaving little room for electives. Juniors and seniors participate in preceptorials, in which students select a book or topic to study in-depth with a tutor.

The selectivity rating given to St. John's by college guides is deceptively low; the school tends to attract a small core of exceptional students and frightens away all other applicants. The SAT and other standardized tests are not required. The core of the St. John's application is a set of essays requiring a great deal of work from the applicant. The school states, "In writing their application essays, many determine their own appropriateness as St. John's students... for the most part, they select themselves." Many students also decide to leave the school once matriculated.

St. John's has no "transfer student" status; all new students enter as freshmen, no matter how many years of college work they've completed. However, students may transfer at any time to the Annapolis campus, since the curriculum is identical. The school offers nothing remotely resembling a preprofessional track. 75 percent of St. John's grads head to grad school shortly after graduation, perhaps looking for a career focus.

Those who wish to study something other than the great works of Western Civilization ("dead white European men") will not want to apply here; science students might find it a waste of time to study Ptolemaic astronomy for a year. But those who do stick it out emerge as true scholars, receiving a remarkable education while learning to think for themselves.

Campus Environment

To avoid increasing in size at Annapolis, St. John's opened the 250-acre Santa Fe campus in 1964. The campus has a distinctive Southwestern flavor, from its architectural style to its spectacular mountain and desert views. Located at an elevation of 7,300 miles in the Sangre de Cristo Mountains, the campus is near the Santa Fe National Forest and about an hour away from Albuquerque. Buildings are all made of adobe, including dorms (most of the two-story dorms have balconies). 75 percent of students live on campus, and stay on campus unless they have a car.

Multicultural Santa Fe has a population of about 65,000, with Native American, Hispanic and anglo residents. The town is a haven for artists of all kinds, and for practitioners of "alternative" lifestyles: holistic medicine and new age philosophies abound. The nearby artists' colony at Taos adds to the bohemian atmosphere. Off-campus dining is excellent, with a wide selection of good restaurants. Town-gown relations have been strained, however. St. John's is making efforts to lose its "Ivory Tower" image through community service and increased contact with townspeople.

Student Life

St. John's is a close-knit community of scholars where intellectual discourse is recreation. It's not uncommon to find Johnnies, often under the influence, hotly debating "the true, the good, and the beautiful." There are no fraternities or sororities, but there are no lack of parties. Drinking and drugs, particularly pot-smoking, are reportedly common on campus.

At a school where missing classes isn't done, an automatic excuse for absence is a search-and-rescue mission. St. John's College Search and Rescue team responds to 25–30 wilderness emergencies a year, including lost hikers, injured back-country travelers, and even light plane crashes, and is considered one of the best in New Mexico. The team's membership is half students and half townspeople, fostering stronger town-gown ties.

There are no varsity sports at St. John's Santa Fe; there isn't even a gym or a pool (there are tennis courts). But the amazing range of outdoor sports makes up for it, and students can get gear for skiing, snowboarding, rafting, canoeing, hiking, climbing, biking, backpacking, and camping from the school, which organizes regular trips. About once a month, students gather for waltz parties, a St. John's tradition since the forties. Project Politae is the school's volunteer arm and coordinates student community service, but student government and film screenings generate more interest.

Santa Fe Johnnies are more relaxed and possibly more eccentric than their Annapolis counterparts. Typical students are white (although race is usually less of an issue than where a student stands on Kant), leftist, and sexually liberated. Most were the "weird" kid in high school, the one who would ask the questions the teacher couldn't answer. If you want a community of scholars, intellectual in an unconventional and provocative way, St. John's is for you.

THE EXPERTS SAY...

" The Great Books program meets an incredible outdoors program at SJC Santa Fe. "

" Kant is fine, but if you want a job outside of academia, St. John's may not be your place. Of course, if you can afford St. John's, you might not need a job. "

SAINT LAWRENCE UNIVERSITY

23 Romoda Dr., Canton, NY 13617
Admissions Phone: (315) 229-5261; (800) 285-1856 Fax: (315) 229-5818
Email: admissions@stlawu.edu
Website: www.stlawu.edu

General Info

Type of School: private, coed

Setting: rural

Academic Calendar: semester

Student Body

Full-Time Undergrads: 2,114
    Men: 47%, Women: 53%

Part-Time Undergrads: 34
    Men: 38%, Women: 62%

Total Undergrad Population:
    African American: 2%
    Asian American: 1%
    Latino: 3%
    Native American: 1%
    Caucasian: 69%
    International: 4%
    In Fraternities: 15%
    In Sororities: 23%

Graduate and First-Professional
    Students: 129

Academics

Full-Time Faculty: 161
    With Ph.D.: 98%

Part-Time Faculty: 42
    With Ph.D.: 31%

Student/Faculty Ratio: 12:1

Most Popular Majors:
    psychology and English (tied)
    government
    economics
    history
    biology

Completing 2 or More Majors: 18%

Graduation Rates:
    69% within four years
    74% within six years

Admissions

Regular Application Deadline: 2/15

Early Decision Deadline(s): 11/15,
    1/15

Fall Transfer Deadline: 4/1

Spring Transfer Deadline: 11/1

Total # of Students Applied: 3,082
    Admitted: 1,767
    Enrolled: 566

# of Students Waitlisted: 476
    Students Accepting Place: 249
    Waitlisted Students Admitted: 23

Inside the Classroom

An excellent small liberal arts school (though not well known outside the Northeast), St. Lawrence's strength is its environmental studies program. In the school's Adirondack semester, students live in "yurts"—circular tents made of hides—in the mountains. Outdoor classes in music and writing are held in the rural upstate New York area. There are over thirty majors and the school's English writing program is a standout.

Students rave about the faculty, who are deeply involved in the St. Lawrence community. "I think one of the strong points of St. Lawrence is how accessible professors are," comments a junior. "All of my professors have been willing to meet with me outside of their office hours, and our conversations can last close to one hour!" Courses are often team-taught by professors from different disciplines, so it's possible to get to know instructors from many fields. A student states, "Most of our classes are small, so class discussions are frequent and most students speak up in class. If someone wanted to just hide in a class of 400 people—this is not the school!"

The coursework is fairly challenging, but it's nothing the students can't handle. "I think people work hard if they want good grades and do nothing if they want to barely get by," an English/theater double major explains. "I know people who spend a good four hours a day studying; you need to put effort into your classes in order to do well." But, "there isn't a cutthroat mentality here at all with regards to competitiveness."

All first-year students participate in the First-Year Program—intensive team-taught interdisciplinary courses in academic thinking and writing. Requirements include courses in arts/expression, humanities, social science, mathematics or foreign language, natural science/science studies, and diversity. St. Lawrence is particularly known for its international programs, and students list them as one of the best things about the school; St. Lawrence's oldest program, in Rouen, France, is even open to freshmen. St. Lawrence's influential alumni network is small but extremely active in helping student locate internships around the world. There's also a Service Learning Program that links students with internships that are tied to coursework

Campus Environment

"The biggest news on the St. Lawrence University campus," reports a school official, "is what's happening to the campus itself—a building boom that is transforming our setting." A student raves, "We have an amazing fitness center that is brand-new, as well as a climbing wall. We have a brand-new squash facility as well." In the planning or construction stages are a student center and three new townhouse-style residences for upperclassmen. Also coming: a multisite outdoor geologic laboratory (only natural for a school that has treehouses in its library).

St. Lawrence is located in Canton, New York, near the Canadian border, and winters are frigid. "Canton is a small town, but there are businesses that cater to college students," a junior notes. "There are a few good coffee/sandwich shops including one, The Harvest Moon Café, that brings in bands," but "there's not a whole lot to do in

KAPLAN

town." A guidance counselor notes that St. Lawrence's rural isolation is "not a shortcoming to all," and a student concurs: "As a female, I have never felt unsafe here; it helps that the town of Canton has a practically nonexistent crime rate."

All first-year students are assigned to coed "first-year colleges" in which 40 to 50 students live together and take one course in common, taught by two or three faculty members. "Personally, I've had amazing rooms," exclaims a writing student. "I have a good-sized single room in a suite as a junior! My first-year room was bigger than any other dorm room I saw at other schools." One dorm is actually a self-sustaining ecohouse. Housing is guaranteed for all four years and 95 percent live on campus.

"Downtown Canton is about a 10-minute walk from campus, although most students find it is easier to have a car," a student informs us. The school offers free airport transportation, a subsidized bus service at vacation period to New York City, Boston, and Buffalo, and subsidized taxi service within the village and to Ottawa, 90 minutes away.

Student Life

The SLU campus is friendly and close-knit, and even the academic achievers love to party. "Most people head to one of the bars on the weekend, and some weekdays, too. There is a bar for underage people," an English major explains. "If we are looking for a change of pace, we head up to Ottawa [for] skating on the Canal, shopping, or going out… The drinking age in Ontario is 19; St. Lawrence is lucky to be so close to the border." "Many people do drink," another student acknowledges, "but there are lots of things to do for the people who don't. There is a grant from the school for students who want to sponsor a non-alcoholic event. We also have an alcohol-free nightclub that brings in comedians and entertainers."

The Adirondacks offer "tons of outdoor activities," and there's "great canoeing right next to campus, and an 18-hole golf course to cross-country ski on during the winter." "Men's hockey is extremely popular!" exclaims a student. "Soccer just received a brand-new field, as did baseball and softball. Sports are popular; if you aren't an athlete; you usually try to make it to your friend's game for support." St. Lawrence competes in 32 varsity sports, and offers 10 intramural sports and 10 club sports.

SLU students tend to be conservative, although there is a contingent of environmentalists. "Northface and Patagonia make huge profits off of St. Lawrence students," quips a junior, adding, "I really appreciate having a campus where complete strangers always smile at each other." The majority of students "are white and relatively well off, although many people are here because St. Lawrence offered them huge amounts of financial aid." The St. Lawrence network of students, faculty, and alumni is a strong one; as members of this community, students are, say college officials, "assisted for life."

Other schools to check out: Hamilton, Colgate, Skidmore, Union, Hobart & William Smith, College of the Atlantic.

Applied Early Decision: 163
Early Decision Admitted: 134

Test Scores (middle 50%):
SAT Verbal: 520–620
SAT Math: 520–630
ACT Comp: 22–27

HS Rank of Entering Freshmen:
Top 10%: 36%
Top 25%: 68%
Top 50%: 96%

Avg. HS GPA: 3.37

THE EXPERTS SAY…

" St. Lawrence's diverse interdisciplinary environmental program combines coursework with amazing Adirondack experiences and field research at the Ecological Sustainability Landscape, a 200-acre facility adjacent to campus. "

" If the isolated campus gets claustrophobic, you can take advantage of an extensive study abroad program. Or, you can drink. Party or passport, it's up to you. "

Costs (2003–04)

Tuition and Fees: $28,190

Room & Board: $7,775

Payment Plan(s): installment plan

Inst. Aid (est. 2003–04)

Institutional Aid, Need-Based: $23,041,020

Institutional Aid, Non-Need-Based: $2,277,325

FT Undergrads Receiving Aid: 70%
Avg. Amount per Student: $26,013

FT Undergrads Receiving Non-Need-Based Scholarship or Grant Aid: 10%
Avg. Amount per Student: $9,151

Of Those Receiving Any Aid:

Rec. Need-Based Scholarship or Grant Aid: 99%
Average Award: $18,585

Rec. Need-Based Self-Help Aid: 91%
Average Award: $6,971

Upon Graduation, Avg. Loan Debt per Student: $23,091

Financial Aid Deadline: 2/15

Graduates

Going to Graduate School: 20% Within One Year

Companies Recruiting On Campus: 9

SAINT LOUIS UNIVERSITY

221 N. Grand Boulevard, St. Louis, MO 63103
Admissions Phone: (314) 977-2500; (800) 758-3678 Fax: (314) 977-7136
Email: admitme@slu.edu Website: www.slu.edu
Application Website: www.slu.edu/admissions

General Info

Type of School: private, coed, Roman Catholic

Setting: urban

Academic Calendar: semester

Student Body

Full-Time Undergrads: 6,341
 Men: 46%, Women: 54%

Part-Time Undergrads: 594
 Men: 35%, Women: 65%

Total Undergrad Population:
 African American: 7%
 Asian American: 4%
 Latino: 2%
 Native American: <1%
 Caucasian: 73%
 International: 2%
 Out-of-State: 49%
 Living Off-Campus: 46%
 In Fraternities: 21%
 In Sororities: 18%

Graduate and First-Professional
 Students: 4,126

Academics

Full-Time Faculty: 629
 With Ph.D.: 94%

Part-Time Faculty: 304
 With Ph.D.: 36%

Student/Faculty Ratio: 12:1

Most Popular Majors:
 biology (6%)
 psychology (6%)
 nursing (5%)
 communications (4%)
 marketing (3%)

Completing 2 or More Majors: 5%

Freshmen Retention Rate: 88%

Graduation Rates:
 55% within four years
 71% within six years

Admissions

Regular Application Deadline: 12/1

Fall Transfer Deadline: 2/1 (priority)

Total # of Students Applied: 6,405
 Admitted: 4,500
 Enrolled: 1,377

Inside the Classroom

"Saint Louis University is an up-and-coming university that will shine in the coming years," a proud student predicts. "[It is] a Jesuit institution that strives for the best. The selection of professors is excellent and the student body is quite motivated."

The College of Arts and Sciences and the John Cook School of Business are by far the largest of SLU's nine undergraduate schools. The other seven schools are: allied health professions; engineering and aviation; nursing; philosophy and letters; professional studies; public service; and social service. Preprofessional programs are the strongest, including physical therapy, aerospace engineering, mathematical computer science, psychology, and biology (premed). "A good, full curriculum in all areas of study, plus an excellent school of medicine," says one Missouri guidance counselor; other counselors take note of SLU's forensic science program (which is suddenly trendy, probably due in part to the popular CBS program, *CSI*).

Students rave about their professors, calling them "outstanding," "professional," and very accessible. "The TA's are actually undergraduate students instead of graduate students, which is a benefit," says a student majoring in biology. "These TA's can relate to the students better and know the information better because it is only a year or less since they have had the class." As at most Jesuit institutions, students here must fulfill broad general education requirements in the arts, English, foreign languages, history, math, philosophy, sciences, social sciences, and theology.

There are many school-sponsored research opportunities for undergraduates. For example, every academic unit within the College of Arts and Sciences provides opportunities for advanced independent study/research. There are also numerous internship and co-op programs available.

Campus Environment

SLU is located near downtown St. Louis, "yet the campus abounds with flowers, trees, fountains, and grass, and is almost entirely pedestrian," says a college official. A student specifies: "[Walking] from one end to the other takes a maximum of eight minutes." All students are allowed to have cars on campus, but one student complains that "parking seems to be a problem once in a while." For students without wheels, the university offers a shuttle system to navigate around campus; public rail and bus systems are also available to navigate around the city. A student notes that the campus "has an excellent view of the St. Louis Arch."

"The on-campus housing situation has finally increased in comfort!" declares a student. All of the residence halls were upgraded as part of Project SLU2000, a $100 million initiative to improve academics, housing, and information systems. All residence halls now have air conditioning, and one (Reinert Hall) even has its own swimming pool. "Pretty much everything is brand-new or no more than four years old," says a junior. Freshmen have seven halls open to them, which are integrated with students from all classes. Approximately 80 percent of freshmen live in university housing. "The main controversy at Saint Louis University is the food," gripes one student, "but there is hope. The company's contract is up at the end of this year."

Housing is not guaranteed for four years, and upperclassmen usually move off campus—often to university-owned apartment buildings. "The off-campus housing is quite nice," says an upperclassman. "Most apartments are close and the cost is lower than what an on-campus apartment would be." The biggest concern: safety. "One must know the [neighborhoods] of St. Louis to know where the best area to choose is," warns one student.

While the school is surrounded by some "not-so-good neighborhoods," students say they feel safe on campus. "The Department of Public Safety has done an excellent job of creating a safety bubble around the campus so that area crime is quite low," says one student. "The main offenses are car break-ins and stealing from unlocked dorms/apartments." However, students do suggest you use caution (and common sense) if you are walking around off-campus at night.

Student Life

"The students here are quite friendly and carry the Jesuit Catholic spirit with them," says a student. "It should be noted, though, that Saint Louis University accepts any student of any religion and race." Only half the students are actually Catholic; around 17 percent are Protestant, and only around one percent are Jewish. But there is some cultural diversity: Minority and international students constitute approximately one-fifth of the undergraduate population.

A junior tells us that one of SLU's most appealing aspects is its medium size: "The size of our school is big enough to not know everyone but yet have enough [students] to choose from to have very close friends." The administration has started working with the students more closely, involving them in university policies. "The act of shared governance is an up and coming thing at Saint Louis University, where a student sits on almost every advisory board or committee," confirms a student.

With 13 frats and five sororities, Greek life is popular here. "The Greeks have many events and are quite popular to join because of the many activities that they do," explains a student. "The non-Greeks on campus do not feel like outsiders, though, because many events include them in some fashion." Drinking is popular, though students agree it doesn't usually get out of hand. A student explains: "There are many parties on and off campus, but the size and extent of them are limited."

"Outside of clubs/organizations, community service is an indicator if a student is truly thriving here," says a university official. "The Saint Louis University Christian in Action Program (SLUCAP) is very popular among students as a form of community service and opportunity to travel. In addition, the Bigs/Littles program, tutoring, food drives and other community outreach programs find many students getting involved."

While SLU fields 16 varsity teams, there's no football ("the only major flaw I can think of at this university," notes one student). But "the popularity of varsity sports on campus is increasing," insists a student. No one can dispute the popularity of intramurals, in which 65 percent of men and 60 percent of women participate.

The school mascot is the Billiken—an elfin creature that sort of looks like a friendly Grinch. Says a college official: "The legend goes: To buy a Billiken gives the purchaser luck, but to have one given to you is better luck." It's a tradition for students on their way to finals to line up in front of the Billiken statue on campus and rub his stomach for good luck.

Other schools to check out: Marquette, Loyola of Chicago, Notre Dame, Creighton, Boston College.

Test Scores (middle 50%):
SAT Verbal: 540–650
SAT Math: 550–660
ACT Comp: 23–29
ACT English: 23–29
ACT Math: 22–28

HS Rank of Entering Freshmen:
Top 10%: 31%
Top 25%: 63%
Top 50%: 90%

Avg. HS GPA: 3.6

Costs (2004–5)

Tuition and Fees: $22,218
Room & Board: $7,740
Payment Plan(s): installment plan, deferred payment plan

THE EXPERTS SAY...

" Guidance counselors have told us that the admissions staff and financial aid office at SLU are very responsive to individual student needs. This supportive, humanistic attitude can be found throughout SLU. "

" If you happen to be a Midwestern, Catholic, premed frat boy, you're in luck. "

Inst. Aid (est. 2003–04)

Institutional Aid, Need-Based:
$39,717,816

Institutional Aid, Non-Need-Based:
$8,648,221

FT Undergrads Receiving Aid: 70%
Avg. Amount per Student: $18,526

FT Undergrads Receiving Non-Need-Based Scholarship or Grant Aid: 17%
Avg. Amount per Student: $8,692

Of Those Receiving Any Aid:

Rec. Need-Based Scholarship or Grant Aid: 95%
Average Award: $12,459

Rec. Need-Based Self-Help Aid: 82%
Average Award: $2,748

Upon Graduation, Avg. Loan Debt per Student: $22,247

Financial Aid Deadline: rolling, 3/1 (priority)

Graduates

Going to Graduate School:
28% Within One Year

Companies Recruiting On Campus:
216

Alumni Giving: 15%

SAINT MARY'S COLLEGE OF CALIFORNIA

P.O. Box 4800, Moraga, CA 94575-4800
Admissions Phone: (925) 631-4224; (800) 800-4SMC Fax: (925) 376-7193
Email: smcadmit@stmarys-ca.edu Website: www.stmarys-ca.edu

General Info

Type of School: private, coed, Roman Catholic

Setting: small town

Academic Calendar: 4-1-4

Student Body

Full-Time Undergrads: 2,406
  Men: 42%, Women: 58%

Part-Time Undergrads: 931
  Men: 37%, Women: 63%

Total Undergrad Population:
  African American: 6%
  Asian American: 9%
  Latino: 15%
  Native American: 1%
  Caucasian: 47%
  International: 2%
  Living Off-Campus: 61%

Graduate and First-Professional
Students: 1,149

Academics

Full-Time Faculty: 208
  With Ph.D.: 90%

Part-Time Faculty: 316

Student/Faculty Ratio: 12:1

Most Popular Majors:
  business (22%)
  psychology (11%)
  communications (11%)
  liberal and civic studies (7%)
  English (6%)

Freshmen Retention Rate: 89%

Graduation Rates:
  66% within four years
  69% within six years

Admissions

Regular Application Deadline: 2/1;
  11/30 (priority)

Early Action Deadline: 11/30

Fall Transfer Deadline: 7/1, 2/1
  (priority)

Spring Transfer Deadline: 1/1

Total # of Students Applied: 3,172
  Admitted: 2,590
  Enrolled: 562

# of Students Waitlisted: 208
  Students Accepting Place: 104
  Waitlisted Students Admitted: 49

Inside the Classroom

A small Roman Catholic college near San Francisco, Saint Mary's College of California integrates liberal arts and professional education. With about 2,500 undergrads and another 2,000 grad students, there's a lot of personalized attention here. Under the direction of the Christian Brothers, the Lasallian teaching philosophy at SMC is "transformative"—a.k.a. holistic—and reinforces core human values. "It's attractive for its family atmosphere," says one guidance counselor we spoke to. With undergraduate programs in liberal arts, nursing, science, education, and economics/business administration, the most popular majors are business, psychology, communications, liberal/civic studies, and English.

Entrance to Saint Mary's is somewhat competitive, with three out of four applicants accepted. The school's "High Potential" program offers admission to students who, because of adverse factors, do not meet the traditional indicators of regular admission. Students come here for intensive interaction with professors, and as such, the administration expressly puts teaching above all else. Teaching assistants are not used. Most students here are serious about their education, and make good use of their time. With an average class size of 21 students, any student absent from class is always missed. One guidance counselor recommends Saint Mary's for its "supportive atmosphere and curriculum, if you don't mind the suburban isolation."

The SMC academic calendar is two four-month semesters, with a one-month term in January. A highlight for most everyone, "Jan Term" allows students to pursue interesting fieldwork—whether it's exploring limestone caves throughout California, studying detective novels, or staging a children's theater production. General education requirements include four "Great Books" courses, devoted to the great writers of the western world; two religious studies courses; and one course in multiculturalism. As for the religious component of the school, there's no required attendance at religious functions, though there are plenty of campus ministry events. We're told the workload is "medium," as is competitiveness, though one student feels that "those who aren't serious [about academics] are pressured by those who are." In other words, those not willing to put in the effort here might have a hard time.

In spite of its tremendous reputation for cultivating well-rounded thinkers, Saint Mary's has seen some leadership problems since the late 1990s: Seven deans have resigned or retired from their posts since 1997, as have eight administrators. A number of faculty members have also left, in part because of the school's emphasis of "teaching over research," we hear.

Campus Environment

The environment at Saint Mary's is calm and serene—"like a country club." Located in Moraga, about 20 miles east of San Francisco, the campus has mission-style architecture and beautiful landscaping. Though it's just a few minutes drive to the local shops, the 420-acre campus is fairly isolated in the hills. One California guidance counselor raves about the "small, beautiful campus, though the need to leave the campus for activity tends to be great." Downtown Moraga is a small, affluent town of several thousand residents who have a great relationship with the school—so much so, that after SMC realized the local fire station didn't have a ladder tall enough to attend to the new science center, it paid for a new fire truck.

About two-thirds of undergrads live on campus. Freshmen are guaranteed housing, and have first priority for dorms, which are set up with one floor for men and another floor for women. Christian Brothers live there as well, as residence hall counselors. Sophomores and upperclassmen are offered dorm rooms and suites through a lottery process, though off-campus apartments in Moraga and nearby Walnut Creek are plentiful (if a bit pricey) for those who want them. The student population also includes a fair number of commuter students who live at home.

Student Life

Sixty percent of the students at SMC are women; 60 percent are Catholic; and almost 50 percent are Caucasian. Minority students comprise around 30 percent of the student body, and apart from some social challenges, they feel "it's worth it." Though to call the campus politically active would be an overstatement, students here have been known to stand up for their needs: In 1998, they protested about the on-campus security system, and in 2001, they staged a hunger strike to force school policy changes about sexual assault.

On weekends, the social activities tend to be rather "wholesome," (there's no Greek life here), though off-campus bars with lax carding policies tend to attract a lot of undergrads. The range of clubs and activities is broad: from the campus TV station to the swing dancing club to the pep band to the Liberal and Civic Studies Club. Saint Mary's also has 16 Division I varsity sports teams, the most popular of which is basketball (women's basketball, in particular). Club teams include lacrosse, volleyball, ice hockey, water polo, cycling, wrestling and water skiing. Intramural sports are divided into leagues (such as flag football, coed soccer); tournaments (such as air hockey, badminton, Frisbee gold); and weekly events (such as inner tube water polo and whiffle ball).

Test Scores (middle 50%):
SAT Verbal: 510–600
SAT Math: 510–600

Avg. HS GPA: 3.3

Costs (2004–5)

Tuition and Fees: $25,150

Room & Board: $9,530

Payment Plan(s): installment plan

THE EXPERTS SAY...

" Saint Mary's integrates liberal arts, professional training, and humanistic values in a family atmosphere. Diversity is a strong suit at this supportive school. "

" The good news is that Saint Mary's emphasizes teaching over research. The bad news is that faculty are leaving to do research elsewhere. "

Inst. Aid (est. 2003–04)

Institutional Aid, Need-Based:
$12,792,948

Institutional Aid, Non-Need-Based:
$396,000

FT Undergrads Receiving Aid: 62%
Avg. Amount per Student:
$20,460

FT Undergrads Receiving Non-Need-Based Scholarship or Grant Aid: 3%
Avg. Amount per Student: $7,944

Of Those Receiving Any Aid:

Rec. Need-Based Scholarship or Grant Aid: 89%
Average Award: $15,625

Rec. Need-Based Self-Help Aid: 99%
Average Award: $5,957

Upon Graduation, Avg. Loan Debt per Student: $21,165

Financial Aid Deadline: 3/2 (priority)

Graduates

Going to Graduate School:
14% Within One Year

Accepting Job Offer:
42% at time of graduation

Companies Recruiting On Campus: 74

SAINT MARY'S COLLEGE OF MARYLAND

18952 East Fisher Road, St. Mary's City, MD 20686
Admissions Phone: (240) 895-5000; (800) 492-7181 Fax: (240) 895-5001
Email: admissions@smcm.edu Website: www.smcm.edu Application Website: www.smcm.edu/application/

General Info

Type of School: public, coed

Setting: rural

Academic Calendar: semester

Student Body

Full-Time Undergrads: 1,793
  Men: 40%, Women: 60%

Part-Time Undergrads: 54
  Men: 33%, Women: 67%

Total Undergrad Population:
  African American: 6%
  Asian American: 4%
  Latino: 3%
  Native American: <1%
  Caucasian: 81%
  International: 1%
  Living Off-Campus: 20%

Academics

Full-Time Faculty: 116
  With Ph.D.: 97%

Part-Time Faculty: 80
  With Ph.D.: 53%

Student/Faculty Ratio: 13:1

Most Popular Majors:
  psychology (15%)
  English (15%)
  biology (12%)
  economics (11%)
  political science (15%)

Completing 2 or More Majors: 19%

Freshmen Retention Rate: 85%

Graduation Rates:
  67% within four years
  75% within six years

Admissions

Regular Application Deadline: 1/15;
  12/1 (priority)

Early Decision Deadline(s): 12/1,
  1/15

Fall Transfer Deadline: 2/15

Spring Transfer Deadline: 10/15

Total # of Students Applied: 2,262
  Admitted: 1,243
  Enrolled: 421

# of Students Waitlisted: 443
  Students Accepting Place: 387
  Waitlisted Students Admitted: 83

Applied Early Decision: 304
  Early Decision Admitted: 163

Inside the Classroom

Don't let the name confuse you: St. Mary's College of Maryland is a state-supported, coed institution—not a private, religious, women's college. Founded as a "female seminary" by the Maryland state legislature in 1839, St. Mary's became a junior college in 1930 and didn't begin offering bachelor's degrees until 1971. Designated a "public honors college" by the governor in 1991, St. Mary's today is one of only a few state-supported liberal arts colleges in the entire country. Yet because the college is not run by Maryland's Board of Regents, it has the power to set its own tuition and its own admissions and personnel policies. The result: "St. Mary's is an 'Ivy'-level liberal arts college with a public school price tag," explains one guidance counselor.

St. Mary's offers 21 majors (many of which are humanities-based), plus 4 interdisciplinary study areas (African and African Diaspora Studies; East Asian Studies; Environmental Studies; and Women, Gender, and Sexuality Studies), a teacher certification program, and several preprofessional programs (including a 3-2 engineering program). In addition, students have the opportunity to design their own major (recent examples of student-designed majors include historical archeology and Web design and entrepreneurship). General education requirements include courses in the following: English composition, history, art, literature, math, physical science, biological science, behavioral science (psychology or sociology), policy science (economics or political science), values inquiry (philosophy or religion), foreign language proficiency, and at least one science lab.

All courses at St. Mary's are taught by faculty members. The low student-faculty ratio allows for close interaction between students and faculty, both inside and outside the classroom. St. Mary's is known for its individualized instruction; the majority of students work one-on-one with a faculty member at some point in their undergraduate experience. The St. Mary's Project (SMP), a research or creative project containing elements of a senior thesis, provides an ideal opportunity for students to engage in research in their chosen area with a faculty member. A large number of grads go on to pursue graduate or professional study.

St. Mary's is known for its willingness to take chances on disadvantaged students who might not normally be accepted at an institution that bills itself as an honors college. A recent example of the college's academic and fiscal generosity: When a foundation promising the students of Bruce Monroe Elementary School in Washington, DC full-tuition scholarships to a college of their choice went bankrupt during the students' senior year of high school, St. Mary's stepped in and offered scholarships to all eligible students.

St. Mary's reluctantly became the center of a national media frenzy in 1998 when a group of 13 students and 3 faculty members from the college were attacked by roadway bandits while on a faculty-led study trip to Guatemala over Winter Break. This case was reportedly "a wake-up call" for many U.S. colleges, who have since implemented stricter procedures for the approval of faculty-led study trips.

Campus Environment

All residence halls are integrated with students from various classes; freshmen may be assigned to any residence hall except the townhouses or apartments. "The two single-sex residence halls have more first-year students assigned to them than the coed residence halls," a college official informs us. Housing is guaranteed for any first-year student who applies for housing by the deadline. Although living on campus is not required, 80 percent of SMCM's full-time students choose to do so.

SMCM is located in historic St. Mary's City, the fourth oldest permanent English settlement in North America. Town-gown relations are reportedly good: The College acts as a resource to the surrounding community by providing athletic facilities to local teams, extensive community swim hours in its pool, reception and convention facilities, and informal gathering places. The campus occupies a beautiful waterfront location on the St. Mary's River, near the Chesapeake Bay. The setting is rural, and yet the campus is still within a 90-minute drive of Washington, DC. Still, the setting may be too isolated for some students: There are no shops, clubs, malls, or restaurants within walking distance.

Student Life

So what type of student is likely to thrive at St. Mary's? A college official answers, "Typically, students who thrive at St. Mary's are bright, self-motivated, and value a broad liberal arts education. They are academically and/or artistically oriented and are concerned about the environment and community service. They welcome the opportunity to work one-on-one with faculty in research and enjoy small classes and group discussions." The college actively recruits students of a variety of different socioeconomic and religious backgrounds, ethnicities, and races.

Thanks to some great faculty connections, St. Mary's has become known as "a musical incubator," where accomplished artists can try out new material. Since 1998, the River Concert Series has offered exciting outdoor, family-friendly concerts overlooking the scenic St. Mary's River. The arenas of literature and drama are also well-represented, giving St. Mary's a reputation as an "artist's colony."

St. Mary's sponsors more than 70 clubs and organizations. Some of the more popular clubs are the following: For Goodness' Sake (community service), Black Student Union, *The Point News* (campus newspaper), Feminist Majority Leadership Alliance, and club sports. St. Mary's has no fraternities or sororities. St. Mary's competes in 13 NCAA Division III sports, and its national champion women's and coed sailing teams compete in ICSA competitions. The college offers more than 20 intramural and recreational sports, and over 40 percent of students participate in some type of sport or organized recreational activity.

Students also have fun with St. Mary's quirky campus traditions, such as the annual cardboard boat race, the May Day bike ride, the shoe tree, the annual chili cook-off, World Carnival, Frisbee golf, bonfires on the St. Mary's River, and "ponding" (when your friends throw you into St. John's Pond to celebrate your birthday).

Other schools to check out: College of William and Mary, Mary Washington College, College of New Jersey, U of Maryland—Baltimore County, Salisbury U.

Test Scores (middle 50%):
SAT Verbal: 590–690
SAT Math: 570–670
HS Rank of Entering Freshmen:
Top 10%: 47%
Top 25%: 76%
Top 50%: 94%
Avg. HS GPA: 3.5

Costs (est. 2004–05)

Tuition and Fees, In-State: $9,680
Tuition and Fees, Out-of-State: $17,160
Room & Board: $7,400

THE EXPERTS SAY...

" As one of only a handful of selective public liberal arts colleges in the country, St. Mary's College of Maryland offers a tempting combination of intimacy and affordability. "

" St. Mary's retains and graduates almost 70 percent of its students in four years—a respectable rate for any college, let alone a public school. "

Inst. Aid (est. 2003–04)

Institutional Aid, Need-Based: $1,057,484
Institutional Aid, Non-Need-Based: $2,774,108
FT Undergrads Receiving Aid: 44%
Avg. Amount per Student: $7,195
FT Undergrads Receiving Non-Need-Based Scholarship or Grant Aid: 32%
Avg. Amount per Student: $4,500
Of Those Receiving Any Aid:
Rec. Need-Based Scholarship or Grant Aid: 58%
Average Award: $4,000
Rec. Need-Based Self-Help Aid: 58%
Average Award: $5,500
Upon Graduation, Avg. Loan Debt per Student: $17,128
Financial Aid Deadline: 3/1 (priority)

Graduates

Going to Graduate School: 46% Within One Year
Companies Recruiting On Campus: 78
Alumni Giving: 42%

SAINT OLAF COLLEGE

1520 St. Olaf Avenue, Northfield, MN 55057
Admissions Phone: (507) 646-3025; (800) 800-3025 Fax: (507) 646-3832
Email: admissions@stolaf.edu Website: www.stolaf.edu/admissions/
Application Website: www.stolaf.edu/admissions/onlineapp/

General Info

Type of School: private, coed, Evangelical Lutheran Church

Setting: small town

Academic Calendar: 4-1-4

Student Body

Full-Time Undergrads: 2,917
Men: 41%, Women: 59%

Part-Time Undergrads: 3
Men: 33%, Women: 67%

Total Undergrad Population:
African American: 1%
Asian American: 4%
Latino: 1%
Native American: <1%
Caucasian: 87%
International: 1%
Out-of-State: 54%
Living Off-Campus: 4%

Academics

Full-Time Faculty: 206
With Ph.D.: 91%

Part-Time Faculty: 128
With Ph.D.: 52%

Student/Faculty Ratio: 12:1

Most Popular Majors:
biology (12%)
psychology (9%)
English (9%)
mathematics (6%)
economics (6%)

Completing 2 or More Majors: 33%

Freshmen Retention Rate: 92%

Graduation Rates:
75% within four years
81% within six years

Admissions

Regular Application Deadline: 2/1 (priority)

Early Decision Deadline(s): 11/15, 12/5

Early Action Deadline: 12/15

Total # of Students Applied: 2,517
Admitted: 1,894
Enrolled: 720

# of Students Waitlisted: 252
Students Accepting Place: 182
Waitlisted Students Admitted: 53

Applied Early Decision: 139
Early Decision Admitted: 115

In the Classroom

One high school guidance counselor calls St. Olaf "the best of a liberal arts education in a caring Christian community." Indeed, the Lutheran faith of St. Olaf's founders remains a strong influence on college life today. Along with the standard liberal arts curriculum, students must take courses in Biblical and Theological Studies in order to graduate, and many other classes draw on Christian perspectives. About half the students are Lutheran, although the college "warmly welcomes individuals of all faiths." When asked to identify their religious background in a recent survey, the student body listed more than 50 religious groups.

St. Olaf has notable programs in many traditional liberal arts areas; the most popular majors are biology, English, economics, mathematics, and psychology. The college also has highly regarded music, dance, and fine arts programs. Qualified students can take advantage of such innovative programs as the two-year Great Conversation program, an in-depth exploration of great works of literature and philosophy. In addition to the spring and fall semesters, students select one class for the January "interim." Many select a study abroad or independent study program that allows them to escape the Minnesota winter.

Tests are unproctored; students sign a pledge binding them to academic honesty. And many teachers here know their students by name. A recent grad reflects, "I felt that most professors were accessible, but you had to use their system." Overall, good relationships with their profs help students through the somewhat grueling academic requirements and heavy workload. But the students at St. Olaf are committed to their studies. "Weekends are lively, but most students are here to learn," a student explains.

Campus Environment

St. Olaf is situated on a hill outside the town of Northfield, which promotes itself as the town of "cows, colleges, and contentment." At the heart of the 1,000-acre campus is the "Green," a wooded lawn surrounded by the oldest buildings. The rest of the campus has been restored to woodland (volunteers have planted 20,000 trees in the past 10 years), prairie, and wetland, offering opportunities for student research and natural areas for jogging and walking.

Students are required to live on campus unless residence halls are filled. When that happens, students may apply to live off campus, although a very small percentage of students are normally allowed to do so. Most undergrads live in "spacious" dorms; one student suggests that "getting a pod [made up of four singles, two doubles, and a common area] is the easiest way to secure a coveted single." Returning students may apply to live in one of the 14 "Honors Houses" that provide a more intimate residential setting. These are reportedly "very competitive" to get into. St. Olaf is even strict about student vehicles: With little exception, only seniors are allowed to have cars. The college provides shuttle service into Northfield, and bus service to Minneapolis–St. Paul is available.

Student Life

A student says, "The 'Minnesota nice' attitude is apparent, as random people will say 'hi' to you whether you know them or not." In fact, he continues, "Minnesota culture can take some getting used to, making it harder to adjust for non-Midwest students." Indeed, more than half the student body is from Minnesota and most of the rest are from other states of the Upper Midwest. Minorities are a rarity, though St. Olaf is making an effort to recruit a wider range of students—but "this is easier said than done." In general, students fall into two groups: "devoted Lutherans" and "more secular students."

St. Olaf's location limits entertainment options, although the college's website tries to make the case that the college is not so isolated: "Students at St. Olaf will find coffee shops, ethnic restaurants, a movie theater, and a bowling alley. Not to mention a Target where you can pick up anything that you forgot to pack from home!" One recent grad confirms, "There is not a lot to do in town, but it is very quaint." In September, Northfield (whose claim to fame is the site where Jesse James and his gang were captured) holds "The Defeat of Jesse James Day" festival, with rides, reenactments, and a rodeo. "It's a great time!" we're told. Students can head to Carleton College, also in Northfield, for more varied social activity. The Twin Cities, only 40 miles away and accessible by bus, provide a wide range of social, cultural, and entertainment options.

On campus, there's not much of a party scene. The college's church ties have influenced rigid guidelines regarding student life, including strict policies against alcohol and drug use—it's a dry campus—and regulations governing visitors of the opposite sex after hours. However, one student says, "people still drink, and if you know where to look, you can find quiet parties with people sitting around, talking and drinking. The smart people know that if you're loud, you're busted!" Students do become deeply involved in a number of extracurricular activities and organizations, and activism is big here, especially volunteer work. And we hear, not surprisingly, that religious clubs are very popular. A music major says, "Two-thirds of the school is involved in the music department, so most of the school sings or plays an instrument." Students enjoy hanging out at the Pause, the campus club located in the beautiful student union, where dances and live performances crop up every weekend.

Sporting types enjoy the sparkling new state-of-the-art recreation and fitness center that boasts modern training facilities, tennis courts, and a 48-foot-high rock-climbing wall. St. Olaf competes in NCAA Division III and offers a variety of men's and women's teams, although one student says, "Many [students] choose not to play a varsity sport because of the time commitments." Hockey is the most popular among Ole spectators. Many students participate in intramural and club sports, including "broomball," which is played with brooms on ice… but without skates. When spring comes, the Frisbees fly on the Green and on the campus's Frisbee golf course. And twice a year, the library staff at St. Olaf plays miniature golf. (What's unusual about that, you ask? They play inside the library!)

Other schools to check out: Gustavus Adolphus, Carleton, Lawrence, Goshen, Earlham.

Test Scores (middle 50%):
SAT Verbal: 580–700
SAT Math: 580–690
ACT Comp: 25–30
ACT English: 24–30
ACT Math: 24–30

HS Rank of Entering Freshmen:
Top 10%: 47%
Top 25%: 80%
Top 50%: 98%

Avg. HS GPA: 3.64

THE EXPERTS SAY...

" While not as well known as Carleton, St. Olaf offers an excellent liberal arts education with some outstanding special study options. "

" Use St. Olaf's awesome study abroad programs to spread the joy of broomball to all corners of the globe! "

Costs (2004–5)

Tuition and Fees: $25,150
Room & Board: $5,800
Payment Plan(s): installment plan, pre-payment plan

Inst. Aid (est. 2003–04)

Institutional Aid, Need-Based: $18,816,132

Institutional Aid, Non-Need-Based: $3,230,150

FT Undergrads Receiving Aid: 63%
Avg. Amount per Student: $18,172

FT Undergrads Receiving Non-Need-Based Scholarship or Grant Aid: 19%
Avg. Amount per Student: $5,717

Of Those Receiving Any Aid:

Rec. Need-Based Scholarship or Grant Aid: 100%
Average Award: $12,210

Rec. Need-Based Self-Help Aid: 100%
Average Award: $5,364

Upon Graduation, Avg. Loan Debt per Student: $18,024

Financial Aid Deadline: rolling, 2/15 (priority)

Graduates

Going to Graduate School:
25% Within One Year

Companies Recruiting On Campus: 104

Alumni Giving: 50%

SALISBURY UNIVERSITY

1101 Camden Avenue, Salisbury, MD 21801-6862
Admissions Phone: (410) 543-6161 Fax: (410) 546-6016
Email: admissions@salisbury.edu
Website: www.salisbury.edu

General Info

Type of School: public, coed
Setting: small town
Academic Calendar: 4-1-4

Student Body

Full-Time Undergrads: 5,422
  Men: 43%, Women: 57%

Part-Time Undergrads: 452
  Men: 42%, Women: 58%

Total Undergrad Population:
  African American: 7%
  Asian American: 3%
  Latino: 2%
  Caucasian: 81%
  International: 1%
  Out-of-State: 14%
  Living Off-Campus: 60%
  In Fraternities: 5%
  In Sororities: 5%

Graduate and First-Professional
Students: 407

Academics

Full-Time Faculty: 299
  With Ph.D.: 82%

Part-Time Faculty: 199
  With Ph.D.: 14%

Student/Faculty Ratio: 16:1

Most Popular Majors:
  business administration (11%)
  education (10%)
  communication arts (7%)
  biology (6%)
  nursing (5%)

Completing 2 or More Majors: 3%

Freshmen Retention Rate: 80%

Graduation Rates:
  46% within four years
  67% within six years

Admissions

Regular Application Deadline: 1/15;
  12/1 (priority)

Transfer Application Deadline: rolling

Early Action Deadline: 12/1

Total # of Students Applied: 6,550
  Admitted: 2,882
  Enrolled: 950

# of Students Waitlisted: 1,251
  Students Accepting Place: 657
  Waitlisted Students Admitted: 32

Inside the Classroom

Undergrads at Salisbury University are offered degrees through the colleges of liberal arts, science and technology, business, and educational and professional studies. All four undergraduate schools at this public university have generous endowments. The core curriculum has a minimum of 47 credit hours in approved general education courses. Requirements are divided into four groups, with English and History 101 and 102 requirements, and a broad spectrum of options in arts, humanities, mathematics and lab sciences. Also, you have to take a course in health fitness. Notable programs are in athletic training, biology, business, communication arts, elementary education, environmental sciences, geography-geosciences, management information sciences, philosophy, physics/engineering, psychology, and social work. Preprofessional programs are in chemistry, law, health, dental, optometry, osteopathic medicine, pharmacy, physician's assistant, physical therapy, podiatric medicine, and veterinary medicine.

Average class size is 24 for lectures, and 20 for other classes. It's small for a state school, and students like the low tuition combined with a more intimate community than larger public schools. Also, they find the instructors to be pretty accessible and friendly.

Salisbury is known for its undergraduate research and service learning programs. Each spring Salisbury hosts a campus-wide student research conference. The school explains, "In addition to earning credit for their research projects, students can also earn summer stipends. Many students are co-authors with faculty at regional and national meetings, and in scholarly journals." All academic programs offer internship opportunities at Salisbury University. The Applied Business Learning Experience (ABLE) is required for all business majors. Many programs also offer independent studies, directed research and practicums that allow students, with special permission, to study topics in-depth.

The honors program at Salisbury "is designed to bring together high-achieving students and dedicated faculty in a small university environment within the diversity of opportunity of the larger university community," and includes honors courses, research/creative projects, and a senior honors thesis opportunity.

Campus Environment

The landscape at Salisbury is a learning experience in itself. The school was awarded University Arboretum status by the American Association of Botanical Gardens and Arboreta. The campus is "a place for the scientific study and public display of various species of woody and herbaceous plants." Many students are hired in the summer to maintain the campus arboretum and grounds. However, the surrounding community is pretty small-town.

New student halls house first-time freshmen and transfers under age 21. Housing is provided on a space-available basis, but is guaranteed for freshmen. There are many types of housing, including traditional residence halls (single-sex and coed), single-room clusters (sorry, shared bathrooms), wellness, living-learning, and international.

University Park, a 576-bed residence hall, twice the size of any of the other University dorms, is located a half mile from the main campus. This newly built residence offers private bedrooms in shared apartments with many amenities (air conditioning, café, fitness center, study area, campus shuttle service, etc.) You'll have to acquire 24 credit hours before you can move here, though. It's like living off-campus, but through the school, without the hassle of difficult landlords, arbitrary rent and locked-in group leases.

Freshmen residents are not allowed to keep a car at Salisbury; after your first year, you can register to register a car to park on campus. In the meantime, the Gus Bus will take you to the mall on Saturdays, and the SU shuttles go to U. Maryland Eastern Shore, to the off-campus housing complexes Sea Gull Village and University Park, and to off-campus classrooms. And, we've been told, "limited mass transit services are available." So make sure you have what you need, or learn to meet people with cars.

Student Life

Large student groups include the Student Government Association, WSUR Student Radio, Greek Council, Union of African-American Students, and the Outdoor Club. There are nine frats/sororities, and beyond the social aspects, Greeks participate in many community service initiatives. However, we are told, "Greeks don't rule" here, and the students pursue other social outlets. "Nearly everyone participates in out-of-the-classroom activities," says the school, "from intercollegiate sports to intramurals, from student government to affinity clubs (Outdoor, French, Surf), from Greeks to Sophanes (theatre)." Further, we are told, "Expect the quarterback on the football team to be sharing his accounting expertise at tax time with the elderly. Look for the DJ on the student-run radio station to also be an officer in Zeta Tau Alpha sorority and a member of the summer paint crew."

Salisbury is a NCAA Division III member, and also affiliates with the Capitol Athletic Conference, the Atlantic Central Football Conference, and the Eastern College Athletic Conference. There are nine men's intercollegiate sports and ten for women. There are 22 intramural sports each for men and women, and nine coed intramurals. More than 1,800 SU students (undergrad and grad) participate in athletics.

The Spring Olympics are "an off-beat competition between dormitory residents featuring games such as tug-of-war, egg toss and fireman's relay." And for the past 15 years, SU has hosted the Annual Sea Gull Century, a nationally acclaimed bicycle tour of Maryland's Eastern Shore with over 7,000 participants, the largest ride of this type on the East Coast.

Test Scores (middle 50%):
SAT Verbal: 510–600
SAT Math: 530–620

HS Rank of Entering Freshmen:
Top 10%: 18%
Top 25%: 52%
Top 50%: 89%

Avg. HS GPA: 3.48

THE EXPERTS SAY...

" If public university tuition with small school class size appeals to you, take a look at Salisbury. Service learning, internship, and research opportunities abound. "

" Bring your bike for the Annual Sea Gull Century and get ready for the Spring Olympics egg toss. "

Costs (2004–5)

Tuition and Fees, In-State: $6,994

Tuition and Fees, Out-of-State: $13,882

Room & Board: $6,900

Payment Plan(s): installment plan, pre-payment plan

Inst. Aid (2002–03)

Institutional Aid, Need-Based: $293,690

Institutional Aid, Non-Need-Based: $793,994

FT Undergrads Receiving Aid: 40%
Avg. Amount per Student: $5,629

FT Undergrads Receiving Non-Need-Based Scholarship or Grant Aid: 7%
Avg. Amount per Student: $3,129

Of Those Receiving Any Aid:

Rec. Need-Based Scholarship or Grant Aid: 54%
Average Award: $3,467

Rec. Need-Based Self-Help Aid: 80%
Average Award: $3,481

Upon Graduation, Avg. Loan Debt per Student: $14,759

Financial Aid Deadline: 5/1

Graduates

Going to Graduate School: 29% Within One Year

Companies Recruiting On Campus: 250

Alumni Giving: 10%

SAN DIEGO STATE UNIVERSITY

5500 Campanile Drive, San Diego, CA 92182-7455
Admissions Phone: (619) 594-7800 Fax: (619) 594-1250
Website: www.sdsu.edu
Application Website: www.sdsu.edu/apply

General Info

Type of School: public, coed

Academic Calendar: semester

Student Body

Full-Time Undergrads: 21,697
  Men: 41%, Women: 59%

Part-Time Undergrads: 5,648
  Men: 42%, Women: 58%

Total Undergrad Population:
  African American: 4%
  Asian American: 15%
  Latino: 21%
  Native American: 1%
  Caucasian: 45%
  International: 3%
  Out-of-State: 7%
  Living Off-Campus: 89%
  In Fraternities: 7%
  In Sororities: 6%

Graduate and First-Professional
  Students: 6,331

Academics

Full-Time Faculty: 1,002
  With Ph.D.: 79%

Part-Time Faculty: 682

Student/Faculty Ratio: 19:1

Most Popular Majors:
  business administration (10%)
  psychology (7%)
  liberal studies (7%)
  biology (4%)
  nursing (4%)

Completing 2 or More Majors: 0%

Freshmen Retention Rate: 82%

Graduation Rates:
  9% within four years
  44% within six years

Admissions

Regular Application Deadline: 11/30

Early Action Deadline: 11/30

Fall Transfer Deadline: 11/30

Total # of Students Applied: 29,129
  Admitted: 14,454
  Enrolled: 3,730

Inside the Classroom

San Diego State prides itself on offering a global perspective in education, a good asset in today's growing global society. SDSU is well known for international education—the International Business Program was named the best study abroad program in the country for 2002 (in any area of study) by the Institute of International Education. Also, the undergrad program in international business is the largest of its kind in the country, and also requires foreign language skills. "Through transnational programs with Mexico and Canada, 180 international exchange programs in 40 countries, and a nationally-recognized international business program, SDSU will equip you to succeed in a global society," states a university official.

SDSU's seven undergraduate schools include the schools of arts and letters, business administration, education, engineering, health and human services, professional studies and fine arts, and sciences. The College of Business is recognized nationally as a leading business school that features faculty excellence, successful alumni, a springboard for entrepreneurs, and a bridge to the international economy. There are 87 bachelor's degree programs; nursing, biology, psychology, and geography are among the strongest. According to the school, "the average class size at SDSU is 32 students in lecture classes, and only 15 in lab classes—smaller than classes at many other universities." (But some general ed classes can get much bigger, so don't be too taken in by "average" size!) The honors program offers even smaller classes to qualified students who are "pursuing an education, not just a degree."

Students can broaden their practical education through research with faculty members, internships, and many service learning opportunities. The school explains, "Many SDSU faculty are dedicated to integrating 'service learning' in the classroom." A nearby inner-city neighborhood offer students and faculty such opportunities and "engages the entire community in such issues as business and economic development, crime and law enforcement, education, health, immigration and cultural diversity, poverty, recreation, technology, and urban planning."

We hear that with more popular programs like business, engineering, and psychology, it's often hard to get into overpopulated prerequisites. This can make it hard to graduate in four years for the less clever or less motivated student. In such a large university, those in the honors program or involved in another program that offers preferential registration have a better chance of getting the classes they want when they want them. Students often scramble to get into "crash" courses, competing to land one more spot from a sympathetic teacher in a closed class.

Campus Environment

The urban San Diego campus is located on the Pacific rim, bordering Mexico; think warm weather, sun, and sand. San Diego itself has much to offer in terms of nightlife. You can also drive just a few hours to Los Angeles, or even less to Mexico.

On-campus housing is neither required nor guaranteed. Students living on campus are housed in traditional residence halls—singles and doubles—along with eight-person suites. There are coed or single-sex floors, study-intensive floors, substance-free floors, and other types of specialized housing. The recently finished Cuicacalli Residence Hall offers all suite-style housing to 686 residents, and includes an in-house dining room, study area, coffee cart, swimming pool, and sand volleyball court. If the newer dorms are full, you might want to consider moving off-campus; we hear that the older dorms aren't too comfortable. The off-campus housing office aids students in finding apartments near campus (yes, you can live at the beach!).

We've noticed some mixed feelings from students about campus safety. While there is a moderate amount of crime on campus, students say that it often comes in the form of non-students from the urban community coming on to the campus. There are also reports of student-on-student assaults, especially in relation to Greek life and parties.

There are many bus routes that service the school, so public transportation can get you just about anywhere. Parking can be very difficult, as the university serves a large proportion of commuters. However, parking difficulties aside, you should consider a car for speed and convenience, especially for getting to the beach (about a half-hour away) or to nearby shopping and restaurants. Scheduled to open in early 2005, the Mission Valley East Light Rail Extension includes a 5.9-mile, $431 million underground trolley station (and a trolley to go with it!) with three-quarters of a mile of tunnels that loop under the central campus. It will ease traffic and parking congestion near campus, and further connect students to the rest of the city and surrounding area.

Student Life

Students and guidance counselors admit that SDSU has a reputation for being a "party school." Some students describe a pretty heavy party scene, especially among the 40+ fraternities and sororities. But students also warn that you should have some perspective: with more than 30,000 students, the partygoers may make the most noise, but the thousands of other students certainly find other things going on at night and on weekends besides frat parties. SDSU has more than 200 student clubs and organizations, so any student can find his or her niche. Diversity is among SDSU's strengths: "SDSU ranks among the top 10 universities of its type in the nation for bachelor's degrees awarded to minority students," says a university official. In fall 2002, SDSU became the first university in California to post important admissions guidelines and requirements in Spanish on its website.

The San Diego State Aztecs participate in the Mountain West Conference with NCAA Division I membership. There are 18 varsity sports; noteworthy teams include softball, baseball, women's volleyball, men's basketball, men's golf, women's water polo, women's track, and both men's and women's tennis. The Aztec Recreation Center on campus offers fitness and recreation facilities including indoor climbing and weight training. Also, there are numerous intramural and club sports opportunities.

SDSU can boast of having many successful alumni, including: Julie Kavner (voice of Marge on *The Simpsons*), Kathy Najimy (*Sister Act*), Gary David Goldberg (executive producer/co-creator of *Spin City*), R. Andrew Rathbone (creator, *...for Dummies* book series), Timothy J. Muris (Chairman, Federal Trade Commission), and Julia Stewart (CEO, International House of Pancakes).

Other schools to check out: UC San Diego, California Polytechnic State University, CSU Chico, UC Irvine, UC Davis.

Test Scores (middle 50%):
SAT Verbal: 480–580
SAT Math: 490–600
ACT Comp: 20–25
ACT English: 19–25
ACT Math: 20–26
Avg. HS GPA: 3.52

Costs (2003–04)

Tuition and Fees, In-State: $2,488

Tuition and Fees, Out-of-State: $10,948

Room & Board: $8,787

Payment Plan(s): installment plan

THE EXPERTS SAY...

" SDSU offers an excellent international business program in a beautiful setting at a reasonable price. "

" A program in international business is valuable only if you are able to buckle down and actually get your degree. Otherwise, you'll just be a very well-educated, well-traveled beach bum. "

Inst. Aid (est. 2003–04)

Institutional Aid, Need-Based: $8,920,000

Institutional Aid, Non-Need-Based: $1,010,000

FT Undergrads Receiving Aid: 43%
Avg. Amount per Student: $8,500

FT Undergrads Receiving Non-Need-Based Scholarship or Grant Aid: 1%
Avg. Amount per Student: $1,400

Of Those Receiving Any Aid:

Rec. Need-Based Scholarship or Grant Aid: 78%
Average Award: $4,000

Rec. Need-Based Self-Help Aid: 90%
Average Award: $4,000

Upon Graduation, Avg. Loan Debt per Student: $13,000

Financial Aid Deadline: rolling, for Cal Grants 3/2

Graduates

Companies Recruiting On-Campus: 230

SANTA CLARA UNIVERSITY

500 El Camino Real, Santa Clara, CA 95053-0925
Admissions Phone: (408) 554-4700 Fax: (408) 554-5255
Website: www.scu.edu

General Info

Type of School: private, coed,
Jesuit/Catholic

Setting: suburban

Academic Calendar: quarter

Student Body

Full-Time Undergrads: 4,160
Men: 45%, Women: 55%

Part-Time Undergrads: 99
Men: 54%, Women: 46%

Total Undergrad Population:
African American: 2%
Asian American: 19%
Latino: 14%
Native American: 1%
Caucasian: 58%
International: 3%
Out-of-State: 31%

Graduate and First-Professional
Students: 3,496

Academics

Full-Time Faculty: 416
With Ph.D.: 92%

Part-Time Faculty: 279
With Ph.D.: 53%

Student/Faculty Ratio: 12:1

Most Popular Majors:
finance (11%)
marketing (9%)
communication (8%)
psychology (7%)
accounting (6%)

Completing 2 or More Majors: 9%

Freshmen Retention Rate: 92%

Graduation Rates:
76% within four years
85% within six years

Admissions

Regular Application Deadline: 1/15

Early Action Deadline: 11/15

Fall Transfer Deadline: 5/15, 3/15
(priority)

Spring Transfer Deadline: 10/1

Total # of Students Applied: 6,388
Admitted: 4,223
Enrolled: 897

# of Students Waitlisted: 483
Students Accepting Place: 134
Waitlisted Students Admitted: 133

Inside the Classroom

Located in the heart of California's Silicon Valley, just south of San Francisco, Santa Clara is California's oldest institution of higher learning. Established by Jesuit priests during the Gold Rush, SCU was an all-male school until 1961. That year, it became the first coed Catholic university in California. Today it enrolls 4,300 undergrad and 3,500 grad students. And while religion is definitely part of the academic landscape here, it is not imposed on anyone. In fact, only around half the students are Roman Catholic (there's a sizable number of Muslims here, as well). The school legally separated from the Jesuit community in the 1960s, and though there are plenty of spiritual retreats and activities to choose from, its only religion requirement is three courses in religious studies.

The three undergraduate divisions are the College of Arts and Sciences, the School of Business, and the School of Engineering. One thing that sets the university apart from others like it is the required core curriculum: The first 'theme' focuses on developing a sense of person and place; the second focuses on methods of inquiry and analysis; and the third focuses on integration and perspective. And in a unique joint program with the Smithsonian Institution, one program studies Hispanic, Mexican American, and Latino heritage in the context of California missions. The school recently received a large grant to strengthen undergrad courses in the biological sciences, with which it is providing students research projects and internships with Silicon Valley biotech firms.

Students say the workload is heavy ("no slacker classes/majors," according to one) and incredibly intense. But in spite of this, few feel any real competition, perhaps because "the school is based on the promotion of justice, not beating out each other," explains one sophomore. Several students spoke to us about the appeal of the school's focus on social justice and volunteerism. Whether it's attending "Social Justice Mondays," a lunchtime series on contemporary social justice issues, or a class in business ethics in the 21st century, Santa Clara prides itself on teaching with "compassion and conscience." Additionally, almost everyone raves about the small classes, though the flip-side of this is that it can be very tough to get into preferred classes.

Campus Environment

There's virtually unanimous agreement about the campus at SCU: It's gorgeous. Built on the grounds of the Mission Santa Clara de Asis in 1851, the 104 acres are "like a mini-country club," according to one student. Students tend to be happy with the facilities, though some say the library is unappealing. In the center of campus is the famed Mission Church, with its Spanish colonial facade, surrounded by roses and palm trees.

On-campus housing for first year students is considered very comfortable. After that, it gets tight; we're told that some students have been housed in a motel. Most upperclassmen live off-campus, though housing is neither inexpensive nor of particularly good quality.

Student Life

Commonly referred to as "the Bubble," because the school is so separated from the rest of the world, the community at SCU is tight-knit and friendly. One student comments, "I'd say one out of five people I pass by will avoid eye contact. I'll run into at least two or three people I know on the way to class." We've heard from a few students that "there's not too much school spirit." There's not much to do for fun right on campus, nor does the surrounding city have much for those under 21, but with San Francisco and the beach so close, this doesn't seem to be a problem for most students.

Santa Clara students tend to be "cliquish" and—judging by the comments we received—don't seem to realize just how ethnically diverse their student body actually is. "Many students are upper-middle class whites," says one student. Another says, "The people here could all be models. Tall, thin, usually blond, gorgeous. Poor students might find the school snobby because so many of the students are very wealthy and trendy." According to the school's media relations office, several hundred students here are foreign nationals who are combining work in Silicon Valley with business or engineering studies here at the school.

While the school works hard to promote a feeling of social justice, the atmosphere at the school is somewhat conservative, with "little diversity in the ideas people hold," according to one junior. Says another, "There's a lack of political expression." In fact, many agree that an extremely liberal thinker would not do well here. On the other hand, the administration has gone to great lengths to support open academic inquiry and free speech—even at a cost. Last year, the Muslim Student Association (MSA) was even allowed to host "Anti Zionism Week," propelling the entire campus community into heated debate.

As for a social culture here, we've been told that many undergrads are "conformists," so those who resist going along with the group might not fit in. Yet when need arises, students here will jump to activism: Not long ago, they protested in favor of a San Jose homeless shelter.

The social life at SCU can tend to get rowdy, though a recent crackdown by police with a number of arrests at off-campus parties has curbed that to some degree. Some say the school's relationship with the local police has gone too far: "The off-campus atmosphere is overprotective... A police force is basically enforcing [the] school," says one senior. The school recently opened an on-campus bar, though we're told the administration is "too strict on underage drinking." To the outrage of many, the administration kicked off (or rather, stopped funding for) all fraternities and sororities from campus in 2001. Interestingly, one student tells us, "this seems to have made them even more popular," though they're not highly visible on campus.

Other schools to check out: Gonzaga, Pepperdine, Loyola Marymount, Pacific Lutheran.

Test Scores (middle 50%):
SAT Verbal: 530–630
SAT Math: 560–650
ACT Comp: 23–28

HS Rank of Entering Freshmen:
Top 10%: 38%
Top 25%: 65%
Top 50%: 94%

Avg. HS GPA: 3.53

THE EXPERTS SAY...

" Undergrads can get research funding and internships in the Silicon Valley's booming biotech industry. And Santa Clara's innovative core curriculum is a definite attraction. "

" Nonconformists looking for a spirited campus may be disappointed by the Santa Clara 'Bubble.' "

Costs (2003–04)

Tuition and Fees: $25,365

Room & Board: $9,336

Payment Plan(s): installment plan, deferred payment plan, pre-payment plan

Inst. Aid (est. 2003–04)

FT Undergrads Receiving Aid: 43%
Avg. Amount per Student: $17,699

FT Undergrads Receiving Non-Need-Based Scholarship or Grant Aid: 10%
Avg. Amount per Student: $5,106

Of Those Receiving Any Aid:

Rec. Need-Based Scholarship or Grant Aid: 93%
Average Award: $12,374

Rec. Need-Based Self-Help Aid: 70%
Average Award: $5,137

Upon Graduation, Avg. Loan Debt per Student: $25,492

Financial Aid Deadline: rolling, 2/1 (priority)

Graduates

Going to Graduate School:
38% Within One Year

Accepting Job Offer:
29% at time of graduation

Companies Recruiting On Campus: 207

Alumni Giving: 36%

SARAH LAWRENCE COLLEGE

1 Mead Way, Bronxville, NY 10708-5999
Admissions Phone: (914) 395-2510; (800) 888-2858 Fax: (914) 395-2515
Email: slcadmit@slc.edu Website: www.sarahlawrence.edu
Application Website: slc.edu/undergrad/admission/apply_online.html

General Info

Type of School: private, coed

Setting: suburban

Academic Calendar: semester

Student Body

Full-Time Undergrads: 1,138
  Men: 27%, Women: 73%

Part-Time Undergrads: 59
  Men: 15%, Women: 85%

Total Undergrad Population:
  African American: 5%
  Asian American: 5%
  Latino: 4%
  Native American: 1%
  Caucasian: 75%
  International: 2%
  Out-of-State: 81%
  Living Off-Campus: 13%

Graduate and First-Professional
  Students: 314

Academics

Full-Time Faculty: 180

Part-Time Faculty: 56

Student/Faculty Ratio: 6:1

Freshmen Retention Rate: 93%

Graduation Rates:
  61% within four years
  72% within six years

Admissions

Regular Application Deadline: 1/1

Early Decision Deadline(s): 11/15

Fall Transfer Deadline: 3/1 (priority)

Spring Transfer Deadline: 11/15
  (priority)

Total # of Students Applied: 2,672
  Admitted: 1,107
  Enrolled: 322

# of Students Waitlisted: 480
  Students Accepting Place: 150
  Waitlisted Students Admitted: 35

Applied Early Decision: 181
  Early Decision Admitted: 100

Test Scores (middle 50%):
  SAT Verbal: 600–700
  SAT Math: 540–640
  ACT Comp: 24–29
  ACT English: 25–32
  ACT Math: 21–28

Inside the Classroom

The SLC academic atmosphere is, as a junior says, "intense, personal, and pervasive." A freshman lauds "the academic freedom.... Sarah Lawrence students are not required to declare a major, or even encouraged to do so." While one guidance counselor worries that Sadie Lou might be "too non-traditional for many students," a student counters, "It is a school where undergraduates receive the individual attention and guidance that is peculiar to graduate students at other institutions." There are no "formal" majors here. Each student works closely with a "don," or faculty adviser, to design an individual program that includes courses in the humanities, creative and performing arts, social sciences, and natural sciences and math. The don then remains available for personal and academic advisement.

At SLC, "class doesn't end when you leave the classroom." In its seminar-conference system with small, highly interactive classes and private tutorials, students take only three courses per semester. However, in each course students are required to complete substantial independent projects ranging from traditional papers to creative works. All students do research, and writing is a way of life (several 20–30-page papers a term are not uncommon). Warns a junior, "One thing anyone thinking about SLC should know is that no one can just not do their work and expect to get by, because your classmates and your professor will know, being as SLC is discussion- and paper-driven."

All courses at Sarah Lawrence are taught by full professors. (The student-faculty ratio is 6:1.) Says a senior, "The academic atmosphere is very low key. We call our professors by their first names, we meet with them every other week to discuss independent projects, and classes are usually no larger than 15 people." Although grades are kept on file, they're not considered as important as the detailed written evaluations students receive from their teachers.

Sarah Lawrence emphasizes creative work as integral to liberal education and is particularly known for its programs in creative writing and the performing arts, as well as for, as a junior raves, "internships you couldn't get anywhere else." Comparing SLC with other schools, a student states, "I felt like I'd just be bogged down with prerequisites... I wouldn't grow as much, or have as much freedom to take the classes I want... I couldn't justify the amount of student loans I'm taking out if I didn't feel it was the best, most challenging college possible."

Campus Environment

Housing, enthuses a junior, ranges "from old, beautiful houses to modern 'bathroom-down-the-hall' style residence halls, to the 'old dorms' (suite-style), to apartment-style living. You're guaranteed a single your junior year, and about 80 percent of sophomores have singles." First year students are placed in doubles or triples, which are "spacious," compared to other colleges. "Our housing director works really hard to match roommates well," a student says. "You take a very comprehensive sort of survey before placement on everything from the type of music you listen to to your diet." Ninety percent of students live on campus, and while housing is guaranteed for all four years, some upperclassmen live off campus in Yonkers and the surrounding suburbs for economic reasons.

SLC itself is located in suburban Bronxville, which one senior calls "an awful town populated by rich, racist senior citizens," adding: "There is nothing to do and I would never go there if it weren't for one good pizza restaurant and the train station to go into the city." Less affluent Yonkers, a junior reports, "is diverse economically, ethnically, racially, and politically." First-year students aren't allowed to have cars, but a major mall, eateries, and "bars that really love the students" are within walking distance. NYC is thirty minutes away.

Student Life

"Weeknights are usually spent on campus, either studying, attending campus events, or throwing illegal parties," we're told. "Weekends many students go into New York City to get out of the 'Sarah Lawrence Bubble.'" The annual Coming Out Dance [the oldest student AIDS fundraiser] is huge. "It's just about the only school event that brings the entire campus out of their rooms," a senior remarks. "This year there was overcrowding and several close calls with alcohol poisoning. It was a blast, though: good music and lots of public displays of... well, everything." Another proudly adds, "We host some of the greatest, most raucous drag shows in the world."

With so many artists around, there are always live performances, poetry readings at the Coffeehaus, and exhibits at the popular A*Space (student-run art gallery). There is an active gay community that has been known to bump heads with the administration, but a senior laments "the surprisingly small activist community." Hot issues include recent student expulsions ("It takes a lot to be expelled from Sarah Lawrence," a junior explains) and the administration's toughening stance on drugs.

"We aren't a very athletic bunch at Sarah Lawrence," a junior confesses, "although I think the introduction of the new sports center three or four years ago has begun to change that. We got our first men's basketball team the year before last and that was pretty exciting." Gym classes include fencing, karate, kickboxing, and belly-dancing, and "people have even been rumored to have gotten gym credit for smoking cessation."

"Friendliness isn't the first thing that comes to mind when I think of Sarah Lawrence," a junior muses. "It's just that I think we were all the nerds and freaks in high school and that can make people sort of awkward or reclusive." A senior lambastes the "stifling on-campus social scene," adding, "in the winter no one talks to anyone else." Also: "Ethnic diversity is not a strong point; my first year, there was one male Asian student." The male student population remains steady at 25 percent. A junior calls the typical SLC student "a middle to upper-middle class white female with leftist politics and a vegetarian diet." But a senior warns: "A student that desperately wants to 'fit in' will not fit in here. You have to be comfortable with whomever you are or you will drown."

Other schools to check out: Smith, Vassar, Reed, Oberlin, Hampshire, Bard.

HS Rank of Entering Freshmen:
Top 10%: 36%
Top 25%: 77%
Top 50%: 97%

Costs (2004–5)

Tuition and Fees: $32,416

Room & Board: $10,918

Payment Plan(s): installment plan, pre-payment plan

THE EXPERTS SAY...

" Where else outside of Oxford do you get a don? Close personal guidance from professors makes all that SLC academic freedom more manageable. "

" Sarah Lawrence men secretly want to go to a school named 'Max Lawrence.' "

Inst. Aid (est. 2003–04)

Institutional Aid, Need-Based: $10,724,715

Institutional Aid, Non-Need-Based: $9,000

FT Undergrads Receiving Aid: 49%
Avg. Amount per Student: $25,826

FT Undergrads Receiving Non-Need-Based Scholarship or Grant Aid: 12%
Avg. Amount per Student: $6,418

Of Those Receiving Any Aid:

Rec. Need-Based Scholarship or Grant Aid: 100%
Average Award: $21,014

Rec. Need-Based Self-Help Aid: 99%
Average Award: $4,738

Upon Graduation, Avg. Loan Debt per Student: $15,023

Financial Aid Deadline: 2/1, 2/1 (priority)

Graduates

Going to Graduate School: 10% Within One Year

Accepting Job Offer: 5% at time of graduation

Alumni Giving: 35%

SCRIPPS COLLEGE

1030 Columbia Avenue, Claremont, CA 91711
Admissions Phone: (909) 621-8149; (800) 770-1333 Fax: (909) 607-7508
Email: admission@scrippscollege.edu
Website: www.scrippscollege.edu

General Info

Type of School: private, all women

Setting: suburban

Academic Calendar: semester

Student Body

Full-Time Undergrads (2002): 805
  Women: 100%

Part-Time Undergrads (2002): 5
  Women: 100%

Total Undergrad Population (2002):
  African American: 3%
  Asian American: 13%
  Latino: 5%
  Native American: <1%
  Caucasian: 61%
  International: 2%
  Out-of-State: 56%
  Living Off-Campus: 4%

Graduate and First-Professional
Students (2002): 15

Academics

Full-Time Faculty: 61
  With Ph.D.: 97%

Part-Time Faculty: 28
  With Ph.D.: 68%

Student/Faculty Ratio: 11:1

Most Popular Majors:
  politics and international relations
  (11%)
  psychology (10%)
  studio art (10%)
  biology (7%)
  English (4%)

Freshmen Retention Rate: 94%

Graduation Rates:
  76% within four years
  79% within six years

Admissions

Regular Application Deadline: 2/1

Early Decision Deadline(s): 11/1,
1/1

Fall Transfer Deadline: 4/1

Spring Transfer Deadline: 11/15

Total # of Students Applied: 1,378
  Admitted: 747
  Enrolled: 210

# of Students Waitlisted: 287
  Students Accepting Place: 119
  Waitlisted Students Admitted: 8

Inside the Classroom

For the woman who wants to attend an all-women's school within a coed surrounding, Scripps might be just the place: As part of the acclaimed Claremont College system, students can freely take courses, use the facilities, and attend social activities at the four other schools—Pomona, Harvey Mudd, Pitzer, and Claremont McKenna.

Some of Scripps' strongest programs include those in the humanities and interdisciplinary programs such as women's studies. The three-semester Core in Interdisciplinary Humanities ("the Core") is considered to be one of the most progressive, interesting, and rigorous programs at the Claremont Colleges. All students must also complete a senior thesis, project, or recital in their major.

The overall atmosphere on campus is, as one sophomore says, "democratic, moderately competitive, generally warm, and safe." Classes average around 18 students. One student tells us, "The small size of the classes forces you to participate and do the work, and really, to understand." In addition to their close interaction with students in classes, professors are available for extra help and guidance. The workload can be heavy: "I feel like I have more work from my classes at Scripps than from my classes at other Claremont Colleges," says a junior. At the same time, there isn't a sense of competitiveness here, because Scripps breeds the attitude that students are here for themselves, not to see what kind of grades they get. This junior goes on to say that "it's kind of an unspoken rule to not talk about grades. We talk about it only in the vaguest sense."

By and large, the students are happy with the administration, though some have had some bad experiences with the financial aid office. "It gives students a decent financial aid package so they'll come to the school, but then drastically cuts funding each year after that," says one student.

Campus Environment

Although the five Claremont colleges are right on top of each other, they're surprisingly distinct. The Scripps campus, with Spanish Mediterranean architecture and Southern California greenery, is "absolutely one of the most beautiful college campuses around, and it breeds a sense of friendliness and serenity."

The eight residential houses are the center of the social life here. Students say that the residences are among the nicest features at Scripps. As one student says, "Some rooms are better than others, but they're still superior to other schools. Some students have rooms with balconies or French doors. Others have singles with their own bathroom. Some of the residence halls are breathtaking." All freshmen are required to live on campus, and most students remain in the residential houses until they graduate. In fact, you must get permission to live off campus.

Scripps is also the lead college in the consortium for the instruction of music and music performance. With a newly received gift of $7 million, the school was able to build a performing arts center. And as the home to the European Union Center of

California, students can meet many international political figures and conduct internships.

An hour from Los Angeles, the town of Claremont is an idyllic community, though one student feels "it attempts to be an eastern college town. Most places in town close at 5:00 p.m. and Claremont itself if pretty conservative, meaning it tries to shut down parties early and such." Students at Scripps are far from isolated; even if they tire of attending social events at the other Claremont schools, they can easily escape to the beaches, ski resorts, and other California schools nearby.

Student Life

A Hawaii guidance counselor observes that Scripps gives "a woman's attention to the well-being of others." Each first-year student is assigned a Peer Mentor, usually a sophomore, who will help her transition into the Scripps community. Incoming freshmen can also attend Outdoor Orientation, a hiking trip that allows them to get to know fellow students before the school year begins.

Scripps women are generally liberal and outspoken about political issues, particularly feminism and multiculturalism. One student cautions, "If someone is strongly against feminism, she might have difficulty here, because so many women are outspoken about feminist ideas here." One student commented, however, that Scripps "wasn't as feminist as I thought it would be. Not at all radical, although certainly not conservative, either." The school boasts a large number of minority students as well as a surprising percentage of out-of-state students. We're told that Republican groups on campus aren't very popular, unlike the National Organization for Women.

Some have complained that the school doesn't fully recognize the needs of women of color. When the Asian American Student Union office, historically funded by the Dean of Students office, was eliminated for consolidation purposes, there were strong protests. As a result of these controversies, the administration has tried to seriously address diversity issues, and to date things are improving. In fact, because of these efforts, the administration is now sensitive about "students accusing it of not listening to those of different cultures," according to one student.

As for the quality of the social life, one student calls it "average, but improving." Another describes it as "not very exciting." For social events, many head over to the other Claremont schools. While some students complain about the lack of social opportunities on their own campus, others seem to enjoy the separation between their studies on campus and social lives off campus. While many of the activities involve students from all of the Claremont colleges, Scripps does have its own student newspaper, literary magazine, and other organizations.

Scripps athletic programs take place, for the most part, in conjunction with Claremont McKenna and Harvey Mudd Colleges. While many students do engage in sports here, athletics are not the most popular activity. We're told that "the pool is gorgeous," and the school is building a new full-service athletic center. And the trademark Scripps tradition of the "weekly tea," unbroken since the founding of the college, brings together students, staff, and faculty for informal discussions.

Other schools to check out: Claremont McKenna, Mills, Mount Holyoke, Wellesley, Bryn Mawr, Smith.

Applied Early Decision: 81
 Early Decision Admitted: 47

Test Scores (middle 50%):
 SAT Verbal: 620–710
 SAT Math: 610–690
 ACT Comp: 28–31

HS Rank of Entering Freshmen:
 Top 10%: 67%
 Top 25%: 93%
 Top 50%: 100%

Avg. HS GPA: 3.9

THE EXPERTS SAY...

" As part of the Claremont system, Scripps students have the advantages of an all-women's school, but can cross-register at Pomona, Harvey Mudd, Pitzer, and Claremont McKenna. "

" If these feminists are too demure for your tastes, check out the more liberal Bryn Mawr, Smith, and Wellesley. "

Costs (2003–04)

Tuition and Fees: $27,100

Room & Board: $8,600

Payment Plan(s): installment plan

Inst. Aid (2002–03)

Institutional Aid, Need-Based:
 $5,694,417

Institutional Aid, Non-Need-Based:
 $764,157

FT Undergrads Receiving Aid: 49%
 Avg. Amount per Student: $23,861

FT Undergrads Receiving Non-Need-Based Scholarship or Grant Aid: 8%
 Avg. Amount per Student: $12,790

Of Those Receiving Any Aid:

Rec. Need-Based Scholarship or Grant Aid: 99%
 Average Award: $18,691

Rec. Need-Based Self-Help Aid: 93%
 Average Award: $5,170

Upon Graduation, Avg. Loan Debt per Student: $14,362

Financial Aid Deadline: rolling, 2/1 (priority)

Graduates

Going to Graduate School:
 39% Within One Year

Accepting Job Offer:
 31% at time of graduation

Companies Recruiting On Campus:
 480

Alumni Giving: 88%

SIMMONS COLLEGE

300 The Fenway, Boston, MA 02115
Admissions Phone: (617) 521-2051; (800) 345-8468 Fax: (617) 521-3190
Email: ugadm@simmons.edu
Website: www.simmons.edu

General Info

Type of School: private, all women

Setting: urban

Academic Calendar: semester

Student Body

Full-Time Undergrads: 1,090
  Women: 100%

Part-Time Undergrads: 134
  Women: 100%

Total Undergrad Population:
  African American: 7%
  Asian American: 6%
  Latino: 3%
  Native American: <1%
  Caucasian: 71%
  International: 4%
  Out-of-State: 43%
  Living Off-Campus: 41%

Graduate and First-Professional
  Students: 2,116

Academics

Full-Time Faculty: 175
  With Ph.D.: 65%

Part-Time Faculty: 176

Student/Faculty Ratio: 12:1

Most Popular Majors:
  psychology (8%)
  nursing (8%)
  English (6%)
  communication (5%)
  health/pt (5%)

Freshmen Retention Rate: 82%

Graduation Rates:
  70% within four years
  72% within six years

Admissions

Regular Application Deadline: 2/2

Early Action Deadline: 12/1

Total # of Students Applied: 1,704
  Admitted: 1,158
  Enrolled: 298

# of Students Waitlisted: 59
  Students Accepting Place: 34
  Waitlisted Students Admitted: 26

Test Scores (middle 50%):
  SAT Verbal: 500–600
  SAT Math: 490–590
  ACT Comp: 19–25

Inside the Classroom

Simmons College is a small, private school located in the king of all college towns, Boston. It is all-female (though the grad school is open to men) and offers a liberal arts-based education with a decidedly professional influence: The school was founded by a tailor, so vocational training was a priority right from the get-go. Simmons graduates are well-rounded at the end of their four years of study, and they leave campus ready for the real world. All of this takes quite an effort, though, and as one student puts it, "You have to outdo yourself every day."

Nursing is a clear favorite among Simmons majors, with English, psychology, and physical therapy vying for a distant second. Preprofessional tracks are strong here, with programs in law, medicine, veterinary science, pharmacy, and dentistry available to students. Dozens of other majors include foreign languages, area studies, management, education, liberal arts, mathematics, social sciences, and women's studies. Practical majors like graphic design and retail management are also offered.

The 12:1 student-faculty ratio at Simmons means that small-group learning is valued here; no student is just a number. The approach seems to be working, given the school's 82 percent freshman retention rate. "If you want a positive and encouraging atmosphere, then choose Simmons," says one student.

Special programs include an honors program, a study abroad program in Spain, and some undergrad-to-grad programs for students wishing to earn their masters at Simmons. The honors program is particularly worthy of distinction: Its curriculum includes a first-year multidisciplinary course that emphasizes intensive writing; a sophomore interdisciplinary seminar; a junior-year 300-level, advanced course in the student's area of specialization; and a senior-year independent project.

Adding a great deal of value to the Simmons experience is the school's membership in the Fenway Colleges Consortium. If you can't find a course you want at Simmons, you can cross-register at consortium member schools, which include Emmanuel College, Hebrew College, the New England Conservatory of Music, and Wheelock College.

Campus Environment

The campus at Simmons is divided into two subcampuses located about a block from each other in the city. The residence campus contains the nine residence halls, the dining hall for resident students, the campus health center, the Holmes Sports Center, and Alumnae Hall. The main campus holds all of the academic buildings. Both campuses are designed to feel like a small-town college, complete with a manicured-grass quadrangle.

Most first-year students live in South, Arnold, Smith, and Dix Halls, which also house transfer students. Some undergraduates also live on the first floor of Simmons Hall, which is otherwise a residence for grad students. The coveted Evans Hall is a senior-only dorm. Lifestyle options for all students include quiet floors, limited visitation floors, wellness areas, and South Hall's smoke-free environment.

The Park Science Center is where science students spend most of their time. This large, well-equipped building features classrooms, more than 50 laboratories, a molecular biology lab, faculty and student research facilities, and a nuclear magnetic resonance spectrometer. In addition, the Park Science Center is home to Simmons' Technology Resource Center. All non-science classes are held in the Main College Building (MCB), which also contains the Trustman Art Gallery, art studios, music practice rooms, the college bookstore, and the Fens Cafeteria. The MCB is also the location of the new College Center, which provides students with community gathering space, a coffee bar, and high-technology classrooms. The Beatley Library is right next door to the MCB; it has about 300,000 books lining its shelves and tries to acquire about 5,000 new books each year. The library is also the site of the campus media center, the career resource library, and computer lab classrooms.

Meeting people of the opposite sex is often a problem at single-sex colleges, but Simmons students have the good fortune of living in the heart of the country's premier college town, Boston. With its excellent public transportation system, the city beckons as a place where shopping, entertainment, dining, and having a good time are all minutes away. One student said that living in the campus dormitories is the perfect best-of-both-worlds arrangement, since the campus is a refuge from the city, and vice versa. The school is located within easy walking distance of Boston's Museum of Fine Arts and—for an occasional baseball game—Fenway Park.

Student Life

Going to school in an all-women environment is a supportive experience for students, and many appreciate the respite from male competitiveness that they will face after graduation. "I can do anything that I want to," says one student. "I know I'm just as good as the next person, and if I work hard, I know I can succeed."

Simmons's eight varsity teams include basketball, crew, field hockey, soccer, softball, swimming, diving, tennis, and volleyball. Painted on a wall of the athletic complex are the words, "Even on land you can be attacked by Sharks," and the nervousness of Simmons's opponents is justified since the school actively recruits players. Tennis, field hockey, and volleyball are perennial Division III standouts.

Given the school's Boston locale, it should not surprise you that tea plays an important role at Simmons: Once a week, resident students gather in their living rooms to socialize, listen to guest speakers, meet with faculty on an informal basis, and, of course, drink tea. Other Simmons traditions: Women's Legacy Weekend, held during the Fall semester for seniors and the influential women in their lives; and Tribute Weekend, held at the beginning of the second semester for sophomores and seniors and their fathers or other special male role models.

Other schools to check out: Wheaton (MA), Chatham, Hollins, Mills.

HS Rank of Entering Freshmen:
Top 10%: 24%
Top 25%: 56%
Top 50%: 88%
Avg. HS GPA: 3.13

Costs (2003–04)

Tuition and Fees: $23,550

Room & Board: $9,450

Payment Plan(s): deferred payment plan

THE EXPERTS SAY...

" Simmons is a proving ground for tomorrow's professional leaders. "

" A New England women's school without the snootiness (or, unfortunately, the national reputation) of the Seven Sisters. "

Inst. Aid (2002–03)

Institutional Aid, Need-Based: $7,852,200

Institutional Aid, Non-Need-Based: $441,625

FT Undergrads Receiving Aid: 66% Avg. Amount per Student: $16,119

FT Undergrads Receiving Non-Need-Based Scholarship or Grant Aid: 3% Avg. Amount per Student: $10,216

Of Those Receiving Any Aid:

Rec. Need-Based Scholarship or Grant Aid: 95% Average Award: $12,136

Rec. Need-Based Self-Help Aid: 89% Average Award: $1,735

Upon Graduation, Avg. Loan Debt per Student: $19,970

Financial Aid Deadline: 3/1 (priority)

SKIDMORE COLLEGE

815 North Broadway, Saratoga Springs, NY 12866
Admissions Phone: (800) 867-6007; (518) 580-5570 Fax: (518) 580-5584
Email: admissions@skidmore.edu
Website: www.skidmore.edu

General Info

Type of School: private, coed

Setting: small town

Academic Calendar: semester

Student Body

Full-Time Undergrads: 2,286
  Men: 42%, Women: 58%

Part-Time Undergrads: 246
  Men: 33%, Women: 67%

Total Undergrad Population:
  African American: 3%
  Asian American: 5%
  Latino: 4%
  Native American: 1%
  Caucasian: 72%
  International: 1%
  Out-of-State: 70%
  Living Off-Campus: 23%

Graduate and First-Professional
  Students: 52

Academics

Full-Time Faculty: 193
  With Ph.D.: 85%

Part-Time Faculty: 8
  With Ph.D.: 63%

Student/Faculty Ratio: 11:1

Most Popular Majors:
  business (.13%)
  English (10%)
  art (9%)
  psychology (8%)
  government (6%)

Completing 2 or More Majors: 13%

Freshmen Retention Rate: 90%

Graduation Rates:
  75% within four years
  80% within six years

Admissions

Regular Application Deadline: 1/15

Early Decision Deadline(s): 12/1,
  1/15

Fall Transfer Deadline: 4/1

Spring Transfer Deadline: 11/15

Total # of Students Applied: 5,903
  Admitted: 2,724
  Enrolled: 642

# of Students Waitlisted: 901
  Students Accepting Place: 308
  Waitlisted Students Admitted: 101

Inside the Classroom

"Skidmore's curriculum emphasizes integrative learning and breadth," states a college official. Taking a heavily interdisciplinary approach, the curriculum encourages students to bring a global perspective to their studies and to make connections between subjects. "I got a true liberal arts experience at Skidmore," states a proud alumna. "I came into the 'real world' with a broad variety of experiences, from theater to physics to constitutional law to a semester abroad."

Students can choose from more than 60 majors, both in the traditional liberal arts and in preprofessional fields. The all-college requirements, which make up roughly one-third of a student's coursework, include the following: expository writing and quantitative reasoning; natural sciences, social sciences, arts, humanities, and culture-centered inquiry; and interdisciplinary study, beginning with the College's signature course, "Liberal Studies 1: The Human Experience," taken by all first-year students and team-taught by some 25 faculty members from across the disciplines. "The school really gives students the ability to pursue a variety of interests," confirms a recent grad. "I came to Skidmore determined to do theater, but through a variety of electives and their unique liberal studies program, I developed a true interest in politics, and graduated with a double major in theater and government." (However, one Massachusetts guidance counselor frets that Skidmore places too much of an emphasis on the arts and not enough on science and engineering.)

Each year, Skidmore sponsors a Summer Collaborative Research Program for faculty-student research teams that often leads to published papers, artistic exhibits, or presentations at professional conferences. A college official stresses, "Students are junior colleagues, not research assistants." Teams are selected based on proposals, and a broad range of disciplines is represented each year.

By the time they graduate, more than half of Skidmore's students will have taken advantage of an internship. The Office of Career Services maintains an online library of internship opportunities, and you can apply to take the introductory course, "Exploration Internship," as well as more advanced professional internship courses in many departments. Internships are available in a range of employment sectors, including government, industry, banking, publishing, law, the media, and the arts.

Campus Environment

The 850-acre Skidmore campus offers striking views of the Adirondack mountains, plenty of flowers and trees, and its own pond. All students may have cars on campus: "Vehicles must be registered, but there are no fees for registration or parking," states the college. "There is a bus that runs hourly to downtown Saratoga," an alum tells us, "but once it's moderately warm out, it's a great 15 minute walk from campus to the heart of town." Saratoga Springs, known for its racetrack, is "a fun, hip town full of great shopping, eating, and clubbing," says one student.

There are no freshman dorms; new students are assigned housing and roommates based on date of enrollment deposit, housing questionnaire, and space available. Theme housing includes a substance-free floor and a multicultural floor. All full-time students are required to live on campus except for seniors and a limited number of juniors who receive permission through the off-campus room-drawing process. Many upperclass students choose Skidmore's on-campus apartments in Scribner Village, or else move to nearby off-campus apartments.

The college's and the city's first art museum, the Tang Teaching Museum and Art Gallery, opened on campus in fall 2000. Fall 2001 marked the debut of the newly renovated and expanded Case Center, bringing under one roof offices for student government and organizations, an intercultural center, snack bar, post office, book store, campus information desk, and cybercafé.

Approximately 1,000 students work through the Student Employment Program each year, either in Federal Work Study or Skidmore Work Study jobs. "First-year students accepting a full work award are assigned to essential college services such as food service," says a college official. "Upperclass students may work in any area of the college offering student employment—admissions, the library, the computer center, academic and administrative departments, and more—and those on Federal Work Study are eligible for community service placements as well."

Student Life

According to the college, Skidmore students tend to be "intellectually curious and open-minded, with a strong sense of initiative and concern for others." Praising the college's nurturing, relaxed atmosphere, an alum says that "Skidmore is the perfect school for students who are creative and eager to learn, but are intimidated, perhaps, by their own potential." Skidmore's laid-back atmosphere is evident even in the students' choice of attire. "Clothing-wise, you have a small group of rather overdressed trendy girls, but other than that, everyone is in jeans," explains a former student. "You very often see students in early morning classes in pajama pants and baseball caps." While most students are from out-of-state, a total of 85 percent are from the Northeast.

The party scene at Skidmore is pretty tame: There's no Greek system and no football, for starters. A student tells us, "Mostly, underclassmen hang out in the dorms or go to parties in other students' apartments." (A warning for prospective freshmen: We hear that while a few bars are lax about IDs, for most you really do have to be 21.) Upperclassmen usually hang out in downtown bars rather than on campus.

Skidmore has its own thriving cultural scene; among the school's many clubs and activities, artistic and performing groups abound, including several high quality singing and theater groups. Major campus events often feature live music by such well-known artists as George Clinton, G-Love, and Blues Traveler.

Among the school traditions are annual theme weekends organized by each of the four classes: Oktoberfest (seniors), Junior Ring Weekend (juniors), Winter Carnival (sophomores), and Spring Fling (freshmen). And Skidmore's Ultimate Frisbee team has a unique tradition, as well: a nude, coed frisbee tournament!

Other schools to check out: Connecticut College, Vassar, Hamilton, Muhlenberg, Colgate, Middlebury.

\# Applied Early Decision: 383
Early Decision Admitted: 223

Test Scores (middle 50%):
SAT Verbal: 580–670
SAT Math: 590–670
ACT Comp: 25–29

HS Rank of Entering Freshmen:
Top 10%: 38%
Top 25%: 75%
Top 50%: 97%

Avg. HS GPA: 3.29

THE EXPERTS SAY...

" Each summer, Skidmore offers a 5-week liberal arts program for high school juniors and seniors—a great way to sample the campus and the academics (and get college credit!). "

" For a college that pushes a 'global perspective,' the student body isn't very diverse. You might learn more by actually interacting with people who are different from you. "

Costs (2003–04)

Tuition and Fees: $29,630

Room & Board: $8,300

Payment Plan(s): installment plan, pre-payment plan

Inst. Aid (est. 2003–04)

Institutional Aid, Need-Based: $15,326,908

Institutional Aid, Non-Need-Based: $310,000

FT Undergrads Receiving Aid: 42%
Avg. Amount per Student: $24,114

FT Undergrads Receiving Non-Need-Based Scholarship or Grant Aid: 1%
Avg. Amount per Student: $10,000

Of Those Receiving Any Aid:

Rec. Need-Based Scholarship or Grant Aid: 100%
Average Award: $18,765

Rec. Need-Based Self-Help Aid: 100%
Average Award: $5,349

Upon Graduation, Avg. Loan Debt per Student: $16,228

Financial Aid Deadline: 1/15

Graduates

Going to Graduate School:
16% Within One Year

Alumni Giving: 43%

SMITH COLLEGE

7 College Lane, Northampton, MA 01063
Admissions Phone: (413) 585-2500 Fax: (413) 585-2527
Email: admission@smith.edu Website: www.smith.edu
Application Website: www.smith.edu/admission

General Info

Type of School: private, all women

Setting: small town

Academic Calendar: semester

Student Body

Full-Time Undergrads: 2,641
 Women: 100%

Part-Time Undergrads: 41
 Women: 100%

Total Undergrad Population:
 African American: 6%
 Asian American: 10%
 Latino: 6%
 Native American: 1%
 Caucasian: 55%
 International: 7%
 Out-of-State: 76%
 Living Off-Campus: 12%

Graduate and First-Professional
 Students: 477

Academics

Full-Time Faculty: 285
 With Ph.D.: 95%

Part-Time Faculty: 20
 With Ph.D.: 95%

Student/Faculty Ratio: 9:1

Most Popular Majors:
 government (11%)
 economics (8%)
 psychology (8%)
 English (6%)
 biology (5%)

Completing 2 or More Majors: 16%

Freshmen Retention Rate: 92%

Graduation Rates:
 80% within four years
 86% within six years

Admissions

Regular Application Deadline: 1/15

Early Decision Deadline(s): 11/15,
 1/2

Fall Transfer Deadline: 6/1, 2/1
 (priority)

Spring Transfer Deadline: 11/15

Total # of Students Applied: 3,304
 Admitted: 1,705
 Enrolled: 635

Inside the Classroom

Smith has long been one of the most highly respected women's colleges in the United States. Alumnae—such as Sylvia Plath, Betty Friedan, Gloria Steinem, and Barbara Bush—come away not only with an outstanding liberal arts education, but also with a real sense of empowerment. It's not surprising to hear from students that, at Smith, "politics are always on the forefront—in the classroom and on campus."

With 45 majors and more than 50 minors from which to choose, students work closely with "extremely accessible" faculty advisers to create a course of study that suits their own academic goals. There is no core curriculum, as Smith believes in providing students with the freedom to discover their own talents and abilities. However, first-year students must take a writing-intensive course, chosen from a number of options. The honor code, which permits students to schedule their own examinations, further fosters maturity and self-reliance.

The average class size at Smith is 15 students, and many upper-level courses and labs reportedly have as few as 5 students. "The level of competitiveness varies according to department (higher in the sciences) but is overall very low," claims a senior. The workload, a student warns us, is "very, very difficult," but serves as "preparation for anything you choose to do in the future." Another student insists, "The amount of work and reading assigned surpasses that at most other schools of similar caliber." While Smithies who choose a preprofessional track are well prepared for careers or grad school, Smith women also recognize the value of learning as an end in itself: Classroom debates frequently carry over to informal discussions with professors and fellow students outside of class.

More than 75 percent of Smith students participate in internships, including the Semester-in-Washington and the Smithsonian Internship programs. The unique Praxis program offers students a paid stipend to fund summer internships. STRIDE (Student Research in Departments) offers top first- and second-year students the opportunity to become paid research assistants to Smith professors. About 30 percent of each junior class studies abroad, often in Smith's own programs in Florence, Geneva, Hamburg, or Paris. Smithies also have the option of taking up to half their classes at Amherst, Hampshire, Mount Holyoke, and the University of Massachusetts at Amherst, which are all connected by shuttle bus.

Campus Environment

Smith's unique housing system plays a key role in students' social lives. Students are assigned to one of 35 self-governing houses, each with its own living room, fireplace, piano, dining room, and kitchen. "The houses are gorgeous for the most part, and extremely comfortable," says a student. All four classes are housed together, providing a sense of family among the residents. "During the week, most people attempt to do work but are most often distracted—in the best and most healthy of ways—by house community." Traditions associated with Smith houses include Thursday night candlelight dinner and Friday afternoon tea.

First-year students aren't allowed to have cars on campus, and limited parking discourages most other students from having cars, but the free Five College bus service "can get you almost anywhere you need to go" (though students complain that "it doesn't go all night"). The town of Northampton provides a nice respite from campus life, with restaurants, cafés, and movie theaters all within walking distance of campus. "Northampton is an amazing city to live in," says one student. "Art, dining, theater, etc. is all very much alive despite its size. It's a very safe place to be."

Student Life

Smith isn't a heavy-duty party school ("drinking is common, but drinking to excess is not"); those looking to meet men or party hearty might find things slow on campus until the weekends, when many students travel to parties at nearby schools or welcome visitors. "On weekends there are parties but, as those tend to get boring, hanging out in smaller groups to drink, etc., is more popular," says a student.

But there are enough clubs, organizations, and extracurricular activities, as well as on-campus cultural events, to keep everyone but the most diehard party freaks happy. Some of the most popular clubs are the community service organizations, varsity crew, intramurals, the Outdoors Club, the Debate Society, and *The Sophian* (the student newspaper). Smith offers 14 varsity sports, in which a total of 300–400 students compete. "Rugby and crew are extremely popular," a student tells us.

The student body has become more mixed in terms of class, religion, and ethnicity; the Asian American population, in particular, is growing. Students and administrators are committed to creating an environment in which differences are valued and respected. The lesbian community, for example, is visible and accepted. "You won't find a more progressive or tolerant atmosphere," a senior tells us. Most students are very liberal, proud to be PC, and outspoken about many topical issues, particularly feminism. However, some students complain that this liberal environment can feel oppressive and isn't conducive to real discourse, as it stifles opposing opinion. But "there are *so* many different forums for debate that this is hardly the case," retorts one student, who believes that conservatives "might feel a little displaced and disempowered" simply because they "are not in the majority, as they are in the larger society."

Other schools to check out: Wellesley, Bryn Mawr, Mount Holyoke, Vassar, Barnard.

# of Students Waitlisted: 311
  Students Accepting Place: 133
  Waitlisted Students Admitted: 42

Applied Early Decision: 211
  Early Decision Admitted: 152

Test Scores (middle 50%):
  SAT Verbal: 580–700
  SAT Math: 570–670
  ACT Comp: 25–30
  ACT English: 25–31
  ACT Math: 23–28
  (Average Test Scores Represent Applicants)

HS Rank of Entering Freshmen:
  Top 10%: 59%
  Top 25%: 88%
  Top 50%: 99%

Avg. HS GPA: 3.8

THE EXPERTS SAY...

" In February 1999, Smith launched the Picker Program in Engineering and Technology, the first engineering program at a women's college. "

" Sylvia Plath, Betty Friedan, Gloria Steinem—do you sense a pattern here? Smith produces strong women with great minds. "

Costs (2003–04)

Tuition and Fees: $25,986

Room & Board: $8,950

Payment Plan(s): installment plan, pre-payment plan

Inst. Aid (est. 2003–04)

FT Undergrads Receiving Aid: 56%
  Avg. Amount per Student: $27,378

FT Undergrads Receiving Non-Need-Based Scholarship or Grant Aid: 4%
  Avg. Amount per Student: $8,943

Of Those Receiving Any Aid:

Rec. Need-Based Scholarship or Grant Aid: 100%
  Average Award: $20,988

Rec. Need-Based Self-Help Aid: 100%
  Average Award: $6,390

Upon Graduation, Avg. Loan Debt per Student: $20,570

Financial Aid Deadline: 2/1

Graduates

Companies Recruiting On-Campus: 45

Alumni Giving: 64%

SOUTHERN METHODIST UNIVERSITY

P.O. Box 750221, Dallas, TX 75275-0221
Admissions Phone: (214) 768-2058; (800) 323-0672 Fax: (214) 768-0202
Email: enrol_serv@mail.smu.edu Website: www.smu.edu Application Website: smu.edu/apply

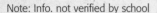

Note: Info. not verified by school

General Info

Type of School: private, coed, Methodist

Setting: suburban

Academic Calendar: semester

Student Body

Full-Time Undergrads: 5,798
 Men: 47%, Women: 53%

Part-Time Undergrads: 228
 Men: 46%, Women: 54%

Total Undergrad Population:
 African American: 6%
 Asian American: 6%
 Latino: 8%
 Native American: 1%
 Caucasian: 74%
 International: 5%
 Out-of-State: 36%
 Living Off-Campus: 52%
 In Fraternities: 37%
 In Sororities: 38%

Graduate and First-Professional
 Students: 4,745

Academics

Full-Time Faculty: 535
 With Ph.D.: 84%

Part-Time Faculty: 241

Student/Faculty Ratio: 12:1

Most Popular Majors:
 business (6%)
 finance (6%)
 psychology (6%)
 advertising (5%)
 political science (5%)

Freshmen Retention Rate: 86%

Graduation Rates:
 56% within four years
 70% within six years

Admissions

Regular Application Deadline: 1/15

Early Action Deadline: 11/1

Fall Transfer Deadline: 6/1 (priority)

Spring Transfer Deadline: 11/1
 (priority)

Total # of Students Applied: 6,152
 Admitted: 4,059
 Enrolled: 1,380

Inside the Classroom

SMU has four undergraduate schools: business and management, engineering and applied science, humanities and science, and fine arts. Most students are on a preprofessional track, and the undergraduate schools offer strong programs in several areas that prepare students for career success, particularly in the highly rated school of business and management. Considered one of the best schools in the country for performing and theater arts, the Meadows School of Art utilizes first-rate facilities, including the Bob Hope Theater and an art museum that boasts a fine collection of Goya's works. The English, history, natural sciences, and psychology departments at Dedman College, the liberal arts school, are also excellent. A junior says, "If you're majoring in the humanities expect an easy workload. Premed is quite competitive and difficult, as is the business school."

Overall, SMU has "very high standards," stresses a Louisiana guidance counselor. A recent grad states that "an unmotivated student" might not fit in at SMU because he or she "would get lost in the hustle and bustle of a fast-paced learning environment."

SMU's curriculum is designed to accommodate students' individual interests within structural guidelines. Students take specific classes, such as writing seminars and courses in race, ethnicity and gender, as well as longer sequences in their chosen disciplines. One unusual school feature: Most students are required to include a liberal arts minor in addition to their major field of study. There are several academic options available to qualified students, including dual degrees, interdisciplinary majors, self-designed majors, study abroad, and even field work at the school's New Mexico campus. Dallas offers students many opportunities to gain work experience and find internships.

Since SMU is not a terribly large university, it offers a "small classroom environment" typically with 25–30 students, and interaction with professors is easy. One student says, "Professors are extremely nice, personable, and truly care about your well being, not only as a student but as a person. Plus most come from Ivy schools and are leaders in their respective fields of research." Students are also proud of the school's long list of famous alumni. "Aaron Spelling graduated from here! And Laura Bush. So did Kathy Bates and the guy that started '7 Eleven.'" The list also includes Pulitzer Prize-winning playwright Beth Henley, four of the seven justices on the Supreme Court of Texas, and Robert Dennard, inventor of the dynamic random access memory chip (RAM) used in virtually every computer in the world.

Campus Environment

SMU offers a beautiful, traditionally collegiate campus that is ten minutes from downtown Dallas. Students have good things to say about their pretty, tree-lined campus, with its Georgian and Jeffersonian architecture. One student raves, "The architecture and the layout of campus are just beautiful." SMU invests a lot of its endowment into the school, both in maintaining the immaculate campus and facilities as well as constructing additions.

All freshmen must live in one of the 14 residence halls on campus, many of which have a festive, party atmosphere. A recent grad tells us, "The dorms are extremely nice—all renovated within the last five years." The campus is described as very safe: "It is landlocked and well-lit. It is a beautiful place to call home!" Another student says, "The campus is beautiful and in one of the safest (and richest) cities in the U.S."

Most upperclassmen move off-campus to fraternity or sorority houses or to area apartments. Because the school is located in an affluent suburb, however, off-campus housing can be expensive. An alum tells us, "The apartments/houses are very nice and close in proximity—however, they are very expensive because the Highland Park area is typically exclusive."

Students generally feel that having a car makes life easier in Dallas. "Definitely need a car," one junior agrees. "Public transportation is horrible and not very accessible in Dallas." Public transportation is available, though, in the form of DART (Dallas Area Rapid Transit) at no cost to students, and Mustang Express, the school's shuttle bus service.

Student Life

SMU welcomes students from all 50 states and over 100 countries. Students have all of Dallas as their playground, giving them lots of opportunities for clubbing and bar hopping. "There are lots of coffeehouses, theaters around town, Dallas-area professional sporting events, as well as good restaurants/bars," says one student. A student says, "Dallas is always awake...there are scenic areas, beautiful homes, crowded streets, and great restaurants. I love living in Dallas for four years." Another students shares the sentiment, saying, "Every Dallasite respects SMU because of the prestige and money associated with students/alums."

SMU offers more than 150 student organizations; a recent grad tells us that "students are *very* programmed at SMU—so after classes people were generally in some type of meeting or club." More than one-third of students join frats or sororities. One student says, "If you're not into the Greek scene or don't have any friends that are Greek, expect on Thursday, Friday, Saturday, and Sunday to be in a library or surfing the net.... [Greeks] have all the major parties plus all the 'cool' people are in them." Another student disagrees, saying, "For the crowd that joins, they are very influential. For those who aren't inclined to join, they probably never miss it much." Sports are fairly popular, according to one student, who says, "Intramurals are pretty involved but no one cares about varsity sports unless the teams such as basketball or football are doing well."

One complaint some students have about SMU is that the student population can be homogeneous in certain respects. A junior describes the typical student at SMU as "white" and "rich, beautiful, drives a BMW." He adds that there is an overall atmosphere on campus of "snobs, snobs, and more snobs. Rich elites abound at SMU—detracts from overall diversity. Most are right-wingers in terms of political ideology... It's too much like high school, it's easy to find gossip about anyone on campus." On the flip-side, though, another student says that the average student at SMU is "unique, yet very normal for a college scene," and sums it up by saying, "SMU perfectly balances life, school, growing up, and career advising. It was a great start for the rest of my life."

Other schools to check out: Tulane, Emory, Texas Christian, Baylor, Southwestern.

# of Students Waitlisted: 773
  Students Accepting Place: 353
  Waitlisted Students Admitted: 55

Test Scores (middle 50%):
  SAT Verbal: 540–630
  SAT Math: 550–650
  ACT Comp: 23–28
  ACT English: 23–28
  ACT Math: 23–28

HS Rank of Entering Freshmen:
  Top 10%: 35%
  Top 25%: 65%
  Top 50%: 91%

Avg. HS GPA: 3.48

THE EXPERTS SAY...

" If you plan to live and work in the Dallas area (or anywhere in Texas), you'll surely benefit from SMU's excellent academic reputation and active alumni network. "

" How many SMU students does it take to screw in a lightbulb? None—who needs light when you're having this much fun! "

Costs (2003–04)

Tuition and Fees: $23,588
Room & Board: $8,391

Inst. Aid (est. 2003–04)

Institutional Aid, Need-Based: $23,587,977

Institutional Aid, Non-Need-Based: $9,927,252

FT Undergrads Receiving Aid: 37%
  Avg. Amount per Student: $20,885

FT Undergrads Receiving Non-Need-Based Scholarship or Grant Aid: 33%
  Avg. Amount per Student: $5,033

Of Those Receiving Any Aid:

Rec. Need-Based Scholarship or Grant Aid: 86%
  Average Award: $13,014

Rec. Need-Based Self-Help Aid: 82%
  Average Award: $5,201

Upon Graduation, Avg. Loan Debt per Student: $18,693

Financial Aid Deadline: rolling, 2/1 (priority)

SOUTHWESTERN UNIVERSITY

P.O. Box 770, Georgetown, TX 78626-0770
Admissions Phone: (512) 863-1200; (800) 252-3166 Fax: (512) 863-9601
Email: admission@southwestern.edu Website: www.southwestern.edu
Application Website: www.southwestern.edu/admission-finaid/message-admission.html

General Info

Type of School: private, coed, Methodist

Setting: suburban

Academic Calendar: semester

Student Body

Full-Time Undergrads: 1,237
    Men: 42%, Women: 58%

Part-Time Undergrads: 28
    Men: 39%, Women: 61%

Total Undergrad Population:
    African American: 3%
    Asian American: 4%
    Latino: 14%
    Native American: <1%
    Caucasian: 77%
    Out-of-State: 6%
    Living Off-Campus: 18%
    In Fraternities: 35%
    In Sororities: 33%

Academics

Full-Time Faculty: 114
    With Ph.D.: 88%

Part-Time Faculty: 51
    With Ph.D.: 47%

Student/Faculty Ratio: 10:1

Most Popular Majors:
    communication (10%)
    biology (10%)
    business (10%)
    psychology (10%)
    political science/Spanish (each) (5%)

Completing 2 or More Majors: 17%

Freshmen Retention Rate: 86%

Graduation Rates:
    63% within four years
    74% within six years

Admissions

Regular Application Deadline: 2/15; 1/1 (priority)

Early Decision Deadline(s): 11/1

Fall Transfer Deadline: 6/1, 4/1 (priority)

Spring Transfer Deadline: 11/1, 10/1 (priority)

Total # of Students Applied: 1,765
    Admitted: 1,115
    Enrolled: 343

Inside the Classroom

In Texas, the general attitude has always been "bigger is better." But Southwestern University is one glaring exception to the rule. Unlike its fellow Texas universities, whose student populations are in the tens of thousands, SU is home to about 1,200 students, who become immersed in their liberal arts studies within a friendly environment. "The best thing here," a student told us, "is the intimacy of the campus and the ease with which you can make friends."

Affiliated with the United Methodist Church, Southwestern University is composed of the Brown College of Arts and Sciences and the Sarofim School of Fine Arts. Southwestern is a highly selective university; typically, about half the students admitted were in the top 10 percent of their high school class. Texas guidance counselors don't understand why this university doesn't get more national recognition. Southwestern's liberal arts and science departments are strong across the board, from biology to psychology to music. The preprofessional and interdisciplinary programs are also well regarded, including communication, business, animal behavior, and premed.

The extensive general education requirements encompass nine hours of first-year Foundation courses and 30 hours of Perspectives on Knowledge courses ("POKs"). The general education requirements are intended to help students improve skills that are considered valuable by employers and grad schools, including problem solving, communication, cross-cultural understanding, and global awareness. Freshmen must also take a first-year seminar; a wide range of topics is offered each year.

SU has a large endowment (one of the highest endowments per student in the nation) that goes into maintaining its exceptional facilities, which in turn draw many renowned faculty members. With a student/faculty ratio of only 10:1, students enjoy an intimate academic environment. The school states that its small size gives students the opportunity to "interact with faculty one-to-one, not one-to-many," and that it "fosters the development of an intellectual and social community where students are known for their individuality instead of being just another face in the crowd." One of the more prestigious events associated with Southwestern is the annual Brown Symposium. Every spring, prominent speakers visit the campus for a three-day conference on a particular subject. The Symposium is open to the public without charge, and classes are cancelled so that students may attend.

Campus Environment

There have been many improvements to the campus in the past few years, including the addition of a new campus center, and expanded science and fine arts centers. The school owns 500 acres, including a 100-acre tree-covered academic campus, a 75-acre nine-hole golf course, and 325 additional acres.

First-year students are typically required to live on campus, and are housed in separate men's and women's residence halls. Coed halls and a male-only residence hall are available for upperclassmen, as are the options of suite- and apartment-style housing. While students are permitted to move off campus after their freshman year, the vast majority opt to remain on campus, where they can live in a traditionally collegiate environment and enjoy a central dining location. Each hall develops its own character based on tradition and the personalities of residents, and the school states that "most students develop a strong feeling of affection for their residence hall community."

Southwestern is located in Georgetown ("the *other* Georgetown," a student clarifies), a quiet town with few student hangouts. Students say that although the school and town are safe and friendly, the town offers little to do. As a result, students take advantage of the school's close proximity to Austin, just 30 minutes away by car. Austin has a thriving music and culture scene, as well as the kinds of restaurants, bars, and clubs that cater to young student crowds. Many Southwestern students feel as though they enjoy the best of both worlds; they can head into an exciting city when they want to, and then return to a tranquil, intimate campus.

Student Life

Students find ways to enjoy an active social life on campus. "Because there is so much stress due to the heavy workload, people need an outlet, so there's a lot of 'adult beverage' drinking," a student tells us. The active Greek system drives much of the campus social scene. But there are certainly things to do at Southwestern besides partying.

Southwestern offers more than 100 activities and clubs that are divided into eight general categories: governing bodies, departmental, scholastic/honorary, Greek/social, religious, special interest, sports, and student publications. There are music groups of all kinds, and professional, political, and public service groups, as well as cheerleading, an independent film club, and a club that focuses on deaf culture. The Union Program Council, or UPC, is a student organization that coordinates campus entertainment events; these have included concerts, comedians, films, and lectures. In addition to attending parties and other fraternity and sorority events, students go to smaller and more informal gatherings and attend movies, concerts, and dances on campus.

Southwestern competes at the Division III level and offers seven men's and seven women's sports, several of which are conference champions. Nearly a fifth of SU students participate in athletics, and over half of them manage a 3.0 grade point average. Students also play a number of intramural sports, such as basketball and softball. And the almost year-round warm weather is perfect for outdoor activities, everything from horseback riding, canoeing, and hiking to cycling, camping, and rock climbing. The university offers equipment and programs for outdoor activities at reduced prices, and students can also take advantage of some of Texas's best parks, rivers and lakes, Gulf of Mexico beaches, and Hill Country trails and climbing spots.

Other schools to check out: Southern Methodist, Austin, Trinity U, Texas Christian, Rhodes.

# of Students Waitlisted: 155
Students Accepting Place: 43
Waitlisted Students Admitted: 11

Test Scores (middle 50%):
SAT Verbal: 570–670
SAT Math: 580–670
ACT Comp: 24–29

HS Rank of Entering Freshmen:
Top 10%: 47%
Top 25%: 83%
Top 50%: 98%

Avg. HS GPA: 3.6

THE EXPERTS SAY...

" This intimate and selective university is a Texas treasure. The facilities are top-notch, and Austin is just half an hour away. "

" Don't be fooled by the high percentage of fraternity/sorority members: Southwestern is for top students only. "

Costs (2004–5)

Tuition and Fees: $20,220
Room & Board: $6,870
Payment Plan(s): installment plan

Inst. Aid (est. 2003–04)

Institutional Aid, Need-Based:
$5,298,492

Institutional Aid, Non-Need-Based:
$2,127,581

FT Undergrads Receiving Aid: 55%
Avg. Amount per Student: $17,781

FT Undergrads Receiving Non-Need-Based Scholarship or Grant Aid: 23%
Avg. Amount per Student: $6,259

Of Those Receiving Any Aid:

Rec. Need-Based Scholarship or Grant Aid: 100%
Average Award: $10,653

Rec. Need-Based Self-Help Aid: 85%
Average Award: $5,438

Upon Graduation, Avg. Loan Debt per Student: $16,301

Financial Aid Deadline: 3/1

Graduates

Going to Graduate School:
23% Within One Year

Accepting Job Offer:
19% at time of graduation

Companies Recruiting On Campus: 17

Alumni Giving: 65%

SPELMAN COLLEGE

P.O. Box 277 350 Spelman Lane SW, Atlanta, GA 30314-4399
Admissions Phone: (404) 270-5193; (800) 982-2411 Fax: (404) 270-5201
Email: admiss@spelman.edu
Website: www.spelman.edu

General Info

Type of School: private, all women

Setting: urban

Academic Calendar: semester

Student Body

Full-Time Undergrads: 1,980
  Women: 100%

Part-Time Undergrads: 83
  Women: 100%

Total Undergrad Population:
  African American: 95%
  International: 2%
  Out-of-State: 68%
  Living Off-Campus: 41%

Academics

Full-Time Faculty: 158
  With Ph.D.: 84%

Part-Time Faculty: 69
  With Ph.D.: 45%

Student/Faculty Ratio: 11:1

Most Popular Majors:
  biology (28%)
  psychology (15%)
  English (10%)
  political science (10%)
  economics (6%)

Completing 2 or More Majors: 3%

Freshmen Retention Rate: 91%

Graduation Rates:
  64% within four years
  76% within six years
  note: 5-yr. programs affect grad rates

Admissions

Regular Application Deadline: 2/1

Early Action Deadline: 11/15

Fall Transfer Deadline: 2/1 (priority)

Spring Transfer Deadline: 11/1
  (priority)

Total # of Students Applied: 4,345
  Admitted: 1,689
  Enrolled: 493

Waitlist Available

Test Scores (middle 50%):
  SAT Verbal: 500–580
  SAT Math: 490–580
  ACT Comp: 20–24

Avg. HS GPA: 3.4

Inside the Classroom

Spelman College is a private, historically black women's college dedicated to academic excellence and service to the community. Founded in 1881 by former slaves determined to learn to read and write, Spelman today boasts famous and highly successful graduates in all walks of life, ranging from writer Alice Walker and Children's Defense Fund founder Marion Wright Edelman to actress (and former *Cosby* kid) Keshia Knight Pulliam. Spelman recently installed a new president, Dr. Beverly Daniel Tatum, a critically acclaimed author and lecturer on race relations. Spelman's commitment to women's studies along with its pride in its African American heritage combine to create a unique learning environment. A senior sums up her experience: "It's inspiring and empowering for young black women to be surrounded by other young women of color who are inspired [to do] something positive for themselves, their families, and the community."

With 26 majors, Spelman offers its students strong academics across the board. Interestingly, majors in traditionally male-dominated fields, such as biology and economics, are among the strongest and most popular at Spelman. Students also have the option of cross-registering at the five other Atlanta University Center colleges (including Morehouse, Morris Brown, and Clark Atlanta University), enabling them to take courses in business administration, mass communication, social welfare, and other areas. The core curriculum is rigorous and comprises about one-third of a student's education; it includes the usual liberal arts–based courses as well as a two-semester interdisciplinary course called "The African Diaspora in the World."

"There is no easy class at Spelman," senior tells us. As is usually the case, workload depends on a student's major and interests. Spelman's relatively small size contributes to a manageable, student-oriented academic setting. The average class has about 20 students, and 35 is considered large. Students say "the classes are challenging and the professors are approachable." The option to cross-register at nearby schools significantly broadens the school's more intimate academic boundaries. "You get the individual attention of a small school and the opportunities of a large one," confirms one student. But another says that Spelman doesn't provide the same kind of hand-holding that goes on at some other small colleges, for better or worse. "You really get to make your own way here," she explains. "No one's going to do it for you—kind of like the real world."

Campus Environment

There are 10 residence halls, which house about 1,200 students. Most first-year students live in freshmen-only dorms, and all freshmen are guaranteed housing. After that, placement works on a lottery system, and we've heard a few gripes about temporary housing. Among other campus buildings are a student center, gym and weight room, swimming pool, bowling alley, dance studio, and tennis courts. Thanks to a highly publicized multimillion-dollar grant from Bill and Camille Cosby, Spelman has a new academic center, as well as other campus improvements.

By and large, students enjoy living on campus, finding the dorm environment comfy and supportive. Says one Spelman woman, "Living on campus was the absolute best.

The sisterhood was definitely there." Another fan of on-campus living at Spelman says, "It is the best way to learn [about] your community and basically how to handle an array of situations." That said, one senior tells us that "many students prefer to live off-campus," although the cost of housing in the city of Atlanta is "about as much as can be expected." Students say dining hall food is acceptable, but complain that limited mealtime hours force students to spend extra money on meals off-campus.

Student Life

One Spelman woman described the overall feeling at the college as "strong African American women bonding to achieve success." The atmosphere is supportive, and a number of women stress "the sisterhood." Students note the confidence they get from being among other African American women. Says one, "I encourage all African American women to engage themselves in the Spelman experience because the development of sisterhood, the confidence of knowing one's heritage, and the realization of one's own strength provide us with the necessary tools to become successful in any field." (On the flip-side, the student body has been called "cliquish," and one high school guidance counselor warns of "mean-spirited women" there.) The typical Spelman coed is "relatively spiritual and well-grounded," we're told, and overall it's a politically liberal environment. A philosophy major insists, "Students come from a plethora of walks of life; the differences found here are unimaginable." Adds another: "Even though 99 percent of Spelman students have some African ancestry, it is an extremely diverse campus. The women have many different attitudes, are from a variety of backgrounds, practice different cultures and faiths, and generally see life from many different aspects."

The social scene at Spelman benefits from its proximity to other schools in the Atlanta University Center. Morehouse, an all-male historically black college, is literally across the street; as one student tells us, the entire area often feels "just like one big campus." Morehouse fraternities team with Spelman sororities to sponsor events and throw parties. First-year students are even paired with "big brothers" from Morehouse. Although there are no sorority houses on campus, the Greeks are a major social force, and "there is no bidding like at larger schools," a student tells us. Clubs also attract high numbers of participants, especially community service groups. But "sports are not very popular," we hear.

"The social life here is what you make it," explains a sophomore. Says a senior, "The overall campus atmosphere is laid-back… On Fridays, we have a DJ, vendors, and students from other schools come over to chill in a 'TGIF' atmosphere called Market Friday." And, of course, Atlanta is a vibrant city with a strong African American presence, and Spelman students enjoy hitting the multitude of clubs, restaurants, museums, and shops there. But if drinking and drugs are your thing, you'll be sorely disappointed at Spelman. "There is no drinking on campus, period," a student says. "Some folks drink on the weekend at house parties off campus or at a club, but not on campus." Another student explains, "Most women who come to Spelman are mature enough to make decisions that do not impede their physical or mental progress and long-term goals."

Other schools to check out: Hampton, Fisk, Howard, Tuskegee, Agnes Scott.

Costs (2003–04)

Tuition and Fees: $14,125

Room & Board: $7,625

Payment Plan(s): deferred payment plan

Inst. Aid (2002–03)

Institutional Aid, Need-Based: $4,563,454

FT Undergrads Receiving Aid: 90%
Avg. Amount per Student: $9,500

FT Undergrads Receiving Non-Need-Based Scholarship or Grant Aid: 21%
Avg. Amount per Student: $2,000

Of Those Receiving Any Aid:

Rec. Need-Based Scholarship or Grant Aid: 100%
Average Award: $2,000

Rec. Need-Based Self-Help Aid: 93%
Average Award: $4,000

Upon Graduation, Avg. Loan Debt per Student: $16,500

Financial Aid Deadline: rolling, 3/1 (priority)

THE EXPERTS SAY...

" Spelman attracts African American women who are eager to develop strong leadership skills and embrace tradition. "

" Spelman alumnae typically speak of their days at their beloved alma mater as a life-transforming experience. "

STANFORD UNIVERSITY

Undergraduate Admission, Old Student Union, Stanford, CA 94305-3005
Admissions Phone: (650) 723-2091 Fax: (650) 723-6050
Email: admission@stanford.edu
Website: www.stanford.edu

General Info

Type of School: private, coed

Setting: suburban

Academic Calendar: quarter

Student Body

Full-Time Undergrads: 6,436
    Men: 52%, Women: 48%

Total Undergrad Population:
    African American: 10%
    Asian American: 25%
    Latino: 12%
    Native American: 2%
    Caucasian: 41%
    International: 6%
    Out-of-State: 51%
    Living Off-Campus: 4%

Graduate and First-Professional
    Students: 10,769

Academics

Full-Time Faculty: 1,714
    With Ph.D.: 99%

Part-Time Faculty: 35
    With Ph.D.: 91%

Student/Faculty Ratio: 7:1

Most Popular Majors:
    biology or human biology
    economics
    computer science
    international relations
    political science

Completing 2 or More Majors: 10%

Freshmen Retention Rate: 98%

Graduation Rates:
    80% within four years
    94% within six years

Admissions

Regular Application Deadline: 12/15

Early Action Deadline: 11/1

Fall Transfer Deadline: 3/15

Total # of Students Applied: 18,628
    Admitted: 2,343
    Enrolled: 1,640
    Waitlisted Students Admitted: 95

Test Scores (middle 50%):
    SAT Verbal: 660–770
    SAT Math: 680–790
    ACT Comp: 28–34
    ACT English: 28–34
    ACT Math: 28–34

Inside the Classroom

If Duke is the Ivy League of the South, then Stanford can certainly lay claim to being the Ivy League of the West. Home to 17 living Nobel laureates and 23 MacArthur ("Genius") Fellows, Stanford—renowned as a research institution with cutting-edge facilities—has a stellar reputation in all areas: academic, social, and financial. One guidance counselor gushes that Stanford, with its "unlimited resources," is "what Harvard wishes it was."

Biology, computer science, economics, English, and psychology are the most popular of Stanford's roughly 60 majors, though incoming freshmen are discouraged from declaring a major before they've had a chance to explore various academic areas. The university's main strengths are in the sciences and engineering, due in part to the high-tech facilities available, but the humanities programs are also excellent. Be forewarned: there is little hand-holding here. Bright students who yearn for a more personalized education may try for one of 400 slots in the "Sophomore College" program, which consists of three weeks of intensive, small-group studies in the summer. Recently, Stanford announced the launch of a similar program, this time overseas, with seminars in China, Belgium, Russia, and South Korea.

The preeminent professors and researchers the school consistently attracts not only teach undergraduate courses but also use undergrads to assist them with research projects. Nearly 800 undergrads receive grants each year to design their own projects under faculty supervision. Professors are available—even excited—to work with students, and as one student says, "They encourage their students to go in and talk about anything—even if it's unrelated to school."

Recently, Stanford's administration—concerned about the pressure that faces high school seniors—took the bold step of dropping the early decision process. From now on, students who apply early to Stanford are not automatically committed to attend if they are accepted. These students will be allowed to apply to other colleges (though they can't apply early to other colleges once they apply early to Stanford), and will not have to make a final choice until May.

Campus Environment

Stanford may resemble the Ivies academically, but it is distinctively Western in style, layout, and attitude—and it boasts, of course, a "climate to die for," as one guidance counselor puts it. The school's sprawling 8,200-acre campus, known as "the Farm," features Spanish-style buildings and courtyards amid lush gardens and palm trees. There is also an "extensive collection of outdoor art." Facilities are top-notch, and renovations are always underway. The dorms vary in style and personality, and include some academic and ethnic theme houses. Students also have the option of living in "the Row," where 30–65 students live in a house with their very own chef. The campus is so safe that students go jogging at all hours of the night. Off-campus housing is considered prohibitively expensive, with little availability, so most people live on campus.

Stanford students are able to get around easily without a car, mostly using bicycles to navigate the massive campus and get to class on time. As one student says, "There are as many bikes on campus as you'd find in Beijing." A free shuttle bus service takes students all around campus and to neighboring communities. Nearby Palo Alto features movie theaters, shops, and restaurants, though it's expensive and has few student hangouts. Some students complain that this "yuppie Silicon Valley" isn't very friendly to college students, though the more affluent types seem to like it. San Francisco is only a short train ride away, and students often go there on weekends.

Student Life

A recent editorial in the student newspaper describes "the key part of Stanford: the spontaneity, energy, dweebiness, rebellion, corniness, and amazing talent rolled into every single student on campus." The school attracts top students who are innovative and accomplished in many areas, and who enjoy challenging themselves intellectually and personally. As one sophomore says, "Every student here has done something with his life that I've never heard about—something unusual—but the great thing is, nobody flaunts it." A guidance counselor tells us, "It's a 'moving' college with great spirit." Diversity is clearly a high priority here: "Stanford walks the talk about diversity, with over half the freshman class nonwhite," one guidance counselor tells us. (However, another counselor claims that Stanford is "hypocritical about minorities," with most coming from a "privileged background.")

While the students are "intense and always busy with something, they're definitely laid back and friendly," according to a sophomore. Interestingly, given the caliber of student the school attracts, there's no real intense competition or cutthroat rivalry. Stanford students, notes a guidance counselor, are "top kids who are not full of themselves." Instead, there's a general sense that community, approachability, and fun are important. So much fun, in fact, that "70 percent of the students marry someone else from Stanford," according to one junior.

During the week, students spend most of their free time studying (and fountain-hopping, we hear). On the weekends, students attend casual dorm parties that, while not exactly wild bashes, provide a chance to relax and hang out. Frat parties certainly do exist, but the Greeks don't dominate the social scene. One student feels "the Greeks are not very well-liked at Stanford. They're seen as feeble attempts to hide their members' dorkiness or weak intellect." He goes on to say, however, "Most academics-related Greek organizations like the engineering groups are considered more reputable and useful." In all, students can participate in more than 500 student organizations. One guidance counselor reports, "Students do a lot of community service." Offbeat clubs like ballroom dancing, a capella singing, and wind ensemble are quite popular, as is the yearly all-night dance. One student says, "It's not a terribly politically active school, but there's a club to promote every political view one can think of."

Sports are huge at Stanford, and very well funded. The facilities are first-rate, and Stanford varsity teams are among the best in the nation. Stanford recently won its eighth consecutive Sears Directors Cup, which is awarded to the most successful Division I athletic program, and Cardinal teams have won a total of 79 NCAA championships, second best in the nation. One highlight is the "Big Game," when Stanford's football team takes on rival UC Berkeley. The game is both school tradition and social event, especially when the offbeat (and occasionally raunchy) Stanford marching band takes the field.

Other schools to check out: Harvard, Yale, Princeton, UC Berkeley, Duke.

HS Rank of Entering Freshmen:
Top 10%: 90%
Top 25%: 97%
Top 50%: 100%
Avg. HS GPA: 3.9

Costs (2004–5)
Tuition and Fees: $29,847
Room & Board: $9,500

THE EXPERTS SAY...

" Stanford blends excellence in education and athletics better than just about any university in the country. "

" Be inspired (or intimidated) by big-shot alumni like Tiger Woods, John Elway, Ted Koppel, Sandra Day O'Connor, ... the list goes on and on. "

Inst. Aid (2002–03)
Institutional Aid, Need-Based: $53,914,816

Institutional Aid, Non-Need-Based: $1,824,075

FT Undergrads Receiving Aid: 46%
Avg. Amount per Student: $25,634

FT Undergrads Receiving Non-Need-Based Scholarship or Grant Aid: 10%
Avg. Amount per Student: $2,760

Of Those Receiving Any Aid:

Rec. Need-Based Scholarship or Grant Aid: 98%
Average Award: $22,356

Rec. Need-Based Self-Help Aid: 69%
Average Award: $3,380

Upon Graduation, Avg. Loan Debt per Student: $16,045

Financial Aid Deadline: 2/1 (priority)

Graduates
Going to Graduate School:
30% Within One Year

Accepting Job Offer:
31% at time of graduation

Companies Recruiting On Campus:
410

Alumni Giving: 71%

STATE UNIVERSITY OF NEW YORK—ALBANY

1400 Washington Avenue, University Administration Building 101, Albany, NY 12222
Admissions Phone: (518) 442-5435; (800) 293-7869 Fax: (518) 442-5383
Email: ugadmissions@albany.edu Website: www.albany.edu
Application Website: www.albany.edu/main/index_admissions.html

General Info

Type of School: public, coed

Setting: suburban

Academic Calendar: semester

Student Body

Full-Time Undergrads: 10,621
 Men: 50%, Women: 50%

Part-Time Undergrads: 622
 Men: 48%, Women: 52%

Total Undergrad Population:
 African American: 8%
 Asian American: 6%
 Latino: 7%
 Native American: 1%
 Caucasian: 65%
 International: 2%
 Out-of-State: 5%
 Living Off-Campus: 42%
 In Fraternities: 4%
 In Sororities: 5%

Graduate and First-Professional
 Students: 5,202

Academics

Full-Time Faculty: 598
 With Ph.D.: 97%

Part-Time Faculty: 339

Student/Faculty Ratio: 20:1

Most Popular Majors:
 psychology (14%)
 business administration (12%)
 English (10%)
 communications (9%)
 sociology (7%)

Freshmen Retention Rate: 84%

Graduation Rates:
 53% within four years
 66% within six years

Admissions

Regular Application Deadline: 3/1;
 12/1 (priority)

Early Action Deadline: 12/1

Fall Transfer Deadline: 7/1, 3/1
 (priority)

Spring Transfer Deadline: 1/1, 12/1
 (priority)

Total # of Students Applied: 17,328
 Admitted: 9,672
 Enrolled: 2,161

Waitlist Available

Inside the Classroom

One of the largest schools within the acclaimed New York State system, SUNY Albany offers students a variety of academic choices and opportunities. Albany is a Carnegie Research II Research University, where students can both study and conduct research alongside the experienced faculty. Additionally, Albany has a high acceptance rate to law, medical and other professional schools. More than two-thirds of Albany students earn graduate or professional degrees. One student tells us that he initially chose SUNY Albany because he felt it would "more adequately prepare me for graduate school, which it certainly has, since I am a research assistant in a lab where I get to work right alongside with graduate students." Within Albany's five undergraduate schools, students can find a wide variety of academic programs, including some that are considered among the best in the SUNY system. Albany students can choose their major from over 100 bachelor's degree programs. Opportunities exist for combined bachelor's/master's programs in many disciplinary areas, and students can take advantage of interdisciplinary majors such as human biology, information science, and urban studies. Albany's many strong departments include biology, business and accounting, earth and atmospheric sciences, political science, psychology, and sociology. The core curriculum includes courses in natural science, fine arts and literature, and world cultures.

As with other large state schools, most freshmen-level classes can tend to be on the large side. A senior says, "One of UAlbany's core strengths is its terrific academic atmosphere. This is hindered, however, by large class sizes in which a close relationship with professors requires effort." Class sizes, which average 35 students at the introductory level, do get smaller as you work into your major. Freshmen are encouraged to participate in Project Renaissance, a year-long living and learning program involving team-taught, interdisciplinary general education led by distinguished faculty.

Campus Environment

SUNY Albany has an uptown campus (the main campus), a downtown campus, and an east campus, each of which serves the different needs of the university system and the student body. The main campus is essentially a large quadrangle, with the four dormitories, known as quads, at each corner and the academic buildings in between. Mostly made of concrete, the campus isn't exactly pretty, but it is certainly functional, as students can easily move back and forth between their rooms and their classes. Entering freshmen are required to live on campus for their first two years. The downtown campus has the more traditional and collegiate red brick residence halls, and "free buses that are conveniently close to popular social events such as bars and clubs." There are housing options ranging from "double or suite-style rooms, and the choice between on-campus three-story low rises or 22-story towers," says one student. "Also, there are on-campus apartments with full kitchens and a whole complex of brand new dorms are being built right now." Off-campus housing ranges from apartments "deep in the city that are cheap yet dangerous, to upscale neighborhoods with safe and friendly side streets."

If students are not entirely thrilled about the appearance of their concrete campus, they do like the enormous podium and fountain at its center, which provides optimal hanging-out space in a central location. And when the fountain is turned on each spring, students have the perfect excuse to let loose. "It's usually fun and extremely wet," is one student's description.

A student says that while having a car isn't absolutely necessary, it's "highly advisable, since many places of interest such as restaurants and businesses are not in the heart of the city." Students appreciate going to school in the state's capital as well. "The nearby city of Albany is both easily accessible and offers terrific diversity from cultural foods to cultural events and museums."

Student Life

The student body is very diverse. A senior says, "Even though it is a larger school there is plenty of room for individualism and uniqueness... The type of student that would *not* fit in at UAlbany is one who holds many prejudices or is racist." Because Albany is a large school, the social life tends to be fractured; students socialize with people in their suites and halls, or with groups sharing common interests. Albany offers a wide array of student clubs and organizations that cater to many interests. The typical academic/professional, political, ethnic, and religious groups are offered alongside clubs for paintball, Japanese animation, and ballroom and Latin dancing. A student tells us more: "UAlbany's Student Association sponsors dances for the electronic music community that are New York City-quality events with renowned DJs playing at a club or rave-like event."

Intramural sports are quite popular as well. Albany is a member of the America East Conference; additionally, SUNY Albany serves as the summer training camp of the New York Giants football team. Weekends are usually spent socializing at "house parties, dorm parties, or going to one of the local bars or clubs." Though Albany has at times been considered a "party school," students seem to have struck a nice balance. "We were rated both the No. 1 party school and the No. 1 politically involved campus in the U.S. in successive years," a student says. Drinking is common at Albany; one student claims, "The student body seems to come together to celebrate the love of life through alcohol."

Fraternities and sororities are popular as well, and there are 20 fraternities and 19 sororities with chapters on campus. One student tells us that their influence is limited, however, possibly due to "the individualistic characteristic of the general population. The social activities are interesting and frequent enough to not need an organized social group to meet new people and make new friends."

Test Scores (middle 50%):
SAT Verbal: 510–610
SAT Math: 520–620

HS Rank of Entering Freshmen:
Top 10%: 19%
Top 25%: 55%
Top 50%: 94%

Avg. HS GPA: 3.34

Costs (2003–04)

Tuition and Fees, In-State: $5,770

Tuition and Fees, Out-of-State: $11,720

Room & Board: $7,181

Payment Plan(s): installment plan, deferred payment plan

THE EXPERTS SAY...

" One of the gems of the SUNY system, U Albany offers superb undergrad research opportunities, plus a ticket into grad school. "

" To avoid the huge freshmen classes, enroll in Project Renaissance and meet some top professors and fellow students. "

Inst. Aid (est. 2003–04)

Institutional Aid, Need-Based: $477,745

Institutional Aid, Non-Need-Based: $3,380,757

FT Undergrads Receiving Aid: 56%
Avg. Amount per Student: $8,251

FT Undergrads Receiving Non-Need-Based Scholarship or Grant Aid: 5%
Avg. Amount per Student: $3,534

Of Those Receiving Any Aid:

Rec. Need-Based Scholarship or Grant Aid: 89%
Average Award: $4,456

Rec. Need-Based Self-Help Aid: 85%
Average Award: $4,583

Upon Graduation, Avg. Loan Debt per Student: $16,700

Financial Aid Deadline: 3/15 (priority)

STATE UNIVERSITY OF NEW YORK— BINGHAMTON UNIVERSITY

P.O. Box 6000, Binghamton, NY 13902-6000
Admissions Phone: (607) 777-2171 Fax: (607) 777-4445
Email: admit@binghamton.edu Website: www.binghamton.edu

General Info

Type of School: public, coed

Setting: suburban

Academic Calendar: semester

Student Body

Full-Time Undergrads: 10,238
Men: 49%, Women: 51%

Part-Time Undergrads: 190
Men: 36%, Women: 64%

Total Undergrad Population:
African American: 5%
Asian American: 16%
Latino: 6%
Native American: <1%
Caucasian: 54%
International: 3%
Out-of-State: 5%
Living Off-Campus: 44%
In Fraternities: 8%
In Sororities: 7%

Graduate and First-Professional
Students: 2,822

Academics

Full-Time Faculty: 504
With Ph.D.: 93%

Part-Time Faculty: 200

Student/Faculty Ratio: 22:1

Most Popular Majors:
management (11%)
psychology (10%)
English (8%)
biology (7%)
computer science (6%)

Completing 2 or More Majors: 8%

Freshmen Retention Rate: 92%

Graduation Rates:
70% within four years
80% within six years

Admissions

Regular Application Deadline: 1/15
(priority)

Early Action Deadline: 11/15

Fall Transfer Deadline: 2/15 (priority)

Spring Transfer Deadline: 11/15
(priority)

Total # of Students Applied: 19,076
Admitted: 8,521
Enrolled: 2,291

Inside the Classroom

Binghamton has five undergraduate colleges: engineering; management; education and human development; nursing; and the acclaimed Harpur College of Arts and Sciences, where liberal arts programs are strong across the board. Biology, chemistry, English and psychology have particularly large enrollments. Binghamton also offers several good interdisciplinary programs, including women's studies; American and Caribbean area studies; Asian and Asian American studies; and philosophy, politics, and law. Students are required to take courses in the following five areas: language and communication; creating a global vision; natural sciences, social sciences, and mathematics; aesthetics and humanities; and physical activity/wellness.

Class sizes at the introductory level can be large, but students regularly break into smaller discussion sections taught by graduate students. For the most part, professors do the teaching and class sizes average about 20 students. According to one junior, making contact with faculty, even in larger classes, is easy: "The professors are always there; even if it is not their office hours, you can swing by and they are willing to talk." The grad-level teaching assistants also hold regular office hours to assist students.

The workload varies by program, but "most classes require a lot of work to earn that A," stresses one student. Of course, hard work is nothing new for these students: More than half of Binghamton's students graduated in the top 10 percent of their high school class.

Campus Environment

Binghamton University is actually located in Vestal, NY, just outside the Binghamton city limits in the Southern Tier of upstate New York. The institutional look of the campus—its functional buildings are arranged in a circular pattern—is alleviated by the beautiful natural surroundings. The Nature Preserve (190 acres of land established in 1970 to protect natural areas, plants and wildlife) and an additional 160 acres of natural land make a beautiful campus backdrop. The University Union, the main student thoroughfare, has recently been renovated and expanded to include a $19.4 million addition. A Field House for sports and other events is nearing completion, and new housing accommodations have recently opened or are underway to accommodate the steady influx of students to Binghamton each year. One junior says, "Moving around can be hard. Space has been really limited and there have been cases where people were tripled, even moved into makeshift dorms."

The dormitories are grouped into four residential communities, each with a distinct personality—or stereotype. One recent alum says, "Each of the four complexes has its own reputation: Newing is considered the Greek/partying dorm; Dickinson is the quiet/studying dorm; College-in-the-Woods is kind of the artsy dorm; and Hinman is maybe the student-government-type kids. But realistically, all different types of people live in each of the complexes, these aren't steadfast rules." Each residence complex has its own dining hall, and there is also a "mini-mall" in the University Union that offers more options—everything from pasta and salads to Taco Bell and Chinese food. Wok, Wild and Wings is a fast food service in the Union that's a student favorite since they deliver until the early morning hours; each residence complex also has its own Nite Owl Café that serves up those late-night essentials until midnight.

Many upperclassmen opt for on-campus, fully-furnished apartments in one of two apartment complexes, which typically feature two-to-six bedrooms, a full kitchen, living/dining room area, and one and a half bathrooms. Half of the undergraduate population chooses to live off-campus in houses or apartments, which are typically quite reasonably priced. Freshmen are not permitted to have cars on campus. A good number of upperclassmen do have cars, and one student claims that while parking is generally sufficient, "it can be a pain." A car is not a necessity, though. Off Campus College Transport is a student-owned, student-run shuttle bus system ("the blue buses") that runs past midnight seven days a week, and takes students both around campus and around town. The extensive Broome County Transit buses are widely used as well. Both services are dependable and free to students with ID cards. Taxis are also constantly shuttling to and from campus; most students know the phone numbers of the various cab services by heart and, as one sophomore tells us, "are on a first-name basis with many of the drivers."

Student Life

One student complains that college guides "totally misrepresent" the social scene at Binghamton. Greek life is popular with 35 fraternities and sororities on campus, but according to one student, "Fraternity parties are big for underclassmen, mostly freshmen. It gets old pretty quick." House parties are popular, and upperclassmen usually go to State Street, where most of the bars and clubs can be found, or to the many restaurants and coffeehouses downtown.

Binghamton competes at the Division I sports level and is a member of the America East Conference. More than 150 student organizations are available, including more than five newspapers/magazines, ethnic clubs, political/social awareness clubs, a capella music groups, and a radio station, WHRW—noted for having the largest music library in the Southern Tier. Binghamton also boasts its own television station (Binghamton Television, or BTV), which is one of only a few independent, student-run television stations in the country. BTV has featured comedy and call-in talk shows, independent movies created by students, *BTV News*, and even its own dramatic series, aside from regularly airing popular movies. There are many shopping centers and a large mall nearby, as well as the Broome County Arena, which hosts sports events and concerts. The Roberson Museum, the Kopernik Observatory, and several theaters are also near campus. Though Binghamton may not be "the most exciting town on earth," according to one student, "the students are fun people and there's always something going on." Binghamton is also relatively close to other college towns, such as Ithaca and Syracuse.

# of Students Waitlisted: 382
  Students Accepting Place: 105
  Waitlisted Students Admitted: 105

Test Scores (middle 50%):
  SAT Verbal: 560–640
  SAT Math: 590–680
  ACT Comp: 25–28

HS Rank of Entering Freshmen:
  Top 25%: 85%
  Top 50%: 99%

Avg. HS GPA: 3.6

THE EXPERTS SAY...

" If you can't make up your mind among all the academic choices at Binghamton, the excellent biology and psychology programs at the Harpur College of Arts and Sciences are great places to start. "

" This college guide won't 'misrepresent' the social life at Binghamton—if you're a freshman, you'll be partying at a frat (until you outgrow it). "

Costs (2003–04)

Tuition and Fees, In-State: $5,687

Tuition and Fees, Out-of-State: $11,637

Room & Board: $7,100

Payment Plan(s): installment plan, deferred payment plan

Inst. Aid (est. 2003–04)

FT Undergrads Receiving Aid: 50%
  Avg. Amount per Student: $10,629

FT Undergrads Receiving Non-Need-Based Scholarship or Grant Aid: 2%
  Avg. Amount per Student: $2,471

Of Those Receiving Any Aid:

Rec. Need-Based Scholarship or Grant Aid: 90%
  Average Award: $4,752

Rec. Need-Based Self-Help Aid: 93%
  Average Award: $4,646

Upon Graduation, Avg. Loan Debt per Student: $14,531

Financial Aid Deadline: 3/1 (priority)

Graduates

Going to Graduate School:
  39% Within One Year

Accepting Job Offer:
  82% at time of graduation

Companies Recruiting On Campus: 92

Alumni Giving: 23%

STATE UNIVERSITY OF NEW YORK— COLLEGE AT GENESEO

1 College Circle, Geneseo, NY 14454
Admissions Phone: (585) 245-5571; (866) 245-5211 Fax: (585) 245-5550
Email: admissions@geneseo.edu Website: www.geneseo.edu

General Info

Type of School: public, coed

Setting: small town

Academic Calendar: semester

Student Body

Full-Time Undergrads: 5,201
   Men: 37%, Women: 63%

Part-Time Undergrads: 106
   Men: 35%, Women: 65%

Total Undergrad Population:
   African American: 2%
   Asian American: 5%
   Latino: 3%
   Native American: <1%
   Caucasian: 88%
   International: 2%
   Out-of-State: 1%
   Living Off-Campus: 46%
   In Fraternities: 10%
   In Sororities: 12%

Graduate and First-Professional
   Students: 243

Academics

Full-Time Faculty: 246
   With Ph.D.: 85%

Part-Time Faculty: 103
   With Ph.D.: 21%

Student/Faculty Ratio: 19:1

Most Popular Majors:
   education (17%)
   business administration (9%)
   biology (8%)
   psychology (7%)
   English (6%)

Freshmen Retention Rate: 92%

Graduation Rates:
   62% within four years
   77% within six years

Admissions

Regular Application Deadline: 1/15

Early Decision Deadline(s): 11/15

Fall Transfer Deadline: 1/15

Spring Transfer Deadline: 10/1

Total # of Students Applied: 8,783
   Admitted: 3,684
   Enrolled: 990

# of Students Waitlisted: 1,738
   Students Accepting Place: 707
   Waitlisted Students Admitted: 176

Inside the Classroom

SUNY Geneseo is one of the most selective of the State University of New York's comprehensive colleges. The school boasts that they offer an education "comparable in quality to the educational experience available at many of the nation's finest private colleges and universities." Geneseo certainly has developed a respectable reputation for itself, and is among the most highly regarded public universities in the nation.

SUNY Geneseo offers 54 degree programs and 48 undergraduate majors. The general education requirements, known as the Common Core, include courses in interdisciplinary humanities, fine arts, social sciences, numeric and symbolic reasoning, foreign language, and non-Western ideas. Special education, biology, psychology, and English are among the most popular majors. The School of Business offers three excellent majors in accounting, business administration, and economics. The School of Education offers majors in elementary education and special education. And the School of Performing Arts has degree programs in music, theater, and dance.

There are fewer than 5,000 full-time undergraduates, and students are able to get a good amount of individual attention from professors. The average class holds 25 students, and the student-to-faculty ratio is 19:1. The professors do the teaching here—not grad students. There's no grade inflation either: Students at Geneseo have to work extremely hard to get high grades.

Students are able to interact with professors on a one-on-one basis when it comes to research opportunities as well. The school encourages undergraduates to participate in research projects with faculty, and opportunities abound especially for geological sciences majors, for whom there are two courses designed for undergraduate research. Students are also encouraged to participate in internships, which are available for the full year, for a semester, or during the summer. 350 students per year participate in internships.

Campus Environment

The SUNY Geneseo campus encompasses 220 acres, and includes 39 buildings and 15 residence halls. The campus offers a traditionally collegiate atmosphere, with "brick sidewalks, shady oaks, and ivy-covered buildings" coming together to create an "idyllic atmosphere." Students generally consider their campus and fellow students to be friendly and approachable, and the school describes students as "interesting people who thrive in an environment where creativity, independent thinking, and cooperative learning are a way of life."

The school is located in the historic village of Geneseo. Geneseo embodies the spirit of small-town America and is listed in the National Register of Historic Places. Geneseo features Victorian homes and a thriving Main Street with an assortment of restaurants and interesting shops. The scenic Genesee Valley is a great place for outdoor activities, including camping, hiking, golfing, fishing, swimming, canoeing, sailing, cross-country skiing, and biking. Conesus Lake is nearby, which serves as a practice and competition site for SUNY Geneseo's Crew Club. Letchworth State Park and major ski slopes are also nearby, and Rochester—New York's third largest city—is only a half-hour away. Rochester makes for a good destination spot since it's also somewhat of a college town, and is a great place for sporting events, shopping, museums, historic attractions, and nightlife.

Freshmen are required to live on campus in one of the 15 coed residence halls, each of which houses roughly 200 students. The halls offer both suite and corridor-style living. There is also a townhouse complex on campus, though there is no fraternity/sorority housing. Many upperclassmen choose to live off campus in apartments or houses in the Geneseo area. All students, even freshmen, are permitted to have cars on campus, though there is an additional parking fee. However, cars are not at all a necessity in Geneseo, since Main Street is only a short walk away from campus.

Student Life

The homogeneous student body is often described as "cliquey" and "image-conscious," and there's not a lot of intermingling between ethnic groups. Common complaints about the student body include the lack of school spirit and the uneven male/female ratio.

SUNY Geneseo offers more than 180 student clubs and organizations, in which 75 percent of the student body participate—which means that one-quarter of the student body doesn't participate in campus life at all. There are academic groups, event planning/programming groups, media organizations that include school newspapers and a television station (Geneseo Student Television, or GSTV), drama and music groups, social service groups, and special interest organizations.

The school is a Division III member of the National Collegiate Athletic Conference and the Eastern Collegiate Athletic Conference. There are 19 intercollegiate sports teams (11 women's and 8 men's), and roughly five percent of the student body are involved. Intramural sports are very popular, with 126 teams (54 women's and 72 men's). 80 percent of the student population participate in intramural sports at some point before graduating; teams often represent residence halls or Greek organizations.

Fraternities and sororities are fairly popular as well. There are 20 Greek organizations in total on campus: 15 local organizations, three national sororities and two national fraternities. Roughly ten percent of students are involved in Greek life. Almost twice that number of students takes part in volunteer work. The school's Volunteer Center helps students to find and coordinate volunteer opportunities that suit their interests and passions.

\# Applied Early Decision: 242
Early Decision Admitted: 133

Test Scores (middle 50%):
SAT Verbal: 580–660
SAT Math: 600–670
ACT Comp: 25–29

HS Rank of Entering Freshmen:
Top 10%: 48%
Top 25%: 86%
Top 50%: 99%

Avg. HS GPA: 3.7

THE EXPERTS SAY...

" SUNY Geneseo offers the faculty attention of a private school at a public school price. Geology majors should investigate the research opportunities here. "

" Urbanites beware: Geneseo is the quintessential quaint small town. And with the lopsided male/female ratio, women may find it hard to get a date. "

Costs (2004–5)

Tuition and Fees, In-State: $5,390

Tuition and Fees, Out-of-State: $11,340

Room & Board: $6,350

Payment Plan(s): installment plan

Inst. Aid (est. 2003–04)

Institutional Aid, Non-Need-Based: $582,850.00

FT Undergrads Receiving Aid: 48%
Avg. Amount per Student: $8,555.00

FT Undergrads Receiving Non-Need-Based Scholarship or Grant Aid: 11%
Avg. Amount per Student: $1,060.00

Of Those Receiving Any Aid:

Rec. Need-Based Scholarship or Grant Aid: 94%
Average Award: $3,340.00

Rec. Need-Based Self-Help Aid: 94%
Average Award: $3,950.00

Upon Graduation, Avg. Loan Debt per Student: $15,500.00

Financial Aid Deadline: 2/15 (priority)

Graduates

Going to Graduate School:
36% Within One Year

Accepting Job Offer:
53% at time of graduation

Companies Recruiting On Campus: 41

Alumni Giving: 35%

STATE UNIVERSITY OF NEW YORK— PURCHASE

735 Anderson Hill Road, Purchase, NY 10577-1400 Admissions Phone: (914) 251-6300
Fax: (914) 251-6314 Email: admissn@purchase.edu Website: www.purchase.edu
Application Website: www.purchase.edu/admissions/adm_applyonline.asp

Note: Info. not verified by school

General Info

Type of School: public, coed

Academic Calendar: semester

Student Body

Full-Time Undergrads: 3,072
  Men: 45%, Women: 55%

Part-Time Undergrads: 281
  Men: 38%, Women: 62%

Total Undergrad Population:
  African American: 8%
  Asian American: 4%
  Latino: 9%
  Native American: <1%
  Caucasian: 69%
  International: 3%
  Out-of-State: 15%
  Living Off-Campus: 41%

Graduate and First-Professional
  Students: 143

Academics

Full-Time Faculty: 136

Part-Time Faculty: 197

Student/Faculty Ratio: 17:1

Freshmen Retention Rate: 72%

Graduation Rates:
  25% within four years
  42% within six years

Admissions

Regular Application Deadline: 3/1
  (priority)

Early Decision Deadline(s): 11/1

Total # of Students Applied: 7,102
  Admitted: 2,636
  Enrolled: 689

Applied Early Decision: 19
  Early Decision Admitted: 11

Test Scores (middle 50%):
  SAT Verbal: 500–600
  SAT Math: 470–580
  ACT English: 20–24
  ACT Math: 17–24

Costs (2003–04)

Tuition and Fees, In-State: $4,350

Tuition and Fees, Out-of-State:
  $10,300

Room & Board: $7,272

Inside the Classroom

Purchase College is uniquely able to offer students three performing arts conservatories (dance, music, and theatre arts and film), a critically acclaimed School of Art and Design, and a top liberal arts and sciences program (in its School of Humanities and School of Natural and Social Sciences), all on one intimate campus. Purchase alumni rank at the top of their fields, and include two MacArthur "genius" award winners, a Pulitzer Prize winner, world-class jazz musicians, Broadway directors, and actors Stanley Tucci, Edie Falco, Wesley Snipes, and Parker Posey. Only a very small number of talented individuals are admitted into the prestigious conservatories, and once accepted, conservatory students report that it's demanding, challenging, and well worth the effort.

"The workload at Purchase is completely dependent on the professor and even more so on the program," a creative writing major says, adding that Design Technology students "are generally overburdened with schoolwork most of the year." Core requirements also vary by school. All liberal arts and sciences students must take courses in Western culture, writing, and diversity. Seniors culminate their studies in a senior project, which is worked on in conjunction with a faculty member; a typical senior project might be a research paper, a collection of original stories or poems, a translation of foreign language literature, or an original scientific investigation. All students in one of the Conservatory Programs take 90 credits, out of 120 needed to graduate, in their major. To receive a B.F.A. at the School of Art and Design, students must take a few art history courses and some "additional liberal arts courses," and complete a senior project. First-year students are also required to complete an Art and Design core program that includes courses in Seeing, Composition, History, and Imaging. And, much to their dismay, all Purchase students are now required to fulfill a two-credit phys ed requirement; the fairly limited and offbeat phys ed offerings include Lifeguard Training, Mideastern Belly Dancing, and Personal Defense.

Purchase College encourages all students to participate in their various study abroad programs, including summer programs in France, Spain, and Italy. Academically motivated liberal arts and sciences freshmen have the opportunity to take part in one of three brand-new Learning Communities—focusing on Natural Sciences, Media and Literature, or American Culture—or a Freshmen Semester Abroad Program in Burgos, Spain. Led by a professor-in-residence, students in the learning community live together, take some of the same courses, and participate in academic and extracurricular activities.

Campus Environment

The arts facilities on campus are virtually unrivaled for a state school. Art and Design students are greatly aided by various studios in the 160,000 square-foot Art and Design building, one of the largest educational facilities of its kind in the Northeast. The Neuberger Museum of Art, the eighth largest university museum in the country, was recently awarded accreditation by the National Association of Museums— something only 750 of the nation's 8,000 museums can boast. Those in the Conservatory of Dance find a second home on campus in the unique, award-winning building that includes ten fully equipped studios, saunas, and a Dance Theatre Lab.

Housing gets so-so marks from Purchase students. For one thing, there seems to be the constant problem of overcrowding. "We have twice the amount of students living on campus most of the time than can actually fit," gripes a student. Rooms meant for two are often tripled-up, and some feel these are pretty small rooms to begin with. The school is attempting to alleviate these issues with new construction, and recently, 200 students moved into a state-of-the-art dormitory, said to be the first phase of a new $20 million student housing project. When it is completed, Purchase promises that more than 400 students will be housed in the 13 two-story, garden-style modular apartment complexes. (One area will be "reminiscent of a New England Green with a traditional quad," we hear.) Most new freshmen are assigned to traditional residence halls, with mostly double/triple-occupancy rooms and a few suites with private baths. Many upperclassmen choose to live in one of two apartment complexes on campus. The "Olde" apartments are in a more convenient location, we hear, but the Commons complex is nicer. "Off-campus housing is nearly impossible to get," according to one student.

The campus is fairly safe—though "graffiti is a big problem," we're told—and students have mixed feelings about the school's location. Manhattan is a short train ride away, and students often take advantage of all the culture and nightlife the city offers. But as for the immediate area, take it from this recent grad: "Purchase students don't really utilize any of the town's 'resources' (there aren't any)." The nearby cities of Port Chester and White Plains fare better in student opinion, being more student budget–friendly (the former) and having more places to hang out (the latter). And be forewarned: "You're immobile without a car," says one student.

Student Life

SUNY Purchase is populated with nonconformist, unique students. "It's a community full of artists, dreamers, marijuana activists, feminists, drama queens, drag queens, writers, musicians, etc.," a student tells us, adding slyly: "All the kids who didn't want to play gym in high school." Indeed, there isn't a sorority girl or a jock in sight—there have been no Greek organizations in decades, and, says one student, "We have a few sports teams, but no one goes to the games. It's really, really sad." It's all for the best, though, since Purchase students tend to be those who didn't quite fit in in high school, and most love that their campus is brimming with people just like them. It's a very PC campus, we hear, and one that's very gay-friendly. And, with such a small, tight-knit community, gossip is rampant: Everybody knows everybody else's business.

There are a handful of special-interest student organizations, including Latinos Unidos, Organization of African People in America, Gay/Lesbian/Bisexual/Transsexual Union, the Purchase Biological Society, Philosophy Club, the Commuter Student Association, X-stream Generation, SISTAS, and the AIDS Task Force. The Campus Centers feature a game room, nighttime pub, and fireside lounge where students spend time between classes and projects. But mostly, when they're not heading to Manhattan for fun, Purchase students behave surprisingly like most college students: They party. In keeping with the school's "hippie" image, "both drugs and alcohol are very prominent on campus," a student says.

Other schools to check out: SUNY Geneseo, NYU, Ithaca, Eugene Lang, Bard.

Inst. Aid (est. 2002–03)

Institutional Aid, Need-Based: $42,780

Institutional Aid, Non-Need-Based: $734,820

FT Undergrads Receiving Aid: 48% Avg. Amount per Student: $7,235

FT Undergrads Receiving Non-Need-Based Scholarship or Grant Aid: 14% Avg. Amount per Student: $11,242

Of Those Receiving Any Aid:

Rec. Need-Based Scholarship or Grant Aid: 87% Average Award: $3,975

Rec. Need-Based Self-Help Aid: 96% Average Award: $3,919

Upon Graduation, Avg. Loan Debt per Student: $13,873

Financial Aid Deadline: 3/15 (priority)

THE EXPERTS SAY...

" SUNY Purchase offers unique academic programs and an artsy environment at an affordable price. "

" Artsy, but sheltered. An option for those who aren't quite ready to try to make it on their own in Manhattan. "

STATE UNIVERSITY OF NEW YORK— STONY BROOK

Admissions Building Room 118, Stony Brook, NY 11794-1901
Admissions Phone: (631) 632-6868; (800) 872-7869 Fax: (631) 632-9898
Email: ugadmissions@notes.cc.sunysb.edu Website: www.sunysb.edu

General Info

Type of School: public, coed

Setting: suburban

Academic Calendar: semester

Student Body

Full-Time Undergrads: 12,647
  Men: 52%, Women: 48%

Part-Time Undergrads: 1,172
  Men: 47%, Women: 53%

Total Undergrad Population:
  African American: 10%
  Asian American: 23%
  Latino: 8%
  Native American: <1%
  Caucasian: 36%
  International: 4%
  Out-of-State: 2%
  Living Off-Campus: 44%

Graduate and First-Professional
  Students: 8,272

Academics

Full-Time Faculty: 872
  With Ph.D.: 95%

Part-Time Faculty: 461

Student/Faculty Ratio: 18:1

Most Popular Majors:
  psychology
  biology
  economics
  computer science/
    information systems
  business management

Freshmen Retention Rate: 87%

Admissions

Early Action Deadline: 11/15

Fall Transfer Deadline: 3/1 (priority)

Total # of Students Applied: 16,909
  Admitted: 8,564
  Enrolled: 2,181

Test Scores (middle 50%):
  SAT Verbal: 540–630
  SAT Math: 570–670

HS Rank of Entering Freshmen:
  Top 10%: 32%
  Top 25%: 71%
  Top 50%: 97%

Inside the Classroom

Because of its top-notch facilities and resources as well as its distinguished faculty, Stony Brook is the major research campus in the SUNY system. While its strongest programs are in the sciences, engineering, and health professions, a number of Stony Brook's arts programs are also well respected, particularly theater and music. Over 50 majors are offered through the College of Arts and Sciences, the College of Engineering and Applied Sciences, the Health Sciences Center, Marine Sciences Research Center, and the W. Averell Harriman School for Management and Policy.

Students feel that the intensity of the workload varies. "The workload depends on the area of study. It's pretty reasonable for non-scientific fields, otherwise it can get pretty intense," says one student. A junior majoring in neurobiology agrees: "The academic atmosphere is variable among majors and disciplines at Stony Brook. Science and Computer Science majors are extremely academically challenging and programs such as nursing and physical therapy are very competitive and hard to get into." The Diversified Education Curriculum ensures that all students receive a broad liberal arts background before specializing; students are required to take courses in 11 academic areas, which may vary by major or college.

Most Stony Brook classes are big lectures. Students who want attention from professors may have to seek it out: "The professors are generally quite enthusiastic and accessible during office hours; if not, appointments can be made for further inquiry." Around 90 percent of Stony Brook professors are engaged in active research leading to publication, resulting in frequent opportunities for undergraduates to collaborate with faculty in research projects and creative activities. Premed students can find research opportunities within Stony Brook's prominent university hospital and research center. Students also find ways to interact academically with one another: "Despite the competition, it is possible to foster a close-knit network with your peers via study groups ... More often than not, they will form spontaneously in locales such as the library during finals week."

Campus Environment

Stony Brook's sprawling campus features a nature preserve, bicycle paths, an apple orchard, and a duck pond, all interspersed among the spacious plazas, modern laboratories, and classroom buildings. The six residential quads are the basic social units for the on-campus population. Since Stony Brook is a big commuter school, dorm life helps students "make more friends and get to know more about people on and around campus." Housing for undergrads includes suites with kitchens, and apartment-style living—although one student tells us that upperclassmen usually get the apartments "because it's decided who gets the room by the point system they have." Stony Brook does have its housing woes, however. One student says, "On-campus is as follows: small rooms, two people per this tiny room, suite-style or corridor-style, extremely expensive, bathrooms are shared, not much privacy, but convenience because of proximity to campus." Another student tells us, "Stony Brook does seem to have had housing problems in the past. In fact, freshmen have sometimes been temporarily tripled up in rooms meant only for two students. However, the University recently built four new dorm buildings which should help alleviate the problem."

Stony Brook isn't quite a typical college town. "Off campus is suburbs ... not very lively, no college life atmosphere." Nonetheless, students find the area still has its merits. "Stony Brook is a quiet town," a student says. "However, there are local clubs, a mall, a movie theater, restaurants, etc., nearby. If that isn't enough, the university is an hour away from Manhattan [and] is also close by Port Jefferson Harbor, the Long Island Sound, and many beaches."

A car isn't necessary for getting around campus; one student says, "Nothing on campus is more than a 10 minute walk from anything else on campus." Public and school-sponsored buses are available to students for their off-campus needs, but "a car is really rather essential to get around town."

Student Life

Stony Brook offers more than 100 students clubs and organizations. Although they've just turned Division I, sports are not extremely popular. A junior says, "Most students don't spend any time following the teams." She adds, though: "Intramural is excellent, a lot of variety." Fraternities and sororities are among the more popular activities, and are responsible for "a decent amount of social events as well as those that benefit the community." A student says, "Stony Brook is awesome in this respect. Yes, we have Greek life for those who want to experience it, but we also have non-Greek life. No one has ever been harassed for not being part of a sorority of fraternity on campus ... The reason Stony Brook is able to maintain a balance of Greek and non-Greek is because of the diversity of students and their varying interests."

Speaking of diversity, Stony Brook students represent all backgrounds. There is no "typical student" at Stony Brook, according to a pharmacology major. "Every one fits. There are clubs and organizations for every belief, religion, orientation, and anything you can imagine." Another student says Stony Brook "fosters a tolerant environment. People are free to express themselves ... provided it is in a safe and productive manner." The only drawback is the cliques: "We have great diversity, but the groups all tend to stick together."

Stony Brook is a big commuter school; most students go home on weekends, making Thursdays important. "Thursday night is designated party night at Stony Brook. Most students attend off-campus parties and on-campus get-togethers." The commuter aspect can make it hard at times to meet people, though. A student says, "People are very friendly around campus when approached but since most people are commuters, you do not see the same people over and over, or around in your class as you see around campus." Still, another student says, "Although Stony Brook has lots of students who commute to and from school both on weekdays and weekends, it's easy to find a friendly face to pass the time with."

Costs (2003–04)

Tuition and Fees, In-State: $5,316

Tuition and Fees, Out-of-State: $11,266

Room & Board: $7,458

Payment Plan(s): installment plan

THE EXPERTS SAY...

" Stony Brook, SUNY's science and research star, is a tremendous place for premeds and bio students. The research opportunities at the University hospital are outstanding. "

" To get into the school spirit, remember that Thursdays are the party night at this commuter school. "

Inst. Aid (est. 2003–04)

Institutional Aid, Non-Need-Based: $2,894,692.00

FT Undergrads Receiving Aid: 58% Avg. Amount per Student: $9,281.00

FT Undergrads Receiving Non-Need-Based Scholarship or Grant Aid: 2% Avg. Amount per Student: $1,842.00

Of Those Receiving Any Aid:

Rec. Need-Based Scholarship or Grant Aid: 15% Average Award: $2,638.00

Rec. Need-Based Self-Help Aid: 84% Average Award: $2,115.00

Upon Graduation, Avg. Loan Debt per Student: $15,747.00

Financial Aid Deadline: 3/1 (priority)

Graduates

Alumni Giving: 5%

STATE UNIVERSITY OF NEW YORK— UNIVERSITY AT BUFFALO

15 Capen Hall, Box 601660, Buffalo, NY 14260-1660 Admissions Phone: (888) UBA-DMIT;
(716) 645-6900 Fax: (716) 645-6411   Email: ubadmit@buffalo.edu
Website: www.buffalo.edu Application Website: www.admissions.buffalo.edu

General Info

Type of School: public, coed

Setting: urban

Academic Calendar: semester

Student Body

Full-Time Undergrads: 16,132
  Men: 55%, Women: 45%

Part-Time Undergrads: 1,257
  Men: 52%, Women: 48%

Total Undergrad Population:
  African American: 7%
  Asian American: 9%
  Latino: 3%
  Native American: <1%
  Caucasian: 66%
  International: 6%
  Out-of-State: 2%
  Living Off-Campus: 62%
  In Fraternities: 2%
  In Sororities: 4%

Graduate and First-Professional
  Students: 9,437

Academics

Full-Time Faculty: 1,121
  With Ph.D.: 97%

Part-Time Faculty: 522
  With Ph.D.: 97%

Student/Faculty Ratio: 16:1

Most Popular Majors:
  business, management (19%)
  engineering (all types) (19%)
  health professions—clinical sciences
    (11%)
  psychology (8%)
  social sciences (6%)

Completing 2 or More Majors: 11%

Freshmen Retention Rate: 85%

Graduation Rates:
  33% within four years
  57% within six years

Admissions

Regular Application Deadline: 11/1
  (priority)

Early Decision Deadline(s): 11/1

Total # of Students Applied: 17,448
  Admitted: 10,890
  Enrolled: 3,593

Applied Early Decision: 415
  Early Decision Admitted: 296

Inside the Classroom

The University at Buffalo is the largest school in the SUNY system, featuring 11 undergraduate colleges and awarding the largest number of bachelor's degrees of any school in the state. The school offers more than 100 bachelor's degrees, and boasts that "with over 300 bachelor's, master's and doctoral degree programs, we have more academic opportunities than any other public institution in New York or New England." Buffalo's total enrollment is roughly 24,000 students, over two-thirds of which are undergraduates.

Like any large school, Buffalo's size presents some inherent problems, such as enormous introductory classes, difficulty getting into popular courses, frustrating registration and administration procedures, and red tape. Students must take it upon themselves to develop relationships with faculty. One student says, "The teachers will help out if they can see the desire of the student." A recent graduate tells us that "some professors are very accessible; some don't give a damn about their students." On an interesting side note, a student informs us that "the mayor of Buffalo teaches a course here."

The advantage to the school's size, however, is the wealth of academic and social choices. Business, engineering, and premed are among Buffalo's more well-known and popular programs. Buffalo also has a range of strong liberal arts departments as well as more specific preprofessional training programs, such as its acclaimed programs in physical therapy and architecture. There are many special academic options as well, including internships, accelerated and dual degrees, an honors program, and opportunities for research work and off-campus study. A New York guidance counselor describes the faculty as "good and steadily improving" and says, "research projects are expanding."

General education requirements include courses in math and computer science, literature, writing, social sciences, and natural sciences. Graduate TA's teach a lot of these courses, but the students seem to be fine with this. "They teach well and work with the students well," says a student.

Campus Environment

The school, divided between two campuses, features many modern buildings. Buffalo has added several impressive new buildings and facilities in recent years, including a fine arts center, sports stadium, and science and math buildings. According to one student, the UB North area is generally considered safer than the University Heights, or South campus, area.

While Buffalo winters are notorious for subzero temperatures, the school makes a lot of accommodations to the climate. All the buildings are connected by either tunnels or covered bridges, or both. "I never have to go outside to get to class or to another dorm in the winter," one student tells us.

The dorms here are pretty standard; rooms are offered as singles, doubles, triples, or quads, though a student adds that "dorms are getting harder to get into as an upperclassman." There are on-campus apartments and townhouses available to upperclassmen, as well as the option of off-campus housing. A student tells us there is a "good variety" when it comes to off-campus living. "Many students live in the area near South campus, in the city of Buffalo, very popular because of access to bars and restaurants, as well as to other students; also very affordable. Still others live in Amherst and surrounding suburbs; nicer apartments, a little more pricey."

The city of Buffalo offers many cultural attractions including museums, performing arts theaters, symphonies, a variety of architecture and landscapes, and the beauty of the nearby Niagara Falls. A student says Buffalo offers "plenty to do, whether it is nightlife, or concerts, restaurants, shopping, other events." The city is able to offer something for everyone, even among the diversified student body at this large university. Students do feel that having a car is a big advantage here. "Definitely need a car to get around," one student says, adding that most students do have one. There are bus services, however, to transport students both around campus and around the city.

Student Life

A recent grad tells us that there is no such thing as a "typical" SUNY Buffalo student, since there are "too many races, nationalities, socioeconomic levels, religions, [and] intelligence levels." The social options at Buffalo are as plentiful and varied as the academic ones. There are tons of clubs and organizations that meet just about any kind of political or social interest, and the Greek system, while small, is active. (One recent grad says, "The school is too big and too diverse and athletes are too visible to make fraternities and sororities important to anyone but the Greeks themselves.") Despite the wealth of social opportunities, the sheer number of students and organizations can make it difficult for students to pull together as one student body. When asked about the campus atmosphere, a student replies, "It is kind of divided between the different groups and the different interests among the students."

Intramural and intercollegiate sports are both popular and benefit from an enormous sports center. The school boasts that "UB's rise from the ranks of Division III to Division I-A in less than ten years is unprecedented in modern-day NCAA history. As a new member of the prestigious Mid-American Conference, UB is the only institution in Western New York to have all intercollegiate sports competing at the highest level of intercollegiate competition." Some students feel, though, that a problem with the administration is that "millions are spent on athletics at the expense of academics."

A student says that on weekday nights, students typically "study, go out to eat, [participate in] student organizations." Weekends are described as "the same thing, but more drinking and shopping." The city of Buffalo offers a number of social venues, including several popular bars and other hangouts, shopping centers, and Buffalo Bills football. "It's a big sports town," comments one student. Students also rave about the Buffalo theater district, which draws many Broadway shows either in preview or on tour. "You'd be really surprised how good it is," says one student. "Buffalo students love it." Buffalo students also love the city's major claim to fame—eating buckets full of the best wings you'll ever taste.

Test Scores (middle 50%):
SAT Verbal: 500–600
SAT Math: 530–630
ACT Comp: 24–28
HS Rank of Entering Freshmen:
Top 10%: 22%
Top 25%: 56%
Top 50%: 91%
Avg. HS GPA: 3.1

THE EXPERTS SAY...

" With more than a hundred different bachelors' degrees awarded, Buffalo is more than the largest school in the SUNY system—it has the most programs of any school in New York. "

" Preprofessionals beware: The business, engineering, premed and architecture classes are great, but registering for them gives the words 'red tape' a whole new meaning. "

Costs (2003–04)

Tuition and Fees, In-State: $5,856

Tuition and Fees, Out-of-State: $11,806

Room & Board: $6,816 (varies)

Payment Plan(s): installment plan

Inst. Aid (est. 2003–04)

Institutional Aid, Need-Based: $1,958,059

Institutional Aid, Non-Need-Based: $1,789,710

FT Undergrads Receiving Aid: 52%
Avg. Amount per Student: $7,520

FT Undergrads Receiving Non-Need-Based Scholarship or Grant Aid: 2%
Avg. Amount per Student: $2,930

Of Those Receiving Any Aid:

Rec. Need-Based Scholarship or Grant Aid: 68%
Average Award: $3,573

Rec. Need-Based Self-Help Aid: 100%
Average Award: $4,450

Upon Graduation, Avg. Loan Debt per Student: $16,418

Financial Aid Deadline: rolling, 3/1 (priority)

Graduates

Going to Graduate School: 36% Within One Year

Companies Recruiting On Campus: 570

Alumni Giving: 21%

STETSON UNIVERSITY

421 N. Woodland Blvd, Unit 8378, DeLand, FL 32723
Admissions Phone: (386) 822-7100; (800) 688-0101 Fax: (386) 822-7112
Email: admissions@stetson.edu Website: www.stetson.edu
Application Website: www.stetson.edu/admissions/apply/onlineapp.html

General Info

Type of School: private, coed

Setting: suburban

Academic Calendar: semester

Student Body

Full-Time Undergrads: 2,042
  Men: 43%, Women: 57%

Part-Time Undergrads: 85
  Men: 38%, Women: 62%

Total Undergrad Population:
  African American: 3%
  Asian American: 2%
  Latino: 5%
  Native American: <1%
  Caucasian: 84%
  International: 3%
  Out-of-State: 20%
  Living Off-Campus: 35%
  In Fraternities: 33%
  In Sororities: 29%

Graduate and First-Professional
  Students: 1,278

Academics

Full-Time Faculty: 186
  With Ph.D.: 90%

Part-Time Faculty: 65

Student/Faculty Ratio: 11:1

Most Popular Majors:
  business (9%)
  education (7%)
  psychology (6%)
  music (6%)
  political science (5%)

Completing 2 or More Majors: 9%

Freshmen Retention Rate: 81%

Graduation Rates:
  56% within four years
  68% within six years

Admissions

Regular Application Deadline: 3/1
  (priority)

Early Decision Deadline(s): 11/1

Fall Transfer Deadline: 3/15 (priority)

Spring Transfer Deadline: 12/15

Total # of Students Applied: 1,992
  Admitted: 1,510
  Enrolled: 529

Applied Early Decision: 65
  Early Decision Admitted: 63

Inside the Classroom

Stetson University is a relatively small school located in DeLand, Florida. One guidance counselor calls it "a Northeastern college in a Southern setting," and guidance counselors across the country told us that Stetson deserves more national recognition. Its three undergraduate schools are the College of Arts & Sciences, the School of Business Administration, and the School of Music. Business in particular is well respected, since business and accounting are two of the few undergraduate programs in the country to be accredited by the prestigious American Assembly of Collegiate Schools of Business. In addition to the standard host of academic majors, Stetson also offers preprofessional programs in dentistry, engineering, forestry, law, medicine, and veterinary medicine.

Stetson is also one of the few schools to offer a digital arts major, in which the boundaries between music, sound design, fine art, commercial art, science, sociology, literature, and psychology become blurred. Designed to prepare students for new media careers and for graduate study in the arts and technology, the highly creative program requires students to work alone and collaboratively on hybrid forms of visual art, programming, and music composition. Another unusual major offered by Stetson is aquatic and marine biology, focusing on both saltwater and freshwater species. Sport and exercise science is another popular Stetson major.

Core requirements for the College of Arts & Sciences include coursework in three broad areas: "Foundations," "Breadth of Knowledge," and "Bases of Ethical Decision-making." "Foundations" include two first-year English courses, one oral communication course, one math course, and modern language proficiency. "Breadth of Knowledge" includes a civilization course, two natural science lab courses, two social science courses, a fine arts course, a religious heritage course, and a course in contemporary culture. "Bases" denotes a course in ethics. Business and music students have different core requirements. In addition to the core academic coursework, all students are required to attend a certain number of cultural events on campus for each semester of enrollment (three events for business and arts and sciences students; 14 events for music students).

Small classes are the norm at Stetson, which has a remarkable 11:1 student/faculty ratio. "I really like how small the classes are," said one student." You can be more comfortable. It's easier to ask questions." The lack of many classmates can have its drawbacks, however, as this student points out: "Because it's a small school with small classes, you will be expected to write a lot of papers and have essay tests. Also, your teachers notice if you skip a lot, and if you live on campus, they'll see you around." Stetson provides a "stress-free zone" for students during final exams, including massages, snacks and other stress-relieving activities.

Stetson also has a thriving Center for International Education that sponsors study abroad programs in other countries. Current offerings for students include programs in Guanajuato, Mexico; Nottingham, England; Madrid, Spain; Hong Kong, China; Freiburg, Germany; Moscow, Russia; and Avignon, France. Students interested in experiential learning and the environment can also participate in a volunteer reforestation project in Guatemala.

Campus Environment

Stetson's 165-acre campus in DeLand is resplendent with Florida greenery: palm, oak, and pine trees; wide lawns, winding walkways, and fountains. Its nearness to Daytona (25 miles) means that the beach is always a possibility, and the city of Orlando, with its myriad entertainment venues, is just 35 miles away. Natural sites for recreation and education include the nearby St. Johns River and the Ocala National Forest.

Freshmen are housed in dorms, and their rooms are clustered together to foster a sense of community. Although housing isn't guaranteed for all four years, the administration does its best to accommodate everyone, even to the point of housing non-Greek students in university-owned Greek houses until other spaces become available. Students cannot live in Greek housing until sophomore year. Students report that the nicer dorms are located near the student union, and that Stetson Hall has larger rooms than the others.

A new gem on campus is the recently completed Hollis Center. Containing a wood-floored gymnasium, a cardiovascular exercise room, an aerobics and dance studio, an Olympic-size pool, and classrooms, the center serves as the hub of student fitness and the headquarters for intramural sports on campus. The conjunction of the Hollis, Wilson, and Edmund Centers forms a three-building athletic complex that few schools of this size can match.

A notable campus landmark is the Holler Fountain, located in the center of the quadrangle between Sampson Hall, Elizabeth Hall, and DuPont Library. Sitting in the middle of a circular pool, the fountain is lit beautifully at night and is the focal point of a student tradition of birthday dunkings.

Student Life

There are 13 Greek organizations on the Stetson campus: 7 fraternities and 6 sororities, with over a third of undergraduates affiliated. Their houses are grouped together in the Greek Village section of campus and serve as the party hub when the weekend rolls around. "Greek life on campus is big," says one student. "They add a lot to college life."

A guidance counselor raves about Stetson's NCAA Division I sports, which include basketball, crew, cross country, golf, soccer, and tennis for both sexes. Men can also play baseball, while women may compete in softball and volleyball. The list of intramural sports features inner-tube water polo, flag football, indoor volleyball, tennis, basketball, bowling, soccer, table tennis, dodgeball, racquetball, sand volleyball, ultimate frisbee, softball, billiards, and swimming.

Stetson also plays host to several popular festivals during the year. At the annual International Guitar Workshop, musicians, teachers, and classical guitar students converge on the campus for four days of music making. Holiday season brings the annual Christmas Candlelight Concerts, in which the University Concert Choir pays tribute to the season with a concert held in a century-old chapel decorated with pine and poinsettias. On your birthday, get ready for a "fountain dunk," courtesy of your friends.

Stetson also has over 100 clubs and societies on campus. Some, like the Catholic Campus Ministry, are religious in nature, while others are centered around athletic or academic themes. Preprofessional societies like the Association for Computing Machinery are also in residence here, and music majors can find a generous selection of organizations like Sigma Alpha Iota and Phi Mu Alpha Sinfonia.

Test Scores (middle 50%):
SAT Verbal: 520–620
SAT Math: 510–610
ACT Comp: 21–27
ACT English: 21–27
ACT Math: 20–26

HS Rank of Entering Freshmen:
Top 10%: 32%
Top 25%: 58%
Top 50%: 87%

Avg. HS GPA: 3.54

THE EXPERTS SAY...

" Stetson University has very strong business and music programs. Its innovative digital arts major is a rarity in academia and proves that the university is interested in preparing students for 21st-century careers. "

" If the social life at Stetson is a little too Greek-centered for you, take a look at Eckerd College. If the Greek scene is what you crave, check out Furman University and Trinity University. "

Costs (2003–04)

Tuition and Fees: $22,640
Room & Board: $6,855
Payment Plan(s): installment plan

Inst. Aid (est. 2003–04)

Institutional Aid, Need-Based: $9,534,799

Institutional Aid, Non-Need-Based: $6,264,680

FT Undergrads Receiving Aid: 58%
Avg. Amount per Student: $19,406

FT Undergrads Receiving Non-Need-Based Scholarship or Grant Aid: 32%
Avg. Amount per Student: $11,283

Of Those Receiving Any Aid:

Rec. Need-Based Scholarship or Grant Aid: 100%
Average Award: $14,369

Rec. Need-Based Self-Help Aid: 71%
Average Award: $6,052

Upon Graduation, Avg. Loan Debt per Student: $20,000

Financial Aid Deadline: 3/15 (priority)

Graduates

Going to Graduate School: 35% Within One Year

Companies Recruiting On Campus: 100

STONEHILL COLLEGE

320 Washington Street, Easton, MA 02357-5610
Admissions Phone: (508) 565-1373 Fax: (508) 565-1545
Email: admissions@stonehill.edu
Website: www.stonehill.edu

General Info

Type of School: private, coed, Roman Catholic (Holy Cross Fathers)

Setting: suburban

Academic Calendar: semester

Student Body

Full-Time Undergrads: 2,219
  Men: 43%, Women: 57%

Part-Time Undergrads: 255
  Men: 27%, Women: 73%

Total Undergrad Population:
  African American: 3%
  Asian American: 3%
  Latino: 2%
  Native American: <1%
  Caucasian: 91%
  International: 1%
  Out-of-State: 38%
  Living Off-Campus: 24%

Graduate and First-Professional Students: 15

Academics

Full-Time Faculty: 130
  With Ph.D.: 82%

Part-Time Faculty: 109
  With Ph.D.: 39%

Student/Faculty Ratio: 14:1

Most Popular Majors:
  psychology (11%)
  communication (7%)
  biology (7%)
  English (6%)
  accounting (6%)

Completing 2 or More Majors: 12%

Freshmen Retention Rate: 91%

Graduation Rates:
  81% within four years
  85% within six years

Admissions

Regular Application Deadline: 1/15

Early Decision Deadline(s): 11/1, 12/15

Fall Transfer Deadline: 4/1

Spring Transfer Deadline: 11/1

Total # of Students Applied: 4,808
  Admitted: 2,366
  Enrolled: 568

Inside the Classroom

Founded by the same Roman Catholic order that brought the University of Notre Dame onto the education scene, Stonehill College is a small liberal arts school located just south of Boston that offers 30 high quality programs in the liberal arts, natural sciences, education, and business. "The goal of a Holy Cross Fathers education is to cultivate the mind as well as the heart," explains a Stonehill official. A high school guidance counselor praises the school's propensity for accepting "high-caliber students." Coursework is described by students as "heavy… but rewarding." "Stonehill has an amazing academic environment," an English major tells us. "Classes are very challenging and stimulating with a demanding workload. The majority of students here at Stonehill take their classes and their GPA seriously."

Classes are small (they range from "15 to 25 students per class," we hear) and strong, successful student-professor relationships are the norm. "My favorite aspect of Stonehill is the professors," an accounting major says. A marketing student agrees, "The majority of the professors are here because they are passionate about the subjects and issues they are teaching. They live for the students and love what they are doing, so they are available at all times for any additional help or advice." Mohammed el-Nawawy, assistant professor of communication at Stonehill, is a leading expert on Al-Jazeera, the Arabic news network; el-Nawawy's expertise has recently been sought by news outlets such as *Nightline*, the *Boston Globe*, and the *Associated Press*.

Stonehill recently put in motion the General Education Cornerstone curriculum, designed to produce higher quality and more well-rounded graduates. During their freshman year, all students take a series of first-year humanities courses. Sophomores enroll in what the school calls "Learning Communities," where faculty from separate disciplines team-teach a course. Juniors select a course from a range of options in moral reasoning, and seniors take a culminating course that combines mastery of the student's major with the content of the Cornerstone program.

Special study options abound at Stonehill. The Stonehill Undergraduate Research Experience (SURE) Program provides an opportunity for students who have completed their first year at Stonehill to perform significant, publishable research under faculty guidance; all SURE Scholars receive a stipend for an eight- or ten-week summer session. International internships are offered in Brussels, Dublin, London, Montreal, Paris, and Zaragoza for the spring of junior year or the fall of senior year. Elementary ed majors may even student-teach abroad.

Campus Environment

Nearly all of students we spoke to list the "beautiful campus" as one of the best aspects of Stonehill. "With the blooming flower gardens, state-of-the-art buildings, picturesque lawns, the variety of different residence areas, and 'the mansion' (a renovated mansion over a century old), Stonehill has one of the most unique and impressive campuses in the United States," one student gushes. (Interesting fact: The school "used to be an estate that made shovels," we're told. "There is a shovel museum on campus dedicated to this.")

Massachusetts guidance counselors have good things to say about Stonehill's on-campus housing, which is guaranteed for all four years. The rooms are large, comfortable, and available in a variety of setups. "To have on-campus housing is a privilege," a student says. We're told that all residential buildings have been built or renovated within the last few years. Freshmen are nearly always assigned to halls that house both first- and second-year students. Students of all classes can choose to live in the five dorms that comprise the Pilgrim Heights complex, where suite-style residences are centered around common lounges. Juniors and seniors can also live in the townhouses of Commonwealth and Colonial Courts. Interestingly, Stonehill uses a merit-based lottery system for housing that is jointly administered by a student lottery committee and the residence life office.

The center of student activity is the Roche Dining Commons, which houses the main eatery, student mail services, and a social hub named "The Hill" that contains a pub, a snack bar, a fireplace, a stage, and a dance floor. A conspicuous gem on campus is the recently completed MacPhaidin Library: In addition to its stacks and stacks of books, the library contains computer labs, small-group study rooms, and Internet ports.

The "upscale town" of Easton gets high marks from many Stonehill students. "It is a quaint little town that offers a variety of restaurants, coffee shops, and shopping plazas that welcome Stonehill students," a junior says. But another warns, "Easton isn't much of a college town; in fact, you might say that it closes down at 10 P.M. Fortunately, it's close enough to Boston and Providence that people have access to fun places off-campus." Most students, we hear, get around by car, though "parking is a major issue." The school just introduced a new shuttle system "that takes students to the train station, bus stations, and area malls and eateries."

Student Life

Stonehill students praise their campus as a friendly one: "The people here truly care about one other," a junior tells us. "We really are like a family here." Though the typical coed can be summed up by one student's description—"a liberal, white, Irish-Catholic, affluent student who is very well-dressed, well-groomed, and involved"—we're told that "the college has done a great job in improving the international and ethnic ratios over the past two years."

The administration has strict policies governing alcohol use, but this doesn't stop weekend bar-hopping from happening. "While Stonehill has a 'rowdy' reputation on the weekends, I would not consider it a party school," a student tells us. "Stonehill is a drinking school, though." The Courts (upperclass townhouses) are "packed on the weekend with students and parties," and people "do take advantage of the numerous bars, pubs, and clubs in Providence and Boston," a junior says. "Mostly, though, on the weekends, the majority of students simply sit in their rooms and drink with their friends."

"School events that people enjoy and are highly attended are the Mr. Stonehill Pageant, the Halloween and New Year's Mixers, and Spring Weekend," a student tells us. There are more than 60 student organizations, and Stonehill has 20 NCAA Division II teams, though we hear that, with the exception of women's basketball, games are "not well-attended." But with an extensive indoor/outdoor intramural sports program for students at all levels of ability, it's no surprise that more than 80 percent of students at Stonehill participate in intramurals.

Other schools to check out: Providence, St. Anselm, Villanova, Boston College.

# of Students Waitlisted: 723
　Students Accepting Place: 204
　Waitlisted Students Admitted: 53

Applied Early Decision: 91
　Early Decision Admitted: 50

Test Scores (middle 50%):
SAT Verbal: 550–630
SAT Math: 560–640
ACT Comp: 24–27

HS Rank of Entering Freshmen:
Top 10%: 49%
Top 25%: 86%
Top 50%: 100%

Avg. HS GPA: 3.53

THE EXPERTS SAY...

" While the liberal arts are at the core of its identity as a Catholic college, Stonehill offers strong programs in business administration and in education. "

" Stonehill encourages participation in extracurriculars to help cultivate the entire person... much as the shovels in its shovel museum once helped cultivate the crops. (Ouch, that's a real stretch...) "

Costs (2004–5)

Tuition and Fees: $23,008

Room & Board: $10,206

Payment Plan(s): installment plan, pre-payment plan

Inst. Aid (est. 2003–04)

FT Undergrads Receiving Aid: 66%
　Avg. Amount per Student: $15,639

FT Undergrads Receiving Non-Need-Based Scholarship or Grant Aid: 22%
　Avg. Amount per Student: $10,069

Of Those Receiving Any Aid:

Rec. Need-Based Scholarship or Grant Aid: 95%
　Average Award: $10,999

Rec. Need-Based Self-Help Aid: 90%
　Average Award: $5,736

Upon Graduation, Avg. Loan Debt per Student: $17,444

Financial Aid Deadline: 2/1

Graduates

Going to Graduate School:
　16% Within One Year

Companies Recruiting On Campus: 74

Alumni Giving: 54%

SUSQUEHANNA UNIVERSITY

514 University Avenue, Selinsgrove, PA 17870-1040
Admissions Phone: (570) 372-4260; (800) 326-9672 Fax: (570) 372-2722
Email: suadmiss@susqu.edu
Website: www.susqu.edu

General Info

Type of School: private, coed, Lutheran (ELCA)

Setting: suburban

Academic Calendar: semester

Student Body

Full-Time Undergrads: 1,904
  Men: 44%, Women: 56%

Part-Time Undergrads: 29
  Men: 34%, Women: 66%

Total Undergrad Population:
  African American: 2%
  Asian American: 2%
  Latino: 2%
  Native American: 1%
  Caucasian: 93%
  International: 1%
  Out-of-State: 40%
  Living Off-Campus: 80%
  In Fraternities: 25%
  In Sororities: 25%

Academics

Full-Time Faculty: 118
  With Ph.D.: 90%

Part-Time Faculty: 68
  With Ph.D.: 26%

Student/Faculty Ratio: 13:1

Most Popular Majors:
  business (23%)
  communications (15%)
  biology (7%)
  psychology (6%)
  elemetary education (6%)

Freshmen Retention Rate: 88%

Graduation Rates:
  76% within four years
  78% within six years

Admissions

Regular Application Deadline: 5/1

Early Decision Deadline(s): 11/15, 1/1

Fall Transfer Deadline: 7/1

Spring Transfer Deadline: 12/1

Total # of Students Applied: 2,373
  Admitted: 1,660
  Enrolled: 499

# of Students Waitlisted: 272
  Students Accepting Place: 130
  Waitlisted Students Admitted: 17

Inside the Classroom

Susquehanna lets students enjoy "university" qualities in a smaller "college" environment. Students may choose from more than 50 majors in three undergraduate schools, or they may design their own major or complete an interdisciplinary program. Preprofessional programs, such as business, education, and communications, are the school's greatest strengths. The Sigmund Weis School of Business is the most prestigious school on campus. Science programs (particularly biology) in the School of Natural and Social Sciences are increasingly cited among the school's best, and we hear that the English department in the School of Arts, Humanities, and Communications is strong as well.

The school prides itself on providing excellent experienced-based, "real-world" learning—taking this principle so far as to have a couple of mandatory business ethics classes taught by white-collar criminals, so students get a firsthand look at "successful" professionals who took it too far and were caught. Nearly half of all SU students take advantage of the numerous opportunities for internships and independent study.

With its small class sizes (averaging 20 students), impressive student/faculty interaction, and strong programs (in business and science especially), SU draws raves from students, parents, alumni, and peers. "It is competitive," says one student, "but not overwhelming. The pressure to do well is significant, however most stress is placed on the idea that you've done your best." All students must fulfill a comprehensive core curriculum; the "personal development" part of the core includes fitness, career planning, and College 101. Professors are helpful, and "go out of their way to offer extended office hours and are always willing to give extra help when possible."

Susquehanna applicants who are in the top 20 percent of their high school class can take advantage of the unique Write Option during the application process: An alternative to the SAT or ACT, qualified students may choose to submit two graded writing (not creative) samples instead of standardized test scores. About ten percent of first-years are offered admission to the challenging, individualized Honors Program, cited by the National Collegiate Honors Council as a model for selective colleges.

Campus Environment

Students brag that theirs is one of the prettiest campuses in the country, especially during the fall. The campus—and the surrounding area—is quite safe and well lit. It's also a friendly place, according to a senior: "When walking around campus most people have a smile on their faces and most say hello in passing, even if you don't know them."

The majority of students live on campus. In fact, Susquehanna requires that nearly all students who aren't commuting from their parents' home live in university housing, which, according to an upperclassman, "sucks. They put three people in rooms for two and can't build fast enough to support the increase in class size." There are six coed halls, two for first-year students; a women's dorm; a scholars' house; an upperclass apartment and townhouse complex; and many small university-owned homes next to campus. One popular option is the Project House system, where students who live together also work together on a volunteer community project. A lottery is held for those who have been granted special permission to move off-campus (seniors get first shot).

SU's campus is just a few blocks from downtown Selinsgrove, a sleepy, quaint town. There are a handful of shops, restaurants, and businesses, and while we heard of no animosity between the locals and the students, the town is hardly geared toward entertaining nearly 2,000 undergrads. Selinsgrove is located on the shores of the Susquehanna River, and so there are opportunities for boating, swimming, and ice skating, but not much else. It's in the heart of Pennsylvania, which means it's about a three-hour drive from Philadelphia, DC, and New York City. Speaking of which, many students have cars, and "there is no public transportation beyond Chuck's Sports Bar's 'Drunk Bus' on Thursday nights for 25 cent drafts," according to an upperclassman. "You can walk to the post office, but you need a car to get to Walmart or the mall or a pharmacy, etc." If it's city life you're looking for, you'd best look elsewhere (though, much like in the city, parking can be a problem here).

Student Life

It's a close-knit, friendly community, but not very diverse; SU's campus is awash in white, well-to-do preppies. The Greek system is a considerable force on campus; about one-quarter of all students join a frat or sorority (plus some "underground fraternities" which were causing problems for the administration last year, we hear). For many students—especially freshmen—frat parties are the only game in town on the weekends. However, while a student says that frats "supply parties—that's about it," still "everyone pretty much mingles with one another." We are told that "anyone could attend Susquehanna and find a place among its students." There are off-campus parties (drinking on campus is asking for trouble) and, if you're 21, there are a few local bars.

There are 23 NCAA Division III varsity teams—the golf, softball, football, field hockey, and men's and women's basketball teams are nationally ranked—and numerous club and intramural sports. Sixty percent of the student body plays on one team or another (about a third are varsity athletes), and we hear the turnout for games is pretty decent. However, according to one student, "sports are not the heart and soul of the campus."

SU has more than 100 clubs and organizations, and a strong tradition of community service; two-thirds of Susquehanna students reportedly volunteer at some point. The Campus Center is home to many student groups, as well as a coffeehouse ("There is always a movie being shown at Charlie's on Friday nights" one student tells us), a 450-seat theater, the campus radio station, and more. One student explains the unique requirements of expanding your personality in a small-town atmosphere: "[Students] must be resourceful and open to trying new things: tubing on the river, visiting the reptile farm, attending faculty readings, getting involved in the many school activities and clubs." The graduating senior adds, "It's about broadening your horizons in the middle of nowhere." Though it doesn't hurt to bring some acts in from the outside—"We've had Cypress Hill, the Roots, Jon Stewart, Adam Sandler, Smashmouth, Rusted Root, and this spring Dave Chappelle and Jim Breuer are performing!"

Other schools to check out: Juniata, Ursinus, Allegheny, College of Wooster, Hiram.

Applied Early Decision: 133
  Early Decision Admitted: 102

Test Scores (middle 50%):
  SAT Verbal: 530–610
  SAT Math: 530–630

THE EXPERTS SAY...

" Susquehanna's comprehensive core curriculum—covering intellectual skills, perspectives on the world, and personal development—lays a solid foundation for success in the real world. "

" 'Broadening your horizons in the middle of nowhere' can be quite a trick. Wise students will rely on Susquehanna's real-world learning opportunities for some perspective. "

HS Rank of Entering Freshmen:
  Top 10%: 30%
  Top 25%: 65%
  Top 50%: 95%

Costs (2004–5)

Tuition and Fees: $24,810

Room & Board: $6,840

Payment Plan(s): installment plan, pre-payment plan

Inst. Aid (est. 2003–04)

Institutional Aid, Need-Based: $12,724,126

Institutional Aid, Non-Need-Based: $4,635,761

FT Undergrads Receiving Aid: 65%
  Avg. Amount per Student: $17,158

FT Undergrads Receiving Non-Need-Based Scholarship or Grant Aid: 24%
  Avg. Amount per Student: $8,143

Of Those Receiving Any Aid:

Rec. Need-Based Scholarship or Grant Aid: 99%
  Average Award: $13,319

Rec. Need-Based Self-Help Aid: 85%
  Average Award: $4,734

Upon Graduation, Avg. Loan Debt per Student: $16,756

Financial Aid Deadline: 5/1, 3/1 (priority)

Graduates

Going to Graduate School:
  16% Within One Year

Accepting Job Offer:
  20% at time of graduation

Companies Recruiting On Campus: 45

SWARTHMORE COLLEGE

500 College Avenue, Swarthmore, PA 19081
Admissions Phone: (610) 328-8300; (800) 667-3110 Fax: (610) 328-8580
Email: admissions@swarthmore.edu Website: www.swarthmore.edu
Application Website: www.commonapp.org

General Info

Type of School: private, coed
Setting: suburban
Academic Calendar: semester

Student Body

Full-Time Undergrads: 1,477
  Men: 47%, Women: 53%

Total Undergrad Population:
  African American: 7%
  Asian American: 16%
  Latino: 8%
  Native American: 1%
  Caucasian: 53%
  International: 5%
  Out-of-State: 84%
  Living Off-Campus: 7%
  In Fraternities: 6%
  In Sororities: 0%

Academics

Full-Time Faculty: 168
  With Ph.D.: 99%

Part-Time Faculty: 35
  With Ph.D.: 74%

Student/Faculty Ratio: 8:1

Most Popular Majors:
  economics
  political science
  English literature
  biology
  psychology

Completing 2 or More Majors: 20%

Freshmen Retention Rate: 97%

Graduation Rates:
  83% within four years
  92% within six years

Admissions

Regular Application Deadline: 1/1

Early Decision Deadline(s): 11/15,
  1/1

Fall Transfer Deadline: 4/1

Total # of Students Applied: 3,908
  Admitted: 920
  Enrolled: 368
  Waitlisted Students Admitted: 21

Applied Early Decision: 304
  Early Decision Admitted: 138

Test Scores (middle 50%):
  SAT Verbal: 670–770
  SAT Math: 670–760

Inside the Classroom

Swarthmore is consistently rated as one of the best liberal arts colleges in the country. It's certainly one of the toughest. Classes are described by some as "intense" and "challenging," by others as "a real pressure cooker." And this seems to be exactly what Swarthmore's highly motivated students want. The grading system here is no joke: As one high school guidance counselor sums it up, it's "much harder than most other colleges." Most "Swatties" take pride in their school's tough standards—after all, there's a reason why the T-shirts that read "Anywhere else it would have been an A ... really" sell so well at the campus bookstore.

Almost all departments and programs are first-rate, from English to engineering to political science. The distribution requirements ensure that students take at least 20 credits outside their major department, including three credits in each of the three divisions of the College: humanities, natural sciences, and social sciences. These requirements are usually completed in the first two years. Incoming students will probably be happy to learn that freshmen are graded on a pass/fail basis for their first semester to help them get used to the school's rigorous academics. The course offerings are a bit limited, and it can be tough to get into certain courses. However, students can cross-register with nearby Haverford, Bryn Mawr, and the University of Pennsylvania, all of which have their own excellent academic offerings.

The "intentionally small" campus population cultivates a feeling of being immersed in a closely knit, highly intellectual community. Students work with fellow students as well as the faculty. The professors teach all the classes, even for freshmen, and are extremely involved with their students' education. Many students have stories of profs holding their final seminar classes over dinner in their homes. But the professors demand a lot from their students in return. A New Jersey guidance counselor notes that the students all have type-A personalities and that there are "too many chiefs, not enough Indians."

For the extremely well-motivated (or "masochistic," according to one student), Swarthmore offers a special program called the External Examination Program, particularly recommended for those looking to continue their education after graduation. Here, honors students take eight seminars, with very limited enrollments, during their last two years, but don't take any exams until the end of senior year, when they're subjected to a difficult comprehensive written and oral examination. It's not for everyone, but those who participate in it find it very rewarding (though a guidance counselor calls it "a bit elitist").

So okay, we know its academics are superb, but what is it that separates Swarthmore from the rest of the pack? Perhaps it's the "successful combination of academic rigor with social responsibility," as their PR office says. Through its Summer of Service program, the college pays a student-worker wage to students (100–150 a year) who perform otherwise unpaid community service internships. Swarthmore also has endowed support for more than 60 students to do summer research each year. Special grants provide an additional 30–40 summer research opportunities on a regular basis.

Campus Environment

Saying that Swarthmore has "a lovely suburban campus" may be a bit of an understatement—a "living museum," as school literature puts it, may be more like it. The campus features over 330 wooded acres that are maintained by staff horticulturists as a nationally registered arboretum. As part of a major improvement in athletic facilities, Swarthmore recently opened the popular Mullan Tennis Center, which includes indoor courts for intercollegiate and recreational tennis and a state-of-the-art fitness center, and is constructing a new science center.

Freshmen live in buildings that house all four classes. More than 90 percent of the student body lives on campus for all four years, and tends to stay around on weekends. This really has the effect of creating a family-like atmosphere on campus. Such a small student population has its positive aspects, but it also has some drawbacks. "Our community makes it possible to maintain a rumor mill whose efficiency rivals the Internet!" a student declares. Swatties may also apply for a housing exchange to live on the Bryn Mawr or Haverford campus, but they might be more interested in staying put now that coed rooms have been introduced on campus ("on a small scale").

You can forget about bringing a car: Parking is very limited, and the required permits are scarce and generally issued only to seniors and those with disabilities. But the school runs shuttles between Swarthmore and its tri-college partners, Bryn Mawr and Haverford, and there is a train station on the edge of campus for trips to Philadelphia and beyond.

Student Life

True to its Quaker roots, Swarthmore attracts a diverse, largely liberal student body. (Although in recent years it has mellowed in its leftist extremism, the school is still sometimes dubbed "The Kremlin on the Crum," referring to its liberal politics and the Crum Creek, which runs along the campus.) Administration and students alike place a high value on what the school's president calls "ethical intelligence."

In general, social life takes a back seat to academia at Swarthmore. If you're looking for a traditional college party scene, you'd better look elsewhere. There are no sororities, and only two fraternities. Most of Swat's social scene takes place on campus, with school-sponsored events like concerts, parties, dances, and movies, which are all free for students. In addition to the 12 popular intramural teams, athletes may participate in Swarthmore's 21 varsity and five club sports. Altogether, roughly half the student population plays some form of organized athletics. But don't expect to spend your fall Saturdays cheering on the football team—Swat doesn't have one (football, along with wrestling, was dropped from the roster in late 2000).

The school does have its wackier special events, too. There's the McCabe Mile, an 18-lap race through—no kidding—the basement of the library (the winner gets a roll of toilet paper); the Crum Regatta, where students race handmade boats; and the fundraiser called "Dash for Cash," where the men's and women's rugby teams take off their clothes and take off running.

Other schools to check out: Amherst, Haverford, Carleton, Bryn Mawr, University of Chicago, Wesleyan.

HS Rank of Entering Freshmen:
Top 10%: 92%
Top 25%: 99%
Top 50%: 100%

Costs (2003–04)

Tuition and Fees: $30,094

Room & Board: $8,314

Payment Plan(s): installment plan

THE EXPERTS SAY...

"Intellectuals: Swarthmore's rigor and intensity may be just what you're looking for."

"Swarthmore's grade deflation is legendary. An A anywhere else is a B here."

Inst. Aid (est. 2003–04)

Institutional Aid, Need-Based: $14,584,493

Institutional Aid, Non-Need-Based: $273,375

FT Undergrads Receiving Aid: 49%
Avg. Amount per Student: $26,088

FT Undergrads Receiving Non-Need-Based Scholarship or Grant Aid: 1%
Avg. Amount per Student: $28,500

Of Those Receiving Any Aid:

Rec. Need-Based Scholarship or Grant Aid: 100%
Average Award: $22,251

Rec. Need-Based Self-Help Aid: 95%
Average Award: $4,039

Upon Graduation, Avg. Loan Debt per Student: $13,533

Financial Aid Deadline: 2/15 (priority)

Graduates

Going to Graduate School: 29% Within One Year

Accepting Job Offer: 43% at time of graduation

Companies Recruiting On Campus: 84

Alumni Giving: 66%

SWEET BRIAR COLLEGE

P.O. Box B, Sweet Briar, VA 24595
Admissions Phone: (434) 381-6142; (800) 381-6142 Fax: (434) 381-6152
Email: admissions@sbc.edu Website: www.admissions.sbc.edu
Application Website: www.admissions.sbc.edu/apply/

General Info

Type of School: private, all women

Setting: rural

Academic Calendar: semester

Student Body

Full-Time Undergrads: 514
  Women: 100%

Part-Time Undergrads: 10
  Women: 100%

Total Undergrad Population:
  African American: 3%
  Asian American: 2%
  Latino: 2%
  Native American: 1%
  Caucasian: 88%
  International: 3%
  Out-of-State: 51%
  Living Off-Campus: 10%

Academics

Full-Time Faculty: 71
  With Ph.D.: 97%

Part-Time Faculty: 30
  With Ph.D.: 37%

Student/Faculty Ratio: 7:1

Most Popular Majors:
  psychology (6%)
  biology (5%)
  government (5%)
  international affairs (3%)
  history (3%)

Completing 2 or More Majors: 11%

Freshmen Retention Rate: 79%

Graduation Rates:
  64% within four years
  67% within six years

Admissions

Regular Application Deadline: 2/1

Early Decision Deadline(s): 12/1

Fall Transfer Deadline: 7/1

Spring Transfer Deadline: 11/15

Total # of Students Applied: 404
  Admitted: 355
  Enrolled: 133

Applied Early Decision: 45
  Early Decision Admitted: 42

Inside the Classroom

Sweet Briar College offers some very strong programs, including psychology, government, English and creative writing, environmental science, biology, and chemistry. Students can design an interdisciplinary major focused on a topic of special interest or construct individualized majors. The college recently announced some new programs, including a B.A. degree in business management, an interdisciplinary Bachelor of Fine Arts degree, and a preprofessional certificate program in equine studies.

The low student to faculty ratio means that classes average 12 students—small enough to encourage active learning in many lecture, seminar, and discussion groups. "You can't hide, and you're forced to get involved in the community," one student tells us. The faculty members are dedicated to teaching and often establish relationships with students that extend beyond the classroom. "Most Sweet Briar professors live on campus and attend campus events; as a result, it is not unlikely that a student will run into her professors at the gym, at the Bistro, or at the Laundromat," an international affairs major tells us. "In addition, Sweet Briar professors take the initiative to call or email students if a student has missed several classes or is doing poorly in a class."

Sweet Briar's Honor System means self-scheduled (and sometimes unproctored) exams. Every paper that a student turns in and every exam a student completes is signed with an honor pledge. "Sweet Briar women are the epitome of honorable," says a proud senior.

One of the special study options at Sweet Briar is the Honors Summer Research Fellowships, a competitive, eight-week on-campus summer program that allows students from all disciplines to conduct independent research. Students also have the option of taking courses at the other colleges in the Seven College Exchange (Hampden-Sydney, Hollins, Mary Baldwin, Randolph Macon, Randolph Macon Woman's College, and Washington and Lee) or participating in a study abroad program.

Campus Environment

Sweet Briar's 3,300-acre campus in the foothills of Virginia's Blue Ridge Mountains is criss-crossed with hiking, biking, and riding trails through woodlands and dells and around small lakes that provide spectacular outdoor recreational activities. Sweet Briar's riding center, one of the largest and best-designed college facilities in the country, attracts both competitive and recreational riders. Getting to and from the riding center is easy, thanks to van service.

The campus is located on the outskirts of Lynchburg, about 45 miles south of Charlottesville, in a secluded and rural environment. "Most Sweet Briar women venture into the nearby towns of Madison Heights (15 minute drive) and Lynchburg (20 minute drive) for only three reasons: Wal-Mart, movies, or a dinner off campus," claims a senior. Students looking for city excitement can travel to Richmond and DC, two and three hours away by road to the east and northeast. Safety is not an issue here: "We are a very safe campus, because everyone watches out for everyone else," says a student.

The lack of men on campus has led some students to nickname Sweet Briar "The Four-Year Slumber Party." Unless you are 23 years old, married, living with a parent or guardian, or financially independent, you're required to live in on-campus residences, each of which house between 30 and 200 women each. First-year students are housed in double rooms; sophomores, juniors, and seniors may choose to live in single rooms or triple and quad suites. The guest option hours for male guests in student rooms range from Option 1 (most restrictive) to Option 3 (least restrictive). Only a few first-years choose Option 1, where men are only allowed until around 10 p.m. on the weekends and not at all during the week. (None of the options permit overnight male guests.)

Student Life

Sweet Briar has come a long way since the days it had the reputation of being a finishing school for dainty Southern belles. Today, the women of Sweet Briar are encouraged to develop their academic and personal strengths. A student puts it more bluntly for us: "I used to think the stuff about women being around other women making them better leaders was bull, but it's totally not." The typical Sweet Briar woman, according to one senior, is "white, from an upper-middle class to affluent family, more conservative than liberal, and generally self-confident." But another student notes, "Over the last 4 years, they have done a good job of making the campus more diverse." And a senior majoring in environmental journalism chimes in, "Lots of girls ride horses and live for Vera Bradley bags, but there is an emerging group that is environmentally oriented."

Sweet Briar College is not a party school by any stretch of the imagination, but a young woman will find plenty to do after study hours if she looks. The weekend social scene consists of dorm parties or going off-campus to visit male friends at other colleges, including the all-male Hampden-Sydney college about an hour away. "Underclassmen go to other colleges to see guys or to frat parties," explains a student. "Juniors and seniors get a little tired of that scene. They stay on campus and entertain themselves." Students report that the administration has really cracked down on partying in the last couple of years, now strictly enforcing the drinking policies on campus—"basically, no drinking in public places, except at the campus Bistro."

Sweet Briar has an outstanding riding program that can teach students all they want to learn and enough to fit right into the demands of the horse industry without the need of a typical B.S. degree in equine science. About half of the students participate in NCAA Division III sports or in Sweet Briar's club sports.

There are no sororities at Sweet Briar, but plenty of clubs and activities in lieu of Greek societies. The most popular clubs are the Bum Chums (service organization with local outreach), Habitat for Humanity, Amnesty International, Young Democrats, and College Republicans. Students are self-governed through the Student Government Association, and all subscribe to and abide by the Honor System. Students say that their campus traditions, such as Lantern Bearing and Step Singing, are *extremely* important to them. Other activities include dell parties on fall and spring nights, formals, Junior Banquet, and bands in the Bistro.

Other schools to check out: Randolph-Macon Woman's College, Mt. Holyoke, Agnes Scott, Hollins, Chatham.

Test Scores (middle 50%):
  SAT Verbal: 500–620
  SAT Math: 490–570
  ACT Comp: 20–26
  ACT English: 21–28
  ACT Math: 18–24

HS Rank of Entering Freshmen:
  Top 10%: 23%
  Top 25%: 58%
  Top 50%: 90%

Avg. HS GPA: 3.39

THE EXPERTS SAY...

"No doubt the stellar relationships between students and professors at Sweet Briar are a huge asset to these students as they apply to graduate programs at top schools around the country."

"Are campus traditions and horseback riding adequate substitutes for male companionship? (The answer: probably!)"

Costs (2004–5)

Tuition and Fees: $21,080

Room & Board: $8,520

Payment Plan(s): installment plan

Inst. Aid (est. 2003–04)

Upon Graduation, Avg. Loan Debt per Student: $17,250.00

Financial Aid Deadline: 2/1

Graduates

Going to Graduate School: 30% Within One Year

Accepting Job Offer: 64% at time of graduation

Companies Recruiting On Campus: 69

SYRACUSE UNIVERSITY

200 Tolley Administration Building, Syracuse, NY 13244
Admissions Phone: (315) 443-3611
Email: orange@syr.edu Website: www.syr.edu
Application Website: admissions.syr.edu

General Info

Type of School: private, coed

Setting: urban

Academic Calendar: semester

Student Body

Full-Time Undergrads: 10,746
 Men: 44%, Women: 56%

Part-Time Undergrads: 94
 Men: 57%, Women: 43%

Total Undergrad Population:
 African American: 6%
 Asian American: 6%
 Latino: 4%
 Native American: <1%
 Caucasian: 71%
 International: 3%
 Out-of-State: 56%
 Living Off-Campus: 27%
 In Fraternities: 12%
 In Sororities: 16%

Graduate and First-Professional
 Students: 4,758

Academics

Full-Time Faculty: 864
 With Ph.D.: 87%

Part-Time Faculty: 498

Student/Faculty Ratio: 12:1

Most Popular Majors:
 psychology (5%)
 political science (4%)
 management & technology (4%)
 marketing (4%)
 architecture (4%)

Completing 2 or More Majors: 27%

Freshmen Retention Rate: 91%

Graduation Rates:
 69% within four years
 81% within six years
 note: 5-yr. programs affect grad rates

Admissions

Regular Application Deadline: 1/1

Early Decision Deadline(s): 11/15

Fall Transfer Deadline: 1/1 (priority)

Spring Transfer Deadline: 11/15
 (priority)

Total # of Students Applied: 14,144
 Admitted: 8,718
 Enrolled: 2,650

Inside the Classroom

A senior raves about the "academic opportunities" and the "vast number of majors" (more than 200) at Syracuse. Among Syracuse's 11 undergraduate schools are the School of Architecture, College of Engineering and Computer Science, School of Management, and College of Visual and Performing Arts. Syracuse is particularly known for its prestigious S. I. Newhouse School of Communications, considered one of the best communications programs in the nation. The pioneering School of Information Studies is top ranked. The College of Arts and Science has many strong programs, particularly in the natural sciences; social science courses are taught by the faculty of the esteemed Maxwell School of Citizenship and Public Affairs.

With the goal of becoming the finest student-centered research university in the nation, Syracuse emphasizes teaching and state-of-the art facilities (Syracuse is a member of the Internet 2 consortium). A psych major says, "Professors are available a fair amount," and a New York guidance counselor notes, "The class size has gotten smaller and they deal with students one-on-one." All of Syracuse's schools participate in the Freshman Forum advising system, in which 15 students work with a professor and one another for two years, and first-year students have the opportunity to study with distinguished professors in small classroom settings. (Some profs collaborate on research with undergrads.) However, a junior complains, "During registration, classes often fill up very quickly, leaving people stranded without being able to take required classes. Many classes are taught by graduate TA's, many who don't speak English, much to the anger of students."

A political science major reports, "Certain classes are known to be easier than others... classes like Public Affairs are known for [their] heavy workload." Says a senior, "Competitiveness is really only seen in the 'prestigious' majors such as Newhouse and VPA." One student complains of the "mandatory writing classes." A junior concludes, "I chose Syracuse because of the scholarship and financial aid I was offered... but if I could do it again, I wouldn't change anything. I've made too many friends and have had a great academic experience."

Campus Environment

Syracuse students have concerns about crime off campus. "Very dangerous lately," declares a senior. "[I] can't even walk to my boyfriend's; violence and crime are high and college students are targets." Adds a junior: "Cops are more worried about busting off campus parties than they are about protecting the neighborhoods." However, "Downtown Armory square and Marshall street have the bars and the social life; Carousel Mall, expanding again, has *everything*."

"Syracuse University's Hall of Languages building was the design basis for the Addams Family house," a student informs us. The student center is new, and in the works is a Center of Excellence in Environmental Systems (CoE-ES), which will be headquartered at Syracuse's Center for Science and Technology; the center will be dedicated to developing new environmental technologies.

Students are required to live on campus for two years. Housing is "very available" but "certain places are NOT easily available if you are an underclassman." The room sizes are "average" in dorms, and the apartments on South Campus are recommended. A senior advises: "Watson suites are worth it." Also: "Many like BB [the Brewster-Boland complex] as freshmen; first two years all your friends are from your dorms." Housing is guaranteed for all four years. Syracuse was recently ranked third by the People for the Ethical Treatment of Animals for the vegan and vegetarian selections found in campus dining halls; for nonvegans, there are brand restaurant chains in the food court.

"Off campus housing is popular with juniors and seniors," says a junior, but a senior warns, "The trek to campus can be brutal; people hate their landlords." Costs are "pretty reasonable with a lot of people." Students say a car is "nice" but not necessary; freshmen are not allowed to have cars. (Adds a senior: "Parking can be a bitch.") Students call the steep hills daunting, and hop the campus bus during the cold and snowy Syracuse winters.

Student Life

"People who aren't even sports fans are sports fans when Syracuse is doing well," declares a student. Hordes crowd the cavernous Carrier Dome to cheer on the Orangemen at intercollegiate events: "Basketball and football are huge," a senior reports. But "lacrosse needs attention."

Besides sports, there are 300 other activities and clubs. Newhouse students help make the school newspaper, three on-campus radio stations, and TV station excellent; VPA students provide frequent performances. Also, major rock groups often make the Dome a stopping point on their tours. And the wired student body creates its own entertainment: At least 16 students recently had their network ports closed for making illegal movies and music available online after SU was hit with copyright violation complaints.

The campus atmosphere is "very rowdy, party school, very college-like spontaneous drinking and fun," says a senior, but there's tension due to the "Greek versus non-Greek thing." A student describes a typical week: "Drink-drink-movies-drink-parties-Marshall Street-library-drink." Another declares, "Even students who come in as freshmen not drinking end up drinking by senior year." Some do make it to the library: "The library (especially 4th floor) is known to be a popular pick-up place and the myth is that you meet a future boyfriend/girlfriend [there]."

The SU "stereotype" is "frat boy/sorority girl... who dress alike in expensive clothing, Abercrombie and Fitch-type"... "Most noticed: Northface fleece, Tiffany bracelets, long straight highlighted hair, too-tan face, scowl, NY accent." Fraternities and sororities are a "big influence" due to their "tons of events," says a senior, but a junior counters, "Greek life is fairly popular, however, [it] only accounts for a minority of the school population."

While a senior cites "the diversity of people" as a Syracuse strength, a political science major comments, "Students self-segregate themselves by race." A recent controversy "involved a fraternity brother who, during a senior dress-up day, put black face on and dressed as Tiger Woods. The student was white, and caused more tension between the races at school." A psychology major complains of "students' lack of interest in campus happenings." A move for a revote in a controversial Student Association election was rejected, according to the *Daily Orange*, because of expected voter apathy and because it was too near the holidays.

Other schools to check out: Boston U, Georgetown, Ithaca, Northeastern, American U.

Applied Early Decision: 748
  Early Decision Admitted: 492

Test Scores (middle 50%):
  SAT Verbal: 570–640
  SAT Math: 580–670

HS Rank of Entering Freshmen:
  Top 10%: 44%
  Top 25%: 80%
  Top 50%: 98%

Avg. HS GPA: 3.6

THE EXPERTS SAY...

" The prestigious S. I. Newhouse school has a strong alumni network, and graduates get media jobs (Ted Koppel and Bob Costas are alums). "

" Diversity doesn't mean unity, as the SU student body demonstrates. At least the students can all get behind the Orangemen. "

Costs (2003–04)

Tuition and Fees: $25,130

Room & Board: $9,590

Payment Plan(s): installment plan

Inst. Aid (est. 2003–04)

Institutional Aid, Need-Based: $70,575,719

Institutional Aid, Non-Need-Based: $13,656,309

FT Undergrads Receiving Aid: 58%
  Avg. Amount per Student: $18,720

FT Undergrads Receiving Non-Need-Based Scholarship or Grant Aid: 17%
  Avg. Amount per Student: $7,240

Of Those Receiving Any Aid:

Rec. Need-Based Scholarship or Grant Aid: 89%
  Average Award: $12,793

Rec. Need-Based Self-Help Aid: 89%
  Average Award: $6,800

Upon Graduation, Avg. Loan Debt per Student: $19,000

Financial Aid Deadline: 2/1

Graduates

Going to Graduate School:
  17% Within One Year

Accepting Job Offer: 78%

Companies Recruiting On Campus: 280

Alumni Giving: 21%

TEMPLE UNIVERSITY

1801 N. Broad Street (041-09), Philadelphia, PA 19122-6096
Admissions Phone: (215) 204-7200; (888) 340-2222 Fax: (215) 204-5694
Email: TUADM@temple.edu Website: www.temple.edu
Application Website: www.temple.edu/UGAPP

General Info

Type of School: public, coed
Setting: urban
Academic Calendar: semester

Student Body

Full-Time Undergrads: 18,830
  Men: 43%, Women: 57%

Part-Time Undergrads: 2,628
  Men: 40%, Women: 60%

Total Undergrad Population:
  African American: 21%
  Asian American: 8%
  Latino: 3%
  Native American: <1%
  Caucasian: 56%
  International: 4%
  Out-of-State: 23%
  Living Off-Campus: 79%
  In Fraternities: 1%
  In Sororities: 1%

Graduate and First-Professional
  Students: 10,662

Academics

Full-Time Faculty: 1,311
  With Ph.D.: 75%

Part-Time Faculty: 1,050

Student/Faculty Ratio: 12:1

Most Popular Majors:
  elementary, early childhood
    education (6%)
  journalism (6%)
  psychology (5%)
  biology (4%)
  marketing (4%)

Freshmen Retention Rate: 82%

Admissions

Regular Application Deadline: 4/1

Fall Transfer Deadline: 6/15

Spring Transfer Deadline: 11/1

Total # of Students Applied: 16,758
  Admitted: 10,058
  Enrolled: 3,606

Test Scores (middle 50%):
  SAT Verbal: 490–590
  SAT Math: 490–590
  ACT Comp: 20–24

Inside the Classroom

Temple offers an impressive variety of academic programs and research facilities, with preprofessional fields accounting for the highest undergraduate enrollments. There are a dozen undergraduate colleges, including the College of Allied Health Professions, the Tyler School of Arts, and the Richard J. Fox School of Business and Management. In total, Temple offers 125 different majors, including highly rated programs in business and communications. Among the more popular majors are elementary/early childhood education, journalism, psychology, computer and information sciences, biology, and film and media arts. The school's African American studies program is considered excellent, and there are many popular course offerings in Asian and Latin American studies as well. All undergrads must take the rigorous core curriculum, which includes English composition, the arts, foreign language, math, science, and technology, and courses in such interesting areas as intellectual heritage, American culture, race and racism, and the individual and society.

For such a large research institution (Temple is actually the largest provider of professional education—law, dentistry, medicine, pharmacy, and podiatry—in the country), undergrads receive a surprising amount of attention. "Teachers make us feel like we're people, not statistics. They're always willing to get to know us and to help us meet other students," a junior tells us. The average undergraduate class size is 25, and even freshmen have access to top faculty members. Freshmen may participate in a Freshman Seminar or one of 30 different Learning Communities—two or three courses scheduled in a block, which 20–30 students take together as a group.

Going to school in the fifth-largest U.S. city gives Temple students ample opportunities for internships and co-ops. "Philadelphia is a living laboratory," a university rep asserts. Ambitious types can participate in the Temple Undergraduate Research Forum (TURF), which gives students the opportunity to conduct research and then present their results to an audience of peers, faculty, family, and friends. The school boasts that 96 percent of students who have participated in TURF have gone on to grad school.

Campus Environment

Temple has five regional campuses, as well as international campuses in Tokyo and Rome. The Main Campus, where over 20,000 students attend, consists of 114 acres in North Philadelphia. There, the new Tuttleman Learning Center encourages students to meet and interact on campus. The center features 2,000 student computer workstations, numerous study lounges and social lounges, two teleconferencing classrooms, a 39,000 square-foot fieldhouse, an indoor-outdoor café, and a new 500-bed residence hall.

Housing problems plague the university. Widely known as a commuting school, Temple doesn't guarantee on-campus housing even for freshmen, although it has been continuously building new residential facilities in recent years. In Fall 2001, the Main Campus saw the opening of "1300," a complex with suites and apartments for 1,000 students, a convenience store, fitness center, computer lab, and lounges. Even so, about one-third of freshmen live off-campus or commute. The numbers for sophomores, juniors, and seniors who choose to live elsewhere are much higher.

For $60 a month, all students may leave a car on campus. But be warned: "A car is not the best means." The university provides free shuttle service, and access to public transportation is just steps away. While parents may have some concerns over the questionable safety of Temple's North Philadelphia neighborhood, be assured that Temple's 200-member university police force patrols all campuses 24 hours a day.

Philadelphia is an interesting and exciting city to live in, with attractions from the Liberty Bell and Independence Mall, to the Eagles, Phillies, Flyers, and 76ers, to the funky nightlife on South Street and in Old City. Bars restaurants, shops, museums, theaters—you name it, Philly's got it in spades. "There is so much to do there," one student tells us. "I love that."

Student Life

Temple isn't your average all-white upper-class college. The remarkably diverse population features far more than the average percentage of minorities—nearly half of the student body self-identifies as "other than white." Students here report how people from all geographic, cultural, and ethnic backgrounds become part of a generally friendly and easygoing student body. Students hail from 48 states and 100 countries, and almost half have transferred from other colleges. In fact, about 20 percent of all undergrads are age 25 or older, lending a "more mature, experienced" feel to the classroom. As one junior puts it, "We have a mini 'real world' on campus." Students aren't shy about saying hello or sparking conversations with others in class or around the campus, we hear. "What I like about Temple is that it has the opportunities of a big university but the feel of a small college," a student says. "It's very easy to meet people here."

It isn't much of a party school, probably owing to the fact that most of the student body are scattered throughout the metropolitan area. A very small percentage of men and women join fraternities and sororities, and for these students Greek life functions as a kind of community within the larger university. In addition to hosting parties and special events, many houses are committed to community service in the city. Annual events like Spring Fling and Cherry & White Day liven up the campus, as well.

Temple has more than 160 student clubs and organizations, including several major cultural groups, such as the African American Student Union, and student associations for Hispanic, Caribbean, Korean, and Chinese students. The Owl Team (a leadership organization), the student government, and various sports clubs are also popular. More than 500 students participate in one of 20 varsity sports; thousands more play on intramural and club teams. The Owls' NCAA Division I basketball team attracts the most—and most rabid—fans, with students, parents, alumni, and Philadelphians regularly packing the 10,200-seat stadium.

Other schools to check out: Drexel, Northeastern, Rutgers, University of Pittsburgh, University of Cincinnati.

HS Rank of Entering Freshmen:
Top 10%: 17%
Top 25%: 50%
Top 50%: 90%

Avg. HS GPA: 3.25

Costs (2003–04)

Tuition and Fees, In-State: $8,594

Tuition and Fees, Out-of-State: $15,354

Room & Board: $7,318

Payment Plan(s): installment plan, deferred payment plan, pre-payment plan

THE EXPERTS SAY...

" Unlike other large research institutions, undergrads get personal attention from professors at Temple. There are a dozen undergraduate schools, a diverse student body, and all of Philadelphia to explore. "

" Temple still has a rep as a commuter school, and housing is not guaranteed, even for freshmen. You may have to work at meeting people (try Owl basketball games). "

Inst. Aid (2002–03)

Institutional Aid, Need-Based: $15,239,306

Institutional Aid, Non-Need-Based: $5,392,845

FT Undergrads Receiving Aid: 63%
Avg. Amount per Student: $11,416

FT Undergrads Receiving Non-Need-Based Scholarship or Grant Aid: 18%
Avg. Amount per Student: $3,130

Of Those Receiving Any Aid:

Rec. Need-Based Scholarship or Grant Aid: 100%
Average Award: $4,310

Rec. Need-Based Self-Help Aid: 85%
Average Award: $3,394

Upon Graduation, Avg. Loan Debt per Student: $22,041

Financial Aid Deadline: 3/1 (priority)

TEXAS A&M UNIVERSITY

P.O. Box 30014, College Station, TX 77842
Admissions Phone: (979) 458-0427; (979) 845-3741 Fax: (979) 847-8737
Email: admissions@tamu.edu Website: www.tamu.edu
Application Website: www.tamu.edu/admissions

General Info

Type of School: public, coed

Setting: suburban

Academic Calendar: semester

Student Body

Full-Time Undergrads: 32,818
  Men: 51%, Women: 49%

Part-Time Undergrads: 3,248
  Men: 54%, Women: 46%

Total Undergrad Population:
  African American: 2%
  Asian American: 3%
  Latino: 9%
  Native American: <1%
  Caucasian: 82%
  International: 1%
  Out-of-State: 3%
  Living Off-Campus: 73%
  In Fraternities: 4%
  In Sororities: 7%

Graduate and First-Professional
  Students: 8,747

Academics

Full-Time Faculty: 1,813
  With Ph.D.: 93%

Part-Time Faculty: 341
  With Ph.D.: 64%

Student/Faculty Ratio: 21:1

Most Popular Majors:
  business administration (5%)
  biomedical sciences (5%)
  psychology (4%)
  interdisciplinary education (3%)
  biology (3%)

Freshmen Retention Rate: 90%

Graduation Rates:
  32% within four years
  75% within six years

Admissions

Regular Application Deadline: 2/1

Early Action Deadline: 12/1

Fall Transfer Deadline: 3/15

Spring Transfer Deadline: 10/15

Total # of Students Applied: 17,250
  Admitted: 11,639
  Enrolled: 6,726

# of Students Waitlisted: 5,595
  Students Accepting Place: 2,057
  Waitlisted Students Admitted: 149

Inside the Classroom

Texas A&M has nine colleges: agriculture and life sciences; architecture; business; education; engineering; geosciences; liberal arts; science; and veterinary medicine. While the university is known for its programs in agricultural sciences and engineering, all of its science and technology courses are good, and the business school is excellent. The veterinary school is "second to none," says a guidance counselor. Adds another, "I had a student who wanted to work with horses, caring for their medical needs, yet she had no previous experience or had even been around horses. They provide hands-on, guided experience from the very beginning of a student's college career."

Students generally feel that although the "workload is very intensive," difficulty and competitiveness vary from course to course. As for studying, Texas A&M students—known as "Aggies"—do lots of it. "During test weeks, the libraries are always packed, there is literally no place to sit, but going to the library is not a drag, the atmosphere is very lively." Class sizes, especially at introductory levels, often number in the hundreds. Though classes get smaller as you work in your major, you won't necessarily have professors who know your name. Nonetheless, "professors are extremely accessible," says one student. "Not always the most accommodating, but very accessible." Another student agrees, with this qualification: "I have found that they can still be helpful and display their huge egos at the same time!"

TAMU gets kudos for its engineering and agriculture summer programs for high school students, and a Texas counselor gives high marks to improvements in financial aid. However, some counselors call TAMU "overrated," and one gripes that the "admissions department is slow and disorganized, and they lose things."

Campus Environment

Guidance counselors tell us that TAMU one of the most beautiful campuses in the country. According to one student, "Dorms are divided by campus, familiarly known as North Side (older, proud dorms) and South Side (newer, proud dorms)." While one senior says, "Everyone I know who ever lived on campus has nothing but great things to say," another states, "I personally hate our dorms. They remind me of jail cells." And availability is "not great," says a recent grad.

Off-campus housing is more popular. A student elaborates: "Accommodations vary from properties that are barely standing to properties with swimming pools and security guards. My apartment is three bedrooms, two baths, about 1,100 square feet for $780 a month!" But a former student complains, "Housing is expensive in this area."

Students say that the immediate area of "Aggieland" offers few attractions "This is the pitfall of TAMU," says one student. But, "a major plus is that TAMU is located in the middle of a tri-city area, with Dallas and Waco to the north, Houston and the beach to the southeast, and Austin and San Antonio to the southwest. These cities are all within a one- to three-hour drive."

Student Life

"The atmosphere at TAMU is the reason I chose this school!" one student raves. Friendliness and school pride are notorious Aggie qualities. "Everyone is very friendly; 'howdy' is the common greeting around campus. Although the university has a large student population, you get a sense of being in a small town." Another student agrees: "The campus really pulls together in a way that wouldn't be expected with 50,000 students."

Most students are "conservative, enough said!" says a grad, and students say that at times "ignorance gets disguised as conservatism." Some find this atmosphere stifling: "The typical student here is the average white male. I'm not so happy about this trait." An alum comments that a "gang-type student with baggy pants and black lipstick," might not fit in. In this vein, TAMU administrators recently cracked down on white students planning an off-campus "Think Ghetto" party on Martin Luther King Day. The event involved students dressing in gangsta-rap outfits and allegedly planning to wear blackface.

Greek life is popular, but "not a social must." The Corps of Cadets is a prestigious military training group that "attracts a different type of male than would a fraternity." There are over 700 student organizations, including the nationally known Aggie Wranglers, a country and western exhibition dance group that has performed for President Bush. Sunday nights offer concerts at the Dixie Chicken Bar; karaoke at Shadow Canyon is popular on Wednesdays; and the weekends are typically reserved for dancing and Northgate, the "oh-so-popular" bar district. There is "lots of social drinking," an alumna reminisces. Volunteer designated drivers are available through CARPOOL (Caring Aggies 'R' Protecting Over Our Lives).

TAMU is a school rich in traditions, many of which revolve around sports. "A&M football is perhaps the biggest event in any Aggie's fall schedule," a student says. Another student cites a football game as the deciding factor in her college search. "It sounds silly but football games at Kyle Field are one of the only places where over 80,000 people are all singing the same song and doing the same thing. Whether or not you are an Aggie, it's an amazing sight." Baseball and intramurals are also popular.

One of the school's most cherished traditions, the bonfire built by students before the annual football game against archrival University of Texas, resulted in tragedy in 1999 when the stack of several thousand logs collapsed, killing 12 students and injuring 27 others. The question of whether to reinstate the bonfire tradition has been a hugely controversial issue on campus ever since. Singing the Texas A&M fight song, a group of students and alumni recently ignited a "traditional"—but supposedly safer—bonfire off campus.

Students love TAMU so much that they have trouble leaving it in four years, and alums are extremely loyal. One student sums up the TAMU experience: "It truly makes you feel like you are part of this huge family… when you leave town and meet former students who will say, 'Beat the Hell Outta TU' (University of Texas)… it's their way of expressing their love for this place 20, 30, 50 years after they have left."

Test Scores (middle 50%):
SAT Verbal: 520–640
SAT Math: 550–660
ACT Comp: 23–28
ACT English: 22–28
ACT Math: 22–28

HS Rank of Entering Freshmen:
Top 10%: 53%
Top 25%: 87%
Top 50%: 100%

THE EXPERTS SAY...

" Already the best in Texas, Texas A&M's Vision '2020' is to be one of the ten best public universities in the nation. "

" 'Aggie' sure doesn't stand for 'agoraphobic': If singing fight songs in a crowd of 80,000 people excites you, saddle up and head on over to TAMU. "

Costs (2003–04)

Tuition and Fees, In-State: $5,051

Tuition and Fees, Out-of-State: $12,131

Room & Board: $6,030

Payment Plan(s): installment plan

Inst. Aid (2002–03)

Institutional Aid, Need-Based: $7,965,731

Institutional Aid, Non-Need-Based: $10,807,517

FT Undergrads Receiving Aid: 27%
Avg. Amount per Student: $8,115

FT Undergrads Receiving Non-Need-Based Scholarship or Grant Aid: 6%
Avg. Amount per Student: $4,079

Of Those Receiving Any Aid:

Rec. Need-Based Scholarship or Grant Aid: 100%
Average Award: $4,644

Rec. Need-Based Self-Help Aid: 80%
Average Award: $2,312

Upon Graduation, Avg. Loan Debt per Student: $15,670

TEXAS CHRISTIAN UNIVERSITY

2800 S. University Drive, Fort Worth, TX 76129
Admissions Phone: (817) 257-7490; (800) 828-3764 Fax: (817) 257-7268
Email: frogmail@tcu.edu
Website: www.tcu.edu

General Info

Type of School: private, coed

Setting: suburban

Academic Calendar: semester

Student Body

Full-Time Undergrads: 6,348
  Men: 40%, Women: 60%

Part-Time Undergrads: 417
  Men: 42%, Women: 58%

Total Undergrad Population:
  African American: 5%
  Asian American: 2%
  Latino: 6%
  Native American: <1%
  Caucasian: 79%
  International: 4%
  Out-of-State: 22%
  Living Off-Campus: 53%
  In Fraternities: 34%
  In Sororities: 38%

Graduate and First-Professional
  Students: 1,342

Academics

Full-Time Faculty: 420
  With Ph.D.: 91%

Part-Time Faculty: 283
  With Ph.D.: 37%

Student/Faculty Ratio: 15:1

Most Popular Majors:
  nursing (5%)
  biology (4%)
  psychology (4%)
  advertising/public relations (4%)
  political science (3%)

Freshmen Retention Rate: 81%

Graduation Rates:
  64% within six years

Admissions

Regular Application Deadline: 2/15

Early Action Deadline: 11/15

Fall Transfer Deadline: 8/15, 4/15
  (priority)

Spring Transfer Deadline: 12/15,
  11/1 (priority)

Total # of Students Applied: 7,654
  Admitted: 4,971
  Enrolled: 1,596

Inside the Classroom

Texas Christian University is composed of seven schools and colleges: the AddRan College of Arts and Science; the M.J. Neeley School of Business; the School of Education; the College of Fine Arts, which houses the School of Music; the College of Communication; the College of Health and Human Sciences, which contains the Harris School of Nursing; the College of Science and Engineering; and the Brite Divinity School. The areas of study offered, which number more than 100, even include a Ranch Management Program for students interested in agricultural resource management.

Students say the preprofessional programs are "very competitive," and describe the workload in other classes as being "average." Premed programs are widely considered to be "intense." One student says, "I am in the premedical track so it is rather competitive and the workload is HIGH. Organic Chemistry is brutal and most medical schools acknowledge that a C in Organic at TCU is quite acceptable." A recent graduate tells us that "the workload is as heavy as you make it for yourself" and that there is "not a lot of competition among students."

Texas Christian University is not a huge school, with a total enrollment of under 8,000 and, according to one student, "relatively small classes, with the largest having no more than 200 students." The student/faculty ratio is 15:1, and the average class size numbers around 30 students, "making it easy for the professor to get to know you," a freshman says. Professors are widely considered to be very accessible to students who need assistance. One high school guidance counselor praises TCU for its "wonderful support of students," adding that the "faculty mix well with students." A junior tells us, "My trig class ended up with only two students (including myself!) in it. Other classes were quite large (up to 85 students in chemistry) but the professors had LONG office hours, [and] were accessible by email or home phone."

Campus Environment

Approximately half the undergraduate population lives on campus in one of TCU's 11 residence halls, eight fraternity houses, or ten sorority houses. Freshmen are required to live on campus, and most rooms are carpeted and come with two phone lines and two ethernet connections. While a recent grad tells us that the "freshmen dorms are terrible," a junior describes the dorms as "incredible! Nice, refurbished ... a must see!" A Texas guidance counselor feels as though TCU offers the best freshman housing. On-campus apartments are also available, and one junior describes them as "beautiful but a bit expensive." Off-campus housing is popular for upperclassmen. "There are lots of apartments nearby that are reasonably priced and all 5–15 minutes from campus," a student tells us. "Really a nice environment."

The Fort Worth area is described as safe and "not your typical city," with a large police presence that is "rarely ever needed!" Downtown is nearby, and the school is a mere 40 minutes from Dallas—which is "a bit more city-like than Fort Worth!" Students feel as safe in Fort Worth as they do on their campus, where "you need an ID card just to get into the library." Having a car is a definite plus here. "Yes, you really do need a car to get around town, although some do ride the buses," a student says. A recent grad concedes, "You can maybe get by without a car your freshman year."

Student Life

TCU is a very friendly campus; a freshman says, "The guys have a good reputation for ALWAYS holding doors open and generally being polite. It's also a very spirited and social campus, with lots of activities planned for everyone, such as bands in the student center and campus-wide volunteer opportunities." The campus, however, is not generally considered to be especially political or diversified. "No rowdiness or politics!" one student says. Another agrees, describing the student body as "wonderfully apathetic. We are very homogenous, with little protesting, etc." However, one Missouri guidance counselor views the "conservative campus atmosphere" as a possible shortcoming. Preprofessional organizations and "anything Bible-related" tend to be popular here, while political groups and "student government and things about diversity typically aren't." A junior describes the "typical student" as "a rich sorority girl whose dad is paying her tuition by check, or the rich fraternity jock." Another student comments that "a very poor student might feel uncomfortable. Additionally, a very strong political activist would have no platform!"

TCU offers more than 160 clubs and activities, but Greek life is by far the most popular. A freshman says that "anyone who absolutely despises the Greek system might not like the fact that it is a rather large part of the TCU campus." She adds that "the majority of the parties on the weekends are Greek, but most of them are nondiscriminatory against non-Greeks, so anyone can attend." Drinking is common among students at TCU, although the administration frowns upon underage drinking. "The campus police have been known to violate basic rights in pursuit of this," a student tells us, "but this is what happens at a private university." Another student says, "The school enforces the Texas state policy that any minor who is in the presence of alcohol, even if they are not drinking, will have consequences. This means that students can be fined for an alcohol violation if their roommate has it in their room." Nonetheless, students say off-campus is "a different story. It's pretty easy to drink underage without being caught."

TCU has NCAA Division I football, basketball, track, tennis, baseball, soccer, golf, and swimming. The home football games are a very popular student pastime, and a student says, "There are many loyal TCU alumni and other supporters in the Dallas/Fort Worth metroplex." Additionally, one junior claims that some varsity athletes get "huge benefits including money on their meal tickets, money for bookstore purchases, free tutoring, etc."

While many students opt to "carpool to Dallas to go clubbing on a Wednesday or Thursday College Night," they also enjoy the attractions of Fort Worth. "Fort Worth has many unique places for students to enjoy," a freshman says. "The historic downtown is festively lit, and the Stockyards offer a Western alternative to the club scene."

Other schools to check out: Baylor, Southwestern, Southern Methodist, Trinity U.

# of Students Waitlisted: 689
  Students Accepting Place: 334
  Waitlisted Students Admitted: 76

Test Scores (middle 50%):
  SAT Verbal: 520–620
  SAT Math: 540–640
  ACT Comp: 23–28

HS Rank of Entering Freshmen:
  Top 10%: 33%
  Top 25%: 67%
  Top 50%: 95%

THE EXPERTS SAY...

" Students get the support they need from faculty at TCU, along with a choice of more than 100 areas of study. The preprofessional programs are tough but solid. "

" The typical student is rich, in a frat, and in a Bible studies club. Political activists, don't even think of applying here. "

Costs (2003–04)

Tuition and Fees: $16,340

Room & Board: $5,300

Payment Plan(s): installment plan, pre-payment plan

Inst. Aid (est. 2003–04)

Institutional Aid, Need-Based: $11,391,570

Institutional Aid, Non-Need-Based: $11,152,673

FT Undergrads Receiving Aid: 43%
  Avg. Amount per Student: $12,614

FT Undergrads Receiving Non-Need-Based Scholarship or Grant Aid: 20%
  Avg. Amount per Student: $7,979

Of Those Receiving Any Aid:

Rec. Need-Based Scholarship or Grant Aid: 99%
  Average Award: $8,877

Rec. Need-Based Self-Help Aid: 86%
  Average Award: $6,219

Financial Aid Deadline: 5/1

TEXAS TECH UNIVERSITY

Box 45005, Lubbock, TX 79409-5005
Admissions Phone: (806) 742-1480 Fax: (806) 742-0062
Email: admissions@ttu.edu Website: www.ttu.edu
Application Website: www.srel.ttu.edu

General Info

Type of School: public, coed
Setting: urban
Academic Calendar: semester

Student Body

Full-Time Undergrads: 21,030
  Men: 54%, Women: 46%

Part-Time Undergrads: 2,565
  Men: 58%, Women: 42%

Total Undergrad Population:
  African American: 3%
  Asian American: 2%
  Latino: 11%
  Native American: 1%
  Caucasian: 82%
  International: 1%
  Out-of-State: 5%
  Living Off-Campus: 75%
  In Fraternities: 10%
  In Sororities: 14%

Graduate and First-Professional
  Students: 4,954

Academics

Full-Time Faculty: 978
  With Ph.D.: 93%

Part-Time Faculty: 92
  With Ph.D.: 41%

Student/Faculty Ratio: 21:1

Most Popular Majors:
  human development & family
  studies (4%)
  psychology (4%)
  mechanical engineering (3%)
  early childhood (3%)
  exercise and sport sciences (3%)

Completing 2 or More Majors: 7%

Freshmen Retention Rate: 82%

Graduation Rates:
  24% within four years
  54% within six years

Admissions

Total # of Students Applied: 13,755
  Admitted: 9,257
  Enrolled: 4,445

Test Scores (middle 50%):
  SAT Verbal: 500–600
  SAT Math: 520–620
  ACT Comp: 21–26
  ACT English: 20–26
  ACT Math: 20–26

Inside the Classroom

Texas Tech University—"a big school with small school qualities," according to a Texas guidance counselor—is comprised of eight colleges: agricultural sciences and natural resources, architecture, arts and sciences, business administration, education, Engineering, honors, and human sciences. The law school is also on the main campus, and "boasts the highest number of students passing the bar exam in Texas." There's also the Texas Tech University Health Center with its schools of medicine, nursing, pharmacy, and allied health.

The College of Arts and Sciences is the largest at Tech, with 120 degree programs in 22 schools and departments. The College of Arts and Sciences offers six distinct bachelor's degrees: the bachelor of arts, bachelor of science, bachelor of general studies, bachelor of fine arts, bachelor of science in international economics, and bachelor of music. The university's core requirements ensure that each student receives a well-balanced education and are incorporated directly into the various degree programs. Freshmen develop their programs with the help of an academic advisor. Required freshmen courses are taken during the first year, and any core requirements are typically completed by the end of the sophomore year. A student says the workload at TTU is "not too much to handle, but it is rather intense."

New students should not be too intimidated by the school's size. A guidance counselor says that the university offers real help when it comes to course selection and career planning. A freshman says that professors "keep in mind what level of students they are teaching," and that they "are readily available pretty much any time you need them." Depending on a student's course of study, class sizes can range vastly at this very large school (with over 20,000 undergrads alone!). For instance, there might be 400 students in a lower-level lecture course, and 10 in an upper-division seminar. A freshman tells us that the people at TTU "are all so nice, and so welcoming to all of the new students … After being here for a while, you will feel like part of a big family."

Campus Environment

Freshmen and students with fewer than 30 credit hours must live on campus. Texas Tech offers traditional residence halls as well as suite-style living, and apartments for upperclassmen. Most halls are air-conditioned, and both single-sex and coed living arrangements are available. There are other options too, including honors housing, intensive study, nonsmoking, and substance-free floors, and the Living/Learning Communities. The university states that these Communities "offer students a collaborative environment, meaningful student-faculty interactions, and academic and social opportunities which foster student success, and a sense of belonging within the Texas Tech University community." The Tech Connections program is designed for freshmen, offering services and programs to help ease the transition from high school to college life. A freshman says, "On-campus housing is readily available; however, it is rather costly. The rooms are not that bad, they are not too small. Apartment-type housing is also offered for upperclassmen; it is very easy to get to class and the library, etc., when you live on campus."

Once a student has earned 30 or more credits, he or she is allowed to move off campus, and living in Lubbock is fairly inexpensive compared to other parts of the United States. A student describes off-campus living as a "popular" option, and says, "There are tons of apartment complexes, availability isn't all that bad, but you do need to start looking the semester before you expect to move in … The cost is about the same as the dorms when you add up food, furniture, bills, etc."

Students consider both their campus environment and the town of Lubbock to be friendly. "Everyone is friendly, that is what attracted me most to this school," says a freshman. "You will not find one person that will not help you with a heavy load, lend you a pen, or hold the door for you." The town is described as "about the same as the campus. Everyone is generally very friendly and would be willing to help out with anything. Everything in the town is very accessible and it is very easy to get around. We are also home to a lot of famous people!" Students say that although most students have cars, they're not a necessity here. "There are free buses that go all over campus and all over the town … Parking is very hard to find."

Student Life

A freshman says that the only type of student who would not fit in on the TTU campus is someone "who either studies too much and focuses only on school, or the type who parties too much and focuses only on social life. You must be balanced out." This student tells us that Sunday and Monday nights are usually spent studying, and that Thursday nights through Saturday nights are for partying. "This helps control some of the stress that comes with all of the work to be done in college." The campus and the city are both "dry," but a student tells us that alcohol "can be purchased right outside the city, which is about a 15-minute drive" and that "most of the drinking goes on off campus."

Fraternities and sororities are described as "a very big part of Tech, especially in the party scene. Most of the houses are where all of the parties are at on the weekends." There are about 40 national and local fraternities and sororities with chapters on campus.

Sporting events are very popular on the weekends, namely football. "When it comes to football we are a very rowdy group of fans," a freshman admits, "but that makes it all the more fun!" Rushing the field and tearing down the goal post after a big win is a campus football tradition. The Saddle Tramps contribute to the Red Raider Spirit as well; the Saddle Tramps are an all-male spirit group that attends sporting events in red T-shirts and can be found next to the band cheering and generally making as much noise as possible. They also do community service and hold annual Saddle Tramp reunions. Basketball is also popular at Tech, as is intramural flag football. "The spirit here at Tech is contagious," a student says. "Once you feel it you will never want to be without it."

HS Rank of Entering Freshmen:
Top 10%: 21%
Top 25%: 52%
Top 50%: 86%

Costs (2003–04)

Tuition and Fees, In-State: $4,445

Tuition and Fees, Out-of-State:
$11,525

THE EXPERTS SAY...

" Students at Texas Tech receive tremendous support from the faculty, the administration, even the townspeople. "

" If you think you'd feel overwhelmed by the hugeness of Texas A&M (or if you know you couldn't get in), Texas Tech is a safe alternative. "

Regional or 'good neighbor' tuition available

Room & Board: $6,023

Payment Plan(s): installment plan, deferred payment plan

Inst. Aid (2002–03)

Institutional Aid, Need-Based:
$9,434,832

Institutional Aid, Non-Need-Based:
$4,717,371

FT Undergrads Receiving Aid: 39%
Avg. Amount per Student: $6,421

FT Undergrads Receiving Non-Need-Based Scholarship or Grant Aid: 27%
Avg. Amount per Student: $2,194

Of Those Receiving Any Aid:

Rec. Need-Based Scholarship or Grant Aid: 75%
Average Award: $3,458

Rec. Need-Based Self-Help Aid: 76%
Average Award: $3,591

Upon Graduation, Avg. Loan Debt per Student: $15,780

Financial Aid Deadline: 5/1 (priority)

Graduates

Companies Recruiting On-Campus:
608

TRINITY COLLEGE

300 Summit Street, Hartford, CT 06106
Admissions Phone: (860) 297-2180 Fax: (860) 297-2287
Email: admissions.office@trincoll.edu
Website: www.trincoll.edu

General Info

Type of School: private, coed

Setting: urban

Academic Calendar: semester

Student Body

Full-Time Undergrads: 1,992
  Men: 50%, Women: 50%

Part-Time Undergrads: 153
  Men: 37%, Women: 63%

Total Undergrad Population:
  African American: 5%
  Asian American: 6%
  Latino: 5%
  Caucasian: 66%
  International: 1%
  Out-of-State: 78%
  Living Off-Campus: 8%
  In Fraternities: 20%
  In Sororities: 16%

Graduate and First-Professional
  Students: 183

Academics

Full-Time Faculty: 187
  With Ph.D.: 90%

Part-Time Faculty: 50
  With Ph.D.: 64%

Student/Faculty Ratio: 10:1

Most Popular Majors:
  political science (16%)
  economics (12%)
  English (9%)
  history (9%)
  psychology (7%)

Completing 2 or More Majors: 1%

Freshmen Retention Rate: 91%

Graduation Rates:
  77% within four years
  84% within six years

Admissions

Regular Application Deadline: 1/15

Early Decision Deadline(s): 11/15,
  1/15

Fall Transfer Deadline: 4/1

Spring Transfer Deadline: 11/15

Total # of Students Applied: 5,510
  Admitted: 1,993
  Enrolled: 550

Inside the Classroom

Students rave about Trinity College, and resent its image as the "safety school" of would-be Ivy Leaguers. Trinity offers an intense, well-rounded academic program, with 35 majors, including nine interdisciplinary programs. Guidance counselors praise the "outstanding liberal arts" curriculum; the "excellent" programs in history, English, economics, political science, philosophy, and psychology are particularly popular. All of the interdisciplinary programs—such as Asian studies, American studies, and women's studies—are highly regarded. The Human Rights Program, launched in 1998, was the first of its kind in the nation. The engineering department offers something rarely found at small liberal arts colleges: accredited degrees. Students in the new environmental studies program benefit from a wealth of research opportunities at the Church Farm field station in nearby Ashford.

A school official tells us that Trinity is committed to "providing a classical education that is rooted in reality, pursuing a commitment to both intellectual exploration and civic engagement, and expanding its close connections to the urban community in which it is located." The distribution requirements are tough, and include one course each from five areas: arts, humanities, natural sciences, numerical and symbolic reasoning, and social sciences. The First-Year Program offers courses in a range of topics and allows students to work closely with fellow first-years and professors who also serve as their advisers. Qualified students can also devote an entire semester to the study of a single subject area, combining course work and seminars with independent study and research. The school tells us that more than 30 percent of Trinity undergrads participate in a research project of some kind.

Students have terrific things to say about their professors, who "are very accessible and friendly." Except for introductory courses, classes are small (usually fewer than 25 students). Trinity's proud of its size, saying, "The heart of Trinity's educational experience is the personal encounter between professor and student." Professors almost always know students by name and frequently meet with students over coffee, lunch, or dinner.

About 65 percent of students take up an internship and there are hundreds to choose from, including many in state government or at local industries in Hartford. Nearly half of the students at Trinity study abroad at some point, often at Trinity's own campus in Rome, and at the growing number of "global learning sites" in such places as South Africa, Trinidad, and Nepal. Those looking to stay a little closer to home join the programs in San Francisco or New York City, where theater and dance majors can study their art.

Campus Environment

A self-contained, separate entity from the capital city of Hartford, the pretty 100-acre Trinity campus features Victorian Gothic buildings on "The Long Walk" surrounding a tree-lined central quad. While students like their collegiate-looking campus, they don't find the city itself very appealing. For a long time, town-gown relations were strained, but they have greatly improved, due in large part to an extensive, highly active student community outreach program and a $175 million neighborhood revitalization initiative that Trinity is leading. The school has done some major renovating and construction on campus in recent years, and continues that trend with the new $35 million Library and Information Technology Center.

As part of the First-Year Program, all freshmen live in one of six residence halls grouped by seminar and by theme. All dorms on campus are coed, though some have single-sex floors, and we didn't hear many complaints about them. More than 90 percent of all undergrads live on campus; housing is guaranteed for all four years. Not too many students—and no freshmen—bring cars to campus; instead, most students walk to classes and downtown, or take the Campus Shuttle.

Student Life

The majority of the 2,000 Trinity undergrads hail from the New England and Mid-Atlantic states, but there is a remarkably large percentage of Californians. Not surprisingly, you'll find a lot of white preppies here. In fact, one guidance counselor lists the "homogenous student population" as the biggest shortcoming of the school. Most descriptions of Trinity students include the words "laid back" and "fun-loving"—after all, they affectionately refer to their school as "Camp Trin-Trin," since most of the time, it seems more like summer camp.

Trinity College can be defined as a work-hard, play-hard school. While most students study long hours, they are also ready for fun (and beer) outside of class and the library. Although there's no explicit peer pressure to drink, students who don't may have a hard time fitting into the social scene. Despite the administration's constant efforts at cracking down on alcohol consumption, weekends for many students begin on Wednesday night. There are early-evening parties sponsored by student government, which students often "pre-load" for, followed by fraternity and dorm parties or visits to local music and comedy clubs or bars such as the Tap Cafe or the View. (We hear the bouncers are strict, so if you're not 21, beware.) Greek organizations—which are all coed—attract around one-quarter of the student body, and are considered a major force in the social scene, but not the only one, we hear. There are lots of clubs to choose from, including several musical groups, cultural organizations, and outreach programs; a high school guidance counselor gives Trinity high marks for its "new emphasis on community service."

The campus itself has many other social opportunities. Students hang out on the quad lawn and in the Koeppel Student Center, where there's a popular bistro and an underground coffeehouse featuring live music and acts. The Trinity Activities Council invites major bands and performers to campus, and the Arts Center produces plays and dance and music concerts on a regular basis. Sports, both intercollegiate and intramural, receive lots of attention; approximately half of the student body plays on Trinity's 29 varsity teams. Basketball, football, and hockey are the spectator sports of choice, and any games against their conference rivals draw huge crowds.

Homecoming is one of the biggest events of the year, and it's tradition that before the game, students burn the varsity letter of their opposing school. Another Trinity tradition: Class Day, which includes handing down, from class to class, a large wooden lemon squeezer that was first used to make the punch served during the first Class Day in 1855.

Other schools to check out: Colby, Bates, Skidmore, Dickinson, Hamilton, Gettysburg.

# of Students Waitlisted: 1,377
  Students Accepting Place: 364
  Waitlisted Students Admitted: 7

Applied Early Decision: 452
  Early Decision Admitted: 271

Test Scores (middle 50%):
  SAT Verbal: 590–700
  SAT Math: 620–710
  ACT Comp: 25–29
  ACT English: 24–29
  ACT Math: 24–29

HS Rank of Entering Freshmen:
  Top 10%: 51%
  Top 25%: 81%
  Top 50%: 95%

THE EXPERTS SAY...

" This superb liberal arts school offers an accredited degree in engineering, 35 majors, and 9 interdisciplinary programs, including the innovative Human Rights Program. Students have transformed relations with Hartford through community outreach. "

" Life at 'Camp Trin-Trin' is a work-hard/play-VERY-hard affair. "

Costs (2003–04)

Tuition and Fees: $30,230

Room & Board: $7,810

Payment Plan(s): installment plan, pre-payment plan

Inst. Aid (est. 2003–04)

Institutional Aid, Need-Based: $16,045,011

Institutional Aid, Non-Need-Based: $128,627

FT Undergrads Receiving Aid: 42%
  Avg. Amount per Student: $25,648

FT Undergrads Receiving Non-Need-Based Scholarship or Grant Aid: 0%
  Avg. Amount per Student: $12,927

Of Those Receiving Any Aid:

Rec. Need-Based Scholarship or Grant Aid: 96%
  Average Award: $22,337

Rec. Need-Based Self-Help Aid: 83%
  Average Award: $5,003

Upon Graduation, Avg. Loan Debt per Student: $11,632

Financial Aid Deadline: 2/1

Graduates

Going to Graduate School: 68% Within One Year

Alumni Giving: 78%

TRINITY UNIVERSITY

715 Stadium Drive, San Antonio, TX 78212-7200
Admissions Phone: (210) 999-7207; (800) TRI-NITY Fax: (210) 999-8164
Email: admissions@trinity.edu Website: www.trinity.edu
Application Website: www.trinity.edu/departments/admissions/apply3.htm

Inside the Classroom

Don't let the size fool you: Trinity University offers an impressive range of opportunities. Trinity offers undergraduate programs leading to the bachelor of arts, bachelor of science, and bachelor of music degrees, with majors in 26 departments and several additional interdisciplinary programs. Trinity also has the resources that are typical of a much larger institution, especially when it comes to research opportunities. As early as the first year, students are "encouraged and welcomed" to participate in research projects, and some students stay at Trinity during the summer to do so as well. It is not uncommon for students to present their findings at professional conferences or to have them published in professional journals or presented at conferences around the nation. Internship opportunities are also plentiful; students are "strongly encouraged" to participate in at least one internship experience during their years at Trinity.

Trinity's biggest strength is arguably its faculty. High school guidance counselors rave about the individual attention Trinity students receive from their professors. A student agrees: "I find that most, if not all, my professors have been easily accessible and most of the time are more than willing to bend over backwards to help a student." With an average class size of about 20 students, the academic atmosphere is a tight and cozy one. Professors are roundly praised as knowledgeable and passionate about the subjects they teach. Students here are bright and successful, and they don't let the workload and stress get the best of them. There's competition, we hear, but it's not cutthroat. "But," a communications major warns, "it's definitely not a school full of lazy bums, either."

The core curriculum seeks to introduce students to "the common life of learning, reflection, and discussion in which they are expected to share during their university years." The core curriculum—or Common Curriculum—includes the First Year Seminar Program (which covers various themes in all disciplines), a Writing Workshop, and courses in foreign language, computer skills, math, Western culture, and phys ed.

Campus Environment

Trinity's 117-acre Skyline Campus is largely notable for its beautifully landscaped grounds. One student jokes, "You know, Trinity has a 11:1 student to gardener ratio." It was originally modeled on an Italian village, as evidenced by its distinctive architecture and the showpiece fountain (where students are usually dunked on their birthdays). Marrs Mclean, home of the departments of Mathematics, Physics, and Geosciences, was recently renovated and now boasts a state-of-the-art exterior to complement its impressive facilities inside.

Students are required to live on campus for their first three years because the school believes that a residential campus is an integral part of the learning environment. Say officials: "We believe this 'community' of scholarship is important to the development of superb critical thinking skills." All residence halls are suite-style with two double rooms connected by a bathroom—and they all have access to an outdoor walkway or balcony. (Some even have walk-in closets!) First-year students are housed together. Though housing is not "explicitly" guaranteed for all four years, the school stresses that seniors have first priority for reserving rooms, and no one who wants to live on campus has ever been turned away. (This will disappoint at least one student we spoke to, who dismissed her dorm as "awful and extremely old and dilapidated.")

Most students bring their cars to Trinity, if only for show or off-campus travel. "While parking on campus would be characterized as tight by the student body," a college official argues, "there is ample parking, as there are currently more spaces than issued tags." We hear that there are two bus stops on the edge of campus for easy access to public transportation throughout the city, though most students venturing off campus will drive or carpool with friends.

San Antonio, with its "plethora of multicultural events and celebrations," gets high marks from Trinity students; a junior tells us there are "a lot of unique and interesting places to go and visit." There's the famous River Walk, where many restaurants and shops can be found, and which is a short distance from a mall and an historic district area. The Alamo is nearby, as well as a Six Flags, a Sea World, and the San Antonio Zoo. The Alamodome features sporting events, and the Gulf Coast beaches and Mexico are to the south.

Student Life

By and large, Trinity students are white, Texan, Christian, and affluent. (The school has been battling a reputation of being a rich kids' country club.) One student, who describes many of her classmates as "snotty," nonetheless admits the student body gives Trinity an overriding atmosphere of "tolerance and acceptance of diversity." That said, there still aren't a whole lot of "alternative types" running around campus.

Greek life seems to reign supreme here. "Unfortunately, unless you join a sorority or fraternity, you really don't get to know that many people," a disgruntled independent tells us. When they're not studying, Trinity students blow off a fair amount of steam the way many college kids do: drinking and more drinking, in dorm rooms, off-campus houses, and San Antonio bars and clubs. "San Antonio also has a decent nightlife," a student says, "although everything pretty much shuts down between 10 P.M. and midnight."

The school offers plenty of groups and organizations for students to get involved in. Popular school-sponsored clubs include: Trinity Activities Council, or TAC, which plans social events and campus traditions; Trinity University Voluntary Action Center, or TUVAC, which coordinates over 10,000 volunteer hours of community service by students; and Trinity Multicultural Network. The performing arts are also popular here.

Trinity is an NCAA Division III school that competes in the Southern Collegiate Athletic Conference. "Football is becoming increasingly popular as they continue to do better each season," a student tells us. About three-quarters of Trintonians play on one of 20 intramural teams. Annual events—such as Tigerfest (a semi-formal dance), the "armadillo hunt," a golf cart parade, and the student talent show—are big hits on campus as well.

Other schools to check out: Washington and Lee, Richmond, Rice, Tulane, Southwestern.

Applied Early Decision: 57
Early Decision Admitted: 40

Test Scores (middle 50%):
SAT Verbal: 600–690
SAT Math: 620–690
ACT Comp: 27–31
ACT English: 26–32
ACT Math: 26–31

HS Rank of Entering Freshmen:
Top 10%: 51%
Top 25%: 81%
Top 50%: 97%

Avg. HS GPA: 3.5

THE EXPERTS SAY...

" Trinity offers extensive undergraduate research opportunities on a residential campus in a culturally rich city. "

" Trinity doesn't have the party atmosphere that some other Texas schools have. Only you can decide if that's a good thing or not. "

Costs (2004–5)

Tuition and Fees: $19,176
Room & Board: $7,290

Inst. Aid (est. 2003–04)

Institutional Aid, Need-Based: $6,849,592

Institutional Aid, Non-Need-Based: $5,425,461

FT Undergrads Receiving Aid: 41%
Avg. Amount per Student: $15,486

FT Undergrads Receiving Non-Need-Based Scholarship or Grant Aid: 37%
Avg. Amount per Student: $6,358

Of Those Receiving Any Aid:

Rec. Need-Based Scholarship or Grant Aid: 94%
Average Award: $10,905

Rec. Need-Based Self-Help Aid: 79%
Average Award: $5,162

Financial Aid Deadline: 4/1, 2/1 (priority)

Graduates

Going to Graduate School:
31% Within One Year

Accepting Job Offer:
23% at time of graduation

TRUMAN STATE UNIVERSITY

McClain Hall 205, 100 East Normal, Kirksville, MO 63501
Admissions Phone: (660) 785-4114; (800) 892-7792 (in-state) Fax: (660) 785-7456
Email: admissions@truman.edu Website: www.truman.edu
Application Website: admissions.truman.edu/Applying_to_Truman/application.stm

General Info

Type of School: public, coed

Setting: small town

Academic Calendar: semester

Student Body

Full-Time Undergrads: 5,338
  Men: 41%, Women: 59%

Part-Time Undergrads: 141
  Men: 52%, Women: 48%

Total Undergrad Population:
  African American: 4%
  Asian American: 2%
  Latino: 2%
  Native American: <1%
  Caucasian: 84%
  International: 5%
  Out-of-State: 28%
  Living Off-Campus: 54%
  In Fraternities: 31%
  In Sororities: 22%

Graduate and First-Professional
  Students: 233

Academics

Full-Time Faculty: 354
  With Ph.D.: 86%

Part-Time Faculty: 23
  With Ph.D.: 22%

Student/Faculty Ratio: 15:1

Most Popular Majors:
  business administration (13%)
  biology (9%)
  psychology (7%)
  English (7%)
  communications (5%)

Completing 2 or More Majors: 8%

Freshmen Retention Rate: 85%

Graduation Rates:
  42% within four years
  64% within six years

Admissions

Regular Application Deadline: 3/1;
  11/15 (priority)

Early Action Deadline: 11/15

Fall Transfer Deadline: 4/15 (priority)

Spring Transfer Deadline: 11/15
  (priority)

Total # of Students Applied: 4,334
  Admitted: 3,622
  Enrolled: 1,317

Inside the Classroom

Guidance counselors in the Midwest agree that Truman State University is a hidden treasure. "Graduates have a leg up because of the school's reputation," says an Iowa counselor. Truman offers a quality liberal arts education at a relatively low cost, with 43 undergraduate and 9 graduate areas of study in 12 academic divisions. The five most popular majors at Truman are business administration, biology, English, psychology, and communication.

All students must take the coursework prescribed in the Liberal Studies Program, TSU's general education curriculum. The program focuses on three broad areas: "Essential Skills," which encompass writing, speech, elementary functions, statistics, computer literacy, and personal well being; "Modes of Inquiry," which include communication, physical sciences, life sciences, history, social sciences, philosophy and religion, the fine arts literature, and mathematics; and "Interconnecting Perspectives," which includes interdisciplinary courses, foreign languages, and writing-enhanced courses.

For students seeking a challenge that will add prestige to their résumé, Truman offers a General Honors Program in arts and sciences, humanities, mathematics, social science, and science. Instead of the usual introductory-level courses in liberal arts, General Honors students can select from a list of courses that explore in-depth topics or encourage a more sophisticated viewpoint.

Part of what makes the difference at Truman is the quality of the faculty. "My history professors make everything they teach interesting," says one history major. "Plus, they try to get to know their students as people, not just as students. They are great lecturers and great discussion facilitators."

One high school guidance counselor from Illinois praised Truman for its journalism program, saying that its courses were better than most schools'. A Missouri counselor told us that Truman's mission is to give students a high-quality education, adding, "They recruit our top kids." Another Illinois counselor acknowledged Truman's "prestige" and "excellent reputation" but criticized its admissions requirements, saying, "They're not flexible enough. They look only at scores, and not the whole person."

Campus Environment

TSU's 140-acre campus is located in Kirksville, Missouri, a town of about 17,000 located 90 miles north of the city of Columbia. The campus is relatively compact, with most of the 40 buildings within easy walking distance of each other. "When I came to visit, I fell in love with the university," says one student. "Primarily, I noticed the beautiful campus and buildings. The people were friendly, the atmosphere was energetic, and I knew it was the place for me."

Conventional coed housing is found in Dobson Hall, Missouri Hall, and Ryle Hall, while Centennial Hall offers suite-style housing. Blanton, Nason, and Brewer Halls make up the all-female BNB complex, housing 372 women on three floors in a suite-style room configuration. Hispanic housing is located in Centennial Hall, and nonsmoking rooms are located in Grim Hall. The Campbell Apartments, Randolph Apartments, and Fair Apartments house both married students and undergraduates of the same sex in apartment-style living quarters.

The newly renovated Fine Arts Center added a new wing in 2001 and now features classrooms, gallery space, art studios, shops, practice rooms, an instrumental rehearsal room, computer-aided design rooms, an art gallery, two theaters, an acting studio, and a music performance hall. The recently renovated Pickler Memorial Library is another remarkable structure, with the huge building enveloping the structure of the previous library, facade and all. Elevated walkways on the second and third floors cross the sunlit atrium between the old building and the newer addition.

Students wishing to keep in shape can do so at the Student Recreation Center, a large facility that houses a three-court, wood floor main gym suitable for basketball, volleyball, or badminton; a small gym with a multipurpose floor that can accommodate roller hockey, indoor soccer, ultimate Frisbee, basketball, or volleyball; a weight room; an aerobics room; an elevated three-lane jogging track; cardiovascular machines; locker rooms; and a lounge with a large screen television and vending area.

Student Life

Truman runs a dry campus and preaches actively about the dangers of alcohol, but the presence of fraternities and sororities tends to offer a counterbalancing effect. One student writer for *The Index*, the campus newspaper, stated his opinion rather eloquently: "I'm not saying drinking is required to have fun—if you don't like to drink, don't. I'm just saying that if I want to go shooting down five tequila poppers in three minutes and then dance badly at a bar, I should be allowed to do so without the fear or insult of dragging my half-dead body to class the next day, where I may be subjected to innovative speakers discussing, 'Alcohol: The Silent Killer,' or 'Weed: Gateway Drug to Obesity.' I don't want to see a mouse pad that taunts me about my hangover."

The Truman Bulldogs compete at the NCAA Division II level, with varsity sports for both sexes including basketball, cross-country, golf, soccer, swimming, tennis, and track and field. Men can also compete in baseball, football, and wrestling, while women can play softball and volleyball. Recently the women's swimming team brought home the Division II national championship for the first time. A large roster of intramural sports programs are also open to students.

Clubs and organizations on campus include notables like the Truman Swingers, a swing dance club; Iguana's Paintball Club, for those who like getting spattered with paint in the woods; and the Toastmasters, an organization dedicated to the development of communication and leadership skills. A number of cultural, preprofessional, honorary, and religious groups exist on campus as well.

Test Scores (middle 50%):
  SAT Verbal: 550–680
  SAT Math: 560–670
  ACT Comp: 25–30
  ACT English: 25–31
  ACT Math: 24–29
HS Rank of Entering Freshmen:
  Top 10%: 50%
  Top 25%: 84%
  Top 50%: 98%
Avg. HS GPA: 3.77

THE EXPERTS SAY...

" Truman represents an outstanding value for students seeking a liberal arts education. "

" Students bright enough to get accepted here have a good chance at being accepted to schools with bigger names and more prestige. "

Costs (2004–5)

Tuition and Fees, In-State: $5,466
Tuition and Fees, Out-of-State: $9,566
Room & Board: $5,250
Payment Plan(s): installment plan

Inst. Aid (2002–03)

Institutional Aid, Need-Based: $308,807
Institutional Aid, Non-Need-Based: $12,657,183
FT Undergrads Receiving Aid: 48%
  Avg. Amount per Student: $5,774
FT Undergrads Receiving Non-Need-Based Scholarship or Grant Aid: 39%
  Avg. Amount per Student: $4,242
Of Those Receiving Any Aid:
Rec. Need-Based Scholarship or Grant Aid: 30%
  Average Award: $3,262
Rec. Need-Based Self-Help Aid: 58%
  Average Award: $3,878
Upon Graduation, Avg. Loan Debt per Student: $15,655
Financial Aid Deadline: rolling, 4/1 (priority)

Graduates

Going to Graduate School: 44% Within One Year
Companies Recruiting On Campus: 300
Alumni Giving: 22%

TUFTS UNIVERSITY

Bendetson Hall, Medford, MA 02155
Admissions Phone: (617) 627-3170 Fax: (617) 627-3860
Email: admissions.inquiry@ase.tufts.edu Website: www.tufts.edu
Application Website: admissions.tufts.edu

General Info

Type of School: private, coed

Setting: suburban

Academic Calendar: semester

Student Body

Full-Time Undergrads: 4,800
    Men: 46%, Women: 54%

Part-Time Undergrads: 74
    Men: 42%, Women: 58%

Total Undergrad Population:
    African American: 7%
    Asian American: 13%
    Latino: 8%
    Native American: <1%
    Caucasian: 55%
    International: 6%
    Out-of-State: 75%
    Living Off-Campus: 25%
    In Fraternities: 15%
    In Sororities: 4%

Graduate and First-Professional
    Students: 4,617

Academics

Full-Time Faculty: 583

Part-Time Faculty: 306

Student/Faculty Ratio: 9:1

Most Popular Majors:
    international relations (12%)
    economics (11%)
    biology (7%)
    English (6%)
    psychology (6%)

Freshmen Retention Rate: 96%

Graduation Rates:
    82% within four years
    90% within six years

Admissions

Regular Application Deadline: 1/1

Early Decision Deadline(s): 11/15,
    1/1

Fall Transfer Deadline: 3/1

Spring Transfer Deadline: 11/15

Total # of Students Applied: 14,528
    Admitted: 3,830
    Enrolled: 1,282

Waitlist Available

Applied Early Decision: 1,313
    Early Decision Admitted: 508

Inside the Classroom

Once considered a safety school, Tufts now offers powerhouse academic programs that demand respect. Benefiting from their affiliation with Tufts's graduate schools, undergraduate programs in preprofessional areas are very strong. "More than 98 percent of enrolling students expect to pursue graduate or professional study," boast school officials.

"Students at Tufts take their classes seriously and work hard; most log a lot of hours at the library," a recent grad tells us. "We get swamped with work," a student complains, but then adds, "As long as you make the effort, you stay on top of it." Another student emphasizes, "It's a fun place to be, but students are committed to study."

Undergrad students can earn their degree from the College of Liberal Arts or the College of Engineering. The tough liberal arts core requirements include courses in humanities, arts, social sciences, math, natural sciences, writing, and foreign language, as well as a course in world civilization. Requirements are slightly different for engineering students. The College of Special Studies also offers an undergraduate degree program in conjunction with the School of the Museum of Fine Arts.

Class sizes vary, and some courses are taught by graduate teaching assistants. Some students say they like having TAs, who are often younger and easier to talk to than their professors. One student notes, "There are a lot of big-name professors here who aren't around much." However, most students report that when they make appointments to see professors, they often find their professors friendly and helpful. "I was never just a number (even in my larger lecture classes)," says a young alumna, "and if there was a class you really wanted to take, most professors would let you in even if it was filled."

Tufts offers its students several interesting academic programs and opportunities, including an extensive study abroad program ("Tufts likes to portray an international spirit and therefore there are a lot of options for going abroad and it is really encouraged"). A summer program is available at the Tufts University European Center in Talloires, France, and year-long or semester-long programs are available in France, Germany, Spain, Great Britain, Russia, Ghana, Chile, and Japan.

Another interesting study option is the Experimental College: "Students and people from the community are invited to design and teach their own courses on topics that range from the ethics of genetics research to creating a photo journal and the history of Boston," explains a recent grad. "Many students take these courses pass/fail as an extra course."

Campus Environment

Complementing its splendid New England setting, the Tufts campus has a large central green, around which various academic buildings are situated. "It's a pretty self-contained campus," comments one student. However, some students say the location is not all that easy on the leg muscles when they have to negotiate the New England hills.

Housing is guaranteed for freshmen and sophomores only. In addition to the traditional residence halls, there is the all-freshman Tilton Hall (highly recommended by a young alum we spoke to); the Bridge program, which houses students interested in creating an intentional learning community; 16 theme houses; and an all-female house. After freshman year, fraternity members can live in Greek housing. Most juniors and seniors share apartments in the surrounding community; be warned, however, that off-campus housing is expensive and "incredibly difficult to find." Some seniors choose to move back on-campus—in singles or in co-ops—after spending a year off-campus.

Tufts students are able to take advantage of Boston's cultural and social opportunities, not to mention the work and internship possibilities, thanks to easy access via the T, the city's mass-transit system. At the same time, they can return to the quiet and serenity of their own quaint New England campus—"a bastion of intellect and beauty," as one overly poetic student calls it.

Student Life

The student body at Tufts is friendly, but cliquey. A recent grad notes "a lot of racial/ethnic self-segregation" on campus. But a student who likes the "large number of close-knit communities" within the student population says, "Being part of a larger student body with a happy clique atmosphere is cool." Students represent a range of political views and can be vocal about various issues.

When we ask about the social life, one student replies, "There really isn't much of a social scene outside of Greek life." Another student objects: "There are many different things! We enjoy drinking and smoking . . . We go to parties in fraternities and off-campus housing parties . . . People gather together at midnight and read poetry." However, most students agree that "Tufts is certainly not a party school."

Tufts offers 31 varsity sports for men and women. However, says one student, "school spirit is a little lacking at Tufts. There is not much support for sports." Perhaps this is because of the school's unflattering team name: the Jumbos. (The bizarre history of the mascot: Jumbo was the star elephant in the Barnum and Bailey circus. After he was hit by a train and killed in 1885, his stuffed hide was donated to Tufts by P.T. Barnum, an original trustee of the college. Jumbo stood in Barnum Hall until destroyed by a fire in 1975. Today, his ashes remain on campus in a peanut butter jar.)

"While there may not be a lot of school spirit for the sports teams, Tufts has a lot of fun traditions," says a young alum. "There is a really nice candlelight ceremony at the beginning of freshman year called the 'light on the hill ceremony,' and one again right before graduation." Another Tufts tradition is the "naked quad run," followed, naturally, by "midnight pancakes." A student explains: "It happens every year before finals. Students run around while 4,000 people watch them. It is clean fun with a nudity aspect!"

Other schools to check out: University of Pennsylvania, Dartmouth, Brandeis, Johns Hopkins, University of Chicago.

Test Scores (middle 50%):
SAT Verbal: 610–700
SAT Math: 640–720
ACT Comp: 27–31
HS Rank of Entering Freshmen:
Top 10%: 70%
Top 25%: 93%
Top 50%: 99%

Costs (2003–04)

Tuition and Fees: $29,593

Room & Board: $8,640

Payment Plan(s): installment plan, pre-payment plan

THE EXPERTS SAY...

" 98 percent of Tufts students plan to go to graduate or professional school, and they are well prepared to do so. "

" The 'Jumbos'? Stuck with that team name, no wonder there's no school spirit. "

Inst. Aid (est. 2003–04)

Institutional Aid, Need-Based: $31,946,762

Institutional Aid, Non-Need-Based: $40,000

FT Undergrads Receiving Aid: 41%
Avg. Amount per Student: $24,084

FT Undergrads Receiving Non-Need-Based Scholarship or Grant Aid: 2%
Avg. Amount per Student: $500

Of Those Receiving Any Aid:

Rec. Need-Based Scholarship or Grant Aid: 92%
Average Award: $20,932

Rec. Need-Based Self-Help Aid: 93%
Average Award: $5,171

Upon Graduation, Avg. Loan Debt per Student: $14,925

Financial Aid Deadline: 2/15

Graduates

Going to Graduate School:
35% Within One Year

TULANE UNIVERSITY

6823 St. Charles Avenue, 210 Gibson Hall, New Orleans, LA 70118
Admissions Phone: (504) 865-5731 (in-state); (800) 873-9283 Fax: (504) 862-8715
Email: undergrad.admission@tulane.edu Website: www.tulane.edu
Application Website: www.tulane.edu/admission/applicantsonline_fresh.ht

General Info

Type of School: private, coed
Setting: urban
Academic Calendar: semester

Student Body

Full-Time Undergrads: 5,989
 Men: 49%, Women: 51%

Part-Time Undergrads: 1,873
 Men: 41%, Women: 59%

Total Undergrad Population:
 African American: 8%
 Asian American: 4%
 Latino: 4%
 Native American: <1%
 Caucasian: 71%
 International: 3%
 Out-of-State: 70%
 Living Off-Campus: 40%
 In Fraternities: 33%
 In Sororities: 37%

Graduate and First-Professional
 Students: 4,581

Academics

Full-Time Faculty: 1,049
 With Ph.D.: 90%

Part-Time Faculty: 46
 With Ph.D.: 80%

Student/Faculty Ratio: 10:1

Most Popular Majors:
 business/marketing
 social sciences/history
 engineering
 psychology
 biological/life sciences

Freshmen Retention Rate: 86%

Graduation Rates:
 62% within four years
 74% within six years

Admissions

Regular Application Deadline: 1/15;
 11/1 (priority)

Early Decision Deadline(s): 11/1

Early Action Deadline: 11/1

Total # of Students Applied: 13,931
 Admitted: 7,801
 Enrolled: 1,684

# of Students Waitlisted: 485
 Waitlisted Students Admitted: 6

In the Classroom

One student cuts to the chase about Tulane's excellent academic reputation and its equally excellent party reputation: "Many people think they can come to New Orleans, party for four years and then graduate. Those people usually don't make it through their first semester." The school is a highly respected academic and research institution with high academic standards, and students who spend all their time partying will quickly find themselves in danger of flunking out.

Tulane's undergraduate schools include business, architecture, engineering, and two schools for arts and sciences: Tulane College for men and Newcomb College for women. (The two schools are essentially the same, and men and women take their classes together; only the administration buildings and governing bodies are separate.) Due to its strong academic programs, top faculty members, and superb facilities, Tulane is considered one of the best universities in the South. A recent grad tells us, "The faculty is outstanding." A premed/finance major concurs: "The academic atmosphere is great. The highly qualified professors make themselves accessible to the students and really want to see the students succeed. The workload is average and although students can be competitive, it never reaches the cutthroat level I've heard of at other colleges." A senior explains, "I chose Tulane for its reputation in the sciences and its academic reputation."

The core curriculum for liberal arts students includes courses in humanities, fine arts, social sciences, natural sciences, and math, and requirements in writing and foreign languages. Courses in Western and non-Western civilization are also required.

Campus Environment

"New Orleans is an incredibly dangerous city and Tulane is not an exception but the campus police department is very good," says an alum. Another student talks about security: "Tulane's campus feels very safe—you always see TUPD officers on bikes patrolling 24 hours a day." Tulane has many security measures, including campus-wide blue-lit emergency telephones, 24-hour escort service, and a self-defense program.

On-campus housing seems to be luck of the draw. One student tells us, "On-campus housing is adequate in terms of comfort ... The rooms are small and you have no control over temperature—my room was always freezing, my neighbors lived in a sauna." However, another student says there is "plenty of on-campus housing, and the rooms are usually nice, roomy, comfortable, and there are many different dorms." A senior adds, "The all-girls dorm, Josephine Louise (JL), is the nicest freshman dorm physically, but it's very quiet and you miss out an a lot of the memorable moments that you get in the coed dorms." One student comments, "The administration seems to honestly care about the welfare of the students first and everything else second. Last year there was a lot of tension because the administration was struggling to make the freshmen dorms dry while many students opposed this."

As for off-campus housing, it's affordable ("$300–$600"), nearby, and pretty popular. Like many urban colleges, "many of the houses are very old, which can cause problems, and some landlords are unresponsive." Explains a history/Italian major,

"Nearly everyone moves off campus after freshman year because there is so much cheap housing around campus. A lot of people find that it is actually cheaper to live off campus than on." A senior elaborates: "In my experience, living with two or three other people is cheapest (but can drive you crazy); living alone can get very expensive."

If it's your first, year, leave the car at home and make some friends in the upper classes. "Freshmen can't have cars, but it is not a problem. Cabs are very available and relatively cheap; the street car runs right in front of the campus and costs $1.25 per ride, but it isn't the most dependable mode of transportation late at night. Most upperclassmen have cars, which is the easiest means for getting around quickly." A recent grad reassures, "There are so many students with cars so students who don't have them usually don't have problems."

Student Life

"I am sure that everyone loves college and has fun in college but no one has as much fun as a Tulane student," raves a grad. A senior tells us, "It isn't 'stodgy' or caught up in academia. Students know how to have a great time while getting a great education." Not surprising, considering the school is located in New Orleans, famous home to Mardi Gras and the hip French Quarter. The city is a center for entertainment and culture and Tulane students take advantage of it. "The population of the campus triples during Mardi Gras," says a senior. "Everybody's friends invite themselves down!" "Wednesday through Saturday are big nights for going out to bars and clubs, but every night is fair game for partying," one student tells us (another explains, "Monday and Tuesday are optional"). While drinking is big, a grad tell us, "there are plenty of people who neither drink nor use drugs at Tulane and they have just as much of a social life as anyone else," and "even the non-partiers (yes, there are some in New Orleans) find their group." And Tulane students do come out in the daylight. "Downtime is often spent just hanging out with friends, going to Audobon park, or the levee when the weather's nice."

On campus, the Greek system is fairly popular, but students tell us that "they have very little influence on the rest of Tulane because there is so much to do in the city and at the school so social life does not depend on them. There is plenty of Greek/non-Greek interaction." Besides hosting parties and frequenting the many bars and clubs, "the sororities and fraternities are also involved in the community, doing service projects, cleaning up Broadway (a major street next to campus and the residential areas)." Tulane also offers its students many other options: "There are a million other clubs at Tulane including sports clubs, religious and political clubs, cigar-smoking clubs, and really anything else you could think of."

Other schools to check out: Southern Methodist, Trinity U, Vanderbilt, University of Richmond, Furman.

Applied Early Decision: 147
 Early Decision Admitted: 98

Test Scores (middle 50%):
 SAT Verbal: 610–730
 SAT Math: 630–690
 ACT Comp: 28–32

HS Rank of Entering Freshmen:
 Top 10%: 65%
 Top 25%: 91%
 Top 50%: 100%

Costs (2004–5)

Tuition and Fees: $31,210

Room & Board: $7,925

Payment Plan(s): installment plan

THE EXPERTS SAY...

" Tulane combines the unique and lively atmosphere of New Orleans with a great research repuatation. "

" Mardi Gras, cajun and creole cooking, jazz music, and the French Quarter all make New Orleans an excellent choice for a 4-year vacation—I mean, college experience. "

Inst. Aid (2002–03)

FT Undergrads Receiving Aid: 42%
 Avg. Amount per Student:
 $24,688

Of Those Receiving Any Aid:

Rec. Need-Based Scholarship or Grant Aid: 97%
 Average Award: $17,282

Rec. Need-Based Self-Help Aid: 70%
 Average Award: $6,370

Upon Graduation, Avg. Loan Debt per Student: $20,983

Financial Aid Deadline: 2/1

TUSKEGEE UNIVERSITY

102 Old Administration Building, Tuskegee, AL 36088-1920
Admissions Phone: (334) 727-8500; (800) 622-6531 Fax: (334) 724-4402
Email: adm@acd.tuskegee.edu Website: www.tuskegee.edu
Application Website: www.abwwed.tuskegee

General Info

Type of School: private, coed
Setting: small town
Academic Calendar: semester

Student Body

Full-Time Undergrads: 2,296
  Men: 44%, Women: 56%

Part-Time Undergrads: 95
  Men: 48%, Women: 52%

Total Undergrad Population:
  African American: 72%
  Asian American: <1%
  Latino: <1%
  Native American: <1%
  Caucasian: 2%
  International: 3%
  Out-of-State: 59%
  Living Off-Campus: 46%
  In Fraternities: 6%
  In Sororities: 5%

Graduate and First-Professional
  Students: 372

Academics

Full-Time Faculty: 218
  With Ph.D.: 71%

Part-Time Faculty: 32
  With Ph.D.: 28%

Student/Faculty Ratio: 12:1

Most Popular Majors:
  engineering (17%)
  biology (11%)
  veterinary medicine (9%)
  computer science (7%)
  business administration (6%)

Completing 2 or More Majors: 2%

Freshmen Retention Rate: 71%

Graduation Rates:
  25% within four years
  51% within six years

Admissions

Early Decision Available

Fall Transfer Deadline: 7/15 (priority)

Total # of Students Applied: 1,326
  Admitted: 1,068
  Enrolled: 528

Test Scores (middle 50%):
  SAT Verbal: 340–540
  SAT Math: 370–550
  ACT Comp: 17–20

Inside the Classroom

Founded by Booker T. Washington in 1881, Tuskegee University boasts high quality academics, groundbreaking research, and a tremendous sense of history. Undergraduates may choose from a variety of programs offered in five colleges: Agricultural, Environmental, and Natural Sciences; Business, Organization, and Management; Engineering, Architecture, and Physical Sciences (the largest college at Tuskegee); Liberal Arts and Education; and Veterinary Medicine, Nursing, and Allied Health. Tuskegee's main strengths lie in its science, preprofessional, and engineering programs. It is, in fact, the leading producer of African American engineering graduates in chemical, electrical, mechanical, and aerospace engineering, as well as the only historically black college in the nation designated as the location for a National Center for Bioethics in Research and Health Care. We hear that there are plans in the works for unique undergrad programs in bioethics and airways science. The veterinary program is unparalleled; nearly 75 percent of all African American veterinarians in the United States are Tuskegee graduates.

Research opportunities abound. Among the impressive "Centers of Excellence" are the Center for Integrated Study of Food Animal and Plant Systems, Center for Biomedical Research, Center for Plant Biotechnology, NSF Center for Research Excellence in Science and Technology, and the George Washington Carver Agricultural Experimental Station. In addition, the university has one of only two NASA-funded centers to develop technology for growing food in space during human space missions. As proud home of the legendary Tuskegee Airmen, TU—which has graduated more African American generals than any other university—offers strong Army and Air Force ROTC programs. School officials have recently announced the return of flight training to the university at the C. Alfred "Chief" Anderson Department of Aviation Science.

Aside from coursework in their major, students must complete a core curriculum that includes credits in English, math, history, political science, the humanities, and the natural sciences. Classes at TU are small and intimate, just the way the students like it. Students have good things to say about their professors; unfortunately, the administration doesn't fare as well in student opinion. We heard complaints about registration and bursar issues in particular. There is no hand-holding at Tuskegee: Students should expect to shoulder a lot of classwork as well as a lot of responsibility for their own education. But they're usually up to the challenge. If you haven't guessed already, Tuskegee graduates tend to be leaders in their fields. Noteworthy alumni include *Invisible Man* author Ralph Ellison, Grammy Award–winning singer/songwriter Lionel Richie, and General Daniel "Chappie" James, the first black four-star general in the armed forces. (Two recent Tuskegee graduates became somewhat famous this past fall, as they were winners of a *Today* show wedding series that culminated with their being married live on the program.)

Campus Environment

Located about 40 miles from Montgomery, Alabama, Tuskegee's sprawling 5,000-acre campus—once the site of an abandoned plantation—is a pleasant mix of contemporary and historic architecture. Tuskegee was the first black college

KAPLAN

designated as both a Registered National Historic Landmark and a National Historic Site. (Tuskegee enjoys the unique position of being a private university with state land-grant status.) Many of the buildings were built by students, including Tompkins Hall (the "social mecca of campus," featuring a cafeteria upstairs and a student union rec area downstairs) and White Hall. The so-called "architecture jewel" in Tuskegee's crown, White Hall, once a women's residence hall, has been in a state of disrepair and as such has been closed of late, but due to the school's successful fundraising campaign, it has been completely renovated and reopened.

On-campus housing options include 16 traditional residence halls and university apartments (additional apartments are under construction, we hear). All freshmen, sophomores, and first-year transfer students are required to live in the dormitories. And, according to the school's cryptic website, the university "recently completed five miles of sophisticated fencing surrounding the campus hailed by many as the 'boundaries of the estate.'"

Other campus highlights include Band Cottage, the oldest building on campus (1889), the luxurious Kellogg Conference Center, the Oaks, and the University Chapel with its "Singing Glass Windows," inscribed with lyrics from Negro spirituals. And students, visitors, and school officials all consider the Booker T. Washington Monument, titled "Lifting the Veil"—a sentiment the school imparts often—the centerpiece of Tuskegee.

Student Life

The predominantly African American student body hails largely from the South, and there is the sense of one big extended family. More than 100 student groups of all kinds are active on campus, including the chess club, the International Students Association, and the Future Business Leaders of America. The prestigious Tuskegee University Golden Voices Choir has performed at the White House and Radio City Music Hall. Socially, Greeks rule the school. Fraternity and sorority parties are often the only thing going on, we hear. Indeed, the small town of Tuskegee is far from a hotbed of activity. Students who have cars—or who have friends with cars—often head to Atlanta for city fun, or to Auburn University for big-campus fun. Several popular on-campus events keep them happy, especially the "celebrity-filled, fun-filled week" during Homecoming.

Men's varsity teams include football, basketball, baseball, track and field, and tennis; women's teams include basketball, softball, volleyball, track and field, and tennis. The Tuskegee Relays, the annual track-and-field event, is a spring highlight for many. And athletes are students first: Tuskegee notes with pride that it is the only HBCU to maintain academic excellence while supporting a football program with a career record of 500-plus wins. Recently, two Tuskegee football stars were chosen in the 2003 NFL Draft. And cheering them on for sure is the huge, crowd-pleasing Marching Crimson Piper Band, who are known as much for their unique marching style and intricate dance steps as they are for their musical arrangements; they perform all over the nation as well as at Golden Tigers matchups.

Other schools to check out: Howard, Hampton, Fisk, Spelman, Morehouse, Xavier.

HS Rank of Entering Freshmen:
Top 10%: 20%
Top 25%: 44%
Top 50%: 82%
Avg. HS GPA: 3.2

Costs (2003–04)

Tuition and Fees: $11,310

Room & Board: $5,940

Payment Plan(s): installment plan

THE EXPERTS SAY...

" Tuskegee respects its past while also looking forward, becoming a training ground for 21st century African American scientists and engineers. "

" Some students might prefer to 'lift the veil' in a more urban setting. "

Inst. Aid (est. 2003–04)

Institutional Aid, Need-Based: $1,205,834

Institutional Aid, Non-Need-Based: $46,675

FT Undergrads Receiving Aid: 77% Avg. Amount per Student: $10,794

FT Undergrads Receiving Non-Need-Based Scholarship or Grant Aid: 30% Avg. Amount per Student: $5,181

Of Those Receiving Any Aid:

Rec. Need-Based Scholarship or Grant Aid: 85% Average Award: $6,319

Rec. Need-Based Self-Help Aid: 85% Average Award: $4,655

Upon Graduation, Avg. Loan Debt per Student: $20,000

Financial Aid Deadline: 4/1, 3/31 (priority)

Graduates

Going to Graduate School: 21% Within One Year

Accepting Job Offer: 70% at time of graduation

Companies Recruiting On Campus: 100

Alumni Giving: 75%

UNION COLLEGE

807 Union Street, Schenectady, NY 12308-2311
Admissions Phone: (518) 388-6112; (888) 843-6688 Fax: (518) 388-6986
Email: admissions@union.edu Website: www.union.edu
Application Website: www.union.edu/Admissions/Applying/Applications.php

General Info

Type of School: private, coed
Setting: suburban
Academic Calendar: trimester

Student Body

Full-Time Undergrads: 2,135
  Men: 53%, Women: 47%

Part-Time Undergrads: 12
  Men: 67%, Women: 33%

Total Undergrad Population:
  African American: 3%
  Asian American: 5%
  Latino: 4%
  Caucasian: 84%
  International: 2%
  Out-of-State: 55%
  Living Off-Campus: 20%
  In Fraternities: 29%
  In Sororities: 26%

Academics

Full-Time Faculty: 192
  With Ph.D.: 94%

Part-Time Faculty: 26
  With Ph.D.: 38%

Student/Faculty Ratio: 11:1

Most Popular Majors:
  political science (10%)
  psychology (9%)
  economics (9%)
  history (7%)
  biology (6%)

Completing 2 or More Majors: 5%

Freshmen Retention Rate: 93%

Graduation Rates:
  77% within four years
  83% within six years

Admissions

Regular Application Deadline: 1/15

Early Decision Deadline(s): 11/15, 1/15

Fall Transfer Deadline: 5/1

Spring Transfer Deadline: 2/1

Total # of Students Applied: 4,159
  Admitted: 1,822
  Enrolled: 559

# of Students Waitlisted: 912
  Students Accepting Place: 301
  Waitlisted Students Admitted: 41

Inside the Classroom

When you look at its academic offerings—nearly 1,000—and particularly at its science and research facilities, you might think Union is a large research university. In actuality, it's a small liberal arts college, one of the oldest in the country, with an undergraduate enrollment that's kept to just over 2,000 students. "We have a lot of students who are motivated in their education," says one student proudly.

Union was the first liberal arts school to offer study in engineering, and that discipline, termed "liberal education for a technological world," remains strong. Social sciences and physical sciences are the most popular courses of study. Union is known for its strengths in the premedical science departments; students are able to make use of superb laboratories and equipment and are encouraged to conduct their own scientific research. Many of its liberal arts departments are highly regarded; English, history, and political science are very popular majors as preparation for law school. Interdisciplinary study is encouraged; students can design their own majors. Ambitious students can receive an M.S. or M.B.A. through Union's accelerated programs. Cooperative programs also allow students to receive M.D. and J.D. degrees from local medical and law schools.

Union's General Education Curriculum includes courses in history, literature, civilization, mathematics, the natural sciences, and the social sciences. The curriculum has strong "incentives" to study a foreign language, embark on a Term Abroad, or study a non-Western cultures. The College's Writing Across the Curriculum program requires all students to take a certain number of courses that use writing as a key element. Most classes at Union are small (under 20 students, on average); students become deeply immersed in their studies and get to work closely with their professors. Guidance counselors praise the "attentive profs" at the school; there are no teaching assistants.

Union promotes independent study and student research, which has sometimes led to joint publication with faculty. Union regularly sends one of the largest groups to the National Conference on Undergraduate Research and more than 250 students present their research at Union's annual Steinmetz Symposium. During the summer, about 50 students receive research fellowships to work with faculty members.

Union is one of the few schools to operate on a trimester system, and students generally take only three courses a term. While this isn't as stressful as a quarter system, students still have a long academic year in which exams and paper deadlines come up frequently. "The academics are challenging," admits a student. And many students are kept even busier by taking up an internship or gaining work experience off campus during their six-week break between Thanksgiving and the New Year. Many departments offer internships; one popular one is in Washington, DC, where students work for a term in congressional offices or government agencies.

A substantial number of students take advantage of Union's extensive Term Abroad program. The College also offers a term in marine studies in Bermuda and along the coastal United States and a 10-week field study of the national health systems of England, the Netherlands, and Eastern Europe.

Campus Environment

The city of Schenectady doesn't hold many charms for students, who don't venture off campus often. Fortunately, the campus, with its ivy-covered walls, gardens, and woods, is much more scenic and stately than the city outside its walls. Union College administrators boast that their school was the first higher learning institute in the country to have a unified campus plan integrating architecture and landscape design—this is no motley group of buildings converted from other uses.

Most students live on campus, and there are many housing options, including several special-interest houses. Union is also developing apartment complexes for additional student housing as part of a campaign to revitalize the area surrounding the campus. One-fifth of the student body lives off campus, braving Schenectady's postindustrial atmosphere.

Parking poses a problem, according to the student newspaper, which states there are adequate spaces, but not many convenient ones. The paper points out that one student lot is located directly behind the Richmond dorm, which houses freshmen who are not allowed to have cars on campus. Students have concerns about the safety of parking at night and in the cold Schenectady winters. On average, 15 to 20 parking tickets are given out each day to vehicles parked illegally on Union's campus.

Student Life

"Union is an upbeat campus with very active students," a student informs us. Union was the first school to have fraternities, and the Greek system remains a prominent part of student life. Fraternities draw over a fifth of the men, and sororities attract about the same number of women. Although the college strictly regulates all parties, the Greeks manage to maintain a healthy party scene; a California guidance counselor says there's "lots of alcohol" on campus. Sober or drunk, streaking around the 16-sided Nott Memorial is a hallowed student tradition.

Many Union students are also interested in sports, both intramurals and varsity. Of the 25 varsity teams, the most successful in recent years have been men's and women's swimming, both of which are nationally ranked. Varsity football and Division I hockey also have strong records, and the Union's Division III basketball team keeps the bleachers full.

Student clubs range from ballroom dancing to professional engineering organizations, of which there are a number for minority students and women. Chet's, a campus hangout, offers entertainment including musical performances, food, and beverages. The Coffeehouse also provides live entertainment and a place to talk. The college newspaper, *Concordiensis*, or "Concordy," is "the voice of the students amplified to an audible pitch." Mountebanks is the oldest continually operating student theatre organization in the country. While social options are adequate—parties, concerts, plays, movies, and the like—the academic opportunities and facilities are mostly what bring students to Union, and in that sense, they are far from disappointed.

\# Applied Early Decision: 262
Early Decision Admitted: 194

Test Scores (middle 50%):
SAT Verbal: 560–660
SAT Math: 590–690

HS Rank of Entering Freshmen:
Top 10%: 58%
Top 25%: 82%
Top 50%: 97%

Avg. HS GPA: 3.49

THE EXPERTS SAY...

" There are 2,000 students and nearly 1,000 courses. The research and science facilities are amazing for a small liberal arts school. "

" Schenectady is awful; luckily, there's a lot to do on campus. For one thing, you can watch your friends streak around a 16-sided monument. "

Costs (2004–5)

Comprehensive Fees: $38,703

Payment Plan(s): installment plan

Inst. Aid (2002–03)

Institutional Aid, Need-Based:
$16,372,900

Institutional Aid, Non-Need-Based:
$1,043,612

FT Undergrads Receiving Aid: 52%
Avg. Amount per Student: $22,601

FT Undergrads Receiving Non-Need-Based Scholarship or Grant Aid: 2%
Avg. Amount per Student: $13,200

Of Those Receiving Any Aid:

Rec. Need-Based Scholarship or Grant Aid: 99%
Average Award: $18,007

Rec. Need-Based Self-Help Aid: 85%
Average Award: $4,798

Upon Graduation, Avg. Loan Debt per Student: $14,673

Financial Aid Deadline: 2/1, 2/1 (priority)

Graduates

Going to Graduate School:
30% Within One Year

Companies Recruiting On Campus: 43

UNITED STATES AIR FORCE ACADEMY

2304 Cadet Drive, Suite 200, USAFA Academy, CO 80840
Admissions Phone: (719) 333-2520; (800) 443-9266
Website: www.usafa.edu

General Info

Type of School: public, coed
Setting: urban
Academic Calendar: semester

Student Body

Full-Time Undergrads: 4,157
  Men: 83%, Women: 17%

Total Undergrad Population:
  African American: 5%
  Asian American: 5%
  Latino: 6%
  Native American: 1%
  Caucasian: 80%
  International: 1%
  Out-of-State: 96%

Academics

Full-Time Faculty: 531
  With Ph.D.: 57%

Student/Faculty Ratio: 8:1

Most Popular Majors:
  engineering
  management
  social sciences
  psychology
  biology/life sciences

Completing 2 or More Majors: 2%

Freshmen Retention Rate: 82%

Graduation Rates:
  97% within four years
  100% within six years

Computers: Computer Required

Admissions

Regular Application Deadline: 1/31

Fall Transfer Deadline: 1/31

Total # of Students Applied: 13,068
  Admitted: 1,948
  Enrolled: 1,302

Test Scores (middle 50%):
  SAT Verbal: 590–670
  SAT Math: 620–700
  ACT English: 26–31
  ACT Math: 28–32

HS Rank of Entering Freshmen:
  Top 10%: 57%
  Top 25%: 85%
  Top 50%: 98%

Avg. HS GPA: 3.85

Inside the Classroom

The USAFA education is one of the best in the country, and it's free. Cadets receive a monthly stipend, plus books, supplies, and a top-of-the-line computer. However, there's a catch: a military obligation of five years, with a good chance of service in "hot zones." In the academy, you'll pay for your education through incredibly challenging academics, physical training, and military exercises; this isn't college life as most students imagine it. But what other college campus has jets sitting right in the middle of it?

USAFA is highly selective, admitting only 17 percent of applicants. The admissions process is a long and arduous one. Applicants must be nominated by at least one member of Congress and/or have a military-affiliated parent meeting certain criteria (children of a parent who has received the Congressional Medal of Honor are eligible, for example). High SAT/ACT scores are a must, and applicants must pass a battery of physical exams.

The life of a cadet is rigorous, but cadets cite the chance to fly or to join the space program as big motivators. Cadets may select one of 31 academic majors (including non-science or engineering-related areas such as English and social sciences). The workload is extremely heavy, and the academy recommends that cadets spend 100 minutes preparing for each 50-minute class (the average course is 18 hours). The demanding core curriculum at USAFA consists of 96 semester hours in the sciences, aerospace engineering, management, law, foreign languages, and the liberal arts. There are no electives until second degree (junior year).

Class size is small, usually 15–20 cadets. The academy's faculty consists of about 75 percent Air Force officers and 25 percent civilian professors. Faculty members are teachers rather than researchers, and there are no graduate assistants. The faculty is extremely accessible; full professors often spend hours tutoring students who need help. Faculty members also "adopt" squadrons.

Future air and space leaders get a rigorous military education from day one at the academy. All cadets participate in some form of airmanship activity each of their four years at the academy. Basic Cadet Training, or "Beast," takes place the first summer, and is a grueling boot camp experience. The way cadets live and work is organized along military lines; the cadet wing is organized into squadrons commanded by a first-class (senior) cadet. Undergraduate Flying Training is conducted after graduation at several U.S. bases and prepares qualified graduates for flying careers in airlift, bomber, fighter, special operations, or transport aircraft. About half of USAFA graduates go on to become pilots or navigators.

Campus Environment

USAFA, which opened its doors in 1958, is the youngest of the service academies. It is located in Colorado Springs on 18,000 acres at the base of the Rocky Mountains. Colorado Springs has a growing downtown with restaurants and entertainment, but cadets fourth class (first-year students) are pretty much confined to campus, and are likely to spend more time in Jack's Valley, 2,000 wooded acres used for training.

Cadets are housed in two dormitories, Vandenberg Hall and Sijan Hall. Inspections of dorm rooms occur every Saturday, and woe to the cadet who is less than spotless. Taps means lights out. Cadets march to breakfast and lunch, which is served by waiters; the food is decent and plentiful. Dinner is served buffet style. Only juniors and seniors can have refrigerators. Upperclassmen are also allowed to have cars, and use them to take advantage of outdoor sports in the Rockies and for trips to Denver, about an hour away.

The academic facilities are cutting edge. In addition to a sophisticated computer lab with war gaming software, the aeronautics laboratory features two wind tunnels, operational turbojet engines, and rocket test cells. Three astronautics laboratories provide facilities for small satellite design, fabrication and testing, rocket design, and orbital analysis software. There is an on-site planetarium for astronomy and navigation. Even the foreign language learning center is state-of-the art.

Student Life

Make no mistake about it: The life of a first-year student, or "doolie," is hard (not coincidentally, "doolie" comes from the Greek work for "slave"). Hazing is common: Doolies are asked for "knowledge" (military protocol and history), and can spend long hours marching in circles if they can't answer. Once a year, however, doolies get some payback. "Every year we have an activity called '100 Nights,' meaning 100 nights till graduation," an Air Force cadet informs us. "The first-year students get to decorate while the seniors are away celebrating. The seniors' rooms get decorated with black lights, desert camouflage, etc.—the sky is the limit! It's their big opportunity to blow off steam."

When do cadets fourth class get time for extracurricular activities? "They do not have much free time," admits an Air Force cadet, "but they do the same type of fun things other students do." Free-fall parachuting and community service are popular, as is fishing on the campus grounds. All cadets can join the Cadet Aviation Club and fly light aircraft as a member of the Aero Club during all four years. Recreation is largely dry: Underage drinking is strictly prohibited, and can be punished by 80 hours of marching plus probation. There are dances, and the Academy sponsors social events, although there are prohibitions against underclassmen socializing with upperclassmen.

Athletics aren't just entertainment at the academy—they're a requirement. Sports Illustrated even named the U.S. Air Force Academy the "most athletic school in the country." Every cadet takes two phys ed courses each semester (if your 1.5-mile aerobics run time is slower than 11:15 for men or 13:31 for women, you're flunking phys ed) and is required to participate in either intercollegiate or intramural sports. The Division I Falcons compete in 17 men's and 10 women's intercollegiate sports.

The academy has been the focus of media attention for months, since dozens of female cadets came forward to say that they were reprimanded or ostracized after reporting to academy administrators that they'd been raped by male cadets. The Air Force and the Defense Department are currently conducting investigations.

Costs (2004–05)

Fees: $2,500 (one-time, first year)
  note: for uniforms and computer

Graduates

Going to Graduate School:
  3% Within One Year

Accepting Job Offer:
  100% at time of graduation

THE EXPERTS SAY...

" A ROTC program at a civilian college might be better idea for some, but if you are willing to work harder than you ever have in your life, the Air Force Academy may be for you. "

" As long as you know what you're getting into (both in terms of service obligation and campus safety), graduating from the Air Force Academy is an admirable goal. "

UNITED STATES
COAST GUARD ACADEMY

31 Mohegan Avenue, New London, CT 06320
Admissions Phone: (860) 883-8724; (860) 444-8500 Fax: (860) 701-6700
Email: admissions@cga.uscg.mil Website: www.cga.edu

General Info

Type of School: public, coed
Setting: suburban
Academic Calendar: semester

Student Body

Full-Time Undergrads: 1,016
  Men: 70%, Women: 30%

Total Undergrad Population:
  African American: 4%
  Asian American: 5%
  Latino: 5%
  Native American: 1%
  Caucasian: 83%
  International: 2%
  Out-of-State: 93%

Academics

Full-Time Faculty: 98
  With Ph.D.: 55%

Part-Time Faculty: 18
  With Ph.D.: 67%

Student/Faculty Ratio: 10:1

Freshmen Retention Rate: 81%

Graduation Rates:
  55% within four years
  57% within six years

Computers: School provides individual computer/laptop

Admissions

Regular Application Deadline: 1/31

Early Action Deadline: 11/1

Total # of Students Applied: 6,028
  Admitted: 429
  Enrolled: 305

Waitlist Available

Test Scores (middle 50%):
  SAT Verbal: 571–650
  SAT Math: 600–680
  ACT Comp: 25–28
  ACT English: 24–30
  ACT Math: 26–30

HS Rank of Entering Freshmen:
  Top 10%: 58%
  Top 25%: 90%
  Top 50%: 100%

Costs (2004–05)

Tuition, Room & Board paid by U.S. Government

Inside the Classroom

The smallest of the five federal service academies, the U.S. Coast Guard Academy offers a four-year Bachelor of Science program with a full scholarship for each individual. Unlike the other federal service academies, there are no Congressional appointments: "We accept young men and women solely on the basis of their own merits, not on nominations. So you make it—or not—on your own." But making it isn't easy, to say the least: CGA accepts a mere seven percent of its applicants, making it more selective than all of the other service academies (not to mention all of the Ivies!).

Cadets earn their B.S. degree in one of eight engineering or professional majors: naval architecture and marine engineering, civil engineering, mechanical engineering, electrical engineering, operations research and computer analysis, marine and environmental science, government, and management. Cadets are required to take a rigid core curriculum, plus physical education courses such as Intermediate and Advanced Swimming, Personal Defense, Physiology of Fitness, and First Aid/CPR.

All cadets adhere to the Honor Concept: "We neither lie, cheat, steal, nor attempt to deceive." Breaches of the Honor Concept are considered to be Class I Offenses. Contrary to what may be popular belief, cadets are reportedly able to rely on their instructors for guidance and support. "I have found that the instructors at the Academy are always more than willing to take time out of their schedule to help clear up any confusion," says a third class cadet on the CGA website. "Many instructors have even given their home phone numbers to be contacted during weekends or after hours."

Obligated to serve five years, graduates of the Academy are commissioned as Ensigns in the Coast Guard and are assigned to ships as Deck Watch Officers or Engineers in Training for their first two-year tour. Following their first tour, other opportunities are available, such as applying for Advanced Degree Programs paid for by the Coast Guard (though this comes with an additional service obligation of two months for every one month of education received). "In the last ten years, every Academy engineering graduate who has applied for an engineering postgraduate program has been accepted and has gone on to complete their master's degree," brags the Academy. Another highly prized option: applying for Flight School and becoming a member of the Coast Guard's elite community of aviators.

After 9/11 and the increased focus on homeland security, the Coast Guard's motto of Semper Paratus ("Always Ready") became even more significant. In February 2003, at a historic "Change of Watch" ceremony, U.S. Secretary of Transportation Norman Mineta transferred leadership of the U.S. Coast Guard to U.S. Secretary of Homeland Security Tom Ridge.

Campus Environment

The Academy lies next to the Thames River in New London, Connecticut. All cadets are required to live Academy grounds for all four years in the Chase Hall dormitory and wardroom. The Academy grounds are open to the public year-round, and visitors are welcome to take a self-guided tour. (Admissions briefings and cadet-guided tours are held on Fridays; call the Admissions Office for an appointment.)

CGA facilities include some of the most sophisticated labs in the world, such as the Ship Control and Navigation Training Simulator. Waesche Hall contains a state-of-the-art library and is also the home of the Coast Guard Museum. Roland Hall is one of the finest, well-equipped athletic centers in New England. Jacobs Rock, the seamanship center, features "watercraft of every size and stripe." The Coast Guard Cutter Eagle, known as "America's Tall Ship," acts as the cadets' main training ship.

One of the best things about being a cadet is getting to travel the world for free. Much of this travel takes place during the four-year Summer Training Program. "Swab Summer," the seven-week traditional military indoctrination before cadets' first academic semester, is notoriously tough ("Be prepared to memorize tons of Coast Guard and Coast Guard Academy information, including the Coast Guard Mission and other facts, such as the daily menu," advises the U.S. Coast Guard Academy Parents' Association). But each successive summer sees the cadets learning and applying new skills in a hands-on environment around the globe.

THE EXPERTS SAY...

" CGA also offers two excellent summer programs geared for high school students the summer between their junior and senior year: Academy Introduction Mission (AIM) and Minority Introduction to Engineering (MITE). "

" Great for law enforcement types seeking an academic, physical, and psychological challenge... not to mention job security after graduation. Women are better integrated into the CGA than they are in the other academies. "

Student Life

The Corps of Cadets is organized into eight companies which form one regiment. Cadets run the Corps themselves through their regimental chain of command. First class (fourth-year) cadets fulfill roles as Regimental Staff Officers, Company Commanders, Department Heads and Division Officers. Second class (third-year) cadets have overall responsibility for the fourth class (first-year, also known as "swabs") training program. Third class (second-year) cadets serve as mentors, each providing personal oversight of one or two fourth class cadets.

Swabs value their free time with good reason: During the academic year, liberty is generally authorized only on Saturdays from noon until 1:00 A.M. and resumes at 7:30 A.M. Sunday through early evening. As a cadet progresses through four years at the Academy, he becomes eligible for Friday night and eventually some weeknight liberty. Leave is authorized for Thanksgiving, Christmas, Spring Break, and for only about 16 days in the summer.

There is a strong emphasis on teamwork at the Academy. CGA offers 23 Division III intercollegiate sports teams, and all cadets are expected to participate in either a varsity or intramural sport each year during two of the three sports seasons (fall, winter, and spring). In addition, cadets may join any of the 18 additional clubs and activities, many of which are musical (e.g., Jazz Band, Glee Club, Gospel Choir, etc.). Then there's the mandatory Cadet Social Program, which has two main components: the Etiquette Training Program, involving instruction of the rudiments of military protocol and proper comportment in any social situation, and the Social Activities Program, involving the planning of activities such as formal dinner dances, mixers, concerts, and pep rallies.

Women have a long and proud history of service in the Coast Guard, and nearly 30 percent of the corps of cadets are female. "I loved the idea of going out to save lives and stopping the importation of drugs," explains a female fourth class cadet on the GCA website. Among the reasons a female third class cadet gives for enrolling in the Academy: "It offers every cadet a great education as well as letting them participate in varsity sports at the college level, which I knew I wanted to do."

UNITED STATES MERCHANT MARINE ACADEMY

300 Steamboat Road, Kings Point, NY 11024-1699
Admissions Phone: (516) 773-5391; (866) 546-4778 Fax: (516) 773-5390
Email: admissions@usmma.edu Website: www.usmma.edu

General Info

Type of School: public, coed
Setting: suburban
Academic Calendar: trimester

Student Body

Full-Time Undergrads: 952
  Men: 87%, Women: 13%

Total Undergrad Population:
  African American: 2%
  Asian American: 4%
  Latino: 4%
  Native American: <1%
  Caucasian: 89%
  International: 2%
  Out-of-State: 86%

Academics

Full-Time Faculty: 85
Part-Time Faculty: 10
Student/Faculty Ratio: 11:1
Freshmen Retention Rate: 74%
Graduation Rates:
  84% within four years
  16% within six years

Admissions

Regular Application Deadline: 3/1
Early Decision Deadline(s): 11/1
Fall Transfer Deadline: 3/1
Total # of Students Applied: 1,919
  Admitted: 388
  Enrolled: 303
# of Students Waitlisted: 293
  Waitlisted Students Admitted: 3
Test Scores (middle 50%):
  SAT Verbal: 575–690
  SAT Math: 580–665
  ACT Comp: 25–30
  ACT English: 24–28
  ACT Math: 28–32
HS Rank of Entering Freshmen:
  Top 10%: 26%
  Top 25%: 68%
  Top 50%: 95%
Avg. HS GPA: 3.6

Costs (2003–04)

Comprehensive Fees: $3,500
  note: Tuition, Room & Board paid
  by U.S. government

Inside the Classroom

The United States Merchant Marine Academy educates professional officers for the U.S. merchant marine, the armed forces, and the transportation system. Graduates receive bachelor of science degrees and U.S. Coast Guard licenses as deck or engineering officers (or both), and a commission in the U.S. Naval Reserve or another uniformed service reserve. And the education is free and features a year at sea. If that weren't enough, a guidance counselor notes, midshipmen are "guaranteed world travel as a student," visiting on average 18 countries.

Yes, there is a catch: Kings Pointers are committed to a five-year maritime service obligation and a concurrent eight-year armed forces reserve commitment. The service obligation may be satisfied as an officer aboard U.S. merchant ships, or in shoreside maritime or intermodal transportation industry positions if employment at sea is not available. Active military duty in the U.S. armed forces or in the National Oceanic and Atmospheric Administration also satisfies the obligation.

Kings Pointers learn early that "graduation is by cooperation," and teamwork is instilled in midshipmen from drilling to the classroom. The workload is rigorous and is combined with military duties and required sports participation. However, the student/faculty ratio is low, and there's strong academic support to help midshipmen succeed. The school is "high tech in every aspect," an Alabama guidance counselor raves, noting that this is an education of "practical applications [and] on-the-job experience."

The core curriculum includes courses in firefighting, naval operations, self defense, aquatic survival, swimming, naval science, physical education and ship's medicine, and computer science, along with other more typical courses like math and English. There are seven major programs: marine transportation, marine operations and technology, logistics and intermodal transportation, marine engineering, marine engineering systems, marine engineering and shipyard management, and dual license. (A guidance counselor lauds the "outstanding engineering, logistics, and intermodal transportation programs.")

USMMA midshipmen say "the world is our campus." In the Shipboard Training Program, students spend part of their sophomore and junior years at sea (a total of 300 days). Students are assigned to two or three different types of ships on each tour, working at everything from cargo loading and navigation to engine maintenance. At sea, students continue with their academics. At the end of training, midshipmen complete a two- to six-week internship with a marine-related organization.

Admission requirements to USMMA are steep. Candidates must be nominated by a member of Congress from their residential district; unlike the other academies, there are no exceptions for military-affiliated candidates or even presidential nominees. SAT and ACT scores must be high, and applicants must pass a battery of physical tests.

While USMMA may lack the cachet of Annapolis, the Academy has a tradition of valor—142 midshipmen died in World War II while on shipboard training, and USMMA is the only service academy allowed to carry a battle standard in its color guard. Midshipmen have participated in every major sealift since Korea; after the attack on the World Trade Center, some 90 students and faculty conducted a sealift with Academy vessels in New York Harbor, ferrying NYC police, firefighters and medical personnel, as well as supplies to the WTC site. The training that USMMA students receive in combating piracy on the high seas—a growing threat to world shipping—was featured on the ABC-TV news program *Downtown*.

Campus Environment

USMMA is located in Kings Point, Long Island, on a picturesque waterfront that serves for both maritime training and recreation. A guidance counselor calls it a "small, safe, beautiful campus overlooking the water only minutes away from NYC." The Academy is on Long Island's legendary Gold Coast, the site of the mansions depicted in The Great Gatsby, and has a magnificent view of the New York skyline across Long Island Sound. Unfortunately, plebes (freshmen) are pretty much confined to campus, so sightseeing is limited to the occasional liberty. Only first class students (seniors) are allowed to have cars.

Plebes are integrated into dorms that include first- through fourth-year students (first class students in effect command the plebes). Students are assigned two to a room; all dorms are coed. On-campus housing is required for all four years except during shipboard training. Says a guidance counselor, "This U.S. academy gets the least amount of funding by the Congress; some facilities are in poor repair and student housing is substandard."

Student Life

From the moment you enter the Academy, you are in the military. Plebes are at the beck and call of midshipmen first class, and there can be hazing and abuse. There are strict hair and uniform dress codes, and an endless round of assemblies, inspections, marching, and drilling. However, there are rewards. One of the greatest moments in any Kings Pointer's life is when he or she gets their Class Ring, representing three years of hard work. To celebrate, there is a formal dance and dinner. There's also a Christmas Ball, as well as other formal events throughout the year (although, with a 10:1 male/female ratio, it can be hard to get a date).

Sports are the main form of recreation; participation in intramural or varsity sports is required of all midshipmen. There are 17 intercollegiate sports for men and 10 for women. The Academy competes at the NCAA Division III level, and Kings Point teams and individuals have made it to the championships in a number of conferences. Not surprisingly, sailing is huge at Kings Point, as are crew and swimming. There are 45 different student organizations. The USMMA Regimental Band has participated in the Macy's Thanksgiving Day Parade, presidential inauguration parades, and the U.S. Tennis Open. Choral groups are enormously popular, as are instrumental music ensembles. Other popular organizations include student government, the student newspaper, religious organizations, debating, and professional groups. Noted alums include Mark Kelly, pilot of the space shuttle Endeavor; Graham Buschor, the air rescue helicopter pilot featured in The Perfect Storm; and Robert Kiyosaki, author of the bestseller, Rich Dad, Poor Dad.

Inst. Aid (est. 2003–04)

FT Undergrads Receiving Aid: 13%
Avg. Amount per Student: $1,381

Rec. Need-Based Scholarship or
Grant Aid: 14%
Average Award: $1,111

Rec. Need-Based Self-Help Aid:
69%
Average Award: $2,429

Upon Graduation, Avg. Loan Debt
per Student: $9,000

Financial Aid Deadline: 5/1

THE EXPERTS SAY...

" No one should attend USMMA solely for the tuition break. It's a tough go while you're in school, and that's before the service commitments following graduation. However, if you want the adventure, and you have the stamina and qualifications, you won't find a better education for the price. "

" USMMA is not strictly free—unlike the other academies, your life could be on the line in a military sealift as a student, so think carefully before you commit. "

Graduates

Going to Graduate School:
2% Within One Year

UNITED STATES MILITARY ACADEMY—WEST POINT

606 Thayer Road, West Point, NY 10996-1797
Admissions Phone: (845) 938-4041
Email: admissions@usma.edu Website: www.usma.edu

Note: Info. not verified by school

General Info

Type of School: public, coed

Setting: small town

Academic Calendar: semester

Student Body

Full-Time Undergrads: 4,088
 Men: 84%, Women: 16%

Total Undergrad Population:
 African American: 8%
 Asian American: 5%
 Latino: 6%
 Native American: 1%
 Caucasian: 77%
 International: 1%
 Out-of-State: 92%

Academics

Full-Time Faculty: 580
 With Ph.D.: 40%

Admissions

Regular Application Deadline: 3/21

Early Action Available

Total # of Students Applied: 10,890
 Admitted: 1,529

Test Scores (middle 50%):
 SAT Verbal: 570–670
 SAT Math: 570–680
 ACT Comp: 26–26

HS Rank of Entering Freshmen:
 Top 10%: 50%
 Top 25%: 81%
 Top 50%: 93%

Costs (2004–05)

Tuition, Room & Board paid by U.S.
 government
 One time deposit of $2,400 to
 help cover initial expenses

Graduates

Going to Graduate School:
 2% Within One Year

Accepting Job Offer:
 98% at time of graduation

Inside the Classroom

The "West Point Experience" lasts about ten years: one devoted to the application process, four in the academy, and five in military service. The top-notch education is free, but the military obligation (now including the very real possibility of active duty in war zones), the strict admissions standards, and the rigorous academic, physical, and mental requirements can all make you forget you're going for free in a hurry. Most cadets at West Point didn't go there for the free education. As one cadet said, "I'm at West Point because I always wanted to go to West Point." After 9/11, applications to the Point are up, but grads recommend you not apply unless you really—really—want to be in the Army.

Because USMA is devoted to training cadets to serve as officers, it is highly selective in its admissions standards. An applicant must be nominated by a member of Congress or by the Department of the Army; children of a parent who has received the Congressional Medal of Honor are also eligible. There are rigorous academic requirements—SAT/ACT scores are quite high—and extensive physical testing.

Life as a cadet involves studying, exercising, and plenty of drilling, with little time for anything else. The academic workload is strenuous, and consists of a core of 31 courses in the arts and sciences, with a required sequence of engineering classes. About 75 percent of cadets select one of 22 majors, and follow a structured series of "electives" in their discipline ("you pick the major, the military will pick your electives"). West Point's engineering programs are "the best in the U.S.," according to an Alabama guidance counselor, and programs in natural sciences, political science, history, and government are quite strong. Classes at West Point are small, usually less than 18. Cadets rave about the attentiveness of the faculty, which includes both senior commissioned officers with Ph.D.'s and civilian professors. Cadets receive a bachelor of science degree, and earn a commission as a second lieutenant upon completion. West Point ranks in the top four in both Rhodes and Hertz Scholarships.

Cadets learn basic military skills, including leadership, through a demanding military program which begins on their first day. Most military training takes place during the summer, with new cadets undergoing Cadet Basic Training (fondly nicknamed "Beast Barracks"), the same basic training that soldiers get in boot camp. The grueling basic is followed the next summer by field training. Cadets spend their third and fourth summers serving in active Army units around the world; attending advanced training courses such as airborne, air assault, or northern warfare; or training the first- and second-year cadets. Military training is combined with military science instruction and a thorough grounding in the West Point ethical code, stated in the Academy's motto, "Duty, Honor, Country."

Campus Environment

The Academy, a landmark for over 200 years, is located at West Point—about 50 miles north of New York City on the Hudson River. The beautiful campus is a history buff's dream, with monuments and a military museum. There is little to do in the nearby town of Highland Falls, but for plebes and yuks (freshmen and sophomores), who need special permission to leave the campus, it doesn't much matter.

Upperclassmen, especially those with cars, have more freedom, and take the occasional trip to New York City.

Although they are called barracks, the cadet dormitories are similar to those at a civilian college. There are generally two or three cadets to a room. Cadets live with other members of their class within their cadet company. Each cadet's desk is equipped with a private telephone line and Internet access. Unlike the more spartan olden days, plebes may now have televisions in their rooms. All of the cadets eat together. West Point rewards the hard physical labor with decent and plentiful food (every other Thursday is steak night).

Student Life

From the minute you arrive at the Academy, you're in the Army. A first-year cadet is given the rank of cadet fourth class, and to upperclassmen there is no lower creature on Earth. Cadets fourth class are at the beck and call of the cadets first class. This system is encouraged by the administration as a way of orienting new cadets to military life, and while there are occasional abuses, this system usually works. "You have to remember when you were a plebe (cadet fourth class), and it gives you a level of compassion," says a West Point upperclassman. "By the time you're a cadet first class you know and believe in the system, and you're less likely to abuse it."

THE EXPERTS SAY...

" West Point has been a legendary alma mater for leaders for over 200 years. One of the best engineering degrees in the nation—and it's free. "

" 'Beast Barracks,' hazing, and marching in circles in the rain— it's great to be a plebe! "

Much of a cadet's day is devoted to academic and military exercises, which does limit social opportunities. Sports are the primary form of extracurricular activity, largely because exercise is a required part of the program. Every cadet participates in an intercollegiate, club, or intramural level sport each semester, and cadets are regularly tested to ensure they remain in prime physical condition. Sports also reinforce the all-important concept of teamwork. About a third of the cadets participate in Army's 25 men's and women's varsity teams, and the annual Army-Navy ("Squid School") game is a traditional grudge match.

The Cadet Honor Code, which states "A cadet will not lie, cheat or steal, or tolerate those who do," is strictly observed. Pointers are largely sheltered from the college temptations of drinking, drugs, and sex, which allows them to devote what little leisure they have to 100 extracurricular activities like the campus radio station WKDT and Big Brother-Big Sister. Religious activities are also popular. West Pointers are receiving more support than ever for choosing a military life: as a recent *U.S. News & World Report* article states: "It's cool to be a soldier again." West Pointers seem to agree that the hard four years is worth the lifetime of pride of joining the Long Gray Line.

UNITED STATES NAVAL ACADEMY

117 Decatur Road, Annapolis, MD 21402-5017
Admissions Phone: (410) 293-4361 Fax: (410) 293-4348
Email: webmail@gwmail.usna.edu
Website: www.usna.edu

General Info

Type of School: public, coed
Setting: small town
Academic Calendar: semester

Student Body

Full-Time Undergrads: 4,335
 Men: 84%, Women: 16%

Total Undergrad Population:
 African American: 7%
 Asian American: 4%
 Latino: 8%
 Native American: 2%
 Caucasian: 78%
 International: 1%
 Out-of-State: 95%

Academics

Full-Time Faculty: 533
 With Ph.D.: 63%

Part-Time Faculty: 24
 With Ph.D.: 33%

Student/Faculty Ratio: 7:1

Most Popular Majors:
 political science (13%)
 economics (10%)
 systems engineering (10%)
 history (9%)
 mechanical engineering (7%)

Freshmen Retention Rate: 96%

Graduation Rates:
 86% within four years
 86% within six years

Computers: Computer Required;
 School provides individual com-
 puter/laptop

Admissions

Regular Application Deadline: 1/31

Early Action Available

Total # of Students Applied: 14,101
 Admitted: 1,479
 Enrolled: 1,228

Test Scores (middle 50%):
 SAT Verbal: 590–680
 SAT Math: 620–700

HS Rank of Entering Freshmen:
 Top 10%: 57%
 Top 25%: 84%
 Top 50%: 96%

Inside the Classroom

The United States Naval Academy is the undergraduate college that prepares young men and women to become professional officers in the U.S. Navy and Marine Corps. As with the other service academies, the competition for admissions is keen: Those selected to become midshipmen must have the drive and motivation to accept a four-year challenge that is both intellectual and physical. If you can make the grade, however, your tuition is free, and your employment in either the Navy or Marine Corps is not only guaranteed, it's mandatory.

The Academy offers a choice of 18 majors grouped into three academic divisions: humanities and social sciences, mathematics and science, and engineering and weapons. All graduates receive a B.S. degree, regardless of their major, due to the curriculum's technical nature. Minors programs are also available in French, German, Japanese, Russian, and Spanish. Core requirements for all majors include courses in engineering, natural sciences, social sciences, the humanities, professional military subjects, and physical education.

Basic eligibility requirements are that incoming "plebes" be U.S. citizens of good moral character, between 17 and 23 years of age, unmarried, not pregnant, and with no dependents. Each applicant's high school record is carefully scrutinized in an effort to select well-rounded students who excel in both academics and sports, and who display leadership in their extracurricular activities.

Each incoming class brigade starts the Naval Academy education with Plebe Summer, a seven-week experience designed to transform civilians into midshipmen with a minimum of gentleness. Perhaps the Academy's website describes this ordeal best: "You start your days at dawn with an hour of rigorous exercise and end them long after sunset, wondering how you will make it through the next day. Forget television, leisure time, or movies. You will have barely enough hours in the day to finish your assigned plebe tasks." In addition to the general military lessons of discipline, time management, and physical conditioning, the Academy also uses this time to instruct students on fundamental naval subjects like seamanship, navigation, boat handling, and the use of weapons.

Campus Environment

The Naval Academy's 338-acre campus, referred to as "The Yard," is located at the mouth of the Severn River in Annapolis, Maryland. Established in 1845, the campus is a beautiful landmark that was designated a National Historic Site in 1963, and it receives more than a million visitors each year. Pathways paved in brick and lined with trees connect the buildings, whose stately appearance reflects French Renaissance and contemporary architecture.

All midshipmen reside in Bancroft Hall, a huge dorm complex where they are assigned to a room with one or more midshipmen. Each class is divided into groups of 130 midshipmen of both sexes: Each group forms a company (according to the military definition), and each company has its "wardroom," or common area, for the purposes of meetings and recreation.

Campus facilities are top-of-the line, but be careful how you use them: In November 2002, the computers of 92 midshipmen were seized in a raid after they were caught downloading copyrighted movies, music, and computer games onto their computers using the school's T3 Internet connection. (The midshipmen involved were disciplined, but none were court-martialed or expelled since the matter was treated as a "conduct offense," which is less serious than an "honor offense" would be.)

Student Life

The Naval Academy is most different from other schools of higher education in the area of student life. The most important social unit is the company, whose members eat, study, drill, play, and compete as teams together. The midshipman's day is strictly regimented, and he is expected to be present for reveille, meals, classes, formations, sports, and training at precise times. Three-and-a-half hours are allotted every day for study, and plebes must be in bed an hour before everyone else. (And that's assuming you haven't gotten into any trouble: A midshipman "on restriction" is forbidden to leave campus for anything other than sports competitions and is required to report to superiors five times a day in an inspection-quality uniform.)

Time is allotted, however, for extracurricular activities. Midshipmen can join musical groups like the gospel choir of the Drum and Bugle Corps; recreational groups like the amateur radio and scuba clubs; academic organizations like the astronomy club and the forensic society; brigade support clubs like the cheerleaders and the silent drill team; and others. All midshipmen must participate in athletics, in the form of either the 21 varsity sports for men and 9 for women or at the club and intramural level. All sports teams have a fierce rivalry with the U.S. Military Academy at West Point, and the annual Army-Navy football game is televised nationally and scrutinized endlessly at The Yard.

The Brigade Activities Committee also sponsors social events on weekends, including the annual International Ball with young guests from foreign embassies in Washington. The highlight of each midshipman's social calendar is Commissioning Week in May, with its five days of dances, garden parties, parades, concerts, sailing, and a Blue Angels flight demonstration leading up to graduation and commissioning of the senior class.

A revered Naval Academy tradition is the Herndon Monument Climb, an occasion held at the end of each class's first year. At the sound of a cannon blast, 1,000 screaming plebes dash towards a 21-foot stone obelisk and attempt to climb to the top. Complicating their task is about 200 pounds of lard that is smeared on the monument by upperclassmen prior to the ceremony. The resulting mess is described in lurid detail on the Academy's website: "The smell of the melting lard permeates thousands of cheering spectators. Bodies turn red with beads of sweat dripping down the tower of people. Agony shows on the faces of those at the bottom of the pyramid as they support upon their shoulders three or four tiers of muscular bodies. As the crowd yells in anticipation, the class gets excited and 'They're gonna make it' is heard all around. Crash. The bodies collapse like dominoes."

Midshipmen on leave or liberty often take advantage of the city of Annapolis's recreational venues. In warm weather, the city dock is the scene of concerts, boat shows, and festivals that mix midshipmen and local citizens with thousands of tourists. Annapolis also boasts restaurants, boutiques, art galleries, museums, and a repertory theatre. Midshipmen can also make the 30-mile trip to Baltimore for some big-city R-and-R.

Costs (2004–5)

Fees: $2,500
Tuition, Room & Board paid by U.S. government

Graduates

Going to Graduate School:
7% Within One Year

Accepting Job Offer:
99% at time of graduation

THE EXPERTS SAY...

" The Naval Academy has the highest admissions yield rate of all the U.S. service academies: 83 percent of the applicants who've been accepted into the Naval Academy actually enroll. "

" At the Naval Academy, you'll get a taste of what it means to lead and to serve. (You might also get a taste of lard in your mouth when you're trying to climb that greased-up Herndon Monument...) "

UNIVERSITY OF ALABAMA

Box 870132, Tuscaloosa, AL 35487-0132
Admissions Phone: (205) 348-5666; (800) 933-BAMA Fax: (205) 348-9046
Email: admissions@ua.edu Website: www.ua.edu/
Application Website: www.ssc.ua.edu/application/

General Info

Type of School: public, coed
Setting: urban
Academic Calendar: semester

Student Body

Full-Time Undergrads: 14,145
  Men: 46%, Women: 54%

Part-Time Undergrads: 1,403
  Men: 49%, Women: 51%

Total Undergrad Population:
  African American: 14%
  Asian American: 1%
  Latino: 1%
  Native American: 1%
  Caucasian: 82%
  International: 1%
  Out-of-State: 20%
  Living Off-Campus: 76%
  In Fraternities: 7%
  In Sororities: 9%

Graduate and First-Professional
  Students: 4,402

Academics

Full-Time Faculty: 896
  With Ph.D.: 92%

Part-Time Faculty: 188
  With Ph.D.: 70%

Student/Faculty Ratio: 19:1

Most Popular Majors:
  nursing (4%)
  public relations (3%)
  advertising (2%)
  biology (2%)
  telecommunication & film (2%)

Completing 2 or More Majors: 5%

Freshmen Retention Rate: 84%

Graduation Rates:
  33% within four years
  62% within six years

Admissions

Regular Application Deadline: 8/1;
  3/1 (priority)

Total # of Students Applied: 8,298
  Admitted: 7,194
  Enrolled: 3,077

Test Scores (middle 50%):
  SAT Verbal: 490–610
  SAT Math: 500–610
  ACT Comp: 21–26

Inside the Classroom

The University of Alabama's undergraduate schools include the schools of Arts and Sciences, Commerce and Business Administration, Communication and Information Sciences, Education, Engineering, Human Environmental Science, Nursing, and Social Work. "The university offers a wide range of majors but most students concentrate in business, education, and the engineering schools," says a marketing major. Guidance counselors tell us that the business program is "one of the premier in the nation," and at least one raved about the "outstanding" medical, law, and engineering schools. A senior tells us that the "academic atmosphere varies from one section of campus to another. While the premedical students are quite competitive, the business students are generally much more laid-back."

UA has many unique academic programs, including several honors programs and the interdisciplinary New College, where students take small, independent seminars and can major in things such as Sound Recording Studies, Pharmaceutical Marketing, and Nanotechnology. The Rural Science Scholars Program encourages students "to return to rural areas as teachers, pharmacists, and technicians as well as health care providers," according to the university. The Blount Undergraduate Initiative (BUI) "offers highly motivated students the intensive learning experience of a small liberal arts college as well as the advantages of a major comprehensive university. BUI members reside, debate, and study together in academic houses and a living-learning center specifically created to enhance their development as a community of scholars."

One student tells us, "Most of the professors are accessible and enjoy talking with the students, though some of the older Ph.D. professors could care less." Another adds, "Professors are generally accessible, however, graduate students often teach in place of professors." The same student chose Bama "because of the location, a strong science and music program, a great scholarship, and the chance to study abroad."

Campus Environment

"Set in the deep South, Alabama is a very friendly campus. It is rather conservative as college campuses go," a biological sciences major explains. One student tells us that "safety is pretty tight on and off campus," while another says, "safety has been an issue. While serious crimes are rare, several cars have been broken into, and campus police are criticized for their apathy."

Freshmen live in a variety of on-campus housing. A young alum warns, "Comfort might be questionable depending on what a student is used to." The majority of the student body moves off-campus after their first year, "unless they live in a sorority or fraternity house later," a student explains. (Only upperclassmen are allowed to live in Greek houses.) We hear that "there are many neighborhoods [off-campus] that cater to the students" and "most apartment costs are moderate." A student sounds off on Tuscaloosa safety: "The only thing I have to worry about living off-campus is some loner stealing my lawnmower." A recent grad reports that Tuscaloosa residents are "very welcoming" and that "the city is pretty well built around the students and their interests." While the campus is walkable, a student explains, "Most students have cars. Even though the campus isn't overly spread out, there are many things you would want to do across Tuscaloosa that you couldn't walk or bike to."

Student Life

"The University of Alabama certainly has a party atmosphere," a student tells us. "There's always something interesting going on socially, never a dull moment, especially during football season." There's no denying that athletics (okay, football) are big at Bama. "Football is life," says one student. When asked about the academic environment, one devoted fan responds, "Academics really pick up in the spring semester. Football is priority in the fall semester." Students celebrate "Game Day," during which a Crimson Tide celebration is held on the quad before all home football games. The Tide has brought home 12 national championships, and been to more bowl games than any other team (though the school is quick to point out that their debate team has won more trophies). The flip-side to all this attention: The football program has been under the microscope lately, and in February 2002, it was slapped with some penalties from the NCAA; the latest disappointment occurred in May 2003, when the new coach was fired after barely four months on the job. But football is not the only standout sport at Bama: In 2002, the Alabama gymnastics team captured its fourth NCAA women's gymnastics championship; in 2003, they came in a respectable second, right behind UCLA's Olympian-filled team.

Greeks are the other major players on campus. "Greeks are very much in control over much of the social life," we hear (though, to be fair, less than a quarter of the student body pledges). According to one obviously biased student: "There are two types of students here, Greeks and whiners. Greeks party, have fun, and still make the grade. [Guys] wear khaki pants and collared shirts. Girls wear skirts and nice tops, never baggy. Whiners are the other 90 percent who constantly protest anything and everything the Greeks do." When they're not at frat parties, Bama students also frequent two sets of bars nearby. There's the infamous "Strip," plus numerous "downtown" bars, which we hear "play host to most of the local crowd and have more of a jazz atmosphere." And even here, Greeks are inescapable: "Many students resent the fraternities that sometimes 'take over' a bar," a student tells us.

Greek–Independent wars aside, most students we spoke to agreed their campus was "really friendly." "Though I cannot imagine any student not fitting in at all at a campus of 14,000 students, I would imagine that very liberal-dressing and acting students would probably have the hardest time," muses a senior. "Most students blend in, and even those with liberal views do not dye their hair strange colors or pierce themselves in strange places or try to express themselves that way… We try to not follow urban trends on purpose. We take pride in being Southern, polite, and classy."

As can be expected in a school of this size, there are plenty of organizations on campus for most any interest you could possibly think of. A student tells us, "Many Christian organizations are popular, such as Campus Crusade for Christ." An impressive selection of club and IM sports is available as well. Says a young alum, "Most students enjoy participating in sports somehow, whether it's actually playing or just being a devoted fan."

ACT English: 21–28
ACT Math: 19–26
HS Rank of Entering Freshmen:
Top 10%: 24%
Top 25%: 51%
Top 50%: 77%
Avg. HS GPA: 3.33

Costs (2003–04)

Tuition and Fees, In-State: $4,134

Tuition and Fees, Out-of-State: $11,294

Room & Board: $4,906

Payment Plan(s): installment plan, deferred payment plan, pre-payment plan

THE EXPERTS SAY...

" Alabama rewards those who take the initiative. Take advantage of one (or many) of the special study options, such as New College, the Blount Undergraduate Initiative, or the many honors programs and leadership development opportunities. "

" As a major Southern campus, it should come as no surprise that UA is steeped in Southern tradition: Football and the Greek system rule, dominating campus life. "

Inst. Aid (2002–03)

Institutional Aid, Need-Based: $297,928

Institutional Aid, Non-Need-Based: $5,806,315

FT Undergrads Receiving Aid: 39% Avg. Amount per Student: $7,549

FT Undergrads Receiving Non-Need-Based Scholarship or Grant Aid: 28% Avg. Amount per Student: $4,126

Of Those Receiving Any Aid:

Rec. Need-Based Scholarship or Grant Aid: 63% Average Award: $3,355

Rec. Need-Based Self-Help Aid: 83% Average Award: $4,262

Upon Graduation, Avg. Loan Debt per Student: $19,319

Financial Aid Deadline: rolling, 3/1 (priority)

Graduates

Going to Graduate School: 27% Within One Year

Alumni Giving: 32%

UNIVERSITY OF ARIZONA

P.O. Box 210040, Tucson, AZ 85721-0040
Admissions Phone: (520) 621-3237 Fax: (520) 621-9799
Email: appinfo@arizona.edu Website: www.arizona.edu
Application Website: admissions.arizona.edu

General Info

Type of School: public, coed
Setting: urban
Academic Calendar: semester

Student Body

Full-Time Undergrads: 24,105
 Men: 47%, Women: 53%

Part-Time Undergrads: 3,659
 Men: 47%, Women: 53%

Total Undergrad Population:
 African American: 3%
 Asian American: 6%
 Latino: 15%
 Native American: 2%
 Caucasian: 67%
 International: 3%
 Out-of-State: 28%
 Living Off-Campus: 82%
 In Fraternities: 7%
 In Sororities: 11%

Graduate and First-Professional
 Students: 8,601

Academics

Full-Time Faculty: 1,362
 With Ph.D.: 99%

Part-Time Faculty: 46
 With Ph.D.: 91%

Student/Faculty Ratio: 20:1

Most Popular Majors:
 psychology (6%)
 political science (4%)
 elementary education (2%)
 studio art (2%)
 communication (2%)

Freshmen Retention Rate: 77%

Graduation Rates:
 29% within four years
 55% within six years
 note: 5-yr. programs affect grad rates

Admissions

Regular Application Deadline: 4/1;
 10/1 (priority)

Fall Transfer Deadline: 6/1

Spring Transfer Deadline: 10/1

Total # of Students Applied: 21,224
 Admitted: 17,796
 Enrolled: 5,958

Inside the Classroom

The University of Arizona is huge, with more than 26,000 undergraduates, and several thousand more graduate students. U of A consists of 14 undergraduate colleges: agriculture and life sciences; architecture; business and public administration; correspondence; education; engineering and mines; fine arts; health professions; humanities; nursing; science; social and behavioral sciences; Arizona International College (which is closing); and the University College, as well as the graduate, law, medicine, and pharmacy schools.

The engineering, business, astronomy, cell biology, chemistry, nursing, and English programs are all well-regarded. A California guidance counselor tells us that the university also offers "good programs for students with learning disabilities."

The intensity varies according to department, but students say that in general, the academic atmosphere is "not very competitive or difficult, except in upper-level classes." A senior majoring in communications explains, "Most classes have a curve to help students, not hurt them." Not all students are particularly serious about their studies; says one grad student TA, "Partying is more important here than good grades, and good grades are more important than learning." On the other hand, he notes, "If you're motivated, you can get a top-notch education." Another student agrees, saying, "This is not the place for people who are not self-motivated."

An Arizona guidance counselor believes that "the faculty is available to students." But a humanities major tells us that while her professors were "very accessible," friends in other majors had less luck in reaching their professors when needed. Another student had very positive things to say about the U of A faculty: "I love my professors; they are understanding and open to suggestion and make a serious effort to help me in any way they can." And a recent grad who double-majored in German and women's studies declares, "The Women's Studies Department has fabulous, amazing, famous scholars and professors that should really be someplace like Stanford or Berkeley."

Campus Environment

Students say they like the look of the red-brick buildings that make up the campus, and that the grassy mall in the campus' center is a great place to catch some sun, people-watch, and just hang out. Students have good things to say about computing resources; a few mentioned the really high speed Internet connections. But U of A students have mixed things to say about the dorms. We heard some complaints about older, run-down dorms on campus. Yet one student told us that living in the dorms was "a blast and surprisingly comfortable." But on-campus housing is limited, and the majority of students live off campus. Says one recent grad, "Living on campus is pretty stupid, because you can live very close to the university and pay a whole lot less." For better or worse, campus dining seems to be more restaurant-like than cafeteria-like, which one student says makes it harder to eat healthy food for cheap. Not everyone minds this: Several students say they thought the variety of food was better than at most schools.

From what we hear, many students have a car after freshman year, although some rely on public transportation, and not all students agree that you need a car to get around. Parking on campus is severely limited; commenting on the parking situation, one student griped, "Don't get me started here." Biking around is popular, and pretty easy to do in flat Tucson.

Campus safety seems to be an issue: One woman complained that bike theft was common, and that the campus could be better lit; another said she felt safe in the daytime but preferred to walk with others at night. Still, the administration offers a "Safe Ride" service so students don't need to walk alone on campus at night. Also, says one student, "the U of A has something called a Cat Tran, which drives around campus to neighborhoods where students live."

The town of Tucson gets mixed reports. One student called it a "fantastic small town with lots of culture around the university." But most students aren't that positive. A recent grad groused that there was nothing much to do off campus: "Tucson is NOT what you'd call a 'happening' town." But students agree that if you're into hiking and exploring the natural world, you only need to travel 20 minutes to hit some amazing scenery. A big plus for most folks is the Tucson weather— nonstop sun most of the time, balmy winters, but blazing summer heat.

Student Life

Most students are from Arizona, though guidance counselors in California often recommend the U of A to their students, too. Some Arizona guidance counselors worry that the school's size may be too much for some students to handle: "Coming from a small town, it's a large campus and students go through cultural freak-outs," says one. Despite the size, quite a few students told us that Arizona is a very friendly school, with a great sense of community. "It is a very welcoming campus and one that I just love," says one enthusiastic student (though a senior warns that "very 'yuppie' kids won't fit in, because the school is laid back and casual"). And guidance counselors applaud the fact that the university actively recruits a multicultural population: The school's minority population hovers around 25 percent, more than half of which are Latino students.

The Greek system is popular at Arizona. One female student said that fraternities are especially popular because women can go to house parties without belonging to a sorority, but men cannot. But we hear that you can have a pretty active social life even if you're not involved in Greek life (and the majority of students are not). "It is a raging place to have some fun," raves one recent grad. In fact, we heard a few warnings from students that "you could party your life away here" if you were so inclined (and plenty of U of A students are, seemingly). However, lately the police have been "focusing on the bars, trying to prevent minors from being out," says one student.

Sports are huge at Arizona, particularly football and basketball; the school belongs to the PAC-10 conference. Notes one student, women's sports—especially basketball, softball, and volleyball—are "awesome." Intramural sports are popular, and one student says that "the relatively new student rec center is definitely a great facility, though sometimes overcrowded."

Test Scores (middle 50%):
SAT Verbal: 490–610
SAT Math: 500–630
ACT Comp: 21–26
ACT English: 20–26
ACT Math: 20–27

HS Rank of Entering Freshmen:
Top 10%: 34%
Top 25%: 62%
Top 50%: 89%

Avg. HS GPA: 3.4

THE EXPERTS SAY...

" There are 14 undergraduate schools to choose from; engineering, astronomy, English, and cell biology are strengths. Students with learning disabilities should check out U of A's programs. "

" Guidance counselors as far away as Ohio and Wisconsin say that the U of A is a trendy choice for their students. What, there are no parties in the Midwest? "

Costs (2004–5)

Tuition and Fees, In-State: $3,603

Tuition and Fees, Out-of-State: $12,373

Room & Board: $6,810

Inst. Aid (2002–03)

Institutional Aid, Need-Based: $5,495,205

Institutional Aid, Non-Need-Based: $4,681,100

FT Undergrads Receiving Aid: 46%
Avg. Amount per Student: $9,993

Upon Graduation, Avg. Loan Debt per Student: $16,881

Financial Aid Deadline: 3/1 (priority)

UNIVERSITY OF ARKANSAS

232 Silas Hunt Hall, Fayetteville, AR 72701
Admissions Phone: (479) 575-5346; (800) 377-8632 Fax: (479) 575-7515
Email: uofa@uark.edu Website: www.uark.edu
Application Website: www.uark.edu/application

General Info

Type of School: public, coed
Setting: small town
Academic Calendar: semester

Student Body

Full-Time Undergrads: 10,865
  Men: 51%, Women: 49%

Part-Time Undergrads: 1,855
  Men: 50%, Women: 50%

Total Undergrad Population:
  African American: 6%
  Asian American: 3%
  Latino: 2%
  Native American: 2%
  Caucasian: 83%
  International: 2%
  Out-of-State: 12%
  Living Off-Campus: 66%
  In Fraternities: 14%
  In Sororities: 19%

Graduate and First-Professional
  Students: 3,322

Academics

Full-Time Faculty: 792
  With Ph.D.: 92%

Part-Time Faculty: 47

Student/Faculty Ratio: 17:1

Most Popular Majors:
  marketing (5%)
  journalism (4%)
  psychology (4%)
  finance (4%)
  biology (3%)

Completing 2 or More Majors: 6%

Freshmen Retention Rate: 48%

Graduation Rates:
  23% within four years
  48% within six years

Admissions

Regular Application Deadline: 8/15;
  11/15 (priority)

Early Action Deadline: 11/15

Fall Transfer Deadline: 8/15, 3/15
  (priority)

Spring Transfer Deadline: 1/1,
  11/15 (priority)

Total # of Students Applied: 5,491
  Admitted: 4,661
  Enrolled: 2,357

Inside the Classroom

The University of Arkansas is best known as a research university, and offers numerous research opportunities for undergraduates. A student majoring in chemical engineering defends her school: "It is not just a school for people who can't get in anywhere else—that is what I used to think." An Arkansas high school guidance counselor agrees, praising the "state-of-the-art business and technology" programs and facilities.

The University of Arkansas consists of eight schools: The Dale Bumpers College of Agricultural, Food, and Life Sciences; the School of Architecture; the J. William Fulbright College of Arts and Sciences; the Sam. M. Walton College of Business; the College of Education and Health Professions; the College of Engineering; the School of Law; and the Graduate School. With over five thousand students, the Fulbright College is the largest, and has a well-regarded honors program that enrolls about 450 students at a time. UA's premed program is particularly strong. Students give high marks to engineering, architecture, biochemistry, nursing, education, and agricultural sciences programs. In addition, the popular College of Engineering offers co-op partnerships for students.

As with all undergrads in the state, University of Arkansas students are required to take a wide range of courses spread among six academic areas, including English, math, and the sciences. Not surprisingly, intro classes can be huge, with more than a hundred students, but class size diminishes as you move up in your major; over 70 percent of classes have fewer than 29 students. The faculty-student ratio is a manageable 16:1. "Most of the teachers are extremely helpful and accessible," says a junior.

The university has a number of programs geared toward freshmen. The New Friends Program matches all new UA students with a faculty or staff member who serves as a friend/mentor. There are also several programs available minority engineering students to help boost skills and present career opportunities. Students also have good things to say about tutoring programs that are available, some conveniently located within the dorms.

Nearly every student we heard from mentioned money as a deciding factor in attending the University of Arkansas. Tuition is low: In-state students pay annual tuition of less than $4,000, while out-of-staters pay less than $11,000 per year. And incoming students from the neighboring states of Texas, Mississippi, Missouri, Oklahoma, Louisiana, and Kansas who meet certain GPA and ACT score requirements can enroll at in-state costs. Scholarships abound; in an effort to attract high-achieving students, the university offers incredible aid packages, including stipends for books and living, to incoming students with top high school records. Says one student, "I got a first-rate education at the U of A, and it didn't cost me or my family a truckload of money."

Campus Environment

The campus is spread out over 345 acres, and a few students describe the campus as "beautiful." UA has 11 residence halls. All freshmen are required to live in a dorm, fraternity, or sorority, or at home with parents. Dorms get fairly high marks, and are described as "enjoyable, comfortable, and convenient." Still, more than half of the student population (undergraduate and graduate) lives off campus.

Students can have cars on campus, and some we talked to insisted that cars really are necessary for getting around about town (although campus parking is a problem). The university operates Razorback Transit, a public mass transit system, which students rely on to get around campus as well as to parts of the city of Fayetteville. By all accounts, Fayetteville is a particularly livable city. "It's small enough to have that small town atmosphere, but large enough to still find plenty to do," says one graduate. Town-gown relations are good, too: "Most of the businesses offer discounts to college students," a junior reveals.

Student Life

Although the UA is a large school, students describe it as "extremely friendly." Says one junior, "I can never walk to class without seeing at least three people that I know." Still, students say that "it's easy to get lost" in the crowd, and recommend joining any organization that interests you in order to get rooted. Greek life is popular—about 20 percent of students join fraternities or sororities—but "not overwhelming," says one student.

While the large majority of students are from Arkansas, the population is fairly diverse. "I don't think there is a 'typical student' because there are so many majors, clubs, and activities to chose from that it is impossible to find two people involved in the exact same things," comments a junior. Sports, particularly football and basketball, are huge; UA students love their "Hogs." As you might expect at a large university, there is a wide variety of extracurricular activities available. A student insists, "There are so many things to get involved in that there is somewhere for everyone to fit in." One student reports that religious organizations of all kinds are popular on campus, as are intramural sports.

Students spend most weeknights doing homework or relaxing with friends in front of the TV. "Hardly anyone does homework on Friday or Saturday, and mostly we try to see the friends we didn't get to see all week and forget about school," a student informs us. "Sunday is reserved for church and homework."

Test Scores (middle 50%):
SAT Verbal: 530–650
SAT Math: 520–650
ACT Comp: 22–28
ACT English: 22–30
ACT Math: 20–27
HS Rank of Entering Freshmen:
Top 10%: 36%
Top 25%: 63%
Top 50%: 91%
Avg. HS GPA: 3.6

THE EXPERTS SAY...

" Low expenses, excellent financial aid, and regional tuition make UA a real educational bargain. Premeds should investigate the honors program for its high med school acceptance rates. "

" UA isn't just a safety school anymore. Get hooked up by participating in extracurriculars to avoid getting lost in the crowd. Go Hogs! "

Costs (2003–04)

Tuition and Fees, In-State: $4,768

Tuition and Fees, Out-of-State: $11,518

Regional or 'good neighbor' tuition available.

Room & Board: $5,087

Payment Plan(s): installment plan, deferred payment plan

Inst. Aid (2002–03)

FT Undergrads Receiving Aid: 43%
Avg. Amount per Student: $8,052

FT Undergrads Receiving Non-Need-Based Scholarship or Grant Aid: 20%
Avg. Amount per Student: $5,179

Of Those Receiving Any Aid:

Rec. Need-Based Scholarship or Grant Aid: 68%
Average Award: $3,562

Rec. Need-Based Self-Help Aid: 69%
Average Award: $4,359

Upon Graduation, Avg. Loan Debt per Student: $14,029

Financial Aid Deadline: 3/15 (priority)

Graduates

Going to Graduate School: 25% Within One Year

Companies Recruiting On Campus: 200

Alumni Giving: 20%

UNIVERSITY OF CALIFORNIA— BERKELEY

110 Sproul Hall #5800, Berkeley, CA 94720-5800 Admissions Phone: (510) 642-6000
Email: ouars@uclink.berkeley.edu Website: www.berkeley.edu
Application Website: www.universityofcalifornia/admissions

General Info

Type of School: public, coed

Setting: urban

Academic Calendar: semester

Student Body

Full-Time Undergrads: 21,941
 Men: 46%, Women: 54%

Part-Time Undergrads: 1,264
 Men: 49%, Women: 51%

Total Undergrad Population:
 African American: 4%
 Asian American: 41%
 Latino: 11%
 Native American: 1%
 Caucasian: 30%
 International: 3%
 Out-of-State: 11%
 Living Off-Campus: 65%
 In Fraternities: 11%
 In Sororities: 10%

Graduate and First-Professional
 Students: 9,870

Academics

Full-Time Faculty: 1,462
 With Ph.D.: 98%

Part-Time Faculty: 420
 With Ph.D.: 98%

Student/Faculty Ratio: 16:1

Most Popular Majors:
 electrical engineering and computer science (4%)
 political science (3%)
 English (3%)
 architecture (3%)
 business admin (2%)

Completing 2 or More Majors: 8%

Freshmen Retention Rate: 97%

Graduation Rates:
 52% within four years
 85% within six years

Admissions

Regular Application Deadline: 11/30

Fall Transfer Deadline: 11/30

Total # of Students Applied: 36,976
 Admitted: 8,832
 Enrolled: 3,653

Test Scores (middle 50%):
 SAT Verbal: 570–700
 SAT Math: 620–740

Inside the Classroom

One of the most prestigious public schools in the country and the oldest university in California, Berkeley combines superb faculty with a unique student environment. "The atmosphere is vibrant," raves a history major. "The workload is intense, but the material is interesting and the professors are amazing." Virtually all departments are superb, but the sciences, English, and history have particularly strong reputations. "It is a first-tier academic institution and boasts more top ten programs than any other school in the nation," brags a junior.

Berkeley is the most selective of all the UC schools. It also has the largest percentage of out-of-state students, making acceptance even tougher for the many California residents who want to attend. And it doesn't get any easier once you're accepted: Students report that competition is brutal. As one biology student explains, "There exists a 'survival of the fittest' atmosphere here... The school is known to be a GPA killer. But that's okay, because many graduate admissions officers take into account that the school is hard, and so give us an extra 10 percent on our GPA when comparing us to students from other universities."

Unfortunately, Berkeley's "large size and impersonal feeling" can be offputting, says a guidance counselor. Undergrads must grapple with huge classes and red tape, and "the administration is a maze," gripes a student. Says a young alum, "The intro classes are always packed and usually can be described as 'weeder' classes. They are excessively competitive and there is nearly no professor contact unless one makes the effort personally." Another student observes, "The professors are great researchers, but that doesn't necessarily translate into good teaching ability." Faculty and graduate research tend to be the top priority in many departments. A senior explains, "Berkeley is a place where you have to fight for your classes and your rights, but it teaches you many things about life."

Campus Environment

"Everything can be found in and around Berkeley: rowdiness on Telegraph Avenue, politics on campus, serenity in Oakland Hills, shopping and excitement in San Francisco; the Bay is just around the corner, and skiing is just a couple hours drive away," raves one student. Students say that safety is a concern, and the streets surrounding the school can be rather dirty. There's never a dull moment: "The local street performers duke it out every lunch hour in Sproul Plaza, surrounded by students of all persuasions." Telegraph Avenue is known for its vendors of jewelry, hemp, and pot ("Berkeley is well known for the availability of good pot," a senior tells us.) Many aging hippies still live here, and according to one student, "You haven't seen weird until you reach Berkeley."

Buildings on the beautiful Berkeley campus range from ivy-covered stone buildings to ultra-contemporary structures. Approximately 70 percent of freshmen live on campus in the seven dorms (many of which we're told are seriously overcrowded). Theme housing includes a student cooperative that runs entirely on "green" electricity (generated solely from renewable resources). Off campus housing is "expensive and hard to find."

Student Life

A North Carolina guidance counselor says Berkeley is hot because "students are aware of it from the 60s." "Students feel this is an 'action' school," adds a Texas guidance counselor. A California guidance counselor cites Berkeley's "openness to new ideas, thoughts, and opinions" as a big draw. The home of the free speech movement and political activism in the Vietnam era, Berkeley continues to be more progressive than the rest of society, though not nearly as radical as it was in the past. But one student insists, "There is no typical Berkeley student. There are just as many Bible-believing conservative students as there are communists, hippies, radicals, etc." Another student's opinion: "Many protests are staged here because Berkeley is supposed to be political, and not for actual passion." In 2002, Berkeley "made the news because our student government didn't want to distribute red, white and blue ribbons on [the anniversary of] September 11th," says a student. (University officials also made the news recently when they "edited" a fund-raising appeal for the Emma Goldman Papers Project, housed at Berkeley for 23 years. In one of the stricken quotations, the socialist called on people "not yet overcome by war madness to raise their voice of protest." Berkeley officials said the quotations could be construed as a political statement by the university in opposition to United States policy toward Iraq.)

While students at Berkeley are serious about their studies, they do like to relax on weekends. "Lots of studying," says a junior. "But there are tons of concerts, sporting events, cultural and artistic shindigs in Berkeley and the Bay Area." Berkeley students are very passionate, so lots of time is spent volunteering and "making a difference," though huge crowds do turn out for football and basketball games. "We won the Big Game against Stanford," exults a junior. "That was the biggest."

The Greeks host large parties every weekend, but they don't dominate the social scene. "Those who drink heavily and do drugs often have problems keeping up with Berkeley's intense academics," a history major comments. "But there are tons of great bars and pubs." Although guidance counselors call Berkeley an "Animal House" school, a student demurs. "Berkeley is not known as a tremendous party school, but you can find pretty much whatever you are looking for."

Diversity of all kinds is evident in the Berkeley student population, which ranges from artsy bohemians to serious preprofessionals; this creates a "pretty electric" atmosphere. "Living at Berkeley is a cultural lesson every day," says a student. Berkeley is also one of the few top schools in which Caucasians constitute a minority; the largest percentage of undergraduate students are Asian Americans. A biochemistry major muses, "All students are united by their intensity, though students focus on very different areas or interests... Some are intensely academic, some are intensely involved in extracurricular activities, and some are intense partiers... Most are a combination of all three." A recent graduate adds, "This is a place for someone open and willing to explore, discover facts of life, and find a niche all his or her own."

HS Rank of Entering Freshmen:
Top 10%: 98%
Top 25%: 100%
Avg. HS GPA: 3.94

Costs (2003–04)

Tuition and Fees, In-State: $5,858

Tuition and Fees, Out-of-State: $20,068

Room & Board: $11,212

Payment Plan(s): deferred payment plan

THE EXPERTS SAY...

" Current faculty at Berkeley include eight Nobel laureates, 19 MacArthur Fellows, 87 Fulbright Scholars, three Pulitzer Prize winners, and 138 Guggenheim Fellows. "

" Located in a canyon with a gorgeous view of San Francisco Bay, there is no more idyllic setting for a big university. One surprise is that today's students are often far more conservative than their radical forbearers from the 1960s. "

Inst. Aid (2002–03)

Institutional Aid, Need-Based: $33,255,720

Institutional Aid, Non-Need-Based: $1,940,745

FT Undergrads Receiving Aid: 45%
Avg. Amount per Student: $11,952

FT Undergrads Receiving Non-Need-Based Scholarship or Grant Aid: 12%
Avg. Amount per Student: $2,355

Of Those Receiving Any Aid:

Rec. Need-Based Scholarship or Grant Aid: 94%
Average Award: $8,283

Rec. Need-Based Self-Help Aid: 77%
Average Award: $5,346

Upon Graduation, Avg. Loan Debt per Student: $14,990

Financial Aid Deadline: 3/2 (priority)

Graduates

Going to Graduate School:
20% Within One Year

Accepting Job Offer:
40% at time of graduation

Companies Recruiting On Campus: 275

UNIVERSITY OF CALIFORNIA—DAVIS

175 Mrak Hall, 1 Shields Avenue, Davis, CA 95616
Admissions Phone: (530) 752-2971; (530) 752-1011 Fax: (530) 752-1280
Email: freshmanadmissions@ucdavis.edu Website: www.ucdavis.edu
Application Website: www.ucop.edu/pathways

General Info
Type of School: public, coed
Setting: small town
Academic Calendar: quarter

Student Body
Full-Time Undergrads: 20,962
    Men: 44%, Women: 56%
Part-Time Undergrads: 2,510
    Men: 44%, Women: 56%
Total Undergrad Population:
    African American: 2%
    Asian American: 37%
    Latino: 10%
    Native American: 1%
    Caucasian: 41%
    International: 2%
    Out-of-State: 3%
Graduate and First-Professional
    Students: 6,757

Academics
Full-Time Faculty: 2,194
Part-Time Faculty: 278
Student/Faculty Ratio: 20:1
Freshmen Retention Rate: 93%
Graduation Rates:
    32% within four years
    78% within six years
Computers: School provides
    individual computer/laptop

Admissions
Regular Application Deadline: 11/30
Fall Transfer Deadline: 11/30
Spring Transfer Deadline: 10/31
Total # of Students Applied: 32,506
    Admitted: 19,367
    Enrolled: 4,786
Test Scores (middle 50%):
    SAT Verbal: 510–630
    SAT Math: 570–670
    ACT Comp: 21–27
HS Rank of Entering Freshmen:
    Top 10%: 96%
    Top 25%: 100%
    Top 50%: 100%
Avg. HS GPA: 3.72

Inside the Classroom

Founded as the "University Farm School" in California's Central Valley, UC Davis is now considered a top research institution. Funding for research is currently in excess of $356 million. The school boasts one of the largest academic internship programs in the country, and 50 percent of students work on a research project in the course of their undergraduate education. "There's a lot of learning outside the classroom as well as in the classroom," asserts one student.

Davis offers more than 100 undergraduate majors in the colleges of Agricultural and Environmental Sciences, Engineering, and Letters and Science. One guidance counselor recommends Davis for its "many strong majors, though high school students tend to think it has only farming and vet." The agriculture and engineering programs are particularly strong, as is the division of biological sciences. There's even a major in viticulture and enology, the sciences of grape-growing and winemaking (thanks to a recent grant from the Robert Mondavi family, Davis is establishing a state-of-art institute for wine and food sciences). One guidance counselor tells us that the outstanding premed and science programs make the school highly attractive (though he did add that the rural area might scare kids away). Another approves of Davis's "good curriculum."

Davis uses a quarter system, which means lots of exams and due dates. "It's intense," a student says. "The first midterm is often only a few weeks after classes start." One student we spoke to commented on the "flexibility" of the general ed requirements. Although the workload can be heavy, one student assures us, "If you're used to AP courses in high school, you should do fine here. I have more time now than I ever did in high school, even with a full load of courses." But a recent grad counters, "The workload was very demanding. For every hour you spent in class listening to the professor, you would have to do two or more hours of studying/homework."

Campus Environment

With 5,300 acres, Davis has the largest campus in the UC system, and while it's not necessarily beautiful, one student insists that it's "better than it looks when you drive by." Most students do this by bicycle, in part out of concern for the environment, but mostly because it's the easiest way to get around. As many as 16,000 bicyclists travel along the bike paths each day. Buses (including some red double-deckers from London) are free for undergrads. Sacramento is just 15 miles away.

Campus highlights include an arboretum with thousands of trees and plants, and a brand-new, state-of-the-art performing arts center. To combat recent problems with overcrowding, the school has begun construction on a 400-bed residence hall as well a new dining commons. Freshmen are guaranteed on-campus housing, and students give the dorms average marks. There are residence halls with different themes, "such as an international house, a Latino house, a sports house, an outdoors adventure house, and so on," a student offers. Off-campus housing is very popular, if only because apartments tend to be cheaper than dorms (assuming you have roommates). A recent grad warns, "The best places to live are taken up very fast. Students even camp outside the night before because they want to make sure they get a good place to live."

Davis, a quiet town with its share of student hangouts ("There's not much to do since it's located in farming area," says a senior), is a progressive community noted for its small-town style, energy conservation, environmental programs, and preservation of trees. A student describes the town as "very safe and outgoing," with "a lot of people out on the streets at all hours of the night either hanging out, walking, running, or riding bikes." The surrounding area has some of the most productive agriculture land in California. But be forewarned: Some find the smell of cows to be fairly strong!

Student Life

In 2002, UC Davis found itself in the blazing MTV spotlight, as one of its Jewish-interest sororities, Sigma Alpha Epsilon Pi, was featured on the channel's Sorority Life reality series. Though some Sigma sorority sisters have protested that the show misrepresented them, there's no denying that the MTV exposure gave Davis "a lot of popularity all around the world," according to a student. One student we spoke to last year told us that there wasn't "an extremely strong Greek system," and that there was little pressure to pledge. But now, a student says, "Because of the MTV coverage, many students are more interested in sororities and fraternities because they think it's the cool thing to do or the popular thing to do."

Students may also choose from more than 300 clubs of all types. Sports are always popular; Davis has one of the largest intramural programs in the country. And the school recently made the move to Division I varsity competition, a decision students largely support. Davis boasts the only outdoor roller hockey rink on a U.S. campus to meet official NHL specifications.

As for drinking, it's "not much of a problem," a student says. "We even have a poll that was taken and most students have 0–3 drinks during the week." One guidance counselor recommends the school as "the most wholesome, down-to-earth of the UC campuses, though some might find it too unsophisticated." The students, overall, are relaxed and laid-back. As a student explains, "Politics do play a role, but we definitely do not have the political movements of UC Berkeley."

"Everyone is very friendly, and always willing to lend a helping hand," one young alum says, though she nonetheless takes issue with the cliques on campus. "Racial groups tended to stick with one another in big groups," she says. There does seem to be a lot of concern over diversity issues here, which is not surprising given the large numbers of Asian American and Latino students. "We have a very diverse student body, which makes everybody fit into the crowd," a student says. The school hosts a number of cultural celebrations, including Native American Culture Days, Asian Pacific Culture Week, and Black Family Week. And UC Davis also celebrates itself during "Picnic Day"—an open house of sorts, said to be the largest student-run event in the country, featuring a parade, a Battle of the Bands, and a wide variety of academic exhibits, from a chemistry magic show to robot races.

Other schools to check out: UC Irvine, UC San Diego, UC Santa Barbara, UC Santa Cruz, California Polytechnic State University.

Costs (2003–04)

Tuition and Fees, In-State: $6,438

Tuition and Fees, Out-of-State: $20,648

Room & Board: $9,410

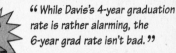

THE EXPERTS SAY...

" While Davis's 4-year graduation rate is rather alarming, the 6-year grad rate isn't bad. "

" Don't go to UC Davis expecting to become MTV's next reality TV star: The disgruntled sisters of Sigma Alpha Epsilon Pi aren't likely to invite camera crews back to campus anytime soon. "

Inst. Aid (est. 2003–04)

Financial Aid Deadline: 3/1 (priority)

UNIVERSITY OF CALIFORNIA— IRVINE

204 Administration Building, Irvine, CA 92697-1075
Admissions Phone: (949) 824-6703 Fax: (949) 824-2711 Email: admissions@uci.edu
Website: www.uci.edu Application Website: www.ucop.edu/pathways/

General Info

Type of School: public, coed

Setting: suburban

Academic Calendar: quarter

Student Body

Full-Time Undergrads: 19,201
Men: 49%, Women: 51%

Part-Time Undergrads: 766
Men: 56%, Women: 44%

Total Undergrad Population:
African American: 2%
Asian American: 50%
Latino: 11%
Native American: <1%
Caucasian: 24%
International: 3%
Out-of-State: 2%
In Fraternities: 8%
In Sororities: 8%

Graduate and First-Professional
Students: 4,907

Academics

Full-Time Faculty: 966
With Ph.D.: 98%

Part-Time Faculty: 304
With Ph.D.: 98%

Student/Faculty ratio: 18:01

Most Popular Majors:
biological sciences (16%)
information and computer sciences (11%)
economics (7%)
psychology and social behavior (5%)
computer engineering (5%)

Completing 2 or More Majors: 5%

Freshmen Retention Rate: 92%

Graduation Rates:
39% within four years
79% within six years

Admissions

Regular Application Deadline: 11/30

Fall Transfer Deadline: 11/30
(priority)

Spring Transfer Deadline: 10/31
(priority)

Total # of Students Applied: 34,417
Admitted: 18,517
Enrolled: 4,043

Inside the Classroom

A large research institution, UCI is well-known for its School of Biological Sciences; the School of Engineering, with prominence in biomedical engineering; and the School of Management, top for its focus on information technology. (Though one word of caution: There's no undergraduate major in business, so if you're interested in that area of study, your only option is to minor in management.) The biology programs are outstanding, and many students go on to medical school. Most students are professionally oriented, and you'll be hard pressed to find many "undecided majors" or free spirits.

With around 20,000 undergrads, many classes are large, and for these, there's little professor contact. "Professors are readily available to answer questions, but it is up to the students to take advantage of their professors. They aren't going to plead with you to come to their office hours," warns a young alumna. Large classes also mean lots of multiple-choice tests for easy grading, which can be good news or bad, depending on your perspective. Most students say the workload is average, though if you're in the sciences, it can be grueling. As one student explains, "This is a research school: The classes require that the reading or work must be done. There is no easy 'A.'" General ed requirements can be taken in any academic year (with the exception of the lower-division writing course): writing, natural sciences, social and behavioral sciences, humanistic inquiry, math, foreign language, and multicultural studies/global issues.

Though in many ways a traditional research institution, Irvine has pioneered some unique and progressive programs: First, after hundreds of students protested in the early 1990s, it created an Asian American Studies department (more than half the students here are of Asian descent). Second, students are allowed to vote for one subject in which the school will bring in a lecturer (recently, that was a Filipino studies course). And third, UCI created the ArtsBridge program, now adopted by many other universities, which grants college students scholarships to teach art in K–12 classrooms.

Campus Environment

With a 21-acre park in the middle, the campus is laid out in concentric circles—a ring, so to speak—with the undergraduate buildings on the inner circle and the graduate facilities radiating outward ("an awesome, centralized campus with groovy architecture" says one California-sounding student). The property is home to 11,000 trees (including 33 species of eucalyptus), not to mention 75 "test tube" redwood trees, and a freshwater marsh reserve.

About 75 percent of freshmen live in on-campus housing: "As far as dorms go, they're as comfortable as you get," we're told. Off-campus housing is popular after the first year—even in the face of spiraling costs. Four or five people often share a two-bedroom apartment. As if that's bad enough, the student population is expected to explode over the next 10 years. Some new residences are being built, though many are concerned it's not enough to meet demand.

Although the city of Irvine is hardly oozing with charm, it's considered one of the safer cities in America. As a "planned community," with every store and structure regulated, there are few student hangouts. Almost everyone we heard from complained about how boring Irvine was, calling it "stuffy" and "sterile," though most everyone says it offers at least some level of entertainment. One student from Canada tells us, "While it's not comparable to what's offered in Los Angeles, I think it's for the better. It helps keep my mind on studying and away from play!"

Student Life

Thrill-seeking high schoolers looking for a wild social life need not apply to UCI: This is not a rowdy school. "We have a Pub on campus, but they are very strict about the legal drinking age. Drinks can only be consumed in the Pub," explains a recent grad. We've heard that school spirit is virtually nonexistent. The atmosphere can be better described as relaxed and laid-back, with a lot of self-focus. One student explains, "The atmosphere on campus is very soothing."

UCI also has a large commuter population, which adds to the "no social life" equation: In addition to those who live at home, many others live on campus but go home on weekends. Those who do stick around usually head to the nearby malls, the famed beaches of Newport and Laguna (a 10-minute bike ride), or the mountains two hours away.

Nearly all undergrads here are Southern California residents; there are very few out-of-state or foreign students. Asian Americans make up 50 percent of the population, with Caucasians a fairly distant second. "The typical student is an Asian female with a wealthy family," one senior tells us. "Bookish" and "electronically adept" are used to describe the students here. As the chancellor for student affairs explains, "Many of UCI's Asian students come from immigrant families who live locally and don't tend to venture far from home." The administration has recently made real efforts to diversify: In 2001, UCI had the largest percentage increase in African American applicants of the UC schools, as well as an influx of transfer students from community colleges. The numbers of Latino and Chicano students is also increasing, to about 11 percent of the population.

Some of the more popular clubs are the Filipino-American Club, with its award-winning hip-hop dance group, Kaba Modern; intramural martial arts; and the Flying Sams, student volunteers who assist in a medical clinic in Mexico. The annual campus highlight is the Wayzgoose Medieval Faire, where members of the Society for Creative Anachronism dress up as knights, damsels, and dragons. Greek and Asian-Greek fraternities and sororities are popular, though with no frat row, they're not a huge presence. And though UCI is a Division I school, we're told that varsity games are poorly attended, with the exception of the ever-popular basketball (perhaps because there's no football team). After a 10-year absence, the baseball program was resurrected in 2000: Today, the school is rated the eighth-best recruiting class in the country by *Baseball America* magazine.

Test Scores (middle 50%):
SAT Verbal: 519–620
SAT Math: 567–675
HS Rank of Entering Freshmen:
Top 10%: 96%
Avg. HS GPA: 3.61

THE EXPERTS SAY...

" UC Irvine offers excellent preprofessional programs to an unusually diverse student body. "

" Intense academics and tons of commuters make for a pretty sad social scene. Premed students wanting a cozy campus atmosphere should check out UC Santa Cruz instead. "

Costs (2004–5)

Tuition and Fees, In-State: $6,165

Tuition and Fees, Out-of-State: $16,104

Room & Board: $7,520

Payment Plan(s): installment plan

Inst. Aid (2002–03)

Institutional Aid, Need-Based: $16,450,476

Institutional Aid, Non-Need-Based: $2,435,389

FT Undergrads Receiving Aid: 47%
Avg. Amount per Student: $10,021

FT Undergrads Receiving Non-Need-Based Scholarship or Grant Aid: 7%
Avg. Amount per Student: $3,535

Of Those Receiving Any Aid:

Rec. Need-Based Scholarship or Grant Aid: 87%
Average Award: $7,128

Rec. Need-Based Self-Help Aid: 81%
Average Award: $4,680

Financial Aid Deadline: 5/1, 3/2 (priority)

Graduates

Going to Graduate School:
34% Within One Year

Accepting Job Offer:
33% at time of graduation

Companies Recruiting On Campus:
100

Alumni Giving: 16%

UNIVERSITY OF CALIFORNIA— LOS ANGELES

405 Hilgard Avenue, Los Angeles, CA 90095 Admissions Phone: (310) 825-3101
Fax: (310) 206-1206 Email: ugadm@saonet.ucla.edu Website: www.ucla.edu
Application Website: www.saonet.ucla.edu/uars/infoprospective.htm

General Info

Type of School: public, coed
Setting: urban
Academic Calendar: quarter

Student Body

Full-Time Undergrads: 24,598
  Men: 43%, Women: 57%

Part-Time Undergrads: 1,117
  Men: 48%, Women: 52%

Total Undergrad Population:
  African American: 3%
  Asian American: 38%
  Latino: 15%
  Native American: <1%
  Caucasian: 33%
  International: 3%
  Out-of-State: 7%
  Living Off-Campus: 70%
  In Fraternities: 12%
  In Sororities: 9%

Graduate and First-Professional
  Students: 12,883

Academics

Full-Time Faculty: 1,871
  With Ph.D.: 98%

Part-Time Faculty: 591
  With Ph.D.: 98%

Student/Faculty Ratio: 18:1

Most Popular Majors:
  psychology (18%)
  political science (16%)
  economics/business (13%)
  biology (12%)
  English (11%)

Freshmen Retention Rate: 96%

Graduation Rates:
  53% within four years
  87% within six years

Admissions

Regular Application Deadline: 11/30

Fall Transfer Deadline: 11/30

Total # of Students Applied: 44,994
  Admitted: 10,581
  Enrolled: 4,268

Test Scores (middle 50%):
  SAT Verbal: 560–690
  SAT Math: 600–720
  ACT Comp: 23–29

Inside the Classroom

Always a popular choice for undergraduate applicants, UCLA is "the premier university in the nation, with something for everyone," says a guidance counselor. "For students who like 'big and busy,' it's ideal."

The College of Letters and Science houses most of the undergraduate programs at UCLA (social sciences, life sciences, humanities, and physical sciences). Undergraduate degrees are also offered in engineering, and the visual and performing arts and culture. A university official informs us, "Many of UCLA's most popular departments for undergraduates are ranked in the top 10 in their fields, and virtually all of the most popular majors are ranked in the top 20; more than 90 percent of UCLA undergraduates receive a degree from a department ranked among the best. Among these majors are psychology, English, sociology, history, chemistry, philosophy, geography, biology, physics, political science, economics, mathematics, astronomy, engineering, anthropology, classics, linguistics, computer sciences, film, geosciences, music, and Spanish." Several of UCLA's graduate professional schools offer popular courses or academic minors for undergraduates, including the schools of management, education, and public policy.

The academic year is divided into quarters, which creates a lot of stress for students as exams and papers roll around more frequently than with the semester calendar. UCLA recently revamped its general education requirements by reducing the number of required courses to focus on writing, discussion, and broad theory in three "foundation" themes: arts and humanities, society and culture, and scientific inquiry. Freshmen now have the option of starting their UCLA experience with a First-Year Cluster: a year-long course on a single broad theme, team-taught by the university's senior faculty from several fields.

UCLA attracts some of the most distinguished professors in the world, including Nobel Prize winners and Guggenheim Fellows, some of whom teach undergrads in small honors seminars. Professors are available and eager to help during office hours (though one junior complains that some professors' office hours may be "filled with students and just turn into another lecture, rather than dealing with each student's specific concerns"). The university's Student Research Program, one of the largest of its kind, links students with faculty in one-on-one research projects. UCLA also houses two centers to support undergraduate research.

While the intensity of coursework varies by major, we're told that competition is especially fierce in math, science, and engineering. A neuroscience major confesses, "Coming from a high school where I was valedictorian, I thought college would be a breeze. I've never experienced such difficulty in my schoolwork in my life … What a teacher in high school would spend a week explaining and practicing, you cover in one lecture—with no further practice." Students agree that "slackers would not fit in here."

Campus Environment

With its brick and terra cotta Italian Romanesque buildings, the UCLA campus is quite beautiful; it is frequently chosen by movie production companies for its stunning non-West Coast appearance ("Stars are found on campus very often!" says a student). The campus and upscale surrounding areas are considered extremely safe.

The guidance counselors we surveyed say UCLA has the best academic facilities in the country. A student agrees: "UCLA is really modern and up to date." UCLA set the standard for computing services at the nation's universities by creating websites for every course (more than 3,000), as well as the groundbreaking "my.ucla" personalized academic homepage for every student.

More than 90 percent of freshmen choose to live on campus. Overcrowding has been a problem in the past, but the university assures us that "facilities for another 2,000 undergraduate students and another 2,000 graduate students are in the works." A junior gives us the inside scoop on housing: "The general rule is this: If you're a first-year and want to meet people, live in the dorms, they're much more social, especially Dykstra Hall. If you're older than a first-year, or just want more privacy and don't care too much about meeting people, live in Sunset or DeNeve." A senior exclaims, "The dorms tend to be really, really nice and have the most amazing food! Everyone misses dorm food once they move out!"

Student Life

What does it take to be a UCLA student? "UCLA seeks the nation's finest students who are committed to learning in a public university environment, who will pursue their academic goals with enthusiasm, and who will contribute actively to the campus community," says a university official. At any one time, one-third of UCLA students are involved in community service programs—from social work in prisons to clean-up projects and environment support.

UCLA has a "really relaxed" feel: "The whole campus walks around in flip flops," says a sociology major. "It's not like the stuck-up East Coast schools. People are friendly." Drinkers and teetotalers alike can find a niche at UCLA. "I think it is the same at every school," a student muses. "If you want to drink and do drugs, you can find a place and people to do it with. If you are not into it and aren't looking for it, then you won't find it."

One sorority member explains the appeal of Greek life at UCLA: "Being in the Greek system is a way to make the campus a little smaller and avoid feeling like you are being swallowed up by such a large school." However, the vast majority of UCLA students do not go Greek, perhaps finding the same sense of community in one of the other 500-plus student organizations. "As you walk down Bruin Walk, it's clogged with people handing out fliers and trying to recruit you for their organization," says a student. "At first it's kinda cool, but after a few weeks, you quickly learn how to not make eye contact and race by them all."

UCLA's 22 varsity sports for men and women have won more national championships than any other university. The programs for women athletes are considered phenomenal. Football and basketball are hugely popular; the players "are definitely mini-celebrities," says one student. The annual football game against archrival USC is actually a week-long event ("Beat SC Week"), with a bonfire, blood drive, and "car smash."

ACT English: 22–30
ACT Math: 24–31
HS Rank of Entering Freshmen:
Top 10%: 97%
Top 50%: 100%
Avg. HS GPA: 4.13

Costs (2004–5)

Tuition and Fees, In-State: $4,878

Tuition and Fees, Out-of-State: $17,257

Room & Board: $10,452

THE EXPERTS SAY...

" With more than 3,000 undergraduate courses, world-class faculty across all disciplines, a campus residence community nestled in the Bel-Air hills, the top college athletic program in the country, and a reasonable price tag—what more could a student want? "

" Be inspired by the scores of successful UCLA alums, including Carol Burnett, Francis Ford Coppola, Kareem Abdul-Jabbar, Troy Aikman, and many, many more. "

Inst. Aid (2002–03)

Institutional Aid, Need-Based: $32,435,336

Institutional Aid, Non-Need-Based: $1,759,819

FT Undergrads Receiving Aid: 51%
Avg. Amount per Student: $10,634

FT Undergrads Receiving Non-Need-Based Scholarship or Grant Aid: 7%
Avg. Amount per Student: $2,244

Of Those Receiving Any Aid:

Rec. Need-Based Scholarship or Grant Aid: 90%
Average Award: $7,641

Rec. Need-Based Self-Help Aid: 79%
Average Award: $4,740

Upon Graduation, Avg. Loan Debt per Student: $12,775

Financial Aid Deadline: rolling, 3/2 (priority)

UNIVERSITY OF CALIFORNIA— SAN DIEGO

9500 Gilman Drive, 301 University Center, La Jolla, CA 92093
Admissions Phone: (858) 534-4831 Fax: (858) 534-5723 Email: admissionsinfo@ucsd.edu
Website: www.ucsd.edu Application Website: www.ucop.edu/pathways/aapctr.html

General Info

Type of School: public, coed
Setting: suburban
Academic Calendar: quarter

Student Body

Full-Time Undergrads: 18,795
  Men: 48%, Women: 52%

Part-Time Undergrads: 293
  Men: 51%, Women: 49%

Total Undergrad Population:
  African American: 1%
  Asian American: 36%
  Latino: 10%
  Native American: <1%
  Caucasian: 36%
  International: 3%
  Out-of-State: 2%
  Living Off-Campus: 66%
  In Fraternities: 10%
  In Sororities: 10%

Graduate and First-Professional
  Students: 3,851

Academics

Full-Time Faculty: 965
  With Ph.D.: 98%

Part-Time Faculty: 184
  With Ph.D.: 98%

Student/Faculty Ratio: 19:1

Most Popular Majors:
  biology (15%)
  economics (9%)
  psychology (6%)
  electrical & computer engineering
  (6%)
  computer science & engineering
  (5%)

Freshmen Retention Rate: 94%

Graduation Rates:
  50% within four years
  81% within six years

Admissions

Regular Application Deadline: 11/30

Fall Transfer Deadline: 11/30

Total # of Students Applied: 41,354
  Admitted: 17,092
  Enrolled: 4,243
  note: numbers for 2002

Inside the Classroom

According to many, UCSD is a "sink-or-swim type of place," where you can excel—or fail—depending on your initiative. The atmosphere is "very academic" and admission here has gotten more competitive over the last several years, due in part to what a guidance counselor calls the "trendy" factor of San Diego. And if you apply, be prepared to stand behind your application. Recently, UCSD officials asked a randomly chosen group of admitted students for evidence to verify self-reported information about family income, honors, achievements, and community service.

"Oxford on the Pacific" is the model UCSD sets for itself. While Oxford never saw this much sunshine, the British university is the model for UCSD's academic structure. The school is actually made up of six colleges, each with its own requirements, curriculum, and character, allowing students to experience an intimate academic community within a large institution.

UCSD is known as an exceptional research institution, particularly strong in the sciences, engineering, and theatre/dance. A San Diego guidance counselor observes that UCSD is "adding more majors in the sciences, and building new buildings to accommodate these majors." UCSD celebrated the opening of two brand new schools recently, the new Management School and the School of Pharmacy and Pharmaceutical Sciences, additions sure to attract even more of the ubiquitous companies that recruit on campus.

The faculty here is a high-powered one and includes several Nobel laureates. While some students reported that this does not necessarily correlate to teaching excellence, others disagree: "Professors are extremely accessible, friendly and helpful (unless you're going to whine and complain)," a senior comments. "Unfortunately, many of the undergrad classes are taught by lecturers and not by faculty." (Interestingly, in spite of very limited office hours, it's often the professors who complain that students here don't visit enough.) Workload is "average but the quarter system is more stressful than a semester system," remarks an economics major. "Courses are fairly difficult and require consistent studying to keep up."

Campus Environment

UCSD is in La Jolla, a well-known beach resort town. Aside from being upscale and exclusive, it's also known for its conservatism and "spanking clean" image. "La Jolla is a very posh town," an alumna states. "Community of La Jolla really didn't welcome the students... On the other hand, La Jolla is very safe and one of the most beautiful places in the world. So, now that I am older, I can appreciate the town's reaction to a bunch of young freedom-loving students.

The campus boasts the acclaimed Stuart outdoor sculpture collection, and is home to an aquarium and the Theodore Geisel Library, named for "Dr. Seuss." Off-campus, 30 minutes in any direction leads to someplace beautiful: Mexico, the beach, Orange County. The spectacular beaches act as the school's outdoor annex, given the number of students who head there after class. As one former student told us, "People go all year round. I can't tell you how many sunsets I saw there!"

"All I know about campus housing is that there's not enough of it," quips a senior. Few students live on campus, and with high rents in the surrounding area of La Jolla, most must seek housing farther out. "Housing close to campus (within two miles) is extremely expensive, the cheapest running at about $900 for a one bedroom apartment," laments a senior. Campus parking is horrendous, so much so that some students have resorted to counterfeiting parking passes, we hear.

Student Life

UCSD students aren't exactly a bunch of beach bums. A sophomore says, "Often confused with San Diego State University, UCSD might give the impression that it's a party school, being right near the ocean. It's anything but! Resident advisors and campus security strictly enforce the alcohol regulation and noise rules. The party scene here is pretty much dead, so rowdiness is not a problem." One student comments, "Students from the northeastern part of the country, and large cities like New York and Philly, will need to adjust to the easygoing, neutral atmosphere here." However, the "campus atmosphere is not so great," a senior remarks. "Students are not exactly unfriendly but neither are they friendly either. It is difficult to meet other students as most are very unresponsive to efforts at communication."

"Neo-liberal" is how some students described the school to us. "There are pockets of activists who are changing the world, but most students are apathetic to real social issues." (However, one genuine area of controversy is The Koala, a student newspaper that publishes racist jabs against most minority groups, now suing the USCD administration for infringement of its First Amendment rights.) Explains one senior, "It's a very antisocial atmosphere, with lots of racial cliques."

UCSD is a dry campus (with strict enforcement), so if you're under 21, Tijuana, Mexico offers the only place where you can go and dance the night away. And if you're over 21, there's Gaslamp Quarter in downtown San Diego. While the fraternities and sororities are the few (if only) organizations that throw parties, there's no "fraternity row."

One common complaint about UCSD is that there's no school spirit. "There isn't a close-knit community on campus, everybody does their own thing or in little groups, so organizations don't have much influence," a senior says. The typical student? "There are two types: one is the Californian type with shorts, t-shirt, flip flops, and a skateboard. The other is the rich type: perfect clothes, make-up (if girl), expensive car, arrogant. The 'rebel types' probably would not fit as well. The school is fairly 'proper' in general."

With the exception of a football team, UCSD has many varsity and intramural sports, but "UCSD is not known for any of its intercollegiate sports," an economics major confesses. The school prefers to be known for its academics, and does not grant athletic scholarships (though, with its recent switch from a Division III school to a Division II school, it could do so). The "Triton Tide" pep club was created four years ago to boost sagging school spirit, but most students prefer intramurals and the great outdoors. Whether jogging or surfing, UCSD students love being outside. As one student aptly puts it, "San Diego has four seasons: summer, summer, summer, and spring."

Test Scores (middle 50%):
SAT Verbal: 540–650
SAT Math: 600–700
ACT Comp: 26–29

HS Rank of Entering Freshmen:
Top 10%: 99%
Top 25%: 100%

Avg. HS GPA: 3.9

THE EXPERTS SAY...

" With a new pharmacy school on campus, there will be more biotech recruiters on campus than ever before. "

" Don't let the perfect weather or beach resort atmosphere fool you: Academics are way more important than surfing at UCSD. "

Costs (2003–04)

Tuition and Fees, In-State: $5,150

Tuition and Fees, Out-of-State: $18,630

Room & Board: $8,622

Payment Plan(s): installment plan, deferred payment plan, pre-payment plan

Inst. Aid (est. 2003–04)

Institutional Aid, Need-Based: $15,171,535

Institutional Aid, Non-Need-Based: $1,775,789

FT Undergrads Receiving Aid: 46% Avg. Amount per Student: $10,405

FT Undergrads Receiving Non-Need-Based Scholarship or Grant Aid: 9% Avg. Amount per Student: $3,143

Of Those Receiving Any Aid:

Rec. Need-Based Scholarship or Grant Aid: 91% Average Award: $6,794

Rec. Need-Based Self-Help Aid: 82% Average Award: $5,090

Upon Graduation, Avg. Loan Debt per Student: $13,808

Financial Aid Deadline: 6/1, 3/2 (priority)

UNIVERSITY OF CALIFORNIA—
SANTA BARBARA

University of California, Santa Barbara, CA 93106
Admissions Phone: (805) 893-2881 Fax: (805) 893-2676
Email: appinfo@sa.ucsb.edu Website: www.admit.ucsb.edu

General Info

Type of School: public, coed

Academic Calendar: quarter

Student Body

Full-Time Undergrads: 16,985
  Men: 46%, Women: 54%

Part-Time Undergrads: 731
  Men: 53%, Women: 47%

Total Undergrad Population:
  African American: 3%
  Asian American: 14%
  Latino: 15%
  Native American: 1%
  Caucasian: 56%
  International: 1%
  Living Off-Campus: 79%
  In Fraternities: 8%
  In Sororities: 10%

Graduate and First-Professional
  Students: 2,649

Academics

Full-Time Faculty: 792

Part-Time Faculty: 171

Student/Faculty Ratio: 19:1

Freshmen Retention Rate: 91%

Admissions

Regular Application Deadline: 11/30

Fall Transfer Deadline: 11/30

Total # of Students Applied: 34,022
  Admitted: 17,018
  Enrolled: 3,649

Test Scores (middle 50%):
  SAT Verbal: 530–630
  SAT Math: 560–670
  ACT Comp: 22–27

Costs (2001–02)

Tuition and Fees, In-State: $3,841

Tuition and Fees, Out-of-State:
  $11,074

Room & Board: $7,891

Inst. Aid (1999–2000)

Institutional Aid, Need-Based:
  $14,201,523

Institutional Aid, Non-Need-Based:
  $517,346

FT Undergrads Receiving Aid: 43%

Inside the Classroom

Santa Barbara offers students a wide scope of quality academic programs combined with terrific research opportunities. Utilizing cutting-edge facilities, the science and technology departments, particularly in physics, biology, chemistry, and engineering, are among UCSB's best. As home to eight national research centers, six of which are sponsored by the National Science Foundations, the school receives large numbers of grants and research opportunities in many disciplines. The school has recently received a $300 million grant to start a nanosytems institute with UCLA, which will focus on developing miniaturized technologies beneficial for health and science. And the school's most recent "point of pride" is that it is home to three Nobel Prize winners in chemistry and physics. Other strong departments are marine biology—not surprising given the school's oceanfront property—accounting, and anthropology. Requirements vary by college but usually include humanities, art and literature, social science, natural science, English, writing, and an ethnic studies course. UCSB also offers an extensive study abroad program, with programs at more than 100 foreign universities.

As a medium-sized research institution, UCSB is more manageable than most large universities but still poses certain challenges. With 18,000 undergraduates, getting into certain courses can be tough, and classes at the introductory levels are large. Receiving individual attention from professors, especially from those focused on their own research, can be difficult. One junior claims that "some professors have made it quite apparent that they're there primarily for the research opportunities, and not to teach others. But for the most part, they're laid back and understanding."

UCSB is on a quarterly system, which means that exams and deadlines come up frequently—much more frequently than most students would like. Yet as one student says, "The quarter system is very fast so there's no room for procrastinating, but I've found this to be a good thing because it keeps you on track." While the workload can be heavy, the amount of studying required largely depends on individual student commitment. One student told us, "You can easily remove yourself from the party scene. But there are also people who party a lot and just do enough work to get by."

Campus Environment

While their friends in the Northeast are freezing their butts off, UCSB students enjoy their own beautiful beach, complete with surfing, playing volleyball, and working on a tan all year long. The school's "feel" is that of a small community, set 100 miles north of Los Angeles, just 10 miles from beautiful Santa Barbara, a world-famous tourist spot known for its beauty and Spanish architecture. The town of Santa Barbara is "bicycle friendly" and has many cafes and shops.

"On-campus housing is definitely lacking," says a young alum. "The rooms in the on-campus dorms are very small, and the food at the dining halls is bad. Most students choose to live in off-campus private dorms their freshman year and move to apartments in Isla Vista for subsequent years." The social atmosphere in nearby Isla Vista is like living in Animal House without having to wear Greek letters. "There's rarely a night when there isn't a party. The streets are filled with hundreds of people as you go from one house to the next," one student tells us. Some over-the-top incidents have occurred there recently, prompting the administration to seriously address drinking and safety issues. As for the apartments themselves, be prepared for true college-town conditions: One junior claims, "Isla Vista is the most densely populated square mile in the country, second only to Manhattan. The apartments there are subpar: expensive and unkempt." However, another student says, "off-campus housing is very nice, spacious, and clean."

Student Life

With over 90 percent of the students here coming from California, the fact that some say the typical student is a "Britney Spears and Backstreet Boy wannabe" isn't surprising. Some graduate and older students have been disappointed in the consistently "young, immature, mainstream crowd." The school does attract large numbers of Chicano/Latino and Asian American populations, however, as well as international students, which "add excitement to an otherwise monotonous, senseless, young crowd," according to one grad student.

Given its beautiful locale, sports are not surprisingly favorite activities here. UCSB intercollegiate teams compete in the NCAA Division I, with strong teams in basketball, water polo, baseball, and volleyball. Some claim that "men's athletics are pretty weak aside from baseball, though women's sports like volleyball and basketball are pretty big." There's a whole range of varsity sports to choose from, though one student claims, "Most of my friends would rather go to a UCLA game than a UCSB one." Intramurals get a lot of participation.

Almost all students comment on how laid-back UCSB is. It even seems to be the polar opposite of one of its fellow UC schools, the politically active UC Berkeley. "It's fun-loving," says a Santa Barbara student. "It is apathetic as far as protesting . . . People are happy with who they are. They're happy with how life is."

UCSB has a reputation for being a party school, and "although UCSB students are studious, they also live up to their reputation," according to one senior. Drinking occurs on a frequent, if not daily, basis for many. Most of the partying takes place off-campus but is entirely open to students living on-campus as well. Fraternities and sororities, while not the only game in town, do sponsor a large number of parties and events. One senior claims "they're like a disease. They inhibit every part of Santa Barbara life."

Many students, however, express concern that UCSB's reputation as a party school eclipses the school's other offerings, particularly in various academic fields. As part of the acclaimed University of California system, Santa Barbara maintains high academic standards. As a student told us, "There are a lot of people who've worked hard to get in and continue to work hard once they get here."

Avg. Amount per Student: $8,851
FT Undergrads Receiving Non-Need-Based Scholarship or Grant Aid: 10%
Avg. Amount per Student: $4,236
Of Those Receiving Any Aid:
Rec. Need-Based Scholarship or Grant Aid: 78%
Average Award: $5,923
Rec. Need-Based Self-Help Aid: 87%
Average Award: $3,935
Upon Graduation, Avg. Loan Debt per Student: $16,426
Financial Aid Deadline: 3/2 (priority)

THE EXPERTS SAY...

" Physics, biology, marine biology, chemistry, engineering—UCSB offers cutting-edge facilities for science and technology majors. There are three Nobel Prize winners in chemistry and physics on the faculty. "

" Even though it has its very own beach, UCSB isn't the party school it's reputed to be. You'll have to do some work while you're working on your tan. "

UNIVERSITY OF CALIFORNIA— SANTA CRUZ

1156 High Street, Santa Cruz, CA 95064

Admissions Phone: (831) 459-4008 Fax: (831) 459-4452 Email: admissions@ucsc.edu
Website: admissions.ucsc.edu Application Website: https://my.ucsc.edu

General Info

Type of School: public, coed

Setting: small town

Academic Calendar: quarter

Student Body

Full-Time Undergrads: 12,967
Men: 45%, Women: 55%

Part-Time Undergrads: 654
Men: 53%, Women: 47%

Total Undergrad Population:
African American: 2%
Asian American: 17%
Latino: 14%
Native American: 1%
Caucasian: 52%
International: 1%
Living Off-Campus: 55%

Graduate and First-Professional
Students: 1,337

Academics

Full-Time Faculty: 516
With Ph.D.: 98%

Part-Time Faculty: 201
With Ph.D.: 98%

Student/Faculty Ratio: 19:1

Most Popular Majors:
psychology
business management economics
biology
literature
sociology

Freshmen Retention Rate: 87%

Graduation Rates:
42% within four years
65% within six years

Computers: Computer Required

Admissions

Regular Application Deadline: 11/30

Fall Transfer Deadline: 11/30, 11/1
(priority)

Spring Transfer Deadline: 7/31, 7/1
(priority)

Total # of Students Applied: 21,525
Admitted: 17,284
Enrolled: 3,729

Test Scores (middle 50%):
SAT Verbal: 510–630
SAT Math: 520–630
ACT Comp: 21–27

Inside the Classroom

Founded in the radical 1960s, UC Santa Cruz remains one of the more progressive schools within the UC system, attracting a politically active and socially aware student body. One California guidance counselor calls it "the jewel of the UC crown." This is a school where it's hard to tell the students from the faculty. Everyone here seems to be open to ideas and bent on disproving status quo beliefs. As one student describes, "I turned down Berkeley and UCLA, and every day I'm glad I did. As I sit here reading dissident literature, I love how UCSC teaches us to unlearn what we thought we already knew."

UCSC offers 50 majors in the arts, engineering, humanities, natural sciences, and social sciences. The sciences—especially physics and biology—are particularly strong. The school also has several research institutes, in nonlinear sciences, tectonics, and particle physics, among others. There's even a popular program in science illustration. UCSC recently added a new health sciences major for students who are interested in going on to med school or working in other healthcare professions.

In a unique arrangement, UCSC is not broken down by academic division, as are most universities, but rather uses a system of ten residential colleges. Every undergrad, whether living on or off campus, is affiliated with one of these residential colleges, each of which has its own philosophy and feel.

Another unique facet of UCSC is its performance evaluation system for every class. In addition to letter grades, students receive written descriptions of their academic strengths and weaknesses as part of their official transcripts. (Several smaller liberal arts colleges use this approach, but it is virtually unheard of at large research universities.) Students also have the option of taking up to 25 percent of their courses on a pass/fail basis. Many find the professors entirely accessible, though others complain that, other than email, some professors offer only one office hour per week. The administration does try to ease this by providing occasional course tutors.

The academic year is organized on a quarter system: Three quarters (fall, winter, and spring) constitute the regular academic year. We're told by one sophomore that "quarters are very intense (they go by very fast), so people have very little time," yet another tells us that "the workload can be painfully light if you know how to cut corners." One guidance counselor we know recommends UCSC "for the easy-going, not grade-driven student." According to one senior, "UC Santa Cruz is a school where everyone seems to be in their own world; people are running here and there to work or class. Study groups are hard to put together." All students must complete a senior thesis or pass a comprehensive exam in order to graduate. Internships and fieldwork are an integral part of some majors, and international field study is actually required for those majoring in global economics.

Perhaps because of the size of the school and the fact that it's part of a statewide school system, it's also said there's a lot of bureaucracy here: Long lines are not unusual, and with a large number of administration and academic offices, students frequently have to visit four or five different offices to resolve paperwork. Moreover, the administration at UCSC can be tough on students. "They send out bills every month, and they're due within three weeks—no excuses," complains one sophomore. However, one high school guidance counselor we spoke to insists that the UCSC "administration has heart."

Campus Environment

Located 75 miles south of San Francisco, the campus offers breathtaking views of Monterey Bay and the Pacific Ocean. Its 2,000-acre landscape combines lush redwood forests with open meadows and hills ("You see deer all the time," points out a young alum). San Jose, Monterey, and Carmel are within an hour's drive, and Big Sur is within two hours' drive. Downtown Santa Cruz is a short bike ride or hitchhike away. A quiet town ("no gangs," says one student), Santa Cruz is considered enticingly mellow and progressive. Students spend a lot of time in its coffee shops and cafés before heading out to the beautiful beaches.

The campus is extremely safe, though one student claims, "people love to pretend that it's not." Freshmen are guaranteed housing on campus, but sophomores enter a lottery, and upperclassmen usually go off campus. A Holiday Inn ("the Ho") was recently converted into a school dorm, though students had been housed there for a few years prior. For those looking off campus, it might take months to find housing—the Santa Cruz housing market can be brutal.

Student Life

With around 12,000 full-time undergrads, the student body at UCSC tends to consist of mostly northern Californian hippie/outdoors types. One literature major colorfully describes the range of typical UCSC students: "the hippie; the white boy who smokes too much weed; and the ultra-hip hipster. And there are lots of intellectual lesbians." Another student argues, "I don't believe there is a 'typical student' at my school, for Santa Cruz is full of weird and bizarre people, ranging from the dorky nerd to tanned surfers to tree-hugging hippies… Anybody will fit in as long as they're okay with the diversity at this school." The student body is ethnically diverse, with 17 percent Asian American and 14 percent Chicano/Latino (though less than three percent African American). Prominent UCSC alumni include TV stars Camryn Manheim (*The Practice*) and Maya Rudolph (*Saturday Night Live*), Pulitzer-winning journalists Laurie Garrett and Martha Mendoza, and NASA astronaut Kathryn Sullivan.

Most students are politically active and are on the far left of the political spectrum, though there are some "mainstream conservatives" on campus as well. One student describes it as "a very friendly campus with the politics very, very liberal en masse, though individuals still carry with them their own conservative views." We're told that drinking and drugs are not a real problem here, but rather that people do very much their own thing.

UCSC has a most unusual mascot, chosen by the student body in 1986: "the Banana Slug," a bright yellow, shell-less mollusk found in the campus's redwood forest. UCSC's men's and women's intercollegiate teams compete in basketball, soccer, swimming and diving, tennis, volleyball, rugby, and water polo.

HS Rank of Entering Freshmen:
Top 10%: 90%
Top 25%: 100%
Avg. HS GPA: 3.48

THE EXPERTS SAY...

" Devoted mainly to undergraduate education, UCSC is a smart and affordable choice for alternative types who are looking for an education that goes 'outside the box.' "

" 'Slugs' is a misnomer: In their free time, UCSC students are more likely to spend hours arguing politics in a café than to lie out in the sun doing nothing. "

Costs (2002–03)

Tuition and Fees, In-State: $5,829

Tuition and Fees, Out-of-State: $23,938

Room & Board: $10,314

Payment Plan(s): deferred payment plan

Inst. Aid (2002–03)

Institutional Aid, Need-Based: $14,929,701

Institutional Aid, Non-Need-Based: $1,132,389

FT Undergrads Receiving Aid: 42%
Avg. Amount per Student: $11,124

FT Undergrads Receiving Non-Need-Based Scholarship or Grant Aid: 6%
Avg. Amount per Student: $3,305

Of Those Receiving Any Aid:

Rec. Need-Based Scholarship or Grant Aid: 87%
Average Award: $7,568

Rec. Need-Based Self-Help Aid: 89%
Average Award: $5,065

Upon Graduation, Avg. Loan Debt per Student (2002): $13,282

Financial Aid Deadline: 3/2 (priority)

Graduates

Companies Recruiting On-Campus: 131

UNIVERSITY OF CHICAGO

1116 East 59th Street, Chicago, IL 60637
Admissions Phone: (773) 702-8650 Fax: (773) 702-4199
Website: www.uchicago.edu
Application Website: uncommonapplication.uchicago.edu

Note: Info. not verified by school

General Info

Type of School: private, coed

Setting: urban

Academic Calendar: quarter

Student Body

Full-Time Undergrads: 4,191
  Men: 50%, Women: 50%

Part-Time Undergrads: 45
  Men: 58%, Women: 42%

Total Undergrad Population:
  African American: 4%
  Asian American: 15%
  Latino: 7%
  Native American: <1%
  Caucasian: 65%
  International: 8%
  Out-of-State: 78%
  Living Off-Campus: 34%
  In Fraternities: 12%
  In Sororities: 5%

Graduate and First-Professional
  Students: 8,941

Academics

Full-Time Faculty: 1,600
  With Ph.D.: 100%

Part-Time Faculty: 260
  With Ph.D.: 100%

Student/Faculty Ratio: 4:1

Most Popular Majors:
  economics
  biological science
  English
  psychology
  political science

Freshmen Retention Rate: 95%

Graduation Rates:
  78% within four years
  85% within six years

Admissions

Regular Application Deadline: 1/1

Early Action Deadline: 11/1

Fall Transfer Deadline: 4/1

Total # of Students Applied: 8,139
  Admitted: 3,379
  Enrolled: 1,114

# of Students Waitlisted: 1,497
  Students Accepting Place: 754
  Waitlisted Students Admitted: 72

Inside the Classroom

The University of Chicago is dedicated to the pursuit of ideas, and attracts the kind of student who draws energy from and takes great pride in that premise. Chicago is probably the premier institution for the study of economics; sociology and political science programs are among the best in the nation, as are the hard sciences. The school has a reputation for being an academic pressure cooker. "The U of C is a terribly intense place," says a student. "Students spend an average of five to seven hours a day doing homework outside of class time." Professors have high expectations and competition is fierce. "Competitiveness is strongest in the sciences, law, and economics departments, cutthroat, in fact," warns a junior, adding: "A 4.0 average is obviously too low."

Classes at Chicago are generally small and seminar-oriented, adding to the stress and intensity as well as to the quality of the academic experience. The professors are very accessible, even if some seem arrogant and condescending. The student body ("nerds," says one guidance counselor) seems to thrive in this environment rather than wilt, even under a quarter system that crams a semester's worth of work into 10 weeks. Students don't mind spending time engaged in study and research, and many go on to make it a career.

While graduate students outnumber the undergrads, the latter have the same access to state-of-the-art facilities and world-class faculty (including six Nobel Prize winners). They can also enroll in graduate courses. At least one student reported that "there is really no line between graduate and undergraduate students in terms of what they can and cannot do on the campus." But another reports that, although undergrads are "treated well," graduate students take priority with professors.

Chicago's stiff core curriculum, called the Common Core, was recently restructured and is now considered easier. Students take required sequences in humanities, social sciences, physical sciences, biological sciences, math, and art or music; there is also a requirement in civilization, which includes study of a Western or non-Western culture, as well as a foreign language requirement. (There's even a phys ed requirement.) Students are expected to perform as well in these courses as they would in the courses in their major.

Campus Environment

The Chicago campus is an architecture buff's paradise, with Gothic structures and buildings by noted architects, like Frank Lloyd Wright's Robie House. One side of the campus borders Lake Michigan, where there are parks and a beach, and students can bike and swim. The school's many exceptional facilities include the fantastic Regenstein library, known by students as "The Reg."

The quality of the housing varies. "A fair number of upperclassmen take apartments off-campus to escape the dorm system," says one student. Another says that while "some are nice, some are definitely below standard." One of the favorite dorms is Shoreland Hall, a converted hotel with spacious rooms that have incredible views of the lake; students also have high praise for the much smaller Breckinridge. (A typical

KAPLAN

Chicago student enthuses: "Enrico Fermi conducted the first chain reaction in my dorm, Snell-Hitchcock.") Housing is guaranteed, and students agree that dorms, and the campus as a whole, are safe. Off-campus housing is "cheap and available," notes a religion major. "However, often times the conditions of apartments are pretty deplorable." First-year students are required to take the freshman meal plan, choosing between two options.

Chicago's location in the Hyde Park area of the South Side has its ups and downs. Most students have great things to say about Hyde Park, and many play down the disadvantages, such as the surrounding area's reputation as a high-crime area. A student says, "The U of C owns a majority of the real estate in Hyde Park and so employs most of the community. This causes major problems since the university is the island of white rich kids in the middle of south side Chicago." The city of Chicago is 20 minutes away by train, and students have "marvelous fun" in town. Transportation is by foot or public transportation. Some students have cars but parking is a "problem."

Student Life

Because most students are so devoted to their studies, the social life at Chicago is not exactly booming. "The overall atmosphere is one of scholarly zeal," says an art history major. "Since we are in the Midwest, there is a generally friendly attitude, but workload tends to keep students locked in their dorm rooms." During the week "students work like dogs." However, the weekend is a different story. "Dorms provide wonderful city activities like opera, symphony, and museum trips," says a student. On campus, "fraternities have parties, [there are] apartment parties, major drinking, dancing, and pot smoking." Still, many students prefer quieter activities, and many friendships are formed by bonding over calculus and philosophy books.

There are many forms of entertainment on campus, including visiting speakers, student and professional performances, and a student-run movie theater. The Model United Nations is popular, as are student newspapers and cultural clubs. Varsity sports "are terrible. We play pool and Frisbee," states a junior. Politics vary from opposite ends of the spectrum. "There are militant communists and militant fundamentalists," says a student. However, the activity is "relatively low-key." The Greeks provide some social life, but not a substantial part and what they do offer is, in the words of one student, "for a limited audience." "They [fraternities] account for the drinking scene. However, the cultural scene is just as popular," adds another.

Most Chicago place a high value on the education they receive at Chicago and the way it develops them as intellectuals. "Typical student: nose in book, glasses, bad breath? No, no. The population is wonderfully diverse," jokes a student. But "everyone is a dork, so everyone fits ... and despite the apparent dorkiness of the population, you can have fun here!"

Other schools to check out: Cornell, University of Pennsylvania, Brown, Washington U in St. Louis, Johns Hopkins.

Test Scores (middle 50%):
  SAT Verbal: 660–750
  SAT Math: 650–750
  ACT Comp: 28–32
  ACT English: 28–34
  ACT Math: 27–33
HS Rank of Entering Freshmen:
  Top 10%: 79%
  Top 25%: 94%
  Top 50%: 100%

THE EXPERTS SAY...

" Chicago may offer the best economics degree in the world. This institution graduates leading social theorists. "

" Chicago is an academic pressure cooker. Get ready to work like a dog and fight for every point of your G.P.A. "

Costs (2003–04)

Tuition and Fees: $29,238
Room & Board: $9,165
Payment Plan(s): installment plan

Graduates

Going to Graduate School:
  33% Within One Year

UNIVERSITY OF CINCINNATI

P.O. Box 210091, Cincinnati, OH 45221-0091
Admissions Phone: (513) 556-1100; (800) 827-8728 Fax: (513) 556-1105
Email: admissions@uc.edu
Website: www.uc.edu

General Info

Type of School: public, coed
Academic Calendar: quarter

Student Body

Full-Time Undergrads: 15,576
  Men: 53%, Women: 47%

Part-Time Undergrads: 2,938
  Men: 45%, Women: 55%

Total Undergrad Population:
  African American: 14%
  Asian American: 3%
  Latino: 1%
  Native American: <1%
  Caucasian: 77%
  International: 1%
  Out-of-State: 8%
  Living Off-Campus: 83%

Graduate and First-Professional
Students: 7,658

Academics

Full-Time Faculty: 1,115
  With Ph.D.: 64%

Part-Time Faculty: 58
  With Ph.D.: 2%

Student/Faculty Ratio: 15:1

Most Popular Majors:
  marketing (3%)
  criminal justice (2%)
  mechanical engineering (2%)
  early childhood education (2%)
  finance (2%)

Freshmen Retention Rate: 76%

Graduation Rates:
  15% within four years
  49% within six years

Admissions

Application Deadline: varies by college

Total # of Students Applied: 10,958
  Admitted: 9,673
  Enrolled: 3,724

Test Scores (middle 50%):
  SAT Verbal: 460–600
  SAT Math: 460–610
  ACT Comp: 18–26
  ACT English: 17–25
  ACT Math: 17–26

Inside the Classroom

The 17 colleges that make up the University of Cincinnati offer more than 500 degree programs to more than 18,000 undergraduates. The College of Design, Architecture, Art, and Planning (DAAP) is the only college in the nation where industrial design students can create "to size" auto parts in a Rapid Prototyping Center and has top ranked architecture and interior design programs. Three out of the last four years, 100 percent of all grads from the College of Applied Science have found employment within weeks of graduation. The College of Engineering offers the first program in cooperative education in the country: The co-op program went from serving 40 students in its first year (1906) to almost 4,000 students working for more than 1,300 employers in 32 states and many foreign countries today. The renowned College-Conservatory of Music is the largest venue of performing arts presentations in the state of Ohio, with more than 900 events per year. The McMicken College of Arts and Sciences is the largest college at the university, with over 5,000 students enrolled there. One guidance counselor recommends its "excellent deaf education program." The College of Pharmacy has a 100 percent placement rate prior to graduation. Notable alumni of the university include former U.S. President William Howard Taft and the legendary Hall of Fame pitcher Sandy Koufax.

Core requirements in English composition, qualitative reasoning, diversity and culture, and social and ethical issues, along with 8 courses in 5 distribution areas (such as humanities, social sciences, and natural sciences), are what all students must complete to fulfill general education requirements at the University of Cincinnati.

The most popular majors are business and marketing, education/teacher education, architecture, social sciences and history, and health sciences. With a student/faculty ratio of 15:1, classes at the University of Cincinnati tend to be on the large side, and students have complained of the lack of individual attention. "In some cases you are 1 in 400," a student gripes. Classes run on a quarterly schedule, with three 10-week terms from September to June, plus one 10-week term in the summer. The quarter system provides students with multiple chances to take more diverse classes, and the university obliges by offering everything from Mythology to Accounting to Chemical Engineering to Trimnastics.

Campus Environment

The main campus is situated on almost 200 acres near downtown Cincinnati and features a mixture of traditional and modern architecture. The state of Indiana is only a few miles away, and Kentucky is just across the Ohio River. Cincinnati offers visitors and residents a vibrant city with a wide range of amenities, including an abundance of galleries and performance spaces and exciting downtown festivals, including one of the country's best fireworks shows. Cincinnati is the home of major league baseball and football teams (Reds, Bengals) as well as a fair number of large corporations (such as Proctor & Gamble, Chiquita Brands International, and Kroger), with lots of internships and cooperative education opportunities nearby. The campus is close to a number of interesting little stores and shops and is very close to the downtown club district. For those who want to walk on the wild(er) side, there are also some 18-and-up bars and clubs within walking distance from the campus.

The University of Cincinnati is known as a "commuter campus," admits an Indiana guidance counselor, who also knocks the quality of the four undergraduate dorms on campus. The good news: a 12-year $151 million housing plan has been underway since 2000 to build and update dorms. All first-year students outside of a 50-mile radius of the school must live in the dorms and have a meal plan. We hear that parking is definitely a problem. "If you don't live nearby," says one student, "it can be 30–40 minutes some days looking for a spot if you can't afford the garages." Some students claim to have even skipped class because they were so frustrated by the parking situation.

The largest construction project in progress at the University of Cincinnati is Main Street, billed by the administration as a hub for events, services, and gathering. Main Street is designed to create a pedestrian corridor running diagonally through the heart of campus and feature a sloping, paved concourse and granite steps to provide connections across campus. The process of building Main Street, due to be completed in 2005, is causing a major stir on campus—as areas are blocked, buildings are torn down and facilities are moved—that has led to some student grousing.

Student Life

Because the University of Cincinnati is so large and has so many students who are older and who commute, there is not much of a sense of community. "At about five o'clock almost everyone leaves and the campus dies. If you want to meet any people you need to live in the dorms for a year or so," a student advises. Yet the student community can come together, as it did to join in protests of the police shooting of an unarmed black man in April 2001.

Greek life is popular at the university—with 35 social fraternities and sororities how could it not be?—but students say that it does not dominate social life. As alternatives, there are more than 200 clubs, organizations, and extracurricular activities available. The university has an organization that sets up some really neat events, such as movie screenings, comedy shows (drawing such famous comics as Margaret Cho), and other nightly activities that students can do free of charge.

College sports are big at the University of Cincinnati. Varsity teams in 18 sports (10 for women and 8 for men) compete at the NCAA Division I-A level. Fans revere the Bearcats as much as they adore Cincinnati's professional teams, such as the Bengals and the Reds. (A bit of sports trivia: The University of Cincinnati became the first school to make five consecutive appearances in the NCAA basketball tournament's Final Four [1959–63].) Additionally, more than 20 intramural sports are offered, including flag football and bowling.

HS Rank of Entering Freshmen:
Top 10%: 13%
Top 25%: 34%
Top 50%: 65%

Avg. HS GPA: 3.09

THE EXPERTS SAY...

" The University of Cincinnati attracts a wide range of extremely talented students, from musicians to athletes. "

" Architecture, engineering, and science students might also want to look at Carnegie Mellon. Musicians: Take a look at Indiana University. Athletes: Stay put. "

Costs (2003–04)

Tuition and Fees, In-State: $7,623

Tuition and Fees, Out-of-State: $19,230

Room & Board: $7,113

Inst. Aid (est. 2003–04)

Institutional Aid, Need-Based: $18,440,870

Institutional Aid, Non-Need-Based: $2,163,344

FT Undergrads Receiving Aid: 48% Avg. Amount per Student: $7,524

FT Undergrads Receiving Non-Need-Based Scholarship or Grant Aid: 4% Avg. Amount per Student: $4,111

Of Those Receiving Any Aid:

Rec. Need-Based Scholarship or Grant Aid: 69% Average Award: $3,325

Rec. Need-Based Self-Help Aid: 97% Average Award: $2,798

Financial Aid Deadline: rolling

UNIVERSITY OF COLORADO— BOULDER

552 UCB, Boulder, CO 80309-0552
Admissions Phone: (303) 492-6301 Fax: (303) 492-7115
Website: www.colorado.edu Application Website: colorado.edu/admissions/apply.html/

General Info

Type of School: public, coed
Setting: urban
Academic Calendar: semester

Student Body

Full-Time Undergrads: 23,618
  Men: 52%, Women: 48%

Part-Time Undergrads: 1,785
  Men: 57%, Women: 43%

Total Undergrad Population:
  African American: 2%
  Asian American: 6%
  Latino: 6%
  Native American: 1%
  Caucasian: 79%
  International: 1%
  Out-of-State: 33%
  Living Off-Campus: 77%
  In Fraternities: 9%
  In Sororities: 14%

Graduate and First-Professional
  Students: 5,855

Academics

Full-Time Faculty: 1,176
  With Ph.D.: 90%

Part-Time Faculty: 561
  With Ph.D.: 39%

Student/Faculty Ratio: 17:1

Most Popular Majors:
  psychology (8%)
  pre-journalism & mass
    communication (4%)
  molecular, cellular &
    developmental biology (4%)
  English (4%)
  political science (3%)

Completing 2 or More Majors: 7%

Freshmen Retention Rate: 83%

Graduation Rates:
  37% within four years
  68% within six years

Admissions

Regular Application Deadline: 1/15

Fall Transfer Deadline: 4/1

Spring Transfer Deadline: 10/1

Total # of Students Applied: 20,920
  Admitted: 16,790
  Enrolled: 5,592

Inside the Classroom

The University of Colorado—Boulder (also known as "CU") is the best of the state's public schools, but with over 25,000 students and 2,500 courses in 150 programs, it can feel overwhelming. The student-faculty ratio is 17:1, but introductory classes are large. A guidance counselor bemoans the "poor freshman counseling," though the FallFest program tries to compensate by providing a prepackaged core curriculum for first-year students. "The accessibility of professors is actually great once you start attending major courses," a student says. "However, in large lecture classes (requirement courses) it is almost impossible to meet with your professor." A senior adds, "Sometimes you have to bug them… Email is the prime form of communication." But the effort to get to know your professors is worth it: The faculty includes two recent Nobel laureates (physics), a MacArthur Fellow (linguistics and computer science), and four recipients of the Presidential Early Career Award for Scientists and Engineers. We also hear that "the English undergraduate director is fabulous," even if certain "hippie instructors" can be offputting.

CU has five undergraduate schools: business, engineering and applied science, environmental design, music, and arts and sciences. Preprofessional programs are among the school's best offerings, particularly in business, engineering, and hard sciences. A guidance counselor cites the "excellent opportunities beyond the classroom for assertive students who want to get a head start in a career." The humanities departments, despite a new building, get low marks, but the department of molecular, cellular, and developmental biology is outstanding. CU Boulder has the only student-run satellite in the nation (11 of its graduates have been in space), and government satellite networks support undergrad study in earth sciences. Undergrad research opportunities abound, including the Summer Multicultural Access to Research Training (SMART) program, which prepares minority students for research careers.

The workload "can be tough and very challenging," an English literature/German major comments. "As far as competitiveness goes, you are your worst competition; it's all about how far you want to go… Everyone else pretty much stays out of other people's business as far as grades, though when offered, people are more than happy to take a look." Others demur: "Most of the campus is not academically focused; many students come to CU just for the party atmosphere… a few come to CU for the academics, mostly the science majors and engineers." But a student retorts, "It's a high-ranked school for a fraction of the cost of many private schools. Also, it's beautiful."

Campus Environment

The spectacular 600-acre CU campus is nestled in foothills of the Rocky Mountains. Boulder is an ideal college town, with trendy cafés, shops, restaurants, bars that support an active music scene. "Boulder definitely has its own 'personality'," a student explains, "which consists of a population of yuppies and hippies … eating organic food and exercising outdoors a lot."

Freshmen are required to live on campus, and the school provides housing for just over 6,000 students in 22 residences. Overflow sometimes occurs. "The dorms at CU are really small rooms," says a senior. "Most of the dorms are off-campus at Williams Village and you have to take a school bus to get to campus." On the plus side, most dorms have computer labs and cafeterias and offer tutoring. Says a student, "They look a lot better than some other campus dorms I've seen." Most upperclassmen live on "The Hill"—a residential area near campus with frat houses, theaters, restaurants, and student hangouts. "Off-campus housing, well, it's very expensive," a student comments. "It's easy to locate, but Boulder is an expensive city to live in." Denver is a quick 30 minutes away.

Student Life

What makes CU such a trendy choice? A Kansas counselor lists the main reasons: "Party school; well-publicized; beautiful; skiing and recreation, clean air, hiking, etc. High-quality academics, too." CU is a Big 12 school, and skiing and football are huge ("I think a lot of the football obsession also has to do with the weekend-long parties that often accompany the football games," a student observes). Intramurals and club sports are also very big. UC students love to ski and take advantage of student discounts at nearby resorts. For climbers, there are the foothills and the Flatirons (which feature a famous 5.5 with a big "CU" painted on it). "The typical UC student is a free-spirited, liberal outdoor-lover," remarks a student. (Or "dirty hippie," in the words of another.)

The off-campus atmosphere is "just about the same as the on-campus atmosphere: friendly, relaxed, happy." Outside of class, students "read Plato, drink coffee, drink period, drugs, movies, hang out." "Parties are the number one," proclaims one student. "Thursday nights are the biggest party night in Boulder, with most of the student population hanging out at bars (Tulagi's, Foundry, Rio, etc.)." "It is a very laid-back campus, so drugs are commonly used," another student claims. Greek houses are officially dry, and around 10 percent pledge. Barbecues are popular and there is an Alfred Packer Day which features raw meat eating and belching contests (Packer was convicted of cannibalism in 1883).

Students lean heavily to the left, especially on environmental issues. "CU is a political campus; i.e., protests, marches, picketing [are] common," reports a student. Another claims that friction occurs whenever the administration does "anything that affects the liberal standpoint this school generally offers." "CU is known for its riots," a student explains. "Students at CU rioted in 1997 due to the fact that CU became a dry campus." Another adds, "Safety is only questionable during football season when one is on the Hill and there is a riot."

The highly active Student Union is the nation's largest student government and operates major centers and services on campus. One-third of the students are from out-of-state; 15 percent are minorities. Who wouldn't fit in? "Someone with no money, sad to say," a senior responds. CU students are friendly, but "you have to be outgoing," says a science major. "The shy, reserved student who isn't willing to sit at someone else's table during lunch may have a harder time enjoying college life at CU."

# of Students Waitlisted: 1,007
  Students Accepting Place: 263
  Waitlisted Students Admitted: 186

Test Scores (middle 50%):
  SAT Verbal: 530–630
  SAT Math: 550–650
  ACT Comp: 23–28
  ACT English: 22–28
  ACT Math: 23–28

HS Rank of Entering Freshmen:
  Top 10%: 24%
  Top 25%: 57%
  Top 50%: 91%

Avg. HS GPA: 3.52

THE EXPERTS SAY...

" CU Boulder actually has very strong science and pre-professional programs, just in case students want a break from the ski slopes. "

" Many non-skiers are drawn to the sheer beauty of the Boulder campus, not to mention the fun atmosphere. And where else can you celebrate cannibalism? (Why you'd _want_ to is a separate issue...) "

Costs (2003–04)

Tuition and Fees, In-State: $4,020

Tuition and Fees, Out-of-State: $20,336

Room & Board: $6,754

Payment Plan(s): deferred payment plan

Inst. Aid (est. 2003–04)

FT Undergrads Receiving Aid: 27%
  Avg. Amount per Student: $9,962

FT Undergrads Receiving Non-Need-Based Scholarship or Grant Aid: 19%
  Avg. Amount per Student: $5,210

Of Those Receiving Any Aid:

Rec. Need-Based Scholarship or Grant Aid: 69%
  Average Award: $4,740

Rec. Need-Based Self-Help Aid: 91%
  Average Award: $4,572

Upon Graduation, Avg. Loan Debt per Student: $16,002

Financial Aid Deadline: rolling, 4/1 (priority)

Graduates

Companies Recruiting On-Campus: 400

Alumni Giving: 19%

UNIVERSITY OF CONNECTICUT

2131 Hillside Road Unit 3088, Storrs, CT 06269-3088
Admissions Phone: (860) 486-3137
Email: beahusky@uconn.edu
Website: www.uconn.edu

General Info

Type of School: public, coed

Setting: rural

Academic Calendar: semester

Student Body

Full-Time Undergrads: 14,251
  Men: 47%, Women: 53%

Part-Time Undergrads: 506
  Men: 50%, Women: 50%

Total Undergrad Population:
  African American: 5%
  Asian American: 6%
  Latino: 5%
  Native American: <1%
  Caucasian: 75%
  International: 1%
  Out-of-State: 24%
  Living Off-Campus: 25%
  In Fraternities: 8%
  In Sororities: 6%

Graduate and First-Professional
  Students: 6,869

Academics

Full-Time Faculty: 842
  With Ph.D.: 95%

Part-Time Faculty: 256
  With Ph.D.: 95%

Student/Faculty Ratio: 17:1

Most Popular Majors:
  psychology (6%)
  political science (5%)
  pre-teaching (4%)
  human development & family
    relations (4%)
  nursing (4%)

Freshmen Retention Rate: 88%

Graduation Rates:
  46% within four years
  70% within six years

Admissions

Regular Application Deadline: 2/1

Early Action Deadline: 12/1

Fall Transfer Deadline: 4/1

Spring Transfer Deadline: 10/15

Total # of Students Applied: 17,666
  Admitted: 9,287
  Enrolled: 3,208

# of Students Waitlisted: 2,096
  Students Accepting Place: 837
  Waitlisted Students Admitted: 715

Inside the Classroom

The University of Connecticut is a large university with 10 undergrad schools offering eight kinds of undergraduate degrees, more than 100 majors, and an extensive list of course offerings. Because the school was originally founded as an agricultural college, the agricultural program is a UConn mainstay. In the College of Liberal Arts, English, psychology, economics, history, and political science are all popular programs of study. One student told us that the theater program, after having been significantly developed in recent years, is also quite strong; there's even a puppetry major available. The core curriculum includes broad requirements in fields including math, literature and the arts, philosophical and ethical analysis, social science, science and technology, foreign language, expository writing, and culture and modern society.

With an enrollment of over 15,000 undergraduates, it's inevitable that there will be problems getting into certain courses and that required classes will be large. "The mass amounts of students in each undergraduate class makes it difficult to make yourself known," notes a recent grad. Still, many classes have only 20 to 30 people. When it comes to advising, professors generally need to be sought out. Students who make it a point to go to see professors during office hours or after class will usually find them very approachable. "Overall, our professors are excellent," a student assures us.

As can be expected at such a large and diverse school, workload and competition among classmates varies greatly. "The atmosphere is all what you make it at UConn," a junior says. "There are the students that just get by and the ones who strive for the 4.0. Many find that getting by isn't as easy as they thought." As a high school guidance counselor warns, "it takes a mature freshman to do well."

Campus Environment

Students complain that the main campus in rural Storrs, Connecticut is "in the middle of nowhere." The university is in the midst of the "UConn 2000" initiative, a $1 billion, 10-year program enacted by the state to rebuild and improve campus facilities. Among the renovated buildings is the Northwest Quad, which is home to more than 900 first-year residents as part of the unique "Northwest Experience." The Northwest Experience is designed to help new students adjust to college life by combining academics, activities, upperclass mentoring, and living arrangements. Altogether, UConn houses 8,500 students in 72 residence halls, mostly coed dorms. Arrangements vary in quality and style, with the general rule of thumb being that they improve as you get older. For upperclassmen, off-campus housing is "prevalent and inexpensive."

Students aren't allowed cars until they've taken 54 credits (usually, junior year). A recent graduate notes, "Although you can walk from one class to another or from your dorm and apartment to class, most people use a car because it is faster, easier, and people are lazy."

Student Life

UConn students praise their peers for being diverse and fun-loving. "The students vary from pot heads to frat guys, to sorority chicks, to meat heads, to jocks, to library dwellers," says a young alum. Although statistics show that most undergrads are white and from Connecticut, "there is a general sense of acceptance," a student tells us. "There is a place for everyone and many people who would normally not mix are close friends. There is an attitude of work hard, party hard."

"UConn has a tendency to get a little rowdy," admits a young alum. "We have a reputation for setting things on fire." Its rep as a party school is not unfounded. According to one senior, "Weeknights are really Monday night to Wednesday night." (He goes on to add that some Wednesday nights actually feel like a weekend as well.) Students boast of partying and drinking nightly in dorms, off-campus apartments and houses, downtown bars (fake I.D.s abound), and frat houses. Less than 10 percent of students join one of the 30 fraternities or sororities. "Some people join them and find a lot of fun to be had by them. Others think they are silly," one student offers. Another mentions, "The Greek sororities and fraternities do a good job in community service work."

There are more than 250 clubs and organizations for students to join, including SUBOG, a student-run group that puts together entertainment programs for the school. "It is a very self-motivated school, in the sense that there is a lot available to those who get out of their dorms and find it," says a junior. Several campus-wide social events throughout the year attract students in large numbers. One undergrad tells us, "Spring Weekend is a big party tradition. There are cookouts, a fair, and parties everywhere." Another student is glad for the on-campus events, because, she laments, "there is nowhere else to go."

The town of Storrs offers few diversions, mostly in the form of a few local bars and hangouts; we hear that Thursday's dollar draft night is a particular favorite among students. For a temporary break from Storrs and the campus, Boston and New York are each less than three hours away by train. And, of course, students can always follow the Huskies to their many out-of-town championship tournaments.

UConn students depend on the Huskies for more than entertainment and excitement—they use sports to give them a common identity. "The importance we place on sporting events is unique," says a student. "It is good for school spirit; it is something really strong." When asked to comment on his school's athletic environment, another student sums it up nicely: "Sports scene? Well, it's UConn!" With both men's and women's basketball teams in regular contention for the NCAA championship, UConn students are understandably enthusiastic about supporting their Huskies. Crowds of student fans regularly flock to the Gampel Pavilion, the university's sports center, to scream their lungs out for their beloved team. Although basketball has long been UConn's number-one sport, many other intercollegiate sports teams are also considered powerhouses, including men's football, field hockey, baseball, and both men's and women's soccer. And when they're not watching a sport, chances are UConn students are playing one as part of the university's extensive intramural program. As one undergrad puts it: "Physical activity huge at UConn. The gym is packed, the stadiums are packed, the intramurals run out of space."

Test Scores (middle 50%):
SAT Verbal: 530–620
SAT Math: 550–640

HS Rank of Entering Freshmen:
Top 10%: 30%
Top 25%: 72%
Top 50%: 97%

Costs (2004–5)

Tuition and Fees, In-State: $7,308

Tuition and Fees, Out-of-State: $19,036

Room & Board: $7,300

Payment Plan(s): installment plan

THE EXPERTS SAY...

" Great athletics, a large variety of academic programs, and an affordable price tag make UConn a popular choice for high school students in the Northeast. "

" Many high school students use UConn as one of their safety schools. Not that there's anything wrong with that... "

Inst. Aid (est. 2003–04)

Institutional Aid, Need-Based: $15,295,184

Institutional Aid, Non-Need-Based: $5,598,841

FT Undergrads Receiving Aid: 45%
Avg. Amount per Student: $8,358

FT Undergrads Receiving Non-Need-Based Scholarship or Grant Aid: 11%
Avg. Amount per Student: $5,359

Of Those Receiving Any Aid:

Rec. Need-Based Scholarship or Grant Aid: 73%
Average Award: $5,316

Rec. Need-Based Self-Help Aid: 85%
Average Award: $3,708

Upon Graduation, Avg. Loan Debt per Student: $17,185

Financial Aid Deadline: rolling, 3/1 (priority)

Graduates

Going to Graduate School: 35% Within One Year

Companies Recruiting On Campus: 330

Alumni Giving: 24%

UNIVERSITY OF DALLAS

1845 East Northgate Drive, Irving, TX 75062-4736
Admissions Phone: (972) 721-5266; (800) 628-6999 (out-of-state) Fax: (972) 721-5017
Email: ugadmis@acad.udallas.edu
Website: www.udallas.edu

General Info

Type of School: private, coed, Roman Catholic

Setting: suburban

Academic Calendar: semester

Student Body

Full-Time Undergrads: 1,119
  Men: 44%, Women: 56%

Part-Time Undergrads: 131
  Men: 44%, Women: 56%

Total Undergrad Population:
  African American: 1%
  Asian American: 7%
  Latino: 15%
  Native American: <1%
  Caucasian: 65%
  International: 2%
  Out-of-State: 37%
  Living Off-Campus: 38%

Graduate and First-Professional Students: 1,907

Academics

Full-Time Faculty: 125
  With Ph.D.: 92%

Part-Time Faculty: 90
  With Ph.D.: 33%

Student/Faculty Ratio: 12:1

Most Popular Majors:
  English (9%)
  biology (8%)
  business leadership (6%)
  politics (6%)
  history (5%)

Freshmen Retention Rate: 73%

Graduation Rates:
  52% within four years
  60% within six years

Admissions

Regular Application Deadline: 8/1; 1/15 (priority)

Early Action Deadline: 12/1

Fall Transfer Deadline: 7/1

Spring Transfer Deadline: 12/1

Total # of Students Applied: 1,080
  Admitted: 966
  Enrolled: 299

Inside the Classroom

The University of Dallas consists of Constantin College (the undergraduate program), the Graduate School of Management, and the Braniff Graduate School of Liberal Arts. The core curriculum requires all students to take classes in the following disciplines: philosophy, English, math, fine arts, science, classics and modern languages, American civilization, Western Civilization, politics, economics, and theology. Majors are offered in art and art history, biology, chemistry, classics (Latin and Greek), computer science, drama, economics, economics and finance, education, English, history, mathematics, modern languages, philosophy, physics, politics, psychology, and theology. The university also offers a number of preprofessional programs. These include pre-architecture, predentistry, pre-engineering, prelaw, premedicine, pre-physical therapy, and Business Through Plan, an accelerated B.A./M.B.A. plan that enables students to earn an M.B.A. in half the time.

The university also offers a popular Rome program, in which students spend part of their sophomore year in Rome. According to the university, the Rome program is premised on the idea that "Rome brought together the Judeo-Christian revelation and the classical wisdom to form that Europe which was the progenitor of American ideals. Thus, to be a student in the Western World—to seek one's true heritage in the liberal arts—is to follow the path to Rome." The curriculum of the Rome program is designed to be congruous with the undergraduate educational experience offered at the university, and courses are selected from the core curriculum and taught primarily by UD professors. The university also offers summer programs in Rome for high school students, and the Eternal Cities Tour, which studies the art and architecture of Greece and Rome.

Roughly half of all UD students graduated in the top 10 percent of their high school classes and had respectable SAT and ACT scores. With fewer than 1,200 undergraduates in this private, Catholic school, making personal contact with professors is not a problem; the student/faculty ratio is a cozy 12:1. The school states that the phrase "the Catholic university for independent thinkers" best expresses the essence of the nationally respected university. The school is consistently ranked highly, and is in fact "one of only eight in Texas to receive Phi Beta Kappa status, and is one of 124 schools nationwide recognized for stressing character development among students."

Campus Environment

The 225-acre UD campus is located in Irving, Texas and is a mere 15 minutes away from downtown Dallas and 40 minutes from Fort Worth. Texas Stadium, home of the Dallas Cowboys, is located only four blocks away. Cars are permitted on campus for students in all grade levels, though the parking situation can get congested. All cars must be registered with the Campus Safety Office. The university has steadily grown since its founding in 1956, and there are currently 28 buildings on campus.

Students under the age of 21 are required to live on campus in one of the eight residence halls, or in the apartment complex, which is generally for upperclassmen. All incoming freshmen are placed in double rooms with a roommate. All eight halls are air-conditioned. The school states that six of the eight feature "two common corridors, two common bathroom facilities, a lounge/TV area, and a laundry room with coin-operated washers and dryers." The other two halls "consist of one floor each with one common corridor and bathroom facilities." Most halls have kitchen facilities for students' convenience. The university apartment complex "offers 22 two-bedroom (four-student occupancy) units, 11 one-bedroom (two-student occupancy) units and 1 (one-student occupancy) efficiency unit." The twelve three-story buildings within the complex are connected by exterior catwalks, and the apartment complex features a common laundry area, a central courtyard, and parking. All apartments are fully furnished with the exception of microwave ovens.

Student Life

University of Dallas offers a diverse array of clubs and organizations for students to get involved in. There are professional, departmental, political, and international organizations, as well as a number of volunteer/service groups like Best Buddies and social awareness organizations like Amnesty International. Among the more unique clubs are the Irish Ceili Dancing Club, Operation Starfish (volunteers through the arts and through an interfaith perspective), and the Dragon Role-Playing and Gaming Organization (which geekily explores "all types of role-playing and encourages fantastic creativity"). The student government communicates students concerns to the administration and works with the programming board to plan events and entertainment for campus. The Photography Club chronicles the happenings on campus and the lives of the students for the Crusader Yearbook.

The University of Dallas offers 15 intercollegiate sports for men and women at the Division III level. Soccer, volleyball, cross-country, basketball, softball, tennis, track and field, and golf are offered for women. Men's sports include soccer, cross-country, basketball, baseball, tennis, track and field, and golf. The athletics clubs include rowing, rugby football, sailing, a tactical operations club (paintball), and the Ultimate Frisbee and Rhetoric Club. This last club "seeks to promote good karma, foster community spirit, provide a forum in which students can hone their rhetorical skills, and to fulfill the great need of the students for Ultimate Frisbee."

Students take advantage of the fun and nightlife that can be found off campus as well, especially since they are in such close proximity to the Dallas/Fort Worth area. Texas Rangers baseball games and Dallas Stars hockey games are popular pastimes, and some students occasionally go to the Dallas Symphony and the Fort Worth Zoo. The Fort Worth Stockyards Station is a popular place, with 85,000 square feet of shopping, restaurants, and other forms of Texas-style fun.

Test Scores (middle 50%):
SAT Verbal: 540–680
SAT Math: 520–640
ACT Comp: 23–28
ACT English: 23–28
ACT Math: 22–28

HS Rank of Entering Freshmen:
Top 10%: 42%
Top 25%: 72%
Top 50%: 93%

THE EXPERTS SAY...

" The program in Rome is a wonderful option and much less jarring than many other study abroad programs, since courses are selected from the UD curriculum and are taught mostly by UD professors. "

" Shouldn't it be called the University of Irving? Southern Methodist University (which is actually in Dallas) is more fun. "

Costs (2004–5)

Tuition and Fees: $19,162

Room & Board: $6,736

Payment Plan(s): installment plan

Inst. Aid (2002–03)

Institutional Aid, Need-Based: $4,513,626

Institutional Aid, Non-Need-Based: $3,776,364

FT Undergrads Receiving Aid: 65%
Avg. Amount per Student: $14,144

FT Undergrads Receiving Non-Need-Based Scholarship or Grant Aid: 28%
Avg. Amount per Student: $9,352

Of Those Receiving Any Aid:

Rec. Need-Based Scholarship or Grant Aid: 69%
Average Award: $11,108

Rec. Need-Based Self-Help Aid: 76%
Average Award: $5,289

Upon Graduation, Avg. Loan Debt per Student: $20,836

Financial Aid Deadline: rolling, 3/1 (priority)

Graduates

Going to Graduate School: 43% Within One Year

Accepting Job Offer: 15% at time of graduation

Companies Recruiting On Campus: 38

Alumni Giving: 42%

UNIVERSITY OF DAYTON

300 College Park, Dayton, OH 45469-1300
Admissions Phone: (937) 229-4411; (800) 837-7433 Fax: (937) 229-4729
Email: admission@udayton.edu Website: admission.udayton.edu
Application Website: admission.udayton.edu/apply/application_login.asp

General Info

Type of School: private, coed, Roman Catholic

Setting: suburban

Academic Calendar: semester

Student Body

Full-Time Undergrads: 6,576
Men: 50%, Women: 50%

Part-Time Undergrads: 391
Men: 57%, Women: 43%

Total Undergrad Population:
African American: 5%
Asian American: 1%
Latino: 2%
Caucasian: 87%
International: 1%
Out-of-State: 34%
Living Off-Campus: 21%
In Fraternities: 15%
In Sororities: 18%

Graduate and First-Professional Students: 3,181

Academics

Full-Time Faculty: 401
With Ph.D.: 94%

Part-Time Faculty: 421

Student/Faculty Ratio: 15:1

Most Popular Majors:
communication (8%)
teacher education (8%)
economics and finance (5%)
marketing (4%)
psychology (4%)

Completing 2 or More Majors: 8%

Freshmen Retention Rate: 86%

Graduation Rates:
57% within four years
76% within six years

Computers: Computer Required

Admissions

Regular Application Deadline: 1/1 (priority)

Fall Transfer Deadline: 6/15

Total # of Students Applied: 7,626
Admitted: 6,247
Enrolled: 1,884

# of Students Waitlisted: 15
Students Accepting Place: 7
Waitlisted Students Admitted: 6

Inside the Classroom

The largest private university in Ohio and the tenth-largest Catholic university in the country, the University of Dayton offers 70 academic programs in its four divisions: arts and sciences, business, education and allied professions, and engineering. Standout programs include engineering, sports management, management information systems, teaching, and music therapy. Known for its campus-wide commitment to social advocacy, UD was the first university in the country to offer an undergraduate degree in human rights.

"The academic atmosphere is serious but not oppressive," says a biology/religious studies major. Another student comments, "Sometimes it is hard to balance out academics and involvement in organizations. However, the programs are centered around what happens in the real world and acclimates us to that." Says a senior, "The only competition at UD is positive competition that serves to push people to succeed." But some students object to a new grading scale: "It will just take some getting used to."

Students rave about their close "collaboration" with their professors." The workload at times can get overbearing," says a student, "but most of the professors will work around your schedule to do what they can to help you out." A senior remarks, "All my professors in four years have known my name and most have been more than willing to help me outside of class." A guidance counselor lauds the individual attention here, and class sizes in this "nurturing, caring environment" are small—27 students on average. Dan Curran, UD's new and first non-Marianist president, "makes sure that he makes himself available to all the students," says one student.

The University Special Admits Program serves entering students who need additional support to realize their full potential. For honors students, "the Berry Scholars program is absolutely AMAZING!" raves a senior. In business, 15 undergraduate finance students manage a university investment portfolio of $3 million, putting UD in the top ranks of schools that give students real money to manage. UD also provides "many, many service opportunities and studies in foreign countries." A senior states, "UD has funded me to study in Cameroon (Africa), Guatemala, Haiti, and Mexico... It has challenged to live a life dedicated to scholarship, leadership, and service."

Campus Environment

An Ohio counselor lauds UD's "friendly, compact, beautiful campus" and the 16-block "ghetto" area where students move in junior and senior year. "More than 90 percent of the students live on campus all four of their years while at Dayton," a student explains. "Wherever you live your first year, you are going to love that place. Everyone on campus is biased towards their first-year resident hall because they had such an awesome experience their first year."

For upperclassmen, "The university owns more than 400 houses that surround the main campus that range from 2–12 person houses," a student tells us. "These student-housing communities, the Ghetto and the Darkside, create an extremely friendly and fun environment for all students." Adds another, "The houses are old and worn, but it is a great environment to have a whole neighborhood of houses all together, living next door to your friends."

The campus has some outstanding facilities, including a 1.3 million-volume library with the largest collection of published material on the Virgin Mary in the world ("the Vatican is number 2," brags a junior). A new living and learning arts complex called ArtStreet that will combine residences and art spaces is slated for fall 2005. UD is also one of the most wired universities in the nation. "Before students move to campus, they meet their roommates online and get a head start on their first-year humanities classes," explains a school official. "The day they move to campus, their computer is waiting, loaded with Microsoft and Lotus Notes software and connected to the Internet."

Student Life

UD students are definitely a close-knit group. "Community is probably the most emphasized word at UD," agrees a senior. "Everyone here at UD is friendly, from the students to the administrators to the cafeteria ladies," we're told, "always open to knowing new people." Even that special someone: "A large number of the student population meet their future spouse while here at UD." Students usually come from Catholic high schools and middle and upper class backgrounds. "It's not the most diverse crowd, but we're working on it," says a history major. A biology/religious studies major admits, "A totally alternative, punk type student might feel a little lonely here." But politics are said to be "liberal for a Catholic university."

Students blow off steam at local bars like BW3s, Tim's, Flanagan's, Fieldhouse and dance clubs like Have a Nice Day Café or Pearl, but on the weekends, the nightlife "mostly consists of spending time with friends and cruising around the ghetto, jumping from one student house to the next." Rowdiness in the ghetto has led to friction between students and the administration: "Homecoming had been banned because there were some outrageous events that took place," reports a student. Another student comments, "The alcohol scene is really improving in recent years though, so administration won that battle." Some students resent UD's "party school reputation," but nondrinkers needn't worry: UD sponsors "a ton" of non-alcoholic events. About 20 percent of students join fraternities and sororities, which include professional and academic organizations. (But students cannot join a fraternity or sorority until their second semester and cannot live in Greek housing during their first year.)

UD competes at the NCAA Division I level (except for football, which is NCAA Division I-AA). "Basketball unites the UD campus more than almost anything else," a student comments. "Our soccer teams are also in the tops in attendance in the country as well." More than 70 percent of students participate in intramurals, which are "huge, with over 100 activities offered."

UD is proud of its religious traditions. On December 8 (Feast of the Immaculate Conception), the University celebrates its traditional "Christmas on Campus," where students "adopt" area children and treat them to seasonal shows, displays, and food. For religious services, there's the "Ghetto Mass" with a live band (bongos included). More than 1,000 students perform some sort of community service each year. "The campus is extremely into social activism, such as the School of the America's protest, Iraq issues, etc.," comments a student. UD has the largest campus ministry program in the country ("it is outstanding, constantly involved, and the best thing at UD in my opinion," one student asserts).

Test Scores (middle 50%):
SAT Verbal: 510–620
SAT Math: 520–640
ACT Comp: 22–28
ACT English: 21–28
ACT Math: 21–28
HS Rank of Entering Freshmen:
Top 10%: 19%
Top 25%: 46%
Top 50%: 79%

Costs (2004–5)

Tuition and Fees: $20,250
Room & Board: $6,300
Payment Plan(s): deferred payment plan, pre-payment plan

THE EXPERTS SAY...

" UD's endowment has grown dramatically due to successful fundraising on the part of the school. Good to know that $37 million of that money is earmarked for scholarships. "

" UD students form a tight community, drawn together by technology, community service, and life in 'the ghetto.' "

Inst. Aid (2002–03)

Institutional Aid, Need-Based: $23,976,946
Institutional Aid, Non-Need-Based: $9,019,008
FT Undergrads Receiving Aid: 58%
  Avg. Amount per Student: $13,258
FT Undergrads Receiving Non-Need-Based Scholarship or Grant Aid: 31%
  Avg. Amount per Student: $4,399
Of Those Receiving Any Aid:
Rec. Need-Based Scholarship or Grant Aid: 98%
  Average Award: $8,254
Rec. Need-Based Self-Help Aid: 99%
  Average Award: $4,807
Upon Graduation, Avg. Loan Debt per Student: $21,467
Financial Aid Deadline: 3/31 (priority)

Graduates

Accepting Job Offer: 26% at time of graduation
Companies Recruiting On-Campus: 275

UNIVERSITY OF DELAWARE

116 Hullihen Hall, Newark, DE 19716-6210
Admissions Phone: (302) 831-8123 Fax: (302) 831-6905
Email: admissions@udel.edu Website: www.udel.edu
Application Website: www.udel.edu/apply

General Info

Type of School: public, coed

Setting: suburban

Academic Calendar: 4-1-4

Student Body

Full-Time Undergrads: 14,816
  Men: 42%, Women: 58%

Part-Time Undergrads: 992
  Men: 41%, Women: 59%

Total Undergrad Population:
  African American: 6%
  Asian American: 3%
  Latino: 3%
  Native American: <1%
  Caucasian: 85%
  International: 1%
  Out-of-State: 58%
  Living Off-Campus: 53%
  In Fraternities: 15%
  In Sororities: 15%

Graduate and First-Professional
  Students: 3,301

Academics

Full-Time Faculty: 1,111
  With Ph.D.: 83%

Part-Time Faculty: 260
  With Ph.D.: 38%

Student/Faculty Ratio: 13:1

Most Popular Majors:
  business administration (7%)
  elementary teacher education
  (5%)
  psychology (5%)
  biological sciences (5%)
  English (4%)

Completing 2 or More Majors: 6%

Freshmen Retention Rate: 90%

Graduation Rates:
  57% within four years
  74% within six years

Admissions

Regular Application Deadline: 2/15;
  1/15 (priority)

Early Decision Deadline(s): 11/15

Fall Transfer Deadline: 5/1

Spring Transfer Deadline: 11/15

Total # of Students Applied: 22,020
  Admitted: 9,267
  Enrolled: 3,440

Inside the Classroom

"One of the top universities in the nation!" declares an overenthusiastic New Jersey guidance counselor, who further describes the University of Delaware as "similar to Princeton." Before you dismiss this claim out of hand, consider some of this state-assisted, privately controlled university's special study options, such as a highly selective Honors Program. Students decide each semester, in consultation with their faculty and program advisers, where and how they'd like to pursue Honors work in the classroom. Freshmen only take about half their work in Honors, and upperclassmen take as many or as few Honors courses as they want. Honors enrolls 500 new freshmen per year.

There's also the Undergraduate Research Program, in which undergrads work as research assistants for faculty members. Approximately 600 students—including freshmen—participate in the research program each year; many students progress to heading their own projects, under the tutelage of a faculty member.

Another option that sets UD apart: More than 65 UD-sponsored study abroad programs are offered in more than 30 subjects in 25 countries (not even counting programs in other parts of the United States). (An interesting fact: The University of Delaware was the first U.S. school to offer a study abroad program, back in 1923.)

Students at UD can choose from more than 120 majors in six undergraduate colleges: arts and science; agriculture and natural resources; business and economics; engineering; health and nursing; and human resources, education, and public policy. The college of engineering is a real standout, say students and high school guidance counselors; engineering students "get tons of respect for the amount of work they do," according to one chemical engineering major.

Freshman lectures tend to be "huge, with little student–teacher interaction," notes a recent grad, who quickly adds that this situation greatly improves after the students' first year. In fact, 79 percent of UD classes have fewer than 40 students; junior- and senior-year seminars may have fewer than 10 students. And technology can help bring students and teachers closer together: "Our school is really net-friendly, so professors are usually very accessible, and tend to post notes and assignments online—a huge help," says a junior.

Students agree that the academic atmosphere at UD "is pretty laid-back." "There was a lack of intensity with most classes which was quite refreshing," a recent grad comments. Of course, workload and competitiveness do vary by major.

Campus Environment

Campus housing holds over 7,000 students—barely. Overcrowding is a big problem here, maybe because students are guaranteed housing through senior year. Unfortunately, freshmen are the ones who suffer: Students tell us that the school has been crowding double rooms with three freshmen instead of two, and even putting groups of students in the lounges of some dorms on a temporary basis. (The university's response: "Each student in extended housing will receive a 25 percent rebate on housing costs for each full week of residence until a permanent space is offered.") Most juniors and seniors escape to on- and off-campus apartments, even though, as one student warns, "apartment housing within walking distance of campus is EXTREMELY expensive." Fraternity and sorority housing is available to those students involved in Greek life. Honors housing is another attractive option: Honors freshman halls house around 65 percent Honors and 35 percent non-Honors students.

The beautiful 2,346-acre campus is pretty spread out, but shuttle buses loop around the campus to transport students. Other shuttle buses go from the campus to various points in Newark. "Students don't need cars to get around," affirms a recent graduate. "There's tons of public transportation." I-95 is just minutes from campus, and it's easy to catch a ride with someone on weekends into Philly or D.C.

Newark measures just nine square miles, with a population of under 30,000 (including the 14,000 UD undergrads). The townspeople, many of whom are UD alumni, are very involved in all types of school events. They also reap the benefits of UD's on-campus Ice Arenas, which happen to be the training spot for some of the world's top figure skaters, and regularly host national and world figure skating exhibitions.

Student Life

Asked why she would recommend UD to high school seniors, a loyal alum simply answered, "The people!" There's certainly an open and friendly atmosphere both on campus and in the charming town of Newark. Townies and students alike take special pride in UD's winning football team; the Blue Hens are consistently ranked among Division I-AA's top 20. Fans go wild when the UD cheerleaders ring the Victory Bell in the southwest corner of Delaware Stadium each and every time the Blue Hens score. And "many people like to tailgate before the football games," we hear. Basketball is also very popular, and many students take part in intramural sports.

The administration has done a lot recently to try to eradicate alcohol and drugs from the dorms, and students agree that the crackdown has been pretty successful. However, alcohol still flows freely off campus and remains "the main way of entertaining the students." One student tells us that "drugs (especially marijuana and prescription drugs) are very accessible to anyone and everyone who wants them and is willing to pay," but another student insists that "drugs aren't really a factor" at UD.

"Fraternities and sororities have a large amount of influence over the overall social life," states a recent grad. Another student explains: "It's an easy way for people to make friends." While the Greeks do throw parties, "not too many people attend," says a student. "People usually opt out to go to house parties hosted by friends." Other popular student groups include religious groups ("they advertise and try to recruit people constantly"), political and cultural clubs, and comedy and singing clubs.

The student body is not very diverse—"mostly preppy kids from Delaware, South Jersey, and Maryland," says a young alum. Another student's colorful description: "Everyone's concerned with image, driving around expensive cars or talking on a cell phone while smoking their cigarette." The administration, through its Commission to Promote Racial and Cultural Diversity, hopes to change the homogeneity through programs such as the Center for Black Culture, which provides support for African American students, and the English Language Institute, which aids international students.

# of Students Waitlisted: 3,577
 Students Accepting Place: 1,601
 Waitlisted Students Admitted: 138

Applied Early Decision: 1,519
 Early Decision Admitted: 792

Test Scores (middle 50%):
 SAT Verbal: 540–620
 SAT Math: 550–650
 ACT Comp: 24–28
 ACT English: 23–28
 ACT Math: 24–29

HS Rank of Entering Freshmen:
 Top 10%: 35%
 Top 25%: 73%
 Top 50%: 96%

Avg. HS GPA: 3.5

THE EXPERTS SAY...

" With an excellent honors program, undergrad research opportunities, and 65 study abroad programs, UD is gaining national prominence. The engineering program is top-notch. "

" Freshmen beware: Dorms are over-crowded and you might get stuck in a lounge. "

Costs (2003–04)

Tuition and Fees, In-State: $6,498

Tuition and Fees, Out-of-State: $16,028

Room & Board: $6,118

Payment Plan(s): installment plan

Inst. Aid (est. 2003–04)

FT Undergrads Receiving Aid: 39%
 Avg. Amount per Student: $9,750

FT Undergrads Receiving Non-Need-Based Scholarship or Grant Aid: 20%
 Avg. Amount per Student: $4,070

Of Those Receiving Any Aid:

Rec. Need-Based Scholarship or Grant Aid: 75%
 Average Award: $5,600

Rec. Need-Based Self-Help Aid: 72%
 Average Award: $5,000

Upon Graduation, Avg. Loan Debt per Student: $13,806

Financial Aid Deadline: 3/15, 2/1 (priority)

Graduates

Going to Graduate School:
 18% Within One Year

Companies Recruiting On Campus:
 300

UNIVERSITY OF DENVER

2197 South University Boulevard, Denver, CO 80208
Admissions Phone: (303) 871-2036; (800) 525-9495 Fax: (303) 871-3301
Email: admission@du.edu Website: www.du.edu
Application Website: www.du.edu/admission/apply.html

General Info

Type of School: private, coed

Academic Calendar: quarter, the College of Law is on the semester system

Student Body

Full-Time Undergrads: 3,959
  Men: 48%, Women: 52%

Part-Time Undergrads: 473
  Men: 18%, Women: 82%

Total Undergrad Population:
  African American: 3%
  Asian American: 5%
  Latino: 7%
  Native American: 1%
  Caucasian: 80%
  International: 4%
  Out-of-State: 50%
  Living Off-Campus: 51%
  In Fraternities: 23%
  In Sororities: 22%

Graduate and First-Professional Students: 5,065

Academics

Full-Time Faculty: 439
  With Ph.D.: 92%

Part-Time Faculty: 486

Student/Faculty Ratio: 9:1

Freshmen Retention Rate: 85%

Graduation Rates:
  54% within four years
  69% within six years

Admissions

Regular Application Deadline: 1/15

Early Action Deadline: 11/15

Fall Transfer Deadline: 2/1 (priority)

Total # of Students Applied: 4,334
  Admitted: 3,405
  Enrolled: 1,021

Waitlist Available

Test Scores (middle 50%):
  SAT Verbal: 510–620
  SAT Math: 520–630
  ACT Comp: 22–27

HS Rank of Entering Freshmen:
  Top 10%: 35%
  Top 25%: 60%
  Top 50%: 88%

Avg. HS GPA: 3.49

Inside the Classroom

The University of Denver is known for its business programs—almost as much as for its skiing. *Forbes* magazine recently ranked the Daniels College of Business among the top 25 regional business schools for salary return on educational investment. Hotel, restaurant, and tourism management programs are strong, with hands-on training in a four-star restaurant in downtown Denver and a multibillion dollar ski resort in Vail. Digital media, international studies and foreign languages, communications, and psychology programs are also excellent; DU's creative writing program, which celebrated its 50th anniversary in 1997, is nationally ranked. Atmospheric physics studies benefit from the Rocky Mountain environment. DU's Meyer-Womble Observatory on Mount Evans, a 14,148-foot peak, has the second-highest vantage point of any telescope on Earth and a resolution near that of Hubble Space Telescope's.

Although some say the liberal arts have been eclipsed by preprofessional training at DU, the newly revised core curriculum provides a true liberal education. General education requirements include foundation courses in the arts and humanities, creative expression, English, foreign language, mathematics and computer science, natural science, and social sciences. The core component consists of interdisciplinary courses in three broad themes: Communities and Environments, Self and Identities, and Change and Continuity.

DU runs on a quarter system, which means that midterms and finals come up fast. Students seem to handle the workload pretty well, knowing when to hit the books and when to put them down. Students like DU's relatively small size. With 4,000 undergrads, classes are small, and faculty are accessible: The student/faculty ratio is 9:1. Students meet up with professors starting at freshman orientation. The University of Denver Campus Connections (UDCC) program is a required course for first-year students, who select faculty mentors at seminars given during the lively SOAR (Student Orientation and Registration) period. Pioneers in the Rockies, DU's retreat in the Rocky Mountains, also gives first-year students the chance to meet classmates and faculty.

DU is big on combining classroom study with practical experience. The Global Scholars program gives students the chance to study abroad for a quarter. DU's Women's College offers weekend classes for working women. The Partners in Scholarship program offers research grants for undergrads. Outside of the classroom, Denver itself provides a wealth of jobs and internships.

Campus Environment

DU's 125-acre high-altitude campus is located within the city limits of Denver in the Rocky Mountains. While not a college town, Denver offers just about anything students might want in terms of shopping, food, and entertainment. The campus is about an hour away from some of the best skiing in the world, and students take advantage of nearby Echo Lake and Estes Park for hiking and camping.

DU is investing more than $350 million in new and refurbished buildings as part of a plan to unite all university programs on its University Park campus. One of the jewels of these efforts is the new Ritchie Center for Sports & Wellness, a facility that rivals the nation's best health clubs.

DU's housing include traditional residence halls, two-to-five person suites, apartments, and living-learning communities. The five living and learning communities are located on designated floors in the residence halls, with the themes of leadership, global studies, wellness, the environment, and scholarly pursuit. Freshmen live in either Johnson-McFarlane ("J-Mac") or Centennial Hall. J-Mac gets better marks for its location near classrooms and its surrounding residential area; rooms are also larger than in Centennial. The school does guarantee housing, but 57 percent of students live off-campus, since housing in Denver is available and good. Freshmen and sophomores are required to live on campus. Freshmen must purchase one of two meal plans, both providing a certain number of all-you-can-eat meals and meal plan "cash" to purchase snacks and food at the school's pubs and cafeterias.

Parking is a problem at DU. While freshmen are allowed to have cars, permits are required and are given out by lottery. Although Denver transit is good, most students do risk the parking tickets for the essential skiing trips and the occasional trip to CU Boulder, 30 minutes away.

Student Life

There's no football at DU, but the hockey fans and skiers barely notice. DU's ski team recently received a record 17th NCAA Division I national title. Skiing is a passion with DU students, and many choose the school for its location. During the school's Winter Carnival in January, students ski, snowboard, and enjoy all the outdoor activities the Rockies have to offer. Pioneers hockey is nothing if not huge, with an award-winning coach and team. Students turn out in droves for the game against archrival Colorado College. DU fields 19 varsity teams and has 23 club sports and 18 intramural sports. And students don't have to go off campus for big-name entertainment: The Ritchie Center's Magness Arena hosts major concerts, as well as sports competitions.

Greek life is a major force on campus, and 31 percent of men and 22 percent of women pledge. Greek houses are on campus for the most part, and the Greeks provide entertainment for the Pioneer partygoers. Annual homecoming week is a big to-do. With a host of microbreweries in Denver, there's also great bar scene for students in town. There are over 120 clubs and student organizations to get involved in.

DU's student body is fairly homogeneous; more than three-quarters of the student body is white, and most come from upper-middle-class backgrounds. There are some nontraditional students: 16 percent are over 25. There's a visible contingent of 21st century hippies to counterbalance the Greeks and ski jocks. All Pioneers value the connectedness of DU life, where professors know students by name, and students say hello to one another on campus. But unlike many small schools, there's also the big city life of Denver to offer all kinds of entertainment, and the slopes are just an hour away.

Costs (2004–5)

Tuition and Fees: $26,610

Room & Board: $8,363

THE EXPERTS SAY...

" A perfect fit for the business major who loves to ski. The hotel management and creative writing programs are top of the line. "

" If you don't know how to ski, you'll have to learn. If you don't like hockey, you're out of luck. "

Inst. Aid (2002–03)

Institutional Aid, Need-Based: $15,796,454

Institutional Aid, Non-Need-Based: $6,730,158

FT Undergrads Receiving Aid: 41% Avg. Amount per Student: $17,271

FT Undergrads Receiving Non-Need-Based Scholarship or Grant Aid: 24% Avg. Amount per Student: $4,839

Of Those Receiving Any Aid:

Rec. Need-Based Scholarship or Grant Aid: 97% Average Award: $12,743

Rec. Need-Based Self-Help Aid: 79% Average Award: $5,004

Upon Graduation, Avg. Loan Debt per Student: $23,138

Financial Aid Deadline: 2/15 (priority)

UNIVERSITY OF FLORIDA

201 Criser Hall, Box 114000, Gainesville, FL 32611-4000
Admissions Phone: (352) 392-1365 Website: www.ufl.edu
Application Website: www.reg.ufl.edu/apppath.html

General Info

Type of School: public, coed
Setting: suburban
Academic Calendar: semester

Student Body

Full-Time Undergrads: 30,977
  Men: 46%, Women: 54%

Part-Time Undergrads: 2,478
  Men: 53%, Women: 47%

Total Undergrad Population:
  African American: 9%
  Asian American: 7%
  Latino: 12%
  Native American: 1%
  Caucasian: 70%
  International: 1%
  Out-of-State: 5%
  Living Off-Campus: 79%
  In Fraternities: 15%
  In Sororities: 15%

Graduate and First-Professional
  Students: 13,876

Academics

Full-Time Faculty: 1,679
  With Ph.D.: 92%

Part-Time Faculty: 41
  With Ph.D.: 93%

Student/Faculty Ratio: 22:1

Most Popular Majors:
  business administration
    management (9%)
  finance, general (5%)
  psychology, general (5%)
  political science & government (4%)
  public relations & org.
    communications (3%)

Completing 2 or More Majors: 3%

Freshmen Retention Rate: 93%

Graduation Rates:
  50% within four years
  77% within six years

Admissions

Regular Application Deadline: 1/12

Early Decision Deadline(s): 10/1

Total # of Students Applied: 22,973
  Admitted: 12,029
  Enrolled: 6,596

Applied Early Decision: 2,836
  Early Decision Admitted: 1,792

Inside the Classroom

The University of Florida offers more than 100 undergraduate majors, from agricultural operations management to zoology. Its 20 colleges and schools include journalism and communications, engineering, education, business administration, and liberal arts and sciences. Preprofessional and career-oriented majors are among the school's strongest and most popular programs. There are many special academic options available as well, including internships, study abroad in more than 30 countries, and an excellent honors program.

All students must fulfill the 36-hour General Education Program, which requires courses in the following areas: composition; mathematical sciences; humanities; social and behavioral sciences; physical and biological sciences; and cultural diversity. The university also has what it calls the Gordon Rule, a measure to ensure that all students show proficiency in writing and math. Guidance counselors praise the high-tech advances UF has made in recent years, increasing students' computer access.

Introductory-level courses are, as one student puts it, "a piece of cake." The difficulty rises considerably, however, in certain courses and programs. "Competition is always very high among premed students," said one student. "But some of the professors realize that we all want to be doctors or work in health care helping others, so in turn we should learn to help out each other rather than work against each other."

With so many students, it's difficult for professors to provide much individual attention. "You can establish one-on-relationships, but you have to go the extra mile and seek out the professor," said one student. "Otherwise you're just a number." There are many advantages to the university's large size, however, including the variety of courses and the availability of high-quality resources and facilities for undergraduates. For example, the University Scholars Program gives undergrads the opportunity to work one-on-one with UF faculty on selected research projects.

Campus Environment

The sprawling, 2,000-acre campus, while located in the midst of lush Floridian foliage, actually looks like a small, quaint city. Prominent features include the cavernous Ben Griffin Stadium, which seats over 72,000 and is referred to affectionately as "The Swamp"; the health science complex, which houses Shands Hospital; and Lake Alice, which separates the buildings on the southwestern fringes from the main campus. The lake and its surrounding grounds are a source of caution and curiosity, since alligators live in the waters. Towards dusk, a huge cloud of bats emerges from a lakeside bathhouse to feed on airborne insect life ... reportedly a remarkable sight.

With the addition of three new dorms in recent years, housing options have improved. Housing options range from suite-style living in the high-rise Beaty Towers and the more stately Keys Complex to more conventional dorms like Riker and North Halls. The only single-gender dorm is Mallory Hall, which houses about 160 women. And in case you ever decide to fly directly over campus in a plane, the linking of Fletcher, Sledd, and Murphree Halls forms the shape of a giant "UF" that's easily visible from the air. According to one senior, availability can be a problem: "Lots of students get turned away, even though more dorms are always being built."

Fortunately, off-campus housing is plentiful for those with the initiative to look for it. "There are tons of apartment complexes and houses off campus," said one student. Another adds, "Some students who can afford the price tag live in luxurious new complexes. It's almost like vacationing. And the free bus service to campus also makes living off-campus a feasible arrangement." Fraternity and sorority housing is also available.

Many students don't pull their punches when they decribe the town of Gainesville. "It's a small town consisting mainly of rednecks—there's no other way to describe them—with a university smack in the middle," said one. Another had issues with the town's crime rate. A third student, however, said, "The campus itself is safe enough. I've never had any problems, and neither have my friends."

Student Life

Guidance counselors around the country acknowledge UF's rep as a party school. "If you're looking for rowdiness," said one junior, "this is the school for you." Finding a party on a Saturday night can be as simple as walking in a straight line. Downtown Gainesville also offers bars and nightclubs that are popular with students. "There are always clubs and bars open every night 'til 2 a.m. with different specials every night," said one knowledgeable senior. "After a while you learn the rotation as to which clubs are good on which nights." Football games tend to bring out the best—or the worst, depending on your point of view—in the school's partygoers. As one sophomore puts it, "If you need to do work on a game weekend, leave town."

The social scene, while active, is as mixed as the student population. "You'll always have a mixture of personalities everywhere you go. You just have to find your niche and fit in where you can," said one student. However, one guidance counselor chides the administration for "their lack of pursuing minority enrollment." About 15 percent of the student body joins fraternities and sororities, which provide an easy way to make friends in a sea of college-aged humanity. "The frats and sororities are active in their recruitment of freshmen," said one student, "and a lot of extroverted and sociable people are drawn to this." Frats are not the only option, however, with over 450 student clubs and organizations available.

One thing that unites the student body is a swelling pride in UF's sports teams. There's a reason why "Go Gators!" is a rallying cry heard beyond the state of Florida: Great facilities and a whopping budget earmarked for sports attract the best athletes in the country. Football and basketball are the headline-making teams to watch, and alumni descend upon the school in hordes for games. "I was born a Gator," said one. "My crib was actually orange and blue." In 2002, *Sports Illustrated* ranked the university second in the nation in its list of the best colleges for women athletes, and for good reason: The school spends lavishly on sports for women, and the athletes return the favor in victory. In the 1990s, three NCAA Division I titles were earned by its women's tennis team alone.

Test Scores (middle 50%):
SAT Verbal: 560–660
SAT Math: 580–680
ACT Comp: 24–29

HS Rank of Entering Freshmen:
Top 10%: 79%
Top 25%: 90%
Top 50%: 97%

Avg. HS GPA: 3.9

Costs (2003–04)

Tuition and Fees, In-State: $2,780

Tuition and Fees, Out-of-State: $13,808

Room & Board: $5,800

Payment Plan(s): pre-payment plan

THE EXPERTS SAY...

" The variety of majors and strong research facilities make UF an attractive option for almost any student. And the Gators are second to very few, if any, in the country. "

" Gators and Greeks will provide distractions galore for the undisciplined student. Play hard if you must, but work hard, too. "

Inst. Aid (2002–03)

Institutional Aid, Need-Based: $9,860,373

Institutional Aid, Non-Need-Based: $13,248,826

FT Undergrads Receiving Aid: 38%
Avg. Amount per Student: $9,380

FT Undergrads Receiving Non-Need-Based Scholarship or Grant Aid: 43%
Avg. Amount per Student: $3,622

Of Those Receiving Any Aid:

Rec. Need-Based Scholarship or Grant Aid: 64%
Average Award: $4,577

Rec. Need-Based Self-Help Aid: 59%
Average Award: $3,660

Upon Graduation, Avg. Loan Debt per Student: $14,449

Financial Aid Deadline: 3/15 (priority)

Graduates

Companies Recruiting On-Campus: 608

Alumni Giving: 21%

UNIVERSITY OF GEORGIA

212 Terrell Hall, Athens, GA 30602-1633
Admissions Phone: (706) 542-8776 Fax: (706) 542-1466
Email: undergrad@admissions.uga.edu Website: www.uga.edu
Application Website: www.admissons.uga.edu/app_info/

General Info

Type of School: public, coed
Setting: suburban
Academic Calendar: semester

Student Body

Full-Time Undergrads: 22,814
  Men: 43%, Women: 57%

Part-Time Undergrads: 2,160
  Men: 47%, Women: 53%

Total Undergrad Population:
  African American: 5%
  Asian American: 4%
  Latino: 2%
  Native American: <1%
  Caucasian: 88%
  International: 1%
  Out-of-State: 11%
  Living Off-Campus: 71%
  In Fraternities: 18%
  In Sororities: 22%

Graduate and First-Professional
  Students: 8,463

Academics

Full-Time Faculty: 1,689
  With Ph.D.: 94%

Part-Time Faculty: 335
  With Ph.D.: 60%

Student/Faculty Ratio: 14:1

Most Popular Majors:
  biology (3%)
  political science (3%)
  psychology (3%)
  art (2%)
  finance (2%)

Freshmen Retention Rate: 93%

Graduation Rates:
  40% within four years
  72% within six years

Admissions

Regular Application Deadline: 2/1

Early Action Deadline: 11/1

Fall Transfer Deadline: 4/1 (priority)

Spring Transfer Deadline: 10/1 (priority)

Total # of Students Applied: 11,813
  Admitted: 8,885
  Enrolled: 5,190

Inside the Classroom

Schools within the university include the College of Agriculture and Environmental Sciences; the Franklin College of Arts and Sciences; the Terry College of Business; the College of Education; the School of Environmental Design; the College of Family and Consumer Sciences; the School of Social Work; and the Grady College of Journalism and Mass Communication. The preprofessional programs are strong: One Georgia guidance counselor tells us the journalism and veterinary programs are excellent, while another counselor praises the business college.

Like the campus itself, UGA's academic offerings are vast: Students choose from 171 different majors. Some freshman classes can number over 300 students, and may be taught by graduate TA's; guidance counselors worry about their kids "getting lost in the crowd." Although exposure to professors can be somewhat limited in the huge intro classes, many students say that professors are accessible, especially by email. UGA has a renowned honors program, which admits less than ten percent of incoming freshmen. In addition to its academic excellence, a perk of the honors program is smaller classes. "My introductory classes mostly had about 20 people," said one student in the program, "while my roommate's had over 100." Students in the honors program also work more closely with professors and advisors than do other students. "I've received more individual attention here than I would have received at any of the other schools I applied to," said one junior in the program.

Students call the workload "moderate" (involving "more studying than actual homework"), but note that it can be more intense in the sciences. A junior premed student says that the academic atmosphere is very competitive, and that for many students, "a B is just as bad as an F."

Students who live in Georgia and maintain a B average through high school can attend state schools tuition free and receive a stipend each semester to help with the cost of books through Georgia's HOPE scholarship. Matriculated students need to maintain good academic standing, and a junior notes that "because of the HOPE scholarship, the university has many students who take academics seriously, and in almost any given class, you can expect to see many overachievers and driven students."

Campus Environment

Spread over 600 acres, UGA's campus is sprawling. Students call the campus "gorgeous," and seem to find it a friendly and manageable place, despite its size. Just about everybody gushes about the surrounding town of Athens, where students spend much of their free time. As one junior puts it, "The people are friendly, the music scene is renowned, the bars are numerous, and every night is a party." Though small and friendly, Athens offers a "big-city feel," with the cultural, artistic, and social offerings of a larger city.

Housing is a sore point. There's a shortage of on-campus housing now, which the administration is trying to remedy, but which leaves students grousing. "Housing is cramped and rarely available," grumbles one senior. Dorms vary in acceptability, with recently renovated dorms scoring high marks, and older, un-air conditioned dorms riling students assigned to them. Off-campus housing offerings are varied, and while some students think housing off campus is overpriced, others say that you can find really nice digs if you look early enough.

The campus bus system is extensive, and students rely on it to get around campus. "You definitely do not need a car," says one junior, "but it does make life easier." The town of Athens has a bus service, but many off-campus students have cars. The campus is described as "very safe" and "well lit, with call boxes all over campus and a very obvious police presence." Students feel safe in downtown Athens, but some prefer to travel in groups at night.

The campus has a new, state-of-the-art athletic center, rated by *Sports Illustrated* as one of the best in the country. One junior describes it as "incredible, with indoor swimming pools and a climbing wall, weight room, basketball courts, and classes in yoga, martial arts, and dancing."

Student Life

No doubt about it: Football is huge at Georgia. During the season, weekends are dominated by home games. Most students seem to love the great parties and school spirit that football mania brings, but a few complain that on gameday weekends, "the campus is bombarded with tailgaiters, alumni, and lots of boozing Bulldog fans." Intramural sports are popular as well.

As you might expect at a huge school like UGA, there are hundreds of clubs and activities available, and students say that joining clubs helps make a giant school seem more personal. While a few students believe that Greek life is losing popularity, fraternities and sororities are still a major presence on campus. A (non-Greek) junior's explanation: "They are popular because they all are rich kids and it provides instant security at such a big school." But another student notes, "Although it may seem like everyone is in a fraternity or sorority, the actual number is around 18 percent of the student body. There are so many other clubs to join that it is possible to have fun and not be Greek."

While students focus on academics during the week, one senior describes the prime weekend activity as "drinking, drinking, drinking." The administration strictly prohibits alcohol in the dorms, but students report that keg parties abound in the fraternities and sororities, and that the town of Athens has dozens of student-dominated bars. "Drugs, on the other hand, are more popular with the area high schoolers than with the college crowd," reveals a senior.

Most students seem to agree that at a school of this size, you are bound to find like-minded people and carve out a niche for yourself. Says a UGA junior, "I honestly can't think of someone who wouldn't fit in. Whatever your interests are, there is bound to be at least one student organization involved in it." Still, students note a lack of diversity, and describe the typical student as "from the Southeast, middle class, and somewhat conservative." There's not a huge minority presence at Georgia, and since a recent federal court decision knocked down race-based admissions in Georgia, UGA's administration is debating ways to recruit more minorities.

THE EXPERTS SAY...

" Bulldog football, 171 different majors, and hundreds of activities: This big school offers a lot of options. Recommended: The honors program for smaller classes and individual faculty attention. "

" If your high school average is a B, the Georgia HOPE scholarship will pay your tuition at U Georgia. So apply: They need the brainy types here. "

UNIVERSITY OF HAWAII—MANOA

2600 Campus Road, Room 001, Honolulu, HI 96822
Admissions Phone: (808) 956-8975; (800) 823-9771 Fax: (808) 956-4148
Email: ar-info@hawaii.edu Website: www.hawaii.edu
Application Website: www.hawaii.edu/admissions/

General Info

Type of School: public, coed

Setting: urban

Academic Calendar: semester

Student Body

Full-Time Undergrads: 11,008
  Men: 44%, Women: 56%

Part-Time Undergrads: 2,062
  Men: 47%, Women: 53%

Total Undergrad Population:
  African American: 1%
  Asian American: 56%
  Latino: 2%
  Native American: <1%
  Caucasian: 19%
  International: 5%
  Out-of-State: 16%
  Living Off-Campus: 87%

Graduate and First-Professional
  Students: 6,108

Academics

Full-Time Faculty: 1,124
  With Ph.D.: 82%

Part-Time Faculty: 91
  With Ph.D.: 70%

Most Popular Majors:
  biology (7%)
  psychology (5%)
  computer science (4%)
  business (4%)
  art (4%)

Completing 2 or More Majors: 6%

Freshmen Retention Rate: 77%

Graduation Rates:
  11% within four years
  53% within six years

Admissions

Regular Application Deadline: 6/1;
  3/1 (priority)

Fall Transfer Deadline: 6/1, 3/1 (priority)

Spring Transfer Deadline: 11/1

Total # of Students Applied: 6,028
  Admitted: 3,566
  Enrolled: 1,996

Inside the Classroom

Located in the exciting city of Honolulu, within miles of the famed surfing beaches of Waikiki, the University of Hawaii at Manoa offers the recreational activities of a vacation resort. However, the workload may surprise those few mainlanders who come looking for a four-year vacation, especially if new president Evan S. Dobelle has his way about it. Called a "tsunami" by the *New York Times*, Dobelle seeks to create a world-class institution to attract more students from the mainland and abroad, with academics and facilities on par with such bastions of public education as the University of Michigan and Cal Berkeley.

As the major research institution of the University of Hawaii system, the Manoa campus offers 85 majors in its 13 undergraduate schools, which range from the College of Arts and Humanities and the College of Natural Sciences to the School of Hawaiian, Asian, and Pacific Studies and the College of Tropical Agriculture and Human Resources. It may take up to two years to fulfill the stiff general education requirements, including courses in expository writing, math, world civilization, arts and humanities, and natural and social sciences. Students must also study a foreign language—interestingly, according to a school official, "more languages are taught at UH than at any other U.S. institution outside of the U.S. Department of State."

UHM views itself as a "bridge between East and West," and multiculturalism is the norm in courses as well in as the student body. UHM is known for programs such as geology, geophysics, and zoology, as well as Hawaiian, Asian, and Pacific Studies, and Hawaiian and Indo-Pacific Languages and Literatures. It's often the programs that draw on the school's location that attract mainlanders ("That, and the great beaches," admits one mainland junior).

"Studying for the test and the curve is intense," a biology major reports, adding that classes become competitive at the upper levels, especially in the sciences. A criminal psychology major adds, "I work at my own pace with no competition from other students." Overall, "the professors are generally very accessible," a senior says. "They usually make every effort to meet with their students in my experience." As of late, UH astronomers are set to develop new telescopes for killer asteroid searches, and the Hawaii undersea research lab at UH recently found the 1941 Japanese midget sub involved in Pearl Harbor.

Campus Environment

Manoa Valley is a "good city/hometown mix," according to one student, but has little to offer students. Most head to metropolitan Honolulu for shopping and entertainment. The campus is "generally amiable" and the students are "laid-back," claims one upperclassman, who adds when asked who might not fit in here, "uptight students—it's too hot to get uptight."

Campus housing can accommodate only a small percentage of undergrads. Space is offered first to regular freshmen and then to first-year students according to geographic priority, and dorms can be crowded. Housing "can be comfortable with an extra personal touch." A student tells us, "Student housing is convenient when it comes to classes, but parking is a problem if you have a car." There is some apartment-style housing for upperclassmen, but most students live at home or search for off-campus housing, which can be very pricey in this tourist-trade city. Security is "low class," at least one student complains. "Things (especially bikes) get stolen." For transportation, cars are good to have, but not essential and we hear parking can be a nightmare; students also use bicycles, mopeds, skateboards, and the city bus system for transportation.

Student Life

The UHM campus is diverse, with many cultures and ethnicities represented. According to one student, the administration most frowns upon "anything that does not embrace diversity." Approximately 56 percent of the students are of Asian or Pacific Islander descent; white students account for about 20 percent. (An interesting fact: UH gives students the option to receive their graduation diplomas in Hawaiian or in English.) Most students attending UHM are Hawaiian residents; the high cost of living and expensive flights back and forth to the continent help to keep the out-of-state student population at a minimum. There's a large percentage of older students (graduation rates at UHM are low, possibly because of the lure of the beaches). But incoming students need not worry about having difficulty making friends; the general atmosphere of the school is remarkably friendly and relaxed, in true Aloha spirit. "I can't imagine a friendlier group of people!" remarks one student.

The athletic facilities at UH Manoa are exceptional and, not surprisingly, athletics are a major part of student life; just be prepared to sweat in this climate! The intercollegiate games are usually well attended, especially football games waged against archrival Brigham Young. The school's baseball, basketball, football, swimming, and volleyball teams have all done well and draw respectable crowds. There are more than 200 organizations and clubs in which students may participate; student government and major-related clubs are popular.

Other than major athletics events and the Hawaiian music festival, most social activities don't draw huge crowds. Some complain that UHM lacks the feel of a major state university. Because so many students live off-campus, there's a tendency for weeknights and weekends to be quiet. Plus, "most students have at least one job." A student tells us, "I spend my time (when not in class) working, studying, hanging out with friends and family, recreational outings, shopping, and of course, in traffic!" Greek life is small; one student cites the "bad reputation" of frats due to arrests and drinking, and a perception of the Greeks as "losers." Another student explains that "a lot of people commute so there isn't a 'house' society here." Drinking is not big on campus, a senior says, and happens "mainly at night in dorms;" drugs are even less of a presence. Small dorm and apartment parties are common, though, and students take advantage of Honolulu nightlife and restaurants for fun. And when prompted for an interesting fact about the school that potential applicants may not know: "We have mongooses," answers a student. "They're really cute."

Other schools to check out: University of Florida, Florida State, UC Santa Barbara, UC Berkeley, Occidental.

Test Scores (middle 50%):
SAT Verbal: 480–580
SAT Math: 510–620
ACT Comp: 20–24
ACT English: 20–24
ACT Math: 20–25

HS Rank of Entering Freshmen:
Top 10%: 26%
Top 25%: 57%
Top 50%: 91%

Avg. HS GPA: 3.37

THE EXPERTS SAY...

" UH Manoa is making inroads into becoming a top state university. It is also a land, sea, and space grant institution. "

" No, you can't major in sunbathing, although all the UHM students who don't graduate in four years may be trying to. "

Costs (2004–5)

Tuition and Fees, In-State: $3,561

Tuition and Fees, Out-of-State: $10,041

Regional or 'good neighbor' tuition available

Room & Board: $5,675
note: Tuition is 2004–05, Fees, Room & Board are 2003–04

Inst. Aid (2002–03)

Institutional Aid, Need-Based: $397,390

Institutional Aid, Non-Need-Based: $663,400

FT Undergrads Receiving Aid: 32%
Avg. Amount per Student: $6,092

FT Undergrads Receiving Non-Need-Based Scholarship or Grant Aid: 4%
Avg. Amount per Student: $5,700

Of Those Receiving Any Aid:

Rec. Need-Based Scholarship or Grant Aid: 81%
Average Award: $3,203

Rec. Need-Based Self-Help Aid: 68%
Average Award: $3,786

Upon Graduation, Avg. Loan Debt per Student: $13,707

Financial Aid Deadline: rolling, 3/15 (priority)

Graduates

Alumni Giving: 17%

UNIVERSITY OF HOUSTON

122 East Cullen Building, Houston, TX 77204-2023
Admissions Phone: (713) 743-1010 Fax: (713) 743-9633
Email: admissions@uh.edu Website: www.uh.edu
Application Website: www.uh.edu/enroll/admis

Note: Info. not verified by school

General Info

Type of School: public, coed
Setting: urban
Academic Calendar: semester

Student Body

Full-Time Undergrads: 18,346
  Men: 47%, Women: 53%

Part-Time Undergrads: 6,989
  Men: 50%, Women: 50%

Total Undergrad Population:
  African American: 15%
  Asian American: 21%
  Latino: 21%
  Native American: <1%
  Caucasian: 37%
  International: 4%
  Out-of-State: 2%
  Living Off-Campus: 91%
  In Fraternities: 3%
  In Sororities: 3%

Graduate and First-Professional
  Students: 8,160

Academics

Full-Time Faculty: 1,052
  With Ph.D.: 85%

Part-Time Faculty: 535
  With Ph.D.: 30%

Student/Faculty Ratio: 21:1

Most Popular Majors:
  business (24%)
  social science (11%)
  engineering and related
    tech (10%)
  sciences (biological and
    physical) (6%)
  visual and performing arts (5%)

Freshmen Retention Rate: 79%

Graduation Rates:
  11% within four years
  37% within six years

Admissions

Regular Application Deadline: 5/1;
  1/15 (priority)

Fall Transfer Deadline: 5/1

Spring Transfer Deadline: 12/1

Total # of Students Applied: 8,175
  Admitted: 6,380
  Enrolled: 3,457

Inside the Classroom

The University of Houston comprises 13 schools and colleges, which include architecture; business; education; engineering; honors; hotel and restaurant management; liberal arts and social sciences; law; natural sciences and mathematics; optometry; pharmacy; social work; and technology. The College of Liberal Arts and Social Sciences is the product of a recent merger of the College of Humanities, Fine Arts & Communication, and the College of Social Sciences, and is the largest and most diverse college in the university. The myriad of academic options aside, the low price tag is another big bonus at this school. One student says, "I chose UH because of its good academic programs and low cost... I would not choose to go anywhere else."

Because the University of Houston is such a large school with over 24,000 undergrads, the student/faculty ratio isn't that great, at roughly 21:1. However, a high school guidance counselor praises the "outreach for students" and the "one-on-one" contact offered at this university. "I've found professors to be very accessible," says one student, who also grants that the school's "large size can be intimidating until you become comfortable." The size of the school also contributes to its overall diversity, which naturally extends to the classroom dynamics. A senior says, "The large student population and tremendous diversity means a classroom of 20–30 students will have as many 18-year-old students as 30- or 40-year-old students."

The university's core curriculum, which was revamped in 1999, requires that students take courses in the following areas: communications, math/reasoning, humanities, visual and performing arts, natural sciences, social sciences, history, and government. The school states that its "new 42-hour core curriculum is informed by a series of basic intellectual competencies—reading, writing, speaking, listening, critical thinking, and computer literacy—that are essential to the learning process in any discipline."

Campus Environment

The university offers several types of on-campus housing. Moody Towers are two 18-story buildings that offer corridor-style arrangements; the Towers are the largest of the residence hall complexes and are single-gender by floor. The Quadrangle consists of five coed halls, which offer four-person, suite-style living. Single rooms are available in Cougar Place, a ten building complex generally reserved for upperclassmen and grad students. There are also the Cambridge Oaks and Cullen Oaks on-campus apartment complexes. Fraternity and sorority housing is also available, as is the option of off-campus housing—something quite a large number of students take advantage of. A senior tells us that "living in Houston is moderately expensive, however affordable."

Many students feel as though having a car is somewhat of a necessity in Houston, though for students without cars, there are also Metro bus routes that service the campus. The school even provides free shuttle bus service to the outlying parking lot areas on campus in an attempt to resolve student concerns about the parking situation on campus. The administration is clearly concerned about students' happiness—something made apparent by the recently created Presidential Task

Force on Student Friendliness. The goal of this Task Force was to determine how "friendly" the university is perceived to be by students, parents, alumni, and the public, and the report was then used to enhance the campus environment.

Student Life

A senior proudly states that "there is not a typical UH student" and that "there are no students that would not fit in" here, thanks to the diversity and size of the student body. The student body at the University of Houston is as diverse and multifaceted as the population of Houston itself, and students seem to appreciate this. "UH has a large commuter, nontraditional student population which makes for a mixed bag of racial and ethnic diversification. Overall, the campus is a very friendly environment."

Students are never at a loss for things to do outside of class, whether they're on or off campus. The University of Houston has tons of student groups and organizations that cater to all sorts of interests, including a wide array of academic, honors, ethnic and religious groups. The 15-sport intercollegiate athletics program is popular, and many students participate in intramurals. The Student Program Board is a student-run group that works to plan campus events and entertainment. Past events have included Homecoming, seasonal arts and music festivals, and a fall concert series, as well as bringing guests to campus such as comedians and well-known speakers. There are 26 national general fraternities and sororities on campus that sponsor a number of social events. And for students interested in making the world a better place, the Metropolitan Volunteer Program helps students volunteer their time in various ways, from tutoring kids to visiting the elderly to feeding the homeless.

Houston is full of places to go and things to do. One senior raves, "Houston is a great place to live and be a student. There are countless places of interest in and around the city. UH is located in the heart of it all!" There are countless restaurants catering to every culture and palate. And the nightlife is rich and varied, from the bars and clubs along Richmond Avenue to the downtown Theater District to the great live music venues. There's also the Houston Zoo and the expansive Museum District.

Test Scores (middle 50%):
SAT Verbal: 450–560
SAT Math: 470–590
ACT Comp: 18–23
ACT English: 17–23
ACT Math: 18–25

HS Rank of Entering Freshmen:
Top 10%: 21%
Top 25%: 46%
Top 50%: 79%

Avg. HS GPA: 3.1

THE EXPERTS SAY...

" The large percentage of commuters and older students makes for a diverse student body in a diverse and exciting city. "

" Is the Presidential Task Force on Student Friendliness for real, or is it part of a 'Saturday Night Live' skit? "

Costs (2003–04)

Tuition and Fees, In-State: $3,258

Tuition and Fees, Out-of-State: $8,922

Room & Board: $5,870

Payment Plan(s): installment plan, deferred payment plan

Inst. Aid (est. 2003–04)

FT Undergrads Receiving Aid: 56%
Avg. Amount per Student: $11,340

FT Undergrads Receiving Non-Need-Based Scholarship or Grant Aid: 17%
Avg. Amount per Student: $2,730

Of Those Receiving Any Aid:

Rec. Need-Based Scholarship or Grant Aid: 81%
Average Award: $6,200

Rec. Need-Based Self-Help Aid: 73%
Average Award: $6,820

Upon Graduation, Avg. Loan Debt per Student: $12,988

Financial Aid Deadline: rolling, 4/1 (priority)

Graduates

Going to Graduate School: 18% Within One Year

Accepting Job Offer: 72% at time of graduation

Companies Recruiting On Campus: 329

Alumni Giving: 27%

UNIVERSITY OF ILLINOIS— URBANA-CHAMPAIGN

901 West Illinois Street, Urbana, IL 61801-3028 Admissions Phone: (217) 333-0302
Fax: (217) 244-0903 Email: undergraduates@admissions.uiuc.edu
Website: www.uiuc.edu Application Website: www.apply.uiuc.edu

Inside the Classroom

At Illinois, "Few students are used to doing less than 'A' work," says a student, "However, because the campus requires one to have initiative to succeed, it is possible to set oneself apart from the crowd." Another adds: "It's a lot more challenging academically than you would think," although: "Nonscience majors seem to have much less competitive and intense schedules." Professors are "very strict about schoolwork and can be a little uncaring," observes a student, concluding: "It's not the place to go if you're looking for a comforting environment."

Illinois' eight undergraduate colleges are liberal arts and sciences; agricultural and consumer and environmental sciences; engineering; education; communications; applied life studies; commerce and business administration; and fine and applied arts. Undergraduate programs are also available in veterinary medicine, social work, and aviation (Illinois's Institute of Aviation operates the university-owned Willard Airport.) With over 150 majors, Illinois is best known for engineering, computer science, architecture, agriculture, veterinary medicine, and business; biology and psychology are among the most popular majors. According to Standard & Poors, U of I grads lead more major corporations than do grads from any other school; alums include *Playboy*'s Hugh Hefner and John Welch of General Electric. *Mosaic*, the first popular Web browser, was developed at Illinois by then undergraduate student Marc Andreessen, who went on to found Netscape.

With over 28,000 undergrads, introductory classes are large, and guidance counselors gripe that there is no help for freshmen. "Professors who teach large classes do not even know their students exist," comments a junior, "but if you are in a small class, they're usually helpful." U of I's First-Year Discovery Program helps some freshmen get to know professors through small classes and involvement in faculty research. But, warns a bio major: "If you need help, you need to go to your professor and ask him or her. No one will approach you and ask you if you're doing OK." Illini's teaching assistants went on a two-day strike recently.

Campus Environment

The 1,450-acre campus is located between the twin cities of Champaign and Urbana, which have a combined population of around 100,000. "The University very much controls the atmosphere and the town graciously caters to student and faculty needs," one student says. The strip of bars and fast-food joints along Green Street, known as Campustown, is popular with students. "Champaign-Urbana has a fair amount of crime," a junior comments. "Some areas are good, some are not. There aren't a great deal of places of interest off campus, except for the mall and movie theaters."

The campus has the largest public university library collection in the nation and its Morrow Plots are oldest experimental agricultural fields. Many facilities have recently been built, including an $80 million computer sciences building. "The campus is very safe and I always find it easily convenient to forget this thriving, exciting campus is surrounded by cornfields," a student quips. (Urbanites take heart: Chicago, Indianapolis, and St. Louis are only two hours away.)

Freshmen are guaranteed housing and are integrated with all classes into all halls. Each quad is its own community, but as a rule, Champaign dorms party, while the Urbana dorms are more studious. "There's a lot of variety," a sophomore reports. "The University dorms are not beautiful but they are comfortable." On-campus housing is available all four years, and freshmen are permitted to live in Illinois' huge selection of frat housing. Many upperclassmen move off-campus. "Off-campus housing is really nice and much more affordable," a bio major says. "Availability is pretty good, too. "

Students are allowed to have cars and can purchase semester permits at campus lots, but "the U of I is really a pedestrian campus," a junior explains. "A lot of people walk to class, or bike, or rollerblade. Since campus is so big, there's a good bus system, too. The buses can take you across campus, or into town, or to the mall or restaurants … You would probably only use a car to go off campus, but the buses can take you there too."

Student Life

For students looking for the traditional college experience, U of I is it: This is school that invented Homecoming. Illinois's Greek system is the largest in the nation and "it defines the social scene on campus," says one student. "It partitions the campus into 'popular' and 'unpopular' factions." The Greeks ensure that large blowout parties and other social events keep coming throughout the year. "I don't think that the University is a rowdy place in general, though the weekend bar/party scene can be wild," a sophomore comments. Alcohol is much more visible than drugs on campus. ("Too many distractions," mutters one Illinois counselor.)

This Big Ten school's students are fanatical about their sports teams, especially in football and basketball (there is continuing controversy over whether the school mascot, Chief Illiniwek, is a "traditional" or a "racist" symbol). "The biggest registered student organization is Illini Pride," a premed tells us. "It's the student pep club … we have a great time making noise at games." U of I's extensive intramural program is also extremely popular.

There are 850 campus activities and clubs. A junior lists some of the most popular: "Student government, career fairs, religious study groups, community projects … bowling [and] swing dancing." "There's something for everyone," adds a human development and family studies major. "Like the Jimmy Buffett Fan Club, underwater hockey club, or card playing clubs." There's even a John Phillip Sousa museum.

Students are "probably more conservative than at many other schools," a sophomore says; otherwise, it is a "typical" school, a bio major comments. However: "Someone who is used to being the center of attention at their high school might have problems. Here at Illinois, there are hundreds of former prom queens, football team captains, and valedictorians. It can be very humbling," a junior concludes.

Test Scores (middle 50%):
SAT Verbal: 570–670
SAT Math: 620–720
ACT Comp: 25–31
ACT English: 25–30
ACT Math: 25–31

HS Rank of Entering Freshmen:
Top 10%: 57%
Top 25%: 86%
Top 50%: 99%

THE EXPERTS SAY…

" For students looking for a traditional college experience, this Big Ten has it all: sports, a wide variety of programs, and the biggest Greek system in the nation. "

" Great college experience, if you can get your professor to remember your name. "

Costs (2004–5)

Tuition and Fees, In-State: $7,476

Tuition and Fees, Out-of-State: $19,504

Room & Board: $6,848

Payment Plan(s): installment plan, pre-payment plan

Inst. Aid (est. 2003–04)

Institutional Aid, Need-Based: $13,242,856

Institutional Aid, Non-Need-Based: $3,582,638

FT Undergrads Receiving Aid: 42%
Avg. Amount per Student: $8,521

FT Undergrads Receiving Non-Need-Based Scholarship or Grant Aid: 12%
Avg. Amount per Student: $3,172

Of Those Receiving Any Aid:

Rec. Need-Based Scholarship or Grant Aid: 63%
Average Award: $6,195

Rec. Need-Based Self-Help Aid: 78%
Average Award: $3,753

Upon Graduation, Avg. Loan Debt per Student: $15,100

Financial Aid Deadline: rolling, 3/15 (priority)

Graduates

Companies Recruiting On-Campus: 1,000

Alumni Giving: 11%

UNIVERSITY OF IOWA

107 Calvin Hall, Iowa City, IA 52242-1396
Admissions Phone: (319) 335-3847; (800) 553-4692 Fax: (319) 335-1535
Email: admissions@uiowa.edu Website: uiowa.edu
Application Website: uiowa.edu/admissions

General Info

Type of School: public, coed

Setting: small town

Academic Calendar: semester

Student Body

Full-Time Undergrads: 17,701
  Men: 46%, Women: 54%

Part-Time Undergrads: 1,700
  Men: 44%, Women: 56%

Total Undergrad Population:
  African American: 2%
  Asian American: 3%
  Latino: 2%
  Native American: <1%
  Caucasian: 87%
  International: 1%
  Out-of-State: 31%
  Living Off-Campus: 73%
  In Fraternities: 9%
  In Sororities: 13%

Graduate and First-Professional
  Students: 9,512

Academics

Full-Time Faculty: 1,623
  With Ph.D.: 96%

Part-Time Faculty: 82
  With Ph.D.: 98%

Student/Faculty Ratio: 15:1

Most Popular Majors:
  psychology (5%)
  English (4%)
  communication studies (4%)
  art (3%)
  biology (3%)

Freshmen Retention Rate: 83%

Graduation Rates:
  38% within four years
  65% within six years

Admissions

Regular Application Deadline: 4/1;
  2/1 (priority)

Fall Transfer Deadline: 4/1

Spring Transfer Deadline: 11/15

Total # of Students Applied: 13,337
  Admitted: 10,979
  Enrolled: 4,083

Inside the Classroom

The University of Iowa has a history of innovation: It was the first school to offer programs in speech pathology and audiology, and was also the site of the first Writers Workshop. Many students are on a preprofessional track, and almost all the preprofessional departments are good. As one student says about "Little Athens," "Iowa turns out a lot of fine scholars. This school is best for people who want to go on to graduate school."

The largest of the university's eleven colleges is the liberal arts school, whose students must fulfill stiff general education requirements, classes that tend to be "spread out all over" Iowa's sprawling campus. The English program (playwright Tennessee Williams was an Iowa alumnus) is remarkable. Raves one student, "The English program is incredible, overshadowed only by the Creative Writing graduate program that it is affiliated with." Iowa has one of the nation's strongest public university medical programs, and with one of the largest teaching hospitals in the country, "a fine medical education is guaranteed," as one student boasts. The library system is "the greatest research library in all of Iowa ... hands down."

"There's a strong academic atmosphere," remarks a political science major. "Workload is not too overwhelming, fair amounts of reading and usually one paper around seven pages due per class." The student body "is concentrated on receiving good grades." It should come as no surprise that classes—particularly introductory ones—can be huge, with more than 300 students in some sections. As one student warns, "If you want super-personalized attention, this is not the college for you." But a junior says, "Professors are willing to take time to talk to students and offer adequate office hours [and] make appointments." Programs such as Courses in Common and First-Year Seminars bring small groups of incoming students together with faculty. For top students, the University Honors Program offers students one-on-one research opportunities with a faculty mentor.

With an undergraduate enrollment of almost 20,000, some classes inevitably fill up quickly, but even the largest lectures will break down into small discussion groups. Students seem to like their professors; one woman said that hers were "thoughtful, intelligent, generous, and civic-minded." Still, a few students complain that professors are better researchers than teachers and that some teaching assistants leave much to be desired.

Due to state budget cuts, Iowa has been increasing tuition. Even so, guidance counselors mark this school as a "best value;" notably, financial aid budgets were not cut. Not surprisingly, David J. Skorton, the new university president, is a proven fundraiser.

Campus Environment

Housing is reputedly in short supply, and the majority of students look for housing off campus. "Off-campus housing isn't that difficult to find, but it is pricey to live close to campus," we're told. "Many students live in nearby towns and commute." Freshmen are not required to live in the residence halls, but 90 percent do. "There are several dorms, but people can be put on waiting lists for rooms," says a junior. "They then will set up temporary housing in different lounges in the dorms." One student says, "Students are usually put on a floor with students of their age and interests—freshmen typically meet other freshmen, sophomores are with other sophomores." As for the dining hall food… well, one student quips, "It probably won't kill you."

The university recently finished rebuilding the Old Capitol building's golden dome (the Iowa City "icon" was destroyed in a fire in 2001). "In the middle of conservative Iowa, Iowa City is a liberal mecca," an Iowa senior tells us. "The town is proud of and supports the college," a junior comments, and there's "an active nightlife" with bars and clubs geared to the student population. "Coffeehouses are becoming huge here," reports one journalism major. But a junior observes, "It is Iowa, and no, it's not heaven."

Student Life

One Iowa guidance counselor claims that the U of I is a hot pick for in-state students because "friends and parties are there." "Iowa provides a friendly campus atmosphere with people that are willing to help each other," says a junior. "I think people take school very seriously here," remarks another student, "but there are also people that have a little bit too much fun." While not "overly rowdy," drinking has a distinct place in student social life. In an effort to curb binge drinking and drinking by minors, the university now notifies parents of students who are found passed out in a public area of campus, hospitalized for alcohol intoxication, or arrested for public intoxication.

Fraternities and sororities keep things hopping, but they don't dominate campus life. According to one student, "If you're not in a house, it doesn't mean you're missing out on anything." Another student elaborates on the lack of cliques: "Athletes hang out with non-athletes, fraternity and sorority members don't limit themselves to their houses when making friends, people introduce themselves when standing in line at the Memorial Union, parties are thrown that basically invite the entire campus and people just get along." The typical student "would be white and Midwestern," comments a junior. "Many of the students are from Iowa or Illinois… It isn't an extremely diverse campus ethnicity-wise, so minority students may not feel they fit in."

Campus controversy this year surrounded a basketball player who was alleged to have raped a former girlfriend and pled guilty to a lesser charge. Reports a political science major, "Many, including myself, didn't feel he received a tough enough punishment. He was able to maintain his scholarship and stay in school." But Iowa still has the Big 10 "mystique." "The student body really rallies around its sports and supports all the teams," says a proud junior.

Test Scores (middle 50%):
SAT Verbal: 530–640
SAT Math: 540–660
ACT Comp: 22–27
ACT English: 21–27
ACT Math: 22–27

HS Rank of Entering Freshmen:
Top 10%: 21%
Top 25%: 48%
Top 50%: 92%

Avg. HS GPA: 3.54

THE EXPERTS SAY…

" English majors, preprofessionals, and premeds really ought to give Iowa a try. "

" With its great college town atmosphere, Big 10 sports, and artistic events, Iowa's an awesome place to spend your college years. "

Costs (est. 2004–05)

Tuition and Fees, In-State: $5,396

Tuition and Fees, Out-of-State: $16,048

Room & Board: $6,350

Payment Plan(s): installment plan, deferred payment plan, pre-payment plan

Inst. Aid (est. 2003–04)

Institutional Aid, Need-Based: $8,182,126

Institutional Aid, Non-Need-Based: $7,134,380

FT Undergrads Receiving Aid: 52%
Avg. Amount per Student: $7,386

FT Undergrads Receiving Non-Need-Based Scholarship or Grant Aid: 21%
Avg. Amount per Student: $4,273

Of Those Receiving Any Aid:

Rec. Need-Based Scholarship or Grant Aid: 56%
Average Award: $4,497

Rec. Need-Based Self-Help Aid: 76%
Average Award: $3,861

Upon Graduation, Avg. Loan Debt per Student: $16,500

Financial Aid Deadline: rolling, 1/3 (priority)

UNIVERSITY OF KANSAS

1502 Iowa Street, Lawrence, KS 66045-7576
Admissions Phone: (785) 864-3911; (888) 686-7323 (in-state) Fax: (785) 864-5006
Email: adm@ku.edu Website: www.ku.edu
Application Website: www.admissions.ku.edu

General Info

Type of School: public, coed

Setting: urban

Academic Calendar: semester

Student Body

Full-Time Undergrads: 18,238
  Men: 48%, Women: 52%

Part-Time Undergrads: 2,528
  Men: 50%, Women: 50%

Total Undergrad Population:
  African American: 3%
  Asian American: 4%
  Latino: 3%
  Native American: 1%
  Caucasian: 84%
  International: 3%
  Out-of-State: 24%
  Living Off-Campus: 78%
  In Fraternities: 14%
  In Sororities: 20%

Graduate and First-Professional
  Students: 7,714

Academics

Full-Time Faculty: 1,194
  With Ph.D.: 92%

Part-Time Faculty: 138
  With Ph.D.: 36%

Student/Faculty Ratio: 19:1

Most Popular Majors:
  biological sciences (9%)
  engineering (8%)
  psychology (8%)
  journalism (6%)
  business (5%)

Completing 2 or More Majors: 6%

Freshmen Retention Rate: 82%

Graduation Rates:
  29% within four years
  58% within six years
  note: 5-yr. programs affect rates

Admissions

Regular Application Deadline: 4/1;
  1/15 (priority)

Fall Transfer Deadline: 6/1

Spring Transfer Deadline: 12/1

# of Students Waitlisted: 249
  Students Accepting Place: 249
  Waitlisted Students Admitted: 249

Inside the Classroom

Some call the University of Kansas "the best of the Big 12," offering tremendous athletics and a great assortment of majors. "The colors are crimson and blue," says a student, "and the crimson was taken from Harvard, because it was considered the Harvard of the West." To prove the point, a KU graduate, Vernon Smith, recently received the Nobel Prize for economics. The only catch is that admissions standards have gone up, so it's harder to get in, and the traditionally reasonable tuition is rising. "The current thing that is on the mind of almost everyone around campus is the constant tuition increases that we have recently undergone and are planning to undergo again," says a student.

KU has 11 undergraduate schools: liberal arts and sciences, allied health, architecture and urban design, business, education, engineering, fine arts, journalism and mass communications, nursing, pharmacy, and social welfare. Students apply to the school of their choice; if they aren't admitted, they are automatically considered for the College of Liberal Arts and Sciences. KU's best programs are in architecture, premed studies, nursing, pharmacy, engineering, and journalism; the Spanish and Portuguese programs are also notable. Online registration has been launched and is expected to make the notorious KU system easier; still, an education major bemoans "enrollment procedures." Each school has it's own distribution requirements, but a guidance counselor remarks, "The students can basically pick their own courses, curriculum, and schedule."

For such a large school (over 20,000 undergrads), KU's professors are remarkably accessible (11 Fulbright awards were offered in 2002–03 alone to KU faculty members). An education major raved, "Accessibility of professors is amazing, they are almost always willing to meet in/out of the classroom, during office hours and at nearly any other time of day." The workload is "fair," but a sophomore warns, "There is no such thing as an easy A. Grades are earned not given away." Students highly recommended KU's honors program for its small class sizes and caring advisers.

Campus Environment

KU is located in Lawrence, a small liberal town in the midst of conservative Kansas. The area is hilly, also unusual for Kansas, and KU's campus sits atop Mt. Oread. Students enjoy Lawrence for its live music scene; for more entertainment options, Kansas City is about an hour away.

Freshmen are not required to live on campus, but are encouraged to do so. Calling housing available and affordable, a sophomore tells us, "There are nine residence halls and two apartment living complexes on the KU campus... The variety is great... Some are geared towards certain majors, females, or upperclassmen." A senior comments, however, "The on-campus apartments could use improvement." Dining services also get a thumbs-down. KU's scholarship halls, in which 50 residents share living space and cooking, are recommended: a good grade point average is required to get in, but board fees are reduced. Freshmen are allowed to live in fraternity and sorority housing. Housing is not guaranteed for all four years, and most students move to very affordable off-campus housing in Lawrence after their first year; "it is usually easy to find future roommates," we're told.

Freshmen are allowed to have cars, but the "parking department is terrible," says a business administration major. Said a sophomore. "Freshman year, I did not have a car and if I needed to go anywhere, there are always people who are willing to drive you around. We have many grocery stores, a Wal-Mart, Target, and such, all within walking distance or on the KU bus route."

Student Life

"Our basketball program is typically in the top 25, if not the top 10 and the enthusiasm is crazy," said a sophomore. "The success of the basketball team is a major factor to most if not all KU students." (In March 2002, the men's basketball team advanced to the Final Four for the first time since 1993. In March 2003, the men's basketball team recorded its 20th straight NCAA Tournament first-round win.) Students are guaranteed tickets but not seats, and have to "camp out" in teams at Allen Fieldhouse. "For big games such as Missouri, our rival, we may have to camp out for up to eight days or more," said an education major. "Football is popular for the tailgating… our football program is undergoing some new changes with a new coach and such so there is not as much strong support." But all Jayhawk sports are big events. (The Jayhawk is a mythical bird; the traditional KU chant at is "Rock Chalk, Jayhawk," repeated faster and faster.)

The typical student is "a white, middle-class person from the Midwest." A student calls the campus "extremely friendly," adding: "Wescoe Beach is always active even during the winter (Wescoe Beach is a 'meeting' place on campus)." While a guidance counselor criticizes KU's "heavy emphasis on Greek system," a student countered: "It is not necessary to be Greek to be involved at KU… Some schools you need to be in a fraternity/sorority in order to know about parties or activities, and that's not at all true of KU."

There is no drinking on campus, but "the bar scene is huge on weekends," said a student "Since Kansas City is so close, a lot of students will head up there and either go out in Westport, shop on the Plaza, go to Chiefs or Royals games." There are hundreds of clubs at KU and intramurals, especially basketball, are big. The Student Union produces special events on campus and the Panhellenic Association sponsors the Rock Chalk Revue, in which frats team up to produce original musicals, raising thousands for charity.

Notable KU alumni include actors Scott Bakula and Mandy Patinkin, basketball legend Wilt Chamberlain, former U.S. Senator Bob Dole, and Netscape cofounder Lou Montulli. KU is rich in folklore: "If a student walks into the Campanile and out the opposite door before graduation, they will never graduate; if a virgin ever graduates from KU, the bronze Jayhawk located in front of Strong Hall will fly away; and prior to a test a student can rub the nose of a statue in front of the Study Abroad office for good luck." A student concludes, "I know that this is the right place for me… Everyone tells me that I have a HUGE smile on my face when I talk about it here."

Other schools to check out: Kansas State University, University of North Carolina—Chapel Hill, University of Colorado—Boulder, University of Missouri, University of Illinois—Urbana-Champaign.

Test Scores (middle 50%):
ACT Comp: 21–27

HS Rank of Entering Freshmen:
Top 10%: 28%
Top 25%: 54%
Top 50%: 86%

Avg. HS GPA: 3.4

THE EXPERTS SAY…

" Now's the time to apply: With tuition and admissions standards rising, getting into KU may soon be harder than getting a seat at a Jayhawks game. "

" Don't let the Greeks, sports, and partying mislead you: KU is also home to Merit, Truman, Rhodes, and Fulbright scholars (who just happen to know how to have a good time). "

Costs (2003–04)

Tuition and Fees, In-State: $4,101

Tuition and Fees, Out-of-State: $11,577

Room & Board: $4,822

Payment Plan(s): installment plan

Inst. Aid (2002–03)

Institutional Aid, Need-Based: $6,214,809

Institutional Aid, Non-Need-Based: $6,734,686

FT Undergrads Receiving Aid: 33%
Avg. Amount per Student: $6,445

FT Undergrads Receiving Non-Need-Based Scholarship or Grant Aid: 12%
Avg. Amount per Student: $3,764

Of Those Receiving Any Aid:

Rec. Need-Based Scholarship or Grant Aid: 85%
Average Award: $2,976

Rec. Need-Based Self-Help Aid: 81%
Average Award: $3,744

Upon Graduation, Avg. Loan Debt per Student: $18,721

Financial Aid Deadline: rolling, 3/1 (priority)

Graduates

Going to Graduate School: 28% Within One Year

Companies Recruiting On Campus: 500

UNIVERSITY OF KENTUCKY

100 W.D. Funkhouser Building, Lexington, KY 40506
Admissions Phone: (859) 257-2000; (800) 432-0967 (in-state) Fax: (859) 257-3823
Email: admissio@pop.uky.edu Website: www.uky.edu
Application Website: www.uky.edu/UGAdmission/applicants/application.html

General Info

Type of School: public, coed
Setting: urban
Academic Calendar: semester

Student Body

Full-Time Undergrads: 16,234
  Men: 48%, Women: 52%

Part-Time Undergrads: 1,517
  Men: 49%, Women: 51%

Total Undergrad Population:
  African American: 5%
  Asian American: 2%
  Latino: 1%
  Native American: <1%
  Caucasian: 89%
  International: 1%
  Out-of-State: 14%
  Living Off-Campus: 75%
  In Fraternities: 18%
  In Sororities: 22%

Graduate and First-Professional
  Students: 7,289

Academics

Full-Time Faculty: 1,209
  With Ph.D.: 88%

Part-Time Faculty: 516

Student/Faculty Ratio: 16:1

Most Popular Majors:
  biology (5%)
  psychology (4%)
  business (4%)
  marketing (4%)
  elementary teacher education
  (3%)

Freshmen Retention Rate: 77%

Graduation Rates:
  27% within four years
  61% within six years

Admissions

Regular Application Deadline: 2/15

Fall Transfer Deadline: 8/1 (priority)

Spring Transfer Deadline: 12/1 (priority)

Total # of Students Applied: 9,418
  Admitted: 7,603
  Enrolled: 3,688

Test Scores (middle 50%):
  SAT Verbal: 510–620
  SAT Math: 510–630

Inside the Classroom

The University of Kentucky's ten colleges for undergraduates—agriculture; architecture; arts and sciences; business and economics; communications and information studies; education; engineering; fine arts; human environmental sciences; and social work—offer a staggering array of 98 bachelor's degree programs. There's even a special "topical studies" major for students who want to mix and match classes from different departments or colleges to build a customized major. In short, if you can't find the subject you're looking for here, you must have missed something.

As might be expected with so many colleges and majors, the workload depends on the student's course of study. One student said that competitiveness between students was "relatively intense," while a broadcast journalism major described the academic atmosphere as "generally laid-back. The workload is not too heavy. We do have a slight problem with grade inflation: While A's are hard to get, B's are given frequently and often undeservingly."

All of the colleges have core requirement programs to ensure that students are well-rounded. Some students voice great satisfaction with the breadth of their studies. Others, like this down-to-earth biology major, feel differently: "One example of the program's problem is that a student must take four semesters of a foreign language but no math. I can't do calculus but I sure can speak Latin! Perfect for the real world."

As with most big land-grant universities, attending UK is not a solitary experience. "The bad thing about UK is that, at first, you feel like a number," says a recent grad. "So many freshmen will drop out at the end of their first semester. Don't! Give it at least a year. That's really the only downside." Another piece of good news for Southern students is that UK is a member of the Academic Common Market, in which colleges located in 14 states throughout the South charge in-state tuition fees to students who come from those states.

One guidance counselor from Kentucky tells us that UK has "excellent premed, prelaw, and nursing programs." Another Kentucky guidance counselor calls UK a "top-rated research institution," and notes that the university is "kind of selective in choosing students; [they] want at least a 3.2 GPA or higher."

Campus Environment

If Kentucky has a bluegrass belt, Lexington's right smack in the middle of it. This is horse racing country, and it's impossible to attend UK without admiring it. "The beauty of Lexington and the surrounding counties is one of the school's most appealing things," says one senior. "The drive from Louisville, passing all of the horse farms, is breathtaking."

The campus is divided roughly into three parts. The north campus contains primarily residence halls. The central campus is home to classrooms, offices, and the various library branches. Finally, the south campus features additional residence halls, athletic and recreational facilities, the medical center, and the college of agriculture.

The William T. Young library is a particular standout on campus. Considered one of the world's most advanced research university libraries, the facility offers 640 computers for use by students, faculty and staff and 3,000 Internet-connected ports for anyone bringing their own laptop. UK's library system already ranked 32nd among the 67 public research libraries in the U.S. before the Young facility opened in 1998.

According to one student, on-campus housing is "fairly nice. Rooms are medium to small on the south campus, where most people want to live. The rooms are much larger on the central and north campuses; however, these rooms are in far less demand." Many students also rent off-campus houses. "Houses further off campus are much nicer and are often brand new," says a political science major. "However, the drive can be bad during rush hour and parking is a nightmare."

Town-gown relations hit bottom recently with a debate concerning a new ordinance that would limit late-night parties. "The UK student government has been extremely active in combatting this ordinance," says one student. "They have held rallies, bought commercial air time, and plastered propaganda all over the city. The student body has followed their lead."

Student Life

Many students at UK seek their fun by following the bouncing ball. "Varsity sports are the lifeblood of much social activity," said one senior. "Students must wait—often close to four or five hours—for free Wildcats tickets in a lottery distribution. However, watching the 'Cats play in Rupp Arena is well worth it," Basketball is the runaway favorite, although one student says that "people will even travel to see a losing but exciting football program." Intramural sports are also popular, with the Greeks fielding teams that are locked in old rivalries. Enthusiasm for intramurals will undoubtedly rise more when a new intramural center is completed.

Like many campuses these days, the University of Kentucky is officially dry. "Students get around this by sneaking beer into the dorms," said one student. "But all the fraternity and sorority houses are dry. Parties must be off campus." Another student offered this observation: "On game days, interestingly enough, rules rarely apply. Students often drink freely in the Commonwealth Stadium parking lot and sneak a pint of bourbon into the game."

The town of Lexington is small, but students often walk off campus for the restaurants and bars. "Two Keys is the most frequented bar for UK students," says a senior. "There are comedians there on Tuesday nights, and Thursday nights are big." Don't look for mobs of students on nights before games, though. "If there's a football game on Saturday, few students go out. Many just rest up for the game." However, every cloud has its silver lining: "Tailgating starts early and after the game you can find may people back at the Keys." Another student names a coffee shop called Common Grounds as a popular hangout.

ACT Comp: 22–27
ACT English: 21–28
ACT Math: 21–27
HS Rank of Entering Freshmen:
Top 10%: 28%
Top 25%: 57%
Top 50%: 87%

Avg. HS GPA: 3.56

THE EXPERTS SAY...

" Big-name basketball and an endless choice of academic options makes the University of Kentucky a one-size-fits-all school for anyone. "

" Choosing your major and your friends at a school this big can sometimes feel like playing the horses. If you don't want the odds to be 17,000 to one, get to know your adviser well and become active in clubs or sports. "

Costs (2003–04)

Tuition and Fees, In-State: $4,547

Tuition and Fees, Out-of-State: $11,227

Room & Board: $4,285

Payment Plan(s): installment plan

Inst. Aid (est. 2003–04)

Institutional Aid, Need-Based: $16,690,767

FT Undergrads Receiving Aid: 38%
Avg. Amount per Student: $7,421

FT Undergrads Receiving Non-Need-Based Scholarship or Grant Aid: 4%
Avg. Amount per Student: $3,728

Of Those Receiving Any Aid:

Rec. Need-Based Scholarship or Grant Aid: 76%
Average Award: $4,533

Rec. Need-Based Self-Help Aid: 67%
Average Award: $3,153

Upon Graduation, Avg. Loan Debt per Student: $16,584

Financial Aid Deadline: rolling, 2/15 (priority)

Graduates

Companies Recruiting On-Campus: 520

UNIVERSITY OF MAINE

5713 Chadbourne Hall, Orono, ME 04469-5713
Admissions Phone: (207) 581-1561; (877) 486-2364 Fax: (207) 581-1213
Email: um-admit@maine.edu Website: www.umaine.edu
Application Website: apply.maine.edu

General Info

Type of School: public, coed
Setting: rural
Academic Calendar: semester

Student Body

Full-Time Undergrads: 7,334
 Men: 51%, Women: 49%

Part-Time Undergrads: 1,638
 Men: 35%, Women: 65%

Total Undergrad Population:
 African American: 1%
 Asian American: 1%
 Latino: 1%
 Native American: 2%
 Caucasian: 93%
 International: 2%
 Out-of-State: 15%
 Living Off-Campus: 43%

Graduate and First-Professional
 Students: 2,250

Academics

Full-Time Faculty: 508
 With Ph.D.: 86%

Part-Time Faculty: 218
 With Ph.D.: 32%

Student/Faculty Ratio: 15:1

Most Popular Majors:
 business administration (9%)
 nursing (5%)
 elementary education (5%)
 psychology (4%)
 secondary education (3%)

Completing 2 or More Majors: 5%

Freshmen Retention Rate: 78%

Graduation Rates:
 30% within four years
 60% within six years

Admissions

Total # of Students Applied: 5,540
 Admitted: 4,204
 Enrolled: 1,698

Test Scores (middle 50%):
 SAT Verbal: 480–590
 SAT Math: 490–600
 ACT Comp: 20–27

HS Rank of Entering Freshmen:
 Top 10%: 22%
 Top 25%: 54%
 Top 50%: 88%

Avg. HS GPA: 3.25

Inside the Classroom

The names of its undergraduate schools speak volumes about the University of Maine's interdisciplinary strengths. There's the College of Business, Public Policy, and Health; the College of Education and Human Development; the College of Engineering; the College of Liberal Arts and Sciences; and the College of Natural Sciences, Forestry, and Agriculture. The acclaimed engineering programs are among the most popular and arguably the toughest; forestry, business administration, marine science, nursing, education, and performing arts are strong as well. The English program boasts best-selling author Stephen King as an alumnus. Interdisciplinary programs in new media and Canadian studies are growing steadily. The Honors College offers 500 motivated students the opportunity to challenge themselves academically and work closely with the most distinguished faculty. UMaine prides itself on offering many opportunities for students who wish to pursue research projects, internships, co-ops, and international studies.

The core curriculum at UMaine forms nearly one-third of a student's education. Students choose from a variety of courses in each of six broad categories: science, mathematics, human values and social context, writing, ethics, and the senior capstone experience. We hear the workload can be taxing but is ultimately manageable, and, of course, is largely based on the student's major. Engineers seem to have it the worst, "but each major and class has a fairly good amount of work," a student tells us. The average class size hovers around 30 students; labs are much smaller. The faculty here is praised for their accessibility and willingness to help anyone, anytime.

Campus Environment

Surrounded by the Penobscot and Stillwater rivers, the university is actually located on a large island. The campus itself is 660 acres, with 161 buildings including the largest library in the state, three museums, a concert hall, a planetarium, and 16 residence halls. More than 3,500 students reside in campus housing, and all freshmen must, unless they live with their family within commuting distance. We didn't hear any major complaints about the on-campus housing, and were assured that you will never have more than one roommate in a dorm room. Special-housing options exist for those in the Honors College or students interested in living with other engineering or science majors, and freshmen who choose to rush may also live in Greek houses, which are located on or next to campus. More than half of all UMaine undergrads move off-campus eventually.

All students may park their cars on campus, once they've obtained a permit for a small fee. "A lot of students have cars," a junior says, "but you don't need one." The university provides "The Maine Bus," a shuttle service for destinations on- and just-off-campus, and students may ride some public transportation for free with an ID card. There's also a terrific bicycle program: the university makes bikes available for students to pick up at one campus location and leave at another.

Orono is described as a "classic college town," and students rave about its natural beauty, serenity, and safety. There may not be a whole lot to do ("you have to make your own fun" in these rural parts), but if you're looking for outdoor activities, the location can't be beat. It's within an hour's drive of Acadia National Park, Baxter State Park and Mt. Katahdin, and Squaw Mountain Ski Resort. Bangor, the state's second largest retail center, is just a 10-minute drive down the road.

Student Life

UMaine is a notoriously friendly campus; freshmen are treated to a "Maine Hello" from day one, as administrators, faculty, and staff greet and assist new students as they move in to their dorm. Diversity isn't the school's strong suit; 93 percent of the student body is white, and well over three-quarters hail from within the state (almost all come from the Northeast). Besides that, most students are typically described as "well-balanced"— meaning they heartily subscribe to the work hard/play hard school of thought. UMaine has been labeled a "party school," but one current undergrad tells us that "drinking is not as bad as it has been in past years."

The university recently added onto its student union building, "the physical and social center of the UMaine campus," to include a bookstore, a career center, and a marketplace, with restaurants, a coffee shop, and pub. It's a "great location" for the hundred-plus student clubs and organizations offered. "There are more activities than ever before," a student gushes. Maine Bound, UMaine's outdoor recreation program, attracts a large number of students, as do ROC (Residents on Campus), the entertainment committee, the community service programs, the women's and professional associations, and the Greek organizations. Fraternities and sororities have a "large influence on social life on campus," one student says, since they're the ones who have the alcohol and the parties. "This is a small town," she continues. "There aren't too many places to hang out or go to."

Indeed, the off-campus atmosphere is "pretty quiet." Aside from a few bars, restaurants, and clubs, town life is pretty limited. Highlights of the social calendar include "Maine Day" in the spring, when all of UMaine participates in community improvement projects, capped off by a picnic and games such as "Oozeball," a volleyball tournament played in a mud pit. The annual music festival "Bumstock" is a big hit as well, with students and New Englanders in general flocking to campus for a weekend of "food, dancing, and good times."

Most students take advantage of their location and enjoy a variety of winter sports and activities. University-sponsored athletics "are a big deal" as well. The school has ten varsity women's teams and nine men's. Women's basketball "has been a fixture in the NCAA tournament for most of the past eight years," and the men's champion ice hockey team "is considered one of the nation's premier programs." Intramural sports are huge, with nearly three-quarters of all undergrads participating in one of the 85 programs offered. "Almost everyone I know is involved in some sort of sport on campus," a student says. "You name the sport, we've got it."

Costs (est. 2004–05)

Tuition and Fees, In-State: $6,328

Tuition and Fees, Out-of-State: $15,658

Regional or 'good neighbor' tuition available

Room & Board: $6,402

Payment Plan(s): installment plan

THE EXPERTS SAY...

" The engineering programs are a standout at this scenic and friendly university; programs ranging from forestry to the performing arts are strengths. "

" You think Stephen King, an Orono alum, was inspired by the annual 'Oozeball' game? "

Inst. Aid (est. 2003–04)

Institutional Aid, Need-Based: $5,750,971

Institutional Aid, Non-Need-Based: $839,847

FT Undergrads Receiving Aid: 65% Avg. Amount per Student: $8,853

FT Undergrads Receiving Non-Need-Based Scholarship or Grant Aid: 17% Avg. Amount per Student: $5,096

Of Those Receiving Any Aid:

Rec. Need-Based Scholarship or Grant Aid: 77% Average Award: $4,931

Rec. Need-Based Self-Help Aid: 88% Average Award: $4,659

Upon Graduation, Avg. Loan Debt per Student: $18,922

Financial Aid Deadline: 3/1 (priority)

Graduates

Going to Graduate School: 25% Within One Year

Companies Recruiting On Campus: 196

Alumni Giving: 17%

UNIVERSITY OF MARYLAND—BALTIMORE COUNTY

1000 Hilltop Circle, Baltimore, MD 21250 Admissions Phone: (410) 455-2291;
(800) UMBC-4U2 Fax: (410) 455-1094 Email: admissions@umbc.edu
Website: www.umbc.edu Application Website: www.umbc.edu/Admissions/undergrad

General Info

Type of School: public, coed

Setting: suburban

Academic Calendar: 4-1-4

Student Body

Full-Time Undergrads: 8,024
  Men: 53%, Women: 47%

Part-Time Undergrads: 1,622
  Men: 51%, Women: 49%

Total Undergrad Population:
  African American: 15%
  Asian American: 20%
  Latino: 3%
  Native American: <1%
  Caucasian: 56%
  International: 5%
  Out-of-State: 8%
  Living Off-Campus: 67%
  In Fraternities: 3%
  In Sororities: 3%

Graduate and First-Professional
  Students: 2,226

Academics

Full-Time Faculty: 464
  With Ph.D.: 85%

Part-Time Faculty: 238
  With Ph.D.: 39%

Student/Faculty Ratio: 18:1

Most Popular Majors:
  information systems (11%)
  computer science (9%)
  biology (8%)
  psychology (6%)
  visual and performing arts (5%)

Completing 2 or More Majors: 6%

Freshmen Retention Rate: 53%

Graduation Rates:
  28% within four years
  53% within six years

Admissions

Regular Application Deadline: 2/1;
  11/1 (priority)

Early Action Deadline: 11/1

Fall Transfer Deadline: 5/31, 3/15
  (priority)

Spring Transfer Deadline: 12/1,
  11/1 (priority)

Total # of Students Applied: 5,501
  Admitted: 3,167
  Enrolled: 1,505

Inside the Classroom

UMBC is strongly committed to providing students with opportunities for hands-on research. UMBC offers 37 majors and 32 minors or certificate programs; new degree programs include environmental science, financial economics, and a B.F.A. in acting. Particularly strong in the sciences, UMBC is a two-time winner of the U.S. Presidential Award for Excellence in Science, Mathematics, and Engineering Mentoring.

Several of the UMBC students we surveyed cited the high quality of the faculty as one of the best things about the university. "UMBC is an extremely rigorous academic school," says a senior psychology major. "My professors have always wanted class participation and involvement from students. Professors are always available, and a high workload is encouraged." A junior adds, "UMBC stresses the importance of research to all its students, no matter what field that research may be in. I am an English Lit major, and I am always reading, writing papers, and doing research." Another junior agrees that the workload is heavy: "I am an animation major and spend an average of 20 hours in the computer labs on weekends working on projects." But a junior double-majoring in biology and math assures us that the academic environment "is not cutthroat at all."

Many top high school students are attracted to UMBC's merit-based programs such as the Meyerhoff Scholarship Program—"for high-achieving high school seniors who have an interest in pursuing doctoral study in the sciences, mathematics, computer science, and engineering"—and Linehan Artist Scholars, Humanities Scholars, and Public Affairs Scholars Programs.

A wide array of research and preprofessional opportunities are available at UMBC. The Goddard Earth Science and Technology Center brings NASA scientists and UMBC professors and students together to study the earth's surface, atmosphere, and oceans. The Imaging Research Center gives students professional experience in computer animation and production with companies such as The Discovery Channel, CNN, and PBS. The Shriver Center links the resources of the campus to urgent social problems. And many students participate in co-ops and internships in the Baltimore-Washington area and abroad.

Campus Environment

Housing is guaranteed for freshmen. A junior states, "Of all the housing I have seen at other campuses, I have to say that UMBC has the best in terms of comfort, variety, affordability, availability, and convenience." Upperclassmen can live in the on-campus apartment communities of West Hill, Terrace, and Hillside, but they often move off campus.

UMBC's research facilities are top-notch, as are other campus facilities. The Commons—the new $35 million, 148,000-square-foot community center—is the hub of campus life. And an English major reveals, "The Albin O. Kuhn Library [commonly known as 'the A-OK Library'] is a great place to study—it has very comfortable chairs."

"It is an extremely safe campus, and most of the students will admit that they feel completely fine with walking around alone late at night," insists an American studies/elementary ed major. Another student reveals, "Off-campus safety is not a problem. We are about 15 minutes from downtown Baltimore City, but that part of Baltimore is quite safe, as it is the tourist part of town. One would rarely trek to the bad parts of the city on purpose."

Most students have a car to get around town. Lack of parking seems to be a major complaint among students, but a junior concedes, "After months of complaining, parking is no longer such a headache. Many strides were made by the administration to improve student parking." Shuttle service is provided to and from the lots, as well as around campus and to the train station. There are also frequent bus and shuttle trips to the Inner Harbor and Washington, DC.

Student Life

Besides having strong science and research programs, UMBC may be best known as a chess powerhouse: In January 2003, UMBC won the Pan-American Intercollegiate Team Chess Championship for a record sixth time in seven years. If you're looking to work up more of a sweat, the UMBC Retrievers play 9 men's and 11 women's Division I sports (a point of contention: there's no football team); there are also 25 club sports and 11 intramural sports.

Students tell us that fraternities and sororities don't play a major role in campus life. And UMBC has never been known as a party school. A junior tells us, "Drinking is not that big of a factor unless it's the day of Quadmania (a huge concert/carnival once a year). Drugs also are not really a factor." A Resident Assistant agrees: "As an RA, I have not had too many incidents involving alcohol, and none involving drugs."

"The students who make the most of UMBC have a sense of personal mission; they aim to get the most out of their education," observes a school official. "Many students lead complex lives, juggling part-time jobs, classwork, and extracurricular activities." UMBC students are certainly a diverse bunch, with African Americans and Asian Americans making up a large percentage of the student body. "Diversity is celebrated here and is never an issue of conflict," says a proud sophomore.

A freshman notes, "It is a quiet school, especially on weekends since most students live in the area and go off campus." So what do UMBC students do with their free time? A junior answers, "On weeknights, students usually can be found studying or perhaps attending a meeting of a club or organization. Thursdays are the one exception: it's the one day that many students go to Baltimore City for College Night, when the clubs are open to students over the age of 18." Students also often head to Arundel Mills, a large mall that just opened up two years ago and is just 10 minutes away. And according to a sophomore, "Many students go to DC on the weekends for parties at popular clubs such as Dream and VIP."

Other schools to check out: St. Mary's College of Maryland, Salisbury University, University of Delaware, SUNY Albany, James Madison University.

Waitlisted Students Admitted: 40

Test Scores (middle 50%):
SAT Verbal: 540–640
SAT Math: 580–670
ACT Comp: 22–28
ACT English: 21–28
ACT Math: 23–29

HS Rank of Entering Freshmen:
Top 10%: 33%
Top 25%: 60%
Top 50%: 88%

Avg. HS GPA: 3.53

THE EXPERTS SAY...

" Whether you're interested in science, IT, or public affairs, UMBC is a great value for your tuition dollar. More than one-third of UMBC students go right on to graduate or professional school. "

" UMBC does a great job of encouraging minorities to pursue careers in the sciences. Students here celebrate intelligence, diversity, and chess. Go team! "

Costs (2003–04)

Tuition and Fees, In-State: $7,388

Tuition and Fees, Out-of-State: $14,290

Room & Board: $7,530

Payment Plan(s): installment plan

Inst. Aid (2002–03)

FT Undergrads Receiving Aid: 53%
Avg. Amount per Student: $6,023

FT Undergrads Receiving Non-Need-Based Scholarship or Grant Aid: 17%
Avg. Amount per Student: $6,341

Of Those Receiving Any Aid:

Rec. Need-Based Scholarship or Grant Aid: 68%
Average Award: $3,677

Rec. Need-Based Self-Help Aid: 89%
Average Award: $3,895

Upon Graduation, Avg. Loan Debt per Student: $14,500

Financial Aid Deadline: 2/15 (priority)

Graduates

Going to Graduate School: 37% Within One Year

Companies Recruiting On Campus: 421

Alumni Giving: 15%

UNIVERSITY OF MARYLAND—COLLEGE PARK

Mitchell Building, College Park, MD 20742-5235 Admissions Phone: (301) 314-8385;
(800) 422-5867 Fax: (301) 314-9693 Email: um-admit@uga.umd.edu
Website: www.umd.edu Application Website: www.uga.umd.edu

General Info

Type of School: public, coed
Setting: suburban
Academic Calendar: semester

Student Body

Full-Time Undergrads: 22,881
  Men: 50%, Women: 50%

Part-Time Undergrads: 1,950
  Men: 55%, Women: 45%

Total Undergrad Population:
  African American: 12%
  Asian American: 14%
  Latino: 6%
  Native American: <1%
  Caucasian: 59%
  International: 2%
  Out-of-State: 24%
  Living Off-Campus: 64%
  In Fraternities: 9%
  In Sororities: 9%

Graduate and First-Professional
  Students: 9,883

Academics

Full-Time Faculty: 1,575
  With Ph.D.: 94%

Part-Time Faculty: 522
  With Ph.D.: 57%

Most Popular Majors:
  criminology/criminal justice (5%)
  computer science (5%)
  psychology (3%)
  government and politics (3%)
  economics (3%)

Completing 2 or More Majors: 5%

Freshmen Retention Rate: 93%

Graduation Rates:
  41% within four years
  69% within six years

Admissions

Regular Application Deadline: 1/20;
  12/1 (priority)

Early Action Deadline: 12/1

Fall Transfer Deadline: 7/1, 3/1
  (priority)

Spring Transfer Deadline: 12/1,
  11/1 (priority)

Total # of Students Applied: 25,028
  Admitted: 10,679
  Enrolled: 4,063

Inside the Classroom

With a choice of 97 undergraduate programs, UMD students have many options, including numerous preprofessional and interdisciplinary programs. Undergraduate schools include agriculture and natural resources; arts and humanities; behavioral and social sciences; business; computer, math, and physical sciences; education; engineering; health and human performance; and life sciences. UMD's computer science department is one of the best in the country; its physics and business programs are also particularly strong. In the last few years, the school's reputation has improved, and guidance counselors are taking note. It has "upped its standards for admission, and weeded out old majors and added new ones."

"The workload is fair, however it can be highly competitive," a senior says. As might be expected, workload varies according to department. One double major explains, "The psychology department is very easy with a light workload, but the professors are often brought in for the sole purpose of teaching a particular class and may have other jobs in nearby cities. Thus, they are inaccessible. The biology department is more difficult, but the professors are all on campus and so are easy to track down." Because there are so many students at UMD, we're told that personalized attention is not the norm. "If you miss the lectures, you may not be able to catch up." A business-decisions and information-systems major explains, "Professors are accessible if you make it a point to get to know them during office hours. If not, you will feel like a number in the large lecture halls, especially during the first two years." Until recently, a common practice at College Park was for professors to post answer keys outside their offices or online after giving an exam so that students can immediately see how they did; however, after a dozen students allegedly used the text-messaging function on their cell phones to cheat on their exams in fall 2002, this practice ended.

Campus Environment

It's no surprise that with such a large student population, the campus itself is large, too. Says one junior, "The campus is so large that you will be walking about two miles a day easily, without really noticing it." People often congregate on the outdoor campus mall when it warms up. As for getting around, one student tells us, "Most students have a car, but freshmen do not. However, the campus has a subway stop so it's no problem." The school runs a great bus system, and there are shuttles everywhere. Location is an added academic bonus, as a recent grad explains: "Because of its close proximity to Washington, DC, I was able to do an internship during the semester and take the metro into the city."

"I was initially attracted by the campus," one sophomore tells us. "It's beautiful—it looks like a gameboard." Still, only about one-third of undergrads live on campus, due partly to overcrowding. One senior warns, "Big time housing squeeze. If you transfer, better start looking off-campus. Freshmen, send in your deposits early." Says a junior, "Campus housing is nearly impossible to get, and while upperclassmen dorms are much nicer than the dirty, old, hot freshman dorms, the administration kicks upperclassmen off campus. The only people who actually live there are athletes." Students tell us it's common to move off campus after freshman year, but "this makes finding acceptable housing difficult. Rents are high as well—averaging about $550 a month."

A junior tells us, "The campus is not incredibly safe—we are near DC and in Prince Georges county, which is the poorest county in the state. We've had about a dozen armed robberies this semester." The university provides many safety measures, though, including 24-hour security and sworn police officers. One student explains, "The university's on- and off-campus escort services are pretty commonly used, especially by females walking at night by themselves."

Student Life

The College Park campus is "generally considered a liberal campus that has strong political roots with a close proximity to DC." One guidance counselor we heard from praised the school's recruiting of minorities. "Diversity is one of the school's prides." Socially, students can be found studying or watching TV in big groups. Says one senior, "Students attend parties on the weekend and might go to one of the three bars in College Park." The same student explains, "Maryland is not the party school it was in the early '90s and '80s. As admission became more selective, the campus expects a different type of student. So drinking is not that big, less than other big 'party schools.'" Another tells us, "The city of College Park has really enforced the 21+ age requirement at bars nearby. You can find a party if you know people but if you're just randomly looking on a weekend night for a party, you won't get much luck."

Greek life has its place on campus but doesn't seem to dominate. A student explains, "A very small percentage of the population is Greek, and while they do throw the biggest parties, they are not that important. Again, in a school of my size, they are prevalent, but you could be living on campus and not even ever go to a frat party." We are also told that "the university has really cut down on the number of fraternity parties it allows."

Athletics at UMD are huge. Sporting events can be all-day events. Says one junior, "There is always so much buzz going on about basketball and football. It is really neat because the sports layers are like gods, but they walk among us and are as nice as can be. You don't notice any special treatment from the teachers, and they pull their own weight in the classrooms." UMD's sports teams, the Terrapins, have an active and enthusiastic following. The basketball team has just made its tenth straight NCAA tournament appearance, and for the past two years, the football team has gone to the Orange Bowl. Sometimes, the excitement can get out of hand. According to one student, "The events surrounding certain sporting events tend to get really rowdy, and there is a stupid tendency to start fires and destroy things when we lose," though others say that people are tolerant and not nearly as rowdy as the media think.

# of Students Waitlisted: 2,614
   Students Accepting Place: 2,489
   Waitlisted Students Admitted: 173

Test Scores (middle 50%):
   SAT Verbal: 570–660
   SAT Math: 600–700

HS Rank of Entering Freshmen:
   Top 10%: 56%
   Top 25%: 89%
   Top 50%: 99%

Avg. HS GPA: 3.88

THE EXPERTS SAY...

" UMD has definitely changed for the better, raising their admissions standards and drawing a much less party-oriented student body. "

" The student body is fairly diverse, both ethnically and geographically. But if you're looking for personalized attention, St. Mary's College of Maryland is a better bet. "

Costs (2003–04)

Tuition and Fees, In-State: $6,758

Tuition and Fees, Out-of-State: $17,432

Room & Board: $7,608

Payment Plan(s): installment plan, deferred payment plan, pre-payment plan

Inst. Aid (2002–03)

FT Undergrads Receiving Aid: 39%
   Avg. Amount per Student: $8,344

FT Undergrads Receiving Non-Need-Based Scholarship or Grant Aid: 6%
   Avg. Amount per Student: $3,854

Of Those Receiving Any Aid:

Rec. Need-Based Scholarship or Grant Aid: 70%
   Average Award: $4,120

Rec. Need-Based Self-Help Aid: 77%
   Average Award: $3,722

Upon Graduation, Avg. Loan Debt per Student: $14,076

Financial Aid Deadline: rolling, 2/15 (priority)

Graduates

Companies Recruiting On-Campus: 331

Alumni Giving: 24%

UNIVERSITY OF MASSACHUSETTS— AMHERST

37 Mather Drive, Amherst, MA 01003-9291
Admissions Phone: (413) 545-0222 Fax: (413) 545-4312 Website: www.umass.edu
Application Website: www.umass.edu/admissions/

General Info

Type of School: public, coed

Setting: small town

Academic Calendar: semester, winter and summer sessions also available

Student Body

Full-Time Undergrads: 17,039
Men: 50%, Women: 50%

Part-Time Undergrads: 1,025
Men: 45%, Women: 55%

Total Undergrad Population:
African American: 4%
Asian American: 7%
Latino: 3%
Native American: <1%
Caucasian: 76%
International: 1%
Out-of-State: 17%
Living Off-Campus: 41%
In Fraternities: 3%
In Sororities: 7%

Graduate and First-Professional Students: 5,592

Academics

Full-Time Faculty: 1,077
With Ph.D.: 94%

Part-Time Faculty: 200
With Ph.D.: 61%

Student/Faculty Ratio: 18:1

Most Popular Majors:
psychology (6%)
biology (4%)
communication (4%)
English (4%)
sociology (4%)

Freshmen Retention Rate: 84%

Graduation Rates:
44% within four years
64% within six years

Admissions

Regular Application Deadline: 1/15

Fall Transfer Deadline: 4/15

Spring Transfer Deadline: 10/15

Total # of Students Applied: 16,427
Admitted: 13,461
Enrolled: 4,077

Waitlist Available

Inside the Classroom

UMass has around 18,000 undergraduate students, but don't let the big numbers fool you: The average student-to-faculty ratio is 18:1, and 70 percent of classes (including labs and discussions) have fewer than 30 students. Of course, introductory lectures can be huge, but classes grow much smaller as students progress in their majors. "In my experience, the professors are easily accessible," an English major comments.

Guidance counselors tell us that UMass has "raised the academic bar" in recent years, making admissions "very competitive." The incredible extent of academic offerings at UMass is a big draw. The University has nine individual colleges (education; engineering; food and natural resources; humanities and fine arts; management; nursing; natural sciences and mathematics; public health and health sciences; social and behavioral sciences) which collectively offer more than 90 undergraduate programs. Nationally recognized programs include music, computer science, linguistics, polymer science, psychology, engineering, business management, and hotel, restaurant, and travel administration.

General education requirements ("Gen Eds") are extensive: two writing courses; six social world courses (two of which must fulfill a cultural diversity requirement); three biological and physical world courses; one math course; and one analytic reasoning course. In most cases you'll have specific college requirements to fulfill as well.

If you're an outstanding high school student, you might want to apply to the Commonwealth College, offering both the advantages of a small honors college and the wide-ranging opportunities of a nationally recognized research university. Another study option: Residential Academic Programs (RAPs), which offer opportunities to learn in a residential hall setting.

Because UMass Amherst is part of the Five Colleges, you can take courses for credit at the other four colleges (Amherst, Hampshire, Mount Holyoke and Smith) without paying additional tuition or fees. UMass also offers more than 70 study-abroad programs—18 percent of UMass students participate every year.

Campus Environment

Naturally, this huge university is located on a huge campus. "The campus sometimes feels too spread out when trekking from one side of campus to the other for class—from one side of campus to the other is about a 20-minute walk," a student complains. With more than five million books, periodicals, and government documents, UMass also has the largest library system of any state-supported institution in New England.

The 41 residence halls are divided into five areas, each with its own ambience: Southwest provides "an urban-type environment for those who enjoy the hustle and bustle of city life"; Northeast is "more laid back and located close to the mathematics and science buildings"; Central is "most easily accessible from campus because it is equidistant from most academic buildings"; Sylvan is "a quiet location for those who enjoy suite life"; and Orchard Hill is "a lot like rural New England life because it is on top of a hill, has an apple orchard, and has a great view of campus from the observatory."

Students are required to live on campus for their first two years, and overcrowding is a major problem. "The lounges in most dorms, especially in Orchard Hill, are converted into triples or quads to accommodate the huge number of enrolled students," a junior explains. "But, by the spring semesters, there always seems to be enough room for everyone and lounges free up again." The university claims that approximately 80 percent of freshmen are placed in their first or second choice of residence hall. Sophomores can escape to fraternity or sorority housing.

"Off-campus housing is generally very affordable, depending on proximity to school," says one student. "However, because UMass is such a large school, students have to act quickly and find a place to live because by mid-semester, most off-campus housing is full."

Amherst—"a very homey college town"—is about two hours from Boston. A student lists the local hangouts: "On weeknights, if students need a break from studying, Rao's Coffee shop is a good place to go in the center of Amherst, or Starbucks. On the weekends, the Cineplex in the Hampshire Mall houses many movies or students can dine and drink at the Hangar, the Pub, or Charlie's." Many students have a bike or a car, but it's not a necessity, says one student: "The center of Amherst is about a mile from any dorm area on campus, so walking is easy and many students choose to walk, bike, or take a bus rather than drive."

Student Life

If you're looking for the fast-paced, party-filled, "ZooMass" social life of yesteryear, beware: The administration has recently taken a hard line on drinking, instituting and enforcing strict sanctions that have curtailed the on-campus party scene. However, one student assures us that "there are a lot of off-campus parties and there's a bar scene." Because the school is so large, the 22 fraternities and 13 sororities don't really influence the social scene all that much—"they have their own way of life and have parties where mostly other Greek members attend," another student tells us.

One student sums up UMass in the following way: "It is fairly liberal and has a friendly atmosphere. It is intense if you want it to be, or it is relaxed if you want it to be." Another student's view: "Students and faculty at UMass are friendly and very concerned with politics and freedom of expression. Very often there are students, faculty, or guest speakers introducing new political ideas in the student center or at other various gathering spots around campus."

With more than 250 Registered Student Organizations (RSOs), UMass has one of the most unique and diversified student activities programs in the country: student-run businesses, student government organizations, cultural and religious activities—not to mention a nationally acclaimed marching band. And The Stonewall Center—"a lesbian, bisexual, gay, and transgender educational resource center"—has served as a model for many colleges and universities across the country.

It seems as if everyone at UMass either watches a sport or plays one. The NCAA Division I athletic teams include 15 for women and 14 for men. Men's basketball is a perennial favorite; students flock to the 10,000-seat Mullen Center to support their beloved team, a regular contender for the NCAA championship. There are also 17 club sports, and more than 8,000 students participate in intramural programs.

Test Scores (middle 50%):
SAT Verbal: 520–630
SAT Math: 510–610
HS Rank of Entering Freshmen:
Top 10%: 16%
Top 25%: 44%
Top 50%: 85%
Avg. HS GPA: 3.28

Costs (2004–5)

Tuition and Fees, In-State: $9,008

Tuition and Fees, Out-of-State: $17,861

Room & Board: $6,189

Payment Plan(s): installment plan, pre-payment plan

THE EXPERTS SAY...

" This superb public school is part of the Five Colleges, and students can take credits at Amherst, Hampshire, Mount Holyoke, and Smith. Political give and take thrives on campus. Gay students: Check out the Stonewall Center. "

" Party animals, take heed: ZooMass is cleaning up its act. The band is still great, though. "

Inst. Aid (2002–03)

Institutional Aid, Need-Based: $12,728,572

Institutional Aid, Non-Need-Based: $2,563,866

FT Undergrads Receiving Aid: 48%
Avg. Amount per Student: $9,422

FT Undergrads Receiving Non-Need-Based Scholarship or Grant Aid: 4%
Avg. Amount per Student: $3,526

Of Those Receiving Any Aid:

Rec. Need-Based Scholarship or Grant Aid: 96%
Average Award: $6,167

Rec. Need-Based Self-Help Aid: 88%
Average Award: $4,509

Upon Graduation, Avg. Loan Debt per Student: $15,374

Financial Aid Deadline: 3/1 (priority)

Graduates

Going to Graduate School:
16% Within One Year

Accepting Job Offer:
38% at time of graduation

UNIVERSITY OF MIAMI

P.O.box 248025, Coral Gables, FL 33124
Admissions Phone: (305) 284-4323 Fax: (305) 284-2507
Email: admission@miami.edu Website: www.miami.edu
Application Website: www.miami.edu/apply

General Info

Type of School: private, coed

Setting: suburban

Academic Calendar: semester

Student Body

Full-Time Undergrads: 9,075
  Men: 42%, Women: 58%

Part-Time Undergrads: 554
  Men: 34%, Women: 66%

Total Undergrad Population:
  African American: 10%
  Asian American: 6%
  Latino: 24%
  Native American: <1%
  Caucasian: 51%
  International: 7%
  Out-of-State: 45%
  Living Off-Campus: 59%
  In Fraternities: 14%
  In Sororities: 12%

Graduate and First-Professional
  Students: 4,239

Academics

Full-Time Faculty: 853
  With Ph.D.: 88%

Part-Time Faculty: 341
  With Ph.D.: 52%

Student/Faculty Ratio: 13:1

Freshmen Retention Rate: 87%

Graduation Rates:
  53% within four years
  67% within six years

Computers: Computer Required

Admissions

Regular Application Deadline: 2/1

Early Decision Deadline(s): 11/1

Early Action Deadline: 11/1

Fall Transfer Deadline: 3/1 (priority)

Spring Transfer Deadline: 11/15
  (priority)

Total # of Students Applied: 16,854
  Admitted: 7,490
  Enrolled: 2,078

Applied Early Decision: 790
  Early Decision Admitted: 244

Inside the Classroom

The University of Miami is the largest private research university in the Southeast. According to the National Science Foundation, it ranks 22nd of all private universities in expenditures of federal funds for research and development. The main campus in Coral Gables is home to nine colleges: architecture; arts and sciences; business administration; communication; education; engineering; international studies; music; and nursing. The college of marine and atmospheric science, located on its own campus in Biscayne Bay, is one of the top oceanographic institutions in the country. UM also excels in several preprofessional areas, particularly law and medicine (a new major in neuroscience allows undergrads to collaborate with faculty at UM's prestigious School of Medicine). Some of the more unique programs at UM are the centers for contemporary Judaic studies, for Cuban studies, and for research on sports in society. With the installment of former Secretary of Health and Human Services Donna Shalala as the school's fifth president in 2001, the University has attracted a great deal of renewed attention—not to mention renewed support for the Hurricanes' athletic program, for which Shalala has enormous enthusiasm. (However, her recent decision to fold the entire School of International Studies into the College of Arts and Sciences has angered many students.)

The workload at Miami is heavy enough to prevent students from becoming complete beach bums. Serious about their studies and their future careers, most students put in a decent amount of study time per week. In the last few years, entrance has become increasingly competitive, with fewer than one out of two applicants accepted—over half of recent freshmen graduated in the top 10 percent of their high school class. One guidance counselor we know is impressed with the improvements in the school's academic reputation.

With around 2,000 new freshmen each year, UM undergrads encounter the problems typical of major research universities, including large lecture classes and professors who might seem more interested in research than in teaching. But the student/faculty ratio is a low 13:1, and most upper-level courses have fewer than 26 students. One upperclassman states, "For the most part, you're able to talk to professors. You'll find some that really care about students." Undergrads are actively encouraged to get involved in research—not only ongoing research projects, but also workshops and training sessions pertinent to their discipline.

Campus Environment

Miami has a unique housing system that helps students feel as though they're attending a small college. Students live in one of five residential colleges, each housing three faculty members, a residence coordinator, and student resident assistants to create a living–learning community. Each college forms its own community, hosting social, cultural, and educational events. We've heard that the dorms are decent, though one guidance counselor told us that many students are disappointed that the school's living quarters—not to mention the labs—are not as modern as they would have hoped. Recently, as a result of increased enrollment, space got so tight that some students were temporarily housed in converted study lounges; the school is now in the process of building another dorm. Although the residential college setup is popular and around 75 percent of freshmen live on campus, most students eventually move off campus, as quality housing is readily found in surrounding areas.

Not every day at UM is picture perfect (hence the name of the school team, the Hurricanes). But if you can get a great education in a place where you're able to study outside under a palm tree as easily as in the library, why not go for it? On campus, there's no shortage of spots to hang out and relax, including the outdoor pool, perfect for sunning, swimming, and—for some—studying. The campus has recently been revamped with a sophisticated wireless network, allowing students to access the school network from their laptops—even from outside. The campus is also home to several arts centers, including an art museum, theatre, cinema, and concert hall, which are popular with students and community residents alike.

The University is based in Coral Gables, a beautiful if formal suburb community just south of Miami's Little Havana neighborhood. With Mediterranean architecture and perfectly manicured landscapes, Coral Gables combines old world charm with a lush tropical environment. Just to the east is Coconut Grove, a funky, offbeat neighborhood popular for shopping. We're told it really helps to have a car here: Sun worshippers can easily get to the beach or to trendy South Beach. As for crime worries, several students note that while some parts of Miami may be bad, Coral Gables is considered safe, requiring only the amount of vigilance necessary in any other American suburb.

Student Life

Miami is a highly diverse school: Almost half the undergrad population are minorities, with Latinos the largest group, followed by African Americans. Additionally, 45 percent of students are from out of state—and many of the remaining 55 percent are commuter students, living at home and traveling to campus daily. "We're still very much a Florida and Washington, D.C.–Boston corridor-type school, but there's a dramatic shift occurring," according to the director of admission. "We're having a lot of success in the Midwest, Southwest, and West." What's more, international enrollment continues to rank among the nations' highest, and not just the obvious South America—there are significant numbers from Europe and Asia as well. In fact, one guidance counselor we heard from in England recommends Miami to her students for the cost, location, and large population of international students.

While most students complain that there's not a lot of school spirit at Miami, the sports teams certainly get a lot of attention. The Miami Hurricanes have won the NCAA football and baseball championships several times, and students are rabidly devoted followers, filling the stands to cheer and show their school spirit, especially for games against rival Florida State.

Greek life is extremely popular; in fact, approximately 85 percent of the leadership positions on campus are held by members of the Greek community. Officially, the membership rate is around 15 percent of students participating, so while there are always some great frat parties going on, they don't dominate the social scene. Two of the ten fraternities have dry housing, and those are becoming increasingly popular with new pledges.

Test Scores (middle 50%):
SAT Verbal: 550–660
SAT Math: 570–680
ACT Comp: 25–30
ACT English: 25–30
ACT Math: 24–30

HS Rank of Entering Freshmen:
Top 10%: 60%
Top 25%: 87%
Top 50%: 98%

Avg. HS GPA: 4.04

THE EXPERTS SAY...

" Anyone interested in studying marine science should definitely look at Miami's Biscayne Bay campus. The main Coral Gables campus should appeal to premed and music majors, among others. "

" Strike a balance—do your neuroscience reading under a palm tree! "

Costs (2003–04)
Tuition and Fees: $26,280
Room & Board: $8,328

Inst. Aid (est. 2003–04)
Institutional Aid, Need-Based: $51,979,478
Institutional Aid, Non-Need-Based: $26,591,173
FT Undergrads Receiving Aid: 55%
  Avg. Amount per Student: $22,940
FT Undergrads Receiving Non-Need-Based Scholarship or Grant Aid: 21%
  Avg. Amount per Student: $12,776

Of Those Receiving Any Aid:

Rec. Need-Based Scholarship or Grant Aid: 98%
  Average Award: $16,363
Rec. Need-Based Self-Help Aid: 82%
  Average Award: $6,944
Upon Graduation, Avg. Loan Debt per Student: $29,046
Financial Aid Deadline: 2/15 (priority)

Graduates
Companies Recruiting On-Campus: 110

UNIVERSITY OF MICHIGAN—ANN ARBOR

1220 Student Activities Building, 515 East Jefferson Street, Ann Arbor, MI 48109-1316
Admissions Phone: (734) 764-7433 Fax: (734) 936-0740
Website: www.admissions.umich.edu

General Info

Type of School: public, coed
Setting: suburban
Academic Calendar: trimester

Student Body

Full-Time Undergrads: 23,253
 Men: 49%, Women: 51%

Part-Time Undergrads: 1,095
 Men: 51%, Women: 49%

Total Undergrad Population:
 African American: 8%
 Asian American: 13%
 Latino: 5%
 Native American: 1%
 Caucasian: 64%
 International: 5%

Graduate and First-Professional
 Students: 14,514

Academics

Full-Time Faculty: 2,280
 With Ph.D.: 91%

Part-Time Faculty: 647
 With Ph.D.: 76%

Most Popular Majors:
 psychology (4%)
 business administration (3%)
 political science (2%)
 economics (2%)
 English (2%)

Freshmen Retention Rate: 96%

Graduation Rates:
 64% within four years
 84% within six years

Admissions

Regular Application Deadline: 2/1

Fall Transfer Deadline: 2/1

Spring Transfer Deadline: 2/1

Total # of Students Applied: 25,943
 Admitted: 13,814
 Enrolled: 5,553

# of Students Waitlisted: 4,100
 Students Accepting Place: 997

Test Scores (middle 50%):
 SAT Verbal: 580–690
 SAT Math: 620–720
 ACT Comp: 26–30
 ACT English: 25–31
 ACT Math: 26–32

Inside the Classroom

Says one senior, "University of Michigan excels at most of their programs, so you are getting the best of everything, in and out of your major, and if you don't know what you want to do, it's a great school because you can figure it out and end up in a good program." With more than 200 majors, Michigan's undergraduate colleges are: art and design; engineering; kinesiology; literature, science, and the arts; music; and nursing. This is the school where valedictorians and class presidents go, say guidance counselors, and that makes for some stiff competition. "BIG; tough to get in—highly selective," one warns, but another states, "They are more open to letting all types of students attend. Their great academics are finally open to everyone!" A bio major explains, "University of Michigan has a very competitive atmosphere... Many of the 101 classes are extremely large and there is not a lot of personal attention. These classes become 'weeder' courses." A preprofessional chimes in, "There is a high level of competitiveness here, as most students are premed, prelaw, or engineering."

The university recently appointed its first female dean, a talked-about event on campus. Michigan's prestigious professors "are not always very accessible because of the many students attending here," says a computer science major. A guidance counselor gripes: "Lots of grad assistants." Says a science major, "At the higher-level classes there is more professor/student interaction, but the student must be proactive to have this kind of relationship." Although Michigan is trendy, many guidance counselors call it "overrated." "Too impersonal, students have to fend for themselves," says one. Student peeves include "the language barrier between some professors/GSIs and students," the "intimidating" class size, and the "major scheduling problems." Still, students love Michigan—so much so that many don't graduate in four years.

Campus Environment

Freshmen are guaranteed campus housing, but are not required to live on campus (though the majority do). According to one junior, "The dorms are very old and all have community bathrooms, so be prepared for that." An optimistic student comments, "The housing rates low on the comfort scale as the rooms are pretty small and close together. However, it makes life interesting and it lets everyone get to know each other better."

Most Michigan students live off campus. "Right now, my house is a three-bedroom with four people living in it and it runs $1,615 in rent alone without any utilities," a psych major laments. Apartments are "available but run-down and old and WAY EXPENSIVE!" exclaims a political science major. And some housing "does get to be quite a distance from campus."

With an undergraduate enrollment of more than 24,000 students, to call the University of Michigan big is an understatement. But the Ann Arbor campus ranks as one of the most beautiful in the nation. "I think the campus is very safe, although there are a number of homeless people and that makes some people uncomfortable," a psychology major relates. "Ann Arbor kicks butt!" exclaims a political science major. "Friendly students, lots of shops, downtown area has a little bit of everything, there is ALWAYS something to do in Ann Arbor!" Adds a junior, "There are two movie theaters and numerous restaurants, bookstores, and small markets that are within walking distance. Also, there are a number of places that deliver food until the wee hours of morning. Also, Detroit is only about 30 minutes away."

Student Life

"Wolverine spirit!" a guidance counselor exclaims. "Ranked in top 25; athletic programs and facilities are top-notch!" "The athletics at U of M are amazing," raves a bio major. "This is a definite highlight for many students considering Michigan. The varsity athletic teams are some of the best in the country, bringing home national championships all the time." A recent grad elaborates, "Football games are big and the campus is inundated with locals and other Michigan residents who come into Ann Arbor for each game." The stellar athletics program received a black eye recently due to improper loans made to four men's basketball players in the 1990s. President Mary Sue Coleman announced the forfeiture of all games won while the four players were ineligible.

"I think that U of M is extremely diverse… ethnically, politically, and financially," a junior says. "I think this diversity is a direct result of the school's attempt to have this kind of atmosphere." A freshman explains, "We have musicians, athletes, academics, party people, and everything in between. Anyone can find people with similar interests here." But another states, "I think that affirmative action causes a lot of friction between students and the administration."

On weeknights, students "honestly study… and that's no joke. They'll take occasional breaks to go to coffee shop and of course they'll procrastinate, but writing papers, completing problem sets, and executing their Web-based computer homework is always on the agenda." Weekends "are used for studying during the day and partying at night." There are 37 fraternities and 23 sororities on campus and "all the houses are not alike, so someone rushing can find the house that meets their needs," says a student. A junior adds, "Since a lot of in-state people come here, it is apparent that a lot of people come here already with their own groups of friends."

Some campus traditions: "If you kiss someone under the engineering arch before your 21st birthday, you will marry them," we're told. "If you step on the M of our Diag before your first bluebook exam you will fail it. There is a large fountain that freshman walk through every year during freshman orientation, and then after you graduate, you walk through the same fountain again. A tradition to mark the beginning and end of your time at U of M!" Declares a junior, "I would choose U of M again in a heartbeat."

Other schools to check out: U of Illinois—Urbana-Champaign, Northwestern, UCLA, Michigan State, U of Minnesota—Twin Cities.

Avg. HS GPA: 3.73

Costs (2003–04)

Tuition and Fees, In-State: $7,975

Tuition and Fees, Out-of-State: $24,777

Room & Board: $6,704

Payment Plan(s): installment plan

THE EXPERTS SAY…

" This public Ivy has a great mix of serious academics, Wolverine sports, and weekend fun. "

" Students must be proactive about their education to make it at big, impersonal U. Mich. "

Inst. Aid (2002–03)

Institutional Aid, Need-Based: $33,398,996

Institutional Aid, Non-Need-Based: $23,729,173

FT Undergrads Receiving Aid: 40% Avg. Amount per Student: $11,375

FT Undergrads Receiving Non-Need-Based Scholarship or Grant Aid: 21% Avg. Amount per Student: $4,794

Of Those Receiving Any Aid:

Rec. Need-Based Scholarship or Grant Aid: 59% Average Award: $7,512

Rec. Need-Based Self-Help Aid: 100% Average Award: $6,141

Upon Graduation, Avg. Loan Debt per Student: $19,407

Financial Aid Deadline: 4/30, 2/15 (priority)

Graduates

Companies Recruiting On-Campus: 1,500

UNIVERSITY OF MINNESOTA— TWIN CITIES

100 Church Street SE, Minneapolis, MN 55455-0213 Admissions Phone: (612) 625-2008;
(800) 752-1000 Fax: (612) 626-1693 Email: admissions@tc.umn.edu
Website: www.umn.edu/tc/ Application Website: www1.umn.ed/twincities/admissions.html

Note: Info. not verified by school

General Info

Type of School: public, coed

Setting: urban

Academic Calendar: semester,
3-week spring intersession,
8-week summer session

Student Body

Full-Time Undergrads: 24,485
Men: 48%, Women: 52%

Part-Time Undergrads: 3,618
Men: 48%, Women: 52%

Total Undergrad Population:
African American: 4%
Asian American: 8%
Latino: 2%
Native American: 1%
Caucasian: 80%
International: 2%
Out-of-State: 26%
Living Off-Campus: 78%

Graduate and First-Professional
Students: 16,220

Academics

Full-Time Faculty: 2,730
With Ph.D.: 91%

Part-Time Faculty: 406
With Ph.D.: 78%

Student/Faculty Ratio: 15:1

Most Popular Majors:
psychology (5%)
biology (3%)
English (2%)
journalism (2%)
political science (2%)

Freshmen Retention Rate: 84%

Graduation Rates:
26% within four years
54% within six years

Admissions

Regular Application Deadline: 12/15
(priority)

Fall Transfer Deadline: 3/1 (priority)

Spring Transfer Deadline: 10/15
(priority)

Total # of Students Applied: 14,746
Admitted: 10,973
Enrolled: 5,188

Waitlist Available

In the Classroom

Generally regarded as one of the top public universities in the country, the University of Minnesota—one of the largest universities in the U.S.—offers 161 bachelor's degree programs to pick from. One student summed it up in a phrase: "top-ranked programs and a world of opportunities."

Freshmen are admitted into one of the following colleges: liberal arts, biological sciences, management, human ecology, natural resources, technology, and agricultural, food, and environmental sciences. Bachelor degree programs are also offered by the colleges of architecture, education, medicine, dentistry, and nursing; however, these do not admit freshmen—you must apply for admission sometime after your first year. The General College, with no degree programs of its own, admits highly motivated freshmen who do not meet the university's admission requirements and then provides special help to prepare them for transfer into one of the regular undergraduate colleges. About 1,600 students are enrolled in the General College at any given time, and the program has become a nationally recognized model.

In spite of the university's size, most students find the individualized help they need. A fisheries and wildlife major said, "I have never had any problems meeting with professors; they have office hours available, and TA's also have office hours to help students." Academic expectations depend on the program, but, all in all, plan to do some serious studying. A microbiology major says, "Although Minnesota students enjoy having fun sometimes, that is not any student's main focus."

All undergrads must obtain a prescribed number of credits in the physical and biological sciences, the social sciences and humanities, historical perspectives, and math. In addition, students must take one course in each of the following themes: Environment, Cultural Diversity, International Perspectives, and Citizenship and Public Ethics. There is also a writing requirement—four writing courses, including two upper division courses, one in the student's major.

Undergrad as well as grad students can take advantage of the facilities and faculty of one of the nation's leading research universities, where such things as the pacemaker, the flight recorder black box, and Uranium 235 were first created. The Undergraduate Research Opportunities Program offers financial awards twice yearly for research, scholarly, or creative projects undertaken in partnership with a faculty member. A guidance counselor in Kaplan's national survey noted the "thousands" of internship opportunities offered, many in nearby downtown Minneapolis. Another special study option is the university's Global Campus, one of the largest study abroad programs in the United States with more than 170 programs in 60 countries.

Campus Environment

The Twin Cities campus is really two campuses—the main one in Minneapolis and one in St. Paul several miles away. The Mississippi River cuts the Minneapolis campus into two sections: East Bank and West Bank. University buses provide transportation between and within the St. Paul and Minneapolis campuses. With this 24-hour service and the Twin Cities' regular urban bus system, many students find having a car is more of a hassle than a help. "Parking is such as issue that not many people have cars here," explained a sophomore, and a senior says, "I've been here four years and never had a car. I've never had a problem getting to where I needed to be."

There are ten residence halls; all are located on the East Bank except for one on the West Bank and one on the St. Paul campus. Students may select a freshman-only dorm or choose from among many theme-housing options. Freshmen are encouraged to live on campus and those who get their housing applications in on time are guaranteed housing. One freshman categorizes his dorm experience as "OK, but loud." Most upperclassmen live off campus, many nearby, but others scattered all over the Twin Cities.

One drawback to having such a large, spread-out campus is a lack of closeness among students. "It's not always easy to find a community to fit into," admits a student. The high percentage of part-time students and the low percentage of students who actually live on campus also contribute to the sense of detachment felt by many students.

Student Life

The university's setting in the heart of a major urban center provides a life beyond the campus like few other Big 10 universities can. The Twin Cities (in the words of one guidance counselor, "a cultural Mecca for the Midwest") offer first-rate museums, jazz clubs, comedy shows, plays, independent films, concerts, and dance clubs. "I am never bored," says a freshman.

With more than 400 student clubs and organizations, there is always something happening on campus as well. "Minnesota Nice" is the prevailing atmosphere, although as one student points out, the university has "many different groups representing a wide range of political views."

"Fraternities and sororities are popular but I think a lot of people are surprised to hear that only 4–5 percent of our student body is a part of that system," one student says. Opinions vary widely: One student said, "They have a strong effect on social life," but another held that "They really have no influence on overall social life here." A third student explains, "I think it's a personal choice; there's room for everyone here."

According to one undergrad, "Drugs are an incredibly small factor. Drinking is a factor, but with such a diverse student body, it's easy to find a group that makes the same choices that you have made." The consensus of the students surveyed: There are those that party excessively, but they don't represent the majority. As one student said, "The majority of students do not party every weekend. There are so many other things to do."

"Students at the U are passionate about their sports teams," a freshman said. Gopher varsity sports, especially Division I football, basketball, and hockey, are very popular spectator events. Club sports offer an alternative for students who want athletic competition but not the demands of varsity athletics, and numerous intramurals, offered at three levels from beginning to advanced, enjoy widespread participation. According to one student, "The atmosphere is generally relaxed, but some leagues can get pretty intense and competitive."

Test Scores (middle 50%):
SAT Verbal: 540–660
SAT Math: 550–670
ACT Comp: 22–28
ACT English: 21–27
ACT Math: 21–28

HS Rank of Entering Freshmen:
Top 10%: 30%
Top 25%: 65%
Top 50%: 92%

Costs (2003–04)

Tuition and Fees, In-State: $7,116

Tuition and Fees, Out-of-State: $18,746

Room & Board: $6,044

THE EXPERTS SAY...

" The opportunities for learning and research are amazing at the U! "

" Don't expect too much individual attention here. They do everything big at this Big 10 school—classes, campuses, sports, parties... "

Inst. Aid (est. 2003–04)

Institutional Aid, Need-Based: $15,941,773

Institutional Aid, Non-Need-Based: $8,505,349

FT Undergrads Receiving Aid: 46%
Avg. Amount per Student: $8,496

FT Undergrads Receiving Non-Need-Based Scholarship or Grant Aid: 11%
Avg. Amount per Student: $4,089

Of Those Receiving Any Aid:

Rec. Need-Based Scholarship or Grant Aid: 74%
Average Award: $6,008

Rec. Need-Based Self-Help Aid: 87%
Average Award: $5,691

Financial Aid Deadline: rolling, 1/15 (priority)

UNIVERSITY OF MISSOURI— COLUMBIA

230 Jesse Hall, Columbia, MO 65211
Admissions Phone: (573) 882-7786; (800) 225-6075 (in-state) Fax: (573) 882-7887
Email: MU4U@missouri.edu Website: missouri.edu

General Info

Type of School: public, coed
Setting: small town
Academic Calendar: semester

Student Body

Full-Time Undergrads: 18,993
  Men: 49%, Women: 51%

Part-Time Undergrads: 1,034
  Men: 47%, Women: 53%

Total Undergrad Population:
  African American: 6%
  Asian American: 3%
  Latino: 2%
  Native American: 1%
  Caucasian: 85%
  International: 1%
  Out-of-State: 12%
  Living Off-Campus: 58%
  In Fraternities: 20%
  In Sororities: 25%

Graduate and First-Professional
  Students: 6,361

Academics

Full-Time Faculty: 1,477
  With Ph.D.: 93%

Part-Time Faculty: 50
  With Ph.D.: 94%

Student/Faculty Ratio: 18:1

Most Popular Majors:
  journalism (5%)
  biological sciences (5%)
  business administration (5%)
  psychology (4%)
  political science (2%)

Freshmen Retention Rate: 84%

Graduation Rates:
  37% within four years
  67% within six years

Admissions

Regular Application Deadline: 4/1
  (priority)

Total # of Students Applied: 10,449
  Admitted: 9,327
  Enrolled: 4,669

Waitlist Available

Test Scores (middle 50%):
  ACT Comp: 23–28
  ACT English: 23–29
  ACT Math: 22–28

Inside the Classroom

The University of Missouri at Columbia was the first public university west of the Mississippi River and is the flagship campus of the University of Missouri system. Undergrads can attend any of Mizzou's five colleges (agriculture, food, and natural resources; business; education; engineering; human environmental sciences) and nine schools (health professions; natural resources; nursing; social work; music; accountancy; undergraduate teacher development center; journalism; fine arts). The school of journalism is easily one of the best in the country, and guidance counselors also praise Mizzou's veterinary science program.

As a major research university, MU offers undergrads plenty of opportunities to get involved in research. The Honors College also offers special opportunities for select freshmen to engage in mentored studies with individual faculty in their primary area of interest.

"There's a real competitive feel at Mizzou, and the classes here are considered the most difficult in the state," says a senior. A recent grad agrees: "There was a definite level of competitiveness in classes, especially the large classes, because most professors graded on a bell curve." One unusual aspect of MU is that, unlike at most other schools, you are more likely to find your classes taught by TA's as you work your way up: "When you get into your major, the school likes to keep groups small. So if there are too many people in your class, the professor will break the class into smaller groups and have the TA's run the group." It can be a fifty-fifty split on classes taught by faculty and classes taught by TA's, another student reports. But students do describe most professors as "generally very approachable people."

MU's general education requirements are extensive; "Mizzou's strong research programs and professional schools add another dimension to general education, taking the program beyond what liberal arts colleges are able to offer undergraduates," explains a school official. One aspect of the program that has drawn national attention is the incorporation of writing across the undergraduate curriculum; more than 120 sections of writing-intensive courses are offered each semester, representing every department in every undergraduate division at the institution.

Campus Environment

Campus housing is guaranteed for freshmen only, with many housing options available, including Greek houses. A very popular option is MU's "living-learning communities," which bring students together who have similar interests, often enrolling them in the same classes. About 70 percent of the 5,200 students living in residence halls choose one of the living-learning options (approximately 90 Freshman Interest Groups, 25 sponsored learning communities, and three residential colleges). A young alum recommends the learning communities because they "can help you meet people during your first couple years of college."

Most students move off-campus after their first year. A senior explains: "Rent in Columbia is ridiculously cheap. Several areas in Columbia are predominantly housing for college students." Another senior breaks it down for us: "There are whole subdivisions that are mostly students such as Southridge and Pear Tree Village. There are also huge apartment complexes such as Tiger Village, Jefferson Commons, and College Park."

Students all rave about the small city of Columbia: "Columbia is a great college town (not too big and not too small)." The town has lots of bars, coffeehouses, restaurants, shops, and clubs, many of which offer student discounts. "The students and the people in town like each other; there's an easy interaction," reports one student. Another student agrees: "The citizens are well-educated, friendly people, and they rarely go a month without coming up with some reason for a parade."

Walking and biking are the major modes of transportation on campus. "You can walk around most of campus and downtown, but the public transportation here is horrible. There are buses, but hardly anyone uses them," says a student. Freshmen are allowed cars on campus, and students say that a car is an absolute necessity if you live off-campus. But "if you don't have a car, you can usually bum a ride off someone if you want to stock up at the grocery store, Wal-Mart, or go to the mall."

Student Life

The Greeks play a major role in the Mizzou social life, but the party atmosphere was greatly affected recently when the administration convinced the Greek organizations to ban alcohol in all their houses by threatening to prohibit freshmen from living in the alcohol-abundant frat houses. "If there are no freshmen in the houses, they can't pay the rent," a student explains. "They have no choice but to go dry." Another student agrees: "There is a lot of disagreement about the 'dry campus' issue, but I think the administration has won that one." Of course, students aren't exactly sitting around studying on Saturday night—there are still parties and bars aplenty. "Drinking is a major factor in off-campus activites, not so much with the on-campus anymore," says a student. However, "Drugs are not a very big factor. Availability of drugs other than marijuana just isn't very prevalent."

Those tired of the party scene can also take advantage of the many concerts and shows on campus. Sports are also huge at Mizzou, as the school belongs to the powerful Big 12 conference and fields a number of powerful teams, including football and men's and women's basketball. But with more than 400 student organizations on campus, there's something for almost any interest.

While several students describe the typical Mizzou student as "a middle-class person from either St. Louis or Kansas City," a senior disagrees: "Mizzou is large enough and attracts enough students nationally (mostly for the journalism program) that it would be difficult to say that there's a specific sort of mold that most students fit into." Notable alums include Grammy-winning musician Sheryl Crow and an impressively long list of prominent print and TV journalists, such as Lisa Myers (NBC's chief Congressional correspondent), Russ Mitchell (CBS anchor), and Elizabeth Vargas (ABC reporter). Brad Pitt attended in the mid-'80s, but never graduated.

HS Rank of Entering Freshmen:
Top 10%: 29%
Top 25%: 58%
Top 50%: 88%

Costs (2003–04)

Tuition and Fees, In-State: $6,558

Tuition and Fees, Out-of-State: $16,005

Regional or 'good neighbor' tuition available

Room & Board: $5,770

THE EXPERTS SAY...

" Students who are competitive and self-reliant will do well at MU. The school of journalism is outstanding. "

" To feel like a real person and not just a statistic, make sure you sign up for one of Mizzou's 'living-learning communities.' "

Inst. Aid (est. 2003–04)

Institutional Aid, Need-Based: $12,517,156

Institutional Aid, Non-Need-Based: $10,103,276

FT Undergrads Receiving Aid: 43%
Avg. Amount per Student: $9,278

FT Undergrads Receiving Non-Need-Based Scholarship or Grant Aid: 24%
Avg. Amount per Student: $4,497

Of Those Receiving Any Aid:

Rec. Need-Based Scholarship or Grant Aid: 84%
Average Award: $5,417

Rec. Need-Based Self-Help Aid: 82%
Average Award: $4,267

Upon Graduation, Avg. Loan Debt per Student: $20,428

Financial Aid Deadline: 3/1 (priority)

Graduates

Companies Recruiting On-Campus: 245

Alumni Giving: 14%

UNIVERSITY OF MISSOURI—ROLLA

106 Parker Hal, Rolla, MO 65409-1060
Admissions Phone: (573) 341-4165; (800) 522-0938 Fax: (573) 341-4082
Email: admissions@umr.edu
Website: www.umr.edu

General Info

Type of School: public, coed
Setting: small town
Academic Calendar: semester

Student Body

Full-Time Undergrads: 3,667
 Men: 78%, Women: 22%

Part-Time Undergrads: 281
 Men: 74%, Women: 26%

Total Undergrad Population:
 African American: 5%
 Asian American: 3%
 Latino: 2%
 Native American: 1%
 Caucasian: 83%
 International: 3%
 Out-of-State: 22%
 Living Off-Campus: 44%
 In Fraternities: 25%
 In Sororities: 23%

Graduate and First-Professional
 Students: 1,370

Academics

Full-Time Faculty: 304
 With Ph.D.: 91%

Part-Time Faculty: 88
 With Ph.D.: 64%

Student/Faculty Ratio: 14:1

Most Popular Majors:
 mechanical & aerospace engineering (20%)
 electrical & computer engineering (16%)
 civil, architecture, environmental engineering (10%)
 computer science (7%)
 chemical engineering/engineering management (tie) (5%)

Freshmen Retention Rate: 83%

Graduation Rates:
 15% within four years
 60% within six years

Admissions

Regular Application Deadline: 7/1, 12/1 (priority)

Fall Transfer Deadline: 5/1 (priority)

Spring Transfer Deadline: 12/1 (priority)

Inside the Classroom

Originally established as the Missouri School of Mines and Metallurgy in 1871, the University of Missouri at Rolla has changed its focus over the years to its current strengths of engineering, math, and science programs. Rolla is the most technological of the four U of M campuses. Mining and metallurgical engineering are still offered, of course . . . but so are eight other types of engineering, plus a great deal more.

UMR offers bachelor's degrees in 35 fields of engineering, science, humanities, and social sciences. Its general education requirements are grouped into five broad categories: sciences, humanities, social sciences, composition, and foreign language. "It's a tough school, with plenty of work," said one student. "If you want to go clubbin' every weekend, go somewhere else. If you want to meet intelligent, hard-working individuals, this is your place. You'll work your ass off, but it's worth it."

Since U of M is a land grant school, research plays an important role on campus. Emphasis is focused on five areas of study: environmental engineering and science, geotechnical engineering, infrastructure engineering, manufacturing engineering, and materials engineering and science. Undergraduates can benefit from UMR's land-grant status through the Opportunities for Undergraduate Research Experience (OURE) or—with faculty guidance—independent research.

For those looking to get an edge on the competition after graduation, a number of co-op and internship opportunities with local companies are available. If you play your cards right, you can also find decent pay, too: According to UMR's admissions office, the average salary for co-op students is $2,600 per month. Over 500 companies recruit on campus each year, including Boeing, Ford, Raytheon, and Sprint. Job fairs held in fall and spring allow students to gain face-to-face contact.

Campus Environment

The 284-acre campus at UMR looks rather like a corporate park, with most buildings reflecting a variety of modern styles. McNutt Hall, site of the School of Mines and Metallurgy, is designed to look like a huge brick cliff with a mine entrance at its base. Trees, lawns, and benches line the walkways, softening the businesslike look and providing places for students to gather and hang out.

Freshmen and sophomores are required to live on campus in one of the six dorms and two apartment complexes. Conventional dorms with double and single rooms include Jefferson, Altman, Kelly, and McAnerney Halls. Holtman Hall also contains conventional rooms, but is designated as a 21-and-over residence. Farrar Hall contains five cooperative suites consisting of five double bedrooms, a bath, a kitchenette, and a living room. Rounding out the school-administered housing options are the two apartment complexes, Nagogami Terrace Apartments and Stuart Apartments; Nagogami features unfurnished and furnished double-bedroom apartments, while the apartments in Stuart are one-bedrooms and efficiencies.

The student center is split into two adjacent buildings, University Centers East and West. The eastern building is where students can find conference and meeting facilities, a snack shop called The Canteen (a cafeteria that can be used with the UMR meal plan), and a large game room with pool tables, ping pong tables and video games. The University Center West contains the campus bookstore and the offices of the student organizations. Renovations are due very soon, as the school received a $5 million pledge for this purpose from an alumnus.

One fascinating place on campus is Stonehenge, a partial reconstruction of its larger, mysterious namesake in England. Incorporating many features of the original rock structures, the 160-ton granite structure can be used to note the time and date and also has a few astrological features that the original Stonehenge didn't have.

Student Life

UMR's 20 fraternities and five sororities serve as a driving force for the social life. The party scene is definitely active, although a hazing incident that got coverage in *The Missouri Miner*, the campus newspaper, in spring 2002 may be an indication that the Greeks' less pleasant side is still evident. "Being in a fraternity helps out a lot," said one student. "It gives me something to do." As for the dating scene, he adds, "There are some great people here, but not a lot of women."

The UMR Miners and Lady Miners compete at the NCAA Division II level. Sports for both sexes include basketball, cross-country, soccer, and track and field. Men also play baseball, football, golf, swimming, and tennis, while women compete in softball. Swimming has been particularly strong lately, with two members capturing national titles in spring 2002. Club sports include lacrosse, cycling, fencing, rugby, and racquetball. Students can also play in one of 17 intramural sports.

The town of Rolla doesn't seem to get rave reviews from students. "If you want to have fun here," said one student, "it is dependent on the people around you, not the actual town. There are no clubs; there are four bars, two of which students go to." Joining a student organization is always an option, of course. The list represents a wide variety of interests, including recreational options like juggling, caving, war gaming, and in-line skating. Some of the more interesting special interest clubs are the concrete canoe team, the solar car team, and the robotics competition team.

Popular traditions include the annual five-day St. Patrick's celebration in March, featuring St. Pat's Follies on the university mall. In honor of the patron saint of engineers, classes have been cancelled on the Thursday and Friday before the holiday for the past 100 years so that everyone can celebrate with games, a parade, concerts, dances and coronation ceremonies.

Total # of Students Applied: 1,887
  Admitted: 1,488
  Enrolled: 878

Test Scores (middle 50%):
  ACT Comp: 25–30
  ACT English: 23–30
  ACT Math: 25–31

HS Rank of Entering Freshmen:
  Top 10%: 40%
  Top 25%: 71%
  Top 50%: 94%

Avg. HS GPA: 3.5

THE EXPERTS SAY...

" The University of Missouri at Rolla is one of the foremost engineering and science schools. "

" The campus isn't as picturesque as some, and the gender imbalance can make dating harder. "

Costs (2003–04)

Tuition and Fees, In-State: $6,839

Tuition and Fees, Out-of-State: $16,286

Room & Board: $5,453

Payment Plan(s): installment plan

Inst. Aid (2002–03)

Institutional Aid, Need-Based: $9,787,172

Institutional Aid, Non-Need-Based: $20,106,895

Upon Graduation, Avg. Loan Debt per Student: $17,991

Financial Aid Deadline: 3/1 (priority)

Graduates

Going to Graduate School: 19% Within One Year

Companies Recruiting On Campus: 501

UNIVERSITY OF NEBRASKA—LINCOLN

RVB, 313 N. 13th, Lincoln, NE 68588-0256 Admissions Phone: (800) 742-8800;
(402) 472-2023 Fax: (402) 472-0670 Email: nuhusker@unl.edu
Website: www.unl.edu Application Website: www.unl.edu/unlpub/admissions.shtml

General Info

Type of School: public, coed

Setting: urban

Academic Calendar: semester

Student Body

Full-Time Undergrads: 16,219
  Men: 52%, Women: 48%

Part-Time Undergrads: 1,632
  Men: 56%, Women: 44%

Total Undergrad Population:
  African American: 2%
  Asian American: 2%
  Latino: 2%
  Native American: <1%
  Caucasian: 86%
  International: 3%
  Out-of-State: 12%
  Living Off-Campus: 74%
  In Fraternities: 14%
  In Sororities: 18%

Graduate and First-Professional
  Students: 4,708

Academics

Full-Time Faculty: 1,010
  With Ph.D.: 96%

Part-Time Faculty: 12
  With Ph.D.: 100%

Student/Faculty Ratio: 16:1

Most Popular Majors:
  business admin (4%)
  psychology (4%)
  biological sciences (3%)
  management (2%)
  English (2%)

Freshmen Retention Rate: 80%

Graduation Rates:
  21% within four years
  59% within six years

Admissions

Regular Application Deadline: 6/30;
  3/15 (priority)

Fall Transfer Deadline: 6/30

Total # of Students Applied: 7,375
  Admitted: 5,586
  Enrolled: 3,679

Inside the Classroom

Stand in the middle of Nebraska's flatlands and your choices of direction are endless: It looks like you could walk to anywhere. The same is true for the University of Nebraska. Years ago the university's most noteworthy offering was—surprise, surprise—its agricultural program, but now its undergraduate colleges include agricultural sciences and natural resources, architecture, arts and sciences, engineering and technology, fine and performing arts, journalism and mass communications, and education.

Each incoming freshman class is subdivided into University Learning Communities with common academic themes, where a group of students take at least two of the same classes and share extracurricular activities. The members of these communities are usually clustered together in the residence halls, allowing them to make friends quickly and provide mutual support for projects and exams.

Students in the arts and sciences school have 27 standard majors to choose from (such as English, Spanish, chemistry, political science, and meteorology/climatology), as well as a number of interdisciplinary majors (such as medieval and Renaissance studies, Great Plains studies, women's studies, and Latin American studies). The university also offers an Individualized Program of Studies option that lets students build their own major from coursework in one or more of the colleges. For example, a student majoring in Great Plains studies might take courses ranging from English, anthropology, biological sciences, and other disciplines.

Students are generally happy with the administration's recent change to a plus-minus grading system (for example, before there was no B+ or A– between a B and an A) to assess students' learning more accurately. At least one senior worries about having two grading systems reflected on his transcript: "You don't want graduate [admissions] committees thinking of you as the guy who made them sit for an hour to figure out your transcripts." For incoming freshmen, however, this won't be a problem.

Campus Environment

The Lincoln campus is divided into two sub-campuses on opposite sides of town. Most of the colleges are located in the larger City Campus, which is closer to the businesses and amenities of Lincoln. On the outskirts, the East Campus is home to the agricultural studies division, the colleges of law and dentistry, the school of continuing studies, the Barkley Memorial Center for Hearing and Speech Disorders, and the Nebraska Educational Television Network.

Students have a variety of options in residence hall living, including dorms that are all-male, all-female, and coed. For groups of students sharing an interest, the school has a number of special program floors for engineering and technology, journalism, educational occupations, music, psychology, business, and academic scholarship that provide common learning and socializing opportunities. Upperclassmen, international students, nontraditional students, and grad students can also have exclusive floors. Dorms range in size from tiny Husker Hall, which houses 37, to Abel Hall, a human warehouse of 949 bodies and souls.

KAPLAN

An interesting component of residence life is the university's Faculty Fellows Program, in which a participating faculty member meets with residents of a floor, has lunch with them, and accompanies them at social events. The idea is to foster mentor-mentee support and build a sense of community at a school where students can feel lost in the crowd.

The University of Nebraska's student union was recently expanded and renovated to include a 325-seat auditorium, additional lounge and food court dining space, expanded facilities for the Student Involvement Center, new facilities for the *Daily Nebraskan* student newspaper, and several new meeting rooms. A 24-hour Student Computing Services room and an art gallery for display of student work are now located on the first floor, with significant expansion of the student lounge areas.

Think they're not serious about agriculture here? Two facilities that set the University of Nebraska apart from other schools in the state—not to mention the country—are the Larsen Tractor Test Museum and the tractor test laboratory. Museum exhibits include over 40 historic tractors tracing developments in power, safety, and innovation, and the lab carries out the necessary performance tests to allow tractors to be sold in the state of Nebraska.

Student Life

There are 26 fraternities and 16 sororities in the university's Greek system, with the majority owning their own houses. According to one frat officer, the frats are well-behaved: "Because we are a dry campus, we follow all local rules." A frat member agrees, saying, "We want to provide options. You don't need alcohol to have a great time, and you don't need alcohol to have a good life." Not every Greek is so pious, however, as this quote by a frat member in the student newspaper indicates: "If you put a bunch of meatheads, a couple cases of Old Milwaukee Light, and a pledge paddle in the same room, something's going to happen."

Sports have a large following on campus, with the Huskers competing at the NCAA Division I level. Options for both sexes to wear the scarlet-and-cream include basketball, cheerleading, cross-country, diving, golf, gymnastics, swimming, tennis, and track and field. Men can play baseball, football, and wrestling, while women can compete in bowling, riflery, soccer, softball, and volleyball. There are also 150 intramural and club sports; nearly 80 percent of the student body plays at least one. Some of the more colorful options are broomball, inner-tube basketball, flickerball, and turkey trot. Off campus, there are plenty of flat roads and prairie for bicyclists, runners, and cross-country skiers.

Most college campuses have ghost stories, but there's a persistent one at the Lincoln campus that has a former theater professor haunting the Tower Theater. Infamous for throwing chairs across the room to rouse inattentive students, the long-deceased professor, named Dallas Williams, reportedly still throws chairs when no one is looking. Of the unexplained crashing sounds, one student said, "We don't even get frightened anymore. We say, 'It's just Dallas.'"

Test Scores (middle 50%):
SAT Verbal: 520–650
SAT Math: 520–660
ACT Comp: 21–27
ACT English: 20–27
ACT Math: 21–27

HS Rank of Entering Freshmen:
Top 10%: 25%
Top 25%: 53%
Top 50%: 84%

THE EXPERTS SAY...

" The days when the University of Nebraska–Lincoln was just a school for farmers are long gone. Agriculture is still big, but so is everything else. "

" It's a big school with sports and frats. Why go all the way to Nebraska for that? "

Costs (2003–04)

Tuition and Fees, In-State: $4,771

Tuition and Fees, Out-of-State: $12,353

Room & Board: $5,204

Inst. Aid (2002–03)

Institutional Aid, Need-Based: $8,052,349

Institutional Aid, Non-Need-Based: $10,058,390

FT Undergrads Receiving Aid: 44%
   Avg. Amount per Student: $6,947

FT Undergrads Receiving Non-Need-Based Scholarship or Grant Aid: 6%
   Avg. Amount per Student: $3,102

Of Those Receiving Any Aid:

Rec. Need-Based Scholarship or Grant Aid: 72%
   Average Award: $4,142

Rec. Need-Based Self-Help Aid: 82%
   Average Award: $4,027

Upon Graduation, Avg. Loan Debt per Student: $16,376

Financial Aid Deadline: rolling

Graduates

Companies Recruiting On-Campus: 189

Alumni Giving: 12%

UNIVERSITY OF NEVADA—LAS VEGAS

4505 Maryland Parkway, Box 451021, Las Vegas, NV 89154-1021
Admissions Phone: (702) 774-UNLV Fax: (702) 774-8008
Email: Undergraduate.Recruitment@ccmail.nevada.edu Website: www.unlv.edu
Application Website: https://ecoms.nevada.edu/app/index.html

General Info

Type of School: public, coed

Setting: urban

Academic Calendar: semester

Student Body

Full-Time Undergrads: 14,183
  Men: 44%, Women: 56%

Part-Time Undergrads: 5,342
  Men: 45%, Women: 55%

Total Undergrad Population:
  African American: 8%
  Asian American: 14%
  Latino: 10%
  Native American: 1%
  Caucasian: 55%
  International: 4%
  Out-of-State: 22%
  Living Off-Campus: 96%
  In Fraternities: 5%
  In Sororities: 3%

Graduate and First-Professional
  Students: 5,069

Academics

Full-Time Faculty: 766
  With Ph.D.: 91%

Part-Time Faculty: 659

Student/Faculty Ratio: 20:1

Most Popular Majors:
  hotel administration (9%)
  psychology (5%)
  elementary education (5%)
  communication studies (5%)
  bioogy (4%)

Freshmen Retention Rate: 72%

Graduation Rates:
  12% within four years
  38% within six years

Admissions

Regular Application Deadline: 4/2

Fall Transfer Deadline: 4/2 (priority)

Spring Transfer Deadline: 11/1 (priority)

Total # of Students Applied: 6,162
  Admitted: 4,938
  Enrolled: 2,976

Inside the Classroom

UNLV is a school on the rise. The Carnegie Foundation for the Advancement of Teaching recently reclassified UNLV, placing it in the category of Doctoral/Research University-Intensive—a substantial jump from its previous classification as a Master's Comprehensive I institution. UNLV's Honors College—an academic enrichment program open to the university's best students—has grown from 38 students in 1985 to more than 581 students today. And the city of Las Vegas has been in the spotlight lately as the backdrop for the way-popular CSI as well as the latest season of The Real World.

UNLV offers more than 150 degree programs in its colleges of business, education, engineering, fine arts, health sciences, honors, hotel administration, liberal arts, sciences, urban affairs, graduate college, dentistry, and law. Students say that the academic load at UNLV isn't too heavy and that "competitiveness is not visible on the UNLV campus." "Many of the students slack so much that you really have hardly anyone to compete against if you are one of those that makes the extra effort," says one student.

A junior majoring in criminal justice tells us, "The accessibility of the professors is great. The professors are always easy to find in their offices and are always willing to speak with you and help you with any problems that you encounter." If you're having ongoing academic difficulties, UNLV offers tutoring through the Learning Enhancement Services. Most tutoring is done in groups. Math Express is an open math lab that is also available through the Learning Enhancement Services. The Writing Center offers four free services to students: face-to-face writing consultations, online writing consultations, a computer lab, and writing workshops.

UNLV offers a variety of programs and classes to help freshmen succeed in their transition to college. Orientation is the best way to get familiar with the campus and begin making the transition to UNLV. The Rebel Peer Mentor program matches new students with an upperclassman to answer questions and just be there for new students. Students can also sign up for EPY 101, a 2-credit class designed to assist students with succeeding in college.

Campus Environment

Most students assure us that the 337-acre campus itself is quite safe: The grounds are always well lit, and call boxes are located across campus in case of emergency. In addition, there is a shuttle service in the evenings, and residence halls feature state-of-the-art security. However, many students don't seem all that comfortable in the area surrounding the campus. "It is in the middle of urban Las Vegas and located on two of the busiest streets in Las Vegas," a student tells us. "There are many restaurants, bars, and shops for the college students, but the public bus system after dark can be frightful; also, walking alone after hours off-campus is not very safe."

Campus housing is nice, but scarce. "The freshman dorms [in the South Freshman Complex] are simple and comfortable, but the upperclassman dorms [in the Upper Class Complex] are the best because they are bigger, [with] a balcony and a wall dividing the room into two," says a junior. "They have also built a brand-new dorm building for mixed students [in the Tonopah Living Learning and Scholarship Complex] that is very nice." Study Intensive Floors are available in all complexes, for honors students and others who request them. Freshmen are required to live on campus, unless they commute from home.

Las Vegas offers a variety of housing options from apartments to condos, to houses for rent. UNLV maintains a computerized database that allows students to search for housing vacancies based on the type of housing and the location.

There are a few different eating options on campus. The Dining Commons is a buffet style eating facility open to students with a meal plan or paying for an individual meal. The Union Café (located in the MSU) offers a variety of food options from pre-prepared choices or made-to-order items. The Sidewalk Café offers a variety of grab-and-go food choices. The newest facility is the Book and Bean at the Lied Library featuring Seattle's Best coffee.

The university recently added a number of new campus facilities, including the 30,000-square-foot Beam Music Center, a 433-bed expansion to Tonopah residence hall, and Eller Media Softball Stadium. The Lied Library (which is "frequently used on Sundays," according to one undergrad) "contains 302,000 square feet of research potential and over 200 computers equipped with full Internet access and much more."

Student Life

"UNLV is a very diverse school with students of every nationality and culture. There are a lot of preppy white guys and girls who belong to the Greek system, yet there is also a very large Asian population along with many African Americans," observes a junior. But it's actually pretty hard to come up with a description of a "typical" UNLV student. UNLV has about 5,000 nontraditional students (age 25 or older)—about one-third of the undergraduate population. These students are not pushed to the side, as happens at many universities; UNLV offers several nontraditional student programs and organizations such as Beta Theta Gamma and the Older, Wiser, Learners Program (OWLs). There are also special programs specifically for commuters and minorities.

Because UNLV is mainly a commuter campus, one student notes that "it's hard to get to know people unless you are Greek, live in the dorms, or are in any clubs." Well, that shouldn't be too hard, since there are more than 120 student clubs to pick from. Students can participate in more than 20 kinds of intramural sports or 16 "very popular" intercollegiate sports at the NCAA Division I level. "The football and basketball stadiums are always full of students cheering on our varsity teams," relates one student. The university claims that the overall participation rate in athletics for women is 49 percent.

Students looking for fun don't need to look far. Both on-campus and off-campus parties are thrown fairly frequently. We hear that alcohol and marijuana are readily available, but there's not a lot of peer pressure to participate if you don't want to. And hey, it's Vegas, with its dizzying array of concerts, clubs, and casinos. Students say they enjoy "cruising the strip" (which can and should be done without losing your shirt at the craps table).

Other schools to check out: U of Nevada—Reno, Indiana U of Pennsylvania, Kansas State, Northern Arizona U, Florida State.

Test Scores (middle 50%):
SAT Verbal: 450–560
SAT Math: 450–580
ACT Comp: 18–24
ACT English: 17–23
ACT Math: 17–24

HS Rank of Entering Freshmen:
Top 10%: 17%
Top 25%: 47%
Top 50%: 83%

Avg. HS GPA: 3.23

THE EXPERTS SAY...

" In spite of its large size, UNLV is very student-centered. The administration and the faculty are ready and willing to help you if you ask. "

" Though the odds are against you, bet your parents that you will graduate in only four years. This will be one bet they'll be more than happy to lose. "

Costs (2004–05)

Tuition and Fees, In-State: $2,946

Tuition and Fees, Out-of-State: $11,620

Room & Board: $8,258

Payment Plan(s): installment plan, deferred payment plan

Inst. Aid (est. 2003–04)

Institutional Aid, Need-Based: $308,000

Institutional Aid, Non-Need-Based: $10,000

FT Undergrads Receiving Aid: 40%
Avg. Amount per Student: $6,911

FT Undergrads Receiving Non-Need-Based Scholarship or Grant Aid: 27%
Avg. Amount per Student: $2,094

Of Those Receiving Any Aid:

Rec. Need-Based Scholarship or Grant Aid: 58%
Average Award: $3,030

Rec. Need-Based Self-Help Aid: 68%
Average Award: $5,057

Upon Graduation, Avg. Loan Debt per Student: $13,860

Financial Aid Deadline: rolling, 2/1 (priority)

UNIVERSITY OF NEVADA—RENO

Mail Stop 120, Reno, NV 89557
Admissions Phone: (775) 784-4700; (866) 2NE-VADA Fax: (775) 784-4283
Email: asknevada@unr.edu Website: www.unr.edu
Application Website: www.ss.unr.edu/admissions/

General Info

Type of School: public, coed
Academic Calendar: semester

Student Body

Full-Time Undergrads: 9,456
  Men: 45%, Women: 55%

Part-Time Undergrads: 2,149
  Men: 47%, Women: 53%

Total Undergrad Population:
  African American: 2%
  Asian American: 7%
  Latino: 7%
  Native American: 1%
  Caucasian: 73%
  International: 3%
  Out-of-State: 18%
  Living Off-Campus: 86%
  In Fraternities: 7%
  In Sororities: 6%

Graduate and First-Professional
Students: 3,416

Academics

Full-Time Faculty: 682
  With Ph.D.: 88%

Part-Time Faculty: 452
  With Ph.D.: 31%

Student/Faculty Ratio: 15:1

Freshmen Retention Rate: 76%

Graduation Rates:
  15% within four years
  47% within six years

Admissions

Regular Application Deadline: 3/1
  (then first-come, first-served)

Total # of Students Applied: 4,024
  Admitted: 3,551
  Enrolled: 2,097

Test Scores (middle 50%):
  SAT Verbal: 470–590
  SAT Math: 480–600
  ACT Comp: 20–25
  ACT English: 19–25
  ACT Math: 19–26

Avg. HS GPA: 3.36

Inside the Classroom

UNR has nine undergraduate schools: agriculture, biotechnology, and natural resources; arts and science; business administration; education; engineering; extended studies (combines continuing education, distance learning, and an extensive independent study program); human and community sciences; the Mackay School of Mines; and the Reynolds School of Journalism. (The administration is planning to separate the College of Arts & Science into two new colleges—the College of Liberal Arts and the College of Science—and place the Mackay School of Mines within the newly formed College of Science as the Mackay School of Earth Sciences and Engineering.) Engineering, journalism, and the mining program are nationally ranked. The university's logistics program in the College of Business Administration is rated among the nation's top ten, and the Reynolds School of Journalism has produced six Pulitzer Prize winners. UNR is also the premier school for gaming management (think casinos), with a major in the subject.

Students like the value of a UNR education. Financially speaking, in-staters should consider staying in-state to take advantage of Nevada's Millenium Scholarship (though one student complains of a freshman class that "does not really know why they came to college, exaggerated by large, low-requirement scholarships given to in-state students"). A Nevada guidance counselor raves about UNR's "caring faculty," and students agree. "The workload can be pretty heavy sometimes, depending on the course, but the professors are always willing to explain things," a junior comments, adding, "The classes are fairly competitive, although not so much that it is really stressful." Another student states, "I like the class size (pretty small), the availability of the professors to help us, and the smaller-sized campus." A journalism major raves, "The professors in my program are amazing! They draw from real world experience and are always available to help students learn and grow."

The core curriculum includes English composition, mathematics, natural science, social science, fine arts, diversity, and courses in the Western tradition. UNR undergraduates can participate in major research, such as studies to reverse the decline in Lake Tahoe's clarity, experimentation on large-scale structures with the $10 million earthquake-shaking tables in the College of Engineering, and interdisciplinary work at the Sanford Center for Aging. The mathematics department and the schools of journalism, engineering, and business administration are reportedly quite active in helping students get internships.

Campus Environment

The university is set in Reno, just east of the rugged Sierra Nevada range. A speech pathology major says, "Everyone thinks of Reno as a 'bad' town because of the gambling, but it is a very nice, beautiful, friendly town. It's very close to a lot of places of interest like Lake Tahoe and is only a few hours from the ocean. Reno's also nice because lots of things are open 24 hours." Another student adds, "Freedom is very apparent with countless bars, casinos, and brothels on the outskirts of the city." A biochemistry major explains, "Reno is fairly safe as long as you stay away from downtown areas and lock your doors."

KAPLAN

Students love their beautiful, 19th-century campus with Manzanita Lake right on the grounds. There are seven residence halls. One student comments, "Quality ranges from pampered to punished." Another adds, "The dorms are the ideal way to meet a huge variety of people." But the vast majority of students live off campus. "Off-campus housing is readily available for relatively cheap prices. Also, there is a broad range of quality to choose from," explains a sophomore.

UNR students are allowed to have cars on campus; parking permits must be purchased (parking availability and fees reportedly cause some friction between students and the administration). A student notes, "Most students have cars. UNR is on a hill, so if you don't live fairly close, riding a bike or walking can get tiring." A journalism major adds, "Just about everything you need is within two miles of campus… It just depends if you are willing to walk two miles in 30-degree weather."

Student Life

One junior describes social life at UNR this way: "The weekend starts on Thursday night, and with casinos and clubs and fraternities, Reno has a pretty exciting nightlife." Another junior comments, "Where else do you have desert, mountain, and lake recreation all within 20 minutes of each other?! Lake Tahoe is gorgeous and the outdoor recreation is endless." However, one undergrad laments the "remoteness in terms of music tours and such." The Greek system has a noticeable impact on social life and "a lot of history," with about 8 percent of the student body pledging. ("There is always a party somewhere, especially during rush," one student tells us.) On a grimmer note, last fall, fraternity Pi Kappa Alpha lost its recognition by the university after a pledge drowned in a campus lake.

The Wolf Pack competes in NCAA Division I in seven men's sports and eleven women's sports. A student tells us, "Although athletics are important, some of our students are not as involved as they should be. The university needs to spend more money on promotional events, music at games, and [other] ways to involve the fans in the season." UNR offers 18 intramural sports, and one student notes "more and more well-run programs." Popular clubs include the Student Ambassadors, the International Club, Campus Greens, the Sagens, the cycling and boxing teams, and Christian organizations; one student complains that service-oriented groups aren't well attended.

Students disagree about drinking at UNR. "Lots of students drink socially, but it has never been a problem," comments a student. "The only issues are with beer at football games. Drugs are not a problem at UNR." But we are also told that "drinking is a big factor because it is part of the Nevada lifestyle… There is never a last call." Students agree that "everyone is very friendly at UNR." Says a sophomore, the typical student "thinks like a Westerner. That is not to say he's rural, necessarily, just that he thinks of life as a mixture of urban and rural." Another mentions UNR's "eclectic mix" of students. A junior agrees: "UNR has many nontraditional students with full-time jobs and family." "I think most people would fit in at UNR as long as you do what you are interested in," a student concludes. "I like the fact that it is not too big of a campus, but it is big enough to get a good education and meet some great people."

Other schools to check out: U of Nevada—Las Vegas, Oregon State, U of Hawaii—Manoa, Arizona State, U of Wyoming.

Costs (2004–05)

Tuition and Fees, In-State: $2,862

Tuition and Fees, Out-of-State: $11,536

THE EXPERTS SAY…

" UNR is a good buy for in-state students and a good choice for nontraditional students. "

" More than five million people visit the Reno/Tahoe area every year. Just remember that you're a student, not a tourist—don't go gambling away your tuition money or letting your grades slide down a ski slope. "

Inst. Aid (2002–03)

Institutional Aid, Need-Based: $1,198,430

Institutional Aid, Non-Need-Based: $2,510,579

FT Undergrads Receiving Aid: 30%
Avg. Amount per Student: $7,003

FT Undergrads Receiving Non-Need-Based Scholarship or Grant Aid: 39%
Avg. Amount per Student: $2,754

Of Those Receiving Any Aid:

Rec. Need-Based Scholarship or Grant Aid: 56%
Average Award: $3,296

Rec. Need-Based Self-Help Aid: 66%
Average Award: $4,101

Upon Graduation, Avg. Loan Debt per Student: $15,548

Financial Aid Deadline: rolling, 2/1 (priority)

UNIVERSITY OF NEW HAMPSHIRE

4 Garrison Avenue, Durham, NH 03824-3510
Admissions Phone: (603) 862-1360 Fax: (603) 862-0077
Email: admissions@unh.edu Website: www.unh.edu
Application Website: www.unh.edu/admissions/apply.html

General Info

Type of School: public, coed

Setting: small town

Academic Calendar: semester

Student Body

Full-Time Undergrads: 10,558
  Men: 43%, Women: 57%

Part-Time Undergrads: 379
  Men: 43%, Women: 57%

Total Undergrad Population:
  African American: 1%
  Asian American: 2%
  Latino: 1%
  Native American: <1%
  Caucasian: 88%
  International: 1%
  Out-of-State: 46%
  Living Off-Campus: 44%
  In Fraternities: 4%
  In Sororities: 4%

Graduate and First-Professional
  Students: 2,324

Academics

Full-Time Faculty: 589
  With Ph.D.: 92%

Part-Time Faculty: 105
  With Ph.D.: 36%

Student/Faculty Ratio: 14:1

Most Popular Majors:
  business administration (10%)
  English (6%)
  psychology (6%)
  biology; political sci.; communications; each: (4%)

Completing 2 or More Majors: 6%

Freshmen Retention Rate: 85%

Graduation Rates:
  49% within four years
  72% within six years

Admissions

Regular Application Deadline: 2/1

Early Action Deadline: 12/1

Fall Transfer Deadline: 3/1

Spring Transfer Deadline: 11/1

Total # of Students Applied: 10,798
  Admitted: 7,502
  Enrolled: 2,452

In the Classroom

At UNH, "If you hate your major, you can take your pick from about 100 others!" UNH's 100-plus majors are offered through seven colleges: arts and sciences, life sciences and agriculture, the Whittemore School of Business, health and human services, engineering, and physical sciences; the Thompson School of Applied Science, and UNH at Manchester (the urban campus). The school received a top ranking for its geoscience programs from the Institute for Scientific Information, and a guidance counselor lauds the business school. The university is also known for its programs in history, creative writing, journalism, performing arts, hospitality management, engineering, and occupational therapy.

One recent grad says academics vary "from college to college, major to major. Some majors were ridiculously easy while others were more demanding than Ivy League med schools!" "The workload is good, keeps you occupied but with plenty of time for sports and socializing," says a philosophy major. A junior notes "I think that it is competitive to a certain extent and that is according to the student." A freshman boasts, "UNH is one of the top ten schools for sending pilots to the military." But don't think bootcamp: the school, a student reassures us, has "overall, a pretty laid-back atmosphere."

A major research institution, programs such as the Undergraduate Research Opportunities Program and International Research Opportunities Program provide more than 100 research grants each year for undergraduates to work closely with faculty on campus or abroad. Research-oriented students can access the Institute for Policy and Social Science Research; the Institute for the Study of Earth, Oceans, and Space; the Interoperability Lab; and the Isles of Shoals Marine Laboratory (a few miles off the New Hampshire coast). A microbiology grad tells us, "The undergraduate research opportunities at UNH are unlike most other schools around."

The faculty/student ratio is 1:14 at this school of 11,000 students, and UNH has a reputation of strong student-faculty interaction. "There are some GREAT faculty members there who are willing to take part in your decision making and shape who you become," says a student. A freshman agrees: "If you need them they give out their office hours, email addresses, and both office and home phone numbers." However, some of those 11,000 students can find themselves in "too large" classes where "you feel as if you get lost in the shuffle."

In 2002, UNH inaugurated a new president, Ann Weaver Hart, who has outlined four challenges UNH faces: competitive salaries for faculty; maintenance of facilities; providing state-of-the-art instructional facilities; and securing financial aid for students. One student states that the issues with administration are "power and more of a voice in the university," but another says that "student groups on campus are very effective through programming and getting their voice heard."

Campus Environment

Most first-year students at UNH live on campus. You're guaranteed campus housing (which can be "very loud and obnoxious") for two years, and after that you enter a lottery system. "Comfort level is great, no problems," says a junior. "They just opened up a new dorm, very nice, suite-style living." (UNH has undertaken extensive campus building and renovation projects, including a new residence hall and dining hall.) Theme housing includes, according to a student, "a substance-free dorm, athlete's dorm close to the field house, and mini-dorms for the tree-hugging potheads." Some upperclassmen live off campus in Durham or nearby areas, and off-campus housing can be "very popular and very UNavailable and VERY expensive!"

Affluent Durham "is pretty dead," states a student. "The town is considered one block." Durham is close to the ocean, and to the town of Portsmouth, NH, and there are "some great outlet stores in nearby Maine." "Skiing and hiking mountains are only an hour away," exults a freshman. Boston and Portland are each less than two hours away. "You could get by without a car," we're told, "but then you couldn't go to the beach!"

Student Life

"In general, UNH students are active and outdoorsy," says the university. UNH is popular with out-of-staters, who make up more than 40 percent of its undergraduate population. There are tons of school-sponsored activities: "the UNH Celebrity Series, the Art Gallery, and the departments of music, dance, art, and art history bring artists of international stature to campus." The sports center also hosts rock concerts, and students can bar-hop and check out local bands in nearby Portsmouth.

"Making friends is easy, everyone here is open to each other," a freshman comments, and a guidance counselor remarks that this "good-sized campus" has a "small community feel." Also, there is a place for everyone from "the granola-eating, overall-wearing vegetarian to the Gucci-wearing sorority girl." Greeks are active on campus, with "the best-looking guys and the prettiest girls," according to one admittedly biased member. The typical student is "white middle class," but "it is becoming more diverse every day," states a junior, reporting that the recent Martin Luther King celebration was a major hit.

"During warm weather, students can just pick up and go to the ocean in the middle of the day," a student says. This isn't the school for "someone who doesn't like snow in the winter. We tend to get about 3–4 feet." "Lots of parties, some good, some bad," says a student. During the weekends, "some students just partied hard every night, stopping only to refuel or watch a movie in their room. Other students studied during the weekend to stay ahead or catch up." "The campus can be dead when a lot of people go home," a junior complains. Drinking can be a "huge factor because there is little to nothing else to do in Durham." ("Of course there is some drinking, it's a college campus!" a junior exclaims.) Drugs appear less frequently. "We like to relax," remarks a political science major.

UNH is nationally ranked for athletics, and a guidance counselor loves this "great hockey school!" where men's and women's ice hockey reign supreme. "We are going to beat Maine at the hockey game!" raves a freshman, adding, "Intramural sports are popular with most everyone else that doesn't play a sport for a varsity team." There are 23 different sports and activities for intramural play, including ice skating in the Whittemore Center arena and sailing and canoeing on Mendum's Pond.

# of Students Waitlisted: 200
  Students Accepting Place: 137
  Waitlisted Students Admitted: 137

Test Scores (middle 50%):
  SAT Verbal: 500–610
  SAT Math: 510–620

HS Rank of Entering Freshmen:
  Top 10%: 20%
  Top 25%: 59%
  Top 50%: 97%

Costs (est. 2003–04)

Tuition and Fees, In-State: $8,664

Tuition and Fees, Out-of-State: $19,024

Regional or 'good neighbor' tuition available

Room & Board: $6,234

THE EXPERTS SAY...

" There are over 2,000 courses offered at this large research university, but it still has feel of a New England liberal arts school with a faculty dedicated to teaching. "

" New UNH president Ann Weaver Hart has stated her commitment to securing financial aid for students. Couldn't come at a better time. "

Inst. Aid (est. 2003–04)

Institutional Aid, Need-Based: $11,974,268

Institutional Aid, Non-Need-Based: $11,945,656

FT Undergrads Receiving Aid: 57%
  Avg. Amount per Student: $14,267

FT Undergrads Receiving Non-Need-Based Scholarship or Grant Aid: 20%
  Avg. Amount per Student: $5,414

Of Those Receiving Any Aid:

Rec. Need-Based Scholarship or Grant Aid: 63%
  Average Award: $2,281

Rec. Need-Based Self-Help Aid: 94%
  Average Award: $2,928

Upon Graduation, Avg. Loan Debt per Student: $20,701

Financial Aid Deadline: 3/1 (priority)

Graduates

Going to Graduate School:
  25% Within One Year

Companies Recruiting On Campus: 200

Alumni Giving: 13%

UNIVERSITY OF NEW MEXICO

Student Services Center 140, MSC06-3720, Albuquerque, NM 87131-2046
Admissions Phone: (505) 277-2446; (800) CALL-UNM Fax: (505) 277-6686
Email: apply@unm.edu Website: www.unm.edu
Application Website: www.unm.edu/preview/na_admis.htm

General Info

Type of School: public, coed

Academic Calendar: semester

Student Body

Full-Time Undergrads: 14,029
  Men: 43%, Women: 57%

Part-Time Undergrads: 3,413
  Men: 40%, Women: 60%

Total Undergrad Population:
  African American: 3%
  Asian American: 3%
  Latino: 34%
  Native American: 7%
  Caucasian: 49%
  International: 1%
  Living Off-Campus: 89%

Graduate and First-Professional
  Students: 7,754

Academics

Full-Time Faculty: 908
  With Ph.D.: 86%

Part-Time Faculty: 505
  With Ph.D.: 39%

Student/Faculty Ratio: 19:1

Freshmen Retention Rate: 76%

Graduation Rates:
  15% within four years
  46% within six years

Admissions

Regular Application Deadline: 6/15;
  12/1 (priority)

Total # of Students Applied: 6,752
  Admitted: 5,095
  Enrolled: 3,004

Test Scores (middle 50%):
  SAT Verbal: 480–600
  SAT Math: 460–590
  ACT Comp: 19–24
  ACT English: 18–24
  ACT Math: 17–24

HS Rank of Entering Freshmen:
  Top 10%: 17%
  Top 25%: 44%
  Top 50%: 79%

Avg. HS GPA: 3.31

Inside the Classroom

The University of New Mexico offers a rich diversity of cultures—Latino, Native American, and Anglo—as well as a wide range of programs. Along with students of different cultures are students with different lifestyles, and UNM accommodates its working students by offering evening and weekend classes (not enough, some students say). Students find the value of a UNM.education—rich course selection and low cost—very appealing, and the academic atmosphere is relaxed and supportive. An Idaho guidance counselor calls the school a "good alternative to CU Boulder and the University of Arizona."

The workload "is bearable for the most part, yet, there are a few classes that require a lot of work," a senior says. "There is not a lot of competitiveness here; with all the tutoring and mentoring available, it is obvious that people want others to succeed." While many introductory classes are taught by TAs,"professors have office hours and are usually there whenever they say that they will be," a student comments. "Most professors are also willing to make appointments outside of their office hours, and most professors are very friendly and approachable." "The teachers are great!" exclaims one student.

UNM's undergraduate schools are: arts and sciences, the Anderson School of Management, education, engineering, fine arts, nursing, architecture, dental, health sciences, and University College, which offers a way for students to explore college before specializing. UNM has the only law, medical, and architecture schools in the state. UNM is known for its outstanding rural medicine program, and premed studies in family medicine and primary care are strong. Photography and art history programs are nationally ranked, and the School of Engineering is considered one of the top 50 schools nationwide. In addition, UNM's anthropology, biology, flamenco dance, and Western history programs have respected national reputations; a New Mexico guidance counselor raves about the "wonderful archaeology and Latin American studies" programs. Field work for anthropology, archaeology, and volcanology students abounds, and UNM students work on a variety of solar energy research projects. The school's Tamarind Institute offers a unique programs in fine-art lithography.

Campus Environment

The University of New Mexico occupies 600 acres along old Route 66 in Albuquerque, a city of half a million people surrounded by magnificent mesas to the west and the Sandia Mountains to the east. Students find much to do in the city, exploring nightlife and enjoying a wide range of outdoor sports. Santa Fe is about an hour away. UNM's unique adobe campus has a Spanish Pueblo architectural theme and a stunning arboretum. The campus is nearly a mile high, and it's possible to ski in the morning and play golf in the afternoon.

Nearly 90 percent of the student body lives off campus or commutes. A guidance counselor says that "dorms have not been kept up to date all the time," but "this is being addressed." A senior says, "I lived on campus for three years and it was very comfortable, but I just wanted to get off campus to feel a little more independent." A new dorm, Redondo Village Apartments, offers four-bedroom suites with kitchens and living rooms. Freshmen are integrated with all classes in residence halls, and are allowed to live in frats. On-campus housing is guaranteed for four years. Off-campus housing is available and affordable. "There are several apartment complexes near UNM and I love my apartment. It is only five minutes away and it is cheaper than being on campus," a student comments.

Freshmen are permitted to have cars, but parking is a big problem. Says a senior: "The only friction between [students and administration] is parking problems, but everyone hates that—not just the students." Shuttle busses are available from many parking lots and students use the city bus, bicycles, and carpools to get around. "A lot of people ride bikes or walk around campus," notes a student. "Some people ride skateboards. This is all fine to get around campus, but to get around the city, you need a car, or a bus pass."

Student Life

With so many commuters, the sprawling UNM campus can seem a bit deserted on weekends. There's a small but active Greek scene: "Homecoming queens and kings are usually fraternity or sorority members," comments a student. Annual school traditions include Welcome Back Days and Fiesta, and the busy International Center hosts numerous dances and functions. Popular student groups include the student government, the Muslim student organization, and various Christian groups. "El Centro de la Raza is a Chicano mentoring group, but it is open to everyone. It is a good program," adds a senior.

There are 9 men's and 10 women's varsity sports; basketball and football are strong due to UNM's generous athletic scholarships, and even ice hockey has a following. "Varsity sports are pretty popular. The men's sports are more popular, but the women are making their way up there," a student observes. "Intramural sports exist, but aren't really too popular." There are 12 intramural men's and 11 women's sports. Outdoor lovers take advantage of the school's location to go skiing, camping, and hiking.

Students take advantage of city life in Albuquerque: "Albuquerque has a lot of clubs, movie theaters, restaurants, and places to hang out," a senior notes. Typically, "students go to clubs or parties on the weekends. During the weeknights, students might go out and have a drink or go bowling. Students are always attending games, no matter if it is the weekend or weeknight." Drinking "is prevalent on and off campus," says one student. "Drugs are not really talked about, but I think that they must be around, as well."

The people at UNM represents a wide cross-section of cultures and backgrounds. "Anybody would fit in at UNM because it is so diverse," says a criminology and political science major. Forty-five percent of students are members of minority groups, primarily Latino and Native American. Students at UNM are older than average: 24 percent are 25 or older, and many nontraditional students juggle families, work, and school. UNM is only homogeneous in one area: About 85 percent of students are home staters. "There is not a 'typical student' because it is totally acceptable to be whoever you are at UNM and everyone is different," a senior concludes.

Costs (2003–04)

Tuition and Fees, In-State: $3,313

Tuition and Fees, Out-of-State: $11,954

Room & Board: $5,450

Inst. Aid

Financial Aid Deadline: 3/1 (priority)

Graduates

Alumni Giving: 9%

THE EXPERTS SAY...

" UNM has an exciting diversity of cultures, and a relaxed, supportive atmosphere. Nontraditional students can really find a home here. "

" If you can't afford—or get into— CU Boulder or the University of Arizona, try here. "

UNIVERSITY OF NORTH CAROLINA— CHAPEL HILL

Campus Box 2200, Jackson Hall, Chapel Hill, NC 27599-2200
Admissions Phone: (919) 966-3621 Fax: (919) 962-3045 Email: uadm@email.unc.edu
Website: www.unc.edu/ Application Website: www.admissions.unc.edu/

General Info

Type of School: public, coed

Setting: suburban

Academic Calendar: semester

Student Body

Full-Time Undergrads: 15,353
 Men: 41%, Women: 59%

Part-Time Undergrads: 358
 Men: 49%, Women: 51%

Total Undergrad Population:
 African American: 11%
 Asian American: 6%
 Latino: 2%
 Native American: 1%
 Caucasian: 76%
 International: 1%
 Out-of-State: 18%
 Living Off-Campus: 56%

Graduate and First-Professional
 Students: 10,215

Academics

Full-Time Faculty: 1,296
 With Ph.D.: 84%

Part-Time Faculty: 112
 With Ph.D.: 57%

Student/Faculty Ratio: 14:1

Most Popular Majors:
 journalism & mass communication
 (10%)
 psychology (10%)
 biology (9%)
 business administration (8%)
 communication studies (7%)

Completing 2 or More Majors: 23%

Freshmen Retention Rate: 95%

Graduation Rates:
 69% within four years
 83% within six years

Computers: Computer Required

Admissions

Regular Application Deadline: 1/15

Early Action Deadline: 11/1

Fall Transfer Deadline: 3/1

Total # of Students Applied: 17,591
 Admitted: 6,441
 Enrolled: 3,516

# of Students Waitlisted: 1,671
 Waitlisted Students Admitted: 209

Inside the Classroom

As the oldest state university in the country, the University of North Carolina has a long history of providing superior academics and excellent facilities at a great price. Almost every student—and every guidance counselor—we spoke to cited the great value of the school, given the superb quality of the education. One student even goes on to say, "I would definitely come here again, even if I had the money to go to any Ivy League school." And another says, "Low cost and high return is what sets the school apart." There's definitely a place for fun here, but academics are the priority by far.

Undergraduates at Carolina have a choice of more than 50 majors. For the first two years, all undergrads are enrolled in the General College, filling most General Education requirements. Then they go on to the College of Arts and Sciences or to one of the professional schools such as Business, Education, or Journalism and Mass Communication. The academic atmosphere is challenging, to say the least (though one senior tells us "there are a good number of 'cupcake' courses"). Even if the workload is small, the amount—and quality—of work required to get an A is significant. Students are fairly competitive: "They're always curious as to how they measure up against their peers," explains one student.

Carolina is huge, which enables students to select from hundreds of course offerings; the problem, however, is getting into some of them. Introductory lectures can enroll as many as 400, though most undergraduate classes have fewer than 30 students. "We don't have a good professor-to-student ratio," a student admits, "but there are some professors who do care and get to know their students." We hear that some of the math and science professors have a limited knowledge of English, creating some communication challenges for students. Explains one student, "It doesn't matter if they're the best at what they do if their students cannot understand them." We're told that professors here keep a vigilant eye on grade inflation.

The "Carolina Computing Initiative" requires all freshmen to own a laptop computer (with financing available), so that all students have equal resources. Almost certainly due to its size, some say the school's bureaucracy can get unwieldy: "The politics involved in everything—from class availability to basketball ticket distribution—is one of the least appealing things about the school." Some students have also complained that in spite of the fantastic curriculum, the school's advisers and career services need improvement. In April 2002, the administration made national news by abolishing early decision admissions.

Campus Environment

The spacious campus, arranged in quadrangle formation, is "pedestrian friendly, with older brick buildings, tree-lined paths, 200-year-old oak trees, lots of azaleas, and open green spaces," according to one student. At the heart of campus stands the beloved Old Well: "Students can bring good luck with a drink from the Old Well on the first day of classes," we are told. We're also told that safety has improved tremendously as a result of past problems. Athletic facilities include outdoor and indoor pools, a golf course, and "all the equipment you'd expect to find at a great health club."

Housing can be hit or miss at Carolina. South Campus, where freshmen and sophomores live, is not terribly convenient to classes (maybe a 30-minute walk)—though to the delight of many, the dorms and facilities there are now being redone. Some dorms are without air conditioning, which can make warm weather a challenge. Off-campus living in Chapel Hill is very expensive, but continues to be popular with upperclassmen. Few underclassmen have cars, and those that do need to buy a parking pass (ironically, at a parking lot to which they'll most likely have to walk).

Chapel Hill, a small city smack in the middle of the state, has largely been built around the school. One junior tells us, "Despite what you'd think, Chapel Hill is not a 'Southern' city. It's Southern by geography only—meaning, you'll be surrounded by many liberal, progressive minds and attitudes, despite traditional North Carolina politics."

Student Life

"This is a very liberal school, so everyone has an opinion on everything. This can create some tension on the campus when heated debates come up, but overall, it adds to the diversity," explains a biology major. Heated discussions frequently unfold courtesy of the student newspaper. Even the written Honor Code has been controversial. The school seems to attract many preppy upper-middle-class Southerners ("Expect to see a lot of J. Crew," says one senior), and many political activists. Having said that, this is an incredibly diverse school where just about anybody can find his niche.

Students at Carolina are known for a "study hard, play hard" attitude. As explained by one student, "People worry about you if you 'study too much.' There's a lot of peer pressure to go out." Greek life is huge: Even though fewer than 20 percent of students join Greek houses, many more than that are informally involved. Explains one junior, "It's a defining factor for many people on the campus. Aside from bars, they ARE the social life." One student tells us that drugs are more accessible here than at other schools. As for organized clubs, Christian organizations, political clubs, and music clubs are very popular, as are the Black Student Movement and the Campus Y, a social justice awareness group. Guest performers and groups frequently appear on campus, and a professional repertory company uses faculty and outside talent to present plays. One Carolina student sums it up this way: "Anything you want to do, you can do here."

Students share an enthusiasm for Carolina's powerhouse Division I sports teams. The school consistently attracts top athletes into its programs—sports god Michael Jordan was once a Carolina Tar Heel. "If you're looking for a place to paint your entire body blue and go to games almost naked, you've come to the right place," quips one senior. "Even intramural sports are competitive." Basketball is so popular that it's hard to get game tickets, and football has been rising in popularity. In fact, at one [winning] football game, students showed their excitement by storming the field and pulling down the goalpost.

THE EXPERTS SAY...

" One of the top educational values in the market, Carolina is academically challenging, has terrific facilities, offers hundreds of courses—and you get to paint yourself blue for Tar Heel games. "

" If you're looking for a conservative Southern school, this ain't it. Politics are well left of center at Carolina. "

UNIVERSITY OF NOTRE DAME

220 Main Building, Notre Dame, IN 46556
Admissions Phone: (574) 631-7505 Fax: (574) 631-8865
Email: admissio.1@nd.edu Website: www.nd.edu
Application Website: admissions.nd.edu

General Info

Type of School: private, coed, Roman Catholic

Setting: suburban

Academic Calendar: semester

Student Body

Full-Time Undergrads: 8,285
  Men: 53%, Women: 47%

Part-Time Undergrads: 18
  Men: 67%, Women: 33%

Total Undergrad Population:
  African American: 4%
  Asian American: 5%
  Latino: 8%
  Native American: 1%
  Caucasian: 80%
  International: 4%
  Out-of-State: 87%
  Living Off-Campus: 19%

Graduate and First-Professional
  Students: 3,104

Academics

Full-Time Faculty: 783
  With Ph.D.: 98%

Part-Time Faculty: 304
  With Ph.D.: 68%

Student/Faculty Ratio: 13:1

Most Popular Majors:
  political science (7%)
  finance (6%)
  preprofessional studies (6%)
  psychology (6%)
  English (5%)

Completing 2 or More Majors: 15%

Admissions

Regular Application Deadline: 1/9

Early Action Deadline: 11/1

Fall Transfer Deadline: 4/15

Spring Transfer Deadline: 11/1

Total # of Students Applied: 12,095
  Admitted: 3,524
  Enrolled: 1,996

# of Students Waitlisted: 840
  Students Accepting Place: 572
  Waitlisted Students Admitted: 142

Inside the Classroom

Notre Dame "gets better academically every year," claims one Ohio counselor. The university administration agrees: "Some of our own graduates are not aware of the improved quality of our programs in art, computer science and computer engineering, languages, music, social sciences, and theater." Actually, Notre Dame offers a number of outstanding academic programs in its five undergraduate colleges: engineering, science, business, architecture, and arts and sciences.

Instead of declaring a major during the first year, you explore the subjects available and can declare a major when the time seems right. "Competitiveness varies between majors," says a premed student. "Engineers always help each other out, while premeds tend to keep their info to themselves." Another student says, "People are fairly competitive, especially in majors where they'll be competing for a limited number of graduate positions. But it's definitely not cutthroat and a lot of cooperating goes on." For all students, the basic curriculum includes courses in sciences, humanities, history, math, writing, and philosophy, as well as theology.

One definite plus for Notre Dame students is the expectation of a loyal alumni network after graduation. "The alumni tend to be a fanatical bunch, and they hire their own. Particularly in the business school, there is a serious recruiting effort by alums for ND grads." Another student who manned the phones for alumni donation campaigns says, "So many times the alumni would bring up memories of dorm life, school traditions, coursework. We felt such a cross-generational connection just because of the university. The power of the alumni network is what I believe is one of the top benefits of the university."

Campus Environment

The Notre Dame campus, graced by two lakes, revolves around the impressive gold-domed administration building. One student's description of the campus: "spectacular, especially in the fall," with architecture that includes "very old brick, ivy-covered buildings" as well as "newer buildings that were built to look like the old ones, except they haven't gotten the ivy to hang just right yet." The campus also has a grotto, modeled on Lourdes Cathedral, where Mass is sometimes held.

In terms of location, the Notre Dame campus is fairly isolated. South Bend "isn't exactly Chicago" in terms of entertainment options, and the bitter winter weather can force students to stay close to campus. Still, it can do wonders for a student's concentration. "I personally prefer big cosmopolitan cities like Chicago," says one alumna. "But the remote locale of the school turned out to be perfect for me. I would have been extremely distracted from being studious had I studied in Chicago or Atlanta, as I almost did."

All 27 dormitories mix all four years of students together. "All dorms are single-sex," says one student. "This sounds like a drag, but the dorms end up serving as sort-of fraternities and sororities." Interhall sports and competitions are fought with great passion, and it's common for a student to spend all four years in one dorm. Not every student, however, supports the single-sex concept. "The gender relations are really screwed up," says one junior. "There are a lot of kids coming from single-sex schools who don't seem to realize that members of the opposite sex are human. Having single-sex dorms only adds to the problem."

Student Life

Notre Dame football is the stuff dreams are made of. With 11 national championships, 39 Hall of Famers (to date), and 7 Heisman trophy winners on record, the Fighting Irish are perhaps the most storied and successful team in college football history. A junior premed student likens it to a campus religion: "Worshipping God and worshipping football is synonymous. Saturday games and Sunday services. Chants at games, hymns at church. The similarities go on and on." The hoopla can get tiresome for a few, including this senior: "Yes, this is the home of the college football hall of fame, but really, folks? Perspective? It is just a game."

Other sports are taken seriously too. The women's soccer and basketball teams have won national championships, and even the club and intramural sports are immensely popular. One sophomore says, "Most students played at least one sport in high school. It's great for people who don't want to play varsity but still enjoy participating as a much less competitive level."

Inevitably, such hardworking and hard-playing students blow off steam during weekends. "The majority of ND students work with great intensity five days a week, and then for the two days of the weekend let loose and go crazy," says one student. "Drinking and parties are permitted in the dorm rooms, so many underclassmen participate here. Upperclassmen frequent local bars, clubs, off-campus apartment parties, and team houses."

The student body is fairly homogenous, with most students leaning to the political and social right. The resulting unity of spirit is pleasant for most: "People smile at each other here and say hello. It's like a family." With this conservatism comes a complacency that might irk more liberal students. "The last time I remember seeing students band together and become active about something was when they removed Captain Crunch cereal from the dining hall," quips one student. "Students held a protest until they returned it. And the world is a better place for it."

Because it's a Catholic university, religion influences the social atmosphere in many ways. A majority of the students are Catholic, and a number consider themselves fairly religious. "The priests are great," says one student. "Most people have a faith here, though it's not all the same faith." Yet some students feel that the school's policies, which adhere to the doctrines of the Church, can "limit growth." Foremost among these are "parietals"—the rules governing the visiting hours in dorms for people of the opposite sex. "Parietals cause the biggest friction between the students and the administration," says one student. "The students don't deem them necessary, but the administration just won't budge due to the university's strong Catholic tradition."

Other schools to check out: Georgetown, Duke, Northwestern, Stanford, Villanova, Syracuse.

Test Scores (middle 50%):
SAT Verbal: 620–720
SAT Math: 650–740
ACT Comp: 30–33
HS Rank of Entering Freshmen:
Top 10%: 83%
Top 25%: 95%
Top 50%: 100%

THE EXPERTS SAY...

" The rich traditions and powerful alumni network make Notre Dame a sure bet for tomorrow's professionals. "

" For some students, the combination of sports, study, and chastity builds character. Others may only end up tired, brainy, and frustrated. "

Costs (2004–5)

Tuition and Fees: $29,512
Room & Board: $7,418
Payment Plan(s): installment plan

Graduates

Going to Graduate School:
34% Within One Year

Accepting Job Offer:
51% at time of graduation

Companies Recruiting On Campus:
340

Alumni Giving: 44%

UNIVERSITY OF OKLAHOMA

1000 Asp Avenue, Norman, OK 73019-4076
Admissions Phone: (800) 234-6868; (405) 325-2252 Fax: (405) 325-7124
Email: admrec@ou.edu Website: www.ou.edu
Application Website: www.ou.edu/admrec/

General Info

Type of School: public, coed

Setting: suburban

Academic Calendar: semester

Student Body

Full-Time Undergrads: 17,464
  Men: 51%, Women: 49%

Part-Time Undergrads: 2,511
  Men: 53%, Women: 47%

Total Undergrad Population:
  African American: 6%
  Asian American: 5%
  Latino: 4%
  Native American: 7%
  Caucasian: 74%
  International: 4%
  Out-of-State: 21%
  Living Off-Campus: 80%
  In Fraternities: 17%
  In Sororities: 25%

Graduate and First-Professional
  Students: 4,229

Academics

Full-Time Faculty: 971
  With Ph.D.: 88%

Part-Time Faculty: 220
  With Ph.D.: 48%

Student/Faculty Ratio: 21:1

Most Popular Majors:
  psychology (4%)
  sociology (3%)
  marketing (3%)
  management information
    systems (3%)

Completing 2 or More Majors: 6%

Freshmen Retention Rate: 83%

Graduation Rates:
  19% within four years
  54% within six years

Admissions

Regular Application Deadline: 6/1

Fall Transfer Deadline: 6/1

Spring Transfer Deadline: 11/1

Total # of Students Applied: 8,140
  Admitted: 6,638
  Enrolled: 3,808

# of Students Waitlisted: 706
  Students Accepting Place: 706
  Waitlisted Students Admitted: 190

Inside the Classroom

The University of Oklahoma's main campus in Norman offers a whopping 143 degree programs for undergrads. In the University College, where all first-years start out, students take two courses specifically designed to provide support for freshmen as they adjust, both academically and socially, to college life. Freshman and sophomore year are also largely spent fulfilling several broad general education requirements in fields such as English composition, foreign language, communications, mathematics, humanities, and the natural and social sciences. Students then choose from among several well-regarded undergraduate colleges, including architecture, arts and sciences, education, and journalism and mass communication. The Michael F. Price College of Business is quite popular, and the engineering school is top-notch, particularly the petroleum program. The school of meteorology is recognized as one of the best in the world, and the college of fine arts receives national kudos, with one of the oldest collegiate ballet programs in the country.

Although workload and competitiveness in the classroom varies wildly across the university, most OU students agree that the general academic atmosphere is, as one student says, "relaxed and easygoing." To be successful at such a big school, students have to work hard to get noticed and stay focused. Class size can number in the hundreds, especially for general education courses, and it's not uncommon to have more TAs than professors giving the lectures and tests. There's "not a lot of individual attention," agrees an Oklahoma high school guidance counselor. The official student/faculty ratio is 21:1, although some students say it feels much bigger than that. These complaints, typical of large state universities, lessen as students move into their majors and class sizes and professor interaction become more intimate. Top students can take part in the prestigious Honors College, where classes are capped at 22 and the faculty is acknowledged as outstanding.

Campus Environment

The campus spreads out over 2,000 acres, with permanently endowed gardens and Prairie Gothic architecture. "Nice scenery," a student agrees. OU is home to one of the largest university-affiliated natural history museums in the world, and the art museum "just received the single most important gift of art to a pubic university in U.S. history"—a collection of 33 French Impressionist paintings by artists such as Van Gogh and Monet.

The university is undergoing extensive construction and renewal, having recently added onto its student union center, physics building, and various lounges and athletic facilities. Another OU project is the Faculty-in-Residence program; there are six living quarters in the residence halls and university apartment complexes where the faculty and their families live among the students.

All freshmen must live on campus; housing options range from towers and quads to community centers and special-interest houses. "The desks and closets and beds are built in, so rearrangement of furniture is not an option," warns a junior. "Apartments are definitely the way to go," she continues, and most of the student body agrees with her: About 80 percent of all undergrads move off-campus after freshman year. All students may bring cars to campus (once they've obtained the requisite parking permit), which is a good thing, since "everyone and his brother drives," students claim. Parking is a major headache, however, so some students opt for the metro bus system, CART, which runs five city routes and two campus routes.

Student Life

It's not surprising that more than three-quarters of OU students hail from Oklahoma. Undergrad enrollment at the Norman campus tops 18,000, and the school is proud of the "diversity" of its student community. OU's Native American enrollment is number one in the Big 12, and the numbers of African American, Asian American, and Latin American students are growing. One high school guidance counselor says that OU has a "tremendous program" of recruitment incentives for African Americans.

Such a large student population calls for a wide variety of student groups and organizations, which OU has in spades ("a lot of distractions," a counselor tells us). There are hundreds of clubs on campus; among the more popular groups are the Campus Activities Council, RUF/NEKS (the oldest spirit organization in the nation), and the Student Union Programming Board. The "Big Event" is also popular, "the day every organization gets together and does community service work for our city."

Greek life is a force to be reckoned with on campus, with 42 national fraternities and sororities claiming a good portion of the student body. Though some claim the Greeks' impact depends upon the people you hang out with, one student insists that your fraternal brothers and sorority sisters shape your social life: "These are the people who you talk to on campus, who you sit with for lunch, and [who you] go to parties and get wasted with." OU has quite a reputation as a party school, and the weekend festivities start as early as Wednesday night here. Students drink at apartment parties and frat parties, and in celebration of a Sooner football victory (or in mourning of a loss, for that matter).

Football is huge here, and students, alumni, and hundreds of other Oklahoma fans regularly pack the OU stadium on fall Saturdays. Hordes of students make the annual trek to Dallas for the Red River Shootout against Texas, and one of the biggest events of the year is the Big Red Rally, where students can show their intense school spirit and support for their beloved Sooners. "There is a lot of school loyalty and tradition here," a student boasts. When football season's over, OU students can turn their attention to 9 other men's and 10 women's varsity teams. There are also 70 intramural sports, which can get "pretty competitive and fun"; about 50 percent of men and 30 percent of women participate in IMs.

Although most of OU's social activities revolve around campus and student parties, the city of Norman—the third largest in the state, but "more like a small town"— offers shopping, museums, theaters, restaurants, and bars.

Test Scores (middle 50%):
ACT Comp: 24–28
HS Rank of Entering Freshmen:
Top 10%: 36%
Top 25%: 73%
Top 50%: 92%
Avg. HS GPA: 3.59

THE EXPERTS SAY...

" 143 majors, with top-flight meteorology, business, and petroleum engineering programs —UO's offerings are as diverse as its student body. Native American and African American students are made welcome here. "

" 42 frats, football, and hundreds of clubs— there are a lot of 'distractions', and with a student/faculty ratio of 21:1, you'll have to stay focused to get noticed in the classroom. "

Costs (2003–04)

Tuition and Fees, In-State: $3,741
Tuition and Fees, Out-of-State: $10,254
Room & Board: $5,485
Payment Plan(s): installment plan

Inst. Aid (2002–03)

Institutional Aid, Need-Based: $2,030,175
Institutional Aid, Non-Need-Based: $1,923,908
FT Undergrads Receiving Aid: 46%
Avg. Amount per Student: $7,421
FT Undergrads Receiving Non-Need-Based Scholarship or Grant Aid: 10%
Avg. Amount per Student: $1,073
Of Those Receiving Any Aid:
Rec. Need-Based Scholarship or Grant Aid: 43%
Average Award: $3,591
Rec. Need-Based Self-Help Aid: 68%
Average Award: $4,302
Upon Graduation, Avg. Loan Debt per Student: $17,444
Financial Aid Deadline: rolling, 3/1 (priority)

Graduates

Companies Recruiting On-Campus: 1,120
Alumni Giving: 22%

UNIVERSITY OF OREGON

240 Oregon Hall, Eugene, OR 97403
Admissions Phone: (541) 346-3201; (800) BEA-DUCK (out-of-state) Fax: (541) 346-5815
Email: uoadmit@oregon.uoregon.edu
Website: www.uoregon.edu

General Info

Type of School: public, coed

Setting: urban

Academic Calendar: quarter

Student Body

Full-Time Undergrads: 14,452
    Men: 47%, Women: 53%

Part-Time Undergrads: 1,531
    Men: 50%, Women: 50%

Total Undergrad Population:
    African American: 2%
    Asian American: 6%
    Latino: 3%
    Native American: 1%
    Caucasian: 75%
    International: 5%
    Out-of-State: 24%
    Living Off-Campus: 81%
    In Fraternities: 8%
    In Sororities: 10%

Graduate and First-Professional
    Students: 4,009

Academics

Full-Time Faculty: 793
    With Ph.D.: 97%

Part-Time Faculty: 338
    With Ph.D.: 86%

Student/Faculty Ratio: 19:1

Most Popular Majors:
    business (14%)
    journalism (9%)
    psychology (6%)
    biology (4%)
    political science (4%)

Completing 2 or More Majors: 10%

Freshmen Retention Rate: 83%

Graduation Rates:
    37% within four years
    61% within six years

Admissions

Regular Application Deadline: 1/15

Fall Transfer Deadline: 5/15

Spring Transfer Deadline: 1/18

Total # of Students Applied: 10,193
    Admitted: 8,602
    Enrolled: 2,865

Test Scores (middle 50%):
    SAT Verbal: 490–609
    SAT Math: 499–613

In the Classroom

The University of Oregon offers 77 majors within 7 different colleges: the School of Architecture and Allied Arts; Charles H. Lunquist College of Business; College of Arts and Sciences; College of Education; School of Journalism and Communications; and the School of Music. The university's programs in journalism, international economics, business, music, psychology, cellular biology, mathematics, and interior architecture rank among the best in the nation. The most popular majors among undergraduates are: business administration, economics, English, environmental studies, fine arts, international studies, journalism, political science, psychology, and sociology. The university is "great for California students not getting in to UC's [University of California schools]," notes a California guidance counselor.

The university offers approximately 2,800 classes each term. Of these, about 95 classes have more than 100 students. But the median class size is only 20. "You won't find the same small-town feeling like you would at Reed or Amherst," remarks one student, "but you get to know a lot of people here quickly. That includes faculty."

To provide a more personalized learning experience, a number of "Learning Communities" have been set up. The Honors College is a small, liberal arts college within the university. "Freshman Interest Groups" (FIGs) place a small group of freshmen with similar interests together in the same series of theme-related courses for the fall term. "Pathways" allow students in some of the FIGs to continue to take some of their courses together, giving them, in the words of a professor, "a carefully designed, small-college educational experience in a major research university with all of its resources [and] excitement."

The school is nationally recognized for its research work in biomechanics, computers, genetics, lasers, and neuroscience. The academic departments and research institutes of the university support a variety of "Participatory Learning Experiences" for undergraduate students.

Campus Environment

The 283-acre campus is located a five-minute walk from downtown Eugene. This small city may be the perfect college town—small enough to be friendly and easy to navigate; big enough to support its own professional ballet, opera, and symphony orchestra companies; and hip enough to offer a lively alternative music scene and a range of other entertainment options. Add in the low crime rate and inexpensive rents and complete the picture with easy access to the Cascade Mountain wilderness and Pacific Coast beaches nearby. Too good to be true? Well, remember the unrelenting winter rain.

Two-thirds of the freshmen live in university residence halls. Dorm selection is based on themes, which for 2002–03 include community service, creative arts, cyber technology, health and fitness, intensive academics, international, multicultural, and music. There is also a substance-free hall, an honors hall, and a 24-hour quiet hall. Most dorms are coed but have same-sex floors. Oregon also offers the option of selecting a residential FIG, so that you not only study but also reside with the same group of freshmen.

Beyond the freshman year, nearly all students live off campus; in fact, only 4 percent of juniors and 2 percent of seniors stay on campus. One option is the 18 fraternities and 10 sororities, but most simply find their own apartments in Eugene.

An automobile is not necessary for getting around. Bicycles provide a popular alternative and the city of Eugene boasts more than 100 miles of paved bicycle paths. And students, armed with their IDs, can board Eugene's bus system free of charge.

Student Life

The UO, where about 12 percent are students of color, offers as much diversity as can be found in the Pacific Northwest. An additional 6 percent of the students are international students, representing 83 different countries. This diversity is reflected in the 250 student organizations active on campus, which include cultural groups, international student clubs, fraternities and sororities, student government, campus ministries, professional organizations, performing arts ensembles, honor societies, and political and environmental action groups. You should have no trouble finding other students who share your interests.

Oregon's student body is one of the most politically active in the nation—more left than right, though the conservatives make their voices heard as well. "You can't go a day without hearing about or seeing a demonstration, march, protest, or petition drive," a student says. Green isn't just the school team's color here, it's an attitude. "We're lucky to be going to school in one of the most beautiful regions in the country," another student said, "and students here, whether they're from Oregon or not, tend to get very protective of it." But other issues are also the focus of campus activism, and the independent daily student newspaper, the *Oregon Daily Emerald*, is not afraid to take on issues uncomfortable to the administration (tuition hikes, faculty salaries, and deals with the food service are just a few) as well as national issues.

Due to its location near mountains and ocean, Oregon attracts a large number of students who want a large helping of outdoor recreational activities with their education. In fact, student dues include membership in the university's outdoor program co-op, which provides equipment, training, and organized outings at all skill levels. Skiing at Willamette Pass, rafting the McKenzie River, rock climbing at Smith Rocks, and ocean sports at Oregon Sand Dunes National Recreational Area are among the most popular activities nearby.

For those more artistically inclined, the Craft Center provides studios and classes even for those not enrolled in an academic course in fine arts. Artists and non-artists alike go to downtown Eugene's quirky outdoor Saturday Market, which offers proof hippies are alive and well and living in Oregon. You can shop for locally produced crafts and organic foods or just enjoy the music of street musicians.

Pac-10, Division I sports produce big events at Oregon and the school has traditionally had standout men's and women's track and cross-country programs. However, more recently, the Ducks' success in men's basketball and football have garnered the most national attention. Other intercollegiate sports include basketball, golf, softball, tennis, soccer, and volleyball for women and golf, tennis, and wrestling for men. In addition, the club sports program includes 19 other sports from aikido to juggling and ultimate Frisbee to surfing. A popular intramural sports program completes the picture.

HS Rank of Entering Freshmen:
 Top 10%: 22%
 Top 25%: 56%
 Top 50%: 91%
Avg. HS GPA: 3.54

Costs (2003–04)

Tuition and Fees, In-State: $4,914

Tuition and Fees, Out-of-State: $16,350

Room & Board: $6,565

Payment Plan(s): installment plan

THE EXPERTS SAY...

" Many state schools can feel like degree factories, but the University of Oregon has a real sense of community, due in part to its highly committed student body. "

" If pickets and protests are your thing, be sure to also check out Cal Berkeley. "

Inst. Aid (est. 2003–04)

Institutional Aid, Need-Based: $138,500

Institutional Aid, Non-Need-Based: $8,327,252

FT Undergrads Receiving Aid: 44%
 Avg. Amount per Student: $8,058

FT Undergrads Receiving Non-Need-Based Scholarship or Grant Aid: 6%
 Avg. Amount per Student: $1,753

Of Those Receiving Any Aid:

Rec. Need-Based Scholarship or Grant Aid: 57%
 Average Award: $3,779

Rec. Need-Based Self-Help Aid: 90%
 Average Award: $5,111

Upon Graduation, Avg. Loan Debt per Student: $17,111

Financial Aid Deadline: 3/1

Graduates

Going to Graduate School:
 20% Within One Year

Companies Recruiting On Campus: 185

UNIVERSITY OF PENNSYLVANIA

1 College Hall, Philadelphia, PA 19104-6376
Admissions Phone: (215) 898-7507 Fax: (215) 898-9670
Email: info@admissionsug.upenn.edu Website: www.upenn.edu
Application Website: www.upenn.edu/admissions

General Info

Type of School: private, coed
Setting: urban
Academic Calendar: semester

Student Body

Full-Time Undergrads: 9,448
  Men: 50%, Women: 50%

Part-Time Undergrads: 388
  Men: 48%, Women: 52%

Total Undergrad Population:
  African American: 6%
  Asian American: 17%
  Latino: 5%
  Native American: <1%
  Caucasian: 50%
  International: 11%
  Out-of-State: 81%
  Living Off-Campus: 37%
  In Fraternities: 23%
  In Sororities: 16%

Graduate and First-Professional
  Students: 9,592

Academics

Full-Time Faculty: 1,382
  With Ph.D.: 100%

Part-Time Faculty: 497
  With Ph.D.: 100%

Student/Faculty Ratio: 6:1

Most Popular Majors:
  finance (8%)
  nursing (8%)
  economics (6%)
  history (5%)
  bioengineering (5%)

Completing 2 or More Majors: 26%

Freshmen Retention Rate: 97%

Graduation Rates:
  79% within four years
  92% within six years

Admissions

Regular Application Deadline: 1/1

Early Decision Deadline(s): 11/1

Fall Transfer Deadline: 3/15

Total # of Students Applied: 18,831
  Admitted: 3,837
  Enrolled: 2,423

# of Students Waitlisted: 1,085
  Students Accepting Place: 533
  Waitlisted Students Admitted: 18

Inside the Classroom

The University of Pennsylvania has four undergraduate schools: the Wharton School of Business, the School of Nursing, the School of Engineering and Applied Science, and the College at Penn (liberal arts and sciences), which is the largest, and, some say, weakest, of the schools. Wharton is indisputably the star and is considered one of the top business schools in the country, particularly known for its emphasis on financial analysis. Finance is a popular major here, as is biology in the College (Penn has an excellent medical school and teaching hospital). Core requirements vary by school, but all students take some kind of basic curriculum with courses in areas such as the humanities and sciences, and must demonstrate proficiency in writing and a foreign language.

Make no mistake: Penn students are intense, competitive ("ruthless," one premed tells us), and focused on the future. "Everyone takes everything and everyone seriously," says an undergrad. "They have to make sure that they secure a job for when they get out there to the real world." Another agrees: "Penn students really seem to be on a mission." The best of the best at Penn can participate in one of several honors programs, such as General Honors, University Scholars, or Benjamin Franklin Scholars. Many ambitious students opt for cross-disciplinary programs and joint and dual degree programs. As this is primarily a teaching and research institution, Penn's renowned faculty boasts Nobel laureates, recipients of the Pulitzer Prize, Fulbright Fellows, MacArthur Fellows, and Guggenhein Fellows, among others. And they're not just distinguished, but accessible—if, warn students, "you make an appointment."

But Penn students also appreciate learning for its own sake. For instance, many undergrads take Preceptorials: short, fun, non-credit seminars led by some of Penn's most-lauded faculty on topics ranging from "Team Dynamics and Paintball" to "Magic and Marketing: Reading *Harry Potter*."

Campus Environment

West Philadelphia isn't the safest of neighborhoods, but Penn's "lovely" campus is self-contained and certainly collegiate in appearance, with academic buildings separated by grass and trees, especially along Locust Walk. Campus is heavily patrolled ("I have never felt unsafe in any terms," a junior tells us) and students at this "urban Ivy" tend to be active participants in improving their surrounding community.

Each of Penn's 12 residential communities (called "college houses") has its own distinctive personality. Most freshmen live in the four college houses that make up the Quad, known for being pretty noisy and highly sociable. The school, however, does not guarantee housing for any students. Many upperclassmen move into one of the "not particularly attractive" high-rises in the Hamilton Village section of campus, described as "definitely apartment-type living, with more space but fewer social opportunities than in the dorms." About 40 percent of students live off-campus altogether, and then it's usually in a fraternity house, or less commonly, a sorority house.

You'll probably want to leave your car at home. Everything on campus is within walking distance, and the school offers van transportation to nearby neighborhoods.

And here's where being in a city works in your favor: Cabs are plentiful, and Philly has an extensive mass transportation system ("shabby but effective," sniffs one student) for outings downtown or out of town.

Student Life

Nestled in a city "rich in culture and diversity," it's not surprising that the 9,700-member student body is generally described in similar terms. Ask a Penn student to define a typical classmate, and you'll probably get a response of "friendly." Unfortunately, though, the school does have a reputation of attracting its fair share of "snotty" coeds. "There is a lot of money at Penn," says one student; another adds, "people are very conscious of how they look."

What do Penn students do outside the classroom? Anything and everything. The Van Pelt Library, identified by the sculpture of a giant button in front, is a popular meeting site ("I'll see you at the Button" is a common refrain). The hundreds of campus clubs and organizations include many professional and honors societies, as well as several culturally oriented groups; student theater and musical groups are also popular.

Drinking, certainly, is a popular extracurricular activity. ("This is undoubtedly 'the party Ivy,'" one student exclaims.) Fraternities and sororities "dictate social life," with about one-quarter of the student body joining the Greek system. If you're not 21, and not studying, you're "drinking heavily at a frat house." Twenty-one year-olds (or those with "a good fake ID") head to local hangouts, such as Smoky Joe's, a college bar tradition. Those who are looking for something outside the usual college social scene don't have to look far: Philadelphia is a "huge, sprawling city full of culture, food, and nightlife."

Sports are also popular ("but not as popular as at other schools," notes one student). About 10 percent of the student body plays on one of 33 varsity teams (17 men's, 16 women's); thousands more participate in club or intramural sports. The football team, a frequent contender for Ivy League champion, is far and away the school's pride and joy. Franklin Field, where Quaker football games are waged, is one of the oldest stadiums in the country.

Penn is filled with tradition—it was, after all, the first university in the colonies. Spring Fling, a carnival-type event capped off with a live concert by a major popular band, is one of the biggest weekends of the year. One of Penn's unique traditions is Hey Day, celebrated on the last day of class when juniors become the "kings of the school" at a large party. "The juniors march together down Locust Walk with hats and canes," a student describes. "After they are declared seniors at the quad, they tap each other's canes like mad and bite chunks out of each other's hats."

Other schools to check out: Columbia, Duke, Georgetown, Johns Hopkins, UC Berkeley.

Applied Early Decision: 3,390
Early Decision Admitted: 1,122

Test Scores (middle 50%):
SAT Verbal: 650–750
SAT Math: 680–760
ACT Comp: 28–32
ACT English: 28–33
ACT Math: 28–34

HS Rank of Entering Freshmen:
Top 10%: 93%
Top 25%: 99%
Top 50%: 100%

Avg. HS GPA: 3.84

THE EXPERTS SAY...

" Penn's competitive programs in biology and finance are nationally ranked. And a degree from Wharton is a sure-fire ticket to an M.B.A. "

" The students are career-oriented, ambitious, and competitive—and that's just when they're partying. Be ready to work like a dog and drink like a fish. "

Costs (2003–04)

Tuition and Fees: $29,318

Room & Board: $8,642

Payment Plan(s): installment plan, pre-payment plan

Inst. Aid (2002–03)

Institutional Aid, Need-Based: $64,866,000

FT Undergrads Receiving Aid: 42%
Avg. Amount per Student: $25,740

Of Those Receiving Any Aid:

Rec. Need-Based Scholarship or Grant Aid: 100%
Average Award: $20,437

Rec. Need-Based Self-Help Aid: 91%
Average Award: $6,766

Upon Graduation, Avg. Loan Debt per Student: $19,579

Financial Aid Deadline: 2/15 (priority)

Graduates

Going to Graduate School: 23% Within One Year

Accepting Job Offer: 47% at time of graduation

Companies Recruiting On Campus: 490

UNIVERSITY OF PITTSBURGH

Alumni Hall, 4227 Fifth Ave., Pittsburgh, PA 15260
Admissions Phone: (412) 624-7488 Fax: (412) 648-8815
Email: oafa@pitt.edu Website: www.pitt.edu
Application Website: www.admissions.pitt.edu/freshapp/freshman.asp

General Info

Type of School: public, coed

Setting: urban

Academic Calendar: semester

Student Body

Full-Time Undergrads: 15,110
  Men: 48%, Women: 52%

Part-Time Undergrads: 1,803
  Men: 43%, Women: 57%

Total Undergrad Population:
  African American: 9%
  Asian American: 4%
  Latino: 1%
  Native American: <1%
  Caucasian: 82%
  International: 1%
  Out-of-State: 15%
  Living Off-Campus: 59%
  In Fraternities: 6%
  In Sororities: 6%

Graduate and First-Professional
  Students: 9,382

Academics

Full-Time Faculty: 1,439
  With Ph.D.: 92%

Part-Time Faculty: 475

Student/Faculty Ratio: 17:1

Most Popular Majors:
  engineering (10%)
  business (10%)
  social sciences (8%)
  psychology (4%)
  nursing (4%)

Completing 2 or More Majors: 16%

Freshmen Retention Rate: 88%

Graduation Rates:
  40% within four years
  63% within six years
  note: 5-yr. programs affect rates

Admissions

Application Deadline: rolling

Total # of Students Applied: 17,494
  Admitted: 8,445
  Enrolled: 2,914

Test Scores (middle 50%):
  SAT Verbal: 550–650
  SAT Math: 570–660

HS Rank of Entering Freshmen:
  Top 10%: 43%

Inside the Classroom

The University of Pittsburgh offers an amazing 178 baccalaureate degree programs. In keeping with its reputation as a top research center, the school's strongest programs and best facilities are those that prepare students for professional careers. Premed students, for example, are able to observe and study at the university's acclaimed medical center. While Pitt is particularly known for its schools of engineering and health and rehabilitation sciences, the college of business continues to attract more and more students. The college of arts and sciences also has several excellent departments. Other undergraduate schools include those of education, dental medicine, information sciences, pharmacy, and social work. Degree requirements vary by school, with most students taking an assortment of general education classes in the sciences, humanities, and arts during their first two years.

Students rate the academic atmosphere as anywhere from "rather laid back" to "great" to "extremely intense." It all depends on your major, of course. As a large university, Pitt presents its challenges for undergrads, including large classes and limited interaction with professors. As one senior puts it, "Your workload and relationships with professors are what you make them." In an intro class you may find yourself in a lecture hall with hundreds of others; upper divisions are thankfully smaller. But the prestigious honors college offers top students the opportunity to study in a more intimate, intense academic environment, with an average class size of 18 students.

Students who take the initiative and seek out opportunities can receive an excellent undergraduate education. In fact, an impressive number of Pitt graduates earn Rhodes and Marshall Scholarships. There are many special academic options available, including opportunities for independent study and research, extensive study abroad programs, and the unique Semester at Sea, which combines world travel and coursework aboard a ship, and which more than 600 undergrads take advantage of each term. Although students from all over the country line up to do Semester at Sea, Pitt students get some preferential treatment since their university is in charge; a few full scholarships (i.e., free round-the-world cruise) are available only to Pittsburgh undergrads.

Campus Environment

The university's main campus is located on a hill in the Oakland district, Pittsburgh's cultural and medical center, near the beautiful, 456-acre Schenley Park. "We don't have a gorgeous, bucolic campus," a senior tells us, "but the advantage is that everything is close." There are approximately 100 academic, research, and administrative buildings and residence halls on the 132-acre campus, including the 42-story Cathedral of Learning, the tallest academic building in the western hemisphere. Despite its urban setting, the school gets high marks for its security measures. "They should be commended for having a very low crime rate [for] a campus inside a major city," an undergrad says proudly.

On-campus housing is available, but limited. "The dorms are nice, clean, and spacious," we hear. Most freshmen live in the Litchefield Towers ("they are ugly but the social community attracts people," according to one student); the school even offers the option of a first-year single. After their freshman or sophomore year, most students choose to move off-campus to "very popular," "cheap" apartments in Oakland. The general consensus regarding cars is that you don't need one. Most Pitt students take advantage of the free bus service.

For some outsiders, the name "Pittsburgh" still conjures up images of an industrial wasteland. But how wrong that image is: People coming here for the first time are always amazed at how pleasant the city has become, with friendly residents, surrounding mountains, and clean water. "Pittsburgh has more to offer than most people think in terms of culture and things to do," asserts one student. Another agrees: "I love Pittsburgh. There is so much to do here." The city boasts upscale shopping districts, museums and galleries, an excellent symphony and opera, and a decent selection of nightlife and restaurants. One student even lists the "O"—the renowned Original Hot Dog Shop in South Oakland—as one of the most appealing things about going to school at Pitt.

Student Life

With more than 15,000 undergrads—most of whom hail from Pennsylvania—it's not surprising that there is no one "type" of student here. When pressed to generalize, one student allows that "most Pitt students enjoy drinking; are concerned, but not overly so, with their studies; are into football; and are middle class." She goes on to praise the "lack of pretentiousness" here, attributing it to the "working-class ethic of the city." Another student agrees, adding, "This school is not a country club." Some complain of a meager minority presence; school figures cite an 82 percent white population.

Because of Pitt's large enrollment and urban setting, there's not a real feeling of community, especially since most upperclassmen don't live on campus. Students tend to hang out in small, isolated groups depending on common interests or backgrounds. There are about 300 student organizations, including a black action society, a student-run newspaper and radio station, and a volunteer outreach program. Pitt also has a long history of devotion to its varsity athletic teams, especially Panthers football and basketball. "The football players are almost celebrities," a student says. Another notes that "the other sports get attention mainly when they are winning." More than half the student body participates in the extensive intramural sports program.

"There is a rather large party scene here at Pittsburgh," a freshman tells us. "There is always an opportunity to get drunk most nights of the week." On weekends most students hit the party circuit, either at houses in Oakland, "where you pay about $3 for a bottomless cup of beer," or at fraternities. The Greek system is active, with over 30 fraternities and sororities, but, we're told, "they are not as popular as they used to be."

Costs (2003–04)

Tuition and Fees, In-State: $9,274

Tuition and Fees, Out-of-State: $18,586

Room & Board: $6,800

Payment Plan(s): installment plan, deferred payment plan

THE EXPERTS SAY...

" With initiative, you can get a great education at Pitt. Engineering, premed, and health and rehabilitation sciences are strong here, and you can take a Semester at Sea—literally. "

" Pitt is like a relaxed Carnegie Mellon with major parties and real sports. Middle class students feel at home here. And believe it or not, Pittsburgh is a pretty nice town. "

Inst. Aid (est. 2003–04)

Institutional Aid, Need-Based: $2,657,746

Institutional Aid, Non-Need-Based: $17,127,378

FT Undergrads Receiving Aid: 56% Avg. Amount per Student: $10,003

FT Undergrads Receiving Non-Need-Based Scholarship or Grant Aid: 12% Avg. Amount per Student: $7,188

Of Those Receiving Any Aid:

Rec. Need-Based Scholarship or Grant Aid: 67% Average Award: $5,183

Rec. Need-Based Self-Help Aid: 94% Average Award: $5,290

Upon Graduation, Avg. Loan Debt per Student: $20,154

Financial Aid Deadline: 3/1 (priority)

Graduates

Going to Graduate School: 43% Within One Year

Companies Recruiting On Campus: 400

Alumni Giving: 16%

UNIVERSITY OF PUGET SOUND

1500 North Warner, Tacoma, WA 98416-1062
Admissions Phone: (253) 879-3211; (800) 396-7191 Fax: (253) 879-3993
Email: admission@ups.edu
Website: www.ups.edu

General Info

Type of School: private, coed
Setting: suburban
Academic Calendar: semester

Student Body

Full-Time Undergrads: 2,457
  Men: 41%, Women: 59%

Part-Time Undergrads: 44
  Men: 52%, Women: 48%

Total Undergrad Population:
  African American: 2%
  Asian American: 9%
  Latino: 3%
  Native American: 1%
  Caucasian: 76%
  International: 1%
  Out-of-State: 71%
  Living Off-Campus: 38%
  In Fraternities: 18%
  In Sororities: 21%

Graduate and First-Professional
  Students: 244

Academics

Full-Time Faculty: 214
  With Ph.D.: 86%

Part-Time Faculty: 45
  With Ph.D.: 36%

Student/Faculty Ratio: 11:1

Most Popular Majors:
  business (8%)
  psychology (6%)
  biology (6%)
  English (5%)
  politics and government (4%)

Completing 2 or More Majors: 9%

Freshmen Retention Rate: 85%

Graduation Rates:
  67% within four years
  77% within six years

Admissions

Regular Application Deadline: 5/1;
  2/1 (priority)

Early Decision Deadline(s): 12/15,
  1/15

Fall Transfer Deadline: 7/1, 3/1 (priority)

Total # of Students Applied: 4,237
  Admitted: 3,022
  Enrolled: 641

In the Classroom

Compared to other small, private, liberal arts colleges, the University of Puget Sound is somewhat larger than most. Thus, you'll find greater student diversity and more academic courses and majors than you might first expect. Among the academic disciplines the school is most known for are Asian Studies and International Political Economy—majors most small liberal arts schools don't even offer. Of course, standard majors like business administration, English, biology, and psychology are also popular and of high academic quality. Guidance counselors we interviewed also recommended this school for its arts and music programs.

All students complete the core curriculum, including courses in written communication or foreign language, mathematical reasoning, historical and humanistic perspectives, society, the natural world, the fine arts, comparative values, international studies, and "science in context." Classes tend to be small, except for a few freshman classes such as chemistry and English, where the total can reach 100. Students generally find the professors accessible and helpful.

The university offers opportunities for students to engage in research, whether in the natural sciences, the social sciences, or the humanities. In fact, programs in most majors require—or at least provide the option of—a research-based thesis in the senior year. Approximately 45 summer research grants ($3,000–$3,500) and 50 smaller research grants (up to $500) during the school year are made available to undergrads by the school.

Numerous internship and co-op education opportunities are also available. In the internship program, juniors and seniors from any major may earn regular course credit by working 10 hours per week and attending a weekly seminar. The co-op education program is offered to sophomores and above who seek paid work experience—and a head start launching their career while still in school. One-quarter to one-half of the regular course credit is given based on the student's job performance and written analysis of the work experience. In special placements that include academic seminars, full course credit is granted.

The Campus Environment

The mild, wet weather has produced the quintessential Pacific Northwest campus with towering evergreen trees and views of nearby snow-capped mountains. However, the campus, located in an attractive, older residential area of Tacoma, is not directly on Puget Sound as the name might imply. With its trees, ivy, and lawns, the campus is overwhelmingly green; although UPS students report their school's initials precipitate a lot of jokes and, no, the UPS school color is not brown.

The dorms are mainly for freshmen with the exception of one residence hall reserved for upperclassmen. One student reports, "After freshman year, you have to scramble around to find a living situation." Additional options for upperclassmen include fraternities/sororities, other on-campus houses, and a rented apartment or house off campus. Sororities and fraternities have a deferred rush so students don't move in with their "sisters and brothers" until their sophomore year. There is one central eating area for students on campus, officially named the Wheelock Student Center but commonly called the SUB.

Everything on campus is within walking distance; for getting around Tacoma, students bike, take the bus, or drive. Automobiles are especially useful for travel beyond Tacoma. Freshmen are allowed to have cars on campus although parking permits are required.

"Tacoma isn't the greatest college town," one student says. "There're of course a mall, bowling, movie theaters, and the like. But . . . I wouldn't rate it so high." Most students would probably agree with that assessment but still say that the location is ideal; after all, it's within an hour of the Cascade Mountains, the Olympic Mountains, the Pacific Coast, and Seattle. Even university officials say little about Tacoma and a lot about Seattle; one says, "Seattle, 30 miles to the north, is a world-class city that provides social and professional contacts that span the globe."

Student Life

UPS offers more diversity than most private colleges in the West. The school recruits ethnic minorities (the largest is Asian American) and is one of only a few U.S. schools offering a leadership scholarship earmarked for LGBT students. The diversity of backgrounds and interests is reflected in a list of the school's most active campus organizations: the Repertory Dance Group, multicultural student organizations, Lighthouse Christian Fellowship, Understanding Sexuality (a LGBT group), and the school's outdoor recreational programs. Many other student clubs and organizations are also active, so, whatever your background and interests, you shouldn't have much trouble finding people who share those. However, at UPS it's likely you'll also get to know people with different interests and backgrounds than your own.

Fraternities and sororities are strong and a sizeable percentage of students get involved in Greek life. One student who didn't pledge writes: "The Greek community meshes well with everyone else. There's no real hostility amongst the students and everyone's pretty much welcome at their parties." For students that want more entertainment choices, nearby Seattle—with its coffee bars, clubs, music scene, and big sports and entertainment events—is easily accessible.

UPS sponsors 23 intercollegiate sports, 11 for men and 12 for women. Approximately 450 students participate in the intercollegiate sports program. The Loggers compete in the Northwest Conference (NCAA Division III); 2001–02 conference championships (including ties) included men's and women's swimming, women's cross country, women's volleyball, men's soccer, and football. In addition there's an active intramural program that consists of 12 to 15 sports and approximately 1,750 students get involved. Outdoor recreational activities are very popular among UPS students, especially skiing and snowboarding.

Another attribute, which sets student life at UPS apart, is a focus on volunteerism. According to a college official, "75 percent of the Puget Sound student body volunteers in the community." In fact, UPS ranks ninth among all small colleges in the country in number of graduates who have joined the Peace Corps.

# of Students Waitlisted: 266
  Waitlisted Students Admitted: 19

Applied Early Decision: 163
  Early Decision Admitted: 143

Test Scores (middle 50%):
  SAT Verbal: 575–685
  SAT Math: 570–660
  ACT Comp: 24–29
  ACT English: 24–30
  ACT Math: 24–29

HS Rank of Entering Freshmen:
  Top 10%: 39%
  Top 25%: 73%
  Top 50%: 95%

Avg. HS GPA: 3.53

THE EXPERTS SAY...

"UPS offers majors you won't find at other small schools. Other schools you should look at are Whitman, Carleton, and Hamilton"

"LGBT students will feel comfortable at UPS—assuming they want no part of city life. Seattle is close, but not _that_ close."

Costs (2003–04)

Tuition and Fees: $23,945

Room & Board: $6,140

Payment Plan(s): deferred payment plan

Inst. Aid (est. 2003–04)

FT Undergrads Receiving Aid: 59%
  Avg. Amount per Student: $19,217

FT Undergrads Receiving Non-Need-Based Scholarship or Grant Aid: 26%
  Avg. Amount per Student: $6,766

Of Those Receiving Any Aid:

Rec. Need-Based Scholarship or Grant Aid: 97%
  Average Award: $13,011

Rec. Need-Based Self-Help Aid: 85%
  Average Award: $7,763

Upon Graduation, Avg. Loan Debt per Student: $23,782

Financial Aid Deadline: rolling, 2/1 (priority)

Graduates

Going to Graduate School:
  34% Within One Year

Accepting Job Offer:
  13% at time of graduation

Companies Recruiting On Campus:
  102

Alumni Giving: 42%

UNIVERSITY OF REDLANDS

1200 East Colton Avenue, P.O. Box 3080, Redlands, CA 92373-0999
Admissions Phone: (909) 335-4074 Fax: (909) 335-4089
Email: admissions@redlands.edu
Website: redlands.edu

General Info

Type of School: private, coed
Setting: suburban
Academic Calendar: 4-4-1

Student Body

Full-Time Undergrads: 2,192
  Men: 41%, Women: 59%

Part-Time Undergrads: 20
  Men: 45%, Women: 55%

Total Undergrad Population:
  African American: 2%
  Asian American: 5%
  Latino: 12%
  Native American: 1%
  Caucasian: 61%
  International: 1%
  Out-of-State: 18%
  Living Off-Campus: 25%
  In Fraternities: 3%
  In Sororities: 4%

Graduate and First-Professional
Students: 88

Academics

Full-Time Faculty: 156
  With Ph.D.: 86%

Part-Time Faculty: 119
  With Ph.D.: 36%

Student/Faculty Ratio: 12:1

Most Popular Majors:
  business administration/manage-
  ment (5%)
  liberal arts and sciences, general
  studies (3%)
  sociology (3%)
  communicative disorder (2%)
  psychology (2%)

Freshmen Retention Rate: 86%

Admissions

Regular Application Deadline: 6/1;
  12/15 (priority)

Fall Transfer Deadline: 6/1, 3/1 (priority)

Spring Transfer Deadline: 11/15

Total # of Students Applied: 2,669
  Admitted: 1,890
  Enrolled: 574

Inside the Classroom

The University of Redlands, a great liberal arts school with a quality curriculum, is home to one of the great educational experiments of all time: the Johnston Center for Integrative Studies. Founded in the 1960s as one of the first alternative education programs in the country, Johnston students design their own educational experience through a process called "contracting"—defining educational goals and a strategy for meeting those goals. Combining "high-quality education with minimal formality," Johnston students "negotiate" their education; that is, design courses and requirements around a personalized Graduation Contract. Whether it's changing a final exam into a final project or reading different books from the ones outlined for class, students "self-direct" their education. To top it off, there are no letter grades, only narrative evaluations. (It's worth noting that Johnston courses are available to all Redlands students on an individual basis.) Though Johnston students make up only a fraction of the undergraduate population, they're "a small minority with a very loud voice," explains one freshman. "Other than formal activist organizations, Johnston students are the most politically vocal group on campus."

Traditional residential students enroll in the university's College of Arts and Sciences. The basic areas of liberal arts and sciences are the school's strong points. Though Redlands has a solid conservatory program at the School of Music (with one guidance counselor citing it as one of the most attractive features of the university), we've heard that music has recently been overshadowed by the university's focus on the sciences.

With a total enrollment of 2,000, classes are small—you might have 8 people in your microbiology class. One student tells us that "the relationship that students can have with their teachers" is what sets the school apart. Another adds, "Accessibility of professors is, in my opinion, the biggest bonus to attending the University of Redlands. The student/teacher ratio is phenomenal." According to a high school guidance counselor, "Redlands develops students who have not yet reached their potential."

Another thing that students love about Redlands is the administration. "Administration 'ease' is one of the biggest pluses about this university. I am always treated with respect. People are almost without exception friendly and go out of their way to help you solve any problem," says one student. (On the other hand, it can take a while for larger projects to get done: One junior cites Internet access in dorm rooms as an example. "It's been a big project since I've been here, and it's taking forever.") Awarding $16 million in financial aid and merit scholarships, Redlands provides about 85 percent of its students with tuition assistance. "Financial aid packages are very enticing," one musical theater major tells us.

All Arts and Science students are required to complete one course in each of 13 liberal arts categories, as well as an 80-hour community service requirement. Students often complete this during the month-long Interim program, where they participate in a travel program, internship, or research project. In 2002, this term was moved from January to May, pleasing many: The general consensus had been that a January term caused the spring semester to end too late.

KAPLAN

Campus Environment

Located inland, roughly 100 miles east of San Diego, the University of Redlands campus is 140 stunning acres surrounded by the San Bernardino Mountains. All freshmen must live on campus and participate in the school's meal plan. Though upperclassmen and transfer students can petition to live off campus, almost 85 percent of all students choose to remain on campus. Residential options range from single-sex dorms to substance-free dorms to honors houses to the Johnston Center complex. Many students complain about the variety and cost of the food—especially those who are vegetarian or have dietary requirements. "The university makes very little room for people [in this area]" explains one student.

Since the University is so small, cars aren't a necessity, though many students (including freshmen) do bring them. On-campus parking is free. The nearby city of Redlands is small, traditional, and sleepy, with little to do, though town-gown relations are superb. Certain parts of town are safer than others: According to one student, those living off campus might find themselves in a less-than-ideal neighborhood: "I hear gunshots in the San Bernardino area just about every time I go near there, which is only five miles from where I live." Overall, however, students love the location: San Diego and Los Angeles are just over an hour away (though we're told by one student that "trips to Los Angeles are not as frequent as we'd like").

Student Life

Students say that the atmosphere at Redlands is "very friendly and not superficial. There are cliques, but that has a lot to do with how small it is." Thirty-five percent of students here are from outside of California, with more women than men. There's not a huge number of minority students (there are more Latinos than African Americans), and very few foreign students.

We're told that fraternities and sororities dominate the social scene and hold almost all the parties. Drinking is very popular, and at times a problem: Explains one biology major, "Probably three-quarters of the people I have met drink very heavily, and not just on weekends." As for other extracurriculars, the Outdoor Club is one of the most popular (and the Chess Club is one of the least, struggling to get even three members).

In the area of athletics, the school has several varsity teams, including lacrosse, water polo, soccer, and swimming/diving. Some favorite intramural sports are flag football and life vest water polo. "Sports aren't too big here. We struggle to fill our small gym every game," suggests one varsity basketball player, though he goes on to say that he appreciates the school's 'student before athlete' policy. "The university's policy is to reinforce the idea that 'student' comes before 'athlete' in the term 'student-athlete,' so the coaches don't care so much if you have to miss a practice because you have a big test the next day. I have been very appreciative of this. You don't find this attitude at too many universities."

Test Scores (middle 50%):
SAT Verbal: 530–620
SAT Math: 530–620
ACT Comp: 22–27

HS Rank of Entering Freshmen:
Top 10%: 32%
Top 25%: 66%
Top 50%: 90%

Avg. HS GPA: 3.52

Costs (2003–04)

Tuition and Fees: $24,096

Room & Board: $8,480

Payment Plan(s): installment plan

THE EXPERTS SAY...

" The Johnston Center is an appealing feature, particularly since its courses are open to all Redlands students. Every student at Redlands receives a great deal of individual attention from both the faculty and the administration. "

" A 'self-directed education' may sound great ... until you realize the huge amount of work you'll need to put into it. Maybe you can 'negotiate' your way into a life-vest-water-polo major. "

Inst. Aid (est. 2003–04)

Institutional Aid, Need-Based: $18,014,404

Institutional Aid, Non-Need-Based: $2,317,375

FT Undergrads Receiving Aid: 69%
Avg. Amount per Student: $23,120

FT Undergrads Receiving Non-Need-Based Scholarship or Grant Aid: 6%
Avg. Amount per Student: $9,525

Of Those Receiving Any Aid:

Rec. Need-Based Scholarship or Grant Aid: 98%
Average Award: $13,162

Rec. Need-Based Self-Help Aid: 94%
Average Award: $6,029

Upon Graduation, Avg. Loan Debt per Student: $22,358

Financial Aid Deadline: rolling, 2/15 (priority)

UNIVERSITY OF RICHMOND

28 Westhampton Way, University of Richmond, VA 23173
Admissions Phone: (804) 289-8640; (800) 700-1662 Fax: (804) 287-6003
Email: Admissions@richmond.edu
Website: Richmond.edu

General Info

Type of School: private, coed

Setting: suburban

Academic Calendar: semester

Student Body

Full-Time Undergrads: 2,835
  Men: 49%, Women: 51%

Part-Time Undergrads: 26
  Men: 62%, Women: 38%

Total Undergrad Population:
  African American: 5%
  Asian American: 4%
  Latino: 1%
  Native American: <1%
  Caucasian: 83%
  International: 5%
  Out-of-State: 84%
  Living Off-Campus: 8%
  In Fraternities: 32%
  In Sororities: 49%

Graduate and First-Professional
  Students: 700

Academics

Full-Time Faculty: 290
  With Ph.D.: 89%

Part-Time Faculty: 76
  With Ph.D.: 66%

Student/Faculty Ratio: 9:1

Most Popular Majors:
  business/accounting (27%)
  political science/history (20%)
  biology/physics (9%)
  English (9%)
  leadership studies (6%)

Freshmen Retention Rate: 92%

Graduation Rates:
  76% within four years
  84% within six years

Admissions

Regular Application Deadline: 1/15

Early Decision Deadline(s): 11/15,
  1/15

Fall Transfer Deadline: 4/15, 2/15
  (priority)

Spring Transfer Deadline: 11/1

Total # of Students Applied: 6,079
  Admitted: 2,560
  Enrolled: 845

# of Students Waitlisted: 1,229
  Students Accepting Place: 940

Inside the Classroom

The University of Richmond has exceptional academic programs set in a comfortable and beautiful environment for its 3,000 undergraduates. The university consists of the School of Arts and Sciences, the Robins School of Business, and the Jepson School of Leadership Studies. The Robins School of Business has an innovative student portfolio program that allows students to document goals, action plans, and work samples that reveal their track towards program completion. These portfolios are made available online for employers during senior year and give students a competitive advantage upon entering the workforce or applying to graduate schools. The Jepson School of Leadership Studies is the first undergraduate school in the country established for the study of leadership.

Richmond students can choose from more than 60 majors. The undergraduate business program is exceptionally strong: The passage rate for accounting graduates who take the CPA (Certified Public Accountant) exam is frequently among the top ten in the nation. The passage rate for UR students taking the CFA (Chartered Financial Analyst) exam is 95 percent compared to the national pass rate of 56 percent.

Students say that the classes are challenging and the grading is fair. With a student/faculty ratio of 9:1 and average class size of 18, faculty members are able to nurture student learning and exploration in individual projects. Students thus become partners in scholarship and research projects conducted by faculty members. There are no teaching assistants at Richmond; all classes are taught by qualified faculty. Many of the professors allow students to contact them at home, and a few may even be spotted socializing with students.

All first-year students enroll in the First-Year Core Course, which "explores some of the fundamental issues of human experience through a close analysis of relevant texts drawn from a number of cultures, disciplines, and historical periods." The two-semester course includes out-of-classroom activities that illuminate the classroom discussion that students must attend. Students must also fulfill general education requirements in the areas of Communication Skills, Wellness, and Fields-of-Study.

Students at Richmond run and abide by the Honor System, which promotes an atmosphere of trust and contributes to the close relationships with the faculty. All incoming students participate in one of two ceremonies intended to formally initiate them into the Honor System. Women are inducted during Proclamation Night, where they sign the Honor Pledge and reflect upon their first three weeks of school by writing letters to themselves that they will read three years later when they are seniors. For men, formal induction to the Honor system comes with the Investiture Ceremony, in which members of sophomore, junior, and senior classes speak to first-year men and challenge them to make the most of their years at the University.

A university official describes a unique academic opportunity at Richmond: "The Richmond Quest is a competition for undergraduates held every two years to determine the best question the entire campus can study over a year. Courses, symposia, and guest speakers are built around the question. The winning student receives a year's free tuition and room and board or $25,000."

Campus Environment

The gorgeous 350-acre campus, set amid rolling hills and tall trees, features red-brick gothic-style buildings and a man-made lake at the center. This lake had always figured prominently in Richmond's distinctive gender-based coordinate college system, in which each undergrad is a member not only of an academic division of the university (Arts and Sciences, Business, or Leadership) but also one of the "coordinate colleges" (Richmond College for men and Westhampton College for women, each with its own campus on either side of the lake). Until fall 2002, men and women had been housed on the separate coordinate campuses, with men living on one side of the lake and women on the other side. Now, although each residence hall remains single-gender and the coordinate college system remains intact, both men's and women's halls are scattered on both sides of the lake. Students are reportedly thrilled with this change, since the old system made normal male-female interaction difficult.

The university is located in the suburban section of the city of Richmond, only minutes away from a great mall and city shopping. Broad Street is a long road that has every sort of restaurant and shopping anyone could imagine and it is only three or four minutes from the school. Downtown Richmond is only six miles away. Many students have cars, and those without can easily get rides to and from places of interest.

Student Life

Richmond students are a "work hard, play hard" bunch. Students can choose from over 200 clubs and activities to get involved with. Among the most popular are the Student Government, Volunteer Action Council, and the Intervarsity Christian Fellowship. There is a strong Greek presence with fifteen organizations (eight fraternities and seven sororities) on campus. One of the fraternities, Sigma Phi Epsilon, was founded on the University of Richmond campus a century ago (1901). During the weekend, frat parties draw in hundreds of students looking for a good time. There is no fraternity or sorority housing.

University of Richmond students are actively involved in sports, with more than 90 percent of the students visiting the recreational facilities each year. Over 21 intramural sports are offered. The most popular activity is basketball, with more than 60 men's, women's, and co-recreational teams competing. There are 25 active club sports, including crew, equestrian, ultimate Frisbee, volleyball, and soccer. UR is a member of the NCAA Division I conference, with ten varsity sports for men and nine for women. The football stadium is off-campus, and we hear that everyone tailgates and dresses up for the games, as the students love their Spiders. (In fact, UR has the only college team with a spider mascot. In 1894, a sportswriter reported spectators yelling that Richmond's baseball players looked "like a bunch of Spiders trying to play ball," and the name stuck.)

An interesting bit of trivia for those of you who watch reruns on cable: Earl Hamner, creator of The Waltons, is a UR alum, and the college that "John Boy" attended, "Boatwright University," was modeled after the University of Richmond.

Other schools to check out: Washington and Lee, Furman, Wake Forest, Davidson, Rice, College of William and Mary.

Applied Early Decision: 403
Early Decision Admitted: 204

Test Scores (middle 50%):
SAT Verbal: 610–690
SAT Math: 630–700
ACT Comp: 27–30

HS Rank of Entering Freshmen:
Top 10%: 60%
Top 25%: 87%
Top 50%: 99%

Avg. HS GPA: 3.53

THE EXPERTS SAY...

"The Jepson School of Leadership Studies, the portfolio plan for business students, the Honor System, and the Richmond Quest all give the University of Richmond a unique academic environment."

"Students no longer have to cross an entire lake to see members of the opposite sex. Kudos to Richmond for recognizing that it's a university, not a summer camp, and updating its coordinate college system accordingly."

Costs (2004–5)

Tuition and Fees: $26,520

Room & Board: $5,390

Payment Plan(s): installment plan, deferred payment plan

Inst. Aid (est. 2003–04)

FT Undergrads Receiving Aid: 31%
Avg. Amount per Student: $19,220

FT Undergrads Receiving Non-Need-Based Scholarship or Grant Aid: 13%
Avg. Amount per Student: $12,929

Of Those Receiving Any Aid:

Rec. Need-Based Scholarship or Grant Aid: 98%
Average Award: $15,685

Rec. Need-Based Self-Help Aid: 76%
Average Award: $3,871

Upon Graduation, Avg. Loan Debt per Student: $16,370

Financial Aid Deadline: 2/25

Graduates

Going to Graduate School:
26% Within One Year

Accepting Job Offer:
57% at time of graduation

Companies Recruiting On Campus:
150

Alumni Giving: 35%

UNIVERSITY OF ROCHESTER

Wallis Hall, P.O. Box 270251, Rochester, NY 14627-0251
Admissions Phone: (585) 275-3221; (888) 822-2256 Fax: (585) 461-4595
Email: admit@admissions.rochester.edu
Website: www.rochester.edu

General Info

Type of School: private, coed

Setting: urban

Academic Calendar: semester

Student Body

Full-Time Undergrads: 4,440
    Men: 55%, Women: 45%

Part-Time Undergrads: 225
    Men: 27%, Women: 73%

Total Undergrad Population:
    African American: 5%
    Asian American: 12%
    Latino: 4%
    Native American: <1%
    Caucasian: 63%
    International: 4%
    Out-of-State: 50%
    Living Off-Campus: 20%
    In Fraternities: 26%
    In Sororities: 19%

Graduate and First-Professional
    Students: 3,686

Academics

Full-Time Faculty: 499
    With Ph.D.: 90%

Part-Time Faculty: 53

Student/Faculty Ratio: 9:1

Freshmen Retention Rate: 95%

Graduation Rates:
    62% within four years
    75% within six years

Admissions

Regular Application Deadline: 1/20

Early Decision Deadline(s): 11/15,
    1/20

Fall Transfer Deadline: 6/15 (priori-
    ty)

Spring Transfer Deadline: 10/1 (pri-
    ority)

Total # of Students Applied: 10,930
    Admitted: 5,372
    Enrolled: 1,153

# of Students Waitlisted: 1,227
    Students Accepting Place: 336
    Waitlisted Students Admitted: 1

Applied Early Decision: 375
    Early Decision Admitted: 194

Inside the Classroom

The University of Rochester is unusually small for a top-rated research institution. The main undergraduate college is named simply "The College," which includes the School of Arts and Sciences and the School of Engineering and Applied Sciences. UR's science, premed, and engineering programs are especially strong; the optics program may be unparalleled. Other undergraduate schools are the School of Nursing and the renowned Eastman School of Music.

Students in The College take part in two core programs. The Quest Program, designed to introduce students to college-level thinking, emphasizes small classes and primary research rather than textbooks. The Rochester Curriculum divides The College's courses into three main subject areas: humanities, social sciences, and natural sciences. Students must choose a major plus two "clusters" of three related courses in each of the other two main subject areas.

The word for the academic atmosphere at UR is "intense," especially in the sciences. "Academics are the number one priority at school. You will find kids in the library all day every day; over finals week, people were sitting on the floor," says a neuroscience major. "No one is satisfied with a B." Many classes are graded on a curve, which increases competition. "We call each other 'dorks' a lot because everyone cares about grades way too much," says a junior.

UR's preprofessional bent can be seen in its 14 different "3–2" programs (combined bachelor's and master's degree). A "4–4" option, the Rochester Early Medical Scholars Program (REMS), allows exceptionally talented freshmen to enter the university with admission to UR's School of Medicine and Dentistry guaranteed. Another special study option is the Take Five Scholars Program, which allows students to take a tuition-free fifth year to pursue broader academic interests.

UR's faculty include Pulitzer Prize winners, Guggenheim Fellows, and MacArthur ("genius grant") award recipients, but the availability of professors varies: "The ones involved in research don't have much time for anything else," a science major complains. A senior agrees: "This is one of the downsides to going to a research-based university." The upside is an abundance of undergraduate research opportunities.

Campus Environment

UR's 85-acre main campus, known as the River Campus, is located two miles south of downtown Rochester, in a bend in the Genesee River. "Rochester is not really one of those college towns," explains a senior. "It's a medium-size city, not too much to do, but enough for someone who really looks and can find the best in a situation." Jobs and internships can be found, though. Downtown is "as safe as any typical city Rochester's size," but there is an area across the river from the campus that causes some students concern. Students often prefer to go to a complex known as the Commons on campus for services such as food, entertainment, even hairstyling.

Freshmen and sophomores are required to live on campus. A controversial freshmen housing initiative gives incoming students "the best rooms on campus," an upperclassman gripes. Another student adds, "All of the upperclassmen are very bitter about it." All dorms have Ethernet (UR is considered one of the most wired schools in the nation). Students, particularly upperclassmen, complain of long walks to campus buildings from dorms, especially in the winter. The campus is considered safe.

Off-campus housing is available in Rochester and relatively inexpensive. There's a public bus system but many students bike or walk, which is tough in the long, snowy winters. Campus shuttles go downtown twice a week. A car helps to avoid feeling isolated on campus, but students say that parking is a hassle. Students also don't rate the food at UR very highly, citing the expense, a limited selection (especially at the Danforth and the Pit eateries), and a lack of flexibility. "The administration changes about everything related to food once every two to three years," says one student, "[but] nothing seems to get better."

Student Life

Students have mixed feelings about what some perceive as UR's bid "to become Harvard" and school spirit can sometimes run low. "The atmosphere on campus is rather apathetic, sometimes you get the feeling that no one wants to be there," a senior comments. The campus is far from dead, though. The campus comes alive for Dandelion Day (the school flower) in the spring ("one of the best parties around; people come out of the woodwork and everyone has a good time," a science major says). There are over 150 student organizations, with club sports, music groups, and the radio station among the most popular; student government ranks among the least popular. Music lovers can take a campus shuttle to the Eastman School of Music, which hosts hundreds of performances each year. Varsity sports (there are 22 teams) are not well attended, although there are more fans now than there were a few years ago. The new gym and intramurals, with 300 teams competing in 8 sports, are very popular.

"[UR] is not much of a party school," says one student. There are 17 fraternities and 10 sororities, and "to have a decent social life at the U of R, you have to either be part of a fraternity/sorority or have friends in them," a student asserts. "Most people frequent the fraternity quad on a regular basis in freshman and sophomore years. The bar scene is more popular with juniors and seniors." Recently, the administration has been cracking down on drinking. "Although UR isn't a dry campus, it seems like it is going in that direction," says a premed.

What's the typical UR student like? "Rich and from New York state," a math major says. A senior adds: "Very preppie ... sporting North Face and Abercrombie." In terms of diversity, one student claims that "although the school is pretty diverse in respect to ethnicity, it is not diverse in regards to sexual orientation." Although cliques form, there are opportunities for a good social life "if you know where to look." But beware: "A student who is looking to party and to do as little work possible to get by is not the type of student that would fit into UR. They wouldn't survive the rigorous life of a UR student."

Other schools to check out: Case Western Reserve, Carnegie Mellon, Washington U in St. Louis, Brandeis.

Test Scores (middle 50%):
SAT Verbal: 600–700
SAT Math: 620–710
ACT Comp: 27–32

HS Rank of Entering Freshmen:
Top 10%: 60%
Top 25%: 88%
Top 50%: 99%

THE EXPERTS SAY...

" This near-Ivy offers a great preprofessional education, especially in the sciences. The optics program may be the best in the world. "

" Grade-grubbers, this is your element. There's not much school spirit, but you'll be too busy studying to notice. "

Costs (2003–04)

Tuition and Fees: $27,628

Room & Board: $8,770

Payment Plan(s): installment plan, pre-payment plan

Inst. Aid (est. 2003–04)

FT Undergrads Receiving Aid: 60%
Avg. Amount per Student: $21,627

FT Undergrads Receiving Non-Need-Based Scholarship or Grant Aid: 37%
Avg. Amount per Student: $9,519

Of Those Receiving Any Aid:

Rec. Need-Based Scholarship or Grant Aid: 99%
Average Award: $16,984

Rec. Need-Based Self-Help Aid: 83%
Average Award: $4,851

Upon Graduation, Avg. Loan Debt per Student: $20,998

Financial Aid Deadline: 2/1

UNIVERSITY OF SCRANTON

800 Linden Street, Scranton, PA 18510
Admissions Phone: (570) 941-7540; (888) 727-2686 Fax: (570) 941-5928
Email: admissions@scranton.edu Website: www.scranton.edu
Application Website: www.scranton.edu/admissions/fa_ao_applyonline.asp

General Info

Type of School: private, coed,
  Roman Catholic

Setting: small town

Academic Calendar: semester

Student Body

Full-Time Undergrads: 3,772
  Men: 43%, Women: 57%

Part-Time Undergrads: 257
  Men: 38%, Women: 62%

Total Undergrad Population:
  African American: 1%
  Asian American: 2%
  Latino: 3%
  Native American: <1%
  Caucasian: 85%
  International: <1%
  Out-of-State: 48%
  Living Off-Campus: 53%

Graduate and First-Professional
  Students: 606

Academics

Full-Time Faculty: 247
  With Ph.D.: 85%

Part-Time Faculty: 149
  With Ph.D.: 15%

Student/Faculty Ratio: 13:1

Most Popular Majors:
  biology (8%)
  elemetary education (7%)
  communication (7%)
  nursing (5%)
  accounting (4%)

Completing 2 or More Majors: 10%

Freshmen Retention Rate: 89%

Graduation Rates:
  71% within four years
  82% within six years

Admissions

Regular Application Deadline: 3/1

Early Action Deadline: 11/15

Total # of Students Applied: 5,669
  Admitted: 4,270
  Enrolled: 983

# of Students Waitlisted: 677
  Students Accepting Place: 440
  Waitlisted Students Admitted: 108

Test Scores (middle 50%):
  SAT Verbal: 510–600
  SAT Math: 520–610

Inside the Classroom

As one of 28 Jesuit colleges in the country, the University of Scranton is dedicated to developing "the whole person" in a nurturing environment. Such characteristics as respect, faith, self-knowledge, service, dignity, justice, and truth are highly regarded in and out of the classroom. One of Scranton's biggest strengths lies in its student-faculty interaction. Classes are small (the average size is 23 students), and with one professor for every 13 students, there's a clear emphasis on personalized education. "The vast majority of professors make an obvious effort to develop a good relationship with their students," a sophomore says. Indeed, students often remark about how much their school cares for them.

A high school guidance counselor raves about Scranton's "excellent, top-notch programs." Approximately 57 majors—including several newer programs such as electronic commerce, exercise science, and media and information technology—are offered through the College of Arts and Sciences and the Kania School of Management. We hear that the biology and other science programs are particularly strong. The school boasts more than 100 Fulbright scholars, a number unsurpassed by any school of similar size, and in 2002, medical and allied-health professional schools accepted 100 percent of Scranton's graduating seniors.

Special academic offerings are impressive, including the highly selective Business Leadership Program, which accepts just 15 sophomores each spring. The Faculty/Student Research Program gives students in all fields an opportunity to participate in faculty research. Language, business, English, and communications majors, among others, study abroad in more than 45 countries. Incoming freshmen may also enroll in Scranton's five-year, entry-level physical therapy or occupational therapy program. The prestigious Special Jesuit Liberal Arts program (SJLA), available to freshmen by invitation, is an alternative way of fulfilling the general education requirements. Most of the SJLA courses stress philosophy and theology, as is the traditional path for Jesuit education.

Campus Environment

High school guidance counselors cite the attractive 50-acre hillside campus as one of Scranton's selling points, and most students agree. Constantly improving itself (the school has added a new building each year since the mid-1980s), the university has invested millions of dollars in creating and improving facilities all over campus. Scranton also owns the Chapman Lake Retreat Center, located 20 minutes away on a picturesque lake. Students, faculty, alumni, and administration use the Conference and Retreat Center regularly. "It isn't 'uncool' to go on a couple of retreats," a student says.

All freshmen and sophomores are required to live in university housing, unless they commute from home. More than 30 small-to-medium-size residences are available, ranging from traditional and suite-style halls to theme houses and apartments/townhouses. Freshmen are housed together in one of 13 smaller residence halls. There are no fraternities or sororities. Juniors and seniors tend to move to places in nearby neighborhoods, such as the "Hill" section of Scranton. "I think, though, that on-campus housing is a lot nicer," one student tells us.

Overall, students are not big fans of the town of Scranton. Even a high school guidance counselor admits that it's "a depressed city [with] nothing to offer," though a sophomore assures us, "The University is slowly resurrecting the area, and the students do literally countless hours of community service." The townspeople aren't crazy about the students, and vice versa. It's not a booming metropolis by any means; the weather is pretty lousy most of the time; nightlife and cultural venues are fairly limited. A mall, a movie theater, and a cultural center are within walking distance from campus, and several ski resorts are a short drive away. And both Philadelphia and New York City are just two hours away.

Scranton is in the Pocono Mountains, and therefore receives tons of snow, which may be good for skiers, but bad for walkers and drivers. And, as one student jokes, "Somehow, some way, Scranton manages itself so that no matter where you walk, you're always walking uphill."

Student Life

Size does matter at Scranton. The university likes its small enrollment, because it makes the campus seem like one big family. Students report having a close bond with their peers, teachers, advisors, etc. "The students feel at home," a New York guidance counselor observes. "Scranton is the friendliest campus I have ever been on," one student gushes. "The Christian values of community and service are evident here." It's not a terribly diverse campus, with the majority of students coming from white, middle to-upper-middle class, Catholic families in Pennsylvania, New Jersey, and New York. About a quarter of all students hail from the immediate Scranton area. And "Democrats are relatively nonexistent," a student tells us in something of an overstatement. The school, however futilely, continues to encourage diversity—there's even a mosque on campus.

Another thing most Scranton students have in common: They like to party. Kegs are banned from campus, as is underage drinking, of course. (The official policy: "Intoxication is not permitted.") But off-campus bars and "keg parties in the basements of student-rented houses" are popular ways to celebrate the weekend—and a few weeknights, too. "Drinking goes on probably just as much as any other campus," a student tells us. "On the other hand," she continues, "student government always has fun things planned… Thursday we have something called 'Coffee House' where they provide coffee and snacks and have a band or a singer come in." The Scranton party scene hits its high point around St. Patrick's Day, when it hosts the fourth largest parade in the nation and tens of thousands of residents and students flock to the downtown area to listen to bagpipes and go on a daylong bar tour.

There are a number of clubs and organizations to join. Students get involved in all sorts of volunteer and community service projects throughout the year; each fall, for example, students convert a now-unused local zoo into a haunted house to raise funds for scholarships. The University Players theater group attracts a lot of attention, and there are great opportunities for anyone interested in music—no audition is required to be part of the University Bands and Singers. And "intramural sports are huge on campus," we hear. Scranton also offers Division III athletics in ten sports for men and nine for women. There is no football team; the basketball teams are the standouts here.

Other schools to check out: Villanova, Fairfield, Loyola College (MD), Providence, Fordham.

HS Rank of Entering Freshmen:
 Top 10%: 23%
 Top 25%: 58%
 Top 50%: 87%
Avg. HS GPA: 3.35

Costs (est. 2004–05)

Tuition and Fees: $21,408
Room & Board: $9,335

THE EXPERTS SAY…

" Students at Scranton—even those who follow a preprofessional track—receive a well-rounded, value-laden education in the liberal arts. "

" Scranton's not actually in the middle of nowhere… it just seems like it is. How many days until St. Patrick's Day? "

Inst. Aid (est. 2003–04)

Institutional Aid, Need-Based:
 $22,246,442
Institutional Aid, Non-Need-Based:
 $2,483,449
FT Undergrads Receiving Aid: 66%
 Avg. Amount per Student:
 $14,666
FT Undergrads Receiving Non-Need-Based Scholarship or Grant Aid: 5%
 Avg. Amount per Student: $8,085
Of Those Receiving Any Aid:
Rec. Need-Based Scholarship or Grant Aid: 97%
 Average Award: $10,625
Rec. Need-Based Self-Help Aid: 85%
 Average Award: $4,725
Upon Graduation, Avg. Loan Debt per Student: $15,800
Financial Aid Deadline: rolling, 2/15 (priority)

Graduates

Going to Graduate School:
 35% Within One Year

UNIVERSITY OF SOUTH CAROLINA— COLUMBIA

University of South Carolina, Columbia, SC 29208
Admissions Phone: (803) 777-7700; (800) 868-5872 Fax: (803) 777-0101
Email: admissions-ugrad@sc.edu Website: www.sc.edu Application Website: www.sc.edu/admissions

General Info

Type of School: public, coed

Setting: urban

Academic Calendar: semester, Maymester

Student Body

Full-Time Undergrads (2002):
 14,789
 Men: 45%, Women: 55%

Part-Time Undergrads (2002):
 1,525
 Men: 50%, Women: 50%

Total Undergrad Population (2002):
 African American: 15%
 Asian American: 3%
 Latino: 1%
 Native American: <1%
 Caucasian: 73%
 International: 1%
 Out-of-State: 12%
 Living Off-Campus: 60%
 In Fraternities: 17%
 In Sororities: 17%

Graduate and First-Professional Students (2002): 8,155

Academics

Full-Time Faculty: 1,099
 With Ph.D.: 87%

Part-Time Faculty: 362
 With Ph.D.: 41%

Student/Faculty Ratio: 17:1

Most Popular Majors:
 biology (6%)
 psychology (5%)
 nursing (5%)
 criminal justice (4%)
 journalism (3%)

Completing 2 or More Majors: 14%

Freshmen Retention Rate: 84%

Graduation Rates:
 36% within four years
 61% within six years

Admissions

Regular Application Deadline: 12/1

Fall Transfer Deadline: 6/1, 3/1
 (priority)

Spring Transfer Deadline: 12/1
 (priority)

Inside the Classroom

The University of South Carolina at Columbia, founded in 1801, is the flagship campus and major research center of a huge eight-campus system with strong professional and liberal arts programs. Eighty-one undergraduate degree programs are offered through the colleges of business; criminal justice; education; engineering and information technology; hospitality, retail, and sport management; journalism and mass communications; liberal arts; music; nursing; pharmacy; public health; and science and mathematics. The School of the Environment offers a minor in environmental studies, and the Colleges of Library and Information Science and Social Work offer courses for undergraduate credit, but no degrees.

The international business specialty is a particularly strong, and the engineering, biology, and English programs are reportedly excellent as well. All students must take courses that fulfill the general education requirements in English, numerical and analytical reasoning, history and fine arts, the natural sciences, and foreign language. The renowned "University 101" first-year seminar is designed to help new students learn the ins and outs of college life.

As with most large universities, the workload is what you make of it. Motivated freshmen who are eligible can be part of the distinguished Honors College—touted as an Ivy League education for state-school tuition—where students work more directly with top-notch faculty. Otherwise, at least in your first year, you may often find yourself in large lecture halls with hundreds of your closest friends, being taught by a TA; you may also have trouble getting into all the classes you need. The official student/faculty ratio is 17:1, and instructors are generally considered praiseworthy. One student confides, "Most professors are pretty cool about everything, but there are a few who need to retire."

The university's large size and status as a leading research institution can frustrate undergrads who need more personal attention, but it does have its perks, mostly in the form of facilities. Students enjoy several distinguished research bureaus and centers, including those for marine biology and coastal research, information technology, earth sciences, and international studies.

Campus Environment

The parklike centerpiece of the 290-acre campus is the historic "Horseshoe," a tree-shaded quad surrounded by restored 19th-century buildings, many of which serve their original functions. The rest of campus, by contrast, is made up of contemporary facilities. The school is just a few blocks from the state capitol in downtown Columbia. Students like Columbia, complimenting its beauty, safety, weather, and variety of things to do and see. There are several large lakes and rivers nearby, and the mountains and the ocean are each about three hours away.

All freshmen are required to live on campus (unless they live at home with their parents or guardians) in "Freshmen Centers," traditional double-occupancy dorms with community bathrooms. There are more than 27 residence halls on campus, in a variety of styles and themes: coed, honors, Greek, international, apartment, special interest, etc. Students looking for a more intimate, small-college experience can apply to Preston, a residential college where about 240 undergrads of all classes live, learn, and eat together. Size, location, and quality of the dorms vary widely, but we hear that most are old and small. Just under half the entire student body lives on campus; many upperclassmen choose rent one of the "many, many" apartments and houses in town. Take it from this junior: "The best part of on-campus housing is the location. Everything else doesn't quite measure up."

We heard many complaints about the parking situation—even the school admits there's a critical shortage of space. Although it technically permits cars on campus, the school discourages students from bringing them. Students here walk, bike, or take the shuttle.

Student Life

Not surprisingly, nearly 90 percent of the "very friendly" student body is from South Carolina; the rest are largely from the Southeast. With about 13,000 undergrads enrolled, the university attracts all kinds, and the prominent minority population (22 percent) is larger than at most of its peer institutions. Students are pretty laid back, and there's a lot of school spirit at the Columbia campus—"the *real* USC." One undergrad sums up what sets her school apart by saying, "I feel at home here."

Greek life is popular, with 17 percent of the student body pledging a fraternity or sorority. They have a pretty tight rein on the campus social life, serving as hosts of the biggest, best, and most frequent parties, but their influence goes far beyond the beer. "Southern Greeks are a way of life, not just a group to party with," we're told. For those who are not such fans of the Greek system, or are looking for a break from the scene, there are always drinks to be had in dorm rooms, off-campus apartments, or city hangouts. Students say that alcohol is available to anyone who's interested, as are pot and ecstasy. It's "not an out-and-out party school," one undergrad says, "but certain groups definitely try."

One type of party is legendary at USC: the tailgate. Students are crazy for their football team, and, regardless of their record or their opponent, loyal Gamecock fans flock to the Williams-Brice Stadium to cheer on their players and enjoy the major tailgating scene. In addition to football, there are many other well-played and well-attended Division I varsity athletics. The sports atmosphere trickles down to its myriad club and IM teams, in which over half the student body participates.

There are literally hundreds of student-run clubs and organizations—political, ethnic, religious, cultural, academic, social—you name, USC's got it. Students say you'd be hard-pressed not to find your niche ("There is something for everyone"). Off-campus, the city of Columbia has a thriving arts community and a hip music scene, and is home to the renowned Riverbanks Zoo. For bars, clubs, restaurants, and trendy shops, students flock to the areas called "Five Points," which is sort of like the Greenwich Village of Columbia, and "the Vista," the newest hot spot in town.

Total # of Students Applied: 12,817
  Admitted: 8,260
  Enrolled: 3,491

Test Scores (middle 50%):
  SAT Verbal: 510–620
  SAT Math: 520–630
  ACT Comp: 22–27

HS Rank of Entering Freshmen:
  Top 10%: 26%
  Top 25%: 59%
  Top 50%: 90%

Avg. HS GPA: 3.77

THE EXPERTS SAY...

" The Honors College is the best of both worlds: You get the individual attention of a small school plus the resources and opportunities of a large university. "

" If you have to ask what a tailgate is, USC may not be the place for you. "

Costs (est. 2003-4):

Tuition and Fees, In-State: $5,778

Tuition and Fees, Out-of-State: $15,116

Room & Board: $5,327

Payment Plan(s): installment plan, deferred payment plan, pre-payment plan

Inst. Aid (est. 2003–04)

Institutional Aid, Need-Based: $3,497,817

Institutional Aid, Non-Need-Based: $4,206,910

FT Undergrads Receiving Aid: 45% Avg. Amount per Student: $9,371

FT Undergrads Receiving Non-Need-Based Scholarship or Grant Aid: 43% Avg. Amount per Student: $4,037

Of Those Receiving Any Aid:

Rec. Need-Based Scholarship or Grant Aid: 100% Average Award: $3,060

Rec. Need-Based Self-Help Aid: 53% Average Award: $4,273

Upon Graduation, Avg. Loan Debt per Student: $16,105

Financial Aid Deadline: 4/1 (priority)

UNIVERSITY OF SOUTHERN CALIFORNIA

700 Childs Way SAS 208, Los Angeles, CA 90089-0911
Admissions Phone: (213) 740-1111 Fax: (213) 740-0680
Email: admitusc@usc.edu   Website: www.usc.edu

General Info

Type of School: private, coed

Setting: urban

Academic Calendar: semester

Student Body

Full-Time Undergrads: 15,644
  Men: 49%, Women: 51%

Part-Time Undergrads: 596
  Men: 56%, Women: 44%

Total Undergrad Population:
  African American: 7%
  Asian American: 21%
  Latino: 13%
  Native American: 1%
  Caucasian: 48%
  International: 8%
  Out-of-State: 33%
  Living Off-Campus: 63%
  In Fraternities: 16%
  In Sororities: 17%

Graduate and First-Professional
Students: 15,224

Academics

Full-Time Faculty: 1,450
  With Ph.D.: 86%

Part-Time Faculty: 891

Student/Faculty Ratio: 10:1

Most Popular Majors:
  business (25%)
  visual & peforming arts (14%)
  engineering (10%)
  communications (10%)
  psychology (5%)

Completing 2 or More Majors: 20%

Freshmen Retention Rate: 94%

Graduation Rates:
  61% within four years
  81% within six years
  note: 5-yr. programs affect rates

Admissions

Regular Application Deadline: 1/10;
  12/10 (priority)

Fall Transfer Deadline: 3/1

Total # of Students Applied: 29,278
  Admitted: 8,753
  Enrolled: 2,976

Inside the Classroom

Once known as a party school with mediocre academics, USC's programs have improved tremendously over the last few years. "They got rid of mediocre programs and poured money into film, communications, science, and business," explains a Los Angeles guidance counselor. The school is generous in giving out financial aid: "Tremendous fundraising has been done and [there are] many endowed scholarships." Admission at USC has gotten more competitive recently: "USC has become more selective, looking for higher GPA's," notes another guidance counselor, who also likes the fact that USC is now "checking on student progress" and has "recruited some top professors." "They are making a bigger commitment to undergrads and have much better student guidance," says another California guidance counselor.

In all, students may choose from 100 majors in 17 schools. The most renowned schools at USC are the Annenberg School for Communication, Marshall School of Business, and School of Cinema-Television. The engineering program is also considered excellent, as are political science and the natural sciences.

A university official explains USC's educational philosophy: "We encourage students to combine liberal arts education in the College of Letters, Arts, & Sciences with a more applied course of study from one of our professional schools." In what the school calls a "breadth with depth" approach, undergrads are encouraged to double-major or major/minor in disparate fields (e.g., biomedical engineering and Russian, or engineering and cinema). In fact, students who distinguish themselves academically in widely separate fields of study are deemed "Renaissance Scholars" and may receive a $10,000 award.

While admissions procedures and general education requirements vary by program, all undergrads must take the "USC Core"—courses in general education, writing, and diversity. All general education courses are taught by senior faculty. A small number of outstanding incoming freshmen are invited to enroll in Thematic Option ("T.O.," or "Tortures and Ordeals," depending on whom you ask), a demanding honors program that teaches critical thinking.

Although introductory lectures can be huge (up to 400 students), USC manages to keep many upper-level classes below 30 students. Professors are also reportedly highly accessible, though students have to take the initiative. As a junior tells us, "Once you reach upper-division courses, class sizes drop dramatically and it becomes much easier to get to know your professors."

Campus Environment

USC sits in the South Central section of Los Angeles, an area high in crime, and students are encouraged to be extremely careful in that neighborhood. But looking at the campus from the inside, you'd never know that you were in the middle of a city: The beautiful campus has courtyards, trees and grass everywhere, and many buildings of Italian Romanesque design. The security on campus is tight, and for the most part, students feel safe. The library was recently renovated and earthquake-proofed, and a new digital production facility for film and television was built, featuring state-of-the-art equipment not currently offered at other school.

More than 90 percent of USC freshmen live on campus. A wide variety of housing types is available, including apartments, special interest halls, and a new international theme hall. Most upper-division students choose to live off campus, many in apartments close to campus. Although L.A. is known for its car culture, there is actually an extensive city bus system, as well as some light rail systems. Many students rely on bicycles for getting around campus and/or between campus and nearby student housing—there are bike racks in front of every building.

Student Life

Guidance counselors applaud the fact that USC makes an effort to attract a diversified student body. Because USC is a large school, it's easy for students to feel isolated or lost. Many find that extracurriculars help to counter that feeling. There are literally hundreds of clubs and activities, from a Bible study group for African American Christians to human rights organizations to music groups. The theater group provides live improv on campus every Friday afternoon. According to the university, 60 percent of USC students volunteer in community service programs.

With roughly 18 percent of students in a sorority or frat, the Greek system is very strong (some say to a fault), though it doesn't completely dominate the social scene. One student tells us, "A lot of people complain about the Greek system ruling the social life, but it's not true. One of the best things about the school is the diversity of the student population in terms of their interests." There are a few Greek houses for African Americans, but they have noticeably few members.

Around half of all USC undergrads participate in some kind of organized sport. As one student says, "This school definitely has lots of 'rah rah.'" A guidance counselor agrees: "Best school spirit, bar none!" Trojan football is a central part of USC's identity, and many school traditions revolve around it, including a week-long rivalry of events against their archrival, the UCLA Bruins. USC football games are also known for the appearance of Traveler, a white horse bearing a "Trojan warrior" into the arena. A favorite stunt of fans from rival schools is to wave their car keys and credit cards in cadence to the Trojan Marching Band as it plays "Tribute to Troy," in a ritual meant to symbolize that USC is the "University of Spoiled Children."

USC could also be called the "University of Social Contacts." Among USC's greatest strengths is its huge alumni network, the "Trojan Family." Many USC alumni have managed to attain a great deal of prestige and success, from professional sports superstars (such as Mark McGwire) to corporate CEOs (including Sol Price, founder of the Price Club) to movie moguls (such as George Lucas). "Getting a degree here opens many doors," affirms a California guidance counselor. And as one recent grad explains, "You get a sort of 'secret handshake' [with respect to jobs] when dealing with alumni, but this secret society is highly concentrated in Southern California." Being one of the top three U.S. universities in terms of international enrollment (large numbers come from Taiwan, China, Hong Kong, and South Korea), USC also has a lot of international alumni, with active alumni clubs in such places as Bangkok, Beijing, Jakarta, and Seoul.

Other schools to check out: UCLA, UC Berkeley, NYU, Northwestern, Georgetown.

Test Scores (middle 50%):
SAT Verbal: 610–700
SAT Math: 640–720
ACT Comp: 27–31
ACT English: 26–32
ACT Math: 27–32
HS Rank of Entering Freshmen:
Avg. HS GPA: 3.99

THE EXPERTS SAY...

" USC has made great improvements in its academics, its selectivity, and particularly its increased focus on undergraduate students. "

" You'll never lack for job connections as a graduate of the 'University of Social Contacts.' Think of hobnobbing with all these bigwigs at an alumni event: George Lucas, Ron Howard, and Neil Armstrong. "

Costs (2003–04)

Tuition and Fees: $28,692

Room & Board: $8,632

Payment Plan(s): installment plan, pre-payment plan

Inst. Aid (2002–03)

Institutional Aid, Need-Based: $95,586,289

Institutional Aid, Non-Need-Based: $27,140,952

FT Undergrads Receiving Aid: 49%
Avg. Amount per Student: $25,521

FT Undergrads Receiving Non-Need-Based Scholarship or Grant Aid: 16%
Avg. Amount per Student: $12,288

Of Those Receiving Any Aid:

Rec. Need-Based Scholarship or Grant Aid: 97%
Average Award: $19,235

Rec. Need-Based Self-Help Aid: 99%
Average Award: $7,885

Upon Graduation, Avg. Loan Debt per Student: $19,176

Financial Aid Deadline: 2/28, 1/20 (priority)

Graduates

Companies Recruiting On-Campus: 600

Alumni Giving: 34%

UNIVERSITY OF TENNESSEE

320 Student Services Building, Knoxville, TN 37996
Admissions Phone: (800) 221-8657; (865) 974-2184 Fax: (865) 974-6341
Email: admissions@utk.edu Website: www.tennessee.edu
Application Website: admissions.utk.edu/undergraduate/ugadmissions.html

General Info

Type of School: public, coed
Setting: urban
Academic Calendar: semester

Student Body

Full-Time Undergrads: 17,935
    Men: 49%, Women: 51%

Part-Time Undergrads: 1,645
    Men: 49%, Women: 51%

Total Undergrad Population:
    African American: 7%
    Asian American: 3%
    Latino: 1%
    Native American: <1%
    Caucasian: 87%
    International: 1%
    Out-of-State: 14%
    Living Off-Campus: 68%
    In Fraternities: 15%
    In Sororities: 20%

Graduate and First-Professional
    Students: 8,015

Academics

Full-Time Faculty: 1,398
    With Ph.D.: 84%

Part-Time Faculty: 93
    With Ph.D.: 71%

Student/Faculty Ratio: 18:1

Most Popular Majors:
    psychology (5%)
    architecture (4%)
    journalism (3%)
    mechanical engineering (3%)
    child development (3%)

Freshmen Retention Rate: 76%

Graduation Rates:
    28% within four years
    58% within six years

Admissions

Regular Application Deadline: 2/1;
    11/1 (priority)

Early Action Deadline: 11/1

Fall Transfer Deadline: 6/1

Spring Transfer Deadline: 11/1

Total # of Students Applied: 9,724
    Admitted: 5,629
    Enrolled: 3,682

Waitlist Available

Inside the Classroom

Students at the University of Tennesssee at Knoxville can choose from more than 300 degree programs in ten academic schools: agriculture and natural resources; architecture and design; arts and sciences; business administration; communications; education; engineering; human ecology; nursing; and social work. The arts and sciences, business administration, and engineering colleges boast the largest enrollments, in that order. Among the most popular majors are business, psychology, architecture, English, agriculture, and engineering. The curriculum requirements vary by college, but generally cover such broad areas as English composition, foreign language, math, natural science, social science, humanities, and history.

As a "Carnegie I Research Institution"—the only one in the state classified as such—the University of Tennessee provides students with an "unbelievable opportunity to research with their professors," a school rep says. Students have the chance to study cutting-edge techniques and developments in such areas as biotechnology, energy, and robotics. UTK is one of the leaders in the development of Internet2, "the second-generation Internet." Other groundbreaking research programs include waste management, materials processing, and veterinary medicine. The university's largest research partner is the prestigious Oak Ridge National Laboratory, a U.S. Department of Energy facility which is managed by UT students and faculty.

Unfortunately, such a concentration on research and a high student/faculty ratio (18:1) are signs that most undergrads will have to deal with teaching assistants and lines outside their professor's doors throughout the first half of their college careers. One junior assures us, however, that "every professor whose class [she has] attended has been very accessible." Exceptional students who are invited to participate in the university's honors program will benefit from more personal interaction with faculty; honors courses and seminars are generally limited to 25 students and are taught by faculty from all ten undergraduate colleges.

Campus Environment

Freshmen must live either on campus or with a parent or guardian in town. The university maintains 13 residence halls (none are freshman-only), mostly coed, that are set up community-style, as a suite, or as an apartment. "Many students choose to live off-campus after their first year," we're told, and the numbers bear this out: Approximately 90 percent of freshmen live on campus, but only one-third of all undergraduates elect to stay there. "Dorm security has been increased," a junior tells us. "Your student ID is needed to gain access into dormitories, and visitors must sign in and be escorted to your room." One sophomore cited cramped and noisy dorms as the cause of the mass exodus off-campus. Most students take advantage of the abundance of inexpensive housing in Knoxville or move into a fraternity or sorority house.

The 500-plus acre campus is easily walkable, and with the city of Knoxville right there, getting around isn't a major headache. "As long as you don't act stupid, Knoxville is a very safe city (so girls, don't walk alone at night)," advises a female student. Freshmen are permitted cars; however, the annual fee to park it on campus will run you more than $200. In addition to bicycles, rollerblades, and the like, public transportation is popular; Knoxville has an extensive bus system, and there is a free campus trolley. For those who plan to spend time outside the Knoxville campus, "a car would be very useful," students advise. Nature lovers need not worry about being trapped in an urban environment: the city is surrounded by three national parks (including the Great Smoky Mountains and Cumberland Gap), seven state parks, seven lakes, and 25 golf courses.

Student Life

With a student body of over 26,000, you'd be hard-pressed to define the quintessential Knoxville undergrad, but the population is overwhelmingly white (86 percent) and from Tennessee (about 85 percent). And nice: "UT Knoxville is quite a friendly place," says a student. School spirit runs high here, adding to the cheery and amiable atmosphere of the place. Making friends and having a good time are high on the average UTK student's agenda.

The University of Tennessee at Knoxville has the dubious distinction of being a party school. "Many people party every night of the week," agrees one student. Alcohol use is rampant, especially on football weekends and at frat parties. The Greek system has a strong presence on campus: There are 24 fraternities and 17 sororities on campus, although only about 20 percent of the students are active members. Nonetheless, the Greeks are responsible not only for the majority of the partying, but also for welcoming the students to campus (freshmen are permitted to rush). "I thought I'd be lost here, but when I joined my sorority I got to be part of a big family," a student says. Non-Greek students attend open parties when they occur. Off-campus, the entertainment options are considerably broader, but still centered on the same thing: drinking. The city of Knoxville features numerous historical attractions, museums, performing arts venues, restaurants, shopping, and more, but the majority of students flock to "the strip," an avenue of popular bars and clubs such as the Old College Inn (OCI), Moose's Music Hall, Boogie's Good Times Bar and Grill, and Mike & Willies.

At UTK, students like to party almost as much as they like their sports teams, and the two often go hand-in-hand. Students sing the school's fight song enthusiastically (and with little provocation) at every sporting event and most parties. Football and women's basketball are the most popular sports, and have been national title contenders for several years now; their games are always packed and "fairly rowdy." Neyland Stadium is able to seat more than 100,000 Vols fans, ensuring students will always be able to get to see the game. A full range of intramural sports are offered as well, and many students take advantage of them year-round. There are several hundred student clubs and organizations to choose from, and students looking for entertainment can head over to the 25,000-seat Thompson-Boling Arena, where major recording artists regularly perform.

UTK underclassmen always look forward to "the passing of the torch." A school official explains: "On campus, there is a statue called 'The Torchbearer' that has a gas flame that burns all the time. Each year, the upperclassmen pass torches to the underclassmen to signify the changing of the ranks."

Test Scores (middle 50%):
SAT Verbal: 500–600
SAT Math: 500–610
ACT Comp: 21–26
ACT English: 21–27
ACT Math: 20–26

HS Rank of Entering Freshmen:
Top 10%: 27%
Top 25%: 54%
Top 50%: 83%

Avg. HS GPA: 3.38

THE EXPERTS SAY...

" Out-of-state students should also look at the University of Florida and the University of Georgia. "

" If you're looking for a big school with big research opportunities (not to mention big parties), come on down to UTK. "

Costs (2003–04)

Tuition and Fees, In-State: $4,370

Tuition and Fees, Out-of-State: $13,202

Room & Board: $5,110

Graduates

Going to Graduate School:
20% Within One Year

Accepting Job Offer:
46% at time of graduation

Companies Recruiting On Campus:
400

UNIVERSITY OF TEXAS AT AUSTIN

P.O. Box 8058, Austin, TX 78713-8058
Admissions Phone: (512) 475-7440; (512) 475-7399 Fax: (512) 475-7475
Website: www.utexas.edu

General Info

Type of School: public, coed

Setting: urban

Academic Calendar: semester

Student Body

Full-Time Undergrads: 34,234
  Men: 48%, Women: 52%

Part-Time Undergrads: 3,246
  Men: 54%, Women: 46%

Total Undergrad Population:
  African American: 4%
  Asian American: 17%
  Latino: 14%
  Native American: <1%
  Caucasian: 61%
  International: 3%
  Out-of-State: 5%
  Living Off-Campus: 82%
  In Fraternities: 9%
  In Sororities: 14%

Graduate and First-Professional
  Students: 13,043

Academics

Full-Time Faculty: 2,432
  With Ph.D.: 91%

Part-Time Faculty: 214
  With Ph.D.: 61%

Student/Faculty Ratio: 19:1

Most Popular Majors:
  biological sciences (7%)
  electrical engineering (5%)
  government (4%)
  computer sciences (4%)
  psychology (4%)

Freshmen Retention Rate: 92%

Graduation Rates:
  36% within four years
  71% within six years

Admissions

Regular Application Deadline: 2/1

Fall Transfer Deadline: 3/1

Spring Transfer Deadline: 10/1

Total # of Students Applied: 24,519
  Admitted: 11,504
  Enrolled: 6,544

Test Scores (middle 50%):
  SAT Verbal: 540–660
  SAT Math: 570–690

Inside the Classroom

Like its home state, the University of Texas at Austin is big. The biggest school in the nation, in fact, with more than 38,000 undergraduates. While the large size presents its challenges, it also means that UT has an incredible range of academic offerings. There are hundreds of majors and 11 undergraduate schools. These include schools for business (one of the most popular), engineering, education, architecture, communications, natural sciences, fine arts, nursing, pharmacy, social work, and of course, liberal arts.

The requirements vary according to the program, as does the workload. One junior tells us, "The academic atmosphere at UT really depends on what you are studying." Another student gets more specific: "Liberal arts students study about 4 to 5 hours a week, but engineering students study about 40 to 50 hours a week."

The classes, not surprisingly, are often huge lectures; introductory-level classes can have as many as 500 students. The school's size means it can take some creativity, not to mention aggressive measures, to get into popular classes, to see professors, and to cut through the miles and miles of red tape. Teaching assistants are great resources for students who have trouble getting a professor's attention. "The most accessible people are TAs," according to one senior majoring in biochemistry. But a freshman majoring in biology and Spanish says that "although UT is one of the largest schools in the nation, I have found the professors very easy to talk to, and they will go out of their way to make one-on-one appointments." And yet another student finds that UT manages to maintain intimacy through distinct classes and programs: "UT may be a large school but there are ways to make it seem smaller. We have a few freshman-oriented programs that get the new students involved from the beginning so they don't get lost in the crowd … [Freshman Seminars] are classes that have less than 30 students and have very interesting topics from coin collecting to … the history of rock and roll."

Many high school guidance counselors claim that their students view UT as a "hot and trendy" college choice. One counselor says UT has "a wonderful facility, very high esteem, great curriculum" and describes the school as being "ahead of the times." Others describe the business school as "world class," laud the "diversity of majors offered," and praise its "big city" advantages.

Campus Environment

The 11 dorms on campus can hold only a small percentage of students. A student tells us, "70 percent of the dorm space is reserved for freshmen, and 30 percent is reserved for others. Even then, not all freshmen can get housing that want it." Some dorms are older than others, and each offers its own atmosphere. Jester Dorm holds 5,000 students and while one student describes it as "kind of old and dirty," another says that "Jester is huge, but it has a fun atmosphere and there are always people around." The San Jacinto Dorm is the newest and a current student favorite: "Students tend to put it as their first choice for housing."

Off-campus housing can be tricky, too. While there are many apartments available in the area, they vary wildly in price, quality, and distance from campus. Generally, apartments that are close to campus are most expensive, and apartments that are not as close "cost significantly less but are a hassle because they are inconveniently far away." Another student says, "If you're willing to take the shuttle to campus, you'll have a better chance of getting a newer, bigger, and cheaper place to live."

The vast majority of students seem to love the city of Austin as much as they love their school. "Austin is a super-cool place to live during college years and beyond. Beautiful rolling hills, hike-n-bike trails, river tubing, the growing film industry, live music … and we know how to party on the famous Sixth Street." As for transportation: "Parking is crazy in Austin and at UT. The city bus system and UT shuttle buses can take you everywhere you want to go."

Student Life

Sixth Street is where you'll be most likely to encounter UT students on weekend nights. The downtown street is renowned for live music events and the multitude of bars, clubs, and restaurants. Austin has scads of live music venues to accommodate its ever-thriving music scene; scoping out up-and-coming bands at local clubs is a major part of student life. "Thursday night is College Night on Sixth Street so many people spend their Thursdays there," a student says. As for the rest of the weekend, another says that "a lot of students take the opportunity to party on the weekends, either at apartments, fraternity houses, or downtown." Though one can literally find something social to do every night, many people choose to "study at the library or coffeehouses" during the week. A freshman stresses that "you have to learn to find a healthy balance. UT is challenging and demanding, so if you are ONLY looking for fun, it is the wrong school."

The phrases most commonly used by UT undergrads to describe their fellow students are "laid-back," "down-to-earth," and "open-minded" (and as one student reminds us, "Texans are known for their friendliness"). Since the weather in Austin is great, students spend a lot of time "laying outside studying, playing guitar, or just relaxing." Minorities make up over 30 percent of the undergraduate population, and students appreciate the diversity. "One thing you have to have when you come to school here is an open mind." A senior concurs: "A close-minded or sheltered person might not feel comfortable here. There are many different cultures and beliefs visibly expressed on campus."

UT offers hundreds of organizations and activities for just about every interest. Intercollegiate and intramural sports are extremely popular; UT's football and basketball teams are national powers, and games regularly draw crowds of adoring fans ("Football is big. Well, everything is big in Texas! Go Longhorns!"). Student Council and preprofessional/honor societies are popular, and many students join one of the 20 fraternities or 14 sororities. One student says, "Greek life is huge at UT, but I don't think it influences the overall social life. I think they are popular because people join so they can meet people in such a huge school."

ACT Comp: 23–28
ACT English: 21–28
ACT Math: 23–29
HS Rank of Entering Freshmen:
Top 10%: 69%
Top 25%: 94%
Top 50%: 99%

Costs (2003–04)

Tuition and Fees, In-State: $4,547

Tuition and Fees, Out-of-State: $11,667

Room & Board: $6,081

Payment Plan(s): installment plan

THE EXPERTS SAY...

" With 38,000 undergrads, UT Austin is the largest school in the nation, and the diversity of programs is fantastic. Head for Sixth Street in Austin for live music and great clubs. "

" There's a diversity of programs and a diverse student body, but the big classes and bureaucracy are monolithic. Make sure you take the Freshman Seminars, or you'll be talking to TA's more than to professors. "

Inst. Aid (est. 2003–04)

Institutional Aid, Need-Based: $22,320,000

Institutional Aid, Non-Need-Based: $37,300,000

FT Undergrads Receiving Aid: 49%
Avg. Amount per Student: $8,750

FT Undergrads Receiving Non-Need-Based Scholarship or Grant Aid: 26%
Avg. Amount per Student: $4,560

Of Those Receiving Any Aid:

Rec. Need-Based Scholarship or Grant Aid: 67%
Average Award: $5,450

Rec. Need-Based Self-Help Aid: 91%
Average Award: $4,650

Upon Graduation, Avg. Loan Debt per Student: $16,500

Financial Aid Deadline: rolling, 4/1 (priority)

UNIVERSITY OF THE PACIFIC

3601 Pacific Avenue, Stockton, CA 95211
Admissions Phone: (209) 946-2211; (800) 959-2867 Fax: (209) 946-2413
Email: admissions@pacific.edu
Website: www.pacific.edu

General Info

Type of School: private, coed

Setting: suburban

Academic Calendar: semester, trimester, quarte

Student Body

Full-Time Undergrads: 3,225
  Men: 42%, Women: 58%

Part-Time Undergrads: 112
  Men: 57%, Women: 43%

Total Undergrad Population:
  African American: 3%
  Asian American: 27%
  Latino: 11%
  Native American: 1%
  Caucasian: 47%
  International: 3%
  Out-of-State: 13%
  Living Off-Campus: 41%
  In Fraternities: 20%
  In Sororities: 21%

Graduate and First-Professional
Students: 2,764

Academics

Full-Time Faculty: 389
  With Ph.D.: 92%

Part-Time Faculty: 238
  With Ph.D.: 79%

Student/Faculty Ratio: 14:1

Most Popular Majors:
  business (15%)
  engineering (15%)
  biology (11%)
  education (6%)
  sports science (5%)

Completing 2 or More Majors: 3%

Freshmen Retention Rate: 85%

Graduation Rates:
  45% within four years
  68% within six years

Admissions

Regular Application Deadline: 1/15
  (priority)

Early Action Deadline: 12/1

Fall Transfer Deadline: 6/1

Spring Transfer Deadline: 1/10,
  12/1 (priority)

Inside the Classroom

With several professional schools ranging from pharmacy to music, the University of the Pacific offers undergraduates broad exposure to professional areas. For those high-achieving students who know before leaving high school that they want to pursue professional degrees, Pacific may be just the place.

Building on the strength of its fine professional schools, Pacific has developed several accelerated programs for undergrads—in dentistry, business, pharmacy, and law, among others. These allow freshmen to enter into professional programs ahead of schedule (though for dentistry and pharmacy, it's possible to change the designated time of study if the program proves too rigorous). The renowned dentistry school has five-year, six-year, and seven-year programs leading to the D.D.S. degree, while the business school offers qualified undergrads an M.B.A. with only one additional year of study. The pharmacy and health sciences school allows freshmen to pursue Doctor of Pharmacy degrees in just three years—one year earlier than other California schools. And in law, there's a six-year bachelor's and J.D. degree: Students take three years of undergraduate study and then three years of law.

As if those aren't enough disciplines to choose from, the Pacific campus also has a highly acclaimed engineering school, where students alternate between terms in the classroom and periods of full-time, paid work; a school of education, which trains students as elementary and secondary school teachers; a school of international studies (one of only six undergraduate schools of international studies), which requires a semester abroad; and a music conservatory, which focuses on everything from composition to music therapy to music management. With a student/faculty ratio of 14:1, three quarters of the classes have fewer than 30 students.

Guidance counselors have told us that the university is sensitive to students' financial needs. In fact, Pacific was the first California school to commit to matching Cal Grants—dollar for dollar—for incoming freshmen. More than 75 percent of incoming freshmen receive financial aid from the school. And in a unique offer to the local community, first-generation college students who are active in Stockton community service may receive scholarships to attend Pacific (in return, they must do volunteer community service while attending school).

So confident is the school of its curriculum design that it offers a four-year guarantee: As long as students meet certain basic requirements, they are assured completion of a bachelor of arts degree in four years (five for engineering and pharmacy majors). If a student is unable to graduate in four years due to reasons beyond his control, no additional tuition will be charged. Also incorporated into the education is an experiential learning guarantee, which includes any learning situation outside of the classroom, such as co-ops, work-study, research or study abroad.

Campus Environment

Pacific's campus looks it's set in New England, complete with old brick buildings, ivy, and a lot of green spaces. Located in a residential section of Stockton, the campus is home to almost all the professional colleges—only the schools of law and dentistry

KAPLAN

are in nearby cities. Though the campus has over 175 acres total, the main academic area is quite small.

Stockton is a low-key industrial city in the middle of farm country that has seen its share of crime and decline. While not the most beautiful city, it has worked hard over the last few years to renew itself: Revitalization has begun, and crime rates have dropped. Unknown to most is the fact that Stockton is a deep-water port, providing access to the San Francisco Bay. More than 75 languages are spoken here, reflecting its history as an immigrant town. As far as student life, however, "boring" is how we've heard it described. For this reason, around half of Pacific students bring cars. With Sacramento under an hour away and Lake Tahoe four, there's always the urge to just get up and go. Fortunately, parking isn't a problem on campus, although it isn't free.

For the first two years, students are required to live on campus. Red-brick and ivy covered dorms are home to more than 1,100 first-year, transfer, and returning students, while the apartments house upper-level students in studio, one-, two-, and three-bedroom units. Seven of the Greek organizations offer housing as well.

Student Life

The Stockton campus has about 5,000 students total, 3,000 of whom are undergraduates. With the overwhelming majority from California, the student body is quite diverse, with 10 percent Latino, 3 percent African American, and 27 percent Asian/Pacific Islanders. (Interestingly, the largest group of out-of-state students is from Hawaii, and the Hawaii Club hosts a popular luau each year.) Though Pacific was founded by Methodists and does have a full-time chaplain and several religious-oriented clubs, students of other faiths are welcome: Campus religious groups include the Jewish Students' Association, Muslim Students' Association, and Christian Life Center. We hear that the student body is fairly conservative.

At Pacific, one out of four undergrads is involved in Greek life. One of the more bold Greek events is an annual fundraiser held by one fraternity: Students themselves live in the streets for a couple of days in order to draw attention to the problem of homelessness. As for other extracurricular activities, the theatre arts department and the music conservatory present numerous shows and concerts each year, and the student radio station was recently updated and put back on the air. There's also a movie theater right on campus.

Pacific has seven men's and nine women's Division I intercollegiate teams, along with many intramural and club sports. Though the school had a football team for many years, the cost proved too prohibitive, and it was discontinued: Interestingly, the San Francisco 49ers' Summer Training Camp is held on (or as some think, takes over) the campus in July and August.

Total # of Students Applied: 4,501
  Admitted: 3,173
  Enrolled: 818

Waitlist Available

Test Scores (middle 50%):
  SAT Verbal: 510–618
  SAT Math: 540–660
  ACT Comp: 22–27

HS Rank of Entering Freshmen:
  Top 10%: 37%
  Top 25%: 70%
  Top 50%: 93%

Avg. HS GPA: 3.45

THE EXPERTS SAY...

" The University of the Pacific offers a surprisingly wide range of academic programs for such a small school. Students here are happy, thanks to the beautiful campus, the active social scene, and the individual attention they receive. "

" Let's clarify Pacific's four-year degree guarantee: Failing to complete your requirements because you're lazy or hung-over does not constitute 'reasons beyond your control.' "

Costs (est. 2004–05)

Tuition and Fees: $23,600

Room & Board: $7,490

Payment Plan(s): installment plan, deferred payment plan

Inst. Aid (est. 2003–04)

Institutional Aid, Need-Based: $21,698,083

Institutional Aid, Non-Need-Based: $2,790,977

FT Undergrads Receiving Aid: 68%
  Avg. Amount per Student: $22,096

FT Undergrads Receiving Non-Need-Based Scholarship or Grant Aid: 10%
  Avg. Amount per Student: $7,766

Of Those Receiving Any Aid:

Rec. Need-Based Scholarship or Grant Aid: 96%
  Average Award: $17,379

Rec. Need-Based Self-Help Aid: 92%
  Average Award: $5,691

Financial Aid Deadline: rolling, 2/15 (priority)

UNIVERSITY OF THE SOUTH

735 University Avenue, Sewanee, TN 37383-1000
Admissions Phone: (800) 522-2234; (931) 598-1238 Fax: (931) 538-3248
Email: collegeadmission@sewanee.edu Website: www.sewanee.edu
Application Website: https://app.applyyourself.com/?id=uots-u

General Info

Type of School: private, coed, Episcopal

Setting: small town

Academic Calendar: semester

Student Body

Full-Time Undergrads: 1,348
  Men: 46%, Women: 54%

Part-Time Undergrads: 1
  Women: 100%

Total Undergrad Population:
  African American: 4%
  Asian American: 1%
  Latino: 2%
  Native American: <1%
  Caucasian: 91%
  International: 1%
  Out-of-State: 76%
  Living Off-Campus: 6%
  In Fraternities: 45%
  In Sororities: 43%

Graduate and First-Professional Students: 109

Academics

Full-Time Faculty: 133
  With Ph.D.: 95%

Part-Time Faculty: 39
  With Ph.D.: 62%

Student/Faculty Ratio: 10:1

Freshmen Retention Rate: 84%

Graduation Rates:
  78% within four years
  83% within six years

Admissions

Regular Application Deadline: 2/1

Early Decision Deadline(s): 11/15

Fall Transfer Deadline: 4/1

Spring Transfer Deadline: 12/1

Total # of Students Applied: 1,825
  Admitted: 1,316
  Enrolled: 427

# of Students Waitlisted: 109
  Students Accepting Place: 47
  Waitlisted Students Admitted: 6

Applied Early Decision: 92
  Early Decision Admitted: 89

Inside the Classroom

At the University of the South, known to many as "Sewanee," you'll find a formal respect for, reverence for, and involvement in serious academics. The school turns out a large number of Rhodes Scholars, and a high percentage also go on to law, medical, veterinary, education, and technical graduate programs.

The university is composed of the undergraduate College of Arts and Sciences and the graduate School of Theology. Besides its strong preprofessional programs, Sewanee also offers well-respected programs in music and forestry. Popular majors include English, history, natural resources, and psychology. "My school is academically challenging," a biology major says. "No one major is extremely easy." Regardless of what career they are planning, all students receive a solid liberal arts education. The extensive distribution requirements include courses in math and science, literature, history and social science, fine and performing arts, foreign language, philosophy and religion, writing, and physical education (the phys ed credit can be earned at Sewanee's on-campus Equestrian Center). Students have the option of taking an interdisciplinary humanities program—four team-taught, chronologically arranged courses—that fulfills several of the distribution requirements listed above.

Classes are intense, and most have fewer than 20 students. Professors get high marks for accessibility and helpfulness. "They will give you their home numbers," a student tells us. "Many students form great friendships with their professors."

Certain things are taken very seriously at Sewanee. One is the Honor Code, which condemns dishonesty of any kind, particularly cheating or stealing. Academics are also highly valued and deeply respected. Although not an actual rule, students dress formally for class (men in coats and ties, women in skirts or dresses) to demonstrate their high regard for their peers and teachers, as well as their reverence for academic study. Students with outstanding GPAs become part of the prestigious Order of the Gownsmen, who, along with the faculty, wear black flowing garments to class.

While they are as committed to their studies as students at other preprofessional schools, most Sewanee students aren't as prone to stress about their work. The Honor Code fosters a sense of respect among students, and there's no cutthroat competitiveness. Students offer one another advice and support, and frequently help one another prepare for examinations.

Campus Environment

Located atop Tennessee's Cumberland Plateau, Sewanee's campus, known as "the Domain," is a whopping 10,000 acres—the second biggest in the country. Most find it an idyllic setting, "beautiful" and "very safe." The breathtaking natural scenery creates a serene and comfortable environment that helps minimize school-related stress. The acres of forest are functional, too, serving as a natural laboratory for many courses.

As most Sewanee students will tell you, if you come to this school, you'd better love the outdoors. The wildly popular Sewanee Outing Program (SOP) takes full advantage of the gorgeous surroundings by regularly hosting numerous canoeing,

616 **KAPLAN**

climbing, biking, backpacking, and caving expeditions. Sewanee's 21-mile Perimeter Trail is a well-marked and maintained multiple-use path that follows the property boundary around the Domain. The bike trails on the mountain are ranked as some of the best in the country.

More than 90 percent of the 1,300 undergrads live on campus in one of the 18 residence halls, all of which are wired for Internet access ("a data port for every pillow!" the school likes to say). Undergraduate housing options, all of which are described as "comfortable," include coed and single-sex dorms, a women's center, language houses, special halls for student emergency personnel, and two sorority houses. Only seniors may live off campus after receiving special permission. Off-campus houses are of limited availability but are popular, so "there is always a wait."

As you can probably tell from a tradition like the Gownsmen, Sewanee models itself in part on Oxford; if not for the beautiful Tennessee mountains, the impressive Gothic architecture could convince visitors they were visiting Great Britain. A new dining hall was recently completed, as well as a new residence hall.

Student Life

The student body "on the mountain" is anything but diverse; only a small number of minorities attend the school. As you might guess, given its name, most students are Southern. Students we talked to corroborate the stereotype of the undergraduate body as generally conservative in their politics and values. Founded by Episcopalian church leaders and maintaining its church affiliation though 28 Church dioceses, the school attracts a number of religious students.

The formal environment may throw some for a loop at first. As this junior warns, "If you are taken aback by guys wearing bowties, plaid pants, and pink shirts, this school will be mind-boggling for you." Due to the small size, there's a warm and friendly sense of community; the "hello rule"—with students greeting everyone they pass— is in full force here.

The formal academic atmosphere doesn't prevent students from having fun, however. Students spend most weeknights studying and hanging out in their rooms with friends. As at any other college, weekends mean partying and drinking. "Drinking is a big deal here," we're told. And at the center of most parties lie the frats. Sewanee's 12 fraternities and 7 sororities draw well over half the student body and hold themselves responsible for keeping the on-campus social scene active. "Off-campus parties are common especially for the upperclassmen who have grown tired of frat parties," one student says. Stirling's Coffee House and the Tiger Bay Pub are popular hangouts as well.

More than 70 percent of the student body participates in some form of athletics, whether on an intercollegiate or intramural level. There are 10 men's and 11 women's varsity sports, including equestrian teams. Club sports, particularly crew and rugby, are big here as well. For more sedentary activities, students can choose from more than 100 clubs and organizations. There are a wide variety of community service and outreach programs, honorary and academic clubs, religious groups, and social and environmental organizations.

Test Scores (middle 50%):
SAT Verbal: 580–660
SAT Math: 580–660
ACT Comp: 25–29

HS Rank of Entering Freshmen:
Top 10%: 45%
Top 25%: 76%
Top 50%: 94%

Avg. HS GPA: 3.41

Costs (2003–04)

Tuition and Fees: $24,135
Room & Board: $6,720

THE EXPERTS SAY...

" The respect that Sewanee's students show their professors and their school is refreshing. The Greek organizations and the Sewanee Outing Program help the students unwind. "

" There's a fine line between a charming environment and a pretentious one. Does Sewanee recognize the difference? "

Inst. Aid (est. 2003–04)

Institutional Aid, Need-Based:
$7,615,419

Institutional Aid, Non-Need-Based:
$2,199,675

FT Undergrads Receiving Aid: 45%
Avg. Amount per Student: $19,633

FT Undergrads Receiving Non-Need-Based Scholarship or Grant Aid: 13%
Avg. Amount per Student: $12,155

Of Those Receiving Any Aid:

Rec. Need-Based Scholarship or Grant Aid: 100%
Average Award: $16,520

Rec. Need-Based Self-Help Aid: 83%
Average Award: $4,996

Upon Graduation, Avg. Loan Debt per Student: $14,441

Financial Aid Deadline: 3/1 (priority)

UNIVERSITY OF TULSA

600 South College Ave., Tulsa, OK 74104
Admissions Phone: (918) 631-2307; (800) 331-3050 Fax: (918) 631-5003
Email: admission@utulsa.edu
Website: www.utulsa.edu

General Info

Type of School: private, coed,
  Presbyterian Church (USA)

Setting: urban

Academic Calendar: semester

Student Body

Full-Time Undergrads: 2,439
  Men: 50%, Women: 50%

Part-Time Undergrads: 165
  Men: 47%, Women: 53%

Total Undergrad Population:
  African American: 7%
  Asian American: 2%
  Latino: 3%
  Native American: 5%
  Caucasian: 65%
  International: 10%
  Out-of-State: 28%
  Living Off-Campus: 42%
  In Fraternities: 21%
  In Sororities: 23%

Graduate and First-Professional
  Students: 1,400

Academics

Full-Time Faculty: 304
  With Ph.D.: 96%

Part-Time Faculty: 108
  With Ph.D.: 96%

Student/Faculty Ratio: 11:1

Most Popular Majors:
  biology (5%)
  management (5%)
  computer science (4%)
  mechanical engineering (4%)
  petroleum engineering (4%)

Completing 2 or More Majors: 10%

Freshmen Retention Rate: 78%

Graduation Rates:
  37% within four years
  54% within six years

Admissions

Regular Application Deadline: 2/1

Total # of Students Applied: 2,292
  Admitted: 1,747
  Enrolled: 590

In the Classroom

One satisfied TU student tells us: "The University of Tulsa is academically rigorous, while still being personally nurturing. Those two things can and do coexist!" With 58 undergraduate majors, 3 undergraduate colleges, a law school, several graduate programs, and a set of pretty demanding core requirements, the University of Tulsa asks its students to set high academic goals. The core curriculum is comprised of course work in the humanities, writing, mathematics, and, for most students, foreign languages, allowing TU students to leave campus with a well-rounded education. TU is recognized for majors in engineering (computer science, chemical, petroleum, electrical, and mechanical), accounting, psychology, anthropology, and English. As for being "personally nurturing," students rave about the faculty: "The professors are extremely accessible; all have office hours, almost all have open door policies on office visits, and many will even put their home phone number on syllabi." With a student to faculty ratio of 11:1 and an average class size of 19, professors and students are able to build strong personal relationships.

The McFarlin Library, located in the heart of campus, houses the general computing laboratory, and is both TU's academic centerpiece and one of the grandest examples of architecture on the campus. Media savvy students have the opportunity to work on *The Collegian*, TU's student run newspaper, which received 13 awards in 2003 alone. There are also plenty of opportunities to study abroad—TU administers its own study abroad programs in Argentina, Canada, France, Germany, Ireland, Italy, Russia, Spain, Switzerland, and the United Kingdom.

Campus Environment

On-campus housing at the University of Tulsa is not only guaranteed for first- and second-year students, but it's also required of all TU students under 21 unless they're married or living at home; most students seem okay with that. One second year business management major said, "There is always enough room for people to switch if they need to or move if they just want a change. They are fairly comfortable, and the university has done a good job at offering a lot of different options for your residence hall experience." Currently some upperclassmen have "double-as-a-single" rooms (a double occupancy room issued to one student), which makes for a nice and roomy housing experience. If that's not enticing enough, TU is making improvements. During the past 7 years over $35 million has been spent on renovation of University housing facilities and new student apartment construction.

For students seeking that "friendly midwestern experience," Tulsa is the right town, and TU is the right college. One student notes, "Midwestern friendliness pervades this campus. Even your morning walk to class will be marked with smiles and hellos from fellow students." Tulsa and TU are taking cues from each other, and they're getting along just fine. The campus itself is "very secure," an applied mathematics major tells us: "Of course, there are criminal acts that occur at times, but no campus can be expected to be free of all crime. I feel very safe when I am walking back to my dorm room late at night." Recently TU has completed a 34-acre campus expansion that includes a soccer field, softball field, track, multi-purpose recreational field, The Michael D. Case tennis center (which was recognized as the nation's best collegiate tennis facility by the U.S. Tennis Association and was the site of the 2004 NCAA Men's Tennis Championships), the Fulton and Susie Collins fitness center, student apartments, and additional campus parking.

Student Life

Outside the classroom, a sophomore tells us "many students choose to be active in our wide variety of student interest groups and organizations." According to one finance major, people "who simply want to 'blend in' and hide in the background may not find what they are looking for at the University of Tulsa." In other words, no wallflowers need apply here. A management, marketing and economics major exclaims, "If you are bored on TU's campus, you simply haven't looked in the right place! Our Student Association does an extraordinary job bringing entertainment to campus. And if there isn't a major event to entertain you, your friends are just down the hall." Prominent alumni include Steve Largent (former U.S. congressmen and NFL Hall of Fame inductee), Gordon Matthews (inventor of voice mail), Mary Kay Place (actress), S.E. Hinton (author of *The Outsiders*), Howard Twilley (former Miami Dolphin wide receiver and founder of "The Athlete's Foot"), and Mark Radcliffe (the producer of the phenomenally successful first two *Harry Potter* films).

TU's athletics teams, nicknamed "The Golden Hurricane," play Division I-A. The football team is gearing up for some excitement in the coming years as the most recent recruiting class has been rated as the best among Western Athletic Conference schools, and one of the best TU has had in a long time. Students are equally excited about varsity sports at TU. "To me, one of TU's best features is the availability of free student tickets to any athletic event," says one avid game attendee.

Students seem to feel that Greek life has a place on campus, but doesn't necessarily run life on campus. "Greeks are very involved in student government organizations as well and can be very influential on the social scene, however, a lot of the Greek parties are open to the entire campus, so those who just want a little taste of Greek life can get their fill." Most students we heard from agreed that alcohol can be a part of the social life, but only if you want it to be. "Just because some students are allowed to drink on campus, doesn't mean that all do. It is definitely a part of the social life here, but does not determine it."

Test Scores (middle 50%):
SAT Verbal: 530–690
SAT Math: 530–670
ACT Comp: 22–29
ACT English: 22–30
ACT Math: 21–28
HS Rank of Entering Freshmen:
Top 10%: 60%
Top 25%: 79%
Top 50%: 100%
Avg. HS GPA: 3.7

THE EXPERTS SAY...

" Tulsa has the second highest grad rate for student athletes in the NCAA Division 1-A (even beating out Stanford, Northwestern, and Duke). "

" And if you're not an athletic student, you can still get free tickets to see the games. "

Costs (2004–5)

Tuition and Fees: $16,830
Room & Board: $5,926
Payment Plan(s): installment plan

Inst. Aid (2002–03)

Institutional Aid, Need-Based: $1,269,680
Institutional Aid, Non-Need-Based: $8,491,263
FT Undergrads Receiving Aid: 49%
Avg. Amount per Student: $13,737
FT Undergrads Receiving Non-Need-Based Scholarship or Grant Aid: 25%
Avg. Amount per Student: $8,285
Of Those Receiving Any Aid:
Rec. Need-Based Scholarship or Grant Aid: 65%
Average Award: $4,234
Rec. Need-Based Self-Help Aid: 76%
Average Award: $5,951
Upon Graduation, Avg. Loan Debt per Student: $14,546
Financial Aid Deadline: rolling, 4/1 (priority)

Graduates

Going to Graduate School: 28% Within One Year
Companies Recruiting On Campus: 212
Alumni Giving: 29%

UNIVERSITY OF UTAH

201 South 1460 East Room 250S, Salt Lake City, UT 84112-9057
Admissions Phone: (801) 581-7281 Fax: (801) 585-7864
Email: uadmiss@saff.utah.edu Website: www.utah.edu
Application Website: www.acs.utah.edu/admissions/

General Info

Type of School: public, coed

Setting: urban

Academic Calendar: semester

Student Body

Full-Time Undergrads: 15,066
   Men: 56%, Women: 44%

Part-Time Undergrads: 6,256
   Men: 54%, Women: 46%

Total Undergrad Population:
   African American: 1%
   Asian American: 4%
   Latino: 4%
   Native American: 1%
   Caucasian: 81%
   International: 3%
   Out-of-State: 7%
   Living Off-Campus: 93%
   In Fraternities: 5%
   In Sororities: 5%

Graduate and First-Professional
   Students: 6,016

Academics

Full-Time Faculty: 1,104
   With Ph.D.: 90%

Part-Time Faculty: 142
   With Ph.D.: 44%

Student/Faculty Ratio: 16:1

Most Popular Majors:
   business (5%)
   communications (4%)
   psychology (3%)
   political science (2%)
   biology (2%)

Completing 2 or More Majors: 0%

Freshmen Retention Rate: 79%

Graduation Rates:
   18% within four years
   54% within six years

Admissions

Regular Application Deadline: 3/1;
   2/15 (priority)

Fall Transfer Deadline: 3/1, 2/15
   (priority)

Spring Transfer Deadline: 11/1

Total # of Students Applied: 5,842
   Admitted: 5,036
   Enrolled: 2,653

Inside the Classroom

Utah's undergraduate colleges include schools of business; education; engineering; health; humanities; mines and earth sciences; nursing; occupational therapy; pharmacy; science; and social and behavioral science. The university is known for its strong engineering program, plus well-respected programs in ballet and the fine arts. The renowned research centers focus on projects including petroleum research, biomedical optics, representation of multidimensional information, and smart sensors, just to name a few.

"All the professors have office hours and can be accessed," says a premed student, who adds that many professors are not accustomed to students being proactive and actually showing up during their office hours, "so when they are visited it is kind of a shock." A Utah guidance counselor says that the administration has been "endeavoring to become more personal with the students' [needs and concerns]."

To fulfill their General Education requirements, students must take two courses in each of the following: fine arts; humanities; social sciences; and life sciences. They must also take one course each in lower-division writing; upper-division writing; American institutions; quantitative reasoning; and diversity.

Students who are undecided about their major, but want to attend a research university, are able to enroll in a first-year learning experience, which allows them to be part of a smaller community of students and teachers. Utah also offers a rigorous Honors Program for select undergrads: Incoming freshmen are invited to join based on their high school record and composite exam scores. No Honors course exceeds an enrollment of 30 students.

The university's Undergraduate Research Opportunities Program (UROP) gives undergrads the chance to work one-on-one with faculty in a laboratory setting or on a research project. Students receive a small hourly wage for the hours they work, and they agree to work with faculty for one or more semesters on investigations in-process. Additionally, the UROP program sponsors an online research journal featuring the research efforts of undergraduate students.

Campus Environment

If you watched the Opening and Closing Ceremonies of the 2002 Winter Olympics in Salt Lake City, then you are already familiar with Rice-Eccles Stadium. Usually able to seat nearly 46,000 Ute football fans, the stadium was temporarily expanded to seat 56,000 for the Olympics. During the Games, students enjoyed an extended Spring Break while their school played host to the world's greatest athletes.

In 2000, construction of 19 suite and apartment-style residential facilities expanded the University of Utah housing options to include over 2,300 graduate and undergraduate students. "There are two housing options for first-year students," a university official explains. "First, there are double suites, which offer first-year students opportunities to live and learn with others who are native Utah students as well as others who may represent a diverse range of countries of origin. Single suites are also available, although these are fewer in number."

Students can also participate in academic enhancement programs, called Living and Learning Communities, which include: First Year Focus, Leadership, Service, Outdoor Adventure, and Undergraduate Traditions of Excellence. In the fall of 2002, a Living-Learning Community initiative was implemented in the historic homes located on Officer's Circle in the old Fort Douglas site. This involved renovating ten historic officer homes, each of which is linked with a different academic program.

Students at the University of Utah can not only park on campus, but also have many parking permit options, ranging in price from $35 per semester to $120 per year. Many University of Utah students travel to and from the campus by using the Utah Transit Authority (UTA) bus lines. Additionally, a free shuttle service that travels the perimeter of the campus, as well as on interior streets, allows many students who live nearby to easily commute from their home to the university. And students who commute from the downtown Salt Lake City area to the university campus are thrilled with the new light rail TRAX lines.

Known mainly as the home of the Church of Latter Day Saints (aka Mormons), Salt Lake City is a pleasant, rather quiet, medium-sized city. "It is easy to find something interesting to do at pretty much any time of day," says an undergrad. Geographically, the University of Utah campus is just two hours from one of the nation's largest mountainous wilderness areas ("the greatest snow on earth"), and just a half-hour from the international airport.

Student Life

"The general atmosphere is friendly and quite active," says one student, "but many times you have to break the ice because too many people seem to mind their own business." While the student body is not diverse compared to public schools in many other states, it is still "generally more diverse than other universities in Utah," notes a guidance counselor. A student describes the political climate (which leans to the conservative side): "There are groups from different political standpoints, but nobody is militant about their views."

Each academic year opens with "RedFest," a "club rush" celebration featuring reps from more than 200 student groups on campus. Popular student organizations include the student government association, the Latter Day Saints Student Association, the Residence Hall Association, and the Cross Cultural Club (for international students). While only a small percentage of students join the eight fraternities and six sororities, their presence is felt on campus, we hear. One guidance counselor tells us that the university has a party-friendly reputation.

Of its nine men's and 11 women's intercollegiate sports, the Utes boast strong teams in women's gymnastics, skiing, and men's basketball. There are also more than 70 intramural teams. Of course, many students forego organized athletics and just grab their skis or snowboards and head for the nearby slopes by themselves or with friends.

Successful Utah alums include Rocky Anderson (Mayor of Salt Lake City), Stephen Covey (author, *The 7 Habits of Highly Effective People*), and 2002 Olympics medalists Shannon Bahrke (silver, women's moguls) and Joe Pack (silver, men's aerials), along with several other Olympic athletes.

Test Scores (middle 50%):
ACT Comp: 22–26
ACT English: 20–26
ACT Math: 19–26

HS Rank of Entering Freshmen:
Top 10%: 25%
Top 25%: 49%
Top 50%: 82%

Avg. HS GPA: 3.48

THE EXPERTS SAY...

" Utah could become trendy, thanks to the picture-postcard setting and friendly atmosphere showcased in the 2002 Winter Olympics. "

" Where else could you find an odd mixture of snowboarders, dancers, and researchers in a conservative atmosphere? "

Costs (est. 2003-4):

Tuition and Fees, In-State: $3,650

Tuition and Fees, Out-of-State: $11,296

Room & Board: $5,036

Payment Plan(s): installment plan

Inst. Aid (est. 2003–04)

Institutional Aid, Need-Based: $760,000

Institutional Aid, Non-Need-Based: $25,000

FT Undergrads Receiving Aid: 36%
Avg. Amount per Student: $7,286

FT Undergrads Receiving Non-Need-Based Scholarship or Grant Aid: 2%
Avg. Amount per Student: $3,127

Of Those Receiving Any Aid:

Rec. Need-Based Scholarship or Grant Aid: 81%
Average Award: $4,075

Rec. Need-Based Self-Help Aid: 68%
Average Award: $5,195

Upon Graduation, Avg. Loan Debt per Student: $12,400

Financial Aid Deadline: rolling, 3/15 (priority)

Graduates

Companies Recruiting On-Campus: 500

Alumni Giving: 9%

UNIVERSITY OF VERMONT

194 S. Prospect Street, Burlington, VT 05401-3596
Admissions Phone: (802) 656-3370 Fax: (802) 656-8611
Email: admissions@uvm.edu
Website: www.uvm.edu

General Info

Type of School: public, coed

Setting: suburban

Academic Calendar: semester

Student Body

Full-Time Undergrads: 7,575
  Men: 44%, Women: 56%

Part-Time Undergrads: 360
  Men: 46%, Women: 54%

Total Undergrad Population:
  African American: 1%
  Asian American: 2%
  Latino: 2%
  Native American: <1%
  Caucasian: 93%
  International: 1%
  Out-of-State: 62%
  Living Off-Campus: 49%
  In Fraternities: 7%
  In Sororities: 6%

Graduate and First-Professional
  Students: 1,733

Academics

Full-Time Faculty: 538
  With Ph.D.: 86%

Part-Time Faculty: 140
  With Ph.D.: 41%

Student/Faculty Ratio: 15:1

Most Popular Majors:
  business administration (12%)
  psychology (8%)
  biology/biological science (7%)
  English (6%)
  political science (5%)

Completing 2 or More Majors: 7%

Freshmen Retention Rate: 84%

Graduation Rates:
  53% within four years
  70% within six years

Admissions

Regular Application Deadline: 1/15

Early Decision Deadline(s): 11/1

Early Action Deadline: 11/1

Fall Transfer Deadline: 4/1

Total # of Students Applied: 10,456
  Admitted: 7,792
  Enrolled: 1,923

# of Students Waitlisted: 931
  Students Accepting Place: 364

Inside the Classroom

UVM offers more than 90 majors in its eight undergraduate colleges and schools: agriculture and life sciences; business; health; nursing; education and social services; engineering and math; natural resources; and arts and sciences. Each of these schools or colleges has its own admissions standards and may have entrance requirements in addition to the general university requirements. The average class size is 22 students, and the student to faculty ratio is 15:1. A recent grad describes the faculty as "very accessible, obviously some more than others," and adds that "UVM is a mid-size school with so many advantages of the bigger and smaller schools in the country: outstanding medical facilities and research, gifted professors, and determined faculty."

Preprofessional majors such as business, management, and premed all have large enrollments. UVM's strongest programs are considered to be in the sciences and environmental fields, which benefit from the surrounding natural resources and wildlife. In addition to these academic programs, interest in nature and the environment at UVM is evident in other ways: A number of students are nature buffs who make the environment a major political issue. UVM takes pride in its status as "Vermont's only comprehensive research university," which offers "specialized laboratories in every school and college, four research farms, nine university-managed natural areas, a waterfront lake research center, and an aquatic research vessel."

There are numerous opportunities for undergraduate research. For example, one-credit mini-courses are offered each semester to freshmen in the life sciences: A scientist actively engaged in research agrees to meet for an hour each week during the semester to provide the students with a more intimate understanding of his or her research. For other programs, undergraduate research credit may be available.

UVM also has an innovative academic program called the Living and Learning Center that combines course work with field trips and independent study. Groups of students with common interests live together, study together, and help one another with independent projects.

Over the last few years, the University of Vermont has made efforts to diversify its student population, which remains overwhelmingly white, much like the overall demographics in the state of Vermont. UVM has formed a relationship with a Bronx high school whereby UVM officials work directly with students of various backgrounds, including immigrant students. The goal is to ensure that these students have the academic skills needed to compete with other college applicants, and to help them with the college admissions process overall through advising sessions. This has attracted many students to UVM who may have never considered applying to a Vermont college. Overall, applications to the University of Vermont have jumped 20 percent.

Campus Environment

With such natural scenery as the Green Mountains (UVM actually stands for *Universitas Viridis Montis*, Latin for 'University of the Green Mountains'), Lake Champlain, and major ski resorts like Stowe and Sugarbush nearby, Vermont is a haven for outdoor activities. Winters are long here, but a young alum adds that "when summer comes (no spring, just mud season!), it is a beautiful and overwhelmingly happy place to be!"

UVM offers three residential campuses: Main Campus (425 acres), East Campus, and Redstone Campus. The campus atmosphere is described as "very laid back and liberal," and there is very little crime both on campus and in the Burlington area. Rooms are available as singles, doubles and triples, and there are a number of options for special interest housing. The aforementioned Living and Learning Center is one of them; there's also The Social Justice Housing Program (which promotes social change), the Outdoor Experience Program, and the Environmental Co-op. Off-campus housing is also available, and UVM provides resources to help students find apartments.

Burlington—Vermont's largest city with a population of only 39,000—is high in New England charm. "Students don't need a car to get around, as long as they're fine with staying in Burlington for long periods of time," says a recent grad. "There is public transportation, but it isn't great." Town/gown relations are not always the friendliest. The administration is making efforts to diffuse the growing battle between the city of Burlington and UVMers regarding the students' noise, partying, and disrespect of city residents.

Student Life

There's no doubt that UVM students know how to have a good time. Unlike at some other reputed party schools, though, the Greeks don't dominate the party scene. (There are, by the way, five sororities and ten fraternities on campus.) If you expect to take full advantage of the party atmosphere here, however, you may hit a bit of a snag. A recent graduate tells us, "There has recently been a major crackdown on off-campus partying in Burlington. The UVM police have a lot more power in the city itself, and can issue noise ordinances, bust people for drinking underage, etc." Parents are notified if a student is found guilty of a drug or alcohol violation—regardless of the amount the student had in his possession or whether it's his very first time. Consequently, many students head to Montreal for the weekend, a recent grad says, where "the drinking age is 18, lots of clubs and restaurants, only one and a half hours away."

As previously mentioned, the student body is predominantly white, and there is a large homosexual population both on and off campus. A recent grad says that everyone is "very concerned with being politically correct—possibly more than being concerned with the actual value of diversity." While not ethnically diverse, the student body is diverse in other ways. The school's location, facilities, and social life attract an interesting mixture of hippies, granolas, nature lovers, and jocks.

There are plenty of student clubs and organizations to choose from at UVM. The Division I athletics are popular, as are intramural sports. The school has just finished construction on a gorgeous new intramural center. Although there's no football team, the well-attended hockey games provide a forum for students to express their school spirit—loudly.

Applied Early Decision: 241
Early Decision Admitted: 187

Test Scores (middle 50%):
SAT Verbal: 530–620
SAT Math: 530–630
ACT Comp: 22–27

HS Rank of Entering Freshmen:
Top 10%: 21%
Top 25%: 56%
Top 50%: 92%

THE EXPERTS SAY...

" Vermont's major research university attracts preprofessionals and students of the environment. The school is making strides in diversifying its student body with an innovative Bronx-based program. Gay students are welcome here. "

" UVM students are an interesting mix of hippies, granolas, nature lovers, and jocks—and they all love to party. "

Costs (2003–04)

Tuition and Fees, In-State: $9,636

Tuition and Fees, Out-of-State: $22,688

Room & Board: $6,680

Payment Plan(s): installment plan

Inst. Aid (2002–03)

FT Undergrads Receiving Aid: 54%
Avg. Amount per Student: $10,781

FT Undergrads Receiving Non-Need-Based Scholarship or Grant Aid: 11%
Avg. Amount per Student: $2,307

Of Those Receiving Any Aid:

Rec. Need-Based Scholarship or Grant Aid: 90%
Average Award: $10,129

Rec. Need-Based Self-Help Aid: 84%
Average Award: $6,000

Upon Graduation, Avg. Loan Debt per Student: $23,167

Financial Aid Deadline: rolling, 2/10 (priority)

Graduates

Going to Graduate School:
21% Within One Year

Accepting Job Offer:
28% at time of graduation

Companies Recruiting On Campus:
164

Alumni Giving: 26%

UNIVERSITY OF VIRGINIA

P.O. Box 400160, Charlottesville, VA 22904-4160
Admissions Phone: (434) 982-3200 Fax: (434) 924-3587
Email: undergradadmission@virginia.edu Website: www.Virginia.EDU
Application Website: www.virginia.edu/undergradadmission/

General Info

Type of School: public, coed
Setting: suburban
Academic Calendar: semester

Student Body

Full-Time Undergrads: 12,790
  Men: 46%, Women: 54%

Part-Time Undergrads: 189
  Men: 51%, Women: 49%

Total Undergrad Population:
  African American: 9%
  Asian American: 11%
  Latino: 3%
  Native American: <1%
  Caucasian: 69%
  International: 4%
  Out-of-State: 28%
  Living Off-Campus: 55%
  In Fraternities: 30%
  In Sororities: 30%

Graduate and First-Professional
  Students: 9,248

Academics

Full-Time Faculty: 1,142
  With Ph.D.: 92%

Part-Time Faculty: 150
  With Ph.D.: 49%

Student/Faculty Ratio: 16:1

Most Popular Majors:
  economics (8%)
  commerce (7%)
  psychology (7%)
  English (6%)
  foreign affairs (5%)

Completing 2 or More Majors: 7%

Freshmen Retention Rate: 97%

Graduation Rates:
  83% within four years
  92% within six years

Admissions

Regular Application Deadline: 1/2

Early Decision Deadline(s): 11/1

Fall Transfer Deadline: 3/1

Spring Transfer Deadline: 11/1

Total # of Students Applied: 14,627
  Admitted: 5,775
  Enrolled: 3,101

In the Classroom

Academics are—and have always been—the number one priority at the University of Virginia. One student explains: "Classes go by 'first, second, third, and fourth years' [rather than 'freshman, sophomore,' etc.] because Thomas Jefferson, the father of UVA, felt one could never be a 'senior' in any area; there was always so much more to be learned."

Guidance counselors say that the competitive nature of the school "makes everyone improve." Also, they warn of "big fish syndrome," where top high school graduates find that they are just one of the tons of top grads when they get here, and must work hard to keep their place. A fourth-year student's view: "UVA is definitely a difficult school, and if you want to get good grades, you are going to have to study hard. In that respect, it is competitive but it is not so in the respect that you feel that you are competing against fellow students."

There are five undergraduate colleges at UVA: architecture; engineering and applied science; commerce; nursing; and arts and sciences. Many students major in preprofessional fields, and high percentages of students go on to law or medical school (one third-year premed student tells us, "the pre-medical program here is *very* competitive. Many students feel it necessary to sabotage others' work in order to gain an advantage"). UVA also has several prestigious honors programs including the Echols Scholars program, in which the top entering first-year students live and study together in an intense, student-driven academic program.

Like most large universities, lower level classes can be large and hard to get into, but one student tells us, "The majority of the professors that I have come across will do what they can to get you into their class if you meet with them or email them." On the downside, we are told of "conflicting office hours and long lines during those hours" and that "a lot of classes have TA's [teaching the class]."

UVA has a strict honor code that has been a source of some controversy recently. A history/economics double major explains, "Over 100 students were brought up on honor charges and there was talk of taking away past students' degrees if their papers showed signs of plagiarism as well. The honor code is taken very seriously at UVA and the only punishment for breaking it is expulsion."

Campus Environment

We are told by an upperclassman, "All first-year students are required to live on campus, with a few exceptions … The old dorms are said to be the more social dorms, although I'm not sure how much truth there really is in that. The old dorms are closer to classes, though. After first year, most students move off campus."

A third-year says, "Off-grounds housing is very popular. It is more available than on-grounds, but it fills up quickly. It costs anywhere from $300–$600 a month." One student explains, "The safety in the town is not as highly regulated as on-grounds, but is still fairly good for such a city." On campus, we are told, "I wouldn't advocate walking alone at night as there have been some incidents in the past, but there are emergency phones all over campus and the school's escort service is available at all hours of the night to drive you where you want to go."

Should you bring your car? Not in the beginning, according to a fourth-year: "First-year students are not allowed to have a car first semester at UVA unless there are extenuating circumstances that require it. After first year though, a large number of students do have cars. It is nicer to have one, but I definitely wouldn't say that it is necessary. Most things that you need to get to are within walking distance (no matter where you live) and UVA bus system, for those that don't want to walk, is reliable."

Student Life

A student describes the student body: "If there is a 'typical guy' at UVA, [he] wears khaki pants, a polo shirt, and baseball hat and is in a fraternity. The girl counterpart wears similar preppy attire and is in a sorority. However, these are the stereotypes and there are many people that do not fit into this mold."

Popular clubs include "the honor and judiciary councils where students brought up on honor charges or less serious offenses (like drinking on campus, for example) are tried before their peers. Also, the Madison House is the popular community service center and offers many ways to get involved." A third-year tells us other popular organizations are the Washington Literacy and Debating Society, the Jefferson Literacy and Debating Society, Black Voices, and a cappella groups such as the Academical Village People. "During the week, many students volunteer, go to the library, eat out, etc. On weekends, there are many people that go to fraternity parties, and the older students tend to go to the bars."

"Fraternities and sororities are very popular at UVA but less so than in the recent past," says a student. "I think that a lot of this has to do with the various regulations passed in regards to Greek organizations. For example, rush is now in the spring semester and upperclass Greeks are not allowed to talk to potential rushees during the first semester. Of course, they still do but still, first-year students are given a chance to build social bases outside of a certain fraternity or sorority." (A bit of trivia: "Dave Matthews started playing at fraternity parties here," says a fourth-year.) We are told that drinking is "not allowed in the dorm rooms, but if students are discreet enough (which basically means they close their bedroom doors) then they can usually get away with it." Says another student, "Drugs are typically just weed. UVA is bigger on drinking than on drugs."

"Varsity sports are popular here and the games are well attended, especially the football games," says one student. "The last game of the season is 'fourth-year fifth,' where tradition has it that fourth-year students drink a fifth of alcohol before the game begins. Not all fourth-years do this, but a fair number do. Basketball games are probably the second most popular sports event to attend."

Other schools to check out: William and Mary, Virginia Tech, UNC Chapel Hill, Duke.

# of Students Waitlisted: 3,888
  Students Accepting Place: 2,863
  Waitlisted Students Admitted: 556

Applied Early Decision: 2,385
  Early Decision Admitted: 918

Test Scores (middle 50%):
  SAT Verbal: 600–710
  SAT Math: 630–720
  ACT Comp: 26–31
  ACT English: 25–32
  ACT Math: 26–32

THE EXPERTS SAY...

" UVA is competitive and tough, but grads of the school Thomas Jefferson founded make it in law and medical school. "

" UVA isn't such a great bargain for out-of-state applicants, but this public Ivy has a national reputation for offering top-notch academics. A bonus: Charlottesville is a great college town. "

HS Rank of Entering Freshmen:
  Top 10%: 85%
  Top 25%: 96%
  Top 50%: 99%

Avg. HS GPA: 4.0

Costs (2003–04)

Tuition and Fees, In-State: $5,964

Tuition and Fees, Out-of-State: $21,934

Room & Board: $5,591

Payment Plan(s): installment plan

Inst. Aid (est. 2003–04)

Institutional Aid, Need-Based: $13,667,714

Institutional Aid, Non-Need-Based: $1,779,962

FT Undergrads Receiving Aid: 23%
  Avg. Amount per Student: $12,408

FT Undergrads Receiving Non-Need-Based Scholarship or Grant Aid: 18%
  Avg. Amount per Student: $5,667

Of Those Receiving Any Aid:

Rec. Need-Based Scholarship or Grant Aid: 83%
  Average Award: $9,564

Rec. Need-Based Self-Help Aid: 77%
  Average Award: $4,640

Upon Graduation, Avg. Loan Debt per Student: $13,522

Financial Aid Deadline: 3/1 (priority)

UNIVERSITY OF WASHINGTON

1410 NE Campus Parkway, 320 Schmitz Box 355840, Seattle, WA 98195-5852
Admissions Phone: (206) 543-9686 Fax: (206) 685-3655
Email: askuwadm@u.washington.edu Website: www.washington.edu
Application Website: www.applyweb.com/aw

Note: Info. not verified by school

General Info

Type of School: public, coed

Setting: urban

Academic Calendar: quarter

Student Body

Full-Time Undergrads: 23,488
  Men: 48%, Women: 52%

Part-Time Undergrads: 3,080
  Men: 49%, Women: 51%

Total Undergrad Population:
  African American: 3%
  Asian American: 24%
  Latino: 3%
  Native American: 1%
  Caucasian: 54%
  International: 3%
  Out-of-State: 15%
  Living Off-Campus: 83%
  In Fraternities: 12%
  In Sororities: 11%

Graduate and First-Professional
  Students: 10,884

Academics

Full-Time Faculty: 2,674
  With Ph.D.: 97%

Part-Time Faculty: 619
  With Ph.D.: 91%

Student/Faculty Ratio: 11:1

Freshmen Retention Rate: 90%

Graduation Rates:
  40% within four years
  70% within six years

Admissions

Regular Application Deadline: 1/15

Fall Transfer Deadline: 4/15

Spring Transfer Deadline: 12/15

Total # of Students Applied: 15,950
  Admitted: 10,884
  Enrolled: 4,771

# of Students Waitlisted: 750
  Waitlisted Students Admitted: 450

Test Scores (middle 50%):
  SAT Verbal: 510–630
  SAT Math: 550–660
  ACT Comp: 22–28
  ACT English: 21–28
  ACT Math: 22–29

In the classroom

"We know it's big, and we like it that way," proclaims the university's website. Students can take advantage of an array of academic opportunities, choosing from 1,800 courses each quarter and 130 majors. The university also provides opportunities to learn—and get credit—outside the classroom through research projects, internships, and community service. "It's so big it offers every student almost every opportunity," a senior says. "You just need to know where to look for it."

On the flip side, a junior explains, "You can have classes with up to 400 students. With so many students, it's very difficult to have much [by the way of] professor-student relations." Getting into the courses you need as prerequisites for your course of study can be difficult; you'll need to plan carefully. It helps to have a pretty good idea what you want before you walk in the door and to be aggressive in pursuing your goals. "This is a self-service university," says a senior. "[Its size] is its greatest strength and its biggest problem. No one will bring what you need to you, you have to go and get it."

Concern about the possibility that freshmen might lose themselves in this environment has motivated the school to set up a couple of innovative programs:

• Freshman Interest Groups (FIGs) consist of three or four courses that freshmen can sign up for as a cluster. Although their classes may be large, the students in a FIG find themselves among a small group of other freshmen taking the same classes and sharing the same interests. The FIG provides both a social support network and a learning community. Over 100 FIGs are offered in the fall quarter.

• Freshman Seminars offer a small-group, discussion-oriented classroom format traditionally open only to upper-division students. Taught by faculty members (not teaching assistants), these seminars meet one hour a week and are limited to 15 students who are graded on a pass/fail basis.

The university is widely regarded as one of the nation's leading state-supported research universities. The undergraduate programs with the greatest national and international recognition include premed, nursing, computer science, architecture, and business. Most undergraduates enroll in UW's College of Arts and Sciences, but most of the university's grad schools offer at least some undergraduate programs.

Campus Environment

The scenic campus on Lake Washington provides exceptional views of Mt. Rainier, but Seattle's cloudy, drizzly weather obscures the mountain most of the year. At the same time, it's an urban campus, providing access to all the entertainment options, cultural events, and work/internship opportunities offered by Seattle.

"On-campus housing is like water in a desert—it is hard to come by and waiting lists are long," a junior says. Although many dorm rooms originally designed for two often hold three students, there still isn't enough on-campus housing for all freshmen who want it. Most students—even many freshmen—live off-campus.

Walking, biking, and riding the bus are the most popular ways of getting around Seattle. With bicycle racks on buses, exclusive bus lanes and tunnels, and a free bus pass included in the cost of tuition, students advise that Metro is the way to go. Many student don't have cars, which are useful mainly for getting to school from the suburbs or getting out of the city on weekends.

Student Life

"No one feels excluded from the main group because there is no such thing," a senior says. Another student explains, "UW is incredibly diverse;" you don't need to worry about "fitting in," you "just need to find others you can get hang out with." Diversity is widely accepted as a positive part of university life.

Another important part of university life is sports. One students says, "I came to UW to watch Husky football and get into med school." There's no doubt that football is big—big games, big money, big student and alumni support. Although football dominates, other Pac-10 men's and women's sports are big too and popular spectator events for students. Many students also get involved in at least one of numerous intramural sports; in this realm, ultimate frisbee is king.

Aside from big games, the campus empties out on weekends. This makes Thursday the night you can expect to find the biggest parties on or near campus. "Fraternities and sororities host many of the parties on campus," a junior says. "However, they do not dominate the social atmosphere due to the fact that the school is located in a major city with a multitude of social outlets."

"Many of the frats and dorms have gone alcohol-free and there's a no-drug policy on campus," a post-baccalaureate student says, "though, off campus, it's another story." Students questioned in Kaplan's survey thought drugs and alcohol were less of a problem at UW than most schools, although "accessibility is good if you want either of them."

Any night of the week, many students make the quick trip into downtown Seattle to hit the clubs, bars, or cafes. "We're not confined to campus and it shows," says a junior. The whole coffee bar craze started in Seattle, as did grunge rock. The city is still a mecca for coffee and music addicts and is well-known for its vibrant youth-oriented scene in general. Flanked by mountains and nearly surrounded by water, Seattle also offers an array of outdoor activities from snowboarding to ocean kayaking. Seattle's offerings may explain why, although UW attracts students from all over the world, most students stay in Seattle upon graduation.

HS Rank of Entering Freshmen:
Top 10%: 44%
Top 25%: 80%
Top 50%: 97%
Avg. HS GPA: 3.66

Costs (2003–04)

Tuition and Fees, In-State: $4,968

Tuition and Fees, Out-of-State: $16,121

Room & Board: $7,968

Payment Plan(s): installment plan, deferred payment plan

THE EXPERTS SAY...

" If you know what you want, you can get it at U Washington. Check out the Freshmen Interest Groups to develop a support network at this big school. "

" Classes with hundreds of students, hassles getting into the courses you need, professors who don't know you exist—and didn't grunge die out with Nirvana? "

Inst. Aid (est. 2003–04)

Institutional Aid, Need-Based: $6,840,600

Institutional Aid, Non-Need-Based: $3,476,000

FT Undergrads Receiving Aid: 40%
Avg. Amount per Student: $9,784

FT Undergrads Receiving Non-Need-Based Scholarship or Grant Aid: 5%
Avg. Amount per Student: $2,290

Of Those Receiving Any Aid:

Rec. Need-Based Scholarship or Grant Aid: 67%
Average Award: $6,909

Rec. Need-Based Self-Help Aid: 85%
Average Award: $4,736

Upon Graduation, Avg. Loan Debt per Student: $14,500

Financial Aid Deadline: 2/28 (priority)

UNIVERSITY OF WISCONSIN—MADISON

Armory and Gymnasium, 716 Langdon Street, Madison, WI 53706-1481
Admissions Phone: (608) 262-3961 Fax: (608) 262-7706
Email: onwisconsin@admissions.wisc.edu Website: www.wisc.edu
Application Website: www.apply.wisconsin.edu

General Info

Type of School: public, coed
Setting: urban
Academic Calendar: semester

Student Body

Full-Time Undergrads: 26,970
  Men: 47%, Women: 53%

Part-Time Undergrads: 1,613
  Men: 48%, Women: 52%

Total Undergrad Population:
  African American: 2%
  Asian American: 5%
  Latino: 2%
  Native American: 1%
  Caucasian: 85%
  International: 3%
  Out-of-State: 29%
  Living Off-Campus: 74%
  In Fraternities: 9%
  In Sororities: 8%

Graduate and First-Professional
  Students: 11,344

Academics

Full-Time Faculty: 2,424
  With Ph.D.: 93%

Part-Time Faculty: 569
  With Ph.D.: 64%

Student/Faculty Ratio: 13:1

Most Popular Majors:
  political science (6%)
  psychology (5%)
  English (5%)
  history (4%)
  communication arts (4%)

Completing 2 or More Majors: 17%

Freshmen Retention Rate: 93%

Graduation Rates:
  42% within four years
  79% within six years

Admissions

Regular Application Deadline: 2/1

Fall Transfer Deadline: 3/1 (priority)

Spring Transfer Deadline: 11/1 (priority)

Total # of Students Applied: 20,601
  Admitted: 13,402
  Enrolled: 5,578

Inside the Classroom

"The most underrated college experience in the U.S.," exclaims a guidance counselor about UW Madison. Guidance counselors agree that Madison has become more selective; one Wisconsin counselor complains of the "hard time getting our kids in." Madison has eight undergraduate colleges: the College of Agricultural and Life Sciences, the School of Business, the School of Education, the College of Engineering, the School of Human Ecology, the College of Letters and Science, the School of Nursing, and the School of Pharmacy. Altogether, there are 140 undergraduate majors available; guidance counselors single out the business and science programs, although English and journalism are also strong.

"Most classes are very large (100–300 students) until you get into specialized upper-classes," a bio major says. Some professors "are really good about being accessible, but others are pretty bad at it," notes a junior. "You have to make a conscious effort to get to know the professor." An English major suggests that Madison needs "more professors, rather than TAs teaching."

Freshmen are assigned an advisor when they enter. One student comments, "With so much to choose from here, it's real important you have an advisor you feel comfortable with. That's why so many of us hit it off with our advisors well." But a junior states, "Students are often frustrated with how difficult it may be to find the answer to a question, meet with an advisor, or find the right person to talk to about financial aid. With such a large school, students are forced to take the initiative on all their affairs." With around a 40 percent four-year graduation rate, Madison introduced graduation contracts in 1998, but the Wall Street Journal reports that there have been few takers.

Students spend a good deal of time studying. "College Library is most popular with the Greek scene, but Memorial, known for it's study cages and having a 24 hour study area, sees a fair amount of students daily," a psychology/legal studies major reports. Warns a junior, "Although the workload is relatively light, the readings are difficult and textbooks are usually written by your professors. You need to be committed to being in school and doing well—or you will fail here at UW." Competitiveness is "prevalent": "Grades are given solely based on your performance in comparison to your fellow students. In most departments, only the top 10 percent of your class will receive A's, so you're constantly at battle with your other classmates."

Campus Environment

A student raves, "This is one of the most gorgeous campuses you'll see at any college in the country." A junior says, "The dorms are pretty nice... They're not too luxurious, but they're not dumps, either." The more expensive "private dorms are filled with East Coast students and generally are like hotel rooms." Off-campus housing is available, but it's hard to find a good deal: "They're beyond affordable unless your parents have a money tree in their backyard."

The liberal city of Madison "is a cool place," says a guidance counselor, and students agree. Says a junior, "Madison is booming with things to do outside the nightlife.

There are several cute shops on State Street to shop at, we have the Monona Terrace which is a great place to study and be on the lake, we have two large lakes to go skiing or boating on." State Street, Madison's main campus town drag, "has about everything you'll need from liquor store to Gap to special collections."

Student Life

There are more than 600 student organizations on campus, and outdoor activities and clubs are popular. "Greek life is relatively large at the UW," says a student. "However, if it is completely not what you're looking for, you'll never notice its presence." Another student offers, "A lot of the kids that are part of them come from the East Coast and use the fraternities and sororities to make new friends once they get to Wisconsin."

"Well," muses an English major, "UW has been known for being a party school, so I think it's safe to say that about everyone you meet is friendly (and will probably invite you to a party on Friday or Saturday night, or even on Thursday night)." "FUN!" exclaims another student. "The bar, Greek and house party scene is huge. Everyone goes out on the weekends—even when it's 20 degrees below!" To curb student drinking, bar owners were pressured by the university into ending drink specials on the weekends. The solution: "Now we simply drink cheap on the weekdays, and drink more expensively on the weekends," says a student. Freshmen and sophomores head to house parties thrown by upperclassmen ("charging five dollars a cup per person," a student notes.) Things can get out of hand on occasion: Riots broke out on State Street after a Halloween "Mardi Gras," leaving many local businesses looted and vandalized.

"We love our Badgers!" exclaims a junior. Wisconsin is a Big 10 powerhouse, and the annual game against archrival Minnesota is a tremendous event. "Game days in the fall are huge!" exclaims a political science/legal studies major. "People wake up at 7 A.M. all over the city to start drinking and BBQing and the city explodes with people from out of town coming in for the game." Adds a junior, "The UW Badgers have been to the Rose Ball twice lately and always seem to produce NFL players like Ron Dayne." Hockey takes over in the winter, with fans a little less numerous, but no less loyal.

Madison students are left-leaning and politically active. Says a junior, "There are tons of environmental and anti-war organizations on campus, and that seems to be the general thinking of the entire campus." While not ethnically very diverse, "there are a great mix of international students here as well as those who wear a collar shirt and tie to class and those who come in their pajamas," says an English major. Says another student, "There may be more undergraduates on campus than people in my hometown, but everyone's attitude helps to make it easier to get your arms around." A junior concludes, "The UW offered me an incredible education without the price of a private school tuition. It's full of school spirit and the students practically run the area. They are everywhere!"

Test Scores (middle 50%):
SAT Verbal: 550–660
SAT Math: 600–710
ACT Comp: 26–30

HS Rank of Entering Freshmen:
Top 10%: 55%
Top 25%: 93%
Top 50%: 99%

Avg. HS GPA: 3.66

THE EXPERTS SAY...

" It's admirable that UW Madison is developing online Advanced Placement courses to help rural and inner-city students in high schools that don't offer AP courses. "

" Madison's a great college town. State Street has lots of cute shops and affordable eateries. Get ready to gorge on cheese, ice cream, beer, and bratwurst (just not all at one sitting, please). "

Costs (2004–5)

Tuition and Fees, In-State: $5,139

Tuition and Fees, Out-of-State: $19,139

Room & Board: $6,130

Inst. Aid (2002–03)

Institutional Aid, Need-Based: $4,574,332

Institutional Aid, Non-Need-Based: $7,186,480

FT Undergrads Receiving Aid: 30%
Avg. Amount per Student: $9,449

FT Undergrads Receiving Non-Need-Based Scholarship or Grant Aid: 16%
Avg. Amount per Student: $2,524

Of Those Receiving Any Aid:

Rec. Need-Based Scholarship or Grant Aid: 41%
Average Award: $6,321

Rec. Need-Based Self-Help Aid: 86%
Average Award: $4,822

Upon Graduation, Avg. Loan Debt per Student: $16,395

Financial Aid Deadline: rolling

UNIVERSITY OF WISCONSIN— STEVENS POINT

Student Services Center, Stevens Point, WI 54481
Admissions Phone: (715) 346-2441 Fax: (715) 346-3296 Email: admiss@uwsp.edu
Website: uwsp.edu Application Website: apply.wisconsin.edu

General Info

Type of School: public, coed

Setting: small town

Academic Calendar: semester

Student Body

Full-Time Undergrads: 7,739
  Men: 44%, Women: 56%

Part-Time Undergrads: 764
  Men: 39%, Women: 61%

Total Undergrad Population:
  African American: 1%
  Asian American: 2%
  Latino: 1%
  Native American: 1%
  Caucasian: 94%
  International: 2%
  Out-of-State: 8%
  Living Off-Campus: 64%
  In Fraternities: 2%
  In Sororities: 1%

Graduate and First-Professional
  Students: 526

Academics

Full-Time Faculty: 362
  With Ph.D.: 86%

Part-Time Faculty: 62
  With Ph.D.: 40%

Student/Faculty Ratio: 20:1

Most Popular Majors:
  education (8%)
  business (7%)
  biology (6%)
  communication (5%)
  psychology (4%)

Freshmen Retention Rate: 77%

Graduation Rates:
  17% within four years
  55% within six years

Admissions

Total # of Students Applied: 4,621
  Admitted: 3,484
  Enrolled: 1,506

Test Scores (middle 50%):
  SAT Verbal: 540–630
  SAT Math: 515–630
  ACT Comp: 21–25
  ACT English: 19–25
  ACT Math: 20–25

Inside the Classroom

Stevens Point, one of the 13 campuses in the University of Wisconsin system, offers nearly 50 undergrad degrees in the College of Fine Arts and Communication, the College of Letters and Science, and the College of Natural Resources. It's this last school that makes Stevens Point especially renowned, since the university has the largest undergraduate natural resources program in North America, with majors in forestry, resource management (including environmental education), soil and waste resources, water resources (including fisheries and limnology and watershed hydrology/management), wildlife, and paper science. In fact, a guidance counselor told us recently that the school's "paper science and natural resource courses are some of the best in the nation." (It even has a fully operational paper machine on site.)

UWSP is also one of only 30 institutions in the country that has accredited programs in art, music, dance, and theater combined. Other points of pride are its nationally recognized benchmark programs in athletic training, communication disorders, and interior architecture. Other strong, popular majors include biology, business administration, and education.

All UWSP undergrads are required to take courses in the following areas: English, writing, communication, mathematics, natural science, non-Western and minority studies, history, humanities, social science, environmental literacy, wellness, and foreign language. "Our students tend to appreciate the value of a strong core curriculum which leads to competencies in all aspects of life during and after college," the school boasts.

Many departments offer internships, and there's a co-op program that sets up students in relevant work situations. There are numerous preprofessional programs available as well, and study abroad is popular, with about 15 percent of undergrads taking the opportunity to do so.

Eighty-four percent of UWSP's 350-plus full-time faculty have doctorate or equivalent degrees. The student/faculty ratio is rather high at 20:1, but we hear you'll never have an assistant as an instructor. Average class size is around 30, but expect large lectures in introductory and popular classes.

Campus Environment

Students attend classes in seven major buildings in a six-square-block area. The campus is compact and easily navigable: Classrooms are in the center, with administrative offices and the University Centers lying to the south and the residence halls to the north. Students are required to live on campus for their first two years, and freshmen are integrated into all 14 residence halls, with the exception of one that is reserved for older (21+) students. Dorms can be single-sex or coed, and vary in arrangement, size, and quality. Although on-campus housing is guaranteed for all four years, upper-division students generally move off campus as soon as the opportunity arises. (Just over a third of the student body calls the dorms home.) Dining options are fairly varied. UWSP's campus is rated one of the safest in the country.

The campus includes a 275-acre nature preserve, with trails for hiking and cross-country skiing, and a large lake. The university also maintains the Central Wisconsin Environmental Station, a large education facility 17 miles east of Stevens Point. On campus, the College of Natural Resources building was enlarged to include greenhouses and state-of-the-art technology for distance-learning education. Computer resources are decent, with workstations in every dorm and academic building.

All students, even freshmen, can park their cars on campus for about $60 a year, but be forewarned: "Currently there about 600 students on the waiting list for parking," a school official tells us. You can manage without a car, though, since academic buildings, as well as local shopping and restaurants, are within walking or biking distance. Stevens Point has a city bus service as well.

Student Life

By and large, students are happy at Stevens Point; in a recent survey, 90 percent said they were satisfied with the university. It's a warm and welcoming place—though this could be attributed to the fact that most coeds are largely from similar backgrounds. The student population is pretty homogeneous: The vast majority of students are from Wisconsin (only eight percent come from out of state), and the minority population is a tiny three percent.

Drinking, of course, is a popular way to pass the time on weekends and the occasional weeknight. It's not your typical Greek party scene, though—just a fraction of the population joins a fraternity or sorority. Booze is officially a no-no for underage students; if you're caught illegally drinking on campus, you will be required to attend a class on alcohol use and abuse. Students still flock to the handful of bars and hangouts in town. A mid-sized city of less than 40,000 residents, Stevens Point is in the center of the state. It's about 160 miles from both Milwaukee and Minneapolis, so you could easily grab some city life on the weekend.

UWSP encourages its students to participate in all sorts of extracurricular activities—preferably those that do not involve beer—and thus offers more than 150 student-run clubs and organizations, from academic and honor societies to religious and multicultural groups. Outdoor activities are particularly popular, as are student government groups, community organizations, and the student newspaper and radio station. WWSP, the campus radio station, sponsors the so-called largest trivia contest in the world, an incredible annual affair in April that's arguably the highlight of the year for students and locals alike, drawing 12,000 people from all over the country for the 54-hour weekend event. The university also sponsors over 200 public events in the arts each year including a major Performing Arts Series.

UWSP is a NCAA Division III school (which means no athletic scholarships) with competitive teams in about a dozen intercollegiate sports and many more club and intramurals. About half the student body participates in athletics in some way, but we hear this isn't a rah-rah sports-centric school.

HS Rank of Entering Freshmen:
Top 10%: 15%
Top 25%: 46%
Top 50%: 95%

Avg. HS GPA: 3.4

Costs (2003–04)

Tuition and Fees, In-State: $4,151

Tuition and Fees, Out-of-State: $14,198

Minnesota Reciprocity

Room & Board: $3,964

Payment Plan(s): installment plan

THE EXPERTS SAY...

" The College of Natural Resources may be the best place in the country to study forestry, resource management, and paper science. "

" Diversity of programs, yes: You can major in athletic training, communication disorders, interior architecture, and any of the arts. Diversity of students, no: Everybody's from Wisconsin, and happy that way. "

Inst. Aid (2002–03)

Institutional Aid, Need-Based: $228,756

Institutional Aid, Non-Need-Based: $667,877

FT Undergrads Receiving Aid: 44%
Avg. Amount per Student: $6,047

FT Undergrads Receiving Non-Need-Based Scholarship or Grant Aid: 6%
Avg. Amount per Student: $1,563

Of Those Receiving Any Aid:

Rec. Need-Based Scholarship or Grant Aid: 55%
Average Award: $4,085

Rec. Need-Based Self-Help Aid: 91%
Average Award: $4,175

Upon Graduation, Avg. Loan Debt per Student: $13,504

Financial Aid Deadline: rolling, 3/15 (priority)

Graduates

Going to Graduate School:
15% Within One Year

Companies Recruiting On Campus:
116

Alumni Giving: 9%

UNIVERSITY OF WYOMING

Dept. 3435/1000 E. University Ave., Laramie, WY 82071-3435
Admissions Phone: (307) 766-5160; (800) 342-5996 Fax: (307) 766-4042
Email: Why-Wyo@uwyo.edu Website: www.uwyo.edu
Application Website: uwadmnweb.uwyo.edu/admissions/apply_now.html

General Info

Type of School: public, coed

Setting: small town

Academic Calendar: semester

Student Body

Full-Time Undergrads: 7,568
  Men: 50%, Women: 50%

Part-Time Undergrads: 1,359
  Men: 33%, Women: 67%

Total Undergrad Population:
  African American: 1%
  Asian American: 1%
  Latino: 4%
  Native American: 1%
  Caucasian: 87%
  International: 1%
  Out-of-State: 27%
  Living Off-Campus: 77%
  In Fraternities: 8%
  In Sororities: 5%

Graduate and First-Professional
  Students: 3,795

Academics

Full-Time Faculty: 624
  With Ph.D.: 86%

Part-Time Faculty: 32
  With Ph.D.: 78%

Student/Faculty Ratio: 16:1

Most Popular Majors:
  elementary education (7%)
  nursing (5%)
  business administration (4%)
  psychology (4%)
  criminal justice (3%)

Freshmen Retention Rate: 75%

Graduation Rates:
  25% within four years
  54% within six years

Admissions

Regular Application Deadline: 8/10;
  3/1 (priority)

Fall Transfer Deadline: 8/10, 3/1
  (priority)

Spring Transfer Deadline: 12/10

Total # of Students Applied: 2,948
  Admitted: 2,796
  Enrolled: 1,416

Inside the Classroom

Guidance counselors say that despite the University of Wyoming's relatively small size, its academic offerings are quite "comprehensive." The school is large enough to offer nearly 90 undergraduate programs of study, but small enough to foster a "small-town environment." The only four-year university in the state of Wyoming, UW consists of the colleges of agriculture; arts and sciences; business; education; engineering; and health sciences. Its best known programs include geology, anthropology, wildlife and fisheries biology, and environment and natural resources. The award-winning Department of Theatre and Dance focuses exclusively on undergraduate education; one student recently was a national winner of an acting competition at the Kennedy Center for the Performing Arts in Washington, D.C. Engineering programs are also strong and popular; the school boasts excellent passing rates on the Fundamentals of Engineering Exam.

All UW students are required to complete a university-wide program in general education called the University Studies program, which encompasses about one and one-half years of study, and transfers to all majors. All freshmen jump right into it with the seminar "Introduction to University Life". The rest of the comprehensive program includes courses in writing, quantitative reasoning, sciences, cultural context, United States and Wyoming constitutions, global diversity, and phys ed.

UW is a well-regarded research university, and research opportunities for undergrads are good; according to one college official, approximately 1,500 undergraduate students participate in research projects each year. The University Honors Programs is touted as one of the best offered at a public institution. "Affordable" and "inexpensive" are two words that students and guidance counselors often use in describing the University of Wyoming. In-state tuition—and, actually, out-of-state tuition, too—is extremely low. We heard good things about the financial aid office ("very helpful and responsive"), and by and large students don't have problems with the school's administration, either; according to one undergrad, registration is "a breeze."

Classes can be large, with some intro lectures topping 300 students, but most other classes have fewer than 40 students. Professors are accessible, and we hear that even in big lectures, instructors take the time to answer questions and pay attention to their students. Classes led by TA's in lieu of profs are rare, but still a possibility. And while we hear some complaints about students who live from party to party, there are plenty of students who "take their education seriously." Classes, especially in the sciences, can be challenging; says one recent grad, "cheap doesn't mean easy."

Campus Environment

The campus is spread out over 785 tree-lined acres. The architecture styles are a pleasant mix of modern and traditional, and the campus is set up so that most academic buildings are within a 10-minute walk of one another. Students have positive things to say about UW's computer resources, as well as the research labs. While we hear that librarians are helpful, the library gets some complaints. A few buildings are undergoing renovations, and a new athletics center was recently completed.

All first-year students are required to live on campus in one of six residence halls including White Hall, which, at 12 stories, is one of the tallest buildings in the state. (All you New Yorkers: Stop laughing!) Most dorms are arranged as doubles, and are coed, with male and female wings on either side of a lobby. Special options include freshmen-interest, substance-free, engineering honors, quiet living, and female-only. A small percentage of first-year students live in Greek houses. Housing is available for most students who want it, but after freshman year, most students hunt for off-campus digs. We hear that finding good, inexpensive housing near campus is tough, but can be done if you start early.

All students are permitted to have cars on campus—and many do, which may be why the parking situation is often bemoaned as "terrible." Students can use a university-run shuttle bus system during class hours, and many bike around campus. There are some underground hallways that connect dorms and dining halls for days when you just don't feel like going outside. Laramie (pop: 30,000) boasts "blue skies, clean air, and 320 days of sunshine"—but don't mistake sunshine for warmth. The winter weather in Laramie is widely thought of as the worst in the state, with subzero temperatures and huge snowfalls.

Student Life

Nearly three-quarters of students come from Wyoming. The minority population hovers around six percent, most of which are Latino students. It can be something of a party school—drinking is a major (and, some say, the only) pastime on weekends and many weeknights. The town of Laramie doesn't have the best reputation for tolerance; it is, after all, where the 1998 murder of gay UW student Matthew Shepard took place. But some call it "warm" and "friendly," although there isn't a whole lot to do aside from drink and ski, it seems. There are bars, cafes, and a few places to go dancing. Feeling stir-crazy? Laramie is 45 minutes from the state capitol of Cheyenne and two hours from Denver, Colorado.

If you're into winter sports, you're in luck: Outdoor recreation is big, with plenty of opportunities to ski, snowmobile, hike, and ride horses. Much of the area surrounding the school is public National Forest land. Guidance counselors gush about the school's "environmentally unique, beautiful" mountain surroundings, and skiers rave about discount skiing available nearby for students. The school's Outdoor Adventure Program offers fun, affordable outings, clinics, and equipment rentals.

Greek life is fairly popular, with nearly 1,000 students joining 14 fraternities and sororities. More than 150 student organizations are offered, as well as 17 intercollegiate sports (eight for men, nine for women). The ice hockey team is the Division III champ, and the rodeo and rifle teams are nationally successful. Intramural sports are big: In a recent year, nearly 6,000 students participated.

Test Scores (middle 50%):
SAT Verbal: 470–590
SAT Math: 490–600
ACT Comp: 20–26
ACT English: 19–25
ACT Math: 19–26

HS Rank of Entering Freshmen:
Top 10%: 19%
Top 25%: 46%
Top 50%: 78%

Avg. HS GPA: 3.41

THE EXPERTS SAY...

" Geology, fisheries and wildlife studies, and environmental programs benefit from UW's location near national forest land. "

" Everyone benefits from underground hallways. With temperatures below zero and tons of snow, it's no wonder students stay inside and drink. "

Costs (2003–04)

Tuition and Fees, In-State: $3,090

Tuition and Fees, Out-of-State: $8,940

Room & Board: $5,546

Payment Plan(s): installment plan, deferred payment plan, pre-payment plan

Inst. Aid (2002–03)

Institutional Aid, Need-Based: $260,586

Institutional Aid, Non-Need-Based: $2,490,108

FT Undergrads Receiving Aid: 47%
Avg. Amount per Student: $8,944

FT Undergrads Receiving Non-Need-Based Scholarship or Grant Aid: 39%
Avg. Amount per Student: $3,421

Of Those Receiving Any Aid:

Rec. Need-Based Scholarship or Grant Aid: 39%
Average Award: $4,030

Rec. Need-Based Self-Help Aid: 89%
Average Award: $1,115

Upon Graduation, Avg. Loan Debt per Student: $15,250

Financial Aid Deadline: rolling, 2/1 (priority)

Graduates

Companies Recruiting On-Campus: 120

URSINUS COLLEGE

P.O. Box 1000, Collegeville, PA 19426-1000
Admissions Phone: (610) 409-3200 Fax: (610) 489-3662
Email: admissions@ursinus.edu Website: www.ursinus.edu
Application Website: www.applyweb.com/apply/ursinus

General Info

Type of School: private, coed
Setting: suburban
Academic Calendar: semester

Student Body

Full-Time Undergrads: 1,465
 Men: 46%, Women: 54%

Part-Time Undergrads: 2
 Men: 100%

Total Undergrad Population:
 African American: 8%
 Asian American: 4%
 Latino: 3%
 Native American: <1%
 Caucasian: 80%
 International: 1%
 Out-of-State: 37%
 Living Off-Campus: 9%
 In Fraternities: 11%
 In Sororities: 19%

Academics

Full-Time Faculty: 110
 With Ph.D.: 90%

Part-Time Faculty: 158
 With Ph.D.: 73%

Student/Faculty Ratio: 11:1

Most Popular Majors:
 business and economics (10%)
 biology (8%)
 psychology (6%)
 English (5%)
 communication studies and
  theater (5%)

Completing 2 or More Majors: 16%

Freshmen Retention Rate: 88%

Graduation Rates:
 75% within four years
 78% within six years

Computers: School provides individual computer/laptop

Admissions

Regular Application Deadline: 2/15

Early Decision Deadline(s): 1/15

Fall Transfer Deadline: 8/1

Spring Transfer Deadline: 12/1

Total # of Students Applied: 1,775
 Admitted: 1,322
 Enrolled: 454

Inside the Classroom

Ursinus College may be small and fairly obscure, but it has an excellent post-graduate record: Three out of four of its students enter grad and professional schools within five years of graduation, and nearly all of its students who apply to medical and other health-related schools gain admission. Indeed, the premedical sciences are far and away the top programs at this small school, especially the popular biology major. Some complain that the school is too focused on these areas, but one French major contends that "while the school is slanted towards the sciences, there is a decided academic atmosphere in all departments."

Labs and professors are reportedly excellent, and the modest class sizes (an average of 15–20 students) promote good faculty-student interaction along with a healthy sense of both competition and cooperation among classmates. Students see one another "more as team members than opponents," we hear. The workload depends on the major (with "sciences holding heavier workload"), but most students feel they have just enough. As one young alum tells us, "Classes are tough... I felt very obligated to study and prepare for class." However, an econ major sniffs, "There are tons of slackers and just about everybody is happy with B's."

All students must complete the "Liberal Studies Curriculum" consisting of three components: The Core, Study in Depth, and the Independent Learning Experience (ILE). The Core contains the usual liberal arts and sciences courses (English, math, humanities, etc.), plus two seminars called the "Common Intellectual Experience." Study in Depth involves taking classes in one of 20-plus majors; as a rule, freshmen do not come to Ursinus already registered for a major. The ILE is usually completed during the senior year, and can be in the form of independent research or a creative project, an internship, study abroad, student teaching, or a fellows program.

Campus Environment

"The campus has a very suburban feel; safe and friendly, if a bit cramped," muses one student. Located on 165 wooded acres, Ursinus is about 30 miles from Philadelphia. Collegeville (pop: 5,000) is quaint and pretty, if not all that action-packed. "The town is the most boring of boring places," one disgruntled student tells us. There are a few shops, restaurants, and bars within walking distance, but for some, the small-town ambience may wear a little thin after a while. "Students who need big-city atmosphere might find Ursinus constrictive," a senior says. "Off-campus interests for Ursinus often require students to have access to a car." In general, only upperclassmen have cars (freshmen must get special permission), and there are widespread complaints about the shortage of on-campus parking.

That said, nearly all students live on or near campus and stay put on weekends. Ursinus practices "Freshman Clustering," which means most, if not all, first-year students live together in an attempt to foster a sense of community. "The housing is exceptionally good," a student says. "The rooms are fairly big, and there are lots of singles." Overall, students are happy with their living quarters, except one: Reimert Hall, the infamous—and infamously dirty—party dorm. (One junior suggests that prospective students ask to see Reimert: "They don't show it on tours because it is so dirty and decrepit.") A new 143-bed residence hall was just completed, although as a freshman, you probably won't get to live there. After their first year, students have the option of living in the Residential Village, a group of beautifully restored Victorian houses along Main Street. "The Main Street houses are the place to live post-freshman year," we're told. The "award-winning" houses are "organized around themes, co-curricular interests, Greek affiliation, and academic interest," the school says.

The campus also boasts state-of-the-art science facilities, a major art museum, and a field house complex for varsity and casual athletes alike. Students give the on-campus dining options decent marks. A major Ursinus perk: As part of a "Dell Initiative," all students receive a laptop computer and color printer to use during their college career.

Student Life

A student sums up her classmates simply: "WASP-y, relatively affluent, but open-minded." Another adds, "The student body is like a walking Abercrombie ad." A majority hails from Pennsylvania; most of the rest are from surrounding states. All of this homogeneity leads to a strong alumni network, and perhaps more: "Apparently there's a really really high percentage of students marrying people they meet at Ursinus," a student tells us.

During the week, students tend to be low-key, spending their time studying or hanging out with friends in their dorms. Weekends—which begin on Thursday nights—mean lots of drinking, and maybe a little getting high. The administration has imposed a tougher, drier alcohol policy, to varying degrees of effectiveness. There are still dorm parties and frat parties, and, for 21-year-olds, a small local bar scene. Greek life is a major force on campus—too major, some complain. "The frats and sororities are everything at Ursinus," a student says. There's no outright pressure to pledge, but we hear that since the school's so small, it feels like everyone's Greek. "It seems like anyone who is popular has pledged," a junior agrees. But another student defends the letter-bent social life, saying the Greeks "provide an open atmosphere at parties that appeals to many students."

When not studying or partying, Ursinus students participate in more than 80 clubs and organizations of every ilk. There are 24 varsity teams that compete in Division III. The college has the oldest field hockey program in the nation (and is home to the Field Hockey Hall of Fame). The majority of the student body plays sports in some form, be it on a varsity, club, or IM team. There are concerts, movies, dances, and comedy shows throughout the year, as well as such popular traditions as Airband, Collegeville Squares, the Mr. Ursinus contest, and Spring Fling. Students who yearn for bigger things are a short distance away from the huge King of Prussia mall, Valley Forge National Park, the Pocono ski resorts, the Jersey shore, and Philadelphia, with its countless bars, clubs, restaurants, museums, shops, and tourist attractions.

Other schools to check out: Juniata, Allegheny, Susquehanna, Muhlenberg, Dickinson.

# of Students Waitlisted: 21
  Students Accepting Place: 12

Applied Early Decision: 168
  Early Decision Admitted: 157

Test Scores (middle 50%):
  SAT Verbal: 550–660
  SAT Math: 560–660

HS Rank of Entering Freshmen:
  Top 10%: 44%
  Top 25%: 76%
  Top 50%: 95%

Avg. HS GPA: 3.5

THE EXPERTS SAY...

" A particularly good choice for future health professionals, Ursinus is a quirky little college filled with bright and focused students. "

" While Ursinus alumni don't complain about the quality of the education they received, they do complain about the total lack of name recognition. "

Costs (2004–5)

Tuition and Fees: $29,780

Room & Board: $7,150

Payment Plan(s): installment plan, external finance plan, credit card payment plan

Inst. Aid (est. 2003–04)

Institutional Aid, Need-Based: $17,861,920

FT Undergrads Receiving Non-Need-Based Scholarship or Grant Aid: 8%
Avg. Amount per Student: $11,500

Of Those Receiving Any Aid:

Rec. Need-Based Scholarship or Grant Aid: 81%
Average Award: $15,874

Rec. Need-Based Self-Help Aid: 100%
Average Award: $6,255

Upon Graduation, Avg. Loan Debt per Student: $18,000

Financial Aid Deadline: 2/15

Graduates

Going to Graduate School: 34% Within One Year

Accepting Job Offer: 20% at time of graduation

Companies Recruiting On Campus: 86

Alumni Giving: 57%

VALPARAISO UNIVERSITY

Kretzmann Hall, 1700 Chapel Drive, Valparaiso, IN 46383-6493
Admissions Phone: (219) 464-5011; (888) 468-2576 Fax: (219) 464-6898
Email: undergrad.admissions@valpo.edu
Website: www.valpo.edu

General Info

Type of School: private, coed, Lutheran

Setting: small town

Academic Calendar: semester

Student Body

Full-Time Undergrads: 2,835
  Men: 48%, Women: 52%

Part-Time Undergrads: 168
  Men: 29%, Women: 71%

Total Undergrad Population:
  African American: 3%
  Asian American: 2%
  Latino: 3%
  Native American: <1%
  Caucasian: 88%
  International: 2%
  Out-of-State: 67%
  Living Off-Campus: 36%
  In Fraternities: 26%
  In Sororities: 19%

Graduate and First-Professional
  Students: 824

Academics

Full-Time Faculty: 232
  With Ph.D.: 88%

Part-Time Faculty: 112
  With Ph.D.: 47%

Student/Faculty Ratio: 13:1

Most Popular Majors:
  elementary education (6%)
  biology (5%)
  nursing (4%)
  communication (4%)
  psychology (4%)

Completing 2 or More Majors: 25%

Freshmen Retention Rate: 86%

Graduation Rates:
  60% within four years
  73% within six years

Admissions

Regular Application Deadline: 8/15;
  1/15 (priority)

Early Action Deadline: 11/1

Total # of Students Applied: 3,576
  Admitted: 2,929
  Enrolled: 795

Inside the Classroom

Perhaps the finest Lutheran school in the country, Valparaiso University is a relatively small institution with a very big name. Lauded consistently in national rankings and by high school guidance counselors interviewed in Kaplan's national survey, Valparaiso—or just plain "Valpo," to those within its walls—offers 60 undergraduate programs through five colleges. The first four colleges offer majors in the arts and sciences, business administration, engineering, and nursing. The fifth, Christ College, is the university's crown jewel: An honors college where the challenging and interdisciplinary curriculum emphasizes liberal arts, the humanities (history, literature, art, music, philosophy, religion), and the social sciences.

Freshman studies at Christ College include the Valparaiso Core Course, a two-semester, interdisciplinary, 10-credit course with the primary subject of the human experience as expressed by great thinkers, writers, and artists. Other general education requirements include two courses in theology, two courses in literature and fine arts, one course in philosophical and historical studies, two courses in social analysis, three courses in the natural and behavioral sciences or mathematics, one course in global cultures and perspectives, and one course in cultural diversity. Certain programs require the study of a foreign language. One significant perk of graduating from Christ College is guaranteed admission to Valparaiso's law school.

"Christ College broadened my academic experiences and helped me apply reasoning and critical thinking skills to my daily life," said one student. "I was challenged to explore my own beliefs and understanding and to further develop as an individual." Another student who participated in the college's Senior Colloquium said, "The colloquium united my discoveries in liberal arts with my spiritual journey, reminding me that character is formed by challenges on all fronts: intellectual, personal, and spiritual."

Valpo is one of the few colleges that operates under a student-run honor code. Examinations aren't proctored unless specifically requested by students, and every piece of written work submitted by students must contain the statement: "I have neither given or received, nor have I tolerated others' use of unauthorized aid." Reportedly, some professors are so serious about this declaration that they want it handwritten on a typed paper and signed. Breaches of the code are deliberated upon by the school's Honor Council. Cheat once, and you fail the course; cheat three times, and you pack your bags permanently.

Campus Environment

All freshmen, sophomores, and juniors are required by decree to live on campus, unless they live with nearby family. The university's 10 dorms are coed by floor, with two dorms offering apartment-style housing for upperclassmen. Two dorms are earmarked almost exclusively for freshmen, and another houses mostly women who are pledged to sororities that don't have houses.

Valparaiso's 310-acre campus is spacious and scenic. One of its signature images is the distinctive Chapel of the Resurrection, which towers above the surrounding landscape. Other buildings of note include the Brauer Museum of Art, which is home to a nationally recognized collection of 19th- and 20th-century American art and includes works by Frederic Edwin Church, Asher B. Durand, Childe Hassam, Georgia O'Keeffe, and Ed Paschke. Other highlights of the collection include world religious art and Midwestern regional art.

Enrollment is small, and the social dynamics at Valpo reflect this. "Rumor-busting is one of the bigger tasks on this campus," said one recent graduate, a former president and vice president of the Student Senate. "Everybody here knows everybody else—and rumors move quickly."

The city of Valparaiso, a residential community with a population of 26,000, is known in the area for its annual popcorn festival in honor of the late Orville Redenbacher, famed popcorn mogul and former Valparaiso resident. When all the corny fun gets to be too much, VU is 15 miles from Merrillville's large Southlake Mall, movie theaters, and restaurant complex; 15 miles south of Indiana Dunes National Lakeshore on Lake Michigan; and 55 miles from the city of Chicago.

Student Life

Freshmen enrolled in Christ College have the dubious honor of staging the annual Freshman Production, a wholly original drama or musical performance based on the themes and ideas they've been discussing in class. A more palatable experience—or perhaps not, depending on the talent involved—is Songfest, the annual musical competition between fraternities and sororities held during Spring Weekend.

Speaking of the Greeks, about 40 percent of students pledge to Valpo's eight frats and seven sororities, several of which have their own houses. In recent years the Greeks have taken a more responsible attitude towards campus life. Students must achieve a certain GPA before they can join a fraternity or sorority, and many VU Greek chapters provide study rooms and tutoring for members.

The social life at VU is par for the course at a small school, with students participating in a range of extracurricular activities and gathering for parties in the late hours. Movies, campus events, and small group gatherings are more the norm than huge, raucous parties.

Valparaiso is a NCAA Division I school, so its Crusaders loom large on campus. Sports for men and women include basketball, cross-country, tennis, swimming, soccer, and track. About 16 percent of undergrads play on Valpo's intercollegiate teams, with football for men and volleyball for women also popular. Men's basketball has been a big draw lately, due to recent successes. "It's insane here," said one senior. "The whole town comes to the games. The whole campus goes. But I'd say there's just as many townspeople who come to the games." A new softball field will be ready for play in spring 2003, and things are looking up for the baseball team, too. A brand-new, state-of-the-art baseball clubhouse is currently under construction, and will be equipped with a weight room, showers, bathrooms, and space for team meetings. About 20 intramural sports are also offered, ranging from badminton to table tennis.

Test Scores (middle 50%):
 SAT Verbal: 520–640
 SAT Math: 530–650
 ACT Comp: 23–29
 ACT English: 23–30
 ACT Math: 23–29

HS Rank of Entering Freshmen:
 Top 10%: 36%
 Top 25%: 67%
 Top 50%: 90%

Avg. HS GPA: 3.37

THE EXPERTS SAY...

" Valparaiso's big-name pedigree carries weight, especially if you can get into Christ College. "

" A small, relatively quiet school in a popcorn-crazy town may not be everyone's idea of a fun time. "

Costs (2003–04)

Tuition and Fees: $20,638

Room & Board: $5,480

Payment Plan(s): installment plan, deferred payment plan, pre-payment plan

Inst. Aid (est. 2003–04)

Institutional Aid, Need-Based: $14,968,298

Institutional Aid, Non-Need-Based: $6,361,345

FT Undergrads Receiving Aid: 68%
 Avg. Amount per Student: $17,404

FT Undergrads Receiving Non-Need-Based Scholarship or Grant Aid: 24%
 Avg. Amount per Student: $7,573

Of Those Receiving Any Aid:

Rec. Need-Based Scholarship or Grant Aid: 99%
 Average Award: $11,310

Rec. Need-Based Self-Help Aid: 78%
 Average Award: $6,288

Upon Graduation, Avg. Loan Debt per Student: $20,270

Financial Aid Deadline: rolling, 3/1 (priority)

Graduates

Going to Graduate School:
 27% Within One Year

Companies Recruiting On Campus: 37

Alumni Giving: 33%

VANDERBILT UNIVERSITY

2305 West End Avenue, Nashville, TN 37203
Admissions Phone: (615) 322-2561; (800) 288-0432 Fax: (615) 343-7765
Email: admissions@vanderbilt.edu Website: www.vanderbilt.edu
Application Website: www.vanderbilt.edu/Admissions/apply.html

General Info

Type of School: private, coed
Setting: urban
Academic Calendar: semester

Student Body

Full-Time Undergrads: 6,212
  Men: 48%, Women: 52%

Part-Time Undergrads: 31
  Men: 71%, Women: 29%

Total Undergrad Population:
  African American: 7%
  Asian American: 6%
  Latino: 4%
  Native American: <1%
  Caucasian: 74%
  International: 2%
  Living Off-Campus: 17%
  In Fraternities: 34%
  In Sororities: 50%

Graduate and First-Professional
  Students: 4,809

Academics

Full-Time Faculty: 713
  With Ph.D.: 97%

Most Popular Majors:
  social services
  engineering
  psychology
  interdisciplinary
  visual & performing arts

Freshmen Retention Rate: 94%

Graduation Rates:
  75% within four years
  83% within six years

Admissions

Regular Application Deadline: 1/2

Early Decision Deadline(s): 11/1,
  1/2

Fall Transfer Deadline: 3/1

Spring Transfer Deadline: 11/1

Total # of Students Applied: 10,960
  Admitted: 4,405
  Enrolled: 1,545

# of Students Waitlisted: 1,130
  Students Accepting Place: 443
  Waitlisted Students Admitted: 32

Applied Early Decision: 1,084
  Early Decision Admitted: 446

Inside the Classroom

"Academically, we are near an Ivy League," declares a proud Vanderbilt student. (One guidance counselor who called the college "little Harvard" would agree.) Students can choose from more than 50 majors in the four undergraduate schools: the College of Arts and Science, the Blair School of Music, the School of Engineering, and the Peabody College of Education and Human Development. The education programs are among the best in the nation. Preprofessional programs are particularly popular, especially in engineering and premed; Vanderbilt is also home to a distinguished medical school. A Nashville guidance counselor raves about the Blair conservatory program, and says about Arts and Sciences: "liberal arts but also has communications and neuroscience."

The core curriculum is broad, and many students satisfy their writing requirement with a freshman seminar, part of the widely praised College Writing Program. These seminars are made up of no more than 15 or 20 students and cover subjects like "Concepts of God" and "Treasure or Trash? Examining Theatrical Credibility." Freshmen with exceptional academic records can participate in the College Scholars Program, in which students do advanced work in honors seminars and independent projects.

Professors at Vanderbilt are known to be casual, friendly, and "exceptionally accessible." A guidance counselor stresses Vandy's "highly personalized" approach. (A junior disagrees: "Professors are often arrogant and though most are somewhat accessible, they are not always fair.") Nearly all undergrad classes are taught by professors, not assistants. The courses are tough, but manageable for the ambitious student. "The workload at Vanderbilt requires a one hour of class to three hours outside of class study ratio," suggests one undergrad. "The competition is extreme in the premedicine area, as all students are bent on beating each other to get into top medical schools," complains a biomedical engineering major. Still, most Vandy students are "willing to help one another out," and they wholeheartedly participate in the school's honor system, which has been in place since 1875.

There's a price for all this: "Cost, cost, cost!" moans a Nashville guidance counselor. Another counselor claims Vandy is "not well-funded." A student agrees about "the overall cost" but counters with some of Vanderbilt's strong points: "The campus is beautiful, the students are smart so you have good colleagues, and [there's] decent financial aid."

Campus Environment

"Residential colleges will be a new thing on campus in '06," a student reports. "Many students are against it. It is guaranteed to change the face of Vanderbilt." Some students are protesting a lack of choice in housing, roommates, and required dining hall attendance in the systems under consideration, but the university stresses vibrant academic communities and increased diversity.

In another controversy, the Tennessee division of the United Daughters of the Confederacy is suing to keep the university from changing the name of the building now known as Confederate Memorial Hall to plain old Memorial Hall. Accusing the school of political correctness, the group's lawyer said the hall was built as monument to Confederate soldiers. The name has stirred debate since African American students refused to set foot there in 1988.

Just a mile and a half from downtown Nashville, the university's secluded 323-acre campus ("the Vanderbubble") has more of a community feel than most urban campuses and was declared a national arboretum in 1988. "When the weather is nice outside, there are always people hanging out on our Alumni Lawn," a student tells us. Only seniors may live off-campus, and they must go through an extensive authorization process to do so. More than 80 percent of the student body lives in the school's small but comfortable campus housing. "Overall, good choices, but restricted more each year because of the increasing volume of students and not-increasing volume of housing," a junior remarks, adding, "The freshmen housing has a good amount of single rooms… at least until 2006." Upperclassmen fill up the other dorms or move into Greek housing. We hear that Vandy gets a thumbs-down on the cafeteria food.

Student Life

Vanderbilt students tend to be conservative in their politics and values; they also tend to be white Southerners. A guidance counselor expresses "some concern about diversity." About half of the roughly 6,000 undergraduates hail from the South. "Vanderbilt is a mid-sized, conservative Southern school with students from just about everywhere in the country," argues one student. But a Missouri guidance counselor believes that the "campus culture may be too traditional and/or Southern for some students." Stereotypes of the "Vandy girl" abound, pegging coeds here as shallow, rich Southern belles. While one undergrad admits that "the typical Vandy student is the beautiful, wealthy, social icon," she dismisses the image as a cliché, saying, "Vanderbilt is a very diverse community." And it is academics, and not social skills, that lands Vanderbilt on this year's guidance counselor Nerd School list.

No doubt about it, at the center of Vanderbilt's social scene lies Fraternity Row: "They have a tremendous impact on social life," a student remarks. "Since half of female population and roughly 30 percent of males are in Greek organizations, it is predominant and obvious." "It's a very image-conscious place," laments one sorority member. The campus is "pretty safe and friendly, but lots of social rifts exist… Goths or people who dress differently, or are not as smart as the others, would be ostracized."

There are more than 300 clubs and organizations of all kinds. Drinking and drugs "are large factors, as students are wealthy enough to afford them," a junior comments. Vanderbilt's intercollegiate sports teams—particularly men's and women's basketball teams, which vie for spots in the NCAA Sweet 16—contribute to the sense of school spirit. According to one high school guidance counselor, "Memorial Gym is the most exciting place in the world to watch basketball." Football "constantly gets a bad rap since the team is not good, but is in SEC and the Greek kids dress up to go to the games."

"Nashville offers a variety of fun and exciting happenings away from Vanderbilt," one student gushes. Another agrees: "Nashville isn't just country music. It's just about everything these days." Country western and bluegrass are most prominent, but decent rock and alternative music venues and a range of bars, clubs, and restaurants are also found. And during a school celebration called Rites of Spring, "we have popular bands come and play for the school."

Other schools to check out: Duke, Johns Hopkins, Emory, Washington U in St. Louis, Wake Forest.

Test Scores (middle 50%):
SAT Verbal: 610–710
SAT Math: 640–720
ACT Comp: 28–32
ACT English: 28–33
ACT Math: 26–32

HS Rank of Entering Freshmen:
Top 10%: 77%
Top 25%: 94%
Top 50%: 100%

THE EXPERTS SAY…

" Vanderbilt tends to catch the admissions overflow from the Ivies, resulting in a very smart, very driven (and very Southern) student body. "

" If you apply to Vanderbilt now, chances are you'll be living (and eating, and studying) in a residential college in 2006. "

Costs (2004–5)

Tuition and Fees: $28,440

Room & Board: $9,457

Payment Plan(s): installment plan, deferred payment plan, pre-payment plan

Inst. Aid (est. 2003–04)

Institutional Aid, Need-Based: $51,399,141

Institutional Aid, Non-Need-Based: $13,378,185

FT Undergrads Receiving Aid: 38%
Avg. Amount per Student: $28,906

FT Undergrads Receiving Non-Need-Based Scholarship or Grant Aid: 16%
Avg. Amount per Student: $15,141

Of Those Receiving Any Aid:

Rec. Need-Based Scholarship or Grant Aid: 93%
Average Award: $20,555

Rec. Need-Based Self-Help Aid: 74%
Average Award: $6,976

Upon Graduation, Avg. Loan Debt per Student: $23,334

Financial Aid Deadline: 2/1 (priority)

Graduates

Going to Graduate School: 38% Within One Year

VASSAR COLLEGE

Box 10, 124 Raymond Ave, Poughkeepsie, NY 12604
Admissions Phone: (914) 437-7300; (800) 827-7270 Fax: (914) 437-7063
Email: admissions@vassar.edu
Website: vassar.edu

General Info

Type of School: private, coed

Setting: suburban

Academic Calendar: semester

Student Body

Full-Time Undergrads: 2,392
  Men: 40%, Women: 60%

Part-Time Undergrads: 24
  Men: 46%, Women: 54%

Total Undergrad Population:
  African American: 5%
  Asian American: 9%
  Latino: 5%
  Native American: <1%
  Caucasian: 75%
  International: 4%
  Out-of-State: 72%
  Living Off-Campus: 5%

Academics

Full-Time Faculty: 254
  With Ph.D.: 94%

Part-Time Faculty: 39
  With Ph.D.: 67%

Student/Faculty Ratio: 9:1

Most Popular Majors:
  political science (11%)
  psychology (10%)
  English (10%)
  economics (8%)
  sociology (7%)

Completing 2 or More Majors: 10%

Freshmen Retention Rate: 95%

Graduation Rates:
  82% within four years
  88% within six years

Admissions

Regular Application Deadline: 1/1

Early Decision Deadline(s): 11/15,
  1/1

Fall Transfer Deadline: 4/1

Spring Transfer Deadline: 11/15

Total # of Students Applied: 6,207
  Admitted: 1,806
  Enrolled: 636

# of Students Waitlisted: 800
  Students Accepting Place: 400
  Waitlisted Students Admitted: 35

Applied Early Decision: 556
  Early Decision Admitted: 245

Inside the Classroom

By giving students a high degree of independence and encouraging them to use it, Vassar attracts free-thinkers who will be motivated to, as one student said, "find a space to grow and excel." Vassar's exceptional liberal arts departments are highly rated; English and the fine arts are especially well regarded and have large enrollments, but the sciences are steadily gaining in reputation. Many students choose a multidisciplinary or interdepartmental major, or design their own. Although there is no core curriculum, students must demonstrate proficiency in a foreign language, take at least one quantitative course (such as math, computer science, or a lab science), and complete a writing-intensive freshman course (chosen from about 20 options). With a student/faculty ratio of 9:1, students receive a great deal of individual attention from professors, most of whom live on campus. While students welcome the small classes because they foster discussion, the enforced small size can make it difficult to get the classes students need or want, a situation at least one student described as "irritating."

Students wanting to study abroad may participate in Vassar's programs in England, France, Germany, Ireland, Italy, Morocco, or Spain, or join programs offered by other colleges. The Undergraduate Research Summer Institute (URSI) pairs students with faculty members for a ten-week, full-time research experience in mathematics, psychology, astrophysics, and other sciences. The Ford Scholars Program provides students in the humanities and social sciences the chance for collaborative scholarship with faculty. Internships, especially in government and community service, are available in nearby Poughkeepsie. Vassar's Powerhouse Summer Theater program apprentices students to professional New York City theater companies; students can earn Actors Equity points through the program.

Academic attitudes at Vassar "can be very lax," reports a recent grad: "Professors are very accessible and a lot of them care, but I didn't feel a lot of pressure or competition. It's very hard to fail." Although some say that there's a big distance between a B+ and an A at Vassar, and that it's hard to get the highest grades, a former student doesn't recommend the school to "anyone who's superambitious and motivated." Vassar alumnae, who include Edna St. Vincent Millay, Katherine Graham, Mary McCarthy, and Meryl Streep, may contradict that statement.

Campus Environment

Students rave about Vassar's beautiful 1,000-acre campus, which is maintained as an arboretum. Housing is guaranteed for all four years (new housing currently is being built), and nearly all students live on campus until graduation. Students from all four classes are housed together in above-average, spacious dormitories. Freshmen usually live in doubles, but it's not hard to get a single in a townhouse or terrace apartment as a sophomore. Off-campus housing varies; one former student says it's "not as available as on-campus housing." There are no fraternity/sororities at the college.

Poughkeepsie, described by one student as a city that "leaves much to be desired," is a blue-collar town, and has little to do with the school. While the Mid-Hudson Civic Center does draw name concerts, there's usually not much to do in town. Luckily, New York City is 75 miles away. All students are allowed to have cars on campus, and parking is free. Bicycles are the number one mode of transportation on campus, and long boards and scooters are also permitted, "but there are some who feel the need to drive their Range Rovers or Benzes to class or the gym," quips a grad. For the town, "you definitely need a car or you may get hit by one." Taxis and buses are available; the college provides a shuttle service around campus and to the local shopping areas and train station.

Student Life

Vassar's dynamic and diverse student body includes various ethnic and cultural groups and a large gay population. The Asian Students' Association, Black Students' Union, Poder Latino and the Student Activists' Union are particularly visible, as is ViCE, Vassar College Entertainment, which mounts concerts and film screenings. Vassar Teknowledgy produces campus events utilizing computer generated music and "some of the best cutting edge graphics available to mankind," says an enthused college official.

A California guidance counselor tells us that Vassar is a good choice for students who are "very open to change and are somewhat nontraditional." (However, a New York counselor points out that Vassar "doesn't make itself stand out from Wesleyan, or stand ahead.") Musicians, actors, writers, and artists abound. Some are put off by the "people-in-black" crowd, but most Vassar students revel in the liberal atmosphere. While the school, which went coed in 1969, is still a popular destination for daughters of the country club set, over 60 percent of the student body went to public high schools. One acerbic alum characterizes Vassar students this way: "1. flakey or 'one' with the environment; 2. anorexic girl; 3. pothead/ druggie; 4. 'typical' liberal arts student, which means fairly intelligent and well-spoken, aware of social issues."

The social scene at Vassar is campus-centered. Matthew's Mug, the college pub, is smoky and quiet during the week, when it has jazz music and poetry readings, but turns into a dance club on weekends; the Aula coffeehouse is popular among the underaged. The Vassar ratio of women to men makes for lopsided social dynamics, however.

Drinking is "a big factor on weekends, but no more than other schools," an urban studies grad remarks. "Drugs are a factor too, among those with money." While there are no frats, "the athletic teams seem to make up for it—the soccer team is pretty much idolized," says an alumna. Vassar competes in NCAA Division III and has 23 varsity teams and intramural sports. (Interesting fact: The earliest documented mention of women playing baseball in the United States is contained in a letter dated April 20, 1866 from a Vassar student).

Traditional events include spring and fall formals, and Founder's Day ("We celebrate the founder's (a beer brewer) birthday by throwing this huge carnival-like party on campus, complete with beer trucks and carnival rides.") In "serenading," seniors go from dorm to dorm, where freshmen sing songs of satire or praise.

Other schools to check out: Oberlin, Swarthmore, Wesleyan, Skidmore, Sarah Lawrence.

THE EXPERTS SAY...

" The quality and prestige of Vassar's academics just keep growing. "

" Hard to get in, hard to flunk out. "

VILLANOVA UNIVERSITY

800 Lancaster Avenue, Villanova, PA 19085
Admissions Phone: (610) 519-4000 Fax: (610) 519-6450
Email: gotovu@villanova.edu Website: www.villanova.edu
Application Website: www.admission.villanova.edu

General Info

Type of School: private, coed,
 Roman Catholic

Setting: suburban

Academic Calendar: semester

Student Body

Full-Time Undergrads: 6,557
 Men: 49%, Women: 51%

Part-Time Undergrads: 323
 Men: 53%, Women: 47%

Total Undergrad Population:
 African American: 3%
 Asian American: 5%
 Latino: 5%
 Native American: <1%
 Caucasian: 83%
 International: 2%
 Out-of-State: 68%
 Living Off-Campus: 34%
 In Fraternities: 6%
 In Sororities: 25%

Graduate and First-Professional
 Students: 3,352

Academics

Full-Time Faculty: 549
 With Ph.D.: 91%

Part-Time Faculty: 424
 With Ph.D.: 58%

Student/Faculty Ratio: 13:1

Most Popular Majors:
 finance (12%)
 communication (11%)
 accounting (7%)

Freshmen Retention Rate: 94%

Graduation Rates:
 80% within four years
 85% within six years

Computers: School provides individual computer/laptop

Admissions

Regular Application Deadline: 1/7

Early Action Deadline: 11/1

Fall Transfer Deadline: 7/15 (priority)

Spring Transfer Deadline: 11/15
 (priority)

Total # of Students Applied: 10,896
 Admitted: 5,781
 Enrolled: 1,557

Inside the Classroom

Villanova students tend to be extremely driven and career-oriented, so it's no surprise that Villanova's preprofessional colleges of commerce and finance, engineering, and nursing are all excellent. But the College of Liberal Arts and Sciences is Villanova's largest college, offering strong programs in political science, psychology, and communication, among others. The four undergraduate colleges offer a total of more than 40 majors.

No matter which undergraduate college they enroll in, all students leave Villanova with a solid liberal arts background. As a Catholic university in the Augustinian tradition, Villanova has a broad core curriculum, with required courses in foreign language, fine arts, history, literature, math, philosophy, theology, social sciences, and natural sciences. Additionally, all freshmen must take a two-semester, interdisciplinary Core Humanities Seminar.

The average class size at Villanova is 23 students, and a "really big" introductory lecture generally has fewer than 100 students. Working with a 13:1 student/faculty ratio, professors are described as "very accessible." The overall workload is "challenging but manageable," according to a young alumna.

Villanova offers several special academic options. The comprehensive, four-year Honors Program involves challenging seminars, research opportunities, and special cultural and social events. Freshmen also have the option of participating in a Learning Community, allowing you to form close friendships with your classmates as you live together and take the same Core Humanities Seminar.

Campus Environment

Over the past six years, Villanova has invested $200 million in campus construction and renovations. The residence halls are generally in good condition, but there aren't enough of them to go around. Most freshmen live in doubles in freshmen-only halls. A university official explains the overcrowding policy: "If freshmen 'tripling' is required, students are offered an opportunity to volunteer to be a part of triple housing for a discount in housing cost. If the number of volunteers does not meet the need of tripling, the University triples students according to their date of deposit, beginning with the latest pay dates, until all freshmen residents are accommodated." (Translation: Pay your housing fee ASAP!) Even though campus housing is guaranteed for three consecutive years, and four additional apartment buildings for upperclassmen were completed in 2000, most upperclassmen still move off-campus with a group of friends. Off-campus apartments are "easy to find" but tend to be expensive.

The beautiful 254-acre campus is located in a quiet, wealthy Philadelphia suburb. "There is a high level of safety on campus with public safety officers constantly patrolling the campus and dorms," says a recent grad. Freshmen and sophomores are not allowed to have cars on campus (unless they commute), but "cars are a necessity" for upperclassmen (although there are two commuter rail lines with stations on campus, plus the city bus and a campus shuttle for the immediate area). Interestingly, while guidance counselors seem to view Villanova's close proximity to Philly as a huge asset, we hear that many students rarely travel into the city.

Student Life

How big is basketball at Villanova? Huge. The Wildcats are NCAA tournament regulars, and students pack the arena at each and every game, home or away. Several players have gone on to the NBA, most notably New Jersey Nets center Kerry Kittles. The men's and women's track programs are also strong and have produced a number of Olympic medal winners. (Little-known fact: A Nova graduate or student has competed in every Olympics since 1948.) Villanova's huge sports complex allows all students to take part in a number of athletic and recreational activities. Intramurals are hot: 75 percent of the student body play at least one of Villanova's 24 IM sports.

Besides basketball, the "very active social life" at Villanova revolves mainly around fraternities and sororities. "There is always a party to go to or something to do every night of the week," a recent grad informs us. The Greek system draws large numbers of underclassmen—about 20 percent of the men and 30 percent of the women—although "many upperclassmen do not stick with their sorority or fraternity," says a former sorority member. Because many of the local bars are very strict about not serving minors, students (at least those without fake ID's) depend on off-campus parties to provide a steady flow of beer. "A lot of people drink here," one student admits. "It's a big activity." A young alum agrees that drinking is "pretty big," but adds that "people who do not drink are not looked down upon."

There's an admitted lack of diversity at Villanova—also known as "Vanillanova." Most students are Catholic, and many come from private or parochial high schools. The typical Novan could be described as "a preppy, upper-middle-class Caucasian who both drinks beer and attends church regularly," according to one source. A recent graduate offers us a similar (if less colorful) description: "a white, middle- to upper-class person who has grown up in the Northeast." However, she adds, "the school is working on becoming more diverse, and students are accepting [of differences]."

On the flip-side, the homogeneity leads to a very "friendly," close-knit student body. As one student says: "It's not too small, but it's small enough to participate in activities. Everyone has an opportunity to get involved." One of the most popular ways to get involved is through community service. Campus Ministry sponsors a wide array of programs, including Hunger Awareness Week, Best Buddies, Bigs and Littles, Service Break trips, and more. A school official boasts, "Villanova has the highest percentage of students, faculty, and staff involved in Habitat for Humanity than any other school in the country."

Even the university's biggest traditions and campus events tend to be service-oriented. Balloon Day—a fun annual event involving approximately 2,000 people—raises money for the poor in the Philadelphia area. Additionally, Villanova recently hosted one of the largest student-organized Special Olympics in the world, drawing thousands of volunteers and participants. An admissions official sums up: "Students who are involved—academically, with extracurricular activities, and with each other—would thrive at Villanova."

Other schools to check out: Bucknell, University of Scranton, Notre Dame, Boston College, Providence, Fairfield.

# of Students Waitlisted: 3,651
Students Accepting Place: 1,489
Waitlisted Students Admitted: 581

Test Scores (middle 50%):
SAT Verbal: 570–660
SAT Math: 590–690

HS Rank of Entering Freshmen:
Top 10%: 45%
Top 25%: 79%
Top 50%: 96%

Avg. HS GPA: 3.63

THE EXPERTS SAY...

" Villanova is a smart choice for students who are intellectually ambitious and socially aware (and are avid basketball fans!). "

" There's just not a lot of individuality or diversity in Villanova's image-conscious student body. "

Costs (2003–04)

Tuition and Fees: $26,223

Room & Board: $8,827

note: Figures represent "typical" tuition which varies by college and class year

Payment Plan(s): installment plan

Inst. Aid (est. 2003–04)

Institutional Aid, Need-Based: $30,591,607

Institutional Aid, Non-Need-Based: $3,256,379

FT Undergrads Receiving Aid: 46%
Avg. Amount per Student: $18,217

FT Undergrads Receiving Non-Need-Based Scholarship or Grant Aid: 5%
Avg. Amount per Student: $10,338

Of Those Receiving Any Aid:

Rec. Need-Based Scholarship or Grant Aid: 83%
Average Award: $11,669

Rec. Need-Based Self-Help Aid: 86%
Average Award: $5,743

Upon Graduation, Avg. Loan Debt per Student: $30,178

Financial Aid Deadline: 2/15

Graduates

Going to Graduate School: 28% Within One Year

Companies Recruiting On Campus: 400

Alumni Giving: 24%

VIRGINIA POLYTECHNIC INSTITUTE AND STATE UNIVERSITY

201 Burruss Hall, Blacksburg, VA 24061
Admissions Phone: (540) 231-6267 Fax: (540) 231-3679
Email: vtadmiss@vt.edu Website: www.admiss.vt.edu

General Info

Type of School: public, coed

Setting: rural

Academic Calendar: semester

Student Body

Full-Time Undergrads: 20,727
  Men: 59%, Women: 41%

Part-Time Undergrads: 616
  Men: 59%, Women: 41%

Total Undergrad Population:
  African American: 6%
  Asian American: 7%
  Latino: 2%
  Caucasian: 77%
  International: 3%
  Out-of-State: 27%
  Living Off-Campus: 61%
  In Fraternities: 13%
  In Sororities: 15%

Graduate and First-Professional
  Students: 4,083

Academics

Full-Time Faculty: 1,259
  With Ph.D.: 95%

Part-Time Faculty: 204

Student/Faculty Ratio: 16:1

Most Popular Majors:
  business
  engineering
  biology
  communication

Freshmen Retention Rate: 90%

Graduation Rates:
  42% within four years
  88% within six years

Computers: Computer Required

Admissions

Fall Transfer Deadline: 3/1

Spring Transfer Deadline: 10/1

Total # of Students Applied: 18,028
  Admitted: 12,387
  Enrolled: 4,837

# of Students Waitlisted: 600
  Students Accepting Place: 300

Costs (2004–5)

Tuition and Fees, In-State: $6,000

Tuition and Fees, Out-of-State:
  $15,934

Inside the Classroom

Students tell us that Virginia Tech is a "great school for the money," with an "excellent education" and a "great faculty." But some are perhaps rethinking this analysis, in light of recent budget cuts that forced the school to hike up tuition more than $5,000, eliminate over 150 teaching positions, and cut nearly 400 course selections. When all is said and done, though, Tech still has a whole lot to offer.

Undergraduate programs are offered through eight individual colleges: agricultural and life sciences, arts and sciences, engineering, human resources and education, architecture and urban studies, natural resources, veterinary medicine, and business. Guidance counselors rave about the "top-notch" engineering and science programs. The school is also known for its architecture and agriculture programs; other popular majors include computer science, biology, business, and communication studies, but you can really study just about anything here. Virginia Tech is one of two universities in the country (Texas A&M being the other) that offers the combined advantages of a military-style leadership development program and a traditional academic and social life through the Corps of Cadets.

With more than 20,000 undergrads and 60 bachelor's degree programs, Virginia Tech is the largest university in Virginia. Freshman classes are rather large, and the size of the school in general can be "overwhelming," warn guidance counselors. There's no hand-holding here, we're told—students need to be self-motivated in order to succeed. While Tech is among the top research institutions in the country, we've heard a few complaints that some professors are more interested in their research than in their students. But most undergrads we spoke to cite "high accessibility" to their professors. And one guidance counselor notes the unique combination of a "large student body [with] a small personal feeling."

The academics can be "challenging," depending on one's major. It's "very competitive in the engineering school," says one student. One chemical engineering major explains, "There are lots of brilliant kids there from all over. Tech is known for its engineering school, so that's what brings everyone in. Some of the classes are pretty intense." Another agrees, but with a caveat: "The workload is pretty rough, but there is plenty of time to have outside interests."

Campus Environment

The biggest complaint we heard from students: overcrowding. One excitable student described on-campus housing as "not available," adding, "This campus cannot support the demand for on-campus housing." (The school says they have accommodations for 8,900 students, so you do the math.) But one student reassures us, "All freshmen have to live on campus and are guaranteed a room." If you can get housing—"there are some nice dorms and some not-so-nice ones," according to a psych major—there are some interesting options. A junior describes a few: "The World, which hosts international students (and American students who want to live there); The Well, which promotes well being (no drugs or alcohol); The Leadership Community, which is a special program in which you live in a newer dorm (with a/c) and have to take a weekly leadership class; The Wing, which is a special program for freshmen orientation; and the women's engineering dorm." For the rest of the students, we're told that off-campus housing "is better because there is almost always availability." Also, "The cost is reasonable, and cheaper if you live here year-round."

Campus safety is described as "average"; one student tells us that Blacksburg is "pretty much a small college town that I feel incredibly safe in." Blacksburg is a small town, with "cute festivals every once in a while that make you forget you're at school," we're told. Most students walk around campus and town. "You really do not need a car if you are planning to stay in Blacksburg," a student says. "There is a bus system which drives around Blacksburg and also to various locales in Christiansburg." If you want to keep a car at Virginia Tech, prepare for some headaches. A forward-thinking junior tells us, "I think they'll build a parking garage or three soon, but right now, they keep taking spots away from the commuters (a.k.a. students) and giving them to faculty." Getting to class by car "really puts the commuters in a sticky situation, especially when parking tickets are $30 a piece."

Student Life

"Virginia Tech is trying to change the atmosphere and make it more diverse," says a student, "but right now a typical student would be a white male, preppy in style, with a middle-class background." Most students hail from Virginia, although one student says, "There are tons of students from various states such as Pennsylvania, New York, and New Jersey." A Virginia guidance counselor praises the school's change for the better, saying, "Their student population has become more diverse."

One student describes the campus atmosphere as "very friendly and welcoming, very safe, and can be rowdy at times but it usually never gets out of control." On weeknights, students "usually behave and spend time studying, hanging out with friends, or going to various meetings." Although there are "many parties, socials, and get-togethers, any day of the week," one student insists "a lot of studying goes on, all the time." Greek life plays the average big-university role: Joining a frat or sorority "is a good way for freshmen to meet people in a school this large," says a student, but it's not a necessity. As another student puts it, "[Greeks] affect only those who want to be affected."

Students here love outdoors activities; one guidance counselor—who points out that the "mountains and scenery are beautiful"—tells us that "everybody wants to go snowboarding and skiing." Also, we hear that "there are over 500 clubs and societies here, catering to every personality and lifestyle, from underwater polo to Latino dance clubs."

And then there's football. "Football is huge—definitely a football school. Basketball is somewhat popular but we are not very good," says one student. The school participates in the Big East Conference in NCAA Division I athletics. There are 11 men's and 10 women's varsity sports. And rooting for them is their adorable(?) turkey mascot, "Hokie Bird." Also, one student tells us, "Intramurals are big for frats and sororities."

Other schools to check out: James Madison, George Mason, West Virginia U, Texas A&M, Georgia Tech.

Room & Board: $4,084

Payment Plan(s): installment plan

Inst. Aid (2002–03)

Institutional Aid, Need-Based: $8,339,088

Institutional Aid, Non-Need-Based: $801,509

Upon Graduation, Avg. Loan Debt per Student: $17,453

Financial Aid Deadline: 3/1, 2/1 (priority)

THE EXPERTS SAY...

" Whether they come for the academics, the social life, or the football games, Virginia Tech students just love being here. "

" Some people call Blacksburg the Gravity Pit—once you get used to life at Tech, you might hardly wish to leave. "

WABASH COLLEGE

P.O. Box 352, Crawfordsville, IN 47933
Admissions Phone: (800) 345-5385; (765) 361-6225 Fax: (765) 361-6437
Email: admissions@wabash.edu
Website: www.wabash.edu

General Info

Type of School: private, all men

Setting: small town

Academic Calendar: semester

Student Body

Full-Time Undergrads: 857
  Men: 100%

Part-Time Undergrads: 1
  Men: 100%

Total Undergrad Population:
  African American: 8%
  Asian American: 3%
  Latino: 5%
  Native American: <1%
  Caucasian: 78%
  International: 4%
  Out-of-State: 27%
  Living Off-Campus: 1%
  In Fraternities: 62%

Academics

Full-Time Faculty: 86
  With Ph.D.: 93%

Part-Time Faculty: 2
  With Ph.D.: 50%

Student/Faculty Ratio: 10:1

Most Popular Majors:
  English (17%)
  history (12%)
  political science (11%)
  psychology (10%)
  biology (10%)

Completing 2 or More Majors: 13%

Freshmen Retention Rate: 87%

Graduation Rates:
  70% within four years
  75% within six years

Admissions

Regular Application Deadline: 12/14
  (priority)

Early Decision Deadline(s): 11/15

Early Action Deadline: 12/15

Fall Transfer Deadline: 12/15 (priority)

Total # of Students Applied: 1,299
  Admitted: 647
  Enrolled: 239

# of Students Waitlisted: 115
  Students Accepting Place: 76
  Waitlisted Students Admitted: 5

Applied Early Decision: 47
  Early Decision Admitted: 37

Inside the Classroom

Students at this all-male college are nothing if not hardworking and well-rounded. Prospective freshmen can look forward to a choice of 21 traditional liberal arts and sciences majors. Of these, the most popular with students are history, English, political science, economics, biology, psychology, and religion. Balance and breadth are provided through the college's stiff core curriculum: All students must demonstrate proficiency in literature and fine arts, a foreign language, behavioral sciences, natural science and mathematics, and quantitative studies. Freshmen choose a special tutorial from a list of interesting subjects, and sophomores take an interdisciplinary course in culture and tradition. "We study every night and every weekend," said one student. "That doesn't mean we don't have fun, but if the work isn't done before you slack off, you will get behind at Wabash."

One requirement that sets Wabash a notch above the ordinary school is a demanding oral and written comprehensive examination that students must pass before graduating. Another is the school's encouragement of original student research. "The opportunities are vast," says one public affairs official. "Students can research subjects collaboratively with faculty, and each year Wabash sponsors a Celebration of Student Research, Scholarship, and Creative Work, at which students present their work to an audience of students, faculty, staff, alumni, and trustees."

With a student/faculty ratio of 10:1, professors usually know all of their students by name, so be prepared to speak up. They're also easy to track down when they're needed . . . and often when they're not needed as well. "Most people have probably eaten a meal or had a beer with their professor," says one student.

Campus Environment

Fortunately, the environment at Wabash lends itself to this kind of intense academic study. The school's high endowment keeps facilities in prime condition; additions and renovations are commonplace, and construction of new buildings is moving at a steady rate. A brand-new Center for Inquiry in the Liberal Arts provides a place for various groups to gather for discussion, exploration, and research issues related to the liberal arts. New academic facilities for Wabash include a completely rebuilt Malcolm X Institute for Black Studies and a new science facility that includes flexible lecture and laboratory spaces, research labs adjacent to faculty offices, and a state-of-the-art infrastructure for modern science programs.

If a small school is your cup of tea, this is the place to go. With less than a thousand undergrads—way less—the faces become familiar very quickly, and getting around is easy. "You can walk around campus with no problem," says one student. "Most people use a car around town, but you can always carpool. I did for two years." Most of the academic and administrative buildings are arranged around the Mall, a central expanse of grass and trees that serves as the focal point of campus activity during the school year. All-campus cookouts, Frisbee, soccer, and the occasional baseball game are common Mall sights.

Housing options for students include four dormitories, fraternity houses, and off-campus housing. Freshmen are guaranteed a place to live on campus, where the rooms are adequate and high-tech: Each is wired with voicemail and at least two Ethernet connections to the campus computing system, and basic cable service is provided for all students.

Student Life

Central to the Wabash experience is what the school calls the "Gentleman's Rule." This dictates that all Wabash undergrads conduct themselves as gentlemen, both on and off campus. Wabash prides itself on shaping character and instilling students with a sense of responsibility—earning respect and guaranteed success go hand in hand. "Everything falls under that rule," says a speech major. "We're always expected to follow it." Having said that, the same student is also frank about what some consider fun. "Alcohol is everywhere at Wabash. Drugs aren't that big of a deal, but pot is fairly common in different circles." Perhaps it's a matter of interpretation.

Frats reign supreme at Wabash: Most of the students join one, and according to one political science major, "They're a huge portion of overall campus life. However, they're not the be-all and end-all. Popularity is based on who you are, not on what group you belong to." Things are certainly looking up for the frats right now: A school official reported that all nine of the college-owned fraternity facilities are undergoing expansion and renovation, with about $2 million being spent on each one.

The absence of the opposite sex doesn't seem to dampen the fun at Wabash. "Since we're an all-male school," one student explains, "most of the frats work with sororities at DePauw, Butler, and Purdue to throw big parties at least every other weekend." Another student chooses to look at the big picture, saying, "We are a college for men; that's not a sexist statement. I work for a domestic violence agency and am a strong feminist. The school simply recognizes what many women's colleges have also recognized: that single-sex education works."

If they're not partying, Wabash students are probably engaged in some kind of athletic activity; varsity teams have good track records, and the well-run intramural sports program consists of 23 teams. Students' enthusiasm for athletics culminates each November in the Bell Game, the big bout for the Monnon Bell waged annually between Wabash and DePauw University. Continuing for over 100 years, it's one of the nation's oldest and fiercest football rivalries. As one student explains, "If we lose every game in every sport but win that one, it's a winning season." If you attend the game, or one of Wabash's many homecoming events, you'll see how much pride Wabash students take in their school—a pride they express loudly but never crudely. After all, they are gentlemen.

Test Scores (middle 50%):
SAT Verbal: 520–625
SAT Math: 550–660
ACT Comp: 23–28
ACT English: 21–27
ACT Math: 24–29

HS Rank of Entering Freshmen:
Top 10%: 38%
Top 25%: 66%
Top 50%: 91%

Avg. HS GPA: 3.6

THE EXPERTS SAY...

" Wabash College is a small, close-knit community for men where high standards are set for both education and character. "

" All that hard work and gentlemanly behavior may earn you an A, but will it get you a date? "

Costs (2004–5)

Tuition and Fees: $22,275

Room & Board: $7,053

Payment Plan(s): installment plan, deferred payment plan, pre-payment plan

Inst. Aid (est. 2003–04)

Institutional Aid, Need-Based: $6,541,986

Institutional Aid, Non-Need-Based: $2,731,897

FT Undergrads Receiving Aid: 70%
Avg. Amount per Student: $19,944

FT Undergrads Receiving Non-Need-Based Scholarship or Grant Aid: 25%
Avg. Amount per Student: $11,261

Of Those Receiving Any Aid:

Rec. Need-Based Scholarship or Grant Aid: 99%
Average Award: $14,921

Rec. Need-Based Self-Help Aid: 94%
Average Award: $4,618

Upon Graduation, Avg. Loan Debt per Student: $17,818

Financial Aid Deadline: 3/1, 2/15 (priority)

Graduates

Going to Graduate School:
37% Within One Year

Accepting Job Offer:
38% at time of graduation

Companies Recruiting On Campus: 40

Alumni Giving: 78%

WAGNER COLLEGE

One Campus Road, Staten Island, NY 10301
Admissions Phone: (718) 390-3411; (800) 221-1010 (out-of-state) Fax: (718) 390-3105
Email: admissions@wagner.edu
Website: www.wagner.edu

General Info

Type of School: private, coed

Setting: urban

Academic Calendar: semester

Student Body

Full-Time Undergrads: 1,780
  Men: 41%, Women: 59%

Part-Time Undergrads: 46
  Men: 28%, Women: 72%

Total Undergrad Population:
  African American: 5%
  Asian American: 2%
  Latino: 5%
  Native American: <1%
  Caucasian: 81%
  International: 1%
  Out-of-State: 52%
  Living Off-Campus: 27%
  In Fraternities: 11%
  In Sororities: 14%

Graduate and First-Professional
  Students: 392

Academics

Full-Time Faculty: 92
  With Ph.D.: 97%

Part-Time Faculty: 94

Student/Faculty Ratio: 16:1

Most Popular Majors:
  business (20%)
  biological sciences (14%)
  psychology (11%)
  sociology (10%)
  theatre (10%)

Freshmen Retention Rate: 81%

Computers: Computer Required

Admissions

Regular Application Deadline: 3/15;
  2/15 (priority)

Early Decision Deadline(s): 12/1

Fall Transfer Deadline: 5/1, 4/1 (priority)

Spring Transfer Deadline: 12/1,
  10/15 (priority)

Total # of Students Applied: 2,425
  Admitted: 1,609
  Enrolled: 534

# of Students Waitlisted: 76
  Students Accepting Place: 52
  Waitlisted Students Admitted: 7

Inside the Classroom

With an undergraduate population of under 2,000 students, Wagner offers a cozy, intimate setting. Class sizes are small, with 20–25 students in a typical freshman class, and an overall student/faculty ratio of roughly 16:1. A high school guidance counselor recommends Wagner specifically for the "great personal attention" it offers. A senior agrees: "Professors are usually extremely accessible and willing to help in any way."

While many students choose to major in the sciences, business, or education, the theater and fine arts programs are also quite strong. Workload tends to vary by program. "Usually, classes aren't too competitive or difficult," says one student.

The Wagner Plan for the Practical Liberal Arts features the typical required courses (in writing, math, sciences, social sciences, and humanities and the arts), as well as classes in subject areas such as speech skills, computer proficiency and "intercultural understanding." The programs in the Wagner Plan are experiential in nature and serve to teach through both conventional and more contemporary strategies. The Learning Communities program combines two courses so that what students learn in one class relates directly to another, and is intended to help students explore the links between various subjects and between ideas and real life problem-solving. The Reflective Tutorial links coursework to experiences outside of the classroom, or "in the field." This may take the form of field trips, independent study, internships, volunteer work, community research, etc., and opportunities for such activities are obviously abundant in New York City. Guidance counselors approve of the way Wagner uses internships and career counseling to help prepare graduates for "the real world."

Campus Environment

The Wagner campus may in fact be more familiar to you than you realize. One senior majoring in theater tells us that "the Channel 7 Sky Cam is on top of Harbor View Hall," and that TV shows such as *The Education of Max Bickford*, and *The Sopranos* actually film on campus. This is most likely in no small part due to the sweeping views of the New York Harbor, the 105-acres of green campus, and older, refined buildings that all give the Wagner campus its flavor.

A New York high school guidance counselor praises the "homey atmosphere" on campus. There are three residential dorms with a certain amount of space reserved for upperclassmen and fraternity/sorority housing, and one of the three dorms has a minimum GPA requirement (3.0). The majority of students opt to remain in the dorms on campus throughout all four years, and housing is also available for graduate students. Generally, though, the good stuff (like suites or single rooms) are reserved for upperclassmen; one student tells us that rooms tend to "vary from on the small side to comfortable" and that "dorms are at maximum capacity with little room to move around in terms of roommate situations." There are apartments available to students for rent very close to campus, though they tend to be "a little on the expensive side."

As at all New York-area schools, the terrorist attacks of September 11, 2001 affected the Wagner campus greatly. "Many students saw the incident from their dorm room windows, while others had families and friends at the Trade Center or in the surrounding areas," a student informs us.

Though the school is relatively small, most students feel this offers a best-of-both-worlds type of scenario, with the thriving heart of Manhattan only 25 minutes away via the Staten Island Ferry. Wagner College is in the Grymes Hill section of Staten Island, an area that was at one time the stomping ground of some of the area's most influential and wealthy families, including the Vanderbilts and the Cunards. Though the Staten Island neighborhood has its fair share of bars, restaurants, clubs, movie theaters and a mall nearby, some students complain that "there's not all that much to do in the area." While many students do have cars on campus (and, incidentally, Wagner does not charge parking fees), having a car is not a necessity to get around town. Wagner provides a shuttle bus and van services that transport students between the school and the mall, the movies, churches, and the Staten Island Ferry, and there's always the extensive New York City public transportation services.

Student Life

Wagner welcomes students from over 30 states and 20 countries, and offers over 60 clubs and organizations. Community service is a big part of life at Wagner, and the Student Government Association encourages such activity by stipulating that each campus organization must sponsor two community service projects each semester. Past projects have benefited the Breast Cancer Awareness Fund, NYC Blood Drive, Adopt a Highway, and the homeless.

Greek life is popular with roughly 12 percent of men and just under 20 percent of women citing membership in the six fraternities and five sororities with chapters on campus. The Greeks have a fair amount of influence on campus due to their active participation in Student Government and through the various social and community events they sponsor, and they contribute greatly to the "big party atmosphere" on campus. One student says, "Greek organizations are always sponsoring parties in the surrounding bars. Fraternities are always throwing parties in the dorms."

While there hasn't always been major student support for sports, interest has increased in recent years, and the administration is quick to fund athletic events ("the administration doesn't like funding things that aren't sports-related," gripes a student). Wagner can now boast the Spiro Sports Center, which was completed in 1999. A dance team, a Fashion Show Committee (which organizes fashion shows as a Wagner fundraiser), and a radio station are all popular. The Student Activities Council arranges trips and outings that take advantage of all the best New York has to offer; past events have included trips to Broadway shows, Yankee and Mets games, various museums, Six Flags, and more. Wagner also has its own planetarium that is open to the public (by reservation only), and Wagner College Theatre puts on a number of quality plays and performances each school year. A student-run coffeehouse on campus is somewhat of a student hangout as well.

Other schools to check out: Drew, Manhattanville, Hobart and William Smith, Fordham, CUNY Baruch.

\# Applied Early Decision: 83
Early Decision Admitted: 29

Test Scores (middle 50%):
SAT Verbal: 515–590
SAT Math: 510–595
ACT Comp: 23–27

HS Rank of Entering Freshmen:
Top 10%: 11%
Top 25%: 51%
Top 50%: 92%

Avg. HS GPA: 88%

THE EXPERTS SAY...

" Experiential and integrative learning, plus Manhattan a ferry ride away, help prepare Wagner grads for the real world. Wagner is a great choice for students who want a personal, intimate college. "

" Get a 'practical liberal arts' education and front row seats to The Sopranos the next time they film on Wagner's campus. "

Costs (2004–5)

Tuition and Fees: $22,600

Room & Board: $7,300

Payment Plan(s): installment plan

Inst. Aid (est. 2003–04)

Institutional Aid, Need-Based:
$7,491,700

Institutional Aid, Non-Need-Based:
$3,668,901

FT Undergrads Receiving Aid: 63%
Avg. Amount per Student: $14,768

FT Undergrads Receiving Non-Need-Based Scholarship or Grant Aid: 26%
Avg. Amount per Student: $7,439

Of Those Receiving Any Aid:

Rec. Need-Based Scholarship or
Grant Aid: 98%
Average Award: $10,955

Rec. Need-Based Self-Help Aid: 77%
Average Award: $5,155

Upon Graduation, Avg. Loan Debt
per Student: $23,144

Financial Aid Deadline: 2/15 (priority)

Graduates

Alumni Giving: 23%

WAKE FOREST UNIVERSITY

P.O. Box 7305, Winston Salem, NC 27109
Admissions Phone: (336) 758-5201 Fax: (336) 758-4324
Email: admissions@wfu.edu Website: www.wfu.edu
Application Website: www.wfu.edu/admissions/

General Info

Type of School: private, coed
Setting: suburban
Academic Calendar: semester

Student Body

Full-Time Undergrads: 3,917
    Men: 48%, Women: 52%

Part-Time Undergrads: 91
    Men: 63%, Women: 37%

Total Undergrad Population:
    African American: 7%
    Asian American: 3%
    Latino: 2%
    Native American: <1%
    Caucasian: 87%
    International: 1%
    Out-of-State: 71%
    Living Off-Campus: 22%
    In Fraternities: 31%
    In Sororities: 53%

Graduate and First-Professional
    Students: 2,407

Academics

Full-Time Faculty: 434
    With Ph.D.: 90%

Part-Time Faculty: 107
    With Ph.D.: 62%

Student/Faculty Ratio: 10:1

Most Popular Majors:
    communication (12%)
    business (12%)
    political science (10%)
    psychology (9%)
    biology (8%)

Completing 2 or More Majors: 9%

Freshmen Retention Rate: 94%

Graduation Rates:
    77% within four years
    87% within six years
    note: 5-yr programs affect rates

Computers: School provides individual computer/laptop

Admissions

Regular Application Deadline: 1/15

Early Decision Deadline(s): 11/15

Total # of Students Applied: 5,752
    Admitted: 2,599
    Enrolled: 1,007

Inside the Classroom

Wake Forest is a relatively small university whose star has been rising faster than most schools in its league. Its academic programs have been gaining visibility in recent years, and the administration's plan of having the rest of the school share the spotlight of its basketball team is gradually coming to fruition.

Wake Forest's seven schools include two for undergraduates: the College of Arts and Sciences and the Calloway School of Business and Accountancy. Calloway's five-year program awards the B.S. and M.S. degrees in accounting, while the college's strongest B.A. degrees include biology, health and exercise science, communications, psychology, English, and political science.

All undergrads receive a solid, well-rounded liberal arts education because of the extensive core curriculum that takes about two years to fulfill. Requirements for all students include history, religion, and philosophy; literature; fine arts; social and behavioral sciences; natural sciences, math, and computer science; health and exercise science; writing; foreign languages; and a first-year seminar. A few WFU students petition for the open curriculum, but it's very difficult to get into the program.

Many students say the workload is tough. "I was not expecting the level of competition or the workload to be as high as it actually was," says one senior. "During the week, a lot of time is spent studying. The library has almost become a place to see and be seen." Another student, however, doesn't see the workload as too over-the-top. "If you're looking for a cutthroat, Duke atmosphere," he says, referring to North Carolina's other big-name university, "Wake Forest is not the place for you."

Campus Environment

If you visit Wake Forest, you might have to remind yourself that it's designated as a university. With a pretty, compact campus and small student population, it has the look and feel of a small liberal arts college. Wake undergrads rave about their "gorgeous" and "immaculate" grounds with their flower gardens, pockets of magnolias and pine trees, and stately Georgian brick buildings.

Construction on campus has added to the university's offerings, including the new Miller Center, which contains an academic service area, practice gyms, meeting and banquet rooms, and a fitness center. Classrooms in Greene Hall feature DVD video and other multimedia equipment for use by the Romance languages, German, Russian, and psychology departments. Recently completed projects include a major addition to Calloway Hall, renamed the Calloway Center, that added classroom space, meeting rooms, and a business incubator for the Calloway School of Business and Accountancy.

A wide range of housing options are available in Wake Forest's dorms, and the room specifications are described in extraordinary detail on the school's website (Need exact dimensions? Type of flooring? Window coverings? That's just the beginning). Most residence halls are coed by floor, with one dorm serving as an all-female option.

Townhouses and apartments are popular with juniors and seniors, while off-campus housing is always an option for those with the initiative to find it. "The cost of living in Winston is dirt cheap," says one sophomore. "There are a bunch of apartment complexes that cater to students. There are also houses for rent . . . they range in condition, but they're also cheap."

Student Life

Students report a decidedly Southern atmosphere at Wake Forest, even though many students hail from northern states and the Midwest. "Students tend to be extremely clean-cut and mainstream," says one junior. "If you're into any kind of 'alternative' lifestyle, I don't think Wake is for you." Another student was less exclusive, saying that people who are "completely comfortable with themselves and make an effort to seek out their interests will find at least a few others like them. It's all a matter of whether you enjoy being in the majority or can be comfortable as a minority."

Wake Forest has 13 fraternities and 9 sororities that pretty much rule the roost when it comes to the campus social life. Between 45 and 50 percent of students join the Greek system, and competition to get into houses is tough. "They have a huge influence on most of the school," one student says. "I think they're popular because Wake is cliquey. If you want to be involved in what most of the campus is doing, you should plan on rushing."

Once you've pledged, though, brace yourself for the usual sorts of Greek antics. One example of this is Vikingfest, a spectator event featuring a pitched battle fought by drunken Sigma Pi pledges with plastic weapons. According to one freshman quoted in the student newspaper, The Old Gold and Black, "It was hideous . . . I saw blood, puke, and gross boys in their underwear—disgusting."

The Wake Forest Demon Deacons play in NCAA Division I-A competition—in fact, they're the second-smallest school to do so. Sports for both sexes include basketball, soccer, cross country, track, tennis, and golf. Sports for men include football and baseball, while women can play volleyball and field hockey. Men's basketball grabs most of the limelight, winning its way into the postseason year after year. "Varsity sports at Wake are almost like their own fraternities and sororities," says one student. "They usually hang out with each other and have their own social scene."

Interesting school traditions include "rolling the quad," where the trees around the main quad are laced with toilet paper (or whatever else is at hand) after Demon Deacon victories. Another tradition is the annual Christmas Lovefeast and Candlelight Service in Wait Chapel—reportedly a standing-room-only event.

There's an extracurricular organization or club for just about everyone at Wake Forest. Some of the more interesting include the Demon Divas, an all-women a cappella group; Wake Radio and Wake TV for those interested in communications; and an aviation club. The university also sponsors movies, fairs, and band concerts for student enjoyment.

Other schools to check out: Vanderbilt, University of Richmond, Davidson, Rollins, Washington and Lee.

Applied Early Decision: 529
 Early Decision Admitted: 293

Test Scores (middle 50%):
 SAT Verbal: 610–690
 SAT Math: 630–700

HS Rank of Entering Freshmen:
 Top 10%: 65%
 Top 25%: 91%
 Top 50%: 98%

Costs (2004–5)

Tuition and Fees: $28,310

Room & Board: $8,000

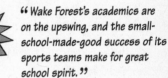

THE EXPERTS SAY...

" Wake Forest's academics are on the upswing, and the small-school-made-good success of its sports teams make for great school spirit. "

" The conservatism of the student body can be seen as its greatest strength or its greatest weakness. "

Inst. Aid (est. 2003–04)

Institutional Aid, Need-Based:
 $13,255,195

Institutional Aid, Non-Need-Based:
 $4,975,823

FT Undergrads Receiving Aid: 33%
 Avg. Amount per Student: $21,413

FT Undergrads Receiving Non-Need-Based Scholarship or Grant Aid: 30%
 Avg. Amount per Student: $10,201

Of Those Receiving Any Aid:

Rec. Need-Based Scholarship or Grant Aid: 96%
 Average Award: $15,699

Rec. Need-Based Self-Help Aid: 82%
 Average Award: $7,785

Upon Graduation, Avg. Loan Debt per Student: $24,549

Financial Aid Deadline: rolling, 3/1 (priority)

Graduates

Going to Graduate School:
 29% Within One Year

WARREN WILSON COLLEGE

P.O. Box 9000, Asheville, NC 28815-9000
Admissions Phone: (800) 934-3536 (out-of-state); (828) 771-2073 (in-state)
Fax: (828) 298-1440
Email: admit@warren-wilson.edu Website: www.warren-wilson.edu

General Info

Type of School: private, coed,
  Presbyterian
Setting: rural
Academic Calendar: semester

Student Body

Full-Time Undergrads: 772
  Men: 39%, Women: 61%

Part-Time Undergrads: 6
  Men: 50%, Women: 50%

Total Undergrad Population:
  African American: 1%
  Asian American: 1%
  Latino: 2%
  Caucasian: 90%
  International: 4%
  Out-of-State: 76%
  Living Off-Campus: 15%

Graduate and First-Professional
  Students: 66

Academics

Full-Time Faculty: 58
  With Ph.D.: 93%

Part-Time Faculty: 16
  With Ph.D.: 50%

Student/Faculty Ratio: 12:1

Most Popular Majors:
  environmental studies (21%)
  outdoor leadership (9%)
  human studies (9%)
  elementary education (8%)
  history/political science (8%)

Freshmen Retention Rate: 55%

Graduation Rates:
  33% within four years
  45% within six years

Admissions

Regular Application Deadline: 3/15

Early Decision Deadline(s): 11/15

Fall Transfer Deadline: 3/15 (priority)

Total # of Students Applied: 753
  Admitted: 595
  Enrolled: 229

Waitlist Available

Applied Early Decision: 78
  Early Decision Admitted: 69

Inside the Classroom

At Warren Wilson, students use their hands as much as their heads. As one of just a few schools in the country with a student–work approach, the students perform almost all the daily tasks needed to operate the college. Originally named the Asheville Farm School, it was later renamed for a Presbyterian missionary who strove to improve the quality of rural life. Today, though it welcomes a diversity of religious perspectives, the school's strong work ethic and community service orientation hasn't changed. Students who go here thrive on the diversity and hands-on activities the school gives them—that is, a nontraditional, vibrant, holistic experience. One Georgia guidance counselor says that in spite of the small size, Warren Wilson has an attractive mix of education, work, and community service, all on a beautiful campus.

Warren Wilson offers bachelor degree programs in the basic areas of liberal arts, and a master of fine arts in creative writing. Environmental studies is its most popular major, followed by English, art, outdoor leadership, and biology. The environmental studies curriculum was recently expanded to include environmental policy, forest resource management, conservation, and sustainable agriculture. Not much about the school could be described as typical. Some of the more unusual programs include Discovery through Wilderness and Peace Studies. In the WorldWide program, every student is given the opportunity to study overseas for a minimal cost. First-Year Seminars include topics such as "Mythic Maps of the Cherokee" and "Around the World Wide Web in 40 Days." Students have easy access to professors, and relations are "very informal, with [professors] often having classes over to their homes for dinner." Not surprisingly, creative projects are encouraged, and projects and papers are stressed more than tests.

At Warren Wilson, students must work 15 hours per week; in exchange, they earn around $2,500 a year, credited toward tuition. "Work" here means actual physical labor, such as bringing compost to the organic garden, working as a carpenter, or chopping firewood. Though upperclassmen get first pick of the tasks, all students appreciate the group effort: "Even if they don't love their jobs, they love working, and are proud of the things they've built and the food they produce," explains one global studies major. In addition to the on-campus work, students must also put in 100 hours of community service throughout their four years.

Campus Environment

Students who come to Warren Wilson love the outdoors. The campus is in a rural valley between the Blue Ridge and Great Smoky Mountains. Over 1,000 acres total, the campus includes a working farm, mountain forest, and an organic garden. Hiking trails cut across the campus, as does the Swannanoa River. In spite of the seeming isolation of the campus, students can travel just 15 minutes to Asheville, the largest city in western North Carolina, where they'll find thrift stores, arts and crafts shops, cafés, theaters, and music clubs. According to one junior, Asheville is a "a very artsy city. Lots of bands come through here and there is of course the traditional Appalachian arts and music all around."

On-campus community is very important to Wilson students: Students love the multigenerational feel of the campus, which has lots of small kids and retired volunteers around. Many faculty and staff live on campus. "We like that it's a quirky school and you see things here that would never happen anywhere else," explains one student. There are nine residence halls: Most are coed, though as there are more women than men here (the official breakdown is around 60 percent women), there are two women's dorms, and one men's dorm. We hear from one student that except for the newer ones, the dorms are "a complete wreck." The Wellness Dorm is totally substance and smoke free, and there is also an Ecodorm with an energy-efficient building design.

Student Life

A junior gives a colorful description of the atmosphere at Warren Wilson: "If you like the city, you won't like it here. If you don't like to get dirty, and have hang-ups about hygiene, you also might not like it. If you are conservative, if you voted for Bush, if you think non-Christians are going to hell, if you are planning on ever joining the armed forces, you'll certainly stick out here, though I can think of people who fit all of these categories and are totally happy."

Wilson isn't your typical college experience. On campus, there are no sororities, no fraternities, no football team. There's no rowdy college town next door. There's partying, yes, and it's not always mellow, but typically, poetry reading, contra dancing, and open mic nights make the evening headlines. Instead of bars and clubs, there are coffeehouses, a drum club, and even a meditation hut in the woods (designed and constructed by students, of course). On weekends you can pretty much roll out of bed and onto a mountain bike—or lace up your boots for a hike. While the environment here is too laid-back for any overt peer pressure to do drugs, there is a lot of pot smoking and a fair amount of experimentation with hard drugs. "Though there are all types of students here, we're seen by outsiders as being a school of 'dirty hippies,'" notes one student.

As it's a very safe campus, administrators "tend to look the other way when broken rules are not causing a safety problem. Politics tend to be to the left here, and environmentalism, to one degree or another, is almost universal." One complaint we hear from students is the lack of minority groups in the study body. And though the school is officially Presbyterian—with Presbyterian students the most active—many students "are generally wary of organized religion, and explore other spiritual paths, such as eastern philosophies."

In keeping with the unorthodox philosophy of the school, the athletics program at Wilson is similarly untraditional. As a leader in outdoor adventure sports, the school conducts joint programs with the state's Outward Bound School, which has its home on the edge of campus. By far the biggest sport is whitewater paddling, followed by mountain biking and Ultimate Frisbee. No athletic scholarships are offered, and the school is just applying for Division III membership. On-campus facilities include a gym, a basketball court, a pool, tennis courts, and a weight room.

Other schools to check out: Berea, Guilford, Antioch, Earlham, Marlboro.

Test Scores (middle 50%):
SAT Verbal: 550–670
SAT Math: 500–620

HS Rank of Entering Freshmen:
Top 10%: 20%
Top 25%: 48%
Top 50%: 73%

Avg. HS GPA: 3.33

THE EXPERTS SAY...

" Warren Wilson offers some truly innovative programs in a unique, hands-on environment. This school's not for everyone, but free spirits can thrive here. "

" A chance to earn your college degree in a hippie commune at practically no cost. Cool. "

Costs (2003–04)

Tuition and Fees: $16,674

Regional or 'good neighbor' tuition available for NC residents

Room & Board: $5,120

Payment Plan(s): installment plan

Inst. Aid (est. 2003–04)

Institutional Aid, Need-Based: $2,281,776

Institutional Aid, Non-Need-Based: $352,692

FT Undergrads Receiving Aid: 52%
Avg. Amount per Student: $12,695

FT Undergrads Receiving Non-Need-Based Scholarship or Grant Aid: 4%
Avg. Amount per Student: $1,664

Of Those Receiving Any Aid:

Rec. Need-Based Scholarship or Grant Aid: 92%
Average Award: $7,372

Rec. Need-Based Self-Help Aid: 96%
Average Award: $5,010

Upon Graduation, Avg. Loan Debt per Student: $14,407

Financial Aid Deadline: rolling, 4/1 (priority)

Graduates

Companies Recruiting On-Campus: 60

Alumni Giving: 34%

WASHINGTON AND LEE UNIVERSITY

Office of Admissions, Washington and Lee University, Lexington, VA 24450-0303
Admissions Phone: (540) 458-8710 Fax: (540) 458-8639
Email: admissions@wlu.edu Website: www.wlu.edu
Application Website: admissions.wlu.edu/app/

General Info

Type of School: private, coed

Setting: small town

Academic Calendar: undergraduate is 4-4-2; law is early semester

Student Body

Full-Time Undergrads: 1,738
  Men: 52%, Women: 48%

Part-Time Undergrads: 2 Women: 100%

Total Undergrad Population:
  African American: 4%
  Asian American: 2%
  Latino: 1%
  Native American: <1%
  Caucasian: 88%
  International: 5%
  Out-of-State: 85%
  Living Off-Campus: 37%
  In Fraternities: 75%
  In Sororities: 70%

Graduate and First-Professional Students: 397

Academics

Full-Time Faculty: 202
  With Ph.D.: 91%

Part-Time Faculty: 1

Student/Faculty Ratio: 11:1

Most Popular Majors:
  business administration (11%)
  politics (10%)
  economics (9%)
  history (9%)
  journalism (7%)

Completing 2 or More Majors: 21%

Freshmen Retention Rate: 95%

Graduation Rates:
  85% within four years
  88% within six years

Admissions

Regular Application Deadline: 1/15

Early Decision Deadline(s): 12/1

Fall Transfer Deadline: 4/1

Spring Transfer Deadline: 11/1

Total # of Students Applied: 3,185
  Admitted: 998
  Enrolled: 453

Inside the Classroom

Washington and Lee University is steeped in history. Named for both George Washington and Robert E. Lee (who served as president of the university immediately after the Civil War), the 250-year-old school offers about 40 majors and 900 undergraduate courses. The school has three divisions: The College; The Williams School of Commerce, Economics, and Politics; and the School of Law. Liberal arts are strong in all areas, especially economics, English, and journalism. Students intent on professional careers often enroll in The Williams School, which provides them with an educational background that would impress many a prospective employer.

General education courses at Washington and Lee take up about a third of the graduation requirements and include English composition, foreign language, literature, humanities, science and mathematics, social sciences, as well as physical education. If you have a water phobia, beware: The phys ed requirements include passing a swimming test.

Washington and Lee has a very strong faculty and small classes. All courses are taught by professors—never teaching assistants or grad students. The student/faculty ratio of 11:1 means that professors are very accessible. "Professors know you by name— some even call you at home if you don't show up to class to make sure you are okay," says a grateful business student. She adds that the academics are "rigorous but not overwhelming… You have to work hard to get an A." A neuroscience major says that "the workload is neverending."

Semesters run on an unusual 4-4-2 calendar consisting of fall and winter terms of 12 weeks, followed by a 6-week spring term. During the spring term, students take only one or two courses, often in a nontraditional field, or use the time for study abroad or internships.

Campus Environment

Washington and Lee has a picturesque campus of white columns and ivy-covered red brick buildings. Located on 50 acres in Lexington, Virginia, in the heart of the Shenandoah Valley, the main campus is surrounded by an additional 300 acres of mostly wooded area where students enjoy jogging and mountain biking.

"On-campus housing is average in comfort for freshmen, above average for sophomores," comments a sophomore. Many freshmen live in single rooms. Students are required to live on campus for two years; most males live in fraternity houses their sophomore year, females live in sorority houses or in campus apartments or suite-style dorms. Off-campus housing is popular for juniors and seniors. There are houses in town and out in the "country" and apartments above stores and in small complexes. The off-campus houses (with names like Pole House, County Seat, Amityville, The Bordello) host parties frequently.

The student-administered honor system is perhaps Washington and Lee's most striking feature. It was established by no less than Robert E. Lee himself and it has been credited with fostering a community of trust between students, faculty, and administrators. The honor system is taken very seriously here and has exactly one penalty: If you have one indictment brought against you for lying, cheating or stealing, you are expelled. The honor system "allows students to take take-home tests and schedule their own exams (it is unbelievable how much of an advantage this can be)," says a student. Doors can be left unlocked and laptops safely placed wherever you so choose. The library assigns each student their own study carrel where they are allowed to leave their books, computer, etc., for the entire year.

Another tradition that makes the Washington and Lee campus a friendly place to be is "the speaking tradition." Students are urged to greet each other and faculty as they pass by on campus. "Whenever I walk down the colonnade or Stemmons Plaza, I can expect to encounter at least ten people that I either say hello to or have a quick conversation with before heading off to class," reports a student.

Student Life

A Washington and Lee student sums up her school: "W&L is a 'work hard, play hard' school. Schoolwork takes priority during the week, but weekends are all play." For the majority of Washington and Lee students, the social scene revolves entirely around the 15 fraternities and the 5 sororities. Most frat parties are open to all, and there is never a charge to get in. "Alcohol is present at generally every off-campus and fraternity party; however, there is definitely a population of W&L students that do not drink and still go out to these parties," says a junior. Most students will party-hop and attend parties at several places each night. "Wednesday nights tend to be nights when there are a lot of parties so students try not to schedule Thursday morning classes," a student confides.

A senior describes the student body: "The typical student attended a private school or a good suburban public school, drives an SUV, shops at J. Crew, wears khakis or pearls, joins a fraternity or sorority, studies hard, drinks a lot, goes on lavish vacations over school breaks. The typical student is friendly, volunteers in the community, is ambitious, voted for Bush, and LOVES Washington and Lee." Even a college official admits, "Some perceive a benefit for coming from politically conservative or upper-middle socio-economic backgrounds."

Popular clubs and extracurricular activities include Nabors Service League (community service), Outing Club, the Generals' Christian Fellowship (GCF), and Habitat for Humanity. Washington and Lee offers 12 varsity men's teams, 10 varsity teams for women and one coed varsity sport (horseback riding). Lacrosse is the sport of choice, but football also draws a decent crowd. Tennis and track are also strong.

There are several dressy date weekends each year, such as Christmas Weekend and Homecoming. These festivities are all sponsored by the fraternities. Everybody loves to get dressed up, and semiformal cocktail parties at the frat houses are commonplace. The biggest date weekend of the year is Fancy Dress Ball in March, consisting of several days of parties and dances culminating in a formal ball for which students dress up in their most dashing formal wear.

Students also organize a realistic presidential nominating convention every four years, in the year of the presidential election, before any actual primaries take place. Students represent the U.S. states and territories in the Mock Convention of the party currently out of the White House. Among the presidents who have spoken at Mock Convention are Harry Truman, Richard Nixon, Jimmy Carter, and Bill Clinton.

Other schools to check out: Davidson, Centre, U of the South, Vanderbilt, Wake Forest.

# of Students Waitlisted: 625
Students Accepting Place: 250
Waitlisted Students Admitted: 34

Applied Early Decision: 426
Early Decision Admitted: 230

Test Scores (middle 50%):
SAT Verbal: 650–720
SAT Math: 650–720
ACT Comp: 28–31

HS Rank of Entering Freshmen:
Top 10%: 78%
Top 25%: 95%
Top 50%: 100%

THE EXPERTS SAY...

" W&L offers outstanding academics and a caring faculty in a tradition-rich environment. Southerners should also look at the University of the South, Davidson, and Vanderbilt. "

" The Confederacy isn't dead! Well, actually, it is: Robert E. Lee, his family, and his horse, Traveller, are all buried on the W&L campus. "

Costs (2003–04)

Tuition and Fees: $23,295
Room & Board: $6,368

Inst. Aid (2002–03)

Institutional Aid, Need-Based: $5,331,854

Institutional Aid, Non-Need-Based: $3,175,651

FT Undergrads Receiving Aid: 27%
Avg. Amount per Student: $16,928

FT Undergrads Receiving Non-Need-Based Scholarship or Grant Aid: 22%
Avg. Amount per Student: $8,162

Of Those Receiving Any Aid:

Rec. Need-Based Scholarship or Grant Aid: 72%
Average Award: $14,773

Rec. Need-Based Self-Help Aid: 45%
Average Award: $4,900

Upon Graduation, Avg. Loan Debt per Student: $15,634

Financial Aid Deadline: 2/1 (priority)

Graduates

Going to Graduate School: 22% Within One Year

Companies Recruiting On Campus: 42

Alumni Giving: 83%

WASHINGTON UNIVERSITY IN ST. LOUIS

Campus Box 1089, One Brookings Drive, St. Louis, MO 63130-4899
Admissions Phone: (800) 638-0700; (314) 935-6000 Fax: (314) 935-4290
Email: admissions@wustl.edu Website: admissions.wustl.edu

General Info

Type of School: private, coed

Setting: suburban

Academic Calendar: semester

Student Body

Full-Time Undergrads: 5,868
  Men: 48%, Women: 52%

Part-Time Undergrads: 365
  Men: 47%, Women: 53%

Total Undergrad Population:
  African American: 9%
  Asian American: 9%
  Latino: 3%
  Caucasian: 66%
  International: 4%
  Out-of-State: 89%
  Living Off-Campus: 20%
  In Fraternities: 25%
  In Sororities: 25%

Graduate and First-Professional
  Students: 5,832

Academics

Full-Time Faculty: 837
  With Ph.D.: 99%

Part-Time Faculty: 263

Student/Faculty Ratio: 7:1

Most Popular Majors:
  biology
  business/finance
  engineering
  English
  psychology

Freshmen Retention Rate: 97%

Admissions

Regular Application Deadline: 1/15

Early Decision Deadline(s): 11/15, 1/1

Fall Transfer Deadline: 4/15

Spring Transfer Deadline: 11/15

Total # of Students Applied: 20,378
  Admitted: 4,080
  Enrolled: 1,367

Waitlisted Students Admitted: 29

Test Scores (middle 50%):
  SAT Verbal: 650–730
  SAT Math: 670–750
  ACT Comp: 29–33
  ACT English: 29–34
  ACT Math: 29–34

Inside the Classroom

When we asked a sophomore at Washington University in St. Louis to describe her fellow students, she replied simply, "Everybody is premed." This claim is not a gross exaggeration: A large number of Wash U students study hard to go to medical school, and an impressive number get accepted each year. Premed students benefit from the numerous research opportunities and fellowships connected with the Washington University School of Medicine—consistently ranked among the top 10 medical schools in the nation.

Wash U offers more than 80 majors in five undergraduate schools: arts and sciences; engineering and applied science; business; art; and architecture. "The quality of programs keeps improving!" exclaims an Indiana high school guidance counselor. Premed is not the only preprofessional route that's popular here; the business and finance programs are very strong, and Wash U has "the best engineering school in Missouri," according to another guidance counselor.

"Well-rounded" is an apt description of the undergraduate curriculum (and the undergrads themselves) at Wash U. A Tennessee guidance counselor approves of the fact that Wash U "emphasizes writing in every department," adding that "engineers get a liberal arts education." Students are actively encouraged to explore their interests; double majors and interdisciplinary programs are quite common here, and changing your major, even from one school to another, is not difficult. All students must take courses in English, humanities, math, science, and social science. Students claim that these distribution requirements are not difficult to fulfill, leaving students with plenty of time to devote to more "serious" courses in their majors.

"The academic atmosphere is intense," admits a senior arts and sciences student. A sophomore double-majoring in Italian and environmental science warns, "People who do not want to work hard and study would not fit in, because the professors expect you to work, and the students do." In preparation for graduate or professional schools, students study like fiends and are very concerned about their grades. A senior double-majoring in anthropology and environmental studies reveals, "In the natural sciences, students are made to compete for grades in order to 'weed out' some individuals." (However, students in the liberal arts are said to be much less competitive.)

While some students complain that professors are involved in their own research and can be inaccessible or remote, others explain that the professors are more than willing to help if you seek them out. And students can gain invaluable experience by working closely with professors on research projects, which are available in all disciplines.

Campus Environment

Located in a suburban section of St. Louis, Washington University's Colonial and Gothic buildings and flower-lined courtyards make for an idyllic, picture-perfect campus. "Not seeing somebody wrestling or playing frisbee in the Quad on a sunny day in between or after classes would be shocking," says a senior. Students say they feel "pretty safe" both on and off campus (though some neighborhoods near campus are said to be safer than others).

KAPLAN

While the university takes great pride in its research facilities, a student double-majoring in political science and Spanish complains to us that "resources are not divided evenly among the five schools." But all students will benefit from the major renovations at the Olin Library, which have added 17,000 square feet and created a cybercafé and 24-hour study space.

All freshmen must live on campus (unless you live with family within a 25-mile radius). Freshmen have the choice of living in a single or double in freshmen-only dorms. "On-campus housing is pretty good—definitely a worthwhile experience," says one senior. Another senior states, "As a result of the recent on-campus development and construction, the on-campus housing situation is wonderful. However, if you get put in an older dorm, get ready for small rooms." The university guarantees housing for all four years, which includes on-campus suites, apartments, and frat houses (there's no sorority housing), or university-owned off-campus housing. Small-group, special-interest housing is also very popular.

Freshmen are not allowed to keep cars on campus. A sophomore reassures us: "It is possible to walk many places off campus, and the school provides a shuttle to the mall, Target, the grocery store, Washington Medical School, off-campus housing, and a few other places." Another student tells us that "the Loop"—with its "bars, boutiques, restaurants, concert halls, music stores, and fruit markets"—is the most popular place for students to go.

Student Life

Wash U students describe themselves as "smart," "mature," friendly," and "very involved in extracurricular activities." A senior goes into detail: "The typical student at Wash U is upper-middle class, usually white, usually aware of public issues, but not very [politically] active." But given its Midwestern location, the student population is surprisingly diverse in terms of geography and ethnicity. "Diversity is a big theme on campus and tolerance is prevalent," agrees a student. Environmentalists on campus are fairly vocal, but there's generally not much activist activity, and the administration is quick to address student concerns.

"During the week, students will often study, work at a job, work in a lab, or play sports in the quad," says one student. "Weeknights are often for homework, socializing, and club meetings." Another student agrees: "It is not typical for students to go off-campus during the week." Thursday through Saturday nights, students (if they're not still studying) might head over to "the row"—the strip of fraternity houses where "there's always a party." Approximately one-third of the student body goes Greek ("if you are not Greek, you are not automatically a geek," a student rhymes), but many frat parties are open to the whole campus. However, one student warns that you "should not expect big, state-school partying when applying." Another student assures us that "it is fine to go to the parties and not drink." Many students also go to smaller gatherings in suites and off-campus apartments.

A few major events bring all the students together, including WILD, an outdoor party with a live band, and the annual student-run carnival. Intramural sports are very popular (75 percent of students participate); a student tells us that "participation is so large that multiple levels/divisions have been created to accommodate different athletic abilities." Volleyball seems to be the most popular of Washington's Division III athletics.

Costs (2004–05)

Tuition and Fees: $30,546

Room & Board: $9,640

Payment Plan(s): installment plan, pre-payment plan

Inst. Aid (est. 2003–04)

Institutional Aid, Need-Based: $44,702,485

Institutional Aid, Non-Need-Based: $6,566,516

THE EXPERTS SAY...

" Most top students—preprofessional or not—have a variety of interests and talents. Washington University understands and encourages this. "

" For those who really enjoy pulling all-nighters—almost every night. "

FT Undergrads Receiving Aid: 45%
Avg. Amount per Student: $24,461

FT Undergrads Receiving Non-Need-Based Scholarship or Grant Aid: 14%
Avg. Amount per Student: $9,231

Of Those Receiving Any Aid:

Rec. Need-Based Scholarship or Grant Aid: 99%
Average Award: $19,641

Rec. Need-Based Self-Help Aid: 78%
Average Award: $7,166

Financial Aid Deadline: 2/15

Graduates

Going to Graduate School: 33% Within One Year

Accepting Job Offer: 62% at time of graduation

Companies Recruiting On Campus: 360

WELLESLEY COLLEGE

106 Central Street, Wellesley, MA 02481
Admissions Phone: (781) 283-2270 Fax: (781) 283-3678
Email: admissions@wellesley.edu Website: www.wellesley.edu
Application Website: www.wellesly.edu/Admission/application.html

General Info

Type of School: private, all women
Setting: suburban
Academic Calendar: semester

Student Body

Full-Time Undergrads: 2,215
    Women: 100%

Part-Time Undergrads: 76
    Men: 32%, Women: 68%

Total Undergrad Population:
    African American: 6%
    Asian American: 26%
    Latino: 5%
    Native American: <1%
    Caucasian: 46%
    International: 8%
    Out-of-State: 83%
    Living Off-Campus: 6%

Academics

Full-Time Faculty: 221
    With Ph.D.: 99%

Part-Time Faculty: 99
    With Ph.D.: 90%

Student/Faculty Ratio: 9:1

Most Popular Majors:
    economics (12%)
    psychology (12%)
    English (10%)
    political science (9%)
    French (7%)

Completing 2 or More Majors: 32%

Freshmen Retention Rate: 95%

Graduation Rates:
    86% within four years
    91% within six years

Admissions

Regular Application Deadline: 1/15

Early Decision Deadline(s): 11/1

Fall Transfer Deadline: 2/10

Spring Transfer Deadline: 11/15

Total # of Students Applied: 3,434
    Admitted: 1,394
    Enrolled: 591

# of Students Waitlisted: 780
    Students Accepting Place: 352
    Waitlisted Students Admitted: 93

Applied Early Decision: 180
    Early Decision Admitted: 123

Inside the Classroom

As one of the remaining Seven Sisters, Wellesley College draws some of the country's most intelligent and motivated women, many of whom go on to impressive professional careers. "I have yet to meet a Wellesley alum (and I'm not just talking about the famous ones) who has not done something really admirable since she graduated," a student says. Just a few of Wellesley's prominent alumnae: Senator Hillary Clinton, journalist Diane Sawyer, former Secretary of State Madeleine Albright, and screenwriter/producer Nora Ephron.

Students are not coddled at Wellesley, but are treated with respect by the faculty and administration. The Wellesley Honor Code allows students to enjoy self-scheduled exams, guests in the residence halls, open-stack libraries, and full use of college resources. But with respect comes heavy responsibility and competition: The academic programs at Wellesley are notoriously tough, and some students find the "catty" atmosphere intimidating. "The academic environment is quite competitive, although students are very focused on their own endeavors," says a senior. "Everyone here is an overachiever. We all pay excessive attention to detail and care a great deal about our work (whether some of us like to admit that is a different question)." Indeed, she continues, this is not a school for everyone: "Someone who cannot comprehend staying in her room one weekend to finish a paper or prepare for a class may not be comfortable here." Many students reportedly consider transferring after their first semester or year. However, by sophomore year, "most students love it!"

While Wellesley's liberal arts and interdepartmental programs are all strong, those in the social and natural sciences are the real standouts. A high percentage of students are accepted into medical, graduate, and law school each year. Professors, not TAs, teach courses. And with around 20 students per class and an incredible student/faculty ratio of 9:1, Wellesley women get tons of individual attention. Not necessarily the "touchy-feely, eat-dinner-at-my-prof's-house" kind of interaction found at other small liberal arts colleges, but a kind of interaction ambitious Wellesley students value even more: professional support. Many students work closely with faculty in independent projects or tutorials in a particular subject of interest. Wellesley alumnae often say that their professors were key in helping them land good jobs and grad school placements.

Wellesley administers programs in Aix-en-Provence, France, and Konstanz, Germany, and has an assortment of other international exchange programs available. Students may also register at nearby colleges, taking advantage of other schools' strengths, such as enrolling in engineering courses at MIT. Wellesley is also part of the Twelve College Exchange program, which allows students to enroll for a semester or year at other top liberal arts colleges such as Amherst and Vassar.

Campus Environment

A student sums up the beautiful Wellesley campus: "We have great facilities, great living situations, beautiful academic buildings, great science equipment. As a student I have felt 'wealthy.'" The lush 500-acre campus situated on Lake Waban, with its "typical New England–style" architecture, is truly one of the loveliest in the country.

(You can view the campus in the recent Julia Roberts picture *Mona Lisa Smile*.) Wellesley women take advantage of well-stocked libraries, a recently built theater, a greenhouse, several cutting-edge science and computer centers, an art museum, and a beautiful sports center.

The dormitories, most of which have been renovated recently, are charming and comfortable; many have common rooms for hanging out. All classes live together; freshmen generally have up to three roommates, while most juniors and seniors have single rooms. Though some complain the rooms are small, one student says, "We are definitely spoiled in terms of living space. Sometimes I think students here fail to appreciate how nice our living conditions are." Students actually enjoy the food and appreciate the availability of the kosher and vegetarian dining halls.

The campus is extremely secure, and students feel comfortable walking around campus at all hours. Students strongly suggest having a car to get around off campus; however, there is a shuttle that regularly runs back and forth to Boston. The upscale town of Wellesley doesn't have many shopping or entertainment options for students, but there are stores, restaurants, and the Natick Mall nearby on Route 9.

Student Life

"Most people find their own niche at Wellesley, and the friends you make become a second family because they share your beliefs and interests in a way that no one really has before," gushes one student. "In general, the women here are considerate and care about one another." A few students describe the atmosphere as "incredibly supportive," but others call it "cliquey." While most students have money and tend to be liberal (and "very opinionated," we hear), there is an unusually large minority population. Wellesley, argues one student, "is one of the most diverse campuses in the country."

Students stress the fact that "you have to make an effort to have a social life." "There's definitely not a wild on-campus social life," comments one student. The social scene for those who stick close to home is quiet and often dull, some complain. Others seem to enjoy the quiet atmosphere, which is conducive to studying. "There are occasional times when one has to forgo socializing and put work first," a senior points out. There's usually some form of campus entertainment such as movies, plays, and concerts. For those who want to party and meet men, Boston—with its hundreds of colleges—is only half an hour away. On weekends, many students head off campus to clubs and parties at neighboring schools, though one student jokes, "Most students go once [to an MIT frat] and never return to frat row again."

As for extracurricular activities, there's no shortage of clubs and organizations, including several elite "societies" for art, music, literature, and other similar interests. Wellesley offers 12 varsity sports; a student says, "Though sports events are not heavily attended, the athletes we have are very passionate about what they do, and our teams are quite successful." Several Wellesley events and traditions spark pride in the school and bring students closer together. On Flower Sunday, each entering first-year student is given flowers by her "big sister." Each May, graduating seniors hold a hoop-rolling race to determine who will be the first person in her class to achieve success; the winner gets tossed into the lake.

Other schools to check out: Smith, Bryn Mawr, Mount Holyoke, Vassar, Wesleyan.

THE EXPERTS SAY...

" If you're a strong young woman who thrives under pressure, a Wellesley education will help you accomplish great things in life. "

" Too often, Wellesley students don't take time to stop and smell the roses. (In fact, they'd be more likely to spend all night doing research on roses and then protest the fact that all roses are not represented equally on campus.) "

WESLEYAN UNIVERSITY

70 Wyllys Avenue, Middletown, CT 06459
Admissions Phone: (860) 685-3000 Fax: (860) 685-3001
Email: admissions@wesleyan.edu
Website: www.wesleyan.edu

General Info

Type of School: private, coed

Setting: small town

Academic Calendar: semester

Student Body

Full-Time Undergrads: 2,704
  Men: 47%, Women: 53%

Part-Time Undergrads: 26
  Men: 31%, Women: 69%

Total Undergrad Population:
  African American: 8%
  Asian American: 8%
  Latino: 6%
  Native American: <1%
  Caucasian: 62%
  International: 6%

Graduate and First-Professional
  Students: 491

Academics

Full-Time Faculty: 329
  With Ph.D.: 93%

Part-Time Faculty: 33
  With Ph.D.: 61%

Student/Faculty Ratio: 9:1

Freshmen Retention Rate: 95%

Graduation Rates:
  84% within four years
  91% within six years

Admissions

Regular Application Deadline: 1/1

Early Decision Deadline(s): 11/15,
  1/1

Fall Transfer Deadline: 3/15

Total # of Students Applied: 6,955
  Admitted: 1,854
  Enrolled: 717

Waitlist Available

Applied Early Decision: 672
  Early Decision Admitted: 298

Test Scores (middle 50%):
  SAT Verbal: 640–740
  SAT Math: 650–720
  ACT Comp: 28–32
  ACT English: 28–32
  ACT Math: 28–32

Inside the Classroom

Wesleyan University is among the most selective academic institutions in the country, providing opportunities and facilities usually found only at larger universities. Students rave about their school's wide choice of academic offerings, its strong and encouraging faculty, and a curriculum with considerable breadth and depth. All courses require a great deal of work, but that doesn't faze Wesleyan students, many of whom were valedictorians or salutatorians of their high school class. "It can get pretty competitive because there are a lot of gifted students who are hard workers," a sophomore tells us.

Undergrads can choose from more than 900 courses and 50 majors in 41 academic departments, all of which are strong. There are several outstanding interdisciplinary programs, including American studies and the humanities program. Aspiring writers should take note of the fact that best-selling novelists Robin Cook (*Coma*) and Sebastian Junger (*The Perfect Storm*) and screenwriters Akiva Goldsman (*A Beautiful Mind*) and Joss Whedon (*Buffy the Vampire Slayer*) are Wesleyan alumni. In the unlikely event students can't find a course they want here, they can easily go elsewhere, thanks to Wesleyan's participation in the Twelve College exchange, which includes such first-rate schools as Dartmouth and Vassar. Although there is no set core curriculum, the General Education Expectations suggest that students complete at least three courses from each of the three broad curricular areas by the time they graduate: arts and humanities, social and behavioral sciences, and natural sciences and math. Freshmen are encouraged, though not required, to participate in the First-Year Initiative (FYI) Program: seminars in various subjects, limited to no more than 20 first-year students, designed to prepare students for advanced work.

Wesleyan students take great pride in their own independence, drive, and passion for learning. Academic and social freedom are central to the educational experience here. Students take a proactive approach to learning, from their classes, teachers, and each other. As one undergrad characterized the school, "It will not hamper those with great initiative, nor will it coddle those who lack it." With a student/faculty ratio of 9:1, students are able to receive a great deal of individual attention from their professors, many of whom are well-known in their field.

Campus Environment

The 120-acre campus features a wide range of architectural styles. Despite its size, Wesleyan has the top facilities of a large university, including the nationally respected Olin Library, tons of lab space with cutting-edge equipment, and an athletic center housing a fieldhouse, natatorium, arena, and fitness center. Brownstone Row, with its ivy-covered buildings, defines the collegiate atmosphere of the campus.

The majority of students live on campus for all four years. Clark Hall, where the majority of freshmen are usually placed (the so-called "party dorm"), recently underwent extensive renovations. All dorms are coed, with single-sex floors available; in some cases, men and women are allowed to share. Program Housing offers upperclassmen the opportunity to live with people who share their interests, background, or identity. The Malcolm X House, the Sign Language House, and the

Eclectic House (known as the "anti-frat") are among the various options. Four fraternity houses are home to a very small percentage of the population. Juniors and seniors generally live in university-owned apartments.

For an annual fee, students may park their cars on campus (even freshmen, unless they are receiving financial aid). But for day-to-day living, most are content to walk or bicycle—the campus is small, and Main Street in Middletown is only a few blocks away—and the school provides a shuttle service.

Student Life

A "warm spirit of community" is how one guidance counselor describes the atmosphere at Wesleyan. With an undergrad population just shy of 2,800, it feels like a small, close-knit family—one that is energetic, diverse, politically active, and liberal. One student describes the archetypal Wesleyan coed as one who "will be protesting something, anything" during his or her college career. Indeed, the school is widely considered one of the most activist in the nation. Wesleyan students are open to many different viewpoints and experiences; most feel that an important part of their education can be found in their interactions with peers. "Wesleyan students like talking about ideas, and many hold strong opinions," a school rep tells us. "There are a lot of good, long conversations in all campus settings."

The student body is ethnically, geographically, and socially diverse; more than 75 percent of Wesleyan undergrads hail from outside New England. There are large percentages of African American and Asian American students enrolled in the school, and the surrounding community of Middletown has a minority population of around 20 percent. The gay and lesbian community has long been an active force on campus.

Aside from diners and a movie theater, Middletown doesn't have much in the way of attractions for students, but there's plenty to do on campus. The Campus Center offers games and discounts on movie tickets, and there are frequent dorm parties and lots of places to hang out. Greek life isn't big at all here: Only five percent of men join a fraternity, and there are even fewer sorority women. That doesn't put a crimp in the weekend party scene, however. "Normally at about 11:00 you begin to see droves of people 'party hopping,'" a student confides.

There are more than 125 clubs and organizations, including many politically oriented groups as well as several theater, dance, and music organizations. The school newspaper, *The Argus*, the Wesleyan Student Assembly, and the QA (Queer Alliance) are among the most popular. The school also offers 15 varsity sports for men and 14 for women, on top of its many intramural and club sports. About three-quarters of the student body participates in one form of athletics or another.

One of the biggest social events of the year, Spring Fling, is a day of partying following the last day of classes. One of the most enduring and celebrated sagas in Wesleyan's history concerns the Douglas Cannon. As part of a Wesleyan tradition, students steal the cannon and hide it in interesting places. Past years have seen the Douglas Cannon presented to Richard Nixon (who declined it), appear in the offices of *Life* magazine, and baked into the school's anniversary cake.

Other schools to check out: Brown, Dartmouth, Swarthmore, Wellesley, Vassar.

HS Rank of Entering Freshmen:
Top 10%: 73%
Top 50%: 100%

Costs (2003–04)

Tuition and Fees: $29,998

Room & Board: $8,226

THE EXPERTS SAY...

" Students who are passionate about learning and driven to change the world will do well at Wesleyan. "

" Activism and intellectualism rule at Wesleyan. "

Inst. Aid (est. 2003–04)

Institutional Aid, Need-Based: $20,993,593

FT Undergrads Receiving Aid: 46%
Avg. Amount per Student: $23,650

Of Those Receiving Any Aid:

Rec. Need-Based Scholarship or Grant Aid: 94%
Average Award: $20,183

Rec. Need-Based Self-Help Aid: 100%
Average Award: $4,101

Upon Graduation, Avg. Loan Debt per Student: $21,389

Financial Aid Deadline: 2/1

WEST VIRGINIA UNIVERSITY

P.O. Box 6009, Morgantown, WV 26506-6009
Admissions Phone: (304) 293-2121; (800) 344-9881 Fax: (304) 293-3080
Email: WVUAdmissions@arc.wvu.edu Website: www.wvu.edu
Application Website: www.arc.wvu.edu/admissions/applications.html

General Info

Type of School: public, coed
Setting: small town
Academic Calendar: semester

Student Body

Full-Time Undergrads: 16,543
  Men: 54%, Women: 46%

Part-Time Undergrads: 974
  Men: 46%, Women: 54%

Total Undergrad Population:
  African American: 4%
  Asian American: 2%
  Latino: 1%
  Native American: <1%
  Caucasian: 91%
  International: 2%
  Out-of-State: 41%
  Living Off-Campus: 72%
  In Fraternities: 5%
  In Sororities: 5%

Graduate and First-Professional
  Students: 6,743

Academics

Full-Time Faculty: 778
  With Ph.D.: 81%

Part-Time Faculty: 283
  With Ph.D.: 24%

Student/Faculty Ratio: 21:1

Most Popular Majors:
  engineering
  nursing
  psychology
  journalism
  exercise physiology

Freshmen Retention Rate: 78%

Graduation Rates:
  27% within four years
  56% within six years

Admissions

Regular Application Deadline: 8/1;
  3/1 (priority)

Fall Transfer Deadline: 8/1

Spring Transfer Deadline: 12/1

Total # of Students Applied: 10,049
  Admitted: 9,281
  Enrolled: 4,415

Test Scores (middle 50%):
  SAT Verbal: 480–570
  SAT Math: 480–580

Inside the Classroom

Through 13 colleges and schools, West Virginia University offers 168 bachelor's, master's, doctoral, and professional degree programs. Its best-known courses of study include health sciences, agriculture and forestry, journalism, engineering, physical education, and the creative arts. What sets this school apart from other large, land-grant universities, however, is the price: Compared to its competition, West Virginia University truly offers more value than most others.

Core requirements are fairly rigorous and include four courses in the humanities, four in the natural sciences and mathematics, and an additional four in social sciences. The reason for this is obvious, and is clearly explained by one student: "I got a very well-rounded education at WVU. You get back what you put in, and if you go after the easy classes, you aren't learning that it takes hard work to succeed."

Freshmen are carefully guided into the collegiate world through the school's "Orientation to University Life" course, which students take pass/fail. Study skills, goal setting, career planning, and other important information are learned by students so that their academic, social, and emotional needs aren't overlooked in the transition from high school.

As is often the case with large, land-grant schools, class sizes can be quite large in introductory-level courses, with faculty difficult to reach. Students report, however, that higher-level courses become much smaller and better. "The school really begins to shine with the upper-level courses," says one journalism major. "I can't say enough good things about my program."

WVU also has an honors program that provides students with the opportunity to engage in undergraduate research, guided study, undergraduate theses, and study abroad. The program attempts to ensure that honors students receive the best instruction in a variety of disciplines, challenging them to make the absolute most of their education.

Campus Environment

The Morgantown campus has 170 buildings on 913 acres in the scenic country just south of West Virginia's northern border with Pennsylvania, but not all of those 913 acres are contiguous. There are three separate subcampuses: Downtown, Evansdale, and the Health Sciences Center. Connecting the three campuses is an odd but effective mass transit system called the PRT, in which van-sized, computer-controlled cars carry students, faculty, and others from place to place. Developed in the 1960s as an alternative mass transit experiment, the system transports over 16,000 people on an average school day.

The Downtown campus is the oldest; its historic buildings serve as the site of the original land-grant university established in 1867. Most of the classes offered on the Downtown campus are undergraduate courses, although the graduate College of Business and Economics is also here.

Through the university's Operation Jump Start program, incoming freshmen are matched with others who share common interests to live in nine residential "houses" that serve as subcommunities within the university. Many dorms are tower-sized blocks of concrete and brick, so this head start on a social life is appreciated by many students. Options available in the dorms include single rooms, doubles, triples, and apartment-style living. (This last option is quite coveted and available only to upperclassmen.)

The university's student center is known as the Mountain Lair, and was named as one of the top student unions in the world by the Association of College Unions International. In addition to the all-important food court, the center contains a movie theater, bowling alley, arcade, convenience store, and a billiards hall with bar and grill. It also serves as the headquarters for the Student Administration, student organizations, and the campus radio station. The school's popular "Up All Night" entertainment series also happens here.

Interesting campus anomalies include two dedicated "free speech zones" near the Mountain Lair. Dating back to before the Vietnam War, the zones serve as places where students may say anything they like, pass out flyers, post signs, and otherwise exercise their First Amendment rights. The constitutionality of the zones has been challenged recently, fueling an ongoing debate as to whether the administration should extend the borders of the zones to the borders of the campus.

Student Life

"The only thing about WVU that I don't like is the city of Morgantown," says one student. "There's next to nothing to do here, unless you like to go out and party and drink every night." Of course, that suits some students just fine, like this one: "The nightlife is great. There are plenty of bars and clubs." A Pennsylvania high school guidance counselor admits that while this may be a "party school," there are "a lot of extracurricular options for new students as well as upperclassmen." For those who prefer quieter recreation, or who are in need of a nice walk or a living laboratory for their biological studies, the Core Arboretum contains 50 acres of old-growth forest, plants, and nature trails. Favorite times to visit are the foliage season in fall and wildflower season in April and early May.

The West Virginia Mountaineers compete at the NCAA Division I level. Sports for both sexes include basketball, soccer, cross-country, gymnastics, swimming, and track. Men also compete in baseball, football, wrestling, and rifle, while women compete in volleyball, rowing, and gymnastics. Fierce rivalries exist with the University of Pittsburgh, Syracuse, and Boston College, spawning massive tailgate parties and a heightened sense of school spirit.

A hallowed campus tradition is Mountaineer Week, a campus-wide celebration. One of the interesting activities is the PRT Cram, in which a PRT car is brought to the Mountain Lair so that student organizations can compete to see how many people they can cram into it. To date, the record is around 100 in a car designed to seat 16.

ACT Comp: 20–25

ACT English: 20–26

ACT Math: 18–25

HS Rank of Entering Freshmen:
Top 10%: 20%
Top 25%: 44%
Top 50%: 76%

Avg. HS GPA: 3.0

Costs (2003–04)

Tuition and Fees, In-State: $3,548

Tuition and Fees, Out-of-State: $10,766

Room & Board: $5,822

THE EXPERTS SAY...

" At this price, you can't beat WVU for both the quality and quantity of educational programs available to students. "

" The student population isn't very diverse, and the surrounding state is one of the poorest in the country. "

Inst. Aid (est. 2003–04)

Institutional Aid, Need-Based: $2,223,030

Institutional Aid, Non-Need-Based: $4,128,485

FT Undergrads Receiving Aid: 47%
Avg. Amount per Student: $8,015

FT Undergrads Receiving Non-Need-Based Scholarship or Grant Aid: 36%
Avg. Amount per Student: $3,324

Of Those Receiving Any Aid:

Rec. Need-Based Scholarship or Grant Aid: 71%
Average Award: $3,327

Rec. Need-Based Self-Help Aid: 84%
Average Award: $4,243

Upon Graduation, Avg. Loan Debt per Student: $20,145

Financial Aid Deadline: 3/1, 2/15 (priority)

WHEATON COLLEGE

501 College Avenue, Wheaton, IL 60187-5593
Admissions Phone: (630) 752-5005; (800) 222-2419 Fax: (630) 752-5285
Email: admissions@wheaton.edu Website: www.wheaton.edu
Application Website: www.wheaton.edu/admissions/UndGrad/applying/forms.htm

General Info

Type of School: private, coed, Christian nondenominational

Setting: suburban

Academic Calendar: semester

Student Body

Full-Time Undergrads: 2,347
Men: 49%, Women: 51%

Part-Time Undergrads: 57
Men: 46%, Women: 54%

Total Undergrad Population:
African American: 2%
Asian American: 7%
Latino: 2%
Native American: <1%
Caucasian: 86%
International: 1%
Out-of-State: 69%
Living Off-Campus: 11%

Graduate and First-Professional
Students: 514

Academics

Full-Time Faculty: 190
With Ph.D.: 93%

Part-Time Faculty: 89
With Ph.D.: 35%

Student/Faculty Ratio: 11:1

Most Popular Majors:
English (8%)
business economics (7%)
communication/music (each) (7%)
biblical studies (5%)
psychology (5%)

Completing 2 or More Majors: 12%

Freshmen Retention Rate: 93%

Graduation Rates:
76% within four years
86% within six years

Admissions

Regular Application Deadline: 1/15;
11/1 (priority)

Early Action Deadline: 11/1

Fall Transfer Deadline: 3/1

Spring Transfer Deadline: 10/1

Total # of Students Applied: 2,170
Admitted: 1,146
Enrolled: 576

# of Students Waitlisted: 410
Students Accepting Place: 330

Inside the Classroom

Wheaton may truly be the Harvard of Christian higher education. This coed, interdenominational, strongly evangelical Protestant institution exists to develop "whole and effective Christians through excellence in programs of Christian higher education." A "Christian commitment" is necessary for admission. The curriculum provides a top-notch liberal arts education, helping students to "think like Christians about what they are studying." The Scriptures are the core of this education, and biblical studies are required. Students aren't shielded from subjects that challenge their faith, like abortion or cloning, although one student reports that a faculty member's contract wasn't renewed because of his views on evolution.

The academic atmosphere "often seems to center on perfection and everyone here is a high achiever, which makes classes and grades very competitive, despite the professors warning to not focus on grades," sighs one Wheatie. Another comments that the workload is "heavier than most state schools and heavier than other Christian colleges in the area, and the competitiveness among the students is incredible." A recent freshman class had 50 National Merit Scholars, and Wheaton College ranks eleventh in the nation in the number of graduates who go on to receive Ph.D.s.

Wheaton offers a wide range of majors along with programs in theology, Christian education, Christian ministry, and biblical studies (the latter include courses in biblical achaeology). The most popular majors include business economics, English, psychology, elementary education, communications, and music. Wheaton also offers preprofessional 3-2 study in education, engineering, and nursing. The nationally recognized Conservatory of Music offers programs that celebrate music as an act of worship and service.

The relationships between students and professors are warm and caring. "Because we are in a Christian environment, there is already assumed trust between us," observes an education major. "They want to be our mentors and make it clear that they are here for us." The student/faculty ratio is 11:1, and the average class size is 23 students. "The professors are very progressive in their evangelical Christian thinking," comments a freshman.

Wheaties study abroad in East Asia, Russia, Western Europe, and the Holy Lands. The Human Needs and Global Resources Program combines third world studies with internships in developing countries. Other off-campus programs are Wheaton's Black Hills Science Station in South Dakota, the Colorado art program, and the Honey Rock Camp in for leadership training in Wisconsin. The campus is the home of the Billy Graham Center, named for the school's most famous alumnus and dedicated to world evangelization.

Campus Environment

Wheaton's 80-acre campus is "near Chicago, but in a quiet, small conservative suburb," says a sophomore. Another student remarks, "Students don't have a whole lot of interaction with the town, but the town seems to have high expectations for Wheaton College students." There is not much to do close to campus, but Chicago is "very accessible," about 40 minutes by train.

Nearly 90 percent of students live on-campus in dormitories or college-owned apartments. "Students have to live on-campus all four years (or obtain special [permission] otherwise)," a Wheatie explains. Dorms "are mostly divided by class... They are pretty comfortable, not much variety. They are also separated by gender and the opposite sex can only come on the other's floor when there are 'open floor hours' about twice a week in the evening." A freshman warns: "A student who wants advanced technology and can't live without TV won't be happy at Wheaton."

Freshman are not allowed to have cars on campus. "Without a car, you can get to the grocery store, pharmacy, and public library, but that's about it," a sophomore notes. At least freshman can eat well. A Wheatie raves: "We have the number one cafeteria in the country and it's really healthy and sometimes there are ice sculptures at dinner!"

Student Life

The central fact of Wheatie student life is "The Pledge," an agreement to live by Christian values as set forth in the Bible. Translated, that means: "can't drink, dance, smoke, or gamble, or 'do' anything gay (it's all right to be gay, otherwise)." The no-dancing issue "seems to come up a lot." Although one student says drinking and drugs are "rarely, rarely factors," another student admits: "Drinking plays a role and it is a touchy issue because we all promised we wouldn't."

A chemistry major gives the campus a "2" (out of 10) for rowdiness and a "9" for friendliness. "Outside of the classroom is very friendly; sometimes it seems fake," comments a student. "To describe Wheaton in one word I would say: 'Pleasantville'." Students are "mostly conservative Republicans—Democrats get flustered/defensive quite easily." Minority issues "have been huge this year," reports a freshman. "There have been several reports of race targeted [name] calling and harassment."

During the week, students "study, study, study." On weekends, students "go into Chicago (eating at the Cheesecake Factory, shopping on Michigan Ave., learning how to use the "L", going to Navy Pier), walk into downtown Wheaton for coffee at Starbucks, and go to church." Wheaton competes in Division III: the teams are now called the Thunders rather than the politically incorrect "Crusaders." The soccer program is "top-notch," says a sophomore. "Our swimming program is good, the basketball team is doing well, and the football team makes itself known, even though it's not on the field." Student ministries are everywhere: "Students [are] called to serve God in many different areas (prison ministry, ski boarding ministry, street evangelism, art evangelism)... tutoring, nursing homes, prisons, orphanages."

Some complain of "close-mindedness", and a "provincial attitude" in the "Wheaton Bubble." "Sometimes it feels like most everyone here comes from one mold," a freshman gripes. "I know they all shop at one store: Abercrombie and Fitch." Wheaton students come "from a good, close family; most likely their parents, grandparents, brothers, sisters, and cousins all have attended Wheaton; many students were home-schooled or are missionary kids. Many students have led very sheltered lives and Wheaton just continues to encourage that." A student who wants diversity, or "punk, Gothic, and liberal" students would not fit in.

But students who appreciate "shared values, awesome professors, and easy access to Chicago" may find a home here. A Wheatie concludes: "Students here do seem to have a genuine love for the Lord, and when it comes down to it we are 'good kids'."

Waitlisted Students Admitted: 60

Test Scores (middle 50%):
SAT Verbal: 620–710
SAT Math: 610–700
ACT Comp: 27–31

HS Rank of Entering Freshmen:
Top 10%: 61%
Top 25%: 87%
Top 50%: 98%

Avg. HS GPA: 3.71

THE EXPERTS SAY...

" Wheaton is the alma mater of Protestant leaders like Billy Graham, offering a top-notch liberal arts education in a safe and nurturing Christian environment. "

" You can't drink, smoke, gamble, or dance at Wheaton. Think Kevin Bacon in 'Footloose'. "

Costs (2004–5)

Tuition and Fees: $20,000

Room & Board: $6,466

Payment Plan(s): installment plan

Inst. Aid (est. 2003–04)

Institutional Aid, Need-Based:
$9,154,708

Institutional Aid, Non-Need-Based:
$831,129

FT Undergrads Receiving Aid: 48%
Avg. Amount per Student:
$16,040

FT Undergrads Receiving Non-Need-Based Scholarship or Grant Aid: 18%
Avg. Amount per Student: $3,702

Of Those Receiving Any Aid:

Rec. Need-Based Scholarship or Grant Aid: 82%
Average Award: $10,582

Rec. Need-Based Self-Help Aid: 91%
Average Award: $5,417

Upon Graduation, Avg. Loan Debt per Student: $16,476

Financial Aid Deadline: 2/15 (priority)

Graduates

Going to Graduate School:
22% Within One Year

Accepting Job Offer:
26% at time of graduation

Companies Recruiting On Campus:
123

Alumni Giving: 63%

WHEATON COLLEGE

26 East Main Street, Norton, MA 02766
Admissions Phone: (508) 286-8251; (800) 394-6003 Fax: (508) 286-8271
Email: admission@wheatoncollege.edu Website: www.wheatoncollege.edu
Application Website: www.wheatoncollege.edu/admission/Applying/

General Info

Type of School: private, coed

Setting: suburban

Academic Calendar: semester

Student Body

Full-Time Undergrads: 1,545
  Men: 37%, Women: 63%

Part-Time Undergrads: 20
  Men: 25%, Women: 75%

Total Undergrad Population:
  African American: 3%
  Asian American: 2%
  Latino: 4%
  Native American: <1%
  Caucasian: 81%
  International: 2%
  Out-of-State: 67%
  Living Off-Campus: 3%

Academics

Full-Time Faculty: 121
  With Ph.D.: 98%

Part-Time Faculty: 41
  With Ph.D.: 61%

Student/Faculty Ratio: 11:1

Most Popular Majors:
  psychology (13%)
  English (13%)
  economics (9%)
  history (6%)
  sociology (6%)

Completing 2 or More Majors: 11%

Freshmen Retention Rate: 89%

Graduation Rates:
  68% within four years
  75% within six years

Admissions

Regular Application Deadline: 1/15

Early Decision Deadline(s): 11/15,
  1/15

Fall Transfer Deadline: 4/1 (priority)

Spring Transfer Deadline: 11/15
  (priority)

Total # of Students Applied: 3,465
  Admitted: 1,492
  Enrolled: 445

# of Students Waitlisted: 1,059
  Students Accepting Place: 341
  Waitlisted Students Admitted: 69

Inside the Classroom

Wheaton College is a liberal arts school that offers 35 major concentrations leading to the A.B. degree. Instead of conforming to the ivory tower stereotype, Wheaton enhances traditional classroom study with real-world experience: Students are required to put learning into practice through a number of options, including internships, community service, research, work, and campus leadership. These experiences are documented in a second transcript for each student, in addition to the customary transcript that contains students' grades. The preparation apparently pays off; the top five career fields reported by Wheaton graduates are finance, law, medicine, media, and advertising. While some universities pay little attention to their mottos, Wheaton College is very serious about theirs: "Learning for Life." A high school guidance counselor approves, saying Wheaton "takes B/C students and makes them feel like A/B students, because that is what they become."

Incoming freshmen take a First-Year Seminar that gives them the opportunity to learn in small classes through reading, regular discussion, and writing. Seminars are available in a variety of topics, sharing the theme of controversy as it shapes human understanding and motivates social and political action. The seminar helps students to develop their own positions on the topic and hone the academic skills needed for a college education.

Students can also pick and choose from the course catalogs of other schools in the area: Wheaton is a member of the Twelve College Exchange, allowing all students to cross-register for courses at Amherst, Bowdoin, Connecticut College, Dartmouth, Mt. Holyoke, Smith, Trinity, Vassar, Wellesley, Wesleyan, and Williams. Cross-registration at Brown University is also possible.

Complementing the real-world experience at Wheaton is the selection of study abroad programs. Students can choose to study in Italy, the United Kingdom, France, Russia, Israel, and Australia. A unique aspect of some of these programs is the availability of internship options, allowing a rare chance to gain work experience in another country and culture.

Campus Environment

Wheaton College's 140-acre campus is located in Norton, Massachusetts, about 35 miles south of Boston and 15 miles north of Providence. Most of its compact campus is contained within the roughly square area bordered by Route 123, Fillmore Drive, Howard Street, and Pine Street, with athletic facilities and parking areas located immediately outside the central campus. A small lake called Peacock Pond and a rectangular lawn named "The Dimple" serve as the school's centerpieces, around which most academic and residential buildings are arrayed.

All formal out-of-classroom experiences like internships are arranged through the Filene Center for Work and Learning, the office that assists students in exploring and integrating these experiences into their education. Located on the second floor of the Admission Building, the center is staffed by advisers and contains resources and program information. It also has information on part-time and summer jobs for students.

All Wheaton students must live on campus in one of the 19 residence halls and 11 theme houses. Most of the dorms are traditional coed buildings with double rooms; all-female living areas include the entire Kilham Hall, the second floor and a section of the fourth floor in Everett Hall, the third and fourth floors of Meadows Hall, and the fourth floor of Stanton Hall. The only all-male living area is a section of the fourth floor of Everett Hall. Larcom and Young Halls are set aside for wellness housing, while Chapin Hall offers an enforced 24-hour quiet atmosphere. In addition to these themes, Emerson Hall is set aside for housing centered around the theme of feminist perspectives.

Students' everyday life involves at least one trip to the Balfour-Hood Center, with its meeting rooms for student groups, TV lounge, fitness center, game room, dance studio, post office, and campus radio station. The center is also home for The Café, an upscale deli eatery, and The Loft, a popular nightspot where pizza, wings, entertainment, and social events are served up.

Most student meals are served at the Emerson Dining Room, with its traditional cafeteria-style menu. A popular alternative to Emerson is the Chase Dining Complex, where the Round Dining Room offers a food-court facility with a deli, grill, pizza by the slice, and a specialty bar, and the Square Dining Room offers food with a theme. Popular Square Room offerings include low-fat and healthy-heart menus, a soup and salad bar, vegetarian offerings, a sauté station, and an international serving area.

Student Life

A number of student clubs and organizations cater to students' academic, recreational, religious, sports, and other interests and pursuits. Some of the more interesting include the Dimple Divers, an improvisational comedy troupe; the Gentlemen Callers, a men's a cappella singing group; the Wheatones and the Whims, two women's a cappella groups; the Hawaii Club, an organization dedicated to Hawaiian culture; and the Wheaton Paintball Club, for people who love being shot at.

Wheaton competes at the NCAA Division III level, with sports for both men and women including basketball, track, swimming, lacrosse, tennis, and soccer. Men also compete in baseball, while women compete in field hockey, volleyball, softball, and synchronized swimming. Intramural sports include basketball, volleyball, badminton, floor hockey, flag football, soccer, tennis, and softball.

Students can also hitch a ride into Boston on one of the school's hired "Boston Connection" buses to enjoy the distractions of the big city. With over 300,000 college students in and around Boston, the city serves as both a playpen for fun-seeking students (being close to Boston "means more [of a] drinking scene," says a high school guidance counselor) and a source of real-world experience, with its high-tech companies, research facilities, cultural organizations.

Applied Early Decision: 262
Early Decision Admitted: 209

Test Scores (middle 50%):
SAT Verbal: 560–640
SAT Math: 570–650
ACT Comp: 25–28

HS Rank of Entering Freshmen:
Top 10%: 43%
Top 25%: 73%
Top 50%: 93%

Avg. HS GPA: 3.45

THE EXPERTS SAY...

" Wheaton's focus on real-world experiences in a liberal arts education makes it a fine place to begin a career. "

" Wheaton's relatively small size limits the specializations to which its real-world experience can be applied. "

Costs (2003–04)

Tuition and Fees: $29,020

Room & Board: $7,430

Payment Plan(s): installment plan, pre-payment plan

Inst. Aid (est. 2003–04)

Institutional Aid, Need-Based: $12,137,289

Institutional Aid, Non-Need-Based: $1,288,612

FT Undergrads Receiving Aid: 58%
Avg. Amount per Student: $21,159

FT Undergrads Receiving Non-Need-Based Scholarship or Grant Aid: 11%
Avg. Amount per Student: $7,625

Of Those Receiving Any Aid:

Rec. Need-Based Scholarship or Grant Aid: 94%
Average Award: $16,164

Rec. Need-Based Self-Help Aid: 95%
Average Award: $6,382

Upon Graduation, Avg. Loan Debt per Student: $20,188

Financial Aid Deadline: 2/1

Graduates

Going to Graduate School:
28% Within One Year

Accepting Job Offer:
20% at time of graduation

Companies Recruiting On Campus: 24

Alumni Giving: 65%

WHITMAN COLLEGE

515 Boyer Avenue, Walla Walla, WA 99362-2046
Admissions Phone: (509) 527-5176; (877) 462-9448 Fax: (509) 527-4967
Email: admission@whitman.edu
Website: www.whitman.edu

General Info

Type of School: private, coed

Setting: small town

Academic Calendar: semester

Student Body

Full-Time Undergrads: 1,408
  Men: 45%, Women: 55%

Part-Time Undergrads: 12
  Men: 83%, Women: 17%

Total Undergrad Population:
  African American: 2%
  Asian American: 8%
  Latino: 3%
  Native American: 1%
  Caucasian: 73%
  International: 2%
  Out-of-State: 44%
  Living Off-Campus: 41%
  In Fraternities: 36%
  In Sororities: 34%

Academics

Full-Time Faculty: 116
  With Ph.D.: 93%

Part-Time Faculty: 69
  With Ph.D.: 62%

Student/Faculty Ratio: 10:1

Most Popular Majors:
  psychology (14%)
  politics (13%)
  biology (13%)
  English (8%)
  history (8%)

Completing 2 or More Majors: 6%

Freshmen Retention Rate: 95%

Graduation Rates:
  74% within four years
  85% within six years

Admissions

Regular Application Deadline: 1/15;
  11/15 (priority)

Early Decision Deadline(s): 11/15,
  1/1

Fall Transfer Deadline: 1/15, 11/15
  (priority)

Spring Transfer Deadline: 11/15

Total # of Students Applied: 2,143
  Admitted: 1,196
  Enrolled: 362

In the Classroom

Whitman's reputation for academic excellence attracts intelligent students enthusiastic about learning. "There's a definite academic standard here—and it's high," one student says. Whitman offers 40 departmental majors; particularly strong are biology, English, and psychology. A guidance counselor also noted its "superb theatric program," and another praised its music program.

Students describe the academic atmosphere at Whitman as "intense but friendly." A student explains, "Students like to do well in class, and strive to, but the atmosphere is not one of fierce competition. Many students form study groups and work together on projects." According to a college official, "Unlike some elite colleges in which cut-throat competition is the norm, Whitman has a culture of cooperation, collaboration and celebration of each other's accomplishments."

This same attitude pervades student/faculty relationships. "I enjoy the professors here at Whitman," says one student. "They make me feel challenged and supported at the same time." Class sizes are small and the professors often get to know their students. Class discussions are an important part of most courses and participation may account for an important part of the student's grade.

Surprisingly, a higher percentage of students at Whitman engage in professional-level research that at most large, state-supported research universities. Since there are no grad students at Whitman to act as research assistants, undergrads are offered these prime positions. A college official states, "Nearly half of all Whitman students have the opportunity to do professional-level research in collaboration with their faculty members."

All first-year students take a two-semester core seminar entitled in "Antiquity and Modernity" that examines the great works of literature from ancient Greece through the twentieth century. To ensure that they receive a broad liberal arts education, students are required to take at least one course in six of the following seven areas: fine arts; history and literature; language, writing, and rhetoric; physical science and mathematics; philosophy and religion; descriptive science; and social science.

Campus Environment

A number of high school counselors questioned by Kaplan spoke of Whitman in glowing terms, but when pressed for possible drawbacks the school might have, all of them needed only one word: location. Walla Walla, an agriculture-based town far from any major urban center, offers lots of sunshine (more than 300 days—this isn't Seattle!) and plenty of peace and quiet. But, as one student put it, "Walla Walla is not terribly exciting." Most students find the town's business, cultural, and entertainment options quite limited. One guidance counselor noted that internship opportunities are constricted by Whitman's location.

Students are required to live on campus for at least four semesters. Freshmen must live in a residence hall; options include co-ed or female-only halls. If overcrowding occurs, student lounges in the residence halls are converted to student rooms. After the freshman year, the on-campus options include housing in residence halls, fraternities, sororities, and special-interest houses that draw together students interested in the following themes: Asian studies, community service, the environment, fine arts, French, German, the global community, Japanese, multiethnic relations, Spanish, and writing. Overall, 60 percent of the students live in on-campus housing.

Student employment is also centered on campus. Approximately half of all Whitman students work on campus. The jobs run the gamut from office work to custodial, from writing articles for the alumni magazine to working in food service positions.

Students generally get around campus by foot and sometimes by bicycle. Access to an automobile opens up more possibilities for weekend activities, which probably explains why most students—including many freshmen—have cars. Student parking is plentiful and free.

Student Life

Guidance counselors praised Whitman's "close-knit community." Whitman students—isolated in Walla Walla—tend to live, study, work, and play together. Students are largely middle class and white, with only small percentages from African, Asian, Latino, or Native American backgrounds.

The Reid Campus Center, completed in January 2002, is the focus of campus social life and base for numerous student clubs and groups from Amnesty International to ballroom dancing. On weekends, there's usually a big party or two on campus, many of these are hosted by the fraternities or sororities. A special night out might include a college music or theater production. But generally, the campus is pretty quiet; when asked about the biggest campus events of the last year, students and university officials most frequently mentioned visits to campus by nationally known figures like Ralph Nader and Maya Angelou.

Whitman offers nine intercollegiate sports for men and women. There's no varsity football, but in tennis and skiing, the Whitman Missionaries are strong. In fact, Whitman's men's and women's alpine ski teams both finished in first place at the U.S. College Ski and Snowboarding Association's national championships in 2001. There are seven intramural sports for men and seven for women as well as eleven sports clubs for women and twelve for men. Approximately 75 percent of the students participate in an organized sport of some kind.

On weekends many students can be found enjoying outdoor activities either with friends or with an organized group. Whitman's Outdoor Program organizes recreational events and rents the equipment you'll need. A popular destination is the nearby Blue Mountains, which offer skiing in winter and a variety of outdoor activities the rest of the year.

Other schools to check out: Carleton, Grinnell, University of Puget Sound, Willamette, Lawrence.

# of Students Waitlisted: 288
 Students Accepting Place: 100
 Waitlisted Students Admitted: 34

Applied Early Decision: 142
 Early Decision Admitted: 116

Test Scores (middle 50%):
 SAT Verbal: 620–730
 SAT Math: 610–700
 ACT Comp: 26–31

HS Rank of Entering Freshmen:
 Top 10%: 59%
 Top 25%: 90%
 Top 50%: 100%

Avg. HS GPA: 3.76

THE EXPERTS SAY...

" If you want an academically challenging school and a supportive environment, Whitman might be a perfect fit. "

" Walla Walla is over four hours from Seattle. The much smaller city of Spokane is closer, but even it is nearly a three-hour drive. Find another college if you crave big city excitement. "

Costs (2003–04)

Tuition and Fees: $25,626

Room & Board: $6,900

Payment Plan(s): installment plan

Inst. Aid (est. 2003–04)

Institutional Aid, Need-Based:
 $8,631,300

Institutional Aid, Non-Need-Based:
 $4,634,750

FT Undergrads Receiving Aid: 42%
 Avg. Amount per Student: $17,750

FT Undergrads Receiving Non-Need-Based Scholarship or Grant Aid: 7%
 Avg. Amount per Student: $7,450

Of Those Receiving Any Aid:

Rec. Need-Based Scholarship or
 Grant Aid: 100%
 Average Award: $12,775

Rec. Need-Based Self-Help Aid: 100%
 Average Award: $5,160

Upon Graduation, Avg. Loan Debt
 per Student: $15,075

Financial Aid Deadline: 2/11, 11/15
 (priority)

Graduates

Alumni Giving: 46%

WILLAMETTE UNIVERSITY

900 State Street, Salem, OR 97301
Admissions Phone: (503) 370-6303; (877) 542-2787 Fax: (503) 375-5363
Email: libarts@willamette.edu Website: www.willamette.edu
Application Website: www.collegenet.com

General Info

Type of School: private, coed, Methodist

Setting: suburban

Academic Calendar: semester

Student Body

Full-Time Undergrads: 1,798
  Men: 44%, Women: 56%

Part-Time Undergrads: 15
  Men: 80%, Women: 20%

Total Undergrad Population:
  African American: 2%
  Asian American: 7%
  Latino: 5%
  Native American: 1%
  Caucasian: 61%
  International: 1%
  Out-of-State: 59%
  Living Off-Campus: 31%
  In Fraternities: 32%
  In Sororities: 32%

Graduate and First-Professional
  Students: 645

Academics

Full-Time Faculty: 185
  With Ph.D.: 88%

Part-Time Faculty: 84
  With Ph.D.: 10%

Student/Faculty Ratio: 11:1

Most Popular Majors:
  politics (5%)
  economics (5%)
  psychology (5%)
  Spanish (5%)
  biology (5%)

Completing 2 or More Majors: 14%

Freshmen Retention Rate: 87%

Graduation Rates:
  76% within four years
  85% within six years
  note: 5-yr. programs affect rates

Admissions

Regular Application Deadline: 2/1

Early Action Deadline: 12/1

Fall Transfer Deadline: 2/1

Spring Transfer Deadline: 11/1 (priority)

Total # of Students Applied: 2,164
  Admitted: 1,603
  Enrolled: 541

In the Classroom

Willamette, the oldest institution of higher learning in the West, was founded in 1842 before the influx of settlers via the Oregon Trail began and before the United States had even clearly established its claim on the Oregon Country. Today the small liberal arts college offers a strong academic program with 34 majors to choose from, the most popular of which are biology, economics, English, politics, and psychology.

The university is known for its programs in the social sciences, and 45 percent of the student body earns a degree in a discipline in this area. The Oregon State Capitol across the street from Willamette provides an unsurpassed political science laboratory, and state government offices and state-run institutions offer an array of interesting internships. Guidance counselors especially recommend the school for students interested in going on to law or business school.

Willamette (the accent's on "lam") provides small classes and close student/teacher relationships. In fact, in a typical semester, about 70 percent of undergraduate classes have fewer than 20 students and only one or two classes have over 50 students.

Graduation requirements, designed to give students a well-rounded liberal arts education, include the World Views freshman seminar, four writing-centered courses (including World Views), two quantitative and analytical reasoning courses, and study in a language other than English. In addition, each student's course of study must encompass six broadly defined areas: understanding the natural world, creating in the arts, analyzing arguments, thinking historically, interpreting texts, and understanding society.

Willamette offers many opportunities for experiential learning. Internships are offered at different levels for different goals: for freshmen and sophomores interested in exploring career possibilities, for upperclassmen desiring work experience related to their major, and, in some fields, for professional, on-the-job training. Four university programs provide funding for undergraduate research. In addition, Willamette encourages study abroad and sponsors or cosponsors programs in more than 30 countries as well as in Chicago and Washington, D.C.

Campus Environment

The campus, complete with salmon-filled stream, reflects the natural beauty of the Pacific Northwest, which in turn is a product of the region's mild, rainy—and in winter, perpetually dreary—climate. Historic buildings house university offices, but most of the school's classrooms, labs, libraries, and sports facilities are housed in new or renovated buildings outfitted with impressive state-of-the-art equipment. However, with such facilities, it's not surprising that the tuition is one of the highest found at any Pacific Northwest college or university.

Freshmen and sophomores are required to live on campus unless they are married, over age 21, or living with parents. The bulk of freshmen live in Belknap and Matthews halls, which offer co-ed and women-only floors. Other options include substance-free residences and theme housing focusing on community service, the international community, or outdoor recreational activities. After freshman year, students may also live with their fraternity or sorority on campus. The majority of juniors and seniors live off-campus, although a new, well-funded university initiative is underway to design and build housing that's more attractive to upperclassmen, thereby encouraging more of them to live on campus.

The university has close ties to its sister school in Japan, Tokyo International University, which, in 1989, built a campus adjoining Willamette's for Japanese students pursuing a degree in American studies. While the two institutions are separate, Japanese students have the option of living in a Willamette dorm and vice versa.

Downtown shopping and entertainment establishments, most government and business offices, as well as bus and train stations are all within easy walking distance from campus. Salem's well-established network of bicycle paths and lanes makes biking a popular alternative. And students get free transit on Salem's urban bus system. You don't really need a car; however, access to an automobile opens up possibilities for travel to the Cascade Mountains, Pacific Coast, and Portland—all of which are within an hour's drive. Freshmen are permitted to have cars and there is an ample supply of on-campus parking.

Student Life

Willamette's population has become increasingly more diverse in recent years. There is a lack of international students here, even with Tokyo International University's adjacent campus. Less than half of the students come from Oregon, with most of the rest from Washington or California. "Intellectually curious—but not quirky nor eccentric—students are the norm here," explains a school official.

Over 90 student clubs offer activities for students sharing the same interests. The new student center provides a base for these activities and a place to hang out. About a quarter of the student body joins sororities or fraternities, which organize a variety of social events for members, including a lot of weekend parties. Traditionally, the biggest campus event of the year is the student-organized WUlapalooza, an outdoor art and music festival that draws a large number of people from the university and the community.

Many students also get involved in athletics; in fact, more than 25 percent participate in a varsity sport sometime during their college career. Willamette participates in NCAA Division III athletics and offers 10 sports for both women and men, including baseball/softball, basketball, crew, football, golf, soccer, swimming, tennis, track and field, and volleyball. In addition there is a popular intramural sports program.

Students often travel to Portland for big-city entertainment, and the Cascade Mountains offer opportunities for skiing and hiking. The Coast is also a popular destination, but don't plan on soaking up some rays on a beach, at least during the school year, when more realistic activities are hiking, crabbing, or storm watching.

# of Students Waitlisted: 182
  Students Accepting Place: 153

Test Scores (middle 50%):
  SAT Verbal: 570–670
  SAT Math: 580–670
  ACT Comp: 25–29
  ACT English: 23–30
  ACT Math: 24–29

HS Rank of Entering Freshmen:
  Top 10%: 49%
  Top 25%: 80%
  Top 50%: 98%

Avg. HS GPA: 3.74

THE EXPERTS SAY...

"If you're interested in the social sciences and want a great deal of individual attention, Willamette could be right for you. Also see Lawrence, Santa Clara, Claremont McKenna, and Lewis & Clark."

"If hiking, crabbing, and storm watching will bore you to tears, the University of Oregon will be a better choice for you."

Costs (2003–04)

Tuition and Fees: $25,432

Room & Board: $6,600

Payment Plan(s): installment plan

Inst. Aid (est. 2003–04)

FT Undergrads Receiving Aid: 64%
  Avg. Amount per Student: $21,027

FT Undergrads Receiving Non-Need-Based Scholarship or Grant Aid: 32%
  Avg. Amount per Student: $10,995

Of Those Receiving Any Aid:

Rec. Need-Based Scholarship or Grant Aid: 100%
  Average Award: $17,365

Rec. Need-Based Self-Help Aid: 87%
  Average Award: $4,267

Upon Graduation, Avg. Loan Debt per Student: $18,689

Financial Aid Deadline: 2/1 (priority)

Graduates

Going to Graduate School:
  25% Within One Year

Accepting Job Offer:
  45% at time of graduation

Companies Recruiting On Campus:
  150

WILLIAMS COLLEGE

P.O. Box 487, Williamstown, MA 01267
Admissions Phone: (413) 597-2211 Fax: (417) 597-4052
Email: admission@williams.edu
Website: www.williams.edu

General Info

Type of School: private, coed
Academic Calendar: 4-1-4

Student Body

Full-Time Undergrads: 1,974
  Men: 50%, Women: 50%

Total Undergrad Population:
  African American: 9%
  Asian American: 9%
  Latino: 8%
  Native American: <1%
  Caucasian: 69%
  International: 6%
  Out-of-State: 80%
  Living Off-Campus: 7%

Graduate and First-Professional
  Students: 57

Academics

Full-Time Faculty: 247
  With Ph.D.: 96%

Part-Time Faculty: 31
  With Ph.D.: 81%

Student/Faculty Ratio: 8:1

Graduation Rates:
  92% within four years
  96% within six years

Admissions

Regular Application Deadline: 1/1

Early Decision Deadline(s): 11/10

Fall Transfer Deadline: 3/1

Spring Transfer Deadline: 12/1

Total # of Students Applied: 5,341
  Admitted: 1,133
  Enrolled: 533

Waitlisted Students Admitted: 39

Applied Early Decision: 559
  Early Decision Admitted: 215

Test Scores (middle 50%):
  SAT Verbal: 650–760
  SAT Math: 660–750

Costs (2004–05)

Tuition and Fees: $28,090

Room & Board: $7,660

Inside the Classroom

Williams College is one of New England's prestigious "little Ivies"—a small, slightly less well-known liberal arts college ("no, we're not William & Mary!") that attracts top students and faculty. An Ohio guidance counselor calls it the "best small liberal arts school" in the nation. Williams has three academic curricular divisions (humanities, sciences, and social sciences), 24 departments, 31 majors plus concentrations and special programs. The science programs are truly excellent—"on par with much larger research institutions," brags one science student—but the academics are strong in all departments.

"The workload is intense both in volume and difficulty," says a biology major. But she insists that the academic environment is "wholly supportive" and that "there is very little competitiveness between students." And students all have good things to say about the faculty: "The professors here are all, every one, brilliant," one student gushes, while another says that the professors "go out of their way to provide help for the students." With a student/faculty ratio of 8:1 and an average class size of 17, professors take the time to get to know their students both inside and outside the classroom.

While Williams provides an excellent education in the traditional liberal arts and sciences, some students complain that the college doesn't offer much beyond that. "Don't come here if you have an offbeat academic interest," one student warns. You can design your own major at Williams, but, as one student points out, this option "is not much help if you cannot find the classes to fill it."

One way students can break free is by taking advantage of the Winter Study Program in January. Most students devote it to completing special projects or studying something a bit off the beaten path, which makes it a nice break from the rigors of the academic year. There's also an unusual program called Free University in which students teach each other a variety of subjects, from cooking various cultural cuisines to dance.

Campus Environment

"The housing at Williams is the best I have seen at any college," says a recent grad. Freshmen are housed together in clusters of 25 students plus two junior advisors. These freshman "entries" fill up six residence halls, with a mixture of singles, doubles, and suites. The 36 residences which house upperclassmen allow 94 percent of these students to live in singles. Students especially love the senior co-ops, which offer "a great transition to the real world." Although housing is guaranteed for four years, a small percentage of seniors live off-campus in nearby houses and apartments—"the cost is moderate to cheap," we are told.

Location seems to be Williams' biggest drawback: "It's in the middle of nowhere!" students whine. Williamstown, in the heart of the Berkshires, is "a beautiful, quaint New England town." But its small size means a very limited number of social choices, and a guidance counselor worries that "some may find it isolated." A young alum warns: "Those who need to be entertained by outside sources may not be very happy at Williams." And its New England location means long, cold winters that one student describes as "lasting from October to May."

One major Williamstown attraction is the annual Theater Festival, where A-list Broadway and Hollywood stars come up for the summer. It is remarkable to see this sleepy Berkshire town turn into a bustling theater mecca every summer, and many students do stick around for it.

If, after a couple of years on campus, you feel yourself getting cabin fever, you can participate in one of the many popular study-abroad programs. One of the best is the Williams-Oxford program, run in association with Exeter College, Oxford, which offers some 30 Williams juniors a year-long immersion in the life of Oxford University.

Student Life

The typical Williams student is down-to-earth, athletic, and intelligent—basically, "traits that come embodied in an L.L. Bean/J. Crew package." "It's extremely laid back," a student tells us. "People do a lot of hanging out. They go to snack bars, mainly because we're in a small town and there aren't a lot of options." But this forced togetherness has resulted in a "tight-knit community" that at least one student believes "doesn't really happen at a lot of other colleges—but it should."

Because Williams has no fraternities, "often sports teams and housing groups function as fraternities and are sources of the typical 'college party,'" says a young alum. However, "Williams is pretty strict on how parties are run, and security checks on them for underage drinking (though, as with any college, people get away with it)" says one student. Things get even more strict in town: Williamstown has a "no open-container policy," and students complain of being stopped by the police for carrying an open beer.

Williams does offer a great deal of activities for students willing to find them and become involved. In addition to many of the standard activity groups, there are several high quality music and theater groups on campus, and one in ten students belongs to one of the excellent a capella singing groups. And with the Theater Festival, aspiring performers have a unique opportunity for exposure.

Sports are at least as popular as the arts at Williams. As one student reports, "Athletics are huge. I would venture to say over half the students compete in some level of athletics." Popular intercollegiate team sports include hockey, skiing, swimming and football, while broomball is the intramural sport of choice. There's also the Outing Club—"They lead hikes, sometimes to see the sunrise in the morning," says one student, who tells us the club also goes camping and cross-country skiing.

"Mountain Day" takes place at Williams each fall semester. One beautiful fall weekend, festivities are held on a nearby mountain. Students go on hikes, and "they always bring cider and doughnuts," a student tells us. "A dozen or so a capella groups sing." Another charming (though strange) tradition: At each Commencement, a watch is dropped from the 80-foot spire of the college chapel. If the watch breaks, tradition holds that the class will be lucky.

Other schools to check out: Amherst, Bates, Middlebury, Dartmouth, Bowdoin.

Inst. Aid (est. 2003–04)

Institutional Aid, Need-Based: $16,639,726

FT Undergrads Receiving Aid: 42%
Avg. Amount per Student: $26,212

Of Those Receiving Any Aid:

Rec. Need-Based Scholarship or Grant Aid: 95%
Average Award: $23,665

Rec. Need-Based Self-Help Aid: 86%
Average Award: $5,253

Upon Graduation, Avg. Loan Debt per Student: $10,627

Financial Aid Deadline: 2/1

THE EXPERTS SAY...

" This 'little Ivy' offers challenging liberal arts programs in a supportive academic environment. Stick around for the summer Williamstown Theater Festival to see Hollywood and Broadway stars. "

" One-tenth of the student body belongs to an a capella group. You can tell there isn't much to do in Williamstown except for that theater festival. "

WITTENBERG UNIVERSITY

P.O. Box 720, Springfield, OH 45504
Admissions Phone: (937) 327-6314; (800) 677-7558 Fax: (937) 327-6379
Email: admission@wittenberg.edu Website: www.wittenberg.edu
Application Website: www4.wittenburg.edu/administration/prospect/apply/

General Info

Type of School: private, coed,
Evangelical Lutheran

Setting: suburban

Academic Calendar: semester

Student Body

Full-Time Undergrads: 2,055
Men: 42%, Women: 58%

Part-Time Undergrads: 97
Men: 36%, Women: 64%

Total Undergrad Population:
African American: 6%
Asian American: 2%
Latino: 1%
Native American: <1%
Caucasian: 84%
International: 1%
Out-of-State: 29%
Living Off-Campus: 30%
In Fraternities: 11%
In Sororities: 21%

Graduate and First-Professional
Students: 37

Academics

Full-Time Faculty: 147
With Ph.D.: 89%

Part-Time Faculty: 53
With Ph.D.: 43%

Student/Faculty Ratio: 14:1

Most Popular Majors:
business management
English
education
biology
psychology

Freshmen Retention Rate: 82%

Graduation Rates:
69% within four years
75% within six years

Admissions

Regular Application Deadline: 3/15;
12/1 (priority)

Early Decision Deadline(s): 11/15

Early Action Deadline: 12/1

Fall Transfer Deadline: 7/15 (priority)

Spring Transfer Deadline: 12/15
(priority)

Inside the Classroom

Affiliated with the Evangelical Lutheran Church, Wittenberg University is a liberal arts school whose strengths are its interdisciplinary programs. Offering 28 majors in the arts and sciences, Wittenberg also offers strong preprofessional programs in prelaw, premedicine, theology, accounting, engineering, and marine/aquatic biology. It is also one of the few schools to require community service for graduation, as part of its Service 100 program: Each student must spend at least 30 hours participating in experiential education and volunteer efforts, rendering assistance in the areas of hunger, the disabled, aging, literacy, environment, homelessness, health, and mentoring. The administration is serious about this requirement, to the point of offering students transportation to and from volunteer sites through its motor pool.

All students take a freshman seminar that is interdisciplinary and focused on contemporary social issues. After the seminar ends, students generally find that small classes with close faculty interaction continues to be the norm at Wittenberg. "The personal relationships I developed with professors really helped me develop as a student," says one senior. Another student says, "I've had professors invite me to lunch at the Commons to discuss a paper or test that was difficult for me, or just to chat. It's simply amazing."

Core requirements include courses in writing, mathematics, a foreign language, speaking, research, and computing. The various academic divisions have other requirements, as well: Those for the arts and sciences include coursework in the diversity of the human experience, integrated learning, natural sciences, social sciences, fine arts, religious and philosophical inquiry, Western history, and non-Western cultures.

A special honors program features seminars, an honors thesis, and other educational activities to the school's most outstanding students. The idea behind the thesis is to train students to produce a significant piece of academic work on a focused question, problem, topic, or means of artistic expression. Membership has its privileges, including the right to use the study lounges and 24-hour computer room in the Matthies Honors House.

Campus Environment

A little over half the students at Wittenberg live on campus in one of the seven dorms, or in Greek housing. All dorms are coed except for Hanley Hall, which is both all-female and a designated quiet dorm. Woodlawn Hall is designated substance-free. Most floors in each dorm have lounges and community bathrooms. To help students decide on housing for future years, the university places the floor plans for each dorm on its website.

The centerpiece of athletic activity is the Health, Physical Education, and Recreation Center, with its three full-size basketball courts, and facilities for racquetball, volleyball, and tennis. A 25-meter swimming pool with one- and three-meter diving boards serves as the site for competitive swimming, complete with a Colorado timing system. The Center, which seats 3,000 for athletic events and 4,300 for social events, doubles as a site for campus lectures, convocations, and concerts.

New additions to the campus will soon include the $23 million Kuss Science Center, which will house the school's science and mathematics departments. When complete, the center will provide a tremendous boost to Wittenberg's science offerings, providing students with access to new cell- and microbiology labs, an environmental resource center, several computer labs, cell and microorganism culturing facilities, audiovisual classrooms, and an auditorium with a flexible design for classes, lectures by visiting scientists, panel discussions, and multimedia presentations.

Wittenberg's 70-acre campus is located in Springfield, Ohio. A small city with nearly 70,000 residents, Springfield offers bars, shops, restaurants, and parks within walking distance. It also provides community service opportunities, internships, and part-time jobs for Wittenberg students. The town-gown relationship is generally good. Wittenberg's proximity to the cities of Dayton (25 miles away), Columbus (45 miles), and Cincinnati (75 miles) gives students other opportunities for exploring and fun.

Student Life

One student described the Wittenberg student body as a mixture of wealthy students, granola crunchers, and fraternity preprofessionals. The student body is overwhelmingly white and largely conservative, but a friendliness and openness characterize the Wittenberg community. A sophomore reports that international students and minority students have no trouble making friends.

Eight fraternities and seven sororities lead an active social life on campus. "We drink a lot," says one student. Campus societies and extracurricular clubs also play a strong—though perhaps less rowdy— role in life at Wittenberg, providing an option for just about anyone. Interesting groups include a caving journal, an East Asian studies club, a swing dancing club, Athletes for Christ, a choir, and an astronomical society. (And some of the societies are reportedly secret, in the tradition of East Coast Ivy League schools... naturally, details are hard to come by.)

Wittenberg's NCAA Division III sports for both men and women include basketball, cross country, lacrosse, soccer, swimming, tennis, and track and field. Men also compete in baseball, golf, and football, while women play field hockey, softball, and volleyball. Club sports include cheerleading, rugby, men's volleyball, ice hockey, cricket, women's crew, and dance. There are also 27 intramural sports open to students, including badminton, frisbee golf, walleyball, table tennis, and many olthers.

Favorite campus traditions include the annual Witt Fest, which is held each spring and includes a number of musical performances and fun entertainment like a Velcro wall, bungie run, off-with-your-head jousting, face painting, and food.

Other schools to check out: Denison, Allegheny, Gustavus Adolphus, College of Wooster.

Total # of Students Applied: 3,048
  Admitted: 2,263
  Enrolled: 570

Applied Early Decision: 49
  Early Decision Admitted: 31

Test Scores (middle 50%):
  SAT Verbal: 520–620
  SAT Math: 520–620
  ACT Comp: 21–26
  ACT English: 20–26
  ACT Math: 20–27

HS Rank of Entering Freshmen:
  Top 10%: 31%
  Top 25%: 60%
  Top 50%: 89%

Avg. HS GPA: 3.43

THE EXPERTS SAY...

" Wittenberg University's community-centered approach to education, in tandem with its interdisciplinary strengths, provide a sound holistic education. "

" Ultraliberal students may not enjoy Wittenberg's religious influences or the conservatism of much of its student body. "

Costs (2004–5)

Tuition and Fees: $26,196

Room & Board: $6,686

Payment Plan(s): installment plan

Inst. Aid (2002–03)

FT Undergrads Receiving Aid: 71%
  Avg. Amount per Student: $21,286

FT Undergrads Receiving Non-Need-Based Scholarship or Grant Aid: 8%
  Avg. Amount per Student: $965

Of Those Receiving Any Aid:

Rec. Need-Based Scholarship or Grant Aid: 100%
  Average Award: $17,056

Rec. Need-Based Self-Help Aid: 94%
  Average Award: $4,769

Upon Graduation, Avg. Loan Debt per Student: $18,623

Financial Aid Deadline: 3/15, 2/15 (priority)

Graduates

Going to Graduate School:
  28% Within One Year

Accepting Job Offer:
  66% at time of graduation

Alumni Giving: 44%

WOFFORD COLLEGE

429 North Church Street, Spartanburg, SC 29303-3663
Admissions Phone: (864) 597-4130 Fax: (864) 597-4147
Email: admissions@wofford.edu
Website: www.wofford.edu

General Info

Type of School: private, coed, United Methodist

Setting: urban

Academic Calendar: 4-1-4

Student Body

Full-Time Undergrads: 1,119
  Men: 49%, Women: 51%

Part-Time Undergrads: 13
  Men: 46%, Women: 54%

Total Undergrad Population:
  African American: 8%
  Asian American: 2%
  Latino: 1%
  Native American: <1%
  Caucasian: 88%
  International: 1%
  Out-of-State: 35%
  Living Off-Campus: 13%
  In Fraternities: 54%
  In Sororities: 64%

Academics

Full-Time Faculty: 82
  With Ph.D.: 91%

Part-Time Faculty: 28
  With Ph.D.: 57%

Student/Faculty Ratio: 12:1

Completing 2 or More Majors: 22%

Freshmen Retention Rate: 93%

Graduation Rates:
  71% within four years
  77% within six years

Admissions

Regular Application Deadline: 2/1

Early Decision Deadline(s): 11/15

Fall Transfer Deadline: 3/1, 2/1 (priority)

Spring Transfer Deadline: 11/15 (priority)

Total # of Students Applied: 1,317
  Admitted: 1,053
  Enrolled: 330

# of Students Waitlisted: 91
  Students Accepting Place: 80
  Waitlisted Students Admitted: 2

Test Scores (middle 50%):
  SAT Verbal: 560–660
  SAT Math: 580–670
  ACT Comp: 22–27

Inside the Classroom

Wofford College likes to say that its average SAT score (1241) is greater than its enrollment (1,133). Indeed, the school has a fine academic reputation and serious students. It was the first independent college in South Carolina to be awarded a chapter of Phi Beta Kappa (1941). Most students here are preprofessionally minded—about one-third of each graduating class goes on to medical, law, business, and divinity schools—and programs that prepare students for these fields are among Wofford's best and most popular. Sciences are particularly outstanding, and almost all of the liberal arts departments are strong, including English, history, philosophy, foreign languages, and religion.

The first two years of a Wofford education are largely devoted to fulfilling extensive core requirements, including courses in science, math, history, philosophy, English, fine arts, foreign language, and a freshman humanities seminar. Additionally, as the school maintains its Methodist affiliation, religious courses are required. During the required interim session in January, students have the opportunity to broaden their educational experiences through independent research and projects or off-campus study. The school has a solid and popular study abroad program, offering students 107 programs in 37 countries. The prestigious Presidential International Scholars program invites a senior to undertake a year of research in developing nations.

Classes at Wofford remain small, challenging students to be active participants in their studies. There are about 13 students to every professor (never a TA), and most classes keep the enrollment under 20. Students work closely with their professors, both inside and outside the classroom, and the profs are praised for being so accessible. One student we spoke with notes the feeling of "equality among students, faculty, and staff—you feel like you're on the same level."

Campus Environment

Founded in 1854, Wofford retains the Old World look and feel of its early days, with its lovely landscape and original buildings still intact. The 140-acre "beautiful, historic campus" is located in the central city Spartanburg and includes several 19th-century buildings as well as a brand new, $14.5 million science center. There are six residence halls, both coed and single-sex, which vary in quality depending on their age, and are said to be friendly and social. All first-year students are assigned to either the Charles F. Marsh men's dorm or the Walter K. Greene women's dorm. About 90 percent of all undergrads remain on campus throughout their college careers. There is a "row" of fraternity and sorority houses, but these are used for meetings and social gatherings.

All students may bring and park their cars if they've obtained the requisite permit. Most students do have cars for off-campus travels, but there is a city bus stop on the edge of campus, and downtown Spartanburg is in the midst of a "Renaissance Project," with plans to construct a cultural center, racing museum, and luxury apartment complex.

Student Life

The student body consists mainly of upper-middle class whites, conservative politically and socially. Roughly two-thirds of the population hails from South Carolina. The college's small size—which is "for some perhaps even claustrophobic"—fosters a real sense of closeness among the students. Most people here know each other, at least by face if not by name. "Everything revolves around the Wofford community," says one student. "It becomes your second family." He adds that this feeling is not just limited to the students: "Everyone knows each other by first name. We go out to lunch with ladies who clean my dormitory!"

The social scene is largely dictated by the Greek system, which draws well over half the student body into one of its eight fraternities and four sororities. Students who choose not to rush may feel left out here. On weekends, students head to parties on Fraternity Row (where "everyone is welcome to come in everyone else's houses," a student assures us) or in off-campus apartments. Those itching to get away for the weekend can travel to nearby Charlotte or Atlanta, but "most weekends, people stay at Wofford," a student tells us. Spring Weekend involves many fun traditions, including an all-out "water fight." A student explains, "We get out to Fraternity Row and take couches out on the front lawn . . . People start to show up . . . We get shaving cream and water guns—it's a water fight between the whole school . . . The roads look like they're completely covered in snow!"

The sports program at Wofford is particularly impressive given its size. A member of the Southern Conference, Wofford offers eight varsity sports for women and eight for men, including an NCAA Division I football team. Like David versus Goliath, Wofford's teams often pummel their bigger rivals. They're called the Terriers—small, but fierce. (School legend has it that the name comes from a former professor's dog who lept onto the baseball field during a game and drove off an opponent.) There are numerous intramural sports, and the Richardson Physical Activities Center, with its dance studio, weight room, and handball courts, gets a lot of use. Outdoor activities, such as hiking in the Appalachian Mountains, are also popular with students.

Besides joining fraternities and playing sports, Wofford students immerse themselves into a number of clubs and organizations, including honor and professional societies, media and performing arts groups, student government associations, and religious and service organizations. The latter are particularly popular; notables include the Twin Towers project, a volunteer service program, and the "active Chaplain's office and campus ministry." As one senior puts it, "Wofford is a community-oriented college dedicated to our overall growth."

Wofford's long history and many traditions, along with its friendly collegiate environment and academic programs that lead to professional success, give its students and alumni a deep sense of pride. "Our alumni support is extensive," affirms one student. "It's meaningful to them to give back some of their time and money. You can't walk away at graduation—you're always going to be a part of it!"

HS Rank of Entering Freshmen:
Top 10%: 53%
Top 25%: 79%
Top 50%: 97%

Costs (2004–5)

Comprehensive Fees: $28,740

Comp. Fees for Commuters: $22,300

Payment Plan(s): installment plan

THE EXPERTS SAY...

" Wofford is an excellent choice for serious students who appreciate tradition and history. Faculty, students, and alumni are a close-knit community. "

" Some students may not want to take religion courses or deal with Southern conservative values, even if the SAT scores here are higher than the enrollment. "

Inst. Aid (est. 2003–04)

Institutional Aid, Need-Based: $4,532,068

Institutional Aid, Non-Need-Based: $2,608,009

FT Undergrads Receiving Aid: 52% Avg. Amount per Student: $20,014

FT Undergrads Receiving Non-Need-Based Scholarship or Grant Aid: 21% Avg. Amount per Student: $8,268

Of Those Receiving Any Aid:

Rec. Need-Based Scholarship or Grant Aid: 100% Average Award: $14,581

Rec. Need-Based Self-Help Aid: 52% Average Award: $4,371

Upon Graduation, Avg. Loan Debt per Student: $12,281

Financial Aid Deadline: rolling, 3/31 (priority)

Graduates

Going to Graduate School: 35% Within One Year

Alumni Giving: 78%

XAVIER UNIVERSITY OF LOUISIANA

One Drexel Drive, New Orleans, LA 70125
Admissions Phone: (504) 520-7388 Fax: (504) 520-7941
Email: apply@xula.edu Website: www.xula.edu
Application Website: www.xula.edu/Admissions.html

General Info

Type of School: private, coed,
  Roman Catholic

Setting: urban

Academic Calendar: semester

Student Body

Full-Time Undergrads: 3,000
  Men: 24%, Women: 76%

Part-Time Undergrads: 77
  Men: 36%, Women: 64%

Total Undergrad Population:
  African American: 85%
  Asian American: 4%
  Latino: <1%
  Native American: <1%
  Caucasian: 1%
  International: 2%
  Out-of-State: 49%
  Living Off-Campus: 73%
  In Fraternities: 2%
  In Sororities: 6%

Graduate and First-Professional
  Students: 768

Academics

Full-Time Faculty: 236
  With Ph.D.: 90%

Part-Time Faculty: 48
  With Ph.D.: 27%

Student/Faculty Ratio: 15:1

Most Popular Majors:
  biology (33%)
  pre–pharmacy (11%)
  psychology (9%)
  chemistry (7%)
  business (7%)

Freshmen Retention Rate: 73%

Graduation Rates:
  38% within four years
  50% within six years

Admissions

Regular Application Deadline: 7/1;
  3/1 (priority)

Early Action Deadline: 1/15

Total # of Students Applied: 4,172
  Admitted: 3,508
  Enrolled: 917

# of Students Waitlisted: 187
  Students Accepting Place: 135
  Waitlisted Students Admitted: 52

Inside the Classroom

Xavier University of Louisiana is truly unique, being "the only historically black, Catholic university in the Western Hemisphere." While Xavier attracts a number of high-achieving students, it also admits some underprepared students "and provides workable ways for them to succeed." And because many of its students have limited financial resources, Xavier maintains a policy of low tuition—unusual for a private school that receives no funding from the Catholic Church.

Xavier's specialty has been in educating health professionals. "Attending Xavier is the closest you can get to a guarantee that you'll get into medical school," says one high school guidance counselor. That's no exaggeration, since according to the AAMC, Xavier ranks first in the nation (as it has for the last ten years) in placing African American students into medical schools. Xavier officials brag that the 77 percent acceptance rate of Xavier graduates by medical schools is almost twice the national average, and 92 percent of Xavier grads who enter med schools complete their degree programs. (Additionally, Xavier's College of Pharmacy reportedly ranks first in the nation in the number of Doctor of Pharmacy degrees awarded to African Americans; since 1927 it has graduated nearly one-quarter of the total number of African American pharmacists practicing in the United States.)

Part of the secret of Xavier's success: Not waiting for students to enroll in college to prepare them to be health care professionals and scientists. The university is able to connect with high school students through its renowned Summer Science Academy. Other measures taken by the university include standardizing its freshman premed math and science curricula. Freshmen at Xavier reportedly spend twice as much time in mathematics and science courses as most freshmen elsewhere; to help them cope, the school has an intensive tutoring program in these subjects, and faculty members encourage freshmen in chemistry and biology to form study groups. However, some students complain that if you're not a science major, your department won't get the same kind of resources (though no Xavier student in any major complains of a lack of attention from faculty).

All undergrads at Xavier enroll in the College of Arts and Sciences to earn a B.A., B.S., or B.M. degree. According to the U.S. Department of Education, Xavier ranks first nationally in the number of African American students earning undergraduate degrees in both the biological/life sciences and the physical sciences. It also ranks high in psychology, computer science and information, and mathematics. (Incidentally, Xavier was the nation's first HBCU to offer its own degree in computer engineering.) Students who are undecided about their major are admitted into the "Deciding Majors" department, where they can stay for up to two semesters. Another option: Through the New Orleans Consortium's Unique Major plan, students may pursue a major not available at Xavier but offered by Loyola University.

Each student must take both a major and a minor, "so that the student may be introduced to scholarly work in at least two areas." Certain programs have a "built-in" minor; Xavier has recently added a minor in African American Studies. The core curriculum includes courses in English, fine arts, foreign languages, history, African American studies, math, natural sciences, philosophy, religion, and social sciences; computer competency is also required in many programs. All students must pass a written comprehensive examination in their major in order to graduate.

Campus Environment

Xavier's campus has been dubbed "Emerald City" because of the prevalence of tall buildings sporting aqua-green roofs. Freshmen who live on campus are not allowed to have cars; for a small annual fee, limited student parking is available for upperclassmen living on campus.

Current students are upset about a "drastic" rise in room and board costs for the 2003–2004 school year. Luckily, nearly three-quarters of the student body live off campus. First-year females are assigned to double-occupancy rooms in either Katherine Drexel Hall or St. Joseph Hall, while all first-year males are assigned to doubles or singles in St. Michael Hall. Housing is not guaranteed, but is assigned on a first-come, first-served basis using the date on which the housing application form and deposit are received in the Office of Admissions. Xavier University scholarship recipients get the highest priority for campus housing, while local students who live within commuting distance of the campus and transfer students get the lowest priority.

Student Life

While Xavier is dedicated to serving the African American, Catholic community, students of any race or religion are welcome. In fact, approximately 70 percent of Xavier students are of other religious affiliations, and close to 10 percent are of other races. Recent years have seen a growing number of out-of-state students, now representing some 40 states and 20 foreign countries.

One complaint that some Xavierites have is over the huge imbalance of women to men on campus. Luckily, there are several other universities in the area to open up the dating pool a bit. Students say that the style on campus tends to be "neat but informal," and casual clothes are worn to class. Alcohol is prohibited on campus, but it flows quite freely around New Orleans, which is also one of the world's premier culinary hot spots.

Xavierites participate in a variety of religious organizations, honor societies, dormitory councils, departmental clubs, regional organizations, student publications, fraternities and sororities (including professional, service, and social), musical groups and various other societies. Students can contact the Volunteer Services Center to get involved in an array of volunteer and community outreach programs, including several mentoring and literacy programs. Xavier offers the following intercollegiate sports within NAIA and the Gulf Coast Athletic Conference: men's and women's basketball, cross country, tennis, men's and women's track and field, and volleyball.

Fun campus traditions include the annual five-day Spring Fest, which includes a wildly popular step show, a fashion show, a "regional fest" ("all regional organizations on campus will have food representing their area, from cajun cuisine to Chicago's deep dish pizza"), and a basketball tournament. Off campus, the biggest and most anticipated tradition is, of course, Mardi Gras.

Other schools to check out: Howard, Hampton, Fisk, Spelman, Morehouse, Tuskegee.

Test Scores (middle 50%):
SAT Verbal: 440–550
SAT Math: 430–550
ACT Comp: 18–23
ACT English: 18–24
ACT Math: 17–23

HS Rank of Entering Freshmen:
Top 10%: 18%
Top 25%: 35%
Top 50%: 51%

Avg. HS GPA: 3.05

THE EXPERTS SAY...

" Kudos to Xavier for creating a premed program whose goal is to get students into medical school, and once there, to have them succeed. "

" If med school is your goal, put yourself on the road to success early by enrolling in Xavier's Summer Science Academy. (A bonus: Getting to enjoy the food, music, and nightlife in the Big Easy!) "

Costs (2003–04)

Tuition and Fees: $11,400

Room & Board: $6,200

Payment Plan(s): installment plan, deferred payment plan, pre-payment plan

Inst. Aid (est. 2003–04)

FT Undergrads Receiving Aid: 80%
Avg. Amount per Student: $4,695

FT Undergrads Receiving Non-Need-Based Scholarship or Grant Aid: 3%
Avg. Amount per Student: $3,046

Of Those Receiving Any Aid:

Rec. Need-Based Scholarship or Grant Aid: 70%
Average Award: $3,886

Rec. Need-Based Self-Help Aid: 68%
Average Award: $2,166

Upon Graduation, Avg. Loan Debt per Student: $15,292

Financial Aid Deadline: rolling, 1/1 (priority)

Graduates

Going to Graduate School:
49% Within One Year

Accepting Job Offer:
20% at time of graduation

Companies Recruiting On Campus: 75

Alumni Giving: 15%

YALE UNIVERSITY

38 Hillhouse Avenue, New Haven, CT 06520-8234
Admissions Phone: (203) 432-9316 Fax: (203) 432-9392
Email: student.questions@yale.edu Website: www.yale.edu/admit
Application Website: www.yale.edu/admit/freshmen/application/index.html

General Info

Type of School: private, coed

Setting: urban

Academic Calendar: semester

Student Body

Full-Time Undergrads: 5,278
  Men: 50%, Women: 50%

Part-Time Undergrads: 9
  Men: 22%, Women: 78%

Total Undergrad Population:
  African American: 8%
  Asian American: 13%
  Latino: 6%
  Native American: 1%
  Caucasian: 52%
  International: 9%
  Out-of-State: 93%
  Living Off-Campus: 13%

Graduate and First-Professional
  Students: 6,117

Academics

Full-Time Faculty: 1,061
  With Ph.D.: 90%

Part-Time Faculty: 396
  With Ph.D.: 71%

Student/Faculty Ratio: :1

Most Popular Majors:
  history
  political science
  economics

Completing 2 or More Majors: 13%

Freshmen Retention Rate: 98%

Graduation Rates:
  88% within four years
  95% within six years

Admissions

Regular Application Deadline: 12/31

Early Action Deadline: 11/1

Fall Transfer Deadline: 3/1

Total # of Students Applied: 17,735
  Admitted: 2,014
  Enrolled: 1,353

# of Students Waitlisted: 814

Test Scores (middle 50%):
  SAT Verbal: 690–790
  SAT Math: 690–770
  ACT Comp: 30–34

Inside the Classroom

A Florida guidance counselor explains what makes Yale such a hot and trendy choice for high school students: "If they get in, it says a lot about them—[it's a] status statement." The workload at Yale is heavy, the pressure is intense, and if you don't keep up, you get left behind quickly. After all, according to one undergrad, "the students are the best and the brightest." Another comments, "Yale has lots of overachievers pushing one another." Many report that the pressure is self-inflicted rather than the result of cutthroat competition. A recent grad agrees: "Students are, on the whole, both cooperative and studious, with study groups cropping up throughout the library."

Yale touts itself as an undergraduate college first and foremost, which sets it apart from some of its Ivy League counterparts. Yalies can choose from a staggering 2,000 courses in 70 majors. Instead of preregistration, students can shop around for courses during the first two weeks of the semester and then sign up for the ones that interest them. Yale's best and most popular departments include the humanities, particularly English and history, as well as social, biological, and physical sciences. "Yale has no preprofessional majors (like advertising or prelaw) because it believes in education as preparation of the mind for life, not for a specific career," a junior explains. Students are required to take 36 courses to graduate, compared to the 32 of other Ivy League schools. First-year classes may number hundreds of students, but by the time you graduate, you will have been in many small seminar classes taught by the school's finest faculty. Yale boasts a student/faculty ratio of 7:1, and a senior says, "The professors are more accessible than one might think."

"They dropped their Early Decision!" a Colorado guidance counselor exclaims joyfully. The school now offers early action, in which early applicants will be told in December whether they have been admitted, but will be allowed to apply to other colleges and will not have to make a final choice until May. (However, Yale will still bar its early action applicants from applying to other early admissions programs.)

Campus Environment

Over 80 percent of Yalies live on campus, mostly in the school's distinctive residential college system. Incoming students are randomly assigned to one of 12 colleges, each of which houses 375–475 undergrads, a master, and a dean. "Each college is a mini-community with its own dining hall, small gym, computer cluster, etc., so that if you wanted to, you wouldn't have to leave your college save for going to class," a recent grad tells us. "The residential college system does an excellent job of fostering community within Yale and making the college feel much smaller," another student says admiringly.

As for food, it's not mystery meat. Writes the New York Times, "At Berkeley College [one of Yale's residential colleges]…we settled into huge red-leather chairs beneath chandeliers… the roasted portobello and tofu salad was subtly spiced, and crusty French loaves were accompanied by a roasted garlic spread, plus olive oil for dipping." The campus is a guidance counselor favorite, but New Haven is not particularly attractive or safe. "Town-gown is hard," admits one student. "Yale is rich, liberal, educated; New Haven is a rough, hard-pressed inner city."

Student Life

A California guidance counselor complains that Yale continues "to raise tuition at a soaring rate, to the point that only the rich [can afford it], and it's terrible." While "preppy" may describe some of the undergrads here, Yale prides itself on being diverse. The school has a 28 percent minority population, and over half of its students come from public high schools. "I feel as though all walks of life are represented," a student assures us. Politically, "Yale is a very liberal place, although the cluster of conservatives stick together," says a poly sci major. "It's the cool, fun Harvard," quips another student. There are quite a few famous faces on campus, including Claire Danes, Jordana Brewster, and Barbara Bush.

As classic overachievers, Yalies are always eager to dive into a bunch of extracurricular activities. Yale is particularly known for its theater and performance groups, including the acclaimed Yale Repertory and the world-famous Yale Whiffenpoofs a capella group. The popular Yale Daily News is the oldest college daily in the country; a column discussing sex is a surprising but wildly popular section in the paper and on the paper's website (though the columnist herself admits that there tends to be "a lot more talk than action" on college campuses). Yale has 33 intercollegiate teams; the Harvard-Yale football battle—a.k.a. "The Game"—is one of the biggest events of the year. About 70 percent of all undergrads participate in athletics in one form or another; as one student says, "Everyone has a roommate on a team."

"The residential college system minimizes the need for a Greek system," a student observes. There are just a few sororities and fraternities (plus a few legendary "secret senior societies" such as "Skull and Bones," which allegedly engage in "naked parties" and other debauchery), and the majority of brothers are athletes.

Each weekend, a residential college hosts a theme dance, such as "Casino Night" and "Exotic Erotic." And despite rampant bad-mouthing of New Haven, students find plenty to do there. Tradition dictates that freshmen spend their Thursday nights at Naples Pizzeria. Yalies flock to Mory's, the oldest and most famous tavern, to "do cups" (drinking champagne-based beverages from large silver goblets); clubbers can head to Toad's Place, where many top rock-and-roll acts got their start. However, "weeknights are largely spent studying," warns a young alum. "By Thursday, students start to loosen up… [but] by Sunday afternoon, most are back to the books."

Other schools to check out: Harvard, Swarthmore, Stanford, Princeton, Brown.

HS Rank of Entering Freshmen:
  Top 10%: 99%
  Top 25%: 100%

Costs (2004–05)

Tuition and Fees: $29,820

Room & Board: $9,030

Payment Plan(s): installment plan

THE EXPERTS SAY...

" By eliminating early decision, Yale has taken the pressure off of students and has created a more financially level playing field: Now kids can apply here early action and still be able to look at all their financial aid offers before they commit. "

" Naked parties and labor strikes aren't what immediately leap to most people's minds when they think of Yale, but it's all part of the Yale 'mystique.' "

Inst. Aid (est. 2003–04)

Institutional Aid, Need-Based: $44,313,097

FT Undergrads Receiving Aid: 40%
  Avg. Amount per Student: $26,978

Of Those Receiving Any Aid:

Rec. Need-Based Scholarship or Grant Aid: 100%
  Average Award: $23,574

Rec. Need-Based Self-Help Aid: 100%
  Average Award: $3,659

Upon Graduation, Avg. Loan Debt per Student: $16,911

Financial Aid Deadline: 3/1 (priority)

Graduates

Going to Graduate School:
  31% Within One Year

Accepting Job Offer:
  64% at time of graduation

Companies Recruiting On Campus: 100

YESHIVA UNIVERSITY

500 West 185th Street, New York, NY 10033-3201
Admissions Phone: (212) 960-5277 Fax: (212) 960-0086
Email: admission@yu1.yu.edu
Website: yu.edu

Note: Info. not verified by school

General Info

Type of School: private, Yeshiva College for men, Stern College for Women

Setting: urban

Academic Calendar: semester

Student Body (2002)

Undergrads: 2,798
  Men: 56%, Women: 44%

Total Undergrad Population
  Caucasian: 84%
  International: 7%

Academics

Graduation Rates (1996 cohort)
  60% within four years
  88% within six years

Admissions

Regular Application Deadline: 2/15 (priority)

Costs (2003–04)

Tuition and Fees: $21,730
Room & Board: $6,980

Inside the Classroom

The two single-sex undergraduate colleges at Yeshiva University are Yeshiva College and Stern College for Women; both men and women attend the Sy Syms School for Business but on separate campuses. Students take a dual curriculum, attending intensive Torah and Talmud classes in the morning, and a full regimen of liberal arts, science, and business courses in the afternoon. The philosophy behind these programs is called Torah Umadda (Torah and "worldly" learning). Jewish studies courses are Yeshiva's strength and a main reason students decide to attend. Students choose from courses in a comprehensive curriculum featuring Hebrew, Bible (Tanakh), Talmud (Gemara), Jewish history, Jewish philosophy, and Judaic studies. Although courses range from beginner through advanced levels, and one student contends that "you don't have to already be well-versed in Judaism to come here," most Yeshiva students do come from an orthodox background and have had prior religious education. The S. Daniel Abraham Israel Program offers first-year students the experience of studying biblical history and contemporary Jewish culture in Israel.

Students at Sy Syms School of Business major in accounting, finance, information systems, management, or marketing. Notable programs at this college include the Rennert Entrepreneurial Institute, which offers entrepreneurship courses, and the Contemporary Problems in Business course, which features a top CEO as guest lecturer each week. Sy Syms students participating in the Charno Fund research the stock market and, supervised by a faculty member, run a stock portfolio.

The liberal arts departments and the courses offered in Yeshiva's Sy Syms School of Business have good reputations, and YU is highly rated as a research university. The student body itself is a strong educational resource. As one senior points out, "Students here are extremely intelligent. About half of them turned down admission to higher ranked schools to come here." The students who choose to come to Yeshiva "have the need to know about their religion," according to a political science and business double major, "but most don't go on to become rabbis." Most Yeshiva students, in fact, are on a preprofessional track, and the corresponding programs are particularly popular.

The dual curriculum makes for a particularly heavy workload. Students spend long hours in class and hitting the books at home. Most classes are small with highly approachable teachers who know their students by name. "You get lots of attention here," says one senior, "and you have a greater opportunity to participate in campus life." The downside of this small size is the less diverse range of academic offerings than one might find at a larger school. However, for most students this is more than offset by the strong Judaic studies curriculum and YU's spirit of Torah Lishmah—the love of learning for its own sake.

Campus Environment

YU's main campus is located in the (way) uptown Washington Heights section of Manhattan, and is home to Yeshiva College. Washington Heights ranges from quiet to high crime. Stern College buildings are clustered in the Murray Hill section of Manhattan in midtown, in the heart of the city's many stores, sights, and cultural activities. Men and women study and live on the separate campuses, connected by shuttle bus. Business school students live and attend classes on the same-sex campus. Dorms are single sex, and freshmen are integrated with students from all classes. Housing options include singles, doubles, and apartments for upper-class students. Housing is not guaranteed, but YU states that it accommodates all students seeking on-campus housing. While most students live on campus, many commuters head home right after class. Due to increased enrollment, a new women's residence with mostly single-room housing recently opened at Stern; the midtown campus also has a new cultural center and many expanded facilities.

Because Yeshiva University is located in an urban setting, students can park their cars on the street—if they can find parking, always a problem in Manhattan. Some students bite the bullet and use local parking lots, or rent night parking from the University. The University provides a frequent van service around the campuses and between the main and Midtown campuses. Public transportation by bus and subway is easily accessible at both YU undergraduate campuses.

Although the food is kosher and the service is pleasant, food at YU is not highly rated. "The Caf," as the Furman dining hall is called, is the worst culprit in terms of taste, small portions, and high prices. Local Kosher takeout alternatives are available, but can become monotonous.

THE EXPERTS SAY...

" Yeshiva's spirit of Torah Lishmah—love of learning — attracts students away from the Ivy League. "

" Torah and Talmud in the morning, and everything else other students have to do in the afternoon. It's a schmertz. "

Student Life

While Yeshiva and Stern have no fraternities or sororities, there are numerous clubs and organizations. The most active student organizations include the Israel Club, which organizes and supports rallies, brings speakers to campus, and arranges Israeli Independence Day celebrations. Recently it organized a 10-day solidarity mission to Israel for 200 students. The Student Organization of Yeshiva (SOY) initiates religious-content programming, features noted rabbis and scholars as event speakers and organizes celebrations of religious holidays. At the Stern College campus, the Torah Activities Council oversees an array of clubs and activities that revolve around religious life and often involve community service. After September 11, Stern College women performed shemirah services (Jewish commandment to watch over a dead body from the time of death until burial) for victims of the World Trade Center.

The Yeshiva College Dramatic Society and the Stern College Dramatics Society each mount theatrical productions during the year. Basketball, both at the varsity and intramural levels, is the most popular sport. Many students take advantage of Manhattan's museums, concerts, and plays. The big night to go out is Thursday, since many students spend the Sabbath off-campus (though students and faculty members, along with their families, are always welcome to celebrate the Sabbath together on campus). School work must be balanced with daily religious practices, and these are woven into daily life; a student seeking an excellent liberal arts or business education in an environment that supports the totality of Jewish life will likely feel at home at YU.

SECTION III:

INDEXES

ALPHABETICAL INDEX

North Carolina State University	NC	Syracuse University	NY	University of Oregon	OR
Northeastern University	MA	Temple University	PA	University of Pennsylvania	PA
Northern Arizona University	AZ	Texas A&M University	TX	University of Pittsburgh	PA
Northwestern University	IL	Texas Christian University	TX	University of Puget Sound	WA
Oberlin College	OH	Texas Tech University	TX	University of Redlands	CA
Occidental College	CA	Trinity College	CT	University of Richmond	VA
Ohio State University	OH	Trinity University	TX	University of Rochester	NY
Ohio University	OH	Truman State University	MO	University of Scranton	PA
Oklahoma State University	OK	Tufts University	MA	University of South Carolina—	
Oregon State University	OR	Tulane University	LA	Columbia	SC
Pacific Lutheran University	WA	Tuskegee University	AL	University of Southern California	CA
Parsons School of Design	NY	Union College	NY	University of Tennessee—Knoxville	TN
Pennsylvania State University—		United States Air Force Academy	CO	University of Texas—Austin	TX
University Park	PA	United States Coast Guard Academy	CT	University of the Pacific	CA
Pepperdine University	CA	United States Merchant		University of the South	TN
Pitzer College	CA	Marine Academy	NY	University of Tulsa	OK
Pomona College	CA	United States Military Academy—		University of Utah	UT
Princeton University	NJ	West Point	NY	University of Vermont	VT
Providence College	RI	United States Naval Academy	MD	University of Virginia	VA
Purdue University—West Lafayette	IN	University of Alabama	AL	University of Washington	WA
Randolph-Macon Woman's College	VA	University of Arizona	AZ	University of Wisconsin—Madison	WI
Reed College	OR	University of Arkansas—Fayetteville	AR	University of Wisconsin—	
Rensselaer Polytechnic Institute	NY	University of California—Berkeley	CA	Stevens Point	WI
Rhode Island School of Design	RI	University of California—Davis	CA	University of Wyoming	WY
Rhodes College	TN	University of California—Irvine	CA	Ursinus College	PA
Rice University	TX	University of California—Los Angeles	CA	Valparaiso University	IN
Ripon College	WI	University of California—San Diego	CA	Vanderbilt University	TN
Rochester Institute of Technology	NY	University of California—		Vassar College	NY
Rollins College	FL	Santa Barbara	CA	Villanova University	PA
Rose-Hulman Institute of Technology	IN	University of California—Santa Cruz	CA	Virginia Polytechnic Institute	
Rutgers University	NJ	University of Chicago	IL	and State University	VA
Saint Anselm College	NH	University of Cincinnati	OH	Wabash College	IN
Saint John's College—Annapolis	MD	University of Colorado—Boulder	CO	Wagner College	NY
Saint John's College—Santa Fe	NM	University of Connecticut	CT	Wake Forest University	NC
Saint Lawrence University	NY	University of Dallas	TX	Warren Wilson College	NC
Saint Louis University	MO	University of Dayton	OH	Washington and Lee University	VA
Saint Mary's College of California	CA	University of Delaware	DE	Washington University in St. Louis	MO
Saint Mary's College of Maryland	MD	University of Denver	CO	Wellesley College	MA
Saint Olaf College	MN	University of Florida	FL	Wesleyan University	CT
Salisbury University	MD	University of Georgia	GA	West Virginia University	WV
San Diego State University	CA	University of Hawaii—Manoa	HI	Wheaton College (IL)	IL
Santa Clara University	CA	University of Houston	TX	Wheaton College (MA)	MA
Sarah Lawrence College	NY	University of Illinois—		Whitman College	WA
Scripps College	CA	Urbana-Champaign	IL	Willamette University	OR
Simmons College	MA	University of Iowa	IA	Williams College	MA
Skidmore College	NY	University of Kansas	KS	Wittenberg University	OH
Smith College	MA	University of Kentucky	KY	Wofford College	SC
Southern Methodist University	TX	University of Maine	ME	Xavier University	LA
Southwestern University	TX	University of Maryland—		Yale University	CT
Spelman College	GA	Baltimore County	MD	Yeshiva University	NY
Stanford University	CA	University of Maryland—			
State University of New York—		College Park	MD		
Albany	NY	University of Massachusetts—			
State University of New York—		Amherst	MA		
Binghamton University	NY	University of Miami	FL		
State University of New York—		University of Michigan—Ann Arbor	MI		
College at Geneseo	NY	University of Minnesota—Twin Cities	MN		
State University of New York—		University of Missouri—Columbia	MO		
Purchase	NY	University of Missouri—Rolla	MO		
State University of New York—		University of Nebraska—Lincoln	NE		
Stony Brook	NY	University of Nevada—Las Vegas	NV		
State University of New York—		University of Nevada—Reno	NV		
University at Buffalo	NY	University of New Hampshire	NH		
Stetson University	FL	University of New Mexico	NM		
Stonehill College	MA	University of North Carolina—			
Susquehanna University	PA	Chapel Hill	NC		
Swarthmore College	PA	University of Notre Dame	IN		
Sweet Briar College	VA	University of Oklahoma	OK		

KAPLAN Indexes

STATE INDEX

Alabama
Auburn University
Birmingham-Southern College
Tuskegee University
University of Alabama

Arizona
Arizona State University
Northern Arizona University
University of Arizona

Arkansas
Hendrix College
University of Arkansas—Fayetteville

California
California Institute of Technology
California Polytechnic State University
California State University—Chico
Claremont McKenna College
Harvey Mudd College
Loyola Marymount University
Mills College
Occidental College
Pepperdine University
Pitzer College
Pomona College
Saint Mary's College of California
San Diego State University
Santa Clara University
Scripps College
Stanford University
University of California—Berkeley
University of California—Davis
University of California—Irvine
University of California—Los Angeles
University of California—San Diego
University of California—Santa Barbara
University of California—Santa Cruz
University of Redlands
University of Southern California
University of the Pacific

Colorado
Colorado College
United States Air Force Academy
University of Colorado—Boulder
University of Denver

Connecticut
Connecticut College
Fairfield University
Trinity College
United States Coast Guard Academy
University of Connecticut
Wesleyan University
Yale University

Delaware
University of Delaware

District of Columbia
American University
Catholic University of America
Gallaudet University
George Washington University
Georgetown University
Howard University

Florida
Eckerd College
Embry-Riddle Aeronautical University-FL
Flagler College
Florida State University
New College of Florida
Rollins College
Stetson University
University of Florida
University of Miami

Georgia
Agnes Scott College
Berry College
Emory University
Georgia Institute of Technology
Morehouse College
Spelman College
University of Georgia

Hawaii
University of Hawaii—Manoa

Idaho
Albertson College

Illinois
Bradley University
DePaul University
Illinois Institute of Technology
Illinois Wesleyan University
Knox College
Lake Forest College
Loyola University of Chicago
Northwestern University
University of Chicago
University of Illinois—Urbana-Champaign
Wheaton College

Indiana
DePauw University
Earlham College
Goshen College
Hanover College
Indiana University—Bloomington
Purdue University—West Lafayette
Rose-Hulman Institute of Technology

University of Notre Dame
Valparaiso University
Wabash College

Iowa
Cornell College
Grinnell College
University of Iowa

Kansas
Kansas State University
University of Kansas

Kentucky
Berea College
Centre College
University of Kentucky

Louisiana
Louisiana State University—Baton Rouge
Loyóla University New Orleans
Tulane University
Xavier University

Maine
Bates College
Bowdoin College
Colby College
College of the Atlantic
University of Maine

Maryland
Goucher College
Johns Hopkins University
Loyola College
Saint John's College—Annapolis
Saint Mary's College of Maryland
Salisbury University
United States Naval Academy
University of Maryland—Baltimore County
University of Maryland—College Park

Massachusetts
Amherst College
Babson College
Bentley College
Berklee College of Music
Boston College
Boston University
Brandeis University
Clark University
College of the Holy Cross
Emerson College
Hampshire College
Harvard University
Massachusetts Institute of Technology
Mount Holyoke College
Northeastern University
Simmons College

Smith College
Stonehill College
Tufts University
University of Massachusetts—Amherst
Wellesley College
Wheaton College
Williams College

Michigan
Albion College
Calvin College
Kalamazoo College
Kettering University
Michigan State University
Michigan Technological University
University of Michigan—Ann Arbor

Minnesota
Carleton College
Gustavus Adolphus College
Macalester College
Saint Olaf College
University of Minnesota—Twin Cities

Mississippi
Millsaps College

Missouri
College of the Ozarks
Saint Louis University
Truman State University
University of Missouri—Columbia
University of Missouri—Rolla
Washington University in St. Louis

Nebraska
Creighton University
Hastings College
University of Nebraska—Lincoln

Nevada
Deep Springs College
University of Nevada—Las Vegas
University of Nevada—Reno

New Hampshire
Dartmouth College
Saint Anselm College
University of New Hampshire

New Jersey
College of New Jersey
Drew University
Princeton University
Rutgers University

New Mexico
Saint John's College—Santa Fe
University of New Mexico

New York
Alfred University
Bard College
Barnard College
City University of New York—
  Baruch College
City University of New York—
  Brooklyn College
City University of New York—John Jay
  College of Criminal Justice

Colgate University
Columbia University—Columbia College
Cooper Union for the Advancement
  of Science and Art
Cornell University
Culinary Institute of America
Eugene Lang College
Fashion Institute of Technology
Fordham University
Hamilton College
Hobart and William Smith Colleges
Hofstra University
Ithaca College
Juilliard School
Manhattanville College
New York University
Parsons School of Design
Rensselaer Polytechnic Institute
Rochester Institute of Technology
Saint Lawrence University
Sarah Lawrence College
Skidmore College
State University of New York—Albany
State University of New York—
  Binghamton University
State University of New York—
  College at Geneseo
State University of New York—Purchase
State University of New York—
  Stony Brook
State University of New York—
  U. at Buffalo
Syracuse University
Union College
United States Merchant
  Marine Academy
United States Military Academy—
  West Point
University of Rochester
Vassar College
Wagner College
Yeshiva University

North Carolina
Davidson College
Duke University
Elon University
Guilford College
North Carolina School of the Arts
North Carolina State University
University of North Carolina—Chapel Hill
Wake Forest University
Warren Wilson College

Ohio
Antioch College
Case Western Reserve University
College of Wooster
Denison University
Hiram College
Kenyon College
Miami University
Oberlin College
Ohio State University
Ohio University
University of Cincinnati
University of Dayton
Wittenberg University

Oklahoma
Oklahoma State University
University of Oklahoma
University of Tulsa

Oregon
Lewis and Clark College
Oregon State University
Reed College
University of Oregon
Willamette University

Pennsylvania
Allegheny College
Bryn Mawr College
Bucknell University
Carnegie Mellon University
Chatham College
Dickinson College
Drexel University
Duquesne University
Franklin and Marshall College
Gettysburg College
Haverford College
Indiana University of Pennsylvania
Juniata College
Lafayette College
Lehigh University
Muhlenberg College
Pennsylvania State U.—University Park
Susquehanna University
Swarthmore College
Temple University
University of Pennsylvania
University of Pittsburgh
University of Scranton
Ursinus College
Villanova University

Rhode Island
Brown University
Providence College
Rhode Island School of Design

South Carolina
Citadel
Clemson University
College of Charleston
Furman University
University of South Carolina Columbia
Wofford College

Tennessee
Belmont University
Fisk University
Rhodes College
University of Tennessee—Knoxville
University of the South
Vanderbilt University

Texas
Austin College
Baylor University
Rice University
Southern Methodist University
Southwestern University
Texas A&M University
Texas Christian University
Texas Tech University
Trinity University

University of Dallas
University of Houston
University of Texas—Austin

Utah
Brigham Young University
University of Utah

Vermont
Bennington College
Marlboro College
Middlebury College
University of Vermont

Virginia
College of William and Mary
George Mason University

Hampden-Sydney College
Hampton University
Hollins University
James Madison University
Mary Washington College
Randolph-Macon Woman's College
Sweet Briar College
University of Richmond
University of Virginia
Virginia Polytechnic Institute
 and State University
Washington and Lee University

Washington
Evergreen State College
Gonzaga University
Pacific Lutheran University

University of Puget Sound
University of Washington
Whitman College

West Virginia
West Virginia University

Wisconsin
Beloit College
Lawrence University
Marquette University
Ripon College
University of Wisconsin—Madison
University of Wisconsin—Stevens Point

Wyoming
University of Wyoming

SIZE INDEX

This index is based on the total number of degree-seeking undergraduates (full-time and part-time).

25,000 or More Undergraduates

Arizona State University	AZ
Brigham Young University	UT
Florida State University	FL
Indiana University–Bloomington	IN
Louisiana State University	LA
Michigan State University	MI
Ohio State University, The	OH
Pennsylvania State University– University Park	PA
Purdue University–West Lafayette	IN
Rutgers University	NJ
San Diego State University	CA
Texas A&M University	TX
University of Arizona	AZ
University of California–Los Angeles	CA
University of Colorado-Boulder	CO
University of Florida	FL
University of Houston	TX
University of Illinois-Urbana at Champaign	IL
University of Minnesota–Twin Cities	MN
University of Texas–Austin	TX
University of Washington	WA
University of Wisconsin–Madison	WI

20,000–24,999 Undergraduates

North Carolina State University	NC
Temple University	PA
Texas Tech University	TX
University of California–Berkeley	CA
University of California–Davis	CA
University of Georgia	GA
University of Kansas	KS
University of Maryland–College Park	MD
University of Michigan–Ann Arbor	MI
University of Missouri–Columbia	MO
University of Utah	UT
Virginia Polytechnic Institute and State University	VA

15,000–19,999 Undergraduates

Auburn University	AL
Boston University	MA
California Polytechnic State University	CA
George Mason University	VA
Kansas State University	KS
Miami University	OH
New York University	NY
Ohio University	OH
Oklahoma State University	OK
State University of New York– University at Buffalo	NY
University of Alabama	AL
University of California–Irvine	CA
University of California–San Diego	CA
University of California–Santa Barbara	CA
University of Cincinnati	OH
University of Delaware	DE

University of Iowa	IA
University of Kentucky	KY
University of Massachusetts–Amherst	MA
University of Nebraska–Lincoln	NE
University of Nevada–Las Vegas	NV
University of New Mexico	NM
University of North Carolina– Chapel Hill	NC
University of Oklahoma	OK
University of Oregon	OR
University of Pittsburgh	PA
University of South Carolina– Columbia	SC
University of Southern California	CA
University of Tennessee	TN
West Virginia University	WV

10,000–14,999 Undergraduates

Baylor University	TX
California State University–Chico	CA
City University of New York–Baruch College	NY
City University of New York– Brooklyn College	NY
City University of New York–John Jay College of Criminal Justice	NY
Clemson University	SC
Cornell University	NY
DePaul University	IL
Drexel University	PA
George Washington University	DC
Georgia Institute of Technology	GA
Indiana University of Pennsylvania	PA
James Madison University	VA
Northeastern University	MA
Northern Arizona University	AZ
Oregon State University	OR
Rochester Institute of Technology	NY
State University of New York–Albany	NY
State University of New York– Stony Brook	NY
State University of New York– Binghamton University	NY
Syracuse University	NY
University of Arkansas	AR
University of California–Santa Cruz	CA
University of Connecticut	CT
University of Hawaii–Manoa	HI
University of Nevada–Reno	NV
University of New Hampshire	NH
University of Virginia	VA

5,000–9,999 Undergraduates

American University	DC
Boston College	MA
Bradley University	IL
Brown University	RI
Carnegie Mellon University	PA
College of Charleston	SC

College of New Jersey	NJ
College of William and Mary	VA
Duke University	NC
Duquesne University	PA
Emory University	GA
Fashion Institute of Technology	NY
Fordham University	NY
Georgetown University	DC
Harvard University	MA
Hofstra University	NY
Howard University	DC
Ithaca College	NY
Loyola Marymount University	CA
Loyola University of Chicago	IL
Marquette University	WI
Michigan Technological University	MI
Northwestern University	IL
Rensselaer Polytechnic Institute	NY
Saint Louis University	MO
Salisbury University	MD
Southern Methodist University	TX
Stanford University	CA
State University of New York– College at Geneseo	NY
Texas Christian University	TX
Truman State University	MO
Tulane University	LA
University of Dayton	OH
University of Maine	ME
University of Maryland Baltimore County	MD
University of Miami	FL
University of Notre Dame	IN
University of Pennsylvania	PA
University of Vermont	VT
University of Wisconsin–Stevens Point	WI
University of Wyoming	WY
Vanderbilt University	TN
Villanova University	PA
Washington University in St. Louis	MO
Yale University	CT

1,000–4,999 Undergraduates

Albion College	MI
Alfred University	NY
Allegheny College	PA
Amherst College	MA
Austin College	TX
Babson College	MA
Bard College	NY
Barnard College	NY
Bates College	ME
Belmont University	TN
Beloit College	WI
Bentley College	MA
Berea College	KY
Berklee College of Music	MA
Berry College	GA
Birmingham-Southern College	AL

Bowdoin College	ME	Knox College	IL	University of Missouri–Rolla	MO
Brandeis University	MA	Lafayette College	PA	University of Puget Sound	WA
Bryn Mawr College	PA	Lake Forest College	IL	University of Redlands	CA
Bucknell University	PA	Lawrence University	WI	University of Richmond	VA
Calvin College	MI	Lehigh University	PA	University of Rochester	NY
Carleton College	MN	Lewis and Clark College	OR	University of Scranton	PA
Case Western Reserve University	OH	Loyola College in Maryland	MD	University of the Pacific	CA
Catholic University of America	DC	Loyola University New Orleans	LA	University of the South	TN
Centre College	KY	Macalester College	MN	University of Tulsa	OK
Citadel	SC	Manhattanville College	NY	Ursinus College	PA
Claremont McKenna College	CA	Mary Washington College	VA	Valparaiso University	IN
Clark University	MA	Massachusetts Institute of		Vassar College	NY
Colby College	ME	Technology	MA	Wagner College	NY
Colgate University	NY	Middlebury College	VT	Wake Forest University	NC
College of the Holy Cross	MA	Millsaps College	MS	Washington and Lee University	VA
College of the Ozarks	MO	Morehouse College	GA	Wellesley College	MA
College of Wooster, The	OH	Mount Holyoke College	MA	Wesleyan University	CT
Colorado College	CO	Muhlenberg College	PA	Wheaton College	IL
Columbia University–		Oberlin College	OH	Wheaton College	MA
Columbia College	NY	Occidental College	CA	Whitman College	WA
Connecticut College	CT	Pacific Lutheran University	WA	Willamette University	OR
Cornell College	IA	Parsons School of Design	NY	Williams College	MA
Creighton University	NE	Pepperdine University	CA	Wittenberg University	OH
Culinary Institute of America	NY	Pomona College	CA	Wofford College	SC
Dartmouth College	NH	Princeton University	NJ	Xavier University of Louisiana	LA
Davidson College	NC	Providence College	RI	Yeshiva University	NY
Denison University	OH	Reed College	OR		
DePauw University	IN	Rhode Island School of Design	RI	**Fewer Than 1,000**	
Dickinson College	PA	Rhodes College	TN	**Undergraduates**	
Drew University	NJ	Rice University	TX	Agnes Scott College	GA
Earlham College	IN	Rollins College	FL	Albertson College of Idaho	ID
Eckerd College	FL	Rose-Hulman Institute of Technology	IN	Antioch College	OH
Elon University	NC	Saint Anselm College	NH	Bennington College	VT
Embry-Riddle Aeronautical University	FL	Saint Mary's College of California	CA	California Institute of Technology	CA
Emerson College	MA	Santa Clara University	CA	Chatham College	PA
Evergreen State College	WA	Sarah Lawrence College	NY	College of the Atlantic	ME
Fairfield University	CT	Simmons College	MA	Cooper Union for the	
Flagler College	FL	Skidmore College	NY	Advancement of Science and Art	NY
Franklin and Marshall College	PA	Smith College	MA	Deep Springs College	NV
Furman University	SC	Southwestern University	TX	Eugene Lang College	NY
Gallaudet University	DC	Spelman College	GA	Fisk University	TN
Gettysburg College	PA	Saint Lawrence University	NY	Goshen College	IN
Gonzaga University	WA	Saint Mary's College of Maryland	MD	Hanover College	IN
Goucher College	MD	Saint Olaf College	MN	Harvey Mudd College	CA
Grinnell College	IA	State University of New York—		Hollins University	VA
Guilford College	NC	Purchase College	NY	Juilliard School	NY
Gustavus Adolphus College	MN	Stetson University	FL	Marlboro College	VT
Hamilton College	NY	Stonehill College	MA	Mills College	CA
Hampden-Sydney College	VA	Susquehanna University	PA	New College of Florida	FL
Hampshire College	MA	Swarthmore College	PA	North Carolina School of the Arts	NC
Hampton University	VA	Trinity College	CT	Pitzer College	CA
Hastings College	NE	Trinity University	TX	Randolph-Macon Woman's College	VA
Haverford College	PA	Tufts University	MA	Ripon College	WI
Hendrix College	AR	Tuskegee University	AL	Scripps College	CA
Hiram College	OH	Union College	NY	Saint John's College	MD
Hobart and William Smith Colleges	NY	United States Air Force Academy	CO	Saint John's College	NM
Illinois Institute of Technology	IL	United States Coast Guard Academy	CT	Sweet Briar College	VA
Illinois Wesleyan University	IL	United States Military Academy—		United States Merchant	
Johns Hopkins University	MD	West Point	NY	Marine Academy	NY
Juniata College	PA	United States Naval Academy	MD	Wabash College	IN
Kalamazoo College	MI	University of Chicago	IL	Warren Wilson College	NC
Kenyon College	OH	University of Dallas	TX		
Kettering University	MI	University of Denver	CO		

TUITION INDEX

This index is based on out-of-state tuition and fees (or "comprehensive fees," where applicable). To find a school's in-state tuition and fees, see the sidebar data in the school's profile in Section II of this book.

$25,000 or More

Allegheny College	PA
American University	DC
Amherst College	MA
Babson College	MA
Bard College	NY
Barnard College	NY
Bates College	ME
Beloit College	WI
Bennington College	VT
Boston College	MA
Boston University	MA
Bowdoin College	ME
Brandeis University	MA
Brown University	RI
Bryn Mawr College	PA
Bucknell University	PA
California Institute of Technology	CA
Carleton College	MN
Carnegie Mellon University	PA
Case Western Reserve University	OH
Claremont McKenna College	CA
Clark University	MA
Colby College	ME
Colgate University	NY
College of the Holy Cross	MA
College of Wooster	OH
Colorado College	CO
Columbia University— Columbia College	NY
Connecticut College	CT
Cornell University	NY
Dartmouth College	NH
Davidson College	NC
Denison University	OH
DePauw University	IN
Dickinson College	PA
Drew University	NJ
Duke University	NC
Emory University	GA
Fairfield University	CT
Franklin and Marshall College	PA
George Washington University	DC
Georgetown University	DC
Gettysburg College	PA
Grinnell College	IA
Hamilton College	NY
Hampshire College	MA
Harvard University	MA
Harvey Mudd College	CA
Haverford College	PA
Hobart and William Smith Colleges	NY
Illinois Wesleyan University	IL
Johns Hopkins University	MD
Kenyon College	OH
Knox College	IL
Lafayette College	PA
Lawrence University	WI
Lehigh University	PA

Loyola College in Maryland	MD
Macalester College	MN
Massachusetts Institute of Technology	MA
Middlebury College	VT
Mount Holyoke College	MA
New York University	NY
Northeastern University	MA
Northwestern University	IL
Oberlin College	OH
Occidental College	CA
Parsons School of Design	NY
Pepperdine University	CA
Pitzer College	CA
Pomona College	CA
Princeton University	NJ
Reed College	OR
Rensselaer Polytechnic Institute	NY
Rhode Island School of Design	RI
Rollins College	FL
Rose-Hulman Institute of Technology	IN
Saint John's College	MD
Saint John's College	NM
Saint Lawrence University	NY
Saint Mary's College of California	CA
Saint Olaf College	MN
Santa Clara University	CA
Sarah Lawrence College	NY
Scripps College	CA
Skidmore College	NY
Smith College	MA
Stanford University	CA
Swarthmore College	PA
Syracuse University	NY
Trinity College	CT
Tufts University	MA
Tulane University	LA
Union College	NY
University of Chicago	IL
University of Denver	CO
University of Miami	FL
University of Notre Dame	IN
University of Pennsylvania	PA
University of Richmond	VA
University of Rochester	NY
University of Southern California	CA
Ursinus College	PA
Vanderbilt University	TN
Vassar College	NY
Villanova University	PA
Wake Forest University	NC
Washington University in St. Louis	MO
Wellesley College	MA
Wesleyan University	CT
Wheaton College	MA
Whitman College	WA
Willamette University	OR
Williams College	MA
Wittenberg University	OH

Wofford College	SC
Yale University	CT

$20,000–24,999

Agnes Scott College	GA
Albion College	MI
Alfred University	NY
Antioch College	OH
Bentley College	MA
Berklee College of Music	MA
Catholic University of America	DC
Centre College	KY
Chatham College	PA
College of the Atlantic	ME
College of William and Mary	VA
Cornell College	IA
Drexel University	PA
Earlham College	IN
Eckerd College	FL
Embry-Riddle Aeronautical University	FL
Emerson College	MA
Eugene Lang College	NY
Fordham University	NY
Furman University	SC
Gonzaga University	WA
Goucher College	MD
Gustavus Adolphus College	MN
Hampden-Sydney College	VA
Hanover College	IN
Hiram College	OH
Hollins University	VA
Illinois Institute of Technology	IL
Ithaca College	NY
Juilliard School	NY
Juniata College	PA
Kalamazoo College	MI
Kettering University	MI
Lake Forest College	IL
Lewis and Clark College	OR
Loyola Marymount University	CA
Loyola University New Orleans	LA
Loyola University of Chicago	IL
Manhattanville College	NY
Marlboro College	VT
Marquette University	WI
Mills College	CA
Muhlenberg College	PA
Pacific Lutheran University	WA
Providence College	RI
Rhodes College	TN
Ripon College	WI
Rochester Institute of Technology	NY
Saint Anselm College	NH
Saint Louis University	MO
Simmons College	MA
Southern Methodist University	TX
Southwestern University	TX
Stetson University	FL
Stonehill College	MA

Susquehanna University — PA
Sweet Briar College — VA
University of California–Berkeley — CA
University of California–Davis — CA
University of California–Santa Cruz — CA
University of Colorado–Boulder — CO
University of Dayton — OH
University of Michigan–Ann Arbor — MI
University of Puget Sound — WA
University of Redlands — CA
University of Scranton — PA
University of the Pacific — CA
University of the South — TN
University of Vermont — VT
University of Virginia — VA
Valparaiso University — IN
Wabash College — IN
Wagner College — NY
Washington and Lee University — VA
Wheaton College — IL
Yeshiva University — NY

$15,000–19,999

Austin College — TX
Baylor University — TX
Belmont University — TN
Berry College — GA
Birmingham-Southern College — AL
Bradley University — IL
Calvin College — MI
Creighton University — NE
Culinary Institute of America — NY
DePaul University — IL
Duquesne University — PA
Elon University — NC
Georgia Institute of Technology — GA
Goshen College — IN
Guilford College — NC
Hastings College — NE
Hendrix College — AR
Hofstra University — NY
Indiana University–Bloomington — IN
Miami University — OH
Michigan State University — MI
Michigan Technological University — MI
Millsaps College — MS
New College of Florida — FL
North Carolina State University — NC
Ohio State University — OH
Ohio University — OH
Oregon State University — OR
Pennsylvania State University–University Park — PA
Purdue University–West Lafayette — IN
Randolph-Macon Woman's College — VA
Rice University — TX
Saint Mary's College of Maryland — MD
Temple University — PA
Texas Christian University — TX
Trinity University — TX
University of California–Irvine — CA
University of California–Los Angeles — CA
University of California–San Diego — CA

University of Cincinnati — OH
University of Connecticut — CT
University of Dallas — TX
University of Delaware — DE
University of Illinois–Urbana-Champaign — IL
University of Iowa — IA
University of Maine — ME
University of Maryland–College Park — MD
University of Massachusetts–Amherst — MA
University of Minnesota–Twin Cities — MN
University of Missouri–Columbia — MO
University of Missouri–Rolla — MO
University of New Hampshire — NH
University of North Carolina–Chapel Hill — NC
University of Oregon — OR
University of Pittsburgh — PA
University of South Carolina–Columbia — SC
University of Tulsa — OK
University of Washington — WA
University of Wisconsin–Madison — WI
Virginia Polytechnic Institute and State University — VA
Warren Wilson College — NC

$10,000–14,999

Albertson College of Idaho — ID
Arizona State University — AZ
Auburn University — AL
California State University–Chico — CA
Citadel — SC
Clemson University — SC
College of Charleston — SC
College of New Jersey — NJ
Evergreen State College — WA
Fashion Institute of Technology — NY
Fisk University — TN
Florida State University — FL
George Mason University — VA
Hampton University — VA
Howard University — DC
Indiana University of Pennsylvania — PA
James Madison University — VA
Kansas State University — KS
Mary Washington College — VA
Morehouse College — GA
North Carolina School of the Arts — NC
Northern Arizona University — AZ
Oklahoma State University — OK
Rutgers University — NJ
Salisbury University — MD
San Diego State University — CA
Spelman College — GA
State University of New York–Albany — NY
State University of New York–Stony Brook — NY
State University of New York–Binghamton University — NY

State University of New York–College at Geneseo — NY
State University of New York–Purchase College — NY
State University of New York–University at Buffalo — NY
Texas A&M University — TX
Texas Tech University — TX
Tuskegee University — AL
University of Alabama — AL
University of Arizona — AZ
University of Arkansas — AR
University of California–Santa Barbara — CA
University of Florida — FL
University of Georgia — GA
University of Hawaii–Manoa — HI
University of Kansas — KS
University of Kentucky — KY
University of Maryland–Baltimore County — MD
University of Nebraska–Lincoln — NE
University of Nevada–Las Vegas — NV
University of Nevada–Reno — NV
University of New Mexico — NM
University of Oklahoma — OK
University of Tennessee — TN
University of Texas–Austin — TX
University of Utah — UT
University of Wisconsin–Stevens Point — WI
West Virginia University — WV
Xavier University of Louisiana — LA

$5,000–9,999

City University of New York–Baruch College — NY
City University of New York–John Jay College of Criminal Justice — NY
Flagler College — FL
Gallaudet University — DC
Louisiana State University — LA
Truman State University — MO
University of Houston — TX
University of Wyoming — WY

Under $5,000

Berea College — KY
Brigham Young University — UT
California Polytechnic State University — CA
City University of New York–Brooklyn College — NY
College of the Ozarks — MO
Cooper Union for the Advancement of Science and Art — NY
Deep Springs College — NV
United States Air Force Academy — CO
United States Coast Guard Academy — CT
United States Merchant Marine Academy — NY
United States Military Academy–West Point — NY
United States Naval Academy — MD

If you are an international student considering attending an American university, you are not alone. Over 586,323 international students pursued academic degrees at the undergraduate, graduate, or professional school level at U.S. universities during the 2002–2003 academic year, according to the Institute of International Education's Open Doors report. Almost 50 percent of these students were studying for a bachelor's or first university degree. This number of international students pursuing higher education in the United States is expected to continue to grow. Business, management, engineering, and the physical and life sciences are particularly popular majors for students coming to the United States from other countries.

If you are not a U.S. citizen and you are interested in attending college or university in the United States, here is what you'll need to get started.

- If English is not your first language, you'll probably need to take the TOEFL® (Test of English as a Foreign Language) or provide some other evidence that you are proficient in English. Colleges and universities in the United States will differ on what they consider to be an acceptable TOEFL score. A minimum TOEFL score of 213 (550 on the paper-based TOEFL) or better is often required by more prestigious and competitive institutions. Because American undergraduate programs require all students to take a certain number of general education courses, all students—even math and computer science students—need to be able to communicate well in spoken and written English.

- You may also need to take the SAT® or the ACT®. Many undergraduate institutions in the United States require both the SAT and TOEFL for international students.

- There are over 3,400 accredited colleges and universities in the United States, so selecting the correct undergraduate school can be a confusing task for anyone. You will need to get help from a good advisor or at least a good college guide that gives you detailed information on the different schools available. Since admission to many undergraduate programs is quite competitive, you may want to select three or four colleges and complete applications for each school.

- You should begin the application process at least a year in advance. An increasing number of schools accept applications year round. In any case, find out the application deadlines and plan accordingly. Although September (the fall semester) is the traditional time to begin university study in the United States, you can begin your studies at many schools in January (the spring semester).

- In addition, you will need to obtain an I-20 Certificate of Eligibility from the school you plan to attend if you intend to apply for an F-1 Student Visa to study in the United States.

Kaplan English Programs*

If you need more help with the complex process of university admissions, assistance preparing for the SAT, ACT, or TOEFL, or help building your English language skills in general, you may be interested in Kaplan's programs for international students.

Kaplan English Programs were designed to help students and professionals from outside the United States meet their educational and career goals. At locations throughout the United States, international students take advantage of Kaplan's programs to help them improve their academic and conversational English skills, raise their scores on the TOEFL, SAT, ACT, and other standardized exams, and gain admission to the schools of their choice. Our staff and instructors give international students the individualized attention they need to succeed. Here is a brief description of some of Kaplan's programs for international students:

General Intensive English

Kaplan's General Intensive English classes are designed to help you improve your skills in all areas of English and to increase your fluency in spoken and written English. Classes are available for beginning to advanced students, and the average class size is 12 students.

TOEFL and Academic English

This course provides you with the skills you need to improve your TOEFL score and succeed in an American university or graduate program. It includes advanced reading, writing, listening, grammar, and conversational English. You will also receive training for the TOEFL using Kaplan's exclusive computer-based practice materials.

SAT for International Students

The SAT is an important admission criterion for American colleges and universities. A high score can help you stand out from other applicants. Kaplan's SAT course for non-native English speakers is specifically designed for to highlight verbal strategies and practice while also covering the math section of the test. This course includes the skills you need to succeed on each section of the SAT, as well as access to Kaplan's exclusive practice materials.

If you will be applying to attend college starting in the fall of 2006 or later, check with the colleges where you plan to apply, and see if they will require you to take the New SAT, which will be offered for the first time in March 2005.

Other Kaplan Programs

Since 1938, more than 3 million students have come to Kaplan to advance their studies, prepare for entry to American universities, and further their careers. In addition to the above programs, Kaplan offers courses to prepare for the ACT, GMAT®, GRE®, MCAT®, DAT®, USMLE®, NCLEX®, and other standardized exams at locations throughout the United States.

Applying to Kaplan English Programs

To get more information, or to apply for admission to any of Kaplan's programs for international students and professionals, contact us at:

Kaplan English Programs
700 South Flower, Suite 2900
Los Angeles, CA 90017, USA
Phone (if calling from within the United States): 800-818-9128
Phone (if calling from outside the United States): 213-452-5800
Fax: 213-892-1364
Website: www.kaplanenglish.com
Email: world@kaplan.com

*Kaplan is authorized under federal law to enroll nonimmigrant alien students. Kaplan is accredited by ACCET (Accrediting Council for Continuing Education and Training).

FREE Services for International Students

Kaplan now offers international students many services online—*free of charge*! Students may assess their TOEFL skills and gain valuable feedback on their English language proficiency in just a few hours with Kaplan's TOEFL Skills Assessment. Log onto www.kaplanenglish.com today.

NOTES

NOTES

NOTES

How Did We Do? Grade Us.

Thank you for choosing a Kaplan book. Your comments and suggestions are very useful to us. Please answer the following questions to assist us in our continued development of high-quality resources to meet your needs. Or go online and complete our interactive survey form at **kaplansurveys.com/books**.

The title of the Kaplan book I read was: _____

My name is: _____

My address is: _____

_____

My e-mail address is: _____

What overall grade would you give this book?   Ⓐ   Ⓑ   Ⓒ   Ⓓ   Ⓕ

How relevant was the information to your goals?   Ⓐ   Ⓑ   Ⓒ   Ⓓ   Ⓕ

How comprehensive was the information in this book?   Ⓐ   Ⓑ   Ⓒ   Ⓓ   Ⓕ

How accurate was the information in this book?   Ⓐ   Ⓑ   Ⓒ   Ⓓ   Ⓕ

How easy was the book to use?   Ⓐ   Ⓑ   Ⓒ   Ⓓ   Ⓕ

How appealing was the book's design?   Ⓐ   Ⓑ   Ⓒ   Ⓓ   Ⓕ

What were the book's strong points? _____

How could this book be improved? _____

Is there anything that we left out that you wanted to know more about?

Would you recommend this book to others?   ☐ YES   ☐ NO

Other comments: _____

_____

_____

Do we have permission to quote you?   ☐ YES   ☐ NO

Thank you for your help.
Please tear out this page and mail it to:

Managing Editor
Kaplan, Inc.
1440 Broadway, 8th floor
New York, NY 10018

KAPLAN

Test Prep and Admissions

Thanks!